# Patterns of
# World History

# Patterns of
# World History

## WITH SOURCES

## Second Edition

**Peter von Sivers**
*University of Utah*

**Charles A. Desnoyers**
*La Salle University*

**George B. Stow**
*La Salle University*

**with the assistance of Jonathan S. Perry**
*University of South Florida, Sarasota-Manatee*

New York     Oxford
OXFORD UNIVERSITY PRESS

Oxford University Press is a department of the University of Oxford.
It furthers the University's objective of excellence in research,
scholarship, and education by publishing worldwide.

Oxford   New York
Auckland   Cape Town   Dar es Salaam   Hong Kong   Karachi
Kuala Lumpur   Madrid   Melbourne   Mexico City   Nairobi
New Delhi   Shanghai   Taipei   Toronto

With offices in
Argentina   Austria   Brazil   Chile   Czech Republic   France   Greece
Guatemala   Hungary   Italy   Japan   Poland   Portugal   Singapore
South Korea   Switzerland   Thailand   Turkey   Ukraine   Vietnam

For titles covered by Section 112 of the US Higher Education Opportunity Act,
please visit www.oup.com/us/he for the latest information about pricing and
alternate formats.

Published in the United States of America by
Oxford University Press
198 Madison Avenue, New York, NY 10016
http://www.oup.com

Oxford is a registered trade mark of Oxford University Press.

**Library of Congress Cataloging-in-Publication Data**
Von Sivers, Peter.
   Patterns of world history with sources / Peter Von Sivers, Charles A. Desnoyers, George B.
Stow. -- Second edition.
      pages cm
   Includes bibliographical references and index.
   ISBN 978-0-19-939978-9 (combined volume : paperback : acid-free paper) -- ISBN 978-0-19-
939979-6 (volume 1 : paperback : acid-free paper) -- ISBN 978-0-19-939980-2 (volume 2 :
paperback : acid-free paper) -- ISBN 978-0-19-939981-9 (volume 3 : paperback : acid-free
paper) 1. World history--Textbooks. 2. World history--Sources. I. Desnoyers, Charles, 1952- II.
Stow, George B. III. Title.
   D21.V67 2015
   909--dc23
                                                                        2014020339

**About the Cover**
This white cotton man's robe was created around 1855 in Lahore, India (present-day Pakistan).
The circular shape of the neck opening, over a flat panel underneath, identifies this as an
*angarkha*, one of the most popular forms of traditional courtly or formal wear in northern India.
The decoration around the back and shoulders is in the unusual form of a draped scarf, a
foliated decorative treatment found in Central Asian garments.

9 8 7 6 5 4

Printed in the United States of America
on acid-free paper

Coniugi Judithae dilectissimae

—Peter von Sivers

To all my students over the years, who have taught me at least as much as I've taught them; and most of all to my wife, Jacki, beloved in all things, but especially in her infinite patience and fortitude in seeing me through the writing of this book.

—Charles A. Desnoyers

For Susan and our children, Meredith and Jonathan.

—George B. Stow

*—I hear and I forget; I see and I remember; I do and I understand*
(Chinese proverb) 我听见我忘记;我看见我记住;我做我了解

# Brief Contents

# Part 5: The Origins of Modernity
1750–1900

# Part 6: From Three Modernities to One
1914–Present

# Contents

## PART ONE

## From Human Origins to Early Agricultural Centers
**PREHISTORY–600 BCE**

**Features:**

**Patterns Up Close:**
The Disappearance of
Neanderthals — 20

**Against the Grain:**
The Hobbits of Flores
Island — 30

**Features:**

**Patterns Up Close:**
Babylonian Law Codes — 44

**Against the Grain:**
Akhenaten the
Transgressor — 64

## Chapter 3
3000–600 BCE

### Shifting Agrarian Centers in India
66

**Features:**

**Patterns Up Close:**

**Against the Grain:**

## Chapter 4
5000–481 BCE

### Agrarian Centers and the Mandate of Heaven in Ancient China
92

**Features:**

**Patterns Up Close:**

**Against the Grain:**

**Chapter 5**
30,000–600 BCE

**Features:**

**Patterns Up Close:**
The Origin of Corn    134

**Against the Grain:**
Thor Heyerdahl    146

**PART TWO**

**The Age of Empires and Visionaries**

**Chapter 6**
600 BCE–600 CE

**Features:**

**Patterns Up Close:**
The Mayan Ball Game    170

**Against the Grain:**
Nazca Lines
and Speculation    178

Features:

**Patterns Up Close:**
The Plague of Justinian  196

**Against the Grain:**
Women in Democratic
Athens                  214

Features:

**Patterns Up Close:**
The Global Trade
of Indian Pepper        236

**Against the Grain:**
India's Ancient
Republics               242

**Chapter 9**
722 BCE–618 CE

## China: Imperial Unification and Perfecting the Moral Order          244

---

Features:

**Patterns Up Close:**

**Against the Grain:**

---

**PART THREE**

## The Formation of Religious Civilizations
**600–1450 CE**                                                    272

**Chapter 10**
600–1300 CE

## Islamic Civilization and Byzantium                              274

**Chapter 11**
600–1450 CE

**Chapter 12**
600–1600 CE

## Chapter 13
550–1500 CE

## Religious Civilizations Interacting: Korea, Japan, and Vietnam

## Chapter 14
600–1450 CE

## Patterns of State Formation in Africa

**Chapter 15**

600–1550 CE

**PART FOUR**

**Chapter 16**

1450–1650

**Chapter 17**
1450–1750

## The Renaissance, New Sciences, and Religious Wars in Europe    494

**Chapter 18**
1500–1800

## New Patterns in New Worlds: Colonialism and Indigenous Responses in the Americas    530

**Chapter 19**
1450–1800

## African Kingdoms, the Atlantic Slave Trade, and the Origins of Black America

**Features:**

**Patterns Up Close:**
Voodoo and Other New
World Slave Religions   590

**Against the Grain:**
Oglethorpe's Free
Colony                 596

**Chapter 20**
1400–1750

## The Mughal Empire: Muslim Rulers and Hindu Subjects

**Features:**

**Patterns Up Close:**
Akbar's Attempt at
Religious Synthesis    608

**Against the Grain:**
Sikhism in Transition  624

**Chapter 21**
1500–1800

### Regulating the "Inner" and "Outer" Domains: China and Japan    626

**Features:**

**Patterns Up Close:**
The "China" Trade    632

**Against the Grain:**
Seclusion's Exceptions    656

**PART FIVE**

# The Origins of Modernity
**1750–1900**    658

**Chapter 22**
1750–1871

### Patterns of Nation-States and Culture in the Atlantic World    660

**Features:**

**Patterns Up Close:**
The Guillotine    668

**Against the Grain:**
Defying the Third Republic    692

**Features:**

**Patterns Up Close:**
Slave Rebellions
in Cuba and Brazil       712

**Against the Grain:**
Early Industrialization
in Chile?               726

**Features:**

**Patterns Up Close:**
Interaction and Adaptation:
"Self-Strengthening" and
"Western Science and
Eastern Ethics"        738

**Against the Grain:**
Reacting to Modernity   758

**Chapter 25**
1683–1908

## Adaptation and Resistance: The Ottoman and Russian Empires

Features:
**Patterns Up Close:**
  Sunni and Shiite Islam   772
**Against the Grain:**
  Precursor to Lenin   788

**Chapter 26**
1750–1914

## Industrialization and Its Discontents

Features:
**Patterns Up Close:**
  "The Age of Steam"   798
**Against the Grain:**
  The Luddites   820

**Chapter 27**
1750–1914

Features:

**Patterns Up Close:**
Military Transformations and
the New Imperialism   832

**Against the Grain:**
An Anti-Imperial
Perspective          852

**PART SIX**

**Chapter 28**
1900–1945

Features:

**Patterns Up Close:**
The Harlem Renaissance
and the African Diaspora 866

**Against the Grain:**
Righteous among
the Nations         892

**Chapter 29**
*1945–1962*

> **Features:**
>
> **Patterns Up Close:**
>   Bandung and the Origins
>   of the Non-Aligned
>   Movement        920
>
> **Against the Grain:**
>   Postwar Counterculture  928

**Chapter 30**
*1963–1991*

> **Features:**
>
> **Patterns Up Close:**
>   From Women's Liberation
>   to Feminism        944
>
> **Against the Grain:**
>   The African National
>   Congress        962

**Chapter 31**
1991–2014

# Maps

# Studying with Maps

## MAPS

World history cannot be fully understood without a clear comprehension of the chronologies and parameters within which different empires, states, and peoples have changed over time. Maps facilitate this understanding by illuminating the significance of time, space, and geography in shaping the patterns of world history.

### Projection

A map *projection* portrays all or part of the earth, which is spherical, on a flat surface. All maps, therefore, include some distortion. The projections in *Patterns of World History* show the earth at global, continental, regional, and local scales.

### Topography

Many maps in *Patterns of World History* show *relief*—the contours of the land. Topography is an important element in studying maps because the physical terrain has played a critical role in shaping human history.

### Scale Bar

Every map in *Patterns of World History* includes a *scale* that shows distances in both miles and kilometers, and in some instances in feet as well.

### Map Key

Maps use symbols to show the location of features and to convey information. Each symbol is explained in the map's *key*.

### Global Locator

Many of the maps in *Patterns of World History* include *global locators* that show the area being depicted in a larger context.

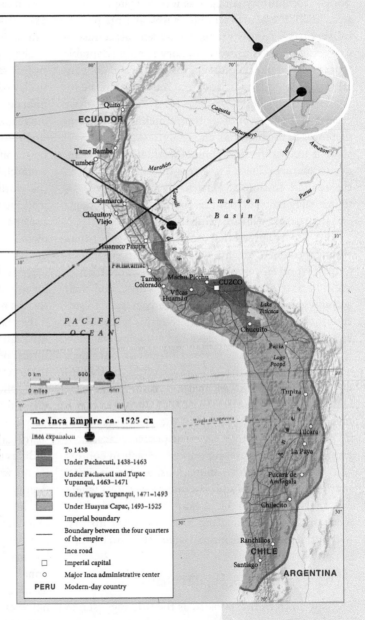

**The Inca Empire ca. 1525 CE**

Inca expansion

| | |
|---|---|
| � | To 1438 |
| | Under Pachacuti, 1438–1463 |
| | Under Pachacuti and Tupac Yupanqui, 1463–1471 |
| | Under Tupac Yupanqui, 1471–1493 |
| | Under Huayna Capac, 1493–1525 |
| — | Imperial boundary |
| —— | Boundary between the four quarters of the empire |
| ---- | Inca road |
| □ | Imperial capital |
| ○ | Major Inca administrative center |
| **PERU** | Modern-day country |

# Preface

The response to the first edition of *Patterns of World History* has been extraordinarily gratifying to those of us involved in its development. The diversity of schools that have adopted the book—community colleges as well as state universities; small liberal arts schools as well as large private universities—suggests to us that its central premise of exploring *patterns* in world history is both adaptable to a variety of pedagogical environments and congenial to a wide body of instructors. Indeed, from the responses to the book we have received thus far, we expect that the level of writing, timeliness and completeness of the material, and analytical approach will serve it well as the discipline of world history continues to mature. These key strengths are enhanced in the second edition of *Patterns* by constructive, dynamic suggestions from the broad range of students and instructors who are using the book.

It is widely agreed that world history is more than simply the sum of all national histories. Likewise, *Patterns of World History*, Second Edition, is more than an unbroken sequence of dates, battles, rulers, and their activities, and it is more than the study of isolated stories of change over time. Rather, in this textbook we endeavor to present in a clear and engaging way how world history "works." Instead of merely offering a narrative history of the appearance of this or that innovation, we present an analysis of the process by which an innovation in one part of the world is diffused and carried to the rest of the globe. Instead of focusing on the memorization of people, places, and events, we strive to present important facts in context and draw meaningful connections, analyzing whatever patterns we find and drawing conclusions where we can. In short, we seek to examine the interlocking mechanisms and animating forces of world history, without neglecting the human agency behind them.

## The *Patterns* Approach

Our approach in this book is, as the title suggests, to look for patterns in world history. We should say at the outset that we do not mean to select certain categories into which we attempt to stuff the historical events we choose to emphasize, nor do we claim that all world history is reducible to such patterns, nor do we mean to suggest that the nature of the patterns determines the outcome of historical events. We see them instead as broad, flexible organizational frameworks around which to build the structure of a world history in such a way that the enormous sweep and content of the past can be viewed in a comprehensible narrative, with sound analysis and ample scope for debate and discussion. In this sense, we view them much like the armatures in clay sculptures, giving support and structure to the final figure but not necessarily preordaining its ultimate shape.

From its origins, human culture grew through interactions and adaptations on all the continents except Antarctica. A voluminous scholarship on all regions of the world has thus been accumulated, which those working in the field have to attempt to master if their explanations and arguments are to sound even remotely persuasive. The sheer volume and complexity of the sources, however, mean that even the knowledge and expertise of the best scholars are going to be incomplete. Moreover, the humility with which all historians must approach their material contains within it the realization that no historical explanation is ever fully satisfactory or final: As a driving force in the historical process, creative human agency moves events in directions that are never fully predictable, even if they follow broad patterns. Learning to discern patterns in this process not only helps novice historians to appreciate the complex challenges (and rewards) of historical inquiry; it also develops critical thinking abilities in all students.

As we move through the second decade of the twenty-first century, world historians have long since left behind the "West plus the rest" approach that marked the field's early years, together with economic and geographical reductionism, in the search for a new balance between comprehensive cultural and institutional examinations on the one hand and those highlighting human agency on the other. All too often, however, this is reflected in texts that seek broad coverage at the expense of analysis, thus resulting in a kind of "world history lite." Our aim is therefore to simplify the study of the world—to make it accessible to the student—without making world history itself simplistic.

*Patterns of World History*, Second Edition, proposes the teaching of world history from the perspective of the relationship between continuity and change. What we advocate in this book is a distinct intellectual framework for this relationship and the role of innovation and historical change through patterns of origins, interactions, and adaptations. Each small or large technical or cultural innovation originated in one geographical center or independently in several different centers. As people in the centers interacted with their neighbors, the neighbors adapted to, and in many cases were transformed by, the innovations. By "adaptation" we include the entire spectrum of human responses, ranging from outright rejection to creative borrowing and, at times, forced acceptance.

Small technical innovations often went through the pattern of origin, interaction, and adaptation across the world without arousing much attention, even though they had major consequences. For example, the horse collar, which originated in ninth-century China and allowed for the replacement of oxen with stronger horses, gradually improved the productivity of agriculture in eleventh-century western Europe. More sweeping intellectual–cultural innovations, by contrast, such as the spread of universal religions like Buddhism, Christianity, and Islam and the rise of science, have often had profound consequences—in some cases leading to conflicts lasting centuries—and affect us even today.

Sometimes change was effected by commodities that to us seem rather ordinary. Take sugar, for example: It originated in southeast Asia and was traded and grown in the Mediterranean, where its cultivation on plantations created the model for expansion into the vast slave system of the Atlantic basin from the fifteenth through the nineteenth centuries, forever altering the histories of four continents. What would our diets look like today without sugar? Its history continues to unfold as we debate its merits and health risks and it supports huge multinational agribusinesses.

Or take a more obscure commodity: opium. Opium had been used medicinally for centuries in regions all over the world. But the advent of tobacco traded from the Americas to the Philippines to China, and the encouragement of Dutch traders in the region, created an environment in which the drug was smoked for the first time. Enterprising rogue British merchants, eager to find a way to crack closed Chinese markets for other goods, began to smuggle it in from India. The market grew, the price went down, addiction spread, and Britain and China ultimately went to war over China's attempts to eliminate the traffic. Here, we have an example of an item generating interactions on a worldwide scale, with impacts on everything from politics to economics, culture, and even the environment. The legacies of the trade still weigh heavily on two of the rising powers of the twenty-first century: China and India. And opium and its derivatives, like morphine and heroin, continue to bring relief as well as suffering on a colossal scale to hundreds of millions of people.

What, then, do we gain by studying world history through the use of such patterns? First, if we consider innovation to be a driving force of history, it helps to satisfy an intrinsic human curiosity about origins—our own and others. Perhaps more importantly, seeing patterns of various kinds in historical development brings to light connections and linkages among peoples, cultures, and regions—as in the aforementioned examples—that might not otherwise present themselves.

Second, such patterns can also reveal differences among cultures that other approaches to world history tend to neglect. For example, the differences between the civilizations of the Eastern and Western Hemispheres are generally highlighted in world history texts, but the broad commonalities of human groups creating agriculturally based cities and states in widely separated areas also show deep parallels in their patterns of origins, interactions, and adaptations. Such comparisons are at the center of our approach.

Third, this kind of analysis offers insights into how an individual innovation was subsequently developed and diffused across space and time—that is, the patterns by which the new eventually becomes a necessity in our daily lives. Through all of this we gain a deeper appreciation of the unfolding of global history from its origins in small, isolated areas to the vast networks of global interconnectedness in our present world.

Finally, our use of a broad-based understanding of continuity, change, and innovation allows us to restore culture in all its individual and institutionalized aspects—spiritual, artistic, intellectual, scientific—to its rightful place alongside technology, environment, politics, and socioeconomic conditions. That is, understanding innovation in this way allows this text to help illuminate the full range of human ingenuity over time and space in a comprehensive, evenhanded, and open-ended fashion.

## Options for Teaching with *Patterns of World History,* Second Edition

In response to requests from teachers who adopted the first edition, we now offer a version of *Patterns of World History* that includes a selection of primary-text and visual sources after every chapter. This section, called "Patterns of Evidence," enhances student engagement with key chapter patterns through contemporaneous voices and perspectives. Each source is accompanied by a concise introduction to provide chronological and geographical context; "Working with Sources" questions after each selection prompt students to make critical connections between the source and the main chapter narrative.

For the convenience of instructors teaching a course over two 15-week semesters, both versions of *Patterns* are limited to 31 chapters. For the sake of continuity and to accommodate the many different ways schools divide the midpoint of their world history sequence, Chapters 15–18 overlap in both volumes; in Volume 2, Chapter 15 is given as a "prelude" to Part Four. Those using a trimester system will also find divisions made in convenient places, with Chapter 10 coming at the beginning of Part Two and Chapter 22 at the beginning of Part Five. Finally, for those schools that offer a modern world history course that begins at approximately 1750, a volume is available that includes only the final two parts of the book.

## Patterns of Change and Six Periods of World History

Similarly, *Patterns* is adaptable to both chronological and thematic styles of instruction. We divide the history of the world into six major time periods and recognize for each period one or two main patterns of innovation, their spread through interaction, and their adoption by others. Obviously, lesser patterns are identified as well, many of which are of more limited regional interactive and adaptive impact. We wish to stress again that these are broad categories of analysis and that there is nothing reductive or deterministic in our aims or choices. Nevertheless, we believe the patterns we have chosen help to make the historical process more intelligible, providing a series of lenses that can help to focus the otherwise confusing facts and disparate details that comprise world history.

*Part One (Prehistory–600 BCE):* Origins of human civilization—tool making and symbol creating—in Africa as well as the origins of agriculture, urbanism, and state formation in the three agrarian centers of the Middle East, India, and China.

*Part Two (600 BCE–600 CE):* Emergence of the axial-age thinkers and their visions of a transcendent god or first principle in Eurasia; elevation of these visions to the status of state religions in empires and kingdoms, in the process forming multiethnic and multilinguistic polities.

*Part Three (600–1450):* Disintegration of classical empires and formation of religious civilizations in Eurasia, with the emergence of religiously unified regions divided by commonwealths of multiple states.

*Part Four (1450–1750):* Rise of new empires; interaction, both hostile and peaceful, among the religious civilizations and new empires across all continents of the world. Origins of the New Science in Europe, based on the use of mathematics for the investigation of nature.

*Part Five (1750–1900):* Origins of scientific–industrial "modernity," simultaneous with the emergence of constitutional and ethnic nation-states, in the West (Europe and North America); interaction of the West with Asia and Africa, resulting in complex adaptations, both coerced as well as voluntary, on the part of the latter.

*Part Six (1900–Present):* Division of early Western modernity into the three competing visions: communism, supremacist nationalism, and capitalism. After two horrific world wars and the triumph of nation-state formation across the world, capitalism remains as the last surviving version of modernity. Capitalism is then reinvigorated by the increasing use of social networking tools, which popularizes both "traditional" religious and cultural ideas and constitutional nationalism in authoritarian states.

# Chapter Organization and Structure

Each part of the book addresses the role of change and innovation on a broad scale in a particular time and/or region, and each chapter contains different levels of exploration to examine the principal features of particular cultural or national areas and how each affects, and is affected by, the patterns of origins, interactions, and adaptations:

- *Geography and the Environment*: The relationship between human beings and the geography and environment of the places they inhabit is among the most basic factors in understanding human societies. In this chapter segment, therefore, the topics under investigation involve the natural environment of a particular region and the general conditions affecting change and innovation. Climatic conditions, earthquakes, tsunamis, volcanic eruptions, outbreaks of disease, and so forth all have obvious effects on how humans react to the challenge of survival. The initial portions of chapters introducing new regions for study therefore include environmental and geographical overviews, which are revisited and expanded in later chapters as necessary. The larger issues of how decisive the impact of geography on the development of human societies is—as in the commonly asked question "Is geography destiny?"—are also examined here.
- *Political Developments*: In this segment, we ponder such questions as how rulers and their supporters wield political and military power. How do different political traditions develop in different areas? How do states expand, and why? How do different political arrangements attempt to strike a balance between the rulers and the ruled? How and why are political innovations transmitted to other societies? Why do societies accept or reject such innovations from the outside? Are there discernible patterns in the development of kingdoms or empires or nation-states?

- *Economic and Social Developments*: The relationship between economics and the structures and workings of societies has long been regarded as crucial by historians and social scientists. But what patterns, if any, emerge in how these relationships develop and function among different cultures? This segment explores such questions as the following: What role does economics play in the dynamics of change and continuity? What, for example, happens in agrarian societies when merchant classes develop? How does the accumulation of wealth lead to social hierarchy? What forms do these hierarchies take? How do societies formally and informally try to regulate wealth and poverty? How are economic conditions reflected in family life and gender relations? Are there patterns that reflect the varying social positions of men and women that are characteristic of certain economic and social institutions? How are these in turn affected by different cultural practices?
- *Intellectual, Religious, and Cultural Aspects*: Finally, we consider it vital to include an examination dealing in some depth with the way people understood their existence and life during each period. Clearly, intellectual innovation—the generation of new ideas—lies at the heart of the changes we have singled out as pivotal in the patterns of origins, interactions, and adaptations that form the heart of this text. Beyond this, those areas concerned with the search for and construction of meaning—particularly religion, the arts, philosophy, and science—not only reflect shifting perspectives but also, in many cases, play a leading role in determining the course of events within each form of society. All of these facets of intellectual life are in turn manifested in new perspectives and representations in the cultural life of a society.

# Features

- **Seeing Patterns/Thinking Through Patterns:** Successful history teachers often employ recursive, even reiterative, techniques in the classroom to help students more clearly perceive patterns. In a similar fashion, "Seeing Patterns" and "Thinking Through Patterns" use a question–discussion format in each chapter to pose several broad questions ("Seeing Patterns") as advance organizers for key themes, which are then matched up with short essays at the end ("Thinking Through Patterns") that examine these same questions in a sophisticated yet student-friendly fashion. Instructors who have class-tested *Patterns of World History* report that the "Thinking Through Patterns" essays, designed to foster discussion, also serve as excellent models for student writing.

- **Patterns Up Close:** Since students frequently better apprehend macro-level patterns when they see their contours brought into sharper relief, "Patterns Up Close" essays in each chapter highlight a particular innovation that demonstrates origins, interactions, and adaptations in action. Spanning technological, social, political, intellectual, economic, and environmental developments, the "Patterns Up Close" essays combine text, visuals, and graphics to consider everything from the pepper trade to the guillotine.

- **Marginal Glossary:** To avoid the necessity of having to flip pages back and forth, definitions of words that the reader may not know, as well as of key terms, are set directly in the margin at the point where they are first introduced.

Today, more than ever, students and instructors are confronted by a vast welter of information on every conceivable subject. Beyond the ever-expanding print media, the Internet and the Web have opened hitherto unimaginable amounts of data to us. Despite such unprecedented access, however, all of us are too frequently overwhelmed by this undifferentiated—and all too often indigestible—mass. Nowhere is this more true than in world history, by definition the field within the historical profession with the broadest scope. Therefore, we think that an effort at synthesis—of narrative and analysis structured around a clear, accessible, widely applicable theme—is needed, an effort that seeks to explain critical patterns of the world's past behind the billions of bits of information accessible at the stroke of a key on a computer keyboard. We hope this text, in tracing the lines of transformative ideas and things that left their patterns deeply imprinted into the canvas of world history, will provide such a synthesis.

# Changes to the Second Edition

**Streamlined narrative** To facilitate accessibility, we have shortened the overall length of the book by 20 percent. This reduction has not come at the expense of discarding essential topics. Instead, we have tightened the narrative, focusing even more on key concepts and (with the guidance of reviewers) discarding extraneous examples.

**Revised and enhanced coverage of the Atlantic World** In response to feedback from both users and nonusers of the text, we have substantially improved Part Five's coverage of the Atlantic World. The former Chapter 27, "Creoles and Caudillos," is now Chapter 23, allowing for a seamless continuation with the discussion of Atlantic revolutions in Chapter 22. "Industrialization and its Discontents," which formerly was Chapter 23, is now Chapter 26, while the former Chapter 26, "The New Imperialism," is now Chapter 27. The overall result of these organizational changes is to substantially enhance the book's coverage of Latin America in the eighteenth and nineteenth centuries. We are indebted to the guidance, scholarship, and close reading of the revised chapters in Part Five provided by Evan Ward of Brigham Young University.

**NEW FEATURE "Against the Grain"** At the end of each chapter, these brief narratives illustrate how the discernment of patterns allows for an appreciation of alternatives, even contradictions, brought about by creative human agency. Topics range from visionaries who challenged dominant religious patterns, including Akhenaten in ancient Egypt and the Cathars in medieval Europe; women who found agency, voice, and even power within patriarchal societies, such as Empress Wu in seventh-century China or Juana Inés de la Cruz in seventeenth-century Mexico; and agitators who fought for social and economic justice, including the outspoken critic of nineteenth-century British imperialism E. D. Morel and the fearless anti-apartheid movement led by the African National Congress.

**NEW FEATURE Pull quotes** The pages of the second edition are enlivened by pithy quotes from a diverse array of contemporaneous voices, lending both context and commentary to the main narrative.

- New **"Patterns Up Close" essays** New topics for this popular feature include recent discoveries about early human/Neanderthal interaction; Islamic influence on European Gothic architecture; comparisons of Byzantine and Islamic art; global innovations in cartography that fueled the age of exploration; the Harlem Renaissance and the African diaspora; and the Non-Aligned Movement.

In addition to the substantive reworking of Part Five, all chapters of *Patterns* have benefited from the thoughtful suggestions of reviewers as well as feedback from instructors who are teaching with the book. Recent discoveries about our past as well as the rapid pace at which our contemporary world is changing are also reflected in the second edition. Here are some of the key changes we made to other parts of the book:

**Part One** Chapter 1 has been revised to incorporate recent scientific discoveries about hominid origins, Asian hominid finds, and the human presence in Beringia. A new "Patterns Up Close" essay considers new evidence about the Neanderthals. In Chapter 2, we expanded discussions of gender roles in early agrarian societies. Chapter 3 takes an enhanced look at the controversy surrounding putative Indo-European migration.

**Part Two** Chapter 6 examines new discoveries by tropical archaeologists that have enhanced our understanding of early plant domestication. Chapter 7 includes a broader discussion of the origins of early Greek literature. Chapter 8 offers a more nuanced discussion of the role of women in Hinduism.

**Part Three** In Chapter 10, discussion of the origins of the Islamic religious civilization has been significantly revised and streamlined, affording both greater clarity and sharper detail; discussion of Eastern Christian civilization and the rise of Byzantium has been enhanced; and a new "Patterns Up Close" essay thoughtfully compares Byzantine icons and Islamic miniatures. In Chapter 11, the "Patterns Up Close" essay has been revised to emphasize the pattern of origins and interactions shaping Gothic cathedrals, especially with Islamic architecture. Chapter 12 includes a refined examination of our interpretation of Indian syncretism. And Chapter 14 considers interactions between Chinese traders and Swahili merchants.

**Part Four** Chapter 16 includes a new "Patterns Up Close" essay exploring the differences between Sunni and Shiite Islam. Chapter 17 has been restructured; it now begins with a discussion of Renaissance culture. In addition, the discussion of Copernicus's connection between the discovery of America and the heliocentric theory of the planetary system has been enhanced, and a new "Patterns Up Close" essay describes the tremendous advances in cartography made by many cultures. Chapter 18 now considers the resistance of Native American peoples to Spanish colonization. Chapter 20 streamlines the discussion of the founding of the Timurids.

**Part Five** In addition to the structural changes described above, Chapter 22 now includes a section on the Haitian Revolution, to emphasize its proper place within the modern constitutional revolutions; new discussions of Native Americans appear throughout. Chapter 23 begins with a new vignette; the entire chapter has been largely rewritten to emphasize the contributions of the indigenous and subaltern populations of Latin America to the process of independence. In Chapter 26, the segment on innovations in communication technology was relocated in order to emphasize their importance.

**Part Six** Chapter 29 now includes a segment on the Central Intelligence Agency, along with a map showing its global involvement in regime change. A new "Patterns Up Close" essay describes the importance of the Bandung Conference. To Chapter 30 we added material in the segment on the American civil rights movement to include civil rights for Native Americans and the gay rights movement. We have also revised the "Patterns Up Close" essay on the women's liberation movement to emphasize global dimensions of the feminist movement. Chapter 31 has been enlarged, to bring world history up to 2014, through sections on Egypt, Syria, Iraq, Nigeria, and the Central African Republic.

# Additional Learning Resources for *Patterns of World History*

**Dashboard:** Dashboard delivers quality content, tools, and assessments to track student progress in an intuitive, Web-based learning environment. Assessments are designed to accompany *Patterns of World History* and are automatically graded so instructors can easily check students' progress as they complete their assignments. The color-coded gradebook illustrates at a glance where students are succeeding and where they can improve so instructors can adapt lectures on the fly to student needs. Dashboard features a streamlined interface that connects instructors and students with the functions they perform most, and simplifies the learning experience by putting student progress first. All Dashboard content is engineered to work on mobile devices, including the iOS operating system. Our goal is to create a platform that is simple, informative, and mobile. Please contact your local Oxford University Press representative for a demonstration of Dashboard.

**Oxford First Source (www.oup.com/us/first-source):** Oxford First Source is an online database, with custom print capability, of primary source documents in world history. The continuously updated collection consists of approximately 300 documents, both textual and visual, selected and organized to complement any world history survey text. These documents cover a broad range of political, social, and cultural topics. The documents are indexed by date, title, subject, and region and are fully searchable. Each is accompanied by a headnote and study questions. Six-month access to Oxford First Source is free when bundled with *Patterns of World History*, or can be purchased standalone for $19.95. Please contact your local Oxford University Press representative for details.

**Asset Resource Center (ARC):** This online resource center, available to adopters of *Patterns of World History*, includes:

**Instructor's Resource Manual:** Includes, for each chapter, a detailed chapter outline, suggested lecture topics, learning objectives, map quizzes, geography exercises, classroom activities, "Patterns Up Close" activities, "Seeing Patterns and Making Connections" activities, "Against the Grain" exercises, biographical sketches, and suggested Web resources and digital media files. Also includes for each chapter approximately 40 multiple-choice, short-answer, true-or-false, and fill-in-the-blank as well as approximately 10 essay questions.

**PowerPoints and Computerized Testbank:** Includes PowerPoint slides and JPEG and PDF files for all the maps and photos in the text, an additional 400 map files from *The Oxford Atlas of World History*, and approximately 250 additional PowerPoint-based slides organized by theme and topic. Also includes approximately 1,500 questions that can be customized by the instructor.

# Additional Resources

- *Sources in Patterns of World History:* **Volume 1: To 1600:** Completely revised, it includes approximately 75 text and visual sources in world history, organized by the chapter organization of *Patterns of World History*. Each source is accompanied by a headnote and reading questions.
- *Sources in Patterns of World History:* **Volume 2: Since 1400:** Completely revised, it includes approximately 90 text and visual sources in world history, organized by the chapter organization of *Patterns of World History*. Each source is accompanied by a headnote and reading questions.
- *Mapping Patterns of World History,* **Volume 1: To 1600:** Includes approximately 50 full-color maps, each accompanied by a brief headnote, as well as Concept Map exercises.
- *Mapping Patterns of World History,* **Volume 2: Since 1400:** Includes approximately 50 full-color maps, each accompanied by a brief headnote, as well as Concept Map exercises.
- **Companion Website (www.oup.com/us/von sivers):** Includes quizzes, flashcards, map exercises, and links to YouTube videos.
- **E-book for Patterns of World History:** E-books of all the volumes are available for purchase at www.coursesmart.com.

# Bundling Options

*Patterns of World History* can be bundled at a significant discount with any of the titles in the popular Very

Short Introductions or Oxford World's Classics series, as well as other titles from the Higher Education division world history catalog (www.oup.com/us/catalog/he). Please contact your OUP representative for details.

# Acknowledgments

Throughout the course of writing, revising, and preparing *Patterns of World History* for publication we have benefited from the guidance and professionalism accorded us by all levels of the staff at Oxford University Press. John Challice, vice president and publisher, had faith in the inherent worth of our project from the outset and provided the initial impetus to move forward. Meg Botteon guided us through the revisions and added a final polish, often helping us with substantive suggestions. Lynn Luecken carried out the thankless task of assembling the manuscript and did so with generosity and good cheer, helping us with many details in the final manuscript. Picture researcher Francelle Carapetyan diligently tracked down every photo request despite the sometimes sketchy sources we provided, Ben Sadock copyedited the manuscript with meticulous attention to detail, and Theresa Stockton steered us through the intricacies of production with the stoicism of a saint.

Most of all, we owe a special debt of gratitude to Charles Cavaliere, our editor. Charles took on the daunting task of directing the literary enterprise at a critical point in the book's career. He pushed this project to its successful completion, accelerated its schedule, and used a combination of flattery and hard-nosed tactics to make sure we stayed the course. His greatest contribution, however, is in the way he refined our original vision for the book with several important adjustments that clarified its latent possibilities. From the maps to the photos to the special features, Charles's high standards and concern for detail are evident on every page.

Developing a book like *Patterns of World History* is an ambitious project, a collaborative venture in which authors and editors benefit from the feedback provided by a team of outside readers and consultants. We gratefully acknowledge the advice that the many reviewers, focus group participants, and class testers (including their students) shared with us along the way. We tried to implement all of the excellent suggestions.

We owe a special debt of thanks to Evan R. Ward, who provided invaluable guidance for the revision of the coverage of Latin America and the Caribbean in Part 5, and to Jonathan S. Perry, who deftly assembled the documents for the "with Sources" version of *Patterns*. Of course, any errors of fact or interpretation that remain are solely our own.

## Reviewers of the Second Edition

Michael Broyles, Macomb Community College Center Campus

Richard Garlitz, University of Tennessee at Martin

Marjorie L. Hilton, Murray State University

Ellen J. Jenkins, Arkansas Tech University

Michael Johnson, Northwest Arkansas Community College

Anthony Makowski, Delaware County Community College

Mary Jane Maxwell, Green Mountain College

Jason McCollom, University of Arkansas

Eva M. Mehl, University of North Carolina, Wilmington

George S. Pabis, Georgia Perimeter College

David Pizzo, Murray State University

Brian M. Puaca, Christopher Newport University

Jason Ripper, Everett Community College

Kira Robison, University of Alabama, Huntsville

Chad Ross, East Carolina University

Casey Schmitt, College of William and Mary

Jonathan Seitz, Drexel University

Teshale Tibebu, Temple University

Annamarie Vallis, California State University, Fresno

Gilmar Visoni, Queensborough Community College

Evan R. Ward, Brigham Young University

James Weiss, Salem State University

## Reviewers of the First Edition

Stephanie Ballenger, Central Washington University

Alan Baumler, Indiana University of Pennsylvania

Robert Blackey, California State University

Robert Bond, San Diego Mesa College

Mauricio Borrero, St. John's University

Linda Bregstein-Scherr, Mercer County Community College

Scott Breuninger, University of South Dakota

Paul Brians, Washington State University

Gayle K. Brunelle, California State University, Fullerton

James De Lorenzi, City University of New York, John Jay College

Jennifer Kolpacoff Deane, University of Minnesota, Morris

Andrew D. Devenney, Grand Valley State University

Francis A. Dutra, University of California, Santa Barbara

Jeffrey Dym, Sacramento State University

Jennifer C. Edwards, Manhattan College

Lisa M. Edwards, University of Massachusetts Lowell

Charles T. Evans, Northern Virginia Community College

Christopher Ferguson, Auburn University

Scott Fritz, Western New Mexico State University

Arturo Giraldez, University of the Pacific

Candace Gregory-Abbott, California State University, Sacramento

Derek Heng, Ohio State University

Eric Hetherington, New Jersey Institute of Technology

Laura J. Hilton, Muskingum University

Elizabeth J. Houseman, State University of New York at Brockport

Hung-yok Ip, Oregon State University

Geoffrey Jensen, University of Arkansas

Roger E. Kanet, University of Miami

Kelly Kennington, Auburn University

Amelia M. Kiddle, University of Arizona

Frederic Krome, University of Cincinnati Clermont College

Mark W. Lentz, University of Louisiana, Lafayette

Heather Lucas, Georgia Perimeter College

Susan Mattern, University of Georgia

Susan A. Maurer, Nassau Community College

Jason McCollom, University of Arkansas

Douglas T. McGetchin, Florida Atlantic University

Stephen Morillo, Wabash College

Carolyn Neel, Arkansas Tech University

Kenneth J. Orosz, Buffalo State College

Alice K. Pate, Columbus State University

Patrick M. Patterson, Honolulu Community College

Daniel Pope, University of Oregon

G. David Price, Santa Fe College

Michael Redman, University of Louisville

Leah Renold, Texas State University

Jeremy Rich, Middle Tennessee State University

Jason Ripper, Everett Community College

Chad Ross, East Carolina University

Nana Yaw B. Sapong, Southern Illinois University

Daniel Sarefield, Fitchburg State College

Claire Schen, State University of New York, Buffalo

Robert C. Schwaller, University of North Carolina at Charlotte

George Sochan, Bowie State University

Ramya Sreenivasan, State University of New York, Buffalo

John Stanley, Kutztown University

Vladimir Steffel, Ohio State University

Anthony J. Steinhoff, University of Tennessee at Chattanooga

Micheal Tarver, Arkansas Tech University

Shane Tomashot, Georgia State University

Kate Transchel, California State University, Chico

Melanie Tubbs, Arkansas Tech University

Andrew Wackerfuss, Georgetown University

Evan R. Ward, Brigham Young University

Joseph K. S. Yick, Texas State University

Please let us know your experiences with *Patterns of World History* so that we may improve it in future editions. We welcome your comments and suggestions.

Peter von Sivers
pv4910@xmission.com

Charles A. Desnoyers
desnoyer@lasalle.edu

George B. Stow
gbsgeorge@aol.com

# Note on Dates and Spellings

In keeping with widespread practice among world historians, we use "BCE" and "CE" to date events and the phrase "years ago" to describe developments from the remote past.

The transliteration of Middle Eastern words has been adjusted as much as possible to the English alphabet. Therefore, long vowels are not emphasized. The consonants specific to Arabic (alif, dhal, ha, sad, dad, ta, za, ʿayn, ghayn, and qaf) are either not indicated or rendered with common English letters. A similar procedure is followed for Farsi. Turkish words follow the alphabet reform of 1929, which adds the following letters to the Western alphabet or modifies their pronunciation: *c* (pronounced "j"), *ç* (pronounced "tsh"), *ğ* (not pronounced but lengthening of preceding vowel), *ı* ("i" without dot, pronunciation close to short e), *i/İ* ("i" with dot, including in caps), *ö* (no English equivalent), *ş* ("sh"), and *ü* (no English equivalent). The spelling of common contemporary Middle Eastern and Islamic terms follows daily press usage (which, however, is not completely uniform). Examples are "al-Qaeda," "Quran," and "Sharia."

The system used in rendering the sounds of Mandarin Chinese—the northern Chinese dialect that has become in effect the national spoken language in China and Taiwan—into English in this book is *hanyu pinyin*, usually given as simply pinyin. This is the official romanization system of the People's Republic of China and has also become the standard outside of Taiwan, Republic of China. Most syllables are pronounced as they would be in English, with the exception of the letter *q*, which has an aspirated "ch" sound; ch itself has a less aspirated "ch" sound. *Zh* carries a hard "j" and *j* a soft, English-style "j." Some syllables also are pronounced—particularly in the regions around Beijing—with a retroflex r so that the syllable *shi*, for example, carries a pronunciation closer to "shir." Finally, the letter *r* in the *pinyin* system has no direct English equivalent, but an approximation may be had by combining the sounds of "r" and "j."

Japanese terms have been romanized according to a modification of the Hepburn system. The letter *g* is always hard; vowels are handled as they are in Italian—*e*, for example, carries a sound like "ay." We have not, however, included diacritical markings to indicate long vowel sounds for *u* or *o*. Where necessary, these have been indicated in the pronunciation guides.

For Korean terms, we have used a variation of the McCune-Reischauer system, which remains the standard romanization scheme for Korean words used in English academic writing, but eliminated any diacritical markings. Here again, the vowel sounds are pronounced more or less like those of Italian and the consonants, like those of English.

For Vietnamese words, we have used standard renditions based on the modern Quốc Ngu ("national language") system in use in Vietnam today. The system was developed by Jesuit missionaries and is based on the Portuguese alphabet. Once more, we have avoided diacritical marks, and the reader should follow the pronunciation guides for approximations of Vietnamese terms.

Latin American terms (Spanish, Nahua, or Quechua) generally follow local usage, including accents, except where they are Anglicized, per the *Oxford English Dictionary*. Thus, the Spanish-Quechua word "Tiahuanacu" becomes the Anglicized word "Tiwanaku."

We use the terms "Native American" and "Indian" interchangeably to refer to the peoples of the Americas in the pre-Columbian period and "Amerindian" in our coverage of Latin America since independence.

In keeping with widely recognized practice among paleontologists and other scholars of the deep past, we use the term "hominins" in Chapter 1 to emphasize their greater remoteness from apes and proximity to modern humans.

Phonetic spellings often follow the first appearance of a non-English word whose pronunciation may be unclear to the reader. We have followed the rules for capitalization per *The Chicago Manual of Style*.

# About the Authors

**Peter von Sivers** is associate professor of Middle Eastern history at the University of Utah. He has previously taught at UCLA, Northwestern University, the University of Paris VII (Vincennes), and the University of Munich. He has also served as chair of the Joint Committee of the Near and Middle East, Social Science Research Council, New York, 1982–1985; editor of the *International Journal of Middle East Studies*, 1985–1989; member of the board of directors of the Middle East Studies Association of North America, 1987–1990; and chair of the SAT II World History Test Development Community of the Educational Testing Service, Princeton, NJ, 1991–1994. His publications include *Caliphate, Kingdom, and Decline: The Political Theory of Ibn Khaldun* (1968, in German), several edited books, and three dozen peer-reviewed chapters and articles on Middle Eastern and North African history, as well as world history. He received his Dr. phil. from the University of Munich.

**Charles A. Desnoyers** is professor of history and director of Asian Studies at La Salle University in Philadelphia. He has previously taught at Temple University, Villanova University, and Pennsylvania State University. In addition to serving as History Department chair from 1999–2007, he was a founder and long-time director of the Greater Philadelphia Asian Studies Consortium, and president (2011–2012) of the Mid-Atlantic Region Association for Asian Studies. He has served as a reader, table leader, and question writer for the AP European and World History exams. He is a lifetime member of the World History Association and served as editor of the organization's *Bulletin* from 1995–2001. In addition to numerous articles in peer-reviewed and general publications, his work includes *A Journey to the East: Li Gui's "A New Account of a Trip Around the Globe"* (2004, University of Michigan Press). He received his PhD from Temple University.

**George B. Stow** is professor of ancient and medieval history and director of the graduate program in history at La Salle University, Philadelphia. His teaching experience embraces a variety of undergraduate and graduate courses in ancient Greece and Rome, medieval England, and world history, and he has been awarded the Lindback Distinguished Teaching Award. Professor Stow is a member of the Medieval Academy of America and a Fellow of the Royal Historical Society. He is the recipient of a National Defense Education Act Title IV Fellowship, a Woodrow Wilson Foundation Fellowship, and research grants from the American Philosophical Society and La Salle University. His publications include a critical edition of a fourteenth-century monastic chronicle, *Historia Vitae et Regni Ricardi Secundi* (University of Pennsylvania Press, 1977), as well as numerous articles and reviews in scholarly journals including *Speculum*, *The English Historical Review*, the *Journal of Medieval History*, the *American Historical Review*, and several others. He received his PhD from the University of Illinois.

# Patterns of
# World History

# PART ONE

# From Human Origins to Early Agricultural Centers

## PREHISTORY–600 BCE

**W**orld history is the discipline that tells us what humans had in common as they evolved both materially and mentally from prehistory to the present. When we study these common patterns, we find that the first period of world history (prehistory–600 BCE) can be subdivided into three wide-ranging phases, which we will discuss very broadly in this part-opening essay. We will return to these same patterns as they develop—and discover new, more complex patterns—in Chapters 1–5.

### The Origins of Modern Humanity

The first phase (6.5 million years ago–8500 BCE) began with the origins and evolution of humanity in Africa. After about 5.5 million years, around 80,000–60,000 BCE, groups of modern humans left Africa and began carrying their civilization of stone tools, shell jewelry, figurines, carvings, rock paintings, and religious symbols across the entire world.

Technologically, the modern humans who left Africa had already acquired the skills to make tools from stone, bone, and wood. Mentally, they were also creating artifacts to which they attributed symbolic meaning, such as seashell necklaces and stone surfaces incised with geometric figures. The tools and artifacts of our earliest ancestors were obviously far less sophisticated than ours today. But they nevertheless defined a fully human civilization that spread across the globe—until the last ice age (32,000–12,000 years ago) put a stop to much of their interactions. Separated by impenetrable ice or desert barriers and existing without much contact for thousands of years, modern human groups developed their own distinct regional technologies and cultures.

Wherever our forager forebears were, they organized themselves into larger lineage societies with shared initiation rites and members who mediated the material and spiritual worlds. Even the stone tools, jewelry, figurines, and rock images displayed remarkable similarities across this region. In short, African-originated material technology and mental culture dominated the world.

**Origins, Interactions, and Adaptations**

| | |
|---|---|
| **7 million years ago**<br>Toumaï, oldest possibly hominin fossil to date | **15,500 years ago**<br>Earliest archaeological evidence of humans in the Americas |
| **200,000 years ago**<br>*Homo sapiens*, or modern human, emerges in East Africa | **9500 BCE**<br>End of last ice age |

## The Origins of Agricultural Centers

The second phase (8500–3300 BCE) began once the global climate normalized, after the "great thaw," when agricultural centers originated in the Middle East, south and east Asia, and the Americas. In the Middle East, foragers resumed their migratory patterns, carrying their languages into regions opened up by receding glaciers and deserts. Between 8500 and 7000 BCE, foragers settled in permanent villages situated below mountain ranges, where seasonal runoff water supported rich forests and meadows. They grew skilled in the collection of plant seeds, which they developed, through selective breeding, into domesticated wheat, barley, rice, millet, and corn. They also captured young animals and domesticated them in their houses and pens for their meat, milk, and hair.

Some of the early hill farmers moved into river valleys and deltas, where they expanded irrigation systems, supporting the rise of cities and kingdoms. The first agrarian-urban centers of the Middle East, India, China, and the Americas originated in irrigated river valleys between 3500 and 2500 BCE. Structured societies emerged in which kings, claiming divine mandates, and administrative and military ruling classes governed craftspeople and farmers.

## The Origins of Empires

In the third phase, people outside the Eurasian agrarian centers adapted to agriculture through interaction with the agrarian-urban centers (3300–600 BCE). Steppe peoples, who controlled the mines containing the raw materials for making bronze alloys, used their horses and bronze weapons to migrate to, conquer, or establish new, distant kingdoms. Through their migrations or conquests, the nomadic steppe peoples of Europe and central Asia connected the three agrarian centers of the Middle East, India, and China. A pattern was established whereby the three centers were continuously adapting to each other's technological and cultural achievements, with steppe nomads functioning as their intermediaries.

From 1100 BCE onward the three Asian agrarian centers gradually replaced bronze with a cheaper metal, iron, as the principal material for weapons and tools. As a result, political and military competitiveness among kingdoms escalated dramatically. The first empires—that is, assemblages of conquered kingdoms under a king-of-kings or emperor—appeared; for example, the Neo-Assyrian Empire in the Middle East. Meanwhile, in some regions of the more sparsely populated continents of Africa and the Americas, agrarian centers grew more slowly, from villages to towns and, in a few places, even small kingdoms.

# Thinking Like a World Historian

▶ What is the best way to describe the three early phases of world history?

▶ Why and how do we differentiate "modern" humans from earlier ancestors?

▶ What adaptations were necessary to improve agriculture? How did improvements in agriculture affect the development of society?

▶ What adaptations changed the methods of early warfare? How did developments in warfare affect regional interactions among civilizations?

▶ How did regional interactions with agricultural centers give rise to early kingdoms?

**8500 BCE**
Beginnings of agriculture in Fertile Crescent

**ca. 7000 BCE**
First evidence of rice cultivation in Yangzi valley

**3000 BCE–200 CE**
Lapita cultural complex in western Pacific

**ca. 2700 BCE**
First American city at Caral-Supé in Peru

**2500–1700 BCE**
Flourishing of Harappan culture in Indus River valley, India

**1766–1122 BCE**
Traditional dates for the Shang dynasty

**1650 BCE**
Hittite Empire

**1200 BCE**
Beginning of Iron Age

**750–600 BCE**
Greek city-states: from aristocrats to citizen assemblies

# Chapter 1 PREHISTORY–10,000 BCE
# The African Origins of Humanity

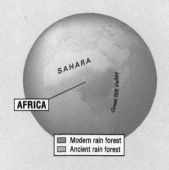

**W**hen Donald Johanson awoke in his tent on the morning of November 30, 1974, he felt that this was the day on which something "terrific" might happen. He and Tom Gray got into their Land Rover and drove for about a half hour to "locality 162" at Hadar in the Afar desert of Ethiopia in northeastern Africa. Once there, the two men walked about, checking the ground carefully for fossils of human predecessors. Members of the expedition had gone over the ground twice before but failed to find anything beyond animal bones.

After 2 hours of fruitless searching, with the temperature now soaring to 110 degrees Fahrenheit, the two took a final glance at a gully the team had visited not long before. Amid the heat waves shimmering off the baked ground, Johanson found himself squinting at something out of place and called out, "That's a bit of a [hominin] arm." With growing excitement, he and Gray began to locate other bones nearby. "An unbelievable, impermissible thought flickered through my mind," Johanson remembered. "Suppose all these fitted together? Could they be parts of a single, extremely primitive skeleton? No such skeleton had ever been found—anywhere." The two raced back to the camp, sharing their excitement with the other scientists and local Afar workers. When night fell and the camp was rocking with joy, a tape recorder was playing the Beatles' song "Lucy in the Sky with Diamonds"; so fossil Hadar AL 288-1, dated to 3.2 million years ago, became known ever after as "Lucy."

*ABOVE:* **Satellite View Southward Across the African Rift Valley.**

Today, a quarter century later, Lucy is neither the oldest nor the most significant skeleton ever found. She remains the most famous, however. Many of the local people in the Afar region still think of Lucy as the ancestor of all humankind. Cafés in Ethiopia carry the name "Lossy" in her honor. Her image has appeared on stamps, and her name is a staple in crossword puzzles. For many people Lucy—the petite female buried for 3.2 million years in a sand bank on the edge of a former lake or stream—is all they know about human origins.

The story of Lucy provides our entry into the study of the origins and evolution of humankind. In the course of millions of years of interactions between cooling climates, more differentiated environments, and genetic changes favoring larger brains, splits among hominin lineages produced lines of early humans who could fashion at first simple, and later more sophisticated, stone tools. From among other lineages back in Africa, finally the line of anatomically and intellectually modern humans evolved who fashioned cultural artifacts such as jewelry, geometric figures cut into stone, and rock drawings. Once more, humans left Africa and settled the world, not only Eurasia but also Australia and the Americas. For the first time in the history of life on earth, a single species was no longer completely bound to the forces of evolution and its interplay between environment and genetics. These first modern humans had become *cultural beings*, by means of which they had acquired a measure of freedom from evolution: Instead of nature writing their history, they could create their own human history—the world history you are about to enter with this book.

## The Origins of Humanity

Becoming human was a long and arduous journey. In the interactions between climate, environment, and genes, every evolutionary step had to build successively on every preceding one so that *anatomically*, as well as *intellectually*, fully evolved modern humans could emerge in Africa about 100,000 years ago. Nothing in this journey was predetermined, but it was also not accidental, given what we know about the genetic architecture of human DNA. It is open-ended, as is the human history which followed the emergence of modern humans. Both evolution and history display recognizable patterns, but these patterns neither were preprogrammed nor occurred by happenstance—they included both predictable and spontaneous occurrences resulting from the constraints and opportunities offered by the interaction of climate, environment, and genes. As we will see throughout this book, however, history equally depends on human agency and its resulting actions. Human prehistory is significant for us today because, thanks to much work done by archaeologists and anthropologists, we are beginning to recognize the complexity of all that had to happen on our evolutionary path to make us fully human: to reach the point where we could become the active creators of our world.

## Seeing Patterns

▶ What made it possible for *Homo sapiens* to survive in a dangerous environment? Why is it difficult to imagine life as a prehistoric forager?

▶ Where did humans go when they left Africa, and what kinds of lives did they establish for themselves in the areas where they settled? Which were the most important social patterns that evolved, and how were the humans impacted by the worsening Ice Age?

▶ Why did early humans create cave paintings and figurines? Do these show patterns that can be interpreted?

**Hominins:** Forerunners of humans after genetically splitting from the chimpanzees.

## Hominins: No Longer Chimpanzees but Not Yet Human

Modern humans are the descendants of long lines of early human-like primates called **hominins**, which in the distant past lived in East Africa. The line of hominins split from that of the other apes sometime around 5 million years ago, but the fossil record is still too poor to allow definite conclusions. Equally unclear is the parentage among the 20 or so species of hominins coming thereafter, which paleo-anthropologists (as the archaeologists and researchers of fossils are called) have discovered so far. The fog begins to lift only around 1.8 million years ago, with the emergence of *Homo erectus*, the first hominin that left Africa and was adaptable to many new environments in Eurasia. It thus took some 3 million years of dead ends as well as environmentally more adaptable forerunners of humans to pave the way for the human species to emerge.

Many historians view the *prehistory* of humans as a field belonging to archaeologists and anthropologists. For these historians, *history* begins only with the rise of the first cities in Mesopotamia around 3500 BCE in which scribes created written documents. This view is unfortunate since historians routinely take the findings of scholars in other disciplines, such as archaeology, anthropology, climatology, geography, medicine, and sociology, into consideration when they write histories on topics after about 3500 BCE. Since written records, furthermore, are highly unreliable documents—subject to manipulation by human hand subsequent to their original production—historians regularly take recourse to the more reliable findings of other disciplines wherever they can. Indeed, in the twenty-first century historians with broad visions have pleaded persuasively for eliminating the artificial distinction between prehistory and history. They speak instead—as the medieval cultural historian Daniel Lord Smail does—of the "deep history" of humanity.

**Who Are Our Ancestors?**    The specific environmental and genetic interactions favorable for the split between hominin and other ape lines are complex. We know that changes in the climate between warm and cool cycles played a part, which were reflected in the African rain forest advancing and retreating. It is also known that it took about 1 million years, from 5 to 4 million years ago according to the genetic clock, and a fairly large population of 50,000–70,000 animals for the split between the chimpanzees in the ape line and the first hominins to begin and be completed. The genetic clock, however, is not only not beyond controversy; it is also not synchronized with the three oldest known tropical African fossils which seem to depart from the rest of the ape line. The Toumaï skull (7–6 million years old), Orrorin femurs (6.1–5.7 million years old), and Kaddaba teeth (5.8–5.4 million years) seem to indicate hominin features. But whether the three can be counted as having belonged to human ancestors is still fiercely debated.

Firmer ground on the road to humanity is reached with Ardi (*Ardipithecus ramidus*, 4.5–4.3 million years ago), a descendant of Kaddaba. If the genetic clock is correct, the members of this lineage lived on the hominin side of the chimpanzee–hominin split. In their home in the tropical rain forests and savannas of East Africa, their capability for straight-limbed tree-walking allowed them to move easily back and forth between these two environments. In the dense rain forest, most apes flexed their hind legs as they stood on branches, hanging on with

**Human Origins.** Donald Johanson with Lucy.

one hand to the tree while reaching with the other hand for fruits or for branches of the next tree to swing to. In the less dense savanna tree stands, hominins could lean over and reach farther by standing on straight legs. Ardis with their straight legs transferred their branch-walking to the ground, which allowed them to step out of the rain forest and walk upright in the savanna for extended periods. They thereby substantially increased their adaptability to a variety of environments, especially during dry periods when the rain forest shrank. Most other apes, by contrast, stayed on their traditional home turf of rain forest, where they learned how to knuckle-walk on the ground for short distances, between more distant trees.

Ardis apparently were not able yet to venture very far into drier environments. After only 200,000 years they were replaced by a different species, the **australopiths** (scientific name *Australopithecus*). These hominins date to 3.9–1.8 million years ago and were widespread, with hundreds of fossil sites ranging from Ethiopia to South Africa (see Map 1.1). We are fairly certain of these date ranges and regional distributions because of a couple of key paleoanthropological finds, which have been widely publicized: (1) a set of fossilized footprints uncovered in Kenya and (2) an almost complete skeleton found in Ethiopia, which has become known as

**Australopiths:**
Prehuman species of the genus *Australopithecus* that existed before those classed under the genus *Homo*.

| | | |
|---|---|---|
| **7–5.4 million years ago**<br>Toumaï, Orrorin, and Kaddaba, possibly hominin fossils | **4.5 million years ago**<br>Ardi hominins, first assumed human ancestor line | **1.8 million years ago**<br>*Homo erectus*, present in Asia and Africa |
| **5 million years ago**<br>Split of the chimpanzee–hominin lines, as indicated by the genetic clock | **4.2–1.8 million years ago**<br>Multiple lines of australopith hominins | |
| **200,000 years ago**<br>*Homo sapiens*, or modern human, emerges in East Africa | **60,000–50,000 years ago**<br>Modern humans migrate to Australia | **13,500–13,000 years ago**<br>Traditional assumption of human arrival in the Americas |
| **80,000–60,000 years ago**<br>Modern humans migrate from East Africa to Asia | **35,000 years ago**<br>Earliest evidence of modern humans in Europe and Siberia | **9,400–9,300 years ago**<br>"Spirit Cave mummy" and "Kennewick man" in the North American West |

"Lucy" (see the vignette at the beginning of the chapter). The footprints reveal how much improved the australopiths were as walkers on the ground, but they were still also very much at home in the rain forest.

**Bipedalism:** The first human characteristic of hominins, specifically, the ability to walk for short periods or distances on hind legs.

**Savanna:** Broken forests with interspersed bush and grasslands.

**Environmental Adaptability**  Improved upright walking, or **bipedalism**, became a key evolutionary advantage to hominins. Walking on two feet is more energy efficient than knuckle-walking and frees the arms to do something else. Being upright exposes a smaller body surface to the sun, a factor important for venturing out from the rain forest and **savanna** into the grasslands. Partaking of the plant resources available in these environments made hominins gradually more flexible than other apes, which were limited to their rain-forest habitat. On the one hand, the rain forest abounded with fruits and nuts, but on the other hand, the woodlands offered grasses and seeds. From the fossil record, it appears that by around 2.4 million years ago, hominins were able to move about equally in the diverse environments of rain forest, savanna, and grassland.

While all australopiths shared basic traits, they were about to become much more varied, primarily because of the new and different environments with which each line interacted. Scholars distinguish among about a dozen or so different australopith lines. In some, brain sizes did not increase much; others reached the volume of half of modern human brains. Indeed, early hominin adaptations to the changing world would later give rise to diverse human cultures; and, as we will see, such different human cultures would, in turn, have a profound effect on our human evolution. This pattern of early human adaptation and cultural diversity is of great importance to historical study because it gives the earliest indications of how humans differentiated themselves—and how they became who we are today.

**Oldowan toolmaking:** The earliest stone-carving technique, which consisted of splitting a stone into two, thereby producing sharp edges on both fragments. See also **Acheulian** and **Levallois toolmaking.**

**Paleolithic:** Old Stone Age, 2.5 million– 11,500 years ago.

**On the Threshold of Humanity**  As hominins moved more and more around in their forest, savanna, and grassland habitats, about 2.5 million years ago an australopith successor lineage (*Australopithecus garhi*) made a major evolutionary step forward. Improved brainpower enabled this lineage to make simple stone tools. Other, younger members of this lineage (*Homo habilis*) fashioned improved tools with sharper edges, called **Oldowan** tools (after the Olduvai region in the Tanzanian Great Rift Valley), with which meat could be removed from the carcasses of animals freshly killed by beasts of prey. Hominins, now able to broaden their diet from vegetarian foods to more or less regular meals of meat, became omnivores, partaking of a broader range of nutrition available in nature. The making of stone tools marks the beginning of the **Paleolithic**, or Old Stone Age, in prehistory, which lasted until about 11,500 years ago. During this time hominins, and later fully evolved humans, made increasingly varied and refined stone tools.

A cool, dry spell of the climate about 1.8 million years ago made mobility again very important. A new hominin line, *Homo erectus*, evolved that no longer climbed trees, was fully stabilized on its feet, and was capable of walking long distances. It could deal equally with the demands of rain forest, savanna, grasslands, and now also steppe habitats. It mastered the control of fire, apparently collecting it from lightning-caused wildfires, possibly 1.5–1.4 million years ago in Africa, as announced in 2004 on the basis of finds in South Africa and Kenya. Small groups of perhaps two dozen hominins, so scholars assume, formed camp groups,

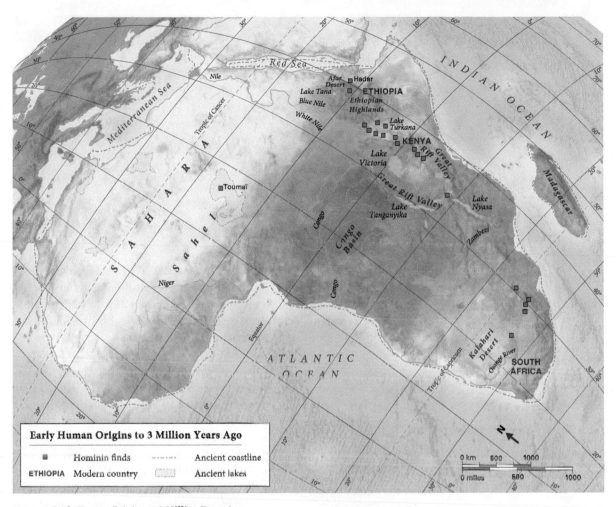

MAP 1.1 **Early Human Origins to 3 Million Years Ago.**

huddling around fires at cave entrances or under rock overhangs. The brain size of *H. erectus* was about half of that of the fully evolved *H. sapiens*. This new line of hominins was the first to adopt habits that we can recognize as human.

*H. erectus* was the creator of vastly improved stone tools in most places where the line lived. Instead of continuing to use the simple Oldowan stones with sharp edges, *H. erectus* created the new **Acheulian** [ah-SHOI-lee-yan] stone technology, around 1.8–1.6 million years ago. (This technology was named after Saint-Acheul, a suburb of Amiens in northern France where the first finds were made in the nineteenth century.) Acheulian tools were oval or pear-shaped hand axes cut with the help of hammer stones from larger cores, or they were one or more flakes split from cores. When the edges of these hand axes became dull, *H. erectus* split further, smaller flakes away to resharpen the edges. A simple visual comparison of Oldowan and Acheulian tools reveals how much the manual skills of early humans advanced in about a million years.

Fossils from around 1.8 million years ago indicate the almost simultaneous presence of *H. erectus* in East Africa, the Caucasus region in eastern Europe, and

**Acheulian toolmaking:** A technique which consisted of flaking a hard piece of rock (especially flint, chert, or obsidian) on both sides into a triangle-shaped hand axe, with cutting edges, a hand-held side, and a point.

**Acheulian Toolkit.** The preferred materials for Acheulian axes were obsidian, chert, and flint. The stone scraper on the right shows the Levallois technique, in which the edges of a stone are trimmed and flaked. Harpoons like the ones shown at the top right were made from reindeer antlers. On the left is a spear thrower from France that dates to about 14,000 years ago. Spear throwers gave hunters the ability to propel their missiles with surer aim. Note the horse-shaped handle.

Java in the southeast Asian archipelago. Stone tools in India, dated to 1.8–1.6 million years ago, can be similarly interpreted as indicators of the presence of *H. erectus* in the subcontinent. Given this astounding simultaneity, scholars are beginning to waver concerning the traditional "out of Africa" theory assumed for *H. erectus*. Until the early 2000s scholars assumed that it was a group of this line that led the first great wave of hominins leaving Africa for the Middle East and Asia. But now it seems possible that one or several of the predecessor lines accomplished this feat several hundred thousand years earlier.

The *H. erectus* fossils from the Dmanisi Cave in Georgia in the Caucasus, discovered in 2005, are of central importance for this revision of the theory of *H. erectus* as the first hominin out of Africa. The cave contained five sets of fully preserved skulls and bones, the anatomies of which were very different from each other. Had they been found individually in caves distant from each other, researchers would have viewed them as belonging to five different lines of early *Homo*. Instead, in an important article of 2013, an international team of researchers came to the conclusion not only that the five fossils belong to the same line but that numerous other fossils found in Africa as well as Asia and dated to around 1.8 million years ago are members of the same hominin line. The ancestor clearly came from Africa, but the line of *H. erectus* itself was perhaps of non-African origin.

**Flores "Hobbits"**   In 2003, shortly before the Dmanisi discoveries, an Australian–Indonesian team unearthed the partial fossils of 13 hominins in a cave on the island of Flores in the southern archipelago of Indonesia. The fossils were of beings that measured only 3–4 feet high, had brains no larger than those of chimpanzees or some australopiths, and were determined by carbon dating to have lived as recently as about 12,000 years ago. Soon after the discovery of the fossils the public dubbed them "hobbits" on account of their seeming similarities with the diminutive characters in J. R. R. Tolkien's *Lord of the Rings* novels. Scholars began to puzzle over the relationship of the "hobbits" with other hominin lines: Did they form a new line, and if not, from which existing lines did they descend? The jury is still out.

# Human Adaptations: From Africa to Eurasia and Australia

*H. erectus* was the ancestor of *H. sapiens* ("the wise man"), the species of modern humans to which we belong. Scholars are far from agreed, however, as to how many intermediate lineages existed between then and now. When *H. sapiens* emerged in East Africa about 200,000 years ago two characteristics distinguished this human being from its less evolved forerunners: (1) rapidly developing *technical skills* and (2) *cultural creativity*. These two characteristics represent a fundamental transformation of humans that placed them on a path toward full liberation from the determinism of nature. The timing of this liberation is still debated by scientists, but world historians generally assume that when *H. sapiens* created a recognizable culture in Africa, it became at least partially the free creator of a new direction in natural history.

## The African Origins of Human Culture

*H. sapiens* appeared around 200,000 years ago in East Africa. (The Latin term "*Homo sapiens*," meaning "wise man," will be used interchangeably with "modern human" in the remainder of this chapter.) The oldest specimen discovered so far is a fossil discovered in 1967 in Ethiopia and dated in 2005 to 195,000 years ago. The archaeological record documenting modern humans in Africa is still spotty, but the 17 sites containing bone and skull remnants of *H. sapiens* as well as a half dozen sites with human artifacts allow for at least one important conclusion: *H. sapiens*, in a process of gradual development in Africa, became physically and intellectually fully human, capable of the basics of culture. While humans continued to remain subject to the natural interaction between environment and genes, requiring constant updates in adaptation, culture gave them the freedom to accept and reject—a completely new dimension largely independent from nature.

**Livelihood**    Early hominins, as discussed earlier, did not hunt; they scavenged meat from animals killed and only partially eaten by predators. Alternatively, hominins purposely followed predators and chased them away after the kill. Stone scrapers, once invented, greatly facilitated the separation of meat from carcasses. An elusive post–*H. erectus* line introduced spears in the form of sharpened sticks some 400,000 years ago and thus allowed the transition from scavenging to hunting. Really effective spears had to await *H. sapiens* as the creator of the much refined new stoneworking technique, the **Levallois** [le-val-WAH], derived from the name of a suburb of Paris, France, where in the nineteenth century the first spear points were found. With this technique, a craftsperson chipped off small flakes from the edges of a prepared stone core and then hammered a larger flake—flat on the bottom, domed on the top, and sharpened by the small flakes around the

**Levallois toolmaking:** A stone technique where stone workers first shaped a hard rock into a cylinder or cone.

edge—from the center of the core, leaving a more or less deep indentation in the spent core. These center flakes could be as large as hand axes and meat cutters or as small as spear points. The appearance of spear points and increasingly large numbers of animal bones in the archaeological sites was an indicator that *H. sapiens* was emerging as an efficient hunter of animals. The hunt, requiring strength as well as endurance, tended to be the province of males—and remained a prestige occupation for much of human history. But it provided no more than a supplement to *H. sapiens'* nutrition.

The combination of the male-dominated hunt with the communal gathering of vegetal foods defines what is called "forager society." Foraging, sometimes called "hunting and gathering," was the dominant pattern of human history for the longest period—several hundred thousand years. It is also the least documented period, requiring for its understanding a combination of archaeology with the anthropological insights gained from observation of surviving foraging societies in the nineteenth and twentieth centuries. Thus, the descriptions of such societies we offer are unavoidably somewhat speculative.

*H. sapiens* continued to live in sheltered places provided by cave entrances and rock overhangs, the source of the popular stereotype of the "caveman." But there were also campsites with hut-like shelters made from branches. Clothing consisted of skins and furs acquired through hunting and slung around the body. Hearths, in which *H. sapiens* could build fires at will, served as places for the roasting of meat or the provision of warmth during cold nights. Anthropological studies suggest that extended families congregated around the hearths to groom each other or give each other comfort and companionship. In the vicinity of the campsite, a dozen or so dispersed families were in touch with one another, forming a clan, among which sexual partners were chosen.

Around 120,000 years ago, food gathering and preparation in the camps appear to have become considerably more varied. *H. sapiens* began to include shellfish collected on beaches and in lagoons in their diets. A little later, humans began catching fish on the coasts and in the lakes and rivers of Africa, using tools carved from bone, such as hooks and barbed points mounted on spears. With the help of grindstones, men and women pulverized hard seeds for consumption or storage. Plaster-lined storage pits appeared in the camps, as did separate refuse dumps. And as the settlements became more numerous, trade networks sprang up, providing toolmakers with obsidian mined as far as 200 miles away. Obsidian is a glass-like hard rock found near volcanoes and therefore relatively rare, so it was much sought after. We may also see this initial period of trade as marking the beginning of thousands of years of increasing human *interaction*—a process vital to the transferring of cultural and technological innovation among human groups.

**Gender Relations**    A central element in human culture is the relationship between men and women. Unfortunately, archaeology is unable to reveal anything decisive about this relationship in Paleolithic forager society. Obviously, the roles of men and women were less specialized among foragers than in agrarian–urban society: Males and females spent most of their time collecting and preparing vegetal foods together, and the male-dominated hunt was a supplemental occupation. But how much these occupations furthered a male–female balance or allowed for one of the two genders to become dominant is not easy to determine.

With the rise of feminism in academia scholars revived the idea, popular in the nineteenth century, of an early female-centered society. Marija Gimbutas (1921–1994), a Lithuanian-born archaeologist, published several books in the 1970s and 80s on what she assumed was a "matristic" society in Russia prior to 4500 BCE. This society, so she asserted, was egalitarian, peaceful, and goddess-oriented. It was by this time agrarian, but by implication matristic culture was assumed to have had deep roots in the preceding forager stage of human life. In her view, aggressive, warlike male dominance came about only with the rise of horseback-riding herders from the southern Russian steppes who were bent on conquest.

Other anthropologists, instead, assumed that male dominance began at about the same time that warring kingdoms emerged in the Middle East. War captives became slaves and elaborate hierarchies emerged in which women, in turn, found themselves relegated to inferior positions. However the origins of patriarchy are explained, there is little controversy over its connection with agrarian–urban life. What came before, however, and was prevalent during the Paleolithic forager period of human history is impossible to determine one way or the other. While patriarchy was part and parcel of the agrarian–urban pattern, what we know of the preceding forager society so far does not indicate a prevalence of matriarchy. In African Paleolithic forager society, females and males differed in their functions but not so decisively that the one or the other could easily become dominant.

**Creation of Symbols**    Parallel to the development of foraging, hunting, and beginning gender roles, there were also first signs of a development of *H. sapiens'* mental life. Activity in the camps expanded from the craftsmanship of tools to that of nonutilitarian objects. This expansion was perhaps the decisive step with which *H. sapiens* left the worlds of animals and other early humans behind and became truly modern. Around 135,000 years ago, humans in what is today Morocco in northwest Africa took seashells and fragments of ostrich eggshell, perforated them, and strung them on leather strips as pendants and necklaces. The significance of this step cannot be overemphasized. By themselves, seashells and ostrich eggshells are natural objects of no particular distinction, but as jewelry they have the unique meaning of beauty for their wearer: In the form of jewelry they are *symbols*, which are clearly distinct from shells found as objects in nature.

Jewelry is more than the material it is made of; its beauty gives it its distinction and makes it a symbol of whatever human emotions it is designed to express. *H. sapiens* was the first and only being that did not think only in the concrete, practical terms of toolmaking but also in *abstract* symbolic terms by using something to express something else, such as jewelry for feelings. This vital transformation may be seen as the root of the human capacity to conceptualize and, with it, the foundation of art, religion, philosophy, science, and all other intellectual pursuits.

Archaeological examples for the emergence of abstract symbolic thinking in Africa are not yet very numerous. But taken together they powerfully suggest an intellectual modernity emerging to match the anatomical modernity of African *H. sapiens*. From about 90,000 years ago, for example, we begin to see grave sites, indicators of reflection on the significance of life, death, ancestral dignity, and generational continuity. Humans added jewelry as the preferred grave gift, suggesting the contemplation of an afterlife or spirit world.

**Apollo 11 Cave, Namibia.**
A rhinoceros depicted on a stone slab, from about 59,000–23,000 years ago, making it contemporary with Australian and European rock art. Together with the Blombos Cave ochre, this artwork is evidence of early humans' ability to create symbols.

Even more recognizably abstract are the early symbols appearing on a 70,000-year-old small piece of ochre excavated in 1991 from Blombos Cave and on 60,000-year-old ostrich eggshell fragments excavated in 1996 from Diepkloof Rock Shelter, both in South Africa. They display geometrically arranged engravings, the significance of which is unknown. Ochre is a soft, reddish form of rock easily ground into powder and as such often found as a gift in prehistoric graves, symbolizing blood with its power of life. Ostrich eggshells served as containers or flasks which could be adorned with engravings similar to etchings on crystal. Even today, engravings or etchings distinguish artistically sophisticate crystal from ordinary glass containers.

Finally, a small stone plaque from Apollo 11 Cave in Namibia discovered in 1969–1972, containing the image of a rhinoceros, is of particular importance for the appreciation of the African origin of *H. sapiens*. The plaque is estimated to be 23,000 years old but, according to some scholars, could date to as far back as 65,000 years ago, if measured by the age of strata found on top of the plaque. If the latter age is true, this would be humanity's oldest pictorial representation found to date. Collectively, these examples can be taken as a confirmation of *H. sapiens* not only as a technically versatile toolmaker but also as the one animal capable of creating symbols that signify something beyond the materials from which they were made.

**Migration from Africa**    Once the *H. sapiens* lineage was fully equipped with practical skills and the foundations of culture, it was adaptable to almost any environment. Genetic research suggests that the first groups of modern humans left Africa between 80,000 and 60,000 years ago. Many scholars assume that these first groups left Africa for Asia by crossing the straits between Ethiopia and Yemen and between Oman and Iran. The members of this group, so it is thought, drifted like beachcombers along the coast, making their way to India, Malaysia, and Indonesia perhaps about 77,000 years ago. Some of their descendants seem to have kept on moving, reaching China about 70,000 years ago, sailing to Australia sometime after 60,000 years ago, and crossing from Korea over a then existing land bridge to Japan about 30,000 years ago. Eventually, modern humans from south Asia migrated northwestward to Europe and northeastward to Siberia, where they arrived around 44,000 years ago. The Siberian groups then made their way to Alaska in North America 16,000 years ago, completing the journey around the world in 70,000 years (see Map 1.2).

## Migration from South Asia to Australia

The migration of human groups from south Asia to Australia deserves a closer look within the context of foraging society as the original mode of human social organization. Australia was the only large world region where foraging remained dominant until the modern scientific–industrial age and, therefore, could be studied almost until today. Largely isolated from the rest of the world until the eighteenth

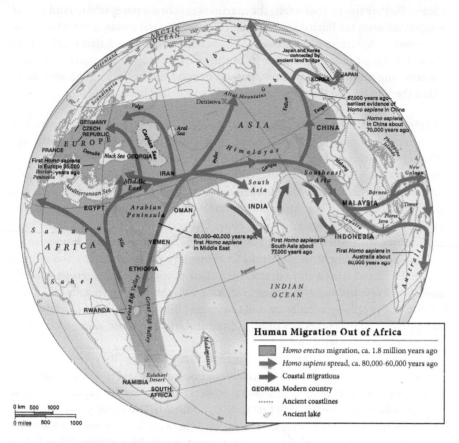

The map legend reads:

**Human Migration Out of Africa**

- *Homo erectus* migration, ca. 1.8 million years ago
- *Homo sapiens* spread, ca. 80,000–60,000 years ago
- Coastal migrations
- GEORGIA Modern country
- Ancient coastlines
- Ancient lake

MAP 1.2 Human Migration Out of Africa.

century, the Australian foragers developed a distinct culture of their own. But since they shared the same *H. sapiens* genes as their hunter-gatherer relatives on the Afro-Eurasian continent, the life patterns of both also remained fundamentally similar, in terms of foraging, social organization, and symbolical expression.

**Geography and Migration**   Although it is the smallest of the earth's continents, Australia extends across a variety of geographical zones. In the north, rain forest became dominant. In the east (today's eastern Australia), various mixtures of forest, savanna, and grassland evolved. The center and most of the west of the continent developed a mixture of grasslands, steppes, deserts, and lakes. The south (today's southeastern Australia and Tasmania) became temperate, with an almost South African or Mediterranean climate. Small pockets of mountain vegetation came into existence only in what are today the central parts of eastern Australia and southern Tasmania. They displayed geological formations and climate zones corresponding to those of Africa south of the Sahara. These geographical environments would become the homes to modern humans, who came originally from Africa and had adapted to life in south Asia.

During an ice age 70,000–60,000 years ago, south Asia and most of the northern islands of Indonesia were connected by land bridges. Farther south, island chains where one could travel by raft without losing sight of land encouraged the idea of further travel. Inevitably, the mariners reached a point where land was no longer visible on the horizon. About 60,000 years ago, the distance from the island of Timor to Australia was 65 miles. Scholars have speculated that smoke rising from lightning-produced brush fires in the south could have suggested to some enterprising mariners that there was land beyond the horizon. Whatever motivated them to take to the sea, they evidently succeeded in crossing it.

**Settlement of the Continent**   As *H. sapiens* groups arrived on the Australian continent, presumably in the northwest, they fanned out eastward and southward, slowly populating it. The descendants of the original settlers became known in our own time as **Aboriginals**. Bringing their African and south Asian foraging customs with them, the settlers hunted the Australian animals and gathered what was edible of its plant life. Australia's animals, as they are today, were very different from those in Africa and south Asia: On account of the continent's early connection with Antarctica and South America, its game animals were largely marsupials, carrying their newborns in protective pouches during the nursing phase. Unlike in Africa and Eurasia, with their profusion of dangerous animals, there were few marsupial predator species to threaten these first humans. The Aboriginal peoples gradually hunted the largest marsupial species to extinction, and by about 16,000 years ago, only medium and small animals, such as kangaroos and wombats, were left to hunt.

As elsewhere in foraging societies, men were the hunters. They used spears and spear throwers—short sticks with a curve or hook on the end to extend the length of the thrower's arm and give additional power to the flight of the spear. Bows and arrows, which appeared for the first time in South Africa 64,000 years ago, probably were too late for the migrants to take with them on their journey to Australia. In southern Australia, eel was a major protein staple. Men trapped this fish in rivers and human-made river basins, using nets made of bulrush fiber. In Tasmania the main meat source was the seal. Once the large marsupials were gone, hunting became a highly diversified set of activities for the Aborigines.

Women, and secondarily men, were responsible for gathering vegetal foods. The basic staples were wild millet and rice. The main fruits and vegetables were the solanum [sow-LAH-num], a tomato-like fruit rich in vitamin C; the yam daisy, a sweet, milky tuber with yellow, daisy-like flowers; and the quandong [KWAN-dong] fruit, also abounding in vitamin C, which was collected from trees and then dried. Women used grindstones to prepare hard seeds and vegetables, such as pine nuts, flax and acacia seeds, as well as bracken (a large fern) and bindweed (a family of vines). Yam, taro, and banana thrived only in the northeast.

Eucalyptus, a native of Australia found nearly everywhere on the continent, served for firewood in the stone-built hearths. People also used fire as a hunting tool and to promote revegetation. Controlled grass and brush fires drove animals in the desired direction where strategically positioned hunting parties could slaughter them. Forest fires were used to synchronize more closely the production and harvest of nuts and fruits on trees, thereby increasing the efficiency of harvests. Over time, the Aborigines developed a keen sense of how to exploit nature efficiently, while consciously setting about preserving it.

Australia was less rich in grasses suitable for grain collection than southwest Asia. For example, Australia had only two types of edible grass seeds; in southwest

**Aboriginals:** The original settlers of Australia, who arrived some 60,000–50,000 years before the arrival of European settlers at the end of the eighteenth century CE.

Asia, there were around 40 types. Thus, it should come as no surprise that foraging remained the dominant mode of subsistence, even if people stayed in their camps for long periods of time before moving them. Only in the south, where eel trapping was the main form of livelihood, did permanent villages appear, similar in many ways to their counterparts in late forager Africa, Europe, North America, and Japan. Aborigines thus remained closely adapted to the basic, relatively modest patterns of forager livelihood until the first English settlers arrived at the end of the eighteenth century CE.

**Social Structures and Cultural Expressions**    Since modern-day Aborigines remained faithful to their traditional forms of life, a great deal about their social structures and organization is known. Australian anthropologists have collected a wealth of data, observing forager culture as it existed in the nineteenth and early twentieth centuries. Unfortunately, today foraging is disappearing before our eyes at an accelerated rate. But the existing literature contains much that is rooted in the distant past, even though, of course, the Aborigines changed in the course of world history just like humans on all other continents.

According to this literature, in the traditional Aboriginal society of the nineteenth century or earlier marriages were predominantly *monogamous*—that is, they consisted of a husband and wife. Some men who not only were successful hunters but also became wealthy through trade could acquire additional wives. Families that camped together and assisted each other in hunting and food gathering formed *clans*, which were units in which all families considered themselves to be descendants of a common ancestor. Groups of clans formed a lineage of between 500 and 1,500 members. Generally, lineages were too large to camp or move about together. They were, rather, loose associations of clans living miles apart but from which they selected their marriage partners. Marriages took place among members of one group of clans and members of another group. Lineages met collectively once a year at one of the sacred places of their land to celebrate shared rituals and ceremonies.

**The Dreamtime**    Despite this loose social organization, lineage members considered themselves trustees of clearly marked parcels of ancestral land. Typical markers were identifiable features of the landscape, such as rocks, rivers, or trees. *Taboos*—things or practices that were forbidden—and myths surrounded both land and markers. People venerated them through rituals, ceremonies, dances, and recounting the myths. Respected elders, who commanded a particularly high degree of regard, presided over the rituals. An elder was venerated when he had a large number of sons, family alliances, and valuable artifacts acquired through trade. The most esteemed elders possessed a deep knowledge of the clan's past in the **Dreamtime**, the name given to the ancient period in which the lineage's past was embedded.

More specifically, the Dreamtime consisted of the stories, customs, and laws which defined the lineage in its original, perfect state at the time of creation. Elders acquired access to this time through trance states, requiring many years of initiation, training, and practice. Their knowledge of the Dreamtime, it was believed, gave them access to creation's hidden powers, enabling them to read other people's minds, recognize their secret concerns, and heal illnesses. Elders, however, did

**Dreamtime:** In the Australian Dreamtime, the shaman constructs an imaginary reality of the lineage's origins and roots, going back to the time when the world was created and the creator devised all customs, rituals, and myths.

not possess a monopoly on knowledge of nature's hidden powers. All members of the clan had access to its sacred heritage and could use it to practice magic, experiment with sorcery, or cast spells.

Aboriginal elders never were able to wield political power through armed force within their own lineages. Since there was no agriculture and, therefore, no agricultural surplus, and since trade did not evolve beyond the exchange of obsidian, tools, and weapons, elders could not acquire enough wealth to pay fighters. Only on the continent's northern coast was there a modest trade in local pearls for knives, pottery, cloth, sails, and canoes from Timor; but it too did not support the rise of powerful chiefdoms. Aboriginal society thus remained "stateless" in the sense of possessing no administrative institutions. Elders in positions of authority used persuasion, not force, to keep the peace.

**Australian Rock Art**    How much the Dreamtime involved rock paintings, existing in large numbers in Australia, is unfortunately not known. Rock art is the one form of cultural expression where historical change in the otherwise slow-paced Aboriginal culture is evident: Contemporary Aborigines are unable to interpret the meaning of early rock paintings. There are many more recent rock paintings, but they are very different in content and style from the earlier ones. Changing climatic conditions leading to different migration patterns are presumably responsible for modern Aboriginals losing their familiarity with the rich culture of ancient Australian rock art.

> "The ca. 28,000-year-old painted rock from Nawarla Gabarnmang [Jawoyn Country, Northern Territory] adds an example from Australia to the world corpus of early pictographs."
>
> —Archeologist Bruno David

The best-known Australian rock paintings are the so-called Bradshaw paintings in the Kimberley Region of northwest Australia, which probably date to a period of 30,000–20,000 years ago. Between two ice ages, this region had a fairly even year-round climate with sufficient rainfall to support foraging and, hence, the presence of human groups practicing rock art. At present, scholars work with a classification dividing the Bradshaw paintings into two major stylistic periods, beginning with (1) indentations, grooves, and animals and followed by (2) elongated human figures with tassels or sashes, fruits and vegetables resembling human figures, and clothespin and stick figures.

The two periods are very difficult to date, since so far none of the places where they have been found have yielded any material that could be reliably carbon dated. Only one Bradshaw painting has been dated so far to more than 17,500 years ago, thanks to a wasp nest on top of it that contained sand grains suitable for thermo-

**Australian Shaman.** A shaman in a trance from a rock carving 30,000–20,000 years ago. This "Bradshaw" figure is usually interpreted as showing movements and communication with the spirits of animated cosmic nature.

luminescent dating. The painting could be much older, of course, depending on when the wasp settled on it. Scholars generally assume that the proliferation of Bradshaws was roughly contemporary with the efflorescence of prehistoric rock art in Europe.

The striking parallelism between Australian and European rock art demonstrates that humans did not have to interact to express themselves culturally in similar ways. Similar forager patterns could evolve without mutual contact. The fact that a great proliferation of paintings occurred simultaneously in Australia and Europe leads to the conclusion that none of the human groups migrating away from Africa was privileged over any other. This cultural parity among foragers needs to be kept in mind as we turn to African *H. sapiens* migrating to Europe.

## Migration from Asia to Europe

There was a gap of at least 30,000 years between groups of modern humans leaving Africa (80,000–60,000 years ago) and migrating to Europe (44,000 years ago). Scholars assume that these humans settled first in central Asia before their descendants fanned out to Europe as well as east Asia. By that time, *H. sapiens* was well adapted to the cool and dry climate of the grasslands and steppes with their large herds of bison, horses, and reindeer. Little is known about the migratory path these descendants chose as they walked across the Asian steppes and grasslands to Europe. It is generally assumed that they moved from the region around the Urals west to the Black Sea and into Europe (see Map 1.2).

**Neanderthals and Other Lines**   When *H. sapiens* arrived in Europe around 44,000–35,000 years ago, this region was already settled by another human line, that of the **Neanderthals** [nay-AN-der-tall, after a valley in northwest Germany where the first specimen was found in the nineteenth century]. This line is assumed to have descended from a successor to *H. erectus* 300,000 years ago, although the exact descent is unclear. In fact, on the basis of fossil finds in Spain (Sima de los Huesos) and Siberia (Denisova), as well as subsequent DNA analyses of these finds during 2010–2013, scholars now speak of several successor lineages, coexisting and interbreeding as well as perhaps even overlapping with *H. erectus* in Europe and Asia.

"Denisovans must have lived over an extraordinarily broad geographic and ecological range, from Siberia to tropical Asia."

—Geneticist David Reich

So far, however, Neanderthals are the best-documented Paleolithic fossil humans in Europe and western Asia, with over 600 finds. The fossils range in age from 230,000 to 24,000 years old and are widely distributed geographically between western Europe, the Altai Mountains in eastern Asia, and the Middle East. Early European *H. sapiens*—or **Cro-Magnon** [crow-man-YON, after the name of the cave in southwestern France where, in the nineteenth century, European *H. sapiens* bones were first found]—was clearly an intruder in an inhabited, if still sparsely settled, human landscape.

Neanderthals were smaller and more heavily boned than modern humans. In their forager livelihood, the two species were very similar. The former, however, buried their dead without the gifts of jewelry or sprinklings of red ochre, a symbol of lifeblood, which modern humans included in the graves. The stone and bone toolkits of the two were also alike, but whether Neanderthals created paintings is at present not certain, in spite of some contrary claims (for example, for the hand stencils and disks in the cave of El Castillo, Spain, redated in 2012 to 40,800 years ago). Paleoanthropologists assume that Neanderthals were able to talk in a rudimentary way but did not yet possess the throat structures of *H. sapiens*. The two species overlapped for about 11,000 (perhaps even 17,000) years. In 2010, the Swedish-born paleogeneticist Svante Pääbo and his team based in Leipzig, Germany, completed an analysis of Neanderthal DNA (from bones from Croatian

**Hybrid Imagery.** Two lion-headed figurines, one apparently dancing, described by the excavator, archaeologist Nicholas Conard, as a "depiction of mythical imagery," although he does not indicate of which myths. The ca. 32,000-year-old figurines were found in two caves in southwestern Germany.

Neanderthals, from which they first removed microbial contamination) and found that there was interbreeding with modern humans: Some 1–4 percent of the genes of this Croatian Neanderthal are shared with the genes of *H. sapiens*. Thus, a small number of Neanderthal genes were absorbed into the modern human genome.

**Rock Paintings and Figurines**    *H. sapiens'* cultural creativity, which had burst forth in Africa, continued after the migration into Europe. There are some 700 caves with rock paintings and engravings, as well as aboveground sites with small figurines. Currently, the oldest known artifacts are the paintings of El Castillo, mentioned above, and a small ivory figurine of a mammoth dating to 35,000 years ago and found in 2007 in Vogelherd Cave in southwestern Germany. Two slightly more recent, equally small ivory statuettes of humans with lion heads, one of them apparently dancing, were also found in southwestern Germany. The mammoth legs have holes, leading to the speculation that this artifact was sewn to garments. Other figurines might have been worn as pendants.

Several thousand years later, an entire class of female figurines, some thin and delicate and others bulging and coarse, called "Venuses," appeared all over western Europe. These figurines were made of stone or bone, and one of them, unearthed in the Czech Republic, was formed of fired clay ca. 26,000 years ago. The creation of the first ceramic pieces was thus a Paleolithic invention, even though the regular production of pottery appeared only some 17,000 years later in agrarian society. All figurines were small, fitting comfortably into the palm of a hand, and therefore easily transportable. The bulging Venuses have been interpreted as fertility goddesses, indicating an early matriarchy, but this interpretation is questionable, given the great variety of female and male figurines of the Venus type. Other scholars view these figurines as dolls for children in the camps or as representatives of relatives or ancestors in camp rituals. Hard proof, however, is still outstanding, if it is even possible.

The great majority of rock paintings in Europe show animals, usually from their most easily identifiable profiles. The animals appear alone or in herds, at rest or in motion, either chasing or fleeing other beasts, or locked in conflict with each other. The oldest paintings found so far are of grass-eating steppe and grassland animals, such as reindeer, horses, cattle, aurochs, bison, mammoths, or rhinoceroses, with which modern humans, migrating from the Russian steppes into central and western Europe, were familiar. Dating to 30,000 years ago, they were discovered in 1994 in Chauvet [show-VAY] Cave in southern France. One intriguing image in this cave depicts a figure with the head and torso of a bison and the legs of a human. A similarly intriguing image from 13,000 years ago, found in the Trois-Frères [trwah-FRAIR] Cave in southwestern France, is known as "the sorcerer," an upright being with human hands and legs but also equipped with reindeer ears and antlers, a bird face, a fox tail, and a phallus. These images of hybrid beings are rare, however; only some 200 are known to exist, in contrast to the tens of thousands of large, mostly herbivore mammals on which the painters concentrated.

Depictions of humans are also rare. The best known, at Lascaux [las-COE] in southwestern France and dated to 17,000 years ago, is that of a bison, perhaps hit by a spear and standing in front of a human stick figure, prostrate with an erect penis. A spear with a bird on top and a rhinoceros (next page) face away from the human. A set of 15,000-year-old engravings on slabs used to cover the floor of La Marche [la-MARSH] Cave in west-central France consists of expertly executed, realistic sketches of young and old males and females, dressed in boots, robes, and hats. These sketches could easily be modern cartoons: They demonstrate that there is little that separates contemporary humans from those who lived 15,000 years ago.

Modern chemical analyses have shown that the rock painters knew how to grind and mix minerals to make different colors. They mixed charcoal and manganese dioxide to outline their paintings in black. To add color, they used other ground minerals, such as hematite for red, mixed in various finely graded proportions. Painters carefully sketched the images before filling them in with paint and shading the figures. They often used protrusions in the rock walls to enhance three-dimensionality and augment the technique of shading. In a number of images, frontal and lateral views are combined. One image depicts a bison with six legs, evidently simulating its swift motion. Thus, the thematic diversity of images had its complement in technical versatility.

The main places with rock art are halls and domes deep inside often miles-long caves. The otherwise complete darkness was illuminated with torches and grease-filled bowls with wicks. Flutes, made of swan bones, and stalagmites, tapped as percussion instruments, testify to the presence not only of painters but also of musicians. To judge by the extant footprints, teenagers as well as adults, men as well as women assembled inside the caves. Modern scholars, such as the South African archaeologist J. David Lewis-Williams, speculate that the caves were places for rituals, perhaps even shamanic assemblies, in which elders, in trance, entered a spiritual world shared with other living beings. Hints of the human mind reflecting on such a shared spiritual world can perhaps be found in the hybrid lion man, bison

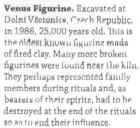

**Venus Figurine.** Excavated at Dolní Věstonice, Czech Republic, in 1986, 25,000 years old. This is the oldest known figurine made of fired clay. Many more broken figurines were found near the kiln. They perhaps represented family members during rituals and, as bearers of their spirits, had to be destroyed at the end of the rituals so as to end their influence.

**Lascaux Cave, France.** This figure shows a bison, apparently disemboweled by a spear and standing in front of a human stick figure, prostrate with an erect penis. This 17,000-year-old image could be interpreted as depicting the scene of a mortally wounded, angry animal attacking a defenseless human. Alternatively, it might also depict a human in deep sleep or trance (hence the erect penis) in the presence of one of the most common steppe animals, also with an enlarged sexual organ.

**"Little Sorcerer."** The meaning of this cave drawing from Trois-Frères, France, continues to baffle. The figure combines traits of a deer, an owl, a fox, and a human. It could be a hunter stalking prey. The combining of animal and human qualities characterizes some 200 examples of Ice Age art.

man, and sorcerer figurines and images. The Australian Bradshaw figures, showing swaying humans with plant-like features, may similarly point in the direction of such a reflection. It is possible to recognize in the Paleolithic artifacts the beginnings of religious thought, specifically the idea of a spiritual nature connecting humans, animals, and plants with each other.

# The Ice Age Crisis and Human Migration to the Americas

In the course of its natural history, the earth has traversed many ice ages. Modern humans experienced two. The first one, 70,000–60,000 years ago, created land bridges that enabled humans to cross much of the Indonesian archipelago on foot and travel the rest of the distance by boat to Australia. This ice age was comparatively mild and brief, in contrast to the last ice age of the world's history, 30,000–13,500 years ago, which severely altered the flora and fauna on all continents. Humans, although suffering through it, exploited it for one major achievement: their migration from Siberia to the Americas.

## The Ice Age

Humans created many of the figurines and cave paintings discussed above when Europe's climate was steadily getting colder. The end of the Paleolithic era occurred during one of the climatically most inhospitable periods in world history. Large parts of the world either descended into a deep freeze or became bone dry. The northern zone of Eurasia, from England to Siberia, changed into a desolate wasteland, partially covered with gigantic ice sheets. The central zone, from southern France to Mongolia, consisted of semiarid steppe lands. The southern zone, from Iberia (today's Spain and Portugal) to southern China, was temperate but semidry, with grasslands and pockets of woodlands.

In Africa and Australia, the rain forest was reduced to a few areas in central Africa and the northern tip of Australia, leaving the rest of those continents largely exposed to drought. The northern Sahara and southern Kalahari in Africa as well as the interior of Australia were giant deserts, cutting deep into what were once rich savannas and rain forest. Life for modern humans in Eurasia, Africa, and Australia during this ice age was an arduous struggle for daily survival (see Map 1.3).

**Difficult Living Conditions** Signs of stress and even desperation testify to the harsh conditions of the Ice Age. For example, human bone remnants from a number of ancient campsites in modern-day Russia display signs of malnutrition and disease. Because of the difficult conditions, humans abandoned the northern European and Russian plains, which remained uninhabited for 15 millennia. Central European settlements were hemmed in between Scandinavian and Alpine glaciers. In an important development, humans domesticated the dog sometime around 15,000 years ago, probably to help in hunting. Many animal species adapted to warmer weather (including Neanderthals; see Patterns Up Close) did not take the Ice Age well, and died out. Species that thrived in colder weather (such as woolly mammoths, mastodons, woolly rhinoceroses, and giant deer) failed to adjust after the end of the Ice Age when the weather became warm again. Whether humans

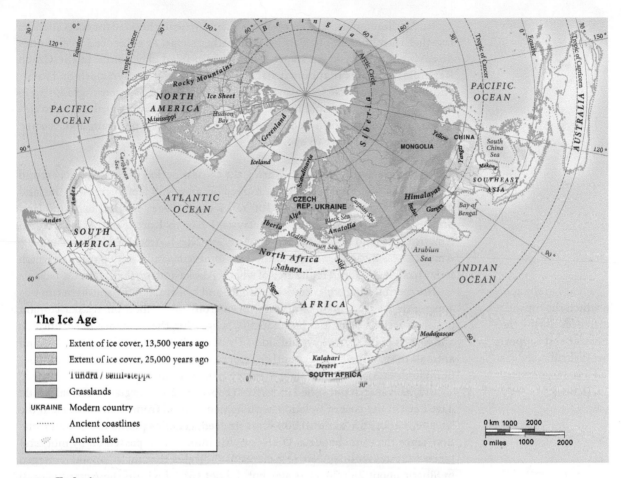

The Ice Age

| | |
|---|---|
| | Extent of ice cover, 13,500 years ago |
| | Extent of ice cover, 25,000 years ago |
| | Tundra / semi-steppe |
| | Grasslands |
| UKRAINE | Modern country |
| ...... | Ancient coastlines |
| ...... | Ancient lake |

MAP 1.3 **The Ice Age.**

hastened the disappearance of the latter animals through overhunting is a matter of dispute among scholars. Ultimately, most of these huge beasts died out around 6,000–4,000 years ago.

Although life was not easy, *H. sapiens* possessed the technological and mental resources to survive even the worst climate conditions. The modern humans had at their disposal a great variety of implements for catching fish, snaring birds, and hunting animals, including harpoons, fishhooks, and darts made of bone; fishnets; and bird traps. Boomerangs, invented independently in Europe and in parallel with their development in Australia, were also used for hunting larger fowl. Wooden handles attached to large stone axe heads increased the efficiency of cutting meat or wood. In a situation of increasingly scarce large animals, *H. sapiens* became efficient at hunting small animals. In this, they were aided by dogs which thus became the earliest domesticated, as mentioned above.

Human mobility increased substantially. Canoes took the form of dugouts or were constructed of bone and wood frames covered with skins. As a result of innovations like the canoe, the range for trading expanded. Baltic *amber* (fossilized tree resin prized for making jewelry) was found 600 miles away in southern Europe, and Mediterranean shells were carried by traders to the Ukraine, 800 miles to the northeast.

Ice Age humans dressed themselves warmly, wearing hooded fur coats stitched together with bone needles, using thin leather strips, as evidenced by figurines discovered in Siberia. An imprint left on kiln-fired clay, found in the Czech Republic, indicates that humans also began to weave woolen cloth on looms, another historical first (see also Source 1.4). No doubt, *H. sapiens* groups were decimated by the impact of the Ice Age, but groups of hardy survivors were still tenaciously hanging on when the world finally warmed up again and became wetter around 14,500 years ago.

**The Beringia Land Bridge**   During the coldest period of the Ice Age, around 19,000 years ago, global sea levels dropped by some 450 feet, increasing the land mass of the continents by about 100 miles in all directions and exposing land bridges connecting Indonesia to Malaysia, Japan to Korea, and Asia to North America. The land bridge connecting Asia and North America to Siberia and the Americas was Beringia, a large land mass of some half a million square miles, which today has been reduced to the area of what is Alaska and northwestern Canada.

**Tundra:** Landscape in which the topsoil unfreezes during the summer and supports dwarf shrubs, sedges and grasses, mosses, and lichens.

Northern Beringia was covered with ice and **tundra**, but the southern rim was apparently ice-free. Sediment cores taken from the seabed off Alaska contain pollen as well as plant and insect fossils, suggesting the existence of shrublands and forests of birch, willow, and alder. Therefore, it was possible for humans and animals to survive along the southern rim of Beringia. A few stone tool and spear point finds in Alaska lend weight to the human survival theory.

But, as research published in *Science* (February 2014) argues, survival would have been at the cost of isolation, with humans cut off from both Siberia and the lower Americas for some 10,000 years. Indeed, genetics points to such an isolation, since the mitochondrial DNA (genetic information passed on by mothers) taken from present-day Native Americans indicates that their genome emerged in Siberia about 25,000 years ago, but did not spread within the Americas until about 15,000 years ago. Thus, Beringia would have been the only refuge for early humans in an otherwise tundra or ice covered, uninhabitable, northern hemisphere stretching from Scandinavia and Siberia to Canada and Greenland.

**Migration to the Americas**   Around 13,500 years ago, it is thought that the ice sheet in what is today the Canadian province of Alberta split, creating a narrow passageway that made a human pathway from Alaska possible. If there was indeed a migration, it must have occurred soon after the passageway opened. Since many of the thousands of spear points that have been found all over North America south of the ice sheet—the so-called Clovis points (see Chapter 5)—go as far back as 13,000 years ago, there were about 500 years for humans to migrate from Alaska to North America. Traditionally, scholars have thought it plausible that it was at this time that humans settled the Americas.

In the 1990s and early 2000s, however, a number of spear points and human settlements older than 13,000 years ago were discovered. Sites at Monte Verde in Chile, Meadowcroft in Pennsylvania, Topper in South Carolina, Cactus Hill in Virginia, Buttermilk Creek in Texas, Taíma Taíma [ta-EE-ma] in Venezuela, and Santana de Riacho [ree-ACHO] and Lapa do Boquete [bo-KET] in Brazil have been reliably dated to 16,000–14,000 years ago. The effect of the new research has been that the arrival of humans prior to 13,500 years ago is no longer mere speculation but is fast becoming the scientific consensus (see Map 1.4).

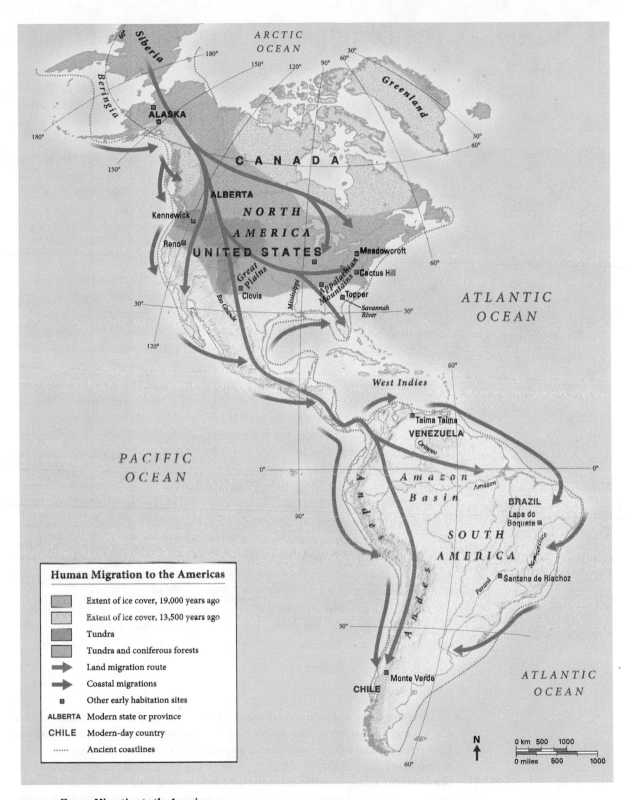

**Human Migration to the Americas**

- Extent of ice cover, 19,000 years ago
- Extent of ice cover, 13,500 years ago
- Tundra
- Tundra and coniferous forests
- Land migration route
- Coastal migrations
- Other early habitation sites
- ALBERTA  Modern state or province
- CHILE  Modern-day country
- ..........  Ancient coastlines

MAP 1.4  **Human Migration to the Americas.**

## Patterns Up Close

# The Disappearance of Neanderthals

The lineage *Homo neanderthalensis* flourished in Eurasia between 300,000 and 110,000 years ago, at a time when (with one interruption around 140,000 years ago) a generally warm and wet climate supported dense woodlands and savanna much more extensive than today. Neanderthals frequently had their camps at the edges of wetlands, lakes, and rivers. As hunters, they typically stalked and ambushed animals from behind trees with thrusting spears. They were therefore not well adapted to the colder and drier steppe lands, which during this time were limited to the eastern reaches of Central Asia and which they generally avoided.

**Donaña National Park in southwestern Spain.**

Beginning about 110,000 years ago the climate gradually changed from warm and wet to cold and dry, bringing about an increase in steppe and open grasslands. This gradual increase, however, often reversed for periods of varying length. During times of greater fluctuation, sometimes within three or four generations, Neanderthals had to adjust their hunting style to open landscapes where larger hunting parties and throwing spears were required. Neanderthals never felt comfortable with throwing spears, however, and certainly did not use bows and arrows, which were developed only later by *H. sapiens*. During a time of respite about 75,000–44,000 years ago when the climate and environment stabilized at a relatively warm and wet level, Neanderthals happily returned to their accustomed forms of livelihood.

Unfortunately, the subsequent period, when the climate resumed its shift from warm and wet to cold and dry, brought havoc to Neanderthal populations in Europe. As open grassland, and eventually steppe, replaced forest and savanna, Neanderthals retreated from north to south. At the same time, *H. sapiens* advanced together with grassland and steppe from southern central Asia and Russia westward into Europe. Scholars assume that the migration of *H. sapiens*, fully adapted to life in open landscapes, into central and western Europe occurred along the Danube valley, around 35,000 years ago. The bone record, however, is still extremely poor, and at present there is only one *H. sapiens* fossil from Romania that has been securely dated to

Long-distance ocean travel in ancient times was perhaps less difficult than has been previously assumed. After all, *H. sapiens* had already traveled by raft or boat from Indonesia to Australia 60,000 years ago. Could modern humans have sailed along the Pacific coastline from Beringia to what is today the state of Washington about 16,000 years ago? Proof of such a journey would, unfortunately, be difficult to come by, since the coastline was some 50 miles farther out in the Pacific than it is today and any settlement traces would now be submerged

34,000 years ago. The earliest western European fossils of *H. sapiens* date to 30,000 years ago, and at present it is impossible to determine who the creators of the figurines and cave paintings during a critical period of about 4,000 years were. *H. neanderthalensis* and *H. sapiens* clearly coexisted, but the fossil record is entirely that of Neanderthals. What the nature of this coexistence was—peaceful or hostile— became a major point of contention toward the end of the twentieth century.

At this time, the general scholarly opinion was that Neanderthals disappeared from the European scene around 30,000 years ago. But in 1999 a Portuguese team published an analysis of a 25,000-year-old fossil of a child discovered at Abrigo Lagar do Velho [VEL-yo] in central Portugal. The team suggested, on anatomical grounds, that this child was born of "admixed" Neanderthal and *H. sapiens* parentage. Apparently the Neanderthals existed for a while longer, in retreat to the far west of the continent.

This impression was confirmed in 2006 when a British team published the results of excavations in Gorham's Cave, Gibraltar, according to which tools found in the cave can be ascribed to Neanderthals who lived there as recently as 28,000– 24,000 years ago. At that time, southern Spain was the last remnant of the warm and wet environment of lush forests and savannas, populated by carnivores (leopards, lions, hyenas, lynxes, and brown bears) as well as herbivores (red deer, boar, aurochs, horse, rhino, and elephant) in which Neanderthals thrived. As always, the Neanderthals of the final years still preferred to hunt smaller to intermediate-sized game, such as rabbits (80 percent of all bones in the Gibraltar cave), birds, mussels, seals, and dolphins. Soon after 24,000 years ago, Gibraltar was hit by the full blast of the Ice Age. Neanderthals could not adjust, but *H. sapiens*—steppe runner and big-game hunter—survived.

Thus it was the environment, not defeat by more resourceful modern humans, that did the Neanderthals in. It just so happened that when climate change resulted in a cold and dry steppe environment, as well as the Ice Age that dominated world history from 30,000 to 13,000 years ago, *H. sapiens* was poised to master the challenge.

## Questions

- Before reading this essay, what misconceptions did you have about Neanderthals?

- Is it important for world historians to study the history of Neanderthals? If yes, for which reasons?

below sea level. In the absence of underwater archaeology so far, nothing is known about such settlements.

**An American Water Nymph**    A possible answer to the question of multiple migrations prior to that of the Clovis spear-point people ca. 13,500 years ago can be gleaned from the genetic study of two human teeth recovered in 2007 from a cavernous sinkhole on the Yucatán peninsula. The teeth were from an almost perfectly preserved skeleton of a 15- or 16-year-old girl named Naia (from Gr., *naias*, water nymph) who had fallen into the sinkhole. According to the study, published in 2014 in *Science*, Naia's skeleton dates to 13,000–12,000 years ago. Her mitochondrial DNA—as well as that of the "Anzick-1" fossil of the same age found earlier in Montana (but published only in 2014, in *Nature*)—is closely related to that of the groups of Siberian *H. sapiens* which had migrated to Beringia during the Ice Age.

It appears, therefore, that members from one single, genetically uniform population in Beringia have populated the Americas from at least ca. 16,000 years ago, that is, if one accepts the pre-Clovis archaeological record, or even earlier, if one prefers the linguistic reconstructions. Prior to 13,500 years ago these Beringians must have traveled by boat along the Pacific coast. Then, around 13,500 years ago they likely walked through the Alberta split in the North American ice shield.

**Paleoindians**    Another conclusion that can be drawn from the 2014 studies is that the Beringian settlers (called "Paleoindians" by archaeologists) are the ancestors of today's Native Americans, or "Amerindians," even though they looked morphologically very different from the latter. In other words, while the Paleoindians still closely resembled early East Asians from a variety of regions, such as Siberia and Japan, genetic and environmental factors *inside* the Americas gradually transformed them into today's Native Americans. Whatever further human migrations occurred during the period 13,000–9,000 years ago, they contributed only in minor ways to the genetic makeup of the population. Thus, Paleoindians formed a transitional population which, ca. 9,000 years ago, was replaced by that of Native Americans.

**Spirit Cave and Kennewick Men**    Among the Paleoindians, two fossil specimens have attracted special attention. The first is the "Spirit Cave mummy," discovered in 1940 near Reno, Nevada, whose true age of 9,400 years was not determined until 1994. The second set of remains is that of "Kennewick man," discovered accidentally in Washington State in 1996 and dated to 9,300 years ago. On the basis of the morphological features of both fossils, paleoanthropologists determined that they were of East Asian descent, perhaps of Ainu (Japanese aboriginal) heritage. On the basis of the 2014 research on Naia, however, one would now have to qualify: a heritage mediated by thousands of years of life in Beringia.

The Spirit Cave mummy was a man about 45 years old when he died, from infection following dental abscesses. His spine was deformed, and as an adult, he must have lived with considerable back pain. A year before his death, he had suffered skull and wrist fractures, but both were healed when he died. Earlier in his life he was an active forager, but later on he depended on the care of his group, which actually fed him his last meal of fish. The group buried him in a cave, laying him on his side in a flexed position, which was typical also among the foragers in Africa, Australia, and Europe. Dry weather mummified his head and right shoulder and preserved the rest of his bones and clothes, including his moccasins and the bulrush mat in which he was wrapped. No doubt we will learn much more about him once scholars have carried out a more detailed study.

By contrast, Kennewick man, also resembling the Ainu of Japan, was tall and robust when he died. He was in good health throughout his youth and died also at the age of about 45 years. Similar to the Spirit Cave mummy, he suffered several major, even brutal external injuries. His forehead, left elbow, and a number of ribs showed signs of healed-over fractures. His worst wound came from a spear, which had been thrust into his pelvis, leaving a fragment of the spear point in his bone, which periodically produced a festering, debilitating bone wound that might have contributed to his death.

The study of humans in the Americas both before and after Clovis is still at an early stage, and much will have to be learned before definitive conclusions can be drawn about who migrated when to the Americas. At present, all that can be said is that small groups trickled in at various times, from at least 16,000 years ago, and that a uniform Native American population emerged only after 9,000 years ago.

## Putting It All Together

The time it took from Ardi to the first modern humans in East Africa was slightly less than 7 million years. Another 100,000 years elapsed before modern humans peopled the earth, down to Clovis and the transition to agriculture in the Fertile Crescent of the Middle East. From there, in another 10,000 years we reached our own time. The time proportions are staggering: The history from Clovis and the Fertile Crescent to the present is a mere 0.02 percent of the time from Ardi to the present and 4 percent of that from the first *H. sapiens* fossil to the present. Practically the entire time we needed to become genetically human is buried in the "deep history" mentioned at the beginning of this chapter.

Reconstruction of the Facial Features of Kennewick Man (9,300 Years Ago).

Nearly as deeply buried is the process during which we began to carve out the space for culture, which we possess within the frameworks of our genes and the environment. Realizing how long these genetic and cultural time spans of prehistory are is what matters for us today: The 10,000 years of history from the shift of forager to agrarian–urban and eventually scientific–industrial society represent a breathtakingly short time of development yet one that is so overwhelmingly complex that we have great difficulty understanding it. When we step back from this frenetically paced world history of the past 10,000 years and consider the much slower deep history of humanity, we become aware that, had it not been for this slow, tortuous, and often dead-end incubation, we would never have been able to sustain the speed of the later history of which we are the current product.

The principal reason for the slow pace of deep history was the conscious effort of foragers to limit population growth as well as the size of their groups. Women as well as men, constantly on the move in search for food, had a strong interest in having few children and nursing them for several years so as to extend birth spacing. Of course, Paleolithic populations grew over the course of the millennia; otherwise, there would not have been a pattern shift from foraging to agrarian–urban life. Thus, even though the culture of foraging sought to inhibit population growth, this culture was not so rigid that people under climatologically and environmentally benign circumstances were not open to material and cultural change. It was under these circumstances at the end of the Ice Age 13,500 years ago that humans in some parts of the world gradually abandoned foraging and began adapting to agriculture.

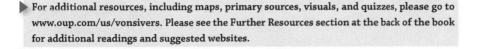

▶ For additional resources, including maps, primary sources, visuals, and quizzes, please go to www.oup.com/us/vonsivers. Please see the Further Resources section at the back of the book for additional readings and suggested websites.

## Against the Grain
# The Hobbits of Flores Island

T he discovery in 2003 of the fossils of *Homo floresiensis*, living as recently as 12,000 years ago on the island of Flores in Indonesia, seemed to contradict much of what was known about human evolution. Never before had archaeologists and paleoanthropologists confronted evidence of hominins apparently evolving backwards into dwarfs. Not surprisingly, scholars offered at first explanations that avoided the question of descent. A first explanation was the assumption of disease. Modern medicine identifies a number of diseases leading to dwarfism. But whether dwarfism can be read into the incomplete fossil record of four Flores individuals is debatable, and scholars quickly doubted whether the hobbits were abnormal hominins.

A second explanation was based on evolutionary theory. Dwarfism is a well-known phenomenon on relatively small islands with limited flora and fauna. On such islands, animals of larger size tend to adapt to their more limited environment And, indeed, archaeologists found fossils of dwarf elephants on Flores, although they also discovered the bones of giant reptiles which did not adapt. Whether this explanation holds true for hominins whose brains allowed them to make stone tools as well as rafts to travel to the island seems questionable. While evolution appears to favor dwarfism for some lines, although not others, it is of dubious applicability to hominins.

A third explanation is the most plausible. What if *H. floresiensis*, on account of its small body and brain size, is the descendant of one of the ancestor lines of *H. erectus*? If so, this would mean that groups of hominins had emigrated from Africa already on one or several occasions between 3.9 and 1.8 million years ago. The theory of *H. erectus* as the first "out of Africa" hominin would have to be revised to account for one or several predecessor hominin groups migrating earlier. Then, after 1.8 million years ago, when *H. erectus* appeared and spread, the earlier hominin lines would have to be assumed to have died out, except on remote islands such as Flores. How long after 12,000 years ago the "hobbits" died out is unknown. A volcanic eruption at that time might be responsible. Intriguingly, oral history among the modern human inhabitants of Flores, recorded by ethnologists, includes stories about small creatures in remote parts of the island stealing food and snatching children around the time of the Portuguese arrival in the sixteenth century.

- **Why were the theories of pathological and evolutionary dwarfism initially *so* attractive as explanations for *H. floresiensis*?**
- **What makes it so difficult to group the hominin lines prior to *H. erectus* together, especially in view of *H. floresiensis*?**

# Thinking Through Patterns

▶ **What made it possible for *H. sapiens* to survive in a dangerous environment? Why is it difficult to imagine life as a prehistoric forager?**

We are twice removed from the world of foragers: After foraging came farming, which is also difficult to understand, because today's pattern of life is part of scientific–industrial civilization. Even those among us who practice wilderness survival still have a lifeline to modern civilization through cell phones, GPS, etc. *H. sapiens* foragers in prehistory, by contrast, relied on their stone tools, bows and arrows, rock shelters, clan members, and unsurpassed knowledge of animals, berry bushes, fruit and nut trees, mushroom patches, and grass fields to guide them through their daily lives. Collecting vegetables, catching fish, and killing the occasional animal did not take as much of an effort as farming later did, and foragers had more leisure time than farmers engaged in the annual agricultural cycle.

After modern humans left East Africa, probably in several waves between 80,000 and 60,000 years ago, in all likelihood they first went to northern India, before fanning out in all directions to Australia, Siberia, and Europe. They encountered *H. erectus* and successors, such as Neanderthals, and interbred with the latter. The modern humans who settled in Australia remained foragers because the Australian flora did not include grasses that could be cultivated through selective breeding into grains. From the complex lineage societies into which they evolved, we can see that forager life could acquire a differentiated culture, expressed in the so-called Dreamtime. However, when the Ice Age hit, forager clans and tribes had to retreat southward and adapt to the harsh environmental conditions. Foremost among the adaptations were the abilities to make protective woolen clothing and build boats with which to travel to more favorable places.

▶ **Where did humans go when they left Africa, and how did they establish themselves in the areas where they settled? How did they adapt to the worsening Ice Age?**

▶ **Why did early humans create cave paintings and figurines? Do they show patterns that can be interpreted?**

The existence of tens of thousands of prehistoric cave paintings and figurines found on all continents attests to the great importance *H. sapiens* gave to the representation of humans, animals, plants, and hybrid figures with which they shared the natural world. The attention they paid to these beings—be they at rest or in motion, alone or in groups, in outline or full detail—shows how important it was to them to identify the inhabitants of their world accurately and to teach the young how to recognize them in nature. Beyond the precise representations, early humans evidently also wanted to demonstrate that their identities were not necessarily fixed. The examples of humans depicted with the features of lions, bisons, stags, or even plants suggests the idea that humans could assume the identity of other beings in nature. In later periods of history, masks of animals or human ancestors, worn by humans in the performance of rituals expressed similar concepts of interchangeable identities. In other words, as important as it was to have an accurate knowledge of visible things, these early humans also conceived of an invisible world in which identities could be exchanged, shared, or merged. In this sense, prehistoric art can be seen as the first expression of religious experience, where humans expressed an awareness not only of the visible world in all its diversity but also an invisible world.

# Patterns of Evidence: Sources for Chapter 1

## SOURCE 1.1

## Shell bead jewelry from the Grotte des Pigeons, Taforalt, Morocco

### ca. 82,000–75,000 BCE

The discovery of 13 shells in a cave in eastern Morocco in 2007 has led to a discussion about the oldest known form of human ornamentation. Because each shell contains a pierced hole and traces of red ochre (a pigment derived from clay), archaeologists concluded that the shells had been strung together as necklaces or bracelets. Another important detail is that the shell is from a genus of marine snail called *Nassarius*. The closest this snail is found to the site (at least today) is an island off the coast of Tunisia, more than 800 miles away.

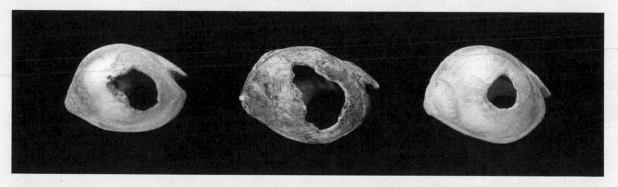

▶ **Working with Sources**

1. Why is the creation of jewelry a significant step in the development of human society?

2. What might this find indicate about trade patterns and networks in northern Africa around 80,000 years ago?

Source: *Smithsonian Institution, National Museum of Natural History*, http://humanorigins.si.edu/category/tags/292

## SOURCE 1.2

# Python-shaped ornamented rock found in the Rhino Cave, Botswana

**ca. 70,000 BCE**

Archaeologists working in the Tsodilo Hills of Botswana in 2006 may have found the oldest evidence of a form of human ritual behavior. One cavern contains a large rock, roughly 20 feet long and 6.5 feet wide, that resembles a giant python, with the natural features of the stone forming its eye and mouth. While its resemblance to a reptile may be natural, there are also several hundred man-made grooves along its side, indicating an attempt to replicate scales with fashioned tools. Spearheads were also found at the site, and similar ones in the area have been dated to 77,000 years ago. Researchers have concluded that this was a worship site for the inhabitants of the region in this period.

▶ **Working with Sources**

1. What symbolic connections might early humans have attributed to snakes, and why might snakes have been depicted and worshipped?

2. What does the growth of "abstract symbolic thinking" suggest about the development of early *H. sapiens* societies?

Source: *National Geographic*, http://news .nationalgeographic.com/news/2006/12/ 061222-python-ritual.html

## SOURCE 1.3

# Paintings in the Cave of Altamira, Santillana del Mar, Spain

### ca. 24,000–16,000 BCE

Inspired by the excitement attending the discovery of prehistoric cave paintings in France, amateur Spanish archaeologist Marcelino Sanz de Sautuola (1831–1888) conducted work on a Spanish cave in which similar paintings had been found. A series of excavations have been undertaken in the years since, leading to the discovery of many objects made from **silex**, bone, and horn at various levels of the cave system. The paintings—of horses, deer, bison, and human hands—were made throughout the cave's occupation, and the images are generally outlined in a black charcoal pigment and filled in with red or yellow paint.

**Silex:** Finely ground stone used as pigment in paint.

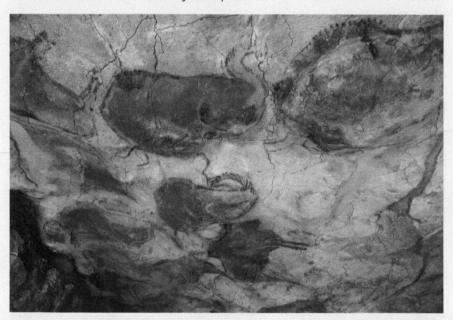

▶ **Working with Sources**

1. What do these images depict, and how can they be compared with the paintings found at Lascaux and Trois-Frères, France (see pp. 20–21)?

2. What do the artistic and technical accomplishments of these artists indicate about the cultural creativity of early humans?

---

Source: *Museo de Altamira*, Spain, http://en
.museodealtamira.mcu.es/Prehistoria_y_Arte/index
.html

## SOURCE 1.4

# Flax fibers found at the Dzudzuana Cave, Republic of Georgia, Caucasus Mountains

### ca. 30,000 BCE

A 2009 paper in *Science* announced the identification of at least 488 fibers of flax attached to clay samples found in a cave in Georgia, in the Caucasus Mountains. Some of these fibers had been spun and dyed, and one of the threads (no. 8 below) had been twisted. The applied colors, ranging from black to gray to turquoise, may indicate that the inhabitants of the cave were engaged in producing colorful textiles. The presence of spores in the cave indicates that fungus was probably already growing on the clothes and progressively breaking them down.

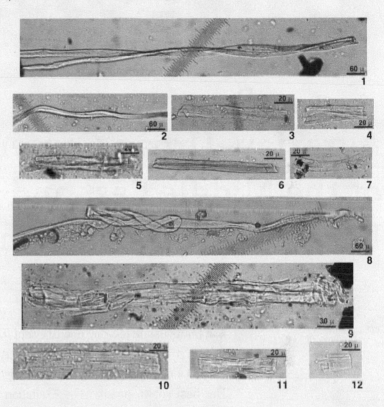

▶ **Working with Sources**

1. What does the manufacture of clothing suggest about the sophistication of Upper Paleolithic human societies?

2. Can the manufacture of textiles in this period be compared to other forms of handcraft in the same era?

Source: *Science Magazine*, 11 September 2009,
http://www.sciencemag.org/content/325/5946/1359
.full#xref-ref-2-1

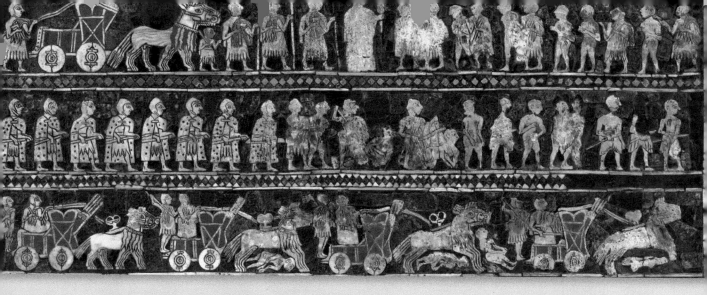

# Chapter 2 11,500–600 BCE

# Agrarian–Urban Centers of the Middle East and Eastern Mediterranean

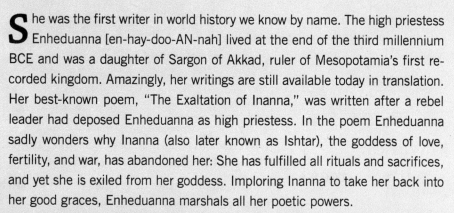

She was the first writer in world history we know by name. The high priestess Enheduanna [en-hay-doo-AN-nah] lived at the end of the third millennium BCE and was a daughter of Sargon of Akkad, ruler of Mesopotamia's first recorded kingdom. Amazingly, her writings are still available today in translation. Her best-known poem, "The Exaltation of Inanna," was written after a rebel leader had deposed Enheduanna as high priestess. In the poem Enheduanna sadly wonders why Inanna (also later known as Ishtar), the goddess of love, fertility, and war, has abandoned her: She has fulfilled all rituals and sacrifices, and yet she is exiled from her goddess. Imploring Inanna to take her back into her good graces, Enheduanna marshals all her poetic powers.

After reciting prayerful poems night and day, Enheduanna finally succeeded. Inanna accepted her priestess' appeals and the rightful ruler returned Enheduanna to her temple position.

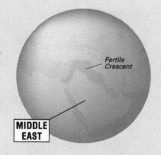

Fertile Crescent

MIDDLE EAST

*ABOVE:* **The Standard of Ur (ca. 2500 BCE), an inlaid wooden box depicting a Sumerian army.**

The end of the third millennium BCE, when Enheduanna lived, was a time when **agrarian–urban society**, with its villages and cities, had become well established in several different areas. Foragers had pioneered agriculture and village settlements during a long period of 5,000 years in the Fertile Crescent of the Middle East, a region particularly favored by climate, vegetation, and animal populations. Once these early inhabitants had become farmers, they began interacting with foragers in the marshes of the Mesopotamian river delta, where—with the help of river water conducted via canals to the fields for irrigation—the groups merged. This combined population used the bountiful harvests for the foundation of cities in which craftspeople, priests and priestesses, merchants, kings, and rebels mingled, creating the fundamentals of the urban amenities of contemporary civilization: comfortable houses, places of worship, administrative centers, public archives, taverns, workshops, and markets. Many of these urban achievements are still crucial to our lives today. This chapter will trace the origins of farming, villages, cities, kingdoms, and empires in the Middle East, the first of the agrarian–urban centers in world history.

## Agrarian Origins in the Fertile Crescent, ca. 11,500–1500 BCE

The movement from foraging to agriculture—one of the most pivotal patterns in world history—was a slow process covering several millennia. During this time, farmers built villages, in which they worked small garden-like plots and depended on annual rains for the growth of their crops. Farming gathered momentum as people mastered increasingly complex methods of irrigation. Farmers began to settle in the two great river valleys of the Tigris–Euphrates [you-FRAY-teez], in present-day Turkey, Syria, and Iraq, and of the Nile in Egypt. In these valleys, irrigation using river water allowed for larger plots and bigger harvests. Nutrient-rich river silt from the regular floods made the fields even more fertile and provided for often considerable surpluses of grain. These surpluses allowed populations to build cities and states, with ruling institutions composed of kings, advisors, armies, and bureaucracies.

### Sedentary Foragers and Foraging Farmers
The region of the Middle East and the eastern Mediterranean stretches over portions of three continents—eastern Europe, southwestern Asia, and northeastern Africa. Historically, this region has always formed a single geographical unit within which there was extensive circulation of goods and ideas, although it did not constitute a single cultural zone. After the rise of the political institution of the empire, from about 1100 BCE, areas in the Middle East and the eastern Mediterranean were often also in competition with each other.

**Geography and Environment**   To understand how people in the Middle East and eastern Mediterranean adopted farming and settlement, we need to look first at the geography of the region. The western half includes Thrace and Greece in the north, together with numerous islands in the Aegean Sea, a branch of the Mediterranean Sea. The terrain on the mainland as well as the islands is mostly mountainous, covered with forests or brushwood. To the east, adjacent to Thrace and Greece, lies Anatolia, which comprises most of modern Turkey. Anatolia is a peninsula consisting of a central high plain which is ringed by mountain chains and traversed by rivers.

## Seeing Patterns

▶ What are the main factors that enabled the transition from foraging to farming?

▶ Where did the pattern of agricultural life first emerge and why?

▶ How did the creation of agrarian–urban society—what we commonly call "civilization"—make for an entirely new pattern of world history?

**Agrarian–urban society:** A type of society characterized by intensive agriculture and people living in cities, towns, and villages.

South of Anatolia and lying on the eastern shore of the Mediterranean Sea is the Levant (from French for "rising [sun]"), encompassing modern Syria, Lebanon, Israel, and Palestine. Along the coastline is a mountain chain reaching from Mount Lebanon in the north to the hill country of Palestine in the south. Mount Lebanon was covered at the time with huge cedars, of which only remnants survive today. The Levant, the Taurus Mountains of southeastern Anatolia, and the Zagros Mountains of southwestern Iran are often referred to as the "Fertile Crescent," to indicate its role as the birthplace of agriculture (Map 2.1).

To the east of the mountain chain extends the Syrian steppe, which gradually gives way on the south to the Arabian Desert. South of the Levant on the African continent are Egypt and Nubia (today's northern Sudan) on both sides of the Nile River. Both are largely covered by desert but bisected by the fertile Nile valley. This valley is wide and swampy in Sudan and narrow in Egypt, except for the Fayyum Depression and the Nile's Mediterranean delta. Also in the Middle East are three smaller regions:

- Persia (modern-day Iran), stretching from the Caspian Sea southward to the Persian Gulf
- Mesopotamia, "the land between the rivers," namely, the Euphrates and Tigris in present-day Iraq and Kuwait
- the Arabian Peninsula, consisting of modern Saudi Arabia, the United Arab Emirates, Qatar, Oman, and Yemen.

Recent historical climate research has established that between the end of the Ice Age (around 11,500 BCE) and 4000 BCE monsoon rain patterns extended

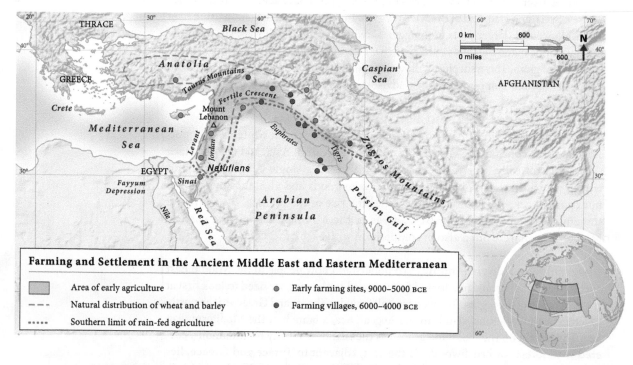

**Farming and Settlement in the Ancient Middle East and Eastern Mediterranean**

| | | |
|---|---|---|
| Area of early agriculture | ● | Early farming sites, 9000–5000 BCE |
| – – – Natural distribution of wheat and barley | ● | Farming villages, 6000–4000 BCE |
| ····· Southern limit of rain-fed agriculture | | |

MAP 2.1 **Farming and Settlement in the Ancient Middle East and Eastern Mediterranean.**

farther west than they do today. Monsoon rain currently forms in the summer in southern Africa and moves northeastward along East Africa before moving to India and China. When the monsoon still covered the Middle East, from the Mediterranean coast to the Persian Gulf, verdant vegetation covered land that is desert today. At present, only the highlands of Yemen and mountain rings around the central salt desert of Iran receive enough rain to sustain agriculture. At the eastern end of the Middle East is Afghanistan, a country with steppe plains and high mountains bordering on India—like the Fertile Crescent and Mesopotamia. It was also a center of early **agrarian society**.

Agriculture first appeared in the Fertile Crescent for several reasons: its moderate climate, its fertile soil, and its access to abundant water sources (the Tigris and Euphrates) for irrigation. Other advantages enjoyed by this region included large areas of wild grains, primarily wheat and barley, as well as a variety of domesticated animals, including cows and sheep, along with donkeys and horses to transport goods from one region to the other. Finally, because of its location, agricultural advances were easily transmitted from the Fertile Crescent to Egypt in the West and to India and China in the East.

**Agrarian society:** At a minimum, people engaged in farming cereal grains on rain-fed or irrigated fields and breeding sheep and cattle.

**The Natufians**   The richness of the Fertile Crescent in plants and animals during the early centuries after the end of the Ice Age seems to have encouraged settlement. Foragers found everything they wanted within a radius of a few miles: wild grains, legumes such as lentils and chickpeas, and game. Nature replenished its ample resources year after year. Semipermanent hamlets, forming the Natufian culture (11,500–9500 BCE), arose in the Jordan and upper Euphrates valleys.

Each hamlet of the Natufians, consisting of about 60 inhabitants, contained a few semicircular pit houses made up of a stone foundation, posts, thatched walls, and a thatched roof. Sometimes their homes would even become their final resting places—the Natufians buried their dead underneath the floors of abandoned houses or along the edges of settlements. Some graves contained ornaments, and at least two persons have been found buried with their dogs. Later Natufians often removed the skulls of their ancestors—whether before or after the burial of the body is unknown—and venerated them in altar niches in their houses. Thus began an important ancestral cult that spread across the Middle East and lasted for several millennia.

To gather food, the Natufians went out into the woods with baskets and obsidian-bladed sickles. Wild cereal grains had evolved over the millennia so that their seeds scattered easily upon ripening, furthering the growth of new crops. Gatherers carefully tapped plants whose seeds had not yet scattered and collected the grains in baskets. Back in the hamlets, the grain was ground with pestles on

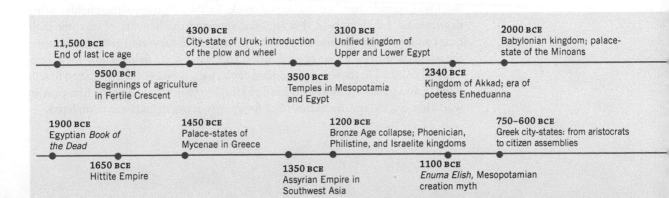

| 11,500 BCE End of last ice age | 4300 BCE City-state of Uruk; introduction of the plow and wheel | 3100 BCE Unified kingdom of Upper and Lower Egypt | 2000 BCE Babylonian kingdom; palace-state of the Minoans |
| 9500 BCE Beginnings of agriculture in Fertile Crescent | 3500 BCE Temples in Mesopotamia and Egypt | 2340 BCE Kingdom of Akkad; era of poetess Enheduanna | |
| 1900 BCE Egyptian *Book of the Dead* | 1450 BCE Palace-states of Mycenae in Greece | 1200 BCE Bronze Age collapse; Phoenician, Philistine, and Israelite kingdoms | 750–600 BCE Greek city-states: from aristocrats to citizen assemblies |
| 1650 BCE Hittite Empire | 1350 BCE Assyrian Empire in Southwest Asia | 1100 BCE *Enuma Elish*, Mesopotamian creation myth | |

grindstones. Storage seems to have been minimal, limited to portable containers, such as baskets. The abundant food supply, however, did not last. A near-glacial cold and dry period from 10,900 to 9600 BCE, called the "Younger Dryas" (named after a cold-resistant mountain flower), caused wild cereal stands to wither and game animals to drift away to warmer climes. Most of the sedentary foragers deserted their hamlets and returned to a fully migratory life of foraging. The short-lived, semisettled culture of the Natufians collapsed.

In the few hamlets that survived, people turned to storing grain in plastered pits or stone silos in order to cope with the harsher winters. In spring, they planted some of their stored grain to thicken the sparse wild stands. When warmer and more humid weather returned, a new era began, the **Neolithic**, or New Stone Age. Scholars use this designation for the period from about 9600 to 4500 BCE in the Middle East because it was characterized by innovations such as polished stone implements (spades and sickles), the introduction of agriculture, animal domestication, sun-dried bricks, plaster, and pottery—in short, most of the key elements of agrarian society.

**Neolithic Age:** Period from ca. 9600 to 4500 BCE when stone tools were adapted to the requirements of agriculture, through the making of sickles and spades.

**Selective Breeding of Grain and Domestic Animals** Climatically, the Neolithic Age began with a metaphorical bang. Within just a few generations, summer temperatures increased by an extraordinary 7 degrees. Thereafter, temperatures continued to rise, at a more modest rate, for another 2,000 years. In this balmy climate, both old and newly established hamlets expanded quickly into villages of around 300–500 inhabitants. People continued to collect grain but also began to plant fields. In the early summer, they waited for the moment when almost all the grain was still in its ears. Through selective breeding, they gradually weeded out early-ripening varieties and began harvesting fields in which all grain ripened at the same time. The kernels of these first wheat and barley varieties were still small, and it took until about 7000 BCE in the Middle East before farmers had bred the large-grained wheat and barley of today.

Parallel to the selective breeding of grain, farmers also domesticated *pulses*—the edible seeds of pod-bearing plants—beginning with chickpeas and lentils. Pulses had the advantage of helping with the refertilization of the grain fields: Pods, stalks, and roots contain nitrogen needed by all plants to grow. Farmers continued to hunt, but they also captured young wild goats and sheep and through selective breeding accustomed them to live with humans in their houses and pens—the first domestication of livestock. For two millennia, this kind of early farming remained essentially garden farming, with hand-held implements, such as digging sticks, spades, and sickles.

The original agriculture—the cultivation of grain and pulses and the domestication of goats and sheep—relied on annual rains in the Fertile Crescent and became more widespread when farmers tapped creeks for the irrigation of their fields during dry months. Inhabitants of this region discovered the benefits of rotating their crops and driving goats and sheep over the stubble of harvested grain fields, using the animals' droppings for refertilization and leaving the fields fallow for a year. Around 6500 BCE, these peoples added cattle, pigs, donkeys (domesticated first in Nubia), and pottery (clay vessels fired in kilns) to their farms. For the first time in world history, the epic transition from foraging to farming had been completed.

## The Origin of Urban Centers in Mesopotamia and Egypt

During the fifth millennium BCE, the climate of the Middle East and eastern Mediterranean changed from one with monsoon rains falling during the summer to one with wet winters and dry summers in the west and north and general dryness prevailing in the east and south. Most of the Arabian Peninsula began to dry up. In lower Mesopotamia, drier conditions forced settlers coming from upstream to pay closer attention to irrigation. All of these changes would contribute to the rise of the first agrarian–urban centers founded along rivers—in the Middle East, Egypt, the Indus valley in the Indian subcontinent, and later the Yellow River valley in China.

**FIRST AGRARIAN-URBAN CENTERS**

**Euphrates and Nile Floods**   The Tigris River in eastern Mesopotamia, with its turbulent waters and high banks, did not lend itself early on to the construction of irrigation canals. The Euphrates River in western Mesopotamia, however, flowed more tranquilly and closer to the surface of the land, providing favorable conditions for irrigated farming. At its lower end, in present-day Iraq, the Euphrates united with the Tigris and dispersed out into swampland, lagoons, and marshes, which supported a rich plant and animal life. It was here that the first farmers from the Fertile Crescent settled, establishing the Ubaid culture of villages (6000–4000 BCE).

The annual snowmelt in the mountains of northeastern Anatolia caused the Euphrates and Tigris to carry often devastating deluges of water down into the plain. The floods arrived in early spring just as the first grain was ready for harvest, forcing the farmers into heroic efforts to keep the ripening grain fields from being inundated by water. And yet the spring floods helped prepare the fields for the growing of smaller crops, such as chickpeas, peas, lentils, millet, and animal fodder. The floods also softened hardened soils and sometimes leached them of salt deposits. Thus, in spite of some drawbacks, irrigated farming in lower Mesopotamia, with its more predictable water supplies, was more productive and reliable than was the more irregular rain-fed agriculture in the Taurus–Zagros–Levant region to the north.

The Egyptian Nile originates in regions of East Africa where the rains hit during the early summer. Much of this rain is collected in Lake Victoria, from which the White Nile flows northward. In the Sudan it unites with the Blue Nile, which carries water and fertile silt from the rains down from the Ethiopian mountains. The Nile usually begins to swell in July, crests in August–September, and recedes during October. For the Neolithic inhabitants of Egypt these late-summer and fall floods created conditions quite different from those of lower Mesopotamia, which depended on the spring floods.

In Egypt, the floods coincided with the growing season of winter barley and wheat. Silt carried by the Nile fertilized the fields every year prior to planting. Because of the steeper descent in both the long valley and short delta of the Nile, the water table was lower and the danger of salt rising to the surface was less than in Mesopotamia, where over time large areas became infertile. The first agricultural settlements appeared in the Fayyum [fay-YOOM], a swampy depression off the Nile southwest of modern Cairo, around 5200 BCE. By about 3500 BCE, agriculture had spread south along the Nile and north into the delta.

**Assembly:** Gathering of either all inhabitants or the most influential persons in a town; later, in cities, assemblies and kings made communal decisions on important fiscal or juridical matters.

**Sharecroppers:** Farmers who received seed, animals, and tools from landowners in exchange for up to two-thirds of their harvest and access to land.

**Nomads:** People whose livelihood was based on the herding of animals, such as sheep, goats, cattle, horses, and camels; moving with their animals from pasture to pasture according to the seasons, they lived in tent camps.

**Early Towns** Between 5500 and 3500 BCE, villages in lower Mesopotamia and Upper Egypt developed into towns. They were composed of a few thousand inhabitants, with markets where farmers exchanged surplus food staples and traders offered goods not produced locally. The Mesopotamian towns administered themselves through local **assemblies**, in Sumerian called *puhrum* [POOH-room]. All male adults came together at these assemblies to decide on communal matters such as mutual help during the planting and harvesting seasons, the digging of canals, punishments for criminal acts by townspeople, and relations with other towns and villages. For nearly two millennia towns in this region regulated their irrigated agriculture through communal cooperation (see Map 2.2).

In Mesopotamian and Egyptian towns an irrigated field produced about twice as much wheat or barley as did a rain-fed field. Indeed, irrigation made it possible for townspeople to accumulate an agricultural surplus that protected them against famines and allowed for population increases. Some people accumulated more grain than others, and the first social distinctions along the lines of wealth appeared. Gradually, wealthy families became owners of land beyond their family properties. **Sharecroppers** who worked these lands were perhaps previously landowners who had fallen into debt and now paid rent (in the form of grain) to the new landowners. Other landless farmers left agriculture altogether and became **nomads**, breeding *onagers* (ancestors of donkeys), sheep, and goats on steppe lands unsuited to cultivation. Wealthy landowners appropriated the places of ritual and sacrifice in the villages and towns and constructed elaborate temples, mansions, workshops, and granaries.

Eventually, the landowning priestly families stopped not only farming their own land but also making tools, pottery, cloth, and leather goods, turning the

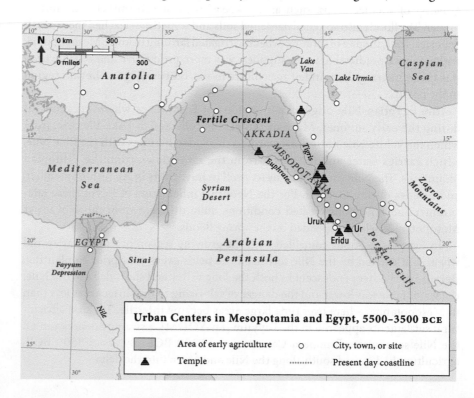

**MAP 2.2 Urban Centers in Mesopotamia and Egypt, 5500–3500 BCE.**

Urban Centers in Mesopotamia and Egypt, 5500–3500 BCE

Area of early agriculture — City, town, or site

Temple — Present day coastline

production of these goods over to specialized craftspeople, such as toolmakers (for stone, bone, or wood tools), potters, weavers, or cobblers, and paying them with grain rations. The landowners employed traders who traveled to other areas with crafts (pottery, cloth, leather goods), trading them for raw materials. Mesopotamian merchants traveled with cloth and tools to villages and towns in the Zagros Mountains and returned with timber, stone, obsidian, and copper. Egyptian villagers traded textiles with villagers in the Sinai Peninsula in return for copper and with Nubian villagers in return for gold.

Around 4300 BCE, some mountain people in the region had mastered the crafts of mining and smelting copper. This metal was too soft to replace obsidian, but the many other uses to which it was put have led scholars to mark the middle of the fifth millennium BCE as the moment when the Neolithic, or New Stone Age of polished stone tools came to an end and the *Chalcolithic*, or Copper Age began.

**Temples**    In the course of the fifth millennium BCE, wealthy landowners gained control over the communal grain stores and clan shrines and enlarged these into town shrines. In Eridu, the shrine, originally a mud brick structure with an offering table for sacrifices, grew over the millennia through a dozen superimpositions into a monumental temple. Adjacent to the early temples were kilns, granaries, workshops, breweries, and administrative buildings. The wealthy landowners, presiding over the temples as priests, were responsible for the administration of all aspects of cult ritual in the temples, as well as the provision of labor in the temple fields, which included the digging and cleaning of irrigation canals; the planting, harvesting, transporting, and storing of crops; and the pasturing, stabling, and breeding of animals.

In Upper Egypt, landowner-priests presided over the construction of the first temples around 3500 BCE, together with elegantly embellished tombs for themselves. The decorations in both temples and tombs depict boats, animals, and humans. One such painting shows a leader carrying out an expedition on the Nile upstream to Nubia, returning with gold, ebony, and diorite (black rock used for statues) to create elaborate ornaments for his temple and tomb. Unfortunately, the sparse archaeological record in Egypt at this point presents few details concerning the transition from village to town.

**The World's First Cities**    In contrast to a town, a **city** (or **city-state**, if the surrounding villages are included) is defined as a place of more than 5,000 inhabitants, with a number of nonfarming inhabitants, such as craftspeople, merchants, and administrators. The latter lived on the food they received in exchange for their own handiwork, such as pottery, textiles, and traded goods. To keep order in such a large place where many people did not know each other, the dominant landowner-priest created a personal entourage of armed men, wielding police power. The first place in Mesopotamia to

**City, city-state:** A place of more than 5,000 inhabitants with nonfarming inhabitants (craftspeople, merchants, administrators), markets, and a city leader capable of compelling obedience to his decisions by force.

**The Temple at Eridu.** Artist's reconstruction of the temple at Eridu. Note the immense platform supporting the temple and the sacred enclosure, which measured 200 square yards.

fit the definition of a city was Uruk, founded near Eridu around 4300 BCE. Within a millennium, it was a city of 50,000–80,000 inhabitants with a mixture of palaces, multistory administrative buildings, workshops, residences, palace estates, and villages clustered around the city with both large and small individual farms.

The people of Uruk were important pioneers of technical and intellectual innovations. It was here that the first known plow was found. Mesopotamian plows were sophisticated wooden constructions with seeder funnels on top and pulled by pairs of oxen or donkeys. Plowing and controlled sowing allowed for much larger harvests. Uruk craftspeople introduced the potter's wheel, which accelerated and made more precise the manufacture of earthenware and ceramics. The sizes of jars, pots, and bowls gradually became standardized, simplifying the storage of grain and its distribution in the cities.

At the same time, two- and four-wheeled carts pulled by oxen expedited the transportation of large quantities of grain from the fields to the city. The grain was made into bread, to conveniently feed the populace, and beer, which like bread became a source of calories and a safe, potable, and easily storable drink of choice among urban dwellers. By some estimates, more than 40 percent of Mesopotamia's grain was committed to beer production, and archaeologists have unearthed numerous recipes for the brew.

Another particularly serviceable invention was bronze, the world's first *alloy*—that is, a blending of two or more metals in the smelting process. Bronze is an alloy of copper and arsenic or tin; it is a hard, although relatively expensive, metal that could be used in tools and weapons. Bronze became so useful in the Middle East and eastern Mediterranean during the following centuries that it replaced stone and copper implements for all but a few purposes in daily life, leading historians to refer to this as the *Bronze Age* (in the Middle East from 3300 to 1200 BCE). Bronze became one of the hallmarks of agrarian–urban life as its use spread or was independently developed in other places in Eurasia.

**Cuneiform Writing**    The administrators in the bureaucracy, who were responsible for the accounting and distribution of grain, animals, ceramics, textiles, and imported raw materials, greatly simplified their complicated tasks around 3450 BCE by inventing a form of writing. Scribes wrote in cuneiform [kyoo-NEE-uh-form] (from the Latin, meaning "wedge-shaped") script on clay tablets, using signs denoting objects and sounds from the spoken language. Small stone or clay tokens indicating different types of grain or goods on baskets or containers had been ubiquitous in the Middle East since the late Paleolithic. These tokens with a variety of engraved or imprinted signs might have been precursors of cuneiform writing. Historians are still researching and arguing these points. However the debate is eventually settled, it is obvious that writing was a major expansion of the conceptual horizon of humankind that reached back to the first flaked stones, ornaments, figurines, and cave paintings in the Paleolithic. For the first time, scribes could not only write down the languages they spoke but also clarify for future generations the meaning of the sculpted and painted artifacts which would otherwise have been mute witnesses of history. With the advent of writing, record keeping, communication, increasingly abstract thought, and, for the first time, history could all be recorded.

## Kingdoms in Mesopotamia, Egypt, and Crete

With the introduction of the plow and increasing numbers of metal tools, city leaders greatly expanded their landholdings. They employed large groups of laborers to cut canals through riverbanks onto virgin lands. Vast new areas of lowlands, situated at some distance from riverbanks, became available for farming. Portions of this land served as overflow basins for floodwaters, to protect the ripening grain fields. Craftspeople invented lifting devices to channel water from the canals into small fields or gardens. As a result of this field and irrigation expansion, the grain surpluses of both temples and villages increased enormously.

**Kingship in Mesopotamia**   A consequence of the expansion of agriculture was the rise of nearly two dozen cities in lower and central Mesopotamia. As cities expanded and multiplied, the uncultivated buffer lands which had formerly separated them disappeared. People drew borders, quarreled over access to water, made deals to share it, and both negotiated and fought over the ownership of wandering livestock.

When it became impossible to contain conflicts and wars broke out, city dwellers built walls and recruited military forces from among their young population. The commanders, often of modest origins, used their military positions to acquire wealth and demanded to be recognized as leaders. They challenged the authority of the priests, who had been the traditional heads of villages and towns. Depending on circumstances, the Mesopotamian city assemblies chose their leaders from either the self-made or the priestly leaders, calling the former "great man" (*lugal*) and the latter "king" (*en*).

Once in power, a royal leader sought to make his position independent from the assemblies and impose dynastic or family rule on the city. To set himself apart from his assembly colleagues, he claimed divine or sacred sanction for his kingship. The King List of 2125 BCE, in which the reigns of all early kings in lower Mesopotamia were coordinated, begins: "After the kingship descended from heaven, the kingship was in Eridu." In other words, the kings argued that as divinely ordained rulers they no longer needed the consensus of the assemblies for their power or that of their sons and grandsons. The earliest king known by name and attested in the archaeological record was Enmebaragesi [en-me-ba-ra-GAY-see] of Kish, who reigned around 2500 BCE. Later kings are known for all the nearly two dozen cities of Mesopotamia.

**Akkadia and Babylonia**   During the 2000s BCE, these Mesopotamian cities began competing against each other for military supremacy. The first royal dynasty to bring them together in a unified territorial state or kingdom—numbering about 2 million inhabitants—was that of Akkadia (ca. 2340–2150 BCE). Sargon, the first major king (r. 2334–2279 BCE), commanded several thousand foot soldiers armed with bronze helmets, leather coats, spears, and battle-axes. At its height, Sargon's Akkadian empire stretched from Mesopotamia into Asia Minor and Syria, earning him the distinction of creating the world's first empire. Sargon's grandson, Naram-Sin, added the Zagros Mountains and Syria to the Akkadian kingdom and claimed to

**Cuneiform Script.** Scribes impressed the syllables on the wet clay with a wedge-shaped reed stylus.

**Empire:** Large multi-ethnic, multilinguistic, multireligious state consisting of a conquering kingdom and several defeated kingdoms.

be the "king of the four (world) shores." He considered his state to be an open-ended kingdom stretching in all four directions and limited only by the sea which surrounded the earth. Naram-Sin was the first king to conceive of a grand imperial design which would lead to the unification of the ethnically, linguistically, and religiously diverse peoples of the Middle East, with or without their consent. However, he did not yet possess the military means to embark on large-scale conquests and **empire** building (see Map 2.3).

A later major Mesopotamian kingdom was Babylonia. Its best-known king was Hammurabi (1792–1750 BCE), who ordered the engraving of the entire code of Babylonian law onto a 7-foot slab of basalt. Like so many rulers in Mesopotamia and, indeed, in cultures around the world, Hammurabi saw himself as the executor of a stern, divinely sanctioned law that punished evildoers and rewarded the righteous. By today's standards, Hammurabi's laws were harsh, threatening severe punishments for crimes against property, land, and commerce. For example, tavern owners who overcharged customers or who failed to notify the police of the presence of criminals on their property were to be drowned. Priestesses caught in taverns were to be burned to death. The law of Mesopotamia was no longer the customary law of villages and towns but the royal writ, divinely ordained and backed by military force (see "Patterns Up Close").

"If a freeman has destroyed the eye of a member of the aristocracy, they shall destroy his eye."

—The Code of Hammurabi

**Patriarchy and Gender** The pattern of state formation from villages to kingdoms contained in itself another pattern crucial in the development of society in the Middle East and beyond: the increasingly pronounced patriarchal structure of society. As we have seen in Chapter 1, the archaeological evidence does not allow many conclusions concerning gender functions in Paleolithic society. The Lascaux image of the injured bull charging its hunter, who is depicted as a stick figure with a phallus, is a rare exception. The gathering and preparation of vegetal food was an occupation that required the communal cooperation of all and probably more than balanced the special occupation of males in the hunt. The Neolithic rise of agriculture does not seem to have changed much in these largely unstructured gender relations.

The wars among the city-states and kingdoms were important events in the creation of new patterns of gender relations. Large numbers of war captives, providing cheap labor as slaves in temple households and wealthy residences, gave the priestly and self-made kings a decisive edge in beginning the restructuring of agrarian–urban society. A ruling class emerged, composed of dynastic families who collaborated with other landowning and priestly families. One rank below the

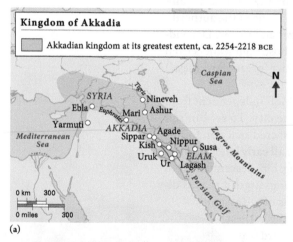

(a)

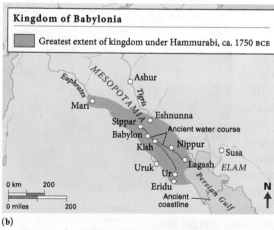

(b)

MAP 2.3 (a) The Akkadian Kingdom. (b) Kingdom of Babylonia.

ruling class were the merchants and craftspeople, who formed a hierarchy among themselves, with merchants and jewelry makers at the top and tanners—because of the unpleasant odor of their manufacturing processes—in the lower ranks. At the bottom of this increasingly structured, hierarchical society were slaves and other marginal urban groups, such as day laborers and prostitutes.

The transition from agrarian societies to urban civilizations had several implications for gender roles. In more egalitarian agricultural societies there was little room for gender distinctions; women served vital roles in the planting and gathering of grains and in caring for children, while men hunted large game. This changed with the growth of urban centers, which resulted in varieties of social stratification. New arrangements were required to accommodate the political, economic, military, and religious changes brought about by urban life. Each of these changing spheres was dominated by males. Men developed and administered military affairs, and fighting forces were restricted to males. Men emerged as rulers and high-ranking administrators, regulated commercial and trading matters, and formed the ranks of scribes, priests, and other functionaries.

Another factor of urban life was the emergence of wealth and property rights, which gave rise to the need to ensure inheritance of private property through male descent. Because this required both establishing and maintaining the legitimacy of the male line, sexual activities of women were restricted. As a result, women's roles were confined to household functions, thereby subordinating their social status to males'.

The formation of hierarchical social structures did not stop with the rise of social classes. As we shall see in later chapters, men assumed legal power over women on all levels of society in nearly every agrarian–urban culture. At first, the patriarchy was still relatively mild. In the ruling classes of Mesopotamia, female members held high positions as priestesses, queen consorts, and in a few cases even queens but only as extensions of male dynastic rule. Enheduanna, in the vignette at the beginning of this chapter, was an example of a highborn woman unhappily dependent on the decisions of the male members of her family. As attested in the law code of Hammurabi, married women enjoyed some legal rights, including the right to sue for divorce if they could prove mistreatment. In general, however, wives were in many ways considered the property of their husbands, who could divorce their wives in cases of neglect of the household without returning dowries, and who could engage in sexual relations with mistresses and prostitutes—while wives caught in adultery were thrown in the river along with their lovers.

Women in Egyptian society fared better in some ways than their Mesopotamian counterparts. Although they existed in a male-dominated society, women were accorded more respect in marriage, and they had more legal rights; they could own and transfer property, and they could sue for divorce. A few women in Egyptian royalty were considered nearly equal to men. In New Kingdom Egypt (1550–1070 BCE), princesses had the same rights of divine descent as princes. Sisters and brothers or half-brothers sometimes married each other, reinforcing the concept that their lineage was divine and pure. A famous example is Hatshepsut [hat-SHEP-soot], who was married to her half-brother. She was a strong-willed woman who became "king" (the title of "queen" did not exist) after the death of her husband, ruling for over two decades (r. ca. 1479–1457 BCE), before a son from one of her former husband's concubines succeeded her.

# Babylonian Law Codes

In addition to the invention of cuneiform writing and the use of the wheel, the Babylonians in lower Mesopotamia produced the earliest known collections of written laws. Because of their formal, written nature, these law codes differed from earlier oral and customary law common to all early cultures. When did these laws originate, how did they develop across time, and what was their influence on later ages?

The origin and evolution of the legal tradition are intertwined with developments associated with the complexity of urban life. In order to sustain sufficient agricultural production, people devised an intricate system of irrigation and drainage canals, along with dikes and dams, to control the often unpredictable flooding of the Tigris and Euphrates Rivers. All of this necessitated not only extensive planning and maintenance but also the allotment of plots of land, some closer and others farther from water sources. In addition, the emergence of complex political, economic, and social relationships—fraught with disputes and inequalities—called for the establishment of a set of centrally administered rules and regulations in order to provide for conflict resolution as well as retribution for wrongdoing.

Across a span of nearly 500 years, from the earliest codification of King Urukagina of Lagash in ca. 2350 BCE to the monumental code of Hammurabi in 1750 BCE, law developed through a successive series of increasingly comprehensive and refined legal codes consistent with developing complexities of urban expansion. Consequently, evolving law codes address correspondingly wider audiences, they cover a broader spectrum of social classes, and they present more complex examples of potential infractions as well as more nuanced resolutions. Most legal codes open with a prologue, which is followed by a body of laws, and close with an epilogue. In terms of format, Sumerian laws follow the format of "if this, then that" regarding violations and ensuing punishments, and punishments are meted out with reference to social status. Finally, they pay growing attention to the importance of irrigation, with more and more references to the maintenance of river dikes and irrigation canals, along with harsh consequences for neglecting this.

In later millennia, after empires formed, noble women disappeared from their male-dependent public positions and lived in secluded areas of the palaces. Men tightened the law, relegating women to inferior family positions. Patriarchy was thus a product not of agrarian but of urban society in city-states and kingdoms of Mesopotamia and, a little later, Egypt.

**Egyptian Kingdoms**   In Egypt, the first city was Hierankopolis [hee-ran-KO-po-lis], founded around 3000 BCE. Smaller cities dotted the river downstream to the delta. As in Mesopotamia, the rulers of cities began to develop into small-scale kings. Among the first of these we know by name were Menes, Narmer, and Aha. Whoever among these three was the first king, he unified all Egyptian lands—stretching from Upper Egypt down the Nile to the delta—and established the first dynasty of Egypt's Early Dynastic Period (ca. 3100–2613 BCE), choosing Memphis, near modern Cairo, as his capital. At first, lesser rulers continued their

The law code of Hammurabi, king of Babylon (r. 1792–1750 BCE), represents the first complete written and well-organized code of law. An amalgamation of earlier Sumerian precepts, the code exceeds them in its extensions and embellishments; whereas earlier codifications list around 40 laws, those of Hammurabi number fully 282. Like earlier models, the code acknowledges distinctions in social categories along with inequalities among them but goes beyond them in addressing more social classes and grouping the classes according to relative wealth and social standing. Also, like previous collections, the code is broken down into several categories, including issues related to property and family law; but here again it covers many more possible scenarios in an effort to close previous loopholes.

Unlike its Sumerian predecessors, however, the code departs significantly when it comes to retribution in that it calls for more extreme punishments according to the principle of *lex talionis* ("an eye for an eye"). Thus, "If a man put out the eye of another man, his eye shall be put out." Further, the importance of maintaining irrigation systems is consistent with earlier themes but expressed in more nuanced terms: "If anyone open his ditches to water his crop, but is careless, and the water flood the field of his neighbor, then he shall pay his neighbor [grain] for his loss."

The long-term influence of Sumerian and Babylonian legal codes—particularly Hammurabi's code—extends far beyond ancient Mesopotamia. Many of its concepts and precepts served as predecessors of Hittite, Egyptian, and Assyrian laws. Instances of its influence appear in the development of biblical law, and striking similarities to the notion of *lex talionis* are found in Jewish law. The code was carried westward across the Mediterranean, where many of its principles found their way into Roman law, especially the organized codification of civil cases.

## Questions

- What do the first law codes tell us about ancient Sumerian and Babylonian societies?

- Are the legacies of these first law codes still evident in modern Western legal practice?

Stele with Hammurabi's Code.

reigns in the other cities. They even rebelled against the king from time to time. Therefore, the early policies of the Egyptian kings were focused almost exclusively on the unification of Egypt. Since it was not easy to subjugate the lesser rulers in a country 650 miles in length, unification was a protracted process.

The first king claimed divine birth from Egypt's founder god, Horus, the falcon-headed deity. As god on earth, the king upheld the divine order (*ma'at* [ma-AHT]) of justice and peace for all. For their part, the inhabitants of his kingdom were no more than humble servants whose duty was to provide for the king's earthly and heavenly life by paying him taxes and constructing an opulent palace and tomb for him. Of course, in practice this royal supremacy was far from complete. Even during times of strong centralization there were always some powerful figures—provincial landowners and governors, for example—who held title to their properties in their own names and collected rents from the farmers working on these properties. As in Mesopotamia, the claim of the kings to divine sanction or

**Egyptian Hieroglyphs, Luxor, Valley of the Kings; Carved into the Wall and Colored.**

even divinity did not keep rivals from bidding for supreme power.

**Hieroglyphs, Bureaucracy, and Pyramids**    As with cuneiform in Mesopotamia, the Egyptian kings were greatly aided in the process of unification by the introduction of a system of accounting and writing. Around 3500–3200 BCE, administrators and scribes developed *hieroglyphic* writing in Egypt. In this system, formalized pictures symbolizing objects and syllables were used to represent words. Hieroglyphic writing was limited to royal inscriptions; *hieratic*, a less elaborate version, was the writing used in bureaucratic documents. The writing material used in Egypt was papyrus, which was more expensive but less cumbersome than the Mesopotamian clay tablets. Papyrus was made from a special kind of Egyptian reed, the core of which was cut into strips, laid out crosswise, and pressed into textured sheets. First documented around 2700 BCE, papyrus became a major export item in the following millennium.

In addition to aiding in communication, writing—as it did in Mesopotamia—lent itself to a larger and more efficient bureaucracy in Egypt. At the beginning of the Old Kingdom (ca. 2613–2160 BCE), heavy Nile flooding enabled the Egyptian kings to expand agriculture on their lands. The royal palace and temple became large, elaborately hierarchical organizations in which everything was minutely regulated, including the food rations distributed to the palace administrators, priests, craftspeople, and laborers. Using arithmetic manuals, scribes calculated the quantities of bread, beer, and meat rations to be distributed; of timber for the shipyards; and of flax for the linen-weaving workshops. For unused fractions of rations a credit system evolved whereby officials traded among themselves what strongly resembled "futures" on a modern commodity market. In its complexity, the Egyptian bureaucratic system of the Old Kingdom easily surpassed that of lower Mesopotamia during the contemporaneous Akkadian period (see Map 2.4).

The most astounding bureaucratic achievement of the Old Kingdom was the construction by Khufu (r. 2589–2566 BCE) of a pyramid near modern Cairo as a funerary monument for himself. Along with two other pyramids, Khufu's Great Pyramid makes up the famous Giza pyramids, which served as tombs for the bodies of later kings. By the orders of Khufu, stone workers quarried local limestone from cliffs along the Nile for the central portion of each of the pyramids. Finer, less brittle casing stones came from quarries upstream on the Nile. Ramparts of chipped stone and other debris, as well as sledges, rollers, and heavy levers made of timber, helped laborers move the stone blocks into place, as much as 479 feet high. After the completion of the pyramid, the construction machinery was dismantled, and today sand covers what were once the workers' camps.

The workforce, perhaps as many as 10,000 laborers, consisted of farmers who were working off their annual 1-month labor service owed to the king. A special labor office made sure that the withdrawal of groups of laborers from the villages was staggered in such a way that regular field labor was disrupted as little as possible. Foremen administered the groups of laborers. Other officials provided

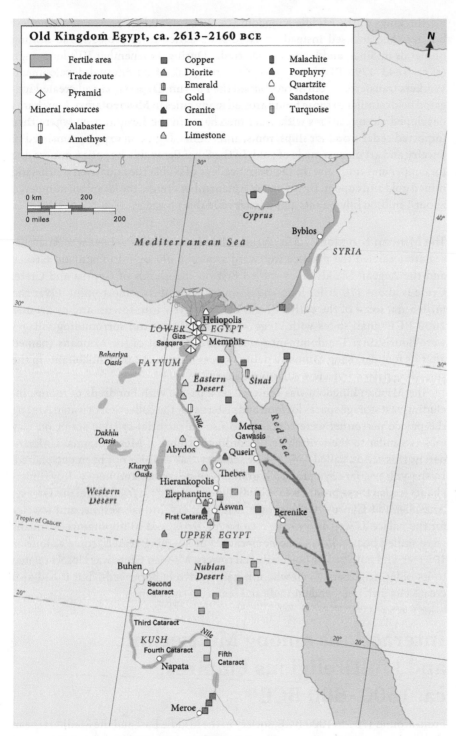

**Old Kingdom Egypt, ca. 2613–2160 BCE**

- Fertile area
- → Trade route
- ◇ Pyramid
- Mineral resources
  - ▯ Alabaster
  - ▮ Amethyst
- ▪ Copper
- ▲ Diorite
- ▯ Emerald
- ▪ Gold
- ▲ Granite
- ▪ Iron
- △ Limestone
- ▮ Malachite
- ▲ Porphyry
- △ Quartzite
- △ Sandstone
- ▯ Turquoise

MAP 2.4  **Old Kingdom Egypt, ca. 2613–2160 BCE.**

rations for them in their camps. Although the workers were strictly supervised, we know that they also occasionally went on strike. Labor unrest, however, could easily be suppressed by the Egyptian army, which was composed of up to 20,000 soldiers, mostly Nubian archers.

The kings of the Middle Kingdom (ca. 2040–1750 BCE) were more modest builders and focused instead on large-scale agricultural projects, the mining of metals in Sinai, and long-distance trade. During Amenemhet III's long reign (r. ca. 1843–1796 BCE), Egypt reached the peak of its internal development. Workers transferred from Syria drained the Fayyum Depression and created irrigated fields similar to those found around many cities in Mesopotamia. Merchants developed close relations with other merchants in the Levant, from where they imported cedar wood for ships, roofs, and coffins. Egyptian exports consisted of jewelry and art objects made of gold. In the Sinai Peninsula Egyptian miners dug for copper and turquoise. In the desert valleys of Nubia they quarried diorite and mined gold and copper. By the end of Amenemhet's reign, the kingdom numbered about 1 million inhabitants and was a formidable power.

**The Minoan Kingdom** After farming had spread from the Levant to Anatolia, seafarers carried the practice westward around 6500 BCE to mainland Greece and the Aegean islands. They settled first on the islands of Cyprus and Crete. Crete is about 170 miles long and 35 miles wide at its widest point. Over the millennia, some of the early villages of Crete grew into towns, and by around 2000 BCE small states with kings, spacious palaces, and surrounding villages were flourishing. The dominant **palace-state** was that of the Minoans (named after its founder, King Minos), a polity with as many as 12,000 inhabitants in the sprawling palace and a few villages outside.

**Palace-state:** A city or fortified palace with surrounding villages.

The Minoan kingdom was centered on a palace with hundreds of rooms, including vast storage spaces for food and cisterns for the collection of water. Among the palace personnel were scribes who used a pictorial-syllabic script on clay tablets similar to the writing and recording systems of Mesopotamia. Unfortunately, this script, called *Linear A* by scholars, has thus far not been deciphered. In the villages, farmers produced grain, olive oil, wine, and honey. Royal merchants traded these products for obsidian, copper, and tin from mainland Greece, Anatolia, and Cyprus. Craftspeople made pottery, bronze vessels, and jewelry for the palace as well as for export to Egypt, Syria, and Mesopotamia. Minoans were skilled boat builders who constructed oceangoing vessels, some as long as 100 feet, and powered by both sails and rowers. Minoan Crete was closely related to its older neighbors, from whom it had creatively borrowed—but it had also created its own independent trade and seafaring traditions.

# Interactions among Multiethnic and Multireligious Empires, ca. 1500–600 BCE

From around 1700 to 1000 BCE, society in the Middle East and the Mediterranean changed in important ways. Chariot warfare, iron tools, and iron weapons were developed and refined. Agriculture spread from the original core of Syria, Mesopotamia, and Egypt to the periphery in Greece, central Anatolia, central Asia, and Arabia. The peoples in this peripheral area adapted the basic agricultural methods acquired from the core area but also introduced contributions of their own, especially military and transport technologies. On the basis of these contributions, conquerors built large empires in which a small, ethnically defined ruling class ruled over collections of other ethnic groups, speaking a multiplicity of languages and sacrificing to a multiplicity of gods.

## The Hittite and Assyrian Empires, 1600–600 BCE

Agriculture spread from the Middle East to foragers in western Europe and Central Asia. Villagers in Central Asia, known as "Proto-Indo-Europeans," domesticated the horse and used it for pulling chariots. Later, Indo-Europeans migrated with their horses and chariots to the Middle East, India, and western Europe, where they settled as ruling classes among the indigenous villagers.

**Horses and Chariots from Central Asia**    The spread of agriculture into Europe and central Asia had major consequences for the Middle East and the eastern Mediterranean. Shortly after 3000 BCE, in the region around the Ural Mountains in central Asia, local Proto-Indo-European villagers domesticated the horse, using it for its meat and for transporting heavy loads. Around 2000 BCE, after villages in the southern Ural Mountains had been transformed into towns through trade, town leaders emerged who were equipped with horse-drawn chariots, as well as with composite bows, made of a combination of grooved wood and horn carefully glued together. With a length of 4 feet and a range of 150 yards, this bow was much more powerful than the existing simpler and shorter bows dating back to the Paleolithic. A chariot could accommodate two or three warriors, one to guide the horses with leather reins and bronze bits and the others to shoot arrows with the composite bow. Around 1700 BCE, both chariot and composite bow made their entry into the Middle East and eastern Mediterranean. They contributed to a major transformation of the kingdoms that had hitherto relied solely on foot soldiers.

**The Hittite Empire**    The first rulers in the Middle East to make use of chariots and composite bows for their military were the Hittites (1650–1182 BCE), Indo-Europeans settling in central Anatolia. This area, one of the richest mining regions in the Middle East, had large iron deposits. Iron was a by-product of copper smelting but was initially considered useless since it manifested itself in the form of "bloom iron," a soft substance with an abundance of ore impurities. Only after prolonged forging (that is, of hammering during which the bloom iron had to be kept red hot) were smiths able to remove the impurities and increase carbon content for hardening. By around 1500 BCE, smiths in Anatolia had fully mastered the art of iron making. The Hittites incorporated iron into the equipment of their chariot armies, in the form of swords, helmets, and protective armor. The combination of these military elements gave the Hittites an early advantage, which they used to become the pioneers of a new type of conquering polity—the multilinguistic, multiethnic, and multireligious empire that was not regionally confined like the kingdom. At its peak, the Hittite Empire stretched from Anatolia to northern Syria, comprising peoples of many languages and religions (see Map 2.5).

To distinguish themselves from ordinary kingdoms, the Hittite kings called themselves "great kings." In their capital, Hattusa, they ruled with an assembly (*panku*) of their principal administrators, recruited from the aristocracy. When

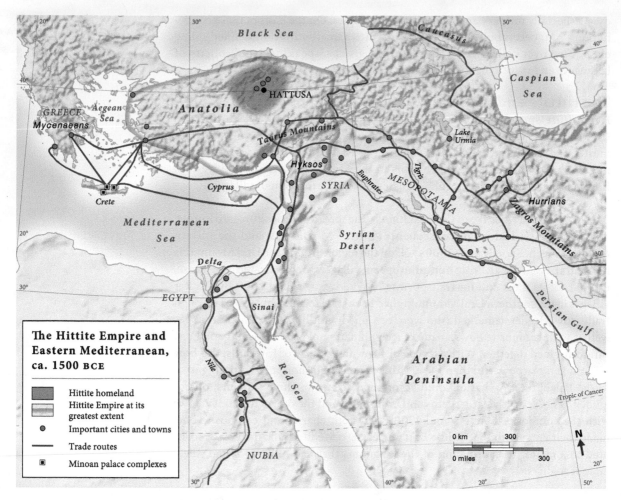

MAP 2.5 **The Hittite Empire and Eastern Mediterranean ca. 1500 BCE.**

they conquered rival kingdoms, they left the lesser, conquered kings in place as provincial rulers. The core of Hittite armies consisted of a nobility of highly trained, disciplined, and mobile chariot warriors. Mercenary foot soldiers, acting as skirmishers, protected the chariots from direct attacks by enemy infantry. These skirmishers were enrolled from among mountaineers, herders, and nomads for the duration of campaigns.

In the conquered lands, the "great kings" placed nobles in strategic garrisons to keep the local, non-Hittite rulers in check. Since the imperial warehouses held limited amounts of foodstuffs, the nobility received land grants, using the rents they extracted from the towns and villages for their livelihood. This Hittite system of employing both its nobility and local rulers was to become the model of organization for all subsequent Middle Eastern and eastern Mediterranean empires.

The practice of imposing an empire on many regional kingdoms did not make for stable politics. People to the east of the Hittites, the Hurrians in the Zagros Mountains, who also had a king and ruling class equipped with chariots, repeatedly

**Tutankhamen (1336–1327 BCE) of Egypt in Full Battle Regalia.** The pharaoh, accompanied by skirmishers (*far left*), is aiming at deer in a herd fleeing from his galloping horses.

invaded their western neighbors. At one point, in the early sixteenth century BCE, they vied with the Hittites for control of Syria. Their struggle dislodged a Syrian, chariot-equipped people, the Hyksos, who migrated to Egypt where they established a kingdom in the Nile delta. As a result of losing the delta, the Egyptians adopted chariot warfare and imperialism as well. Under the eighteenth dynasty, ca. 1550–1086 BCE, they inaugurated the New Kingdom, which devoted its military energies to the conquest of Nubia in the south and Palestine and Syria in the north.

**Imperial Egypt** During the New Kingdom (1550–1070 BCE), the Egyptians vigorously pushed their border with the Hittites as far north as possible, building garrisons and collecting tributes from a number of coastal cities in southern Syria (modern Palestine) and Lebanon. The Egyptians eventually clashed with the Hittites at Qadesh [KAH-desh] in northern Syria (1274 BCE), where they engaged in the largest chariot battle ever fought in the Middle East. Neither side prevailed, and the two empires decided to curb their imperialism and coexist diplomatically with each other, with Syria divided between them.

A short time later, this coexistence was shattered by invasions of the "Sea People" from the Aegean Sea. Originally a mixture of former foot soldiers, mountaineers, and herders from northern Greece had raided the Mycenaean [my-sen-EE-yan] kingdoms of southern Greece, as we discuss later in this chapter. These people, joined by survivors of the collapsing kingdoms, took to the sea (hence their name "Sea People") and sailed to the wealthy kingdoms of the Levant. One group of Sea People, the Ahhiyawa [ah-hi-YA-wah], in Greek "Achaians" [a-KAY-ans], presumably remnants of one of the Mycenaean kingdoms, destroyed the Hittite Empire in 1207 BCE, reducing it to a few small fragments. The Egyptian Empire lost southern Syria to another set of seafaring invaders, the Pelesets [PE-le-sets] (Philistines, or Palestinians), and retreated to Sinai, abandoning its imperial ambitions.

The invasions by Sea People triggered the so-called **Bronze Age collapse** of ca. 1200 BCE with which the **Iron Age** in the Middle East and eastern

**Bronze Age collapse:** Around 1200 BCE, resulting from the collapse of the Hittite Empire and the weakening of the Egyptian New Kingdom; chariot warfare had become unsustainable in these early kingdoms.

**Iron Age:** Around 1500–1200 BCE, smiths were able to produce sufficiently high temperatures to smelt iron bloom, a mixture of iron and a variety of impurities.

Mediterranean began. The collapse is explained as a crisis in which the overextended early empires of the Hittites and Egyptians were unable to sustain the enormous expenses required for chariot warfare. With the decline in the numbers of chariots, large numbers of skirmishers became jobless. Scholars assume that most of the destruction and diminishment of these early kingdoms was due to marauding or migrating skirmishers like the Ahhiyawa and Pelesets who were unemployed.

**The Assyrians**    Emerging after the Bronze Age collapse, the Assyrians (ca. 1350–607 BCE) founded a new empire, which like the Hittite Empire was also based on rain-fed agriculture. Its capital was Assur, a city founded in upper Mesopotamia around 2000 BCE on an island in the Tigris River. Originally, Assur's farming base was too limited to support territorial conquests. Instead, its inhabitants enriched themselves through trade. They built trading outposts as far away as central Anatolia and exchanged textiles for timber, copper, tin, and silver, much of which they sold to the Babylonians in the south. In the fourteenth century BCE, the Assyrian kings began to use Assur's commercial riches to finance their first large-scale conquests.

The Assyrians expanded into both the Zagros Mountains and Syria, reaching the borders of the Hittite Empire and claiming equal status with them. The great king of the Hittites, however, haughtily rejected the upstart's claim: "On what account should I write to you about brotherhood? Were you and I born from the same mother?" Stopped at the Hittite borders, Assyrian troops turned southeastward and expanded into lower Mesopotamia. Here, they occupied Babylon for a short period, humiliating their wealthy neighbors by carrying away the statue of the city god.

**Ashurbanipal Hunting Lions in Chariot.** Note the driver holding the reins, accompanied by the archer, presumably Ashurbanipal. Note also the powerful flex of the composite bow, as well as the quivers of arrows mounted on the sides of the chariot.

After some severe military setbacks, during which Assyria was reduced to its upper Mesopotamian center, ambitious kings renewed Assyrian expansion, creating Neo-Assyria (New Assyria), which lasted from 934 to 607 BCE. They embarked on conquests as had no other kings before them, systematically and ruthlessly conquering the lands around them. The core of the Neo-Assyrian armies consisted of small chariot forces and larger regiments of a new type of warrior—horsemen, chosen from among the nobility. These horsemen rode without stirrups on saddlecloths and fought using bows and arrows. The conquered peoples were forced to contribute soldiers to the Assyrian infantry, thus replenishing and multiplying the ranks of the largest and most expendable forces. Iron swords, iron-tipped lances, full-length scale armor (iron platelets sewn on leather shirts), and iron helmets were now common and helped the Assyrians to become the most formidable empire builders of their day.

In fact, the Assyrians were among the most ruthless campaigners in recorded history. They destroyed temples, razed cities, and forcibly deported the defeated inhabitants of entire provinces to other parts of the empire. Scholars have estimated that hundreds of thousands of deportees, the men among them often in chains, had to walk hundreds of miles through the countryside before being settled in new villages. At the peak of their conquests (745–609 BCE), the Assyrian rulers became the first to unify all of the Middle East, a dream first expressed by King Naram-Sin of Akkad centuries earlier. This same accomplishment would be repeated many more times in years to come (see Map 2.6).

## Small Kingdoms on the Imperial Margins, 1600–600 BCE

Syria was a region between the Hittite (or, later, Assyrian) Empire in the north and the Egyptian Empire in the south. The dominant form of political organization in these regions was the city-state under a royal dynasty. These city-states were located on the coast and had harbors, a number of surrounding villages, and a larger hinterland of independent villages in the hills and mountains. In northern Syria, the city-states were those of the Phoenicians; in southern Syria, they were those of the Pelesets on the coast and the Israelites in the hills. In the eastern Mediterranean, outside the military reach of the Hittite and Assyrian Empires but in commercial contact with them, were the Mycenaean palace states and early Greek city-states.

**The Phoenicians**   The people known in Greek as "Phoenicians" and by the Egyptians as "Canaanites" held the city-states of Byblos (modern Jubeil [joo-BALE]), Sidon, and Tyre (ca. 1600–300 BCE), each with a population of several tens of thousands. The Phoenicians also controlled the slopes of Mount Lebanon, with its famous cedars. These valuable trees, together with timber from Anatolia, were much sought after in the Middle East and eastern Mediterranean as construction material for buildings and ships. No less important was a species of sea snail collected on the beaches, from which a highly valued purple textile dye was extracted. The surrounding villages produced barley and wheat for the cities as well as olive oil, wine, dried fruits, and nuts for export. Urban craftspeople made ceramics, textiles, leather goods, jewelry, and metalware with distinctive Phoenician designs, destined for sale abroad. More than any other territorial states in the Middle East, the Phoenician city-states were engaged in trade.

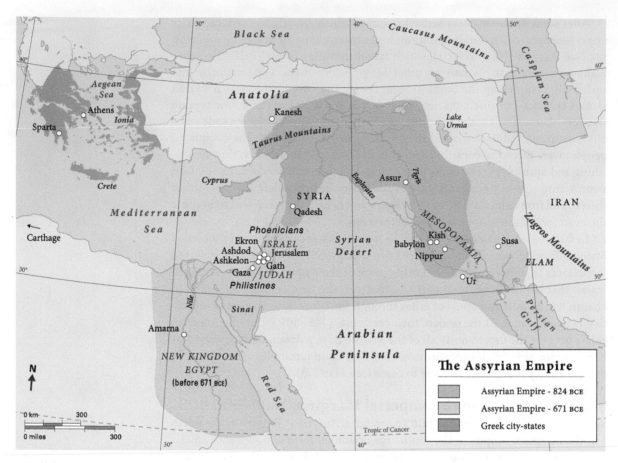

MAP 2.6 **The Assyrian Empire.**

Phoenicians as traders appear in the historical record from 2500 BCE onward. During ca. 1600–1200 BCE, the Phoenicians and Mycenaeans shared the sea trade of the eastern Mediterranean, transporting their own goods as well as metals, timber, and stone. On land, they preferred paying tribute to, and occasionally putting their fleets at the service of, Hittite or Egyptian imperial overlords. When the Mycenaean kingdoms and Hittite Empire collapsed and the Egyptians withdrew around 1200 BCE under the onslaught of the Sea People, the Phoenicians seized their chance. Systematically expanding their reach in the Mediterranean, they established trade outposts on islands and along the Mediterranean coast as far west as modern Morocco and Spain.

In addition to founding numerous ports and outposts around the Mediterranean (one of which, Carthage, would later become the center of a powerful empire on its own), the Phoenicians acquired world-historical importance through their introduction of the letter alphabet. People in Syria had been familiar with the Mesopotamian cuneiform and Egyptian hieroglyphic writing systems for centuries. Both systems were complicated, however, and required many years of training to learn. From rock inscriptions discovered in 1998 in Egypt it appears that Phoenician (or Syrian) merchants began experimenting around 1900–1800 BCE with a much simplified writing system. In this system letters replaced the traditional signs and syllables, with each letter standing for a spoken consonant. Subsequently, in various parts of Syria, fully developed alphabets with letters for about 30 spoken consonants appeared (the vowels were not written). The Phoenician alphabet of ca. 1200 BCE was the most widely used, becoming the ancestor of all alphabetical scripts.

**Phoenician, Greek, and Roman Alphabets.** This illustration reveals similarities among the Phoenician, Greek, and Roman alphabets. Phoenician traders carried the alphabet across the Mediterranean, where it was adopted by Greeks. Subsequent interactions among Greeks, Etruscans, and Romans resulted in the transition to Roman letter forms, which in turn ultimately provided the foundation for English characters.

**The Pelesets and Israelites**     During its imperial phase (ca. 1550–1200 BCE), Egypt controlled the Palestinian towns of Gaza, Ashkelon, Ashdod, Gath, and Ekron. Occasionally, the Egyptian kings aided their governors in these towns by carrying out punitive campaigns. After one such campaign, a defeated people in southern Syria was "stripped bare, wholly lacking seed," as an Egyptian inscription of 1207 BCE recorded. The name used in the inscription for this people was "Israel," the first time this name appeared in the records. "Israel" seems to refer to some sort of tribal alliance among Canaanite villagers and herders in the hills.

When the Pelesets, or Philistines, took over southern Syria and Egypt withdrew a short time later, agriculture and trade quickly recovered from heavy Egyptian taxation. The coastal Philistines established garrisons among the Israelites in order to secure trade routes through the highlands and along the Jordan valley. In response, as is recorded in the Hebrew Bible (the Old Testament in Christian usage), a military leader named Saul and a number of tribal leaders recruited a military force that began a war of liberation against the Philistines. According to this scripture, Saul was killed during the early stages of the war, and his successor, David, completed the liberation, establishing himself as king in Jerusalem shortly after 1000 BCE.

According to the Hebrew Bible, Jerusalem was a town on top of a mountain spur in southern Syria. David's son Solomon is said to have greatly enlarged the town, constructing a palace, the famous temple, and administrative buildings. To date, archaeologists have found few traces of Solomon's constructions except a few foundation walls and terraces on the eastern slope of present-day Jerusalem. Moreover, they have not even been able to confirm the rise of Jerusalem from village to city level. For historians, therefore, the biblical account, like that of many ancient texts, is perhaps best understood not as history but as a religious foundation story, demonstrating God's providence.

According to the Hebrew Bible, the two states that emerged after Solomon, Israel in the north (930–722 BCE) and Judah in the south (930–587 BCE), enjoyed only short periods of independence after being liberated from the coastal Philistines. The empire of Assyria and its successor, Neo-Babylonia (626–539 BCE), conquered the two kingdoms in the eighth to seventh centuries BCE. Thousands of members of the two royal families, priests, scribes, landowners, and craftspeople had to resettle in other parts of Syria or in Mesopotamia. The Philistines, together with people in the Syrian steppes (collectively called "Arabs"), suffered similar fates of defeat and deportation. In their place, Anatolian and Iranian populations settled in Syria. The final wave of Israelite deportations, under the Neo-Babylonians in 597–582 BCE, became the infamous "Babylonian captivity" (*gola*) mourned by several prophets in the Hebrew Bible.

**The Mycenaeans and Early Greeks**    Parallel to the Phoenicians, Pelesets, and Israelites in Syria, the Mycenaeans arose in Greece and the eastern Mediterranean during the middle of the second millennium BCE. After the adaptation to farming, demand for specialized agricultural products (such as olive oil, wine, dried fruits, and nuts) among the villages had advanced sufficiently to result in the emergence of towns and cities which traded in these goods as well as in copper and bronze wares. Around 1700 BCE, in Attica and the Peloponnesus, two peninsulas with relatively large plains suitable for agriculture, leaders built forts as refuges in times of war for their fellow villagers. The best known among these forts were Mycenae, Tiryns, Pylos, Sparta, and Athens.

Two centuries later, the forts evolved into palaces with warrior lords and kings, as well as administrative offices, surrounded by clusters of villages. In these palace-states, scribes introduced a new, cuneiform-derived script, which has been identified as Greek, and unlike the Linear A of the Minoans, has been deciphered. This *Linear B* script provides us with invaluable information for understanding early Greek culture. About 1450 BCE, chariot and bronze weapon–equipped Mycenaean warriors sailed to Minoan Crete and conquered the island. The Mycenaeans were a major seafaring power in the eastern Mediterranean, establishing trading outposts in competition with the Phoenicians.

The Mycenaean palace-states were short-lived. When an earthquake hit around 1250 BCE, the walls of many palaces collapsed. Former mercenaries (skirmishers in the chariot armies of the Hittites) joined by herders from northern Greece raided the weakened Mycenaean palace-states. A century later most palaces had disappeared, together with their administrators, scribes, and archives. The descendants of the kings, however, managed to salvage some wealth, as evidenced by their tombs. Iron swords and jewelry found in these tombs were of Phoenician origin and indicate that some sea trade continued even after the destruction of the Mycenaean states.

A general recovery in Greece began during the eighth century BCE. Trade in agricultural goods such as grain, olive oil, and honey was revived in new market outposts in Anatolia, Syria, and Egypt. The Anatolian craft of ironworking spread to Greece. Literacy returned as the Greeks adopted the Phoenician alphabet, adding vowels to the existing consonants to create the Greek alphabet. The population increased, often so quickly that many people were unable to find employment. After 750 BCE, many unemployed or adventurous Greeks seeking new challenges emigrated to the Anatolian west coast or as far as Italy and the Black Sea to colonize the land and establish new cities. As they developed into city-states of their own, the settlements on the Anatolian coast became known collectively as "Ionia."

The distinctive mark of these new cities was the absence of palaces. Instead, a sacred precinct in a city's center served as an open space for general assemblies. Contained within this space were a temple and administrative buildings with porches supported by rows of pillars. The construction techniques and styles for these temples and pillars came from Egypt. Farmers in villages outside the city walls produced grain, vegetables, olive oil, and wine for the urban dwellers. A city with surrounding villages formed a city-state, or *polis*. Each of these new city-states administered its own internal and external affairs, although they also formed alliances or pursued hostilities with each other.

Initially, kings from among the landowning families were responsible for the administration of the city-states. Their forerunners had been the warrior lords and the landowning families of the post-Mycenaean period and made up what the Greeks called the "aristocracy" of the states. During the period 750–600 BCE, conflict often broke out between the aristocracy and the common folk—merchants, traders, craftspeople, and free farmers—over the distribution of wealth in the growing cities. Some aristocrats exploited these tensions and allied themselves with groups of commoners. Once allied, these aristocrats assumed power as tyrants, who attempted to create family dynasties. Many of the would-be dynasts sponsored festivals, public work projects, and artists; but their popularity rarely lasted beyond the sons who succeeded them.

Other aristocrats opposed the tyrants and agreed to power sharing with the commoners. Through trade, many commoners were becoming wealthier than the aristocrats. Both aristocrats and commoners served as foot soldiers in the city-states' defense forces. These armies relied not on charioteers but on foot soldiers, who were heavily armed with shields, lances, and swords, all made of iron. Their battle order was the *phalanx*— that is, a block of eight or more rows of soldiers marching forward shoulder to shoulder, each man holding a shield in the left hand, helping to guard the man to his left, while in his right hand he held a lance or pike.

> "It is evident that the polis belongs to the class of things that exist by nature, and that man is by nature an animal intended to live in a polis."
> —Aristotle

In the narrow valleys and defiles of Greece and Ionia these bristling "hedgehog" formations were nearly impossible to break with archers, infantry, or cavalry— if each man held his position and the men in the back moved up to take the place of those who fell. In these phalanxes it was not individual aristocratic valor that counted but the courageous willingness of each citizen-soldier to support and protect the other. Thus, as many ordinary city dwellers became the military equals of the aristocracy in the crucible of battle, they quite naturally began to demand an equal share of political power in times of peace.

Political reformers in the sixth century BCE gave commoners their first basic political rights. The best-known reforms were those introduced in Athens and Sparta, the city-states with the largest agricultural territories. In Athens, aristocratic rule was replaced with political rights distributed according to levels of property ownership. The poorest class had the right to participate in the citizen assembly (*ekklesia*), cast votes, and sit on juries; members of the wealthier classes could run for a variety of leadership and temple offices. A written law code curbed arbitrariness. With these assemblies, the Greek city-states continued the Mesopotamian and Hittite systems of assemblies discussed earlier. Whether the Greeks developed their assemblies independently or adopted them from their predecessors is not known. What can be debated, however, is whether the idea of political participation is deeply rooted in the region of the Middle East and the eastern Mediterranean. In Greece, and later Rome, these traditions would evolve into the ancestral forms of many of the political institutions we live under today, particularly **republican** and **democratic** offices.

In Sparta, the traditional rule by two coequal kings was held in check through a newly created board of five officers elected annually from among

**Republicanism:** A system of government in which, in the place of kings, the people are sovereign, electing representatives to executive and legislative offices.

**Democracy:** A system of government in which most or all of the people elect representatives and in some cases decide on important issues themselves.

the popular assembly. These officers were responsible for the administration of day-to-day affairs in Sparta. The assembly was made up of all landowners wealthy enough to live in town because of the revenue they collected from their legally indentured (unfree) tenant farmers in the surrounding villages. These political reforms, however, did not prevent new tyrants from rising up in periodic takeover attempts. Thus, in the middle of the first millennium BCE Greeks were still struggling to find a consistent direction for their political development.

# Religious Experience and Cultural Achievements

By around 5500 BCE, when agriculture had replaced foraging, many human groups began to move from naturalism to polytheism as their new form of religion. In *naturalism* people experience an awe and reverence toward the creatures and forces of the natural world. However, there is no indication in the available archaeological record that people identified these creatures and forces with particular deities. With the rise of cities and the development of writing, these forces received names. *Polytheism* is the general term used to denote religions of personified forces in nature. Artists depicted and sculpted the deities as well as the rulers who derived their mandates from these gods. Writers recorded myths and hymns exploring the relationship between humans and gods. Administrators, responsible for constructing architectural monuments, calculating the calendar, and assessing the taxes laid the foundations of the mathematical and physical sciences. Since many of the religious and cultural achievements were expressed in writing, we can evaluate them today with far better understanding than the culture of the foragers and early farmers.

**Toward Polytheism**    The creators of the Paleolithic rock paintings in Africa, Europe, and Australia (discussed in Chapter 1) have left us few hints of their spiritual preoccupations in their world full of dangerous animals. The depictions of "lionman," "bisonman," and "sorcerer" are but a few examples where the human and animal worlds are merged, presumably with people in the cave rituals experiencing this merger, with the purpose of influencing the animal world. In the Neolithic transition period from foraging to agriculture, the principal change was the transfer of ritual from caves to aboveground sanctuaries and towns.

An example of the transfer to a sanctuary was Göbekli Tepe in southern Anatolia, a place where foragers came together for rituals during 9000–6000 BCE. Excavations begun in 1995 are still in progress, but a rich imagery of animals, mostly in the form of reliefs, has already been unearthed. It shows that naturalism was still in force, even if the venue was no longer a cave. The oldest example documenting the transfer of ritual from the cave to the town is Çatal Hüyük [Tsha-TAL Hoo-YOOK] (7500–5700 BCE) in southern Anatolia, excavated in the 1960s and 1990s. At its height, the town had 5,000 inhabitants, who lived in densely packed houses accessible only from the top with ladders. The inhabitants farmed fields outside of town, using irrigation water from the Taurus Mountains, and hunted extensively. Probably communal rooms in town contained a concentration of artifacts, among which Venus-type figurines and reliefs and wall paintings of animals, especially of *aurochs* (ancestors of cattle), are prominent. The imagery is reminiscent of that of the Paleolithic foragers, but the emergence of urban places of ritual indicates that humans were far along in the transition from nature to civilization.

In Ubaid Mesopotamia (6000–4000 BCE), urban places of ritual evolved into temples. These temples contained figurines of the hybrid human–animal as well as the Venus type of exaggerated female form. Urban dwellers then took the decisive steps of transition from naturalism to polytheism in the period 3500–2500 BCE when writing developed and kings ruled cities.

This connection between writing, kingship, and gods is crucial for an understanding of polytheism and religion in general: Prior to 3500 BCE, religion tended to be an impersonal and nameless naturalism; thereafter, it was the polytheism of kings with often colorful personalities, told in myths and epics. Writing made it possible to record the names of individuals, kings viewed themselves as the guarantors of urban life, and gods were the powers that endowed kings with the authority to prevent urban life from slipping back into preurban culture. In the cities, people were no longer in awe of wild animals, as they had been during forager days. But they were still in awe of nature's powers, as they had been during the earlier Neolithic village life, when nature could be benevolent through bounty and fertility as well as wrathful through floods, storms, droughts, or blights.

Polytheism began when kings became individuals—through adopting patron deities—and associated the awe-inspiring natural powers and phenomena with these deities. Or perhaps polytheism evolved the other way around: Villagers created rituals to please the awe-inspiring anonymous forces of nature, and after the introduction of writing and kingship, these forces became deities. Either way, the rise of polytheism depended crucially on writing and kingship.

In polytheistic empires, rulers were very tolerant toward the phenomenon of multiple gods, even though they had a personal relationship with only one god, their patron deity, and the priesthood of their deity's temple. Even strong rulers never had the power to force the many temple priesthoods of their empire to give up their gods. Egyptian kings, however, unified Egypt more thoroughly than their Mesopotamian counterparts, who never overcame the long city-state tradition of their region. Under royal influence, therefore, Egyptian priesthoods devised a hierarchically organized pantheon of all gods, along with elaborate stories about these gods.

During the New Kingdom period (1550–1070 BCE) kings and priests came into close contact with other empires of the Middle East. They developed an understanding that all gods taken together were really only a few deities, or even only one, with many different manifestations—an understanding quite similar to that of Vedic India. One theologically well-versed king, Akhenaten (1353–1336 BCE), went even further, conceiving of the Sun as the only god, to the exclusion of the pantheon, to whom all Egyptians were henceforth to pray. The new Sun religion—not yet true monotheism, where God the One would have to be invisible—was too radical to survive Akhenaten. But its brief appearance demonstrates the full range of meaning which polytheism as a religion could acquire. (See "Against the Grain.")

**Akhenaten and His Family.**
This wall painting shows Akhenaten, the 18th Dynasty (New Kingdom) Egyptian pharaoh, and his family worshiping Aten. Images like these were designed to broadcast Akhenaten's devotion to the solar disc among his subjects.

## Mesopotamian and Egyptian Literature

Among the earliest writings in the world exploring religious themes are the *Epic of Gilgamesh* and the myth of *Enuma Elish*. These had their origins in third-millennium BCE Mesopotamia but were not recorded for another millennium. The first is the story of Gilgamesh, who was a mythical king in early Sumer. Gilgamesh, according to the epic, ruled Uruk and built its walls. Like the Chinese sage kings we will meet in Chapter 4, he fought many battles and performed heroic deeds in both this world and the underworld but failed in his ultimate quest to find immortality. In the end, Gilgamesh could not escape the fate of all mortals and had to suffer death as well.

Flood stories featured prominently in these early texts; and there are several similarities between those conveyed in the Epic of Gilgamesh and Genesis, the first book of the Old Testament. In each the gods (or God) unleashed a gigantic flood as punishment for sinful behavior, whereupon a righteous figure is directed to build a boat and to fill it with select humans and animals in order to escape the deluge. After they land on a mountaintop, sacrifices are offered, which appease the Creator's wrath.

The myth of *Enuma Elish* (named after its first line, which means "when on high . . .") tells the story of creation, beginning with a time when nothing existed but Father Abzu (the Depth or Abyss) and Mother Tiamat (Ocean) and their numerous children, who were the city gods of Mesopotamia. The raucous behavior of his children enraged Abzu. He tried to kill them but was instead murdered by one of them. Tiamat [tee-ya-MAT] and her second husband continued the violent domestic battle, finally driving the children away. Marduk [MAR-dook], alone among the children, eventually returned and slaughtered both his mother and stepfather. He split Tiamat's body into halves, which became heaven and earth. From the blood of the stepfather he made humankind, whom he predestined to serve the gods. One senses how the unknown authors of this text struggle with the question of power in nature—at times benevolent and at times violent, always unpredictable, even as one sacrifices to please it.

The Egyptian version of the creation myth, like those of the Mesopotamians, also begins with an original ocean. In the Egyptian telling, an island arose from the depth of this ocean. The ruler of this island was the creator god Atum, who contained all the qualities of nature in himself. He created things in pairs, one after the other, beginning with air and water and finishing his handiwork with the male and female of the human race. This Egyptian creation myth is more explicit than its Mesopotamian cousin about the infinity of the original "depth" and "ocean," out of which earth and heaven were created. It is also far less violent, a reflection of the more gradual and harmonious growth of the Egyptian kingdom and empire.

**Sculptures and Paintings**    Mesopotamian and Egyptian rulers wanted to impress those who observed them as severe, powerful, and pious persons. Early Mesopotamian kings had massive statues made of themselves, showing them posed in prayer. In Egypt, compact, block-like royals stand freely or sit impassively on their thrones. Statues in both regions often have wide, oversized eyes that stare sternly at the viewer. On many high-relief sculptures carved into stone, larger-than-life-size kings with bulging muscles trample victoriously over diminutive enemies. In all these sculptures the primary objective of the artists was not photographic realism but a rendering of the gulf between gods and kings on the one hand and subjects on the other.

Wall paintings were highly popular among Mesopotamians, Egyptians, and Minoans. Unfortunately, in the more humid region of lower Mesopotamia, few such paintings survived. By contrast, in the dry climate of Egypt (except for the delta), a large number still exist. Paintings filled the interior of tombs, illustrating scenes from their owners' lives. The painters' point was not only to show their royal features but also to draw them from all angles: Looking at the images from the perspective of eternal life, the kings should be able to see themselves in all their earthly aspects simultaneously. Accordingly, face, arms, and legs were painted in profile; eyes, shoulders, and upper body appear frontally; and the waist was half frontal but turned to reveal the navel. Later, as more nonroyal people built tombs for themselves, the complex multiangled royal perspective gave way to a simpler, single-angle realism.

The Greek arts began in the Minoan and Mycenaean city-states. Minoan wall paintings, stylistically related to those of the Egyptian New Kingdom (1550–1070 BCE), show realistic scenes with vegetation, birds, dolphins, and bulls. The art of Mycenae is mostly known to us from small sculptures, masks, drinking vessels, and jewelry found in the tombs of royal warriors. Through their close contact with the Assyrians, the Greeks in their growing city-states (during the period ca. 750–600 BCE) learned not only about Mesopotamian literature but also about their arts. Winged and fighting animals, as well as muscular gods and heroes, appear in vase paintings. Egypt was the inspiration for the development of sculptures, which initially were block-like, wide-eyed, and stylized. Gradually, however, with the decline of the aristocracy, stylized representation was replaced by realism. By the 500s BCE, the heavy and stern-looking kings were succeeded by well-proportioned, smoothly muscled, and slightly smiling figures depicted as one would encounter them in the market.

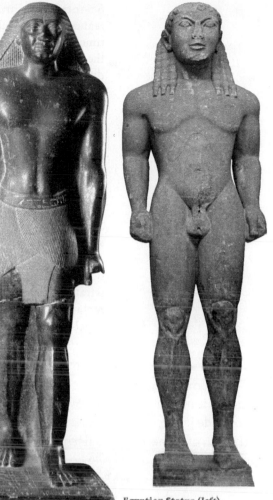

**Egyptian Statue (left) and Early Greek (right) Adaptation.** The Egyptian influence on the Greek cities is striking. Here we have a visual example of the pattern of origins, interaction, and adaptation. The Greek example is a creative adaptation of an Egyptian model.

**Scientific Beginnings**    In both Mesopotamia and Egypt, conceptualization of reality advanced substantially from Old and New Stone Age imagery. For the first time we get glimpses of humans constructing abstract ideas, without recourse to the senses—for example, in mathematics. Mathematical calculations, such as addition and subtraction, began in Mesopotamia even before the first writing system was introduced.

Subsequently, scribes developed tables for multiplication and division, squares, cubes, square roots, cube roots, and reciprocal and exponential functions. They calculated numerical approximations for the square roots of 2 and 3. Exercise texts from the Old Babylonian period (ca. 2000–1600 BCE) pose such problems as: "Beyond the ditch I made a dike, one cubit per cubit is the inclination of this dike. What is the base, the top and the height of it? And what is its circumference?" Babylonian mathematical interests focused primarily on the roots of algebra. Scribes also laid the foundations for geometry and astronomy by devising the system of 60 degrees for arcs, angles, and time—all still in use today.

In Egypt, the *Rhind Mathematical Papyrus* (ca. 1550 BCE) is an early handbook of geometric and algebraic questions typically used by scribes and administrators. It teaches the apprentice scribe how to calculate the volume of rectangles, triangles, and pyramids and how to measure the slopes of angles. Algebraic operations are illustrated through examples such as "[animal] fat [worth] ten gallons [of grain] is issued for one year; what is its share per day?" As in Mesopotamia, Egyptian mathematics implicitly employed important mathematical principles without yet stating them explicitly.

> "As for 'something entering from outside,' it means the breath of an outside god or death, not the intrusion of something his flesh engenders."
>
> —*Edwin Smith Papyrus, Case 8*

The *Kahun* (ca. 1825 BCE) and *Edwin Smith* (ca. 1534 BCE) *Papyri* are the best-known texts on the applied science of medicine. They cover diagnosis, prescriptions, and surgery. In the latter text we find the earliest distinction between supernatural and natural causes of illness, disease, or injury.

A few examples illustrate ancient Egyptian medical standards. Headache is diagnosed as "half head," which the Greeks translated as "*hemikrania*," from which our English word "migraine" is derived. Remedies for treating stiffness of limbs, pregnancy, birth complications, and childhood diseases, as well as advice on birth control and abortion, include mixtures of homeopathic herbs and elements. Surgeons received advice on how to use copper knives for male and female circumcision and needles for stitching up wounds. During their work, physicians were encouraged to repeat magic healing formulas that encouraged their patients to use their own self-healing powers.

# Putting It All Together

The beginning of the agrarian age in the Middle East and eastern Mediterranean was marked by agricultural surpluses, especially in irrigated areas. Depending on the size of the surplus, a pattern of state formation became visible along which city-states, kingdoms, and empires emerged in the various areas of the region. The central concern of the rulers in these small and large states was establishing and maintaining their authority, which included the use of military force—something not always easy to justify, especially when trade and ruling-class cooperation were also important. Therefore, the rulers appealed to gods—that is, personalized forces in nature stronger than rulers. The will of these forces was conceived as being expressed in the law code of each state. Gods were lawgivers, and their law possessed divine authority; thus, rulers became the executers of the god-given law.

Although "divine," the rulers' mandate was never absolute. Popular or aristocratic assemblies from preroyal times of tribal or clan organization survived stubbornly or were revived in the Greek *poleis*. Although the Hittite and Assyrian kings succeeded in marginalizing these assemblies during periods of empire building, the divine mandate was not exclusively theirs, and they had to share power, if only to a limited degree. It is important to note that this tradition of assemblies, which we often associate solely with Greece, was widespread in the Middle East. This awareness is necessary to understand the period after 600 BCE when individuals arose with messages of personal salvation and announced that it was not simply fate or misfortune to live and die under these often harsh imperial powers. Instead, they insisted that the destiny of humanity *transcended* these all-too-human institutions.

▶ For additional resources, including maps, primary sources, visuals, and quizzes, please go to www.oup.com/us/vonsivers. Please see the Further Resources section at the back of the book for additional readings and suggested websites.

# Against the Grain

# Akhenaten the Transgressor

As early as the Old Kingdom (ca. 2686–2181 BCE) Re, the sun god, was well established as the supreme deity (sometimes referred to as the "Father of the Gods") in the Egyptian polytheistic pantheon. Re was closely associated with kings, who were often depicted as his sons. During the Middle Kingdom, Amenhotep III ("Amun is satisfied") (1386–1349 BCE) promoted the worship of Amun-Re as the focus of Egyptian religion. It was therefore assumed that Amenhotep's son and successor, Amenhotep IV (1353–1336 BCE), would follow in his father's footsteps.

For reasons that are not altogether clear, Amenhotep IV took the radical step of repudiating the cult of Amun-Re in favor of a new object of devotion, that of the Aten (the solar disc). To drive home the point, early in his reign **Amen**hotep IV changed his name to Akhen**aten** ("devoted adherent of Aten"). Thus, in place of Amun as the *supreme* god among all the gods, Aten was now designated as the *sole* god for all Egyptians.

Akhenaten quickly instituted policies in order to officially replace worship of Amun-Re with devotion to the Aten. Masons were ordered to chisel out all references to Amun in temples and other monuments, while scribes were directed to delete similar references in official documents. Then, after closing down all temples of Amun, Akhenaten constructed a new capital at Akentaten, hundreds of miles north of Thebes, the center of the priestly cult attending Amun-Re. Here, the new temples to Aten were designed as sun temples, facing east in order to admit the light of the rising sun into the interior. Moreover, in various forms the Aten was depicted as a solar disc, whose rays of light were directed to the hands of Akhenaten and his queen, Nefertiti, who would presumably then share the beneficence of the sun's life-giving rays with their subjects (see page 60).

Akhenaten's experiment at overturning existing orthodoxy was short-lived. His successor (possibly his own son), given the name Tutenkh**aten**, quickly reverted to the previous cult of Amun-Re, taking the name Tutenkh**amen** (1336–1327 BCE). Nevertheless, Akhenaten's radical revolution has generated considerable scholarly conjecture. Among explanations for his motives, it has been thought that his intention was to undermine the growing political power of the priests of Amun-Re. Alternatively, perhaps Akhenaten was determined to replace the former polytheism with a monotheistic religion devoted to *his* power, and not to the solar disc. A more altruistic theory suggests that Akhenaten was interested in opening up religion (formerly restricted to a select few who followed the commands of the priests of Amun-Re) to wider participation by all Egyptians. Perhaps the most provocative of speculations concerns whether Akhenaten was the forebearer of later monotheistic worship in the ancient Near East.

- **Why was Akhenaten's revolt against prevailing religious practices considered so revolutionary?**

- **Are there any possible similarities between Akhenaten's approach to monotheism and later examples found in either early Judaism or Zoroastrianism?**

# Thinking Through Patterns

▶ **What are the main factors that enabled the transition from foraging to farming?**

One crucial factor in this pattern was the environment of the Taurus–Zagros–Levant region, the Fertile Crescent. Adequate rainfall, abundant edible plants suitable for domestication, and several animals that proved useful and easy to domesticate characterized the region. But had it not been for human beings mastering irrigation, such a transition might have remained confined to small microclimatic regions. Populations in the great riverine agricultural areas in Mesopotamia and Egypt (and, as we will see in the following chapters, India and China) took as their task the mastery of the fertility of river valleys and the use of reliable river water for irrigation, rather than relying on rainfall. Here was a system adaptable to a variety of climates, as witnessed by the fact that these four early agricultural civilizations arose in dry climates watered by large river systems.

While scholars still debate the absolute origins of the domestication of plants and animals, most are in agreement that the Fertile Crescent is central to this process. Here, experimentation with local grains, leaf plants, and pulses during the Neolithic helped humans develop more reliable and better-yielding crops, which were then traded locally and, through regional trade, further afield. The climatic zones of Eurasia were especially well suited to this because of the long east–west axis. Animals like sheep, goats, and cattle were similarly found over wide areas and were easy to trade, which led to the sharing of information about raising livestock. Another important factor was that as populations grew as a result of the stability of food production by agriculture, groups split off and started their own communities, carrying the new techniques with them. Thus, by about 5000 BCE, the basic techniques and species of Eurasian and North African domestication were well established.

▶ **Where did the pattern of agrarian life first emerge and why?**

▶ **How did the creation of agrarian–urban society—what we commonly call "civilization"—make for an entirely new pattern of world history?**

The ability of humans to create large food surpluses encouraged a considerable degree of settlement. Such stability enabled the nonproducing part of the population to occupy themselves with creating nonagricultural things—buildings, religious centers, defensive works, dwellings. As these elements of villages and towns grew and became more complex, they allowed the cumulative knowledge and production of human beings to enlarge in these sites. In short, cities created an entirely new kind of society with elaborate class hierarchies built on power and efficiency. Rivalry and competition among cities required ever more powerful defenses to protect the people, their wealth, and their trade. From this period, the patterns of urban life and of state formation were established, patterns we readily recognize today as our own.

# Patterns of Evidence: Sources for Chapter 2

## Law Code of Hammurabi

**ca. 1772 BCE**

In order to "cause justice to prevail in the land" and to "further the welfare of the people," the Amorite King Hammurabi (ca. 1792–1750 BCE), having made Babylon his capital and having conquered Mesopotamia, issued a comprehensive code of laws. He caused them to be inscribed on stones that were erected at crossroads and in marketplaces throughout his kingdom, so that all his subjects would understand the penalties that their actions might incur. This document survives on one of these stones, topped by an illustration showing Hammurabi receiving the order to write as directed by the sun god Shamash. The stone was discovered by French archaeologists in 1901–1902, and it remains one of the treasures of the Louvre Museum in Paris.

**1.** If a man accuse a man, and charge him with murder, but cannot convict him, the accuser shall be put to death.

**3.** If a man in a case before the court offer testimony concerning deeds of violence, and do not establish the testimony he has given . . . the man shall be put to death.

**53.** If a man neglect to strengthen his dike, and do not strengthen his dike, and a break be made in his dike and he let the water carry away farmland, then the man in whose dike the break has been made shall restore the grain which he has damaged.

**54.** If he be not able to restore the grain, they shall sell him and his goods, and the farmers whose grain the water has carried away shall divide the results of the sale.

**104.** If a merchant give an agent grain, wood, oil, or goods of any kind with which to trade, the agent shall write down the money received and return it to the merchant. The agent shall take a sealed receipt for the money which he gives to the merchant.

**105.** If the agent be careless and do not take a receipt for the money which he has given to the merchant, the

Source: Nels M. Bailkey and Richard Lim, eds., *Readings in Ancient History: Thought and Experience from Gilgamesh to St. Augustine*, 6th ed. (Boston: Houghton Mifflin, 2002), 28–36.

money not receipted for shall not be placed to his account.

**196.** If a man destroy the eye of another man, they shall destroy his eye.

**197.** If he break a man's bone, they shall break his bone.

**198.** If he destroy the eye of a common man or break a bone of a common man, he shall pay one *mina* of silver.

**199.** If he destroy the eye of a man's slave or break a bone of a man's slave, he shall pay one-half his price.

**206.** If a man strike another man in a quarrel and wound him, that man shall swear, "I did not strike him intentionally," and he shall be responsible for the physician.

**207.** If he die as a result of the blow, he shall swear as above, and if it were the son of a gentleman, he shall pay one-third *mina* of silver.

**228.** If a builder erect a house for a man and complete it, he shall give him two shekels of silver per *sar* of house as his wage.

**229.** If a builder erect a house for a man and do not make its construction firm and the house which he built collapse and cause the death of the owner of the house, that builder shall be put to death.

**233.** If a builder erect a house for a man and do not surround it with walls of proper construction, and a wall fall in, that builder shall strengthen that wall at his own expense.

**253.** If a man hire a man to oversee his farm and furnish him the seed-grain and entrust him with oxen and contract with him to cultivate the field, and that man steal either the seed or the crop and it be found in his possession, they shall cut off his fingers.

*From the Epilogue:*

The great gods proclaimed me, and I am the guardian shepherd whose scepter is righteous and whose beneficent shadow is spread over my city. In my bosom I carried the people of the land of Sumer and Akkad; under my protection I brought their brethren into security; in my wisdom I sheltered them.

That the strong might not oppress the weak, and that they should give justice to the orphan and the widow. . . .

▶ **Working with Sources**

1. When are financial and capital punishments applied in the code, and is there a consistent principle at work here?

2. Why is Hammurabi concerned with the regulation of business transactions, and particularly when they have to do with agriculture?

## SOURCE 2.2

# Babylonian Poem of the Righteous Sufferer

### ca. 2000–1600 BCE

Composed in Akkadian and consisting of 480 lines distributed over four tablets, this poem is a protest against one man's undeserved suffering. The author is tormented but cannot determine the cause, and he feels that the god Marduk is not responding adequately to his lamentation. Because he has always been faithful to his god and assiduous in his worship, the Sufferer begins to speculate that the gods are not concerned with human pain at all. Even more, they may engage in this sort of torment for their own benefit. The figure of the "Righteous Sufferer" is frequently compared to the Biblical figure Job. While this "Babylonian Job" is eventually delivered from his sufferings, perhaps his complaints linger on.

My god has forsaken me and
  disappeared,
My goddess has failed me and keeps
  at a distance.
The benevolent angel who walked
  beside me has departed,
My protecting spirit has taken
  to flight, and is seeking
  someone else.
My strength is gone; my appearance has become gloomy;
My dignity has flown away, my protecting made off. . . .
The king, the flesh of the gods, the
  sun of his peoples,
His heart is enraged with me, and
  cannot be appeased.

The courtiers plot hostile action
  against me,
They assemble themselves and give
  utterance to impious words. . . .
They combine against me in slander
  and lies.
My lordly mouth have they held as
  with reins,
So that I, whose lips used to prate,
  have become like a mute.
My sonorous shout is reduced to
  silence,
My lofty head is bowed down to the
  ground,
Dread has enfeebled my robust
  heart. . . .
If I walk the street, ears are pricked;

Source: Nels M. Bailkey and Richard Lim, eds., *Readings in Ancient History: Thought and Experience from Gilgamesh to St. Augustine,* 6th ed. (Boston: Houghton Mifflin, 2002), 20–22.

If I enter the palace, eyes blink.
My city frowns on me as an enemy;
Indeed my land is savage and
    hostile.

      . . .

My ill luck has increased, and I do
    not find the right.
I called to my god, but he did not
    show his face,
I prayed to my goddess, but she did
    not raise her head.
The diviner with his inspection has
    not got to the root of the matter,
Nor has the dream priest with his
    libation elucidated my case.
I sought the favor of the **zaqiqu-
spirit**, but he did not enlighten
me;
And the incantation priest with his
    ritual did not appease the divine
    wrath against me.
What strange conditions
    everywhere!
When I look behind, there is perse-
    cution, trouble.

      . . .

For myself, I gave attention to sup-
    plication and prayer:
To me prayer was discretion, sacri-
    fice my rule.
The day for reverencing the god was
    a joy to my heart;
The day of the goddess' procession
    was profit and gain to me.

The king's prayer—that was my joy,
And the accompanying music
    became a delight for me.
I instructed my land to keep the
    god's rites,
And provoked my people to value
    the goddess' name.
I made praise for the king like a
    god's
And taught the populace reverence
    for the palace.
I wish I knew that these things were
    pleasing to one's god!


What is proper to oneself is an of-
    fense to one's god,
What in one's heart seems despi-
    cable is proper to one's god.
Who knows the will of the gods in
    heaven?
Who understands the plans of the
    underworld gods?
Where have mortals learnt the way
    of a god?
He who was alive yesterday is dead
    today.
For a minute he was dejected, sud-
    denly he is exuberant.
One moment people are singing in
    exaltation,
Another they groan like profes-
    sional mourners.

*Zaqiqu*-spirit: The god
of dreams.

▶ **Working
with Sources**

1. **What is the responsibility of the gods to this worshipper, and what can
he do if the gods renege on the contract?**

2. **How are the priestly establishment and the king connected to this man?
Have these institutions also failed him?**

## SOURCE 2.3

# Advice from a royal scribe to his apprentice, Middle Kingdom Egypt, Twelfth Dynasty

### ca. 1878–1839 BCE

The Papyrus Lansing is a letter of instruction from the royal scribe (and "chief overseer of the cattle of Amun-Re, King of Gods") Nebmare-nakht to his apprentice Wenemdiamun. It seems to date from the reign of the pharaoh Senusret III (Sesostris III). The letter conveys a great deal of practical advice to an up-and-coming scribe—as well as warnings about what temptations he must avoid to be successful. While Nebmare-nakht is clearly proud of the status his work has earned him, he also illuminates the specific duties and responsibilities of a royal official in this period.

The scribe of the army and commander of the cattle of the house of Amun, Nebmare-nakht, speaks to the scribe Wenemdiamun, as follows. Be a scribe! Your body will be sleek; your hand will be soft. You will not flicker like a flame, like one whose body is feeble. For there is not the bone of a man in you. You are tall and thin. If you lifted a load to carry it, you would stagger, your legs would tremble. You are lacking in strength; you are weak in all your limbs; you are poor in body.

Set your sight on being a scribe: a fine profession that suits you. You call for one; a thousand answer you. You stride freely on the road. You will not die like a hired ox. You are in front of others.

I spend the day instructing you. You do not listen! Your heart is like an empty room. My teachings are not in it. Take their meaning to yourself!

The marsh thicket is before you each day, as a nestling is after its mother. You follow the path of pleasure; you make friends with revelers. You have made your home in the brewery, as one who thirsts for beer. You sit in the parlor with an idler. You hold the writings in contempt. You visit the prostitute. Do not do these things! What are they for? They are of no use. Take note of it!

Furthermore. Look, I instruct you to make you sound; to make you hold the palette freely. To make you become one whom the king trusts; to make you gain entrance to treasury and granary. To make you receive the ship-load at the gate of the granary. To make you issue the offerings on feast days. You are dressed in fine clothes; you own horses. Your boat is on the river; you are supplied with

Source: Translated by A. M. Blackman and T. E. Peet, *Journal of Egyptian Archaeology* 11 (1925): 284–298, as quoted by Miriam Lichtheim, *Ancient Egyptian Literature*, vol. 2, 171–172.

attendants. You stride about inspecting. A mansion is built in your town. You have a powerful office, given you by the king. Male and female slaves are about you. Those who are in the fields grasp your hand, on plots that you have made. Look, I make you into a staff of life! Put the writings in your heart, and you will be protected from all kinds of toil. You will become a worthy official.

Do you not recall the fate of the unskilled man? His name is not known. He is ever burdened [like an ass carrying] in front of the scribe who knows what he is about.

Come, let me tell you the woes of the soldier, and how many are his superiors: the general, the troop-commander, the officer who leads, the standard-bearer, the lieutenant, the scribe, the commander of fifty, and the garrison-captain. They go in and out in the halls of the palace, saying, "Get laborers!". . . .

His march is uphill through mountains. He drinks water every third day; it is smelly and tastes of salt. His body is ravaged by illness. The enemy comes, surrounds him with missiles, and life recedes from him. He is told: "Quick, forward, valiant soldier! Win for yourself a good name!" He does not know what he is about. His body is weak, his legs fail him. When victory is won, the captives are handed over to his majesty, to be taken to Egypt. The foreign woman faints on the march; she hangs herself on the soldier's neck. His knapsack drops, another grabs it while he is burdened with the woman. . . .

Be a scribe, and be spared from soldiering! You call and one says: "Here I am." You are safe from torments. Every man seeks to raise himself up. Take note of it!

▶ **Working with Sources**

1. How does Nebmare-nakht attempt to make the life of a diligent scribe attractive to his apprentice? How does he use negative examples to steer Wenemdiamun in the right direction?

2. Why is the position of scribe so prominent in Middle Kingdom Egypt? What role does a scribe play in relation to the Pharaoh?

## SOURCE 2.4

# Sketch of the palace complex at Knossos, Minoan Crete

### ca. 1700–1400 BCE

In 1900, Sir Arthur Evans discovered the remains of a vast palace complex on the island of Crete in the southern Aegean Sea. Christening the civilization "Minoan" after the legendary King Minos of Crete, Evans continued to excavate at Knossos and at other sites around the island. The palace at Knossos seems to have contained hundreds of rooms, including a throne

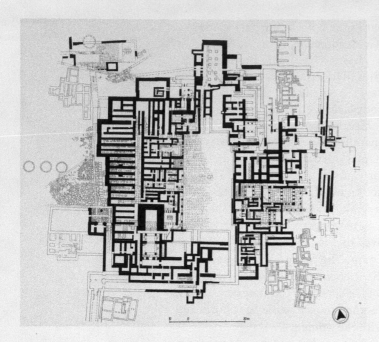

room and storage spaces for food and cisterns for the collection of water. The legacy of Evans's work can be viewed at the visual archive held at the Ashmolean Museum in Oxford, England (http://sirarthurevans.ashmus.ox.ac.uk/), and there is a virtual tour of the site, provided by the British School at Athens (http://www.bsa.ac.uk/knossos/vrtour/).

▶ **Working with Sources**

1. Can the palace complex at Knossos be compared with palace sites in Mesopotamia and Egypt in the second millennium BCE? In what respects?

2. What do you think the palace complex suggests about the structure of Minoan society?

## SOURCE 2.5

# The Great Hymn to the Aten

### ca. 1353–1336 BCE

This hymn to the Egyptian sun god Aten has been attributed to King Akhenaten ("the devoted adherent of Aten"), the pharaoh formerly known as Amenhotep IV. While Akhenaten's experiment in monotheism was short-lived, the poem reflects the connections this revolutionary religious thinker attempted to forge between himself and an all-powerful deity. Note that he also solicits the blessings of Aten for himself, as leader of the Egyptian people, and for his wife, the famous Nefertiti.

Source: Translated by J. A. Wilson, as quoted by Miriam Lichtheim, *Ancient Egyptian Literature*, vol. 2, 96–99.

Splendid you rise in heaven's
  lightland,
O living Aten, creator of life!
When you have dawned in eastern
  lightland,
You fill every land with your beauty.
You are beauteous, great, radiant,
High over every land;
Your rays embrace the lands,
To the limit of all that you made.

. . .

When you set in western
  lightland,
Earth is in darkness as if in death;
One sleeps in chambers, heads
  covered,
One eye does not see another.
Were they robbed of their goods,
That are under their heads,
People would not remark it.
Every lion comes from its den,
All the serpents bite;
Darkness hovers, earth is silent,
As their maker rests in lightland.

. . .

Ships fare north, fare south as well,
Roads lie open when you rise;
The fish in the river dart before you,
Your rays are in the midst of the sea.
Who makes seed grow in women,
Who creates people from sperm;
Who feeds the son in his mother's
  womb,
Who soothes him to still his tears.
Nurse in the womb,

Giver of breath,
To nourish all that he has made.

. . .

You are in my heart,
There is no other who knows you,
Only your son, **Neferkheprure,
  Only-one-of-Re**,
Whom you have taught your ways
  and your might.
[Those on] earth come from your
  hand as you made them,
When you have dawned they live,
When you set they die;
You yourself are lifetime, one lives
  by you.
All eyes are on your beauty until
  you set.
All labor ceases when you rest in
  the west;
When you rise you stir [everyone]
  for the King,
Every leg is on the move since you
  founded the earth.
You rouse them for your son who
  came from your body,
The King who lives by Maat, the
  Lord of the Two Lands,
*Neferkheprure, Only-one-of-Re,*
The Son of Re who lives by **Maat**,
  the Lord of crowns,
Akhenaten, great in his lifetime;
And the great Queen whom he
  loves, the Lady of the Two Lands,
*Nefer-nefru-Aten Nefertiti*, living
  forever.

*Neferkheprure, Only-
one-of-Re*: Akhenaten.

**Maat:** balance, law,
justice.

▶ **Working
with Sources**

1. **How does the hymn reflect on the practical advantages provided by
   the sun?**
2. **How does the hymn reinforce the power of Aten in political terms?**

## Chapter 3  3000–600 BCE

# Shifting Agrarian Centers in India

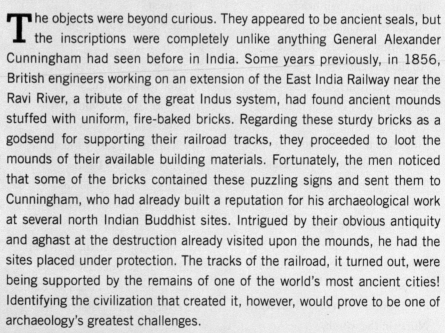

The objects were beyond curious. They appeared to be ancient seals, but the inscriptions were completely unlike anything General Alexander Cunningham had seen before in India. Some years previously, in 1856, British engineers working on an extension of the East India Railway near the Ravi River, a tribute of the great Indus system, had found ancient mounds stuffed with uniform, fire-baked bricks. Regarding these sturdy bricks as a godsend for supporting their railroad tracks, they proceeded to loot the mounds of their available building materials. Fortunately, the men noticed that some of the bricks contained these puzzling signs and sent them to Cunningham, who had already built a reputation for his archaeological work at several north Indian Buddhist sites. Intrigued by their obvious antiquity and aghast at the destruction already visited upon the mounds, he had the sites placed under protection. The tracks of the railroad, it turned out, were being supported by the remains of one of the world's most ancient cities! Identifying the civilization that created it, however, would prove to be one of archaeology's greatest challenges.

It was well into the next century before scholars really began to understand the place of this "lost city" of Harappa—the center of one of the world's oldest and most mysterious societies. And although a full program of archaeological investigation has been under way at Harappa and dozens of similar sites throughout the Indus valley since the 1920s, some of the most basic questions about this society remain to be answered. For example, how

*ABOVE:* **The Ruins of Mohenjo-Daro.**

did their writing system—composed of the symbols carved on the seals first brought to Cunningham—work? Unlike other early civilizations, which endured for thousands of years, Harappan society was relatively short-lived, lasting perhaps 600 years before vanishing almost entirely; why did it disappear? And while scholars believe the structures of Harappan village life set many of the patterns for later Indian rural society, exactly how did these structures develop over the intervening generations? Indeed, how and why did urban societies reemerge later along the Ganges River, setting so many of the patterns of south Asian history? In short, what were the fundamental patterns that marked these founding cultures, and how did these patterns change the lives of the peoples in the region and come to be adopted and adapted by them?

## Seeing Patterns

▶ Who were the Harappans? Where did they come from? What evidence exists for their origins?

▶ What explanations have been offered for the collapse of Harappan society? How well do the rival theories hold up, given what scholars and archaeologists have discovered?

▶ How can we know about the newcomers to northern India? What sources exist for historians to examine?

▶ What patterns can we see evolving in the Ganges River states that will mark the subsequent development of Indian civilization?

One important pattern marking the history of northern India, like that of Mesopotamia, lies in regular rhythms of migration and invasion, interchanges of innovation, assimilation of peoples, and the expansion of ideas. In contrast to the long history of political unification in Egypt or China, all of India did not experience rule by a single regime until the nineteenth century CE. Yet considerable cultural and religious unity had already been created thousands of years earlier under the influence of newly emerging states along the Ganges River. The ability to maintain this cultural continuity while creating social systems with the flexibility to manage innovation from outside has marked India to the present day. Among their most significant achievements, the social, philosophical, and political challenges facing these early Ganges states resulted in some of the world's most important religious movements: Hinduism, Jainism, and the most widespread and influential religious movement in Asia, Buddhism.

## The Vanished Origins of Harappa, 3000–1500 BCE

Since the first intensive archaeological work of the 1920s, the sites of the Indus valley have been imbued with all the romance of "lost civilizations." Unlike Egypt (see Chapter 2), where the patterns of society remained remarkably stable for thousands of years, or Mesopotamia, which spawned a succession of states and empires, the cities of the Indus valley flourished for less than 1,000 years—from about 2500–1700 BCE—before vanishing almost without a trace. Anchored by two major cities—Harappa [hah-RAP-uh] in the north and Mohenjo-Daro [moe-hen-joe DAH-roe] in the southwest—and extending from the upper Ganges River to the Arabian Sea, a dense network of small cities, towns, and villages marked by a remarkable consistency of architecture and artifact occupied the largest cultural area of the third millennium BCE: twice the size of the Old Kingdom of Egypt and four times that of the empire of Sargon in Mesopotamia. Trade with southwest Asia and Egypt extended Harappan influence even farther.

Yet this "Harappan," or "Indus valley," culture, as archaeologists have named it, remains by far the most mysterious of the early centers of agriculturally supported urban society. The sophistication and precision of its urban planning, the standardization of weights and measures, and the attention to cleanliness and comfort all suggest an elaborate system of social organization, yet we know virtually nothing of its arrangement. Scholars have labored for nearly a century to unlock the secrets of the Harappan pictographic symbols, yet they remain mostly undeciphered. Most tantalizing of all is the fundamental question: Why, as the new mode of urban society gathered momentum elsewhere, did the inhabitants of this one abandon their cities and disappear from the historical record? To look at what we can and do know about these mysterious people, we must start with the geography of the Indus and its region.

## The Region and People

Geographers define the region encompassed by the modern states of India, Pakistan, and Bangladesh as a *subcontinent*—a large, distinct area of land somewhat smaller than a continent. While the region is attached to the Eurasian landmass, it is almost completely cut off from it by some of the most forbidding physical barriers on earth. The lower two-thirds of India form a vast peninsula surrounded on three sides by the Arabian Sea, the Indian Ocean, and the Bay of Bengal. To the north of the bay, extending from Bangladesh through the Indian province of Assam to the north and east and deep into Myanmar (formerly Burma), are continuous ranges of heavily forested mountains. Some of the world's highest annual rainfall totals—over 100 inches—are regularly recorded here.

Forming the northeastern border of the subcontinent above the rain belt is the "roof of the world," the Himalayan Mountains. These meet another set of formidable peaks, the Hindu Kush, which extends into Pakistan and, with the Sulaiman and Kirthar ranges, marks the northwestern border of the region. Access to the Indian peninsula by land is thus limited to a handful of mountain passes through the Himalayas and the more substantial Khyber and Bolan Passes of the northwest. Historically, these have been the main avenues of trade, migration, and, frequently, invasion (see Map 3.1).

**Topography:** The physical features—mountains, rivers, deserts, swamps, etc.—of a region.

**The Monsoon System**    As the region is surrounded by water and framed by high mountains, India's internal **topography** also has a considerable influence on its climate. The Deccan Plateau, Vindhya Range, and other internal highland areas tend to both trap tropical moisture against the west coast and funnel it toward the region drained by the Ganges River in the northeast. The moisture itself comes from the summer winds of the monsoon system, a term derived from the Arabic word *mausim*, for "season." The winds carry moisture generated from the heat of southern Africa as they flow southwest to northeast over the Indian Ocean from June through October and govern the climatic cycles of southeastern Asia, Indonesia, and southern China as well as India. In the winter months the winds reverse direction and pull hot, dry air down from central Asia. During this dry season, rainfall is scant or nonexistent over large areas of south Asia.

The extremes of the monsoon cycle, as well as its regularity, exert a powerful influence on Asian agriculture. This is particularly the case in India, where the monsoon rainfall amounts differ widely from region to region. Because even

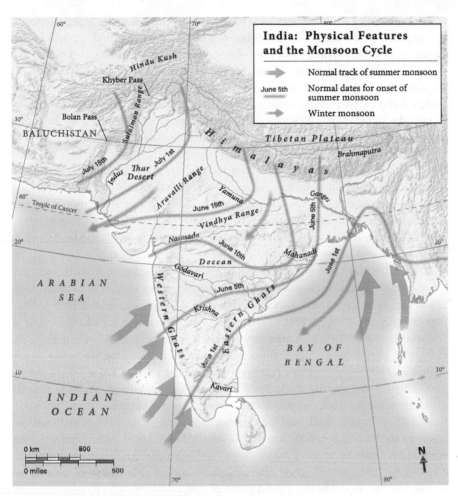

MAP 3.1 **India: Physical Features and the Monsoon Cycle.**

minor variations in the timing of the cycle or the volume of rain may spell potential flood or famine, the arrival of the monsoon is even today greeted with nervous
anticipation. Generally speaking, the subcontinent becomes drier as one moves
farther north and west until one reaches the Thar, or Great Indian, Desert and the
plain of Sind, the site of some of the hottest temperatures ever recorded on earth—
nearly 130 degrees Fahrenheit. It is this arid region bordered by mountains and
watered by the Indus River system that saw the rise of the first Indian cities.

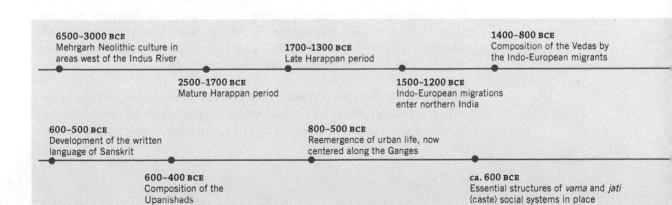

**6500–3000 BCE**
Mehrgarh Neolithic culture in
areas west of the Indus River

**2500–1700 BCE**
Mature Harappan period

**1700–1300 BCE**
Late Harappan period

**1500–1200 BCE**
Indo-European migrations
enter northern India

**1400–800 BCE**
Composition of the Vedas by
the Indo-European migrants

**600–500 BCE**
Development of the written
language of Sanskrit

**600–400 BCE**
Composition of the
Upanishads

**800–500 BCE**
Reemergence of urban life, now
centered along the Ganges

**ca. 600 BCE**
Essential structures of *varna* and *jati*
(caste) social systems in place

As the Greek historian Herodotus called Egypt "the gift of the Nile," so too, as archaeologists have noted, should Harappan civilization be called the "gift of the Indus." A vast river system composed of seven main branches in ancient times, the Indus has a slow, meandering course that for millennia has left behind rich deposits of fertile soil, by some estimates twice as much as the Nile. Moreover, like the Yellow River in China, the constant buildup of silt in the riverbed periodically caused the water to overflow its banks and change course—dangerous for those living close by but an effective means of spreading soil over a wide area.

**Mehrgarh Culture**   Researchers have found a number of Neolithic sites near the river, one of the most productive being Mehrgarh [MARE-gar], located near a strategic mountain pass in Baluchistan. Scholars have dated the Mehrgarh culture to about 6000 BCE, making it perhaps the oldest on the Indian subcontinent. Like the inhabitants of the Fertile Crescent, villagers in Neolithic Baluchistan raised wheat and barley and domesticated sheep, goats, and cattle. As long ago as 5500 BCE pottery was being produced in the area. Also dating from this period are the crafting and trading of fine *lapis lazuli* (an opaque, dark blue gemstone) beadware, or "microbeads," later a coveted item among Harappan luxury goods. Significantly, even the earliest Baluchistani dwellings are made of mud brick, a material that with greater scope and sophistication became a hallmark of the Harappan cityscape. For all of these reasons, some archaeologists have viewed Mehrgarh culture as a possible precursor to Harappa.

Scholars agree that by about 3000 BCE a culture of villages and towns with elaborate trade networks, sophisticated pottery, and a substantial array of domesticated plants and animals had long been established in the hills of Baluchistan adjacent to the Indus and its western tributaries. Attracted, most likely, by the comparative ease of growing staple crops in the reliably fertile river valleys, the inhabitants of these hill sites extended their settlements eastward sometime before 2600 BCE and began a rapid phase of consolidation, which culminated in the region's first cities.

## Adapting to Urban Life in the Indus Valley

By about 2300 BCE the two major cities of Harappa and Mohenjo-Daro—separated by 350 miles—marked the poles of a system of small cities, towns, and villages sprawled across an area estimated to be between 650,000 and 850,000 square miles (see Map 3.2). At its height, the city of Harappa had a population of over 40,000—comparable to that of the largest Mesopotamian cities of the period—and its defensive walls measured 3.5 miles in circumference. The location of these cities on a floodplain, moreover, dictated that they be built on enormous artificial hills to protect them from damage during times that the rivers overflowed their banks. Mohenjo-Daro, for example, with an estimated 3,000 dwellings and a population of about 41,000, was built on two 40-foot mounds separated by a channel 200 yards wide for easy access to the Indus. More remarkable than the sheer size of these cities, however, are their similarities to each other.

**Harappan Uniformity**   While all the cities of Mesopotamia and Egypt contained architectural features that make them a recognizable part of their respective cultures, Harappan cities seem almost to have been designed by the same

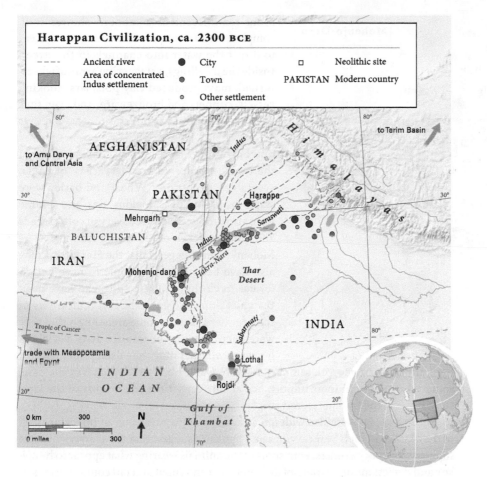

MAP 3.2 **Harappan Civilization, ca. 2300 BCE.**

hand. Harappa and Mohenjo-Daro, as well as several smaller cities and numerous towns, are laid out according to a rigorously surveyed and meticulously planned grid, with major thoroughfares running on north/south and east/west axes and squares, public buildings, temples, and markets at regular, convenient locations. The larger streets are paved with brick and remarkably straight. They are laid out according to standard widths, and most have drains and gutters connected to what may be the most elaborate urban sewer system of ancient times (see Map 3.3). The bricks themselves were produced according to a uniform ratio of 4:2:1. Moreover, the Harappans developed perhaps the world's first decimal system and used it in designing highly refined scales of weights and measures. The smallest scale division yet uncovered among any culture of this period was found in Lothal: 1.704 millimeters.

This uniformity appears to have extended into the personal realm as well. Houses of several stories were made of brick and plastered with gypsum, their floor plans strikingly similar even at widely spaced sites. Many had brick-lined indoor wells and primitive toilets emptying into terra-cotta **cesspits** whose overflow connected to the city's drains and sewers. Nearly all dwellings had a bathing

**Cesspits:** Deep holes or trenches used to deposit human waste and refuse; in the case of Harappa, they were flushed with water into city sewers and drains, ultimately leading to the adjacent river.

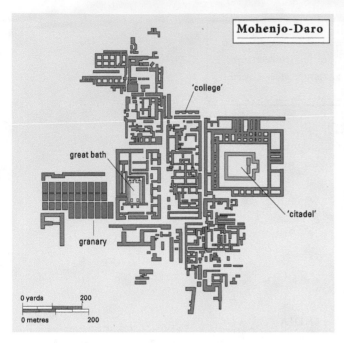

**Mohenjo-Daro**

'college'

great bath

'citadel'

granary

0 yards          200

0 metres         200

MAP 3.3 **Mohenjo-Daro.**

room reminiscent of a modern shower stall, complete with a waterproof floor and drain system to direct the water into channels in the street. Inside the dwellings, a staggering array of wheel-turned, mass-produced clay pots, jars, cooking vessels, copper- and bronzeware, and even toys have been found at various sites.

**The Harappan Diet**    The rich alluvial soil of the region supported a wide variety of fruits, vegetables, and grains. Wheat and barley were staple crops, but peas, melons, figs, and sesame were also produced. The recovery of cotton seeds and small patches of cloth and fishing line at Mohenjo-Daro suggests that the Harappans may also have been the first people to raise cotton for use in clothing. Cattle appear to have been the chief domestic animals, and indications of the large herds kept in some areas imply that they were seen as signs of wealth. It is not clear, however, whether they were used principally for food and milk or as work animals, as were water buffaloes. Whatever the case, some scholars see in their importance at this early time the origins of the later stereotype of the Indian "sacred cow."

Sheep and pigs were also widespread and appear to have been an important part of the Harappan diet. Seal carvings and figurines suggest that the Harappans were sophisticated dog breeders, with some of the animals wearing what appear to be collars and depictions of a variety of different sizes and snout and tail configurations. It is also thought that the chicken was first domesticated here in Neolithic times. Rice, which figures so prominently in later Indian agriculture, may have also been grown but, because of the relatively arid climate, does not appear to have been a staple.

**Harappan Identity and Government**    But who were they? Even today, evidence concerning the identity of the Harappans is obscure and contradictory. Everyday items and statuary offer few clues. Samples of symbols, most of which are found on what are believed to be merchant seals, were once believed to hold some tenuous links to a "Proto-Dravidian" language group distantly related to that of most modern south Indian peoples. Scholars have also suggested that the Harappans may have been an eastern branch of a people called "Proto-Mediterraneans," who ranged widely across southwest Asia. Complicating the matter further, archaeologists have identified an urban society designated as the "Bactria-Margiana Archaeological Complex" (BMAC) to the northwest of the Indus valley culture that shares some technological features with the Harappans but thus far no other obvious connections beyond some evidence of trade. Such findings are thus intriguing, but the uniqueness of Harappan urban life argues against any theory of simple cultural diffusion.

As with other early urban cultures, there appears to have been a close relationship among the religious, political, and social spheres of Harappan society.

Nevertheless, the clues, while suggestive, again yield little that is definitive. For example, the replication of city plans and architecture throughout such a wide area might indicate the kind of strong central authority and bureaucratic control typically found in a kingdom or empire. Yet we know virtually nothing of how it might have been organized. Moreover, some departures from the otherwise rigorous uniformity of previous sites found in recent work at Rojdi [ROEJ-dee] have led scholars to amend this picture in favor of one of overall unity marked by discernible regional styles. This modified view, along with findings that suggest that a number of pockets of Harappan culture survived the collapse of the cities by many centuries, would, in light of the apparent self-sufficiency of these areas, seem to work against theories of highly centralized control.

**Harappan Trade**   The ability to mass-produce a vast array of articles implies specialization, regulation, and an occupation-based class system. Moreover, elaborate port facilities suggest the prominence of a merchant class with overseas connections. Mesopotamian records from about 2300 BCE tell of a people called "Meluha", now believed to be the Harappans, who carried on extensive seaborne trade and maintained colonies of merchants in several of their cities.

Harappan seals have been found at Ur in Mesopotamia, and there is evidence of Harappan merchandise being traded as far away as Egypt and central Asia. Because of the apparent occupational specialization of the Harappans, some scholars have theorized that they may have belonged to *guilds*, organizations whose members all pursue the same trade or craft. However, the plainness and uniformity of Harappan dwellings, in contrast to the pervasiveness of their amenities—generous living quarters, indoor plumbing, and so forth—defy any easy generalizations about class structure.

The Harappans appear to have maintained complex trade networks both within their cultural sphere and outside of it. Fortified border settlements, evidently trading posts, extended their influence to the borders of modern Iran and as far north as the Amu Darya, or Oxus, River, the region of the BMAC. Curiously, however, we see virtually no evidence of foreign trade goods such as handicrafts in the Indus cities, suggesting perhaps tight government control over outside influences. As we have seen, a surprising variety of agricultural products and craft specialties were also created for both internal commerce and overseas export.

In addition to bulk foodstuffs such as grain, the Mesopotamian records of the Meluha note that their merchants dealt in beadwork, lapis lazuli, pearls, rare woods, cotton cloth, and dog and cat figurines. Due in part to our inability to decipher the Harappan symbols, we know much less about their imports, though bulk goods such as foodstuffs, oils, and cloth seem to be among them. The network of cities along the Indus also seems to have been pivotal in the long-distance

**The Horned God.** The figure on this seal found at Mohenjo-Daro may be a depiction of a Harappan deity. Its cross-legged "lotus" position and multiple faces prompted archaeologist Sir John Marshall to theorize in the 1930s that it was an early version of the Hindu god Shiva. More recently, some scholars have moved away from this claim, noting that mention of Shiva does not occur for another 1,000 years during the Vedic years. Above the figure is a typically short sample of the pictographic Harappan script.

**Building Foundations and Street Layout at Lothal.** The precision of Indus urban planning and execution is evident in this photograph of a residential area in Lothal.

"When I first saw them I found it difficult to believe they were prehistoric; they seemed to completely upset all established ideas about early art. . . . Now, in these statuettes, it is just this anatomical truth which is so startling; that makes us wonder whether, in this all-important matter, Greek artistry could possibly have been anticipated by the sculptors of a far-off age on the banks of the Indus."

—Sir John Marshall, Director-General of the Archaeological Survey of India

trade of copper from Baluchistan and in the exchange of gold, silver, semiprecious stones, shells, and timber throughout an extensive area north and west into Afghanistan and east to central Asia. Harappan figurines have been found along a broad front of nomadic routes from the Tarim Basin west. In addition, their sophistication and realism is striking among their contemporaries.

**Lothal**  The complexity of these questions of trade and social organization may be seen quite vividly at Lothal [LOW-tall]. Located several miles up the Sabarmati River from the Gulf of Khambat (Cambay), Lothal was a large—perhaps the chief—Harappan seaport. Recent work has shown it to be not only a vital link in Harappan maritime trade in the Arabian Sea and points west but an important manufacturing center of various trade items as well.

Lothal's central structure is an enormous basin, approximately 120 feet long and 70 feet wide, which was once connected to an inlet of the river. Most researchers believe that this was a dock for oceangoing ships, though some contend instead that it was a reservoir for water storage. Nearby are a number of structures believed to have been warehouses, each with numerous cubicles marked with what appear to be the stamps and seals of various merchants.

But Lothal was also a famous regional craft center, with microbeads used for decorative craft items and jewelry as its chief product for internal trade and export. Indeed, scholars theorize that the city's site may have been chosen precisely because of its proximity to convenient sources of precious stones for bead making. The site, with the precise city planning and water systems typical of Harappan cities, is also notable for its numerous specialized pottery kilns and bead "factories," complete with worker housing. Yet, for all this wealth of artifacts, such questions as who the merchants or workers were, how they were organized and

**Dockyard at Lothal.** While some scholars maintain that this structure was a holding tank or reservoir, the current consensus is that it was in fact a technologically advanced area for loading and unloading oceangoing ships. A sophisticated system of channels kept it flooded to the proper level, prevented overflow, and, with locks and gates, allowed access to the river and sea.

governed, what levels of mobility there might have been among different classes, and even precisely what those classes might have been remain elusive.

**Harappan Religion**    Clues about Harappan religion are equally tantalizing. The swastika, a symbol long associated with the cyclical nature of life in Indian and Buddhist art before its appropriation by the Nazis in the twentieth century, is first found in the cities of the Indus. Moreover, recent scholarship has suggested that the entire Harappan system of symbols, always assumed to be a form of writing, may instead be best understood as a form of religious shorthand for use in the multiethnic and multilingual Indus society. Figurines depicting cows, buffaloes, tigers, crocodiles, elephants, assorted animals from surrounding regions, and even mythical ones such as unicorns have also been found. Along with female figurines and **phallic stones**, these perhaps connote a type of fertility religion. Like many Neolithic and agrarian–urban cultures, the Harappans interred their dead with ornaments and pottery, and perhaps food. Such practices have led scholars to speculate that the Harappans may have believed in an afterlife. All of these finds have also led scholars to see deep continuities with later Hindu practices.

The prominence of such combined dualities as male and female or plant and animal may imply a principal deity embodying a unity of opposites, perhaps prefiguring later Indian religious conceptions. Likewise, the central importance of the Indus River and the considerable attention paid to personal bathing are believed to be symbolically linked with a great ritual bath in the center of Mohenjo-Daro, perhaps adding yet another ritual dimension to the picture. Here again, however, the details are obscure, and, for the moment, the nature of Harappan religion remains an open question.

**Phallic stones:** Stones in the shape of or meant to evoke the male sex organ; Indian religions use a host of phallic images, or *lingams*, in shrines, rituals, and festivals to symbolize the male, or active, forces of both natural and supernatural creation.

## The Collapse of the Cities

Around 1900 BCE the major cities of Harappan society appear to have been in decline. Structures of inferior quality seem to have been constructed on top of earlier buildings, suggesting a drop in population with a consequent loss of maintenance and services. By 1700 BCE the great cities appear to have been all but abandoned, their people moving to smaller outlying towns and villages, many returning to farming or becoming herders.

Some recent interpretations of Harappan urban decline attribute it to ecological collapse. The surrounding land—overgrazed, stripped of trees, and reliant upon the river for fertilization—had reached the limits of its capacity to support large cities. Perhaps increased flooding or weather-related problems stretched these limits even further. One theory holds that a prolonged regional drought—extending even to Mesopotamia—occurred around 2200 BCE resulting in a drying up of vital branches of the Indus watershed. Some scholars have proposed that increasing salt levels in the Indus played a role, perhaps as the result of diverting too much of its water for irrigation and supplying the cities; one study places part of the blame on earthquakes, which may have partially diverted the river's flow around 1800 BCE. We do know that the Hakra-Nara River was abruptly shunted into the Indus by the early eighteenth century BCE, resulting in a progressive drying up of its old watershed and increased flooding on the lower Indus.

Recent work at sites in the area south of the Indus valley indicates a longer period of survival for some of the smaller late Harappan towns in the region. Nevertheless, by about 1500 BCE it appears that remnants of Indus civilization were to be found only within isolated regional cultures that blended Harappan influences with those of neighboring peoples. The expansion of Harappan village agriculture to the east and south, however, continued. Indeed, the firm base that had made Harappan urban life possible—the cultivation of regionally appropriate staple crops and domesticated animals by people organized in villages—might justly be called the foundation of Indian social history. In that sense, though its cities were long since abandoned, the culture that produced this pattern of world history can hardly be considered "lost." It would be centuries, however, before India again saw the rise of cities.

## Interactions in Northern India, 1500–600 BCE

The "villains" of the Harappan collapse were long considered to be Indo-European-language-speaking migrants from the north who called themselves "Aryans" (Sanskrit, "the noble ones")—a term which, through a series of twisted associations and garbled history, Adolf Hitler and the Nazis later identified with Germans. The tales associated with them recount their movement south and east through the Khyber Pass and across the Punjab between 1700 and 1400 BCE. Their accounts of epic battles had formerly been assumed to refer to their conquest of the Harappans. The earliest of their religious texts, the *Rig-Veda* [rig VAY-duh], refers to a short, dark-skinned people whom the Aryans contemptuously called *dasas*, or "the others," a term later used to denote servants or slaves. It also mentions conflicts with sedentary phallus-worshipping people living in cities and manning fortifications, which would certainly seem to describe the Harappans.

These works, however, were not written down until centuries after the events may have occurred, and whether their references date from the mid-second millennium BCE or were added later on is still not resolved. Moreover, while battles undoubtedly did occur, long periods of peaceful migration and settlement appear to have taken place as well. Perhaps the most significant problem, however, is that the Harappan cities appear to have been largely abandoned by the time the newcomers arrived on the scene.

In addition, the relative lack of Aryan artifacts; conflicts of interpretation between archaeologists, classical scholars, and linguists; and a growing body of scholarship by Indian researchers have produced in recent years a comprehensive questioning of the narrative of the role of Aryan migration altogether. Indeed, some scholars have suggested that long-held assumptions about the Aryans grew out of nineteenth-century beliefs of European superiority supported by the British occupation of India. Their contention is that the roots of Vedic society came not with invaders from the north but from peoples—perhaps the remnant of the Harappans themselves—already long established in Punjab and, later, along the Ganges River. Since the debate has loomed increasingly large in revisiting broad currents of Indian history and identity, it most likely will remain unresolved for some time to come.

## The Vedic World, 1750–800 BCE

Most scholars, however, still assign a prominent, if not predominant, role to the Indo-European migrants. While, as we have seen, their exact homeland is unknown, scholars believe it to be in Central Asia in the area around the Caspian Sea. Groups of nomadic peoples speaking a set of languages that linguists have designated "Proto-Indo-European" appear to have migrated along a broad front into Asia Minor, the eastern Mediterranean, Iran, and deep into central Asia, as evidenced by the so-called Tocharian texts and the recent find of the Tarim Basin mummies. In all these areas they proved to be important catalysts in the diffusion of such technologies as ironworking and the use of the horse and chariot.

**Indo-European Origins**   Their ancestors had already played an extensive role in the spreading of items and ideas throughout Eurasia long before the Aryans arrived in India. Indeed, recent European scholarship has suggested that their presence predated the Neolithic settlement of the continent. More recently, branches are believed to have migrated east and west across the continent from perhaps 4000 to 2500 BCE. In the course of their travels they were active agents in collecting, refining, and spreading a host of Bronze Age technologies. They are believed to have been the people who introduced the domestication of the wild horses of the central Asian steppes on a wide scale, along with such items as bridles and weapons for use on horseback. Similarly, it seems likely that they were instrumental in moving the technology of the chariot along a wide front, ranging from the eastern European steppes to China. As we saw in Chapter 2, around 1000 BCE various Indo-European-descended groups, most prominently the Hittites, brought the techniques of ironmaking out of Anatolia, ultimately taking them as far as the western reaches of the Yellow River basin.

Scholars have long identified a Proto-Indo-European language these groups are believed to have spoken as the parent tongue of a family of languages that includes Latin, German, Greek, the Slavic languages, Celtic languages such as Gaelic, and what became the Indian literary language, Sanskrit. A number of words with common roots for certain basic objects or concepts may be found among these languages. Examples include *pater* (Latin), *Vater* (German), and *pitar* (Sanskrit) for "father"; *septem* (Latin) and *sapta* (Sanskrit) for "seven"; and the place name "Iran" (from "Aryan"). The identification of the Indo-European family of languages with the peoples of northern Europe in the nineteenth century, particularly the Germans, prompted the Nazi appropriation of the term "Aryan" for those of Germanic ethnicity in the 1930s and 1940s. However, a new group of scholars has argued for a "Paleolithic continuity theory," in which these groups had already begun to differentiate linguistically by the beginning of the Neolithic period and were not involved in massive "invasions" on the continent from the fifth to the third millennium BCE.

> "Both the spatial and the temporal extent of the Indus civilization has expanded dramatically on the basis of new excavations and the dating of the Vedic age as well as the theory of an Aryan invasion of India has been shaken. We are required to completely reconsider not only certain aspects of Vedic India, but the entire relationship between Indus civilization and Vedic culture."
>
> —Sanskrit and Hindu scholar Klaus Klostermaier

**The Vedas**   Scholars believe that sometime around 2000 BCE a linguistic group designated "Indo-Aryans" had already split off from the Indo-Iranian subgroup and began moving toward the passes leading to northern India. As noted earlier, however, the confusing written record, the lack of firm archaeological sites, and national politics have made this history extraordinarily difficult to unravel. Some scholars see the Indo-Aryans as emerging from the BMAC culture; others see them as engaging in wars within the BMAC against the indigenous settled inhabitants; still others see them as migrating into the Punjab long after the Harappan cites had been in decline. In this context, they view their accounts of great "battles" and storming "citadels" as in reality cattle raids and attacks on village corrals.

In any case, the migrants appear to have carried with them an oral tradition of epic poetry, hymns, prayers, and heavily allegorical myth and history that would be carefully cultivated and preserved until it was committed to writing after 600 BCE. The core works, composed from around 1400 to 800 BCE, are the religious hymns known as the Vedas ("knowledge" or "truths"). Like the *Iliad* and *Odyssey* for Homeric Greece, the Vedas are still the principal window through which we can glimpse the world of early northern India.

The *Rig-Veda*, the earliest of the Vedas, is currently believed to have been composed between about 1400 and 900 BCE. Some scholars, however, have suggested that some of the references contained in it point to much more ancient indigenous origins for it. Its verses were customarily memorized and passed from generation to generation by priests and their successors until after 1400 CE. The oldest recorded poetry in any Indo-European language, the *Rig-Veda*'s 1,028 verses provide an idealized and allegorical vision of a society led by hard-fighting, lusty warrior chieftains and priests, and composed of herders, cultivators, artisans, and servants. These groups became the prototypes of the four early social divisions, or *varnas*—priests, warriors, merchants, and commoners (see Patterns Up Close). Material wealth and skill in battle were the most valued attributes of Vedic culture. This emphasis on struggle and daring is seen as evidence of a strongly *patriarchal*, or male-led, society with an elaborate hierarchy based on kinship and prowess.

Nearly a quarter of the verses of the *Rig-Veda* celebrate the exploits of the god Indra, who is portrayed as the embodiment of the Vedic heroic ideal. In the accompanying quotation, he battles the serpent demon Vritra and triumphantly releases the rivers it had bottled up.

**Early North Indian Society and Economics**   Though a nomadic people, the Indo-Europeans possessed a high degree of technical skill. Not only had they benefited from the diffusion of earlier Bronze Age crafts, but, as we have seen, they were also important agents in distributing these crafts throughout Eurasia. They were particularly proficient in weaponry, and their bronze spear tips, arrowheads, and blades, in addition to the mobility of their chariots and horse-borne warriors, very likely gave them a pronounced advantage over those of the village communities they encountered. After the beginning of the first millennium BCE, they also helped spread the use of iron.

> "Now I shall proclaim the mighty deeds of Indra, those foremost deeds that he . . . has performed. He smashed the serpent. He released the waters. He split the sides of the mountains. . . . So, as king, he rules over the peoples. As a rim in the spokes of a wheel, he encompasses them."
>
> —*Rig-Veda*

Excellent horsemen, the Vedic peoples made extensive use of horse-drawn wagons and chariots in battle. The earliest migrants may have introduced the horse to northern India, and it is likely that they first brought the chariot to late Xia or early Shang China. Elaborate equipment such as bridles, yokes, and harnesses and other items related to the use of horses have been found at a number of sites. The horse was so potent a symbol of power and well-being in Vedic culture and religion that its sacrifice became the most sacred of all ceremonies.

Ranging across vast stretches of grassland, the early Vedic peoples carried much of their food supply with them in the form of domestic animals. As with the Harappans, cattle were the chief measure of wealth, thus continuing the centrality of the "sacred cow" to the Indian religious experience. As skilled cultivators as well as herdsmen, the migrants adapted easily to a wide range of environments. Sheep and goats were also mainstays of their livestock, while milk and butter, particularly the clarified butter called "ghee" [gee, with a hard "g"], occupied a prominent place in their religious symbolism.

As a highly refined product of the cow, ghee came to signify a rain that was at once purifying and fruitful. Even today ghee is used in daily household rituals. In the *Rig-Veda*, it acquired *cosmological* significance; that is, it was seen as something that reveals the underlying meaning and structure of the universe. As with so many aspects of the deeper Indian past, ghee provides tantalizing clues about ancient practices but still leaves a tightly drawn veil over everyday life.

**The Settlement of Northern India**   While the Vedas provide a rich literary account of Indo-European conceptions of society and religion, the history of the settlement of northern India is far more obscure. Evidence from assorted sites suggests that there was a prolonged period of migration and settlement in the northwest of the subcontinent marked by a gradual transition of the Vedic peoples from a nomadic and pastoral life to a settled and agricultural one. As early as 1000 BCE, evidence of large towns appears in the area around present-day Delhi. An important catalyst in bringing about the conditions necessary for the reemergence of large cities, however, was the beginning of widespread rice cultivation in the newly opened lands to the east.

First domesticated in Neolithic southeast Asia and south-central China, rice proved well suited to the warm temperatures, monsoon rains, and high fertility of the Ganges basin once the forests had been cleared. Here, it seems evident that the introduction of iron tools such as plows and axes was instrumental in preparing the land. High yields and a climate warm enough to permit two crops per year helped ensure the surpluses necessary to support an increasingly dense network of villages, towns, and cities, sometimes called by archaeologists India's "second urbanization."

However, the meticulous, intensive labor required at every stage of the rice plant's growth cycle required many hands for its successful cultivation. The plants must be grown in shallow water of a carefully prescribed depth and must be transplanted before the grain is harvested. Hence, the elaborate infrastructure of rice culture—the dikes, drainage ditches, terraces, raised paths, and other items related to water control—demanded a high degree of cooperation and increasingly sophisticated social organization. From roughly 800 BCE, we can trace the development of strong agrarian-based states called *janapadas* [jah-nah-PAH-duhs] ("populated territories" or "clan [*jana*] territories") in northern and northeastern India.

## Statecraft and the Ideology of Power, 800–600 BCE

By the sixth century BCE the *janapadas* had encompassed the entire Ganges valley and were leading the way toward a cultural, if not a military, conquest of the subcontinent. Supported by the growing agricultural wealth and trade of the region, their influence was crucial in spreading their increasingly elaborate religion steadily east and south. Sixteen large states, or *mahajanapadas* [MAH-hah-jah-nah-PAH-duhs], now dominated northern India from the Bay of Bengal to the foothills of the Himalayas. The four largest—Avanti, Vatsa, Kosala, and Magadha—grew increasingly powerful, rich, and contentious along the Ganges. Buoyed by large revenues from agricultural and trade taxes and supported by theories that accorded kingship an almost divine status, their respective quests for domination grew as they absorbed their weaker neighbors. In this respect, as we shall see in Chapter 4, these states shared much in common with their contemporaries, the states of Zhou China.

### Centralization and Power among the Ganges States    The growing power and prosperity of the larger states tended to push them toward increasing centralization so that their resources might be used to maximal effect in the struggle for domination and survival. The two wealthiest *mahajanapadas*, Magadha and Kosala, found the route to consolidation through centralized kingdoms supported by the Brahmans, or priests. By the sixth century BCE this combination of state power and religion had produced kings, or *maharajas* [mah-hah-RAH-juhs], who were accorded godlike stature and wielded power that was seen as both secular and divine. For example, a number of kings, with the sanction of the priestly class, conducted increasingly elaborate horse sacrifices. The king's horse, accompanied by soldiers and royal grooms, was first made to wander the kingdom for a year, during which all land within the borders of its travels was claimed by the ruler. Its sacrifice thus became not only a supremely important religious festival but also a reminder of the king's power.

Other large states retained systems of government in which power was more diffuse, often being ruled by councils of various sorts as opposed to kings; scholars sometimes refer to these states as "republics." The most powerful of the republics, the

Vajjian Confederacy, was ruled by a chief whose authority was derived from a council made up of heads or representatives of the principal clans. The council members were in turn responsible to local assemblies of clan elders and notables.

Even among the republics, the general trend appears to have been that of growing economic prosperity coupled with fierce competition among all the states for domination and survival—requiring ever greater efficiency in collecting revenue and spending for defense—pushing them toward either monarchy or absorption. The Vajjian Confederacy, for example, was eventually absorbed by Magadha during its drive for empire in northern India.

Thus, by the sixth century BCE, these states, like the Greek *poleis* and the states of late Zhou China, found themselves embroiled in continual political crises. Alliances between the states were sought and abandoned as the situation warranted; attempts to create a balance of power repeatedly failed as the largest states relentlessly vied for control. Increasing sophistication in strategy, tactics, and military technology—now including iron weapons, massed cavalry, war elephants, and even giant bows—put a premium on manpower and revenue, thus giving the larger states further advantages. By the late fourth century BCE, when these armies faced the threat of invasion by the forces of Alexander the Great and his successor Seleucus, they would number in the hundreds of thousands of men.

**The Ideology of Rulership**   Warfare conducted by kings vested with godlike status raised a number of ethical and practical questions about the nature of kingship, the responsibilities of rulers to their subjects, and their role as agents of a universal order. For example, how should a ruler monitor the activities of his subjects? What are the bounds of behavior in terms of diplomacy, espionage, the conduct of conflict, and the long-term welfare of the kingdom? Under what conditions may the rules be broken? In short, how should the ideal ruler comport himself for the good of his kingdom, subjects, and himself in accordance with his divine mission?

The growing size, wealth, and power of the Ganges states made these questions increasingly important as all struggled to expand—or merely survive. By 600 BCE, all the Gangetic rulers were, roughly speaking, in the situation later described by the political strategist Kautilya [kaw-TEEL-yuh] of Magadha in his grimly realistic, pioneering political treatise, the *Arthashastra* [ar-tah-SHAS-truh]. In this constant war of all against all, says Kautilya, the wise ruler understands that those who encircle him on all sides and "prevail in the territory adjacent to his are . . . known as the enemy." On the other hand, those who control the territory "that is separated from the conqueror's territory by one [namely, the enemy's territory] is the constituent known as friend." Hence, one's policy toward neighboring states should be opportunistic: Attack the weak, seek allies against the strong, bide one's time with equals, and practice duplicity wherever and whenever necessary. As we shall see, there are many parallels with late Zhou Chinese treatises such as Sun Zi's *Art of War*. The prime purpose of such action, however, must always be the welfare of one's subjects by means of the survival and prosperity of the state.

This grim vision of the evolving world of statecraft was tempered somewhat by the themes depicted in the epics, composed during the Vedic period, though committed to writing only in the third century BCE, of which the two most

**Illustration from the Mahabharata.** The stories of the Mahabharata continue to be among the most popular forms of entertainment in India today. In this 1598 CE painting, Arjuna confronts his relatives on the battlefield.

famous are the Mahabharata [Mah-hah-BAH-rah-tuh] and the Ramayana [Rah-muh-YAH-nuh]. Perhaps the world's longest poem—at 100,000 verses in 18 books, it is many times longer than the Bible—the Mahabharata centers on the struggles among the descendants of the king Bharata, and especially on the conflicting obligations imposed on the individual by state, society, and religion. The sixth book, Bhagavad Gita [BAH-guh-vahd GEE-tuh] (Song of the Lord), has been called the "Indian gospel" because of its concentration on the tense and intricate combination of ethics and action.

On the eve of a battle in which the enemy includes his relatives and former companions, Arjuna, the protagonist, agonizes over fighting against his family and friends. His charioteer—actually the god Krishna in disguise—reminds him of the need to fulfill his duty according to *dharma* [DAR-mah] (literally "that which is firm"). To act according to dharma means following one's prescribed role according to one's place in society and in the natural order. As a warrior and ruler, therefore, Arjuna cannot leave the field of battle because of his personal connections to his opponents. Krishna tells him that the higher law of dharma demands that he put aside his personal reservations and fulfill his larger obligation to fight and win. Hence, Arjuna is urged to perform his duty without attachment as the agent of forces that transcend the immediate ties of friendship or family. Thus, if Arjuna forces himself to do his duty because it must be done, abandoning his attachment to the result—whatever it may be—then, according to Krishna, he is acting wisely and advancing the course of the universe.

By about 600 BCE, the largest of the northern Indian states, especially Magadha and Kosala, were attempting both to expand southward and to absorb their neighbors along the Ganges. In this volatile political environment, they developed ideologies of kingship and power based on a common understanding of the religious and cultural implications of the Vedas and a realistic appraisal of their respective political environments. At once supported and trapped by the idea of dharma as it relates to kingship, they would struggle for the next several centuries until Magadha incorporated the northern third of the subcontinent (see Map 3.4).

# Indian Society, Culture, and Religion, 1500–600 BCE

The first chronicles of Indian history do not make their appearance until well after the beginning of the Common Era. Because of this, such documentary evidence as we have about social history, especially that of families or village organization, is found in religious and literary texts, law codes, and the collections of folktales and genealogies called the *Puranas* [poor-AH-nuhs] ("legends"), which date from about 500 BCE.

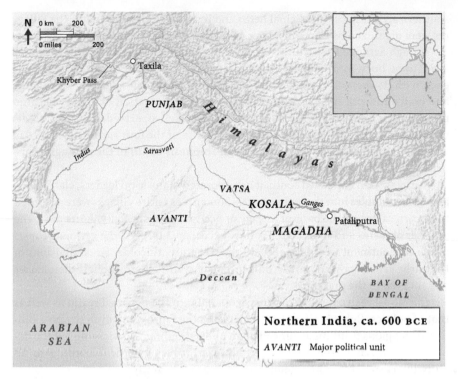

MAP 3.4 **Northern India, ca. 600 BCE.**

## Society and Family in Ancient India

While part of Indian religious thought was becoming increasingly concerned with the nature of the absolute and ways to connect with it, much of the rest dealt with the arrangement of society, law, and duty; the role of the family and its individual members; and relationships between men and women.

**Dharma and Social Class**    For example, the Bhagavad Gita contains numerous illustrations of the dilemmas that come from following one's dharma: duty in accordance with one's capabilities and the requirements of one's place in society. Krishna outlines these duties quite succinctly to Arjuna in the Bhagavad Gita in a set of passages that closely echo the structure of the *varnas*: "Tranquility, control, penance, purity, patience, and honesty, knowledge, judgment, and piety are intrinsic to the action of a priest," he notes, while "heroism, fiery energy, resolve, skill, refusal to retreat in battle, charity, and majesty in conduct are intrinsic to the action of the warrior." The activities that support the subsistence of society such as farming, herding cattle, and commerce "are intrinsic to the action of a commoner," while "action that is essentially service is intrinsic to the servant."

The great majority of Indians followed Krishna's last two sets of injunctions. Although one of the distinctive developments in the rise of the Gangetic states had been the rebirth of urban life in India, the village remained the center of the social world for perhaps 80–90 percent of the subcontinent's inhabitants—as it largely does to this day. In pursuing various tasks such as tending cattle and water buffalo, raising a variety of crops such as rice, wheat, barley, millet, and, in the

**Caste:** A system in which people's places in society—how they live, the work they do, and whom they marry—are determined by heredity.

southern areas , spices, medicinal herbs and barks, and forest products the villagers were organized by clan and *jati*, or **caste** (see Patterns Up Close).

Though arranged according to a rigid hierarchy, the social system based on *jati* ("to be born into") functioned in many ways as a kind of extended family, each with its own clans, villages, local dialects, gods, laws, advisory councils, and craft and work specializations. Thus, as the organization of society became more complex—owing to the demands of increased size, trade, population diversity, and urbanization—the ritual importance of the four *varnas* of the Vedas was slowly giving way to the occupational emphasis of *jati* in the new agrarian–urban order.

As the system expanded south, it incorporated many local leaders, clan elders, and other notables into the higher castes. Sometimes entire villages were accorded their own castes on the basis of lineage or occupational specialty. At its peak, the number of castes and subcastes may have exceeded 3,000. As the various peoples of the subcontinent were brought into the structure, the older ritual divisions of the early Vedic era were slowly broken down even further, though their traces remain even to the present.

The all-pervasive force of dharma extended into the personal realm as well as that of politics. Behavior in village society and the family, and even the possibilities for religious fulfillment, hinged upon understanding and carrying out the demands of dharma. These demands, however, varied greatly according to an individual's social standing, gender, and place in the family.

**Gender Roles: Men and Women in Society**    The importance of family life in India is readily evident in religious scriptures and the law codes, or *smriti* [SHMEER-tee]. By 600 BCE, *artha* [AHR-tah], the pursuit of subsistence and prosperity, was recognized as a moral course of action necessary to sustain family position and harmony. In addition to tending to the extensive ritual demands of daily life, the male householder of the upper caste was expected to "cast food on the ground for dogs, untouchables [the excluded castes], and crows." Moreover, according to the *smriti*, "Children, married daughters living in the father's house, old relatives, pregnant women, sick persons, and girls, as also guests and servants—only after having fed these should the householder and his wife eat the food that has remained." Thus, the male householder must be willing to habitually sacrifice his own needs for those of his family and dependents.

The position of women in the Indian family and in Indian society is more difficult to determine. At once partner and property, the center of the family, yet burdened with complex restrictions over education and marriage, adult women seem simultaneously to occupy several separated rungs on the hierarchies of family and society. Unswerving loyalty and devotion on the part of wives and daughters was demanded and highly prized. For example, a large part of the epic of the Ramayana, an allegorical account of the conquest of the peoples of the south, centers on the obsessive, though ultimately groundless, suspicion of the hero Rama [RAH-mah] about the faithfulness of his kidnapped wife, Sita. The reciprocal aspect of the demand for loyalty and devotion, as the Code of Manu advises, is that, "regarding this as the highest dharma of all four classes, husbands . . . must strive to protect their wives." Thus, a great part of Rama's behavior toward Sita springs from his self-reproach over his failure to fulfill his most basic responsibility of protecting his wife. At the same time, Sita's loyalty to Rama makes her an exemplary model of dharma.

In household matters a wife should be engaged "in the collection and expenditure of . . . (the husband's) wealth, in cleanliness, in dharma, in cooking food for the family, and in looking after the necessities of the household." The position of women in this context, the code says, is "deserving of worship."

Coupled with this ideal of domesticity is a concept of women and women's sexuality as simultaneously compelling and threatening. The idea of kama, as encapsulated in the later *Kama Sutra*, included the enjoyment of a wide variety of sexual pleasures by men and women as part of a balanced social and religious life. Much Indian literature, both sacred and secular, as well as motifs, symbols, and statuary associated with shrines and temples, graphically celebrates the union of male and female as the conduit for the primal creative force of the universe. Female beauty itself is identified with beneficial natural phenomena.

Later on, during the period of Classical Hinduism, numerous temples would have carvings depicting men and women in all phases of sexual activity, and even today small local temples feature phallic stones which worshipers periodically anoint with milk and flowers.

In contrast to this concept of truth and purity arising from naked innocence was the idea that the material world in general, and sexuality in particular as its most enticing aspect, could divert a person from fulfilling his or her dharma. As such, it poses a threat to the social and natural order if not properly controlled. The close relationship between society and religion in this regard provided considerable latitude for men to explore ways of going "beyond" the material and sexual world by engaging in solitary, often celibate, religious practices. On the other hand, it also bolstered the idea that a woman without the protection of a husband or family was a danger to herself and a source of temptation to others. For both men and women, independence from the social system of family, clan, or caste—unless channeled into an approved religious or social practice—was subject to severe sanction. But, because of the concept that the family was the foundation of society as a whole and the place of women was at the center of family life, the burdens of supporting the system and the penalties for failing to do so fell far more heavily on women than on men.

## Cultural Interactions to 600 BCE

The social system of *varna* and *jati* held together as the religion of the Vedas expanded into the diverse body of beliefs, practices, and philosophy that would later be referred to by outsiders as "Hinduism." The term is derived from the Persian word *hindu*, taken from the Sanskrit *sindhu*, or "rivers," in reference to the inhabitants of the Indus valley.

Gods and Priests     Though principally the embodiments or controllers of natural forces, the gods had human personalities as well. Indra, for example, was a swashbuckling warrior with a taste for *soma*, an intoxicating drink used in religious rituals. Varuna was the regulator of cosmic affairs and the lawgiver. Agni encompassed all the forces of light, sun, and fire and was, in a sense, the messenger of the gods, carrying the sacrifices of humans to the other deities.

# The Caste System

More than any other agrarian states, the *janapadas* developed an interlocking social order based on ethnicity and occupation. As the Vedic peoples settled into northern India, the relatively fluid divisions of their nomadic society became more firmly defined according to ritual position and occupational status as the four *varnas* ("form; shape"; though it is also sometimes interpreted as "color"): the first three for priests, warriors, and commoners, respectively, and a fourth that included both servants and laborers. The origin of the *varnas*, according to the *Rig-Veda*, lay in the seminal sacrifice of the cosmic being Purusha, which gave form to the universe: His mouth became the Brahmans, or priests; his arms became the *kshatriyas* [kuh-SHA-tree-yahs]—kings and warriors; his two thighs the *vaishyas* [vy-SHEE-yahs], or merchants; and from his two feet came the *shudra*, or peasants, servants, and laborers.

The newcomers' task of establishing and maintaining themselves as an elite class over the indigenous peoples meant that the system had to be expanded to accommodate all but with tight restrictions placed on social mobility. Thus, it appears that intermarriage was forbidden between the new elites and *dasas*, the term used for non-Aryans, and the latter were incorporated into the peasant/laborer/servant *varna*. By the sixth century BCE it appears that divisions between Aryans and non-Aryans that might have originally been based on ethnicity or locale were giving way to ones based on occupation. An elaborate *jati*, or caste, system—a term derived from the Portuguese word *casta*, for "breed" or "race," which they mistakenly believed governed these social arrangements—was already developing.

Based on the original divisions of the four *varnas*, each caste was theoretically divisible into an infinite number of subcastes finely graded according to hereditary occupations. A new category of "excluded" castes—the so-called untouchables—was added, comprising people whose occupations were considered ritually unclean: butchers,

Brahman

Kshatriya

Vaishya

Shudra

As the members of the most important and respected *varna*, the prestige of the Brahmans (priests) grew as they monopolized the performance of ever more elaborate rituals and sacrifices. The priests carefully maintained the oral tradition of the Vedas, taking extreme care to pass on the exact formulas of the old rituals, while also creating new, increasingly elaborate ones centered on the needs of a more sedentary, agrarian people. The growing emphasis on the precise details of various rituals, as codified in the Vedic commentaries called Brahmanas, spurred the development of education among the men of the upper castes. By the sixth century BCE, the major works of the Vedic and Brahmanic oral tradition were being committed to writing in Sanskrit, from this time forward the sacred language of Indian scriptures.

**Toward New Religious Directions**   At the same time, this trend contributed to an increasing *formalism* within the Vedic-Brahmanic tradition: the belief that

refuse collectors, privy cleaners, leather workers, and those involved with tending to the dead. The excluded castes also came to include "outcasts," people who for various offenses had "lost caste" and were therefore placed on the fringes of society. Perhaps a lingering vestige of early Vedic attempts at ethnic separation, stringent prohibitions were imposed on sexual relations between *shudras* and members of the castes within the first three "twice born" (Aryan) *varnas*—so called because they alone were permitted to undergo the ceremony of the "sacred thread" and be "reborn" as initiates to the mysteries of the Vedic scriptures.

The evolving *jati* system, with its precarious balance of flexibility and stability, expanded southward as the Ganges River states pushed farther and farther into these areas. Eventually, it incorporated villages, clans, and sometimes even entire tribal groups into their own *jatis.* Though highly restricting in terms of social mobility, these arrangements guaranteed a prescribed place for everyone in society, with at least a minimal degree of mutual support. Moreover, the idea of movement between

1805 French Lithograph of Indian Funeral (top) and Upper-Caste Dress (bottom).

castes became a vital part of Indian religious traditions through the doctrines of continual rebirth and the transmigration of souls. Thus, the evolving Indian innovation in response to the problem of incorporating a staggering multiplicity of ethnic, linguistic, and religious groups into its expanding culture was to create a space in society for each, while ensuring stability by restricting the social mobility of individuals and encouraging good behavior through the hope of a higher place in the next life. The fact that the system continues today despite its dissolution by the Indian government is testimony to its tenacious cultural roots and long-standing social utility.

## Questions

- How is the caste system a cultural adaptation?
- How does the persistence of the caste system today demonstrate its social utility?

only the precise observance of all the proper forms of ritual behavior—prayers, sacrifices, daily and seasonal ceremonies—could ensure their effectiveness. Since the formulas for these rituals were for the most part accessible only to the "twice-born" or upper *varnas*, a small percentage of the population, and considered the special province of the Brahmans, there was considerable social and religious exclusiveness attached to the tradition as well.

A movement away from this restrictive formalism was already apparent by 600 BCE. Instead of appeasing the gods through the precise performance of ritual as a means of ensuring the cosmic order, some in the upper *varnas* began seeking the forces behind that order and trying to achieve communion with them. Two paths within the Vedic-Brahmanic tradition became discernible in this regard.

One path was *asceticism*, full or partial renunciation of the material world, which, because of its impermanence, was seen as an impediment to a deeper

**Asceticism.** For millennia great respect has been accorded those who withdraw from the lure of the material world and seek the unchanging within. Here, a modern "world renouncer," or sannyasi, is shown.

**Bathing in the Ganges at Varanasi.** The sacred character of rivers in the Indian religious experience may go back all the way to the Harappans. As the multiple religious traditions we know as Hinduism developed in the Ganges valley, that river assumed a position of central importance in terms of ritual purification. Here, bathers are shown on the ghats—steps built on the riverbank—of the city of Varanasi, also known as Benares, site of some of Hinduism's holiest shrines.

understanding of reality. The Vedic tradition had long held a special reverence for hermits and those who fled society in order to purify themselves. The many schools of ascetic practice held that the multiple distractions of making a living, raising a family, and even the body itself hindered the quest for one's spiritual essence. These schools developed a variety of strategies for uncovering the unchanging, and thus real, "self" removed from a world where everything is impermanent and, hence, illusory.

The practices of certain schools of *yoga* ("discipline"), for example, were based on the belief that mastery of the body allowed the adept to leave the restrictions of the material world and achieve communion with this inner self. Since the body, as part of the physical world, is subject to constant change, the discipline of postures, breathing, and meditation allows the practitioner to go beyond its limitations and find that which is unchanging within.

The other emerging path to a deeper spiritual reality was scriptural. Between the seventh and fifth centuries—though perhaps from as early as 800 BCE—a diverse group of writings called the Upanishads [oo-PAHN-ee-shahds] ("secret knowledge") marked a dynamic new direction within the Vedic tradition. The Upanishads represented the Vedanta, "the end," or "fulfillment" of the Vedas, in which the hidden symbolism was revealed, layer by layer, and apparent inconsistencies were reconciled. While different levels of understanding the "true" principles of the Vedas were to be expected of those with limited access to the scriptures, a slavish reliance on the formal aspects of sacrifice was clearly subject to criticism.

The material world was increasingly regarded as extraneous as well. The individual "self" (*atman*) was ultimately to become identified with the cosmic "essence" (*brahman*—note that this usage is different from the same term used to describe the priestly *varna*).

**Karma-Samsara**    Though the full impact of these trends would be felt only in succeeding centuries, speculation about the nature of individual and universal "essence" was already beginning to be reflected more broadly in culture and society. The elaboration of the idea of caste and its accompanying obligations carried with it the development of *karma-samsara*, the transmigration of souls and reincarnation. Though few references to these concepts are found in the Vedas, by the sixth century BCE the two ideas appear to have been widely accepted. The concept of a nonmaterial essence or "soul" carrying with it the residue of one's deeds—*karma*—is coupled with the idea of the rebirth of the soul into a new body—*samsara*. The fidelity with which a person pursues his or her dharma within the context of the caste system ensures an advance in caste in the next life. Ultimately, the doctrine provided for *moksha*—release from the karmic cycle and the achievement of a state of complete understanding in this world—for those who are fully able to grasp the principles of *atman: brahman* and *dharma*.

# Putting It All Together

In the Indus valley, as we have already seen in Egypt and Mesopotamia, a critical mass of factors required for the transition to agrarian-based cities had come together sometime around 2500 BCE. Yet our inability to decipher the symbols of the Harappans has proven to be a powerful impediment to our understanding of how their society worked and, equally important, why it fell. We are accustomed to thinking of history as a series of thresholds through which human societies pass in linear, progressive fashion—from forager society to agrarian to urban society, for example—without any substantial backtracking. And yet there are the Harappans, who, for whatever reason, abandoned their splendid cities for, we must suppose, village agriculture or life in the forest.

Invasion by mobile nomads had formerly been seen as the cause, and this pattern of struggle between the settled and the nomadic will continue in various parts of the world for thousands of years. For the Harappans, however, the coming of the nomadic Indo-Europeans may not actually have had much of an impact, making the questions of interaction and adaptation that much more intriguing.

In India, the interruption in urban life lasted nearly 1,000 years. When cities again arose, they were centered hundreds of miles from the old, now forgotten Harappan sites. Instead of the apparent uniformity of the earlier society, the new one was to be marked by the struggle of individual states for advantage and supremacy. Yet, although these Gangetic states lacked political unity, their cultural and religious similarity remained an important factor throughout Indian history. Their unique innovation of the *jati* system was to act like a great flexible mold within which Indian society was increasingly cast into ever more complex sections.

Not surprisingly, this unsettled period of interaction and adaptation for the Gangetic societies was marked by widespread questioning of social, political, and religious arrangements. In the India of 600 BCE, the beginnings of an important redirection of the Vedic tradition were already under way through the speculations of the earliest Upanishads, which mark a pivotal development in the history of abstract religious and philosophical conceptualization. Moreover, amid the rich diversity of ascetic religious experience, some were shortly to map the direction of entirely new religious paths. One of these, Buddhism, may be seen as perhaps the first avowedly *universal* religious system and, thus, the beginning of a vitally important new pattern of world history.

▶ For additional resources, including maps, primary sources, visuals, and quizzes, please go to www.oup.com/us/vonsivers. Please see the Further Resources section at the back of the book for additional readings and suggested websites.

## Against the Grain

# A Merchants' Empire?

Despite their unique cultural aspects, patterns of development among the land-based agrarian–urban civilizations we have examined so far share an important quality: the Mesopotamians, the Egyptians, the Gangetic states, and (as we will see in Chapter 4) the states arising in ancient China were all dependent on rivers for the fertility of their soil, for irrigation, and for transport, among other necessities. Indeed, scholars have repeatedly cited the centrality of rivers among these civilizations as a powerful conditioning factor in shaping the form and structure of their early institutions. Such riverine societies, which need large-scale public works projects to control the rivers on which they depend, develop powerful central governments (with kings or emperors wielding power through state bureaucracies or dependent local rulers) capable of directing such enormously complex undertakings. Such governments thus control vast labor resources, and tend to display their power by means of monumental architecture (such as palaces and religious centers) and other visible signs of state and religious unity and harmony.

The great exception to this pattern appears to be the Harappan system of cities in the Indus valley. Although the Indus cities were at least as reliant on the river as the cities of these other agrarian–urban civilizations, we see practically no evidence of a central government of any kind, aside from the striking uniformity of buildings and materials. Apart from what may be modest temples and baths, we see little in the way of any kind of state religion or cult, though religious objects themselves are quite numerous. In other words, we see little that we can point to with certainty to suggest a large state presence of any kind as reflected in the categories of artifacts found in, say, Egypt or Mesopotamia.

So how did things function? One intriguing (if still unproven) theory suggests that, rather than having a powerful central government and bureaucracy to marshal the resources of the state, the Harappan cities were part of a well-integrated merchants' empire. This possibility is supported in part by the vast amount of trade articles recovered in the Indus region, by the many apparent craft factories and warehouses, by the harbor and docking facilities, and by the theory that Harappan writing may in fact be nothing more than a sophisticated shorthand script used principally by merchants.

If this is indeed the case, it not only goes "against the grain" of the early patterns of riverine civilization but against the trends of world history in general. One thinks of the Republic of Venice, three thousand years later, as another trading empire, run by a merchant aristocracy for the benefit of its traders. It may well have been that the Harappan system was organized and run along similar lines. If so, its size and influence make it unique in its mode of operation—as it appears to be in so many other ways.

- **What similarities and differences do you see among the Harappans and other river-based agrarian–urban societies?**

- **Based on your reading of this chapter, is there evidence that works against the theory of a "merchants' empire" to explain the apparent differences between the Indus valley and other early river civilizations?**

# Thinking Through Patterns

▶ **Who were the Harappans? Where did they come from? What evidence exists for their origins?**

The riddle of the origins of the Harappans has remained unsolved for close to 100 years. Most scholars believe their ancestors had been in the Indus region or nearby Baluchistan for millennia. Some also see them as perhaps related to extremely ancient peoples inhabiting the region around modern Kerala. Clues for this include archaic chants still practiced in Kerala that contain words that are believed to be so ancient that no one knows their meaning anymore. Carbon-14 dating, linguistic tracking, DNA surveys, and sedimentary analysis of ruins have all enhanced our understanding. One large impediment, however, remains: deciphering Harappan script—or, as we noted in this chapter, even judging whether the symbols the Harappans left behind are in fact a form of writing. Thus, a powerful analytic tool for understanding any civilization, the literary record, remains elusive.

Why do civilizations rise and fall? This is a key question for archaeologists and historians. Collapse can come from predictable causes—war, famine, ecological degradation—or random ones like earthquakes or volcanic eruptions. For the Harappans, the literary record of the Indo-Europeans long suggested that they conquered the Harappans, but it seems in conflict with more recent discoveries about the flooding patterns of the Indus, the sedimentary analysis of building and rebuilding of structures, and salinization levels at various points in the river. As is most often the case, historians generally expect to find no single *sufficient cause*—one that by itself led to the collapse—but rather a number of *necessary causes*—those that contributed but were not capable of causing the collapse all by themselves.

▶ **What explanations have been offered for the collapse of Harappan society? How well do the rival theories hold up, given what scholars and archaeologists have discovered?**

▶ **How can we know about newcomers to northern India? What sources exist for historians to examine?**

Another ongoing debate revolves around the identity and nature of the newcomers into northern India. Here, as noted in the previous discussion, the literary record of the Vedas, particularly the oldest, the *Rig-Veda*, appears in conflict with much of the archaeological evidence. While the Vedas are quite clear about where the newcomers ended up, they are tantalizingly vague about where they originated. Indo-European-speaking peoples ranged widely across Eurasia, which we can tell from the vast legacy of the spread of their languages, and the kinds of technologies associated with them: horse equipment, chariots, iron. But because they left little in the way of archaeological sites, piecing together their story from their material culture is extremely challenging. For the moment, much of the most productive work is being done through genetic analysis of the area's modern inhabitants, as well as increasingly refined linguistic techniques of *glottochronology*—the tracing of language change over time and space.

Since one of our primary tasks in this text is to help you look for patterns surrounding origins, interactions, and adaptations, the question arises about the nature of patterns we see evolving among the early north Indian states. Not all these states were monarchies, but the religious aura of the monarchs and its relationship to the first stirrings of what will become Hinduism is striking. The permeation of society by religion is certainly a pattern that continues to this day, as is the desire for transcending the bounds of the material world by a variety of ascetic or scholarly methods. The most pervasive pattern lies in the development of the caste system as the basic social structure of society, which tenaciously endures even today in the face of a constitutional ban.

▶ **What patterns can we see evolving in the Ganges River states that will mark the subsequent development of Indian civilization?**

# Patterns of Evidence: Sources for Chapter 3

## SOURCE 3.1

## Hymns to Agni, from the *Rig-Veda*, Book 2

### ca. 1400–900 BCE

The worship of Agni, as the fire principle animating a burnt offering to the gods, features prominently in the *Rig-Veda*. The voice of Agni was thought be heard in the crackling of the fire beneath a sacrifice, and it was a crucial element of Vedic tradition that the priest perform the ritual correctly. Fire was conflated with the emanations of the sun, and the priestly *varna*, or caste, was thought to be the community's best representative to the god.

### HYMN I. Agni.

**1.** THOU, Agni, shining in thy glory through the days, art brought to life from out of the waters, from the stone: From out of the forest trees and herbs that grow on ground, thou, Sovereign Lord of men art generated pure.

**2.** Thine is the Herald's task and Cleanser's duly timed; Leader art thou, and Kindler for the pious man. Thou art Director, thou the ministering Priest: thou art the Brahman, Lord and Master in our home.

**3.** Hero of Heroes, Agni! Thou art Indra, thou art Viṣṇu of the Mighty Stride, adorable: Thou, Brahmaṇaspati, the Brahman finding wealth: thou, O Sustainer, with thy wisdom tendest us.

**4.** Agni, thou art King Varuṇa whose laws stand fast; as Mitra, Wonder-Worker, thou must be implored. Aryaman, heroes' Lord, art thou, enriching all, and liberal Aṁśa in the synod, O thou God.

. . .

**12.** Thou, Agni, cherished well, art highest vital power; in thy delightful hue are glories visible. Thou art the lofty might that furthers each design: thou art wealth manifold, diffused on every side.

**13.** Thee, Agni, have the Ādityas taken as their mouth; the Pure Ones have made thee, O Sage, to be their tongue. They who love offerings cling to thee at solemn rites: by thee the Gods devour the duly offered food.

Source: *The Hymns of the Rigveda*, trans. Ralph T. H. Griffith (Benares: E. J. Lazarus, 1889), 333–338.

**14.** By thee, O Agni, all the Immortal guileless Gods eat with thy mouth the oblation that is offered them. By thee do mortal men give sweetness to their drink. Pure art thou born, the embryo of the plants of earth. . . .

### HYMN II. Agni.

**1.** WITH sacrifice exalt Agni who knows all life; worship him with oblation and the song of praise, Well kindled, nobly fed; heaven's Lord, Celestial Priest, who labors at the pole where deeds of might are done.

**2.** At night and morning, Agni, have they called to thee, like milk-cattle in their stalls lowing to meet their young. As messenger of heaven thou lightest all night long the families of men. Thou Lord of precious boons.

**3.** Him have the Gods established at the region's base, doer of wondrous deeds, Herald of heaven and earth; Like a most famous car, Agni the purely bright, like Mitra to be glorified among the people.

**4.** Him have they set in his own dwelling, in the vault, like the Moon waxing, fulgent, in the realm of air. Bird of the firmament, observant with his eyes, guard of the place as it were, looking to gods and men.

**5.** May he as Priest encompass all the sacrifice. Men throng to him with offerings and with hymns of praise. Raging with jaws of gold among the growing plants, like heaven with all the stars, he quickens earth and sky.

. . .

**12.** Knower of all that lives, O Agni, may we both, singers of praise and chiefs, be in thy keeping still. Help us to wealth exceeding good and glorious, abundant, rich in children and their progeny.

**13.** The princely worshippers who send to those who sing thy praise, O Agni, reward, graced with cattle and horses,—Lead thou both these and us forward to higher bliss. With brave men in the assembly may we speak aloud.

▶ **Working with Sources**

1. Why was the priestly caste so vital to the correct performance of the ritual?
2. How are the powers of the sun and a sacrificial fire conflated in these hymns?

## SOURCE 3.2

# The Bhagavad Gita

**ca. 1750–800 BCE, written down in the third century BCE**

The Bhagavad Gita comprises the sixth book, and is the central component, of the Mahabharata. Because it centers on the struggles between kings and princes, the Mahabharata can be read as a reflection of the ideological components of rulership in ancient India. At its center is a power struggle between the descendants of two brothers, culminating in a comprehensive war that ends in the victory of one branch of the family over the other. Elements of philosophy, religion, and moral behavior appear throughout the poem, and the concepts of *dharma* (natural law, correct behavior) and chaos are introduced by Krishna, the wise sage who appears at critical moments to explain the wider implications of what seems a simple battle narrative. The speakers in the following excerpt are Dhritarâshtra, a blind king in the midst of a succession crisis; Sañgaya, the visionary narrator of the battle; and Arjuna, one of the five sons of Pandu, the Pandava.

## BHAGAVADGÎTÂ. CHAPTER I.

Dhritarâshtra said:

What did my (people) and the Pândavas do, O Sañgaya! when they assembled together on the holy field of Kurukshetra, desirous to do battle?

. . .

Sañgaya said:

Thus addressed by Gudâkesa , O descendant of Bharata! Hrishîkesa stationed that excellent chariot between the two armies, in front of Bhîshma and Drona and of all the kings of the earth, and said O son of Prithâ! Look at these assembled Kauravas.' There the son of Prithâ saw in both armies, fathers, and grandfathers, preceptors, maternal uncles, brothers, sons, grandsons, companions, fathers-in-law, as well as friends. And seeing all those kinsmen standing (there), the son of Kuntî [Arjuna] was overcome by excessive pity and spake thus despondingly.

Arjuna said:

Seeing these kinsmen, O Krishna! standing (here) desirous to engage in battle, my limbs droop down; my mouth is quite dried up; a tremor comes on my body; and my hairs stand on end; the Gândîva (bow) slips from my hand; my skin burns intensely. I am unable, too, to stand up; my mind whirls round, as it were; O Kesava! I see adverse omens and I do not perceive any good (to accrue) after killing (my) kinsmen in the battle. I do not wish for victory, O Krishna! nor sovereignty, nor pleasures: what is sovereignty to us, O Govinda! what enjoyments, and even life? Even those, for whose sake we desire sovereignty, enjoyments, and pleasures, are standing here for battle, abandoning life and wealth-preceptors, fathers, sons as well as grandfathers, maternal uncles, fathers-in-law, grandsons, brothers-in-law, as also (other) relatives. These I do not wish to kill, though they kill (me), O destroyer of Madhu! Even for the sake of sovereignty over the three worlds, how much less then for this earth (alone)?

. . .

Sañgaya said:

Having spoken thus, Arjuna cast aside his bow together with the arrows, on the battle-field, and sat

Source: *The Bhagavadgita, with the Sanatsugatiya and the Anugita*, trans. Kashinath Trimbak Telang (Oxford: Clarendon, 1882), 37, 39–41, 42, 73–75, 87–88, and 91.

down in (his) chariot, with a mind agitated by grief.

## CHAPTER VII.

The Deity said:

O son of Prithâ! now hear how you can without doubt know me fully, fixing your mind on me, and resting in me, and practicing devotion. I will now tell you exhaustively about knowledge together with experience; that being known, there is nothing further left in this world to know. Among thousands of men, only some work for perfection; and even of those who have reached perfection, and who are assiduous, only some know me truly. . . .

There is nothing else, O Dhanañgaya! higher than myself; all this is woven upon me, like numbers of pearls upon a thread. I am the taste in water, O son of Kuntî! I am the light of the sun and moon. I am 'Om' in all the Vedas, sound in space, and manliness in human beings; I am the fragrant smell in the earth, refulgence in the fire; I am life in all beings, and penance in those who perform penance. Know me, O son of Prithâ! to be the eternal seed of all beings; I am the discernment of the discerning ones, and I the glory of the glorious. I am also the strength, unaccompanied by fondness or desire, of the strong. And, O chief of the descendants of Bharata! I am love unopposed to piety among all beings. And all entities which are of the quality of goodness, and those which are of the quality of passion and of darkness, know that they are, indeed, all from me; I am not in them, but they are in me. The whole universe deluded by these three states of mind, developed from the qualities, does not know me, who am beyond them and inexhaustible;

for this delusion of mine, developed from the qualities, is divine and difficult to transcend. Those cross beyond this delusion who resort to me alone. Wicked men, doers of evil (acts), who are deluded, who are deprived of their knowledge by (this) delusion, and who incline to the demoniac state of mind, do not resort to me. But, O Arjuna! doers of good (acts) of four classes worship me: one who is distressed, one who is seeking after knowledge, one who wants wealth, and one, O chief of the descendants of Bharata! who is possessed of knowledge. Of these, he who is possessed of knowledge, who is always devoted, and whose worship is (addressed) to one (Being) only, is esteemed highest.

. . .

## CHAPTER X.

. . .

Arjuna said:

You are the supreme Brahman, the supreme goal, the holiest of the holy. All sages, as well as the divine sage Nârada, Asita, Devala, and Vyâsa, call you the eternal being, divine, the first god, the unborn, the all-pervading. And so, too, you tell me yourself, O Kesava! I believe all this that you tell me (to be) true; for, O lord! neither the gods nor demons understand your manifestation. You only know yourself by yourself. O best of beings! creator of all things! lord of all things! god of gods! lord of the universe! be pleased to declare without, exception your divine emanations, by which emanations you stand pervading all these worlds. How shall I know you, O you of mystic power! always meditating on you? And in what various entities, O lord! should I meditate on you? Again, O Ganârdana! do you yourself declare your powers and emanations; because hearing this nectar, I (still) feel no satiety.

The Deity said:
... I am the rod of those that restrain, and the policy of those that desire victory. I am silence respecting secrets. I am the knowledge of those that have knowledge And, O Arjuna! I am also that which is the seed of all things. There is nothing movable or immovable which can exist without me. O terror of your foes! there is no end to my divine emanations. Here I have declared the extent of (those) emanations only in part. Whatever thing (there is) of power, or glorious, or splendid, know all that to be produced from portions of my energy.

▶ **Working with Sources**

1. **Why does Arjuna feel compelled to act, despite the competing claims of family ties?**

2. **How does the text develop the theme of supreme knowledge and its power?**

## SOURCE 3.3

# The Brihadaranyaka Upanishad

## ca. 600 BCE

A diverse set of writings, the Upanishads were thought to convey secret knowledge and serve as the *vedanta*, or fulfillment, of the Vedic tradition. Among these documents are the Aranyakas ("forest books"), which may have been recited originally by hermits who had retreated to forests. Throughout the Upanishads one can see the full development of the principle of the joining of the individual self (*atman*, or "soul") with the *brahman*, or "world soul"/"soul essence."

### SECOND ADHYÂYA. FIRST BRÂHMANA.

**1.** There was formerly the proud Gârgya Bâlâki, a man of great reading. He said to Agâtasatru of Kâsi, 'Shall I tell you Brahman?' Agâtasatru said: 'We give a thousand (cows) for that speech (of yours), for verily all people run away, saying, Ganaka (the king of Mithilâ) is our father (patron).'

**2.** Gârgya said: 'The person that is in the sun, that I adore as Brahman.' Agâtasatru said to him: 'No, no! Do not speak to me on this. I adore him

Source: *The Upanishads*, vol. 2, trans. F. Max Müller (Oxford: Clarendon, 1884), 100–101 and 103–105.

verily as the supreme, the head of all beings, the king. Whoso adores him thus, becomes Supreme, the head of all beings, a king.'

**3.** Gârgya said: 'The person that is in the moon (and in the mind), that I adore as Brahman.' Agâtasatru said to him: 'No, no! Do not speak to me on this. I adore him verily as the great, clad in white raiment, as Soma, the king.' Whoso adores him thus, Soma is poured out and poured forth for him day by day, and his food does not fail.

**4.** Gârgya said: 'The person that is in the lightning (and in the heart), that I adore as Brahman.' Agâtasatru said to him: 'No, no! Do not speak to me on this. I adore him verily as the luminous.' Whoso adores him thus, becomes luminous, and his offspring becomes luminous.

. . .

**13.** Gârgya said: 'The person that is in the body, that I adore as Brahman.' Agâtasatru said to him: 'No, no! Do not speak to me on this. I adore him verily as embodied.' Whoso adores him thus, becomes embodied, and his offspring becomes embodied. Then Gârgya became silent.

**14.** Agâtasatru said: 'Thus far only?' 'Thus far only,' he replied. Agâtasatru said: 'This does not suffice to know it (the true Brahman).' Gârgya replied: 'Then let me come to you, as a pupil.'

**15.** Agâtasatru said: 'Verily, it is unnatural that a Brâhmana should come to a **Kshatriya**, hoping that he should tell him the Brahman. However, I shall make you know him clearly,' thus saying he took him by the hand and rose.

And the two together came to a person who was asleep. He called him by these names, 'Thou, great one, clad in white raiment, Soma, King.' He did not rise. Then rubbing him with his hand, he woke him, and he arose.

**16.** Agâtasatru said: 'When this man was thus asleep, where was then the person (purusha), the intelligent? And from whence did he thus come back?' Gârgya did not know this?

**17.** Agâtasatru said: 'When this man was thus asleep, then the intelligent person (purusha), having through the intelligence of the senses (prânas) absorbed within himself all intelligence, lies in the ether, which is in the heart. When he takes in these different kinds of intelligence, then it is said that the man sleeps (svapiti). Then the breath is kept in, speech is kept in, the ear is kept in, the eye is kept in, the mind is kept in.

**18.** But when he moves about in sleep (and dream), then these are his worlds. He is, as it were, a great king; he is, as it were, a great Brâhmana; he rises, as it were, and he falls. And as a great king might keep in his own subjects, and move about, according to his pleasure, within his own domain, thus does that person (who is endowed with intelligence) keep in the various senses (prânas) and move about, according to his pleasure, within his own body (while dreaming).

**19.** Next, when he is in profound sleep, and knows nothing, there are the seventy-two thousand arteries called Hita, which from the heart spread through the body. Through them he moves forth and rests in the surrounding body. And as a young

**Kshatriya:** Second highest of the four *varnas* (castes) in Hindu society.

man, or a great king, or a great Brâhmana, having reached the summit of happiness, might rest, so does he then rest.

**20.** As the spider comes out with its thread, or as small sparks come forth from fire, thus do all senses, all worlds, all Devas, all beings come forth from that Self. The Upanishad (the true name and doctrine) of that Self is 'the True of the True.' Verily the senses are the true, and he is the true of the true.

▶ **Working with Sources**

1. How does the text develop the principles of *brahman* and *soma* addressed in Chapter 3?

2. What is the responsibility of the king with respect to knowledge?

## SOURCE 3.4

# *The Code of Manu*

## ca. 100–300 CE

The *Code of Manu* deals with many different features of Hindu life, such as the proper behavior of different castes and methods for ritual purification. The "Manu" referred to in the title is the legendary "first man" of Hindu culture, also recognized as the first lawgiver. Thus, the *Code of Manu* is thought of within Hinduism as a text based on human traditions (*smriti*), but it is also believed to be consistent with the values included in texts that are divinely revealed (*shruti*), such as the "Purusha Hymn." As a result, it restates and reaffirms traditional values and structures, but it does so on the basis of religious authority.

The responsibilities described for women in the *Code of Manu* need to be understood within the context of Hinduism. As was discussed in Chapter 3, a central component of Hinduism is the concept of *dharma* ("that which is firm"). Hindus believe that by living up to the religious and social responsibilities attached to one's social position (caste and gender), one sustains the proper order of the universe and gains good *karma*, moving up the scale of reincarnation toward unity with the *brahman*, or World Soul. Composed following a period of unrest, the *Code of Manu* represents a vigorous attempt to reestablish order within the Hindu world.

Source: *The Law of Manu*, in *The Sacred Books of the East*, vol. 25, trans. G. Bühler (Oxford: Clarendon, 1886), 194–197, 328–330, 332, 335, 344–345.

Hear now the duties of women.

By a girl, by a young woman, or even by an aged one, nothing must be done independently, even in her own house.

Her lord is dead to her sons; a woman must never be independent.

She must not seek to separate herself from her father, husband, or sons; by leaving them she would make both (her own and her husband's) families contemptible.

She must always be cheerful, clever in (the management of her) household affairs, careful in cleaning her utensils, and economical in expenditure.

Him to whom her father may give her, or her brother with the father's permission, she shall obey as long as he lives, and when he is dead, she must not insult (his memory).

[B]etrothal (by the father or guardian) is the cause of (the husband's) dominion (over his wife).

The husband who wedded her with sacred texts, always gives happiness to his wife, both in season and out of season, in this world and in the next.

Though destitute of virtue, or seeking pleasure (elsewhere), or devoid of good qualities, (yet) a husband must be constantly worshipped as a god by a faithful wife.

No sacrifice, no vow, no fast must be performed by women apart (from their husbands); if a wife obeys her husband, she will for that (reason alone) be exalted in heaven.

A faithful wife, who desires to dwell (after death) with her husband, must never do anything that might displease him who took her hand, whether he be alive or dead. . . . [L]et her emaciate her body by (living on)

pure flowers, roots, and fruit; but she must never even mention the name of another man after her husband has died.

Until death let her be patient (of hardships), self-controlled, and chaste, and strive (to fulfill) that most excellent duty which (is prescribed) for wives who have one husband only. A virtuous wife who after the death of her husband constantly remains chaste, reaches heaven, though she have no son, just like those chaste men.

By violating her duty towards her husband, a wife is disgraced in this world, (after death) she enters the womb of a jackal, and is tormented by diseases (the punishment of) her sin. . . .

[A] female who controls her thoughts, speech, and actions, gains in this (life) highest renown, and in the next (world) a place near her husband.

Women must particularly be guarded against evil inclinations, however trifling (they may appear); for, if they are not guarded, they will bring sorrow on two families. . . . No man can completely guard women by force; but they can be guarded by the . . . (following) expedients: Let the (husband) employ his (wife) in the collection and expenditure of his wealth, in keeping (everything) clean, in (the fulfillment of) religious duties, in the preparation of his food, and in looking after the household utensils. Women, confined in the house under trustworthy and obedient servants, are not (well) guarded; but those who of their own accord keep guard over themselves, are well guarded. . . .

Through their passion for men, through their mutable temper, through their natural heartlessness, they become disloyal towards their husbands, however carefully they may be guarded in this (world).

(When creating them) Manu allotted to women (a love of their) bed, (of their) seat and (of) ornament, impure desires, wrath, dishonesty, malice, and bad conduct. . . . The production of children, the nurture of those born, and the daily life of men, (of these matters) woman is visibly the cause.

Offspring, (the due performance of) religious rites, faithful service, highest conjugal happiness and heavenly bliss for the ancestors and oneself, depend on one's wife alone.

He only is a perfect man who consists (of three persons united), his wife, himself, and his offspring; thus (says the Veda), and (learned) Brahmanas propound this (maxim) likewise, "The husband is declared to be one with the wife." . . .

The husband receives his wife from the gods, (he does not wed her) according to his own will; doing what is agreeable to the gods, he must always support her (while she is) faithful.

"Let mutual fidelity continue until death," this may be considered as the summary of the highest law for husband and wife.

▶ **Working with Sources**

1. According to the code, how should men relate to women? In what ways are men asked, in their relationships with women, to keep order?

2. How are women rewarded for behaving the way the code instructs them to? How are the rewards connected with the Hindu belief in reincarnation and *karma*?

## SOURCE 3.5

# Image of Draupadi and the Pandava, from the Dashavatara Temple, Deogarh, India

**Late sixth century CE**

This is an inscribed rendering of some of the major male and female characters of the Mahabharata. According to this legend, a king surrenders power to his blind brother and has five sons (the Pandava) by his queen, Kunti. The five brothers are collectively married to the beautiful princess Draupadi. In Indian tradition, her role is analogous to the way the palm of a hand holds together the hand's five fingers.

Source: Courtesy of Ed Sentner.

▶ **Working with Sources**

1. How is the female principle represented in this collective portrait?

2. Does this image evoke in any way the restrictions on female behavior detailed in the *Code of Manu*?

# Chapter 4 5000–481 BCE

# Agrarian Centers and the Mandate of Heaven in Ancient China

Thousands of miles east of Harappa and several centuries after its decline, the twenty-first Shang king, Wu Ding, prepared to commune with his ancestors in the hope of gaining some insight into the childbearing prospects of his pregnant wife, Fu (Lady) Hao. Fu Hao, his favorite (and most powerful) wife, had come from a noble family outside the Shang capital of Yin, near the modern city of Anyang in northern China. Well educated and highly capable as an administrator, Fu Hao had even on occasion led Shang armies in the field. Now she was entrusted with what Wu Ding and his court considered to be the most important duty of all: continuing the line of Shang kings into the future. For the Shang kings believed that the past, present, and future rulers of their line formed an unbroken continuum, with the deceased existing in a spirit realm accessible to the living by ritual divination. Therefore, Wu Ding, whose concern for Fu Hao and her unborn child was paramount, sought the advice of the ancestors about her condition and that of her child to come. Wu Ding and his chief diviner, Que [chway], scratched their questions into a cleaned and dried shoulder blade of an ox and held it over heat. The diviner then tapped it carefully with a bronze rod and attempted to read the meaning of the cracks as they appeared in the hot bone.

*ABOVE*: **Skeleton and Shang War Chariot, Anyang, China.**

Que's reading of the cracks was "It is bad; it will be a girl." Although this was considered disappointing because the desire for a male heir, Fu Hao remained Wu Ding's most beloved wife until her death. Indeed, after she died, the despondent king frequently sought her advice through oracle bones on matters of state and private affairs. Fortunately for us, her tomb is one of the most completely preserved from the Shang era. Like the vast caches of oracle bones uncovered over the years, it tells us a great deal about society and gender, economics and trade, and the origins and interactions of Chinese states among themselves and with neighboring peoples.

Like Harappa along the Indus, the Shang state had developed in a process of growth and consolidation among the Late Neolithic settlements along China's Yellow River. But the Harappans and the Shang had begun very different historical paths for India and China. Harappa and the other cities of the Indus, as we have seen, all but disappeared, their influence detectable only within the deepest currents of later Indian society. In contrast, the foundations laid by the Shang and subsequent dynasties developing in China's Yellow River valley remained vital into the twenty-first century and profoundly influenced east and southeast Asia. The history of India was one of infusion and synthesis, of cycles of partial political unity punctuated by long stretches of fragmentation. The political and cultural experience of China, however, was marked by relatively little outside influence and thousands of years of centralized rule. Moreover, for the great majority of its history, China would be perhaps the world's greatest exporter of ideas and goods.

# The Origins of Yellow River Cultures, 5000–1766 BCE

The sun beyond the mountain glows,
The Yellow River seaward flows,
If you want an even better sight,
Ascend an even greater height.
"Climbing 'Stork Pavilion,'" Wang Zhihuan (648–742 CE)

An observer at the site of the Stork Pavilion of poet Wang Zhihuan's reverie could justly claim to have gazed upon the heartland of Chinese history. Situated on a high bluff at Yongji in the south of the modern province of Shaanxi, the pavilion marked a celebrated scenic spot commanding a view of the Yellow River as it approaches its great bend to the east. Here it is joined by the Wei River from the west and rolls across the North China Plain in a leisurely but at times fearsome manner for another 500 miles to the Bohai Gulf, an arm of the Yellow Sea.

Over the centuries, our observer might have witnessed the origins and development of some of China's first Neolithic cultures along the river. Sixty miles up the Wei, he or she could have visited China's most famous Neolithic village at

## Seeing Patterns

▶ How did the interplay of environment and climate help to influence the earliest patterns of Chinese civilization? How do historians address the question of whether "geography is destiny" in this case?

▶ What can the remains of Neolithic Chinese settlements tell us about the continuities and disruptions of Chinese history?

▶ How did the Zhou concept of the Mandate of Heaven operate?

Banpo or one of dozens in between. Even today, on every side of the bend lie burial mounds from a wide selection of China's early village and town cultures. Nearby is the modern city of Xi'an [SHE-ahn], the capital of no fewer than 13 Chinese regimes during its long history. And here, too, the richest and most famous site of all attracts visitors by the millions: the sprawling tomb complex of China's first emperor, Qin Shi Huangdi [chin SHUHR hwang-DEE], packed with thousands of life-sized terra-cotta soldiers in perfect ranks marching in timeless close-order drill.

## Geography and Climate

While China's natural boundaries are perhaps less dramatic than those of India, they have had an equally profound effect on its history and society. As with India, the Himalayas and Pamirs along the southern border of Tibet mark one natural barrier. River systems such as the Amur and Ussuri in the north, the Salween in the southwest, and the Red in Vietnam have also represented past borders, though not impermeable ones. The northern and western deserts—the Gobi, Ordos, and Taklamakan—have also served as natural boundaries that frequently passed in and out of the hands of successive Chinese dynasties as their emperors sought to curb the incursions of nomads or control central Asian trade routes.

The chief effect of these features, however, has been to limit the principal avenues of outside interaction to the narrow corridor running west of Xi'an, south of Mongolia, and north of the modern province of Qinghai, spanning the route of the famous Silk Road. Like the Khyber Pass in India, this route has historically been the main avenue into China; unlike the Khyber, however, it has seldom been an invasion route for outsiders. The result of this has been that, on the one hand, the origins and early development of ancient China were more isolated than those of the other Eurasian centers of civilization, but, on the other hand, the absence of outside competitors facilitated both cultural and political unification.

While conditioned by many of the same factors found in India, China's climate is more varied. The area south of the Qin [chin] Mountains marks the northern boundary of the region regulated by the monsoon, with warm temperatures and abundant summer rainfall. Because of the summer monsoon, rainfall amounts can range from about 40 inches per year in the eastern coastal city of Hangzhou [HAHNG-joe] to over 70 inches in the subtropical south. The suitability of the southern regions for rice cultivation, as with the Gangetic societies of India, resulted in rapid growth and high population density there. Above the monsoon line, temperatures and rainfall amounts are influenced more by the weather systems of the Eurasian interior. Thus, northern China is subject to blistering summers and frigid winters with scant and unreliable precipitation.

One result of these conditions has been that China's population has historically been concentrated in the plains along the major river valleys and the coast. Three main river systems have remained the primary avenues of agriculture and commerce: the Pearl River (Zhujiang) in the south, the Yangzi [YAHNG-zuh] River (at 3,988 miles, the third longest in the world), and the Yellow River (Huanghe), where the most influential early Chinese societies developed (see Map 4.1).

**The Yellow River**    Rising in the highlands of Gansu and flowing north to the Ordos Desert, the Yellow River then turns south and east out of Inner Mongolia for 500 miles before making its bend to the east and the sea, a total distance of

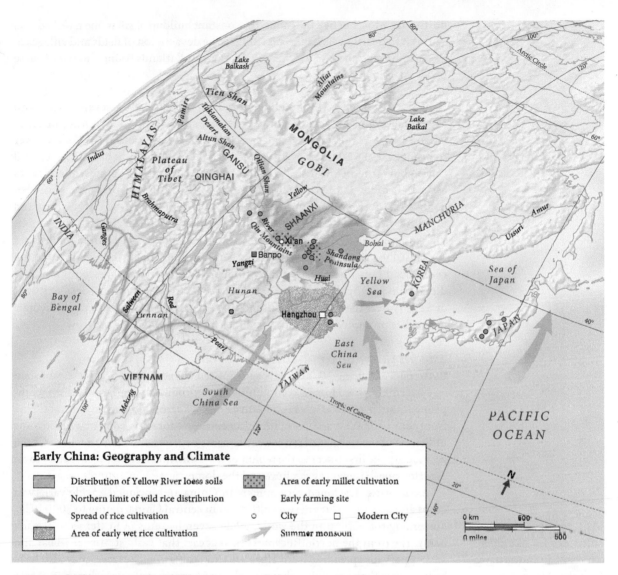

MAP 4.1 **Early China: Geography and Climate.**

about 3,000 miles. The river gets its name as a result of the *loess*—a light, dry, mineral-rich soil deposited by centuries of strong winds—it picks up as it flows, giving it a yellowish tint. As with the Nile in Egypt, the rich, easily worked soil carried by the river has brought abundantly productive agriculture to arid

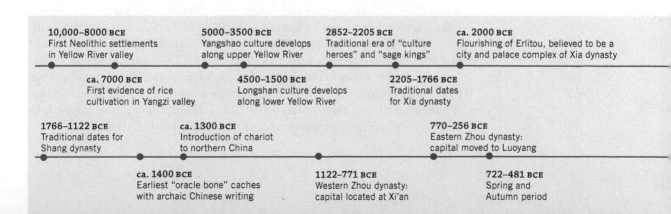

| 10,000–8000 BCE | 5000–3500 BCE | 2852–2205 BCE | ca. 2000 BCE |
|---|---|---|---|
| First Neolithic settlements in Yellow River valley | Yangshao culture develops along upper Yellow River | Traditional era of "culture heroes" and "sage kings" | Flourishing of Erlitou, believed to be a city and palace complex of Xia dynasty |

| ca. 7000 BCE | 4500–1500 BCE | 2205–1766 BCE |
|---|---|---|
| First evidence of rice cultivation in Yangzi valley | Longshan culture develops along lower Yellow River | Traditional dates for Xia dynasty |

| 1766–1122 BCE | ca. 1300 BCE | 770–256 BCE |
|---|---|---|
| Traditional dates for Shang dynasty | Introduction of chariot to northern China | Eastern Zhou dynasty: capital moved to Luoyang |

| ca. 1400 BCE | 1122–771 BCE | 722–481 BCE |
|---|---|---|
| Earliest "oracle bone" caches with archaic Chinese writing | Western Zhou dynasty: capital located at Xi'an | Spring and Autumn period |

northern China, but like the Indus, the constant buildup of silt in the riverbed also causes it to overflow its banks, resulting in the devastation of fields and villages in its path through the North China Plain, the vast flatlands lining the river course on its final run to the sea.

**"China's Sorrow"**   This building up and bursting of natural levees, along with earthquakes and occasional human actions, such as the dynamiting of dikes during World War II to stop the Japanese invasion, have caused the Yellow River to change course 26 times over the last 3,000 years. Its mouth has shifted several times above and below the Shandong Peninsula, assuming its present course to the north following massive floods in 1854–1855. Not surprisingly, efforts to control the river have occupied a prominent place in the mythology, history, and political and social organization of the region from earliest times. For example, Yu, the supposed founder of the Xia dynasty, was said to have labored for decades to control the river's rampages. More recently, some scholars have pointed to the centralized bureaucratic structure of imperial China and suggested that it was dictated in part by the struggle for mastery of its waterways. Thus, despite its gift of fertility over the course of thousands of years, the Yellow River's unpredictable nature has prompted writers to sometimes refer to it as "China's sorrow."

## The Origins of Neolithic Cultures

Between 50,000 and 20,000 years ago modern *Homo sapiens* became established in eastern Eurasia. Human communities that produced small, refined stone implements such as arrowheads and knives ranged across north and central China from about 30,000 years ago, marking an extensive foraging culture. Within a few millennia of the last glacial retreat, settlements began to appear in northern China containing the first traces in the region of the transition from forager society to an agrarian one, based on agriculture and the domestication of animals.

**Millet:** A species of grass cultivated for its edible white seeds and as hay for animal feed.

Agriculture developed very quickly in China and included a wide variety of crops and livestock. Sites of rice cultivation in central China, dating to 7000 BCE, are among the earliest in the world, while several strains of **millet** were already being grown in the north. Recent work suggests that early strains of wheat and barley, perhaps spreading from areas around the Fertile Crescent, may also have been grown. Chickens, pigs, sheep, cattle, and dogs were also widely raised. Areas along the Yellow River contain some of the earliest agricultural villages in China, and several *prototypical cultures*—those that pioneered techniques, institutions, or patterns of social organization widely copied in later years—emerged here and along the North China Plain over the next several thousand years.

**Banpo Village**   Perhaps the most studied of the thousands of Neolithic sites across China is Banpo [BAN-paw] Village, located on the outskirts of Xi'an. Banpo Village is representative of Yangshao [YAHNG-shaow], or "painted pottery," culture, which flourished from 5000 to 3500 BCE. Although the potter's wheel had not yet been introduced from western Eurasia, Yangshao communities like Banpo had sophisticated kilns that fired a wide variety of brightly painted storage pots, vases, etc. decorated with animal and geometric designs. The inhabitants of Yangshao villages also produced stone implements such as axes, chisels, and knives to support the community's hunting, farming, and fishing activities.

The perimeter of the Banpo settlement is surrounded by a defensive ditch, rather than the walls characteristic of later towns and cities, with 40 homes arranged around a rectangular central structure believed to be a clan meeting house or religious site. The homes were supported by vertical posts and had thatched roofs that, along with the walls, were plastered with mud and straw. The village contains a number of features that archaeologists believe to be early forms of certain long-standing patterns of rural life in northern China. For example, some of the huts contain raised clay beds with flues laid through them—an early version of the *kang* [kahng], the heated bed still found in older northern Chinese farming homes today. Also, silkworm cocoons and crude needles suggest the early development of silk weaving. Perhaps the most exciting finds, however, are the pot shards bearing stylized pictures of animals and geometric markings that some Chinese scholars have speculated may be ancestral forms of the Chinese written language.

**Longshan Culture**   Settled life in villages and towns appears to have expanded greatly during the Longshan period, from about 4000 to 2000 BCE. Once thought to have grown out of Yangshao culture as it spread east to modern Shandong Province, the dates of the earliest distinct Longshan artifacts have now been pushed as far back as 4500 BCE. A later branch of Longshan culture based in what is now Henan [HEH-nahn] Province is also believed to have arisen around 2000 BCE, lasting until about 1500 BCE, when it was absorbed by the Shang dynasty.

Like their Yangshao counterparts, Longshan potters were highly skilled and pioneered forms and styles still favored by Chinese artisans today. The black-colored pottery associated with Longshan culture is particularly refined. Some of the pieces are so delicate and nearly transparent that they resemble the famous "eggshell porcelain" of later Chinese imperial pottery works. The introduction of the potter's wheel from the west in the mid-third millennium BCE—one of the earliest indications we have of late Neolithic Chinese interactions with other peoples—permitted unprecedented precision, while improved kilns, reaching firing temperatures in excess of 1,800 degrees Fahrenheit, and

*Top:* Interior View of Banpo Dwelling. *Bottom:* Circular Foundation Showing Postholes.

**Painted Pottery, or Yangshao, Earthenware Basin Found at Banpo Site.** Contrast and compare this piece with the one from Longshan (p. 98). What similarities and differences can you spot?

Longshan (Black Pottery)
Culture Stemmed Beaker (*bei*),
Shandong, ca. 2000 BCE.

experimentation with kaolin clays began a long process of ceramic innovation that ultimately resulted in the first porcelain thousands of years later.

After 2000 BCE, the Longshan and other late Neolithic cultures were at a point where a transition to a society marked by large towns and even small cities supported by agriculture was becoming discernible. Towns of several thousand inhabitants have been uncovered, and a number of sites contain elaborate altars. The use of gold, copper, bronze, and jade in jewelry is also increasingly evident. Craft specialization and embryonic social classes are detectable.

**Beyond the North China Plain**    Given the subtropical environment of the regions below the Yangzi River basin in central China, it would be surprising if archaeologists did not find remains of flourishing cultures there as well. Until recently, however, such artifacts have been marginal and fragmentary. In addition to isolated sites on the western Yangzi River, a few close to modern Shanghai and Hangzhou, and at Dalongtan in Yunnan, the most extensive distinctive culture is that of Dapenkeng [DAH-pen-keng], which flourished from 5000 to 2500 BCE. Artifacts including pot shards, arrowheads, and polished tools and axes indicate a sophisticated coastal and riverine society along an extensive corridor running from the borders of modern Vietnam along the south China coast to Fujian Province and, most strikingly, across the Taiwan Strait to the western coast of that island.

The vast reach of Dapenkeng culture and the similarity of its relatively rare artifacts over a wide area suggest extensive interaction with peoples throughout the region. While the origins of this culture may be obscure, they do appear to be quite different from those of the north. Long and patient work by linguists has established this area as part of a Proto-Austronesian-speaking region, one whose parent language is distinct from the Sino-Tibetan language group that contains the various Chinese dialects and that has strong links to the Austronesian speakers on modern Taiwan. This in turn has prompted scholars studying the origins of the Polynesian language family—which is part of the Austronesian group—to search for possible links with these people on Taiwan and along the China coast.

**Origins of Rice Cultivation**    While the staple grain crops of the north included various strains of millet, with wheat and barley not coming into extensive cultivation until the Zhou period, the most far-reaching innovation in the regions south of the North China Plain was the development of widespread rice cultivation. Two sources have been cited as likely early centers of rice experimentation: southeast Asia and the area extending from China's modern province of Hunan to the coastal reaches of the Yangzi River, where rice grains have been dated to 7000 BCE. While we cannot know with precision which region played the more prominent role in spreading rice cultivation and techniques throughout China, we do know that southeast Asia remained an important source of new rice strains that allowed China's food production to keep pace with its population until well into the nineteenth century. Other food sources domesticated elsewhere making their appearance in Neolithic south China include chickens—perhaps obtained from south Asia via southeast Asia—and cattle, especially the water buffalo. Cattle, however, were raised primarily for farmwork rather than consumption.

**Toward a Chinese Culture**    With these recent finds, the older view of Chinese civilization being the exclusive product of the Yellow River valley cultures, which then expanded to more distant areas, has undergone considerable modification. Instead, scholars now suggest that the area approximating modern China consisted around 3000 BCE of a collection of agrarian communities that remained distinct in their own right but whose interactions with each other began to contribute common cultural elements that ultimately became identified as "Chinese." Indeed, some scholars have adopted a view of China down through the end of the third millennium BCE as being not so far from the mythical period referred to by ancient writers as *wanguo* [WAHN-gwo]—the "ten thousand states."

Though scholars have filled in much of the picture of these ancient cultures, the precise time and duration of their transition to one marked by cities is still very much open to debate. Chinese chroniclers, however, drawing upon the world's largest and longest literary record, have long given pride of place in this regard to their first three dynasties: the Xia, Shang, and Zhou.

## The Age of Myth and the Xia Dynasty, 2852–1766 BCE

The Chinese have been called the most historically minded people on earth. For thousands of years, the use of writing for purposes of record keeping has been of paramount importance, and the written word itself was considered to have a kind of inner power. For millennia, the careful study, writing, and rewriting of history have been vital elements of individual self-cultivation as well as key mechanisms for political and social control (see "Patterns Up Close").

Among the earliest collections of Chinese writings we have are those of the *Shujing* [SHOO-jeeng]. Also known as The *Book of History* or *Classic of Documents*, the *Shujing* is a detailed compilation of ancient material purportedly from 2357 to 631 BCE. Though heavily laden with material of questionable reliability, it remains a principal documentary source for information about the people, places, and events of China's first three dynasties: the Xia [she-AH], Shang [shahng], and Zhou [joe]. In a surprising number of cases, its clues have helped to illuminate the archaeological evidence in recent attempts to establish the historical existence of the Xia dynasty.

**Culture Heroes and Sage Kings**    According to Chinese legend, mythical culture heroes and sage kings reigned from 2852 to 2205 BCE and introduced many of China's basic elements and institutions. Among the contributions attributed to the first culture hero, Fuxi, were medicine, divination, and, according to some stories, writing. His successor, Shen Nong, was credited with developing agriculture. Fire and silkworm cultivation were said to have been introduced during the reign of Huangdi, the "Yellow Emperor," whose reign followed that of Shen Nong. The Yellow Emperor's rule was followed by that of the three sage kings—Yao, Shun, and Yu—who set the example for strong moral leadership and are credited with passing the role of leadership on to the land's most worthy men instead of to their own family members.

"Examining into antiquity we find that the Emperor Yao was called Fangxun. He was reverent, intelligent, accomplished, sincere, and mild. . . . His light covered the four extremities of the empire and extended to Heaven above and the Earth below. . . . The numerous people were amply nourished and prosperous and became harmonious."

—*Shujing*, "The Canon of Yao"

**Between Myth and History**   The *Shujing* acclaims Yu, the last sage king, as the tamer of the Yellow River. He is also traditionally considered to be the founder of the Xia dynasty in 2205 BCE. Because of the difficulty in establishing a clear archaeological record, however, Yu and his successors have largely remained suspended between myth and history.

Moreover, the character of the *Shujing* as a creation of later Zhou chroniclers, with a specific agenda of justifying Zhou rule, has cast a long shadow over events that allegedly took place over 1,500 years before. More generally, as the sole literary account we have of the period, it has naturally assumed a dominant and, most likely, misleading role as the master narrative of ancient Chinese history. Some scholars have even argued that the Xia were an invention of the Zhou. More recently, some have suggested that their rule was in fact a kind of Shang mythology. On the other hand, some, notably a group of Chinese archaeologists, have noted that the relative accuracy of the dates given in the *Shujing* for events in the Shang dynasty suggests a similar level of reliability for its accounts of the earlier Xia.

Recent archaeological work also has moved somewhat closer to confirming the historical existence of a widespread culture, if not yet a state, corresponding to the literary accounts of the Xia. Excavations at Erlitou [AR-lee-toe] in southern Shaanxi Province in the 1950s and 1960s revealed that artifacts at the site fall within the traditional dates given for the existence of the Xia. In addition, artifacts, particularly early bronze ritual vessels virtually identical to those at Erlitou, appear widely throughout regions described in the *Shujing* as belonging to the Xia and, in some cases, considerably beyond it.

**Xia Society**   The small number of purported Xia sites makes it difficult to draw many firm conclusions about their society. Much of what we believe is based on the premise that the Xia was a transitional society, developing and elaborating the material culture of the late Longshan and Yangshao cultural periods. Of particular note in this transition are the growing importance of bronze casting, the increasingly complex symbols on pottery, and the widespread evidence of large-scale communal efforts at flood control, including dams, dikes, levees, and retention ponds.

As we have seen, the Yangshao and Longshan cultures stretched across a continuum from small hunting, fishing, and farming villages to substantial agriculturally supported towns. The Xia, however, though our picture of them is far from complete, appear to have reached the tipping point at which most of the hallmarks of urban society—what we commonly think of as "civilization"—began to appear. For example, excavation at the Erlitou site, dated to perhaps 2000 BCE, reveals a walled city of moderate size containing what is believed to be the foundation of China's first palace: a stamped-earth terrace extending over 100 yards on each side.

Moreover, the layout of the buildings within walled compounds dating from this time began to resemble that of later official residences. Beams supported by large wooden posts carry the weight of moderately sloped roofs with upturned ends, while "curtain walls," which bear little or none of the structure's weight, are built between the posts of plastered brick or masonry. Most of the larger buildings are also built along a north–south axis with their courtyards and entrances facing south, an orientation favored even today by Chinese builders.

Literary evidence suggests that Xia leaders exercised a strong family- or clan-based rule, and the archaeological evidence seems to support this to a considerable degree. Evidence indicating the role of the elites as mediators with the spirit world, and particularly with the ancestors of Xia rulers, is also found in abundance at Erlitou. China's first bronze ritual vessels—wine beakers on tripod stands in shapes favored throughout subsequent Chinese history—as well as jade figurines, turquoise jewelry, the world's earliest lacquered wood items, and cowry shells, a medium of exchange monopolized by the Xia rulers, all testify to their leaders' religious and social roles. Moreover, foundations of workers' residences and workshops for copper and bronze casting have also been found. As with a number of Longshan sites, extensive cemeteries outside the city suggest the development of social classes in the number and kind of burial artifacts and the position and richness of elite plots.

Though the boundaries of Chinese history have been pushed back considerably by such work, the Xia remain, like their contemporaries the Harappans, an elusive, if not perhaps a "lost," civilization. Indeed, much of what we believe about them comes from interpretations extended back in time from the period of documented Shang dominance. Unlike the Xia, however, the written records and artifacts of the Shang dynasty offer a much more complete picture of East Asia's first Bronze Age society.

## The Interactions of Shang and Zhou History and Politics, 1766–481 BCE

The Shang dynasty represents the first genuine flowering of urban society in east Asia. Though this development occurs somewhat later than in the other core areas of Egypt and the Mediterranean, southwest Asia, and the Indus valley, we nevertheless find here all of the attributes of such cultures elsewhere: a high degree of skill in metallurgy, a large and varied agricultural base, an increasingly centralized political and religious system, growing **social stratification**, a written language, and, of course, cities. In all of these areas the Shang made considerable contributions; in some, such as their spectacular bronzes and especially their system of written characters, they were startlingly original.

Social stratification: A hierarchical arrangement of groups or classes within a society—for example, peasants, merchants, officials, ministers, rulers.

### The Shang Dynasty, 1766–1122 BCE

Unlike the idealized rule of the sage kings Yao, Shun, and Yu depicted in the *Shujing*, Shang social and political organization was kinship-based, with an emphasis on military power and efficiency of command. As in Mesopotamia, the advent of cities, with their vastly increased populations, now required rulers to wield greater power for defense and internal regulation, while at the same time appealing to an authority beyond human power for legitimacy. Thus, loyalty was pledged to the Shang king and his family. Members of the king's extended family controlled political and religious power, with more distant relatives acting as court officials.

Among the purported 31 Shang kings mentioned in literary records, rulership often passed from uncle to nephew, though sometimes it went from elder brother

to younger. Unlike the Aryan system of *varna*, there was no rigidly defined priestly class, though spirit mediums and diviners were widely used by Shang rulers—as we saw with Wu Ding—and exercised considerable influence at court. Local leaders who controlled walled cities and towns and their surrounding lands were employed by the ruling families as regional officials, as were specially designated Shang allies, though the exact nature of these arrangements is not clearly understood.

**Shang Weapon.** A bronze ceremonial axe head with intricate decorative markings, from the thirteenth to the eleventh century BCE.

**Shang Armies and Expansion**    Though small compared to the forces commanded by their successors, the armies fielded by Shang rulers were the most powerful of east Asia in their day. One expeditionary force of the late thirteenth-century BCE king Wu Ding and his wife Fu Hao numbered more than 13,000 men and included both paid soldiers and local defense forces recruited from the larger walled towns. Excavations reveal that the armies were organized into companies of 100 men who wielded bronze-tipped spears and pikes topped with crescent-shaped axe heads and spear tips (see Map 4.2).

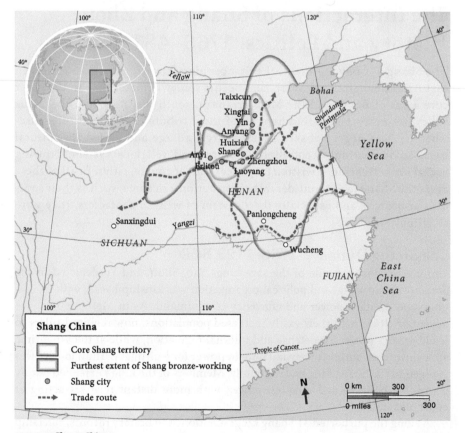

MAP 4.2 **Shang China.**

**Shang Chariot.** Whether used for battle or state functions, Shang-era chariots were distinctive in their wide stance, roominess, and portability. The photograph shows a careful reconstruction of a Shang chariot with authentic bronze decorations and lacquered finish. Note the linchpins holding the wheels to the axles. These could be quickly removed for ease in changing wheels or breaking down the chariot in order to carry its parts separately.

**The Introduction of the Chariot** Another potent weapon used by the Shang was the chariot, possibly introduced to China through interaction with Indo-Europeans around 1300 to 1200 BCE, when these vehicles first make their appearance in Shang burial sites. Chariots seem to have been shortly preceded by the widespread introduction of the horse from the west, an innovation that had already revolutionized transport and warfare through much of Eurasia. Up to this point, the small Mongolian ponies native to the northern reaches of Shang lands seem to have attracted little interest, perhaps because of their limitations as transport and draft animals. The larger and faster steeds of central Asia and the western Eurasian steppes, however, were to remain important items of trade for the Chinese for thousands of years and were celebrated in painting, poetry, and song.

Shang chariots were pulled by two horses and generally held three men. Detachable wheels held by linchpins permitted easy storage and repair. Both charioteers and infantry wielded large composite bows—so called because they were made of wood, cattle horn, and sinew. The bows were curved away from the archer in their unstrung state for additional power. As with other ancient peoples, the combination of archers with the chariot gave Shang forces considerable striking power, especially when employed against slower and more unwieldy infantry formations.

**Shang Politics and Foreign Relations**    Because their prestige depended in large part on their military power and harmony with their ancestors, the Shang rulers constantly mounted campaigns for sacrifice—both material and human. Indeed, the archaeological evidence and oracle bone inscriptions suggest that the greater part of Shang foreign relations with **client states** and allies consisted of setting and enforcing levels of tribute and labor service. Shang kings, especially Wu Ding, continually led expeditions against settled peoples to the west, the most prominent of whom, the Zhou, based around modern Xi'an, were ultimately enlisted as allies and clients. Wu Ding's successors, such as Zu Geng [ZOO-gung] and Di Yin, met with less success, however, and over time shifting coalitions of former allies and client states began to encroach on Shang lands. Significantly, even to the end of the Shang period, the interior lands of the state appear to have been considered secure enough to lack walls and other defensive structures around many major towns.

**Client states:** States that are dependent on or partially controlled by more powerful ones.

**Shang Interactions**    Throughout the span of roughly 1,200 years from the traditional beginnings of the Xia to the end of the Shang, ties between the northern Chinese states and the other Eurasian civilizational cores seems to have been tenuous at best. The most direct links appear to have been through the trade and migrations of an ethnically and culturally diverse group of nomadic–pastoral peoples who ranged along a broad northern tier of Eurasia from the steppes of modern Ukraine to the area of modern Manchuria in the east. Though they left few traces, and early Chinese accounts use a haphazard collection of names for them, scholars have theorized that these nomads included both speakers of Altaic languages—the distant ancestors of the Mongols, Manchus, Turks, and perhaps the Huns—and, perhaps more significantly at this point, the Indo-European peoples who played such an important role in spreading a host of ancient technologies throughout Eurasia.

Though direct mention of these nomadic peoples is almost completely absent from Shang records, a number of objects in Shang tombs carry clear signs of their foreign origins. For example, Fu Hao's tomb contains a number of bronze and jade objects—most significantly, bronze mirrors—which only later would come into widespread use in China. For their part, the Shang circulated local and foreign items such as bronze vessels, weapons, and jade throughout the region and beyond.

Many of these foreign items have been found as far south as northern Vietnam, and the peoples of surrounding areas acknowledged Shang predominance in wealth and culture. The picture is complicated somewhat by the recent work on cultures that show a connection to artifacts uncovered at Shang sites, and even at Erlitou, but have distinct—almost exotic—regional variations. The most intriguing example is that of the strange elongated figurines of Sanxingdui [SAN-shing-dway] in Sichuan [SIH-chwan], well out of Shang-dominated territory. On the whole, however, widespread recognition of Shang sophistication marks, with the ascendancy of the Zhou, an important example of a recurring pattern of world history, as well as that of China: conquerors on the cultural periphery interacting with and adapting to the culture of the conquered.

## The Mandate of Heaven: The Zhou Dynasty to 481 BCE
Unlike the Xia and Shang dynasties, the nearly nine centuries of Zhou rule are extensively documented in such literary works as the *Zuo Zhuan* [ZWOA-jwan]

(*The Commentaries of Mr. Zuo*), the *Chunqiu* [CHWUN-chew] (*Spring and Autumn Chronicles*), and later compilations such as the *Shiji* [SHIH-jee] (*Records of the Historian*) by the second-century BCE historian Sima Qian [sih-ma-CHIEN] in addition to the *Shujing*.

Like the *Shujing*, these other Zhou records contain much of questionable value and uncertain origin. Nevertheless, they suggest both an ongoing quest for social, political, and moral order as well as institutional and intellectual experimentation on a grand scale. They also provide us, in the closing date of the *Spring and Autumn Chronicles* (481 BCE), with an important transition point with which to end this chapter. As we will see in Chapter 9, out of the increasingly fierce competition among the Zhou states for expansion and survival in the succeeding Warring States period (formally 403–256 BCE but used to encompass the entire era from 480 down to the creation of the Qin empire in 221 BCE) came China's greatest flowering of philosophical and political theory and ultimate unification into an empire that would last, with brief interruptions, for over 2,000 years.

**The Mandate of Heaven** By the twelfth century BCE, it appears through the trend of oracle bone inscriptions that the size of the Shang state had shrunk considerably due to encroachment by peoples to the north and west. The oracle bones also suggest an increased concentration of power in the hands of the last Shang kings, a situation depicted in the literary record as coinciding with their dissolution and corruption. Against this backdrop, the state of Zhou to the west—which, as we have seen, had become a Shang dependency—began to take military action. The *Shujing* tells of the Zhou kings Wen, Wu, and Cheng and Cheng's regent, the Duke of Zhou, systematically pushing their holdings eastward from 1122 BCE, taking much of the Shang territory under their control. Sometime around 1045 BCE, Zhou forces captured and burned the last Shang capital and stronghold near Anyang. In doing so, the Zhou sought to portray their conquest as morally justified after an overlong interlude of Shang decadence (see Map 4.3).

Unlike the rise and fall of states in other areas, conquest by one of the three dynasties, as depicted in the literary record, did not mean exile, extinction, or enslavement for those defeated. On the contrary, the conquerors were shown as presenting their victories as acts of moral renewal for those they conquered by ridding them of oppressive or degenerate rulers and restoring leadership to the worthy. Although the attitudes of the common people toward such shifts of power remain unknown, the idealized

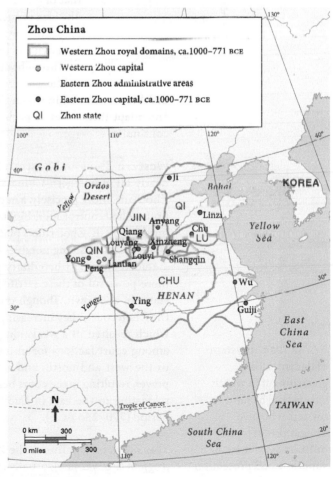

MAP 4.3 **Zhou China.**

speeches of the new rulers in the *Shujing*, for example, attempt to justify their actions and seek the cooperation of all classes in the new order.

As the compilers of this literary record, the Zhou sought to place themselves firmly within it. While it is unknown whether the practices they recorded had been widespread or newly invented by the conquerors, they provided the backdrop for one of China's most enduring historical and philosophical concepts: the Mandate of Heaven.

According to this idea, a dynasty's right to rule depends on the moral correctness of its rulers. Over time, dynasties grow weaker and tend to become corrupt as individual rulers give in to the temptations of court life or different factions seek to manipulate the throne. Under such conditions, rebellion from within or conquest by outside forces becomes morally justified. The success of such actions is then seen as proof that heaven's approval or "mandate" has been taken from the old rulers and bestowed on the insurgents, who may then legitimately found a new dynasty. Ultimately, however, the new dynasty, too, will decline. Thus, the fall of the Shang dynasty, as described in the *Shujing*, sprang from a loss of virtue, similar to that of the Xia, which had earlier resulted in Shang ascendancy. The idea of such a "dynastic cycle" operating as the driving force of history was later codified by court historians during the Han dynasty (202 BCE–220 CE).

Throughout Chinese history, these concepts not only allowed political renewal to take place internally but framed a remarkably durable system within which the Chinese and outside conquerors could interact and adapt themselves to each other in maintaining governmental and societal continuity.

> "We must not presume to suppose that the Yin [Shang] received the Mandate of Heaven for a fixed period of years; we must not presume to suppose that it was not going to continue. It was because they did not reverently care for their virtue that they early let their Mandate fall."
>
> —*Shujing*, "Shaogao"

**Western Zhou and Eastern Zhou**    By the end of the eleventh century BCE, nearly all of northern China as far south as the Yangzi River had come under Zhou rule. More precisely, a network of over 100 smaller territories was organized under Zhou control, marking the beginning of the Western Zhou era, which lasted until 771 BCE. Zhou rulers placed family, distinguished subjects, allies, and even some defeated Shang notables in leadership positions of these territories under a graded system of hereditary ranks. By the eighth century BCE, however, the more powerful of these territories had begun to consolidate their holdings into states of their own. Though the states would continue to pledge their loyalty to the Zhou court, they increasingly worked toward promoting their own interests, which resulted in a weakening of Zhou political power. A half century of war among court factions for ultimate rule, border struggles with nomadic peoples to the west and north, and a devastating earthquake further weakened Zhou power, resulting in the court being driven from its capital at Xi'an in 771 BCE and relocating to the east in Luoyang. This forced move began the Eastern Zhou period (770–256 BCE).

**Feudalism:** A system of decentralized government in which rule is held by landowners who owe obligations of loyalty and military service to their superiors and protection to those under them.

**The Zhou in Decline**    The Zhou system of decentralized government called *fengjian* [FUNG-jien], usually rendered as "**feudalism**," gave considerable autonomy to its local rulers and was thus an important reason for the weakening of the

Zhou central government and the strengthening of its dependent states. As these dependent states grew in power and their economies flourished, local rulers became less loyal to the Zhou leadership, and some rulers even went as far as naming themselves "king" (*wang*) of their own domains.

The prestige of the Zhou court was further weakened after its flight to Luoyang in 770. Continuing border problems with nomadic–pastoral peoples to the north and west around the Zhou home state and the relative isolation of its new capital drastically cut the flow of revenue from the dependent domains. This isolation was especially important since these states were in a period of tremendous economic expansion. Within a few generations of the inauguration of the Eastern Zhou in 770 BCE, Zhou control and power had significantly weakened in absolute as well as relative terms.

The Zhou decline is graphically described in the *Spring and Autumn Chronicles* and its accompanying work, *The Commentaries of Mr. Zuo*. Compiled in the Zhou state of Lu in the modern province of Shandong, these complementary works detail the maneuverings of states and individuals in northern China from 722 to 481 BCE. The world they depict is one in which repeated attempts at creating a stable political and social order among the 15 major Zhou states are frustrated by constantly shifting power dynamics and especially by the rise of dominant states on the Zhou periphery.

Early on, during the mid-seventh century, the most important of these states was Qi [chee], which dominated northeast China and much of Shandong. By shrewd diplomacy and careful use of military power, Qi became the first "senior," or *ba* [bah], state in a system of **hegemony** in which the lesser Zhou states deferred to the *ba* state as the protector of the Zhou system. The successive *ba* states mounted alliances against non-Zhou states and attempted to regulate relations among those within the system. They also presided at conferences held from the mid-sixth century BCE aimed at regularizing trade and diplomacy among the states. Qi was succeeded by Jin, which reorganized the *ba* system and, in 579 BCE, sponsored a truce and disarmament conference among the Zhou states.

By the latter part of the sixth century, a rough balance of power among the four leading states of Jin, Chu [Choo] (the premier state of the southern periphery), Qi, and Qin (a rising force in the old Zhou homeland near Xi'an) held sway. While this system functioned for several decades, new powers on the peripheries, expansion into non-Zhou lands, and civil war in Jin ultimately precipitated the partition of Jin in 403 BCE, marking the formal opening of the Warring States period. By its close, Zhou itself had been absorbed by the combatants (in 256 BCE), and Qin would emerge as not just the dominant state but the creator of a unified empire in 221 BCE.

> **Hegemony:** A system of state relations in which less powerful states directly or implicitly agree to defer to the lead of the most powerful state, which is, thus, the hegemon.

# Economy, Society, and Family Adaptation in Ancient China

From Neolithic times, the Chinese economy has been based on agriculture. Even today, slightly more than half of the country's people are engaged in some variety of farmwork. From early times as well, both the Yellow River states and those in the south of China outside of the control of the Shang and Zhou dynasties relied on a peasant subsistence economy based on family and clan landownership, with much of the local political power diffused to the thousands of villages dotting the landscape. While periodic concentration of landlord power and the problems of land-centered social relationships occupied Chinese rulers over the course of millennia, China, unlike some other agriculturally based societies, never developed an extensive system of slave labor.

Family life played a dominant role among all members of ancient Chinese society. Here, in a way parallel to trends in other agrarian kingdoms, the position of women in power among the elite eroded over time, a process that would be accelerated during the long interval of imperial rule. By the late Zhou period, the hierarchy of patriarchy and the growing influence of notions of *filial piety*—a model of behavior based on relationships among members of a family headed by the father—were on their way to becoming firmly established.

## Shang Society

Though Shang leaders, like those of the Xia and Zhou, frequently moved their headquarters for political and military reasons, nearly all of their newly established capitals swiftly grew to proportions comparable to those developing in India and the Mediterranean.

**Erligang**    The capital city at Erligang [AR-lee-gahng] was characteristic of the late Xia or early Shang period. It had a defensive wall 4.5 miles in circumference, enclosing an urban center of about a square mile. The area within the walls was the province of the rulers, related families, diviners, and bronze casters and craftspeople in the direct service of the elites. Merchants and craftspeople involved in the manufacture of items other than bronze, jade, or ritual objects lived outside the city walls, as did peasants and slaves.

The life of the commoners in Erligang centered largely on communal agriculture. They tilled the soil with small plows, stone-tipped hoes, and assorted wooden implements, bronze being considered too valuable for use in agricultural tasks. They grew millet and vegetables as their staples and raised water buffalo, sheep in the more arid areas, chickens, and pigs. The pig, domesticated since at least Yangshao times, continued to be of central importance in the rural diet. Even today, the written character for "family" or "household" (家, *jia*) is represented by a character depicting a pig under a roof.

**Social Class and Labor**    Within the towns and villages immediately outside the larger cities, a more differentiated social structure was also developing, with artisans of various trades organized according to lineage. Many families and clans tended to pursue the same occupations for generations, and craft guilds and other organizations came to be dominated by family groups, such as potters and ceramics makers, as was the case later in imperial China. The constant warfare of Shang rulers and their increasing interest in monumental projects, such as flood control along the Yellow River and its tributaries, all boosted the need for labor. Professional soldiers and local militia generally satisfied Shang military needs. Conscript labor, however, constituted an increasingly important part of the workforce.

## Interactions of Zhou Economy and Society

The large size of the territory claimed by the Zhou dynasty, and the enhanced trade that this expansion entailed, added to the wealth and power of all the rulers of its increasingly autonomous dependencies. The expansion of these dependencies to the Yangzi River basin brought much of east Asia's most productive farmland under some form of Zhou control and stimulated increased interaction with the inhabitants of the region.

**Innovation and Adaptation in Agriculture**    In the north, the introduction of the soybean from Manchuria, with its high protein content and ability to fix nitrogen in the soil, boosted crop yields and pushed growers to cultivate more marginal lands. The rotation of wheat and different varieties of millet allowed for more intensive farming. The use of more efficient ox-drawn plows and, from the fourth century BCE, iron-tipped tools, as well as increasingly elaborate irrigation and water-conservancy efforts, pushed yields even further. In the south, the Zhou dependencies, like the *janapadas* of India, developed rapidly as rice cultivation facilitated population growth. With the coming of intensive rice farming, the economic and demographic center of China moved steadily southward. By the middle of the sixth century BCE, the Zhou kingdoms taken together constituted the world's most populous, and perhaps richest, agriculturally based urban society.

**Zhou Rural Society**    The Zhou rulers devised a system of ranks for governing their dependencies based on the size of landholdings:

- *hou* [ho], the title given to rulers of the Zhou dependencies
- *qing* [ching], the chief functionaries of the *hou*
- *shi* [shihr], a general category for lower officials, eventually including talented commoners
- *shuren* [SHOO-ren], the remainder of the commoners.

Members of the various ranks of the aristocracy were responsible for collecting taxes from their dependents, and the *shuren* and were required to provide military service to those above in return for support and protection. Peasant cultivators worked their own lands, with the lands of the aristocracy often scattered in plots among those of the commoners.

**The Well-Field System**    In an attempt to untangle the more confusing aspects of this land arrangement, the Zhou were the first among many dynasties to attempt to impose a uniform system of land tenure in China. Later writers, most notably the philosopher Mencius, would look back nostalgically on the idealized *well-field system*—a method of land division said to have been devised by the Duke of Zhou. In this arrangement, each square *li* (one *li* is about one-third of a mile), consisting of 900 *mou* (each *mou* is approximately one-sixth of an acre), was divided into a grid of nine plots. Individual families would each work one of the eight outside plots while the middle one would be farmed in common for the taxes and rents owed the landowner or local officials. The term "well-field" comes from the Chinese character for "[water] well" (井, *jing*), which resembles a grid. Whether the system as idealized by Mencius was ever widely practiced is still a matter of debate among scholars. It did, however, remain the benchmark against which all subsequent attempts at land reform were measured, even into the twentieth century.

By the late 500s BCE, a substantial change had taken place in many of the Zhou states. The needs of individual governments to use the wealth of their states to support their militaries and developing bureaucracies prompted them to institute land taxes based on crop yields and, in some cases, to commute labor obligations to direct taxes payable in kind to the state. Depending on the state and the productivity of the land, these tended to vary from 10 to 20 percent of a family holding's yield. Then, as now, the taxes tended to affect the poor the most.

**The New Classes: Merchants and *Shi***  Further evidence for the decline of the Zhou feudal system is the rise of new classes. For the first time, the literary record now includes references to merchants. The growing power of this new class began, among other processes, a long-term struggle with various governments for control of such vital commodities as salt and iron. It also marked the beginning of the perception of merchants as *usurpers*—a class with no ties to the land and thus no stake in upholding the values of landholders or peasants—whose drive for profit from trafficking in the goods of others endangered the stability of Zhou social institutions. Accompanying the rise of a merchant class was the steady advance of a cash economy. The coining of money was becoming widespread by the late Zhou, including the round copper "cash" with the square middle hole, symbolically depicting heaven and earth, which remained almost unchanged for over 2,000 years.

Though often viewed with distaste by the landed aristocracy, merchants, with their wealth and expertise, were increasingly seen as resources to be tapped. Their rapid rise to economic prominence, however, meant that as a group their social position lay outside the traditional structures of agrarian life. Their independence and mobility, along with the steady growth of cities as centers of trade, helped spur political and economic centralization as the rulers of Zhou territories attempted to create more inclusive systems of administration. Direct taxation by the state, uniform law codes, and administrative restructuring were increasingly altering the old arrangement of mutual obligation between aristocratic landowners and dependent peasant farmers. Here, members of the new *shi* class, drawn from the lower aristocracy and wealthier commoners, who, like merchants, were divorced somewhat from the older structures of rural life, took on the role of bureaucrats and advisors. From the ranks of the *shi* would rise many of China's most famous thinkers, starting with Confucius, and the duties and proper conduct of the *shi* would come to occupy a prominent place in their writings from the late sixth century BCE on.

**Central Asian Interactions**  The growing wealth of north and central China spurred a dramatic increase in trade outside of the Zhou realm as well as among its constituent states, particularly in the south and along well-established routes into central Asia. As one measure of the extent of such interaction, scholars have pointed to silk threads appearing in the bindings of Egyptian mummies dated to 1000 BCE, in Greek gravesites several hundred years later, and even in central and northern European encampments from about 500 BCE. In this interchange, Zhou traders were increasingly helped by the carriers of the central Asian exchange.

By the sixth century BCE, a series of loosely related cultures along this northern front (called *Scythic* because of their broad cultural similarity to the peoples the Greeks called "Scythians") can be clearly discerned. These peoples appear to have taken Zhou goods much farther than originally thought, and scholars are only now beginning to realize the vast extent of their trade relations. What other goods besides silk may have been involved in such exchanges remains unknown, however, until the period of officially sanctioned and better-recorded trade along the Silk Road began in the second century BCE.

## Gender and the Family

While scholars have long explored the role of women and the family during China's imperial era, notably during the Song and Ming dynasties, serious study of gender roles in ancient China has only recently begun. One obvious reason for this is the relative scarcity of records from earlier times. Another is the development of women's instructional literature from roughly the first century BCE to the first century CE, a phenomenon that has provided modern scholars with an important focal point in charting a shift in perspectives of female "virtue" and proper behavior in the home and in public.

**Elite Women of the Shang**    In marked contrast to later Chinese court life, with its tightly prescribed etiquette and seclusion of wives and concubines from the avenues of power, elite women of the Shang often participated in political, and even military, affairs. As we saw in the opening of this chapter, one of the most complete Shang burial sites is that of Fu Hao, discovered in 1975. The most prominent of the 64 wives of Wu Ding, Fu Hao was buried with artifacts—hundreds of bronze, jade, and bone ornaments, as well as the sacrificial skeletons of 16 people and six dogs—that help bring to life a woman whose existence, though well established in written records, has otherwise been elusive.

The artifacts also shed light on a number of questions regarding Shang technology and material culture, court life, and especially the position of women among the aristocracy. For example, inscriptions on oracle bones in Fu Hao's tomb indicate that she wielded considerable power and influence even before becoming Wu Ding's principal wife. Prior to coming to court at the Shang capital of Yin sometime in the late thirteenth century BCE, she owned and managed a family estate nearby and was apparently well educated in a number of areas that would make her well prepared for palace life. She both supervised and conducted religious rituals at court and during military expeditions. As Wu Ding's chief confidant she advised him on political and military strategy and diplomacy. She even conducted her own military campaigns against Shang adversaries. The king apparently considered her so wise and beloved that after her death he frequently appealed to her for guidance through divination with oracle bones.

**Women's Status in Transition**    Elite women like Fu Hao appear to have shared a comparatively equal status with male rulers, even to the point of leading armies and practicing divination. To the extent that such literature as the *Book of History* and the *Poetry Classic* of the early Zhou era addresses issues of women and power, women were still depicted as occupying important positions as mentors and advisors. Women's crafts such as spinning and weaving, and especially the different skills demanded by silk production, were highly regarded. In fact, there were government offices supervised and staffed by women to oversee silk and hemp cloth weaving.

The wives and concubines of rulers in many instances had their own sets of records and genealogies as well, an important asset among the powerful in this family-conscious society. Even by the late Zhou period, as one scholar notes, a "model" woman like Lady Ji of the state of Lu was able to instruct her son, the high official Wen Bo (Earl Wen), in the arts of government by comparing the roles of different officials to the proper arrangement of the components of a loom in the process of weaving. In this role of advisor, she was much praised for her virtue by subsequent thinkers.

Yet it was also true that by this time it was Wen Bo and not Lady Ji who actually held the reins of power. Late Zhou women might be well educated and highly capable, but they seldom ruled in their own right. In fact, the treaties hammered out during the Spring and Autumn period (722–481 BCE) in many cases specifically barred women from involvement in state affairs. The same general trend may be glimpsed at other levels of society as well. The enormously complex web of family, clan, village, and class associations of the Zhou era reflects considerable respect for the wisdom and work of women, but these skills were increasingly seen as best exercised in the home instead of in the public sphere. The later development of state-sponsored Confucianism, with its preponderant emphasis on filial piety, ushered in a markedly secondary role for women.

## Interactions of Religion, Culture, and Intellectual Life in Ancient China

In many respects, the evolution of Chinese religion follows a similar pattern to that of other agriculturally based urban societies. That is, like the gods of the early Mesopotamians, the first Chinese gods were local deities that inhabited a spirit world presided over by a ruling god. In China, the rulers' ancestors occupied the highest rungs of the spirit world, and worship largely consisted of communication with them by various means. Religion was not separate from everyday life but permeated all aspects of it.

While they creatively adapted and adopted many other aspects of Shang culture, the Zhou era marked a turn toward a more abstract, impersonal, and universal concept of religion. As an illustration of this, Shangdi [SHANG-dee], the chief Shang deity, and other beings with superhuman powers but human-like personalities, began to give way to the more distant Zhou concept of "heaven" (*tian* [tien]) as the animating force of the universe. As in other religious traditions, there is a movement to go beyond the invocation of gods through proper sacrifice and divination rituals—*formalism*—in order to seek insight into the forces that control the universe. By the late Zhou era, this concept of heaven as the guiding cosmic force had become central to nearly every major Chinese religious and philosophical tradition.

### Oracle Bones and Early Chinese Writing
Scholars agree that samples of Shang characters found on oracle bones are examples of China's earliest known writing, representing an entirely original system.

One legend has it that the cultural hero Fuxi discovered writing after seeing symbols etched on the back of a turtle, and, indeed, the oracle bones themselves are mostly the undershells of turtles and the shoulder blades of oxen.

As we saw with Wu Ding in the opening of this chapter, those seeking guidance would have a diviner incise questions onto the bones. The bones were then heated and tapped with a rod, and the resulting cracks were interpreted as answers. Several thousand distinct symbols have been identified, and many are clearly ancient versions of modern Chinese characters. More importantly, the principles these symbols employed as a form of writing had already moved away from those of other hieroglyphic or pictographic languages. Chinese characters became increasingly stylized and, after the Qin era (221–202 BCE), put into standard forms. But in most cases, these retained enough of their earlier character to be recognizable to later readers. Moreover, the political and religious significance of Shang and Zhou ritual vessels, which, in many cases, contained inscriptions in archaic characters, ensured that some knowledge of them would be preserved.

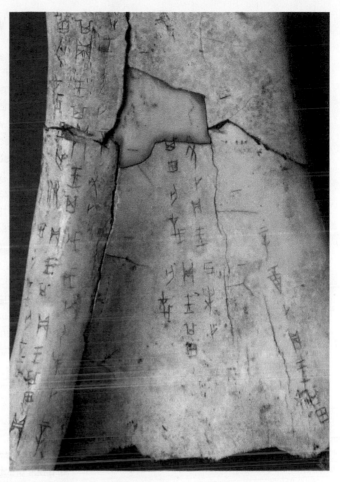

Shang Oracle Bone Inscription on Shoulder Blade of an Ox.

**Shang Bronzes** While it now seems that, like the potter's wheel, some of the early bronze articles and weapons found at late Longshan sites may have come by way of trade routes from western Asia, bronze-casting techniques used in China quite likely diffused northward from southeast Asia at about the same time. The best evidence for this is that the "carved-clay" technique favored by Shang and Zhou casters, in which inner and outer molds of the object are made of clay and molten bronze is poured into the gap between them, is unique to China and radically different from the "lost wax" method of the peoples of western Eurasia. Shang and early Zhou ritual vessels themselves, with their richly stylized *taotie* [TAOW-tea-eh] motifs—fanciful abstract reliefs of real and mythical animals incorporated into the design—are utterly unlike anything outside of east Asia.

**Shang Religion** The use of bronze vessels with their elaborately stylized *taotie* motifs constituted a central part of Shang religious ceremonies among the elites. Offerings of meats, grains (wheat, millet, and occasionally rice), and wine were a regular part of Shang ritual. Except for some limited references in later literature to offerings of wine and millet at local shrines and ancestral graves, we know little about the religious practices of Shang commoners. However, the growing number of artifacts and oracle bones found at the gravesites of elites and at the remains of royal palaces has considerably clarified the belief system of the rulers.

# The Chinese Writing System

Of all the innovations commonly associated with China—paper, gunpowder, tea, the compass—perhaps the one with the longest-lasting impact was its unique writing system. Like many attempts at symbolic communication, such as those of the Egyptians, the Harappans, and, in the Americas, the Mayans, it was originally a system based on pictures. As with these other systems, the pictures became simplified and to some extent standardized for ease of interpretation. In its earliest form, for example, the Chinese character for the sun is a circle with a dot in the center. In its modern form it is still recognizable as 日.

Even in its archaic form, Chinese contained two basic types of characters: *pictographs*—pictures designating particular objects—and *ideographs*—pictures representing ideas—as well as some purely phonetic characters. Both types became increasingly elaborated and stylized, with the most basic characters acquiring phonetic components and compounds of simple characters formed to represent abstract expressions. For example, compounding the character 女, *nu* [neeu] (female or woman), with 子, *zi* [zuh] (child), created 好, *hao* [how] (good), an abstract expression symbolized quite concretely by a mother and child. Similarly, 女, *nu*, placed under the character for roof yielded the character, 安, *an* [ahn], meaning peace or contentment. The characters for sun (日) and moon (月) placed together came to mean bright, 明.

The close association of the written language with early Chinese religious practices, court ceremonial functions, and self-cultivation and character development imbued it over the centuries with a kind of spiritual dimension not usually found among the written languages of other peoples. The patience and discipline demanded by learning the thousands of characters necessary for advanced

**Three Excellences.** Chinese children learn at an early age to combine painting, poetry, and calligraphy in the highest form of self-expression.

The principal deity, Di or Shangdi, presided over the spirit world and governed both natural and human affairs. Shangdi was joined by the major ancestors of the dynastic line, deities believed to influence or control natural phenomena, and local gods appropriated from various Shang territories. The religious function of the Shang ruler, as it appears to have been for the Xia and would be for subsequent Chinese dynasties, was to act as the intermediary between the world of the spirits and that of humanity. Hence, rituals appear to have consisted largely of sacrifices to ancestors to ensure their benevolence toward the living. As we have seen, the Shang sought the guidance of their ancestral spirits through divination on a wide variety of human affairs, such as royal marriages and military campaigns, and on such natural phenomena as

literacy and the artistic possibilities embodied in the brush and ink traditionally used to write them placed calligraphy at the top of Chinese aesthetic values. Thus, wherever written Chinese is used, skill at the three interrelated "excellences" of painting, poetry, and calligraphy is esteemed as the highest mode of self-expression.

The Chinese written language had a tremendous impact on the course of Asian history. While it requires extensive memorization compared to the phonetically written languages of other cultures, it is remarkably adaptable as a writing system because the meaning of the characters is independent of their pronunciation. Thus, speakers of non-Chinese languages could attach their own pronunciations to the characters and, as long as they understood their structure and grammar, could use them to communicate. This versatility enabled Chinese to serve as the first written language not only for speakers of the Chinese family of dialects and languages on the Asian mainland but also for the Koreans, Japanese, and Vietnamese, whose spoken languages are totally unrelated to Chinese. The pattern of interaction and adaptation prompted by the acquisition of the written language allowed the vast body of Chinese literature, philosophy, religion, history, and political theory to tie the literate elites of these states together within a common cultural sphere. In this respect, it functioned in much the same way as Latin among the educated of Europe. Even today, despite the development of written vernacular languages in all these countries, the ability to read classical Chinese is still considered to be a mark of superior education. Moreover, the cultural heritage transmitted by Chinese characters continues to inform the worldviews of these societies.

## Questions

- How did the pattern of interaction and adaptation that characterized the development of the Chinese writing system bring people together into a common cultural sphere?

- How does the impact of the Chinese writing system compare to the impact other writing systems have had in other parts of the world?

droughts, floods, plantings, and harvests. Scholars theorize that many of the animals appearing as designs on ritual vessels represent messengers from the spirit world associated with divination.

As the Shang state grew more powerful and commanded more and more resources, the size and scope of the sacrifices also increased. Like the Xia, the Shang practiced human sacrifice. Excavations at both the early capital in the Erligang district of the modern city of Zhengzhou and later capitals near Anyang have yielded numerous sites containing headless skeletons. The evidence suggests that the death of a ruler was accompanied by the slaughter of hundreds of slaves, servants, and war captives, perhaps to serve the deceased in the spirit world.

**Ritual Vessel with**
***Taotie* Design Pattern.**

## Adaptations of Zhou Religion, Technology, and Culture

The Zhou, like other conquerors after them, sought to give legitimacy to their reign by adopting many of the forms of art and ritual practiced by the defeated Shang. As before, the ruler maintained his place as mediator between the human and divine worlds. But the Zhou also appear to have followed the trend toward more abstract religious ideas we have observed in other early civilizations.

**Heaven**    The Zhou introduced the concept of *tian*, "heaven," as a relatively neutral, impersonal controlling force of the universe, which eventually replaced the more approachable, humanlike Shangdi. It was this more abstract heaven whose mandate gave the right to rule to all subsequent Chinese dynasties. Thus, throughout the long history of imperial China, the emperor retained the title of *Tianzi*, "son of heaven," as a symbol of his cosmic filial piety—his obligation to fulfill heaven's mandate as a son serves his father.

**Iron Casting**    Perhaps the most significant technological innovation introduced during the Zhou period was the use of iron. Some late Shang and western Zhou tombs contained iron objects of foreign origin, probably obtained from Indo-European peoples ranging across central Asia. By the seventh century BCE, basic technologies for mining and working iron are in evidence in western China. Significantly, it appears that the casting techniques of bronze production were adapted to this purpose. When combined with the high-temperature technologies employed by Zhou potters, the Chinese produced the world's earliest cast iron. By the sixth century BCE, cast- and wrought-iron weapons, tools, and farm implements were in common use; even some steel objects, including a sword, have been found. As in Gangetic India, they were instrumental in opening up new lands for cultivation and multiplying the deadliness of warfare.

**Folk Culture: *The Book of Songs***    As noted in the previous section, we know relatively little about the lives of the common people during the period of the Xia, Shang, and Zhou dynasties. One of the few sources that do provide some clues is the *Shijing*, the *Poetry Classic*, sometimes called *The Book of Odes* or *The Book of Songs*. The subject matter covers a wide range of interest and emotion, from homely observations on the cycles of rural life to protests and cleverly veiled satire. It is believed that, in most cases, the verses were meant to be sung.

As historical source material as well as art, the *Shijing*'s songs and poems of the lives and loves, burdens and laments of peasants and soldiers, young wives and old men are still striking in their immediacy today.

"Big rat, big rat,
Don't eat my millet!
Three years I've served you
But you won't care for me."
—Ode 113: "Big Rat," from *The Book of Songs*

# Putting It All Together

The period from the first Neolithic settlements in the Yellow River valley to the birth of Confucius in 551 BCE witnessed the beginning of many of the foundations of the cultures of China and, through interaction with Chinese influences, east and southeast Asia. Like the other agricultural–urban cores in Mesopotamia, along the Nile, and in the Indus valley, the society that emerged in northern China was very much a product of its major river system. As early as 10,000 BCE, the Yellow River basin saw the rise of self-sufficient agricultural villages, marking the transition from forager to agrarian society. It was the early states that developed here that came to dominate the Chinese historical record. With the rise of the Xia dynasty late in the third millennium BCE, the first evidence of Chinese cities and the first people, places, and events traceable through later literary sources all make their appearance.

The Shang conquest of the Xia, traditionally held to be in 1766 BCE, marks the first flowering of China's bronze age. The centering of political, military, and religious authority in one ruler; the development of a unique and versatile form of writing; the growth of cities; and the widespread use of bronze under the Shang in many ways run parallel to developments in the other early centers of civilization. In their casting techniques and design motifs of bronze ritual vessels and their system of writing, however, Shang contributions were original and long-lasting.

The theme of moral renewal came with the rise of the Zhou after 1122 BCE and was perhaps applied retroactively by them as well. Nearly all of China from the Yangzi River basin north was incorporated into a decentralized governmental system centered on the Zhou court at Xi'an. But the growing power of the largest Zhou territories eventually eclipsed that of the court; this began a prolonged era of struggle between the states. The increased wealth and power of rulers, aided by the drive of new social classes such as merchants and the *shi* to share in it, contributed to the breakdown of older feudal social patterns during the Spring and Autumn period from 722 to 481 BCE. Continual warfare stimulated both a drive for political consolidation and a questioning of the foundations of society. With the ideas of Confucius, to whom we turn at the beginning of Chapter 9, a radical direction in conceiving the nature and aims of society would soon take place. His ideas, adopted by a Chinese imperial system that would last over 2,000 years, would profoundly affect hundreds of millions of people inside and outside of China in the centuries to come.

▶ For additional resources, including maps, primary sources, visuals, and quizzes, please go to www.oup.com/us/vonsivers. Please see the Further Resources section at the back of the book for additional readings and suggested websites.

## Against the Grain
# Women's Voices

While scholars still debate the extent to which the Neolithic villages like Banpo may have been matrilineal or matriarchal, there is universal agreement that by the time of the first three dynasties, the northern Chinese states and their successors were creating a rigorously patriarchal society and culture. As we shall see in Chapter 9, this will be considerably reinforced by the uses to which Confucian values were put. Yet it is a mistake to assume that women were without influence or agency in ancient China; indeed, male Confucian writers occasionally noted the exploits of outstanding women of the ancient past, even those who went beyond what ultimately came to be seen as the filial, home-centered core ideals so widely celebrated in manuals of female deportment. One need only look at the enduring tales of the woman warrior Mulan, recently popularized in the West through literature and animated film, to see a powerful counterfoil to the stereotypical subservient Chinese daughter.

Long before this period, however, the *Shijing* (*Book of Songs*), in its collections of sung poems from the common people, contained a number of compositions that, although the individual authors are unknown, show strong evidence of having been composed by women, or perhaps in some cases in the persona of women. In them we have one of the few tools available with which we can discern something of the authentic voices of ancient Chinese women. Consider this lament from a young woman facing the challenges of family expectations for marriage:

> My mind is not a mirror;
> It cannot [equally] receive [all impressions]
> I, indeed, have brothers,
> But I cannot depend on them.
> I meet with their anger . . .
> Silently I think of my case,
> And, starting as from sleep, I beat my breast. (Number 26; "Cypress Boat")

In an almost visceral way, she gives voice to the frustration of the independent mind and heart as it breaks on the shoals of family and social convention. Her song was to be a familiar one over the intervening centuries.

- It often seems as if women had somewhat greater freedom among the earliest civilizations we have encountered than they would in the period after 600 BCE. Do you think this is a fair observation? If so, which of these societies seemed to offer the most agency to women?

- Why did China become increasingly patriarchal over time? Does the development of urban–agrarian society necessarily lead to patriarchy?

# Thinking Through Patterns

▶ **How did the interplay of environment and climate help to influence the earliest patterns of Chinese civilization? How do historians address the question of whether "geography is destiny" in this case?**

The relationship of environment to the ways in which a particular culture lives is at once seemingly obvious and quite complex. In the case of northern China, the river both allows a large, reliably fertile area for cultivation to be maintained and restricts the ability to live close to it because of flooding. Not surprisingly, the collective efforts of the early Chinese states to control the river proved central to the character of these states. But what kinds of larger conclusions can we draw? Some scholars in the past theorized that early civilizations based around rivers developed many similarities in their patterns of governing, such as centralization, bureaucracy, and elaborate labor regulations. But here the key is in the details: How similar can we say Egypt is to Shang-dynasty China? As for the larger question of geography and destiny, most historians would say that geography is an important *conditional* factor, among many others, in determining how a civilization develops. But rarely can it be seen as *destiny—* as a *sufficient cause.*

Among other things, these remains can suggest the kinds of plants and animals that were domesticated, the kinds of shelters that housed people, how gender roles were assigned, how the people living there handled their dead, and how they defended themselves. Many of these things are open to debate, however. Scholars in the People's Republic of China, for example, argued that such Neolithic villages were matriarchal and matrilineal; those from outside are less sure of the evidence for this. If true, the later switch to the strong patriarchal tradition represents an important change in the structure of Chinese families.

▶ **What can the remains of Neolithic Chinese settlements tell us about the continuities and disruptions of Chinese history?**

▶ **How did the Zhou concept of the Mandate of Heaven operate?**

The Mandate of Heaven, as we have seen, was at once a way for the Zhou to retrospectively legitimize their conquests and to create a precedent for future moral renewal. As part of a dynastic cycle, it set the fundamental pattern for the way the Chinese tended to view history. The rule of a particular dynasty was expected to advance in reform and expansion in its early stages, reach a comfortable point of harmony in its middle stages, and go into moral and material decline in its final stages. From that point, revolt breaks out and heaven transfers its mandate to a new dynasty—*if that revolt succeeds.* If not, the rebels have committed the worst of crimes. There is a definite closed logic to this system: Heaven approves, so the rebels succeed; the rebels succeed because heaven approves. This pattern of dynastic cycle and heavenly mandate made China's historical experience—conveniently fitted to the theory—not only comprehensible but also predictable. Alert rulers constantly searched for signs that the mandate was in danger; the people themselves often speculated about portents or natural disasters as presaging dynastic change. Even China's modern rulers are heirs to this pattern: During human-made and natural disasters the Communist Party is even more alert to possible signs that the people are expecting a "dynastic" change.

# Patterns of Evidence: Sources for Chapter 4

## SOURCE 4.1

### *The Zuo Commentary (Zuozhuan)*

**ca. fourth century BCE**

The *Spring and Autumn Annals* (*Chunqiu*), a chronicle covering the years 722–483 BCE and composed at the court of Lu (the home state of Confucius), was acknowledged even at the time to be very difficult reading. Accordingly, scholars began composing commentaries to elucidate its finer points and clarify its meaning. The third orthodox commentary, attributed to "Mr. Zuo," continues to influence historical thought about ancient China. This section concerns a conflict between the states of Qin and Jin in the seventh century BCE.

**Renxu:** The date of the battle.

On **renxu** day, they fought on the plain of Han. The warhorses of Jin were confounded by the mud and forced to halt. The Lord [of Jin] called for Qing Zheng. Qing Zheng said, "You rejected my remonstrance and disobeyed the divination. You were resolutely seeking defeat— why flee from it now?" Then he abandoned [his lord].

Liang Youmi was driving for Han Jian; Guo She was the right-hand man. They came upon the carriage of the Earl of Qin and were about to stop him. [Qing] Zheng misled them by [calling for someone] to save the Lord [of Jin]; thus they lost the Earl of Qin. Qin caught the Marquis of Jin and returned with him. The Grand Masters of Jin followed him, letting their hair loose and camping in the wilderness. The Earl of Qin sent an embassy [asking them] to desist, saying, "Gentlemen, why are you so aggrieved? I am accompanying the Lord of Jin to the west only in order to comply with the ominous dream of Jin. Would I dare do anything excessive?"

The Grand Masters of Jin paid their respects by kowtowing three times and said, "Lord, you tread on the Earth Deity and bear up August Heaven. August Heaven and the Earth Deity have surely heard your words, my Lord, so we, your flock of subjects, dare to be inspired by them beneath you."

When Lady Mu heard that the Marquis of Jin was about to arrive, she ascended a terrace with Heir Apparent Ying, [her other son] Hong, and her daughter Jianbi, and stood upon a pyre there. She sent an embassy clad in mourning cap and gown to meet

Source: Victor H. Mair, Nancy Shatzman Steinhardt, and Paul R. Goldin, eds. *Hawai'i Reader in Traditional Chinese Culture* (Honolulu: University of Hawai'i Press, 2005), 72–76.

[her husband], and then she said, "Heaven Above has sent down catastrophe, causing my two lords to meet each other without jade and silk, and to be aroused to warfare. If the Lord of Jin enters [the capital] in the morning, I and my children will die in the evening; if he enters in the evening, we will die the next morning. Only my Lord can decide [the hour of my death]!" Thereupon [the Lord of Jin] was lodged in the Spirit Terrace.

. . .

Zisang said, "If we send him home but take his heir apparent hostage, that would be the greatest accomplishment. Jin cannot be annihilated, and to kill their lord would only bring about their hatred. Moreover, Historian Yi once said, 'Do not initiate misfortune; do not await [others'] disorders; do not redouble anger.' Redoubled anger is difficult to bear, and to abuse others is inauspicious." Thereupon they granted peace with Jin.

▶ **Working with Sources**

1. **Is this merely a rousing battle story, or does the tale convey a sense of what behavior is proper in the midst of conflict?**

2. **What role does anger play in the narrative? Why?**

## SOURCE 4.2

# Excerpts from *The Book of Odes* (*Shijing*)

**ca. 2852–481 BCE**

O ver 300 poems of various lengths were anthologized and transmitted by Confucius in the early fifth century BCE. Philosophers of the Confucian school (see Chapter 9) cherished the Odes and cited them frequently, and they have continued to entrance readers with their naturalistic imagery and personal voices. Only two samples are given here, but this rich tradition of poetry should be sampled at length.

**Wild and Windy**

Wild and windy was the day;
You looked at me and laughed,
But the jest was cruel, and the
   laughter mocking.
My heart within is sore.

There was a great sandstorm
   that day;

Kindly you made as though
   to come,
Yet neither came nor went away.
Long, long my thoughts.

A great wind and darkness;
Day after day it is dark.
I lie awake, cannot sleep,
And gasp with longing.

Source: *The Book of Songs*, transl. Arthur Waley, edited with additional translations by Joseph R. Allen (New York: Grove, 1996), 27 and 65.

Dreary, dreary the gloom;
The thunder growls.
I lie awake, cannot sleep,
And am destroyed with longing.

**I Beg You, Zhong Zi**

I beg of you, Zhong Zi,
Do not climb into our homestead,
Do not break the willows we
    have planted.
Not that I mind about the
    willows,
But I am afraid of my father
    and mother.
Zhong Zi I dearly love;
But of what my father and
    mother say
Indeed I am afraid.

I beg of you, Zhong Zi,
Do not climb over the wall,

Do not break the mulberry-trees
    we have planted.
Not that I mind about the
    mulberry-trees,

But I am afraid of my brothers.
Zhong Zi I dearly love;
But of what my brothers say
Indeed I am afraid.

I beg of you, Zhong Zi,
Do not climb into our garden,
Do not break the hard-wood we
    have planted.
Not that I mind about the
    hard-wood,
But I am afraid of what people
    will say.
Zhong Zi I dearly love;
But of all that people will say
Indeed I am afraid.

▶ **Working with Sources**

1. **How do the poems deal with the theme of love, whether reciprocated or not?**

2. **What do they suggest about gender relations in ancient China?**

## SOURCE 4.3

# *The Book of Lord Shang (Shangjun Shu)*

### ca. 338 BCE

This collection of sayings and reports attributed to Lord Shang (d. 338 BCE) may have been compiled by later officials, but its vision of a centralized bureaucracy was emulated at many points in China's turbulent history. The work is composed of 25 or more brief sections, some of which are lost, but the remainder address the necessity of good and competent government.

Source: Sebastian De Grazia, ed., *Masters of Chinese Political Thought: From the Beginnings to the Han Dynasty* (New York: Viking, 1973), 339–343.

The guiding principles of the people are base and they are not consistent in what they value. As the conditions in the world change, different principles are practiced. Therefore it is said that there is a fixed standard in a king's principles. Indeed, a king's principles represent one viewpoint and those of a minister another. The principles each follows are different but are one in both representing a fixed standard. Therefore, it is said: "When the people are stupid, by knowledge one may rise to supremacy; when the world is wise, by force one may rise to supremacy." That means that when people are stupid, there are plenty of strong men but not enough wise, and when the world is wise, there are plenty of clever men, but not enough strong. It is the nature of people, when they have no knowledge, to study, and when they have no strength, to submit.

. . .

A sage-prince understands what is essential in affairs, and therefore in his administration of the people, there is that which is most essential. For the fact that uniformity in the manipulating of rewards and punishments supports moral virtue is connected with human psychology. A sage-prince, by his ruling of men, is certain to win their hearts; consequently he is able to use force. Force produces strength, strength produces prestige, prestige produces virtue, and so virtue has its origin in force, which a sage-prince alone possesses, and therefore he is able to transmit benevolence and righteousness to the empire.

. . .

Of old, the one who could regulate the empire was he who regarded as his first task the regulating of his own people; the one who could conquer a strong enemy was he who regarded as his first task the conquering of his own people. For the way in which the conquering of the people is based upon the regulating of the people, is like the effect of smelting in regard to metal or the work of the potter in regard to clay; if the basis is not solid, then people are like flying birds or like animals. Who can regulate these? The basis of the people is the law. Therefore, a good ruler obstructed the people by means of the law, and so his reputation and his territory flourished.

▶ **Working with Sources**

1. Why does Lord Shang assume there will be an antagonistic relationship between a ruler and the ruled?

2. Would he think it preferable for a leader to appear virtuous rather than to actually be virtuous?

## SOURCE 4.4

## *The Canon of Shun*

### Third millennium BCE?

Shun was thought to be one of the three "sage kings" who ruled China between 2852 and 2205 BCE, after the reign of the "Yellow Emperor." The achievements of these kings are recorded—though the exact dating of each strand of material is controversial—in the *Shujing*, or *Book of History*. The material in the compilation purportedly dates from 2357 to 631 BCE, but, regardless of its precise chronology, the "Canon" attributed to Shun reveals increased sophistication in determining the role and proper behavior of a leader.

**1.** Examining into antiquity, we find the emperor Shun was called Chong Hua. He corresponded to the former emperor; he was profound, wise, accomplished, and intelligent. He was mild and respectful, and entirely sincere. The report of his mysterious virtue was heard on high, and he was appointed to occupy the imperial Seat.

. . .

**9.** In five years there was one tour of inspection, and four appearances of the nobles at court. They set forth a report of their government in words. This was clearly tested by their works. They received chariots and robes according to their services.

**10.** Shun instituted the division of the land into twelve provinces, raising altars upon twelve hills in them. He likewise deepened the rivers.

**11.** He gave delineations of the statutory punishments, enacting banishment as a mitigation of the five great inflictions, with the whip to be employed in the magistrates' courts, the stick to be employed in schools, and money to be received for redeemable crimes. Inadvertent offenses and those which might be caused by misfortune were to be pardoned, but those who offended presumptuously or repeatedly were to be punished with death. "Let me be reverent; let me be reverent!" he

said to himself. "Let compassion rule in punishment!"

. . .

**24.** The emperor said, "Kui, I appoint you to be Director of music, and to teach our sons, so that the straightforward may yet be mild, the gentle may yet be dignified, the strong not tyrannical, and the impetuous not arrogant. Poetry is the expression of earnest thought; singing is the prolonged utterance of that expression. The notes accompany that utterance, and they are harmonized themselves by the pitch pipes. In this way the eight different kinds of instruments can all be adjusted so that one shall not take from or interfere with another, and spirits and men will thereby be brought into harmony." Kui said, "Oh! I smite the stone; I smite the stone. The various animals lead on one another to dance."

**25.** The emperor said, "Long, I abominate slanderous speakers, and destroyers of right ways, who agitate and alarm my people. I appoint you to be the minister of Communication. Early and late give forth my orders and report to me, seeing that everything is true."

**26.** The emperor said, "Ah! you, twenty and two men, be reverent, and so shall you aid me in performing the service of heaven."

Source: James Legge, trans., *The Sacred Books of China: The Texts of Confucianism*, vol. 3 (Oxford: Clarendon, 1879), 38, 40–41, and 44–45.

**27.** Every three years there was an examination of merits, and after three examinations the undeserving were degraded, and the deserving promoted. By this arrangement the duties of all the departments were fully discharged. The people of San Miao were discriminated and separated.

**28.** In the thirtieth year of his life, Shun was called to employment. Thirty years he was on the throne with Yao. Fifty years after he went on high and died.

▶ **Working with Sources**

1. How important is effective management of subordinates to the career of a king of Shun's stature?

2. To which particular voices should a wise king give heed?

## SOURCE 4.5

# Iron sword with jade handle, earliest cast-iron object (Western Zhou), from Henan Museum, Guo state, Sanmenxia city

**ca. 1046–771 BCE**

When this sword was discovered in 1990, it challenged conventional wisdom about when and under what circumstances Chinese people made the first cast-iron object. The dating of the object to the Western Zhou period pushed back the earliest date of this kind of manufacture by over 200 years. The sword consists of an iron blade, a bronze handle core, and a jade handle. Embedded turquoises were also found at the joint of the blade and the handle.

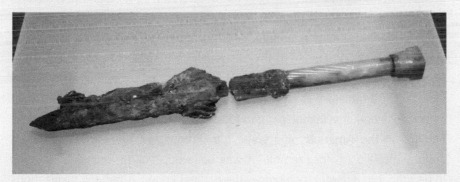

▶ **Working with Sources**

1. What does this object suggest about the casting technology and metalworking prowess of workers in the Zhou dynasty?

2. Why would a cast-iron sword have been an especially effective weapon in this era?

Source: Tim Hulsen - OurTravelPics.com.

# Chapter 5 30,000–600 BCE

# Origins Apart:
# The Americas and Oceania

In a dramatically understated press release from the Chicago Field Museum dated April 26, 2001, anthropological archaeologists Ruth Shady Solis, Jonathan Haas, and Winifred Creamer announced a stunning discovery in the archaeology of the Americas. The scientists had just finished conducting radiocarbon dating tests on plant fibers taken from site excavations of Caral, in the Supé valley in Peru. Though largely ignored for over a century, the site had recently stirred considerable interest because of its immense size (over 200 acres), monumental architecture—pyramids more than 60 feet high and nearly 500 feet square at the base—and evidence of early urban living. The test results, however, now demanded a complete retelling of the main narrative of the history of civilization in the Americas.

Because earlier evidence pointed toward a relatively late arrival for modern humans in the Americas and given the difficulty of domesticating staple grain plants—corn, for example, it was believed, took at least 1,000 years to be bred into a useful food crop—the earliest known American civilizations had been assumed to be much more recent than their earliest Eurasian and African counterparts—until now, that is. For decades, discoveries in North and South America had strongly suggested that humans had migrated much earlier than previously thought, calling into question their puzzlingly swift occupation of the continents.

*ABOVE:* **Ruins at the first Andean city site (c. 2700 BCE) at Caral-Supé.**

But the Caral-Supé [ka-RALL soo-PAY] results, published in the journal *Science*, put the date of the materials tested at 2627 BCE, making the city as old as the pyramids of Egypt and the most ancient Mesopotamian cities. Indeed, work at nearby sites showed that they had been occupied by substantial villages for far longer, that the entire area was supported by elaborate irrigation works, and that Caral-Supé is only one of 18 similar urban sites in the Supé valley. Clearly, the human urge to create cities, monumental architecture, and religious sites ran deep enough to manifest itself thousands of miles away from other early examples.

The Americas represent a vital counterpoint to the development of agrarian-based cities and states in Eurasia and Africa, which we have discussed in earlier chapters. In some ways, the parallels run very close:

- the role of staple food surplus accumulation
- the development of urban centers as religious and trade centers
- the kinds of buildings—pyramids, for example.

Yet some of the differences in the civilizations provide enticing puzzles. For example, Caral-Supé appears to have been thriving long before ceramics turn up in Peru, an innovation that in all cases *predated* cities in Eurasia and Africa. In addition, although there is some evidence of record keeping by *quipú*, the much later system of knotted ropes used by the Incas, there is no writing—again, something the major Eurasian civilizations developed. Finally, as with later American civilizations, there is no evidence of the use of the wheel for transportation or mechanical work. Thus, in our search for patterns of world history, the Americas provide an entirely independent test case for examination and analysis.

- In Chapter 1, we examined the "big bang" of world history: the origins of human society in Africa and the first great pattern of human subsistence: foraging.
- In Chapter 2, we learned about the next great pattern of people moving from foraging to farming societies and some of the consequences that change brought.
- In Chapter 3, we explored how this pattern can be replayed and remixed in different ways—in some cases, like that of the Harappans, moving from an urban society back to village farming or foraging.
- In Chapter 4, we learned more about how civilizations become centralized, while at the same time regional powers can challenge the forces of centralization.

In Chapter 5, we will see examples of all of these patterns but conditioned by the key variable of *separation*. How do we explain these similarities and differences appearing in societies separated by thousands of miles of ocean and with no evidence of contact? A vital part of our examination springs from interactions and adaptations. How did these take place thousands of miles away in the Americas and the islands of the Pacific? (See "Against the Grain.") How do the critical

## Seeing Patterns

▶ What do historians see as the advantages and disadvantages of the separation of the Americas from the societies of Eurasia and Africa?

▶ The wheel is often cited as the most basic human invention, yet large and sophisticated civilizations were able to flourish without this signal innovation. Why do you think it did not develop in the Americas?

▶ Why did no cities develop on the larger Pacific Islands?

*Quipú:* Spanish for Quechua *khipu;* the knots in the strings and the varying distances from each other have supposedly numerical or symbolical meanings.

elements of environment and culture play out in such societies separated from the intense direct contact among societies in Eurasia and Africa? How do they alter the patterns we have examined? How much greater or lesser bearing do environment and culture have on the human societies on the thousands of islands of Oceania? How did the peoples interact with each other and adopt or reject certain innovations? Indeed, how "isolated" were the occupants of these islands from each other and the societies of Asia, Australia, and the Americas? Finally, given the importance that we place on interaction and adaptation among peoples, what advantages and disadvantages did such separateness bring?

# The Americas: Hunters and Foragers, 30,000–600 BCE

The remoteness of human beings on the American continents from the larger and more interconnected societies of Eurasia and Africa raises one of the key questions of world history: What would people do in places far removed from other human communities over long periods of time? The initial great migration out of Africa had equipped human beings with an assortment of tools, practices, and habits that collectively created an effective *foraging*—or hunting and gathering—type of society. As we read in Chapter 1, human foragers spread out to populate the earth in Eurasia and Australia, and the coming of humans to the Americas in many ways represented the final stage of their great migration from Africa.

The advances and retreats of the great ice sheets of the polar region over the last 75,000 years allowed several possible opportunities for humans to migrate from the Eurasian landmass in search of game. Exactly when *Homo sapiens* began to move into these new lands, however, is at present a highly controversial question. Migration might have begun as early as 40,000–30,000 years ago, though only now has enough archaeological evidence accumulated to support dates before about 13,500 years ago. After this date, the number and range of humans grew rapidly on the two continents, with inhabitants forming small, highly mobile forager bands.

Yet, even at this stage, the migrants had begun to adapt the technology of spears, bows, and other hunting equipment to the big game of the new continent with astonishing swiftness. And as the success of their hunting began to reduce the populations of their favored game, a question arises for world historians: Would they now follow the same patterns by undergoing a Neolithic revolution and developing practices and institutions similar to those of humans in Eurasia and Africa?

It does indeed appear that they did. During the period from about 6000 to 4000 BCE, in what is today Mesoamerica (Mexico and Central America) and the Andes Mountains in South America in Ecuador and Peru, people began to settle in villages. They domesticated squash, beans, corn, and, somewhat later, potatoes and founded the first forms of agrarian society in the Americas. Separated by thousands of miles and vast bodies of water from the peoples of Eurasia and Africa, they were nevertheless traveling independently along the same crucial early pattern of world history: moving from foraging to farming and to settled life—until, ultimately, they built great cities, states, and empires. As we will see, however, there were also some important differences in their modes of subsistence and technology and the processes involved in the creation of these new societies.

## The Environment

Next to Eurasia, the two continents comprising the Americas encompass the largest landmass on earth. From the perspective of Europe, they form the Western Hemisphere—that is, the western "half" of the "sphere" or globe. Located north and south of the equator, the Americas resemble geographical mirror images of each other, with somewhat similar types of landscape and climate, though their shapes differ considerably (see Map 5.1).

The Americas' most prominent geographical feature is a contiguous spine of mountain ranges, or **cordilleras** [cor-dee-YEH-ras], near or along the entire western coast. Known as the Rocky Mountains in the north, these ranges become the Sierra Madre in the center and the Andes in the south. Water from these mountains feeds nearly all river systems on the continents, of which there are eight major ones in the north and four in the south. Both continents also share low mountain systems along their eastern coasts. North and South America meet in Mesoamerica near the equator, with North America then reaching northward to the North Pole and South America extending southward almost to Antarctica. Thus, the climatic zones of both South and North America range from extreme cold to subtropical and tropical warmth.

**Cordilleras:**
A continuous spine of mountain ranges near or along the entire western coast of the Americas.

**Geographical Regions**   North America consists of four main geographical regions:

- The Mountain West
- The Canadian Shield, which stretches from today's Canada to Greenland
- The Great Plains and central lowlands in the center of today's United States
- The Appalachian Mountains in the east and the broad coastal plain along the Atlantic Ocean.

The four regions not only are distinct geographically but also vary considerably in precipitation and temperature. Historically, they have produced widely differing modes of subsistence and society among their inhabitants from the time of the first migrants through much of the history of present-day Canada, the United States, and Mexico, as well as among interior regions of all three countries.

Mesoamerica and South America form six distinct geographical regions:

- The Central American mainland and the Caribbean islands
- The Andes Mountain region along the west coast
- The Guyana Shield, a rocky plateau that separates the Amazon River and basin in the south from the Orinoco River
- The Brazilian Shield, a rocky crust in the east jutting into the South Atlantic Ocean

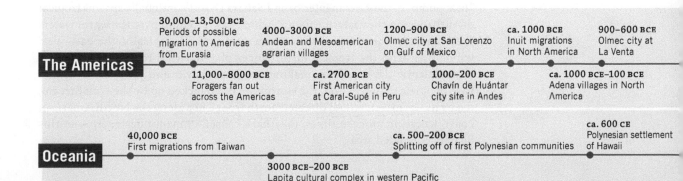

**The Americas**

| 30,000–13,500 BCE Periods of possible migration to Americas from Eurasia | 4000–3000 BCE Andean and Mesoamerican agrarian villages | 1200–900 BCE Olmec city at San Lorenzo on Gulf of Mexico | ca. 1000 BCE Inuit migrations in North America | 900–600 BCE Olmec city at La Venta |
|---|---|---|---|---|
| 11,000–8000 BCE Foragers fan out across the Americas | ca. 2700 BCE First American city at Caral-Supé in Peru | 1000–200 BCE Chavín de Huántar city site in Andes | ca. 1000 BCE–100 BCE Adena villages in North America | |

**Oceania**

| 40,000 BCE First migrations from Taiwan | ca. 500–200 BCE Splitting off of first Polynesian communities | ca. 600 CE Polynesian settlement of Hawaii |
|---|---|---|
| 3000 BCE–200 BCE Lapita cultural complex in western Pacific | | |

- The *Gran Chaco* in the east between the Andes and Paraguay River
- The Patagonian Shield, in the center of the continent's southern tip.

Here, the size of the mountains and the extent of the rain forests dictated even greater regional separation than in North America until recent times.

During winters in North America, freezing winds from the Arctic blow south across the Canadian Shield into the central plains, or American Midwest. By contrast, at the southern tip of South America, air currents are predominantly westerly and more moderate and do not push winter frost very far northward. Thus, apart from the southern tip at Cape Horn and Tierra del Fuego—the site of some of the world's most violent seas and frequent storms—snow and frost are mostly limited to the Andes. In North America, winter and summer temperatures vary greatly, except in Florida and southern California, as do precipitation levels, especially in the western half of the continent. Generally, the eastern and midwestern regions of North America receive regular rainfall throughout the year, while the western regions and lower Pacific coast tend to be drier, with occasional droughts, and intermittently subject to massive forest fires started by lightning strikes.

In Mesoamerica, the Caribbean, and the northern two-thirds of South America, temperatures and humidity levels tend to be relatively high. Large steppe and desert areas cover the western third of North America, while in South America deserts and steppes are more limited and mostly found along the northwestern coast and in the interior of the south. Prior to modern times, large forests covered the eastern two-thirds of North America and the northern half of South America.

**Ocean Currents, Hurricanes, and El Niño**    Like the monsoon system that wields so much influence in the agricultural life of India, China, the Indian Ocean, and western Pacific regions, large-scale weather events governed at least in part by the actions of ocean currents and continental weather systems have played historical roles in the Americas. Unlike the monsoon systems, however, their cycles have only recently come to be understood.

Running roughly parallel to the eastern coasts of northern South America and nearly all of North America, the Gulf Stream current of the Atlantic Ocean moves warm water from the south Atlantic along the Eastern Seaboard of the United States before heading northeast toward the European coast. There, it moderates the climate of northern Europe and the British Isles despite their high latitudes. In the Americas, the Gulf Stream's interactions with changing wind patterns in fall and winter in eastern North America frequently result in large storms called "nor'easters," a phenomenon first studied by the American scientist Benjamin Franklin.

More destructive is the frequency with which the Gulf Stream guides hurricanes into the Caribbean Sea and along the North American coast. The immense "heat pump" of the African interior and Sahara Desert continually spawns tropical disturbances in the eastern Atlantic, which gain strength over the warm waters there and the Caribbean as they move westward. Historically, the east–west winds that drive the tropical disturbances played a vital role in fostering the trans-Atlantic slave trade by making navigation swift and predictable. In the case of hurricanes, however, the storms are often picked up by the Gulf Stream, fed by its warm waters, and directed north from Cuba along the North American coast, where, in modern times, they have caused immense destruction in this heavily populated area.

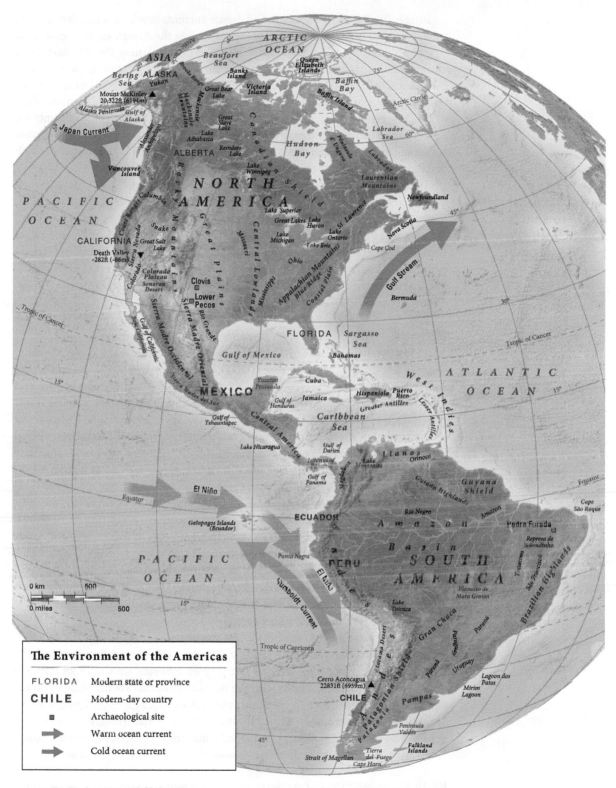

### The Environment of the Americas

| | |
|---|---|
| FLORIDA | Modern state or province |
| CHILE | Modern-day country |
| ■ | Archaeological site |
| → | Warm ocean current |
| → | Cold ocean current |

MAP 5.1  **The Environment of the Americas.**

In the Pacific, the Humboldt and Japan currents work in a similar fashion, though, in relation to the direction of their waters in the Americas, in reverse. That is, warm waters of the western Pacific and along the Japanese Pacific coast move northward toward the Aleutian Islands and then down the west coast of the Americas. Like the Gulf Stream, this has a considerable moderating effect on climate, particularly from the coast of southern Alaska to northern California, home to much of the world's temperate rain forests. From northern California to Chile, the currents are generally cooler than the surrounding ocean and provide important fish and marine mammal habitats. For millennia, these supplied the peoples of the west coast with sustenance and allowed settled life with a minimum of agriculture.

**El Niño:** A periodic reversal of the normal flow of currents in the Pacific, greatly altering weather patterns.

The Pacific region is also home to the **El Niño** phenomenon, which, though little understood until recently, plays an immense role in global climatology. In cycles that vary from 3 to 8 years, large areas of abnormally warm water appear off the coasts of Peru and Chile, which lowers barometric pressures there and raises them in the western Pacific. The results tend to vary but usually alter the jet stream patterns and cause abnormal rainfall and storm levels over large areas of the globe, particularly in the Americas. The reverse phenomenon, La Niña, occurs when the oceans in the region have large areas of abnormally cold water.

## Human Migrations

As we saw in Chapter 1, one of the most hotly contested debates in modern archaeology is who exactly the first people to appear in the Americas were, and where they came from. Part of the debate revolves around the authenticity of sites and the accuracy of techniques used to date them; part of it also arises from legal and political issues of who can claim to be the "first" Americans and have rights to the contents of such sites. Generally, however, scholars agree that the earliest period down to 9000 BCE is that of the *Paleoamericans*, whose remains indicate that they are from different areas in Asia, while later arrivals are classified as *Native Americans* (also often called *Amerindians*).

To give some idea of the scope of the problem, some scholars believe that the earliest immigrants might have been people similar to those migrating to Australia. Genetic evidence, however, suggests that later migrants came from southeast and northeast Asia. Complicating the picture even further, as we saw in Chapter 1, Kennewick man, discovered in 1996 on the banks of the Columbia River in Washington State and dated to ca. 9,300 years ago, has been determined to be genetically close to northeastern Asians. Thus, the earliest populations of the Americas may have been far more ethnically diverse than had previously been supposed.

When the northeast Asians, the ancestors of the Native Americans of today, arrived is difficult to determine and one of the most contentious problems in American archaeology. Researchers working on Siberian sites have so far been unable to establish connections with the Alaskan sites that are assumed to be the places from which people migrated through the Alberta ice gap into North America around 13,500 years ago. What is known, however, is that these Alaskan immigrants, who formed initially only one group among many others, eventually around 7,000 years ago became the dominant population of "Native Americans."

**Early Foragers**    One of the ways in which scientists have attempted to track and date the migrations of early Americans is through their hunting technology. The earliest arrivals hunted with *stabbing spears*—weapons meant to be thrust into an animal's body or thrown from a very short distance. During the period from 11,000 to 8000 BCE, such spears were equipped with a stone point that was grooved, or "fluted," on both sides. These fluted sides allowed the spearhead to be inserted into a groove cut into one end of the spear and fastened there with a leather strip. As in Eurasia and Africa, the size and shape of spearheads and arrowheads provide valuable clues to regional variations in technology and, by tracking these, on migration patterns. In North America, where the spearhead flutes were oval, they are known as "Clovis points," from the town in New Mexico near where scholars identified them for the first time in the 1930s. The pervasiveness of Clovis points in the north and a fishtail style of spear flutes in South America had suggested to scholars until very recently that their users were indeed the first migrants to the continents. It was also widely thought that their close dating and specialized use in big-game hunting indicated that these people had settled both continents within a few years of arriving and had, in short order, killed off most of the prehistoric big game such as mammoths, mastodons, and ground sloths. The absence of Clovis points in Eurasia, and the presence of less sophisticated points and tools at the newly examined earlier sites (such as Buttermilk Creek in Texas), however, now seem to suggest that the Clovis people had already been here for some time. Indeed, these points might be seen as the first distinctively "American" innovations.

Like their counterparts we examined in Chapters 1 and 2, these early American settlers were hunters and gatherers, or *foragers*. They formed groups of extended families and lived in rock shelters, caves, and huts, moving whenever the food resources in a given territory were exhausted. Once a year, during the summer, extended families met to commemorate a common ancestor by sharing food and performing other rituals. Families held initiation ceremonies for adults, arranged marriages, and exchanged goods such as obsidian, copper, mica (a mineral that flakes off in transparent sheets), and seashells. Most of the time families stayed in their own territory, collecting wild foods such as grass seeds, roots, berries, mushrooms, fruits, and nuts.

As we have seen, the fluted spear points were designed specifically for hunting big game, such as mammoths, moose, and bison. Killing these animals would have required repeated stabbing, for which securely fastened points were necessary. The warming climate, however, favored the expansion of forests and was increasingly unfavorable to the survival of big mammal species. As big game became scarce, hunters shifted to smaller spear points and smaller game, such as antelope, deer, and rabbit. By about 8000 BCE most big mammal species were gone from the Americas.

**Toward Settlements** As larger game became increasingly scarce, people in coastal areas began relying more on fish and shellfish, and those in inland regions increased their collection of wild seeds and nuts. Hunters developed the spear thrower, a device for hurling smaller spears from a greater distance at elusive small animals. Obsidian, recovered from volcanic regions and traded over long distances, became the preferred material for spear points. Following a pattern similar to that of their distant relatives in Eurasia and Africa, humans in the Americas learned to grind, groove, and polish stone to make axes, mortars, pestles, and grindstones. Bone became an important material for spears, fishhooks, awls, needles, combs, and spatulas. Humans continued to live in rock shelters and

**Midden:** A refuse pile; archaeologists treasure such piles because a great deal can be learned about the material culture of a society by what the people threw out over long periods of time.

caves, but also increasingly constructed huts made of poles and covered with skins or even more permanent wooden structures. These more permanent dwelling places appeared especially along the seacoasts, the Great Lakes, and large rivers, where there were plentiful resources of fish, shellfish, and waterfowl. The first domesticated animal, the dog, appeared, perhaps descended from the wolves picking through human **middens** or perhaps accompanying hunters migrating to the new continents. As bands of hunters and gatherers acquired more household goods, they became less inclined to move about over large distances. As in Eurasia and Africa, they increasingly tended to stay close to favored long-term food sources and centers of ceremonial life.

**Early Ceremonial Life**   As did their contemporaries in north China, more sedentary foragers began to bury their dead in cemeteries, which soon became territorial centers. Hunter–gatherers in the Americas, like those on the other continents, buried their dead with gifts of ochre, symbolizing the color of life, and tools to help them in the life after death. Leaders of hunter–gatherer bands were often *shamans*, elders with spiritual powers that enabled them to deal with the forces of nature. By donning animal masks, playing music on flutes and drums, and engaging in ritual dance, shamans fell into ecstatic trances. During these trances they experienced themselves merging with powerful animals or other people, charming animals into submission, exorcising evils from humans, or healing afflictions. Leaders worked together with elders, forming councils for the administration of their settlements and hunting grounds.

Shaman-led ceremonies often took place in caves or overhangs, where people painted animals and humans on the rock walls. Probably the oldest paintings are those of Pedra Furada [PAY-drah Foo-RAH-dah] in northeastern Brazil, dating to about 8000 BCE. One of the most distinctive paintings in the ceremonial vein is that of the so-called white shaman at Lower Pecos in Texas, dating to 2000 BCE. He is shown in a trance, leaving his body behind. His feet are feline, his arms are feathered, and he is surrounded during his spiritual journey by animals and humans, both dead (upside down) and alive (upright). Hunter–gatherers possessed a complex culture, ranging from sophisticated gathering and hunting techniques and settlements ordered by elders to shamanic religious ceremonies.

**The White Shaman, Lower Pecos, Texas, ca. 2000 BCE.** The practice of *shamanism*—the belief in the ability of certain individuals to communicate with spirits or inhabit the spirits of people or animals—appears to be a common feature of many widely diverse peoples. Many scholars believe that migrants from Asia carried these religious forms with them to the Americas because of the resemblance to practices among peoples in Siberia and other areas in northern Eurasia.

# Agriculture, Villages, and Urban Life

As we have seen in the preceding chapters, far-reaching changes accompanied human societies that made the transition from foraging to agriculture—from hunting and gathering to relying principally on domesticated plants and animals. The first major change we see associated with this momentous pattern is the ability

**Pedra Furada, São Raimundo Nonato, Piauí, Brazil, ca. 8000 BCE.** One of the earliest cave paintings in the Americas, and particularly striking because of its location in Brazil, this artwork perhaps depicts ceremonies related to warfare.

to maintain large populations: to sustain villages, towns, and cities, developing increasingly complex societies with ever more diverse intellectual, cultural, and religious spheres. The second change is the opposite side of the coin: the creation of the potential for conflict and destruction on an unprecedented scale. Both of these changes grow from the Neolithic revolution (see Chapter 2). In the Americas, however, this grand pattern of world history appears to have begun somewhat later than in many areas of Eurasia and Africa.

## The Neolithic Revolution in the New World

The most noteworthy first steps toward agriculture took place in central and southern Mexico in Mesoamerica and Ecuador and Peru in the Andes. Temperatures in these regions turned warmer after about 4000 BCE. Foragers shortened their annual migrations and extended existing patches of wild bean and **teosinte,** [tay-oh-SIN-tay] (a wild grass precursor of maize [corn]) through purposeful planting. Careful harvesting and replanting, probably with obsidian-spiked sickles, led to early domesticated varieties of these plants, increasingly bearing larger kernels. Beans were domesticated first in Peru, and maize followed somewhat later in southern Mexico. By about 3000 BCE, foragers in these regions had completed their transformation into farmers (see "Patterns Up Close").

**Teosinte:** a wild grass native to Mesoamerica, believed to be ancestral to maize (corn).

**Early Domestication of Plants and Animals**    Humans in Mesoamerica and the Andes exchanged their domesticated species of beans and corn within their regions and began trading other domesticated staples as well. In Mesoamerica these included squash, manioc (a root), avocado, and chili pepper; in the Andes, quinoa (a seed), amaranth (an herb), potatoes, tomatoes, and cotton. In time, these plants spread via trade throughout both regions wherever the climate and soil would support them.

The domestication of animals in the Americas, however, was more modest than that of plants. Unlike in Eurasia and Africa, the majority of large mammals had died out after the last Ice Age, with the result that no draft, pack, or riding animals of sufficient size were left to be domesticated (see Figure 5.1). The Americas thus had no horses or cattle until they were brought by the Spanish in the sixteenth century CE as part of the so-called Columbian exchange of plants, animals, and diseases traveling both directions. The development of the wheel, so intimately connected with draft animals, with its nearly infinite uses on plows, chariots, carts, and other conveyances, never took place in the Americas, though some of the world's best roads were built through the Andes. The only animals suitable for domestication—besides the dog—were the llama, alpaca (both relations of the camel), guinea pig (a rodent), Muscovy duck, turkey, and honeybee. The llama, whose capacity is limited to carrying about 60 pounds for 12 miles per day, was the only animal in pre-Columbian America to provide even modest transportation services. The wool of the alpaca, together with cotton, became an important textile fiber in the Andes. In the relative absence of domesticated animals raised for meat, hunting and fishing remained important methods of obtaining food (see Figure 5.1).

**Early Settlements**    Early agricultural settlements ranged in size from a few extended families to as many as 1,000 inhabitants. As in Neolithic China, the typical dwelling was a round, dome-shaped, wooden house with a sunken floor, stone foundation, and thatched roof. As in southwest Asia, some early American agrarian peoples mummified their dead by salting or smoking them before burial. Others buried their dead in midden piles on the outskirts of their villages or in the sand dunes along the beaches. Funerary gifts were modest, usually consisting only of the cotton clothes worn during life and a red mat—symbolizing the blood of life—wrapped around the body. In contrast to more transient hunter–gatherer settlements, agrarian villages became settled communities of the living and the dead.

Between 3000 and 2000 BCE, villagers in the lowlands along the Andes coast of Peru built rafts of balsa wood, which enabled them to fish farther from shore. They also pioneered the use of irrigation in the dozens of river deltas along the coast. With crop yields boosted by irrigation, the population of the villages increased to 2,000 or 3,000 inhabitants, and the first signs of social stratification and distinctions in wealth appeared. Scholars have speculated that upstream families had more water and thus accumulated greater food reserves than downstream families. Under the leadership of upstream elders, inhabitants of several villages pooled their labor and built monumental plazas, platforms, and terraces in central locations in their settlements.

As had other societies making the agrarian transition, Mesoamerican and Andean societies also began producing pottery, which was used in the preparation and

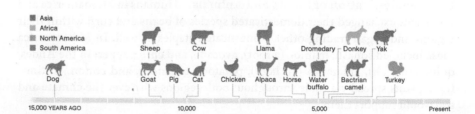

**Figure 5.1** Comparative Timeline for Domestication of Animals.

preservation of food. The earliest known pottery dates to about 3300–3200 BCE on the northern Andean coast; by 1800 BCE pottery making had spread throughout central and southern Mexico. Cotton textiles dating to about 3000 BCE have been found along the coasts of Ecuador and Peru. Richly colored pieces of cloth served as skirts and overcoats. Condors with outstretched wings, double-headed snakes, felines, and human figures were typical motifs on the textiles.

## The Origins of Urban Life

As we saw in the opening vignette to this chapter, in 1994, archaeologists began excavating the ruins of a large, planned city covering over 200 acres at Caral in the Supé River valley in Peru. Caral-Supé was one of at least 18 sites of a culture that flourished in the valleys descending from the Andes to the coast. Researchers were stunned at the monumental stone architecture that included what appeared to be pyramid-shaped temples, plazas, a wide variety of dwellings of different sizes, and, perhaps most intriguing of all, a large amphitheater. As important as the initial survey of the site turned out to be, its significance grew further in 2001 when carbon dating revealed the artifacts at the site to be from 2627 BCE, making this by far the oldest city in the Americas and contemporary with the early Mesopotamian cities and the Great Pyramid of Egypt. As Jonathan Haas, one of the scientists involved in the dating, noted, "This is a project that comes along once in a generation and offers opportunities rarely glimpsed in the field of archaeology."

Caral-Supé    Scholars now theorize that this city, like the similarly mysterious sites along the Indus, was part of a fairly large civilization supported by intensive agriculture and fishing, with extensive trading networks and an incipient class system. They have linked the Caral-Supé culture to the ruins at Aspero, on the Peruvian coast, which contain similar pyramids but had been previously covered by centuries of trash heaps. The varied climate, ranging from the coast through lowland plains and river valleys up to mountain highlands, produced pumpkins, squash, sweet potatoes, corn, chilies, beans, and cotton, while the rivers and sea yielded a variety of edible aquatic life. The agriculture of the valley was supported by a highly complex and sophisticated irrigation system utilizing mountain runoff and directing water to individual plots (see Map 5.2).

Farmers were the largest social class, with merchants, administrators, and priests also in evidence, though it is not clear at this point exactly what constituted the hierarchy. Widely varying sizes of houses suggest disparities of wealth, and the proximity of some of the houses to pyramids seems to indicate a religious or bureaucratic connection, but the exact nature of these remains the subject of speculation. Similarly, the uses to which the amphitheater was put can only be guessed, though pictures of musicians suggest that they were an important part of festivals held there.

Perhaps the most intriguing artifact of all is an intact quipú, a device of elaborate knotted ropes tied together in patterns that form a coded system of communication, a kind of writing system by means of knots. Since the quipú was also used by the Incas over 4,000 years later, it represents not only a direct connection between these two societies but one of the world's first, and oldest, systems of record keeping in continuous use.

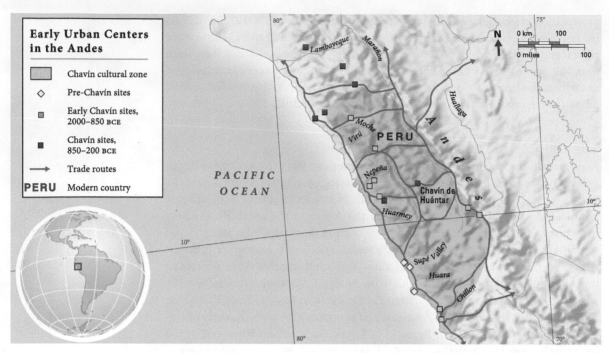

**Early Urban Centers
in the Andes**

Chavín cultural zone

◇   Pre-Chavín sites

▪   Early Chavín sites,
2000–850 BCE

■   Chavín sites,
850–200 BCE

→   Trade routes

**PERU**   Modern country

MAP 5.2 **Early Urban Centers in the Andes.**

**Other Andean Cultures**   Of smaller scale and a somewhat later period are the
structures at El Paraíso, Peru, which date from about 2000 BCE. To construct these
monuments, villagers built large rectangles of locally quarried rock and mud mortar.
They filled the interior of the rectangle with rock rubble encased in large mesh bags,
which may have been used to measure the amount of labor each villager contributed.
Multichambered and multistoried buildings made of stone occupied some of the platforms. Steep staircases led from the lower plazas up to these buildings, which were plastered and painted in primary colors. Wooden beams supported the roofs.

Charcoal-filled pits in the building chambers indicate that some form of sacrifice took place there. The chambers were small, allowing access to no more than a
few prominent villagers or shamans. The rest of the villagers assembled on upper
and lower platforms, according to their social status, to participate in religious
functions and share communal feasts. Early sculptures dating to 1519 BCE depict
ancestral warriors and suggest that villagers might also have come together for
military displays.

Farmers in the Andean highlands also built ceremonial centers in their villages. As in the lowlands, these centers contained fire pits for sacrificial offerings.
The buildings were much smaller, however, with only one or two chambers, and
stood on modest platforms. Highlanders, in addition to farming, engaged in
long-distance trade, exchanging obsidian and cotton from the highlands for lowland pottery. Sometime around 1500 BCE, highlanders developed skills in metallurgy (perhaps including smelting), thus laying the foundation for the development
of exquisitely crafted metalwork, including copper, gold, and silver.

**Chavín de Huántar**   While our understanding of the early Caral-Supé culture
is still in its infancy, more extensive work on the later small highland city of

Chavín de Huántar [Cha-VIN de Oo-WAN-tar] (ca. 1000–200 BCE) has yielded important insights into Andean cultural patterns. Situated in a valley high in the Andes Mountains on both banks of a tributary to the Marañón River, the modern town was dominated by a bridge, which was destroyed in a landslide in 1945. A 3-day journey from both coast and rain forest and at an elevation of 10,000 feet, Chavín carried on an organized long-distance trade, built and graded roads, protected them with retaining walls, and cleared a number of mountain paths to facilitate travel. Residents of Chavín imported obsidian, used in the making of sharp tools, and metals and exported textiles, pottery, and gold and silver artifacts.

Early Chavín was a small place of some 300 inhabitants, most of whom—including priest-rulers and craftspeople—were detached from agriculture. Another 700 full-time farmers and herders lived in outlying hamlets. Farmers grew potatoes, quinoa, and some corn on the slopes and valley floor, supplementing the rainfall with irrigation. Corn was used not only for making bread but also for brewing a type of beer, called *chicha*. On the higher grasslands, herders bred llamas and alpacas. The dried meat and wool of these animals contributed substantially to the village economy, as did the llamas' role as pack animals.

Chavín's ceremonial center consisted of U-shaped ramparts built on a plaza and lined with walls of cut and polished stone. The walls enclosed several partially interconnected underground complexes. Within the U was a round, sunken court accessible via staircase. A cross-shaped, centrally located chamber contained what is assumed to have been the center's main deity, a stone sculpture of a fanged, snarling feline creature, standing upright like a human, with one clawed paw extended upward and the other hanging down. The sculpture might have had a shamanic significance, symbolizing the priest's ability to assume the powers of a wild animal.

Other underground chambers were used for sacrificial offerings. Remnants of pottery once filled with the meat and bones of animals—as well as human bones—found in these chambers suggest animal and human sacrifices. An elaborate system of canals guided water through the underground chambers. Priest-rulers and the assembled villagers used the temple complex to offer sacrifices, observe open-air rituals, celebrate feasts, dance, and perform music.

By around 500 BCE, the population had grown to about 3,000 inhabitants. Artisans living in the town began to specialize in particular crafts. Craftspeople living in one section of town made beads and pendants from seashells; artisans in another section fabricated stone tools; and a third section of the town housed those who made leather goods. Whether these craftspeople had given up agricultural labor completely is not known. Homes for the wealthy were built of stone, while the less well-off lived in houses made of adobe. The rich dined on the meat of young llamas; poorer residents subsisted on the meat of decommissioned pack animals. Around the town, there must have been a number of villages with farmers producing enough food to feed the urban dwellers.

**Chavín de Huántar, New Temple.** Chavín is one of the best-studied sites and over the years has yielded considerable information about town and small-city life in the ancient Americas.

# The Origin of Corn

We have no idea who the originators of corn were nor exactly where they might have lived nor even exactly when the momentous event took place. We do not know

whether the idea occurred to a number of people simultaneously or to one lone experimenter. We assume, given the unprepossessing nature of the plant in question, the *teosinte* grass, that it did not suggest itself as a productive food crop, or even as edible, for quite some time. Yet, when these first bold people began to cultivate it, they were unknowingly taking part in one of the most momentous revolutions in world history: a completely independent chapter in the transition from foraging to agriculture and, ultimately, to agrarian-based urban civilization. The ultimate result of their work, maize, or corn, became the staple of the great Mesoamerican civilizations, sustained the early peoples of North America, and ultimately became the world's most versatile and widely grown food crop (see Map 5.3). Indeed, ancient Mayans believed that humans themselves were made from corn.

**Various Types of Corn.**

The site where we believe the event took place, somewhere in what is now southern Mexico, may have been inhabited by human beings for as few as 7,000 or 8,000 years. And it was here, perhaps 6,000–7,000 years ago, that they began the process of cultivating this unpromising grass into the grain that would shortly sustain vast numbers of people. Yet, to this day, plant geneticists are still not in agreement as to how this transition took place.

It was long assumed that *teosinte* was the sole ancestor of corn and that the process was one of painstaking selection and replanting. That is, people would inspect a group of plants and search for the ones with the largest and most numerous kernels and then plant them and repeat the process over many generations, hoping over time to select for those desirable qualities. Given the *teosinte* limit of eight rows of tiny seeds, it was assumed this process would take hundreds, perhaps thousands, of years. Yet the short time between the known dates of early corn cultivation and the rise of corn-supported societies suggests that the transition was much faster.

The increased population meant larger assemblies, which in turn required bigger platforms and a larger temple for more sacrifices. Laborers added a square, sunken court, a feature common to many Andean and Mesoamerican cities, and additional underground chambers, mostly for storage. By 400 BCE, Chavín had become the culturally dominant center of the region. Large numbers of travelers, traders, and pilgrims from the coast and rain forest visited the temple. Travelers made offerings of seashells, coca leaves, and textiles to the priests in return for receiving temple blessings, presumably for their health, welfare, and safe return. Residents of Chavín provided services for the visitors, such as lodging and meals. Craftspeople produced clothing, wall hangings, banners, and pottery in what were

Because of this, scientists have recently theorized that corn is in fact the result of crossbreeding more than one genus of plants.

The most promising results so far were presented by plant geneticist Mary Eubanks in 2004, who attempted to experimentally trace the origins of corn. Her experiments showed convincingly that *teosinte* was, in fact, an ancestor plant of modern corn but that it had at some point been bred with *gama grass*, which contains key genes for multiplying and enlarging the kernels on each ear. Moreover, her work supported the work of other recent research that suggested that the plant had developed very rapidly into a usable staple, perhaps in less than a century.

We have to assume that this momentous feat was accomplished by plan and experimentation, given its complexity. The result was one that permanently altered the agricultural patterns of world history, particularly over the last 300 years. Corn's versatility allows it to be cultivated on every habitable continent; in dry or moist, hot or cool climates; and often on land too marginal to support any other staple crop. And corn combined with beans provides essential amino acids, which in turn negates the need for domesticated animals as a source of protein. It is widely used as human and animal food and helped to sustain population expansions in North America, Asia, and Europe. It spawned huge industries in such modern foodstuffs as corn syrup and oil and older ones like whiskey and beer. Most recently, and controversially, it has been touted as a biofuel. In short, this American innovation's uses are still unfolding as we wrestle with the problems of population, land use, and energy consumption.

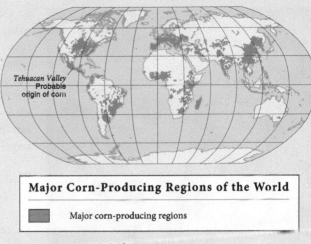

### Major Corn-Producing Regions of the World

Major corn-producing regions

MAP 5.3  Major Corn-Producing Regions of the World.

## Questions

- Why is the innovation of corn a "momentous revolution in world history"?

- How does the fact that this example of bioengineering occurred 6,000–7,000 years ago put today's debate on genetically modified foods into a new perspective?

identifiable Chavín patterns, motifs, and styles. Archaeologists have found Chavín artifacts as far away as 350 miles.

Inhabitants of Chavín pioneered new techniques in the making of textiles and in metallurgy. Textile makers combined the wool from llamas with cotton to create a new blended cloth. They decorated it using new methods of dyeing and painting adapted to wool fibers. Goldsmiths devised new methods of soldering and alloying gold and silver to make large ornamental objects. Small objects, such as golden headbands, ear spools, beads, and pins, signified prestige and wealth. Gold artifacts found in the graves of the wealthy attest to the value residents of Chavín placed on gold.

**Olmec Jade Mask.** Like the Chinese, Mesoamerican peoples appear to have worked jade from very ancient times.

Chavín came to a gradual end, perhaps declining as other centers began producing equivalent pottery, textiles, and gold jewelry, and competing in trade. In any event, sometime after 500 BCE, archaeologists note a decisive trend toward militarization, with the emergence of fortified villages and forts. Possibly, the people of Chavín ultimately fell victim to a military attack. Sometime around 200 BCE, it appears that squatters invaded the largely deserted city, which subsequently fell into ruin.

## The First Mesoamerican Settlements

In Mesoamerica, the first permanent villages appear to date from around 1800 BCE. The first ceremonial centers, the collaborative work of farmers from several villages, appeared along the Pacific coast of southern Mexico and Guatemala around 1500 BCE. As in the Andes, the ceremonial centers consisted of plazas, platforms, and terraces. Metallurgy, however, did not develop here for another millennium, and instead craftspeople used jade for ornaments. (The Spanish believed that this green, translucent gemstone was useful in the treatment of kidney stones.) By around 1200 BCE, agrarian society throughout the Andes and Mesoamerica was characterized by ceremonial centers centrally located among several villages, monumental structures of plazas and platforms, and an emerging craftsmanship in the production of sacred ornaments.

**The Olmec**    The first important Mesoamerican center was that of the Olmecs at San Lorenzo (1200–900 BCE), located on the Gulf of Mexico in hot, humid, and forested coastal lowlands. The name "Olmec" means "rubber people" in the language of the later Aztecs and refers to the rubber-tree farming for which the area was later known. Farmers in these lowlands had to cut down the dense tropical rain forest with stone axes and burn it before they could plant corn. Once the riverbanks had been cleared, the silt deposited by floods during the rainy season and the rich soil created favorable agricultural conditions. As in Mesopotamia, Egypt, India, and China, the rivers here proved marvelously productive. It is estimated that farmers harvested as much as 3,200 pounds of corn per acre from the riverbanks, a yield twice as plentiful as that in the villages of the Mexican valleys and highlands to the west. The high yield allowed for the rise of wealthy ruling families, who assumed a dominant position over small farmers (see Map 5.4).

The ceremonial center of San Lorenzo was located on a plateau overlooking the surrounding rain forest, villages, and fields. On this plateau, archaeologists have so far unearthed some 60 terraced platforms, 20 ponds, countless basalt-lined drainage troughs, and the foundations of dwellings for 1,000 inhabitants. These dwellings were arranged around small family plazas. Among the household goods found in the dwellings were grindstones for preparing corn and tools for making beads and ear ornaments. The dense concentration of dwellings suggests that San Lorenzo was an urban center, inhabited by priests, administrators, and craftspeople. Based on estimates of crop yields in the area and the number of dwellings at the site, scholars believe that this center was surrounded by some 10,000 small farmers dispersed in outlying villages and hamlets and producing the surplus food needed to feed the urban center.

The priest-rulers of San Lorenzo engaged thousands of farmers as laborers to construct the plateau and its terraced platforms. Laborers quarried blocks of basalt from a mountain range 70 miles to the northwest of San Lorenzo. Large groups of workers shouldered beams from which the basalt blocks, weighing 18 tons on average, hung in slings. They carried these blocks to the coast and shipped them to San Lorenzo on rafts. There, sculptors fashioned the blocks into fierce-looking, helmeted heads, kneeling or sitting figures, and animal statues.

It is unknown whether these figures represented priest-rulers, gods, or divine beings.

MAP 5.4 **Olmec Civilization.**

Olmec priest-rulers also commissioned sculptors to craft figurines and masks of clay. Other craftspeople made figurines from jade and serpentine. One jade figurine is that of a jaguar with a human body representing perhaps the rain god. Like the legendary *werewolf*—a human being who is transformed into a wolf when the moon is full—scholars have speculated that these figures might be *were-jaguars*. That is, the figurine might indicate rituals in which priests possessed shamanic powers shared with jaguars and other wild animals. Since jade and serpentine could be obtained only from areas some 200 miles away, San Lorenzo appears not to have been an isolated urban center with surrounding villages but a place with far-reaching trade connections.

**La Venta** Around 900 BCE, a mysterious event took place that destroyed San Lorenzo. Perhaps a religious calendar cycle was completed and a ruler ordered the destruction of the urban center. Perhaps there was an internal uprising, with farmers protesting their oppression by the ruling priests and administrators and then offering ritual atonement. Whatever occurred, the event left San Lorenzo's large stone sculptures mutilated and buried in carefully prepared graves, along with the sculptors' tools used in creating the images.

Following the fall of San Lorenzo, La Venta, 50 miles to the northeast, became the leading Olmec center. The first settlers at La Venta cleared the rain forest from a ridge on a swampy river island in the lowlands and then, like the Harappans on the Indus, graded the ridge to create a plateau. On the plateau they erected terraced platforms and a fluted, 100-foot-high earthen mound to establish an urban center. Burial sites at La Venta contained axes and figurines made of serpentine and jade as well as concave mirrors ground from hematite and other iron-bearing ores. Rulers' regalia included mirrors worn on the chest, but what significance these might have had is unknown.

Three of the burial sites at La Venta each contained 485 pieces of serpentine carefully arranged to form a stylized jaguar face. Only two sites contained human remains, as the extremely acid soil of La Venta dissolved most human bones. The burial gifts in the site included ochre, figurines, beads, ear ornaments, and awls made of jade. About 600 BCE La Venta ended under circumstances as mysterious as those that destroyed San Lorenzo. The next Olmec center was at Tres Zapotes, a more modest complex 70 miles to the northwest. Tres Zapotes endured from about 500 to 1 BCE, when it was eclipsed by new ceremonial centers in the highlands west of the Olmec lowlands.

Through their long-distance trade, the Olmecs left a strong cultural imprint throughout Mesoamerica. Olmec traders, probably accompanied by armed escorts, obtained the obsidian needed for making stone-sculpting tools in Guatemala and jade from mines south of the Mexican Basin and in Guatemala and Costa Rica. In exchange for these raw materials, the Olmecs exported cacao beans (from which chocolate is obtained), pottery, textiles, and jewelry. Along their trade routes, the Olmecs maintained settler outposts to supply the traders, mostly westward toward the Valley of Mexico, to which they exported their artistic styles.

**Olmec Writing**   In 2006 an announcement came that, like the work at Caral-Supé, redefined the archaeology of the Americas. Scientists at Cascajal in Veracruz, Mexico, found a large stone with what is currently believed to be Olmec writing on it. Dating to somewhere between 1100 and 900 BCE, it appears to be the oldest writing in the Americas. Moreover, it is unlike any of the later scripts of the Mayas or Aztecs and thus seems to have died out as a system with the decline of the Olmecs.

Like Egyptian hieroglyphics and Chinese Shang-era scripts, the Olmec characters contain stylized representations of objects like fish, insects, and plants, but there are also some that seem to have a phonetic component. Unfortunately, the corpus contained on the Cascajal stone and a stone roller stamp dating from a few centuries later is simply too small to be deciphered. With the accumulation of other samples in the future it is hoped that the fragments of an Olmec literature may ultimately come to light. In the meantime, like the Linear A script of the Minoans and the seal figures of the Harappans, the Olmec figures present scholars with an important challenge in decoding the past.

"If we can decode their content, these earliest voices of Mesoamerican civilization will speak to us today."

—Archaeologist Stephen Houston

## Foraging and Farming Societies
## Outside the Andes and Mesoamerica

After 2000 BCE, many foragers in the forests, deserts, and tundras in North and South America had adopted agriculture as a full or partial mode of subsistence. While most societies in the Andes and Mesoamerica had become fully agrarian by around 2000 BCE, foraging groups in the places already mentioned continued to persist—in some places down to the present. Using stone tools, they hunted in the extreme north, slowly cleared some of the forests that covered the entire east and midwest of North America, irrigated and farmed arid areas of the southwest, and foraged and farmed in the Amazon basin of South America.

**The Inuit**   The Inuit [INN-ooh-it] from Siberia arrived in the far northern tundra of North America around 2000 BCE. For a long period the Inuit remained traditional hunter–gatherers, hunting mammals on land and fish in the rivers and sea. Much later, during the first millennium CE, they began hunting whales. As many as 20 sailors with paddles manned a boat built of walrus ribs and skin. In the summer, boats sailed the coastal seas for weeks at a time. When sailors spotted a bowhead whale, they shot a toggling harpoon into the animal. The head of the harpoon detached, burrowing into the skin of the animal. After many more harpoon shots and a long struggle, sailors killed the whale, hauled it ashore, and stored the fat and meat in ice. A whale carcass could feed a hamlet for an entire winter.

The Inuit lived in pit houses framed by whale ribs, covered with walrus skin, and piled over with sod. The entrances were long, dipped tunnels that trapped the cold air below the floor of the house. On winter hunts for seals and walruses, people built snow houses, or *igloos*, from ice blocks. During the summer, the Inuit moved from the often waterlogged pit houses to tents. Women were expert seamstresses, using caribou sinew and seal and caribou pelts to make warm and watertight pants, parkas, and boots. For transportation on snow and ice, the Inuit used dog teams to pull sleds made with bone runners. They traded mammal teeth and carved bone artifacts for timber and earthenware from the south. By 1000 CE the Inuit had expanded from the North American Arctic eastward, eventually reaching Greenland, where the Norse from Scandinavia had established their first settlement in 982 CE.

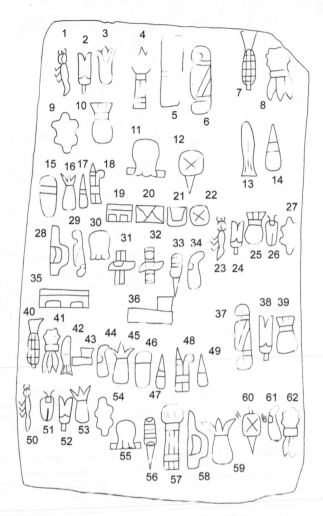

**Cascajal Block.** Currently the oldest example of writing found in the Americas, this sample was created by the Olmecs in the early first millennium BCE. Notice the stylized renderings of objects and placement horizontally, rather than vertically. What kinds of things do they suggest to you?

**Adena and Hopewell**  Agricultural villages appeared in the cleared forest areas of North America by the first millennium BCE. Village inhabitants planted sunflower, goosefoot, sumpweed, and corn. The villagers of the Adena (1000–100 BCE) and Hopewell cultures (200 BCE–500 CE) pooled their labor to build ridges and mounds used in ceremonies and rituals. The phenomenon of mound building, a practice with very ancient roots, seems to have been widespread among peoples living in the east and midwest of North America. A small mound covering a child's grave found in Labrador is estimated to be some 7,500 years old. Others, much larger and more recent (about 4,500 years old), have been found in the lower Mississippi valley; some of these mounds are more than 20 feet high. In the case of the earthworks at Hopewell, large square and circular enclosures contained multiple mounds, tens of feet high, encompassing dozens of acres of land. Research from the mid-1990s suggests that some of the Hopewell settlements were also connected by roads up to 60 miles long, perhaps serving communal purposes such as official visits and gift exchanges (see Map 5.5).

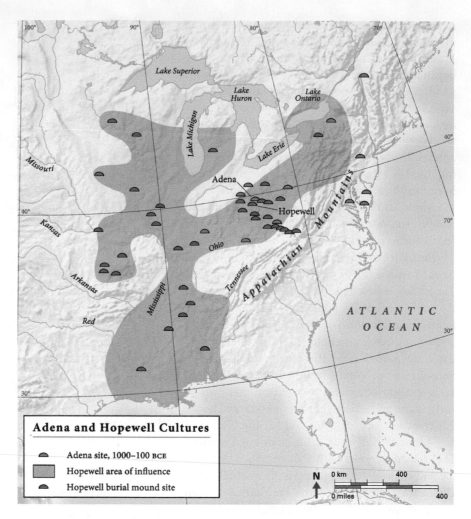

MAP 5.5 **Adena and Hopewell Cultures.**

**Amazonian Peoples**    In the flood plains of the Amazonian rain forest in South America, agricultural villages also date to the first millennium BCE. The best-explored culture is that of Marajó, on a large island in the mouth of the Amazon. At its height in ca. 500 BCE, the Marajó built large funeral mounds 30 feet high and 750 feet long. Depending on their social status, the dead were buried with modest grave gifts or in richly painted, jewelry-filled urns. The cultures of the flood plains in the upper Amazon drainage are still largely unexplored. For example, at an unknown date, the people of the Baures culture in today's Bolivia established a large hydraulic complex of canals, raised fields, moat-enclosed villages with sacred precincts, and causeways connecting the villages. The complexity of this culture left a strong impression on the Spanish missionaries who visited the area in the sixteenth century CE.

**The Islands of the Caribbean**    The earliest hunter–gatherer settlements in the rain forests of the Caribbean islands date to the fourth millennium BCE, but from where on the mainland these first settlers came is unknown. The first agricultural settlements appeared between 500 BCE and 500 CE, when migrants from the rain forests along the Orinoco River in the northeast of South America colonized the eastern Caribbean as far west as Hispaniola (today's Dominican Republic and Haiti). These people built villages and terraces on which they grew manioc. Their ceramics are in the shape of, or painted to display, a variety of animals, such as frogs, bats, and turtles, indicative of a shamanic religion. Beginning in eastern Hispaniola around 500 CE, villagers supported the emergence of the Taíno [Ta-EE-no] chieftain society that by ca. 1500 comprised nearly the entire Caribbean. Influenced by Mayan culture (see Chapter 6), some Taíno chiefs built ball courts and causeways. In their villages, the chiefs employed specialized craftspeople for the production of ceramics and cotton textiles, as well as stone and wood carvings. Sailors using canoes traveled extensively to the mainland and among the islands in search of salt, jade, and metals. These travels connected the Taíno chiefdom society with Mesoamerican societies on the mainland.

# The Origins of Pacific Island Migrations

If the early societies of the Americas show how the great patterns of world history can achieve striking variations in separation from other groups, the peopling of the thousands of islands of Oceania may be seen as an extreme case of the interaction of these patterns with culture and an environment apart. In prehistoric times, Asians traveled in multiple waves not only to the Americas but also to the islands of the Pacific and Indian Oceans (see Map 5.6).

The populating of Oceania must rank as one of humankind's greatest feats. Unlike the comparatively short distances involved in establishing human societies on the islands of the Caribbean or Mediterranean, vast amounts of open ocean had to be routinely crossed between many of the island groups in the Pacific in order to settle them. Such trips were considered epic voyages as late as the eighteenth century. Yet these early seafaring people settled island after island, traveling restlessly until they had discovered nearly every island of Oceania. As we saw in Chapter 4, their homeland appears to have been Taiwan and the Indonesian-Philippine archipelagos. Using computer assisted linguistic analysis, modern scholars have now theorized that the people of Oceania are at least partially related to Taiwan's aboriginal population (about half a million members today), mostly concentrated in the central mountains of Taiwan. About 6,000 years ago, the first seafaring people left Taiwan and, together with subsequent waves of emigrants, spread out in westerly and easterly directions. They settled in the Philippines, Indonesia, and the Malay Peninsula, bestowing their languages and ethnic identities on the aboriginal peoples of these lands.

In later times, descendants of these settlers, all speakers of languages belonging to the Austronesian family, spread farther into the Indian and Pacific Oceans. In the Indian Ocean, they sailed as far west as Madagascar, an island off the east coast of Africa, where they arrived around 200 CE and founded a number of chiefdoms. In the Pacific Ocean, they sailed to the Bismarck Archipelago, off the eastern coast of New Guinea. It was on this archipelago that settlers created the Lapita culture around 1600 BCE, which was the homeland for the colonization of

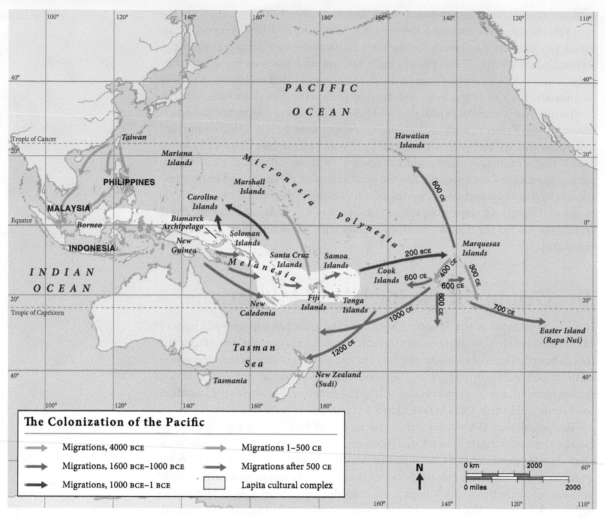

MAP 5.6 **The Colonization of the Pacific.**

Oceania—that is, the islands of Polynesia, Micronesia, and parts of Melanesia. On the map, Oceania forms a huge triangle comprising Polynesia, Hawaii, New Zealand, and Easter Island, with Micronesia and Melanesia to the west.

## Lapita and Cultural Origins

By the fourth millennium BCE, a sophisticated system known as the Lapita cultural complex had already become well established. Named for a site on the island of New Caledonia, the Lapita culture was a system of kinship-based exchanges among the inhabitants of thousands of islands running from Borneo to the edge of Melanesia in the western Pacific. Of particular importance was obsidian, which, as in the Americas, was highly prized as a material for tools and weapons in the absence of workable metals. Another item in demand was a distinctive kind of pottery decorated with stamped patterns called Lapita ware, after shards located at that site.

**Environment and Long-Distance Navigation**    By about 1600 BCE it appears that a number of factors had also come together to allow for decisive innovations in long-distance navigation over hundreds of miles of open sea as well as systematic colonization of otherwise uninhabitable islands. The development of ever larger and more sophisticated sail- and paddle-driven oceangoing canoes, stabilized with outriggers or double hulls, provided reliable craft for such journeys. An extensive, orally transmitted storehouse of navigational information—much of it still retained by Polynesian elders today—enabled sailors to set their courses by the sun and stars, retain elaborate mental maps of islands visited, read winds and currents, and take advantage of seasonal reverses in prevailing wind directions.

Perhaps the most important development centered on supplying such voyages. Here, the cultivation of easily storable root crops, especially yams and taro, proved invaluable in sustaining long voyages. Among other staples circulated about the newly colonized islands were breadfruit, coconuts, and bananas, as well as such domesticated animals as pigs, chickens, and dogs, which entered the trade system from southeast Asia, the Philippines, and Indonesia. Over the centuries from 1600 to 100 BCE, Lapita sailors moved eastward and settled the islands of Vanuatu, Tonga, Fiji, and Samoa. Archaeologists believe that Fiji may be the ultimate source of the culture that sparked the next outward migration: that of the Polynesians.

**Bwaimas, Papua New Guinea.** Some of the earliest known human attempts at agriculture took place in the highlands of Papua New Guinea perhaps 9,000–7,000 years ago. The introduction of yams several millennia later created an enduring staple crop, and their portability allowed their spread as they sustained seafarers throughout the Pacific.

## Creating Polynesia

As populations grew, the primary mode of governmental and economic organization, the kinship-based chiefdom, became increasingly elaborated. On Tonga, the Society Islands, the Marquesas, and later the Hawaiian Islands, the power of local chiefs extended to nearby island systems. Even here, far removed from outside influences, the inclination of human societies toward centralization, as well as tension with smaller regional societies that we saw in Chapter 4, is apparent.

**Conflict, Interaction, and Expansion** What effect such centralization and the increasingly intensified agriculture of staples in the more productive islands may have had on their inhabitants is uncertain. Up to a point, it may have made these societies more efficient as food producers. But the difficulties we have seen in other societies of sustaining large populations on limited amounts of land were undoubtedly intensified in an island society. Some researchers have theorized, for example, that environmental problems related to overpopulation may have developed in the Cook Islands and the Marquesas around 500 BCE and again in 200 BCE. Political disputes arising from the struggles between centralizing and decentralizing factions

**Early Pacific Seafaring Rafts.** During the first millennium CE, Polynesian navigators benefited from advances in ship design as they colonized far-flung island chains. The Norwegian adventurer Thor Heyerdahl demonstrated the seaworthiness of similar designs when he constructed a replica of the type of raft utilized by aboriginal seafaring Peruvians. The raft measured approximately 45 feet by 18 feet and consisted of several large balsa tree trunks arranged in a crisscross design. The craft was outfitted with a 29-foot mast and a huge sail, along with a sizeable cabin to provide shelter for the six-man crew. For sustenance, large quantities of drinking water and food supplies—mostly coconuts, sweet potatoes, and other Peruvian staples—were carried on board.

may have played a role as well. In any case, there seems to have been a break around 500 CE that resulted in the longest period of migration yet: to Hawaii around 600, Easter Island (Rapa Nui) about 700, and New Zealand by 1200. In the cooler climates of Easter Island and New Zealand the introduction of the South American sweet potato—one of the rare examples of hypothetical Polynesian interaction with continental societies—allowed for a diversity of staple crops to support the population.

**Later Interactions**   By the time of the first European contact in the early sixteenth century, nearly every habitable island had been settled, and some, Hawaii and New Zealand perhaps most dramatically, had populations of many hundreds of thousands. As we shall see in subsequent chapters, however, this vast achievement of exploration and colonization would soon be threatened by disease and a new breed of conquerors and colonists. Like the Amerindian cultures of the Americas, disease would reduce the populations in some of these islands by perhaps as much as 80 percent. The next three and a half centuries of European exploration of the Pacific would carry with them untold and, all too often, disastrously unforeseen consequences.

# Putting It All Together

Though separated from each other by thousands of miles of ocean and spawning radically different cultures, the Americas and Oceania share common patterns with each other as well as with the cultures of Eurasia and Africa. The first pattern that historians can see is that even in such widely separated areas human foraging communities at roughly the same time *independently began a process toward the development of agriculture and animal domestication*. While domestication of the first plants and animals and gathering into more settled village life began shortly after the last retreat of the glaciers in Eurasia, it came somewhat later in the Americas, perhaps because human groups were still rather scattered and few in number and could be sustained by large-game hunting. The many different types of plants available as food—especially legumes—were relatively high in protein, an important feature as large game became increasingly scarce. It is also the case that the plant that ultimately became a chief staple of the American societies, corn, required extensive experimentation before becoming domesticated in anything near its present form. Thus, it is only around 4000 BCE that we see its development and the beginning of its extensive domestication.

The second pattern we can see is *growth and sophistication of social structures and the development of the city and of monumental architecture for religious and political purposes.* Even in Oceania, where the critical population levels for cities were never reached, one finds the monoliths of Rapa Nui as evidence of this human pattern. In some cases, the types of structures—pyramids, terraces, and obelisks, for example—seem to follow an almost "universal" pattern, so much so that scholars still struggle to find evidence of contact among widely separated cultures where none appears to have existed.

Recent finds at the Caral-Supé sites show how rapidly the development of astonishingly sophisticated large cities took place once the threshold of plant and animal domestication was crossed. The accomplishments of the society that created Caral and the other sites uncovered so far, like those of the Indus valley, survived in the local practices of Andean peoples long after the cities themselves were abandoned. The settlements of the Olmecs on the southern Gulf coast of Mexico, though coming somewhat later, were equally imposing in their architecture, the efficacy of their farming techniques and irrigation practices, the sophistication of their social structures, and, it now appears, their development of writing. Yet it is also the case that people will not create all the aspects of "civilization" in the same ways and by the same means. One striking example of this is the use of the wheel. Rotation and cyclical motion appear to permeate the ritual lives of people all over the globe, yet the use of the wheel for conveyance and as a basic concept of technology is not universal. Thus, as with so many human innovations, the intersection of need and opportunity led to a crucial breakthrough. Hence, despite the widespread use of ball courts employing spheres of rubber put through circular hoops as a central political and religious ceremony among Mesoamerican peoples and the enormous cyclical mathematical and timekeeping achievements of later peoples like the Mayas (and even the fact that we have evidence that American societies provided their children with toys that had wheels), the need and means for utilizing heavy-wheeled vehicles never occurred and thus never developed as it had in Eurasia and Africa.

In the case of Oceania, the peopling of the innumerable islands of the Pacific was inseparable from trade and cultural connections. Colonizing uninhabited islands could take place only when the plants and animals required could be brought along and provision could be made to trade for unavailable items. Thus, in terms of square mileage, the Lapita system was one of the world's largest trading spheres, stretching thousands of miles and including thousands of islands. Yet, for a variety of reasons— the necessities traded, the remoteness of the islands from other trade centers, the lack of connections to mainland Asia and the Americas, the unique seafaring skills of the island navigators—the peoples of Oceania remained separated from other such systems. Even here, as in the Americas, Eurasia, and Africa, we see yet another pattern emerging within the political behavior of human societies: *centralization and resistance to it.* As with other fundamental patterns of world history, we will see this one emerge repeatedly in a variety of guises as our story proceeds.

▶ For additional resources, including maps, primary sources, visuals, and quizzes, please go to www.oup.com/us/vonsivers. Please see the Further Resources section at the back of the book for additional readings and suggested websites.

# Against the Grain

# Thor Heyerdahl

The early Americas and Oceania present an interesting exception to the principal theme of Patterns of World History. Because they were separated by thousands of miles of ocean from Eurasian and African developments, the peoples of the early Americas and Oceania were denied the benefits of cultural innovations resulting from interactions and adaptations. One might assume, therefore, that these isolated cultures were entirely dependent on indigenous cultural and environmental factors in the development of their emerging civilization.

Although generally accepted, the isolationist theory has not gone entirely unchallenged. Over the last few decades a few unorthodox archaeologists and historians have presented arguments and theories that oppose these traditional views. One of the earliest challengers was Thor Heyerdahl, an amateur Norwegian archaeologist. Heyerdahl set out to demonstrate that South American sailors could have established east-to-west contacts by traversing vast distances across the Pacific solely by relying on prevailing trade winds and ocean currents. In 1947 Heyerdahl successfully sailed across the Pacific from Peru to Polynesia aboard a large balsa raft named the *Kon-Tiki* (after a mythical Peruvian god), similar to those used by ancient Incans. The voyage took 101 days to complete across an expanse of nearly 5,000 miles. This startling achievement convinced Heyerdahl that the original settlers of Polynesia were ancient Peruvians. As additional support for his theory, Heyerdahl pointed out that some modern Polynesians had lighter complexions than others, possible evidence of earlier Peruvian rather than Asian descent. (See photo of Heyerdahl's journey on p. 144.)

Heyerdahl's theory has met with mixed reception. His assumption that some of the early Polynesians were of Peruvian descent has been generally discredited by the academic establishment. By relying on mitochondrial DNA analyses, archaeologists have argued that in fact the first settlers of Polynesia were indeed of Asian—not Peruvian—descent. And yet, intriguingly, recent scholarly opinion—based on more sophisticated genomic HLA typing as well as DNA analysis of a select group of Easter Islanders—indicates the presence of genetic traits found among Amerindians, most likely Peruvians. In addition, recent archaeological investigation has produced linguistic and material evidence in support of the diffusion of agrarian advances carried from Peru westward across the Pacific. For example, the sweet potato, indigenous to Peru, was present in Polynesia centuries before European expeditions across the Pacific. Therefore, despite its controversial approach and results, Heyerdahl's courageous adventure and radical suppositions suggest at the very least the possibility of transoceanic cultural diffusion by prehistoric Peruvian seafarers.

- **In what ways do Heyerdahl's theories represent a good example of thinking "against the grain"?**

- **How do the sorts of evidence Heyerdahl and others have used to question the isolationist theory of early Oceanic and American history provide a different perspective on the types of sources most commonly associated with historical research?**

# Thinking Through Patterns

▶ **What do historians see as the advantages and disadvantages of the separate evolution of the Americas?**

Like the role of geography, this is a question that is often debated. For one thing, we can turn the question around and ask why we should consider the Americas as "isolated," rather than Eurasia and Africa. But it is also true that the societies were not as large or as ethnically diverse as their Eurasian counterparts. Historically, too, scholars still often view the two sets of continents as "old" and "new" and from that perspective view the Americas as "isolated." A big part of how one chooses to look at the question also revolves around how one sees the roles of invasion, infusion of innovation, and cultural competition. Some scholars have argued that the very shape of Eurasia allowed for the brisk dissemination of innovation along broad areas similarly situated in latitude and therefore climate. The Americas, by way of contrast, were more longitudinally oriented, making such diffusion more difficult. Some argue that the separateness of the Americas allowed them to hothouse distinctive cultural traits among their populations. Yet others argue that constant mixing of peoples and ideas accelerates innovation and, hence, "progress." One distinct disadvantage of isolation is that peoples become susceptible to diseases and biological changes suddenly inflicted on them. Thus, from the sixteenth to the early eighteenth centuries, virulent epidemics of Eurasian and African diseases like smallpox devastated the peoples of the Americas when introduced. Though the Americas in all likelihood introduced syphilis in return, it did not cause nearly the devastation in Eurasia and Africa that the Old World diseases did in the New World.

▶ **Why did no cities develop on the larger Pacific Islands?**

While the Pacific Islanders had abundant access to food for immediate consumption, the islands themselves were generally too small to allow the accumulation of enough surplus food to free up the numbers of nonfarmers necessary to build and maintain a city. In addition, the islands themselves contained limited amounts of building materials and fresh water, while their isolation helped guard them against attack. Culturally, the islanders also had grown to *expect* that if their numbers outran the food supply, they could simply find another island to which the excess population could migrate.

▶ **The wheel is often cited as the most basic human invention, yet large and sophisticated civilizations were able to flourish without this signal innovation. Why do you think it did not develop in the Americas?**

Historians looking at this question tend to look at it in one of two ways: culturally or practically. Some cultural scholars see a lack of deep-seated affinities for circular motion in the belief systems of the American peoples as helping to prevent them from relating to the motion of the wheel in the way that Eurasian and African peoples did. Yet American societies had toys with wheels on them, so they were not unaware of the concept of circular motion—indeed, far from it. The scholars favoring a practical or technological approach argue that the environment of the mountains close by seacoasts, rain forests, and dry, hilly regions was not conducive to bulk transport by wheeled vehicles and that the peoples there simply were never forced to look for more efficient means of transport.

# Patterns of Evidence: Sources for Chapter 5

SOURCE 5.1

## Quipú from the Caral-Supé culture, Peru

**2600–2000 BCE**

Recent archaeological discoveries in the Caral-Supé valley have pushed back the timeline of cultural development in the Andes by several millennia. A fixture of later Incan culture, the quipú was an elaborate series of knotted ropes that seemed to serve as a coded system of communication. Excavations have demonstrated that the quipú was used in the region as much as 3,000 years before its earliest previous attestation. Moreover, this quipú was apparently left as an offering on the stairway of a public building when another building was built on top.

▶ **Working with Sources**

1. **What does this object suggest about the continuities among various Andean cultures over several thousand years?**

2. **What does the existence of an object used for accounting suggest about this culture's administrative and bureaucratic sophistication?**

SOURCE 5.2

# Textile fragment from Chavín de Huántar, Peru

### ca. 500–200 BCE

Now housed in the Metropolitan Museum of Art in New York City, this section of an elaborately crafted and painted piece of textile attests the manufacturing prowess of the Chavín people. In the image, a central fanged figure grasps and may be controlling a four-eyed monster. The snake-like elements of this figure have led to the conclusion that he is an ancestor of the *khipucamayuc*, the Inca name for the keeper of a quipú.

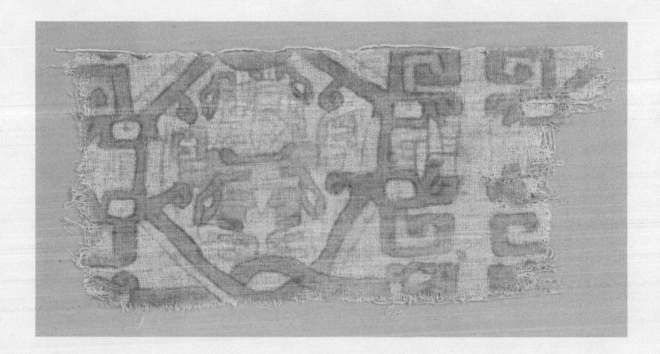

▶ **Working with Sources**

1. **What does the sophistication of this object indicate about the division of labor in Chavín society at its peak?**

2. **What were the likely connections between textile manufacture and the operation of quipú in the period?**

## SOURCE 5.3

# Burial mound at L'Anse Amour, Labrador, Canada

### ca. 5500 BCE

This mound marks the grave of an adolescent boy from the "Maritime Archaic" people of Labrador. Roughly 7,500 years ago, his body was wrapped in a shroud of bark or hide and placed face down in the grave with his head facing to the west. At that point, a large mound of rocks was erected over his burial place.

▶ **Working with Sources**

1. What are the similarities between this burial mound and others found in ancient North America?

2. What seems to have been the status of this boy, judging from the placement and the circumstances of his burial?

Source: Courtesy of Brian Bursey

## SOURCE 5.4

# Lapita pot shards, found in Vanuatu, Western Pacific

### ca. fourth millennium BCE

Named for a site in the archipelago of New Caledonia, the Lapita culture was a system of kinship-based exchanges among the inhabitants of thousands of islands in the western Pacific. Elements of "Lapita ware," decorated with stamped patterns, were in high demand, and pots were exchanged among the inhabitants of the islands.

▶ **Working with Sources**

1. What do the elaborate designs imprinted on this pot suggest about the sophistication of Lapita culture?

2. How can the pot be connected with the themes of navigation and gift exchange in the wider Polynesian culture?

Source: © Philippe Metois

# PART TWO

# The Age of Empires and Visionaries

## 600 BCE–600 CE

**B**y the middle of the first millennium BCE, two major transformations changed the course of world history. First, kingdom formation, which had begun earlier in Eurasia, became a near-universal pattern in the world, including sub-Saharan Africa and Mesoamerica. Second, visionaries emerged in Eurasia whose formulations of monotheism and monism laid the foundations of religious civilizations that eventually emerged in the Middle East, India, China, and adjacent regions after 600 CE.

## Kingdoms and Empires

**Sub-Saharan Africa and the Americas.** Around 600 BCE, improvements in agricultural productivity made it possible for some chiefdoms to expand into kingdoms. In sub-Saharan Africa, the kingdoms were Meroë in the steppes of the middle Nile and Aksum in the highlands of Ethiopia, and in Mesoamerica, the kingdoms were those of the Maya in the Yucatán Peninsula and Teotihuacán in the Mexican Basin.

**The Middle East and the Mediterranean.** After the Hittites and Neo-Assyrians, around 600 BCE the Persian Achaemenids continued the pattern of empire building. The Greeks resisted the Persians for a long time with their alternatives of city-states and elective offices. But eventually the Macedonian Greek Alexander the Great, his Hellenist successors, and the republican Romans in the western Mediterranean also adopted the imperial pattern, expanding into the Middle East. The Roman Empire competed with the two Persian successor empires of the Parthians and Sasanids for dominance of the region. The characteristic pattern of the Middle East and Mediterranean was competitive imperialism.

**India and China.** Intense political–military competition among small states ruled by a military class or royal dynasty led to the elimination of the weakest states and the consolidation of larger kingdoms in both India and China around 600 BCE. In contrast to the Middle East and Mediterranean, the pattern of India and China was one of rising and falling single empires, followed by long periods of decentralization before the rise of new imperial dynasties that unified much or all of the region.

**ca. 800 BCE**
Earliest evidence of
iron smelting in
sub-Saharan Africa

**551–479 BCE**
Traditional dates for
life of Confucius

**550–331 BCE**
Achaemenid Persia

**ca. 427–347 BCE**
Plato, founder of the
first philosophical
school, the Academy

**Interactions in Eurasia and with Africa.** Merchants in the kingdoms and empires of Eurasia and sub-Saharan Africa began to interact during the period 600 BCE–600 CE. They pioneered the sea routes to southern India, China, and eastern Africa and the land routes of the Silk Road through central Asia and across the Sahara from northern to western Africa. Exchanges on these routes were not yet regular enough to lead to adaptations, for example, of technological inventions. But the trade whetted the appetites of rulers for luxury goods, such as spices, ointments, silks, and ceramics, stimulating the rise of merchant classes.

## Visionaries and the Adoption of State Religions

**Visionaries.** At the height of the political–military competition among city-states, kingdoms, and empires around 700–500 BCE, individuals arose in Eurasia to proclaim new visions of reality. In the place of the polytheistic universe in which gods and humans mingled, they proclaimed a transcendent God or "first principle" beyond the universe. Their messages were not bound to the particular kingdoms or empires in which the visionaries lived but were addressed to anyone who would listen.

What difference did their new visions of reality make? For the first time in world history, individuals claimed to have discovered standards of truth and justice that were beyond the ever-changing circumstances of kingdoms and empires and their polytheistic pantheons. An unchanging God or first principle, so these individuals argued, was the measure for what was truthful and just. Not all agreed, however, that this measure could be translated into concrete doctrines, laws, and regulations.

**Empires and the Adoption of State Religions.** In the centuries after the visionaries, small groups of followers popularized the messages of monotheism and monism. They formed priestly classes, churches, and/or schools. Interaction among groups of followers led to the adaptation of some monotheisms and monisms to each other. For example, Jews adopted elements from Zoroastrianism and Greek philosophy, Buddhists influenced Confucianism and Daoism, and a group of Jews founded the reform movement of Christianity and merged it with Greek philosophy.

As one might expect, kings and emperors sought to capitalize on the unifying forces they perceived in monotheism and monism. By 600 CE, monotheism or monism had become the dominant religion, philosophy, and/or ethics of the empires and kingdoms in Eurasia and parts of sub-Saharan Africa.

Previous chapters focused on the patterns of social and political formation, from foraging to agricultural villages, as well as towns and cities, and from there to kingdoms and empires. Now—after the adoption of state religions—kings, emperors, and religious officials laid the foundations for the formation of religious civilizations which, after 600 CE, evolved into social and cultural units that were geographically larger and more enduring than kingdoms and empires—lasting, in most cases, right to the present.

## Thinking Like a World Historian

▶ What is the connection between food, population density, and patterns of social–political formation in world history? Why did these patterns develop later in sub-Saharan Africa and the Americas?

▶ What elements did the visionaries of ca. 700–500 BCE share in common, and what made their visions so decisive in the course of world history?

▶ Which areas in the Americas saw the development of a corn- and potato-based agriculture that did not depend on the plow, the wheel, and ironmaking?

▶ What is the difference between kingdoms and empires, and how did empires change as a result of the adoption of state religions?

**322–185 BCE**
Most of India united for the first time under Mauryan Empire

**196 BCE–284 CE**
Early Roman Empire (including imperial republic)

**250–900 CE**
Classic period of Maya kingdoms

**322–550 CE**
Much of India reunited under Gupta Empire

**221–206 BCE**
First Chinese Empire under Qin

**100–750 CE**
Moche chiefdom in northern Peru

**300–600 CE**
Kingdom of Aksum in northeastern sub-Saharan Africa

**476 CE**
End of western Roman Empire

# Chapter 6  600 BCE–600 CE

# Chiefdoms and Early States in Africa and the Americas

A humble stone carving in Oaxaca, in southern Mexico, carbon dated to about 600 BCE, is the earliest documentation for the existence of a 260-day divinatory calendar in Mesoamerica, which later played a central part in Mayan time reckoning and divination. Mexican archaeologists under the leadership of Alfonso Caso excavated the inscription in the 1930s, and an American archaeological team in the 1990s discovered perhaps an even earlier version of this calendar in Tabasco to the north of Oaxaca. Amazingly, this calendar system is still in use in southern Mexico, making it among the world's longest-lived methods of reckoning time. Similarly, an astronomical observatory in Kenya, carbon dated to 300 BCE, is the earliest example of the so-called Borana lunar calendar of 354 days. It is still in use today among the Kushite herders of East Africa. Two American anthropologists, B. M. Lynch and L. H. Robbins, discovered the observatory in Namoratunga [nah-mow-rah-TOON-ga], Kenya, during fieldwork in 1978. The two calendars not only attest to the cultural prowess of Mesoamerica and sub-Saharan East Africa during the period of 600 BCE–600 CE but, more importantly, are reminders of the diversity and relativity of all calendar systems, including the modern Western one which dominates the world today.

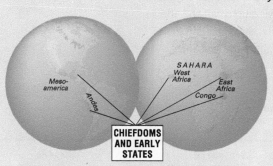

*ABOVE:* **The ruins of Meroitic pyramids at Jebel Barkal in modern Sudan.**

Interest in time reckoning was not the only similarity between the Americas and sub-Saharan Africa. During the period 600 BCE–600 CE, these regions also resembled each other in terms of patterns of agricultural development, spread of villages, emergence of chiefdoms, and early rise of kingdoms. These institutions, results of regional interactions and adaptations, evolved more slowly than in the more populated Eurasia, where kingdoms and empires already proliferated prior to 600 BCE–600 CE. Since there was little contact between Eurasia and the Americas and much of sub-Saharan Africa it is all the more remarkable that the patterns of agriculture and life in villages, chiefdoms, and kingdoms were fairly consistent *within* world regions as much as *across* world regions. People did not need to be in contact with each other across the continents to build their cultures in similar ways. All they needed were sufficiently large populations for similar institutions to arise. Nevertheless, as we saw in Chapter 5, the isolated world regions, through their own internal interactions, adapted to a transition from foraging to agriculture. Indeed, as recent scholarship has revealed, urban centers like Caral-Supé appear to be of the same age as some of the earliest Old World sites.

In this chapter, we will see how, through continued internal interactions, sub-Saharan Africans and Americans blazed indigenous trails in pattern formation, from villages to **chiefdoms** and **kingdoms**. Sharing a common humanity with the Eurasians, they did not need the direct influence of those peoples to develop strikingly similar social and political patterns. The calendars of these two regions, while strikingly similar to Eurasian models in some respects, also illustrate the adaptation of the concept to local needs as well as sophistication.

# Agriculture and Early African Kingdoms

Largely on account of its relative separation and lower population levels, sub-Saharan Africa (like the Americas and Oceania) transitioned from forager society to agrarian–urban society with its patterns of village, city-state, kingdom, and empire formation somewhat less rapidly or completely than Eurasia. However, north of the Sahara Africans interacted with the Middle East and adapted to its agrarian patterns early on. They adopted village life, built cities, and created kingdoms (such as Kush and Nubia along the Nile) well before the period of 600 BCE–600 CE. After 600 CE, the kingdoms of Meroë [ME-ro-way] in the Nile valley and Aksum in the Ethiopian highlands flourished, while Africans farther south shifted from foraging to agriculture, villages, and chiefdoms. By 600 CE, urbanism had spread to West Africa and foraging had shrunk to pockets in the center and south of the continent.

## Saharan Villages, Towns, and Kingdoms
For many millennia, the Sahara was relatively hospitable, with savannas and steppes, furthering the pattern shift from foraging to agriculture. But when the

# Seeing Patterns

▶ How does comparing and contrasting sub-Saharan Africa with the Americas during 600 BCE–600 CE help in understanding the agrarian–urban patterns of social and political development across the world?

▶ Where did chiefdoms, cities, and kingdoms arise in sub-Saharan Africa and why? On which forms of agriculture, urbanization, and trade were they based?

▶ Which areas in the Americas saw the development of a corn- and potato-based agriculture that did not depend on the plow, the wheel, and ironmaking?

Chiefdom: An agricultural village or town of up to 1,000 inhabitants, in which people know each other, requiring a person of authority (an elder or the head of a large family) to keep order as a respected chief.

**Kingdom:** A city-state or territorial state in which a ruler, claiming a divine mandate and supported by a military force, keeps order and provides for the defense against outside attacks.

monsoon rains shifted eastward, around 5000–3000 BCE, the desert expanded, and savannas and steppes retreated southward. Agrarian life relocated to oases and the Nile River valley. In the northeast, the kingdom of Meroë, successor of Napata, established a capital with the same name in the middle Nile basin, between the Nile and the western slopes of the northern Ethiopian highlands. The kingdom received its support from a sufficient, although not abundant, agricultural surplus produced with the help of annual Nile floods and irrigation.

**Saharan Chiefdoms and Kingdoms**    The earliest evidence of Africans shifting from foraging to agriculture comes from the area of the middle Nile around Khartoum, the capital of modern Sudan. Archaeological sites reveal a culture of raising cattle, cultivating sorghum, and shaping distinctive pottery. Sorghum tolerates a climate of less rainfall than wheat and barley, and it is possible that farmers along the middle Nile domesticated it locally, probably after becoming familiar with Middle Eastern farming. By the period between 4000 BCE and the first written records in Egypt in 3100 BCE, a substantial chiefdom of Nilo-Saharan speakers had emerged in northern Sudan, then called "Nubia" (from the Latinized Egyptian word *nebew* for gold, which was found in a valley off the Nile). This chiefdom was based on farming, livestock raising, and trading of gold as well as rain-forest ivory and timber. Archaeologists have noted that even at this early date tombs in Nubia contained objects rivaling those of the Egyptians, including objects from southwest Asia and beyond. Moreover, Nubian military prowess emerged clearly in Egyptian records, with archers especially sought after as mercenaries. Indeed, the bow and arrow, both Paleolithic African inventions, gave their names to the state which the Egyptians called *Ta-Seti* [tah-SAY-tee], the "Land of the Bow."

After 2500 BCE, a kingdom grew in wealth and power in Nubia, building a palace, large tombs, temples, and a wall around its capital city of Kerma, the first African city outside Egypt. During 1850–1400 BCE Kerma and Egypt were rivals for the control of Nile trade, with each conquering and ruling the other for periods of time until Egypt eventually destroyed Kerma and colonized Nubia for about half a millennium. Nubia regained autonomy early in the first millennium BCE, in a state centered around the city of Napata, a new capital at some distance upstream on the Nile. Later, the Napatan kings liberated themselves from Egyptian control and even assumed the throne of their northern neighbor as the twenty-fifth dynasty (ca. 780–686 BCE). But when Assyria, the first empire to unify all of the Middle East, conquered Egypt, the defeated king retreated and relocated himself farther upstream at Meroë, south of the Nile bend in the border zone between the southern Saharan steppe and the savanna.

**The Villages of Tichitt-Oualata**    Contemporaneously with the Nubian kingdoms, villages emerged in the southeastern corner of today's Mauretania. As in Nubia, the climate in the western Sahara had changed during 5000–3000 BCE, away from the monsoon regime which since the end of the last Ice Age (12,500 BCE) had supported a steppe and savanna vegetation in what is desert today. As the monsoon patterns moved eastward, foragers retreated to shallow lakes and oases. They left behind a rich collection of cave paintings in the surrounding mountains

**AFRICA, SHOWING SITES IN MAURETANIA 2000 BCE–600 BCE**

dating to earlier times when the Sahara was still wet. During 3000–2000 BCE, these foragers—perhaps stimulated by the knowledge of Middle Eastern agriculture—domesticated pearl millet, a type of grain requiring less water than wheat or barley to grow.

Archaeological evidence published by a British team in 2004 points to the emergence of a set of sizeable villages at Dhar Tichitt [dar tee-SHEET] and Dhar Oualata [dar wah-LAH-tah] in Mauretania around 2000 BCE, which flourished until 600 BCE. There, the team identified centers with large masonry structures. Corrals held herds of cattle, and granaries held large quantities of millet. Numerous tomb mounds, perhaps for the chiefs in the villages, held beads and copper jewelry. Furnaces contained remnants of charcoal and ore, evidence of craftspeople smelting copper that was mined in the nearby Saharan mountains. While it appears that the social structure was based on wealth in livestock, exactly how society was regulated, what nature of religious order it possessed, and which form of chiefly authority ruled are still unclear. One theory holds that the people eventually retreated farther south, together with the steppe and savanna, as the Sahara continued to dry out. As we shall see in Chapter 14, these migrants might have been the founders of the kingdom of ancient Ghana.

**Meroë on the Middle Nile**    The kings of Meroë were successors of the twenty-fifth Nubia-descended dynasty of Egypt, who, under Assyrian pressure, withdrew to the steppes of the middle Nile, about 100 miles north of present-day Khartoum. Here they built their capital, Meroë. At that time, the floodplain to the south of the capital still received sufficient monsoon rainfall during the summer to support agriculture. In addition, the kings built large water reservoirs to supply the farmers. The latter grew the African cereals sorghum and millet, but archaeological finds also include barley and wheat, all of which were planted with the plow. Presumably, the kingdom financed itself for the most part with the agricultural surplus.

At its height, from the sixth through fourth centuries BCE, the city of Meroë encompassed 20,000 inhabitants, and a substantial population lived in the provincial towns. Although the king was the recognized head of Meroë, the kingdom was largely decentralized. The provinces downstream and upstream along the Nile were autonomous, ruled by their own town chiefs who perhaps sent no more than annual presents to the capital. Outside the limited agricultural area, cattle nomads grazed their herds.

The difference in power between the kings and the chiefs was defined by the royal control over trade. Miners in the desert north of the capital produced iron

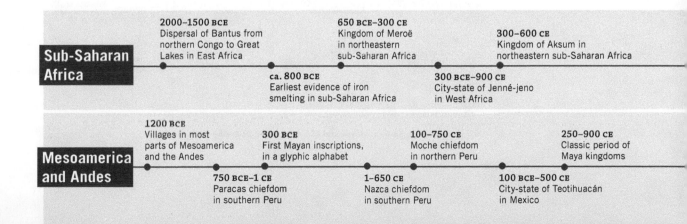

ore and farmers south of the capital grew cotton, both of which were important for the urban crafts. Smiths and weavers in Meroë produced weapons, hoes, utensils, and cloth, both for local consumption and for trade beyond the kingdom. Hunters in the south acquired ivory from elephants and feathers from ostriches hunted in the savanna. Traders carried these goods on donkey and camel caravans on the traditional trade route down the Nile to Egypt or across the Red Sea to Yemen by boat. In return, they brought back olive oil and wine from Egypt and frankincense and myrrh from Yemen (see Map 6.1).

From the kingdom's inception in the seventh century BCE, people in Meroë mined, smelted, and forged iron; they might have been the first to do so in sub-Saharan Africa. However, how and when the knowledge of smelting and forging iron began in sub-Saharan Africa has been a bone of contention among scholars. As is generally agreed, the craft of iron smelting evolved gradually in Hittite Anatolia during several centuries after 1500 BCE (see Chapter 2). To date, the possible spread of ironworking skills from the Middle East to Africa has not been satisfactorily proved. But the independent origin of ironworking in Africa has not been demonstrated conclusively

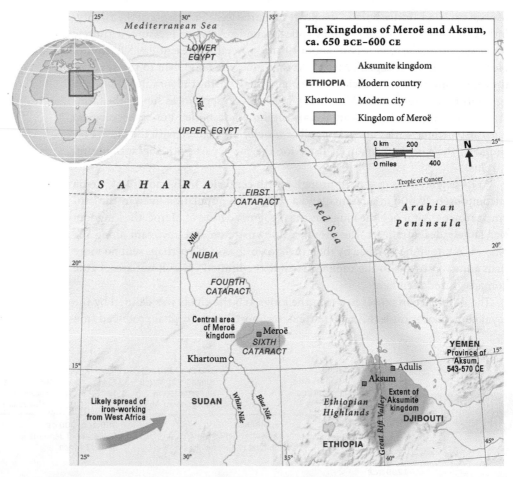

MAP 6.1 **The Kingdoms of Meroë and Aksum, ca. 650 BCE–600 CE.**

either. Researchers such as Stanley Alpern and Jan Vansina, evaluating the evidence in the early 2000s, came to the conclusion that the earliest reliable carbon date for iron production is 839–782 BCE, in the savanna on the border between today's Central African Republic and Cameroon. If this date is correct, Meroë would have received the impetus for iron production from within sub-Saharan Africa.

**Meroë's Cultural Achievements**   In Meroë, the kings adapted their Nubian–Egyptian heritage to the different regional circumstances of the steppe and savanna south of the Sahara. Their monuments acquired a distinct style, as is evidenced by their tombs: pyramids with flat tops and pyramids with steep angles. Although the main temple and its priesthood remained in the north, the priests added native deities to the pantheon, such as the lion god Apedemek. Meanwhile, Egyptian hieroglyphics seem to have "evolved" into an alphabetic script, visible on many monuments, even though at present this script is still undeciphered.

In spite of its regional orientation, Meroë was well known to the outside world. Mediterranean travelers visited it quite frequently. In the early first century CE the kings of Meroë skirmished with Rome over border issues. And in the third century CE, when Meroë's power was already declining, Heliodorus of Emesa, a Hellenistic-Greek writer, made it the stage for the conclusion of his popular romance novel *Aethiopica*. As much as Meroë provided a physical network for regional travelers, it also provided an intellectual link between Eurasia and Africa; the people of Meroë facilitated this important cultural link through their adaptation.

## The Kingdom of Aksum

Meroitic trade with the Red Sea had to cross through the Ethiopian highlands. Exposed to this trade, highlanders gradually acculturated to urbanized Meroë as well as Yemen. Sometime in the early first century CE, a king replaced the chiefdoms of the highlands and established the kingdom of Aksum (300–600 CE). Based on a relatively productive, plow-driven agriculture, this kingdom assumed control of the trade from Meroë, which declined subsequently. Aksum became the major supplier of African goods to the Roman Empire, from where it accepted Christianity in the early 300s.

**Meroë's Decline and Aksum's Rise**   Three factors contributed to Meroë's decline in the third century CE. First, the iron industry devoured immense amounts of charcoal, which is made by burning wood in earth-covered mounds. Once the forests in the east were gone, the iron industry in the capital city was doomed, depriving the kings of a major source of their income. Second, beginning in the late 200s BCE, camel nomads from the deserts east of the Nile raided northern Meroë. Third, the eastern neighbor, Ethiopia, acculturated to Meroë, thanks to the trade that crossed its land. Ethiopian guides and owners of transportation animals became participants in the trade, and then chiefs in the agriculturally rich high plain of Aksum took it over. Aksum was located close to the coast, where the port of Adulis (today Zula) was one of the main transshipment ports in the Red Sea. Thus, a combination of agricultural and commercial wealth enabled the chiefs of Aksum to assume the succession of Meroë.

The agricultural bounty of the Ethiopian highlands southeast of Meroë was due to its plains at 5,000–6,000 feet elevation and surrounding mountains 15,000 feet high. Deep valleys, notably of the Blue Nile and of the Rift Valley, cut into these highlands, which were therefore accessible only over steep ascents. The summer monsoon from the south Atlantic brought sufficient and, in places, abundant rain to the plains and mountains and supported large forests and a productive sub-tropical agriculture in the lower elevations.

As in the Nile valley, agriculture in the Ethiopian highlands was of considerable age, with evidence (from a rock painting and archaeological finds) of the existence of plows, oxen, barley, and wheat going back several thousand years. In higher elevations where barley and wheat did not prosper, farmers grew teff, a high-yielding grain. Plenty of grasslands supported cattle breeding. The Red Sea coast was dry and hot, with today's Djibouti sporting the highest average temperatures in the world. The coast supported only a few ports dependent on their hinterland. Ethiopia was a largely self-contained region in Africa, remaining outside the large population movements and cultural assimilation characteristic of West and East Africa.

**Aksum's Splendor**   Aksum, founded around 100 CE, came into its own around 300 CE. Its king, Ezana (ca. 303–350 CE), adopted Christianity as the state religion in 333 CE, thereby making Aksum the third Christian kingdom, after Armenia (301 CE) and Georgia (319 CE). Like his Armenian and Georgian counterparts and, somewhat later, the Roman emperor, Ezana replaced tolerance for a multiplicity of polytheistic religions with the requirement of conversion to a single faith (see Chapter 7). When the Roman emperors, however, embraced what would become the Roman Catholic interpretation of Christianity at the Church Council of Chalcedon (451 CE), Aksum opted for Coptic Christianity, which was dominant in Egypt. The emperors clearly considered the religious unity of the western and eastern halves of the empire as more important than the religious unity with their Middle Eastern provinces. Aksum, on the other hand, embraced union with the Coptic Church. Although it did not break with the Roman Empire and even sided with it in the second half of the 500s CE against the Sasanid Persians, Aksum kept its distance.

Another centralizing policy characteristic of Aksum was the use of a gold-based currency through which the taxation of the market for the import and export of luxury goods was facilitated. The kings of Aksum acquired their gold by sending merchants, protected by accompanying troops, to the southern highlands outside the kingdom, where the gold was mined. The merchants paid with salt, iron, and cattle. Finally, a small central administration of tax collectors, tax farmers, and provincial tribute collectors ensured delivery of agricultural surplus to granaries in the towns and the capital. The provinces outside the capital, however, were in reality small kingdoms, federated with Aksum through some kind of tribute system, the details of which are unknown. Even though more centralized than Meroë, Aksum was well below the level of administrative coherence of a typical Middle Eastern or Mediterranean kingdom or empire, such as Ptolemaic Egypt (305–30 BCE) or Antigonid Greece (301–168 BCE).

> "I built a shrine in Himyar at 'QNL' [Okelis?], zealous for the name of the Son of God, in Whom I believe, and I built His Gabaz [Cathedral of Aksum?] and sanctified it by the name of God."
>
> —Inscription by King Kaleb of Aksum, celebrating the conquest of Yemen

**Imperialism and Crisis**   In the 500s CE, Aksum briefly engaged in imperialism—the only imperialism coming out of sub-Saharan Africa in its entire history. This century was a time of profound crisis in both the Roman and Sasanid Persian empires, which were under threat by nomadic invaders from the central Asian and Russian steppes (see Chapter 7). Naval trade in the Red Sea declined and the kingdom of Himyar in Yemen increasingly relied on camel caravan trade along the west coast of Arabia. Perhaps under the influence of Jewish communities at the northern end of the caravan route, a Yemeni usurper who had converted to Judaism seized the throne and persecuted the Christians in his land. In response, and with the encouragement of Rome, the Aksumite king invaded Yemen and defeated the usurper. After a period of political instability, Aksum was able to make Yemen a regular province (543–570 CE).

But Aksum eventually lost this province when the Sasanid Persians invaded by land and sea in 570 CE, to establish their own proxy regime at the commercially important entrance to the Red Sea. The Sasanids had recovered earlier than the Romans from nomadic invasions and were determined to turn the long competition between the two empires (discussed in Chapter 7) to their favor. Seizing control over the entire India and East Africa trade was part of the Sasanid strategy to defeat Rome in the Middle East.

As a kingdom dependent to a considerable degree on transcontinental luxury trade, Aksum eventually became a collateral victim of this new Persian ascendancy. After 570 CE, Aksumite trade in the Red Sea declined precipitously. The capital city shrank to a shadow of itself, and in the following centuries provincial rulers in the highlands farther south rose to prominence. In addition, there were signs of internal problems: Timber resources for Aksum's iron industry in the vicinity of the capital became scarce. Although Ethiopia did not disintegrate, as Meroë had done, after 600 CE it played a much more modest regional role.

**Aksumite Stela, pre-400s CE.** This is the largest of hundreds of stone monoliths, some with tombs and altars, attesting to the architectural sophistication of the kingdom. Workmen transported them from quarries 3 miles away, where they had cut the stelae with iron tools. Some of the stelae, like the one above, have false windows and doors, looking like modern Art Deco buildings.

# The Spread of Villages in Sub-Saharan Africa

By about 600 BCE, agriculture and pastoralism were common not only in East Africa but also in West Africa. Both emerged when a majority of people retreated from the increasingly dry Sahara southward into West Africa. They followed the gradual southward shift of West Africa's three ecological zones, stretching from west to east in the form of more or less broad bands. The first and northernmost zone was the steppe, or **Sahel** (Arabic *sahil*, or "coast" of the "sea" of the Sahara Desert). The second zone was the *savanna*, an expanse of grassland with stands of trees. The third zone was a relatively narrow (up to 150-mile-wide) belt of rain forest along the coast from Guinea to Cameroon. Villages were dispersed by 600 BCE over all three zones, although they were most numerous in the savanna, where farming was most productive.

**Sahel:** An area of steppe or semidesert bordering the Sahara.

### West African Savanna and Rain-Forest Agriculture

During the period 600 BCE–600 CE the densest village networks were located in the savannas of the inland delta of the Niger and middle Senegal Rivers. The village of Jenné-jeno [jen-NAY JEN-no] in the delta developed into a major urban center during 300–900 CE. Indications are that it was a chiefdom with a developing regional trade for raw materials and luxury goods. In the rain forest, the evolution of slash-and-burn agriculture is still largely undocumented by archaeology, although its end result, the so-called Bantu dispersal, with its combination of yam, taro, banana, and oil palm village agriculture, is well established.

**Inland Delta Urbanism**    The river Niger originates in the far west of the West African rain forest and flows northeast from the savanna to the Sahel, before turning at a right angle southeastward in the direction of the Atlantic Ocean. Midway along its northeastern leg, it slows and divides into several branches, the 250-mile-long and 50-mile-wide inland delta. In the first millennium BCE, when the climate was still relatively humid, the delta was located entirely in the savanna, forming a huge area of canals, islands, and swamps. Villagers in the delta grew millet and African rice, the latter domesticated around 1500 BCE.

Over time, a dense network of villages developed. After 300 BCE a village division process began, by which some villages, increasing to town size, became the center of satellite villages. This is how Jenné-jeno at the southern end of the delta originated. By 900 CE, so it is estimated, Jenné-jeno was a *city*—that is, a dwelling place for a nonagricultural crafts-based population—of between 5,000 and 13,000 inhabitants. It was surrounded within a circle of half a mile in diameter by 25 villages. Other towns with satellite villages developed farther downstream as well and made the delta the most populated area in West Africa.

Unfortunately, the archaeology of the period under discussion (chiefly explored by Susan Keech McIntosh and Roderick J. McIntosh) has not revealed much yet about the social stratification and power structures of Jenné-jeno. It is clear that this urban–rural center had a line of chiefs, some basic administrative offices, and craftspeople. The strongest evidence is a gold ring and many objects made of copper and bronze dated to 850–900 CE. Copper and iron ore had to be carried in by donkey or camel from a distance of 30 miles or more from the desert and savanna to be smelted and manufactured in town into weapons and implements. Two chemically analyzed glass beads, dated to the pre-600 CE period, seem to have come from overseas, one from India, southeast Asia, or east Asia and the other from Roman Italy or Egypt. Thus, trans-Saharan trade seems to have been in existence, supporting an incipient urban demand for luxuries.

**Rain-Forest Settlements**    The earliest evidence for rain-forest agriculture comes from the Kintampo complex of 2250–750 BCE, located in today's Ghana. Here, archaeologists have found traces of wood and mud huts on stone foundations, domesticated cattle and dwarf goats, rats, pottery, terra-cotta figurines, and polished stone implements. The assumption is that the villagers practiced slash-and-burn farming, growing yams and oil palms. Unfortunately, no archaeological evidence of the cultivation of yams has been found so far, and the earliest evidence for oil palm cultivation dates to an 800 BCE site in the Atlantic Niger delta. Rain-forest archaeology, burdened by the tendency of the environment to break down the organic matter of artifacts, is lagging behind, and archaeologists have begun producing good data only from the 1990s onwards.

**Early Plant Domestication?** A first breakthrough in tropical archaeology came in 1996 at Nkang in the Cameroons. Belgian scholars excavating this site were able to date banana **phytoliths** to about 500 BCE. Phytoliths are silica from soil sediments deposited in bananas. Their dating caused unrest among many Africanists who for decades had thought that the banana had arrived with Indonesian sailors on the East African coast sometime between 200 and 500 CE. The Ugandan scientist B. Julius Lejju caused even more surprise in 2006 when he published findings from Munsa, Uganda, with banana phytoliths dating to the fourth millennium BCE. While discussion about the validity of the new data is still continuing, it is becoming more and more evident that Indian Ocean connections between Southeast Asia and East Africa are of greater antiquity than hitherto assumed. Did domesticated bananas, yams, sugarcane stalks, and rice travel westward and domesticated sorghum and millet travel eastward already thousands of years ago, carried by intrepid Polynesian sailors?

**Phytoliths:** Many plants pick up silica from the soil. After these plants decay, the silica returns to the soil in the form of phytoliths, which can be analyzed microscopically. Carbon dating of soil layers provides approximate dates.

**Village Farming** West African slash-and-burn farming for yam, banana, and oil palm plantations consisted of clearing small areas of rain forest for the establishment of villages of up to 500 inhabitants. Virgin rain forest was relatively easy to cut, even with stone tools, prior to the arrival of iron axes in the 800s BCE. Trees between 80 and 125 feet high formed a thick canopy, allowing relatively little light to penetrate and, therefore, not much undergrowth to develop and obstruct the clearing process. Each clearing was large enough for a village of a few hundred farmers, family fields, communal fallow land, and small numbers of cattle and goats.

If a village grew beyond its population capacity, a group had to depart and select a new site in the rain forest for clearing. Yam fields could be cultivated for up to 3 years and had to lie fallow for 10–15 years. During the fallow years, the rain forest grew back, although it now no longer returned to its virgin state. A secondary rain forest developed, with few tall trees and a proliferation of medium vegetation up to 30 feet high. Given several millennia of slash-and-burn cultivation, over time nearly all virgin African rain forests were replaced by secondary forest. As in so many other places in the world, what many might perceive as pristine "jungle" was in fact the creation of human hands, as emphasized by Jan Vansina in his classic on African rain-forest settlement. The transformation of the environment by humans, for better or worse, is a process that began early on in world history.

## The Spread of Village Life to East and South Africa

Groups of yam, banana, and oil palm farmers of southeast Nigeria, at the eastern end of the West African rain-forest belt, calling themselves "Bantu," meaning "the people," exhausted their area for clearings around 2000 BCE. In contrast to their westerly neighbors, they were fortunate in their search for new spaces to clear because they had the equatorial rain forest of the Congo to the southeast at their disposal. Once there, a northerly group, the Mashariki Bantus, began to disperse around 1500 BCE, this time, however, eastward into the savanna of the Great Lakes in East Africa. On their way, they adapted to the cereal agriculture and iron crafting of the savanna villagers. The Bantu villages of the Great Lakes became the center for one of the great transformation events of history. Under Bantu impact, during 600 BCE–600 CE, nearly all foragers in the southern cone of Africa became either villagers or cattle nomads and adopted Bantu languages and culture (see Map 6.2).

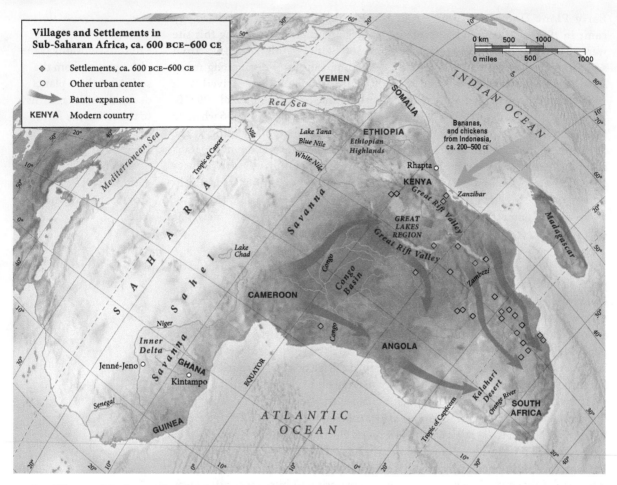

MAP **6.2** **Villages and Settlements in Sub-Saharan Africa, 600 BCE–600 CE.**

**Inland Villagers and Nomads**    At the time of the Mashariki Bantu arrival around 600 BCE, much of the land around the Great Lakes was still heavily forested savanna. As the villagers cleared the forest, the threat of the tsetse fly diminished and nomads from the north were able to expand southward. Many nomads gave up their minimal farming, which they traditionally engaged in from campsites. As in the Middle East, these nomads entered into a symbiotic relationship with the villagers, from whom they acquired their necessary grain supplements. In the meantime, the descendants of the original Bantu dispersal of 2000 BCE had settled the Congo equatorial rain forest and, under the impact of their eastern cousins, had complemented their yam and oil palm agriculture with millet and sorghum, as well as ironworking. Only small pockets of the original Paleolithic foragers of the virgin rain forest, the pygmies, continued their traditional lifestyle, although they eventually adopted Bantu languages.

The conversion of the foragers on the savanna south of the Congo rain forest to farming, from the Great Lakes westward to Angola and southward to the tip of South Africa, was the work of both eastern Great Lakes and western Congo branches of Bantus. The foragers either retreated before the farmers with their iron implements and weapons or adapted voluntarily to farming and speaking a Bantu language. Small numbers of savanna foragers, speaking Khoisan-family languages, retreated into the Kalahari Desert and steppe in western and central South Africa, hanging on to a precarious hunting-and-gathering survival. As could be expected, the process from Mashariki Bantu origins and Bantu interaction with the nomads and foragers of East and South Africa to the eventual mutual adaptations took time and was still incomplete in 600 CE.

**African Traditional Rituals**   The results of an analysis of Bantu linguistic roots and of early Iron Age (350–900 CE) sites in South Africa provide a glimpse into traditional **African spirituality**, summarized by Jan Vansina, a pioneer of Bantu studies. In this perception of reality, Bantus distinguished between the daily world of more or less regular cycles of renewal and disintegration in the village (birth, puberty, adulthood, marriage, old age) and the fields (rain, plantation, harvest, and dry season), and the calendar movements of heaven (described at the beginning of this chapter). Elaborate rituals, including a scrupulous observance of taboos and omens, had to be followed to keep the village and field cycles on their regular paths. For example, South African sites contain stone cairns marking the space of male circumcision lodges, stone-walled pits for rainmaking ceremonies, places with broken pots symbolizing deflowering in female puberty rites, and masks used for the representation of ancestor spirits in village feasts. Rituals guaranteed that the human and field cycles would remain in sync.

Ancestor and nature spirits pervaded the village and fields, and they had to be given their due respect through regular sacrifices, lest they disrupt the cycles of renewal and disintegration. Charms, mixed from herbs, protected against unintended insults of the spirits. The worst disruption, however, threatened to come from male or female witches in the villages who, acting out of envy, vengeance, or malice, could severely harm or even kill their victims. The only way to avoid death from bewitchment was to seek a diviner or healer in the village who, through trances, dreams, oracles, or charms, was able to enter the spirit world, recognize bewitchment, and stop it through **witchcraft**. It appears that in the early African Iron Age the adoption of elaborate rituals involving the human and field cycles—and, in some places, the calendar cycle, as evidenced by the Borana calendar discussed in the vignette at the beginning of this chapter—represented the main changes in the patterns of reality conceptualizations dating back to the African origins of humanity.

**Indonesian Contacts**   Village agriculture received a boost in 200–500 CE when Indonesian sailors brought new species of bananas and chickens to East Africa. These sailors were descendants from Austronesian farmers, who had dispersed to the islands of the Pacific, Philippines, and Indonesia, beginning around 4000 BCE, and who had probably also traveled shortly thereafter to East Africa, as discussed earlier in the chapter. The mariners of 200–500 CE sailed on large outriggers. These watercraft were rigged with canted square sails, which made it possible to sail a course at an angle from the aft wind. Prevailing wind patterns in the southern Indian Ocean would otherwise have made sailing westward from Indonesia to Africa difficult. Where on the African coast the Indonesians landed

**African spirituality:** Perception of reality based on the concept of nature in all its manifestations (planets and stars, landscapes, trees and plants, animals and humans), pervaded by spirits and influencing each other.

**Witchcraft:** A belief in which an evil person (male or female) can harm an innocent victim at a distance and cause the victim to become possessed, with attendant illnesses.

**Stone Relief of a Large Outrigger Merchant Ship, Buddhist Temple of Borobudur, on the Indonesian Island of Java, ca. 800 CE.** This type of ship traveled regularly from Java to East Africa on the cinnamon trade route, with its merchants exchanging spices for ivory, wild animal skins, and slaves during the early centuries of the first millennium.

is unknown, although they definitely settled the still-uninhabited tropical island of Madagascar, the fourth largest island in the world.

**Incipient Urbanism on the East Coast**   East Africans also benefited from trade with the Middle East. Archaeological evidence points to the inclusion of the northern East African coast into the Yemeni commercial network in the last centuries BCE, which connected Meroë, Ptolemaic and Roman Egypt, Parthian and Sasanian Persia, the Indian west coast, Sri Lanka, and (indirectly) Indonesia and China. Remnants of two camps on the northern coast of Somalia, dating to 150 BCE–500 CE, contain shards of ceramics from all these places. But as impermanent fixtures, these camps do not indicate regular commercial journeys.

The mid-first century CE seems to have been the transition point in the construction of permanent ports. The *Periplus of the Erythraean Sea*, a Greek-Hellenistic source describing for the Romans the monsoon winds for journeys to and from India, mentions Yemenis intermarrying with locals in the town of Rhapta along the Kenyan coast.

The archaeological remnants of this place have not yet been located, but Roman glass beads and shards found in digs on the island of Zanzibar and the nearby Tanzanian coast suggest regular journeys beginning around 200 CE. The beads and ceramics were presumably intended to be exchanged for ivory, rock crystal, ostrich feathers, and hardwood. If true, the roots of the later Swahili cities antedated the spread of Islam by several centuries—just as they did in the case of Jenné-jeno in West Africa before the rise of Islamic Saharan kingdoms.

## Patterns of African History, 600 BCE–600 CE

Based on a modestly productive agriculture, sub-Saharan Africa evolved along two basic patterns in the period 600 BCE–600 CE. First, in the northeast Meroë and Aksum adapted themselves to Middle Eastern agriculture, including the plow and irrigation techniques. In addition, both African-domesticated sorghum and millet—and in Aksum teff—were grown. With the help of irrigated farming and long-distance trade, chiefs built kingdoms, which lasted as long as the urban infrastructure could be supported. The exhaustion of timber in the vicinity of the capitals ended the royal pattern of social and political evolution in the sub-Saharan northeast.

Second, in the northwest of sub-Saharan Africa inhabitants pioneered the agricultures of the steppe, savanna, and rain forest on the basis of millet, rice, yam, and the fruit of the oil palm. Millet was productive enough to support the rise of villages. In one steppe region, the inland delta of the Niger, the irrigated farming of millet and rice allowed for the rise of a dense village network, village nucleation, and eventually a city, Jenné-jeno. With its incipient long-distance trade, this city foreshadowed the post-600 rise of Saharan kingdoms. Farther south, in the rain forest, the farming of yam, banana, and oil palm supported the emergence of small and widely dispersed villages. The expansion of the Bantus and their agriculture brought village life as well as iron smelting to all parts of sub-Saharan Africa.

**Africa and the Americas**     The Americas displayed striking similarities to the internal sub-Saharan interactions and adaptations. The latter, as we have seen, were responsible for patterns of village, city, and kingdom formation. In Mesoamerica as well as the Peruvian Andes Mountains, internal processes of interaction and adaptation based on increasingly productive agricultures also supported a pattern of village, city-state, and kingdom development from 600 BCE to 600 CE.

The principal difference, however, was that in sub-Saharan Africa this evolution gradually expanded also to the central and southern regions, whereas in the Americas no such expansion took place until after 600 CE. Social and political formation patterns spread to North America only after 600 CE, as represented by the Pueblo and Cahokia cultures in what are today the US states of Arizona, Utah, New Mexico, and Missouri.

# Early States in Mesoamerica: Maya Kingdoms and Teotihuacán

In Chapter 5 we saw that the chiefdoms of Caral-Supé (2600–2000 BCE) and Chavín de Huántar (1000–200 BCE) in the Andes as well as of the Olmecs (1200–600 BCE) in Mesoamerica represent early examples of social processes of development from agriculture and villages to urbanization, chiefdoms, and kingdoms. In the period 600 BCE–600 CE, in the Yucatán Peninsula of modern southeastern Mexico and the Mexican Basin in south-central Mexico, chiefdoms evolved into full-fledged kingdoms. In the Andes, urban centers continued to form under chiefly rule, although in Teotihuacán and Moche the urban culture was nearly as diversified as in the Mesoamerican kingdoms.

## The Maya Kingdoms in Southern Mesoamerica

Closeness to the equator and a long rainy season supported a dense rain forest in the central Yucatán Peninsula. By creating clear-cuts and heaping up the soil on elevated fields or terraces on hill slopes, Maya villagers built a rich agriculture based on squash, beans, and corn. Around 600 BCE towns evolved into cities, where chieftains transformed themselves into kings. By organizing the labor of the farmers during slack agricultural times in the winter, they created city-states with imposing temple pyramids and palaces, surrounded by outlying villages. Among these city-states, the most powerful during the period 600 BCE–600 CE were Tikal and Kalakmul (see Map 6.3).

**Mayaland on the Yucatán Peninsula**     The climate of the Yucatán Peninsula is subtropical, with a rainy season extending from May to September. The base of the Yucatán Peninsula consisted of rain-forest lowlands and swamps, traversed by rivers. To the south were rain-forest highlands, sloping from a chain of mountains about 80–110 miles wide, which descended gradually toward the lowlands in the

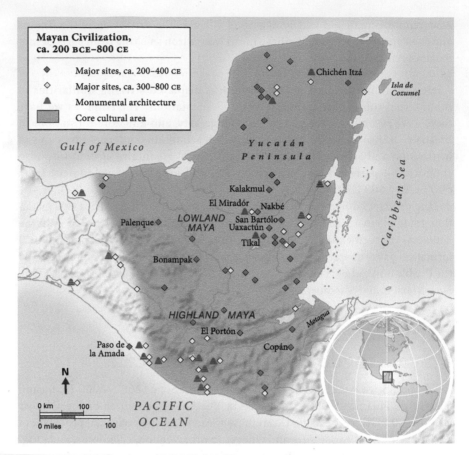

MAP **6.3** **Mayan Civilization, ca. 200 BCE–800 CE.**

north and abruptly to the Pacific coast in the south. The northern region comprised the tip of the Yucatán and consisted of dry and riverless lowlands. Maya culture began in the center and far south and later radiated into the southern mountains and northern lowlands. Underlying the northern lowland areas was a limestone shelf that provided stone for construction. Here, local *chert* (a fine-grained sedimentary silica-rich rock) and flint deposits provided for the fashioning of tools with which to quarry the limestone. The volcanic south was quarried for its lava stone and was also rich in obsidian and jade. Quetzals, birds whose feathers were used for prestigious ornamentation, inhabited this region as well (see Map 6.3).

The people in the Yucatán highlands and lowlands spoke a variety of Mayan dialects. Even though they were exposed early on to Olmec cultural influence, it does not appear that there was much Olmec immigration as Maya culture formed. As the early Mayas became sedentary in the center of the peninsula and along the Pacific, they cut down the rain forest in order to clear fields, drain swamps, and build villages on low stone platforms near water sources. Drainage ditches in fields indicate a beginning intensification of agriculture. By around 1000 BCE, some villages evolved into towns, dominating village clusters around them. Elite lineages under chieftains resided in the towns and controlled the best lands, while more humble lineages in the surrounding villages were on less productive soils. Although society continued to be organized by familial descent, social stratification by wealth began to differentiate the lineages. This stratification is archaeologically recognizable from rich tomb gifts as well as corrective dentistry: Then as now, the wealthy had enhanced means to beautify themselves.

**Early Kingdoms**    As in the agrarian centers of Eurasia, debt dependence was probably the earliest lever of power in the hands of the Mayan chieftains. Poor farmers, it can be assumed, borrowed seeds from rich farmers and during droughts were often unable to return what they had borrowed. Rich farmers had larger families, built bigger homes, and had more domestic workers producing pottery and textiles. They traded manufactured goods for goods not locally available, such as obsidian and jade. Thus, in the period 1000–600 BCE, these wealthy farmers transformed themselves into chieftains, exerting family rule for more or less extended periods over a central town surrounded by satellite villages.

Beginning in the seventh century BCE, chieftains in some agriculturally rich areas increased their wealth so that they could claim to be kings (sing. *ajaw*). Wealthy chieftains were able to surround themselves with military forces through which they made themselves the ultimate arbiters in all town disputes. They began to collect taxes, enlarge their towns into *cities*—that is, centers with craftspeople and merchants who did not practice agriculture—and conquer other villages. During slack times in the agricultural cycle, these kings commanded farmers to construct the first ceremonial monuments—rectangular platforms up to 50 feet in elevation with temples and royal residences on top. Olmec-inspired stone stelae with images of human figures, dressed in Maya-style clothing, were placed around the platforms. Nakbé (700 BCE–150 CE), a city in the north of the central lowlands, was the site of the first temple pyramids on ceremonial platforms. These pyramids were stepped stone structures, as high as 200 feet, with staircases to the temples on top. In those elevated temples, kings conducted their sacrifices in tribute to the gods of the emerging divine pantheon.

A nearby town, El Miradór (600 BCE–150 CE), became a city with surrounding villages about a century after Nakbé. Perhaps favored by better trade connections than Nakbé, El Miradór gradually surpassed its neighbor in size and monumental ambitions. With about 100,000 inhabitants, hundreds of ceremonial and palatial structures on its platforms, and a 216-foot pyramid built around 300 BCE, this Mayan city was the largest early center of what ultimately were more than 4,400 Mayan urban and rural sites. Only the later Tikal (200–600 CE) reached a similar size. El Miradór was explored systematically by archaeologists for the first time only in 1978–1983 and then again beginning in 2003. To their surprise, this site turned out to be as fully Mayan, with its temple pyramids, elite structures, stelae, ball courts, sweat houses, and commoner quarters, as the later and better-known centers of the so-called Early Classic Period (250–600 CE). Maya culture at its peak has to be considered—as it is in this chapter—within the much longer time horizon that began around 600 BCE.

**El Miradór, La Danta Temple, 600 BCE–150 CE.** By height (230 feet), volume, and footprint, this pyramid was the largest of all Maya sacred structures and one of the largest buildings of the premodern world. At present, the site is only partially excavated, and archaeological work is still ongoing. The temple visible atop the pyramid is surmounted by a rooster-like roof comb, once covered by stucco figurines of Maya deities.

Progress made since the 1990s in deciphering the Maya glyphic script has allowed the conclusion that "Mayaland" consisted of some 15–17 fully evolved, dominant kingdoms in the central lowlands during the Early Classic Period, each with a capital and one or more secondary cities, plus countless towns and villages nearby. Marriage alliances among the royal lineages of the capitals and secondary cities served to maintain the cohesion of the kingdom. Rebellions by secondary cities, however, often called the power of the kings into question. Many scholars think that the frequent wars in Mayaland were either intrakingdom rebellions or wars among secondary cities in different kingdoms. The only exception was the direct military competition between the kingdoms of Tikal and Kalakmul, which endured for many centuries.

**Spirituality and Polytheism**   The kings and their royal households lived in palaces adjacent to the temple pyramids. When they ascended the throne, in the tradition of American spirituality, kings often assumed the names of animals or combined them with the names of human-made objects—for example, "Spear-thrower Owl," "Shield Jaguar," and "Smoke Squirrel." Heirs to the throne, usually the eldest son, used the same name but with the suffix II, III, etc. On wall paintings, earthenware vessels, and stelae, kings were recognizable through their elaborate headdresses decorated with quetzal feathers, animal masks, and richly embroidered clothing. When sons were still minors, their mothers assumed the roles of regents. Occasionally, women ruled as queens. After death, kings were buried in pyramids or in separate tombs. Dead kings were assumed to have taken their place among the gods, residing in abodes both above and beneath the earth.

**Polytheism:**
Personification of the forces of nature and performance of rituals and sacrifices to ensure the benevolence of the gods and goddesses.

**Polytheism** had begun to develop on top of traditional spirituality after the emergence of the first villages around 2500 BCE. Gods were the embodiments of forces of nature whose favor had to be curried if rich harvests were to occur. The Mayan kings considered themselves servants of the many animal, nature, star, and war gods which had come to populate the divine pantheon by the time of the Olmecs in the eleventh century BCE and continued to grow during the Maya period. They fulfilled the demands of these gods for sacrifices during daily rituals in the temples atop the pyramids. The main sacrifice was the gift of blood—a heritage from traditional spirituality—which Mayan kings drew from their ear lobes, tongues, and penises. During times of war, captured enemies, from kings to commoners, were also sacrificed. Through their blood, the kings nourished nature and supported the human and divine worlds.

**The Ruling Classes**   Apart from their temple service, kings and leading officials also assembled for the administration of justice, the collection of rents and tributes, commercial exchanges, and diplomatic relations. Many of these functions required expert knowledge of the annual calendar as labor on palaces or pyramids could be required from farmers only during specific times in the agricultural cycle. Other functions, such as military action, required divination to discover the most favorable star constellations under which to proceed. The tracking of these units of times required a specialized group of calendar specialists, mathematicians, and astronomers.

The Mayan calendar was an outgrowth of developments that began sometime after 1000 BCE in Olmec-influenced Paso de la Amada. One calendar was the 260-day, or 9-month, divinatory calendar, which scholars interpret as being related to the human gestation period. A second calendar, based on the solar year of 365 days and important for determining the beginnings of the agricultural seasons, was nearly as old. A third calendar was the Mayan Calendar Round, occurring every 52 years when the divinatory and solar calendars began on the same day. The Mayas believed that this calendar inaugurated cycles of calamitous as well as fortuitous times. The fourth calendar in use among the Mayas was the Long Count Calendar, which counted the days elapsed since the mythical origin of the universe (corresponding to August 11, 3114 BCE, in the Gregorian calendar). A sophisticated mathematics, based on a *vigesimal* system of numbers (base 20, unlike our modern base-10 system), undergirded the calculations necessary for the coordination of these four calendars.

Other occupations of the royal family and leading courtiers consisted of daily processions and feasts during which copious amounts of cacao, spiced with chili, vanilla, and honey, were consumed. Alternatively, the elite consumed chocolate wafers, forerunners of our modern chocolate bars, which were also used as easily transportable nourishment on journeys. Finally, the court attended ball games in stadiums, which formed part of the temple-palace grounds. As in the kingdoms of Eurasia, but without evidence of any influence, in Maya kingdoms the occupations and functions of the ruling class were ritualized, refined pastimes far beyond the reach of common farmers and craftspeople. A stratified social hierarchy typified the Maya kingdoms (see "Patterns Up Close").

**The Commoners** The commoners, whose taxes supported the royal courts, lived in housing compounds of a few thatched huts or clusters of huts erected around courtyards on stone platforms, which allowed them to be above the floodwaters during the rainy season. In these houses, women were in charge of cooking, weaving, pottery making, the growing of garden vegetables and fruits, and the rearing of domestic animals (including dogs, turkeys, and pigeons). Garden fruits included avocado, guava, papaya, vanilla, and pineapple. Within the household, women and men shared the crafts of tool making, fabricating tools from chert, bone, and wood. In larger Maya kingdoms some households seem to have specialized more than others in tool manufacturing and weaving, with both women and men participating.

Men were in charge of growing corn in fields which were cut into the rain forest through slash-and-burn techniques. Fields near rivers and in swamps were "raised fields" (Spanish *chinampas*), rectangular islands on which the mud from adjacent canals had been heaped. The main agricultural implement was the digging stick (Mayan *kool* [kuhl]), with which farmers loosened the soil and dropped corn kernels into a hole. Slopes along river valleys were terraced in order to retain rain or irrigation water. Cotton, cacao, and tobacco fields formed special plantations because of either special soil preparation or intensive labor needs. Hunting and fishing with bow and arrow, blowguns, and harpoons, skills inherited from forager times, remained important occupations among both royals and commoners.

The hard agricultural labor of the commoners produced an agricultural surplus, which supported ruling dynastic families as well as craftspeople in the cities. Craftspeople worked for the construction and maintenance of royal palaces, creating monuments, wall paintings, pottery, and inscriptions on stone pillars or stelae.

**Mayan Writing**   Excavations in El Portón and San Bartolo in the early 2000s suggest that Mayan writing might have begun as early as 400–300 BCE. These early texts—although similar in appearance to the fully evolved script of the later centuries—still await decipherment. Their age raises the important question among Maya specialists of whether the notion of the late Olmecs having developed writing first can still be maintained. The Mayas might very likely have been the originators.

Glyphic script: The Maya developed a script of some 800 images. Some are pictograms standing for words; others are syllables to be combined with other syllables to form words.

Mayan writing is a **glyphic** as well as a syllabic script, numbering some 800 signs. It is structurally similar to Sumerian cuneiform and Egyptian hieroglyphics. The glyphic part consists of *pictograms*, one-word images of the most essential features of what is to be depicted (for example, the glyph for a human being would be a stick figure with body, legs, arms, and a head). Glyphs as syllables consist of one, two, or three signs, which stand for the combination of a consonant and a vowel. Combinations of syllabic glyphs, or *syllabaries*, are pronounced as a series of syllables. Given the mixture of pictograms and syllabaries, which is potentially immense, the complexity of Mayan writing appeared for a long time to be an insuperable obstacle to any effort at deciphering.

A breakthrough came only in the 1960s and 1970s when scholars successfully interpreted a number of stelae monuments for kings recording the dates of their birth, accession to the throne, and death. First, scholars realized that Mayan writing had an important syllabic component; then, the Russian-born American architect and Maya specialist Tatiana Proskouriakoff discovered that the inscriptions on many royal stelae contained information on dynastic dates and events. The final breakthrough came during a conference at the Maya site of Palenque in 1973 when participants recognized the syllables *k'inchi* as referring to the Mayan sun god as well as individual kings. As first in Mesopotamia and then in many other places, kings invoked patron gods that symbolized forces in nature and thereby became founders of polytheism, as mentioned above. In one inspirational afternoon, a working group consisting of the art historian and epigrapher Linda Schele, the linguist Floyd Lounsbury, and the undergraduate Peter Mathews deciphered the king list of Palenque, containing eight rulers. Since then, scholars have assembled a dictionary of as many as 1,000 words, and it has become possible to embark on a systematic chronicling of the dynasties of Maya kingdoms.

**The Crisis of the Kingdoms**   Spectacular building activities characterized Mayaland during the Late Classic Period (ca. 400–600 CE). Ruling classes must have grown to considerable sizes, and it is possible that farmers in some kingdoms were no longer willing to produce food staples as well as provide labor for the pyramid temples and palaces. Destruction identified in some archaeological sites could be interpreted as the result of revolts. In other places, overexploitation of the soil, loss of topsoil on terraces, or salinization of lowland fields as the result of neglected drainage might have increased the imbalance between the peasants and ruling classes. Frequent wars among the kings might have reduced the size of the ruling class, but their wars clearly also had negative consequences for the farmers.

"On July 7, 749, Ruler 4, king of Piedras Negras, completed his first k'atun [7,200-day period] in reign, witnessed by Yo'pat B'ahlam II, king of Yaxchilán. Two days later, on July 29, Ruler 4 performed the descending Macaw dance. That night, he drank fermented cacao."

—Panel 3 Inscription, Piedras Negras

The interplay between the ruling class, farmers, and the environment produced a crisis beginning in the late 500s CE and extending through the mid-600s CE, leading to the collapse of many older Mayan kingdoms and endangering the survival of the strongest newer ones in the southern lowlands. When the crisis ended, the political weight of Maya power shifted to the northern lowlands of the Yucatán Peninsula.

## The Kingdom of Teotihuacán in the Mexican Basin

The subtropical climate of Yucatán extended northward into the highlands, in which the Mexican Basin was the largest agricultural region. Although the high elevation did not allow for the full breadth of Mayan agriculture, the alluvial soil and water from the surrounding mountains supported a productive agriculture of beans, squash, and corn. The northern part of the basin developed a rich village life later than the south, but its closeness to obsidian quarries gave these villages commercial advantages. Militarily and economically, the town of Teotihuacán in the north caught up to the south around the early 100s CE and developed into a city-state that became politically and culturally dominant across all of Mesoamerica.

**The Mexican Basin** The Mexican Basin is a large, 7,400-foot-high bowl without river outlets in southern Mexico. In the center of the bowl was Lake Texcoco [tes-CO-co], nourished by rivers flowing down from 15,000-foot-high mountain chains on the eastern and western sides. As in Mayaland, the basin enjoyed a rainy season from May to September. River water, channeled through irrigation canals to terraces and the flatlands around the central lake, as well as numerous bays, supported a moderately productive agriculture.

During the period of village expansion (1200–600 BCE), many of the slopes surrounding this bowl were forested. There was plenty of firewood and timber for construction, as well as abundant wildlife for the hunt. Fish in the freshwater bays of the lake were another important food source. Clay deposits in the flatlands and obsidian quarries on the slopes of the still active volcanoes in the northeastern mountains provided resources for the manufacture of ceramics, tools, and weapons. However, the high elevation and temperature differences between winter and summer did not allow for cultivation of the cotton, cacao, vanilla, and tropical fruits which enriched lowland Maya agriculture. These latter products had to be acquired by trade.

The principal plant fiber for the weaving of clothes came from the maguey [ma-GAY] plant, a large, deep-rooted, agave-like cactus that could grow in poor soil and did not need much water. The fiber was obtained from scraping the sweet-tasting flesh off the interior of the long, stalk-like leaves. The flesh contained a juice which, in its fermented state, was consumed as an alcoholic drink called *pulque* [Spanish, PULL-kay; Nahuatl, *octli*]. If people wished to manufacture

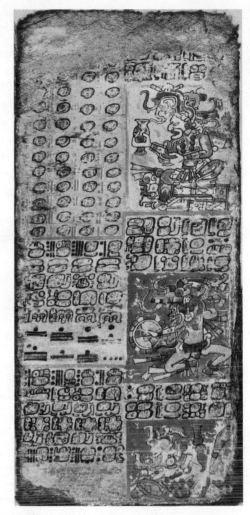

**Mayan Glyphs.** Beginning in the fourth century BCE, scribes in the Maya kingdoms developed a written language composed of pictograms and syllables, eventually numbering about 800 signs. This language allowed communication among educated people in the different Maya kingdoms who spoke often mutually unintelligible local languages. Because of the double meaning of each glyph as pictogram and syllable, it took most of the twentieth century for scholars to decipher the Mayan language. The example shown here is from the Dresden Codex.

# The Mayan Ball Game

One of the most remarkable features in Mesoamerica was the team ball game. Although it shares its ancient age with similar games in China, the Persian Middle East, and the Greek and Roman Mediterranean, only in Mesoamerica was it a game with formal rules, played in stadiums constructed specifically for this purpose. In Mesoamerica, archaeologists in 1985 discovered the oldest stadium to date, from 1400 BCE, in the ruins of Paso de la Amada, a chiefdom town with surrounding villages in the far southeast of today's Mexico. Adjacent to the palace of the chief, this ball court measures 260 by 23 feet, with two 7-foot-high spectator platforms on both long sides. Later on, during the Maya period, these platforms usually rose theater-style on both sides, for better viewing from farther away. Given the proximity of the ball court to the chief's residence, it is possible that other chiefdoms in the area engaged in what we would call today "league tournaments."

The ball was made of solid rubber, from a gum- or latex-producing tree growing in the area of Paso. Balls were around 2 feet or more in diameter and weighed 8 pounds. Given these

**The Mayan Ball Game.** Note the strong body protection around the midsection of the players as well as the elaborate headdresses, symbolizing animals.

clothes from cotton or acquire cacao, vanilla, jade, or quetzal feathers, they had to trade their obsidian. Commercial exchange was a necessary ingredient in the period of village expansion and played a major part in the subsequent pattern of kingdom formation.

**Teotihuacán**   In a wide valley to the northeast of Lake Texcoco, traversed by the San Juan River and endowed with rich alluvial soil, villagers in the early centuries of the Common Era dug a large canal system with raised fields similar to those of the Maya. Around 100 BCE, villages around this canal network began to cluster, eventually forming the city of Teotihuacán. When the transition from chieftains to kings and chiefly dynasties occurred is impossible to determine on the basis of the present archaeological record. The iconic writing system, less developed than that of the Mayas and lacking syllabic elements, does not allow for identification of any rulers or lineages. Teotihuacán was a city-state with an anonymous dynasty, centered in a city and surrounded by villages. In its physical appearance it was even more imposing than most of the Maya kingdoms (see Map 6.4).

In the first century CE, the rulers of Teotihuacán began spectacular building projects. They laid out an urban grid along a north–south axis, dubbed the

dimensions, players often wore protective gear around their hips and helmets on their heads, as shown in murals and on ceramics.

Under the Maya, who called the game *pitz* and built about 1,500 courts, the rules became more formalized. A basic rule was that the ball had to be hit with the hip only and had to remain aloft. But variations are also known in which players struck the ball with forearms, bats, or hand stones. The size of a team extended from one to seven players. The team that lost was the one that dropped the ball most often.

The significance of the Mayan ball game fits into the larger picture of agrarian–urban society and its chiefdom and kingdom patterns when polytheism with its innumerable rituals and sacrificial practices assumed elaborate proportions. Although the archaeological record is debatable, it appears that ball games took place during chiefly or royal festivities and fertility rituals, and perhaps also human sacrifices. The apparent but also disputed role of some players as human sacrifices on a number of murals was a late Mayan phenomenon. Today, in scientific–industrial society, these roots of "games" in past rituals, processions, and reenactments of divine events are largely forgotten. Instead, sports have their own modern rituals, such as flag waving, parading, tailgating, and hooliganism. Whether religious or secular, rituals are permanent fixtures that follow their own patterns, parallel to those of society at large.

## Questions

- How did the ball game serve as a microcosm for larger patterns in Mayan society?
- What function could the ball game have played in relations among the various Mayan chiefdoms?

"Avenue of the Dead" by archaeologists, which included two densely constructed city quarters of some 2,200 housing units. Each unit housed a patrilineal clan of 60–100 members. Near the central avenue, closely packed and plastered adobe houses were divided by alleyways. Some 600 houses have the appearance of workshops, primarily for the making of tools from the gray and green obsidian mined near Teotihuacán. The workshops indicate a degree of nonagricultural crafts specialization, which one would expect from a city. Farther away, houses and fields were interspersed. Canals, reservoirs, and an extensive drainage system facilitated the transportation of food, the provision of drinking water, and the elimination of waste. By around 300 CE, Teotihuacán had grown to as many as 100,000 inhabitants. It was a metropolis easily comparable to Rome, Ctesiphon, and Alexandria in the Roman Mediterranean and Persian Middle East; Pataliputra in Gupta India; and Chang'an in Han China.

An aerial view of Teotihuacán's ruins conveys the vast scale on which the temple pyramids, palaces, markets, and city quarters were built. The Temples of the Moon and the Sun, built at the northern end of the city, represent the earliest structures. They were ceremonial centers which attracted pilgrims from everywhere in the Mexican Basin and beyond. Archaeologists interpret the Temple of the Sun as a construction on top of a cave symbolizing the entrance to the nether

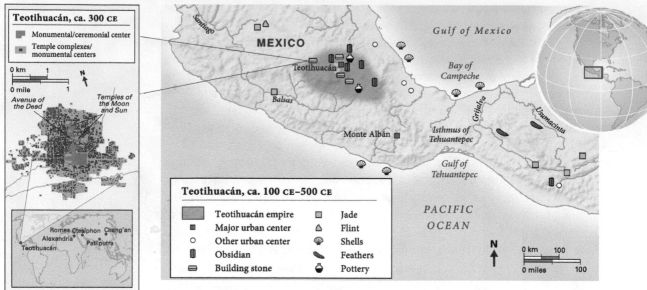

MAP 6.4 **Teotihuacán, ca. 100 CE–500 CE.**

world. In the third century CE, the temple of the god of the feathered serpent (Nahuatl *Quetzalcoatl* [ket-sal-COA]) followed, probably built in honor of the then reigning dynasty. The founding king sacrificed some 260 humans, probably war captives, to garner the good will of the god. After what appears to have been an internal uprising and change in leadership in the 400s CE, the new rulers destroyed the temple's facade and erected an attachment (Spanish *adosada*) in front of it. Colorful wall paintings and pottery, depicting rulers, priests, gods, and mythical figures in processions, rituals, and dances, still survive, attesting to a highly developed aesthetic culture. Today, after a century of intermittent excavations, much has been learned about the city's architecture, but little is yet known about its rulers and inhabitants.

**The Decline of the City**    As in the case of the Maya kingdoms, the balance among the peasantry, urban inhabitants, dynasties, and construction programs was not always easy to maintain. Hints at an internal upheaval in the 400s CE point to the balance being lost for a first time during Teotihuacán's existence. Another such upheaval occurred in the late 500s CE, to judge from fires and destructions along the Avenue of the Dead, possibly in the course of a popular uprising against the rulers. Thereafter, the population of the central city quarters declined rapidly, although the outlying quarters continued to exist, reverting back to the village level as farming communities for centuries to come. The mid-500s CE saw prolonged periods of cooler weather and droughts and were generally a more difficult time for farming in the Americas. As we shall see in Chapter 15, in contrast to the agriculturally richer Maya kingdoms, the less endowed Mexican Basin found a return to urbanism and dynastic states more difficult.

At its height, Teotihuacán exerted a commercial, cultural, and perhaps even political influence considerably greater than the Maya kingdoms. Its trade reached deep into Mayaland and beyond, to the Isthmus of Panama. Teotihuacán exchanged its obsidian for cotton, rubber, cacao, jade, and quetzal feathers from the subtropics. Its gods, especially the deity of the feathered serpent, were sacrificed to everywhere in Mesoamerica. Similarly, Teotihuacán was instrumental in spreading the so-called *talud-tablero* architectural style (sets of inward-sloping platforms, surmounted by temples) from the Basin of Mexico to the Yucatán Peninsula. In the later 300s CE and throughout the 400s CE, Maya rulers of Tikal, Uaxactún [wa-shac-TOON], and other kingdoms claimed descent from rulers of Teotihuacán, evidently seeking to benefit from the city's prestige as a ceremonial center.

# The Andes: Moche and Nazca

In Andean South America, a pattern of chiefdom formation, wherein chieftains controlled urban ceremonial centers and surrounding villages, evolved between 3000 and 2000 BCE, a millennium earlier than in Mesoamerica. Given the absence of large plains and the enormous differences in elevation within short distances, however, relatively small chiefdoms remained the dominant social formation in the Andes. Still, around 1000–200 BCE, a major ceremonial center like Chavín de Huántar (north of present day Lima) was a town with fewer than 5,000 inhabitants, even though it was a pilgrimage site for most of the Andes. Chavín's successors, the chiefdoms of Moche and Nazca, although somewhat larger, remained within the chiefdom pattern during the period 600 BCE–600 CE.

## The Moche in Northern Peru

The Moche Valley was the place of the two largest ceremonial centers in the Andes, the Temple Pyramids of the Sun and the Moon. The power of its main chiefdom must have been impressive, since large numbers of farmers had to be mobilized for the construction of these pyramids. But it remained a federation of village chiefdoms clustered around an urbanized temple center with a dominant chiefly lineage.

**Moche Origins** The Moche Valley was at the center of nine coastal valleys in what is today northern Peru. It had a subtropical climate south of the equator with moderately wet winters from April to November and dry summers from December to March. It was based on an irrigated agriculture of corn, pulses, cotton, and potatoes; llamas and alpacas from the highlands were domesticated for wool and light transportation. Here, the earliest evidence of the emergence of the Moche chiefdoms (100–750 CE) is the tomb of the "Lord of Sipán," dated to 50 CE. The tomb contained the chief's mummy, clad in warrior clothing and richly decorated with gold and silver necklaces, nose rings, earrings, helmets, and bracelets. Eight people were buried with him, including his wife, two other women (perhaps concubines),

**Teotihuacán, Temple of the Feathered Serpent God Quetzalcóatl.** This sculpture of a serpent's head with its exposed, menacing fangs and the collar made of feathers is one of many along the front wall of this temple. The hybrid deity [quetzal bird and snake (*cóatl*)] bridged the fertile Earth and the planet Venus, bringer of rain in the summer.

**Moche Terra-Cotta Portrait Vessel with Handle, ca. 100–800 CE.** Archaeologists assume that the vessel shows a chief. Other types of Moche vessels show deities, animals, ritual objects, sexual acts (for education?), domestic objects, and crafts activities. Potters often used stone molds for making their wares. Among the Andes peoples, the Moche potters were among the most imaginative and versatile.

a military officer, a watchman, a banner holder, a child, and a dog. This chieftain was wealthy and powerful indeed.

**A Federated Chiefdom**   Half a century later, Moche chieftains began the construction of the two Temple Pyramids of the Sun and the Moon, huge stepped structures made of adobe bricks. Markers on the bricks indicate the participation of about 100 village teams in the construction, which lasted intermittently for centuries. The platforms contain the burial places of Moche chieftains and priests and the remains of human sacrifices brought during ceremonies and rituals. At the feet of the two temples was a city that included administrative offices and workshops. Lesser chieftain lineages ruled in the more remote valleys. Altogether the chiefdoms formed a loose federation around a main ceremonial center and pilgrimage place.

None of the participating villages appears to have grown beyond the moderately large spaces at the mouth of valleys, and it seems that they coexisted peacefully for the most part. When the generally cooler and drier climate of the sixth century CE arrived, it had a greater negative impact on the agriculture of the central chiefdom in Moche, closer to the coast and more remote from the river waters, than on the chiefdoms upstream in the adjacent smaller valleys. In the Moche Valley with its two huge temples the balance between chiefly elites and farmers was more difficult to maintain than in the farther valleys with smaller elites and comparatively larger peasantries. Eventually, in the early 600s CE, the Moche elite dissolved, while smaller elites in other valleys carried on and eventually disappeared also, sometime around 750 CE (see Map 6.5).

## Paracas and the Nazca in Southern Peru

Southern Peru was much drier, and its agrarian population density lagged behind that of the north. The chiefdoms were correspondingly more modest. Nevertheless, Paracas [pa-RA-cas] represents one of the earliest burial places for mummies in the world, and Nazca offers the most elaborate petroglyphs of the Americas. The two possess, therefore, considerable cultural significance.

**Paracas Chiefs**   Desert conditions on the southern Peruvian coast and full dependence on runoff water from Andean snowmelt between January and March after the Andean winter required more elaborate irrigation works than on the northern coast. The patterns of social formation from foraging to villages and chiefdoms with ceremonial centers were correspondingly slower and more modest. Shamans and chiefs on the Paracas peninsula and the Ica valley set the pattern in motion when they unified a number of hamlets. Subsequently, other Paracas chiefdoms appeared in neighboring valleys, forming a loose confederation (750 BCE–1 CE).

A necropolis on the peninsula contained hundreds of mummies of chieftains, wrapped in the colorful, high-quality wool and cotton mantles still characteristic of southern Peru today. It was primarily through the icons woven into the mantles and painted on pottery that modern scholars identified the Paracas chiefs. These icons included figures—shamanic ancestors or early agricultural, polytheistic

MAP 6.5 **Andean Centers, 600 BCE–600 CE.**

deities—holding weapons, plants, or skulls. Other icons were felines, birds, or whales, often with human-like features reminiscent of Paleolithic cave paintings in other parts of the world. Although contemporary with the Maya kingdoms in Mesoamerica, the Paracas chiefdoms in the Andes were culturally still compact.

**The Nazca Ceremonial Center**   The transition from pottery painted after firing to predecorated or slipware ceramics defines the shift from the Paracas to the Nazca chiefdoms (1–650 CE). Nazca chiefs built ceremonial centers, not the monumental freestanding ones as on the northern Peruvian coast but more modest adobe structures, which actually covered preexisting mounds. Cahuachi [ca-wooh-WAH-chee], the main pilgrimage center, contained 40 such structures, assumed to represent the contributing chiefdoms.

During the extended cold weather and drought periods of the sixth century CE, when a number of rivers dried out, Nazca chiefs mobilized the villagers in the valleys for the construction of an extensive tunnel network for irrigation. Workers tapped underground water in the mountains and guided it onto the slopes of the valleys and into reservoirs. These highly sophisticated constructions, with intermittent shafts and manholes for cleaning and repair, were built so sturdily that

**Nazca Lines: A Spider.** These lines can only be seen from the air—perhaps by a sky god?

**Geoglyphs:** Long geometric lines and figures as well as outlines of animals formed in the desert by removing darker stones and exposing the lighter sand underneath.

many of them are still in operation today. Called *puquios* [Quechua, POO-kyos], they are reminiscent of the much later *qanat* [Arabic, ka-NAHT] structures of Islamic Iran and Morocco. In the agrarian age, chiefdoms could be technologically just as innovative as kingdoms and empires.

**The Nazca Geoglyphs**   Another Nazca innovation was the so-called Nazca **geoglyphs**, large geometric and animal figures laid out in the dry highlands and on the valley slopes of the chiefdoms. Villagers constructed straight and zigzag lines, triangles and trapezoids, as well as images of a monkey, spider, whale, and several birds with astounding precision by removing dark-colored rocks and exposing the lighter sand underneath. These geoglyphs, totaling some 300, are unique to the Andes, and the closest parallel was not created until nearly a millennium later when the Incas arranged sacred objects (Quechua, *huacas*) outside their capital, Cuzco, in straight lines.

There are, however, vague parallels with a considerable number of undated later geoglyphs in the Great Basin and other western regions of North America. Native Americans under the leadership of shamans used these later geoglyphs during rituals in which they evoked honored figures, animals, and events of the mythical past. Processual archaeologists (archaeologists applying concepts of cultural evolutionism) relate the Nazca symbols to the abstract Paleolithic geometric cave symbols found in Africa, Europe, and Australia (see Chapter 1). But since the purpose of these symbols is also unknown, a fully convincing theory is still elusive. (See "Against the Grain: Nazca Lines and Speculation.")

Eventually, the Nazca came under the influence of the highland state of Wari, a later city-state in the Andes (see Chapter 15). This state expanded its political and cultural influence toward the southern Peruvian coast in the first half of the 700s CE and gradually gave the Nazca chiefdoms a new identity.

## Putting It All Together

In the period 600 BCE–600 CE, agriculture and life in villages became nearly universal in the world. Only Australia remained outside this development from foraging to agrarian settlement. Of course, remnants of foraging societies survived, notably in sub-Saharan Africa and even more so in the Americas. But it is nevertheless striking that humans on the latter two continents developed in the same direction as those in Eurasia toward cities, kingdoms, and long-distance luxury trade.

Agrarian-based urban culture, however, was a fragile achievement in Eurasia and even more so in sub-Saharan Africa, Mesoamerica, and the Andes. Irregularities of the weather and, in the latter regions, the slow improvement of food plant productivity (as revealed by plant archaeologists) meant that agriculture was a tenuous enterprise. Corn, especially, evolved only slowly toward a greater cob length and was still quite short during the Maya period. Only by the time of the Aztecs, selective breeding had produced corn of modern proportions. As a rule, dynastic cities regularly outstripped the natural resources of their local environments, as was the case in Meroë, Aksum, the Maya cities, and Teotihuacán. But once the possibility of urbanization had arrived, this option was usually not lost again and sooner or later new city-based states arose.

As we have seen in this chapter, the primary dynastic urban achievements were monumental architecture, sophisticated metal and textile craftsmanship, and, in some cases, forms of intellectual expression. Typical examples covered in this chapter were the remarkably similar monumental temple pyramids and stelae of the kings in northeastern sub-Saharan Africa, Mesoamerica, and the Andes. Metal and textile craftsmanship, of course, had deep village roots on both sides of the Atlantic. Gold, silver, copper, and bronze jewelry was often exquisite, and the iron manufacturing in African villages was remarkably developed. In cities these crafts became the refined products of specialized workers who did not participate in farming.

Similarly, precocious intellectual achievements appeared both in nomadic contexts (complementary to agriculture), as witnessed by the Borana calendar of the Kushite nomads in Kenya, and in small-town agricultural chiefdoms, as seen in the giant geometric lines and animal outlines created in the desert landscape by the Nazca of Peru. By comparison, the intellectual pursuits in royal cities were on a much larger scale. Here, the Mayas took the prize with their complex calendar and script, as well as their elaborate divine pantheon and cosmogony.

Altogether, evolving largely on their own, both sub-Saharan Africa and the Americas made long strides in the period 600 BCE–600 CE toward expressing the same depth of humanity which was already on display in Eurasia. They did not yet have empires or possess the literary breadth that favored the rise of the visionaries of transcendence, hallmarks of the Middle East, India, and China during 600 BCE–600 CE. But their more compact cultures were not lacking in any of the overall patterns that characterized Eurasia.

▶ For additional resources, including maps, primary sources, visuals, and quizzes, please go to www.oup.com/us/vonsivers. Please see the Further Resources section at the back of the book for additional readings and suggested websites.

## Against the Grain

# Nazca Lines and Speculation

Peruvian archaeologist Toribio Mejia Xesspe was the first scholar to describe the Nazca geoglyphs, which he viewed in 1927 from adjacent hills. The true extent of the glyphs and its many figures, however, became known only once seen from the air. The pioneer of the aerial mapping of the site was Paul Kosok, an American historian interested in ancient irrigation systems who crisscrossed the area by plane during the 1940s. Further mapping was carried out by his assistant, Maria Reiche, a trained mathematician from Germany interned during World War II in Peru. Reiche devoted her life to recording the Nazca lines and protecting them from encroachment by road builders and squatters.

Based on the discovery that a number of lines converged at the winter and summer solstices, Reiche published her theory that the Nazca geoglyphs were elements of a complex astronomical calendar and observatory, and the animal figures represented constellations. This theory did not find much support among later scholars, who demonstrated that only 20 percent of the glyphs had an astronomical significance. Reiche's theory, however, inspired popular writers to engage in frequently outlandish speculation about the site—speculation that has only increased as the centenary of the discovery approaches. For example, some have proposed that extraterrestrials created landing pads among the allegedly primitive Nazca people (Erich von Däniken, 1970 and 1972); others suggested that the Nazca were technically sophisticated people who used hot air balloons to survey the accuracy of their creations (Jim Woodman and Julian Nott, 1977). Still others have speculated that the Nazca lines were a version of GPS coordinates with which ancient civilizations encoded the locations of their sacred sites (Carl Munck, 2005); energy beams locating the earth in space (Alla Belocon, 2007); magnetic strips that in the distant past allowed a group of "Gliptolitic" earthlings to lift off to a space voyage (Kathleen Doore, 2008); or elements of an "exploded planet cult" among the Nazca (Allan Alford, 2000). Like many seemingly impossible large-scale works of engineering or art, the Nazca lines have proven particularly attractive to those who prefer outlandish speculation to evidence-based inquiry.

- Is it important to be aware of purely speculative theories of world history? For what reasons?

- What are some other feats of ancient engineering, architecture, or craft that seem to inspire speculative (or even fantastic) theories? Do historians have a particular responsibility to engage with or dispute "fringe" theories?

# Thinking Through Patterns

▶ **How does comparing and contrasting sub-Saharan Africa with the Americas during 600 BCE–600 CE help in understanding the agrarian–urban patterns of social and political development across the world?**

Innovations in world history usually originated in one specific place and then radiated outward to new populations through interactions among different peoples. Through adaptation, the new populations incorporated innovations into their own cultures. Adaptation was never slavish imitation; it was always a creative process of shaping something from a different culture to the new culture's needs and circumstances. Sub-Saharan Africa and the Americas were partially or entirely limited to their own internal patterns of innovation, given their relative or absolute isolation from Eurasia. Encountering the same experiences and challenges as humans in Eurasia, albeit somewhat later, their responses were remarkably comparable. Thus, the history of the world was not merely the history of peoples coming into more and more intensive contact with each other. It was also the history of peoples experiencing similar challenges without transcontinental interaction.

Agrarian sub-Saharan Africa during 600 BCE–600 CE is an example where interaction with the Middle East—as well as, in some periods, its absence—formed the background for comparable processes of economic, social, and political developments. The middle Nile valley and the highlands of Ethiopia gave rise to the plow-based agrarian kingdoms of Meroë and Aksum, both receiving their original plows and grain from the Middle East and maintaining a lively trade for luxury goods with that region. By contrast, the West African inland Niger delta grew into the urbanized chiefdom of Jenné-jeno without recognizable external interactions. Through interaction and adaptation, forms of farming as well as iron smelting (the latter perhaps received from the Middle East) traveled south in sub-Saharan Africa, together with the Bantu expansion.

▶ **Where did chiefdoms, cities, and kingdoms arise in sub-Saharan Africa and why? On which forms of agriculture, urbanization, and trade were they based?**

▶ **Which areas in the Americas saw the development of a corn- and potato-based agriculture that did not depend on the plow, the wheel, and ironmaking?**

Three regions in the Americas were favorable for the development of densely settled villages, some of which subsequently evolved into cities and kingdoms: Yucatán with its Maya kingdoms, the Mexican Basin with the city-state of Teotihuacán, and Peru with the Moche and Nazca chiefdoms. The Maya kingdoms were economically and culturally the most differentiated polities—and the only ones to record the histories of their kings in writing on stelae and other monuments. Highly productive farming took place on riverbanks or hill terraces, with a surplus that supported the construction of elaborate temple pyramids and structures containing painted ceramics and wall paintings.

# Patterns of Evidence: Sources for Chapter 6

## SOURCE 6.1

## Relief sculpture from Meroë, Sudan

**ca. 600–300 BCE**

The kings of Meroë, successors of the Nubia-descended twenty-fifth dynasty of Egypt, established their capital on the Middle Nile about 100 miles north of Khartoum, Sudan. At its height, the city was home to more than 20,000 people. Its surviving buildings have qualified it as a UNESCO World Heritage Site.

▶ **Working with Sources**

1. How does the relief reflect the ongoing influence of ancient Egyptian iconography and symbolism?

2. What was the extent of the empire around Meroë, and what was the source of its influence?

## SOURCE 6.2

# Cosmas Indicopleustes (Cosmas the India-Voyager), *Christian Topography*

### ca. 550 CE

This remarkable account of a merchant's travels throughout Eastern Africa, the Arabian Peninsula, and India resulted from the singular obsession of a monk in retirement. Determined to prove that a proper understanding of earth's geography would confirm God's creation—and that the earth was a flat, oblong table surrounded by the ocean—the monk Cosmas reflected back on his extensive voyages, which had probably been undertaken to further a spice-import business. Cosmas commented on the trading practices of the Aksumites and on their wealthy culture, providing one of the few available outsider glimpses of Aksum.

The region that produces frankincense is situated at the projecting parts of Ethiopia, and lies inland, but is washed by the ocean on the other side. Hence the inhabitants of Barbaria, being near at hand, go up into the interior and, engaging in traffic with the natives, bring back from them many kinds of spices, frankincense, cassia, calamus, and many other articles of merchandise, which they afterwards send by sea to Agau, to the country of the Homerites [Yemen], to Further India, and to Persia.

This very fact you will find mentioned in the Book of Kings, where it is recorded that the Queen of Sheba, that is, of the Homerite country, whom afterwards our Lord in the Gospels calls the Queen of the South, brought to Solomon spices from this very Barbaria, which lay near Sheba on the other side of the sea, together with bars of ebony, and apes and gold from Ethiopia which, though separated from Sheba by the Arabian Gulf, lay in its vicinity. We can see again from the words of the Lord that he calls these places the ends of the earth, saying: *The Queen of the South shall rise up in judgment with this generation and shall condemn it, for she came from the ends of the earth to hear the wisdom of Solomon* (Matthew 12:42). For the Homerites are not far distant from Barbaria, as the sea which lies between them can be crossed in a couple of days, and then beyond Barbaria is the ocean, which is there called Zingion. The country known as that of Sasu is itself near the ocean, just as the ocean is near the frankincense country, in which there are many gold mines.

The King of the Aksumites, accordingly, every other year, through the governor of Agau, sends thither special agents to bargain for the gold, and these are accompanied by many other traders—upwards, say, of five hundred—bound on the same errand

Source: Cosmas Indicopleustes, *Christianike Topographia*, Book 3, trans. and ed. Christopher Haas, trans., Villanova University; available online: http://www29.homepage.villanova.edu/christopher.haas/cosmas_indicopleustes.htm.

as themselves. They take along with them to the mining district oxen, lumps of salt, and iron, and when they reach its neighborhood they make a halt at a certain spot and form an encampment, which they fence round with a great hedge of thorns. Within this they live, and having slaughtered the oxen, cut them in pieces, and lay the pieces on the top of the thorns, along with the lumps of salt and the iron. Then come the natives bringing gold in nuggets like peas, called *tancharas,* and lay one or two or more of these upon what pleases them— the pieces of flesh or the salt or the iron, and then they retire to some distance off. Then the owner of the meat approaches, and if he is satisfied he takes the gold away, and upon seeing this, its owner comes and takes the flesh or the salt or the iron. If, however, he is not satisfied, he leaves the gold. When the native, seeing that he has not taken it comes and either puts down more gold, or takes up what he had laid down, and goes away.

Such is the mode in which business is transacted with the people of that country, because their language is different and interpreters are hardly to be found. The time they stay in that country is five days more or less, according as the natives more or less readily coming forward buy up all their wares. On the journey homeward they all agree to travel well-armed, since some of the tribes through whose country they must pass might threaten to attack them from a desire to rob them of their gold. The space of six months is taken up with this trading expedition, including both the going and the returning. In going they march very slowly, chiefly because of the cattle, but in returning they quicken their pace lest on the way they should be overtaken by winter and its rains.

For the sources of the river Nile lie somewhere in these parts, and in winter, on account of the heavy rains, the numerous rivers which they generate obstruct the path of the traveler. The people there have their winter at the time we have our summer. It begins in the month *Epiphi* of the Egyptians and continues till *Thoth,* and during the three months the rain falls in torrents, and makes a multitude of rivers all of which flow into the Nile.

▶ **Working with Sources**

1. **How does Cosmas characterize the Aksumites, and to what other peoples does he compare them?**

2. **How and why does Cosmas allude to Old and New Testament accounts in his analysis of cultures adjoining the Red Sea?**

## SOURCE 6.3

# The market at Jenné-jeno, Mali

**founded ca. third century BCE**

After extensive archaeological work was done at the site of Jenné-jeno in the 1980s, researchers concluded that the city was the oldest known in sub-Saharan Africa, and that it flourished throughout the first millennium CE. It is situated on a vast low mound at the heart of the Niger Inland Delta. The site was gradually abandoned in favor of Timbuktu during the Middle Ages.

▶ **Working with Sources**

1. How did the founders of Jenné-jeno capitalize on existing trade networks in western Africa, and what geographic factors were involved?

2. Examining this recent photo of Jenné-jeno, what does it say about the continuity of patterns of trade and urbanism in West Africa?

## SOURCE 6.4

# Limestone panel from a Mayan temple, Palenque

### ca. 490 CE

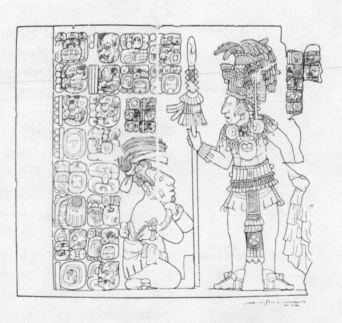

This panel from a temple in the Mayan city of Palenque contains glyphs (forming a caption) and two figures. A captive kneels before a standing warrior who holds a flint spear and wears a war headdress. The large text to the left records an event at Palenque that occurred in 490. The small text above the kneeling figure gives the name of a captive.

▶ **Working with Sources**

1. What are the likely circumstances surrounding the creation of this image?

2. What were the connections between Mayan temples and warfare?

---

Source: (6.3, top) Photo by Rob Dougall. (6.4, bottom) The Linda Schele Drawings Collection, http://research. famsi.org/schele_list.php?_allSearch=118.

# Chapter 7 550 BCE–600 CE

# Persia, Greece, and Rome

PERSIA, GREECE, AND ROME

Mediterranean Sea

At one of his banquets after vanquishing the Achaemenid [a-KEE-ma-nid] Persian Empire in 330 BCE, the world conqueror Alexander the Great (r. 336–323 BCE) had a violent confrontation with one of his leading commanders, Cleitus. Flatterers at the banquet compared Alexander to the gods, and Alexander himself boasted that his conquests were far superior to those of his father, Philip. Cleitus, older than Alexander and an officer in Philip's army who had been engaged in the preparations for the Greek conquest of Persia, angrily interjected. It was the army that was the true victor, he objected, noting that he himself had saved Alexander's life in at least one of the battles against the Persians.

The exchange became heated, fueled by copious amounts of wine. At one point, Cleitus loudly complained about Alexander demanding that everyone, Greek and Persian, fall on their knees when entering his presence. As the shouting match continued, Alexander first threw an apple at Cleitus, then reached for his sword—which guards had prudently removed—and finally grabbed a javelin, killing Cleitus with a lightning-like thrust. Almost before the blow had been struck, Alexander regained his senses. Deeply remorseful, he grieved over the death of his companion; according to one source, he abstained from food and drink for several days, bewailing the loss of his veteran commander.

Although the sources that report the incident vary considerably in detail, they agree that the quarrel was about the question of Alexander remaining

*ABOVE*: **Detail of the Ludovisi sarcophagus (c. 175 CE), depicting battle between Romans and "barbarians."**

true to his Macedonian/Greek heritage or becoming a Persian "king of kings." Was he still a first among equals? Was he still bringing liberty to the Greeks of Asia? Or was he becoming a divinely mandated monarch who could command Persians and Greeks alike to obey him on bended knee? Not surprisingly, these questions arose right at the time that Alexander had completed the liberation of the Greeks from Persian rule, destroyed the Persian Empire, and was about to begin his conquest of India. He was on his way to becoming the exalted single ruler of the then known world, encompassing all nations, languages, and religions on earth, a world similar to that heaven where Zeus ruled all gods and goddesses (or the Libyan god Ammon, from whom Alexander believed he was descended).

The Middle East and Mediterranean during 600 BCE–600 CE was a region that was culturally diverse, as illustrated by Cleitus's contrast between Greek liberties and Achaemenid Persian royal power. It was also an area of intense military rivalry, as we see in Alexander's avenging the Persian dominance of Greece in 386 by his own conquest of Persia in 334. Later on, as we shall learn in this chapter, the successor states of Parthian and Sasanid Persia and Rome continued the rivalry. However, already in the sixth century BCE, Greek, Jewish, and Iranian visionaries introduced very similar *monotheistic* (single personal god) and *monist* (single impersonal principle) forms of thought into the region. Centuries later, in the rivalry between Persia and Rome, the opposing state religions of Christianity and Zoroastrianism also faced off against each other. In short, this chapter focuses on one single region that had evolved from its Mesopotamian and Egyptian agrarian–urban origins and shared such basic patterns as imperialism, monotheism, and monism but was also torn apart by concrete and unbridgeable political and cultural differences. Intense internal interaction and adaptation characterized the Middle East and Mediterranean in the period of 600 BCE–600 CE.

# Interactions between Persia and Greece

The Achaemenid Persian conquest of the Middle East, from Anatolia and Egypt in the west to northwestern India in the east, was a relatively easy affair compared to the conquest of Greece, whose inhabitants resisted fiercely. Although Persia was able to subjugate the Greek city-states of the Anatolian coast, it proved unable to conquer the Greek mainland. A century and a half later, Alexander the Great unified Greece and led it to victory over Persia, establishing a short-lived Macedonian–Greek Empire. Alexander's generals divided the empire into three successor kingdoms under which politics stabilized until the Persians, under the Parthians and Sasanids, renewed the Persian imperial tradition.

## The Origins of the Achaemenid Persian Empire
The Persians originated as agrarian villagers and nomadic horse and sheep breeders during the Bronze Age in central Asia south of the Ural Mountains. Toward the end of the third millennium BCE, groups of nomads migrated from the Urals

## Seeing Patterns

▶ Why should the Middle East and Mediterranean Europe during the period 600 BCE–600 CE be studied as a single unit?

▶ What is transcendence, and why is it important to understand its importance in world history?

▶ Which elements characterize the institutions that grew out of the Middle Eastern monotheisms of Judaism and Christianity and the monism of Greek philosophy and science?

southward and, by the middle of the second millennium BCE, reached the Aral Sea region. From here, some migrants pushed farther, establishing themselves in Upper Mesopotamia and India around 1200 BCE. The Persians were a branch that migrated sometime before the 800s BCE from the Aral Sea region to the southwestern Iranian province of Fars, from which the name "Persia" is derived.

**Persian Conquests**    The first Persians to appear in the historical record were the Medes, who presided over a loosely organized kingdom with provincial vassals adjacent to the Assyrian Empire in Fars. The head of one vassal family, Cyrus II the Great (r. ca. 550–530 BCE) of the Achaemenids, assumed the crown of the Persians in 550 BCE and, in contrast to the Medes, embarked on an ambitious imperial program. Cyrus first expanded into Anatolia (modern-day Turkey), where he conquered the kingdom of Lydia [LIH-dee-ya]. The Lydians are notable for having created in 615 BCE the first minted money in world history, coins made of silver and gold and used in trade. Next, Cyrus turned to the neighboring Greek city-states of Ionia on the southwestern Anatolian coast. His generals besieged these cities one by one, until their inhabitants either surrendered or returned to the Greek mainland.

Cyrus himself was busy with the conquest of the Iranian interior and north, as far as Afghanistan. In 540 BCE he began his campaign against Neo-Babylonia in Mesopotamia, capturing the capital of Babylon a year later. The Phoenician city-states in Syria submitted voluntarily in the following years. Within a little more than a decade, Cyrus had defeated the most important powers of the period and had unified all of the Middle East except Egypt, which Persia conquered a little later, in 525 BCE (see Map 7.1).

**Cataphracts:** Heavily armed and protected cavalry soldiers.

**Persian Arms**    The Achaemenids achieved their conquests with the help of lightly armed, highly mobile mounted archers as well as heavily armored, slow-moving **cataphracts**—horsemen with protective armor consisting of iron scales sewn on leather shirts. The archers fought with composite bows, and the cataphracts with 5-foot-long, iron-tipped lances for thrusting. Saddles and stirrups

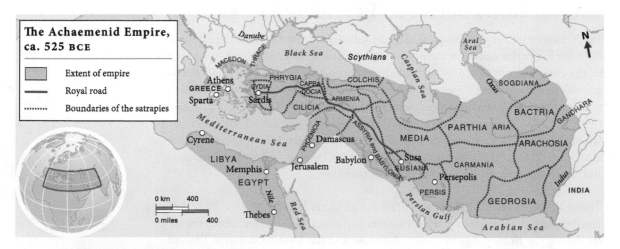

MAP **7.1  Achaemenid Persian Empire.**

The Achaemenid Empire, ca. 525 BCE

Extent of empire

Royal road

Boundaries of the satrapies

had not yet been invented, and hence the lance—requiring the mounted user to have a firm footing with which to brace himself—was still a relatively short, modest weapon. Infantry soldiers armed with bows, arrows, shields, and javelins provided support for the cavalry, complementing its tank-like thrust.

Early on, Persian kings supplemented their armies with heavily armored infantry recruited from among the Anatolian Greeks. These foot soldiers, called **hoplites**, fought shoulder to shoulder in ranks, called "phalanxes." They were equipped with 8-foot-long, iron-tipped thrusting spears, short iron swords, large shields held on the left forearm, helmets, and iron-scale protective armor. In close quarters, hoplite phalanxes were nearly invincible. Even in the open, however, phalanxes were difficult to crack, unless attacked by mounted archers on their unshielded right flank.

**Hoplites:** Greek foot soldiers fighting in closed ranks, called "phalanxes."

The Persian navy comprised as many as 1,200 galleys during its peak in the fifth century BCE. The Ionian and Phoenician provinces of the Persian Empire constructed and staffed these galleys, which were long, narrow ships, approximately 100 feet long and 15 feet wide. Apart from fighting naval battles against the Greeks, the navy also explored the western Mediterranean and even unsuccessfully attempted the circumnavigation of Africa. Altogether, the Persian military was a formidable fighting machine stationed in garrisons and ports in the various provinces of the Middle East and eastern Mediterranean.

**Persian Administration**   The Achaemenid Persian Empire, encompassing not only the Middle Eastern agrarian centers of Mesopotamia and Egypt but also those of the Indus valley, is estimated to have had some 15 million inhabitants. The kings prided themselves on having at their palace in southwestern Iran containers of water from both the Nile and the Danube, which they served at their banquets to demonstrate their vast power. (King Darius I, "the Great" [r. 522–486 BCE], campaigned in 514 or 513 BCE against the Scythians in Russia, on the north shore of the Black Sea.) The enormous size of the Persian territories demanded creative assimilation of the institutions they inherited. The empire consisted of some 70 ethnic groups, hundreds of temple cults, a small Persian aristocracy, and a limited central bureaucracy. Most kings prayed to the god Ahuramazda (Ahu-ra Maz-da) of the Zoroastrians, but others selected other deities from the Persian pantheon. Since the Achaemenids granted considerable autonomy to their 30 provinces, many of which retained their native ruling dynasties, temples, and legal systems, a bewildering number of languages, ethnic groups, and religious pantheons coexisted in the empire.

Around 500 BCE, the empire had become integrated enough that the kings could replace indigenous rulers with their own governors from the Persian

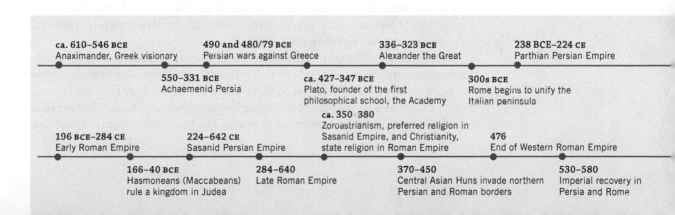

| ca. 610–546 BCE Anaximander, Greek visionary | 490 and 480/79 BCE Persian wars against Greece | | 336–323 BCE Alexander the Great | 238 BCE–224 CE Parthian Persian Empire |
|---|---|---|---|---|
| | 550–331 BCE Achaemenid Persia | ca. 427–347 BCE Plato, founder of the first philosophical school, the Academy | 300s BCE Rome begins to unify the Italian peninsula | |
| | | ca. 350–380 Zoroastrianism, preferred religion in Sasanid Empire, and Christianity, state religion in Roman Empire | | |
| 196 BCE–284 CE Early Roman Empire | 224–642 CE Sasanid Persian Empire | | 476 End of Western Roman Empire | |
| | 166–40 BCE Hasmoneans (Maccabeans) rule a kingdom in Judea | 284–640 Late Roman Empire | 370–450 Central Asian Huns invade northern Persian and Roman borders | 530–580 Imperial recovery in Persia and Rome |

**Persepolis.** This relief from the stairs that approach the royal audience hall shows ambassadors from the various lands under the power of the "king of kings" humbly offering tribute.

**Shahinshah:** "King of kings," the title of Persian rulers.

aristocracy. These provincial governors, or *satraps*, supported by Persian troops in fortresses, were powerful rulers. They administered Persian law, to which all imperial subjects could appeal from their own legal systems. The satraps also collected tributes and taxes, with which they maintained themselves and their troops, forwarding the remainder to the kings. When called upon by the kings, the governors contributed their provincial troops to the royal army. Officially, the Achaemenid king called himself "king of kings" (**shahinshah** [SHAW-in-shaw])—that is, emperor—in order to make his elevated status clear to all princes and governors of regional and Persian aristocratic origin, as well as the populace.

The *shahinshahs* had a number of palaces in Iran and Mesopotamia, among which Persepolis [per-SEH-puh-lis] is the best known. Here, they maintained the central administration with its treasury and archive. The language used for administrative purposes was imperial Aramaic, a special bureaucratic version of the spoken and alphabetically written Aramaic that had become the predominant language of Mesopotamia and Syria in the previous centuries. Clay tablets continued to be used as writing material, particularly in Mesopotamia; but scribes preferred parchment or papyrus scrolls, which offered them more space. A basic principle of the empire's financial administration was the hoarding of all incoming silver and gold. Trade was not yet fully monetized, and the kings minted only small amounts of coins. As elsewhere in Asia, villagers continued to pay taxes or rents in kind, and local markets continued to function primarily on the basis of barter. Enormous quantities of precious metal piled up in the Persian treasuries, with no purpose yet except luxury trade and the giving of presents.

The vast size of the empire dictated that the imperial administration pay close attention to its communication networks. Thus, the Persians created their famous "royal roads," perhaps the first such highways in the world. They consisted mostly of regularly maintained paths connecting Persia with Anatolia and Mesopotamia as directly as possible. Governors provided the roads with distance markers, constructed inns and depots at regular intervals, and protected them through a chain of police and army posts. The roads were intended primarily for quick troop movements, although traders with carts and pack animals used them as well.

## Greek City-States in the Persian Shadow

In the sixth century BCE, while Persia evolved into an empire, hundreds of city-states—cities (singular *polis*; plural *poleis*) with surrounding villages—dotted the landscape in Anatolia, Greece, and Italy. The most populous of these poleis were Athens and Sparta. The two competed for dominance, but neither could overcome the other, and their rivalry eventually benefited Persia in its attempt to assume power over Greece.

**Athens and Sparta**    Most of the hundreds of city-states of which Greece was composed ruled themselves independently. The only common bonds, besides language, history, and culture, were a number of so-called **oracles** and the Olympic Games. Greeks went to the oracles to settle disputes or to divine their future. The Olympic Games, in the polis of Olympia, brought together the Greek youth for athletic competitions. Athens, with 200,000 inhabitants, and Sparta, with 140,000 inhabitants, were the largest city-states and exerted a certain dominance but ultimately accomplished little in terms of unification (see Map 7.2).

**Oracles:** Temples where humans could consult priests or priestesses to determine the will of the gods.

MAP **7.2  Greece in the Sixth Century BCE.**

Athens is located on the small peninsula of Attica in southeastern Greece. Its limited agricultural resources forced inhabitants to specialize in the production of cash crops, such as wine, olive oil, nuts, and dried fruits. They traded these crops, together with woolen textiles and metal goods, for grain and metals from Italy and the Black Sea region. The growing focus on trade helped in the emergence of mercantile interests among the landowning citizenry. Disputes about representation in the ruling council and chronic debt among farmers forced the first among several reforms in 594 BCE under Solon, sole archon, or ruler for one year. In 508 BCE, Cleisthenes, a prominent landowner, forged an alliance between merchant landowners and smallholders to bring about further constitutional reforms, broadening the citizenry to include more modest property owners and ending the arbitrary rule of self-appointed strongmen. He expanded the rights of citizens to sit on juries and participate in the legislative assembly, which was enlarged to 500 members. Proposals adopted by the assembly were to be ratified by the citizenry, and executive power was vested in boards of elected magistrates. The reforms of Solon and Cleisthenes are often cited by scholars as the first steps toward the creation of Athenian democracy in the middle of the next century.

Sparta was another major city-state of Greece and Athens' principal rival. It was located on a plain in the Peloponnesus [peh-lo-po-NEE-sus] Peninsula southwest of Athens. Unlike land-poor Athens, Sparta had room to enlarge its agricultural base before eventually turning to maritime trade. Its constitutional organization preceded that of Athens by a century and, therefore, embodies more traditional traits. Citizenship was based on landownership, and Spartan citizens were entitled to stand for participation in the 30-member Council of Elders and the five-member Board of Overseers, the decisions of which were ratified by the assembly of owners of medium-sized properties. Executive power was in the hands of two hereditary kings.

Army service was of crucial importance in Sparta. At age 7, boys left home and entered military camps to train as hoplites. Until the age of 30, married soldiers were not allowed to live with their wives but received extended military leaves in order to create large families. A thoroughgoing code of male citizen discipline dominated Sparta. Women also received rigorous physical training and were fully imbued with the Spartan military ethic: Wives or mothers seeing their men off to battle customarily handed them their shields with the parting words "Come home with it or on it."

The village farmers who tilled the land in Sparta and the other Greek city-states were noncitizens of unfree status, in contrast to the free farmers in the Middle East. In Athens, as we have noted above, small free farmers were at the center of early reform efforts. In Sparta, however, the farmers, called *helots*, were the descendants of surrounding peoples conquered by Sparta during its years of expansion and tied to the land in perpetuity.

Since, in addition to villagers, women were excluded from political participation, constitutional rule benefited only small minorities in the Greek city-states. This was true even in the mid-fifth century BCE, when the final round of Athenian reforms under Pericles extended voting and office rights to all male citizens. While Athens' "golden age" of democracy was arguably the most open of the ancient world, it was still restricted to no more than one-third of the population at its height. Thus, what has been idealized by people in the modern era as a forerunner of our own institutions was in fact not very different from the urban assemblies in Mesopotamian cities or those of some of the early Indian city-states in the Ganges valley (see Chapter 3). In retrospect, Greece was thus not the only pioneer of constitutional rule: It shared this role with other societies, although each adopted rule by assemblies independently and not as a result of interaction.

**Greece and Persia**    Their maritime commercial wealth made the Greek city-states irresistible targets of Persian imperialism. When Athens supported the Ionian revolt of the Greek city-states in 499–494 BCE, the Persian monarchy found its justification to wage war against the Greeks. They suppressed the revolt and organized two large-scale invasions of the Greek mainland in the following years (492–490 and 480–479 BCE). Both invasions were well planned and included vastly superior land and sea forces. Storms took their toll on these forces, however, and long supply lines further compromised Persian military efficiency. To meet the invasion, the Greek city-states on the mainland united under the joint leadership of Athens and Sparta. In two battles, on land at Marathon (490 BCE) and on the sea at Salamis (480 BCE), the united Greeks took advantage of their better knowledge of local conditions and the utility of the phalanx against larger massed forces in narrow areas and repelled both Persian invasions. Greece managed to preserve its liberty and escape Persian imperial dominance. Soon, however, the Greek world was plunged into a long and devastating internal conflict.

After the repulsion of the Persian invasions, Athenian–Spartan unity fell apart. As a substitute, Athens formed a league with as many as 200 poleis around the Aegean and Black Seas and for about two decades harassed the Persians in the eastern Mediterranean. When Athens diverted a portion of the league's membership contributions to the reconstruction of its Persian War–damaged citadel, the Acropolis, however, anger against this perceived self-service erupted into the Peloponnesian War (431–404 BCE). During this war, Sparta made itself the champion of liberation from what many Greek cities viewed as an Athenian empire. After depleting Athens' land forces, Sparta—with Persian financial support—built a navy, which won a brilliant victory over Athens, forcing the latter to sue for peace in 404 BCE.

> "The real cause I consider to be the . . . growth of the power of Athens, and the alarm which this inspired in Lacedaemon [Sparta]"
>
> —Thucydides

Once involved again in Greek politics, the Achaemenids played their cards carefully, this time stoking fears of Spartan dominance. During yet another round of hostilities, a coalition of city-states led by Athens and backed by Persia defeated Sparta. In the King's Peace of 386 BCE, the Persians granted the Greeks autonomy, or self-rule, according to their city-state constitutions, provided they recognized Persia's overall dominance. Persia held the purse strings, employing some 50,000 Greek hoplite mercenaries who became jobless in Greece after the King's Peace. Persian imperial lordship over Greece had finally become a reality, to last for about half a century.

## Alexander's Empire and Its Successor Kingdoms

The one Greek area that remained outside Persian control was Macedonia, on the northern periphery of the Greek city-states. Although the Macedonians spoke a Greek dialect, the city-state Greeks considered them barbarians—that is, people mired in tribal customs and without an urban culture. In the middle of the

**East Meets West.** A turbaned man stands next to a Corinthian capital in the Hellenistic city of Ai-Khanoum, founded in what is today northern Afghanistan—ancient Bactria—in the fourth century BCE after Alexander's conquests. Ai-Khanoum was one of the focal points of Hellenism in the East. Archaeological excavations in the 1970s revealed a flourishing city, with a Greek-style theater, a huge palace, a citadel, a gymnasium, and various temples.

300s BCE, however, a king, Philip II (359–336 BCE), unified the country and provided it with a disciplined infantry army. He conquered the Greek city-states to the south, and his son Alexander continued the expansion with the conquest of Persia.

**Alexander and His Successors**    In 337 BCE, Philip employed his greatly enhanced military strength to declare war on the Persian Empire, in revenge for the Persian invasion of Macedonia and Greece a century earlier. He made himself the champion of Greek liberty in Asia, the "liberator" of the city-states in Anatolia. Just as Philip was getting ready to invade Anatolia, he was assassinated in a court intrigue. Philip's 20-year-old son Alexander took over both throne and campaign, setting off for Persia in 334 BCE. In three fiercely fought battles (334–330 BCE), Alexander outmaneuvered and defeated the Persian defenders; they prevailed because the Macedonian army was the most proficient and advanced force in the region. The Persian king was the lesser strategist and tactician, but he and the Persian aristocracy resisted tenaciously. The Persian forces retreated slowly into what is today Afghanistan. Alexander occupied the Persian royal towns and confiscated the Persian treasury, including some 7,000 tons of precious metals. During a drunken revelry in the palace town of Persepolis, Alexander had the imperial palace burned down, as a final act of vengeance for the destruction of the Acropolis by the Persians.

After finishing off the Achaemenid forces in Afghanistan and occupying Bactria (modern Uzbekistan) to the northeast, Alexander invaded India. When he reached the Ganges basin, however, persistent monsoon rains and exhausted troops forced him to retreat. As he left, he appointed governors over northwest India. Under these governors, Greek culture entered the subcontinent and exerted a palpable influence even beyond 305 BCE when the expanding Maurya Empire conquered India (see Chapter 8). Alexander returned to the Middle East and made plans to trump the Persians by executing their unfulfilled plan to circumnavigate Africa. Before he could depart, however, a fever seized him; and within 10 days, at the age of 33, Alexander was dead (323 BCE). In the stupendously short time of just 11 years, he had turned the mighty Persian Empire into a Macedonian–Greek one (see Map 7.3).

Not surprisingly, this empire did not hold together. Alexander's one legitimate son was born after his father's death and had no chance to assume the throne. Alexander's generals divided the empire among themselves, founding kingdoms, among which Antigonid Greece (276–167 BCE), Ptolemaic Egypt (305–30 BCE), and Seleucid southwest Asia (305–64 BCE) were the most important.

Altogether, about 1 million Greeks emigrated during the 200s BCE to the Middle East, assimilating gradually into the local population of some 20 million and imprinting their **Hellenistic** (Greek-influenced) culture on urban life. Thus,

**Hellenistic:** Period of Greek history from 323 BCE to 31 BCE.

even though the Macedonian–Greek Empire failed politically almost immediately, its cultural legacy lasted for centuries, even in faraway central Asia and India.

# Interactions between the Persian and Roman Empires

A century after Alexander's conquests, a resurgent Persia—in the shape of Parthia—appeared on the northeastern border of the Seleucid kingdom. This resurgence coincided with Rome's expansion after the unification of Italy. On the periphery of the successor kingdoms of Alexander's Macedonian–Greek Empire,

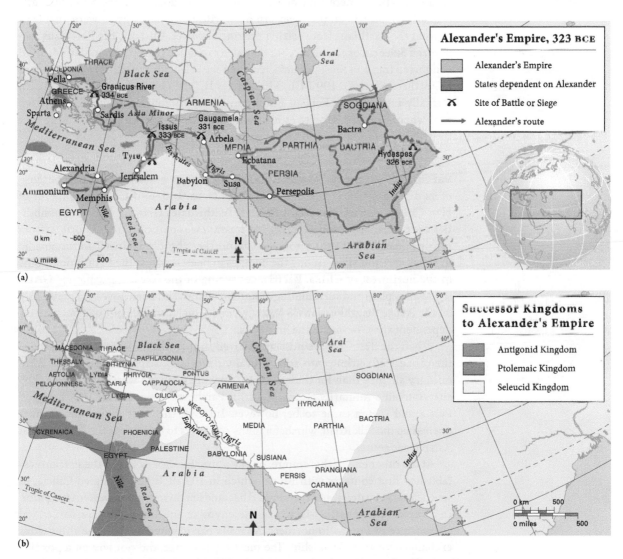

MAP **7.3** **Alexander's Empire (a) and Successor Kingdoms after the Breakup of Alexander's Empire (b).**

both Parthia and Rome pressed against the Antigonids, Seleucids, and Ptolemies. After conquering these kingdoms, Rome and Parthia eventually came face to face in Anatolia and Syria in the early second century BCE. Neither, however, succeeded in eliminating the other, as strenuously as they tried in a long series of wars. As a result, the Middle East and the Mediterranean remained politically as divided as they had been in the previous centuries under the successor states of Alexander the Great.

## Parthian Persia and Rome

Parthia was originally the name of the northeasternmost province of the Seleucid kingdom. In the 240s BCE, the tribal federation of the Parni, distant relatives of the Achaemenid Persians, migrated from the region east of the Aral Sea in central Asia to Parthia, where they defeated the Seleucid governor. The Seleucids, distracted by conflicts on their western front with Ptolemaic Egypt, were unable to prevent the Parthians from seizing provincial power. Initially, the Parthians recognized Seleucid overlordship, but they also expanded their power and in 141 BCE conquered Iran and Mesopotamia, reducing the Seleucids to a small rump kingdom in northern Syria. In 109 BCE, Mithridates II, "the Great" (r. ca. 123–88 BCE), formally renewed the Persian Empire in his newly founded capital Ctesiphon, near where Baghdad is today, by assuming the title "king of kings" and taking over the traditional Iranian pantheon of gods.

**Parthian Diplomacy**     Parthian Persia was a major power, in large part because of its diplomacy. In 115, Wudi [woo-DEE] (r. ca. 140–87 BCE), the emperor of Han China, sent a diplomatic mission to Mithridates II, to explore the possibilities of an alliance as well as trade. The mission was part of Wudi's efforts, lasting nearly a quarter of a century, to secure his northern border against Turkic nomadic invaders and find allies among the nomads in Bactria across the Pamir mountains in the northwest of China. Bactria, consisting of the fertile Fergana [fer-GAH-nah] valley plain and surrounding mountain chains, had been governed previously by the Achaemenid Persians, Alexander, and Greek generals but had become independent after the end of the Seleucids.

When the first Chinese missions arrived in the valley, many nomads were in the process of settling into agricultural villages and displayed less desire for a military alliance than for trade. The missions then moved westward, where they encountered a militarily strong power in Parthian Persia. No alliance between Persia and China came to be, however. Instead, this first diplomatic contact opened up the Silk Road, which, for many centuries to come, was the main central Asian trade route.

At the other end of this empire, on the upper Euphrates River, the Persians established first contacts with Rome, which in 103 BCE had occupied Cilicia, in southeastern Anatolia, and thereby had become Parthian Persia's western neighbor. In a diplomatic meeting, in which the envoy of the small, Persian-descended principality of Pontus in northern Anatolia participated as well, the three sides exchanged vows of friendship. The meeting, however, did not end on a positive note. The Roman governor seated himself in the middle and thereby sought to pull rank on the other two envoys, causing an infuriated Mithridates II to have his ambassador executed for allowing the Roman envoy to claim superiority. Not surprisingly, Rome and Persia soon came to blows.

**Roman Republican Origins**   The western Mediterranean, adapting to agriculture around 3000 BCE and to the Iron Age after 1000 BCE, became part of the Middle Eastern and eastern Mediterranean agrarian centers in the course of the first millennium BCE. Phoenicians from the eastern Mediterranean established ports along the northern shores of Africa, in Spain, and on the islands of Sicily and Sardinia, attracted by the rich mineral resources there. Their principal port at the entrance to the western Mediterranean, in today's Tunisia, was Carthage. Later on, Greeks established city-states in southern Italy and Sicily. In north-central Italy was the kingdom of the Etruscans, a local people who originally came from Anatolia and the Levant and settled in Italy since ca. 2000 BCE. The kingdom included Rome, founded around 1000 BCE.

**Paestum, Southern Italy.** By the sixth century BCE, Greek city-states were flourishing across southern Italy and Sicily, including Paestum, which has some of the best-preserved temples outside of Greece, including the Temple of Hera shown here.

Subsequently, around 500 BCE, the Romans made themselves independent and overthrew their kings. They created a **republic** (from Latin *res publica*, "public matter"), that is, a state without a king, electing leaders and forming a constitutional government. Around 450 BCE, the Romans adopted the Twelve Tablets, a set of laws covering a variety of legal matters, such as procedure, property, inheritance, constitution, due process, family, and crime. A chief priest was responsible for administering the cult of the patron god, Jupiter, and fixing the calendar. Later on, the Romans sacrificed to hundreds of gods, and their polytheistic religious practices acquired a close resemblance to those of the Greeks and Persians.

**Republic:** State without a royal dynasty and with an elected executive.

**Expansion of the Republic**   In the 300s BCE, when Rome began to unify the peninsula, it organized its citizen army more formally into legions. The heavily armed infantry of **legionaries**, forming the center of each legion, consisted of landed citizens able to pay for their swords, javelins, helmets, shields, and scale armor. Wealthy Romans also manned the light and heavy cavalry, including cataphracts, while small landholders made up the light infantry of skirmishers. With the help of these legionaries, Rome unified Italy and in three wars (246–164 BCE) conquered its strongest rival, Carthage, across the Mediterranean in what is today Tunisia.

**Legionaries:** Roman foot soldiers fighting in semiclosed ranks.

Around 200 BCE, during the second war when Carthage was still relatively strong, it sought to protect itself against Rome through an alliance with the kingdom of Antigonid Greece. In a first expansion east, the Romans defeated the Antigonids and, in 196 BCE, issued the Isthmus Declaration, according to which the Greeks of Greece, Anatolia, and farther east were to be "free" of Antigonid overlordship and governed by their own laws. In Roman eyes, the Greek cities were now clients. When the Greeks resented this restriction of their laws and rebelled, in the middle of the second century BCE, they were ruthlessly repressed by the Romans, who eventually reduced Greece to provincial status. The Isthmus Declaration was Rome's decisive step toward becoming an empire. It continued its republican institutions for another two centuries and never formally abolished them. Historians usually date the beginning of the Roman Empire to 27 BCE, when the Senate bestowed the title "Augustus" on Octavian. In the wake of Rome's expansion into North Africa, Greece, and Anatolia during the second and first centuries BCE, a new ruling class of wealthy landowners emerged. These consisted of Italian aristocrats who had appropriated the land of smallholders absent for extended periods during their military service as legionaries, turning these lands into large estates called **latifundia**. Ruling-class members also acquired leases of conquered lands overseas, where they established latifundia with enslaved war captives who grew cash crops. Discharged legionaries and dispossessed farmers crowded Rome, while rebellious slaves on latifundia in southern Italy and Sicily rose up in massive revolts. The most dangerous revolt was that of Spartacus in 73–71 BCE. Spartacus was an army deserter from Thrace who had been recaptured, enslaved, and trained as a gladiator. The sources describe Spartacus as a skillful tactician who devastated latifundia throughout Italy and held the Roman army in check for 3 years before it succeeded in defeating him.

**Latifundia:** Large, ruling class–owned estates with tenant farmers or slaves.

Efforts by a few social reformers at improving the lot of the poor through food subsidies, land reforms, and public work projects failed against the fierce resistance of the landowners. About the only reform that succeeded was that of Marius, who was senator from 107 to 85 BCE and a successful general in North Africa. He opened the army ranks to the landless, equipped them with arms, and enlisted them for up to 20 years of service. Upon retirement, soldiers received plots of land in conquered provinces. This reform greatly benefited imperial expansion and also Romanized conquered provinces through settled veterans. But it also encouraged generals to use the now fully professionalized army for their own ambitions.

**Augustus.** The famous Augustus of Prima Porta dated to 15 CE, and probably a copy of a bronze original commissioned by Augustus at some date after he was honored with the title "Augustus" in 27 BCE. Intended as a representation of the power and authority of Rome's first emperor, the statue depicts Augustus as barefooted, a symbolic image of gods and heroes.

In the middle of the first century BCE, three ambitious generals were vying for control of the empire. One of them was Julius Caesar (r. 60–44 BCE), from a prominent family of administrators and a successful conqueror of northwestern Europe. Recently returned from triumphant conquests in Gaul (modern France), he defeated his two rivals. When he then assumed several offices traditionally held by separate magistrates, including the title "dictator for life," he provoked much opposition. An assassin, Marcus Junius Brutus, eventually struck Caesar down, and a "triumvirate" of generals assumed power.

The triumvirate did not last. Civil war broke out, and the ultimate victor was Octavian (r. 31 BCE–14 CE), a distant younger relative of Caesar whose career the latter had furthered. More subtle than Caesar, Octavian gradually created a new constitutional order with himself as leader, always maintaining the pretense of being merely the executive officer of the state. In practice he possessed unlimited powers under the title of Augustus ("the Revered One"), bestowed on him in 27 BCE.

**The Augustan Age** To consolidate his power, Augustus limited imperial expansion in the north to France and Germany, west of the Rhine and Danube Rivers. He ordered the construction of a wall, called the *limes*, linking the two rivers, to keep the Germanic tribes on the other side at bay. In the east, a series of wars with the Persian Parthian Empire (56 BCE–1 CE) over the control of Armenia, Upper Mesopotamia, and Syria ended inconclusively. Egypt, Syria, and Judea came under direct Roman rule; Armenia became a Roman client state; Upper Mesopotamia east of the Euphrates remained Parthian; and peace reigned between Rome and Parthia for two generations. At this time, the Roman Empire had about 55 million inhabitants (see Map 7.4). It was considerably more populous than its Middle Eastern competitor, Parthia, with 10 million, but less so than its territorially smaller contemporary, Han China (202 BCE–220 CE), with 58 million. In addition, the Roman and Parthian Empires were geographically far less compact and had more vulnerable borders than China, disadvantages which hampered political cohesion.

All 44 Roman provinces outside Italy had to pay heavy poll and agricultural taxes in kind and silver coins, primarily to support a standing army, which Augustus

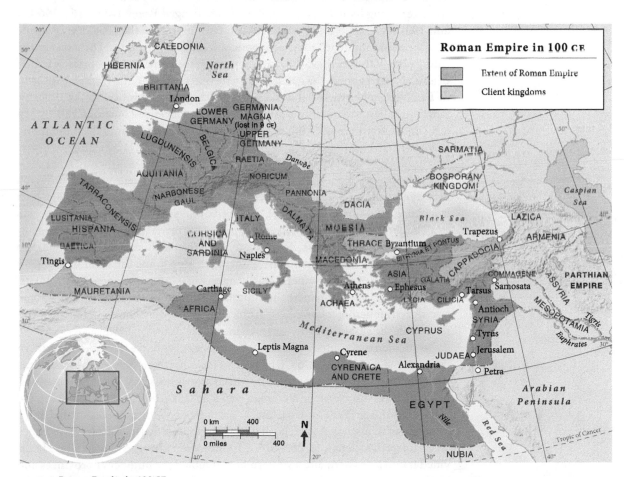

MAP 7.4 **Roman Empire in 100 CE.**

reduced to half to the size of the earlier civil war armies. Legionaries came not only from Italy but also from Gaul and Hispania (modern France and the Iberian Peninsula). In addition, tax money went into the building and upkeep of roads and ports, as well as wheat subsidies and circuses for the inhabitants of Rome and other large cities. In contrast to the huge military, the number of civilian Roman administrators in the provinces was small. The Roman Peace (*pax romana*) clearly rested more on the projection of military might than on a civilian administration, as in Han China.

The Roman Peace on the borders was rarely disrupted during the first two centuries following Augustus. Not surprisingly, the disruptions that did occur were on the border with Parthian Persia. Here, the flashpoint was the kingdom of Armenia, which both Parthia and Rome coveted as a client state. Compromise solutions collapsed twice (54–63 CE and 112–117 CE). On the second occasion, Rome came close to destroying Parthia when it succeeded in occupying Mesopotamia for a short time. The subsequent puppet kingdom, however, was unable to maintain itself, and the Parthians returned to independence.

## The Sasanid Persian and Late Roman Empires

After renewing its independence, Parthia challenged Rome twice (161–166 CE and 193–198 CE). It lost both times and had to give up the province of Upper Mesopotamia and much of its economic wealth to pay tributes. Divisions in the ruling class of the Parthians began to appear. In the early 200s, the priestly family of a temple to Anahita, the goddess of water and fertility in the Iranian pantheon in Fars, assumed provincial leadership functions in opposition to the dynasty. Ardashir, a descendant of this priestly family, finally ended Parthian rule in 224 CE and declared himself king of kings, establishing the Sasanid Persian Empire (224–642 CE).

**Roman Crisis**    Just when Persian imperial power was rejuvenated through a new dynasty, the Roman Empire fell into a political and economic crisis, which lasted half a century (234–285 CE) and profoundly changed its organization. As in all empires, the balance between war booty, tax revenue, and military expenditures was always precarious. Booty acquired in the Parthian wars kept the empire afloat until the 220s, but thereafter emperors had to dilute the silver money paid to the legionaries with cheaper metals. The ensuing inflation angered the soldiers, who supported any claimant to the imperial throne promising higher wages. Some two dozen emperors followed each other in rapid succession on the throne, and for a while the empire even fragmented into three pieces.

In addition to the internal conflicts, Germanic tribes broke through the northern defenses and during 260–276 CE pillaged as far as northern Italy. At the same time, both Rome and Persia were afflicted by what historians of science assume was an outbreak of mass disease along the trade routes in 251–266 CE, foreshadowing the plague of 541 (see "Patterns Up Close"). The number of deaths was estimated in the hundreds of thousands. At the end of the 200s it appeared as if Rome was at its end.

Emperor Diocletian (r. 285–305 CE), however, salvaged the empire. He divided it into an eastern and a western half, doubled the number of provinces and civil administrators, and created a separate set of military districts. In addition, he ended Italy's tax exemption, regularized tax collection, increased the number of legions by one-third, and created a mobile field army under his command. Civil peace returned to the empire, albeit at the price of an increased militarization.

**Adoption of Monotheism**    Since the early Sasanids had to consolidate their rule in a large territory, stretching from Upper Mesopotamia to Uzbekistan and northwestern India, they could not exploit the Roman crisis to the fullest. Although they led lightning invasions into Roman territories in Syria and Anatolia, acquired immense booty, received large indemnity payments, and even captured the Roman emperor Valerian in battle in 260 CE, in the end the Romans always regained control over Armenia and Upper Mesopotamia. Diocletian, after his reforms, was even able to push the border eastward to the Tigris River.

In the first half of the 300s, while the inconclusive wars between the two imperial rivals of Rome and Persia continued, both empires took first, halting steps toward a profound internal transformation—that is, a shift away from polytheism and toward the elevation of monotheism to the status of state religion. During the previous polytheist millennia in the Middle East and the Mediterranean, kings and emperors had supported imperial temple priesthoods in their capitals in return for the justification of their rule. Temples devoted to many other deities existed in their realms, and rulers did not seek their elimination. But when the Romans and Persians suffered their severe internal crises—the former nearly falling apart and the latter changing dynasties—rulers became aware of the need for a unifying single religious bond.

"He himself proceeded . . . like some heavenly messenger of God. . . . It was evident that he was distinguished by piety and godly fear."

—Eusebius

At the beginning of the reign of Emperor Constantine I, "the Great" (r. 306–337 CE), Christianity's adherents numbered about 10 percent of the Roman population. Christianity had begun three centuries earlier with the preaching of Jesus of Nazareth and Paul of Tarsus. Its growth, despite periodic persecutions, was impressive enough for Constantine to take a first step toward making Christianity the state religion by presiding over the Council of Nicaea in 325 CE, which issued **the Nicene Creed** as the common doctrinal platform among Christians, as well as granting tax privileges and jurisdictional powers to the Christian Church. Baptized shortly before his death, Constantine can be considered the first Christian Roman emperor.

**Nicene Creed:** Orthodox Christian doctrine declaring the divinity of Jesus Christ

In Persia, under the sponsorship of Shapur II (r. ca. 307–379), Zoroastrian priests began to write down the Gathas, the oldest holy scripture of Zoroastrianism. In Rome, several pagan emperors succeeded Constantine, and it was only in 380 that Christianity became the sole state religion. Persia, with its large Jewish and Christian minorities in Mesopotamia, took the different route of making Zoroastrianism the preferential religion in ca. 350, with Christianity and Judaism being accorded a protected status. Thus, both empires sought to strengthen internal unity through the adoption of a single monotheistic faith.

**Nomadic Invasions**    The adoption of Christianity and Zoroastrianism to strengthen the cohesion of the Roman and Sasanid Empires came just in time, before the great migration of peoples across Eurasia caused severe disruptions.

## Patterns Up Close | The Plague of Justinian

At the end of the 500s, neither the Roman nor the Sasanid Empire was as populous and wealthy as before the nomadic invasions from the north. For the first time, in 541 CE, a mass epidemic, the bubonic plague, hit the world, breaking out first in the Roman Empire and traveling thereafter to Persia and, in cycles of 15 years, by the 600s CE as far as China and England. This plague, recorded as the "Plague of Justinian"—it sickened the emperor himself for several weeks—dramatically reduced population levels everywhere. The Plague of Justinian originated either in East Africa or in Burma. It reached the Mediterranean through black rats infested with fleas traveling in ships on the Indian Ocean and Red Sea.

Historians know now that for the plague to spread from fleas and rats in one of its endemic regions and become a pandemic the region's average temperatures must have declined. Fleas are most likely to jump from rats to humans at 59–68 degrees Fahrenheit. Such a temperature decline might have occurred a few years prior to 541 CE, with the eruption of the volcano Krakatau in Indonesia in 535 CE, the ashes of which obscured the sun for a number of years. Although the climate returned to normal a few years later, recurrent cycles of the plague every decade or two until well into the 700s CE prevented population levels from recovering.

Observers in various cities of the Roman Empire, some afflicted by the plague themselves,

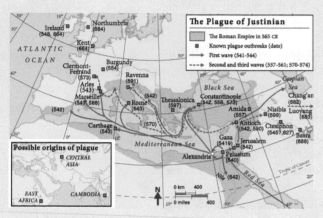

MAP 7.5 **The Plague of Justinian.**

The migration began in the mid-300s CE when the western branch of the Huns—horse- and sheep-breeding nomads in the steppes of central Asia east of the Ural Mountains—moved westward and southward on the Silk Road. As in the case of the previous migrations out of central Asia in the second millennium BCE, the reasons that the western Huns packed up and journeyed westward remain unclear. One possible factor was the success of the Chinese in driving away nomadic invaders from their Great Wall in the north, resulting in a chain reaction of migrations among neighboring tribes, including the Huns. During their journey westward, the Huns grew into a large federation of nomads, farmers, and town dwellers of mixed ethnic and linguistic composition (Turks, Mongols, and Iranians).

As the Huns entered the Russian plains, they encountered local Germanic farming populations, whom they defeated. Other Germanic peoples, such as the Visigoths, fled from the Huns and negotiated their entry into the Roman Empire. In the early 400s CE, both Hunnish and Germanic peoples overcame the defenses

have left us vivid accounts. People infected by the plague bacillus typically developed a high fever, followed by swelling of the lymph nodes in the groin, the armpits, and the neck. In great pain and delirious from fever, most people died quickly after a few days. Although the concept of quarantine was known, there was no known medicine. Survivors tried folk remedies, to no avail. Many clerical observers at the time were convinced that sinfulness was what had attracted God's wrath. For us modern observers, the most important lesson of the Plague of Justinian is the evidence it provides of how interconnected the various parts of Eurasia and Africa were toward the middle of the 500s CE (see Map 7.5).

The Plague of Justinian shows us how climate and disease followed their own natural patterns in world history, patterns different from those of the polytheistic and monotheistic city-states, kingdoms, and empires. By killing up to one-third of the population and keeping population levels low for at least a century, the Plague of Justinian severely impacted city-state, kingdom, and empire patterns. The reduced population levels led to increased labor costs and food shortages; it also made survivors wealthier. On the other hand, since the plagues were equal-opportunity killers, they hit states and societies with impartial ferocity. Justinian's plague favored neither Rome nor Persia and thus had a more quantitative than lasting qualitative effect on the process of world history.

## Questions

- What does Justinian's plague tell us about the interconnectedness of Afro-Eurasia at this time?
- How does understanding the impact of disease and climate on human societies add a new dimension to the patterns of world history?

of the Romans, poured into the western half of the Roman Empire, and eventually ended the western line of emperors, an event remembered as the fall of Rome in 476 CE (see Map 7.6).

The emperors in the eastern half of the empire withstood the migrants' threat, in part because of Constantinople's strategic location. This city, made the capital by Constantine in 330 CE, was relatively close to the endangered northern and eastern borders, allowing for a more rapid deployment of troops than was possible from faraway Rome. The Sasanids initially repelled an attack by another branch of the Huns on their central Asian border in the early 400s CE but succumbed to renewed invasions in 483–485 and were forced to pay tribute for a number of years. A third branch of Huns invaded the Gupta Empire of India toward the end of the 400s CE. In the mid-500s the Sasanids eventually recovered from the invasions, but the Guptas were reduced to small remnants. Further compounding matters, plague struck the Middle East and Europe in 541 BCE (see "Patterns Up Close" on pp. 196–197).

**Roman and Persian Recovery**   The architect of the reconstruction of the Roman Empire was Justinian I, "the Great" (r. 527–565 CE). Although not a military campaigner himself, Justinian employed talented generals who reconquered most shores of the western Mediterranean from the Germanic invaders, including all of Italy. As the empire stabilized, prosperity returned. With improved tax revenues, Justinian was able to finance reform measures. The best known of these reforms was the reorganization of the legal system, based on the codification of the huge body of Roman law that had grown from the initial Twelve Tablets in republican Rome. In addition to the *Codex Justinianus* and *Digests*, he issued an instructional textbook, the *Institutions*, used by law students for centuries after Justinian's death. Originally written in Latin, Justinian's *Codex* was later translated into Greek and became the legal foundation for the Roman Empire's successor, the Byzantine Empire (610–1453 CE), as well as the Islamic empire of the Abbasids (750–1258 CE).

Often considered the crown jewel among Justinian's long-lasting achievements was the construction of Hagia Sophia ("Holy Wisdom"), until the construction of Saint Peter's in Rome the largest Christian church. Begun shortly after deadly riots in 532 had destroyed large portions of Constantinople, Hagia Sophia represents

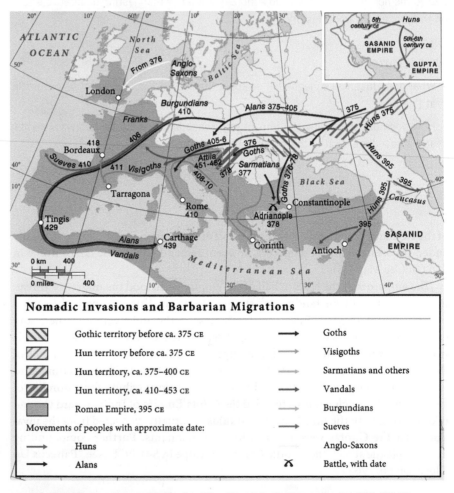

MAP 7.6 **Nomadic Invasions and Barbarian Migrations into the Roman Empire, 375–450 CE.**

Justinian's interest in affairs of the church. A magnificent architectural accomplishment, Hagia Sophia combines Roman features with new elements. It was designed to provide for a large open space, capped by a huge dome surrounded by windows that admitted light into the interior. So stunned was Justinian by the magnificence of the new church that he is said to have blurted out, "Solomon, I have outdone thee!"

In Persia, it was Khosrow I (r. 531–579) who rebuilt the Sasanid Empire (see Map 7.7). He began his rule in the aftermath of a civil war that pitted Mazdak, a renegade Zoroastrian priest and social reformer, and the dynasty against the Zoroastrian priesthood and the ruling class. In this war, the dynasty confiscated landed estates from the ruling class, opened the latter's granaries to the poor, and distributed its lands to small military landowners (*dihqans*). Khosrow, scion of the dynasty but siding with the ruling class, seized power and had Mazdak executed, ending the social reforms. But he maintained the military reforms in favor of the *dihqans*, thereby distancing himself from the traditional ruling class. After a census of the population, which allowed him to raise taxes and hire bureaucrats, he greatly expanded the central administration at the expense of the ruling class.

Like Justinian, Khosrow also pursued military expansion. Acceding to pleas from the Armenians after a revolt against Justinian in 530 CE, Khosrow reopened

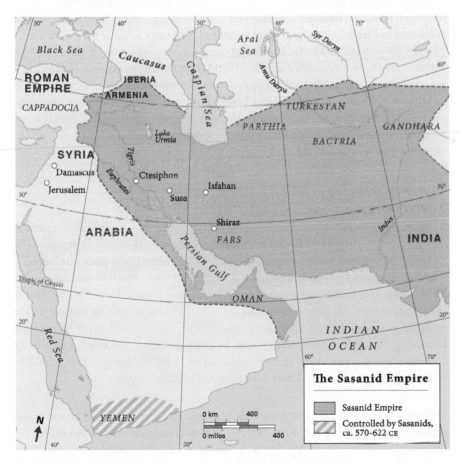

MAP **7.7 The Sasanid Empire.**

hostilities against the Romans. Initially, his armies broke through to the Mediterranean and returned with rich loot, but the campaign stalled and the war once more ended in 577 CE in a draw. The Romans agreed to pay a tribute, and Khosrow returned the conquered territories. In the north, Khosrow defeated European and Turkic tribes, expanding the border eastward to Turkistan. A plea from the king of Yemen in southwestern Arabia to aid him in his efforts to repel a Roman-backed Ethiopian invasion brought Khosrow's fleet to southern Arabia in 575–577 CE. On land, Arab vassal kings established Persian control over much of the rest of Arabia. In contrast to Rome, the reach of Persia was much expanded at the end of the sixth century.

# Adaptations to Monotheism and Monism in the Middle East

Although demographically weakened by plague, Rome and Sasanid Persia were comparatively strong unitary empires at the end of the 500s CE. Both had regained territories lost to the Asian tribal migrations two centuries earlier and were religiously unified through the adoption of the monotheisms of Christianity and Zoroastrianism as obligatory or preferential state religions. The adoption of these religions, however, had been of relatively recent vintage, as we have seen. It came at the end of a lengthy process that originated at the beginning of the Achaemenid Persian Empire (550–330 BCE). At that time, visionaries arose to whom a single god revealed himself or who discovered fundamental truths. At first, these visionaries of religious monotheism and philosophical monism had only small numbers of followers. It took many centuries before followers of each faith became more numerous and organized themselves in local communities dispersed over the empires' territories until the creeds achieved imperial sanction as the preferred or obligatory state religion.

## Challenge to Polytheism: The Origins of Judaism, Zoroastrianism, and Greek Philosophy

Religious visionaries of the sixth century BCE arose in a polytheistic environment, a culture of many gods who embodied overpowering as well as benign natural forces and phenomena. In Egypt and in Mesopotamia these gods numbered in the thousands; in Greece and Rome their numbers were smaller, and among the Persians and ancient Israelites they numbered fewer than a dozen. Regardless of specific numbers, all polytheisms had one basic characteristic in common: The gods all descended from something unnamable that existed prior to creation (Nothing, the Abyss, Darkness, Waste, or Chaos). Unity preceded multiplicity, and even though perceived reality consisted of both, in thought they could be separated from each other. Unity **transcended** multiplicity.

**Transcendence:** Realm of reality above and beyond the limits of material experience.

**Judaism**    Remarkably, the discovery of transcendence occurred more or less simultaneously during the 600s BCE in Mesopotamia, Iran, and Anatolia. The historically most influential case was that of an anonymous Jewish visionary, whom scholars dubbed "Deutero-Isaiah" or "Second Isaiah" (fl. ca. 560 BCE) in

Mesopotamia. After their deportation by the Neo-Babylonians from Palestine (597–582 BCE), as we saw in Chapter 2, a majority of Israelites lived in Babylonian exile, scattered over areas of Upper and Lower Mesopotamia as well as western Iran and earning their livelihood as scribes, craftspeople, and soldiers. After the establishment of the Achaemenid Persian Empire and its subsequent conquest of Babylonia and Syria, including Palestine, these scribes began to compile their Israelite religious traditions from Palestine into larger collections of writings. They became the founders of what is called today "Judaism," and one of them, Deutero-Isaiah, was the first to declare Yahweh [YAH-way], or God, to be the only god of the Jews.

In Deutero-Isaiah's words, there are no gods but Yahweh: "Thus says the LORD the king of Israel, and his redeemer the LORD of hosts; I am the first, and I am the last; and beside me there is no other god" (Is. 44:6–8). Yahweh is completely distinct from the traditional gods of polytheism. Yahweh is invisible and cannot be represented by visible images: "Verily you are a God who hides himself, O God of Israel, the Savior" (Is. 45:15). God in Deutero-Isaiah is the single, invisible creator and sustainer of the world. He is transcendent—a conceptual reality beyond the empirical reality of this world.

Some of Deutero-Isaiah's followers inserted revisions in the corpus of early scriptures that the Jews had brought with them into Babylonian exile to emphasize Yahweh's transcendence, particularly in the book of Genesis dealing with creation. (A new element they also introduced in Genesis was the 7-day calendar, an innovation which is today recognized everywhere.) Other followers petitioned the Persian king to allow them to leave for Jerusalem and restore the temple destroyed by the Neo-Babylonians. The Persian king issued the permit in 538 BCE, and a small but determined group of monotheists returned to Jerusalem to construct the Second Temple (completed in 515 BCE). A new priesthood took up residence in the Temple and, on the basis of new rituals and laws, administered the emerging monotheistic faith of Judaism.

**Zoroastrianism**   Zoroastrians attribute their origin to Zoroaster (also called Zarathustra), who, like Moses of the Israelites, is supposed to have lived around 1200 BCE, long before the rise of monotheism. The earliest recorded references to Zoroaster's teachings, however, date only to the rise of the Achaemenid Persian Empire in 550 BCE. These teachings were handed down orally by a priestly class, the magi. The main oral text is the Avesta, a body of liturgical texts which the magi used in their religious ceremonies.

The earliest text forms the section called "Yasht" in the Avesta. Zamyad Yasht 19, or the "Hymn to the Earth," speaks of the glories of Ahuramazda (God), to whom the priests are bringing sacrifices. The last of his glories, bestowed on humankind at the end of history, is that of the savior (Avestan *saoshyant*).

Other sections of the Avesta describe in considerable detail an additional period of time just prior to the arrival of the savior, a time of trial and tribulation with horrible calamities and devastations, later called the "apocalypse" (Greek *apocalypsis*, revelation). Both themes—Savior or Messiah and apocalypse— are trademarks of Zoroastrian monotheism. In later centuries they became

> He will restore the world "which will [thenceforth] never grow old and never die, never decaying and never rotting, ever living and ever increasing."
>
> —Yasht 15:89–90

**Zoroastrian Fire Temple.**
Consisting of a cube with a superimposed dome, this Zoroastrian temple, one of the best preserved, is located outside Baku in present-day Azerbaijan. Zoroastrianism was prevalent in the Caucasus region until the arrival of Christianity, and then, Islam.

central in Judaism, Christianity, and Islam. They replaced the polytheistic notion of a shadowy afterlife in the underworld with salvation in the righteous in God's transcendent kingdom.

Unfortunately, the extant sources do not present a clear picture of the evolution of Zoroastrian monotheism after the 500s BCE. It appears, however, that under the Parthians the magi introduced traditional Iranian and Anatolian cults of fire, maintained in fire temples, into Zoroastrianism. Similarly, they adopted customs of exposing the dead on rooftops to vultures before burying the bones cleansed of mortal flesh in graves. How far the fire temples evolved into congregational places for priests and laity, however, similar to Jewish synagogues, Christian churches, or Greek philosophical schools, is a matter of conjecture among scholars.

**Greek Philosophy**    While the author of Deutero-Isaiah and the Zoroastrian reformers of the 500s BCE are unknown to us today, the first Greek philosophers are known by name: Thales, Heraclitus, and Thales' pupil Anaximander, who lived during the first half of the 500s in the city of Miletus on the Anatolian coast. Of these, Thales of Miletus is usually credited with beginning the Greek philosophical tradition of divorcing scientific explanations of natural phenomena from mythical, supernatural forces. In contrast to Judaism and Zoroastrianism, Anaximander formulated the impersonal, or *monist*, "principle of the infinite" (*apeiron*) as the invisible cause underlying the world (*kosmos*). A lively debate over principles ensued after Anaximander and his successors, also mostly from Anatolia, proposed several other cosmic principles. This debate became the basis for the rise of the mathematical and physical sciences in the subsequent centuries.

The Athenian Plato (ca. 427–347 BCE) was the first systematic thinker who extended the debate from principles in nature to a principle common to all areas of reality, such as politics, ethics, and the arts, calling it Being (*on*, originally coined by his predecessor Parmenides, fl. fifth century BCE). In his thinking, called "philosophy," meaning love of wisdom, Being is embodied in the three transcendent forms (*eidai*) of Truth, Justice, and Beauty. These forms, so Plato argued, represent objective standards against which all earthly assertions about truth, justice, and beauty in daily life are to be measured. Anaximander's monism thus formed the trunk from which two major branches, science and philosophy, sprouted.

**The Break from Polytheism to Monotheism**  The common thread linking the three visions of transcendence is that they all involve transcendent symbols, such as God or Being, which can only be thought but not experienced. For the Greek, Zoroastrian, and Jewish visionaries, reality consisted of two separate halves, the one that can be comprehended only through abstract thought and the other that can be comprehended concretely by being sensed. Polytheist reality is undivided, with gods and corresponding natural phenomena conjoined. Given this contrast, it is not surprising that monotheism was incompatible with polytheism. Deutero-Isaiah expressed this incompatibility explicitly; in Greek philosophy and Zoroastrianism it was more implicit. Nevertheless, in the long run, polytheism disappeared from the Middle East and Mediterranean, ceding its long reign to monotheism and subsequent religious civilizations.

## Toward Religious Communities and Philosophical Schools

The visionaries were founders of small religious communities and philosophical schools amid an initially continuing polytheism in the Greek city-states and the Persian Empire, both in the Iranian–Mesopotamian imperial center and the Jewish province of Palestine. The small Jewish community that built the Second Temple in Jerusalem grew more rapidly than the Zoroastrian fire temple communities and Greek philosophical schools and led the way to monotheism. It furthermore spawned a Jewish reform movement, Christianity, which in turn changed the Roman Empire from polytheism to monotheism (see Map 7.8).

**Judaism in Palestine**  The Achaemenid Persian kings allowed the Jews, who had moved from Mesopotamia to Palestine and had founded the Second Temple in Jerusalem, a large degree of autonomy. Under their successors, the Ptolemaic and Seleucid kings in Alexander the Great's successor states, this autonomy declined substantially. These kings introduced Greek-Hellenistic institutions and culture into Palestine, forcing the Jews to allow the *gymnasium* (the basic school, which included Olympic sports exercises in the nude) as well as polytheism and philosophy in their midst. A majority resisted the introduction of the gymnasium and Zeus into the temple with fierce and eventually successful rebellions. As a result, the Jews established the autonomous Hasmonean (also called "Maccabean") kingdom (140–37 BCE), which sought to limit the Hellenization of society.

In spite of all Hasmonean attempts to keep Judaism pure, educated Jews learned Greek and read the writings of the Greek philosophers, especially the

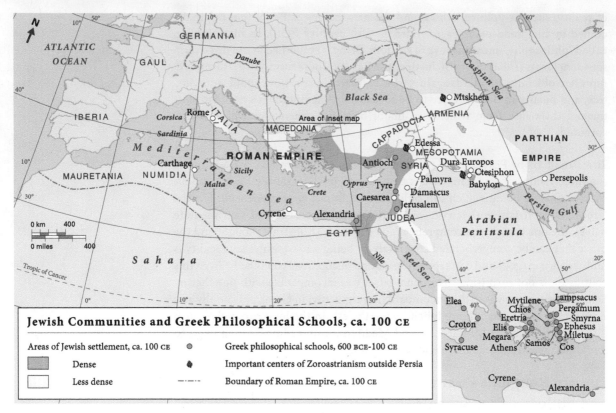

MAP 7.8  **Jewish Communities and Greek Philosophical Schools, ca. 100 CE.**

**Synagogues:** Jewish meeting places for prayer and legal consultation.

so-called Cynics, who advocated the virtues of natural simplicity far removed from power, wealth, and fame. Scribes translated Jewish scriptures into Greek, and in the second half of the 200s BCE prayer houses, called "**synagogues**," emerged in cities and towns for the study of the scriptures and of the new Jewish law that had evolved since the foundation of the Second Temple. The monotheism of Yahweh continued to be exclusively administered by priests. But preachers in the synagogues, called "Pharisees," made this monotheism an increasingly popular faith among ordinary Jews.

In the first century BCE, the Romans and Persian Parthians replaced the Seleucids and the Herodians replaced the Hasmoneans in Palestine. The Jews interacted not only with the culture of Hellenism but also with the culture of the Romans, their new overlords, and the Parthian Persians, their new neighbors to the east. Many Jews adapted to the Roman philosophical school of the Stoics (who, like the Cynics, advocated an ethics in harmony with the laws of nature) and to the Persian Zoroastrian-inspired apocalypse, which predicted God's final war against evil (that is, foreign domination by Rome), the resurrection of the dead, the day of judgment, and salvation in the heavenly kingdom. Elements of philosophy and the apocalypse, coming together in the teachings of the Pharisees in the synagogues, found widespread followers in the Jewish population. Palestine was a cauldron of cultural influences—some monotheistic, others monist, many clashing with polytheism.

**The Origins of Christianity**     It was from this cauldron that the Jewish reform movement of Christianity arose in the first century CE. The earliest scriptures of the Christians, contained in the New Testament, describe the founding figure, Jesus of Nazareth, as a preacher in Galilee in northern Palestine, several miles from Jerusalem. After he was baptized by John, an ascetic preacher on the Jordan River, Jesus is reported to have left the Mosaic as well as the Pharisaic law aside, including the stringent purity laws, and to have preached instead the spirit of the law, which he expressed as the "law of love" (Greek *agape*, Latin *caritas*; Mark 12:29–30). Only if one loved God and one's neighbor as one loved oneself would one acquire the proper understanding of law and be prepared for the apocalypse and salvation in the heavenly kingdom soon to come.

When Jesus is reported to have gone to Jerusalem during Passover, one of three times a year when Jews were enjoined to visit the Temple for sacrifices, he provoked the Temple priests with his ultimate challenge to Jewish law: He overturned the tables of the money changers and sellers of sacrificial birds to Jews performing the required animal sacrifices. For Jesus, obedience to all these detailed laws and regulations was quite unnecessary in the anticipation of the heavenly kingdom. According to the New Testament, his actions in the Temple initiated the chain of events which ended with the priests turning Jesus over to the Roman governor for death on the cross.

Again according to the New Testament, shortly after Jesus' death, the Pharisee, Roman citizen, and philosophically trained Paul of Tarsus in Anatolia converted to Jesus' law of love. Paul dispensed with another Jewish law, circumcision, and thereby liberated Jesus' message from its last tie to Judaism: Henceforth, anyone could become a follower of Jesus. Paul retained the concept of the apocalypse with its tribulations but also argued that salvation had already begun with Jesus' resurrection from death, ascension to heaven, and imminent return—the Second Coming as the Messiah or Christus, hence Jesus' divine name, "Christ"—and ruler of the heavenly kingdom. According to both the Lucan Acts and the letters attributed to his name, Paul traveled widely and preached to numerous small Christian communities, called "churches" (Greek, sing. *ekklesia*), which formed in the Roman Empire during the middle of the first century CE.

**Mural from Dura-Europos on the Euphrates.** The city, founded in 303 BCE, was home to a sizeable Jewish community whose synagogue was adorned with murals in the Parthian-Hellenistic style. Shown here is a depiction of the infant Moses being rescued from the Nile.

**The Christian Church**     Paul trained the first missionaries, and after him proselytizing became a regular feature of the emerging Christian community. The missionaries preached Christianity in the Roman Empire from scriptures which evolved in the first three centuries CE. At this time, the first basic canon of accepted writings, the New Testament, was assembled. A hierarchy of bishops and priests preached from these scriptures to laypeople who congregated in local churches for regular communal services. From an early period, however, Christians were divided on how to understand the New Testament. The philosophically educated tended to interpret it figuratively—that is, by reading their philosophical concepts into scripture. Others, opposed to Greek philosophy, preferred a literal interpretation, even though Paul's Christianity was already philosophically tinged. A long struggle over the integration of scripture and philosophy into a single Christian civilization ensued in the church.

Principal figures in the struggle were theologians, called "church fathers." The earliest among them was Origen of Alexandria (ca. 185–254 CE), who focused not only on the allegorical but also on the ethical interpretation of scripture. The intellectually most versatile church father was Augustine (354–430 CE), from what is today Algeria. His two main works are the *Confessions*, in which he describes his conversion to Christianity and reflections on spirituality, and *The City of God*, in which he defends Christianity against the accusation by many Romans that its adoption as the state religion in 380 contributed to the decline of the empire. Although his philosophical training was limited, he was a strong proponent of the allegorical interpretation, which became a principal pillar of church doctrine. Thanks to the church fathers, the church was set on a path of merging monotheism and philosophy, as the basis for the rise of a Christian civilization.

# The Beginnings of Science and the Cultures of Kings and Citizens

Monotheism and philosophy entered society early on during the Jewish Second Temple kingdom in Palestine. In the Persian and Roman Empires this incorporation, in the form of preferred or state religions, took longer. Greek science became important in Ptolemaic Egypt (305–30 BCE). The Ptolemies provided state support for the development of mathematics, physics, astronomy, and the applied science of mechanics as new and independent fields of culture. The other, inherited forms of cultural expression—painting, sculpture, architecture, and literature—remained within traditional polytheistic confines. Nevertheless, in Greece and Rome these cultural forms underwent substantial innovation and differentiation, influenced by Hellenism as well as Parthian and Sasanid Persia.

## The Sciences at the Library of Alexandria

In Athens and other city-states, citizens supported philosophical schools, such as the Academy of Plato or the Lyceum of Aristotle (384–322 BCE), one of Plato's students and the tutor of Alexander. These institutions were small if compared with the enormous resources the Ptolemies and their Roman successors poured into a new type of institution of Greek learning, the institute for advanced study, as we would say today. Centers of research, principally libraries and museums, flourished at Pergamon, Alexandria, and elsewhere. The Library of Alexandria (280 BCE–ca. 400 CE) was devoted primarily to research in the mathematical and natural sciences. At times, some 100 resident fellows did research in its library holdings of half a million scrolls, performed limited dissection of corpses in laboratories, gazed at the stars in the astronomical observatory, strolled through the botanical gardens, and shared meals.

The most developed branch of the sciences at the museum was geometry. Euclid (fl. ca. 300 BCE), one of the founders of the museum, provided geometry with its basic definitions and proofs in his *Elements*, still important today. In addition to geometry, mathematicians laid the foundations for algebra. The pioneer was Diophantus (ca. 214–284 CE), with his exploration of the properties of algebraic equations. Hypatia (ca. 360–415 CE), the first known female scientist in world history, is said to have contributed further to the development of algebra, but her work is unfortunately no longer extant. In the absence of a practical Greek number system, however, algebra remained ultimately stunted in its growth in Alexandria and had to await the Muslims and the Arabic numeral system—originally devised in India—to evolve fully.

Alexandrian geographers and astronomers, trained in geometry, made important calculations of the earth's circumference and tilt and formulated the first heliocentric astronomical theory, according to which the earth spins around the sun. Unfortunately, this theory was rejected in favor of more commonsensical observations, such as the fact that an arrow shot upward falls to the same spot instead of farther to the west. Therefore, the opposite theory of the earth at the center of the planetary system became dominant. Claudius Ptolemy (ca. 87–170 CE) devised such a detailed and precise geometric system of the planets' movements that his geocentrism reigned for the next millennium and a half in the astronomies of the Islamic Middle East and western European Christianity, dethroned eventually only by Copernicus in the sixteenth century.

In addition to astronomy, physics also flourished at the museum. The outstanding physicist was Archimedes (287–212 BCE), who investigated the behavior of floating bodies in the new science of hydrostatics—bold investigations, which had to wait a millennium and a half before being fully appreciated in the works of Galileo Galilei, one of the pioneers of modern physics.

The museum came to its end under unknown circumstances at the beginning of the 400s CE. Its legacy, however, was such that later Islamic rulers resumed the tradition of sponsoring institutes for advanced study.

## Royal Persian Culture and Arts

The Achaemenid Persians arrived in Mesopotamia with their rich Indo-European traditions of divine and heroic myths, which were also characteristic of Aryan migrants to India. These myths told of deities and heroes mingling in a verdant landscape of mountains, rivers, and pastures. Major themes included the protracted, sometimes noble, and occasionally treacherous struggles between the Persians and their tribal rivals in central Asia, whom they called "Turanians." After 600 BCE, monotheistic Zoroastrians reworked the pagan myths in the Avesta so that under the one, invisible God (Ahuramazda) the other deities became lesser beings, such as angels and demons. The myths and epics were handed down orally until the 400s CE, well after the disappearance of the Achaemenids, before they were finally written down.

As heirs of both Achaemenid Persian and Greek traditions, the Parthians forged a new synthesis between inherited styles and adopted Greek-Hellenistic elements, while maintaining an overall palace-focused culture of their own. For example, courtiers listened to bards who recited the exploits of Hercules and other

Greek heroes, thereby laying the foundations for the Rustam story cycle written down several centuries later. Other bards and minstrels traveled among aristocratic families, composing stories of their masters' courtly loves and intrigues or their exploits in battles against nomadic invaders from central Asia. After the Parthians, these stories were handed down orally and grew in both length and complexity. They exist today in a modern Persian version, called the *Book of Kings* (*Shahname* [Sha-ha-na-MAY]), compiled by the poet Firdosi [Feer-dow-SEE] in the eleventh century CE.

The Sasanids were major transmitters of Indian texts to the Middle East and Mediterranean. The most popular text was a translation of animal fables, known in Sanskrit as the *Five Treatises* (*Panchatantra* [Pan-cha-TAN-trah]) and in Arabic as *Kalila wa dimna* [Ka-LEE-lah wa DIM-nah]. In these fables, animals appear in witty, cleverly constructed stories intended to teach lessons to palace courtiers and retainers. Other texts were instruction manuals on chess, a game which made its way to the West during Sasanid times. Also from India came medical texts complete with discussions of anatomy, diseases, and herbs. All these texts, which were both useful and entertaining, played important roles at the Sasanid court.

In architecture, the characteristic feature of Sasanid palaces was the monumental dome and barrel vault. Arches, domes, and barrel vaulting had been pioneered in Mesopotamia in the second millennium BCE but only for small structures. Sasanid vaults and domes were massive structures. The central audience hall of the palace in the capital, Ctesiphon, built ca. 250 CE, had a barrel vault 118 feet high. Other palaces had "squinched" domes of up to 45 feet across, covering square audience and banquet halls. *Squinches* were curved triangular transition spaces between the dome and the corners of the halls. In order to counter the outward thrust of the dome's weight, buttresses supported the walls on the outside. The techniques of both barrel vaulting and the dome were transmitted

**Barrel Vault of the Sasanid Royal Reception Hall, Ctesiphon.**

from Sasanid Persia to Christian Armenia, Rome, and ultimately western Europe, where they appeared in church architecture.

## Greek and Roman Civic Culture and Arts

The disappearance of kings and aristocracies in the Greek city-states during the sixth century BCE had momentous consequences for Greek culture. Instead of merely a handful of kings and aristocrats sponsoring the arts, thousands of wealthy citizens began to patronize artists or even create works of literature, sculpture, painting, and architecture themselves. A broad civic artistic creativity arose. Although polytheism, myths, and other ancient traditions remained central for the majority of the citizens and only a minority adapted to the new philosophical and scientific monism, the heritage lost its symbolical, stylized, and generic royal orientation. Instead, Greeks began to experiment with a variety of individual shapes, types, and models, seeking realistic representation in their art.

As in Mesopotamia and Egypt, seasonal festivals were of great importance in Greece. In contrast to Mesopotamia and Egypt, however, Greek city culture encouraged personal artistic expression. Given the increasing participation of commoners in the state, festivals in Greece became occasions for the composition of songs and poems whose authors were remembered by name. Festivals often had poetry contests, and Hesiod appears as the earliest winner of such a contest. In the following century, a writer who acquired fame outside the poetry contest circuit was Sappho. She was the instructor of female initiation groups in one of the city-states on the island of Lesbos. Her poetry reflects the experience of erotic experimentation among adolescent girls which was part of their preparation for marriage.

**Greek Literature and Art**    The earliest Greek literature dates to the eighth century BCE. The period 750–600 BCE was a time of close cultural contact between the rising Greek city-states and the Neo-Assyria Empire, which dominated Syria and Anatolia. Not surprisingly, therefore, the Assyrian versions of the Mesopotamian epic and creation myths, *Gilgamesh* and *Enuma Elish*, made their way to the Greeks, where they were incorporated into Greek culture.

This incorporation was the work of two gifted writers, Homer (fl. ca. 730 BCE) and Hesiod (fl. ca. 700 BCE), both from Greek city-states in Anatolia, and both familiar with Mesopotamian literature through interactions with the ancient Near East. Homer composed two epics in the form of extended poems, the tragedy *Iliad* and the narrative legend *Odyssey*. Hesiod's *Theogony* begins with "Chaos, the Abyss," out of which the earth, or Gaia, came into being. The rest of the *Theogony* is devoted to telling the stories of some 300 divinities descended from Chaos and Gaia. Three of the first four generations of deities destroyed each other violently. The fourth, the Olympians, became the present pantheon of gods, with Zeus as the patriarch.

The Greek theater emerged around 500–480 BCE out of the stylized traditions and rituals of the Dionysiac cult. Every year in March, during the Dionysiac processions, competitions took place among groups of citizens (later wealthy non-citizens also competed) for the presentation of the best tragedy or comedy. These competing groups, or *choruses*, dressed in sumptuous robes and elaborate masks

**Greek Realism.** The Greeks used decorated stelae to mark the burial places of the dead in much the same way tombstones function today. This intimate relief, from about 450 BCE, memorializes a young girl. The treatment of the child's body is realistic—note the chubby arms—and the way the girl tenderly holds her pet doves transforms the little scene into a touching story.

to perform the chosen dramatic or comic piece through declamation and dance. In the course of time, individual actors emerged from among the chorus members and presented dialogues on which the chorus commented as the plot evolved. Tragedy developed out of Dionysiac myths and comedy from the Dionysiac processions.

Among the most important writers who composed for the early Greek stage were the tragedians Aeschylus, Sophocles, and Euripides, as well as the comedian Aristophanes. All four authors, and many of their successors, continue to exercise a profound influence on the evolution of Western literature today.

Just as democracy encouraged the exploration of individual character in tragedy and comedy, so it supported the search for character representation in Greek painting and sculpture. Unfortunately, no murals or panels exist today, although a few Roman reproductions survive. Vase painting gives us a good impression of scenes of daily life, even though the medium imposed severe limits of color and composition on artists. Surviving examples of sculptures are plentiful, even if primarily in the form of later Roman copies, which often lack the refinement of the original Greek models.

In the fifth century BCE, sculptors abandoned the last traces of the traditional Middle Eastern symbolic royal style that required figures to be in tranquil repose, projecting dignity and impassivity. Instead, sculptors began to explore physical movement and individual emotional states. In terms of themes, poses, and individuality, Greek vase paintings and sculptures achieved a remarkably wide range, from figures exerting themselves in their chosen sports to serene models of human beauty. Greek sculptors and painters abandoned symbolism and, instead, embraced realism as their style of representation (what we might call today "photographic representation").

**Roman Literature and Art**    Greece influenced Roman culture early on. As early as the middle of the third century BCE, Romans had translated Greek plays and poetry into Latin. After the adaptation of Greek poetic metrical patterns to the Latin language, a long line of poets emerged. Prose writings on political and historical themes, also modeled on Greek precursors, appeared in large numbers. Emperor Augustus and his wealthy friend Maecenas, renowned for his sponsorship of the arts, stimulated an outburst of early imperial pride. For example, in his epic poem *The Aeneid*, Virgil (70–19 BCE) played down the influence of Greece by positing the origins of Rome in Troy, the rival of Greece. In his Odes, Horace (65–8 BCE) glorified courage, patriotism, piety, justice, and a respect for tradition, which he regarded as uniquely Roman virtues. These writers viewed Rome as the culmination of civilization.

Roman sculpture followed the Greek civic style closely by emphasizing proportion, perspective, foreshortening, and light and shadow. Among the earliest sculptures were marble busts which aristocratic Romans had made of their patriarchs, cast from wax masks and plaster models. These busts, kept in family shrines, were a central part of aristocratic life in the republic. During the imperial period prior to the establishment of Christianity as the state religion (31 BCE–380 CE), life-size imitations of Greek and Egyptian statues were commonly found in the

**Scene from the Aeneid.**
According to Virgil's *Aeneid*, on his journey from Troy, Aeneas landed in North Africa and fell madly in love with Dido, the queen of Carthage. One day, as they were hunting, a storm forced the two to seek shelter in a cave. Destiny, however, demanded that Aeneas travel on to Italy and found Rome. In her disconsolate grief of being without Aeneas, Dido committed suicide. The cave episode is illustrated here in a manuscript of the fifth century CE.

**Pompeii: Mural Executed with Careful Attention to Perspective, Light and Shadow, and Foreshortening.**
An eruption of the Vesuvius volcano buried the city in 79 CE in ash and thereby preserved the murals of the city. They provide some of the best evidence we have of life in ancient Rome.

households of the wealthy. On columns and triumphal arches, reliefs similar to those of the Persians celebrated military victories. In contrast to the Parthians and Sasanids, civic Romans adorned their cities with numerous monumental structures and hence provided their empire with much greater visibility.

Roman pictorial art existed mostly in the form of wood panels, wall paintings, and floor mosaics. In the fifth century CE, the first illustrated book appeared, depicting scenes from Virgil's *Aeneid*. Nearly all panel paintings have perished, but wall paintings have survived in larger numbers, ironically due to their preservation in Pompeii and other cities buried by the eruption of Mount Vesuvius in 79 CE. The paintings demonstrate Roman art at a remarkably skilled level, with perspective emphasized and executed just as precisely as in Greek art.

Rome's architecture was initially closely modeled on the Greek and Etruscan heritage in Italy. In the imperial age, when the desire for monumental architecture developed, the Romans—shortly after the Parthians—adopted the elements of arch and dome for large buildings. An example is the Pantheon in Rome, built in 118–126 CE. This building, a temple dedicated to all the Roman gods, consists of a dome placed on top of a drum and lit by a round open skylight at its apex (diameter and height both 142 feet). The circular foundation wall made squinches unnecessary. The courtyard of Emperor Diocletian's palace in what is now Split, Croatia (ca. 300 CE), contains the first example of arches set on pillars, which later acquired crucial importance in Islamic and medieval Christian architectures.

Beginning with the first Christian emperor, Constantine, in the early fourth century CE, there was a return from realistic to symbolical representation in the arts. The rich variety of literature shrank to the one category of religious poetry and hymns. Pagan Greek and Roman realistic artists had emphasized emotional variety in their art, playing with surface detail, perspective, foreshortening, light and shadow, and full and empty space. In contrast, Christian artists began to emphasize what they considered essential. Instead of seeking emotionally diverse forms and expressions, they drew from Middle Eastern models, which retained connections to symbolism. Accordingly, characters and objects became generic and lost their detailed psychological and physical characteristics. Space became two-dimensional and figures were large or small according to their religious importance, not their closeness to or distance from the viewer. What mattered was the paradigmatic saintly comportment of figures, whom the believers were supposed to imitate. Religious uniformity came to dominate culture in the Roman and Sasanid Persian Empires, as it dominated their politics in the form of state religion.

## Putting It All Together

In 590/591 the Sasanid Empire suffered a war of succession during which one of the rivals, King Khosrow II (r. 590–628), fled to the Romans. Before he arrived in Constantinople, he sent an embassy that pleaded for military support: "It is impossible for a single monarchy to embrace the innumerable cares of the organization of the universe. . . . It is never possible for the earth to resemble the unity of the divine and primary rule." As Khosrow had hoped, his ambassadors' arguments were persuasive, and he received Roman military support, with which he defeated his rival and regained the Persian throne.

Khosrow's argument is a fitting conclusion to this chapter on world empires, which began with Alexander's bold quest to unite the Mediterranean, Middle East, and India. For Alexander it was still possible to think in terms of one supreme god in heaven and one empire on earth. But after the introduction of monotheism, the situation changed. For the Persian ambassadors it was impossible for a human empire not only to ever resemble the kingdom of God but also to reign alone on earth. For the Persians and Romans—Theophylactus cites the Persian ambassadors approvingly—the one single God anywhere and nowhere disapproves of all imperial projects on earth and prefers a commonwealth of multiple kingdoms. It is this reevaluation of politics and history which the visionaries can be seen as having contributed to world history. Obviously, many kings and emperors later in history did not accept the idea of the futility of empires. But after monotheism, they had to reckon with forceful critics who would cut their ambitions down to size and remind people of the fundamental difference between the imperfect earthly states and the heavenly kingdom.

▶ For additional resources, including maps, primary sources, visuals, and quizzes, please go to www.oup.com/us/vonsivers. Please see the Further Resources section at the back of the book for additional readings and suggested websites.

## Against the Grain

# Women in Democratic Athens

The word "democracy" is derived from the Greek *demos* ("the people") and *kratia* ("power," or "strength"). Yet even though democratic rule in Athens is usually cited as a model of egalitarian rule, the status of women in Athenian society reflects a glaring contradiction of this ideal depiction.

Several indicators point to policies of marked gender inequality. Athenian women could neither vote nor own property. Their marriages were often arranged, primarily for monetary gain; once married, women could not sue for divorce. Married women were under the constant control of a guardian (*kyrios*), either their husbands or nearest male relatives. While it is true that women were permitted to bring dowries into the marriage, these were immediately assigned to the husband's control.

For the most part, women's roles consisted of bearing and raising children, inculcating in them the moral and ethical values of the polis, and being responsible for managing the household (*oikos*). Because women were believed to be more emotional and driven by sexual passion than men, they were seen to pose a threat to the stability of both *oikos* and polis. Thus, Athenian women were largely confined to the home, although they frequented the marketplace and civic center (*agora*), and occasionally attended festivals. Women were also assigned participatory roles in funerals, weddings, and religious rituals, where they played important roles as priestesses. Educated women routinely accompanied men as companions (*hetairai*) to various social functions, such as plays and dinner parties. At the bottom of the social ladder were slave women and prostitutes (*pornai*).

Why were Athenian women relegated to second-class citizenship? In a patriarchal society like Athens men determined cultural norms, and thus reflected prevailing views of women. For example, in Euripides' *Medea* the protagonist laments "If only children could be got by some other way without the female sex. . . . If women didn't exist, human life would be rid of all its miseries." And in his *Politics* Aristotle observes that "the male is by nature superior, and the female inferior; and the one rules, and the other is ruled; this principle, of necessity, extends to all mankind."

- How does the inferior status of Athenian women represent a contradiction to the prevailing view of Athenian democracy?

- In what ways does this image of women in Athens compare and contrast with women's status in other ancient civilizations?

# Thinking Through Patterns

► **Why should the Middle East and Mediterranean Europe during the period 600 BCE–600 CE be studied as a single unit?**

The sharp division between Europe and the Middle East that exists today is a recent phenomenon. During the period of late multireligious and early monotheistic empires, from 600 BCE to 600 CE, the two regions were tightly intertwined. Initially, the sequence of the multireligious Persian and Macedonian Empires dominated the Middle East and eastern Mediterranean. Later, the competition between the subsequent two empires, Rome and Persia, inaugurated a pattern of urbanization, a deepening gulf between the wealthy and poor, and the immigration of tribal people from central Asia.

The experience of transcendence happens constantly, even if it remains for the most part unexpressed and little thought about. In its most common form, it is encountered as the unknown future: You dream of getting a college degree as the entry ticket to your future academic career. After years of toil, sacrifices, and financial cost, the day of graduation arrives. In one moment, as your name is called, the transcendent expectation becomes a reality: As you clutch the diploma, a thrill goes down your spine. Apart from the future, the past as well as space can be thought of as transcendent. The great visionaries of 700–500 BCE abstracted a separate, transcendent God or first principle from the world where there had been in polytheism a single cosmos in which heaven with its high god, plus all the other gods and goddesses, intermingled with the world. The visionaries did not merely reflect on gods and humans mixing *in* the world, as in the polytheism of the past; they rather directed their focus on God or the first principle *separate from* the world, thereby creating religious monotheism and philosophical monism. Following the visionaries, thinkers explored new, abstract dimensions of thought in the new intellectual disciplines of science, philosophy, and theology.

► **What is transcendence, and why is it important to understand its importance in world history?**

► **Which elements characterize the institutions that grew out of the Middle Eastern monotheisms of Judaism–Christianity and monism of Greek philosophy-science?**

In the Middle East and eastern Mediterranean, visionaries were the creators of bodies of transcendent thought that evolved into the Zoroastrian and Jewish religions as well as Greek philosophy and science. The visionaries and their early followers created scriptures which expounded in great detail the nature of God or the first principle. Anyone could read or listen to the scriptures, and, accordingly, the visionaries and their successors attracted communities of like-minded followers. Zoroastrianism, Judaism, and Christianity were religions of salvation: Firm believers in the power of God's forgiveness would be saved in a transcendent kingdom of heaven. For Zoroastrians, Jews, and Christians—cogs in the giant, brutal, and meaningless multireligious machines of the Persian and Roman Empires—this religious promise of salvation was the only way of making sense out of life. Eventually the emperors themselves converted, making monotheism the state religion.

# Patterns of Evidence: Sources for Chapter 7

## The Cyrus Cylinder

**539 BCE**

Founder of the Achaemenid Persian Empire, Cyrus (Kurosh) the Great rose to the throne of a small kingdom in 559 BCE; by the time of his death in 529, he had brought virtually the entire Near East under his control. In 539, he conquered Babylon and drove out Nabonidus, the last of the Neo-Babylonian kings. However, he was hailed as a liberator by the priests of the Babylonian god Marduk, and he issued a remarkable document, guaranteeing freedom of religion to the subjects whom he had added to his empire. The text, which was publicized in Akkadian, an ancient Mesopotamian language, is preserved on a clay cylinder, today called the Cyrus Cylinder and housed in the British Museum.

. . .

On account of their complaints, the lords of the gods became furiously angry and left their [the Babylonians'] land; the gods, who dwelt among them, left their homes. . . . In all lands everywhere [the god Marduk] searched; he looked through them and sought a righteous prince after his own heart, whom he took by the hand. He called Cyrus, king of Anshan, by name; he appointed him to lordship over the whole world.

The land of Qutu, all the Umman-manda, he cast down at his feet. The black-headed people, whom he gave his hands to conquer, he took them in justice and righteousness. Marduk, the great lord, looked joyously on the caring for his people, on his pious works and his righteous heart. To his city, Babylon, he caused [Cyrus] to go; he made him take the road to Babylon, going as a friend and companion at his side. His numerous troops, in unknown numbers, like the waters of a river, marched armed at his side. Without battle and conflict, he permitted him to enter Babylon. He spared his city, Babylon, a calamity. Nabonidus, the king, who did not fear him, he delivered into his hand.

. . .

Source: Cyrus Cylinder, trans. R. W. Rogers, http://www.kchanson.com/ANCDOCS/meso/cyrus.html.

When I [Cyrus] made my triumphal entrance into Babylon, I took up my lordly residence in the royal palace with joy and rejoicing; Marduk, the great lord, moved the noble heart of the residents of Babylon to me, while I gave daily attention to his worship. My numerous troops marched peacefully into Babylon. In all Sumer and Akkad I permitted no enemy to enter.

The needs of Babylon and of all its cities I gladly attended to. The people of Babylon [and ... ], and the shameful yoke was removed from them. Their dwellings, which had fallen, I restored. I cleared out their ruins. Marduk, the great lord, rejoiced in my pious deeds, and graciously blessed me, Cyrus, the king who worships him, and Cambyses, my own son, and all my troops, while we, before him, joyously praised his exalted godhead.

. . .

And the gods of Sumer and Akkad—whom Nabonidus, to the anger of the lord of the gods, had brought into Babylon—by the command of Marduk, the great lord, I caused them to take up their dwelling in residences that gladdened the heart. May all the gods, whom I brought into their cities, pray daily before Bel and Nabu for long life for me, and may they speak a gracious word for me and say to Marduk, my lord, "May Cyrus, the king who worships you, and Cambyses his son, their [ ... ] I permitted all to dwell in peace [ ... ]."

▶ **Working with Sources**

1. **How and why did Cyrus incorporate local deities into his public image after subjugating Babylon?**

2. **How does this document compare with other instances of Persian tolerance in the historical record?**

## SOURCE 7.2

# Herodotus, *Histories*

**ca. 420s BCE**

H aving failed to defeat the Athenians in their first attempt in 490 BCE, the Persians launched a massive invasion of the entire Greek peninsula in 480, under the leadership of Darius's successor, Xerxes. Thirty-one Greek cities agreed to band together to resist this force of (according to Herodotus) 1,700,000 Persian soldiers, in addition to a sizeable naval contingent. Herodotus envisions a conversation between Xerxes and the Spartan defector Demaratus shortly before the first major confrontation between Persia and the Greeks at Thermopylae. In answer to the king's question, Demaratus claims that the Greeks will prove more difficult to defeat than Xerxes expects.

Having sailed from one end to the other of the line of anchored ships, Xerxes went ashore again and sent for Demaratus, the son of Ariston, who was accompanying him in the march to Greece. "Demaratus," he said, "it would give me pleasure at this point to put to you a few questions. You are a Greek, and a native, moreover, of by no means the meanest or weakest city in that country—as I learn not only from yourself but from the other Greeks I have spoken with. Tell me, then— will the Greeks dare to lift a hand against me? My own belief is that all the Greeks and all the other western peoples gathered together would be insufficient to withstand the attack of my army—and still more so if they are not united. But it is your opinion upon this subject that I should like to hear."

. . .

"I think highly," [Demaratus said,] "of all Greeks of the Dorian lands, but what I am about to say will apply not to all Dorians, but to the Spartans only. First then, they will not under any circumstances accept terms from you which would mean slavery for Greece; secondly, they will fight you even if the rest of Greece submits. Moreover, there is no use in asking if their numbers are adequate to enable them to do this; suppose a thousand of them take the field—then that thousand will fight you; and so will any number, greater than this or less."

Xerxes laughed. "Demaratus," he exclaimed, "what an extraordinary thing to say! Do you really suppose a thousand men would fight an army like mine?"

. . .

"King," Demaratus answered, "I knew before I began that if I spoke the truth you would not like it. But, as you demanded the plain truth and nothing less, I told you how things are with the Spartans. Yet you are well aware that I now feel but little affection for my countrymen, who robbed me of my hereditary power and privileges and made me a fugitive without a home—whereas your father welcomed me at his court and gave me the means of livelihood and somewhere to live. Surely it is unreasonable to reject kindness; any sensible man will cherish it. Personally I do not claim to be able to fight ten men—or two; indeed I should prefer not even to fight with one. But should it be necessary— should there be some great cause to urge me on—then nothing would give me more pleasure than to stand up to one of those men of yours who claim to be a match for three Greeks. So it is with the Spartans; fighting singly, they are as good as any, but fighting together they are the best soldiers in the world. They are free— yes—but not entirely free; for they have a master, and that master is Law, which they fear much more than your subjects fear you. Whatever this master commands, they do; and his command never varies: it is never to retreat in battle, however great the odds, but always to remain in

Source: Herodotus, *The Histories*, trans. Aubrey de Sélincourt (Harmondsworth, UK: Penguin, 1954), 403–405.

formation, and to conquer or die. If, my lord, you think that what I have said is nonsense—very well; I am willing henceforward to hold my tongue. This time I spoke because you forced me to speak. In any case, I pray that all may turn out as you desire."

Xerxes burst out laughing at Demaratus' answer, and good-humoredly let him go.

▶ **Working with Sources**

1. For what reasons does Demaratus think the Spartans will fight so hard to resist Xerxes?

2. What does the passage reveal concerning Herodotus's attitude toward the Greeks—and the Persians?

## SOURCE 7.3

# 1 Maccabees

### ca. 134 BCE

Just before his death in Babylon in June 323 BCE, Alexander the Great was the unrivalled conqueror of an enormous portion of the known world, counting modern Greece, Egypt, the Middle East, Iran, and Afghanistan among his possessions. However, when he died, leaving his kingdom "to the strongest," conflicts immediately broke out among his Macedonian successors to determine who that strongest man was. A part of the military and political struggle that followed was an attempt to Hellenize, with varying levels of success, the older and more entrenched cultures Alexander had defeated as he raced through Africa and Asia. This process continued for the next three centuries. In the mid-second century BCE, one of these successor kings, Antiochus IV Epiphanes, attempted a brutal imposition of Greek cultural values on the Jews in Jerusalem. This effort, and the revolt it triggered, is described in the apocryphal (i.e., not part of the standard canon) Jewish book of 1 Maccabees. Notice that the Hellenistic era did not appear to everyone to have been a fortuitous blending of disparate cultures.

**1** After Alexander son of Philip, the Macedonian, who came from the land of Kittim, had defeated King Darius of the Persians and the Medes, he succeeded him as king. (He had previously become king of Greece.) **2** He fought many battles, conquered strongholds, and put to death the kings of the earth. **3** He advanced to the ends of the earth, and plundered many nations. When the earth became quiet before him, he was exalted, and his heart was lifted up. **4** He gathered a very strong army and ruled over countries, nations, and princes, and they became tributary to him. **5** After this he fell sick and perceived that he was dying. **6** So he summoned his most honored officers, who had been brought up with him from youth, and divided his kingdom among them while he was still alive. **7** And after Alexander had reigned twelve years, he died. **8** Then his officers began to rule, each in his own place. **9** They all put on crowns after his death, and so did their descendants after them for many years; and they caused many evils on the earth.

**10** From them came forth a sinful root, Antiochus Epiphanes, son of King Antiochus; he had been a hostage in Rome. He began to reign in the one hundred thirty-seventh year of the kingdom of the Greeks. **11** In those days certain renegades came out from Israel and misled many, saying, "Let us go and make a covenant with the Gentiles around us, for since we separated from them many disasters have come upon us." **12** This proposal pleased them, **13** and some of the people eagerly went to the king, who authorized them to observe the ordinances of the Gentiles. **14** So they built a gymnasium in Jerusalem, according to Gentile custom, **15** and removed the marks of circumcision, and abandoned the holy covenant. They joined with the Gentiles and sold themselves to do evil. **16** When Antiochus saw that his kingdom was established, he determined to become king of the land of Egypt, in order that he might reign over both kingdoms.

**17** So he invaded Egypt with a strong force, with chariots and elephants and cavalry and with a large fleet. **18** He engaged King Ptolemy of Egypt in battle, and Ptolemy turned and fled before him, and many were wounded and fell. **19** They captured the fortified cities in the land of Egypt, and he plundered the land of Egypt.

**20** After subduing Egypt, Antiochus returned in the one hundred forty-third year. He went up against Israel and came to Jerusalem with a strong force. **21** He arrogantly entered the sanctuary and took the golden altar, the lampstand for the light, and all its utensils. **22** He took also the table for the bread of the Presence, the cups for drink offerings, the bowls, the golden censers, the curtain, the crowns, and the gold decoration on the front of the temple; he stripped it all off. **23** He took the silver and the gold, and the costly vessels; he took also the hidden treasures that he found. **24** Taking them all, he went into his own land. He shed much blood, and spoke with great arrogance. **25** Israel mourned deeply in every community, **26** rulers and elders groaned, young women and young men became faint, the beauty of the women faded. **27** Every bridegroom took up the lament; she who sat in the bridal chamber was mourning. **28** Even the land trembled for its inhabitants, and all the house of Jacob was clothed with shame. **29** Two years later the king sent to the cities of Judah a chief collector of tribute, and he came to Jerusalem with a large force. **30** Deceitfully he spoke

Source: *The Apocrypha: Revised Standard Version of the Old Testament* (New York: Thomas Nelson & Sons, 1957), 190–192.

peaceable words to them, and they believed him; but he suddenly fell upon the city, dealt it a severe blow, and destroyed many people of Israel. **31** He plundered the city, burned it with fire, and tore down its houses and its surrounding walls. **32** They took captive the women and children, and seized the livestock. **33** Then they fortified the city of David with a great strong wall and strong towers, and it became their citadel.

. . .

**44** And the king sent letters by messengers to Jerusalem and the towns of Judah; he directed them to follow customs strange to the land, **45** to forbid burnt offerings and sacrifices and drink offerings in the sanctuary, to profane sabbaths and festivals, **46** to defile the sanctuary and the priests, **47** to build altars and sacred precincts and shrines for idols, to sacrifice swine and other unclean animals, **48** and to leave their sons uncircumcised. They were to make themselves abominable by everything unclean and profane, **49** so that they would forget the law and change all the ordinances. **50** He added, "And whoever does not obey the command of the king shall die." **51** In such words he wrote to his whole kingdom. He appointed inspectors over all the people and commanded the towns of Judah to offer sacrifice, town by town. **52** Many of the people, everyone who forsook the law, joined them, and they did evil in the land; **53** they drove Israel into hiding in every place of refuge they had. **54** Now on the fifteenth day of Chislev, in the one hundred forty-fifth year, they erected a desolating sacrilege on the altar of burnt offering. They also built altars in the surrounding towns of Judah, **55** and offered incense at the doors of the houses and in the streets. **56.** The books of the law that they found they tore to pieces and burned with fire. **57** Anyone found possessing the book of the covenant, or anyone who adhered to the law, was condemned to death by decree of the king. **58** They kept using violence against Israel, against those who were found month after month in the towns. **59** On the twenty-fifth day of the month they offered sacrifice on the altar that was on top of the altar of burnt offering. **60** According to the decree, they put to death the women who had their children circumcised, **61** and their families and those who circumcised them; and they hung the infants from their mothers' necks. **62** But many in Israel stood firm and were resolved in their hearts not to eat unclean food. **63** They chose to die rather than to be defiled by food or to profane the holy covenant; and they did die.

▶ **Working with Sources**

1. To what specific innovations does the writer of this document object? Why?

2. What evidence is contained in this document of cultural misunderstanding?

## SOURCE 7.4

# Graffiti from the walls of Pompeii

## ca. 79 CE

This is a small sample of the array of painted, scratched, and scribbled graffiti archaeologists have discovered on the walls of the city of Pompeii, which was sealed in ash after the eruption of Mount Vesuvius in 79 CE.

I

Twenty pairs of gladiators of Decimus Lucretius Satrius Valens, lifetime flamen [priest] of Nero son of Caesar Augustus [Claudius], and ten pairs of gladiators of Decimus Lucretius Valens, his son, will fight at Pompeii on April 8, 9, 10, 11, and 12. There will be a full card of wild beast combats, and awnings [for the spectators]. Aemilius Celer [painted this sign], all alone in the moonlight.

II

Market days: Saturday in Pompeii, Sunday in Nuceria, Monday in Atella, Tuesday in Nola, Wednesday in Cumae, Thursday in Puteoli, Friday in Rome.

III

6th: cheese 1, bread 8, oil 3, wine 3 [expenses in food, in coins called *asses*]
7th: bread 8, oil 5, onions 5, bowl 1, bread for the slave [?] 2, wine 2
8th: bread 8, bread for the slave [?] 4, grits 3
9th: wine for the winner 1 *denarius* [a higher denomination of coin], bread 8, wine 2, cheese 2
10th: [ . . . ] 1 *denarius*, bread 2, for women 8, wheat 1 *denarius*, cucumber 1, dates 1, incense 1, cheese 2, sausage 1, soft cheese 4, oil 7

IV

Pleasure says: "You can get a drink here for an as, a better drink for two, Falernian [fine quality wine] for four."

V

A copper pot is missing from this sho65 sesterces reward if anybody brings it back, 20 sesterces if he reveals the thief so we can get our property back.

VI

The weaver Successus loves the innkeeper's slave girl, Iris by name. She doesn't care for him, but he begs her to take pity on him. Written by his rival. So long.

[Answer by the rival:] Just because you're bursting with envy, don't pick on a handsomer man, a lady-killer and a gallant.

[Answer by the first writer:] There's nothing more to say or write. You love Iris, and she doesn't care for you.

VII

Take your lewd looks and flirting eyes off another man's wife, and show some decency on your face!

VIII

Anybody in love, come here. I want to break Venus' ribs with a club and cripple the goddess' loins. If she can

Source: Naphtali Lewis and Meyer Reinhold, eds., *Roman Civilization: Selected Readings*, vol. 2 (New York: Columbia University Press, 1990), 276–278.

pierce my tender breast, why can't
I break her head with a club?

But damn it! I don't want to be a god
without you.

IX

I write at Love's dictation and Cupid's
instruction;

X

[A prostitute's sign:] I am yours for
2 *asses* cash.

▶ **Working
with Sources**

1. **Are you surprised by what these graffiti reveal about daily life in
   Pompeii?**

2. **How could this material be used to assess the relative standing of
   women in Roman society? Should it be used in this way?**

## SOURCE 7.5

# The murder of the philosopher Hypatia, Alexandria, Egypt

### ca. 415 CE

Born around 360 CE and instructed by her father, Theon, a mathematician and the last librarian of the famous Library of Alexandria, Hypatia directed the Platonic school in the city, teaching students who were of mixed religious commitments but were, presumably, all men. The few sources that mention her agree that she was abducted, stripped of her clothes, and stoned to death with roof tiles by a fanatical group of Christians, but the precise sequence of events that led to this atrocity has always been controversial.

Because all of these sources were composed by Christians—with the exception of her own correspondence with a former student, the bishop Synesius of Cyrene—the lynching of Hypatia may be interpreted as an instance of fanaticism attempting to destroy reason, or as the elimination of a dangerous pagan influence in the midst of a Christianizing Egypt. The latter approach has, unfortunately, been more common, given Christian influence—and misogyny—in Western societies and the installation of her main opponent, Bishop Cyril of Alexandria, as one of the "fathers of the church."

There was a woman in Alexandria named Hypatia. She was the daughter of the philosopher Theon. She had progressed so far in her education that she surpassed by far the philosophers of her time, and took over the Neoplatonic school that derived from Plotinus, and set forth every philosophical approach to those who wanted to learn them. Accordingly people from all over who wanted to study philosophy rushed to her side. Because of the dignified reputation that derived from her education, she began (with due modesty) to address even the rulers. And she had no hesitation about being in the company of men, since they all respected her more because of her extraordinary chastity.

Then she became the subject of envy. Because she was frequently in the company of Orestes, people in the church began to slander her, as if that were what was preventing Orestes from making friends with the bishop. Some hot-headed men who agreed with this, who were led by a certain Peter the Reader, were on the lookout for the woman when she returned to her house from wherever she had been. They threw her out of her carriage, and dragged her to the church known as Caesarion. They tore off her clothing, and killed her with potsherds. When they had torn her apart limb from limb, they took the pieces of her body to the place called Cinaron, and burned them.

This act did no small amount of damage to Cyril and to the Church at Alexandria. For murder and fighting, and everything of that sort, are totally alien to those who believe in Christ. These events took place after Cyril had been bishop for four years, and Theodosius for ten [c. 415 CE], in the month of March, during Lent.

. . .

About Hypatia the philosopher. An illustration of how disorderly the Alexandrians are. She was born and raised and educated in Alexandria. She inherited her father's extraordinarily distinguished nature, and was not satisfied with the training in mathematics that she received from her father, but turned to other learning also in a distinguished way. Although she was a woman she put on a man's cloak and made her way into the center of the city and gave to those who wanted to listen public lectures about Plato or Aristotle or about some other philosophers. In addition to her teaching she also excelled in the practical arts, being just and chaste, she remained a virgin, though she was so beautiful to look at that one of her pupils fell in love with her. When he was no longer able to control his passion, he let her know how he felt about her. The uneducated stories have it that Hypatia told him to cure his disease through the study of the arts. But the truth is that he had long since given up on culture; instead, she brought in one of those women's rags and threw it at him, revealing her unclean nature, and said to him, "This is what you are in love with, young man, and not with the Beautiful," and in shame and wonder at this ugly display his soul was converted and he became more chaste.

That (according to this account) is what Hypatia was like, skilled in debate and dialectic, intelligent in her conduct and politically adept. The other citizens understandably were fond of her and accorded her the greatest respect, and the current magistrates of the town always went first to her, as used to happen also in Athens.

Source: Socrates, *Ecclesiastical History* 7.15, available online at http://www.stoa.org/diotima/anthology/wlgr/wlgr-religion451.shtml.

For even though the practice had died out, the name of philosophy still seemed distinguished and impressive to the people who had primary charge of the city. It then happened that the man in charge of the opposing sect, Cyril, passed by Hypatia's house and saw a large crowd in front of the door, consisting of men and horses, some arriving, some leaving, and some waiting there. He asked what the gathering was, and why there was commotion in front of the house, and learned from his followers that the philosopher Hypatia was giving a lecture and that this was her house. And when he learned this he was very upset and soon planned her murder, the most unholy of all murders. As she was going out to lecture, as was her custom, a group of bestial men attacked her, true ruffians, who had no respect for God and no concern for men's indignation; they killed the philosopher and brought the greatest pollution and disgrace on their fatherland.

▶ **Working with Sources**

1. Was Hypatia killed principally because she was a female philosopher or because she was a non-Christian philosopher?

2. How did Hypatia both refer to and transcend the boundaries placed upon women in ancient Greco-Roman society?

## Chapter 8 600 BCE–600 CE

# Empires and Visionaries in India

**INDIA,
800 BCE–800 CE**

It was one of the most intriguing meetings of the ancient world, though no one could have foreseen its ultimate significance at the time. One of the participants, Alexander the Great, as we have seen, had already become by the age of 30 the most successful military leader the world had ever seen. His present interest, however—the conquest of northern India—had so far proved difficult in the face of the huge armies and terrifying ranks of war elephants massed by his opponents. Now, as he prepared to invade the most powerful Indian state, Magadha, Alexander's men were growing anxious about the seemingly insatiable ambition of their commander. Given the opposition within his own ranks and on the battlefield, Alexander had retreated to the northern city of Taxila, near the modern capital of Islamabad in Pakistan, to replenish his forces and rethink his situation.

While in Taxila, Alexander met with a man identified by his biographers simply as "Sandrokoptros," who had recently fled the Magadhan court after a failed attempt to overthrow its government. Though we can only speculate about the substance of the talks between the two men, Alexander's use of local politics in his past military campaigns suggests that he sought to take advantage of Sandrokoptros's knowledge of Magadha and its leadership in planning his attack. The intelligence Alexander obtained must have been discouraging, for he soon abandoned his plans to invade India and, facing the possibility of mutiny among his men, withdrew to the safer confines of Persia, where he died in 323 BCE. Following Alexander's death, one of his commanders, Seleucus

*ABOVE:* **Sutra of the 1,000 Buddhas, from a seventeenth-century Tibetan manuscript.**

Nikator [si-LOO-kus Ni-KAY-tor], gained control of the eastern reaches of his empire. By 321 BCE, however, Seleucus Nikator found his territory around the Indus River threatened by a powerful new Indian state created by none other than Alexander's former ally, Sandrokoptros. But it was not until the end of the eighteenth century CE that the shadowy "Sandrokoptros" was identified by English Sanskrit scholars as Chandragupta Maurya [chahn-drah-GUP-tah MOR-y-ah], the founder of India's first and largest indigenous empire.

The meeting between Alexander and Chandragupta was significant for many reasons. For one thing, it took place between two men with similar desires for world empire, whose models of leadership inspired a host of imitators. More significant for our purposes, however, was what this meeting symbolized for the future patterns of Indian history: intensifying exchanges of ideas and goods between peoples of vastly different cultures and beliefs.

Indian visionaries and innovators made contributions that would have a profound effect on patterns of world history as they made their way throughout Eurasia and North Africa. In turn, India's place as a crossroads of trade and invasion continually replenished the subcontinent with innovation from out side. Many centuries later, the lore of India's wealth and culture would fire the imaginations of Europeans and drive them to seek out the connection first established by Alexander and Chandragupta so many centuries before.

## Patterns of State Formation in India: Republics, Kingdoms, and Empires

When Alexander arrived, the pattern of state formation in India had shifted permanently to the plains and hills of the Punjab and Ganges valley. As we noted in Chapter 3, the shift may have begun when tectonic movements in the Himalayas around 1900 BCE caused the drying up of the Sarasvati River in northwest India. People abandoned the agrarian–urban center of the Indus valley and migrated eastward. Much of the land to which they migrated in the Punjab and Ganges valley consisted of rain forest and marshes that required laborious land clearing. But the settlers drew on their past experience as they built the new agrarian–urban centers of northern India. In contrast to Africa and Mesoamerica where the patterns of state formation from villages and chiefdoms to kingdoms developed slowly, state formation proceeded rapidly. The earliest traces of villages date to about 1200 BCE. Thereafter, polities emerged quickly, in the form of warrior republics and kingdoms. Both flourished in the early first millennium BCE.

A gradual consolidation process set in from about 800 BCE onward, with a few kingdoms emerging as the strongest states, while the warrior republics disappeared from the scene. At the height of the wars for predominance, around 700–400 BCE, visionaries similar to those appearing at the same time in the Eastern Mediterranean, the Middle East, and China offered reforms of the Vedic

## Seeing Patterns

▶ Think about the reasons for the spread of Buddhism inside and outside of India. How have historians seen the decline of Buddhism in India?

▶ What do you consider to be the most influential patterns in Indian history to this point? Why?

▶ Do you think some of Ashoka's ideas could be implemented by governments today? Why or why not?

traditions: the Upanishads, Jainism, and Buddhism. The process of state formation reached a first peak with the Mauryan Empire, which united northern and central India and experimented with Buddhism as a privileged religion. A firm marriage between state and religion, however, occurred with the Hindu Gupta Empire (320–550 CE), which, along with its contemporary, Christian Rome, became the first state in world history to lay the foundation for a religious civilization.

## The Road to Empire: The Mauryas

In the early first millennium BCE, the emerging states along the Ganges River valley developed political systems ranging from *gana-sanghas* [GAH-nah SAHN-gahs]—often termed "republics" by scholars—to centralized monarchies whose rulers were accorded god-like status. The agricultural advances made in these formerly forested areas, particularly through the use of iron tools—and the dikes, ponds, flooded fields, and drainage systems necessary for growing rice—resulted in the emergence of wealthy, centralized states led by Magadha and Kosala, along with the lesser kingdoms of Vatsya and Avanti farther west (see Map 8.1).

During the half century before Alexander attempted to expand his empire into northern India, Mahapadama Nanda [mah-hah-PAH-dah-mah NAHN-dah], a member of the *shudra* (or lowest) *varna*, seized power in Magadha and embarked on a series of military campaigns against Vatsya and Avanti, both of which he

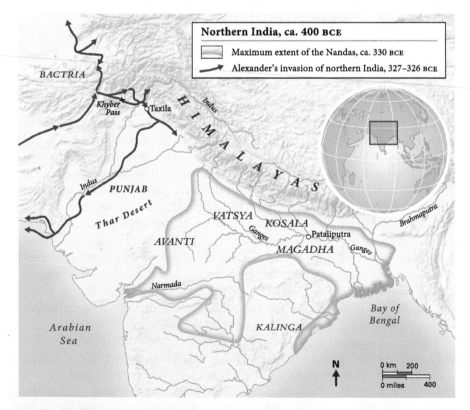

MAP **8.1** **Northern India, ca. 400 BCE.**

conquered. By the 330s BCE, the Magadhan state stretched across the entire breadth of northern India, and the taxes imposed by the Nandas brought unprecedented wealth to their capital of Pataliputra [pah-tah-lee-POO-trah], the modern city of Patna, on the Ganges. The Nandas, however, were not alone in their aspirations for universal empire.

**Chandragupta Maurya**    Little is known of Chandragupta's early life. It is believed that at a young age he was put under the care of the philosopher Kautilya, whose *Arthashastra* became the most influential political treatise in Indian history (see Chapter 3). Contemporary accounts of Chandragupta's court and the structure of his government suggest a strong connection to the political practices of the idealized ruler outlined in the *Arthashastra*. At this stage, however, Kautilya was instrumental in the young Chandragupta's first attempt to seize power from the ruling Nandas. Playing on discontent over Nanda taxation and the threat to religious order posed by rulers from the lowest *shudra varna*, he used his considerable influence to back a palace revolt by the young Chandragupta. When the revolt was unsuccessful, the two fled to Taxila, a dominant trade crossroads strategically located near the Khyber Pass, where they encountered Alexander.

Kautilya and Alexander played important roles in building Chandragupta's empire, though Alexander's role is less obvious. The dislocations in the northwest caused by Alexander's attempted invasions allowed Chandragupta to pursue a patient strategy of securing the most vulnerable and least contented of the Nandas' client states while methodically surrounding and, ultimately, conquering Magadha. By 321 BCE Chandragupta had secured the capital and embarked on a campaign to enlarge his empire. Following a series of battles with Alexander's successor Seleucus Nikator, the Greeks surrendered their north Indian and Indus territories to Chandragupta. Though forced from his Indian holdings, Seleucus and his successors maintained cordial relations with the Mauryas and posted the ambassador Megasthenes to the Mauryan capital of Pataliputra. Though little survives of his reports, Megasthenes' accounts of the enormous wealth and population of the capital and the efficiency of Mauryan government formed the basis of much of the classical and medieval European understanding of India.

Although his motivations for doing so are unclear, Chandragupta stepped down from his throne around 297 BCE and joined an ascetic religious order, the Jains, formed on the basis of the teachings of the visionary Mahavira. Legend has it that he ended his life in the Jain monastery at Karnataka, where, in imitation of the order's founder, he refused all food and starved himself to death rather than consume any living thing. Chandragupta's son continued to expand the Mauryan

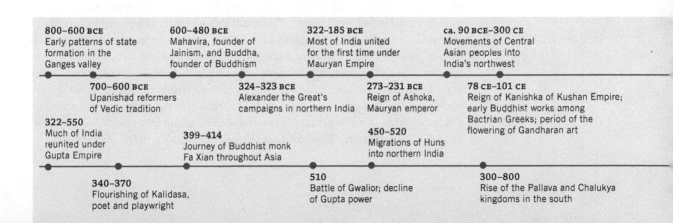

| 800–600 BCE | 600–480 BCE | 322–185 BCE | ca. 90 BCE–300 CE |
|---|---|---|---|
| Early patterns of state formation in the Ganges valley | Mahavira, founder of Jainism, and Buddha, founder of Buddhism | Most of India united for the first time under Mauryan Empire | Movements of Central Asian peoples into India's northwest |

| 700–600 BCE | 324–323 BCE | 273–231 BCE | 78 CE–101 CE |
|---|---|---|---|
| Upanishad reformers of Vedic tradition | Alexander the Great's campaigns in northern India | Reign of Ashoka, Mauryan emperor | Reign of Kanishka of Kushan Empire; early Buddhist works among Bactrian Greeks; period of the flowering of Gandharan art |

**322–550**
Much of India reunited under Gupta Empire

**399–414**
Journey of Buddhist monk Fa Xian throughout Asia

**450–520**
Migrations of Huns into northern India

**340–370**
Flourishing of Kalidasa, poet and playwright

**510**
Battle of Gwalior; decline of Gupta power

**300–800**
Rise of the Pallava and Chalukya kingdoms in the south

domains to the west and south, but it was his grandson Ashoka [ah-SHOW-kah] (r. ca. 273–231 BCE), who emerged as perhaps India's most dominant ruler until the nineteenth century CE.

**Ashoka** Born around 304 BCE, Ashoka may have actually seized the throne from his father. Like his predecessors, he soon began a series of military ventures to drive the Mauryan Empire deeper into the south (see Map 8.2). The climax of his efforts was a fierce war he fought with the kingdom of Kalinga, the last adjacent region outside of Mauryan control, on the eastern coast. Though figures given in ancient sources must always be treated with suspicion, by Ashoka's own admission, 100,000 people were killed in the conflict. Yet it was also here, at the height of his power, that, deeply moved by the carnage in Kalinga, in around 260 BCE he abruptly abandoned the path of conquest, converted to Buddhism, and vowed to rule his kingdom by "right conduct" alone.

Scholars know perhaps more about Ashoka's reign than that of any other ancient Indian monarch. He told much of his own story and outlined his Buddhist-inspired ideas for proper behavior on inscriptions in caves and on rocks and pillars set up in strategic places throughout his empire. Written mostly in Prakrit, the parent tongue of many of the modern north Indian dialects, these inscriptions present a fascinating and human glimpse of the ruler and his personal vision of the idea of dharma (see Chapter 3).

"The Beloved of the Gods [Ashoka] . . . is moved to remorse now. For he has felt profound sorrow and regret because the conquest of a people previously unconquered involves slaughter, death and deportation. . . . But there is a more important reason for the King's remorse . . . all suffer from the injury, slaughter, and deportation inflicted on their loved ones. . . . Thus all men share in the misfortune, and this weighs on King Priyadarsi's [Ashoka's] mind."

—From Ashoka's pillar inscriptions

Departing somewhat from the Bhagavad Gita's concept of dharma as duty (see Chapter 3), dharma for Ashoka was simply "that which is good." Among other things, this involved living a life of "kindness, liberality, truthfulness, and purity." Moreover, he believed that following the path of dharma represented the only way one could achieve happiness. One distinctive innovation growing out of Ashoka's support of dharma was his taking up of the Buddhist concept of *ahimsa*, or nonviolence: People should be kind to the weak and disadvantaged and do no harm to any living creature. By way of setting an example, Ashoka declared dozens of animal species to be under his protection, forbade the wholesale burning of forests, and even warned his people not to burn grain husks in order to avoid injuring any creatures living within them. Ashoka's devotion to dharma even extended to sending his sons as Buddhist missionaries to Sri Lanka, where it has remained the principal faith to this day.

Although Ashoka advocated the peaceful principles of dharma, the records of his reign also indicate that his empire was, in many respects, an early kind of police state. He followed many of the political practices suggested in Kautilya's *Arthashastra*, which emphasizes that a monarch must be alert to the moods of his people, on the lookout for enemies, and ready to capitalize on opportunities to exercise power. While allowing the practice of many religions other than Buddhism, Ashoka kept a tight rein on his officials and people through a vast network of spies and informers, a practice begun by his grandfather Chandragupta. The empire itself was divided into four large regional districts, each with a governor. They and all the officials under them were subject to

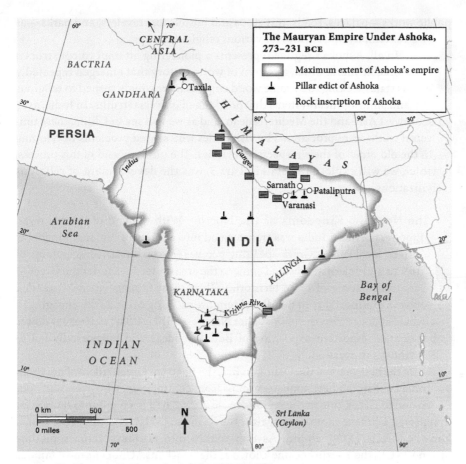

MAP 8.2 **The Mauryan Empire under Ashoka, 273–231 BCE.**

periodic review by roving special commissioners appointed by the throne, whose chief task was to check on everyone's adherence to dharma. Thus, the entire governmental apparatus was now geared toward uplifting the people's morality and supervising their happiness.

Ashoka also encouraged a unified system of commercial law, standardization of weights and measures, and uniform coinage throughout his realm, innovations that greatly facilitated trade and commerce. A majority of state revenues came from taxes on harvests of wheat, rice, barley, and millet plus those on internal and external trade. Under the Mauryans, India was the major crossroads in the exchange of gold and silver sought by the Hellenistic kingdoms and for the expanding maritime trade accompanying the advance of Buddhism into southeast Asia. In the north, Taxila and the cities and towns along the caravan routes from China to the west grew wealthy from the increasing exchange of silk and other luxury goods.

Within India, the circulation of tropical fruits, medicinal barks, and innumerable other forest products augmented trade still further. Thus, the immense wealth and power flowing into Ashoka's court in Pataliputra made that city of half a million perhaps the richest in the ancient world. The wealth at Ashoka's command and his devotion to dharma allowed the government to spend lavishly in sponsoring

**Capital of Ashoka Pillar of Sarnath.** The triple lion motif atop the chakravartin wheel, symbolizing universal kingship, topped one of Ashoka's famous pillars. The one from which this capital was taken had been set up to commemorate the Buddha's first sermon in Sarnath's deer park.

public works—palaces, roads, rest stops and hostels for travelers, and parks—as well as temples and shrines for various religious groups.

In all, Ashoka's regime represents a pioneering attempt to construct a workable moral order, a pattern of world history that emerged repeatedly as states seeking to become world empires increasingly turned to religious and philosophical systems that proclaimed universal truths. In India, as in southwest Asia and the Mediterranean, and as we will see in China, these universal truths were proclaimed by visionaries who sensed problems developing in the old order of their respective societies. The ultimate end of this process, which we will explore in detail in Part 3, was the development of religious civilizations.

**The Nomadic Kingdoms of the North** With the end of the Mauryan Empire, northern India was transformed into a series of regional kingdoms run by local rulers. Greek-speaking peoples from Bactria—descendants of troops and colonists who had come to the area under Alexander the Great—controlled some of these territories. Their most famous ruler, Menander, achieved immortality in Buddhist literature as "King Milinda" by engaging in a debate at court with the philosopher Nagasena. Their talks, as later set down, became an important exposition of Buddhist ideas and purportedly led to Menander's conversion.

By the first years of the Common Era, the Bactrian Greek rulers of northern India confronted new nomadic groups from central Asia, who eventually put an end to Greek rule in the region. These groups had been put into motion by repeated Chinese campaigns against the Xiongnu [SHIUNG-noo] (the Huns) and the Yuezhi [YOO-eh-jih]. As they moved into northern India sometime around 25 CE, the Yuezhi became known as the "Kushans." Under its most famous ruler, Kanishka (r. ca. 78–101 CE), the Kushan Empire expanded into not only northern India but also much of modern Pakistan and Afghanistan. Kanishka, like Menander, adopted Buddhism and actively propagated the faith within his growing kingdom and beyond. Through his efforts, the new religion expanded along the caravan routes of central Asia and shortly afterward appears for the first time in Chinese records.

Although the continual arrival of new groups expanded the cultural resources of northern India and greatly aided the spread of Buddhism, it also worked against the development of stable states in the region. With the intensity of the migrations abating by the end of the third century, however, a new and aggressive line of rulers, the Guptas, established power in the Ganges valley and stood poised to reunite the old Mauryan heartland. Under their rule would come India's great classical age.

## The Classical Age: The Gupta Empire

The origin of the Gupta line is somewhat obscure, though scholars agree that, like the Mauryans, it originated somewhere near Magadha. The first major ruler of the dynasty was Chandragupta I (r. ca. 320–335 CE; no relation to the Chandragupta of the Mauryan Empire), whose new state occupied much of the old heartland of Magadha and Kosala. With recognition of the rising power of the Guptas extending from Nepal in the north to the Shaka territories in the west, the way lay open

**MOVEMENT OF NOMADIC PEOPLES, 300 BCE–100 CE**

for his successor, Samudragupta [sahm-OO-drah-gup-tah] (r. ca. 335–380 CE), to expand the borders of the empire even further.

Under Samudragupta, the Gupta dominion extended both north and south, embracing a swath of territory extending far up the Ganges River to the borders of the Kushans south of Taxila and down the coast deep into the territory of the Pallavas in the south. Like Chandragupta I, he forged ties to regions outside of Gupta control, whose populations in turn pledged their loyalty to him. As was the case of the states of Zhou China, this arrangement has often been characterized as "feudal" in that it resembles the relationships among the states of medieval Europe, though scholars are careful not to push the parallels too far. Samudragupta's son Chandragupta II (r. ca. 380–413 CE) seized the throne from his elder brother and continued to expand the empire, adding the southern and western Gujarati territories of the Shakas. The cumulative effect of this string of conquests over barely a century was that, once again, the Indian subcontinent stood on the threshold of unity (see Map 8.3).

**Court and Culture**    The Gupta era is considered to be the classical age of Indian culture and religion. During the reign of the Guptas, the collection of religious traditions called **"Hinduism"** flourished, becoming the dominant faith of the time. Indeed, the Guptas actively used the gods and practices of Hinduism, particularly in their devotion to Vishnu and Shiva, to extend their legitimacy not just as kings but as universal rulers.

Although the Guptas preferred the king-centered, hierarchical Brahmanic tradition of Hinduism, which they made the privileged religion in the state, they permitted the practice of other faiths, including both Jainism and Buddhism. Under their influence and with their financial support, the first distinctly "Hindu" art was created in the temples and shrines to a variety of deities that were built in staggering profusion. In addition, the era marked a peak of popularity for classical treatises on political and social behavior such as the *Arthashastra* and the *Kama Sutra*, the famous manual of sexual practices and personal deportment, as well as, it is often supposed, the works of the playwright and poet Kalidasa (fl. fifth century CE), sometimes called the "Indian Shakespeare."

**The Waning of Gupta Power**    Gupta power began to fade under the reigns of Chandragupta II's son and grandson, whose weakened authority was challenged by groups seeking greater autonomy in the vicinity of Malwa, in central India. By this time, however, a new wave of central Asian nomads, the Hunas, sometimes called the "White Huns," had appeared. By 510 CE, having defeated the Guptas at Gwalior, some 200 miles south of the modern city of New Delhi, the Hunas established themselves as the dominant force in northwest India, and once again the areas along the Ganges were thrust into political disunity. By 515 CE, the eastern tributary states of the Guptas had broken away, while in the west the kingdom of the Rajputanas emerged in Gujarat by mid-century.

## The Southern Kingdoms, ca. 300–600 CE

Though their states were constantly contending with each other for wealth, power, and territory, the southern regimes of the so-called imperial Pallavas, Pandyas,

**Coins of the Northwest Kingdoms, Second Century BCE and Late First Century CE.** The complex history of the area encompassed by modern Afghanistan and Pakistan has been understood principally through the coins minted by the many rulers of frequently shifting territories. The silver coin (above) was minted by a Bactrian Greek king, probably in the second century BCE. The gold coin (below) with the Greek inscription was the product of the reign of the famous Buddhist king Kanishka (78–101 CE) of the Kushans and depicts the king himself.

**Hinduism:** A convenient shorthand term for the vast multiplicity of religious practices derived from the Vedic, Brahmanic, Upanishadic, and later traditions in India and those places influenced by Indian culture.

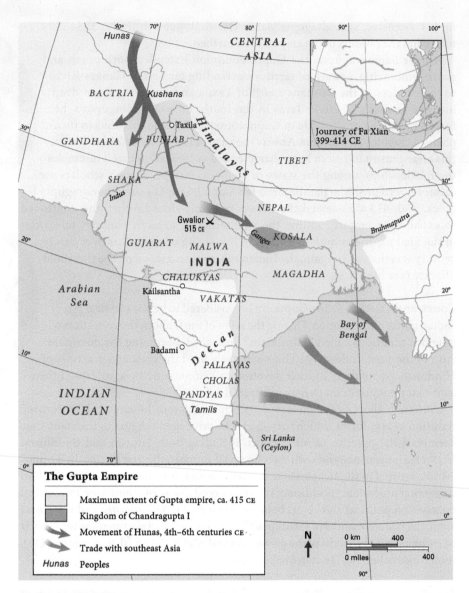

MAP **8.3** **The Gupta Empire.**

**Devotional:** In the context of this chapter, belonging to a branch of Hinduism in which one dedicates oneself to practices that venerate, honor, or adore a particular god or divinity. The largest of these branches are dedicated to Vishnu and Shiva.

Cholas, and Chalukyas of peninsular India were comparatively stable in cultural terms from the decline of the Guptas until the installation of the Muslim sultanates of the north. One reason for this was the absence of a powerful empire pushing south. Freed from the need to defend themselves from incursion from the north, the southern kingdoms could pursue the pacification of their own realms. Their political and religious systems were also still largely dominated by descendants of northern colonists, so their ruling classes shared to some degree a common culture.

In addition, the development of Hinduism among the Tamils, the region's chief ethnic group, contributed to cultural stability, while its synthesis with local traditions inspired a dramatic flowering of literature and art. These include the rise of **devotional** branches of Hinduism and an outpouring of spectacular religious art rarely equaled in any area of the world. Finally, the power and wealth

**The Kailasantha Temple.**
Hewn from a single, solid rock, the Kailasantha Temple, part of an elaborate complex in east-central India, is considered the world's most monumental sculpture. Strongly influenced by south Indian architectural traditions, the temple complex dazzles the visitor with carvings of innumerable deities, mythic figures, and erotic imagery.

of the region was enhanced by the promotion of trade, especially with the established "Indianized" enclaves of southeast Asia and the Indonesian archipelago. As a result of these ties, Indian religions, culture, and economics dominated Indian Ocean trade until it was gradually taken over by the Muslims after the fourteenth century CE.

**Temple Complexes**   The southern kingdoms' most tangible remains are the Hindu temple complexes left behind at a number of sites. The Pallavas, for example, under Mahendra Vikruma Varman I (r. ca. 590–630 CE), constructed the famous Mandapa Temple, carved from solid rock. His descendant Narasimha Varman II (r. 695–728 CE) sponsored the seven rock pagodas of Mahabali Purana. Perhaps most spectacular of all was the eighth-century CE Rashtakutra complex of Krishna I at Kailasantha, again carved from solid rock. The work was so complex, detailed, and painstakingly done that it was said to have moved its master builder to cry, "Oh, how did I do this?"

**Regional Struggles**   The long process of interaction and adaptation in India had already created a recognizably different society as one moved south from the Ganges. In these areas the systems of *varna* and *jati* (see Chapter 3) tended to revolve more around where one lived than they did in the north. For example, there were major differentiations between those living in the cities and flatland farming communities and the "hill peoples" and "forest peoples," still considered largely uncivilized. A major division also existed between the local leaders, whose families had in many cases emigrated from the north and were members of the upper *varnas*, and their subjects. Within these divisions, rulers tended to be more predatory in their efforts to enrich themselves and their kingdoms.

The rise of the Chalukya state on the western side of the peninsula in the mid-sixth century CE, along with that of the Vakatakas of the Deccan Plateau and the Rashtakutras in the early eighth century CE, resumed the struggle for wealth and territory among the older southern kingdoms. As we will see in Chapter 13, by the middle of the eighth century CE, the Chalukya state spawned a potent rival when the areas to the north and west broke away from its grasp. The leaders there became known as the "Rashtakutras" and shortly thereafter captured the capital at Badami.

# The Vedic Tradition and Its Visionary Reformers

Beginning around 700 BCE, visionaries appeared seeking to reform a Vedic tradition that they believed had grown overly formalistic and unresponsive to the needs of the people. As we noted in Chapter 3, the first of these men were the thinkers who created the Upanishads, a set of spiritual writings that laid the foundations of *monism*—the belief in a single transcendent first principle—in Hindu thought. In the next two centuries, Mahavira and the Buddha followed, becoming the founding figures, respectively, of Jainism, a small community in today's India, and Buddhism, today a major religion in southeast Asia, China, and Japan.

## Reforming the Vedic Tradition

The Vedas consisted of 10 books of hymns to the gods and goddesses of the Hindu pantheon and described in detail the rituals and sacrifices required to keep the world in harmony with these deities. They thus framed the culture of the period 1200–600 BCE, when the inhabitants of the Indian subcontinent initiated the pattern of Punjab and Ganges valley state formation. As we saw at the beginning of this chapter, several dozen warrior republics and kingdoms competed against each other for wealth and power, similar to the warring states of China that we will explore in Chapter 9. It was against the backdrop of this competition that visionaries critical of the polytheistic Vedic heritage arose and sought to reform it through the formulation of a single first principle. The main figures of these reform efforts were the authors of the Upanishads (ca. 700–300 BCE), Mahavira (trad. 599–527 BCE), and Gautama, the Buddha, or Enlightened One (trad. 563–483 BCE).

**The Upanishad Visionaries**   Many authors of the more than 100 Upanishads are known to us by name. They were Brahmanic priests—and also the daughter of one—whose principal concern was to penetrate beyond the complexities of the tens of thousands of gods (as one of the Upanishads mockingly asserts) to a vision of cosmic unity. This Upanishadic vision, with its opposition to polytheism and the proclamation of monism, was remarkably similar to those propounded in the Middle East and China during the same time: They proclaimed a transcendent first principle as universal truth, addressed to anyone anywhere.

The Indian visionaries were hermit teachers living in the forests of the Gangetic states seeking to "draw near" to themselves (the meaning of the Sanskrit *upanishad*) disciples who did not want merely to understand the transcendent unity of the universe outside of the individual but also to attain this unity by merging their personal selves (*atman*) into the universal self (*brahman*) and thereby achieving salvation. These visionaries did not develop this theme of the unity of atman–brahman systematically in the form of treatises. Instead, they concentrated on leading their disciples through brief aphorisms, paradoxes, and negations ("not this, nor that") step by step into deep meditation, which they considered the activity through which salvation could be achieved. As time went on, however, contemplation of the Upanishadic scriptures and their hidden meanings concerning the mysteries of atman–brahman also became a vital part of a new evolving tradition. In the highest state of understanding of atman–brahman, one could attain release from the bounds of the cycles of death and rebirth and thus enter into transcendence, or *moksha*.

**Criticism of the Vedic Rituals and Sacrifices**    Although they were advocates of monism, or first principle, the authors of the Upanishads remained faithful to the Vedic rituals, sacrifices, and doctrines. Their reforms were limited to creating a meditative supplement to the Vedic religion. However, as strong kingdoms emerged in the 500s BCE and conquered smaller kingdoms and warrior republics, criticism of religious ritual grew. Urbanization and trade created new classes of inhabitants, such as merchants and craftspeople, to whom rituals and sacrifices meant far less than they did to the kings and the priestly class. The merchants and craftspeople viewed the rituals as formalistic and the sacrifices, consisting of burning large quantities of food and killing many animals, as wasteful. For the kings and priests, these religious practices were essential to legitimize their power. The Vedic doctrine that eventually caused the break between the priests and their strongest critics, however, was that of the cycle of karma–samsara (see Chapter 3), death and rebirth.

**The Ascetic Break: Jainism**    The founder of the Jains, Nigantha Nataputta [nee-GAN-tah nah-tah-POO-tah], whose title of Vardhamana Mahavira means "the great hero," was born the son of a warrior chief perhaps around 540 BCE. At the age of 30 he left home and gave up all his worldly possessions to become an ascetic, and after 12 years he found meditative enlightenment. From this point on he was given the title of *jina*, or "conqueror," and from this his followers became known as Jains. For the next 40 years, he wandered throughout India without clothes or possessions, spreading the new sect's principles and practices. Finally, as the ultimate exemplar of the movement's ideal of not taking the life of any being whatsoever, Mahavira refused all food and performed a ritual fast that led to his death in Pava, near Pataliputra.

While much of the earliest Jain doctrine was lost during its first two centuries of oral transmission, it begins with a universe in which all things possess *jiva*, a kind of "soul" that yearns to be free from the prison of the material world. Jains believe that even inanimate objects, such as stones—as well as plants, human beings, and other animals—possess *jiva*, though at different levels or "senses." These "souls" are governed in turn by the degree to which a thing's past karma stands between it and its release from material bondage. For human beings, karma builds up according to the injuries one does to other beings and objects, intentionally or not. The way to enlightenment is to act in such a way that one acquires as little karma as possible, while performing actions of suffering and self-sacrifice to atone for and reduce the karma one already has. In this sense, karma might be thought of as a kind of weight on the "soul": As karma dissipates, the soul becomes lighter until, finally free, it rises to the very heights of the cosmos and lives for eternity.

**Ahimsa**    Jain monks take extraordinary pains to prevent injury to any object, especially living things. For example, from the first centuries of the movement there has been a **schism** between those who insist on complete nakedness—to

**Schism:** A division; when used in a religious context it usually refers to the splitting of members of a certain religion into two or more camps over matters of doctrine, ritual, etc.

**Statue of the Jain Saint Gomateshwara at Karnataka.** The world's largest statue cut from a single stone, this statue was built at the site of the famous Jain monastery where, it was said, Chandragupta Maurya entered the order and fasted to death, following the example of the sect's founder, Mahavira.

**Atheistic:** Not believing in a god or supreme being.

avoid attachment to worldly possessions as well as not injuring creatures that might be trapped in one's clothing—and those who wear a simple white robe. Other measures include wearing gauze masks to filter out invisible organisms that might be breathed in and carrying brooms to sweep small creatures out of one's path. Monks live by begging food from others—so that they themselves do not have to harvest it—and hence, kill it—and add to their karma. Because suffering reduces karma, some underwent extraordinary ordeals, such as allowing themselves to be covered with biting insects or lying on beds of nails. Such extreme forms of asceticism, especially if done for show or outside the spirit of overcoming the realm of the body, were ultimately condemned as "dark penance." Still, the most dedicated performed the supreme sacrifice and ritually fasted unto death in their later years, which, because of the intense suffering involved and the resolute refusal to harm living things, was seen as the ultimate act of ahimsa, or nonviolence. This is practiced by a handful of devotees even today, despite recent efforts in India to make it illegal.

Not surprisingly, the strict practices of the Jains did not appeal to most people. As a result, an extensive laity, especially among the lower castes who identified more with the sacrifices of the monks, grew to support them. The patronage of kings, most famously Chandragupta Maurya, helped ensure the sect's vitality. As a matter of course, Jains would not take up farming, so monastic and lay followers were often involved in business, study, and writing—occupations they still favor today. The religion's most distinctive element is that it is rigorously **atheistic**, choosing not to worship any god but insisting instead on meditatively merging into an eternal, uncreated, indifferent unity that is both universal and transcendent.

**The Middle Way: Buddhism**   The other major movement, Buddhism, began in part as a reaction against such extreme ascetic practices. Siddhartha Gautama, whose title of "Buddha" means "the Enlightened One," is believed to have been born a prince in the Shakya republic in the Himalayan foothills. His traditional birth date is given as 563 BCE, though recent accounts have moved it to at least the mid-400s BCE. Because of his royal pedigree, he is frequently referred to as "Sakyamuni," or prince of the Sakyas. Seeking to shelter him from the evils of the world, Gautama's father secluded him in the palace. At the age of 29, however, Gautama left his world of privilege and followed the paths of various Vedic schools. At one point, following a discipline of extreme asceticism, his path of self-deprivation led him to fast nearly to death.

During his travels, Gautama was exposed to the entire range of human suffering and death from which his father had tried so hard to shelter him. His shock and compassion for the world around him drove him to find a way to understand the endless round of death and rebirth to which all creatures were apparently subject. According to Buddhist accounts, the insight gained from his experiences and a long period of deep meditation sparked his enlightenment one day under a pipal (fig) tree in the town of Gaya. Shortly afterward, Gautama went to a deer park in Sarnath, close by the great city of Varanasi (Benares), where he found five former disciples and preached a sermon to them outlining what became known as the Middle Way—the path of moderation.

**The Four Noble Truths, the Eightfold Path, and Nirvana**   Gautama believed that the fundamental nature of the perceived universe is change. In a constantly changing world, suffering is the common lot of all beings because they attach themselves to what will ultimately be taken from them. Although they crave permanence, they rely only on their senses, which provide the illusion of stability but actually obscure the true, ever-changing nature of things. Pushed into evil deeds in pursuit of whatever they desire, they accumulate karma. Over many lifetimes, the karma they acquire stays with them even after the separation of the material "soul" from the immaterial at death. It builds up with each life and keeps them from breaking free of the cycle of death and rebirth. In that first sermon in Sarnath, Gautama distilled these insights into what he called the Four Noble Truths:

1. All life is suffering.
2. Suffering arises from craving.
3. To stop suffering, one must stop craving.
4. One stops craving by following the Eightfold Path of right views, right resolve, right speech, right conduct, right livelihood, right effort, right mindfulness, and right concentration.

Later sermons and vast numbers of commentaries outlined the specifics of the Eightfold Path. Essentially, the path represents a course of life in which one avoids extreme behaviors of any kind, adheres to a code of conduct that favors **altruism** and respects the life of all living beings, and through meditation and "right mindfulness" reaches a state of calm nonattachment with an uncluttered mind able to grasp the universal truth. When one reaches this stage, the karmic traces of past lives are "blown out" like a lamp flame, the literal meaning of the Sanskrit word associated with this final state of enlightenment: *nirvana*, or nothingness. In Buddhism, this nothingness is a more explicit version of the logic of *moksha*— transcendence—first explored in the Upanishads.

**Altruism:** The practice of acting in an unselfish manner for the good of others.

Even during the Buddha's lifetime his followers had organized into a brotherhood, despite his dying instruction that the true path to enlightenment resided in them as individuals. As in other movements, the void left by the Buddha's death resulted in disputes about the authenticity of certain teachings and questions about how the group should now conduct itself. Over the following two centuries, several Buddhist councils were held, and during one of these meetings, a division developed, resulting in one group separating from the main body of adherents. The now separate group became known as Theravada [ter-rah-VAH-dah], "the teachings of the elders." Under Ashoka's influence, Theravada Buddhism became the approved sect, with the first complete surviving texts dating from this time.

**Buddhist Texts**   The *Pali Canon*, written in Pali, the sacred language of Buddhism, is a collection of texts that forms the foundation of Theravada Buddhism and serves as the fundamental body of scriptures for nearly all Buddhist schools. The collection consists of the *Tripitaka* [tree-pee-TAH-kuh], or "Three Baskets"; the *Vinaya* [vee-NAI-yah], treatises on conduct and rules of discipline for monks; the *Sutras* [SOO-truhs], or "discourses," of which there are five groups, with most of them believed to have originated with the Buddha; and the *Abhidhamma* [ah-bee-DAH-mah], doctrines of philosophy and metaphysics.

As Theravada Buddhism developed and spread in northern India and beyond, a number of developments changed its character, making it more accessible to a larger group of followers. The rich cultural interaction of the many peoples encountering it resulted in a great number of religious ideas and traditions circulating around the region. Questions and problems among Buddhist adherents from these different areas required broader solutions than in earlier times. For example, stories of the Buddha's last days implied that he would save everyone who followed his path, opening the way for the potential enlightenment of all. Coupled with this was a developing tradition of the Buddha as one in a long line of past and future buddhas, suggesting the potential for a devotional component to the religion. In addition, there was the concept of the *bodhisattva* [boh-dee-SAHT-vuh]—one who, having achieved enlightenment, does not proceed to nirvana but is dedicated instead to helping the suffering achieve their own enlightenment.

**Theravada and Mahayana**    All of these ideas took shape around the first century CE in what became the largest branch of Buddhism, Mahayana [mah-hah-YAH-nah], the "greater vehicle." Dismissing Theravada Buddhism as Hinayana [heen-ah-YAH-nah], or "the lesser vehicle," Mahayana spread along the trade routes into central Asia, into the borderlands of the Parthians, and ultimately to China, Korea, Japan, and Tibet (see Map 8.4). As it spread, its different interpretive schools were, broadly speaking, divided into *esoteric* branches—those seeking enlightenment through scriptural or other kinds of deep knowledge—and devotional branches. Of the devotional schools, that of Amitabha [ah-mee-TAH-bah], the Heavenly Buddha of the Western Paradise, is today the most popular Buddhist sect in both China and Japan (see Chapters 9 and 13).

**Great Buddhist Stupa at Sanchi.** The need for commemorative burial mounds and reliquaries for the Buddha's relics spawned a characteristic structure called a stupa, meaning "gathered" or "heap." Brimming with symbolic motifs representing the stages of enlightenment, the structures changed considerably from this example—built in the first century BCE over an earlier one from the Mauryan period—as they spread through east Asia, where they assumed the shape of the pagoda.

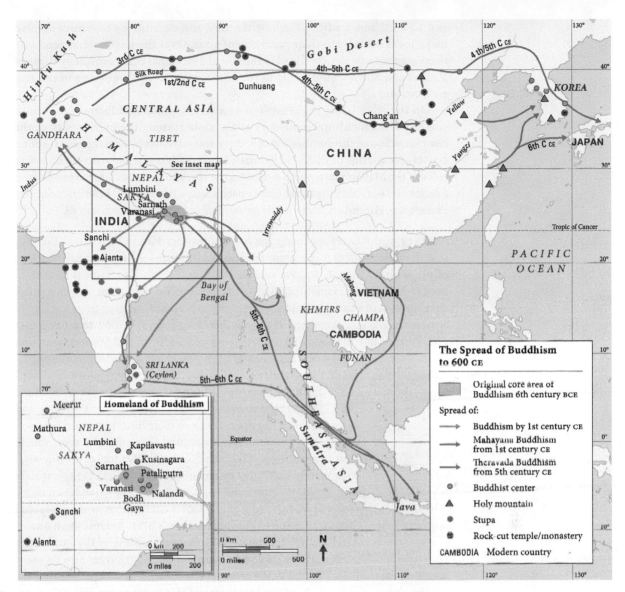

MAP 8.4  **The Spread of Buddhism to 600 CE.**

As Buddhism was spreading across the greater part of Asia, however, its decline had, in a sense, already begun in the land of its birth. With the revitalization and consolidation of the older Vedic and Brahmanic traditions into Hinduism, all the schools of Buddhism were to face strong competition for converts and noble patronage.

## The Maturity of Hinduism:
## From the Abstract to the Devotional

The period from the Mauryans to the rise of the Guptas brought about a number of changes within the orthodox traditions of Indian religion. On the one hand, the continuing push of state formation to the south carried with it the older Vedic and Upanishadic traditions. Along the way, these traditions had incorporated many local deities into their pantheon of gods. Over the next several centuries these southern areas would lead in the rise of devotional cults, especially those of Vishnu and Shiva, culminating in the *bhakti* movements beginning in the seventh century CE.

On the other hand, the growth of new religions like Buddhism and Jainism challenged such cultural mainstays as the caste system, the inevitability of the karmic cycle, and the domination of society and salvation by the traditional ruling classes. As a result of these challenges and through the popularity of the grand epics of the Mahabharata and Ramayana, the spreading of the classical texts of the first and second centuries, and Gupta patronage, a rejuvenated brand of religious experience, Hinduism, is distinctly recognizable by the fourth century CE.

**Avatars and Alvars**    Among the most consistent Hindu beliefs was the idea that the subcontinent was a single land united by faith—*Bharat*—from the name of a legendary king said to have achieved this unification. The name is enshrined even today in India's constitution as an official term for the nation. Another is the development of a full continuum of religious experience, ranging from the highly abstract to the emotional and mystical, springing from devotion to a particular god. Perhaps due to the egalitarian influence of Buddhism and Jainism, salvation was increasingly seen as accessible to all, according to one's abilities and the restrictions of caste and one's social position.

> "Since I transcend what is transient and I am higher than the eternal, I am known as the supreme spirit of man in the world and in sacred love.
>
> Whoever knows me without delusion as the supreme spirit of man, knows all there is, Arjuna— he devotes his whole being to me."
>
> —From the Bhagavad Gita

Of the many gods singled out for special attention, the most important were the so-called Indian trinity: Brahma, Vishnu, and Shiva. Of these, the main divisions of devotion emerged between Vishnu, the beneficent preserver, and Shiva, the powerful, fertile giver and destroyer of life, the "Lord of the Dance" of the universe. Both Vishnu and Shiva can manifest themselves through avatars or incarnations, the most popular of which is Krishna, an incarnation of Vishnu, who plays such a central role in the Bhagavad Gita. In addition to guiding that epic's hero, Arjuna, to an understanding of fulfilling his dharma—regardless of the immediate consequences—Krishna reveals the true power of devotion to him as transcending the transitory nature of the material world.

The ability of the new devotional traditions of Hinduism to appeal to all castes made the religion increasingly popular from the time of the Guptas on. Within the all-encompassing character of Hinduism grew the assumption that one could achieve salvation according to one's caste and ability, whether one was a *shudra*, worshiping Shiva with a pure heart, or a highly educated Brahman, finding liberation within the most profound texts. By the seventh century CE, religious poets were carrying the message of devotional Hinduism to all believers in vernacular languages. *Alvars* and *nayanars*, singers of praise for Vishnu and Shiva, respectively, created some of the most passionate and beautiful religious poetry in any language over the next five centuries and helped bond the people to the orthodox religion as a whole.

**Shakti and Tantra**    A related development was that of Shakti, literally "power," sometimes called "tantra." Shakti practitioners often probed the darker edges of the multiple natures of the gods—especially Shiva and his consort Kali, or

Durga—associated with death and destruction. Toward this end they purposely violated social norms—by eating meat, having illicit sex (even committing incest), eating human excrement, and, on rare occasions, committing ritual murder. The idea behind such perverse behavior was both to prove one's mastery over attachment to the acts themselves and to push beyond the ordinary dualities of good and evil. Such extreme activities were comparatively rare, though the idea of transcending ordinary norms also passed into Buddhism at about the same time, in the fourth and fifth centuries CE. Here, it was also referred to as "tantra" and often as "the vehicle of the thunderbolt." In this modified form it passed into Nepal and Tibet, where its mysticism and interest in magical practices formed important elements of Tibetan Buddhism.

# Stability amid Disorder: Economics, Family, and Society

Despite India's tumultuous political history, the agrarian-based economy of the subcontinent remained for 2,000 years the richest (along with China) in the world. Its agriculture was enormously productive in its most fertile areas, and the topography and climate allowed an astonishing variety of products, from fragrant woods to pepper and other tropical spices, to be produced for domestic consumption and export. As the economy flourished, society as a whole remained relatively stable. The hierarchical nature of the caste system maintained continuity through times of political turmoil, prescribing set duties and standards of behavior according to social position. Although the newly emerged religions of Buddhism and Jainism did not recognize the caste system, their appearance and spread did not fundamentally alter that system.

The relationships between men and women and among family members outlined in Chapter 3 grew increasingly complex, particularly from the classical age of the Guptas onward. Despite the trend in Buddhism—and, as we shall see in Chapters 10 and 12, in Islam—toward greater equality between men and women, beliefs such as the strictly delineated spheres of husband and wife, the idea of the female as a fundamental force of the universe, and a male vision of women as simultaneously desirable and threatening were considerably enlarged during this time.

## Tax and Spend: Economics and Society

By 600 BCE, the inhabitants of the emerging Gangetic states had long since made the transition to being settled agriculturalists. With the vast majority of inhabitants of the new states being peasants from the lowest *shudra varna*, the chief form of revenue was harvest taxes. The average tax levied on the people of these early states appears to have been around one-sixth of their annual harvest.

**Accelerating Taxes**   With the expansion of Magadha in the fifth and fourth centuries BCE, the agricultural tax increased to one-quarter of the harvest and even higher on royal lands—as much as half the cultivable land in the kingdom. By this time, the accelerating pace of urban life, the explosion of trade, and the increasingly differentiated castes expanded the economy even more, allowing whole new classes of items to be taxed. Thus, the immense wealth wielded by the Mauryans was accumulated through harvest taxes as high as one-half of all the produce raised in the empire, as well as taxes on livestock, internal trade, imports and exports, and such commodities as gold, textiles, salt, horses, and a variety of forest products and spices. Moreover, the increase in trade had led to a growing commercial class expanding beyond the traditional *vaisya* (merchant) *varna*, while the growing need for capital and credit was met by guilds of bankers and traders in precious metals.

Agricultural taxes of about one-quarter to one-third of the harvest continued under the Guptas. The various working guilds, or *sreni*, in the major cities were highly organized. As under the Mauryans, bankers and merchants were frequently tapped by rulers for ready cash to fund armies, buy off intruders, or finance other emergency measures. Despite low **tariffs**, the Guptas enjoyed a highly favorable balance of trade. Indeed, the empire's self-sufficiency in nearly all commercial items meant that foreign traders had to pay for their goods in gold or silver. Because of this, the Romans were eventually forced to stop much of their Indian trade because of its drain on their supply of precious metals.

**Trade and Expansion**    By the time of Persia's invasion in the late sixth century BCE, the reputation of the wealth of northern India was already well established among the Greeks. The historian Herodotus (ca. 484–425 BCE), for example, noted that the yearly tribute of gold from the region was several times that of Persian Egypt. Interactions with the expanding Hellenistic world extended the reach of Indian markets and trade through the eastern Mediterranean and, shortly, into the expanding Roman domains.

With the decline of the Mauryans and the adoption of Buddhism by peoples of the northwest, the region around Taxila became the **nexus** of a caravan trade that from the third century BCE to the third century CE linked nearly all of Eurasia from Roman Britain to Han China and beyond through the famous Silk Road (see Chapter 9). In addition, Buddhist, Jain, and Brahmanic religious elements all spread westward over time to enrich in varying degrees the intellectual climate of the Parthians, Greeks, and Romans.

Indians also dominated the region's maritime trade until they were gradually displaced by the Arabs from the ninth to the fifteenth centuries CE and by the Europeans shortly thereafter. The reputations of "Chryse" and "Cheronese," the lands of gold of southeast Asia, were well established among the Romans through Indian trade by the first centuries CE, while Roman and Greek jars and coins could be found as far away as Vietnam, Cambodia, and Java. Colonies of Greek, Roman, Persian, and Arab traders clustered in the western port cities of Broach and Kalliena, trading tin, copper, hides, and **antimony** for the teak, ebony, ivory, spices, and silks available there. A testament to the importance of trade in the Greco-Roman world was the first-century guide to the Indian Ocean, the *Periplus* (marine atlas) *of the Erythrean Sea* (see "Patterns Up Close: The Global Trade of Indian Pepper").

**Indian Influence beyond India**    By the first century CE, this expanding trade region had established a network of outposts in southeast Asia and the Indonesian archipelago. Buddhist influence in the area may have come soon after. Though it is unclear whether merchants or missionaries made the first contacts, a series of small settlements of Indians on the Malay Peninsula launched the founding of the first of the Indianized kingdoms in the area, that of Funan in the Mekong delta of southeast Asia by the Brahmin Kaudinya in the second century CE. The spread of both

**Tariffs:** Taxes levied on imports.

**Nexus:** A connection, a bond or link; also, a series of connections.

**Antimony:** A metal widely used in alloys.

Buddhism and the Indian system of "god-kings" soon reached the nearby Khmers [ke-MARES] and the state of Champa [KAM-puh] in modern Cambodia and Vietnam. By the seventh and eighth centuries CE, these areas became important trade centers in their own right, connecting the Indian states with Tang China and Heian Japan.

In addition, these countries formed important way stations in the expanding traffic of Buddhist pilgrims. The widespread appeal of Buddhism enhanced the Indian economy by both increasing the volume of trade on the subcontinent and providing a uniform structure for its expansion abroad. The mobility of pilgrims and monks, their role as missionaries, and their aversion to a number of lower-caste occupations made them natural candidates to assist in the increasingly far-flung circulation of goods and ideas. Monasteries served as hostels and way stations along well-traveled routes; larger complexes along branches of the Silk Road often had commercial centers grow up around them, particularly if they were destinations for pilgrims as well. The international character of Buddhism also facilitated contacts among long-distance traders. Perhaps most important, it linked India to an emerging cultural sphere that soon spanned Eurasia from the borderlands of the Persian empires to Japan. By the fourth century CE, firm trade ties had been established with the Romans, the Sasanids, the remnant states of Han China, and the Buddhist and Indianizing territories of southeast Asia (see Map 8.5).

## Caste, Family Life, and Gender

As with the economy, the basic patterns of Indian society were already being forged by the seventh century BCE. The integration of the Vedic peoples, those of northwestern India, and the early inhabitants of the Ganges valley had been largely completed. Thereafter, the fusion of Vedic traditions into a distinct form of Hindu culture, drawn heavily from the Brahmanic religious and social practices, proceeded apace. In the Gupta Empire, when Hinduism became the privileged religion of the state and the subcontinent was largely decentralized as regional kingdoms competed with each other, Hinduism evolved into a religious civilization, the pattern of social organization dominant during the period 600–1450 in world history (see Part 3).

**Maturation of the Caste System**    Perhaps the most distinctive marker of Hinduism as a religious civilization is the caste (*jati*) system. Scholars are still uncertain as to whether this system originated with the four *varnas* in the Punjab–Ganges states or whether it evolved later. In any case, varna and caste seem to have merged over time to create a markedly stable, adaptable, yet also repressive system that continues even today, despite being technically unlawful under the Indian constitution. One of the caste system's chief functions was to provide a mechanism for absorbing and acculturating peoples of widely divergent languages, ethnicities, and religious practices into an integrated social whole. Within the framework of caste, all people lived within an interlocking system of reciprocal rights and responsibilities in which even those at the bottom levels had a necessary, if disagreeable, societal function.

During the Mauryan era, Ashoka's advocacy of dharma also reinforced older notions of duty according to social position, while such treatises on proper behavior as the *Code of Manu* (written down by 200 CE) helped solidify concepts of model conduct among the various classes of society. By the Gupta period, renewed interest

# The Global Trade of Indian Pepper

Pepper was perhaps the world's most sought-after commodity for thousands of years. Indeed, its primacy among such other rare spices as nutmeg, ginger, cinnamon, and cloves ultimately drove European adventurers and traders to the Americas as they sought a direct all-water route to its source in India.

The black pepper plant (*Piper nigrum*) is a vine native to the Malabar Coast of India in the modern state of Kerala. The two main varieties of pepper, white and black, are derived from the same berries: white pepper is the product of removing the black skin of the dried seeds (peppercorns) and crushing them, while black pepper comes from soaking and drying the seeds with their fruit coating still attached. As far back as the thirteenth century BCE, Egyptian records show black pepper being used in mummifications, a testament to its early place as a valued import.

By the third century BCE, pepper had become a mainstay of south India's burgeoning Indian Ocean trade, with growing annual cargoes going to China, southeast Asia, and Egypt. The Hellenistic cultural exchange conducted through Ptolemaic Egypt spread the use of pepper throughout the Mediterranean world. By the first century BCE, traders from Egypt, coastal Arabia, and northeast Africa were regularly availing themselves of the monsoon winds to make annual voyages to the Malabar ports for pepper. But it was after the Roman acquisition of Egypt that pepper became the subject of a kind of mania throughout their empire. Contemporary Romans like Pliny the Elder regularly complained of the huge drain of gold required to keep the empire adequately spiced, and the export of gold to India was ultimately curtailed.

How does one account for the huge popularity of a food product that has no nutritive value and burns the tongue? Initially, part of pepper's attraction may have been its exotic quality as a mysterious spice from a faraway land. But it had also long been used for medicinal purposes in India, and from Roman times through the European Middle Ages it was hailed in European and Arab treatises as healthful in a number of ways. Moreover, although pepper's effectiveness as a preservative

**Pepper Pot.** The earliest records of pepper being imported into Britain are from the first century. Discovered in 1992, this exquisite pepper pot—a special container intended to hold this expensive spice—is designed in the shape of an empress and dates to the fifth century CE. Made of gold and silver, it testifies to the high value placed on such a precious commodity, especially in a remote place like Britain.

**Ritual pollution:** The act of someone or something becoming "unclean" in terms of religious taboos or prohibitions.

in societal stability after nearly five centuries of disorder prompted increased attention to stricter boundaries for acceptable behaviors within the different *jati*. Indeed, genetic testing among various modern Indian groups has shown that, while there was considerable fluidity among castes and intermarriage throughout the first millennium BCE, this slowed down considerably after approximately 100 CE, even before the Hindu revival of the Gupta period. Along with this, the idea of **ritual pollution** resulting from unsanctioned contact with lower castes— requiring ever more elaborate purification rites to cleanse oneself after such contact—becomes increasingly common. This increasing trend of social segregation led to such things as small closets, nooks, and other places of concealment built into the houses of the upper castes so that their lower-caste servants could instantly hide themselves if their masters suddenly happened upon them.

Yet such repressive extremes also mask some of the strengths that gave the caste system its vitality and longevity. Like religious organizations and guilds in medieval Europe, *jati* membership provided a kind of extended family, giving

is questionable, it was nonetheless highly useful as a flavor enhancer in a variety of preserved foods.

The Arab occupation of the prime transshipment areas of the eastern Mediterranean and the termini of the Silk Road and, by the fourteenth century, their domination of Indian Ocean trade caused the price of Indian commodities to soar in Europe. The urge to break the Islamic monopoly of the spice trade ultimately drove the Portuguese to sail around Africa, and Columbus to sail into the Atlantic, hoping to go directly to the Malabar Coast. The commercial network built on pepper and other spices was now positioned to drive what would grow into the world's first global trading system.

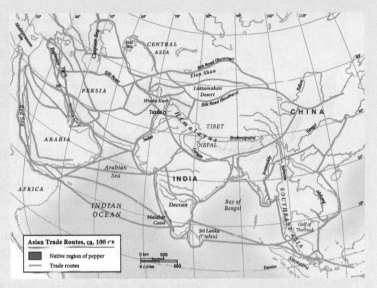

MAP **8.5 Asian Trade Routes, ca. 100 CE.**

## Questions

- How does the global trade in Indian pepper show the connectedness of Eurasia in this period in world history?

- What are the origins of the pepper trade? How did it change over time through interactions? What adaptations, if any, resulted from these interactions?

each person a recognized and valued place in society, despised as they might be by their "betters." In some areas, especially in the south, entire villages or clans were incorporated into their own *jatis*; in others, ethnicity or occupation might be the determining criteria. Although the upper castes dominated the political structure of rural society, social power was in fact more diffuse than is usually appreciated. For example, the members of various caste and guild councils were customarily represented at state functions. In addition, different castes became associated with special feasts and their sponsoring gods or goddesses, giving them a degree of informal power within the larger social structure.

**Jainism, Buddhism, and Caste**    Jainism and Buddhism had a considerable influence on the caste system as well. Although both religions accepted the theory of karma–samsara, their followers saw their own distinct practices as ways to break out of the cycle of death and rebirth. They thus represented powerful alternative traditions to the acceptance of varna and *jati*. Moreover, the potential for anyone, regardless of social position, to practice these methods undermined the hierarchical order of the caste system and made Jain and Buddhist practitioners equals in a society of believers. Their alternative institutions such as monasteries for men and women as well as their self-sufficiency, good works, and commercial expertise also gave them considerable material power in the larger community, particularly when patronized by nobles or monarchs.

**Family Life and Hindu Culture**    As we saw in Chapter 3, the role of women both in the family and in Indian society was perhaps more complex than in any other agrarian-based culture. On the one hand, the idea of female "dependence" was central to the Hindu conception of the family. That is, a woman without the support and protection of a web of family relations was cast adrift in society, a kind of nonperson. Thus, to protect women was to safeguard the family and the social order. It followed from this that obedience and loyalty to senior female and male authority within the hierarchy of the family was the keystone of a woman's dharma, her duty according to her position. This fundamental duty was consistent regardless of her position in the caste system. In some regions, such loyalty found extreme expression in the act of *sati*. This controversial practice of a widow committing suicide by throwing herself on her husband's funeral pyre, however, remained largely confined to northern India and is legally prohibited today.

As in the strict division between men's and women's spheres in Confucian China we will see in Chapter 9, women's education and legal responsibilities in India were considerably narrower than those for men and tended to revolve around maintaining the home. Although in the Tamil areas of the south families remained matrilineal, property rights were limited. Yet wives customarily exercised the important responsibility of controlling the household accounts and supervising servants and hired help. For the more well-to-do, an appropriate knowledge of poetry, literature, and conversational skills was required, along with other attainments necessary for well-rounded, gracious living. And while men were somewhat less restricted in terms of marrying for love, the vast majority of men and women were united through marriages arranged by their families after careful negotiation and often betrothed before adolescence.

A number of texts were devoted to outlining the correct conduct of the "four stages of life" for men: student, householder, hermit, and wanderer. In the first stage, that of the student, boys of the "twice-born" upper castes were to be taken into the household of a *guru*, or teacher, for a minimum of 12 years. During this time, they were expected to study the works of the Vedic–Brahmanic–Upanishadic tradition. Upon entering into the second stage (householder), more mature men with sufficient savings should marry young women of good character and appropriate caste membership. In addition to providing for his household, servants, and relatives, a man should get up before dawn, offer the appropriate sacrifices throughout the day, and busy himself studying the Vedas, Puranas [poor-AHN-ahs] (genealogies and histories), and Itihasas [ee-tee-HAH-sahs] (legendary histories). As old age approaches, he enters the third stage (hermit) and should retreat to the forest, live on the roots and berries he can gather, and work to master the self in preparation for the end. In the final (wanderer) stage, he moves beyond desire for life or death, wandering without home or possessions. Caring not for anything of this world, he returns good for any evil done him and, ideally, attains moksha, or release from the cycle of death and rebirth at his journey's end.

**Balancing Male and Female Roles**    Although women were, for the most part, treated as subservient members of a patriarchal society, they were also seen by men as complementary opposites, as symbols of harmony and balance, though also as real and imaginary temptations and impediments to their ultimate release (moksha). On the one hand, women in epic and popular literature were often depicted as heroic and resourceful—Draupadi in the Mahabharata, for example, married five brothers in the Pandava family and aided all of them in their battles. Moreover, from the Gupta period on, a bewildering number of goddesses were increasingly appealed to by devotees for a variety of reasons. Fertility, sexuality, and growth, largely associated with female-ness, were all celebrated in Hindu literature, statuary, and religious symbolism. The lush depictions of frank sexuality in Hindu temples are among the most erotically charged artworks produced anywhere in the world. In contrast with this celebration of sexuality, on the other hand, was the perception of women as temptresses who anchored men to the sensual world. This in turn diverted them from the fundamental truth of the material world as transitory, thus potentially delaying their release from the karmic cycle through moksha.

The tensions growing from this duality and the difficulties of controlled enjoyment of the senses for both men and women as part of approved religious practice are graphically illustrated in Vatsyayana's [vaht-see-ai-AH-nah] famous *Kama Sutra*, or *Aphorisms of Love*, written perhaps sometime in the first or second century CE. Its frank handling of a multiplicity of sexual practices has created an aura of pornography about it for readers outside of India. Within a wider context, however, it should be seen more as a manual on the everyday worship of living. While the more sensational aspects of the arts of sexual love are certainly present, the majority of the text deals with how to become a well-rounded person of taste and culture. For women, no less than 64 separate skills are detailed, including singing, dancing, cooking, chemistry, first aid, metallurgy, architecture, and even driving horses and elephants. Here, at least, the "proper" sphere for women's activities was greatly expanded.

**Gandharan Buddhas.** One of the most stunning syntheses of artistic and religious traditions occurred in the wake of the decline of the Seleucid states and the invasion of the Kushans. In the area centered around Gandhara (in modern northeast Afghanistan and northwest Pakistan) Hellenistic artistic techniques of realistic human representation fused with the developing practices of Mahayana Buddhism to create sculptures like the head pictured here, from the second or third century CE, believed to be that of a bodhisattva, or perhaps of Siddhartha Gautama.

# Strength in Numbers: Art, Literature, and Science

The vast number of artistic, literary, cultural, and scientific contributions arising from India makes it impossible to do more than hint at their richness here. One area worth noting in terms of its cross-cultural fertilization, however, is that of Gandharan art. During the time of the Kushan Empire, the powerful influences of the old empire of Alexander the Great were meeting the new religious movements arising within Buddhism to create a new "Gandharan" style of art.

Previous representations of the Buddha had not been anthropomorphic but were instead symbols associated with his life and lore: the "wheel of dharma," an empty throne, or a footprint. Around the beginning of the Common Era, perhaps coinciding with the development of Mahayana Buddhism, the distinctly realistic forms of Greek sculpture and the tradition of depicting the Greek gods as human merged with the new Buddhist sensibilities to create the first images of the Buddha, which looked remarkably like the Greek god Apollo. This synthetic Gandharan approach spread across northern India, and soon images of the

Buddha were being turned out in great profusion. Over time, however, the more familiar, stylized, less realistic, and heavily symbolic representations became standard throughout the Mahayana religious sphere.

**The Classical Age**   While relatively little art from the Mauryan era has survived, the Gupta period brought an explosion of art and literature from a multitude of artists patronized by the court and the upper classes. The "perfection" of Sanskrit as the medium of the sacred texts of Hinduism under the scholar and grammarian Panini and its systematic study under the **philologist** Patanjali several centuries later standardized the sacred language and caused it to be viewed and preserved as unchanging. As a classical language, Sanskrit was used in a staggering variety of works of poetry, prose, and drama, as well as in the *Puranas*—religious and secular historical genealogies. Other noteworthy works may include the poems and plays of "India's Shakespeare," Kalidasa (though some scholars place his life in the first century CE), such as the poignant romance *Shakuntala* and the poetic yearnings of *The Cloud Messenger*.

In addition to Sanskrit literature, scholarship of all types, including Buddhist works and scientific treatises, was undertaken at the great Buddhist monastery and university of Nalanda in northeastern India, founded in the fourth century CE.

**Philologist:** A specialist in language study, particularly in the history and provenance of important terms.

"He used to love, when women friends were near, / To whisper things he might have said aloud / That he might touch thy face and kiss thine ear; / Unheard and even unseen, no longer proud, / He now must send this yearning message by a cloud."

—From *The Cloud Messenger*

**Science and Mathematics**   In addition to Buddhism, the most profound intellectual influences from India on the surrounding regions were in science, especially mathematics. Despite the highly sophisticated speculative philosophy of the Upanishads, during the period from the second century BCE until the second century CE India was an importer of scientific and mathematical concepts from the Greco-Roman and Persian spheres. Greek geometry, for example, made its way into northern India during this time. In exchange, however, concepts of Indian health regimens—some involving yoga discipline—along with the vast body of Indian medicine, with its extensive knowledge of herbal remedies, also seem to have moved west. The second-century CE medical text *Charaka Samhita* for example, like its counterparts in the Mediterranean and later European world, taught a health regimen based on the balance of humors.

In the area of mathematics and astronomy an important synthesis of ideas took place from the time of the Mauryans through the twelfth and thirteenth centuries CE. Like the early Chinese methods of reckoning time, the first Indian calendars were based on the lunar months, though a year consisted of six seasons, and an intercalary period was inserted every 30 months to make up the difference with the solar year. During the Hellenistic period, Indians adopted the calendar of the eastern Mediterranean and southwest Asia, which had a 7-day week, a 24-hour day, and a 365-day solar year—along with the 12 zodiacal signs of the Greco-Roman world.

Indian thinkers refined these imported concepts to levels unsurpassed in the ancient world. The subtleties of some of the philosophical schools had already required intervals of time and numbers that still stagger the imagination today. For example, cycles of time marking eternity in some philosophical schools were measured in intervals larger than current estimates of the age of the universe; the shorter *kalpa*, reckoned at about 4 billion years, is only slightly less than current estimates of the age of the earth. Philosophical discussion on the nature of matter in infinitesimal space among some schools anticipated key arguments of modern physicists regarding the principle of indeterminacy.

The ability to conceive of mathematics on at once such a grand and such a tiny scale seems to have also helped Indian mathematicians and astronomers during the Gupta period to calculate a precise length of the solar year. Like the Chinese, they had already developed a decimal system; however, they now employed the first use of the zero, initially marked by a dot, as a placeholder, and developed a system of positive and negative numbers. Their work with the geometry of the Greeks enabled them to calculate pi to four decimal places as well as to develop methods for the solving of certain kinds of algebraic equations. By the eleventh and twelfth centuries CE, the acquisition of these techniques by the Arabs and their transmittal of them to the new universities of Christian Europe gave us the system we still use today, known by the somewhat erroneous name of "Arabic numerals."

# Putting It All Together

In roughly a millennium, a number of important patterns of world history emerged in India. The political, cultural, social, religious, and economic systems of the states along the Ganges River were diffused to all parts of the Indian subcontinent, where they were substantially—though by no means completely—received by the surrounding peoples. With the maturing of these patterns came the tendency to see the subcontinent as a unified entity in nearly every way except in politics. Here, despite the accomplishments of the Mauryans and Guptas, unity would prove elusive—in some respects even to the present day. This would prove particularly true, as we will see in later chapters, with the coming of Islam.

In terms of its regional influence and beyond, India's impact was disproportionately large. By at least the time of Ashoka, the population of the subcontinent was second only to that of China. Within it was contained the world's most active source of religious traditions, next to southwest Asia and the Mediterranean. The influence of one of these religions, Hinduism, spread to Indonesia and southeast Asia; that of the other, Buddhism, could lay claim through this period to be the world's largest religious system as well as the first "universal" one.

Paradoxically, many of the factors that allowed for this tremendous richness of religious, cultural, and intellectual traditions also tended to abet the subcontinent's chronic political instability, particularly in the north. Here, continual migrations of outside peoples cross-fertilized the cultural resources of the region but also impeded political unification.

▶ For additional resources, including maps, primary sources, visuals, and quizzes, please go to www.oup.com/us/vonsivers. Please see the Further Resources section at the back of the book for additional readings and suggested websites.

## Against the Grain

# India's Ancient Republics

As we have seen, in addition to numerous kingdoms, the ancient Gangetic states also counted republics (*ganas*) among them. Accustomed as we are to thinking of such political institutions as exclusive to the Mediterranean world, as with the Roman Republic, representative forms of government have appeared at times in nearly all human societies. Yet until very recent times, as scientific-industrial society and the nation-state have come to dominate global politics and economics, republics had proved short-lived and problematic to sustain. In Greece and Rome, for example, popular-based governments seemed inevitably to descend into factionalism that in the end demanded a strong ruler to restore order.

The early Indian republics of the late Vedic period were also seen by contemporaries to be models of power sharing in some respects, but were always vulnerable to the same weaknesses of internal dissention and factionalism as their counterparts elsewhere. For states moving toward a unified conception of concentrated power and religious unity—particularly when inheriting a tradition of rulers claiming divine sanction—the instability of power sharing seemed increasingly unattractive, even dangerous. Moreover, the requirements of economic stability in agrarian societies and the growing rigidity of caste also militated against the viability of republics.

And yet this form of social organization was discussed a number of times in the Mahabharata, in the accounts of Alexander's expeditions into India, and in a number of Buddhist accounts of northern Indian states as late as the second century CE. Detailed descriptions of their workings occur in the political treatises of Kautilya, and Arrian, the historian of Alexander, notes that republics such as Mallas offered the Greek armies some of the fiercest resistance they encountered. Perhaps here lies a clue to what contemporaries viewed as their true strengths and vulnerabilities: All commentators insist that no form of government works better when the people are unified and have a stake in the existing order; but factionalism and division are in the end fatal. As the Buddha himself notes in the Maha Nirvana Sutra, "So long as the Vajiyyans . . . so frequent the public meetings of their clan, so long they may be expected not to decline but to prosper." As Indian society as a whole became more complex and differentiated by religious tradition, economic station, and caste, the drive for political unity, so it was believed, would become that much stronger. With the creation of empires by the Mauryans and Guptas, the age of the republics in India was to pass—until 1947. Today, with its constitution and representative government, India prides itself on being the world's largest democracy.

- **What difficulties did all republics that sprang from agrarian–urban society face? Were they in the end insurmountable? Why?**

- **Do you think Indian republics were more vulnerable than those elsewhere to problems of disunity and factionalism? What role do you think religion played in sustaining or undermining them?**

# Thinking Through Patterns

▶ **Think about the reasons for the spread of Buddhism inside and outside of India. How have historians seen the decline of Buddhism in India?**

An important historical pattern we examine in this part is that of individuals we call "visionaries"—people who, as the saying goes, "think outside the box" in their own societies. In this chapter, we place the Buddha in this category as a man who sought—and satisfied himself and his followers that he succeeded—to go beyond the Hindu bounds of death and rebirth. Like the other visionaries we examine, however, the Buddha's fundamental message of transcendence and enlightenment can be adapted to any belief system. As his message moves along the trade routes in India, central Asia, and, as we will see in later chapters, China, Korea, Japan, and southeast Asia, it adapts to local customs by borrowing bits of indigenous religious mythology and belief to make it attractive to converts while keeping the fundamental message intact. Local people in turn adapt it to their own beliefs and make it their own. In the case of east Asia, this will receive a large boost from the translation of Buddhist scriptures into literary Chinese and the circulation of Buddhist practitioners, monks, merchants, and pilgrims throughout the Buddhist cultural sphere. Its decline in the place of its birth appears to be due in part to the shift of its cultural center to China and Japan and the official support of the Guptas for Hinduism.

How do historians establish criteria of "importance"? One measure of this is to assess the influence of certain patterns and practices on a culture or society over time. Change over time or the lack of it is an important indicator of the prevalence and kind of innovation taking place in a society. So some influential patterns in Indian history might include the permeation of religion into all aspects of Indian life, the search for transcendence of the material world, the caste system as the social fabric of the subcontinent, and the prominence of India as a crossroads astride the trade routes of the Indian Ocean and the great land routes across Eurasia.

▶ **What do you consider to be the most influential patterns in Indian history to this point? Why?**

▶ **Do you think some of Ashoka's concepts could be implemented by governments today? Why or why not?**

Ashoka's ideas seem quite modern in many ways, and his decrees regarding the protection of animals and ecological matters might certainly have some current application. His ideas of not taking life except in extreme circumstances and of giving prisoners time to repent also parallel modern concepts. Yet it must also be remembered that he is still far removed in time and culture from the modern world. His ideas of dharma as duty might not carry exactly the same import as today. Historians are routinely conscious of the pitfalls of identifying too closely with peoples in very different cultures in the remote past. "The past is a foreign country," it is often said. "They do things differently there."

# Patterns of Evidence: Sources for Chapter 8

## SOURCE 8.1

## The Seven Pillar Edicts of King Ashoka

### ca. 247–246 BCE

The third of the Mauryan kings, Ashoka ruled a vast empire throughout the Indian subcontinent in the period 273–231 BCE. His abrupt conversion to Buddhism in 260 led him to govern according to Buddhist principles—at least as he understood them. His new policies with respect to "righteous" governance were posted in a series of edicts that were engraved on rocks and pillars at strategic spots in his empire. A sample of these contains both very specific injunctions—imposed upon himself and upon his subordinates—and general principles, which could presumably be adapted to changing real-world circumstances.

**1.** Beloved-of-the-Gods speaks thus: This Dharma edict was written twenty-six years after my coronation. Happiness in this world and the next is difficult to obtain without much love for the Dharma, much self-examination, much respect, much fear (of evil), and much enthusiasm. But through my instruction this regard for Dharma and love of Dharma has grown day by day, and will continue to grow. And my officers of high, low and middle rank are practicing and conforming to Dharma, and are capable of inspiring others to do the same. Mahamatras in border areas are doing the same. And these are my instructions: to protect with Dharma, to make happiness through Dharma and to guard with Dharma.

. . .

**4.** Beloved-of-the-Gods speaks thus: This Dharma edict was written twenty-six years after my coronation. My Rajjukas are working among the people, among many hundreds of thousands of people. The hearing of petitions and the administration of justice has been left to them so that they can do their duties confidently and fearlessly and so that they can work for the welfare, happiness and benefit of the people in the country. But they should remember what causes happiness and sorrow, and being

Source: Ven. S. Dhammika, trans. DharmaNet, 1994, http://www.cs.colostate.edu/~malaiya/ashoka.html# PILLAR.

themselves devoted to Dharma, they should encourage the people in the country (to do the same), that they may attain happiness in this world and the next. These Rajjukas are eager to serve me. They also obey other officers who know my desires, who instruct the Rajjukas so that they can please me. Just as a person feels confident having entrusted his child to an expert nurse thinking: "The nurse will keep my child well," even so, the Rajjukas have been appointed by me for the welfare and happiness of the people in the country.

The hearing of petitions and the administration of justice have been left to the Rajjukas so that they can do their duties unperturbed, fearlessly and confidently. It is my desire that there should be uniformity in law and uniformity in sentencing. I even go this far, to grant a three-day stay for those in prison who have been tried and sentenced to death. During this time their relatives can make appeals to have the prisoners' lives spared. If there is none to appeal on their behalf, the prisoners can give gifts in order to make merit for the next world, or observe fasts. Indeed, it is my wish that in this way, even if a prisoner's time is limited, he can prepare for the next world, and that people's Dharma practice, self-control and generosity may grow.

**7.** Beloved-of-the-Gods, King Piyadasi, says: Along roads I have had banyan trees planted so that they can give shade to animals and men, and I have had mango groves planted. At intervals of eight **krosas**, I have had wells dug, rest-houses built, and in various places, I have had watering-places made for the use of animals and men. But these are but minor achievements. Such things to make the people happy have been done by former kings. I have done these things for this purpose, that the people might practice the Dharma.

Beloved-of-the-Gods, King Piyadasi, speaks thus: My Dharma Mahamatras too are occupied with various good works among the ascetics and house-holders of all religions. I have ordered that they should be occupied with the affairs of the Sangha. I have also ordered that they should be occupied with the affairs of the Brahmans and the Ajivikas. I have ordered that they be occupied with the Niganthas. In fact, I have ordered that different Mahamatras be occupied with the particular affairs of all different religions. And my Dharma Mahamatras likewise are occupied with these and other religions.

Beloved-of-the-Gods, King Piyadasi, speaks thus: These and other principal officers are occupied with the distribution of gifts, mine as well as those of the queens. In my women's quarters, they organize various charitable activities here and in the provinces. I have also ordered my sons and the sons of other queens to distribute gifts so that noble deeds of Dharma and the practice of Dharma may be promoted. And noble deeds of Dharma and the practice of Dharma consist of having kindness, generosity, truthfulness, purity, gentleness and goodness increase among the people.

Beloved-of-the-Gods, King Piyadasi, speaks thus: Whatever good deeds have been done by me, those the people accept and those they follow. Therefore they have progressed and will continue to progress by being respectful to mother and father, respectful to elders, by courtesy to the aged and proper behavior towards Brahmans and ascetics, towards the

**Krosas:** Unit of land measure.

poor and distressed, and even towards servants and employees.

Beloved-of-the-Gods, King Piyadasi, speaks thus: This progress among the people through Dharma has been done by two means, by Dharma regulations and by persuasion. Of these, Dharma regulation is of little effect, while persuasion has much more effect. The Dharma regulations I have given are that various animals must be protected. And I have given many other Dharma regulations also. But it is by persuasion that progress among the people through Dharma has had a greater effect in respect of harmlessness to living beings and non-killing of living beings.

▶ **Working with Sources**

1. To what extent did Ashoka claim to be occupying a paternal role in relationship to his people? Is it likely his specific instructions were actually carried out?

2. Are there indications here that Ashoka really aimed at creating what we might perceive as a kind of police state? In what respects?

## SOURCE 8.2

# *The Questions of King Milinda* (*The Milindapanha*)

**ca. 100 BCE**

A series of Greek rulers attempted to maintain the Hellenizing goals of Alexander the Great in Bactria (modern Afghanistan), long after his death in 323 BCE. The most famous ruler in this line was Menander I (ca. 160–130 BCE), who achieved immortality in Buddhist literature by engaging in a debate with the Buddhist sage Nagasena. Their talks, set out as a series of dilemmas to be posed and (if possible) resolved, became an important exposition of Buddhist ideas and supposedly led to the conversion of Menander ("King Milinda") to Buddhism. In any event, *The Milindapanha* reflects the fusion of Greek and Indian traditions of philosophy, in the fascinating cauldron of world contact that existed in Central and South Asia.

Source: *The Questions of King Milinda*, trans. T. W. Rhys Davids, vol. 2 (Oxford: Clarendon, 1894), 4–7 and 20–22.

## DILEMMA THE FORTY-SECOND. MODERATION IN FOOD.

**4.** 'Venerable Nâgasena, the Blessed One said:

"Be not remiss as to (the rules to be observed) when standing up (to beg for food). Be restrained in (matters relating to) the stomach."

But on the other hand he said: "Now there were several days, Udâyin, on which I ate out of this bowl when it was full to the brim, and ate even more."

"Now if the first rule be true, then the second statement must be false. But if the statement be true, then the rule first quoted must be wrong.

This too is a double-edged problem, now put to you, which you have to solve."

**5.** 'He who has no self-control as regards the stomach, O king, will destroy living creatures, will take possession of what has not been given to him, will be unchaste, will speak lies, will drink strong drink, will put his mother or his father to death, will slay an Arahat, will create a schism in the Order, will even with malice aforethought wound a Tathâgata. Was it not, O king, when without restraint as to his stomach, that Devadatta by breaking up the Order, heaped up for himself karma that would endure for a kalpa? It was on calling to mind this, O king, and many other things of the same kind, that the Blessed One declared:

Be not remiss as to (the rules to be observed) when standing up (to beg for food). Be restrained in (matters relating to) the stomach."

**6.** 'And he who has self-control as regards the stomach gains a clear insight into the Four Truths, realizes the Four Fruits of the life of renunciation, and attains to mastery over the Four Discriminations, the Eight Attainments, and the Six Modes of Higher Knowledge, and fulfils all that goes to constitute the life of the recluse. Did not the parrot fledgling, O king, by self-restraint as to his stomach, cause the very heaven of the great Thirty-Three to shake, and bring down Sakka, the king of the gods, to wait upon him? It was on calling to mind this, O king, and many other things of a similar kind, that the Blessed One declared:

"Be not remiss as to (the rules to be observed) when standing up (to beg for food). Be restrained in (matters relating to) the stomach."

**7.** 'But when, O king, the Blessed One said: "Now there were several days, Udâyi, on which I ate out of this bowl when it was full to the brim, and ate even more," that was said by him who had completed his task, who had finished all that he had to do, who had accomplished the end he set before him, who had overcome every obstruction, by the self-dependent Tathâgata himself about himself.

Just, O king, as it is desirable that a sick man to whom an emetic, or a purge, or a clyster has been administered, should be treated with a tonic; just so, O king, should the man who is full of evil, and who has not perceived the Four Truths, adopt the practice of restraint in the matter of eating. But just, O king, as there is no necessity of polishing, and rubbing down, and purifying a diamond gem of great brilliancy, of the finest water, and of natural purity; just so, O king, is there no restraint as to what actions he should perform, on the Tathâgata, on him who hath attained to perfection in all that lies within the scope of a Buddha.'

'Very good, Nâgasena! That is so, and I accept it as you say.'

. . .

## DILEMMA THE FORTY-SIXTH. THE MOCKING OF THE BUDDHA.

**19.** 'Venerable Nâgasena, it was said by the Blessed One of Six-tusks, the elephant king,

"When he sought to slay him, and had reached him with his trunk,
He perceived the yellow robe, the badge of a recluse,
Then, though smarting with the pain, the thought possessed his heart,—
'He who wears the outward garb the Arahats wear
Must be scatheless held, and sacred, by the good.'"

'But on the other hand it is said:
"When he was Gotipâla, the young Brahman, he reviled and abused Kassapa the Blessed One, the Arahat, the Buddha supreme, with vile and bitter words, calling him a shaveling and a good-for-nothing monk."

'Now if, Nâgasena, the Bodisat, even when he was an animal, respected the yellow robe, then the statement that as Gotipâla, a Brahman, he reviled and abused the Blessed One of that time, must be false. But if as a Brahman, he reviled and abused the Blessed One, the statement that when he was Six-tusks, the elephant king, he respected the yellow robe, must be false. If when the Bodisat was an animal, though he was suffering severe and cruel and bitter pain, he respected the yellow robe which the hunter had put on, how was it that when he was a man, a man arrived at discretion, with all his knowledge mature, he did not pay reverence, on seeing him, to Kassapa the Blessed One, the Arahat, the Buddha supreme, one endowed with the ten powers, the leader of the world, the highest of the high, round whom effulgence spread a fathom on every side, and who was clad in most excellent and precious and delicate Benares cloth made into yellow robes? This too is a double-edged problem, now put to you, which you have to solve.'

**20.** 'The verse you have quoted, O king, was spoken by the Blessed One. And Kassapa the Blessed One, the Arahat, the Buddha supreme, was abused and reviled by Gotipâla the young Brahman with vile and bitter words, with the epithets of shaveling and good-for-nothing monk. But that was owing to his birth and family surroundings. For Gotipâla, O king, was descended from a family of unbelievers, men void of faith. His mother and father, his sisters and brothers, the bondswomen and bondsmen, the hired servants and dependents in the house, were worshippers of Brahmâ, reverers of Brahmâ; and harboring the idea that Brahmans were the highest and most honorable among men, they reviled and loathed those others who had renounced the world. It was through hearing what they said that Gotipâla, when invited by Ghatîkâra the potter to visit the teacher, replied: "What's the good to you of visiting that shaveling, that good-for-nothing monk?"

**21.** 'Just, O king, as even nectar when mixed with poison will turn sour, just as the coolest water in contact with fire will become warm, so was it that

Gotipâla, the young Brahman, having been born and brought up in a family of unbelievers, men void of faith, thus reviled and abused the Tathâgata after the manner of his kind. And just, O king, as a flaming and burning mighty fire, if, even when at the height of its glory, it should come into contact with water, would cool down, with its splendor and glory spoilt, and turn to cinders, black as rotten blighted fruits—just so, O king, Gotipâla, full as he was of merit and faith, mighty as was the glory of his knowledge, yet when reborn into a family of unbelievers, of men void of faith, he became, as it were, blind, and reviled and abused the Tathâgata. But when he had gone to him, and had come to know the virtues of the Buddhas which he had, then did he become as his hired servant; and having renounced the world and entered the Order under the system of the Conqueror, he gained the fivefold power of insight, and the eightfold power of ecstatic meditation, and became assured of rebirth into the Brahmâ heaven.'

'Very good, Nâgasena! That is so, and I accept it as you say.'

▶ **Working with Sources**

1. To what extent does this dialogue reflect elements of the Greek philosophical tradition, explored in Chapter 7?

2. How do both speakers deploy real-world examples, in order to enhance their philosophical arguments?

## SOURCE 8.3

# Bamiyan Buddhas, Afghanistan

**Late sixth century CE**

A few months before the 9/11 terrorist attacks, in the spring of 2001, Taliban officials oversaw a series of explosions in the Bamiyan Valley, which deliberately detonated priceless elements of world heritage. Among the victims of this depredation were a set of enormous Buddha statues that had symbolized the unity of peoples in the region across religious lines. The two statues of Buddha (at 35 and 53 meters in height, one was the tallest Buddha in the world until its destruction) were rendered in a blended Hellenistic and South Asian style. Even after the collapse of the Taliban regime in Afghanistan, little has been done to restore the objects. (Next page, top: an 1880 drawing showing how they originally appeared; next page, bottom: what remained of the statues after their destruction.)

▶ Working
with Sources

1. Why and under what circumstances would Buddhas have been carved
   into this mountainside in the first place?

2. Can any monotheistic system tolerate a fusion of cultural and religious
   values?

SOURCE 8.4

# Seated Buddha, from the Gandhara culture, Afghanistan-Pakistan

**second–third centuries CE**

Gandhara became the center of a vibrant artistic tradition for several centuries. As Greek Bactrians merged their cultural values with Buddhists, Hellenistic artistic techniques fused with the practices of Mahayana Buddhism, yielding a renaissance of daring, boldly innovative sculpture. Among the products of this cultural synthesis was a seated Buddha which incorporates both Hellenistic and Indian aesthetic elements.

▶ **Working with Sources**

1. In what specific respects does this object reflect a conflation of Greek and Indian imagery, especially in the styles of clothing and hair?

2. Why is this object in the British Museum in London today?

## SOURCE 8.5

# Kalidasa, *The Cloud Messenger*

### ca. fourth–fifth centuries CE

S ometimes described as the "Shakespeare of India," Kalidasa mastered various literary genres in his lifetime and continued to thrive, even in Western translations, into modern times. He composed three plays, two epic poems, and a series of shorter poems. Among these is *The Cloud Messenger*, in which a man asks a passing cloud to carry a message to his beloved wife, who is awaiting him in the Himalayas. Translated from the Sanskrit into English in the early nineteenth century, *The Cloud Messenger* served as the inspiration for composer Gustav Holst's 1909–1910 choral work *The Cloud Messenger*.

**Yaksha:** A demigod attendant to the god of wealth.

A certain **yaksha** who had been negligent in the execution of his own duties, on account of a curse from his master which was to be endured for a year and which was onerous as it separated him from his beloved, made his residence among the hermitages of Ramagiri, whose waters were blessed by the bathing of the daughter of Janaka and whose shade trees grew in profusion.

That lover, separated from his beloved, whose gold armlet had slipped from his bare forearm, having dwelt on that mountain for some months, on the first day of the month of Asadha, saw a cloud embracing the summit, which resembled a mature elephant playfully butting a bank.

Managing with difficulty to stand up in front of that cloud which was the cause of the renewal of his enthusiasm, that attendant of the king of kings, pondered while holding back his tears. Even the mind of a happy person is excited at the sight of a cloud. How much more so, when the one who longs to cling to his neck is far away?

As the month of Nabhas was close at hand, having as his goal the sustaining of the life of his beloved and wishing to cause the tidings of his own welfare to be carried by the cloud, the delighted being spoke kind words of welcome to the cloud to which offerings of fresh kutaja flowers had been made.

Owing to his impatience, not considering the incompatibility between a cloud consisting of vapor, light, water and wind and the contents of his message best delivered by a person of normal faculties, the yaksha made this request to the cloud, for among sentient and non-sentient things, those afflicted by desire are naturally miserable:

Source: http://allpoetry.com/poem/8526541-The-Cloud-Messenger---Part-01-by-Kalidasa

Without doubt, your path unimpeded, you will see your brother's wife, intent on counting the days, faithful and living on. The bond of hope generally sustains the quickly sinking hearts of women who are alone, and which wilt like flowers.

Just as the favorable wind drives you slowly onward, this cataka cuckoo, your kinsman, calls sweetly on the left. Knowing the season for fertilization, cranes, like threaded garlands in the sky, lovely to the eye, will serve you.

Your steady passage observed by charming female **siddhas** who in trepidation wonder 'Has the summit been carried off the mountain by the wind?,' you who are heading north, fly up into the sky from this place where the nicula trees flourish, avoiding on the way the blows of the trunks of the elephants of the four quarters of the sky....

Even though the route would be circuitous for one who, like you, is northward-bound, do not turn your back on the love on the palace roofs in Ujjayini. If you do not enjoy the eyes with flickering eyelids of the women startled by bolts of lightning there, then you have been deceived!

On the way, after you have ascended to the Nirvandhya River, whose girdles are flocks of birds calling on account of the turbulence of her waves, whose gliding motion is rendered delightful with stumbling steps, and whose exposed navel is her eddies, fill yourself with water, for amorous distraction is a woman's first expression of love for their beloved.

When you have passed that, you should duly adopt the means by which the Sindhu River may cast off her emaciation—she whose waters have become like a single braid of hair, whose complexion is made pale by the old leaves falling from the trees on her banks, and who shows you goodwill because she has been separated from you, O fortunate one.

...

Even if you arrive at Mahakala at some other time, O cloud, you should wait until the sun passes from the range of the eye. Playing the honorable role of drum at the evening offering to Shiva, you will receive the full reward for your deep thunder.

There, their girdles jingling to their footsteps, and their hands tired from the pretty waving of fly-whisks whose handles are brilliant with the sparkle of jewels, having received from you raindrops at the onset of the rainy season that soothe the scratches made by fingernails, the courtesans cast you lingering sidelong glances that resemble rows of honey-bees.

Then, settled above the forests whose trees are like uplifted arms, being round in shape, producing an evening light, red as a fresh Chinarose, at the start of Shiva's dance, remove his desire for a fresh elephant skin—you whose devotion is beheld by Parvati, her agitation stilled and her gaze transfixed.

**Siddhas:** Experts in spiritual matters.

▶ **Working with Sources**

1. How do the places seen by the cloud on its journey relate to the husband's feeling of longing for his wife?

2. How are the outer and inner worlds connected in this poem?

# Chapter 9 722 BCE–618 CE

# China

## IMPERIAL UNIFICATION AND PERFECTING THE MORAL ORDER

"**V**enerable sir, since you have not considered a thousand *li* too far to come, may I presume that you bring something that may profit my kingdom?" Even today one can sense the air of challenge, however polite, as the two men begin to take each other's measure. The speaker, King Hui of Liang, had seen his kingdom steadily eroded by the powerful surrounding states of Chu, Jin, and Qin, vying for supremacy at the height of China's Warring States period (403–221 BCE). Given the increasing desperation of his situation, perhaps he can be forgiven his somewhat sharp tone.

The "venerable sir" to whom he addressed his question, however, was in no mood to banter: "Why must Your Majesty use that word 'profit'? I bring only humanity and righteousness," he thundered. Warming to his topic, the Confucian sage Mencius now laid out his rebuttal:

> If Your Majesty says, "How may I profit my kingdom" the great officers will say, "How may we profit our families"; and the lesser officers and common people will say, "how may we profit ourselves." Superiors and inferiors will try to snatch this profit from each other and the kingdom will be endangered . . . [but] there never has been a humane man who neglected his parents. There never has been a righteous man who made his ruler an afterthought.

—James Legge, trans., *The Works of Mencius*
(New York: Dover Reprint, 1970, pp. 125–126)

THE FIRST CHINESE EMPIRES

*ABOVE:* "**The Admonitions Scroll: The Instructress Writing the Admonitions**," a handscroll painting from the Tang dynasty.

Chastened by this confrontation, but also intrigued, King Hui now sought Mencius out for advice on a number of fronts. Through it all the sage refused to mince words with him about the extent of his misgovernment. Finally, both Hui and his son and successor, Xiang, said, "I wish quietly to receive your instructions."

This story from the opening pages of the fourth-century BCE *Mengzi*, known in English as the *Book of Mencius*, illustrates several important points not only about late Zhou China but also about the role of intellectual innovation, the ultimate direction of Chinese political thought, the way Chinese ideas would influence nearby peoples, and, more generally, the larger pattern of empires and states adopting the ideas of visionary thinkers. As we noted in Chapter 4, the Spring and Autumn and the Warring States periods in China during the final centuries of the Zhou era were socially and politically tumultuous. In spite, or perhaps because, of this, the period was also the most fertile one in China's long intellectual history. As we shall see, starting with Confucius— from whom Mencius drew his ideas—Chinese thinkers suggested ways of looking at the world, how to behave in it, and how to govern it that ranged from radically abstract to firmly practical, from collective to individualistic, and from an absence of active government to near totalitarianism.

From the time of the Han dynasty (202 BCE–220 CE) until the twentieth century, Confucianism, as interpreted by Mencius and adopted as a means of bureaucratic control, would be the governmental system of China. Moreover, as Chinese was adopted as the first written language by the Koreans, Japanese, and Vietnamese, Confucian concepts would be firmly planted in these lands as well. So in China, as in India, Persia, Rome, and eventually the Islamic world, the legacy of innovators we have identified as "visionaries" would be picked up and adopted by rulers as officially approved thought. As we will emphasize in this and the following chapters, an important pattern of world history emerges by the beginning of the Common Era: Large "world" empires utilize religions and systems of thought that have universal application and appeal.

## Visionaries and Empire

The period from the eighth century BCE until the first unification of China under the Qin in 221 BCE is universally regarded as China's most fertile period of intellectual exploration. The foundations of nearly every important school of Chinese philosophy were laid during this era. By the time of the Confucian ethicist and political thinker Mencius in the fourth century BCE, so many competing systems of thought had emerged that Chinese chroniclers refer to them as the "hundred schools." Of these various systems, those that are best known and that had the greatest impact were Confucianism, Legalism, and Daoism.

## Seeing Patterns

▶ Was the First Emperor's ruthlessness justified by his accomplishments in his empire?

▶ How would you compare the values expressed by Confucius and Mencius to those of contemporary society?

▶ How have historians viewed the role of women in early imperial China?

## Confucianism, Legalism, and Daoism

Like so many important figures in the world of ideas, the historical Confucius is an elusive figure. Contemporary researchers have widely differing views on his identity and his works. According to traditional accounts, he was born in 551 BCE to a family named Kong. Even today, the Kong family, some of whose members still live in the original family compound at Qufu [CHOO-foo] in modern Shandong Province, maintains what is claimed to be a continuous genealogy of the sage's descendants, who are now said to number in the millions.

In Confucian texts he is referred to as "the Master" (*zi* or *fuzi*) or "Master Kong" (*Kong fuzi*) [koong FOO-zuh]. European Roman Catholic missionaries in China during the seventeenth century rendered *Kong fuzi* into Latin, where it became "Confucius." As a member of the growing *shi* class of well-to-do, educated commoners and lower aristocracy (see Chapter 4), Confucius spent much of his early career seeking a position as political adviser to the courts of several of the Zhou states in northern China. Though tradition has him holding a minor position in his native state of Lu, his search for employment was largely unsuccessful. As with the visionaries we saw in the previous chapter in India, he ended up spending most of his life as an itinerant teacher, spreading his ideas about ethics and politics to a growing group of followers. Like the Buddha, however, it would be centuries before his ideas were applied on a large scale by a state.

**Confucian Doctrine**   Confucius has been called "China's first great moralist." His teachings—as presented in the *Lunyu*, or *Analects*, the central Confucian text—have at their core a view of human beings as inclined toward ethical behavior and of human society as a perfectible moral order. According to Confucius, there are certain fundamental patterns that are manifestations of the *Dao* ("the Way") of the universal order.

One of these fundamental patterns is the relationship between parent and offspring. A child owes its life and body to its parents. Because of this, a child—even a grownup, who was, after all, once a child—dares not injure him- or herself or others. People develop their moral character to reflect well upon their parents and serve those in higher social or political stations as they serve their own parents. This example of human society as a kind of extended family applies at every level, from the peasant to the ruler—and even beyond: Drawing on the idea of the Mandate of Heaven (see Chapter 4), Confucius makes the ruler himself responsible to heaven for the state of his country. Indeed, emperors in later regimes would habitually refer to themselves as the "son of heaven," to emphasize this filial duty.

Though this view is avowedly hierarchical rather than egalitarian, the mutual obligations present at every level serve as checks for Confucius on the arbitrary exercise of power. Hence, when asked to sum up his thinking in one word, Confucius answered, "**Reciprocity.**" Confucius believed that individuals should strive for the qualities of *ren* (kindness or humaneness toward others) by faithfully following the practices of *li* (the observance of rules of decorum as guides to appropriate behavior toward others). People who did so would not only perfect their own character but also set an example for the rest of society.

**Reciprocity:** Mutual exchange of things, ideas, etc.

"**Reciprocity**" [*shu*]—what you would not want for yourself, do not do to others.

—Confucius, *Analects*

**Confucian Government**    Confucius lived during a time of great social and political disorder, and as a result many of his teachings center on ways to restore order and make government and society more humane. But because Confucian doctrine places great emphasis on personal responsibility, the structure of government is far less important than the ethical fitness of the ruler and the people. Good government, according to Confucius, begins with educated leaders and officials of strong moral character, like the Zhou kings Wen and Wu and the Duke of Zhou (see Chapter 4), who are often cited in the *Analects* as examples. To describe this ideal of behavior, Confucius introduced the concept of the **junzi** ("the superior man" or "gentleman").

**Junzi:** According to Confucius, the "superior man" or "gentleman" who behaves according to an ethical and moral ideal. A society run by *junzi* will foster social institutions that encourage proper behavior.

Those able to attain these ideals would comprise for Confucius a kind of aristocracy of merit, while rulers who possessed these qualities would set a sound example for their subjects to follow.

Just as the *junzi* cultivated his personal ethics and morals, a state run by *junzi* would spread these values to society by fostering social institutions that encouraged proper behavior among the people. In the same way that a musician's consistent practicing of scales eventually makes playing them correctly second nature, the consistent observance of *li* would help make appropriate behavior routine among ordinary people. Not everyone would necessarily develop the high moral standards of the *junzi*, but at the very least, the majority of people would develop a sense of right and wrong and thus acquire a stake in the social order.

By the time Confucius died in 479 BCE, he had attracted a loyal following of adherents to his teachings. Two later students of Confucian doctrine, Mencius and Xunzi [SHWUN-zuh], continued to spread the teachings of the master, though with their own distinctive contributions. Despite challenges from a number of competing philosophical schools, Confucian ideals ultimately became the standard for Chinese politics and scholarship.

**Mencius**    By Mencius's time, in the fourth century BCE, the intensity of the competition and continual warfare among the Zhou states had spawned most of the so-called hundred schools of thought as thinkers questioned fundamental assumptions about the private and social good. Not surprisingly, given the chaotic times, their answers varied from radical individualism to universal love and altruism, with some, like Sun Zi (often spelled Sun Tzu) in *The Art of War*, examining the nature and practice of armed struggle.

Mencius (*Mengzi*, or Master Meng; ca. 385–312 BCE), like Confucius, believed that people were fundamentally good and that individuals must continually work to understand and refine this goodness in order to avoid being led astray by negative influences. Mencius used water, the nature of which is to flow downhill,

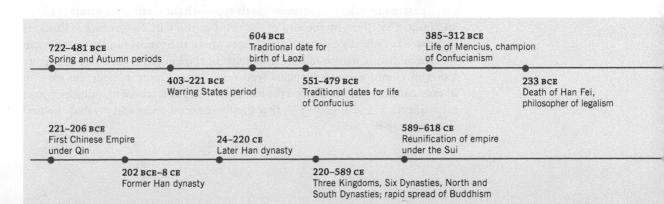

722–481 BCE
Spring and Autumn periods

604 BCE
Traditional date for birth of Laozi

385–312 BCE
Life of Mencius, champion of Confucianism

403–221 BCE
Warring States period

551–479 BCE
Traditional dates for life of Confucius

233 BCE
Death of Han Fei, philosopher of legalism

221–206 BCE
First Chinese Empire under Qin

24–220 CE
Later Han dynasty

589–618 CE
Reunification of empire under the Sui

202 BCE–8 CE
Former Han dynasty

220–589 CE
Three Kingdoms, Six Dynasties, North and South Dynasties; rapid spread of Buddhism

**The Kong Family Mansion in Qufu.** Though scholars have debated many aspects of the life and activities of the historical Confucius, his descendants have maintained the family genealogical records and compound over the centuries at Qufu in modern Shandong province. Since 1055 CE, Chinese emperors have bestowed on the eldest male family member in direct descent from the sage the title of "Duke Yansheng." The most recent holder of the title, Kung Te-cheng (Kong Dezheng), died in October 2008 in Taiwan at the age of 89. He was the 77th direct descendent of Confucius.

as a familiar metaphor for human nature. It is possible, of course, to force water out of this natural tendency, said Mencius; but once such artificial means are removed, it reverts to its original course. Hence, he concluded, the way to proper behavior is through cultivating the Confucian virtues as a bulwark against forces pushing toward "unnatural" behavior.

Mencius traveled throughout China spreading Confucian ideals, especially as a basis for government practice. The *Mengzi,* or *Book of Mencius,* is written in more of a narrative form than the *Analects* and is supplemented by stories, parables, and debates with advocates of other schools of thought. Its most powerful sections deal with the obligations of rulers to their subjects. As the center of power and moral authority, a ruler's primary duty for Mencius is to maintain the "people's livelihood" and uphold the "righteousness" (*yi*—appropriate behavior by and toward all according to social rank) of the state. As an appropriately ideal way to maintain the people's livelihood, for example, Mencius advocated the "well-field" system (see Chapter 4) as a means of ensuring crop surpluses and equality among peasant cultivators.

As for the state, as Mencius said to King Hui of Liang in the chapter-opening vignette, "I bring only humanity [*ren*] and righteousness [*yi*]; why must Your Majesty use that word 'profit'?" Mencius argued that rulers who sought to profit from their states sowed the seeds of their own destruction by encouraging their subjects to profit only themselves. A state ruled by righteousness and humanity, on the other hand, ensured that the people would be prosperous and orderly, which automatically contributed to the "profit" of the ruler. A ruler who abused or neglected his subjects upset the social order and the natural tendency of people toward good. In such a case, the people had not only the right but also the obligation to invoke the Mandate of Heaven and depose him. In the end, said Mencius, anticipating a host of later Chinese thinkers, the people, not the ruler, are the foundation of the state.

**Xunzi**   As states grew increasingly powerful, their armies larger, and warfare more deadly, Mencius's optimistic view of human nature seemed less and less practical to many thinkers. Like Mencius, Xunzi (trad. ca. 310–219? BCE) was also a student of Confucian philosophy but had a much darker view of human nature. Living during the apogee of the Warring States period, Xunzi came to believe that individuals were self-involved creatures with little interest in society as a whole and capable of regulating themselves only through immense effort. Only by enforcing the restraints of civilization, such as ritual, law, and the example of past model rulers, could individuals approach the Confucian ideals of virtue and humanity. Thus, by the end of the third century BCE, Confucian thinkers had come to radically opposed conclusions about their most fundamental premise: the authentic nature of human beings. In the long run, the more moderate views of Confucius and Mencius won out. Xunzi's more pessimistic view of human nature, however, formed the basis of the Legalist school founded by two of his students, Han Fei and Li Si, that finally restored order and created the first Chinese empire.

**Legalism**    The Legalist school is the most severe of the three major schools of philosophical thought that emerged during the Warring States period. For Legalists, building a strong state was of utmost importance. Out of Xunzi's view of human beings as inclined toward evil and drawing on the earlier practices of the Qin minister Lord Shang (d. 338 BCE), Han Fei (d. 233 BCE) and Li Si (d. 208 BCE) developed a system of uniform laws and practices based on the absolute will of the ruler. Order in a state, they claimed, could be implemented only through the institution of strict, detailed, and explicit laws diligently enforced and imposed on all subjects without regard to rank or class. Since Legalists believed that compliance on small matters led to compliance on larger ones, they imposed harsh punishments—forced labor, mutilation, in some cases death—for even the tiniest infractions.

The Legalists argued that the state was all important; therefore, all subjects must serve the state through productive activities. Among these activities, agriculture and military service were the highest priorities. Individuals were encouraged to take up farming or military service as their livelihoods; any other occupation was discouraged. Idlers were put to work by force. Since dissent led to disorder, only government-approved history and literature were tolerated.

Although Legalism had many critics, it was its strict practices, not the more moderate ideals of Confucianism or Daoism, that imposed order on China. The price it exacted for doing so, however, was considered by succeeding generations to have been intolerably high.

**Daoism**    While most Chinese philosophical schools accepted the concept of the Dao as the ordering principle of the universe, they varied considerably as to the best means of achieving harmony with it. For Confucians, as we have seen, study and self-cultivation to the point of intuitive understanding put the individual in tune with the Dao. For followers of the Daoist tradition, attributed to Laozi (Lao Tzu), however, the Confucian path prevented genuine understanding of and harmony with the Dao.

The historical Laozi is even more obscure than Confucius. In fact, many scholars believe Laozi to be a mythical figure. Chinese tradition cites his birth date as 604 BCE and gives his name as Li Er. The honorific title "Laozi" is translated as either "the Old Master" or "the Old Child." The translation "Old Child" captures something of the Daoist belief that only a return to childlike simplicity would lead to union with the Dao.

For Daoists, in contrast to the Confucians, the Dao was not the ordering force *within* the universe but the transcendent first principle *beyond* the universe. The Confucian Dao, dealing with the particulars of this world, can be named; the Daoist Dao, like the relationship between atman and brahman we saw in Chapter 8, transcends all particulars and therefore cannot be named. The Dao is thus beyond all dualities and unifies them in a great oscillating whole.

In fact, the vocabulary Laozi used for this new measure of all phenomena is remarkably similar to that of other Eurasian visionaries discussed previously: Deutero-Isaiah, the Zoroastrian reformers, Anaximander, and the Buddha, as well as the Upanishad writers. All were striving in their volatile kingdoms and empires, many of which worshipped large pantheons of gods, for one, single, unchangeable, and all-encompassing standard for morality and understanding.

Since the Dao transcended the world, including all such opposites as "good" and "evil," no single path of action would lead an individual to union with it. To choose the good, as the Confucians do, is therefore to follow only a limited part of the universal Dao. Instead, the Daoists taught that only through a life of quiet self-reflection and contemplation of opposites and paradoxes might an individual come to know the Dao. A classic tale that expresses this aspect of Daoist thought is the story of the philosopher Zhuang Zhou [JWONG joe], who lived in the fourth century BCE and awoke from a dream unsure of whether he had dreamed he was a butterfly or whether he was a butterfly dreaming he was Zhuang Zhou.

**Daoism and Government**    Daoist political theory held that the best government was that which governed least. Here, the key idea is one from the most famous Daoist work, the *Daode Jing* (*The Classic of the Way and Virtue*, often spelled *Tao Te Ching*): "By non-action there is nothing that is not done." This is not to say that the ruler literally does nothing; rather, his role is to create the conditions that naturally lead to a society in which everyone spontaneously acts in accordance with the Dao. The ruler should not push specific policies but rather let all things take their natural course, for even as they run to extremes they will always reverse. The ruler's understanding of the flow of these universal cycles leads to union with the Dao and keeps the world in equilibrium.

These three schools of thought were all to play a role in the development of China's political and cultural life. Confucianism would provide the basis for the bureaucracy of China's empires and ideals of a perfectible moral order; Daoism would provide the mystical dimension of Chinese culture and a profound love and idealization of nature; finally, Legalism would provide the brute muscle of unifying the last of the warring states into a single structure under the Qin [chin].

## The Qin Dynasty

As the period of the Warring States continued, the Qin state ultimately claimed victory over its opponents and established centralized rule throughout China. At first glance, Qin might seem unpromising as a candidate for empire. It was the smallest and poorest of the Zhou dependencies, located far to the west of most of the other Zhou states. However, Qin had several powerful advantages over its competitors. Its position on the fringe of the Zhou world meant that it was free to expand its economic base by promising land to peasant cultivators as the state seized territory on its western frontier.

**Qin and Zhou**    The agricultural surplus that resulted from these land grants led to increased prosperity for the small but growing state. Qin's location was also a benefit when it came to military preparedness. Many of the warring states were in close proximity to each other, and the constant battles among them depleted their economic and military resources. Qin, on the other hand, did not have to fight off other states at its borders. Consequently, the Qin participated in limited military campaigns, mostly against nomadic groups, which strengthened their fighting skills but did not upset their economy or weaken their army. By 350 BCE, Qin rulers, particularly the famous Shang Yang, reorganized the state by eliminating the last of the old Zhou institutions and replacing them with a uniform, centralized system that anticipated a number of later Legalist principles.

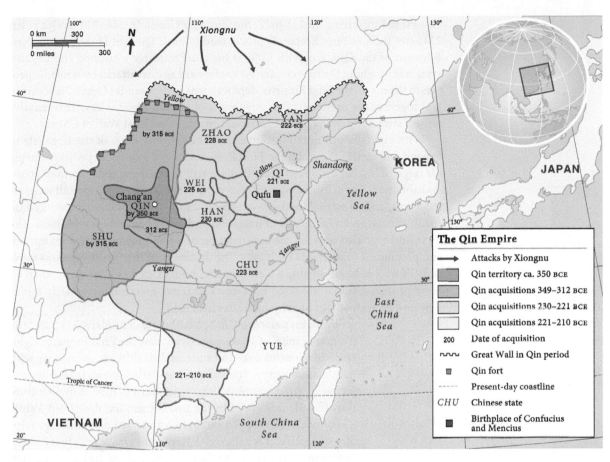

MAP 9.1 The Qin Empire.

In 256 BCE, the Qin conquered Zhou itself and began the drive for empire in earnest (see Map 9.1).

With its strong economy, expert military, and the Legalist theorists Han Fei and Li Si advising the court, Qin took advantage of the collective exhaustion of the other northern Chinese states and conquered them at a pace reminiscent of Alexander the Great's campaigns of the previous century. With stunning swiftness, Qin armies, now swelling to hundreds of thousands of men, drove south and eliminated the opposition of the many tribal peoples below the state of Yue.

The Qin then continued into the northern part of modern Vietnam—thus beginning a long, and often bitterly contested, relationship with southeast Asia. The Chinese would attempt to rule the area with limited success for over 1,000 years and claim it as a protectorate for nearly another thousand until they were ousted by the French in 1885. In the north and west, Qin armies fought a series of campaigns to drive nomadic peoples, especially the Xiongnu, or Huns, from newly established borders and secure the trade routes into central Asia. By the end of the 220s BCE, the Qin had subdued all of the states that would constitute what was about to become the first Chinese empire.

**The First Emperor**   In 221 BCE, the Qin ruler Cheng (r. 246–221 as Qin ruler; 221–209 BCE as First Emperor) proclaimed himself Qin Shi Huangdi, the First Emperor of the Qin, and with Li Si as his chief minister instituted the Legalist system throughout the new empire. As a safeguard against attacks by nomadic peoples in the north, the First Emperor deployed tens of thousands of forced laborers to join together the numerous defensive walls of the old Zhou states. This massive project stretching over 1,400 miles would become the Great Wall of China.

With virtually unlimited resources and the ruthless drive of the Legalists to expand and fortify the state, the First Emperor began a series of projects during his reign of less than a dozen years that are still astonishing today in their scope and ambition. The Chinese writing system was standardized, as were all weights, measures, and coinage. Hundreds of thousands of conscript laborers worked on roads, canals, and a multitude of irrigation and water conservancy projects. The First Emperor also ordered the construction of a tomb for himself, a mammoth complex meant to celebrate his legacy. The discovery of the First Emperor's tomb in 1974 by a peasant digging a well near the modern city of Xi'an unearthed an army of thousands of life-sized terra-cotta warriors marching in orderly ranks, intended to protect Qin Shi Huangdi after his death.

> "Your servant suggests that all books in the imperial archives, save the memoirs of Qin, be burned. . . . Anyone referring to the past to criticize the present should, together with all members of his family, be put to death."
>
> —Li Si, quoted in the Han dynasty–era *Records of the Grand Historian*

From his palace in Chang'an, the site of modern Xi'an and the ultimate capital of 13 separate dynasties, the First Emperor tightened his control over the state and dealt with opponents with ruthless efficiency. Scholars, particularly Confucians, who objected to government policies were buried alive. Any literature not officially sanctioned by the government was destroyed. While it is difficult to assess the extent to which the book burnings actually took place, it is believed that a great many works that existed before the Qin were put to the torch. Writers of the following Han dynasty, emphasizing the horrors of the Qin, have left a number of accounts of mass executions of dissenting scholars.

**Terra-cotta Warriors at the First Emperor's Tomb.** One of the most important archaeological finds of the twentieth century, the Qin burial complex was discovered in 1974 by local farmers digging a well. Over 5,000 figures have been unearthed so far, all with individualized features. The dig has been enclosed and a museum built on site. Along with the Great Wall, it is one of China's most popular tourist destinations.

After a reign of about 12 years as emperor, Qin Shi Huangdi died. His strict laws, severe punishments, and huge construction projects had angered and exhausted the people, and soon after his death the empire erupted in rebellion. Ironically, the government's severe laws and punishments now worked against it as officials attempted to conceal the revolt's severity for fear of torture and execution. At the same time, Minister Li Si provoked additional discontent by conspiring to keep the First Emperor's death a secret in order to rule as regent for the monarch's son. He was captured attempting to flee the rebellion and executed in 208 BCE. In an attempt to make the punishment fit the crime, his captors lashed him to a board and slowly sawed him in half, lengthwise, in accordance with Qin law. After a brief civil war, a general named Liu Bang put an end to the fighting and restored order to the region. He proclaimed himself emperor in 202 BCE and called his new dynasty the Han.

## The Han Dynasty

If the Qin constructed the Chinese empire, the Han perfected it. The Han developed over time a centralized political system of rule that blended the administrative structures of the Qin with more moderate Confucian ideals of government as a moral agent. This model of rule endured—with some interruptions and modifications—for over 2,000 years, by having its power tempered by a bureaucracy that saw its role as both carrying out the will of the court and acting as advocates for the people.

Unlike earlier rulers who came from aristocratic families, Liu Bang, who had taken the reign name Gaozu (r. 202–195 BCE), had been a peasant. Perhaps because of this background, he had little interest in restoring the decentralized system of the Zhou, which favored the aristocratic classes. Instead, he left intact the Qin structure of centralized ministries and regional **commanderies**. This structure seemed the only sensible way to keep such a large empire under control. To mollify advocates of returning to the old Zhou system, Han rulers offered them token distributions of land. They also reduced taxes and labor obligations and rescinded the most severe punishments imposed under the Qin. Han rulers altered the Qin system of leveling social classes by instituting uniform rules for different segments of society—aristocrats as well as commoners. Under the Han, the upper ranks of society were taxed at lighter rates and exempted from most forms of corporal punishment.

**Commanderies:** Districts under the control of a military commander.

As the Han Empire expanded—reaching a population recorded in 2 CE of just under 60 million—so did its bureaucracy. Within a century of Liu Bang's reign, the number of government officials had swollen to 130,000. Officials were divided into graded ranks ranging from the heads of imperial ministries to district magistrates. Below these officials were clan leaders and village **headmen**. Landowners were to collect and remit the taxes for themselves and their tenants, while the lower officials recorded the rates and amounts, kept track of the labor obligations of the district, and mobilized the people during emergencies.

**Headmen:** Local leaders; these are usually chosen by the people of the village, clan, district, etc., rather than appointed by the government.

**Wudi, the Martial Emperor**   A high point of the Han dynasty came during the rule of the emperor Wudi, whose reign name means "Martial Emperor" (r. ca. 140–87 BCE). Like both his predecessors and successors, Wudi faced the complex problem of defending the empire's northern and western boundaries from diverse groups of nomadic peoples, especially the Xiongnu. He therefore

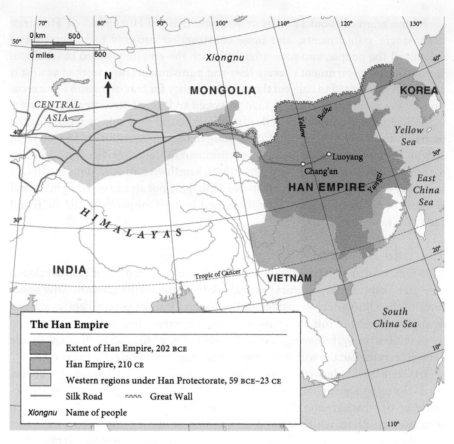

MAP 9.2 **The Han Empire.**

extended the Great Wall begun by the Qin to provide greater protection. Hoping that a strong Chinese presence would discourage potential invasions, Wudi encouraged people to move to areas along the northern and western borders of the empire (see Map 9.2).

In addition to securing the empire, Wudi had to suppress Xiongnu raids on central Asian trade routes, especially the Silk Road. He made diplomatic efforts, offering the Xiongnu food and other necessary supplies, but when those efforts failed, he mounted military campaigns against them. Over the long term, the Han also adopted the practice of "**sinicizing**" the nomadic peoples, a process similar to that pursued by their contemporaries the Romans toward the peoples surrounding their empire. The practice of sinicizing involved encouraging nomadic peoples to assimilate themselves to Chinese culture and identity. Once they had been assimilated, the threat of nomadic invasion would be lessened. Wudi drove his armies into central Asia, where he established a lucrative trade with the peoples there, and again into northern Vietnam and Korea, extending Han rule into those areas. Along with the imposition of Han rule came the Chinese writing system and the infusion of Confucian ideology and practices.

**Sinicizing:** The pattern by which newcomers to areas dominated by Chinese culture were encouraged to adopt that culture for themselves.

**Wang Mang and the Red Eyebrow Revolt**   Lasting more than 400 years, the Han era has traditionally been divided into the Former, or Western, Han

(202 BCE–8 CE) and the Latter, or Eastern, Han (24–220 CE). During the brief interval between 8 and 24 CE, Han rule was temporarily interrupted when a relative of the royal family, Wang Mang (45 BCE–23 CE), seized power. Wang Mang attempted to introduce a number of reforms in land distribution in an effort to reduce the huge disparity between rich landowners and peasants, which had been inherited from the Warring States period. Wang Mang's proposed reforms provoked a revolt led by a Daoist secret society called the Red Eyebrows. The rebels killed Wang Mang and sacked the capital of Chang'an. An imperial relative restored the Han dynasty in 24 CE but moved the capital to Luoyang, where the empire continued in somewhat reduced size.

Wang Mang's attempts at land reform and the Red Eyebrow revolt hastened the collapse of the last of the old aristocratic landholdings. Together with the sense of renewal accompanying the restoration of the Han dynasty, these events helped to temporarily mask the empire's growing weakness.

**Han Decline**   By the late second century CE the Han dynasty was showing signs of strain. Ambitious internal improvements ordered by Han emperors were carried out by *corvée* labor—labor required by the government as a form of taxation. These labor obligations made it increasingly difficult for peasants to tend their lands, and as a result agricultural productivity declined. Furthermore, the loss of some borderland territory reduced the tax base just when the empire required more taxes to maintain the Great Wall and far-flung military outposts also meant to protect the empire from nomadic invasions. Economic crises, however, were not the only threats to the empire. A series of internal battles within the royal family, aggravated by increasing regional power falling into the hands of Han generals and the rise of the Daoist Yellow Turban revolt after 184 CE, finally brought the Han dynasty to an end in 220 CE.

**Between Empires**   Like the Romans of the late fourth century CE, who saw Germanic migrations as temporary disruptions rather than fatal blows to their empire, the Chinese expected that a new dynasty would shortly emerge after the collapse of the Han. Instead, China experienced its most chaotic postimperial political period. This interlude of turmoil is traditionally divided into the era of the Three Kingdoms (220–280 CE), the overlapping Six Dynasties period (222–589 CE), and the also overlapping period of the North and South Dynasties (317–589 CE).

From the initial Three Kingdoms period through the numerous small, weak, and short-lived "dynasties" that followed, the aim of reconstituting the empire was always present. As in so many other respects, the parallels with the problems besetting the Roman Empire at the same time were striking: The growing power of landed elites, the increasing weakness of the bureaucracy, the chronic defense problems of the north and west all continued and even multiplied. In the absence of effective centralized administration, the infrastructure fell into disrepair, the enormous internal economy grew more regionalized, external trade declined, and warfare, famine, and banditry haunted the land.

Unlike the Roman Empire, however, by the fifth century CE the rebuilding process had begun, when an eastern Mongolian people known as the Toba established the state of Northern Wei in northern China. Taking advantage of the possibilities of the new military tactics growing from the development of the stirrup,

# Patterns Up Close | The Stirrup

Given the long list of familiar Chinese pathbreaking technologies such as paper, the compass, printing, the horse collar, and, of course, gunpowder, it may seem strange that we would feature something as simple as the stirrup. Yet the stirrup's understated presence has long been recognized by historians as being of major importance. The reason is that it not only completely changed the way humans used horses but ushered in a new type of warfare that altered the structure of societies and dominated military strategy for 1,000 years.

Despite the fact that the horse had occupied a prominent place in Eurasian warfare for over 2,000 years, its utility had been limited to pulling chariots and supporting mounted archers and riders with light spears. The central problem of using horses in pitched battles was that the back of a horse was a precarious perch: It was difficult to mount a horse when one was weighed down with armor and weapons, but it was easy to be knocked from one, especially when one was engaged in close combat and swift maneuvering.

**Jin Dynasty Iron Stirrups.** Widespread use of the stirrup not only brought the use of cavalry back to the forefront of warfare, it led to a resurgence in power of Eurasian mounted nomadic peoples. The ornate stirrups pictured here helped the nomadic Jurchen people displace the Northern Song dynasty (see Chapter 12) and set up their own Jin dynasty, which lasted from 1127 to 1234. Their downfall was brought about by another mounted nomadic people—the Mongols—who not only displaced the Jurchens but went on to conquer the Southern Song in 1279 and incorporate their new Yuan dynasty into the short-lived Mongol super-empire spanning Eurasia in the late thirteenth and early fourteenth centuries.

Around the beginning of the Common Era the first attempts at saddles with straps for supporting a rider's feet began to appear in northern India. But these employed only a simple toe loop, and the saddle concentrated the rider's weight on a small area of the horse's back, tiring and hurting the animal. This basic idea for the stirrup, however, appears to have spread via the Silk Road, and by the early 300s CE a recognizably modern iron stirrup with a flat bottom and semicircular top began to be used in north and central China; the earliest remains discovered so far date to 302 CE. At about the same time, saddles with a rigid frame to distribute the rider's weight more evenly and better padding to cushion its effects on the horse began to be employed.

The effects of these changes were soon apparent in a China now dominated by feuding states and marauding nomads in the post-Han era. With his legs secured to

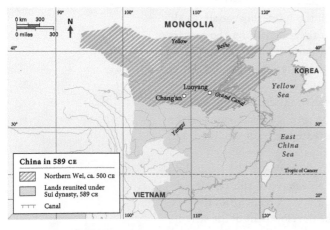

MAP 9.3 **China in 589 CE.**

Northern Wei established itself as a dominant power in the region. By the beginning of the sixth century, the Toba had enacted a formal policy of assimilating into Chinese culture—taking Chinese names, marrying into leading families, reviving old imperial rites, and taking on the perennial problem of land reform. In organizing a program of land redistribution to the peasants, they helped pave the way for the return of centralized administration, military service, and tax collection. A Toba general named Yang Jian succeeded in uniting most of the old Han lands in 589 and called the reunified dynasty the Sui (see Map 9.3).

his mount and a high saddleback to cushion him in combat, a mounted warrior could use a long lance to charge directly into enemy formations without fear of being immediately unhorsed. Furthermore, he could wear a full complement of armor and armor his horse. The stirrup proved so effective that by the fifth century CE the armies of all the states in China had adopted and refined the technology. In China, it helped pave the way for the Sui reunification in 589.

It was in western Eurasia, however, that the new technology saw its greatest impact after its arrival in the seventh century CE. It has even been argued that the feudal society of Europe was ultimately derived from the stirrup. The ability of a heavy cavalry of armored warriors to break infantry formations and fight effectively at close quarters from horseback depended on refining armor and weapons, training warriors, and breeding bigger, faster, and stronger horses. The politically fractured eras of post-Roman and post-Carolingian Europe meant that local elites and regional strongmen had to mount their own defenses. The stirrup and the military innovations it spawned allowed them to do this without heavily equipped armies, while the expenses necessary to adopt the new technology ensured that it would remain a monopoly of the rich and powerful. Thus the relationships comprising feudalism matured as peasants placed themselves in the service of their mounted protectors. The rough parity and independence of this widely dispersed warrior elite proved a powerful obstacle to the patterns of centralized state formation and empire building. Ironically, it would be another Chinese invention that would ultimately end this way of warfare many centuries later· gunpowder.

## Questions

- How does the stirrup show how a technological innovation can lead to cultural and societal adaptations across many regions and across time?

- Which environmental and geographical conditions facilitated the impact of the stirrup across Eurasia in a way that would not have been possible in the Americas?

**The Empire Reclaimed: The Sui**    Like the Qin before them, the forcefulness with which the Sui pursued empire building—particularly in an ill-conceived invasion of the Korean peninsula after their ascension in 589 CE—prompted unrest among the people. The Sui used forced labor for several elaborate construction projects, including palatial palaces, roads, and perhaps the most ambitious project of all, the Grand Canal. Linking the Yangzi River with the Yellow River, the Grand Canal facilitated shipment of large quantities of rice and other food crops from the south directly to the refurbished capital at Chang'an. This was to prove a vitally important highway over the coming centuries as northern capitals increasingly depended on food supplies shipped from the south. The Grand Canal, still in operation today, would eventually be extended all the way to the Beihe River, which leads to Beijing.

The outbreak of rebellion following the death of the second Sui emperor, Yangdi, brought the precocious 16-year-old commander Li Shimin to power.

Li had the Sui emperor killed, placed his own father on the throne, and announced the founding of the Tang dynasty in 618 CE. In less than a decade, he forced his father to abdicate and took power in his own right in 627 CE.

As we will see in the next part, the reconstitution of the Chinese empire under the Sui and its expansion and consolidation under the Tang not only marked a dramatic turning point in Chinese political history but also placed China among the world's regions marked by the ascendancy of religious civilizations. Like Christianity in the late Roman Empire, Buddhism made remarkable inroads in China during the period of fragmentation following the collapse of the Han. Indeed, through the work of Chinese monks it had also become firmly established in the Korean kingdoms and the Yamato state in Japan. The Tang would see the completion and high point of this process.

Buddhism and its institutions permeated Tang China to an extent never surpassed or even equaled in later dynasties. For a period in the late seventh and early eight centuries CE it even became the established Chinese state religion, under the remarkable empress Wu Zetian. In this regard, China became not only part of a giant regional religious and cultural sphere during the Tang but an important part of a new world pattern that would encompass Islamic civilization, orthodox Christianity in the eastern Roman (Byzantine) Empire and much of eastern Europe, and the Christian civilizations of Roman Catholicism and Protestantism.

# The Domestic Economy: Society, Family, and Gender

**Coal Mining.** While the miners shore up a tunnel and gather coal into a basket lowered from above, a large bamboo pipe is thrust into the mine to draw off poisonous gases.

Throughout Chinese history, various dynasties actively encouraged and supported agriculture as the basis of the domestic economy. Yet, from the Han dynasty on, China exported far more in luxury goods and technology than it imported. Unlike the various regimes in India, which actively sought to foster trade, the Confucian view of the pursuit of profit as corrupting meant that Chinese governments seldom encouraged merchants and generally preferred to adopt a passive, but controlling, role in trade. Although merchants were held in low esteem, the state recognized that trade was indispensable to the financial health of the empire and saw it as an expandable source of tax revenue.

## Industry and Commerce

Goods made in and distributed throughout the empire by the time of the Han included some of the best-known items of Chinese production. By the first century CE, Chinese manufacturers were making paper using a suspension of mashed plant fibers filtered through a fine-mesh screen and set aside to dry, a method still considered to produce the highest-quality product for painting or literary work.

Perhaps even more impressive, by this time artisans were also producing a kind of "proto-porcelain" that, with increasing refinement, would be known in the succeeding centuries to the outside world as "china." The earthenware produced during the Tang dynasty is among the most coveted in the world today. In other arts, the use of lacquer as a finish, as well as in artwork created by sculpting built-up layers of it, was also well established. By the second century CE, the Chinese had perfected silk production and had become world leaders in textile weaving. Both treadle- and water-powered looms were in widespread use, and bolts of silk with standardized designs were produced for export. The Chinese supply of silks could barely keep pace with demand, especially from Persia and Rome. But much of the most important domestic production centered on bulk strategic goods that sparked some of the world's first debates on the government's role in economics.

**Iron and Salt**    By the Han period, the Chinese were producing cast iron in huge foundries. According to one estimate, by 2 CE, there were no fewer than 48 major ironworks in north China, while the mining industry as a whole may have employed as many as 100,000 people. The foundries, which produced ingots of standardized sizes and weights, used sophisticated systems of forced-air control, including water-powered bellows. Salt mines employed complex gearing for lifting brine from deep wells, systems of bamboo piping for transferring it, and evaporators fired by natural gas for extracting the salt. Because of the enormous productivity of the iron-making and salt-mining industries, the government continually sought ways to regulate and control them.

Despite the increasing importance of industry and commerce to the imperial economy, the Han and succeeding dynasties continued to view merchants as a parasitic class, with no ties to the idealized relationships of agrarian life. Trade was thus a necessary evil. Nevertheless, government programs aimed at improving the empire's infrastructure facilitated commerce. The unpredictable flow of China's rivers required dikes, dredging, reservoirs, and especially canals to ease transportation. Along with roads, canals grew in importance as the empire relied more and more on the produce of the rich lands of the south to supply the capitals of the north. The Han emperor Wudi, as we have seen, began work on the Grand Canal that linked the Yangzi and the Yellow rivers (see Map 9.4).

**Land Reform**    By the time of the late Han, China's old aristocracy had largely died out, its place at the top of the social hierarchy assumed by the so-called *scholar-gentry*—the educated large landholders who constituted the Confucian bureaucracy. Despite the elimination of the old aristocracy, landlord holdings continued to expand. Since the upper ranks of the landowners and bureaucrats either were exempt from taxes or paid reduced amounts, the tax burden fell increasingly on tenants and owners of small parcels of land. Poor harvests or bad weather, particularly in the arid north and west, made the situation even worse for those already heavily taxed. Because the north, despite its elaborate irrigation works, was far less productive and more prone to crop failure than the south, it was also proportionally more heavily taxed.

Such problems made land reform and redistribution an ongoing concern. The Tang, for example, continued the policy of land redistribution begun during the brief Sui dynasty by allotting each peasant family a tract of 100 *mou*, one-fifth of which was inheritable, while the remainder reverted to the state for redistribution. Although the Tang land redistribution policy resulted in a relatively high level of prosperity, absentee landlordism, tenancy, and usury also rose again, particularly

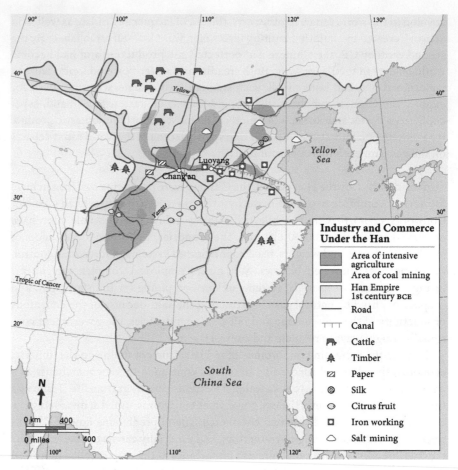

MAP 9.4 **Industry and Commerce under the Han.**

during times of economic stress. The continual problem of land tenure and attempts at reform and redistribution marked every dynasty and modern government down to the People's Republic—where it is even today a major concern.

**Agricultural Productivity**    A number of technical and systemic innovations steadily increased agricultural productivity. In addition to such staples as wheat, millet, and barley in the north and rice in the south, a wide variety of semitropical fruits and vegetables were cultivated within the empire. New strains of rice resulted in larger harvests on more marginal land. Trade with central Asia had introduced wine grapes, and the production of fermented grain beverages had become a substantial industry. New techniques of crop rotation, fertilization, and plowing were gradually introduced, as were the collar for draft animals and the wheelbarrow; oxen-drawn, iron-tipped plows; treadle hammers; undershot, overshot, and other types of waterwheels; the foot-powered "dragon" chain pump for irrigation; and the *fengche*—a hand-cranked winnowing machine with an internal fan to blow the chaff from the grain. With this basic, reliable technology, China led the world in agricultural productivity until the eighteenth century CE.

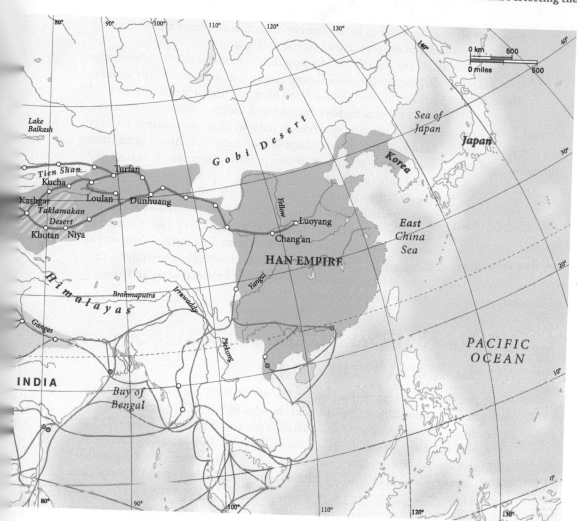

carriers of the ancestral line and their potential to win admission to official state service led to a gradual devaluing of daughters. In times of severe economic stress, when families had difficulty supporting several children, young girls were the first to suffer. Families, especially in rural areas, would sometimes sell their daughters into prostitution or kill female infants. By the Song era (960–1279 CE) problems relating to the treatment of young girls had become so acute that China's first foundling hospitals were opened in 1138.

Although some elite women achieved prominence in intellectual pursuits, like the historian Ban Zhao (48–116 CE), women's education centered primarily on cultivating the domestic virtues of devotion and obedience, as well as mastering crafts such as spinning and weaving. Daughters were expendable in the sense that they would marry or be placed with another family through adoption or servitude. Since these last options often brought advantages to the girl's family, daughters were frequently educated in singing, playing instruments, chanting poetry, etc., in order to make them desirable candidates for placement. Yet, in theory at least,

**The Silk Road**   The dramatic expansion of maritime and caravan trade from the seventh century CE on, particularly within the huge Buddhist cultural sphere, spread Chinese technology abroad and brought new products into the Chinese empire. During the first millennium and a half of its history, China made numerous connections throughout the world and spread its influence in all directions. Early examples of silk appear to have reached the Mediterranean and North Africa through a long train of middlemen as early as the first millennium BCE. By the first century BCE, a variety of artifacts clearly identifiable as Chinese had turned up in Egypt; by the fourth and fifth centuries CE, Indian and Persian middlemen extended the Chinese trade to the African empires of Kush and Aksum.

The principal route connecting the Chinese to the various trading centers of central Asia, and ultimately to the Mediterranean and Rome, was known as the **Silk Road**. Along this route, the Chinese would forever be identified with silk; and though they tried to guard the secrets of its production, the demand was so high that many peoples along the caravan routes were soon engaged in making silk themselves. The techniques of raising silkworms and weaving silk reached

**Silk Road:** Overland trade routes that connected eastern and western Eurasia, beginning at the end of the fourth century BCE.

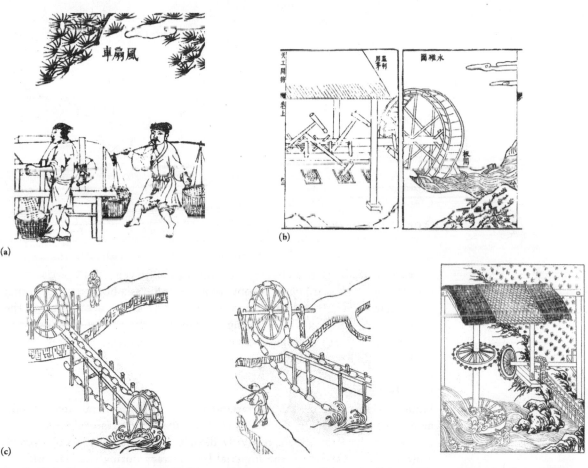

**Han-Era Technology.** By the first century CE, Chinese sophistication in crafts and labor-saving devices could be seen in a number of areas. While the illustrations here are from the famous seventeenth-century compendium of technology *Tiangong kaiwu* (*The Works of Nature and Man*), all of them illustrate techniques in use during the Han period: (*a*) *fengche* winnowing machine; (*b*) undershot waterwheel driving hammers in a pounding mill; (*c*) vertical and horizontal waterwheels driving chain-bucket "dragon pumps" for irrigation.

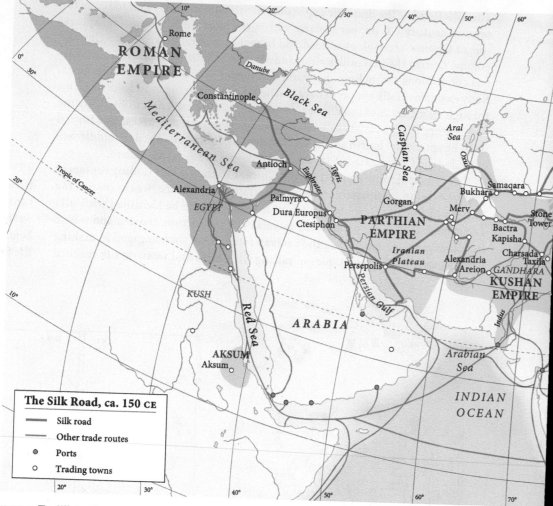

MAP 9.5 **The Silk Road, ca. 150 CE.**

the eastern Mediterranean between the third and fifth centuries CE. Competition among producers and merchants in western Eurasia became so keen that the Roman emperor Justinian allied with the African kingdom of Aksum in the sixth century CE to contest growing Persian dominance of the trade in fine silks. In the process, the Romans created their own silk monopoly to service the western trade.

### Gender Roles

Women in imperial China, as in agrarian-based societies in general, were subordinate to men. Early Confucian works, while emphasizing reciprocal responsibilities within the family, were relatively flexible about the position of women. However, with the rise of the imperial bureaucracy during the Han and the increasing emphasis on filial piety within its new Confucian curriculum, a more rigidly hierarchical, patriarchal model of proper women's behavior gradually developed. At the same time, the emphasis on sons within the extended family as

---

there was always supposed to be an element of complementarity and reciprocity between men and women, especially husband and wife.

From the fifth century CE on, the popularity of monastic Buddhism created attractive alternatives for those fleeing family pressures, especially women. Those women enrolled in Buddhist schools that required extensive scriptural study became highly educated, and the communities themselves, like Christian monasteries in Europe, often owned large tracts of land and wielded considerable local influence. At the same time, the relative strictness of the practices regulating sexual and family life varied, particularly among high officials and the growing urban commercial classes. Foreign influences and fashions also affected behavior, particularly in Chang'an and places engaged in international trade. Tantric Buddhist (see Chapter 8) and Daoist sexual practices, which were used by their followers as a means of spiritual liberation, undoubtedly contributed to a more relaxed approach to relations between men and women during the Tang as well.

> "Yet only to teach men and not to teach women—is this not ignoring the reciprocal relation between them? According to the *Rites [of Zhou]*, book learning begins at the age of eight, and at the age of fifteen one goes off to school. Why, however, should this principle not apply to girls as well as boys?"
>
> —Ban Zhao, *Admonitions for Women*

## Intellectual Trends, Aesthetics, Science, and Technology

As we saw in the opening of this chapter, the period from the sixth century BCE until the first unification of China under the Qin in 221 BCE was marked by a dynamic collision of economic and social forces and is universally regarded as China's most fertile period of intellectual exploration. Long-term contacts with the East Asian Buddhist sphere from the end of the Han through the Tang era resulted in a number of new Buddhist schools being founded and spread throughout east Asia.

### Confucianism, Education, and History during the Han

While the first Han rulers tended to favor a philosophical system that combined a more lenient Legalism with aspects of other surviving schools, over time a form of Confucianism became the preferred governmental doctrine. Confucian emphasis on the ethical correctness of officials, caring for the people, filial piety, and the study of history tended to make it a good fit for Han administrators. By the second century CE, the steadily growing popularity of Confucian academies led to their subsidization by the state, in effect placing all official education in the hands of these academies. Since the purpose of such education was state service, it also made knowledge of Confucianism the principal test for entrance into the bureaucracy. This situation, expanded and elaborated over nearly two millennia, would remain in force until the opening years of the twentieth century.

**The Han Confucian Synthesis**    Although Confucianism served as the foundation for the Han educational curriculum, Confucian doctrine had changed somewhat from the early teachings of Confucius and his disciples. During the Warring States period and the era of Qin rule, much Confucian thought—along with that of other philosophical schools—had been altered to suit the times, while a great many texts had been lost along the way. Thus, the Confucianism that finally received state approval included a number of elements reflecting the new realities of the Han dynasty.

This so-called Han synthesis of Confucian philosophy is evident in the era's chief treatise on government, the *Huainan zi*. In this document, a number of Confucian ideals, rooted in humane, righteous, and filial behavior by the powerful, are linked with Daoist ideas of the ruler as divorced from day-to-day administration and Legalist notions on the role of officials. As the intermediary between heaven, humankind, and earth, the emperor occupied a position of cosmological significance by nourishing the people and holding all in balance. For continuity's sake, a dynasty had to be hereditary—in contradiction to Confucius's ideas. But the idea of dynastic cycles and the Mandate of Heaven became even stronger during this period as they were elaborated by the great Han historians.

**Han Historians**    As we saw in Chapter 4, while there had been no shortage of history writing in the late Zhou period, much of it was seen even by contemporaries as overly partisan, fanciful, or tied to teaching moral lessons at the expense of accuracy. Mencius, for example, doubted the truthfulness of most of The *Book of History*. By the Han period, with the ideal of empire now encouraging a new sense of cultural unity, a series of court historians attempted to collate historical materials that had survived the Qin purges and to unify and systematize the writing of history.

For these men and women, the purpose of history writing, much as it was for the great Greek historians Herodotus (ca. 484–425 BCE) and Thucydides (ca. 460–ca. 395 BCE), was the accurate transmission of information—often with verbatim copies of important documents—and analysis of the events portrayed in terms of a larger vision of the direction and purpose of human history. For the Han historians, as for Chinese historians throughout the imperial era, history was cyclical: Human events, as manifestations of the great universal cycles of being, are a constant succession of birth, growth, decay, death, and rebirth, in which older ideas of the Mandate of Heaven, dynastic cycles, and yin and yang theory are imbedded. The moral lessons learned are therefore tied to actions taken at various stages of these cycles.

The basic format of long-term history was laid out by the father-and-son team of Sima Tan (d. 110 BCE) and Sima Qian (145–86 BCE). Their *Shiji* (*The Records of the Grand Historian*) attempts the first complete history of the Chinese people from the mythical Yellow Emperor to their own time. One particularly valuable section that became a staple of later histories was a survey of non-Chinese peoples encountered along with their habits, customs, religions, geography, and other significant traits. Hence, the Han records give us our first written accounts of Japan and other places on the Chinese periphery.

Like other Chinese officials, the historians took their role of "conscience" of the government seriously, sometimes at severe peril to themselves. As historian to the powerful Emperor Wudi, for example, Sima Qian offended the ruler by exonerating a general in his writings whom the emperor and court had accused of cowardice. Given the choice between execution and castration, Sima chose the latter; if he were dead, he explained, he could not finish his history, which he believed was his highest duty.

Several generations later, the Ban family comprised another dynasty of Han court historians. Writing after the Wang Mang interval, Ban Biao (3–54 CE) and his son Ban Gu (32–92 CE) pioneered the writing of dynastic history with their *Hanshu* (*The History of the Former Han*), which laid out the format followed by all subsequent dynastic histories. Ban Gu's daughters were also scholars and writers, and his sister Ban Zhao (48–116 CE) carried on the family tradition of history writing as well as a treatise on proper women's behavior, *Admonitions for Women*. Interestingly, accounts of the historians' activities themselves may be found in the *Hou Hanshu* (*The History of the Latter Han*), written after the fall of the dynasty by Fan Ye (398–446 CE).

## Buddhism in China

The growth of Buddhism as a universal missionary religion came, at least in part, from the adaptability of its doctrines to widely diverse peoples and belief systems. As we saw in Chapter 8, by the mid-first century CE, when it is first mentioned in Chinese accounts, Buddhism had already split into the major divisions of Theravada (Hinayana), which had established itself in southern India and Sri Lanka and was moving into southeast Asia, and Mahayana, which would be established in China, Korea, Vietnam, and Japan.

The introduction of Mahayana Buddhism into China presents a number of interesting parallels with that of Christianity into Rome, though there are important differences as well. Rather than focusing on the problems of practical government, both religions emphasized instead personal enlightenment or salvation. Both, to some extent, were initially seen as "foreign" systems and subjected to periodic persecution before emerging triumphant. Finally, while both challenged existing political and social hierarchies, the institutions of both were also adopted by rulers who wanted to strengthen or expand their power.

**Bodhisattva Guanyin, Sixth Century CE.** Originally incorporating aspects of both genders, Guanyin (also spelled Kuan-yin) came to be depicted as female as Buddhism became firmly established in China. For Pure Land adherents, she was the bodhisattva invoked in times of extreme peril, and "the miracles of Guanyin" (*Kannon* in Japan) was a favorite theme of both Chinese and Japanese artists.

**Language and Scripture**    The incompatibility of the Chinese written language with Sanskrit and Pali scriptures complicated the introduction of Buddhism to China. The earliest Buddhist missionaries had to rely heavily on transliterations, borrow extensively from Daoist terminology, and invent a new and diverse vocabulary of Chinese terms. Over the next several centuries, this eclecticism resulted in a proliferation of sects and a growing need on the part of Chinese and, later, Korean, Japanese, and Vietnamese converts to travel to India for study and guidance. The travel account of the Chinese monk and early pilgrim Fa Xian (see Chapter 8), who journeyed throughout central Asia and India from 399 to 414 CE in search of Pali copies of Buddhist works, contributed greatly to Chinese understanding of the growing Buddhist world. The most famous pilgrim, Xuan Zang (596–664 CE), went to India in 623 CE and brought back the extensive collection of scriptures still housed in the monastery he founded just outside Xi'an. His travels were later immortalized in the popular collection of fabulous tales called *A Journey to the West*.

**Buddhist Schools**    The period between the dissolution of the Han and the ascendancy of the Tang was also marked by the founding of several of the most important schools of East Asian Buddhism. By the fifth century, the school of popular devotion to Amida, the Buddha of the Pure Land, was spreading rapidly in China. Like the *bhakti* sects in India, no immersion in the texts is necessary for enlightenment for Pure Land followers; merely invoking Amida's name is sufficient for salvation. Even today, it remains the most popular Buddhist sect in both China and Japan. Amida is often pictured with the bodhisattva Guanyin—*Kannon* in Japan—the Goddess of Mercy who, like the Virgin Mary in Catholicism, is frequently invoked during times of peril.

Another influential Buddhist school was Tiantai, centered on the scripture of the *Lotus Sutra*. Tiantai emphasized contemplation of the sutras as the vehicle to enlightenment and later inspired several schools of esoteric (see Chapter 8) paths to enlightenment. These schools exercised considerable influence over both the Tang and the Japanese court at Heian during the eighth and ninth centuries CE.

Finally, one school that later achieved fame, if not widespread popularity, was Chan Buddhism, better known by the name given it in Japan: Zen. As outlined in its central text, *The Platform of the Sixth Patriarch*, by Hui Neng (638–713 CE), enlightenment is transmitted not through scriptural study or personal devotion to a particular figure but rather through the discipline of meditation and the active example of a master. The intense give-and-take between master and pupil, the discipline involved in performing humble tasks, and the contemplation of paradoxical questions are all meant ultimately to generate an intuitive flash of enlightenment. While limited in its influence in China, the emphasis on discipline and obedience made Zen the preferred Buddhist school of Japan's warrior aristocracy after the twelfth century CE.

## Intellectual Life

To a considerable degree, Chinese concepts of **aesthetics** that developed during the first millennium CE became the founding principles for the arts throughout east Asia. The most important developments during this period were the maturation of three disciplines: poetry, painting, and calligraphy. An important part of a well-rounded education even today, these three disciplines are considered to be closely interrelated and governed by the same overriding principles. Central to each discipline is the idea of spontaneous creation as a reflection of the inner state of the artist. The artist in each of these media seeks to connect with the Dao by indirectly suggesting some aspect of it in the work itself. For example, Chinese landscape paintings often feature misty mountains, lone pines, and tiny human figures, with the action and occasion implied rather than detailed, because too much detail would place limits on the illimitable.

**Aesthetics:** The study of the beautiful; the branches of learning dealing with categorizing and analyzing beauty.

**The Sciences**　Because the imperial establishment relied on the prediction of comets, eclipses, and other omens to monitor the will of heaven, astronomy and mathematics were especially important disciplines. Chinese mathematicians had long used a decimal system and had worked out formulas and proofs to figure the areas of most standard geometric forms. They had also calculated pi to four places and were able to solve simultaneous algebraic equations. The astronomers Zhang Heng (78–139 CE) and Wang Chong (27–100) had each championed theories of a universe governed by comprehendible natural forces. Zhang built a water-powered

**Calligraphy.** Detail of calligraphy from Wang Xizhi (303–361). The styles of Chinese characters were standardized for use in formal documents during the Qin and Han eras but have since been endlessly refined as art by master calligraphers. Along with painting and poetry, calligraphy was esteemed as one of the "three excellences" (*sanjue*) of the scholar. Wang Xizhi is revered even today as the master of the *xingshu*, or "running script," a cursive form used for private correspondence. This sample is from an early Tang tracing copy of Wang's hand.

**Earthquake Detector.** One of the more ingenious pieces of high technology to come out of the Han period was a working earthquake detector created by Zhang Heng (78–139 CE) in 134 CE. In the model illustrated here, carefully balanced balls were placed inside the large, hollow egg-shaped vessel. A tremor coming from a particular direction would jar the ball closest to the direction of the quake loose and send it down a track where it would fly from the mouth of one of the dragons on the outside of the "egg" and fall into the yawning mouth of the frog underneath. Thus, anyone checking the device could tell at a glance that a quake had occurred and from what direction by seeing which frog held a ball.

*armillary sphere*—a hollow globe surrounded by bronze bands, representing the paths of the sun, stars, and planets—and, in 134 CE, devised what was perhaps the world's first practical earthquake detector.

**Printing and Proto-Porcelain** One of the signal innovations of Eurasia was printing. Believed to have their origins in the ancient practice of making rubbings on paper or silk of gravestone inscriptions, woodblock prints of popular Buddhist works had become available in major Chinese cities by the eighth century CE. By the end of the Tang and the beginning of the Song dynasties, presses employing both carved block and movable copper type were in regular use in China, Korea, and Japan. As it would later in Europe, the innovation of printing dramatically raised the literacy rates in all the areas it touched. By the beginning of the Song era, China had some of the highest preindustrial literacy rates achieved in human history—despite the difficulties of the written language.

The techniques involved in generating the extremely high temperatures required for casting iron were also transferable to porcelain production. Though there is debate about when the breakthroughs resulting in true porcelain first occurred, by the Tang period, distinctive brown and green glazed figures, often depicting the vibrant parade of peoples and animals of the caravan trade, were widely exchanged. By the Song, delicate white, crackled glaze and sea-green celadon ware were produced and sought by connoisseurs as the height of aesthetic refinement. Today, such pieces are considered to be among the world's great art treasures.

# Putting It All Together

The political and social turmoil of the late Zhou era also marked an enormously innovative period in Chinese intellectual and cultural history. During this era the most important schools of Chinese thought and philosophy developed: Confucianism, Daoism, and Legalism. While Confucianism ultimately triumphed as the ideology of imperial China, it was the Legalist state of Qin that created the empire itself.

When the Qin dynasty fell in 206 BCE, much of the infrastructure of the early empire, including the Great Wall, was in place. The Han dynasty, from 202 BCE to 220 CE, retained the administrative structure of the Qin but softened the harsh laws and punishments of the Legalists. Eventually, the form of Confucianism practiced by the empire's administrators was taught in the imperial schools, becoming in effect the imperial ideology. By the end of the Han, China had created a solid alliance between the state and this all-encompassing ethical and legal system.

Perhaps more important than even the structures themselves, however, was that, like the Egyptians and Romans, the Chinese had become accustomed to what has been called the "habit of empire." As suggested in this chapter, 400 years of unity under the Qin and the Han had conditioned the Chinese to believe that empire was the natural goal of the patterns of political formation in China and that any interruptions in these patterns would be but brief interludes in the dynastic cycle. Thus, Chinese history has been marked by rhythms of inwardness and outwardness, inner renewal and usurpation of rule from the outside. Along with these rhythms came an inherited belief, reinforced by the theories of dynastic historians, that human society and the cosmos were knit together in a moral order, made perfectible by the power of the empire and the dedication of a bureaucracy selected for its understanding of ethics in human affairs. Throughout the imperial era—and even in our own time—the students and scholars of China have tried to keep faith with this heritage by guiding and remonstrating with those in power.

▶ For additional resources, including maps, primary sources, visuals, and quizzes, please go to www.oup.com/us/vonsivers. Please see the Further Resources section at the back of the book for additional readings and suggested websites.

# Against the Grain
# Yang Zhu and Mo Di

The ideas that appeared during the period of the "hundred schools" of thought spread across an extraordinarily wide intellectual continuum, from the deceptively passive mysticism of the Daoists to the totalitarian ambitions of the Legalists. At its height, however, during the time of the Confucian thinker Mencius (385–312), the two schools of thought that he and his disciples considered most influential and dangerous were another exercise in extremes: the radical individualism of Yang Zhu and the advocacy of universal love of Mo Di (often spelled Mozi).

Yang Zhu taught that since life was short and death inevitable, people should take what enjoyment they can while they can. After all, he said, the four great sages (including Confucius) "during their life had not a single day's joy. Since their death they have had grand fame that will last through the ages. . . . Celebrate them—they do not know it; reward them—they do not know it. Their fame is no more to them than the trunk of a tree or a clod of earth." Moreover, the most infamous villains who enjoyed vast wealth and lusts and pleasures went smiling to their graves, caring not at all in death about their ill fame. So one should seize the day and take what enjoyment from it that one can.

Mo Di, on the other hand, taught that the only truly humane way to approach the world was to love all people equally. Everyone has a father and a mother; thus all should be regarded as one would regard one's own family. To do otherwise is to be overly partisan in one's duties to society. The followers of Mo put these ideas into action during the Warring States period by volunteering to help the inhabitants of besieged cities defend themselves.

For Mencius, the era was defined by "lords becom[ing] arbitrary and intemperate, and unemployed scholars [indulging] in uninhibited discussion. The words of Yang Zhu and Mo Di overflow the world; the world's words all go back if not to Yang then to Mo. Yang holds for egoism, which involves denial of one's sovereign; Mo holds for universal love, which entails denial of one's parents. To deny one's sovereign or one's parents is to be an animal."

In the end, the extremes of both systems would undoubtedly have made them unworkable, especially that of Yang, with its complete abandonment of altruism. That of Confucius, with its emphasis on family relationships and duties at the micro and macro levels, was ultimately more in harmony with Chinese society—so much so that it continues to shape that society at its deepest levels even today.

- **The appearance of visionary thinkers appears to have been an extraordinarily widespread phenomenon. Why were the times of great turmoil in these societies such fertile ones for new ideas?**

- **What ideas in other cultures seem to be like those of Yang and Mo? How do they also differ? Do they spring from similar conditions?**

# Thinking Through Patterns

▶ **Was the First Emperor's ruthlessness justified by his accomplishments in his empire?**

Addressing this question raises a very basic problem: Why do we study history? In ancient times, most people studied history for the moral lessons it offered and to avoid making the same mistakes their ancestors did. As we have also seen, some cultures, like the Chinese, studied it in hopes of grasping its basic patterns so as to understand the present and anticipate the future. Modern historians have generally taken their cue from Leopold von Ranke (1795–1886), who felt that scholars should rise above preconceived ideas and simply seek the past "as it really was." For most of the twentieth century, historians have sought to avoid making moral judgments about the past, to see their job as being detectives rather than judges. By that standard, the historian should empathetically enter the past and seek to understand it; to judge it by the standards of the present is to be "presentist." But how does one deal with such things as genocide, extreme cruelty, or slavery? Thus, one way out of this dilemma might be to weigh the actions of the First Emperor against the standards of morality current in *his* day. Yet here, too, we encounter a problem: There were so many new schools of thought emerging in China then that no single one dominated; moreover, the First Emperor himself created his own system of morality based on Legalism. Perhaps, then, the best that we can do at this point, aside from judging him privately by our personal standards, is to note that he set the fundamental pattern for Chinese imperial government for the next 2,000 years—but at considerable cost.

Perhaps the biggest difference between Confucian society and modern American society is in the way both see the ideal forms of societal relations. Americans see the individual, the rule of law, democracy, and equality as fundamental to a good society. The purpose of government is to allow people to do as they wish while stipulating the limits within which they can do so. Confucian concepts of government and society put a premium on holism, hierarchy, and harmony. People are not seen as mere individuals but as part of larger patterns: family, clan, village, society, state. These are seen as part of a hierarchy that stretches from the poorest peasant to the

▶ **How would you compare the values expressed by Confucius and Mencius to those of contemporary society?**

emperor himself. Reciprocal rights and responsibilities are present at every level for protection of the weak, but equality is not seen as important. The role of government itself is seen in large part as being to provide a moral example to the people. If it teaches them well through regulations, customs, and ritual, then the people aspire to be good and will police themselves to a great extent.

▶ **How have historians viewed the role of women in early imperial China?**

One of the most unattractive things about imperial China to the majority of us today is that it often appears that women were held in low regard, abused, denied basic human rights, and even tortured for fashion's sake, as with foot binding. The Confucian emphasis on hierarchy within society and the family tends to reinforce this impression. But scholars have in recent years begun to study the role of women at different times and in different regions of China, and the picture now appears much more complex than before. While scholars agree that in some respects, particularly foot binding from the Song period on, women's roles deteriorated, there were also times when the evidence suggests they exercised considerable freedom and influence, such as during the Tang and early Song periods. The pattern of "inner" and "outer" as it governed the traditional Chinese family is still discernible in many Chinese households today: While husbands go off to work, women definitely hold sway within the "inner" realm of the house.

# Patterns of Evidence: Sources for Chapter 9

## SOURCE 9.1

## *Analects (Lunyu)* of Confucius

**ca. 500–479 BCE**

The details of Confucius's life are murky, especially given the chaos surrounding the declining Zhou period in the 490s and 480s BCE. It is important to take into account the impact of interstate conflict on Confucius's philosophical insights. A commoner who was effectively shut out of power by the three noble clans of Lu, Confucius was eventually driven out and forced to wander among the other states, due to the resentment of this traditional aristocracy. Despite the resistance of warring aristocrats, Confucius advocated a new approach to government, in which respect for the weak, poor, and defenseless would form the basis for civil society.

[12.7] Zigong asked about government. The Master [Confucius] said, "Sufficient food, sufficient arms, and popular trust [in the ruler]."

Zigong said, "If this were impossible, and we would have to dispense with one of these three, which should come first?"

[Confucius] said, "Dispense with arms."

Zigong said, "If this were impossible, and we would have to dispense with one of these two, which should come first?"

[Confucius] said, "Dispense with food. Since antiquity, there has always been death. But people without trust have no standing."

[12.11] Lord Jing of Qi asked Confucius about government. Confucius answered, "The lord acts as a lord, the minister, the father as a father, the son as a son."

The lord said, "Excellent! Surely, if the lord does not act as a lord, nor the minister as a minister, nor the father as a father, nor the son as a son, then although I might have grain, would I be able to eat it?"

[12.13] The Master said, "In hearing litigation, I am like other people. What is necessary is to cause there to be no litigation."

[12.17] Ji Kangzi asked Confucius about government. Confucius answered, "To govern is to correct. If you lead with rectitude, who will dare not be correct?"

Source: Victor H. Mair, Nancy Shatzman Steinhardt, and Paul R. Goldin, eds., *Hawai'i Reader in Traditional Chinese Culture* (Honolulu: University of Hawai'i Press, 2005), 48–49.

[12.18] Ji Kangzi was vexed at the thieving [in his state] and asked Confucius about it. Confucius answered, "If you, sir, were not covetous, then even if you were to reward them for it, they would not steal."

[13.3] Zilu said, "The Lord of Wei is waiting for you to effect government. What will you do first?"

The Master said, "What is necessary is to rectify names!"

Zilu said, "Is there such a thing? Master, you are wide of the mark. Why such rectification?"

The Master said, "You, you are uncouth. A noble man should appear more reserved about what he does not know. If names are not rectified, then speech does not flow properly. If speech does not flow properly, then affairs are not completed. If affairs are not completed, then ritual and music do not flourish. If ritual and music do not flourish, then punishments and penalties do not hit the mark. If punishments and penalties do not hit the mark, the people have no way to move hand or foot. Thus, for the noble man, names must be able to be spoken, and what he speaks must be able to be carried out. With regard to his speech, the noble man's [concern] is simply that there be nothing that is careless."

[13.10] The Master said, "If there were one [among the princes] who would make use of me, within no more than twelve months, [the government] would be acceptable. Within three years there would be success."

▶ **Working with Sources**

1. **To what extent did Confucius expect to be consulted by the leaders of the various states?**

2. **What does he seem to have envisioned as the ultimate basis of proper government?**

## SOURCE 9.2

# *Book of Mencius* (Mengzi)

## ca. 310–289 BCE

A later student of Confucian doctrine, Master Meng (ca. 371–289 BCE) spread the teachings of the master, while also making his own distinctive contributions. Having traveled throughout China spreading Confucian ideals, particularly as a basis for governmental practice, Mencius composed a book that was in more of a narrative form than the *Analects* and was

Source: Victor H. Mair, Nancy Shatzman Steinhardt, and Paul R. Goldin, eds., *Hawai'i Reader in Traditional Chinese Culture* (Honolulu: University of Hawai'i Press, 2005), 60–61.

supplemented by stories, parables, and debates. He often used imagery drawn from the natural world and advocated the rulers' involvement in cultivating a "well-field" system, both literally and metaphorically.

[6A.2.] Master Gao said, "Human *xing* [nature] is like a torrent of water. If you clear a passage for it to the east, it will flow to the east; if you clear a passage for it to the west, it will flow to the west. Human *xing* is not divided into good or not good, just as water is not divided into east and west."

Mencius said, "Water is indeed not divided into east and west, but is it not divided into higher and lower? The goodness of human *xing* is like water's tendency to go downward. There is no person without goodness; there is no water that does not go downward. Now as for water, if you strike it and make it leap up, you can cause it to pass over your forehead; if you dam it and make it move [in a certain direction], you can cause it to stay on a mountain. Is this the *xing* of the water? Or is it force that makes it so? When people are caused to become bad, their *xing* is also like this."

[6A.8.] Mencius said, "The trees of Ox Mountain were once beautiful. Because it was in the suburbs of a great city, with axes and hatchets chopping at it, could it remain beautiful? With the respite that [the mountain] was afforded by the nights, and the moisture of the rain and dew, it was not without buds and sprouts that grew on it; but then the cattle and goats came to pasture there. That is why it is so bald. People see its baldness and suppose that it never had timber on it. Is this the *xing* of the mountain?

"Even what exists within human beings—are we without a mind of humanity and righteousness? The manner in which we let go of our good minds is like axes and hatchets with respect to trees. If [the trees] are chopped down every morning, can they remain beautiful? With the respite that we are afforded by the nights, and the [restorative influence] of the morning airs, our likes and dislikes are close to those of other people. [But the power of this restorative process] is slight, and it is fettered and destroyed by what takes place during the day. When this fettering is repeated again and again, the [restorative] nocturnal airs are insufficient to preserve [our goodness]. If the nocturnal airs are insufficient to preserve [our goodness], then we are not far from being disobedient beasts. People see our bestiality, and suppose that there was never any ability in us. Is this human *xing*?

"Thus, if it obtains its nourishment, no creature will fail to grow; if it loses its nourishment, no creature will fail to decay.

"Confucius said, 'It is to the mind alone that the following refers! If you grasp it, it will be preserved; if you discard it, it will be destroyed. There is no time to its comings and goings, and no one knows its province.'"

[6A.10.] Mencius said, "Fish is what I desire; bear's paw is also what I desire. Of the two, if I cannot have both, I will set aside fish and take bear's paw. Life is what I desire; righteousness is also what I desire. Of the two, if I cannot have both, I will set aside life and take righteousness.

"Life is surely something I desire, but there are things I desire more than life, and thus I will not act improperly in order to retain [life].

Death is surely something I hate, but there are things I hate more than death, and thus there are troubles that I do not avoid.

"If one were to make people desire nothing more than life, then why would they not use every means by which they could retain their lives? If one were to make people hate nothing more than death, then why would they not do anything by which they could avoid trouble?

"There are cases where we do not use some means that would ensure our life, and there are cases where we do not do something that would ensure our avoidance of trouble.

"Therefore, there are things that we desire more than life, and there are things that we hate more than death—and it is not only a moral paragon who has such a mind. All people have it; the moral paragon is able to keep it from perishing."

▶ Working with Sources

1. How does Mencius deploy naturalistic images to illustrate his points?
2. What does the parable of Ox Mountain indicate about the existence of evil people?

## SOURCE 9.3

# Li Si, "Memorial on the Burning of Books," from the *Shiji*

**ca. 100 BCE**

Virtually no records have survived from the period between the unification of China in 221 BCE and the collapse of the Qin Empire 15 years later. Accordingly, historians are forced to rely on documents composed during the Han dynasty for relevant information. Nevertheless, one of the stories passed along, concerning the advice of Li Si to the emperor, is a stark reminder of how fragile learning can be, even in a temporarily successful polity. The *Records of the Grand Historian* (*Shiji*), a lengthy history of China compiled by Sima Qian (ca. 145–86 BCE), also includes a detailed biography of Li Si.

In earlier times the empire disintegrated and fell into disorder, and no one was capable of unifying it. Thereupon the various feudal lords rose to power. In their discourses they all praised the past in order to disparage the present and embellished empty words to confuse the truth. Everyone

Source: *Shih chi* 87:6b–7a, in de Bary and Bloom, comps., *Sources of Chinese Tradition*, vol. 1 (New York: Columbia University Press, 1960), 140–141.

cherished his own favorite school of learning and criticized what had been instituted by the authorities. But at present Your Majesty possesses a unified empire, has regulated the distinctions of black and white, and has firmly established for yourself a position of sole supremacy. And yet these independent schools, joining with each other, criticize the codes of laws and instructions. Hearing of the promulgation of a decree, they criticize it, each from the standpoint of his own school. At home they disapprove of it in their hearts; going out they criticize it in the thoroughfare. They seek a reputation by discrediting their sovereign; they appear superior by expressing contrary views, and they lead the lowly multitude in the spreading of slander. If such license is not prohibited, the sovereign power will decline above and partisan factions will form below. It would be well to prohibit this.

Your servant suggests that all books in the imperial archives, save the memoirs of Qin, be burned. All persons in the empire, except members of the Academy of Learned Scholars, in possession of the *Book of Odes*, the *Book of History*, and discourses of the hundred philosophers should take them to the local governors and have them indiscriminately burned. Those who dare to talk to each other about the *Book of Odes* and the *Book of History* should be executed and their bodies exposed in the market place. Anyone referring to the past to criticize the present should, together with all the members of his family, be put to death. Officials who fail to report cases that have come under their attention are equally guilty. After thirty days from the time of issuing the decree, those who have not destroyed their books are to be branded and sent to build the Great Wall. Books not to be destroyed will be those on medicine and pharmacy, divination by the tortoise and milfoil, and agriculture and arboriculture. People wishing to pursue learning should take the officials as their teachers.

▶ **Working with Sources**

1. **Li Si's advice may seem extreme, but is there a logical element to his reasoning?**

2. **Why was he advocating the destruction of these specific books?**

## SOURCE 9.4

# *Han Shu (History of the Former Han Dynasty)*

### ca. 100 CE

This dynastic history was a continuation of the *Records of the Grand Historian (Shiji)*, originally compiled by Sima Qian (ca. 145–86 BCE), and it repeats many of the phrases and situations Sima Qian had described verbatim. However, these histories provide remarkable insights into the behavior of emperors and their families at court—while also suggesting developing notions of gender and education. This segment of the *Han Shu* covers the reign of Hsiao-Ai (Xiao Ai), in roughly 6–1 BCE.

## The Annals of [Emperor Hsiao]-Ai

Emperor Hsiao-ai was the grandson of Emperor Yüan by a concubine and the son of King Kung of Ting-t'ao, [Liu K'ang(1a)]. His mother was the Concubine [née] Ting. When he was in his third year, he succeeded [his father] and was set up as King. When he grew up, he delighted in words and phrases and in the laws and statutes.

In [the period] Yüan-yen, the fourth year, he came [to Ch'ang-an] to pay court, followed by all [his high officials], his Tutor, his Chancellor, and his Commandant of the Capital. At that time the youngest brother of Emperor Ch'eng, King Hsiao of Chung-shan, [Liu Hsing], also came to pay court, followed [only] by his Tutor. The Emperor thought it strange, and asked [Liu Hsin(5), the future Emperor Ai], about it. The King of Ting-t'ao, replied, "According to the [imperial] ordinances, when vassal kings come to pay court, they are permitted to be accompanied by the [officials ranking at] two thousand piculs in their kingdoms. The Tutor, Chancellor, and Commandant of the Capital are all [officials ranking at] two thousand piculs in a kingdom, hence I am accompanied by them all." The Emperor ordered him to recite from the *Book of Odes*, and he understood and was versed in it, and was able to explain it.

On another day, [the Emperor] asked the King of Chung-shan, [Liu Hsing], in what law or ordinance [it was ordered that he should be] accompanied only by his tutor, and he was unable to reply. [The Emperor] ordered him to recite from the *Book of History*, and he broke off [in the middle of his recitation]. Moreover, [at an imperial feast], when he had been granted food in the presence of [the Emperor], he was the last to finish eating; when he arose, his stockings came down, [for] their ties had become loosened. Because of these [facts], Emperor Ch'eng considered that he was incapable, and esteemed the King of Ting-t'ao, as capable, often exalting his abilities.

At this time the grandmother of the King, the Queen Dowager [of Ting-t'ao, née] Fu, had come with the King to pay court, and privately sent presents to the Brilliant Companion [née] Chao, whom the Emperor favored, and to the Emperor's maternal uncle, the General of Agile Cavalry and Marquis of Ch'ü-yang, Wang Ken. The Brilliant Companion [née Chao] and [Wang] Ken saw that the Emperor had no sons, and also wished beforehand to attach themselves [to the coming ruler] by a plan for the

Source: *Han Shu*, Book 11 (Annals of the Emperor Hsiao-Ai), Chinese text and English translation: http://www2.iath.virginia.edu/saxon/servlet/SaxonServlet?source=xwomen/texts/hanshu.xml&style=xwomen/xsl/dynaxml.xsl&chunk.id=d2.49&toc.depth=1&toc.id=0&doc.lang=bilingual.

distant future, so both in turn praised the King of Ting-t'ao and urged the Emperor to make him his successor. Emperor Ch'eng of his own volition also exalted [Liu Hsin(5)'s] ability, and after having put the bonnet of virility upon him, sent him [back to his kingdom]. At that time he had [reached] his seventeenth year.

. . .

In [the period] Sui-ho, the second year, the third month, Emperor Ch'eng died, and in the fourth month, on [the day] ping-wu, the Heir-apparent took the imperial throne and presented himself in the Temple of [Emperor] Kao. He honored the Empress Dowager [nee Wang] with the title, Grand August Empress Dowager, and the Empress [née Chao] with the title, Empress Dowager. He [granted] a general amnesty to the empire, granted one quadriga of horses to each king's son of the imperial house who was enregistered, to the officials and common people, noble ranks, to [each] hundred households, an ox and wine, and to the Thrice Venerable, the Filially Pious, the Fraternally Respectful, the [Diligent] Cultivators of the Fields, widowers, widows, orphans, and childless, silk.

The Grand Empress Dowager [nee Wang] issued an imperial edict honoring King Kung of Ting-t'ao, [Liu K'ang], as Sovereign Kung [of Ting-t'ao]. In the fifth month, on [the day] ping-hsü, [the Emperor] established the Empress née Fu [as Empress]. An imperial edict said, "[According to the principle of] the *Spring and Autumn*, [in the *Kung-yang Commentary*] that 'a mother becomes honorable because of her son,' [We] honor the Queen Dowager [née Fu] of Ting-t'ao with the title, Empress Dowager Kung, and the Concubine [née] Ting [of Ting-t'ao with the title, Empress Kung, and establish for each an entourage, a Supervisor of the Household, and the income of an estate, like [the occupants of] the Ch'ang-hsin Palace and the Inner Palace. [We] posthumously honor the father of [the Empress Dowager nee] Fu as the Marquis [through Whom the Emperor] Renders Homage to an Ancestor, and the father of [the Empress nee] Ting as the Marquis in Recompense to his Virtue." The maternal uncle [of the Emperor], Ting Ming, had been made the Marquis of Yang-an, his maternal uncle's son, [Ting] Man, was made Marquis of Ping-chou, and [Ting] Man's father, [Ting] Chung, was posthumously [granted] the posthumous name, Marquis Huai of P'ing-chou. The Empress [née Fu's] father, [Fu(4)] Yen, had become the Marquis of K'ung-hsiang, and the younger brother of the Empress Dowager [nee Chao], the Palace Attendant and Imperial Household Grandee Chao Ch'in(b), became the Marquis of Hsin-ch'eng.

In the sixth month, an imperial edict said, "'The melodies of Cheng are licentious' and bring disorder into music. They were banished by the Sage-kings. Let the Bureau of Music be abolished."

▶ **Working with Sources**

1. **What was thought to be the best course of education for the young Emperor?**

2. **What seems to have been the extent of the power of the Empress Dowager? Why?**

## SOURCE 9.5

# Ban Zhao, *Admonitions for Women (Nüjie)*

## ca. 80 CE

Ban Zhao (45–ca. 116 CE) was by far the most educated woman of her day, and she trained many important male scholars. The *Han Shu* (the continuation of Sima Qian's *Shiji*) was originally undertaken by her father, Ban Biao (3–54 CE), and continued by her brother Ban Gu (32–92). Ban Zhao is credited with giving the Han Shu its present shape after the deaths of her father and brother, but she is most famous today for her advice book, directed toward young women.

I, the unworthy writer, am unsophisticated, unenlightened, and by nature unintelligent, but I am fortunate both to have received not a little favor from my scholarly Father, and to have had a cultured mother and instructresses upon whom to rely for a literary education as well as for training in good manners. More than forty years have passed since at the age of fourteen I took up the dustpan and the broom in the Cao family [the family into which she married]. During this time with trembling heart I feared constantly that I might disgrace my parents, and that I might multiply difficulties for both the women and the men of my husband's family. Day and night I was distressed in heart, but I labored without confessing weariness. Now and hereafter, however, I know how to escape from such fears.

Being careless, and by nature stupid, I taught and trained my children without system. Consequently I fear that my son Gu may bring disgrace upon the Imperial Dynasty by whose Holy Grace he has unprecedentedly received the extraordinary privilege of wearing the Gold and the Purple, a privilege for the attainment of which by my son, I a humble subject never even hoped. Nevertheless, now that he is a man and able to plan his own life, I need not again have concern for him. But I do grieve that you, my daughters, just now at the age for marriage, have not at this time had gradual training and advice; that you still have not learned the proper customs for married women. I fear that by failure in good manners in other families you will humiliate both your ancestors and your clan. I am now seriously ill, life is uncertain. As I have thought of you all in so untrained a state, I have been uneasy many a time for you. At hours of leisure I have composed . . . these instructions under the title, "Lessons for Women."

Source: Nancy Lee Swann, *Pan Chao: Foremost Woman Scholar of China* (New York: London Century, 1932), 82–90.

# PART THREE

# The Formation of Religious Civilizations

## 600–1450 CE

**A** vitally important pattern of world history during the period 600–1450 was the emergence and development of what may be called "religious civilizations." By this we mean the formation of religions and cultures in entire world regions, shared by the states and empires in these regions. In all cases, religious, philosophical, and/or ethical traditions based on monotheism or monism helped give legitimacy to the polities that adopted them. They helped link individual states by providing them with a common set of cultural norms and bonds. Six religious civilizations emerged in a relatively short space of time in Eurasia and, to a lesser extent, in Africa during the second half of the first millennium. They were, from west to east, western Christianity (from 476), eastern Christianity (640), Islam (750), Hinduism (550), Buddhism (Korea 550, Japan 594, Vietnam 971), and Neo-Confucianism (China 960, Vietnam 1010). Each occupied a world region.

## Uniqueness and Comparability

**Uniqueness.** The rise of religious civilizations on the continents of Asia, Europe, and Africa is a striking phenomenon that unifies the period 600–1450. In this respect, it may be considered as a continuation of the intellectual and institutional transformations that began with the emphasis on transcendence by the visionaries of the mid-first millennium BCE as a key aspect in understanding the world in which they lived.

**Comparability.** The religious civilizations were not monolithic and displayed many regional variations. Internal diversity notwithstanding, they shared a number of common characteristics:

- Religious civilizations formed in regions which were larger than any single state within them: They superseded empires as the largest units of human organization. They often consisted of commonwealths of competing states sharing common characteristics and even common cultures.

- The civilizations were *scriptural*—that is, based on bodies of texts inherited in most cases from earlier periods. In each religious civilization, followers were

| | | | | | |
|---|---|---|---|---|---|
| **633–651**<br>Arab conquest of Syria, Iraq, Egypt, and Iran | **794–1185**<br>Heian period, Japan | **918–1392**<br>Koryo Kingdom, from which the name "Korea" is derived | **ca. 1000**<br>*Tale of Genji*, perhaps world's first novel, Japan | **1204**<br>Sack of Constantinople by Crusaders | |
| | **618–960**<br>Tang Dynasty in China | **850–1000**<br>Kingdom of Chichén Itzá in northern Yucatán Peninsula | **960–1127**<br>Neo-Confucian synthesis in China | **ca. 1000–1400**<br>Kingdom of Ife in West African rain forest | **1206–1310**<br>Mongol Conquests of Asia, Eastern Europe, and the eastern Middle East |

preoccupied with harmonizing the often conflicting texts into one coherent *canon*: a single, official interpretation adhered to by all.

- The guardians of the canon (clergy, scholars, sages) were members of educated elites who taught and interpreted it to laypeople.

- Despite hostilities among religious civilizations, merchants, missionaries, pilgrims, and travelers visited each other's areas in large numbers. They fostered a lively exchange of innovations from one end of Eurasia and Africa to the other.

## Origins, Interactions, and Adaptations

The era of religious civilizations provides some striking examples of the processes of origins, interactions, and adaptations that we have emphasized in this book.

**Internal Forces.** The elements with which people built their religious civilizations came from the intellectual and institutional traditions of empires and kingdoms from the pre-600 period. These elements were for the most part found inside the territories of the evolving religious civilizations. Some exceptions include Korea, Japan, and Vietnam, which adopted Chinese Buddhist civilization more or less ready-made from the outside.

In the majority of religious civilizations, the scriptural canons were completed within two or three centuries. Thereafter, refinement within the confines set by the canons continued for many more centuries, in some cases even beyond 1450. Without outside challenges, however, these refinements slowed. Over time, scholars, thinkers, and artists tended to exhaust the possibilities which their civilizations offered them.

**External Challenges.** External intellectual challenges contributed to the reshaping of two religious civilizations during the period 600–1450: Neo-Confucian China and western Christianity. China's intellectual foundation from the Han dynasty on was based on Daoism and Confucianism, harmonized with some difficulty during the early centuries of the millennium. Buddhism, coming from India, became a full-blown intellectual and institutional challenge by the 800s. In response, the Chinese reconfigured their canon from the mid-tenth century with the creation of Neo-Confucianism.

In western Christianity, Latin Christians enlarged their canon twice, as a result of adapting to intellectual challenges coming from the outside: first around 1100–1250, after the arrival of Arabic and Greek texts, and second around 1400, after the arrival of another set of Greek and Hellenistic texts.

## Thinking Like a World Historian

▶ How was each religious civilization of the period 600–1450 unique? How were these civilizations comparable?

▶ What impact did internal forces and external challenges have on the patterns of development in the religious civilizations of the period 600–1450?

▶ Why do the civilizations of the Americas fall outside the patterns that characterize Eurasian and African civilizations during this period?

**1206–1526**
Muslim Delhi Sultanate at height of power

**1240–1645**
Empire of Mali in West Africa (rain forest, sahel, and savanna)

**1257–1287**
Vietnamese repel three attempted Mongol invasions

**1336–1564**
Dominance of Hindu state of Vijayanagar in southern India

**1427–1521**
Aztec Empire in Mesoamerica

**1453**
Constantinople falls to Ottoman Empire

**1238–1492**
Muslim kingdom of Granada

**1250–1505**
Kingdom of Great Zimbabwe in southern Africa

**1268**
St. Thomas Aquinas' *Summa theologica*

**1348–1352**
Black Death in Middle East and Europe

**1438–1533**
Inca Empire in Andes

# Chapter 10 600–1300 CE
# Islamic Civilization and Byzantium

Byzantium

Islamic Civilization

**BYZANTIUM AND THE ISLAMIC WORLD, ca. 1000 CE**

One cannot help but feel sympathy for Safra, a jilted wife whose husband left her for a more attractive woman in twelfth-century Cairo. Two letters by Safra to her estranged husband Khidr tell of her deep hurt and bitter anguish. She is offended that Khidr denigrates her as unattractive and reveals marriage secrets to his new lover, who is also married. In her words, his "repulsive, shameless talk" causes her deep suffering. Were she not a good Muslim, she says, she would curse him roundly and loudly, both privately and in public.

The letters also reveal that she was independently wealthy, while her husband was not. She freely admits that when they were married 3 years earlier, she did not realize that he was unreliable. Since he could not pay the obligatory portion of the "bride wealth" payable to her at the time of the wedding, she let it stand as a loan. Not only did he not make payments, but he did not even feed and clothe her or pay the rent. When he began his affair 2 years earlier, she went to the countryside to find distance and rest. But he tortured her with insistent demands to return and promised to leave his mistress. The moment she gave in and returned to Cairo, he went back to his lover. Like a ghost, he slipped into Safra's house at night for a few hours of sleep in his room, only to disappear the next morning. During his nightly visits he stole

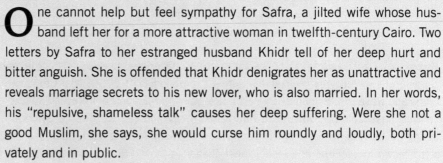

*ABOVE*: The constellation Aries, from *Book of the Fixed Stars* by Abd al-Rahman al-Sufi (903–986).

most of the household furnishings, so that in the end she found herself in an empty house.

Safra's reflections and actions provide an important glimpse into the legal side of Islamic civilization. Contrary to the widely held opinion in the contemporary West, Islamic law afforded women considerable protections. Safra was a woman of property, holding personal title to possessions as well as to debts payable to her. She could go to court, where she had standing as a complainant. She could initiate divorce proceedings, even if a wife's proceedings were more complicated than those of a husband. In short, even though Islamic civilization was as patriarchal as the other religious civilizations of the time, women exercised considerably more rights than in the Persian and Roman Empires.

The central patterns of Islamic civilization flowed from an empire that conquering Arabs from northern Arabia built during 633–750. These patterns would then develop across a 5,000-mile swath ranging from the Iberian Peninsula to Turkestan. The empire, ultimately ungovernable as a single unit, evolved into a **commonwealth** of smaller states. From 750 to 950 it underwent a formative period during which its inhabitants adapted to inherited Greco-Roman and Persian cultures. By the mid-tenth century, historians consider the empire "fully developed," meaning that it was subjected to few outside influences that changed it in substantive ways. After this time, Islamic civilization continued to be shaped by its patterns of characteristic religious, political, and cultural traditions and institutions. These patterns remained largely unchanged and unchallenged by new stimuli coming from the outside until well into the modern period. In this respect, Islamic civilization was similar to Byzantine eastern Christian, Hindu Indian, Neo-Confucian Chinese, and Confucian–Buddhist Japanese civilizations. All of these, after their formation by the end of the first millennium, pursued a course more along their established internal patterns than as a result of innovation, interaction, and adaptation coming from the outside.

## The Formation of Islamic Religious Civilization

Arab conquests and the rise of the religion of Islam were foundational events during the period 600–900. In the 600s, the Arabs carved out a kingdom for themselves by exploiting the preoccupation of the eastern Roman and Sasanid Persian Empires with their destructive wars of conquest in 602–628. Two Arab dynasties, the Umayyads and then the Abbasids, built a vast empire stretching thousands of miles from east to west. Given the enormous distances, the Abbasids were forced to grant autonomy to many outlying provinces. In the process, their empire changed into a commonwealth of many states sharing a single Islamic religion. The pattern which Islamic religious civilization followed during its

## Seeing Patterns

▶ Why can the period 600–1450 be described as the age of religious civilizations? How do eastern Christian and Islamic civilizations fit this description?

▶ Which cultural traditions combined to form Islamic religious civilization during its formative period? What were the most characteristic patterns?

▶ How did eastern Christian or Byzantine civilization evolve over time? On which institutions was this civilization based, and how did it evolve, wedged between Islamic and western Christian civilizations?

Commonwealth: An association of self-governing states sharing similar institutional and cultural traits.

formative period was a variation of what happened in the other parts of Asia and Europe in the first millennium CE: Through conquest or peaceful expansion, regions of religious civilizations emerged which grew much larger than the political units within them, resulting in the appearance of commonwealths (Middle East, Europe, India) or periodic unity and disunity (China).

## The Beginnings of Islam

At the beginning of the 600s, the Sasanid Persian and Roman Empires battled each other in a lengthy war, which left their Arab subjects in Syria and Mesopotamia (which the Arabs subsequently called "Iraq") to their own devices. The Arabs had been nomadic inhabitants of the Syrian-Arabian desert since the domestication of the camel (ca. 2500 BCE) and were founders of sedentary kingdoms and city-states around the rim of the desert on the Arabian Peninsula in the early centuries CE. In the mid-600s Arab leaders declared their rule over Roman Syria, conquered Sasanid Iraq, captured Egypt from the Romans, and destroyed the Sasanid Persian Empire. Through further conquests, the initial Arab realm became an empire, stretching by the mid-eighth century from Iberia (Spain and Portugal) in the west to the Indus River in the east.

**The Final Roman–Persian War** The long history of the Roman–Persian rivalry once more reached a climax during the first three decades of the 600s. In 602, King of Kings Khosrow II (r. 590–628) invaded the Roman Empire, using the pretext of a coup d'état in Constantinople that had brought to power a usurper. Within a little more than a decade his generals had conquered Syria, Egypt, and Anatolia, and the Romans were hard pressed to defend themselves in their capital. In the midst of its bleakest moment, the empire was saved by Heraclius (r. 610–641), a governor from North Africa who seized power in Constantinople in 610. Borrowing huge sums, he reorganized the military and was able to drive the Sasanids back to Iraq. In 628 he achieved his greatest triumph when Khosrow was murdered by rivals and the Sasanids were forced to make peace.

After his victory, Heraclius restored the prewar administrative structures in the province of Syria. He subsidized Arab leaders and reintroduced locally recruited garrisons and bishops in cities. In order to pay back the war debt, he reduced the size of the army. To simplify the central administration, he replaced Latin with Greek as the language of the bureaucracy and the multiple Latin titles of the emperor (*imperator, caesar, augustus*) with the single Greek title of king (*basileus*), Christ's representative on earth. Thus, as many scholars of Byzantine history now emphasize, it was under Heraclius that the Roman Empire became the Byzantine Empire, or Byzantium.

**The Arab Empire of the Umayyads** The reappointment of subsidized Arab leaders to govern Syria was more complicated than Heraclius had anticipated. The Sasanid interlude had shaken up the hierarchy among these leaders, and Heraclius was unable to restore it, even when he withheld subsidies to some leaders and dispatched military forces to subdue others. It was in this context of leadership competition that new Arab leaders emerged in Syria after 633 who were not satisfied with being mere vassals of Byzantium. These leaders conquered Sasanid Persia (633–651) and Byzantine Egypt (639–641). An Arab empire rose which the strongman Muawiya (r. 661–680) consolidated under the dynastic rule of the Umayyads.

**Umayyad Religious Developments**  Under the third Umayyad ruler, Abd al-Malik (685–705), early signs of a religious orientation in the Arab Empire became visible. Arabic inscriptions in and on the Dome of the Rock, dating to 691/692, refer to Muhammad and biblical prophetic predecessors, including Jesus the Messiah, as servants of God. Polemical verses oppose the theology of Jesus as son of God, while other verses describe **Muslims** as believers in the "concordance" (*islam*) among all prophetic messages of the past. By implication this means that following God's commands in this concordance will bring salvation on the Day of Judgment.

**Gold Coin of Abd al-Malik, ca. 696.** This coin displays the characteristics of what were to become Islamic coins; that is, the avoidance of images and the use of religious phrases.

The Dome of the Rock is a splendid, architecturally commanding structure on Jerusalem's Temple Mound which can be viewed as Abd al-Malik's counter monument to the Church of the Holy Sepulcher on the other side of Jerusalem, built on the site of Jesus' tomb. Presumably he saw himself as the true "representative of God" (*khalifa*, or **caliph**) vis-à-vis the Byzantine basileus. Similarly, the emerging Islamic faith of the One God, which he was shaping as the state religion of the Umayyad Empire, was offered as a faith superior to **Trinitarian** Byzantine Christianity. To buttress this state religion, Abd al-Malik created a strong central administration and army, with Arabic as the bureaucratic language and a reformed coinage which renounced any imagery, in contrast to Byzantine coins with their crosses and emperors. Abd al-Malik saw the Umayyad Empire as the true successor of a shrinking, perhaps even dying, Byzantine Empire.

**Muslim:** Initially: believer in the concordance among all prophetic messages from Abraham to Muhammad. Later on: believer who submits to the will of God (*Allah*).

**Caliph:** Representative of God, and later of Muhammad, on earth.

**Trinitarianism:** Christianity based on the doctrine of God the Father, Son, and Holy Spirit.

**Umayyad Conquests in West and East**  Abd al-Malik's successors continued the Umayyad efforts to take over Byzantium. Armies composed of Arabs and Berbers conquered Byzantine North Africa in 686–698, reducing Byzantium to parts of Italy, the Balkans, and Anatolia. Once North Africa was conquered, Abd al-Malik's successors became entangled in western Christian politics. In 711, dissident Visigothic nobles called Berber and Arab troops into the Iberian Peninsula to help them in their bid to oust the dominant Visigothic king. After rising to dominance in the Visigothic kingdom, the Berbers, Arabs, and Visigothic allies divided Iberia among themselves. In the same year, the Umayyads expanded their rule into Central Asia and the Indus Valley, creating an immense empire with copious amounts of booty and masses of enslaved war captives streaming to Syria.

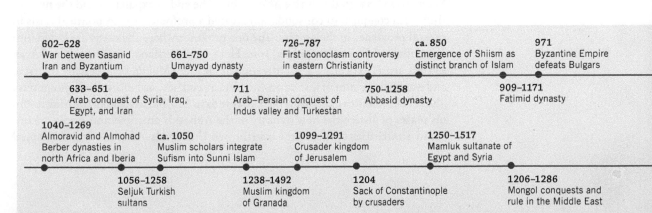

| | | | |
|---|---|---|---|
| **602–628** War between Sasanid Iran and Byzantium | **661–750** Umayyad dynasty | **726–787** First iconoclasm controversy in eastern Christianity | **ca. 850** Emergence of Shiism as distinct branch of Islam | **971** Byzantine Empire defeats Bulgars |
| **633–651** Arab conquest of Syria, Iraq, Egypt, and Iran | **711** Arab–Persian conquest of Indus valley and Turkestan | **750–1258** Abbasid dynasty | **909–1171** Fatimid dynasty |
| **1040–1269** Almoravid and Almohad Berber dynasties in north Africa and Iberia | **ca. 1050** Muslim scholars integrate Sufism into Sunni Islam | **1099–1291** Crusader kingdom of Jerusalem | **1250–1517** Mamluk sultanate of Egypt and Syria |
| **1056–1258** Seljuk Turkish sultans | **1238–1492** Muslim kingdom of Granada | **1204** Sack of Constantinople by crusaders | **1206–1286** Mongol conquests and rule in the Middle East |

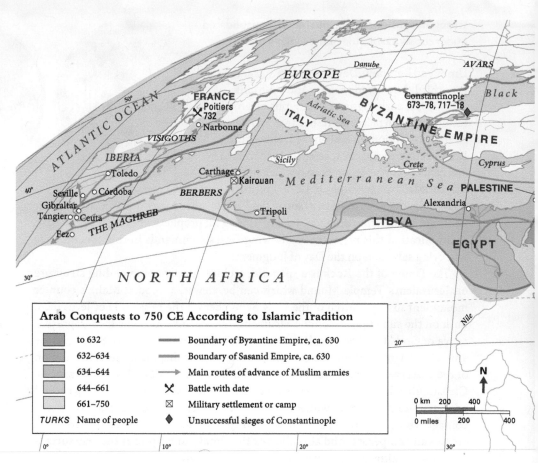

MAP **10.1** **Arab Conquests to 750.**

Two decades later, the Iberian Berbers and Arabs pushed into France. One of these raids was commemorated in western Christianity as the Battle of Tours in central France (732 or 733). Here, the founder of the western Christian Carolingian Empire, Charles Martel (r. 714–741), beat back the invading raiders. Similarly, Arab campaigns in the Caucasus to take the Russian steppes failed around 740. From today's vantage point it looked as if the empire had reached its physical limits: It became evidently impossible to dispatch cavalry armies during summer campaigns from the capital of Damascus any farther than the Pyrenees, Hindu Kush, and Caucasus mountains (see Map 10.1).

**From the Umayyads to the Abbasids**    The end of expansion and the need to shift from conquest to consolidation created a profound religio-political crisis in several provinces of the empire. The one province where the crisis exploded into an uncontrollable revolution was Iran. Here, local Persian military lords and Arab settlers arose, expecting a "rightly guided" leader (*Mahdi*, or Messiah) to arrive and establish a realm of justice on earth at the end of time before God's Judgment. The revolutionaries overthrew the Umayyads in 750, but instead of the Mahdi and his realm of justice the new dynasty of the Abbasids emerged and displayed uncanny similarities to that of the overthrown Umayyads. After moving the capital

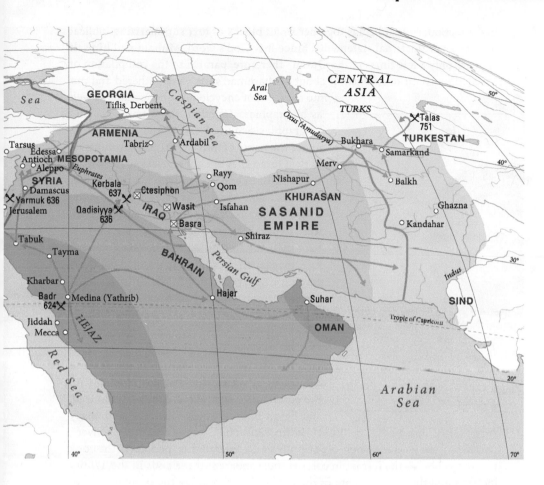

of the empire to Baghdad in Iraq, the Abbasids built the same top-heavy central administration and army which had characterized the Umayyads.

## Islamic Theology, Law, and Politics

In Iraq, the Abbasids completed what the Umayyads had begun in Syria. They enlarged and systematized the state religion, built around the Prophet Muhammad, God's commands, and salvation on the Day of Judgment. They sponsored the translation of scientific, philosophical, legal, and literary works from Syriac and Persian into Arabic. Schools and libraries spread from Baghdad to large and small cities everywhere in the region, from Iberia to northwest India. Many of these cities became cultural and political centers of their own, under autonomous dynasties that recognized the Abbasid caliphs in Baghdad but for all practical purposes were independent. By around 950, an Islamic religious civilization had come into being which was organized into a commonwealth of some two dozen realms under ethnically diverse dynasties.

**Shaping Islamic Theology**   In the 800s, scholars, judges, and bureaucrats in the Abbasid Empire compiled the Quran, the beginnings of which dated back to the later Umayyads. In contrast to the Christian New Testament, the Quran is

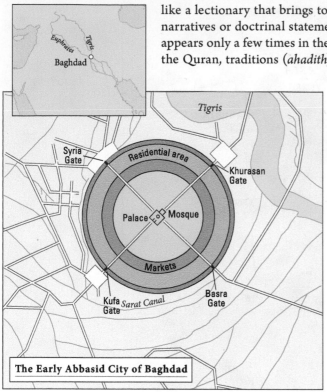

The Early Abbasid City of Baghdad

MAP 10.2 **The Early Abbasid City of Baghdad.**

**Sunna:** The para-digmatic "path" of Muhammad's traditions which, if trodden by believers, will lead to salvation.

**Umma:** Community of all who believe in one God, with Muhammad as his prophet, and reject pagan idolatry (ignorance, *jahiliyya*) or associationism (*shirk*), such as the Christian doctrine of Trinity.

like a lectionary that brings together small blocks of text summarizing biblical narratives or doctrinal statements. Since it is God's word, Muhammad himself appears only a few times in the Quran. Therefore, parallel to the compilation of the Quran, traditions (*ahadith*) about Muhammad's life were gathered and put into the form of encyclopedic collections as well as biographies. Together, these traditions and biographies acquired the status of scripture, under the name of **Sunna**, although in contrast to the Quran they are not revelations.

The Quran and Sunna sketch a theology of of Mecca and Medina as sacred cities in the early 600s in which Muhammad preached God's word to pagan Arabs. Their ancestors in the past had once adhered to Abraham's message but had since fallen back into paganism. After over-coming armed resistance, Muhammad founded a community (**umma**) of Muslims with the mandate to engage in a holy struggle (**jihad**) against all those who "associate" other gods to the one all-powerful God—that is, place other gods next to him. After Muhammad, four close associates as successors in the leadership of the community conquered Arabia, Syria, Iraq, and Egypt in order to establish the supremacy of Islam. Although pagans had to convert, Christians and Jews as owners of Scriptures were tolerated as "peoples of the book [i.e., the Bible]"—the former in spite of their apparent three gods in the Trinity doctrine and the latter in spite of their refusal to recognize the prophethood of Muhammad.

For us today, living in a secularized world, it is crucial not to misunderstand Islamic tradition as history. None of the texts with which Abbasid Muslims shaped their theology in the 800s is based on documents or oral tradition which can be dated to the early 600s. The few Christian and Jewish texts which can be reliably dated to the 600s say nothing about Mecca. The earliest Arab who can be securely identified with the beginnings of Islam is the Umayyad caliph Abd al-Malik, dis-cussed above as the builder of the Dome of the Rock with its early Islamic inscriptions.

We thus can conclude that when the Abbasids and their collaborators in the 800s and 900s shaped the theology of Islam, their endeavor was to date the origins of Islam prior to the Umayyads and place these origins outside the Judaism and Christianity of Syria—deep into what they declared to have been a pagan Arabia. In contrast to the contemporary Carolingian Christians in western Europe who assimilated to Catholicism with only minor modifications, the Abbasids con-sciously created a separate Arabian faith by rejecting major Jewish and Christian doctrines.

This separateness of Islam is most pronounced in the five religious duties which identify a Muslim: the profession of faith, prayer, fasting, alms-giving, and pil-grimage to Mecca. The profession of faith is summed up in the formula "There is no God but God, and Muhammad is his messenger." The five-times-daily prayer requires the washing of hands and feet for ritual cleanliness and the performance of a sequence of bodily motions and prayers. On Fridays the noon prayer is to be performed in the congregational mosque. Fasting means a monthlong abstinence during Ramadan from food, drink, and sex during the daylight hours. Alms-giving is a small (2.5 percent) donation or tax to the poor, and the pilgrimage is a journey made at least once in one's life to Mecca. These duties are very different from those defining Judaism and Christianity and make Islam not merely a denomination but a separate religion.

**Jihad:** Literally "struggle (for the path of God—*fi sabil Allah*)," that can range from personal struggle for faith to war in the name of Islam.

**Creating Islamic Law**     The five religious duties form part of the much larger body of Islamic law. The Abbasids had inherited a judicial system from the Umayyads that was based on the disparate legal traditions of Roman Syria and Sasanid Persia. In the late 700s, the dynasty sponsored the translations of digests of the Justinian Roman law codex in order to create a unified legal system. Since Muslims were at the same time busy compiling the Quran and shaping Muhammadan traditions, it was not surprising that the creation of the legal system of the **Sharia** became part and parcel of the same unification process. When it was completed in the mid-900s, the Sharia encompassed the legal verses of the Quran, the prophetic Sunna, and voluminous legal commentaries.

**Sharia:** The combined body of the legal verses of the Quran, the prophetic Sunna, and the legal commentaries of the 800s and 900s, covering law as well as morality.

**The Separation of State and Religion**     The shaping of Islamic theology and law became a major matter of controversy toward the middle of the 800s. If all theology and law had to be based on the Quran and Sunna, sooner or later every possible moral or legal matter would be unchangeably grounded in God's authority. Nothing could be added to the Sharia or changed in it, and one could only interpret. To preserve their freedom to shape the Sharia, the caliphs instituted a loyalty oath (*mihna*) from 833 to 849 which required all judges, jurists, and jurisconsults employed by the administration or in the courts to support the policy of continued caliphal legislation.

A small but vocal minority refused the oath and found support among the ordinary folk of craftsmen and traders in Baghdad and other cities who were attracted to the idea that God's law should be above human manipulation. After riots the Abbasids gave in and enacted a compromise whereby the religious scholars (*ulama*) became the guardians of the Sharia and the caliphs its executors. This compromise resulted in a separation of religion and state, with the ulama responsible for the judicial system and the state executing the law according to its own often extrajudicial interests.

**Shiite Islam**     The fully evolved Islam under the guardianship of the ulama, in place from about 950 onwards, is known as **Sunni Islam**. It expresses the Sunna of the Prophet and the consensus of the religious community represented by the ulama and laid down in the Sharia. Sunni Islam always encompassed the large majority of Muslims and today amounts to about 90 percent of the totality. The minority of Muslims, followers of **Shiite** [SHEE-ite] **Islam**, make up about 10 percent, although they are the majority in contemporary Iran, Iraq, and Lebanon.

The historical origin of Shiite Islam can be dated to the end of the Umayyads, when revolutionaries proclaimed the imminent arrival of the Mahdi to usher in

God's kingdom of justice on earth (see above, p. 278). Tradition places the Shiite beginnings in the period of the first four caliphs, when Caliph Ali lost his throne and Ali's grandson Husayn lost his bid for power against the Umayyads. According to tradition, Ali was a cousin of the Prophet; the husband of one of his daughters, Fatima; and the founder of the Alid family, where the eldest male in direct descent was entitled to the leadership of the Muslim community in place of the Umayyads.

The main differences between Sunnism and Shiism concern the roles of tradition and authority. The tradition of Husayn's martyrdom near Karbala in Iraq at the hands of the Sunni Umayyads is central for all Shiites and is commemorated during one of the months of the Muslim calendar, Muharram. The authority of the Alid descendants in the past, and today of the leaders of the Shiite clergy, is absolute and infallible. Sunnis, by contrast, reject the Karbala tradition. For them the consensus of the community separate from rulers and the absence of a scholarly hierarchy among the ulama are supreme. In the history of Islamic civilization, Shiite–Sunni differences flared up repeatedly, and, unfortunately, they are acute again today, in the context of Iran's ambitions to become a nuclear power.

When the Abbasids squashed the apocalyptical expectation of God's kingdom at the end of time, apocalypticism went underground. It resurfaced in 874 when the twelfth-generation descendant of Ali was reported to have died without leaving a successor. A radical group formed in Syria around the doctrine that a descendant of the seventh-generation leader would appear soon as the Mahdi. (A dispute concerning the legitimate successor in the seventh generation divided the Shiites. Those who accepted the twelfth-generation descendant remained nonrevolutionary.) The radical group of "Seveners" sent out emissaries who fomented armed rebellions around 900 in a number of outlying provinces of the Islamic commonwealth. The most successful rebellion was that of the Fatimids in Algeria, Tunisia, and Egypt, western Arabia, and parts of Syria. The Fatimids were Shiites who founded a counter caliphate to that of the Abbasids and were major players during the period of the Crusades. Until their end in 1171 they held up their claim of representing God's kingdom on earth through a higher form of justice than that of the Abbasids.

**Abbasid Glory.** Little is left of the Abbasid splendor during the 800s, since Iraq suffered several invasions in later history, in which palaces, mosques, and other structures were destroyed. This is the eighth-century Abbasid palace of Ukhaydir, southwest of Baghdad. The palace included gardens, baths, residential suites, courtyards, and audience halls.

**The Abbasids in Crisis**   In the second half of the 800s, right around the time when the Shiite underground began to reorganize itself, the Abbasids were hit by severe financial problems. The Sasanid Persian expansion of agriculture between the Euphrates and Tigris Rivers, continued by the Abbasids, had reached the limits of its potential. In many places, the soil was too salty due to poor drainage on the flat terrain of lower Iraq. Crop yields declined and agricultural tax revenue shrank. As a result, the administration found it difficult to maintain its lavish palace culture and massive bureaucracy. More acutely, it could no longer pay its palace guards, causing the officers to take over still fertile tax districts directly as personal assignments (sing. *iqta*) in place of direct salaries.

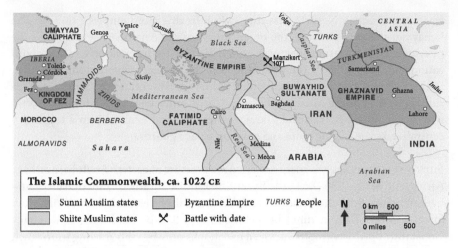

MAP **10.3 The Islamic Commonwealth, ca. 1022 CE.**

By this time, a majority of the soldiers in the guards were Turks, recruited as slaves from Central Asia. Slave-raiding parties captured non-Muslim boys and girls during campaigns into Turkish Central Asia. Merchants sold these youths to the caliphs in Baghdad, where they were converted to Islam and trained as soldiers. From 861 to 945, Turkish slave generals wielded power in Baghdad while retaining the caliphs as titular heads of the government. The main function of the generals was the control of political affairs in Iraq, but they also went on summer campaigns against Byzantium to continue the Umayyad holy war. Apart from the conquest of Byzantine Sicily by an autonomous dynasty in Tunisia, the only active jihad activities were the campaigns of the Turkish palace guards on the Anatolian border with Byzantium. For all practical purposes the conquest period initiated by the Umayyad Arabs had ended.

# Eastern Christian Civilization in Byzantium

Under siege by the Umayyads and Abbasids, the old eastern Roman Empire, now Byzantium, had retreated to Anatolia and parts of the Balkans. It survived because its emperors reconstituted the state on a new military and religious basis: locally organized border defenses and redefinition of Christian doctrine. Similar to the Abbasid Empire, Byzantium evolved into the center of a commonwealth of eastern Christian states reaching deeply into Russia after the conversion of the principality of Kiev to eastern Christianity in 988. Aided initially by the Crusades, later on the Byzantines became their victims. For a brief period, Byzantium was a western Christian realm (1204–1261) before it recovered as a modest eastern Christian realm (1261–1453).

## Byzantium's Difficult Beginnings

While the Arabs created the new identity of Islamic religious civilization for themselves, the Roman transition to the Byzantine eastern Christian civilization was more gradual. Nevertheless, the switch in title from emperor to king, the Umayyad military pressure, the organization of the Anatolian defense, and the interlude of iconoclasm collectively amounted also to the creation of a new civilizational identity. Once this new identity and the recovery from the Muslim (and, in the Balkans, Slavic) onslaughts were achieved, Byzantium followed a pattern similar to that of the Muslims. Eastern Christianity became a commonwealth, with autonomous Balkan and Ukrainian realms, and evolved into a top-heavy centralized state relying more and more on palace guards.

**Survival Strategies**  Under constant Arab pressure in eastern Anatolia, northern Africa, and Sicily (636–863), the Byzantine Empire shrank to a small Anatolian–Balkan realm. Both the Umayyad and Abbasid caliphs either led or sent invasion forces a total of seven times between 653 and 838 by land and sea to attack Constantinople. The empire survived the attacks only by withdrawing from much of the Balkans. Around 580, southern Slavs had begun migrating from the large lowland area extending from Poland eastward across modern Belarus and northern Ukraine into northwestern Russia to settle in the Balkans. Here, the Slavs gradually became the linguistically dominant population, assimilating speakers of other languages, such as Turkish-speaking groups of Bulgars from eastern Russia. These Bulgars migrated in the 500s to the Byzantine lower Danube, where they were influenced by Slavic culture and asserted their independence from Byzantium in 681. As the Byzantines were fighting for survival against the Arabs in Anatolia, the Bulgars became a major power in the Balkans.

Focusing initially almost entirely on Anatolia, the emperors created new, stationary troops known as "themes" (Greek *themata*). New research has demonstrated that the central administration in Constantinople, beginning around 660, recruited the themes from among volunteer foot soldiers in the interior Byzantine provinces, giving them small plots from imperial estates in the exposed provinces of Anatolia (and later also against the Slavs in the Balkans). In addition, it paid them small wages in cash and food provisions, which were collected as taxes from large landowner estates and free farmers. The themes' main task was to shadow and harass their mightier Arab rivals, waiting for a lucky moment to strike back. One effect of these harassment tactics was an impoverishment of southern Anatolia, which suffered harshly from constant Muslim raids. Provincial life in Anatolia became increasingly poor for its Christian inhabitants, and even Constantinople declined in wealth.

**Iconoclasm**  Throughout this difficult period the Byzantine emperors continued to be active in the shaping of religious doctrine and law, similar to the caliphs in the Islamic empire. One of the most important religious disputes to rack the empire was the **iconoclasm** controversy (726–787 and 814–842). Christians of all theological directions had been embroiled for centuries in controversies over the visual depiction of Jesus and Mary. By the eighth century proponents argued for a total ban on holy pictures and statues, based on the biblical injunctions against idolatry. In 726 the emperor Leo III (r. 717–741) decided to reform eastern Christian theology by imposing a ban on all such paintings (*eikons*). He ordered the destruction of religious art, hence the term *iconoclasm*—literally

**Iconoclasm:** Removal of all religious images from churches and monasteries during a period in the Byzantine Empire, under orders of the emperors.

meaning smashing the icons. The reform pitted the emperor and his clerical advisors against the imperial church hierarchy, including the papacy in Rome, which defended what it considered the legitimate tradition of Christian imagery. As in the case of the Islamic traditionalists insisting on the immutability of God's word, eastern Christian traditionalists sided with church practices which were widely shared by ordinary believers.

Even though belief in God *and* divine images violated strict interpretations of monotheism—as with the doctrine of God's transcendence in Islam—for ordinary believers such imagery was seen as a tangible link to the divine. Pressured by popular demand, in 842 the Byzantine emperor, like the Abbasid caliph a few years later, ended his control over religion and law. Although the emperors did not become figureheads like the caliphs, their authority nevertheless was considerably diminished vis-à-vis an invigorated church hierarchy. As we will see in Chapter 11, a similar disengagement between politics and religion occurred in western Christianity after the investiture controversy two centuries later. In this respect, the religious civilizations of Islam, Byzantium, and western Christianity followed similar patterns of development.

**Transformation into a Commonwealth**   As the internal doctrinal quarrel over iconoclasm was being settled in the mid-800s, the strategy of using themes to defend Anatolia finally paid off. By exploiting the fiscal crisis of the Abbasids, theme commanders were able to go on the offensive after ca. 850 and raid Muslim settlements in eastern Anatolia and northern Iraq with increasing frequency. A century later, in 965, Byzantium had regained all of Anatolia and in 969 even retook the northern Syrian gateway of Antioch. The emperors were now able to turn their attention to the Balkans. Here, the Bulgars had converted to eastern Christianity in 864 and, under their own emperors, had forced Byzantium to pay tributes in the early 900s. But in 971, the Byzantines crushed the Bulgars and reintegrated their realm into the empire. Toward the middle of the eleventh century, Byzantium again encompassed a respectably large territory, extending from Belgrade and the Balkans some 1,100 miles southeast to Antioch in northern Syria (see Map 10.4).

**The Byzantine Commonwealth.** Characteristic of eastern Christianity are the many churches dedicated to Hagia Sophia, "Holy Wisdom," which can be found throughout the Byzantine commonwealth, from the Balkans to the Caucasus. Though each region developed its own architectural style, they all organized sacred space in similar ways. A masterpiece of design and engineering based in part on the theories of the third-century BCE mathematician Archimedes, the Hagia Sophia in Constantinople was dedicated in 537 by the emperor Justinian on the foundations of an earlier structure (*a*). Its massive dome was often compared to the great dome of heaven itself, and the church would become the prototype for many others throughout the commonwealth in subsequent centuries, including the Cathedral of Saint Sophia in Kiev, whose foundations were laid early in the eleventh century (*b*). While it exhibits a distinctly Kievan style of church architecture, including over a dozen cupolas, the cathedral nonetheless embodies an unmistakable Byzantine tradition whose roots extend deep into the past.

"Constantine's horse was speedier [than the Muslims' horses], and its rider was a marvelous young man. He charged at the emir and struck him a blow with his stick and then the emir began to tremble and flee."

—*Digenes Akritas*, a novel celebrating the liberation of Anatolia from the Muslims

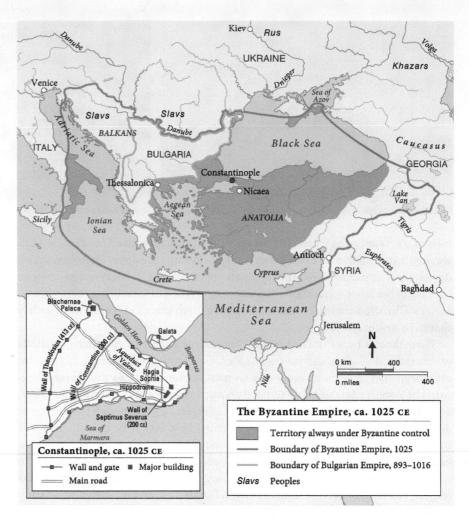

MAP 10.4 **The Byzantine Empire, ca. 1025 CE.**

The reintegration of the Balkans into the empire formed the background for the transformation of Byzantium into a commonwealth of eastern Christianity. In the late 700s, Kiev in what is now the Ukraine was an outpost of the large, ethnically Turkish, and religiously mixed Jewish, Christian, and Muslim Khazar realm in southern Russia. The merchants in Kiev were "Rus" (from which the name "Russia" is derived), of Scandinavian origin. The Rus were active in Russia at the same time as their cousins, the Norsemen or Vikings in western Europe and the Atlantic. By the 800s, most Rus had intermarried with Slavs and had become culturally Slavic. The Rus traded furs from Scandinavia and the Urals and wine from western Europe for Indian spices and Chinese silk, traveling on the Dnieper and Volga Rivers and the Baltic Sea between the Abbasid and Carolingian Empires. In addition to trading, the Rus repeatedly raided Byzantium, thereby adding to the difficulties of the empire during the 800s and early 900s. By the mid-900s, Rus trading and raiding had made Kiev a regional power.

In 988, Grand Prince Vladimir I of Kiev (r. 980–1015) decreed the conversion of his subjects to Christianity. The conversion was part of a deal whereby Vladimir would convert and receive a Byzantine princess for marriage if he would assist the emperor with 6,000 Kievan troops against internal rebels. With this conversion of the Ukraine, eastern Christianity expanded beyond the Byzantine Empire into the much larger region of Russia. An eastern Christian commonwealth of states emerged in this region similar to that of Islam in the Middle East and Mediterranean.

**Military Changes**   The Kievan troops in the service of the Byzantine Empire, called the "Varangian Guard," formed the nucleus of foreign palace guards, recruited later also from among western Norsemen (including Normans—that is, Norsemen settled in France). The Varangian Guards fulfilled functions similar to those of the Turkish slave guards among the Abbasids. In Byzantium, they were added to balance older indigenous regiments (*tegmata*) recruited from among the themes as special crack troops to protect the emperors from rivals for the throne. These rivals were often from provincial landowning families which had succeeded in monopolizing the position of commander (*strategos*) in the themes, responsible for the defense of the empire on the Arab–Muslim and Slavic–Balkan frontiers. The landowning families formed an aristocracy, which in many cases remained prominent until the end of Byzantium in 1453.

In the later 900s, when the empire had recovered, the emperors embarked on a recentralization of the empire. They began to reduce the themes in order to

**Byzantine Woman Defending Her Virtue.** Conscious of their privileged status, the Varangian Guards often mistreated ordinary people in the population. Similar to the Turkish slave guards at the Abbasid court, they had the reputation of being thieves, murderers, and rapists. In this image, Ioannes Skylitzes (ca. 1040–1101), a historian and illustrator, delighted in depicting the story of a woman who not only defended her virtue successfully by killing her attacker but also had the stunned surviving Varangians turn over the clothes of their dead comrade to her.

weaken the power of the aristocracy. In the mid-1000s, they demobilized entire themes, cutting the army by about a fifth. The effect of these changes in the military was a rising dependency of the emperors on palace guards and a serious weakening of the border defenses. The Byzantine Empire experienced the same—albeit milder—phenomenon of a top-heavy state and a power-hungry palace military that had already plagued the Abbasids for two centuries.

## The Seljuk Invasion and the Crusades

The demobilization of the themes happened at precisely the wrong time. Recently Islamized Seljuk Turks migrated in the early eleventh century southwestward from Central Asia. They conquered the shrunken Abbasid realm outright and inflicted heavy land losses on the Byzantines in Anatolia. To beat back the Seljuks, the emperors called on the pope for help, who responded by sending the First Crusaders. The subsequent Crusade Kingdom of Jerusalem was of some help to Byzantium but the latter suffered a severe setback under western Christian occupation for nearly two generations (1204–1261). The Crusader kingdom, severely reduced by the Muslims in 1187, survived precariously for another century (1291).

**The Seljuk Invasion**    The shift from a decentralized theme-located administration to a vastly enlarged central bureaucracy with palace guards in Constantinople was still in full swing during the mid-1000s when the recently converted Muslim Seljuks [sel-JOOKS] appeared on the eastern borders of both the Muslims and eastern Christians. Until this time, the Turks in eastern Russia and Central Asia had been victims of regular slave raids by Muslim rulers in Iran. Gradually, however, nomadic Turkish leaders benefiting from trade along the Volga and the Silk Road developed an interest in the benefits of urbanized Islamic civilization. This interest was similar to that of the Rus of Kiev seeking to adopt eastern Christianity. It was in this context that the Seljuk Turks east of the Volga River, between the Caspian and Aral Seas, converted and began their migration into the Islamic commonwealth.

As newcomers to Islam, the Seljuk leaders made themselves champions of a renewal of jihad. In their eyes, Muslims had grown lax with their holy war against the Byzantines. Furthermore, they considered Shiism an abominable heresy. In Baghdad, freeborn nonrevolutionary "Twelver" Shiites had replaced the Turkish slaves in the palace guards. In Egypt and parts of Syria the revolutionary "Sevener" Fatimids still sought to overthrow the Abbasids in Iraq. Assuming the exalted title "sultan" (from Arabic for power), the Seljuk leaders devoted themselves wholeheartedly to jihad and began their first raids against the Byzantines in the 1040s. By 1059 they had disbanded the guard of Twelver Shiite soldiers and were in full control of Baghdad, as the springboard from which to conduct their double-pronged holy war against Byzantium and the Fatimids (see Map 10.5).

**The Defeat of Manzikert**    Although cognizant of the Seljuk danger, the Byzantine emperors did not have sufficient time to rebuild a coherent army that could stop the Seljuks from full-fledged conquest. An effort in 1071 to drive the Seljuks from recently conquered eastern Anatolia failed miserably, in spite of the assembly of a huge army that was numerically superior to that of the Seljuks. The assortment of remaining theme soldiers and central regiments, as well as

**Battle of Manzikert.** The battle was not only a bitter defeat for the Byzantine army at the hands of Sultan Alp Arslan (1063–1072) and the Seljuks; it was also a personal humiliation for Emperor Romanus IV Diogenes (1068–1071). This humiliation had such repercussions even in western Christianity that Maître de Rohan, the artist of this miniature, in the early fifteenth century still found it worthy of commemoration. Rohan, in the service of members of the French aristocracy, was a major manuscript illustrator of his time.

palace guards and other mercenaries, was unable to hold together for more than a few days of maneuver and battle at Manzikert in eastern Anatolia. In the end the emperor found himself a prisoner of the Seljuk sultan.

The consequences of the defeat were severe. In the following decade and a half the Seljuks occupied most of Anatolia, leaving the Byzantines in command of only a few coastal cities and islands. Normans in the mid-1000s carved out realms for themselves from Byzantine southern Italy and Muslim Sicily. From here they invaded Greece and became a real threat for the empire in the second half of the eleventh century.

The situation improved only in 1092 when the reigning sultan died and the Seljuk Empire broke apart into a dozen or so competing successor states. By this time, a young, energetic, and reform-minded emperor, Alexius I Comnenus

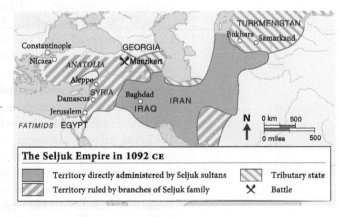

MAP **10.5** **The Seljuk Empire in 1092 CE.**

(r. 1081–1118), had succeeded in driving out the Normans from Greece. He could now begin to turn his attention to his most dangerous Muslim neighbor, the Rum Sultanate in Nicaea, just 60 miles from Constantinople. For dealing successfully with this neighbor he needed more troops than he was able to pay for in the Varangian Guard, his only reliable military force. Relations with western Christianity had returned to near normalcy after the low point of 1054 when the Catholic pope in Rome and the orthodox patriarch of Constantinople had excommunicated each other over doctrine and rank. One pope had even contemplated the delivery of aid in the aftermath of Manzikert. Thus, when Alexius sent an embassy in the spring of 1095 to Rome, he found a sympathetic ear.

**The Crusades**    As it turned out, Alexius received more from the pope than he bargained for. Pope Urban II (r. 1088–1099) issued a brilliantly crafted call for an armed pilgrimage to aid Byzantium and liberate the church from the "abominable" Seljuks, whom he accused of horrible crimes. Well-equipped knights with foot soldiers, as well as poorer folk with few supplies and weapons, responded enthusiastically by the tens of thousands (for more on the Crusades, see Chapter 11). For Alexius, the crusade was an acute embarrassment. It included many Normans who had battled him in Greece. Even if he were able to control them, how much land in Anatolia would the victorious crusaders turn over to him? And even if considerable territory were ceded, how would he be able to defend it by himself? At first, Alexius did indeed receive what he wanted: With the help of the Byzantine navy, the crusaders conquered Nicaea and grudgingly turned it over to him.

In the period thereafter, however, Alexius was under no illusion about the willingness of the crusaders to conquer Anatolia and Syria for him. Even though the emperor made efforts to support to the crusaders during their difficult siege of Antioch (1097–1098), he did not receive the city after the crusaders' victory. Nor did he obtain Jerusalem, which the crusaders conquered from the Fatimids in 1099. Instead, in 1100 the crusaders made Jerusalem the capital of an independent crusader kingdom.

Nevertheless, the reconquest of Nicaea enabled Alexius to retake western Anatolia with its rich agricultural valleys from the Seljuks. Luck helped him also to defeat a renewed effort by Normans, on the way home from the crusader state, to take Greece. For the defeated Turkish emirs the success of the First Crusade, by contrast, was an unmitigated disaster. It took a full generation before new leaders recovered from their defeats. This they achieved in 1144 with the capture of Edessa, an exposed city at the northern end of the crusader kingdom.

Muslim historians in the early 1100s were fully aware of the significance of the Crusades. (The term appeared after 1200 in French chronicles.) In their judgment, the Crusades were delayed Christian jihads in revenge for the great Arab expansion under the Umayyads. They dated the beginning of this revenge to the Norman invasion of Muslim Sicily in 1061 and the Castilian capture of Toledo in 1085. The fall of Jerusalem in 1099 was for them a logical continuation, exposing an alarming laxness of Muslim religious zeal.

The loss of Sicily, Toledo, and Jerusalem was indeed substantial. The agriculturally wealthy Emirate of Sicily had flourished for a century and a half. The Emirate of Toledo had been part of a nearly three-century-old brilliant Islamic culture in Iberia. In its heyday, this culture was even headed by its own caliphs reigning in Córdoba (Umayyad Andalus, 909–1031). The power of the caliphate rested on its gold trade with West Africa through the Sahara and on palace guards manned by Slavic slave soldiers who had been raided as boys by western European Christians in what was then still pagan eastern Europe. The losses of Sicily and Toledo effectively ended Muslim dominance in the Mediterranean.

**Muslim Recovery and Byzantine–Crusader Cooperation**    Imad al-Din Zenki (r. 1127–1146), the victor of Edessa, was a Turkish-descended leader from Upper Iraq who took the admonitions of the historians to heart. He sponsored religious scholars who revived the teaching of the law of jihad and poets who sang his praise as a holy warrior. He, and later his sons, made steady (although slow) progress against the Crusader Kingdom from his principality of Aleppo. He weathered the Second Crusade of 1147–1149 but could not prevent the crusaders from repairing their strained relations with Byzantium. After submitting Antioch to Byzantine overlordship they received much-needed naval support in return. The king of Jerusalem took a Byzantine princess as his wife in 1158, and the emperor himself married a princess from Antioch in 1160. Constantinople and Jerusalem forged a powerful alliance.

The alliance paid off with a bold new initiative in 1169: A Byzantine fleet carried crusaders to agriculturally rich Fatimid Egypt for a full-fledged invasion. The Fatimids had never recovered from the loss of the Palestinian–Syrian coast after 1099 to the crusaders. A number of child caliphs in the 1160s signaled a serious dynastic enfeeblement. Unfortunately for the Byzantium–crusader alliance, however, the Muslims also eyed Egypt for its agricultural wealth. By 1171 Muslims had outfoxed the Christian alliance, ended the Fatimid dynasty, and joined Egypt to Aleppo and Damascus for the establishment of a formidable anticrusader realm.

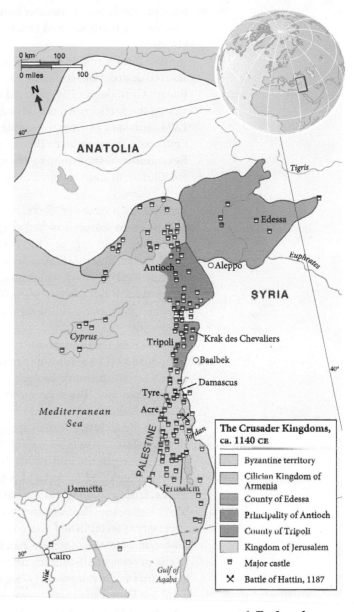

MAP 10.6 **The Crusader Kingdoms, ca. 1140 CE.**

**Jerusalem and Constantinople Lost**    The Sunni Muslim conquest of Shiite Egypt was a turning point for both the crusaders and Byzantium. The Kurdish-descended emir Saladin (Salah al-Din Yusuf Ibn Ayyub, r. 1174–1193), at the head of the new anticrusader realm, parlayed the agricultural wealth of Egypt into a formidable war machine that wore down the crusaders. In 1187 he succeeded in trapping the flower of crusader knighthood in the Battle of Hattin, near the Sea of Galilee. The battle enabled him to reconquer Jerusalem and nearly wipe out the kingdom.

The Third Crusade of 1189–1192 saved the rump kingdom from seemingly assured destruction. Its failure to regain Jerusalem, however, set the stage for the Fourth Crusade in 1204, planned as a mass campaign. But because of scheming among the participants, the crusade became instead a conquest of Byzantium in 1204. This sack of Constantinople underlines how crucial the failure of gaining Egypt as a resource was. The concentrated urban wealth of Constantinople in Byzantium was too tempting as a substitute for Egypt to be resisted, even if eastern Christians were brethren in the faith and Muslims the enemy.

**Precarious Crusader Survival for Another Century**  Not surprisingly, once western Europeans had stripped Constantinople bare and established a precarious Latin regime (1204–1257), the idea of conquering Egypt became an obsession. Five more crusades were launched for the benefit of the Kingdom of Jerusalem (1191–1291), which now was a narrow coastal strip of land with Acre as it capital. Only one of these crusades landed in Acre; all others sailed to, or toward, Egypt without ever yielding significant material returns or leading to permanent conquest.

Ironically, the one crusade that arrived in Acre yielded Jerusalem for a short period (1229–1244) through diplomacy and without the need of either Egypt or even a serious military campaign. But this diplomatic victory was more symbolical than real. The main reason why the kingdom survived as long as it did was that Italian and Syrian Muslim merchants had a common interest in conducting the lucrative Indian spice trade not only through Alexandria but also through Acre.

Beginning in the mid-1200s, however, it was only a question of time before the crusader kingdom would become the victim of new and powerful political forces arising in the Middle East. In 1250 the Mamluks—Turkish military slaves from the Russian steppes and dominant in the armies of Saladin's successors—established their own regime in Egypt (1250–1517). Barely in power, in 1260 the Mamluks had to face the pagan Mongols, who had emerged in the previous half-century under Genghis Khan (r. 1206–1227) and his descendants as a major power (see Chapter 13). The Mongols were conquerors of a giant but loosely organized cavalry-borne empire in central Asia, China, eastern Europe, and the eastern Middle East—so they were tough competition for the Mamluks.

The Mongols stormed into the Middle East in 1255, conquering Iran and Iraq, ending what remained of the Abbasid caliphate in Baghdad in 1258, and advancing into Syria. After conquering Baghdad, they tolerated the weak crusader kingdom, since their main target was the Mamluk Sultanate as the last remaining Islamic power in the Middle East. The Mamluks, however, defeated the Mongols in several battles between 1260 and 1303, thanks to their much heavier cavalry, and pushed them from Syria back into Iraq and Iran. Under the name of Ilkhanids, the Mongols converted to Islam and became linguistically Persian. Finally free of the Mongol threat, the Mamluks terminated the crusader state in 1291 with the conquest of Acre.

# Islamic and Eastern Christian Civilizations at Their Height

By 1300, the borders between western and eastern Christianity as well as Islam were again clearly drawn. The most important state was the Mamluk Sultanate in Egypt, Palestine, and Syria. It had been victorious against the crusaders and the Mongols and was the richest and most powerful state, enduring for nearly three centuries (1250–1517). It represented Middle Eastern Islamic civilization at its peak. Byzantium had been rebuilt as a small but culturally flourishing realm located mostly in the Balkans (1261–1453). Both were eventually succeeded by the Ottoman Empire (Chapter 16), the origins of which date to 1300, and which shifted the center of Islamic civilization from Egypt northward to Anatolia and the Balkans.

## State and Society in Mamluk Egypt

Few in the Mamluk ruling class spoke Arabic or intermarried with the indigenous population of their realm in Egypt and Syria. The indigenous population in turn possessed its own autonomous institutions, such as judicial courts, Sufi (mystics') lodges, and religious endowments. Although the Mamluks provided military protection, especially during the time of the Mongol attacks, the indigenous population had to pay for it dearly with high taxes and often arbitrary rule.

THE MAMLUK EMPIRE, ᴀᴅ. 1300

**The Mamluk Ruling Class**   At the top of the ruling class was the sultan, who controlled the annual purchases of slaves and commanded the largest cavalry regiment. Raiding parties in the Mongol state of the Golden Horde (1241–1502) on the Russian steppes (and later the Caucasus) captured boys and girls from nomadic tribes and sold them to Genoese mariners, who shipped the slaves to Alexandria. The popes protested against the slave trade but to no avail.

**Mamluk Cavalry.** Mamluk horsemen, protected by chainmail armor and wearing helmets, wielded swords and lances similar to the crusaders. Stationed in barracks on Nile islands near Cairo, the Asian-born, originally pagan, Muslim-educated Mamluks formed a standing army of a dozen regiments that trained daily and could be mobilized within a short time. Their children were not slaves but freeborn Muslims, who were admitted only to auxiliary military units. The Mamluks were a one-generation ruling class replenished regularly from the outside.

The Mamluk sultan governed with a council of a dozen or so emirs at his side. Each commanded a cavalry regiment of his own. The lesser emirs in the council were stationed in the provincial cities of Egypt and Syria. Additional auxiliary troops, both infantry and light cavalry, consisted of sons of Mamluks, tribal nomadic contingents, and freeborn Turks. The sultans maintained a lavish court in Cairo, which included a splendid kitchen and some of the finest cooks of their time. A large civilian bureaucracy, composed of Muslim, Coptic Christian, and Jewish scribes and accountants, staffed the three main ministries—correspondence and archives, tax collection, and army administration. Other officials oversaw the construction and/or administration of granaries, oil presses, the mint, hospitals, the postal service (including pigeon courier), water supplies, sanitation, stud farms, horse stables, and the hippodrome (for polo games). The maintenance of a standing, well-supplied army ready for mobilization at any moment was of utmost concern.

Mamluk power was based on a large, state-centered economy. At the center was a rich, irrigated agriculture that did not suffer from the salinization that plagued Iraq. The annual Nile flood at the height of the summer rolled down at a steeper slope than that of the lower Euphrates and Tigris and therefore flushed waste water out into the sea more easily. In the countryside, the top tier of Mamluk officers held tax assignments (*iqta*) in the form of village districts. They used the revenues from these assignments to pay the lower officers and regular soldiers of their regiments wages and food rations. Bureaucrats and managers recruited from the indigenous Arab population aided them in the collection of the taxes in grain and their sale on the market.

In the cities, the same top officers owned buildings and collected rents from residences, mills, ovens, workshops, inns, public baths, and bazaars. They hired large labor forces for the construction or repair of mosques, city walls, fortresses, and waterworks. Sultans and emirs even built entire city quarters. They usually paid regular wages to their workers but occasionally also used forced labor. The sultans had their own permanent labor force, which included prisoners and slaves. Their military campaigns were occasions for large numbers of craftspeople, traders, storytellers, entertainers, prostitutes, and other hangers-on to find additional employment. In short, nearly all economic activities in the villages as well as cities revolved around the demands of the sultans and emirs.

**The Urban Working Population**    Below the Mamluk ruling class and the intermediate urban elite of judges and religious scholars were craftspeople, laborers, domestics, and farmers. Urban working people lived in city quarters, which were organized according to religious (Christian, Jewish), ethnic (Arab, Kurdish, Persian), and, in the case of the Sunni majority, family and clan ties. The city quarters were not closed communities, however, and always contained minorities.

City quarters, crafts clusters, and neighborhood mosques and Sufi lodges were autonomous structures in urban life. Although overseen by appointees of the market inspectors, the residents often engaged in acts of resistance and rebellion against the Mamluks in times of famine, overtaxation, or arbitrary rule. In addition, Syrian cities, such as Damascus and Aleppo, had a long tradition of rebellious youth gangs fomenting unrest in suburbs and adjacent villages outside the city walls. The gang members wore distinctive hairstyles and cloaks and found their recruits mostly from among ditch diggers, canal dredgers, and brick layers as well as from among the occasional discontented cooks, traders, spinners, and carpenters.

During times of peace these gangs collected protection money from owners of workshops and market stalls, inevitably coming into conflict with the market inspectors and their deputies whose turf they invaded. At times of economic or political distress they linked forces across city quarters and transformed themselves into formidable militias, holding down entire Mamluk regiments for days or weeks. The gangs provided a degree of protection for society from the state.

**Divorce Court.** Husband and wife arguing about a divorce before a judge; scene from al-Hariri, *Maqamat* (ms. dated 1222). Hariri's stories, among the most popular during the classical period, involve a poor but eloquent storyteller traveling from town to town in different disguises but being recognized each time by the fictional author. The stories include occurrences of everyday life, like this divorce.

**Gender Relations**   Islamic civilization followed the traditional Middle Eastern patriarchal family system. Within this system, as we saw at the beginning of the chapter, married women had definite rights and were no longer the chattel they had been in the Assyrian Empire. But the Syrian Muslim leader Usama Ibn Munqidh (1095–1188) was shocked when he saw the behavior of the men and women in the crusader kingdom: Husbands allowed their wives to walk around alone in public and shake hands and converse with men to whom they were not married. The patriarchal order in Islamic civilization was clearly stricter than that in western Christianity. Ibn Munqidh had only contempt for crusaders who had such a low sense of honor that they even went home alone when their wives wished to continue their chats (perhaps even flirtations) with other men. Evidently, a significant cultural difference existed between western Christianity and Islamic civilization.

> "The Franks are without any vestige of a sense of honor and jealousy."
> —Usama Ibn Munqidh

## Byzantine Provincial and Central Organization

The one-generational system defining the Mamluk ruling class was a unique form of governmental organization in the history of Islamic religious civilization. Just as unique was the theme organization in the Byzantine Empire. The crucial difference, of course, was the time difference. The Mamluk Sultanate was a phenomenon at the height of Islamic civilization. The theme organization characterized the very beginning of the Byzantine Empire and was in the process of disappearing in 1204 when the empire was disrupted by the Fourth Crusade and subsequent Catholic regime in the Latin Empire (1204–1261). It was absent from the reconstituted Byzantine Empire in all but the name.

**The Rise of the Landed Aristocracy**   In Egypt the requirements of irrigation favored social uniformity and administrative centralization. Byzantium with its rain-fed agriculture oscillated between free smallholder farms and big landlords on one hand and a large central administration on the other. This central administration could grow as large as it did by ca. 1100 under conditions of relative external peace because it was well protected by its maritime location and well connected with most provinces by easy sea and river communication.

When the themes were introduced around 660 the empire still possessed a functional urban system and money economy, in contrast to much of western Europe where Roman urban institutions had withered more dramatically. Granted, the emperors settled foot soldiers and horsemen on plots of land in partial payment for their services. But they also still possessed the means to collect taxes in money and distribute them in the form of stipends among the soldiers. Furthermore, although it is estimated that about a fifth of the Anatolian land was allocated to the themes, mostly from imperial estates, plenty of small freeholders as well as large landlords inherited from the late Roman period coexisted with them.

In the difficult years of defense, the emperor and his central administration were relatively weak. They could protect only the themes but not the small farmers and thereby were unable to prevent the rise of the landed aristocracy. From about the mid-700s, landlords typically began to gobble up small farms and reserve the positions of theme generals for their families: they became a hereditary aristocracy. Free farmers turned increasingly into tenant farmers of the aristocracy, and it is estimated that by 1200 the free farmers (by now also including demilitarized themes) had become a minority. Like the Mamluk emirs a little later, the aristocratic landlords had become the wealthiest segment of imperial society.

**The Recentralization of the Empire**  Generals from the aristocracy were the main competitors for the office of emperor in Constantinople, from the beginning of the themes. But when the empire recovered and the central administration grew again from the 900s onwards, high officials of the bureaucracy developed their own ambitions hostile to those of the aristocracy. An administrative handbook of 899 listed 59 high officials invited to the emperor's banquet table and some 500 additional officials invited to palace receptions. By 1187, as evidenced by a palace muster in that year, the size of the bureaucracy had doubled, mostly through title inflation and the sale of offices. The court of Constantinople resembled that of Versailles many centuries later.

In the eleventh and twelfth centuries the emperors were typically torn between the interests of the aristocracy and the central administration. They shared the interests of the aristocrats by wishing to preserve the themes so that the territorial integrity of the empire would be preserved. But they also sided with the central administration by not wishing to be pawns of the aristocrats, their potential rivals. In the eleventh century few emperors were up to the task of long-term reforms, such as ensuring regular theme training or exercises and prohibiting the acquisition of land by the aristocracy.

The easy way out was to hire mercenaries, beginning with the Varangian Guard. Competent emperors, as from the Komnenos dynasty (1081–1185), however, realized that the financial capacity of the state was insufficient to hire more than small numbers of mercenaries into these guards. They made extensive use of a hitherto seldom used institution, the land assignment (*pronoia*), which allowed an assignee to collect all taxes from a parcel of land in return for military service. This institution, similar to that of the iqta used in Islamic countries (p. 282 above), became the backbone of a vast patronage system of family appointments and other leading families in Constantinople. Scholars have estimated that 90 percent of the upper military positions in the mid-1100s were occupied by members of the Komnenos family, with most paying themselves through assignments.

Of course, after the hiatus of 1204–1261, the court and its top families were largely gone. What were left were the aristocratic families in the reconstituted provinces. Their reluctance to submit permanently to the new Paleologs imperial family of post-1261 eventually doomed Byzantium when the Ottomans decided to end it in 1453.

## Commercial Relations from the Atlantic to the South China Sea

The Persians and Romans had pioneered the trade of gold and silver for subtropical and tropical luxuries during the period 600 BCE–600 CE, as we discussed in Chapter 7. An enormous leap forward in this trade occurred during the Fatimid and Mamluk periods in Egypt. It was clearly facilitated by the existence of a cultural unity in the enormous expanse of Islamic civilization, even if this civilization was politically fragmented into a commonwealth of autonomous realms. In addition,

Byzantium during its heyday (950–1050) and western Europe after the First Crusade (1099) were firmly integrated in this trade for luxuries. An Afro-Eurasian commercial world system, extending from West Africa to China and regularly connected by seasonal travel, linked the Islamic, eastern Christian, and western Christian civilizations to the Indian and Chinese civilizations (see Map 10.7).

**Trade Routes and Commerce**   To understand the West Africa–China world trade, we begin with West Africa. Villagers mined gold in the rain forest on the upper Niger and Senegal Rivers and traded with African merchants from kingdoms located along the middle Niger. The kings sent raiding parties to other regions in the rain forest to capture slaves. Merchants and kings then sold the gold and surplus of slaves not employed in the kingdoms to visiting Muslim merchants from North Africa and Iberia.

The visitors from the north paid with North African and Iberian manufactures and with salt from mines in the Sahara. In the Mediterranean basin, Muslims, Jews, and western and eastern Christians shared the trade of West African gold (minted into coins) and European timber for Indian and Indonesian spices, dye stuffs, ointments, and cottons as well as Chinese silks, porcelain, and lacquerware. The Mamluks did not allow Christians to travel beyond the Mediterranean, and thus Muslims, Jews, and Indians were the only groups who participated in the Indian Ocean and Chinese Sea trade of gold for luxuries.

In addition to these main routes, there were three secondary trade routes. First, there was the overland Silk Road with its gold-for-luxuries trade that connected Iran with China via central Asia, active particularly during the Mongol period. Second, there was the maritime East African trade route, where merchants exchanged manufactures for ivory, gold, and slaves. The latter route connected Egypt and Iraq with the Swahili Muslim city-states along the East African coast and the gold mines of Zimbabwe (see Chapter 14). And third, there was the Volga route, where Rus merchants traded gold, silver, spices, ivory, silk, wine, and fur, connecting the Middle East with western Europe. The Abbasid and Mamluk regiments were major consumers of the goods that flowed down from the Volga trade route, using Russian and Scandinavian furs for the designation of its ranks. Both primary and secondary trade routes yielded immense supplementary tax revenues, which added to the basic and highly dependable agricultural tax income of the Mamluks.

Islamic and Jewish merchants in the Egyptian center of this network were for the most part wholesalers for whom the import and distribution of eastern luxuries formed only a part of their overall commercial activities. They also organized the regional production and distribution of raw materials, such as textile fibers (wool, flax, cotton, and silk), chemicals for dyeing and tanning, metal ingots for making utensils and jewelry, and pitch for caulking ships' planks. They contracted with craftspeople for the production of soap, glassware, candles, and perfume. Tailors, cobblers, and sugar mill owners delivered robes, slippers, and bags of refined sugar to the merchants. To provide their accountants, scribes, porters, and guards with daily food, these merchants had caterers deliver lunches and dinners to their residences and warehouses. Merchants who were also **tax farmers** maintained grain stores, with employees responsible for collecting, shipping, brokering, and marketing the grain. Others farmed the taxes from ports or public

**Tax farming:** A system for collecting taxes and rents from the population, where the state grants the right of collection to private individuals.

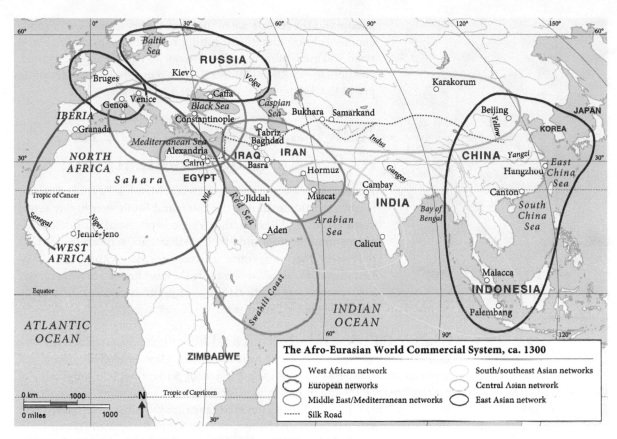

MAP **10.7 The Afro-Eurasian World Commercial System, ca. 1300.**

auction houses. Diversification was the preferred path to consistent profitability in the merchant class.

**The Black Death** Extensive travel, however, yielded not only profits but also unforeseen horrors. The more densely people lived together in cities and the more frequently they traveled, the more often they incurred the risk of spreading terrifying and lethal diseases hitherto confined to small, isolated regions of the world. The Black Death of 1346 was the second time that an outbreak of this ghastly plague occurred in world history (the first was the Plague of Justinian in 541; see Chapter 7). Scholars surmise that the Mongol invasion of Vietnam set off the spread of this horrific mid-fourteenth-century pandemic. The Mongols acquired the bubonic plague bacillus in southeast Asia, one of its permanent breeding grounds, from rodent fleas and dispersed it via China and the Silk Road to the Black Sea area. From here, Genoese merchants carried the virulent disease to the Mediterranean and northwest Europe (see Chapter 11 for a more detailed discussion of ravages of the bubonic plague).

Egyptian sources vividly recount the devastation which the plague wrought on the population. The plague was both sinister and incomprehensible to people at the time who had never experienced it. They possessed no effective medical resources, and thus found themselves powerless to fight it. Similarly difficult to

**Maritime Trade.** This image, an illustration in Hariri's *Maqamat* (ms. dated 1236), depicts a stylized oceangoing sailboat used between Arabia and India.

**Sufism:** Meditative devotion to faith, expressed in the form of prayer, ecstasy, chanting, or dancing.

fathom was the recurrence of the plague every generation or so for another century and a half, hitting rulers and subjects; rich and poor; and men, women, and children with equally appalling force. Not until the 1500s did Middle Eastern population levels recover to pre-1346 levels.

# Religion, Sciences, and the Arts in Two Religious Civilizations

Despite the impact of the Black Death, Mamluk Egypt and reconstituted Byzantium during the 1300s and 1400s were highly active cultural centers. Although they sought or received little further cultural stimuli from outside their civilizations, scholars and artists developed their respective cultures further within traditional boundaries. In Islamic civilization, the most important new cultural phenomenon was mystical (Sufi) Islam, and in eastern Christianity it was a revival of Platonism.

## Islamic Culture: Intellectual and Scientific Expressions

Like a number of other religions we have examined, Islam developed a devotional mystical tradition of its own. Mystical Islam, or **Sufism**, was an outgrowth of meditative thought and practices developed from the Christian, Zoroastrian, and Greek philosophical heritages interacting within the Muslim world. Around 1050 Muslim scholars integrated Sufism into the Sunni-dominated Islamic civilization, and around 1200 Sunni mystics adapted Sufism to popular practice in the form of congregational brotherhoods in lodges. Educated Muslims, in addition, were conversant in philosophy and the sciences, both of which experienced an important flowering in the period 1050–1300.

**Sunni–Sufi Islam** Sufism was a form of meditative practice that went beyond the prayers prescribed in Islam. A Sufi typically went step-by-step through stages to withdraw from sensory experience and arrive at the climax of pure ineffable consciousness. If pushed for words, Sufis identified this consciousness as their experience of the eternal and infinite divine. Since this experience took place within themselves, early Sufis in the 900s were often accused of violating the Islamic doctrine of God's transcendence. It was only in the second half of the eleventh century during the Seljuk-sponsored religious revival that a compromise was reached. The main figure representing this compromise was the Persian Abd al-Hamid al-Ghazali (1058–1111), who introduced a persuasive metaphor to illustrate the compromise: Believers, looking at a glass of red wine from a distance, are unable to decide whether they are not instead seeing an empty red glass. Ineffable experience cannot be expressed unambiguously.

In the 1200s, teachers of Sufism—often revered as saints—founded lodges in which they provided instruction and training in meditative practice for Muslims. With time, these lodges branched out, with hundreds of sublodges organized along the specific practices of its founder saints in urban centers as well as villages and even among nomadic tribes. Sunni Muslims of all walks of life joined, from legal scholars and judges to craftspeople, farmers, and nomads. By around 1450, Islamic civilization was a commonwealth not only of competing states but also of competing Sufi brotherhoods. The Sunni–Sufi compromise dominated in Islamic civilization until ca. 1900.

**Philosophy and Sciences**   As in the case of Sufism, philosophers also encountered opposition from among the proponents of Sunnism and did so for the same reason of violating the transcendence doctrine. Greek philosophical writings were accessible in translation from Syriac since the 800s and had attracted Muslim thinkers well before the emergence of mature Sunnism. A central concern of the Muslim philosophers was the reconciliation of Platonic-Aristotelian thought with Islam. Leading philosophers, such as Ibn Sina (Avicenna, ca. 980–1037) and Ibn Rushd (Averroes, 1126–1198), achieved this reconciliation by viewing philosophy as the discipline of logical concepts and religion its equivalent in images. Philosophy, requiring literacy and extensive education, was practiced by the few, while religion, which relied on imagery, was accessible to the uneducated masses. Ibn Khaldun (1332–1406), a philosopher of history and political theorist, accepted this division between the few and the masses but sided with the latter, finding philosophy and speculative theology incompatible with religion. As in western Christianity, thinkers struggled with the question of compatibility between thought and faith.

As in philosophy, scientific texts were also available in translation. Islamic scientists made major contributions early on, pushing beyond the discoveries of the Greeks. The Greeks had excelled in developing geometry into a mathematical science, but in the absence of a numbering system—they used letters as numbers—they had left algebra undeveloped until the Alexandrian period of Hellenism. The Persian Muhammad Ibn Musa al-Khwarizmi (ca. 780–850) laid the foundations for the conversion of algebra into a science. In his textbooks, computation is based on a decimal system of "Arabic" numerals, from 0 to 9. He borrowed this system from India (where it had been developed 150 years earlier) and introduced algebraic equations for the determination of unknown quantities, expressed through letters, as is still done today.

After Khwarizmi, mathematicians developed decimal fractions, raised numbers to high powers, extracted roots from large numbers, and investigated the properties of complex equations with roots and higher-degree powers. Persian and Arab astronomers simplified the work of the Hellenistic astronomer Ptolemy (d. ca. 168 CE), whose trigonometry operated with a confusing variety of three centers for the planetary system. Physicists elaborated on Archimedes' investigations into the physics of balances and weights and developed the impetus theory of motion (force applied to thrown objects), adopted in western Christian physics and much discussed there until the time of Galileo in the 1500s.

Medicine was based on comprehensive handbooks, with chapters on anatomy, bodily fluids ("humors"), diseases, diagnosis, surgery, therapy, and drugs. Specialized medical fields included ophthalmology (the treatment of eye diseases), obstetrics and pediatrics (which also dealt with sexual hygiene, birth, breast-feeding, childhood, and childhood diseases), as well as pharmacology, with descriptions of medicinal plants. The discovery in the 1200s of the pulmonary circulation system of the body anticipated similar European medical discoveries by several centuries, underlining the high degree of specialization which the sciences had reached in Islamic civilization.

## Artistic Expressions in Islamic Civilization

During the formative period of Islamic civilization (800–950), secular poetry and prose flourished. As Sunni–Sufi Islam fully evolved (1050–1200), religion was interwoven with the telling of stories, the painting of miniatures, and the building of mosques and palaces. Persian artistic traditions reemerged from pre-Islamic times, and Turkish central Asian steppe traditions entered Islamic culture.

**Islamic Literature**    The first extant poems in Arabic were odes celebrating the tribal ethos of courage, trust, generosity, and hospitality in Arabia (800s). They follow the quest theme common to many folktales and myths, with its three distinct stages of loss, marginality, and reintegration that the hero has to experience to find peace. In the cosmopolitan culture of Baghdad, new forms of literature evolved which brought together highly literate secretaries and officials from a variety of non-Arab ethnic backgrounds. They cultivated poetry with urban themes, such as the pleasures of sensual abandonment, seduction, and homosexual love. Essays expressing refined taste, elegance, and wit circulated widely, on topics such as "The Art of Keeping One's Mouth Shut," "Against Civil Servants," "Arab Food," and "Levity and Seriousness." The most popular collection of short stories was the *Maqamat,* about an impersonator telling tall stories to gullible listeners, collecting money for his tales, and traveling from city to city in ever-new disguises. Another collection of stories, the *Arabian Nights*, was first written down in Mamluk Damascus during the 1300s. Even today, one admires the refined taste, elegance, and wit that people of cosmopolitan Islamic urbanity possessed.

Persian and Turkish Muslims preserved their pre-Islamic pasts in epics celebrating the heroic deeds of their ancestral leaders in central Asia. In the case of the Iranian *Shahs*, the poet Firdosi (940–1020) spent a lifetime collecting the traditions of the Persians and rendering them into the 60,000 verses of the *Book of Kings (Shanameh)*. The anonymous epic *Dede Korkut* originated among the central Asian Turks at the time of the Arab conquests and was written down in the 1300s. Both ethnic groups also produced outstanding poets, especially mystical poets, among whom the Afghanistan-born Jalal al-Din Rumi (1207–1273) acquired worldwide popularity. Similar to Ghazali, Rumi sought to illustrate the complexities of God's transcendence-cum-immanence through ambiguities and paradoxes. Although Arabic remained the basic literary language, Persian gained increasingly in popularity.

**Painting and Architecture in Islam**    In the visual arts, Arabs and early Muslims continued to create paintings and sculptures in the hybrid realistic-hieratic style which had become common in the Mediterranean and Middle East during the 300s. The realism of the Greek sculptures and Roman frescoes was mixed with the hieratic figurative art of Sasanid reliefs. In the hieratic style, artists sought to capture the essence of their subjects, often neglecting the light-and-shadow as well as three-dimensional representational style typical of realism. Modern viewers have often described this hybrid style as less artistic and refined than that of Greco-Roman realism. But this description does not take into account the long tradition of Mesopotamian hieratic conventions which culminated with the Sasanid Persians. These conventions constitute an artistic style in its own right, even if it is perhaps less appealing to modern tastes.

Moreover, since Islamic law contains prohibitions against painting and sculpting, similar to Byzantine iconoclasm, the visual arts disappeared entirely from public spaces and retreated to the domestic sphere of the courts of rulers. The Umayyad and early Abbasid caliphs loved frescoes with hunting, drinking, and dancing scenes but confined them to the chambers of their palaces. The rulers of Granada in the 1400s enjoyed scenes of courtly love in their royal chambers. The Seljuk and Ilkhanid rulers were lavish sponsors of miniature painters. They delighted in richly illustrated biographies and histories, which played a role in their libraries similar to that of coffee-table books today.

By contrast, the architecture of mosques and palaces was intended for public use, often in commemoration of their state sponsors. Mosques followed the architectural style of the Arab open courtyard and covered prayer hall or Persian open courtyard with surrounding half domes and galleries, both with roots in the pre-Islamic past of the Middle East. Among the surviving palaces, the best preserved is the Alhambra of Granada (ca. 1350–1450), with its exquisite honeycomb-style decorations. Religious and palace architectures were perhaps the most direct forms in which the identity of Islamic culture was expressed. They are still admired today for their variation and richness.

## Learning and the Arts in Byzantium

In contrast to Islamic civilization, the eastern Christianity of Byzantium was a fully formed religious civilization from its beginning in 640, even if it underwent major doctrinal changes thereafter. The principal institutions of higher learning were the secular Magnaura and the theological Hagia Sophia, which offered the study of the liberal arts and theology. The liberal arts included the preparatory *trivium* (grammar, rhetoric, and dialectics), advanced *quadrivium* (arithmetic, geometry, music, and astronomy), and philosophy as the capstone. During its difficult struggle for survival against the Arabs, Slavs, Bulgars, and Rus, Constantinople declined in both wealth and sponsorship of knowledge and the arts. The copying of texts and teaching survived tenuously.

In the arts, Byzantine iconoclasm during the 700s and 800s caused the destruction of innumerable and irreplaceable icons and mosaics. It also disrupted the transmission of artistic techniques from masters to subsequent generations of artists. When the public display and veneration of images became the officially sanctioned doctrine again in the mid-800s, it took a while for the arts to recover. As artists were relearning their craft, they engaged in much initial experimentation.

**Revival of Learning**    The subsequent mature period of ca. 950–1200 saw a veritable explosion in the production of icons, mosaics, and frescoes as well as the building of new churches and monasteries. Byzantine mosaic craftspeople and painters were also much sought after by the caliphs in Córdoba, who avoided hiring artists from their Abbasid and Fatimid rivals. Byzantine craftspeople were

also popular with the princes of Kiev, who, after their conversion, carried the Byzantine arts into the commonwealth of eastern Christian states, providing it with an immediately visible cultural unity.

Higher learning revived noticeably after 950. The state built a number of public schools of law and philosophy in the middle of the 1000s, followed by a church school for theology at the end of the century. Philosophers revived the tradition of commenting on Plato, Aristotle, and the Neoplatonic synthesis inherited from Hellenistic antiquity. This revival aroused among churchmen the same suspicions as among the Muslim scholars and led to the condemnation of some philosophers. Two outstanding figures were Michael Psellos (ca. 1017–1078) and John Italos (fl. eleventh century). Both taught many students, but church or palace hostility forced them at points in their careers to cease teaching.

**Byzantine Renaissance** The disruption of 1204–1261 by the Fourth Crusade and Latin Empire saw a tremendous loss of Byzantine art as well as manuscripts, this time to Venetian pillage during the Fourth Crusade. When Byzantium was restored Plato scholars initiated a strong recovery of philosophy, which resulted in a return of western Christians, this time peacefully, to that city in search of Platonic writings. The Academy of Florence, a leading institution of the Italian Renaissance (see Chapter 17), invited Byzantine Plato scholars to help in the recovery of the texts of this philosopher. Further scholars emigrated to Italy after the fall of Constantinople to the Ottomans in 1453. Thus, western Christianity renewed its adaptation to stimuli from a neighboring civilization, in contrast to eastern Christianity and Islamic civilization, which continued within their existing traditions.

# Putting It All Together

Both Islamic civilization and eastern Christian civilization were based on a synthesis of religious revelation and Greek philosophy and science. This synthesis had begun in the Roman and Sasanid Persian Empires. Muslims accomplished their cultural synthesis after the period of Arab conquest, roughly during 800–950. Eastern Christians completed their synthesis in the period 950–1050, after their recovery from the Arab, Slav, Bulgar, and Rus onslaughts. Both refined their internal civilizational achievements to a high degree well into the 1400s. Thereafter, they did not absorb substantial new cultural stimuli from the outside until about 1700, when the Muslim Ottoman sultans invited western Europeans to reform their empire.

Islamic civilization was an outgrowth of the Arab conquests in the Middle East, Central Asia, northern Africa, and Europe in the 600s and early 700s. It emerged as an adaptation of the Arabs to the heritages of the Jews, Christians, Greeks, Romans, and Persians. Its core was the monotheism of Allah, and its cultural adaptations were to Greek philosophy and science, Roman law, and Persian statecraft, as well as a variety of artistic and architectural traditions of the Middle East and Mediterranean. At its height, during 950–1450, a commonwealth of competing Islamic states represented Islamic civilization. This ethnically diverse commonwealth with Arab, Turkish, Persian, and Berber rulers and states shared a number of common characteristics, among which were the same canon of scriptures (the Quran and the Sunna), laws and moral norms (Sharia), and religious institutions (separate state and religious authorities as well as Sunni–Sufi brotherhoods). These characteristics endured to 1300.

The Byzantine Empire succeeded the Roman Empire around 640 when the emperors, under attack by the Arabs, reorganized their military forces and redefined the inherited Christian theology. Byzantium recovered politically and culturally in the mid-900s, and the empire changed into a commonwealth when Russian Kievan Rus converted to eastern Christianity. Unfortunately, the recovery lasted only a century. The Seljuk Muslim Turks conquered most Anatolian provinces of Byzantium (1071–1176), and the Venetians conquered Constantinople in the Fourth Crusade and established the Latin Empire (1204–1261). Byzantium recovered thereafter for another two and a half centuries and even flourished culturally, but after 1453 the center of eastern Christian civilization shifted northward to Russia.

▶ For additional resources, including maps, primary sources, visuals, and quizzes, please go to www.oup.com/us/vonsivers. Please see the Further Resources section at the back of the book for additional readings and suggested websites.

## Against the Grain

# Did Ibn Taymiyya "Have a Screw Loose"?

Born in Harran, northern Iraq, Taqi al-Din Ibn Taymiyya (1263–1328) became a refugee as a small child when his family of prominent religious scholars fled from the pagan Mongols, fulfilling their Sharia duty to live in a Muslim-governed country. Ibn Taymiyya grew up in Damascus, then ruled by the Egyptian Mamluks, and became a prominent religious scholar in the Hanbali legal school.

Among the four legal schools, the Hanbali school was the one most devoted to the study of the Quran and prophetic traditions. Ibn Taymiyya invoked these traditions when he dedicated his scholarly career to combating the form of popular brotherhood and saintly Islam dominant in the Islamic world at the time. In his view, Muslims engaged in popular brotherhood activities and devoted to Muslim saints were insufficiently committed to Islam. He did not condemn, however, Sunnis engaging in spiritual Sufi practices as individuals, engaging in retreat, prayer, and meditation—a point often overlooked by modern reformist Muslims, for whom he is a hero.

Most of Ibn Taymiyya's contemporaries would have shrugged off Ibn Tamiyya's rantings against brotherhood members listening to music, dancing, and visiting saints' tombs for blessings, had he not shown exemplary courage during a time of continuing Mongol attacks. Since 1260 the Mongols had tried to conquer Mamluk Syria and Egypt, and in 1299–1303 they succeeded in occupying parts of Syria. At one point during the occupation, the Mamluks sent a mission of religious scholars, including Ibn Taymiyya, to the Mongols to implore their ruler Ghazan (r. 1295–1304) in the name of Islam to end his attacks. Ghazan had officially converted to Islam in 1295 but continued to adhere to Mongol law rather than the Islamic Sharia. Only Ibn Taymiyya had the courage to stand before the Mongol ruler and accuse him of being an infidel, lecturing him sternly on his Muslim duties of adherence to Islamic law and peace. This feat of courage earned Ibn Taymiyya both admiration and resentment from scholars of the other religious schools.

Ibn Taymiyya, a loner since his youth who never married or even had a concubine, apparently had both an aura of self-importance and a short temper—hence the unkind surmise by one contemporary scholar concerning his mental balance. (The rendering of this as "a screw loose" is by the Middle East scholar Donald P. Little.) It was this arrogance which Ibn Taymiyya's detractors confronted, attacking him on his own ground of legalism. They accused him of violating the Islamic unity doctrine himself in his teachings and misinterpreting the doctrine of fighting the infidels as a religious duty.

As a result of these accusations, the Mamluks imprisoned Ibn Taymiyya. In the end, Ibn Taymiyya died in jail, a lone dissenter during a time when the majority of Muslims adhered to the different form of saintly Islam. His teachings were revived, however, in the twentieth century when Islamists reclaimed him as the preacher of an Islamic revolution against their own "Mongol" rulers and Islamic laxity in general.

- **Was Ibn Taymiyya right in standing up against the Muslims of his time and in preaching jihad against Mongols who had converted to Islam? If yes, for which reasons?**

- **Are contemporary Islamists correct in claiming that their present situation in Islamic countries closely resembles that of Ibn Taymiyya facing the Mongols? If yes, are rulers in contemporary Islamic countries similar to the Mongols?**

# Thinking Through Patterns

▶ **Why can the period 600–1450 be described as the age of religious civilizations? How do eastern Christian and Islamic civilizations fit this description?**

The adoption of Christianity and Zoroastrianism as state or privileged monotheistic religions in the Roman and Sasanid Empires was late and ultimately did not prevent these empires from eventual collapse. But both empires helped launch the period of religious civilizations. New empires arose in this period, beginning around 600. Byzantium was Christian from its inception. The Arab Empire adopted Islam early on, initially under the Umayyads and fully in the Abbasid-led commonwealth of states. Eastern Christian and Islamic civilizations were characteristic of religious civilizations because both embraced basic religious scriptures, upheld a form of separation of state and religion, and adapted to inherited cultural traditions.

Specifically, the pattern of Islamic civilization included revealed scripture, a religiously interpreted history, the separation of state and religion, the fusion of revealed religion and Greek philosophy, and the adaptation to the scientific and artistic heritage from Rome and Persia. The pattern was completed early, by about 950 with the emergence of Sunni Islam, but continued to evolve internally, without further outside stimuli, through Sufi Islam and a myriad of Sufi brotherhood lodges. The result was an Islamic civilization around 1300 which was composed of many states and even more autonomous religious congregations existing alongside the mosques.

▶ **Which cultural traditions combined to form Islamic religious civilization? What were the most characteristic patterns?**

▶ **How did eastern Christian or Byzantine civilization evolve over time? On which institutions was this civilization based, and how did it evolve, wedged between Islamic and western Christian civilizations?**

The late Roman Empire achieved a close integration of Christianity, Greek-Hellenistic philosophy and science, and Roman law, but it was hard-pressed for survival by the conquering Arabs. When the eastern Roman, or Byzantine, Empire recovered, it elevated eastern Greek Orthodox Christianity to a supreme position. A powerful recentralization effort strengthened the empire, especially in the Balkans. But in the wake of the Seljuk invasions and western Christian Crusades, the empire weakened again, surviving in a much diminished form until it was conquered by the Ottoman Muslims in 1453. Eastern Christianity survived as a state religion in Russia.

# Patterns of Evidence: Sources for Chapter 10

SOURCE 10.1

## Excerpts from the Quran, *Sura* 2, "The Cow"

**ca. 650 CE**

The name of the most holy book of Islam, the Quran, means "the recital." It contains, according to Islamic theology, the direct words of God (Allah), as told to his prophet Muhammad through the angel Gabriel. Muslims believe that the angel directed Muhammad to "recite" 114 *suras*, or books, beginning around 610 CE. After Muhammad's death in 632, an authorized text of these *suras* was compiled and publicized. The general arrangement of the Quran is according to the length of each document. It is important to note, therefore, that the Quran does not purport to be a continuous narrative, telling a series of stories, as is typical in other religious texts. This means that individual pronouncements can be taken out of context, and that various portions of the document can be quoted to different effects.

**2:177**
Righteousness is not that you turn your faces toward the east or the west, but [true] righteousness is [in] one who believes in Allah , the Last Day, the angels, the Book, and the prophets and gives wealth, in spite of love for it, to relatives, orphans, the needy, the traveler, those who ask [for help], and for freeing slaves; [and who] establishes prayer and gives *zakah* [charitable gifts]; [those who] fulfill their promise when they promise; and [those who] are patient in poverty and hardship and during battle. Those are the ones who have been true, and it is those who are the righteous.

**2:178**
O you who have believed, prescribed for you is legal retribution for those murdered—the free for the free, the slave for the slave, and the female for the female. But whoever overlooks from his brother anything, then there should be a suitable follow-up and payment to him with good conduct. This is an alleviation from your Lord and a mercy. But whoever transgresses after that will have a painful punishment.

**2:179**
And there is for you in legal retribution [saving of] life, O you [people] of understanding, that you may become righteous.

**2:180**
Prescribed for you when death approaches [any] one of you if he leaves wealth [is that he should make] a bequest for the parents and near relatives

Source: Sahih International translation, available online at http://quran.com/4.

according to what is acceptable—a duty upon the righteous.

### 2:181

Then whoever alters the bequest after he has heard it—the sin is only upon those who have altered it. Indeed, Allah is Hearing and Knowing.

### 2:182

But if one fears from the bequeather [some] error or sin and corrects that which is between them, there is no sin upon him. Indeed, Allah is Forgiving and Merciful.

### 2:183

O you who have believed, decreed upon you is fasting as it was decreed upon those before you that you may become righteous.

### 2:184

[Fasting for] a limited number of days. So whoever among you is ill or on a journey [during them]—then an equal number of days [are to be made up]. And upon those who are able [to fast, but with hardship]—a ransom [as substitute] of feeding a poor person [each day]. And whoever volunteers excess—it is better for him. But to fast is best for you, if you only knew.

### 2:185

The month of Ramadhan [is that] in which was revealed the Qur'an, a guidance for the people and clear proofs of guidance and criterion. So whoever sights [the new moon of] the month, let him fast it; and whoever is ill or on a journey—then an equal number of other days. Allah intends for you ease and does not intend for you hardship and [wants] for you to complete the period and to glorify Allah for that [to] which He has guided you; and perhaps you will be grateful.

### 2:186

And when My servants ask you, [O Muhammad], concerning Me—indeed I am near. I respond to the invocation of the supplicant when he calls upon Me. So let them respond to Me [by obedience] and believe in Me that they may be [rightly] guided.

### 2:187

It has been made permissible for you the night preceding fasting to go to your wives [for sexual relations]. They are clothing for you and you are clothing for them. Allah knows that you used to deceive yourselves, so He accepted your repentance and forgave you. So now, have relations with them and seek that which Allah has decreed for you. And eat and drink until the white thread of dawn becomes distinct to you from the black thread [of night]. Then complete the fast until the sunset. And do not have relations with them as long as you are staying for worship in the mosques. These are the limits [set by] Allah , so do not approach them. Thus does Allah make clear His ordinances to the people that they may become righteous.

### 2:188

And do not consume one another's wealth unjustly or send it [in bribery] to the rulers in order that [they might aid] you [to] consume a portion of the wealth of the people in sin, while you know [it is unlawful].

### 2:189

They ask you, [O Muhammad], about the new moons. Say, "They are measurements of time for the people and for Hajj." And it is not righteousness to enter houses from the back, but righteousness is [in] one who fears Allah. And enter houses from their doors. And fear Allah that you may succeed.

### 2:190

Fight in the way of Allah those who fight you but do not transgress. Indeed Allah does not like transgressors.

**2:191**

And kill them wherever you overtake them and expel them from wherever they have expelled you, and fitnah [distress, civil strife, sedition] is worse than killing. And do not fight them at al-Masjid al-Haram until they fight you there. But if they fight you, then kill them. Such is the recompense of the disbelievers.

**2:192**

And if they cease, then indeed, Allah is Forgiving and Merciful.

**2:193**

Fight them until there is no [more] fitnah and [until] worship is [acknowledged to be] for Allah . But if they cease, then there is to be no aggression except against the oppressors.

**2:194**

[Fighting in] the sacred month is for [aggression committed in] the sacred month, and for [all] violations is legal retribution. So whoever has assaulted you, then assault him in the same way that he has assaulted you. And fear Allah and know that Allah is with those who fear Him.

**2:195**

And spend in the way of Allah and do not throw [yourselves] with your [own] hands into destruction [by refraining]. And do good; indeed, Allah loves the doers of good.

▶ **Working with Sources**

1. **What are the requirements of believers, and what benefits and punishments are promised in response to their actions?**

2. **Why is it important to observe the rules regarding fasting and the pilgrimage?**

## SOURCE 10.2

# Documents related to the iconoclasm controversy

### Seventh–ninth centuries CE

The Byzantine Empire was racked by a series of religious disputes that pulled in emperors as well as priests. One of the most significant of these was an ongoing difference of opinion concerning "graven images" of Jesus and other prominent figures in Christian narratives. Was it proper to create and display images of God, and, if so, should existing "icons" be destroyed in order to protect the faithful? These documents represent the two major perspectives on this debate, between the poles of the "iconodule" (pro-icon) position and the "iconoclastic" (anti-icon) position.

Source: Excerpts from Anthony Bryer and Judith Herrin, eds., *Iconoclasm: Papers Given at the Ninth Spring Symposium of Byzantine Studies, University of Birmingham, March 1975* (Birmingham, UK: Centre for Byzantine Studies, University of Birmingham, 1977), available online at http://www.tulane.edu/~august/H303/readings/Iconoclasm.htm.

ICONODULE POSITION:

**1.** Quinsextum Council (in Trullo), 692 CE, ruling by Justinian II (685–695; 705–711):

"Now, in order that perfection be represented before the eyes of all people, even in paintings, we ordain that from now on Christ our God, the Lamb who took upon Himself the sins of the world, be set up, even in images according to His human character, instead of the ancient Lamb. Through this figure we realize the height of the humiliation of God the Word and are led to remember His life in the flesh, His suffering, and His saving death, and the redemption ensuing from it for the world."

**2.** John of Damascus (675–749), Oration (*Patrologia orientalis* 94, cols. 1258C-D):

"When we set up an image of Christ in any place, we appeal to the senses, and indeed we sanctify the sense of sight, which is the highest among the perceptive senses, just as by sacred speech we sanctify the sense of hearing. An image is, after all, a reminder; it is to the illiterate what a book is to the literate, and what the word is to the hearing, the image is to sight. We remember that God ordered that a vessel be made from wood that would not rot, gilded inside and out, and that the tables of the law should be placed in it and the staff and the golden vessel containing the manna—all this for a reminder of what had taken place, and a foreshadowing of what was to come. What was this but a visual image, more compelling than any sermon? And this sacred thing was not placed in some obscure corner of the tabernacle; it was displayed in full view of the people, so that whenever they looked at it they would give honor and worship to the God Who had through its contents made known His design to them. They were of course not worshipping the things themselves; they were being led through them to recall the wonderful works of God, and to adore Him Whose words they had witnessed."

**3.** *Horos* (Definition of Faith) at the Seventh Ecumenical Council, Nicaea, 787 CE:

"We define with accuracy and care that the venerable and holy icons be set up like the form of the venerable and life-giving Cross, inasmuch as the matter consisting of colors and pebbles and other matter is appropriate in the holy church of God, on sacred vessels and vestments, walls and panels, in houses and on the roads, as well as the images of our Lord and God and Savior Jesus Christ, of our undefiled Lady of the Holy Mother of God, of the angels worthy of honor, and of all the holy and pious men. For the more frequently they are seen by means of pictorial representation the more those who behold them are aroused to remember and desire the prototypes and to give them greeting and worship of honor—but not the true worship of our faith which befits only the divine nature—but to offer them both incense and candles, in the same way as to the form and the venerable and life-giving Cross and the holy Gospel and to the other sacred objects, as was the custom even of the ancients."

ICONOCLASTIC POSITION:

**1.** The *Horos* (Definition of Faith) at the Council of Hiera, 754 CE:

"The divine nature is completely uncircumscribable and cannot be depicted or represented in any medium whatsoever. The word Christ means both God and Man, and an icon of Christ would therefore have to be an image of God in the flesh of the Son of God. But this is impossible. The artist would fall either into the heresy which claims that the divine and human natures of Christ are separate or into that which holds that there is only one nature of Christ."

**2.** The *Horos* (Definition of Faith) at Iconoclastic Council of 815 CE:

"Wherefore, taking to heart the correct doctrine, we banish from the Catholic Church the unwarranted manufacture of the spurious icons that has been so audaciously proclaimed, impelled as we are by a judicious judgment; nay, by passing a righteous judgment upon the veneration of icons that has been injudiciously proclaimed by Tarasius [Patriarch, 784–802] and so refuting it, we declare his assembly [i.e., Seventh Ecumenical Council in 787] invalid in that it bestowed exaggerated honor to painting, namely, as has already been said, the lighting of candles and lamps and the offering of incense, these marks of veneration being those of worship. We gladly accept, on the other hand, the pious council that was held at Blachernae, in the church of the all-pure Virgin, under the pious Emperors Constantine V and Leo IV [in 754] that was fortified by the doctrine of the Fathers, and in preserving without alteration what was expressed by it, we decree that the manufacture of icons is unfit for veneration and useless. We refrain, however, from calling them idols since there is a distinction between different kinds of evil."

▶ **Working with Sources**

1. Do you find one of the positions in this theological debate more convincing than the other? Why?

2. Was it necessary for the Byzantine emperors to intervene in this controversy? Why or why not?

## SOURCE 10.3

# Memoirs of Usama Ibn Munqidh

### ca. 1180s

A scholar, a gentleman, and a warrior, Usama (1095–1187) had ample opportunity to meet crusader forces in person on the battlefield and in civilian life. After a distinguished military career, he became a consultant and advisor to Saladin in 1174, and he oversaw the surrender of Beirut, as its governor, to crusader forces. Basking in Saladin's favor, Usama became

Source: *An Arab-Syrian Gentleman and Warrior in the Period of the Crusades: Memoirs of Usāmah ibn-Munqidh*, trans. Philip K. Hitti (Princeton, NJ: Princeton University Press, 1987), 160–161, 162–163, and 164–165.

the center of attention in Damascus. He began a memoir describing the various peoples whom he had encountered during his long and adventurous life. His observations are often humorous, sometimes baffling, but always imbued with curiosity about people whose customs are strange—and intriguing.

Among the Frankish [i.e., Crusaders, known to Arabs as "al-Ifranj"] captives who were carried into my father's home was an aged woman accompanied by her daughter—a young woman of great beauty—and a robust son. The son accepted Islam, and his conversion was genuine, judging by what he showed in the practice of prayer and fasting. He learned the art of working marble from a stonecutter who had paved the home of my father. After staying for a long time with us my father gave him as wife a woman who belonged to a pious family, and paid all necessary expenses for his wedding and home. His wife bore him two sons. The boys grew up. When they were five or six years old, their father, young Rā'ūl, who was very happy at having them, took them with their mother and everything that his house contained and on the second morning joined the Franks in Afāmiyah, where he and his children became Christians after having practiced Islam with its prayers and faith. May Allah, therefore, purify the world from such people!

Mysterious are the works of the Creator, the author of all things! When one comes to recount cases regarding the Franks, he cannot but glorify Allah (exalted is he!) and sanctify him, for he sees them as animals possessing the virtues of courage and fighting, but nothing else; just as animals have only the virtues of strength and carrying loads. I shall now give some instances of their doings and their curious mentality.

. . .

The king of the Franks [Fulk of Anjou, king of Jerusalem] had for treasurer a knight named Bernard, who (may Allah's curse be upon him!) was one of the most accursed and wicked among the Franks. A horse kicked him in the leg, which was subsequently infected and which opened in fourteen different places. Every time one of these cuts would close in one place, another would open in another place. All this happened while I was praying for his perdition. Then came to him a Frankish physician and removed from the leg all the ointments which were on it and began to wash it with very strong vinegar. By this treatment all the cuts were healed and the man became well again. He was up again like a devil.

Another case illustrating their curious medicine is the following:

In Shayzar we had an artisan named abu-al-Fath, who had a boy whose neck was afflicted with scrofula. Every time a part of it would close, another part would open. This man happened to go to Antioch on business of his, accompanied by his son. A Frank noticed the boy and asked his father about him, "Wilt thou swear by thy religion that if I prescribe to thee a medicine which will cure thy boy, thou wilt charge nobody fees for prescribing it thyself? In that case, I shall prescribe to thee a medicine which will cure the boy." The man took the oath and the Frank said:

"Take uncrushed leaves of glasswort, burn them, then soak the ashes in olive oil and sharp vinegar. Treat the scrofula with them until the spot on which it is growing is eaten up. Then take burnt lead, soak it in ghee butter and treat him with it. That will cure him."

The father treated the boy accordingly, and the boy was cured. The sores closed and the boy returned to his normal condition of health.

I have myself treated with this medicine many who were afflicted with such disease, and the treatment was successful in removing the cause of the complaint.

. . .

Here is an illustration which I myself witnessed:

When I used to visit Nāblus, I always took lodging with a man named Mu'izz, whose home was a lodging house for the Moslems. The house had windows which opened to the road, and there stood opposite to it on the other side of the road a house belonging to a Frank who sold wine for the merchants. He would take some wine in a bottle and go around announcing it by shouting, "So and so, the merchant, has just opened a cask full of this wine. He who wants to buy some of it will find it in such and such a place." The Frank's pay for the announcement made would be the wine in that bottle. One day this Frank went home and found a man with his wife in the same bed. He asked him, "What could have made thee enter into my wife's room?" The man replied, "I was tired, so I went in to rest." "But how," asked he, "didst thou get into my bed?" The other replied, "I found a bed that was spread, so I slept in it." "But," said he, "my wife was sleeping together with thee!" The other replied, "Well, the bed is hers. How could I therefore have prevented her from using her own bed?" "By the truth of my religion," said the husband, "if thou shouldst do it again, thou and I would have a quarrel." Such was for the Frank the entire expression of his disapproval and the limit of his jealousy.

▶ Working with Sources

1. What proof does Usama offer of the uncivilized nature of the Christian invaders of the Middle East?

2. How does he demonstrate Islamic cultural, if not always military, superiority in his account?

## SOURCE 10.4

# A Jewish engagement contract from Fustat (Old Cairo)

### 11 November 1146

A treasure trove of letters, contracts, legal instruments, etc., known as the Cairo Geniza, attests to the lives of both prominent and average Jewish people, especially in the eleventh and twelfth centuries. Due to their *dhimma* status (that is, officially recognized religious minorities in a predominantly Muslim state), Jews lived under the constant threat of reprisals and violent raids throughout the Middle East (as well as in Europe) in this period. Nevertheless, they were also able to engage in normal business and personal activities, and these documents provide a welcome window into daily life.

This is a copy of the engagement contract of Abū Mansūr Semah, son of Rabbāna Japheth [known as] the elder Abū 'Alī, the perfumer, to Sitt al-Khāssa, the daughter of the elder Abu 'l-Barakāt Ibn al-Lebdī.

On Monday, the fifth day of the month of Kislev of the year 1458 of the era of the documents, in Fustat, Egypt, which is situated on the Nile River and which is under the jurisdiction of our lord Samuel, the great Nagrid—may his name be forever, M. Semah, the young man, son of M. and R. Japheth the elder, son of M. and R. Tiqvā, the elder, the Friend of the yeshiva—may he rest in Eden—concluded a match with Sitt al-Khāssa, his fiancée, a virgin, the daughter of M. and R. Berakhōt, the elder—may he rest in Eden.

His obligation is a first installment of 40 certified dinars, to be given as a gift at the time of the wedding, and a final installment of 100 certified dinars. Abū Mansūr Semah, the fiancé, presented the 40 dinars of the first installment, and the elder Abu 'l-'Alā' Musallam, the perfumer, son of Sahl, received them from him. The wedding is set for the month of Kislev of the coming year—may we be destined for life in it—which is the coming year 1459 [1147].

Semah assumed these obligations toward Sitt al-Khāssa: She will be regarded as trustworthy in all that concerns food and drink in the house, no suspicion may be cast upon her, nor can he demand from her an oath concerning any of these things, not even a supplementary oath. He may not marry another woman, nor retain a maidservant whom she dislikes. Should he do any of these things, the final installment is hers, and he must release her [from the marriage bond by divorce]. In the case that there are no children, half of what remains of the dowry returns to her family. She may choose the place and the domicile where she wishes to live. The rent

Source: S. D. Goitein, *A Mediterranean Society: The Jewish Communities of the Arab World as Portrayed in the Documents of the Cairo Geniza*, vol. 4 (Berkeley: University of California Press, 1983), 317–319.

of her properties is hers, she may spend it for whatever purpose she prefers; he has no say in the matter.

Should he nullify this engagement contract and not marry her during the said Kislev, she will receive 20 dinars. This is a debt and an obligation, binding [as from now]. We made the symbolic purchase from M. Semah, the young man, for Sitt al-Khāssa, the fiancée, according to all that is recorded above, a purchase which is definite and strict, made with the proper object for such a transaction.

We also made the symbolic purchase from Sitt al-Sāda, the daughter of the elder Abū Nasr, the physician, the mother of Sitt al-Khāssa, the fiancée, in the most rigorous terms, binding as from now: Should her daughter Sitt al-Khāssa nullify the engagement contract and refuse to marry the fiancé during the said month of Kislev, she would owe the fiancé 20 [dinars]. . . . This has taken place after the verification of her identity.

Signatures: Mevōrākh b. Solomon [of] b[lessed] m[emory]. Sadaqa b————.

▶ **Working with Sources**

1. Are the parties to this contract eager to demonstrate, particularly to Muslim officials, that they understand business affairs and can conduct them sensibly among themselves?

2. What differences are reflected in this document between the roles of women and men with respect to marriage?

## SOURCE 10.5

# *The Alchemy of Happiness,* by Abd al-Hamid al-Ghazali

### ca. 1095–1105

**B**orn in 1058 to a family of spinners and sellers of wool in a small village in eastern Iran, Ghazali became one of the most prominent expounders of Islamic theology of his day. Traveling widely, from Persia to Baghdad to Damascus, he mastered a wide range of disciplines, and he energetically engaged in arguments with those he considered extremists. When he died in 1111, he left behind a series of treatises, many of them incorporating autobiographical material, particularly the discoveries he had himself made and was fully capable of defending.

Source: Abū Hāmid Muhammad al-Ghazzālī, *The Alchemy of Happiness*, trans. Claud Field (Armonk, NY: M. E. Sharpe, 1991), 6–7 and 11–13.

The first step to self-knowledge is to know that thou art composed of an outward shape, called the body, and an inward entity called the heart or soul. By "heart" I do not mean the piece of flesh situated in the left of our bodies, but that which uses all the other faculties as its instruments and servants. In truth it does not belong to the visible world, but to the invisible, and has come into this world as a traveler visits a foreign country for the sake of merchandise, and it will presently return to its native land. It is the knowledge of this entity and its attributes which is the key to the knowledge of God.

. . .

A mistake of an opposite kind is made by shallow people who, echoing some phrases which they have caught from Sufi teachers, go about decrying all knowledge. This is as if a person who was not an adept in alchemy were to go about saying, "Alchemy is better than gold," and were to refuse gold when it was offered to him. Alchemy is better than gold, but real alchemists are very rare, and so are real Sufis. He who has a mere smattering of Sufism is not superior to a learned man, any more than he who has tried a few experiments in alchemy has ground for despising a rich man.

Anyone who will look into the matter will see that happiness is necessarily linked with the knowledge of God. Each faculty of ours delights in that for which it was created: lust delights in accomplishing desire, anger in taking vengeance, the eye in seeing beautiful objects, and the ear in hearing harmonious sounds. The highest function of the soul of man is the perception of truth; in this accordingly it finds its special delight. Even in trifling matters, such as learning chess, this holds good, and the higher the subject-matter of the knowledge obtained, the greater the delight. A man would be pleased at being admitted into the confidence of a prime minister, but how much more if the king makes an intimate of him and discloses state secrets to him!

An astronomer who, by his knowledge, can map the stars and describe their courses, derives more pleasure from his knowledge than the chess player from his. Seeing, then, that nothing is higher than God, how great must be the delight which springs from the true knowledge of Him!

. . .

Man has been truly termed a "microcosm", or little world in himself, and the structures of his body should be studied not only by those who wish to become doctors, but by those who wish to attain to a more intimate knowledge of God, just as close study of the niceties and shades of language in a great poem reveals to us more and more of the genius of its author.

▶ **Working with Sources**

1. How does Ghazali demonstrate an understanding of "science," and which specific sciences does he reference?

2. Why is he angry at the Sufis? Is his analysis of the problems posed by some Sufis justified?

# Chapter 11 600–1450 CE

# Innovation and Adaptation in the Western Christian World

Around 575 a casual encounter took place in Rome that had enormous implications for the future of western Europe. While strolling through the forum, a young monk from the monastery of St. Andrew came upon several boys for sale in the slave market. Struck by their fair skin and light hair, he asked about their ethnic origin. He was informed that the youths were from the far-off island of Britain and were called "Angles." The monk replied that because of their angelic appearance they should instead be called "angels." He then asked whether the inhabitants of this far-off land were Christians. When told that they still clung to pagan beliefs, he remarked that it was a pity that such beautiful young persons were not blessed with Christian faith.

In the year 596 the young monk, now elevated to the papacy as Pope Gregory I (r. 590–604), dispatched a group of monks to Britain, led by Augustine (later named the first archbishop of Canterbury), on a missionary campaign of conversion among the Anglo-Saxons of southern England. Throughout the seventh century Roman Christianity slowly spread northward into Anglo-Saxon England, eventually eclipsing the already established Celtic form of the faith brought over from Ireland in the fifth century. During the

LATIN
CHRISTENDOM,
ca. 700–1000

*ABOVE:* Detail from *The Effects of Good Government on Town and Country,* a fresco by Ambrogio Lorenzetti (ca. 1290–1348).

first half of the eighth century English missionary monks, most notably St. Boniface (680–754), carried Christianity to the continent.

The papal reign of Gregory I represents the dawn of a new era in the history of western Europe. By encouraging the conversion of Germanic kings to Christianity in return for the sanction of the church, Gregory studiously advanced the role of the papacy in both ecclesiastical and secular affairs throughout Europe. Thus, Gregory was responsible for making the Roman papacy a significant power in the West. In the process, Gregory inaugurated new links between Rome and northwest Europe that went a long way toward the emergence of a new civilization distant from the Mediterranean. In addition, Gregory's efforts led to the eventual assertion of the independence of **Latin Christendom** from the Eastern Greek Church at Constantinople. Moreover, Gregory established an effective institutional structure and organized a hierarchy that provided the framework for a unified and well-regulated Christian civilization in emerging Europe that would endure until around 1450, when the Renaissance ushered in a new phase in European history.

# The Formation of Christian Europe, 600–1000

During the fifth century, Roman provincial rule in the west collapsed and a new post-Roman period of cross-cultural interactions began, combining Greco-Roman and Germanic traditions, as well as Christian values. Even amid the chaos of the times, the Roman administrative practice of grouping provinces into dioceses formed the foundation of the diocesan system of the early church. Gradually, from these various ways of living emerged a distinctively Christian European civilization. An important feature of this new civilization was the dominance of the church, whose alliance with Frankish kings—particularly Charlemagne—initiated a new church-state relationship in the West. This civilization nearly dissolved during the civil wars among Charlemagne's successors and the ninth-century invasions by non-Christians. During the tenth century, however, the slow process of restoring order was under way in post-Carolingian Europe. Despite the turbulence of the ninth and tenth centuries, a new cultural and religious cohesiveness provided a new sense of forward-looking optimism; Latin Christendom had survived.

## Frankish Gaul and Latin Christianity

Amid the confusion caused by Germanic invasions and the breakdown of Roman rule during the fifth century, the first attempt to restore a semblance of political order appeared in Frankish Gaul. Although Merovingian kings relied on brute force to begin assembling a unified kingdom, they also recognized the importance of the church and its leaders as a unifying force. After a period of political turmoil a new line of Frankish kings, the Carolingians, emerged during the eighth century. At the same time, the Christian Church played an integral role in the shaping of Frankish Gaul and, in a larger sense, early medieval European civilization. It was during this period that the concept of *Christendom* as a common identity through the practice of western Christianity began to take shape.

# Seeing Patterns

▶ How did the Merovingians and Carolingians construct a new Christian European civilization during the seventh and eighth centuries?

▶ What were key factors in the political, economic, and social recovery of Europe during the eleventh and twelfth centuries?

▶ What were some of the cultural and intellectual developments during the "twelfth-century renaissance," and how did they contribute to medieval civilization?

▶ How did the church influence political developments in Europe during the twelfth and thirteenth centuries?

▶ What events made fourteenth-century Europe so dismal? How did these combine to spell the gradual demise of medieval institutions and perspectives?

**Latin Christendom:** Those countries professing Christian beliefs under the primacy of the pope.

**Coronation:** The act or ceremony of crowning a sovereign.

**Unction:** The act of anointing with oil as a rite of consecration.

**The Merovingians**    Unlike other Germanic tribes, the Franks did not invade the western Roman Empire but, rather, expanded from within the confines of its borders. The Franks, unlike most other Germans, became Western Christians. As a result, they were not rejected as heretics by native Gallo-Romans. For these reasons, Frankish Gaul was ideally suited to lay the foundation for the emergence of a Christian state in post-Roman Europe.

The first Frankish dynasty, the Merovingians [mer-oh-VIN-gee-anz], was established by the Frankish king Clovis (r. 481–511), who unified a number of northern Frankish tribes and defeated neighboring Germanic states. At some point in his reign, perhaps in 498, Clovis adopted Christianity, which gave him the backing of Christian bishops in Gaul. As a result, Clovis had powerful allies in his attempt to solidify his control over a unified Christian kingdom. However, because of the Merovingian practice of dividing inheritances among surviving heirs, soon after his death Clovis's kingdom was split up into Austrasia in the east, Neustria in the west, and Burgundy in the southeast.

**The Carolingians**    During the eighth century one aristocratic family, the Carolingians, gradually rose to power in Austrasia and eventually took control of all of the Frankish lands. The power of the Carolingians was greatly enhanced during the eighth century by two outstanding leaders. Charles Martel ("the Hammer") (ca. 714–741) increased the authority of the Carolingians by promoting his ties with the church, such as his affiliation with the abbey church of St. Denis near Paris. His defeat of advancing Muslim armies at the Battle of Tours in 732 made him not only the most powerful man in Frankland but also the leader of the most powerful force in Latin Christendom.

Martel's son, Pepin III ("the Short") (751–768), succeeded his father as mayor of the palace in 741, and enhanced ties with the church in two ways. First, in 751 he was crowned by the reigning pope as the king of the Franks, thereby replacing the former Merovingian line of kings with a new Carolingian dynasty. Second, the **coronation** established a new Franco-papal alliance. One consequence of this was the establishment of a closer affinity between Rome and Frankish Gaul, an important factor in allowing Europe to develop independently of the Byzantine Empire in the East. In addition, the pope included the ceremony of **unction** (used earlier by the Visigoths) in the coronation ceremony, introducing into western European history of the concept of sacred kingship, whereby kings now began to call themselves "kings by the grace of God."

**The Early Medieval Church**    The church contributed greatly to the development of a new era in Western history during this period. The *secular clergy* (from the Latin *saeculum* [CY-cu-lum], or "world") included bishops—among them bishops of Rome, who later became popes—and urban priests. The *regular clergy* (from the Latin *regula*, or "rule") were monks who adopted a particular monastic rule and who lived in rural monasteries. Each of these monasteries made distinctive contributions to early medieval culture.

The model for monastic life was established by St. Benedict (ca. 480–543), whose *Holy Rule* governed such matters as the times for rising, praying, eating, and retiring, all supervised by an *abbot*, or head of the monastery. The daily lives of Benedictine monks were devoted to prayer and manual labor and were regulated by a series of "offices," or times of the day given over to specific tasks.

In economic terms, Benedictine monasteries helped to revitalize rural agricultural production because of their emphases upon economic self-sufficiency and manual labor as a form of prayer. Most monasteries had a watermill and a forge, and their large landholdings produced significant quantities of grain and wine. In addition, Benedictine monks expanded arable lands by draining swamps and clearing forests.

Above all else, monasteries preserved classical and early Christian culture in the midst of a mostly illiterate Germanic population. The limited education available during the early medieval period took place mostly in monasteries. It emphasized study of the Bible, church doctrine, and the "seven liberal arts"— consisting of the *trivium* (grammar, rhetoric, logic) and the *quadrivium* (arithmetic, geometry, music, astronomy). Monks copied and studied the works of the church fathers (such as Augustine, Jerome, and Ambrose), along with texts from the Bible and scattered papal decrees, thus laying the foundation for a new, Christian civilization for medieval Europe.

**The Papacy**　While monks lived and worked in isolated rural monasteries, bishops of the church resided in urban centers. Although major cities throughout the Roman Empire had bishops, the bishop of Rome emerged as spiritual head of the Christian Church in western Europe. The most important of the early medieval popes, and indeed the pope usually credited with the foundation of the medieval papacy, was Gregory I.

In a wider sense, however, Gregory was responsible for making the Roman papacy a power in the West. His letters to Childebert II (r. 575–595), king of the Franks, laid the foundation for the Franco-papal alliance that came to fruition in the eighth century. Gregory also enhanced the prestige of the Roman papacy in Italy, which gave rise to the Papal States and the separation of the Roman and Eastern Roman Church. Finally, by encouraging the gradual mingling of Christian ideals and pagan rituals, Gregory facilitated the conversion of pagans to Christianity.

**The Age of Charlemagne**　Following the death of Pepin III in 768, his son Charlemagne ("Charles the Great") (r. 768–814) inherited the Frankish crown. In his personal preferences and in his official policies, Charlemagne represents the first full synthesis of Roman, Germanic, and Christian elements to forge a unified Christian empire, establishing what many consider the "first Europe." Because Charlemagne raised the status of western Europe to rival the civilizations of Byzantium and Islam, the Mediterranean was no longer the center of civilization in the West.

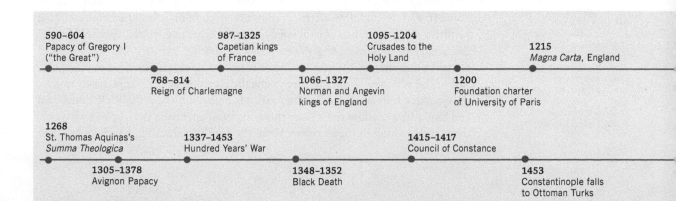

| 590–604<br>Papacy of Gregory I<br>("the Great") | 987–1325<br>Capetian kings<br>of France | 1095–1204<br>Crusades to the<br>Holy Land | 1215<br>*Magna Carta*, England |
| | 768–814<br>Reign of Charlemagne | 1066–1327<br>Norman and Angevin<br>kings of England | 1200<br>Foundation charter<br>of University of Paris |
| 1268<br>St. Thomas Aquinas's<br>*Summa Theologica* | 1337–1453<br>Hundred Years' War | | 1415–1417<br>Council of Constance |
| | 1305–1378<br>Avignon Papacy | 1348–1352<br>Black Death | 1453<br>Constantinople falls<br>to Ottoman Turks |

Through extensive military campaigns and attention to effective rule, Charlemagne constructed and administered the largest empire in Europe since the collapse of Roman rule in 476 (see Map 11.1). An important step was the creation of a magnificent palace complex at Aachen [AH-ken] (Aix-la-Chapelle in French). From here Charlemagne ruled over a highly centralized empire—that is, a polity composed of many different ethnic and linguistic groups. Charlemagne also reformed legal practices by instituting the Frankish inquest, a forerunner of the jury system, which was carried to England at the time of the Norman Conquest.

Charlemagne's reign also resulted in significant intellectual contributions to medieval Europe. In an attempt to revive learning, especially among the aristocracy and the clergy, Charlemagne orchestrated a program of educational reform throughout his empire. Key to this effort was the appointment of Alcuin of York (ca. 735–804), the leading intellect of his age, as master of the palace school. Monks in several monastic schools were instructed to make copies of both Roman and Christian texts, including the Bible and the *Rule* of St. Benedict. This painstaking process produced around 50,000 books over the course of a century, preserving and disseminating many classical authors and texts.

**Charlemagne's Throne.**
Charlemagne frequently traveled throughout his realm, and one place where he stopped several times was Ravenna on the Adriatic coast of Italy, where he would admire the magnificent sixth-century church of San Vitale. Inspired by its harmonious proportions and stunning mosaics, Charlemagne determined to build a replica at Aachen. The Palatine Chapel, the only surviving component of his palace, combines Byzantine and Carolingian architectural styles.

Like his forebears, Charlemagne also took an active interest in affairs of the church, often going beyond mere protection to outright interference. In the Capitulary for Saxony (775–790), for example, he ordered the forced conversion of Saxons to Christian practices. Not only did he promote the interests of Christianity throughout his kingdom, but he also intervened in papal affairs in Rome. In 774 Charlemagne journeyed to Rome to offer protection against the Lombards, and in 800 he gave assistance to Pope Leo III (r. 795–816), who was attacked by rivals. While attending Mass at St. Peter's on Christmas Day, Charlemagne was suddenly crowned "emperor of the Romans" by a grateful Leo III, an event Charlemagne later claimed was orchestrated by the pope without his prior knowledge.

The creation of a new Roman emperor in the West announced the independence of western Europe from the Byzantine East, and it signaled a shift in the center of power away from the Mediterranean and toward Europe north of the Alps. Charlemagne's new imperial status was recognized (reluctantly) not only by the Byzantine court but also by the Abbasid caliph in Baghdad, Harun al-Rashid (r. 786–809).

**Post-Carolingian Europe**    Shortly after his death in 814, Charlemagne's empire was torn apart by internal wars and divisions. Charlemagne's eldest son, Louis the Pious (r. 814–840), followed the Frankish custom of dividing the empire among his three sons, who then squabbled over their respective shares. By the terms of the Treaty of Verdun in 843 the empire was divided into eastern, western, and central portions. At the same time, a series of devastating raids further disturbed the situation. From the north came the Norsemen, or Vikings, motivated by the quest for land and treasure. They sailed from Scandinavia into West Frankland and England in shallow-draft "long ships," causing terror and destruction wherever they landed along Europe's rivers. From the south, marauding bands of Muslim

MAP 11.1 **The Empire of Charlemagne.**

pirates created fear and destruction along the French coast of the Mediterranean and even penetrated inland as far as the Alps and into Rome itself in 846. Magyar horsemen from the plains of Hungary terrorized East Frankland in the same period, although they were more inclined to settle onto farmlands than to merely plunder (see Map 11.1).

**The Feudal Age**    The name traditionally given to the form of governance that arose in West Frankland during the ninth through the eleventh centuries is **feudalism**. But what, precisely, was feudalism? Historians have never fully agreed on a precise definition of the term, and some have suggested abandoning it altogether. Indeed, the term is often (and confusingly) used to describe similar

**Feudalism:** An arrangement in which vassals were protected and maintained by their lords, usually through the granting of fiefs, and required to serve under them in war.

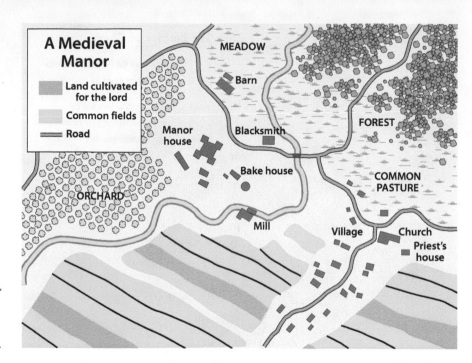

**Figure 11.1 A Medieval Manor.** This illustration shows the layout of a typical manor, with the manor and its satellite buildings next to a village surrounded by fields for planting and common (waste) land.

arrangements that arose, in different periods, in Zhou China and Tokugawa Japan. It is true that feudalism was not a system *per se*; it was based on no theory, and it was nowhere uniform or consistent. Yet, amid the turmoil of the ninth and tenth centuries, feudalism provided security at the local level in the absence of central government.

Essentially, feudalism represented a new form of governance at the regional and local levels instead of from a centralized royal court. Feudalism consisted of powerful landed aristocrats (lords) who assembled small private armies consisting of dependents (vassals) in order to defend against the Norsemen, Muslims, and Magyars. Since wealth and power were now measured in terms of landholdings, vassals were rewarded for their services with grants of land, known as *fiefs*.

Lord–vassal relationships and institutions marked a turning point in European history that led to the later formation of centralized kingdoms. Most important was the concept of loyalty to someone higher in the feudal hierarchy. Even though in *practice* the local aristocratic lords were sometimes stronger than royal figures, in *theory* all land and power was possessed by kings, who stood at the apex of the feudal hierarchy. By using these and other elements of feudal relationships to his advantage, a royal figure could convert the feudal relationships to royal control of his realm.

**Manorialism:**
The medieval European system of self-sustaining agricultural estates.

Whereas feudalism refers to the political and governmental aspects of life in the ninth and tenth centuries, **manorialism** refers to social and economic affairs of the time. Large manorial estates were established in rural areas and constituted self-sustaining agricultural communities. The manorial estate consisted of several build-ings: the castle or manor house, the church, the barn, and the mill (see Figure 11.1).

Peasants lived in small cottages in a confined area of the estate. The typical cottage was windowless, constructed of mud and straw with an earthen floor. Cooking was done over a small stone hearth; a hole in the roof allowed smoke to escape.

Interiors were very dark, and privacy was nonexistent. Surrounding all this were fields for crops, stands of timber for building and fuel, and a fish pond. The fields were arranged into long, narrow strips, some farmed by peasant families and others owned by the lord of the manor. Peasants had to provide free labor, called "boon work," on the lord's fields. The physical pattern of such manors may still be seen in many areas of France.

# Recovery, Reform, and Innovation, 1000–1300

From about 1000 to 1300 Europe experienced a period of revitalization, expansion, and cultural creativity and innovation. The period began with the appearance of several competing, politically centralizing kingdoms and with advancements in agriculture, commerce, and trade. Reforms in the church provided an overarching framework that defined a unified western European Christian religious civilization, culminating in papal supremacy over Europe around the beginning of the thirteenth century. During the so-called twelfth-century renaissance, extending from ca. 1050 to 1250, a cultural revolution in universities produced new philosophical and scientific perspectives that, along with interaction with the Islamic world, came to distinguish western Europe from other world civilizations.

## The Political Recovery of Europe

Europe in the middle of the ninth century was nearly everywhere in turmoil caused by internal civil wars and external invasions. As we have seen, all signs of central government had disappeared as a result of the collapse of the Carolingian empire. In this turbulent setting most people were ruled by local lords. By around 1300, however, most of western Europe was governed by well-run centralized administrations headed by kings, who restored both political and fiscal health to their realms.

**France and England**    The French nobility elected Hugh Capet (r. 987–996) as their king in 987 CE, beginning a long process of restoring centralized monarchy. This event marked the establishment of a new royal dynasty, the Capetians, in place of the former Carolingians. Although relatively weak in relation to powerful lords, the Capetians could claim several theoretical advantages. For one thing, the king's court served as the place where all disputes among his vassals were resolved, and the location of Hugh's royal **demesne** [deh-MAIN] in the lands around Paris meant that he was at the strategic and commercial center of France. Like the Carolingians, the Capetians enjoyed the support of the church. Not only did they have control over dozens of bishoprics and monasteries, they alone were anointed with holy oil (unction) as a part of the coronation ceremony, making their persons sacrosanct and safe from bodily injury.

Over the next 300 years, Capetian kings extended royal control in France. Success in petty wars against the nobles and arranged marriages between Capetian heirs and members of the nobility helped extend the domain and enhance Capetian power. Determined to make France the most powerful country in Europe, Philip IV (r. 1285–1314) established a representative assembly in France, the **Estates-General**,

**Demesne:** All territories within France controlled directly by the king.

**Estates-General:** The French representative assembly, composed of the three social "estates" in France, first convened by Philip IV.

in order to raise needed revenues. Composed of the three social "estates"—the clergy, the nobility, and the townspeople—this body played an important role in later events leading up to the French Revolution.

Compared to the long and slow process of building a centralized monarchy in Capetian France, the establishment of centralized rule in England took place over a much shorter period of time. After the Norman duke William the Conqueror defeated an Anglo-Saxon army at the Battle of Hastings in 1066, he was proclaimed king of England as King William I (r. 1066–1087). William then seized control of all lands in the realm, distributing them to his followers. To secure his claim to the throne, he built castles throughout the country.

William's successors continued his practice of centralizing authority. Henry II (r. 1154–1189), the first of the Plantagenet kings of England, reformed the judicial system by making royal courts the final courts of appeal, particularly in disputes over land, thereby overriding the authority of **baronial** courts. Moreover, Henry established a uniform code of justice (known as English common law) throughout the realm, which replaced the complex and frequently contradictory jurisdictions of baronial and local courts. Even more effective was Henry's reliance upon roving royal justices and the use of royal **writs** and the jury system, which provided justice for all disputants.

Henry's son John (r. 1199–1216), however, alienated the baronage of England, who forced the king to sign Magna Carta ("the Great Charter") in 1215. Magna Carta established several important principles: the king must rule in accordance with established feudal practices; he must consult with the barons before levying taxes; and all free men have the right to trial by jury if charged with a crime. Many of these concepts also contributed to the appearance of a new institution known as **Parliament**.

During the thirteenth century the English Parliament increased its power and scope. It also established certain principles that would be contested periodically by English monarchs over the next five centuries. In order to raise money for an anticipated French attack against England, Edward I (r. 1272–1307) found it expedient to convene in 1295 the so-called Model Parliament, composed of an upper house of nobles and a lower house of "knights of the shires and burgesses of the towns." This precedent established the origin of Parliament's House of Lords and House of Commons, which continues today.

**Germany**  Events in East Frankland, or Germany, took a different turn. One setback to centralized rule was the division of the eastern portion of Charlemagne's realm into five regional groupings, or *duchies*, each under the control of a powerful duke. The result was that successive kings were chosen by the five regional dukes, making it difficult for kings to centralize royal authority.

Furthermore, imperial involvement in papal affairs in Italy provided another impediment to centralization. When Otto I of Saxony (r. 936–973) took power as king of the Germans, he extended Germanic influence in Italy in order to reestablish Charlemagne's protection of the papacy. In 962, Otto put down political disturbances and protests against the church. In gratitude, Pope John XII (r. 955–964) proclaimed Otto "emperor of the Romans," forming the basis of what has been termed the "Holy Roman Empire." Otto's successors continued the policy of interfering in papal affairs, with momentous results for both church and state.

**Baron:** A term initiated by William I to designate feudal vassals who held lands in return for service and loyalty to the king.

**Writ:** A written order issued by a court, commanding the party to whom it is addressed to perform or cease performing a specified act.

**Parliament:** A representative assembly in England that, by the fourteenth century, was composed of great lords (both lay and ecclesiastical) and representatives from two other groups: shire knights and town burgesses.

In ensuing years Otto's successors continued efforts to extend German control south of the Alps into Italy. Through the tireless efforts of Frederick I (1152–1190), the first to bear the title Holy Roman Emperor, German holdings in Italy were greatly expanded in the north, and in 1155 he was named king of Italy. After his later defeat at the hands of a coalition of northern Italian cities in 1176, however, Frederick was forced to grant them quasi-independence, in return for their support against papal interests in the Italian peninsula. In his determination to encircle the Papal States, Frederick turned his attention to Sicily. Following the Norman liberation of Sicily from Muslim control in 1091, the Norman king Roger II (r. 1130–1154) established the Kingdom of Sicily, which included southern Italy as well as Sicily. By marrying his son, the future Henry VI (r. 1190–1197), to Constance of Sicily, daughter of Roger II, Frederick added the Kingdom of Sicily to the lands controlled by the Holy Roman Empire.

## The Economic and Social Recovery of Europe

Yet another area of recovery for Europe around the year 1000 was in economics. At that time there was little manufacturing or commerce in Europe. Agriculture was still the mainstay of the economy, and there were few cities (and even these were underpopulated). Society was divided into three classes: those who worked, those who fought, and those who prayed. By 1300, however, the map of Europe was crisscrossed by scores of trade routes; trade and commerce were important features; urban life was humming; and a new social class of merchants had emerged in cities. How are we to explain this remarkable economic resurgence?

**The Agricultural Revolution**   Developments in agriculture contributed to Europe's economic revival. In addition to land reclamation, as well as deep deposits of topsoil rich in nutrients, an important factor in the agricultural revolution was the heavy-wheeled plow, fitted with an iron blade and a *moldboard* (a curved iron blade to cut through the heavy sod of the region and lift and turn the newly dug soil). The use of new fertilizers and the transition from a two-field to a three-field system also provided a 33 percent increase in crop production. In the three-field system, one field was planted in the spring for a fall harvest, another was planted in the winter for a spring harvest, and the third remained fallow to enable its soil to regenerate nutrients.

It is important to note that the agricultural revolution in Europe was largely due to innovations from elsewhere in Eurasia (perhaps from China), which were transmitted to Europe through cross-cultural interactions (mostly via the Silk Road trade network). Among these innovations were the use of horses with collar harnesses (instead of slower-moving oxen), which provided a fivefold increase in traction, not to mention less injury to the animal; the use of iron horseshoes; the use of the tandem harness, allowing horses to work in pairs and further increasing production; the vertical waterwheel; and the single-wheeled barrow.

Moreover, new forms of mechanical energy—also of Asian origin—were introduced to Europe through interactions with the Islamic world. As early as 1050 watermills were in wide use, and although some historians attribute the watermill's origins to Rome, its design—particularly the incorporation of the trip-hammer—indicates Asian roots. Windmills, which were borrowed from Islamic Iran during the twelfth century, converted the power of water or wind into pounding and grinding motions used for the production of cloth goods, beer, and especially grain products; this in turn led to an increase in food production. Even the first deep-drilled water well, introduced in the twelfth century, was of Chinese origin. Finally, through Muslim Spain the Europeans benefited from several Islamic advances in agriculture, such as improvements in techniques of irrigation and drainage, and the introduction of new crops including rice, sugarcane, watermelons, and bananas.

These new crops and techniques meant an increase not only in the quantity of agricultural production but also, more importantly, in the quality and variety of food. Before the agricultural revolution, the European diet was based mainly on grains. Though rich in carbohydrates, it was low in protein. Peas and beans provided much-needed proteins and, when combined with chicken, fish, and eggs, resulted in a more balanced and nutritious diet. Improvements to the European diet resulted in an increase in population: in 1000, the population stood at about 36 million; by 1100 it had jumped to 44 million, and by 1200 to 58 million. By 1300 the European population reached about 80 million.

**Commerce and Trade**   The revolution in agricultural production sparked in turn a rejuvenation of commerce and trade that spread throughout and beyond medieval Europe. As Europe's population grew, so did the demand for consumer goods, ranging from agricultural implements to household utensils, clothing and shoes, and numerous other commodities. The expansion of mercantile elites in thriving urban centers also provoked a brisk demand for luxury goods from beyond Europe, including silks, spices, and sugar.

One focal point of the revival of trade and commerce developed in northern Europe. Cloth goods, especially woolen products, had been a staple item in Flanders (along the coast of the North Sea in northeastern France) even before the Carolingian era. After the cessation of Viking raids, Flemish weavers began a flourishing exchange with wool-producing centers in England, particularly with monasteries in the north of the island, in the twelfth century. Another very productive source of the commercial trade revival in northern Europe was the importation of French wines into England beginning in the later eleventh century, occasioned by the Norman Conquest in 1066. German merchants established trade routes to London in the west and to Russian cities like Riga and Novgorod in the east.

Far more vital, however, was the remarkable revival of European commerce and trade across the Mediterranean. When Umayyad rulers were displaced by the Abbasids, who ruled from 750 to 1258, maritime contacts between Islamic and Christian merchants resumed. In addition, the Norman conquest of southern Italy and Sicily (1046–1091) afforded the northern Italian maritime cities of Pisa, Genoa, and Venice the opportunity to collaborate with Islamic merchants in Alexandria and the Levant. By the end of the eleventh century, Italian traders had established commercial ties with Constantinople, Syria, and Cairo and had begun the exchange of all manner of goods between Europe and Asia.

The most momentous change in European trade and commerce took place near the close of the thirteenth century. Around 1275, first Genoese and then Venetian maritime traders sailed westward across the Mediterranean, through the Strait of Gibraltar, and then out into the Atlantic. Then, Ferdinand IV (r. 1295–1312), king of Castile and León in Spain, claimed control of Gibraltar from the Muslims in 1309, ensuring full access to the waters of the Atlantic. Before these developments,

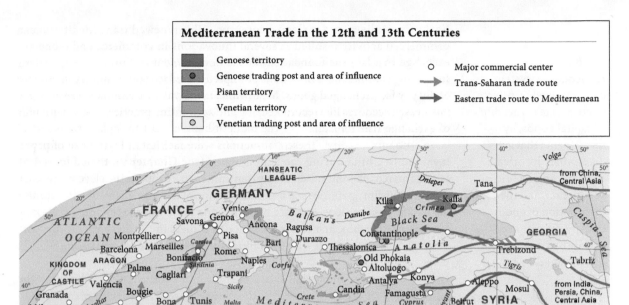

**Mediterranean Trade in the 12th and 13th Centuries**

- Genoese territory
- Genoese trading post and area of influence
- Pisan territory
- Venetian territory
- Venetian trading post and area of influence
- ○ Major commercial center
- → Trans-Saharan trade route
- → Eastern trade route to Mediterranean

MAP 11.2 **Mediterranean Trade in the Twelfth and Thirteenth Centuries.**

trading patterns were primarily of a one-way nature: European merchants imported modest quantities of goods like *alum* (a mineral essential for dyeing cloth), spices, and silks from China and India. Thanks to economic advances in the West, however, European merchants now had products to export to the East: wool and tin from England, finished French and Flemish cloth goods, and manufactured items like iron agricultural and household implements (see Map 11.2).

Cross-Mediterranean trade and commerce were facilitated by several navigational innovations, some of which were assimilated as a result of interactions with Islamic and Byzantine merchants. Navigation was tremendously improved by advances in European ship design. Among the most important was the incorporation of the sternpost rudder. This concept was familiar to Chinese and Muslim sailors, but the European version—in use as early as 1180—was unique in that it used hinged iron plates firmly mounted to the ship's stern. The principal advantage of the stern-mounted rudder was that it allowed for the construction of larger ships, which in turn greatly increased the volume of transported goods. Another improvement was provided by the adoption from Muslim sailors of the *lateen sail*, a front-mounted triangular sail that allowed for tacking into the wind. It was largely owing to this navigational device that Italian ships were able to sail into the westerly winds that had previously prevented their sailing through the Strait of Gibraltar into the Atlantic. Most important was the introduction of the magnetic compass. Whether of independent invention or derived from China, where it was used on Chinese ships as early as around 1090, the magnetic (or mariner's) compass first appeared in Europe in 1190. Use of the compass greatly facilitated maritime travel beyond the sight of land, particularly across the Mediterranean.

**Capitalism:**
An economic system characterized by private or corporate ownership of capital goods, by investments that are determined by private decision, and by prices, production, and the distribution of goods that are determined mainly by competition in a free market.

**Early Capitalism and a Cash Economy**    This renewed trans-Mediterranean commercial activity resulted in several innovations in commerce and monetary exchange that laid the foundation for the development of European **capitalism**. Increasing commercial transactions prompted a need for coined money in order to easily pay for exchanged goods. Meanwhile, medieval fairs gradually created new business procedures like record-keeping and accounting practices, along with bills of exchange (the forerunner of the modern bank check) to replace transport of large amounts of coins. These transactions were facilitated by the use of paper, invented in China during the Han dynasty (see Chapter 9), then adopted by Islamic merchants, and subsequently transmitted to Europe in the eleventh century through Muslim Spain. Several innovative financial and legal instruments were also devised to promote long-distance trade. Among these was the *commenda*, a legally binding partnership, first in use by Venetian traders in the eleventh century and borrowed via interactions with their Byzantine and Islamic counterparts.

**Urban Growth**    The revitalization of trade and commerce contributed to the rejuvenation of urban life in eleventh-century Europe. Although many Roman towns survived the tribulations of the early medieval period, most resembled underpopulated ghost towns. The repopulation of these existing urban sites plus the creation of new cities attests to the influence of the economic revival of the eleventh century. Artisans and merchants were drawn to these vibrant urban centers, along with craftspeople and laborers, many of whom fled rural manors in order to begin new lives in cities. These cities were small by today's standards. Most numbered around 5,000 people, although London and Bruges each held about 40,000 inhabitants, while cities like Venice and Genoa in northern Italy boasted populations of around 100,000. Churches and castles were the most prominent urban buildings. Most urban areas were enclosed within stone walls and surrounded by agricultural fields.

**Bourgeoisie:**
The urban-based middle class between the wealthy aristocracy and the working class.

**Guilds:** Associations of artisans and merchants intended to protect and promote affairs of common interest.

**Social Patterns**    Social patterns within the revitalized urban centers of the eleventh and twelfth centuries underwent change for several reasons. Of primary importance was the return of a money economy, which not only spelled the demise of feudalism—in that kings and nobles could now pay for armies with cash rather than with grants of land—but also resulted in the appearance of a new social class: the military. The effects of a new cash economy were especially noticeable in cities, which benefited from the cash contributions of wealthy businessmen in order to build cathedrals and large town halls. Finally, cities produced a new class of people, the **bourgeoisie** [boor-zhwa-ZEE]. Composed of merchants and artisans who lived in "burghs" (or cities) the bourgeoisie made their livings from producing and selling goods for commercial exchange. This new "middle class" of people was destined to exert an enormous influence on the development of medieval representative governments, primarily because their access to liquid cash made them attractive to European rulers.

Urban women worked in a variety of occupations, especially craft industries. Women were employed in a diverse array of crafts, as butchers, candle makers, metal crafters, silk weavers, and bookbinders. Nevertheless, women were rarely admitted as full members to craft **guilds**, and in the silk industry—the one area where women did predominate—there is no evidence of a guild. For the great majority of working women, better opportunities were available in what were known as "bye industries," or home-based enterprises, like spinning cloth and brewing ale. In some cases widows took over their late husband's trade and worked as single women.

Jews occupied a distinct position in medieval towns and cities during the early years of the urban revival in the eleventh century. Comprising a small but distinct minority of the European population, Jews were spread in communities around the Mediterranean world. Through their travels and interactions with a wide variety of peoples, Jews developed both wide geographical knowledge and the command of multiple languages. For these reasons they sometimes served as diplomats, and they engaged in moneylending and banking.

As the eleventh century unfolded, however, tolerance toward Jews began to wane. Jews were increasingly vilified as murderers of Christ, a sentiment fanned by the First Crusade in 1096. In 1144 a full-scale assault against Jews was unleashed in the English town of Norwich. In many cases Jews were forced to live together in walled-off, gated ghettos in towns, which frequently held charters of liberty separate from those of the towns. Ghettos appeared as early as the thirteenth century in Spain, Portugal, Germany, and elsewhere. Several countries expelled Jews—England in 1290, France in 1306, and a number of continental cities in the early 1400s—resulting in their dispersal throughout eastern Europe.

**The Virgin Mary Knitting.** This fourteenth-century painting of the Virgin Mary knitting a garment for her unborn child is the earliest known representation of knitting, a medieval innovation. Knitwear was unknown in the ancient Mediterranean but was essential in the cold, damp climate of northern Europe.

## Religious Reform and Expansion

During the period from 1000 to 1300 the clerical establishment of medieval Europe underwent dramatic reform as the church struggled to recover from nearly two centuries of decentralization and decline of learning. The reform movement in the church began in monasteries, then spread to the ecclesiastical hierarchy in cities, and eventually resulted in a new age of religious enthusiasm throughout Europe.

**Monastic Reform**    The effort at monastic reform began in France in a monastery founded at Cluny in 910 by Duke William I (875–918) of Aquitaine. Cluny was established as a monastery totally free of obligations to either feudal lords or local ecclesiastical control, and committed to strict adherence to the Benedictine rule. The number of reformed monasteries increased during the eleventh and twelfth centuries. The most successful of new monastic orders was the Cistercians, founded in 1098 in a remote area of France at Citeaux. At its inception the order numbered only a handful of monastic houses, but by 1200 nearly 500 Cistercian monasteries were active throughout France. The appeal of the Cistercian order lay in its simple and austere way of life; Cistercians were enjoined to work and live in poverty and to devote their total beings to "God's work" (*opus Dei*).

**Papal Reform and the Investiture Controversy** As the monastic reform movement progressed, a similar reform effort took place in the papacy. One of the major concerns of the church was to establish its independence from secular influence, particularly the practice by which lay rulers appointed clergy, including the pope, to their offices. Popes, however, believed it was the exclusive right of the clergy to make such appointments. The creation of the College of Cardinals in 1150, followed by the Papal Election Decree in 1059, ensured that only the College of Cardinals was empowered to elect the pontiff of the Holy Catholic Church. The result was the elimination of the role of the Holy Roman (German) emperor in the appointment of popes.

This conflict came to a head in what is known as the "investiture controversy." Pope Gregory VII (r. 1073–1085), a staunch advocate of papal reform, insisted that appointment of the clergy was in future to be controlled solely by the church. When the German emperor Henry IV (1056–1106) openly challenged Gregory's proclamation, the pope excommunicated him. The struggle between popes and emperors dragged on for more than 40 years, until 1122 when an agreement known as the Concordat of Worms (named for the German city where the agreement was made) was reached. This agreement stipulated that German bishops must be elected by church officials.

The investiture controversy produced mixed results. On the one hand, Gregory's actions represented the enhanced power of the church and proved that popes could force emperors to acknowledge papal authority. On the other hand, Henry IV's struggle with the church proved disastrous for his successors. Later German emperors never fully recovered from the distraction of attempting to control matters in both Germany and Italy. Even such otherwise strong figures as Frederick I (r. 1152–1190) and Frederick II (r. 1215–1250) were unable to establish centralized rule in Germany. After Frederick's death, the five Germanic principalities reasserted their independence from royal control, and Germany remained disunited until the later nineteenth century.

**Popular Piety and a Religious Society** As early as the eleventh century Europe experienced a dramatic increase in popular piety, when ordinary people took a more active interest in religion. This movement was caused by several factors. One was the reform movement in the church, which resulted in both higher standards of conduct among regular and secular clergy and the increased visibility and temporal authority of the pope following the investiture controversy. Another factor was the construction of numerous shrines dedicated to Christian saints, whose *relics*—venerated items connected with their lives—were considered powerful aids in the quest for personal salvation.

Another factor that generated renewed enthusiasm for religion was new ways of depicting Jesus and Mary, the mother of Jesus. Whereas in the earliest years of the church the Crucifixion of Jesus was rarely shown—and then only in a stylized, unemotional manner—by the tenth century Christ was depicted as a compassionate figure, whose tragic death on the Cross was portrayed as a reminder of his sacrifice for the redemption of humanity's sins.

(a)

(b)

**Changing Views of Christ.** The Crucifixion scene from the door of the basilica of Santa Sabina, Rome, ca. 430, is formal and stylized; Christ is remote (*a*). In contrast, the Crucifixion commissioned by the archbishop of Cologne, Germany, just before 1000 shows a suffering Christ—a human being in agony and sorrow, hanging from a cross (*b*).

A further contribution of the popularization of Christian piety was the introduction of new concepts of time. One concept derives from the biblical book of Genesis, where the creation of the earth took 6 days, leaving the seventh day as a day of rest. Another concept, the numbering of years in accordance with the Christian era, was introduced in 532 by Dionysius Exiguus (ca. 470–544), a Roman monk. For Dionysius historical time began with the birth of Christ, hence his designation of *Anno Domini* ("in the year of the Lord") to denote a new dating system. The new system was used by the eighth-century Anglo-Saxon scholar Bede (ca. 673–735) in his *Ecclesiastical History of the English People* and then popularized in Europe by Alcuin of York during the reign of Charlemagne.

These Christian influences on the perception of time had several implications for Europeans. For one thing, two crucial Christian feast days now became standard: the birth of Christ was celebrated on December 25 (Christmas) and his resurrection on a movable date called **Easter**. For another, saints' days, set aside for reflection and celebration, became major events around which Europeans' lives centered. Finally, the ringing of church and monastery bells announced the hours of the day, which provided for regulation of daily routines. Mechanical clocks, introduced into Europe in the early fourteenth century—and most likely derived from earlier Chinese models—later provided more precise measurement of time.

A less benign aspect of popular piety was an alarming trend toward the appearance of heretical movements within the church (see "Against the Grain" below, page 342). In an effort to rechannel the devotion of the faithful, particularly in cities, Pope Innocent III (r. 1198–1216) licensed two new religious orders of friars ("brothers"), the Franciscans and the Dominicans. Founded by St. Francis of

**Easter:** Christian celebration of the Resurrection of Christ; celebrated on the Sunday following the first full moon after the vernal equinox.

Assisi (1181/2–1226), the Franciscan order inspired a new dedication to Christianity in the form of living simply among the people, preaching repentance for sins, and aiding the poor and the sick. The Dominicans, founded by St. Dominic (1170–1221) in 1216, also lived among the people, but they were more interested in preaching and teaching, believing that the best way to combat heresy was to teach the doctrines of the church. The Dominican order included many famous medieval theologians in its ranks, such as St. Thomas Aquinas (ca. 1225–1274).

**The Crusades**   A movement that reflects both the growing appeal and power of the church as well as the renewed energy of a revitalized Europe centers on the Crusades. Like the reform movement of the church, the Crusades were in part inspired by the new wave of religious enthusiasm sweeping Europe during the period of recovery from the horrors of the ninth and tenth centuries. But there were other causal factors as well, chief among them the so-called *Reconquista*, or reconquest, of formerly Christian lands that had been taken over by Muslims.

Until the year 1000 Spanish Christians were forced to retreat into the far northwest of the Iberian Peninsula, while the Muslims controlled most of the lands from their capital in Córdoba. In 1031, however, internal squabbling among Muslim factions led to a loosening of Muslim control throughout Spain, which in turn prompted two kings of Christian territories to launch an offensive in order to reclaim land from the Muslims. The breakthrough occurred in 1085 when Toledo was liberated from Muslim control, resulting in almost half of Spain returning to Christian control.

A similar effort to retake Christian territory from Muslim control took place in southern Italy and Sicily. Beginning in 1061, a group of Norman knights began wresting Sicily from the Muslims, resulting in its eventual conquest in 1090. Across the twelfth century their successors established a strongly centralized Norman kingdom in Sicily. The Norman kings of Sicily allied themselves with the papacy. In return for their protection of the papacy, the kings were given the status of permanent papal legates, which in turn gave them total control over all the higher clergy in their realm.

These spectacular successes against the Muslims in the western Mediterranean occurred simultaneously with alarming developments in the eastern Mediterranean. As we have seen in Chapter 10, by the 1180s Seljuk Turks had seized control of substantial territories in the Middle East, prompting Pope Urban II to call for the launching of a crusade to the Holy Land during the Council of Clermont in France in 1095. Anxious not only to liberate the Holy Land but also to enhance papal prestige, Urban called on the great barons of Europe to assemble their feudal armies and march to the east to liberate Jerusalem from Muslim control. For their part, although they may have been partially driven by religious enthusiasm, Europe's feudal nobility most likely saw in this expedition the promise of new lands and a chance to use their military training for a good cause.

In the summer of the following year the main force, consisting of approximately 7,000 mounted knights along with around 35,000 infantry and augmented by thousands of attendants, suppliers, and prostitutes, crossed over into Asia Minor and in 1097 took Nicaea from the Turks. Two years later, in the summer of 1099, Jerusalem was finally freed from Muslim control—but at a horrific cost in human life.

Other crusades followed throughout the twelfth century. In 1144 the fall of the crusader state of Edessa (in present-day Syria) to a resurgence of Islamic militancy caused renewed interest in a second crusade. Called for in a sermon by Bernard of Clairveaux, the crusade, led by King Louis VII of France and Holy Roman Emperor Conrad III, failed to reach Jerusalem. A surge of renewed interest in the crusading movement occurred in 1187, when Jerusalem was overrun by the renowned Muslim leader Saladin. Known as the "Crusade of the Three Kings," the Third Crusade was led by Frederick I of Germany, Philip II of France, and Richard I of England. The accidental drowning death of Frederick I removed the German contingent from the force, but the combined English and French forces managed to capture Acre from the Muslims in 1191. At that point, however, dissension between Philip I and Richard I resulted in Philip's hasty return to France.

Yet another crusading effort, the Fourth Crusade, was instigated by Pope Innocent III. Led by Baldwin IX, count of Flanders (r. 1194–1206), the crusade was launched in 1201. Consisting mainly of French knights, the crusading army contracted with the Venetians for passage by ship to the east. The crafty Venetians, who were quick to realize the advantage of transporting a crusading army, attacked the Adriatic port city of Zara, their commercial rival. Outraged by an attack on a Christian city, Innocent III excommunicated the crusaders, who ignored the papal ban. From Zara the Venetians transported the army to Constantinople in 1204, where they plundered the city, slaughtering innocent Christians in the process. In the long run the Fourth Crusade not only weakened the authority of subsequent Byzantine rulers but also deepened animosities between the Roman and Eastern Orthodox Churches.

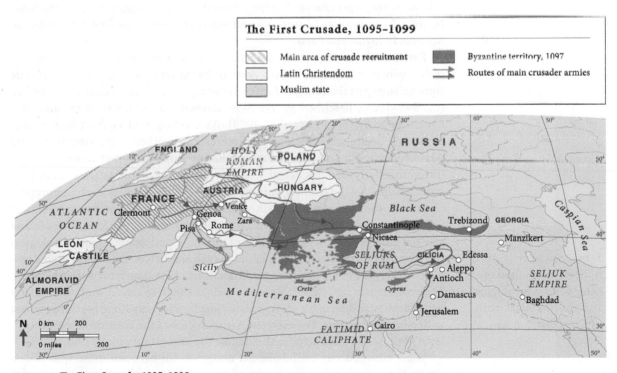

MAP 11.3  **The First Crusade, 1095–1099.**

Although the crusading movement ultimately failed to keep Jerusalem out of Muslim hands and resulted in cumulative casualties estimated in the millions, the Crusades produced some positive achievements for Europeans. The ability of Western popes to organize European knights into armies and to send them far afield in service of the church enhanced their prestige in both the west and the east. The Crusades also helped to establish western Christian dominance of sea traffic in the Mediterranean. In addition, the retaking of Christian territories in southern Italy, Sicily, and Spain gave European scholars access to new sources of Greco-Arabic scientific advances, known collectively as the "New Logic," and it resulted in the transmission of Islamic architectural elements to Western Europe (see "Patterns Up Close," p. 332).

## Intellectual and Cultural Developments

The High Middle Ages (ca. 1000–1300) saw a series of important new directions and institutions reflective of the intellectual and cultural expressions of western Christian religious civilization. Perhaps the two most visible symbols of this civilization—the Gothic cathedral and the university—were born during the "twelfth-century renaissance." It was in the university that the study of Aristotle provoked a renewed interest in science and the natural world.

**Universities**   As a result of the urban revolution of the eleventh century, monastic schools in rural areas began to lose ground to cathedral schools in urban centers, which offered more relevant instruction in reading and writing, mathematical reckoning, and logical reasoning—skills required by the commercial world of the twelfth century. Creative thinkers were now attracted to cathedral schools in the larger cities of Europe, where they in turn began to attract students. In time, larger groups of students and teachers formed the first universities at Salerno, Bologna, and Paris.

Particularly in Paris, the university curriculum began to focus on the philosophy of Aristotle, who had been all but ignored during the early Middle Ages. In large part this renewed focus was owing to the efforts of Gerbert of Aurillac (ca. 946–1003), described as "the most learned man of his century" and later named Pope Sylvester II (r. 999–1003). As a young man Gerbert had studied in Islamic Spain, where he pursued interests in mathematics, astronomy, and Aristotelian logic. Later, as deacon of the cathedral school at Reims, Gerbert introduced both the sciences and Aristotelian logic to his students, many of whom in turn helped spread the new learning throughout cathedral schools in Europe.

During the eleventh and twelfth centuries, two important developments in universities resulted from the growing popularity of Aristotelian logic. One of these was the emergence of a new method of pursuing philosophical and theological truth by use of Aristotelian logic, known as **scholasticism**. Adherents of this new methodology began to subject long-held doctrines of the church to rigorous scrutiny. The problem was that Aristotle posed a serious threat to church authority, since a better understanding of his ideas revealed just how incompatible his thinking was with religious doctrine. For example, Aristotle denied the creation of the world in favor of the world's eternity; he also denied the immortality of the soul.

What emerged was a fundamental disagreement between those who placed the truths of *faith* before the truths of *reason* in attempting to gain knowledge

**Scholasticism:**
A medieval method of determining theological and philosophical truth by using Aristotelian logic.

of God's existence and those who placed reason first. The most famous advocates of these opposing schools of thought were St. Anselm (ca. 1034–1109) and Peter Abelard (1079–1142). Anselm argued that faith must precede reason ("I believe in order that I might understand"). He further argued that proof of God's existence could be deduced by first accepting church doctrine on the basis of faith and then proceeding to support these notions by reasoned argument. Abelard, the most popular teacher at the cathedral school of Notre Dame in Paris during these years, disagreed, arguing, "I understand in order that I might believe." Abelard was particularly famous among twelfth-century scholars because of his tragic love affair with his student Heloise, niece of the canon of the cathedral school of Notre Dame, who became pregnant. The most sensational portion of Abelard's *Historia Calamitatum* (*The Story of My Misfortunes*) concerns his description of how Heloise's uncle took revenge when he discovered that, after their secret marriage, Abelard sent Heloise to a nunnery. As a result, Abelard's apparent favoring of reason over faith tipped the balance in favor of those who were inclined to question traditional Christian doctrine.

> "They had vengeance on me with a most cruel and most shameful punishment, such as astounded the whole world; for they cut off those parts of my body with which I had done that which was the cause of their sorrow."
>
> — Peter Abelard

So popular was Aristotle by the middle of the thirteenth century that in addition to the earlier division between those who advocated either the truths of faith or reason, a third perspective was offered by those who took a middle path. It was to the latter camp that St. Thomas Aquinas (ca. 1224–1274) belonged. In his *Summa Theologica*, Aquinas argued that, instead of considering the truths of reason as being totally irreconcilable from the truths of faith, it was possible to consider a compromise, or a synthesis of the two, that would in the end lead to a knowledge of God's existence and, thus, to personal salvation. According to this construct, one could begin an upward journey to an understanding of God by first relying upon the truths of reason, but at a certain point one would have to abandon pure reason for the more enlightened approach afforded by faith, which would then allow an understanding of the mysteries of Christian doctrine and, thus, of God.

> "Grace (faith) does not destroy nature (reason)—it perfects her."
>
> —St. Thomas Aquinas

**Law and Medicine**   In the twelfth century, universities began to offer training in two more disciplines critical to cosmopolitan urban life: law and medicine. By the early years of the century scholars at Bologna discovered the Roman legal tradition preserved in Justinian's celebrated *Corpus Iuris Civilis*. It was at Bologna around 1140 that the *Corpus* inspired a monk named Gratian to compile a compendium of ecclesiastical law known as the *Decretum*. Gratian's student Peter Lombard's *Book of Sentences*, produced in 1150, served along with the *Decretum* as the foundation for the development of **canon law**, utilized by the papacy in its struggles to contest secular power.

**Canon law:** The law of the church.

Medical studies were taught at Salerno in the late eleventh century. Located in Sicily, Salerno was able to assimilate Islamic and Byzantine medical advances. Serving as the nucleus of medical studies at Salerno were the works of the Roman physician Galen and the *Canon of Medicine* compiled by the Islamic scholar Ibn Sina (or Avicenna, 980–1037). These works formed the foundation of medical studies throughout medieval European universities.

**Medieval Science**    Another consequence of the appeal of Aristotle was a corresponding fascination with scientific texts of the ancient Greeks. The initial impulse in this direction was provided not only by Gerbert of Aurillac but also by Christian advances into Spain and southern Italy during the waning years of the eleventh century. The Christian conquest of Toledo in 1085, followed by the retaking of Sicily in 1090, provided opportunities for scholars from all over Europe to gain access to Islamic treasure troves of scientific learning. Adelard of Bath (ca. 1080–1152) was one of the earliest Western scholars to translate Greek scientific texts from Arabic into Latin. As such, Adelard served as an important bridge between the Islamic and western Christian worlds. It was largely owing to his efforts that a new sense of curiosity about natural science began to circulate in Western intellectual circles.

Adelard contributed to what is often referred to as the age of Latin translators. The most prolific of these translators was Gerard of Cremona (ca. 1114–1187), who provided Latin translations of over 70 Greek scientific texts, including Ptolemy's *Almagest* and most of Aristotle's works on physics, along with numerous mathematical treatises such as Euclid's *Elements* and al-Khwarizmi's *Algebra*, and several medical treatises such as Galen's texts and Avicenna's *Canon of Medicine*.

Perhaps the most important of Adelard's successors in England was Robert Grosseteste (ca. 1175–1253). Grosseteste represented a rare combination of ecclesiastical and secular interests; he was for a time bishop of Lincoln but was also a dabbler in the new scientific studies of natural phenomena. Grosseteste made an important contribution to the advancement of science in that he recognized the value of mathematics. He was also among the earliest scholastics to question the scientific authority of Aristotle. Grosseteste's arguments were developed by his student Roger Bacon (ca. 1214–1294), whose principal contribution to the development of Western science was to emphasize the role of induction and experimentation.

**Merton College Library.**
Merton College was founded as a self-governing academic institution by Walter de Merton in 1264. During the fourteenth century scholars interested in mathematics and physics, known as the Merton (or Oxford) Calculators, produced significant advances that contributed to the European scientific revolution of the sixteenth and seventeenth centuries. In 1373 construction was begun on Merton College Library, but earlier records indicate that scholars at Merton began to build a collection of books as early as 1276.

During the early years of the fourteenth century another "school" of natural scientists, the so-called Oxford Calculators, advanced scientific studies. There were several influential members of this group, and all were associated with Merton College, Oxford. They were united by their interest in and pursuit of abstract mathematics combined with physics. Taken together, they challenged many of Aristotle's mistakes regarding natural science, including his denial of the existence of vacuum, his notion that objects of different weights fall to earth at different speeds (the heavier fall faster), and his theory of motion, which erroneously held that objects remain in motion only through the continuous application of an external force. Perhaps the best known of the Calculators' contributions is the mean speed theorem, which anticipates Galileo's law of falling bodies, stating that objects of different weights in fact fall with uniform rates of acceleration in a vacuum.

# Crisis and Creativity, 1300–1415

The fourteenth century marks the final phase of European Christian civilization and is often considered an age of transition to the European Renaissance. The early part of the century witnessed a series of economic reversals. Near mid-century a devastating plague originating in southeast Asia ravaged Europe, killing as much as one-third of its population and generating further social upheaval. Centralized kingdoms developed a sense of national identity and consolidation; one result was a long, drawn-out period of war between England and France that began in 1337 and ended in 1453. In addition, the authority of the papacy was challenged from without by powerful European secular rulers and weakened from within by a series of internal problems and philosophical disputes. As bleak as things were, however, signs of new creative forces arising from the ashes of the fourteenth century appeared as early as the middle of the century.

## The Calamitous Fourteenth Century

Fourteenth-century Europe experienced all manner of dearth, disease, death, and dissolution. The early part of the century witnessed a series of reversals in the economic and social realms, brought on initially by dramatic climatic change starting in the year 1315 that resulted in a prolonged period of poor harvests followed by famine. Near mid-century a disastrous plague added to the misery of daily life.

**Famine**   During the early years of the fourteenth century Europe was hit by a disastrous combination of factors that produced a prolonged period of famine. One factor was a sudden disparity between an expanding population and its available food supply. From ca. 1000 to 1300 Europe's population had nearly doubled to a total of around 80 million, thanks to advances in agricultural technology. By 1300, however, no new advances were forthcoming. In addition, after centuries of expansion and clearing of lands, Europe suddenly ran out of new frontiers, resulting in a lack of land available for increased agricultural production. To make matters worse, the average annual temperature dropped during this period, which shortened the summer growing season. At the same time, an unusually prolonged series of rainy seasons in the spring and summer planting seasons, followed by a succession of harsh winters, resulted in a famine that extended from 1315 to 1322.

**Plague**   Near mid-century, Europe's already weakened populations suffered a horrific outbreak of plague. The disease originated in Cambodia, Burma, and Vietnam; it was then transmitted across Asia in goods and wares transported by Mongol traders in the 1330s. From there it spread westward along trade routes to the Black Sea. The plague was introduced to the West when grain-carrying Genoese merchant ships, infested with rats, sailed from the Crimea to ports in Sicily and northern Italy in 1346–1347. Within a year, the plague had spread into northern Europe via trade routes, carried by infected rats and fleas, fanning out across Europe north of the Alps. Whereas this pestilence was originally considered to be a version of bubonic plague, recent research has shown that because of its rapid dissemination a more accurate designation is *pneumatic* plague. That is, people with infected lungs inadvertently spread the disease by close contact with others, and by frequent coughing.

# The Gothic Cathedral

Although the Gothic cathedral is the iconic symbol of medieval European Christianity, its origins and evolution are less familiar.

**Nave of the Abbey Church of St. Denis**

The origin of the cathedral can be traced back to late imperial Rome. Following Constantine's Edict of Milan in 313, Christians no longer had to worship in secret, and church leaders sought a public building that could accommodate larger congregations. Many features of the Roman *basilica*, a civic hall traditionally used for public functions, rendered it ideal for early Christian worship. Its design was assimilated by the church and transformed from pagan to Christian usage. The basilica style featured a long central aisle (or nave), roofed over with timber, ending with an intersecting transept and an arched passage into a semicircular *apse* (or sanctuary) with a raised platform where the presiding magistrate sat in judgment.

During the post-Roman early medieval period, other earlier Roman and Christian architectural styles were adapted to European circumstances. The result was the Romanesque style of church architecture, which appeared in different guises from ca. 800 to 1000. A key feature of Romanesque architecture was the replacement of the basilica's low timber roofs with heavy stone barrel vaults, which required massive stone piers and exterior walls to support the weight and resulted in gloomy interiors. In addition, the apse was expanded beyond the transept by the addition of a circular walkway (the ambulatory) to allow crowds of pilgrims to view Christian relics. Finally, the focal point of the exterior was now the western façade, flanked by two towers. The spread of Benedictine monasteries as well as the emergence of powerful German emperors during the tenth and eleventh centuries prompted additional changes in Romanesque churches: the enlargement of interiors, the increased height of the nave—utilizing vaulting and groin arches—and the addition of a clerestory with rounded arches above the nave to admit more light into the interior.

The revitalization of urban life and lay piety in the eleventh and twelfth centuries prompted architects to assimilate some features of the Romanesque into a new design that reflected these changes. The first attempt to open up gloomy Romanesque interiors—and an early expression of the new Gothic style—was made in 1144 at the abbey church of St. Denis in Paris under the direction of Abbot Suger (1085–1151). Suger's intention was to enlarge the interior spaces of Romanesque churches, providing more light and increasing the upward reach of their exteriors.

The disease took its name "Black Death" from the appearance of blackened body sores, called *buboes* (hence the name "bubonic plague"), especially near the lymph nodes, that announced the arrival of the disease. Once the dreaded black sores appeared, infected people suffered horribly with high fevers, swollen lymph nodes, and painfully aching joints and usually died within 3 days. The plague ravaged Europe from 1348 to 1352 and returned sporadically in the 1360s, 1370s, and 1390s.

In order to realize these objectives Suger turned to solutions already in practice in late Romanesque churches: the pointed arch, the ribbed vault, and flying buttresses.

Pointed arches allowed for higher vertical thrusts in weight distribution, resulting in soaring naves. The pointed arch, widely used as early as the eighth century in Islamic architecture, was most likely transmitted to Europe from Sicily. A likely scenario traces a route from Sicily, where the pointed arch was incorporated in the design of Monte Cassino in 1071. After the Norman conquest of Sicily in 1090 the concept of the pointed arch was transmitted to France, where it was used in the construction of the third church of Cluny (1088–1095). Abbot Suger visited Cluny in 1130, and would have been aware of the distinct advantages offered by the pointed arch.

Ribbed vaults were improvements over earlier Romanesque groin vaults in that they provided for elevated vaults while at the same time directing the vertical thrust downward through more slender columns, thus providing greater interior space. Ribbed vaults also allowed for thinner outer walls, which could accommodate large glass windows that allowed in more light. There is considerable conjecture over whether the technique of ribbed vaults may have originated in earlier Islamic architecture. For example, the great mosques at Córdoba in Spain and Tlemcen in Algeria utilized a form of crisscrossing webs in the construction of domes over the *maqsura*; this form may have found its way to European architects as a result of the fall of Toledo in 1085. It has been argued, however, that the earlier Islamic models were of a different sort than those of Christian Europe in that they were primarily used in domes instead of the nave, and in any event were designed for symbolic and decorative purposes, rather than for structural design. The consensus, then, is that the earliest example of a ribbed groin vault over a nave emanating from Romanesque architecture occurred at Durham Cathedral as early as 1093.

Another innovation at St. Denis was the incorporation of stained-glass panels (frequently depicting stories from the Bible) in the outer walls, which provided dazzling arrays of color and light in the interior. Flying buttresses—perhaps the most innovative feature of the Gothic style—were then used to support the thinner outer walls, distributing the thrust of the ribbed vaults and pointed arches away from the outer wall and down toward the ground.

## Questions

- How does the Gothic cathedral demonstrate the origins–interactions–adaptations process in action?
- What types of cultural adaptations are evident in houses of worship built in modern times?

The highly contagious disease was next to impossible to contain for a variety of reasons. For one thing, Europe's population was weakened as a consequence of the great famine. For another, overcrowded European cities, with their lack of sanitation, created ideal breeding conditions for the rapid spread of the disease. Moreover, medieval medicine was woefully backward when it came to the treatment of illnesses and diseases. John of Gaddesden (1280–1361), educated at

"Write these words on the jaw of the patient: In the name of the Father, the Son and the Holy Ghost, Amen.+Rex+Pax+Nax+in Christo Filio, and the pain will cease at once as I have often seen."

—John of Gaddesden

Merton College, Oxford, whose *Rosa Anglica practica medicinae* was widely consulted by physicians (Chaucer lists the book as a staple in physicians' libraries), relies as much on charms and incantations as he does on rational practices for curing illnesses.

It has been estimated that England alone may have lost nearly 1 million from a total population of around 4 million. Urban areas were the hardest hit; Florence suffered losses amounting to around 50,000 out of a total population of 85,000. A reasonable estimate of the number of people who died throughout Europe as a result of the first wave of the plague puts the total loss at about one-third of the entire population (see Map 11.4).

A series of economic and social consequences of the Black Death followed throughout Europe. It was widely believed that the plague was provoked by a wrathful God, who punished Christians for their sins. A more sinister response was another wave of anti-Semitism, seen earlier in the twelfth century. Considered heretics and "Christ killers," Jews were targeted as scapegoats and accused of poisoning wells, perhaps an ominous foreshadowing of the Inquisition (see Chapter 16). The falling off of Europe's population resulted in urban areas in less demand for goods and manufactured items, causing a downturn in commerce and trade, and in rural areas in a similar decline in demand for grain products. Another result of the overall decline in Europe's population was the reduction in the number of agricultural workers, whose labor was suddenly more sought after than before the plague. The result of these increasing tensions between the well-off and those less well-off was a series of social uprisings throughout Europe. In Paris a disturbance known as the Jacquerie broke out in 1358, and in Florence the Ciompi rebellion flared up in 1378. The most serious social revolt occurred in London in 1381. Known as the Peasants' Revolt, the uprising was more broadly based and

**Burial of Plague Victims.** With up to 50 percent of the people in some places in Europe dying of the plague, burial scenes, such as this one depicted in a Flemish manuscript, were common throughout the middle and late fourteenth century.

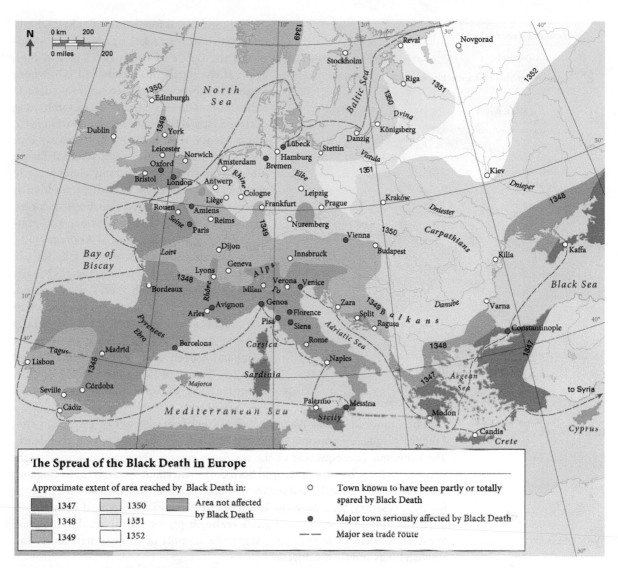

**The Spread of the Black Death in Europe**

Approximate extent of area reached by Black Death in:

| | |
|---|---|
| 1347 | 1350 |
| 1348 | 1351 |
| 1349 | 1352 |

Area not affected by Black Death

○   Town known to have been partly or totally spared by Black Death

●   Major town seriously affected by Black Death

- - -   Major sea trade route

MAP 11.4  **The Spread of the Black Death in Europe.**

included wealthy country residents as well as participants from the ranks of the urban working classes.

**The Hundred Years' War**    From the mid-fourteenth to the mid-fifteenth century, Europe was embroiled in a disastrous conflict, dubbed the "Hundred Years' War" by nineteenth-century historians. At issue was a long-simmering dispute over English landholdings in France, the result of the Norman Conquest. More immediately, when the English king Edward III (r. 1327–1377) laid claim to the vacant French throne in 1328, his claim was rejected in favor of Charles IV (r. 1322–1328), the first of the Valois rulers. These issues came to a head in 1337 when Philip VI (r. 1328–1350) seized control of Gascony and fighting erupted in earnest between the two countries.

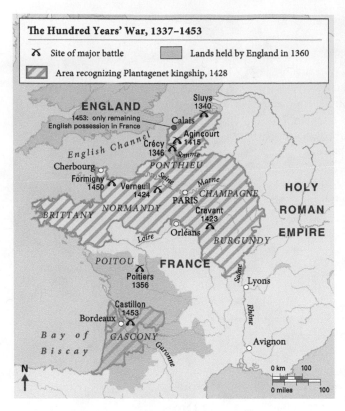

**The Hundred Years' War, 1337–1453**

↗ Site of major battle          Lands held by England in 1360

⬚ Area recognizing Plantagenet kingship, 1428

MAP **11.5** **The Hundred Years'**
**War, 1337–1453.**

The conflict was fought in three phases. Early on, English forces racked up significant victories at the Battle of Crécy in 1346 and then again at the Battle of Poitiers in 1356, where English longbowmen handed smashing defeats to the mounted French knights. The same thing occurred later at the Battle of Agincourt in 1415, where Henry V (r. 1413–1422) led vastly outnumbered English forces (only 6,000 facing 20,000) to score a surprising victory while suffering relatively few casualties. Suddenly, however, when it seemed that English forces were on the verge of declaring victory, a 17-year-old peasant girl named Joan of Arc (ca. 1412–1431) encouraged the uncrowned Charles VII (r. 1422–1461) to relieve the siege of Orleans in 1429, where English forces were routed. The victory at Orleans inspired the French to one success after another. The conflict finally came to an end in 1453, when the English conceded a French victory in terms agreed to in the Treaty of Paris, leaving the English in possession of only the port of Calais (see Map 11.5).

The Hundred Years' War affected almost every aspect of European life. Like the plague, the war was a constant reminder of the omnipresence of death. The economic consequences of the war were equally serious. The war—fought entirely on French soil—destroyed both crops and small farms. In both England and France, financing the war meant new and increased taxes—and further woes for the peasantry, who bore the brunt of these increased financial obligations. The war even affected the religious realm. It prevented the resolution of the **Western Schism** as rival popes sought the support of contending French and English kings and their subjects.

**Western Schism:** The period 1378–1417, marked by divided papal allegiances in Latin Christendom.

**Crises in the Church**    Troubles began during the papacy of Pope Boniface VIII (r. 1294–1303), whose stubborn personality clashed with the ambitious national interests of Philip IV (r. 1285–1314) of France. Philip, desperate for money in order to consolidate royal power, levied a tax on the French clergy. In response, Boniface excommunicated Philip; he retaliated by ordering the imprisonment of the pope in 1303, who subsequently died from the shock of this rude treatment. Boniface's successor, Clement V (r. 1305–1314), left Rome and took up residence in Avignon, on the French border. Clement appointed a number of French clergymen to the College of Cardinals. From 1305 to 1378 successive French popes continued to reside at Avignon, a period known as the *Avignon Papacy*.

In 1378 Pope Gregory XI (r. 1370–1378) returned to Rome, but he died shortly after his arrival there. Perhaps in response to pressure from a Roman mob to elect either a Roman or an Italian as the next pope, the predominantly French College of Cardinals elected an Italian archbishop, Urban VI (r. 1378–1389). Urban badly mistreated the cardinals and insisted on a series of outlandish reforms. The cardinals, regretting their selection of Urban, returned to Avignon and promptly elected a Frenchman as the new pope, Clement VII (r. 1378–1394). An attempt by the Council of Pisa in 1409 to resolve the conflict merely intensified the embarrassment. The council deposed both reigning popes and named a new one, Alexander V (r. 1409–1410). However, the two reigning popes refused to step down, with the result that the church had not one or two but *three* popes.

Adding to the church's problems were several outspoken critics of its doctrine. One of the earliest of these critics was John Wycliffe (ca. 1330–1384), an Oxford theologian. Wycliffe railed against the wealth and abuses of the higher clergy, denied the power of priests to act as intermediaries between believers and God, and disputed the validity of many **sacraments**, including the most central of Christian dogmas, the sacrament of the Eucharist (sometimes referred to as Communion or the Lord's Supper), which holds that Christ's presence is revealed in consecrated bread and wine. Wycliffe also oversaw the translation of the Bible into Middle English. Wycliffe's teachings reached Bohemia in central Europe when the English king Richard II (r. 1377–1399) married the princess Anne of Bohemia. John Huss (1370–1415), a radical religious reformer and preacher at Prague, enthusiastically supported Wycliffe's ideas, especially the English theologian's argument for the primacy of scripture as the basis for all Christian doctrine (see Map 11.6).

**John Wycliffe.** Educated at Oxford during the turbulent fourteenth century, Wycliffe attained the degree of doctor of divinity during the 1370s. In expressing dissident views regarding several doctrines of the church, including transubstantiation and the authority of the priesthood, Wycliffe went so far as to declare the pope an "antichrist." In 1382 Wycliffe completed his translation of the Bible into English. His radical teachings were carried throughout England by his followers, known as Lollards, and eventually to Germany, earning him the title "Morningstar of the Protestant Reformation."

**Sacrament:** An outward and physical sign of an inward and spiritual grace.

## Signs of a New Era in the Fifteenth Century

All of the instances of doom and gloom we have mentioned signaled the waning of earlier medieval values, perspectives, and institutions. Yet, at the same time, dire situations in the fourteenth century prompted adaptations and subsequent transformations in the succeeding century that prefigured the transition to the Renaissance. We can observe these adjustments in political, economic, and cultural aspects of fifteenth-century Europe.

**Political Reorganization in France and England**   Out of the ashes of the Hundred Years' War arose new conceptions of royal authority in both England and France that set the stage for the appearance of the "new monarchies" in the second half of the fifteenth century. In France, for example, fifteenth-century rulers utilized the pressures of warfare as rationales to centralize their authority. One expedient was to overhaul the royal bureaucracy in order to enhance its efficiency and power. Another was the raising of new taxes without consulting the Estates-General.

The state of politics in England was similarly affected by the course of the Hundred Years' War. Across the course of the war English monarchs were repeatedly forced to convene Parliament in order to gain quick access to much-needed funds to prosecute the war effort. Before granting monies to the crown, however, the House of Commons, consisting of merchants and lesser nobility, insisted on "redress of grievances before consent to taxation." As a result, the House of

**The Great Western Schism, 1378–1417**

| | | |
|---|---|---|
| ▨ Center of Hussite activity | ☐ | Areas recognizing Rome-based pope |
| ▨ Area most affected by teachings of John Wycliffe | ▨ | Areas recognizing Avignon-based pope |

MAP 11.6 **The Great Western Schism, 1378–1417.**

**Hanseatic League:**
A trade network of allied ports along the North Sea and Baltic coasts, founded in 1256.

Commons eventually gained the right to introduce all important tax legislation in Parliament; it was granted its first speaker in 1376; and it was given the right to impeach irresponsible members of the king's government.

**European Commerce and Trade**    Europe's fifteenth-century economic recovery was even more pronounced in commerce. When France regained control of Flanders during the course of the Hundred Years' War, England—then at war with the French—was forced to abandon its profitable wool trade with Flemish merchants. As a result, England developed a far more lucrative trade in manufactured cloth products, of which by 1500 it had become a leading exporter.

When the Hundred Years' War disrupted trade in France, new lanes of commerce opened up across Europe. Germanic towns in northern Europe had formed a trading alliance, known as the **Hanseatic League** (from *hansa*, meaning "company"), as early as the thirteenth century. The league reached its peak of influence during the later fourteenth and fifteenth centuries, with trading links from London in the west to Novgorod in Russia. A new commercial axis extended from the cities of the Hanseatic League in the north southward to the northern Italian cities of Venice and Genoa.

Of crucial importance for the future of European trade was the collapse of the so-called Pax Mongolica in 1368. Following the expansion of the Mongol Empire during the thirteenth and fourteenth centuries, travel and trade networks flourished between China and the West across the Silk Road. Thus, the Mongols facilitated the transfer of significant technological innovations from China to Europe. When, however, Mongol rule in China dissolved and was replaced by the Ming dynasty, which was less interested in ties with the West, travel on the Silk Road was no longer safe or profitable. Faced with the necessity of reaching the riches of the East by alternate means, European merchants were forced to resort to southern maritime routes, in use from the 750s onward.

**Innovations in Business Techniques**    Several innovative economic practices contributed to a revitalization of Europe's economy during the fifteenth century. Smaller markets, shrunk by the economic crises of the fourteenth century, brought on increased competition among merchants, who sought ever more creative business methods in order to remain solvent. New accounting procedures, such as double-entry bookkeeping, increased the efficiency of record keeping. In addition, the introduction of maritime insurance, which protected investments in risky seaborne trade, fueled an increase in trans-Mediterranean trade and commerce, while at the same time increasing profits for individual investors.

New banking procedures also facilitated the expansion of Europe's economy by providing loans to merchants and manufacturers. Florence emerged as the center of huge banking partnerships such as the Medici Bank; the Medici family went on to dominate Florentine civic affairs by 1500.

**Developments in the Church**    As a consequence of the disintegration of papal leadership during the fourteenth century, the church was controlled by councils of bishops in the early fifteenth century, a movement known as *conciliarism*. In order to resolve the crises of the fourteenth century, the Council of Constance (1414–1417) was convened by the Holy Roman emperor. Its first order of business was to depose the three reigning popes and to restore papal authority to a single pontiff, who took the name Martin V (r. 1417–1431). Second, to put an end to heretical movements, principally the teachings of John Wycliffe, the council convicted John Huss of heresy and burned him at the stake. The execution of Huss had momentous implications for the future of the church, especially in Germany. Huss's region of Bohemia emerged as a hotbed of heresy, and these anticlerical sentiments helped fuel Martin Luther's Protestant Reformation, which began in neighboring Saxony in the next century. Finally, to improve the management of the church, the council declared that henceforth councils of bishops would meet frequently in order to keep popes under their strict control.

The conciliar movement was an attempt by the bishops to wrest control of the church from popes. The popes resisted the conciliar movement but had to make concessions to secular rulers to gain their support. The result of these concessions was the further weakening of the Roman Church and the creation of national churches, independent of control from Rome.

**Literature**    Significant and widespread changes in literary expression flourished, in large part due to the growing popularity of cultural expression in **vernacular** languages instead of Latin. Although writing in the vernacular first made its appearance in France in the later 1100s, education in the vernacular was especially popular in the city-states of northern Italy, where the emphasis was on educating students for productive careers in the secular world, rather than training them to become priests.

**Vernacular:** The native, common spoken language of a particular region.

A number of Italian authors chose to write in the vernacular rather than in Latin. A particularly noteworthy example is the poet Dante Alighieri (1265–1321), author of *The Divine Comedy*, a long epic poem written in Italian and completed in 1321. Two Italian authors of the next generation continued Dante's legacy. Francesco Petrarch (1304–1374), known as the "father of Renaissance humanism," turned to Roman authors and classical texts, whose values more closely resembled the secular, materialistic world of everyday life in Florence. Petrarch also wrote a series of love sonnets to his beloved Laura, in Tuscan Italian. The *Decameron* of Giovanni Boccaccio (1313–1375), written between 1352 and 1353, represents a further drift away from medieval literary conventions—and toward the Roman classical past—in that it draws its inspiration from the first-century Roman author Petronius and his scandalous *Satyricon*.

English and French writers of the fourteenth century also began to produce works in their native languages. *Piers Plowman*, composed in Middle English by William Langland (ca. 1332–1400), presents a series of complaints and laments about current abuses in late-fourteenth-century England, especially among the aristocracy and the clergy. Geoffrey Chaucer (ca. 1340–1400), a friend and contemporary of Langland's, also wrote in Middle English. Like Langland, Chaucer satirized abuses in contemporary society. His *Canterbury Tales* is a series of stories told by travelers making their annual pilgrimage from London to the shrine of St. Thomas Becket in Canterbury. Christine de Pizan (ca. 1364–1430) of France composed both poetry and prose; she was primarily concerned with advancing the status of women, and for her criticisms of male behaviors is often considered the first feminist writer. In her *Epistle to the God of Love*, for example, she criticizes the Roman poet Ovid for attributing "nasty ways" to women.

> "That women have such vices I deny; I take my arms up in defense of them."
>
> —Christine de Pizan

**Philosophy**   Bold departures in the era's philosophy challenged basic medieval theological beliefs. In place of Aquinas's attempt to reconcile differences between the truths of faith and reason, the intellectuals of the time turned decidedly toward the latter, especially toward Aristotle. The earliest philosopher to take this approach was the Oxford Franciscan John Duns Scotus (ca. 1266–1308). Critical of Aquinas, Scotus argued for the strict separation of reason from theology. William of Ockham (ca. 1285–1349), another Oxford Franciscan, carried the assault on the Aquinas synthesis even further. He argued for extreme nominalism, arguing that only the truths of reason, vested in individual things, could be known for certain. Therefore, no metaphysical knowledge is possible; and, from this, it is impossible to have any sure knowledge of the existence of God. That being the case, only a personal, mystical association with God was available to the believer.

# Putting It All Together

Following the collapse of the united Mediterranean Roman Empire, a new postclassical, Christian religious civilization gradually developed in western Europe during the period ca. 600–1400. The Germanic invasions that brought down Roman rule in the western provinces destroyed imperial unity in the West and created in Europe a series of smaller political entities. After a brief period of centralized imperial rule during the reign of Charlemagne in the later eighth century, medieval Europe fell back in the ninth and tenth centuries into a pattern of decentralized political entities that provided for law and order at the local, instead of empire-wide, level. Feudalism, as this arrangement is known, prevented the reassertion of a centralized European empire and prepared Europe for the appearance of several highly centralized, competing kingdoms. One advantage of this "political pluralism" was the appearance of competition among the states of Europe, which in turn created a sense of vitality and progress in the West.

In terms of cultural developments, the Germanic invasions and subsequent destruction of Roman rule in the West were immensely disruptive, forcing the formation of a new, distinctly European, postclassical culture formed from a blending of three elements that had formerly been antagonistic to each other: Roman legacies, Germanic customs, and Christian institutions. Of these, the Christian Church would prove the most important in shaping a new European religious civilization. In much the same way that Buddhism, Hinduism, Confucianism, and Islam undergirded civilizations in Asia and Africa, Christianity served as the basic unifying force that held together the new European civilization.

During the fourteenth century Europe experienced several transforming events. The horrors of famine and plague, accompanied by over a century of warfare between England and France, cast a pall of gloom over European society, which in turn called into question traditional medieval values and perspectives. In addition, a series of internal problems in the church resulted in a lessening of its authority and prestige. At the same time, however, several developments—particularly in the cultural sphere—prepared Europe for the transition to Renaissance secularism and humanism.

▶ For additional resources, including maps, primary sources, visuals, and quizzes, please go to www.oup.com/us/vonsivers. Please see the Further Resources section at the back of the book for additional readings and suggested websites.

## Against the Grain

# The Cathar Heresy

In 1144, the dedication of the magnificent Gothic abbey church at St. Denis provided a physical manifestation of the power and glory of Roman Christianity in European Christendom. And yet, only one year earlier—in 1143—a heretical cult was identified as posing the most dangerous challenge to Orthodox Christianity in its history.

Known as Cathars ("pure ones"), or Albigensians (from Albi, a region in southwestern France), this heretical movement reflected anticlerical sentiments emanating from mounting discontent among educated urbanites and rural laity alike, dismayed by the materialism, corruption, and increasing worldliness among the clerical establishment. It was derived from a combination of Persian Zoroastrianism and Manichaeanism, dualistic religions in which forces of good and light (represented by God and the spiritual world) struggle against forces of evil and darkness (represented by Satan) for dominance in the universe. Cathars believed that because Satan created the material world and imprisoned human souls within the physical body, the only way to end the cycle of reincarnation in the material world and to escape from Satan's grasp was to forego all material things of this world, including marriage, sex, and certain foods. And because Christ was of the material world, Cathars rejected elements of Orthodox Christianity, including the Trinitarian doctrine, as well as many sacraments, including the Eucharist and baptism.

Alarmed at their growing influence, Pope Innocent III moved to suppress Catharism. His initial response was to try persuasion by enlisting the help of the recently licensed orders of Dominicans and Franciscans. When that failed, Innocent ordered the Albigensian crusade (1209–1229), which resulted in the brutal (even by medieval standards) suppression of the movement. When a force of French knights stormed the center of Cathar resistance at Beziers, they were ordered by the presiding bishop to slaughter all of its inhabitants, both Catholic and Cathar: "Kill them all. God will know His own." Further efforts to eliminate Catharism included the establishment of an Inquisition in 1234, and the final dissolution of the movement in 1329, when the last of the Cathars were burned at the stake.

- In what ways does Catharism represent a contrast to the patterns of development of medieval Europe?

- How does the Cathar heresy compare with other heresies in world religions?

# Thinking Through Patterns

▶ **How did the Merovingians and Carolingians construct a new Christian European civilization during the seventh and eighth centuries CE?**

The Merovingians and Carolingians constructed a new Christian European civilization during the seventh and eighth centuries by utilizing the support of the Christian Church. Through their conversion to Christianity, as well as their support and encouragement of monastic expansion, they earned the support of bishops, priests, and monks in all regions of their kingdom. In addition, the creation of the Franco-papal alliance during the eighth century, followed by Charlemagne's personal involvement in church affairs, ensured the emergence of a new Christian foundation for Europe.

Some key factors in the political, economic, and social recovery of Europe during the eleventh and twelfth centuries included the emergence of centralized kingdoms in France and England, which replaced the decentralized cells of political authority during the ninth and tenth centuries. The expansion of agricultural advances and the development of commerce and trade produced a population surge, which in turn resulted in urbanization and the emergence of a new bourgeois middle class of merchants and traders.

▶ **What were key factors in the political, economic, and social recovery of Europe during the eleventh and twelfth centuries?**

▶ **What were some cultural and intellectual developments during the "twelfth-century renaissance," and how did they contribute to medieval civilization?**

During the "twelfth-century renaissance" urban-centered cathedral schools developed into universities in Europe. In order to serve the needs of an expanding urban and commercial economy, more practical disciplines like law and medicine were developed in revised curricula. The influx of Aristotelian logic and science, assimilated from contacts in Spain and Sicily between Latin scholars—known as the Latin translators—and their Muslim counterparts, resulted in a prolonged debate between the truths of reason and the truths of faith. Although temporarily resolved by Aquinas in the later thirteenth century, Aristotelian nominalism dominated philosophy and theology in the fourteenth century. Another result of the fascination with Aristotle was the development of natural science at Oxford and Paris, which during the later thirteenth and early fourteenth centuries began to uncover flaws in Aristotelian celestial and terrestrial scientific conceptions.

As a result of a series of ecclesiastical reforms in both the monastic and episcopal arms of the church, a series of increasingly powerful popes began to assert papal primacy over secular rulers, and, indeed, over all European institutions. Pope Gregory VII humbled the German emperor Henry IV in the eleventh century, and Pope Innocent III did the same with King John of England in the beginning of the thirteenth century.

▶ **How did the church influence political developments in Europe during the twelfth and thirteenth centuries?**

▶ **What events made fourteenth-century Europe so dismal? How did these combine to spell the gradual demise of medieval institutions and perspectives?**

The "calamitous fourteenth century" witnessed several unprecedented setbacks that, taken together, signaled the end of the medieval era and the early stages of the Renaissance era. Among these events were the Black Death, the Hundred Years' War, and the Avignon papacy followed by the Western Schism, which produced not one, not two, but eventually three popes. At the same time men of letters, philosophers as well as theologians, began to challenge earlier assertions of papal authority, resulting in the Council of Constance (1414–1417), which ultimately replaced papal control of the church with councils of bishops during the fifteenth century.

# Patterns of Evidence: Sources for Chapter 11

## SOURCE 11.1

## Einhard's *Life of Charlemagne*

### ca. 830 CE

The model for Einhard's *Vita Caroli Magni* was Suetonius's biographies of the first 12 Roman emperors, and particularly of Augustus, composed in the second century CE. The biography is thus an example of the general attempt to revive interest in and appreciation for pre-Christian Roman antiquity in the midst of the "Carolingian Renaissance," of which Einhard was both a product and a driving force. Educated at the Palace School at Aachen (Charlemagne's capital), Einhard established a close personal and professional connection with the man himself. Due to his intimate knowledge of Charlemagne's behavior, habits, and outlook, Einhard was ideally placed to write his biography, which was composed after Charlemagne's death but contained pointed advice to the man's successors.

§24: ... His main meal of the day was served in four courses, in addition to the roast meat which his hunters used to bring in on spits and which he enjoyed more than any other food. During his meal he would listen to a public reading or some other entertainment. Stories would be recited for him, or the doings of the ancients told again. He took great pleasure in the books of Saint Augustine and especially in those which are called *The City of God*.

. . .

§25 He spoke easily and fluently, and could express with great clarity whatever he had to say. He was not content with his own mother tongue, but took the trouble to learn foreign languages. He learnt Latin so well that he spoke it as fluently as his own tongue; but he understood Greek better than he could speak it. He was eloquent to the point of sometimes seeming almost garrulous.

He paid the greatest attention to the liberal arts; and he had great respect for men who taught them, bestowing high honours upon them. When he was learning the rules of grammar he received tuition from Peter the Deacon of Pisa, who by then was an old man, but for all other subjects he was taught by Alcuin, surnamed Albinus, another Deacon, a man of the Saxon race who

---

Source: Einhard and Notker the Stammerer, *Two Lives of Charlemagne*, trans. Lewis Thorpe (Harmondsworth, UK: Penguin, 1969), 78–80.

came from Britain and was the most learned man anywhere to be found. Under him the Emperor spent much time and effort in studying rhetoric, dialectic and especially astrology. He applied himself to mathematics and traced the course of the stars with great attention and care. He also tried to learn to write. With this object in view he used to keep writing-tablets and notebooks under the pillows on his bed, so that he could try his hand at forming letters during his leisure moments; but, although he tried very hard, he had begun too late in life and he made little progress.

§26 Charlemagne practised the Christian religion with great devotion and piety, for he had been brought up in this faith since earliest childhood. . . . He donated so many sacred vessels made of gold and silver, and so many priestly vestments, that when service time came even those who opened and closed the doors, surely the humblest of all church dignitaries, had no need to perform their duties in their everyday clothes. He made careful reforms in the way in which the psalms were chanted and the lessons read. He was himself quite an expert at both of these exercises, but he never read the lesson in public and he would sing only with the rest of the congregation and then in a low voice.

▶ **Working with Sources**

1. **How does this passage reflect the attempt to recreate the ancient past during the Carolingian Renaissance?**

2. **Did Charlemagne separate his private life from his public image? Why?**

## SOURCE 11.2

# Feudal contracts and the swearing of fealty

## 1127 and 1219

In the catastrophe brought on by the assaults on all their borders, some European Christians were forced to devise new means of self-protection. Into this vacuum of governmental authority came new "feudal" relationships between lords and vassals. Over time, these contractual relationships became increasingly regularized. The terms of these relationships can be reconstructed through documents describing the ceremonial and formulaic aspects of feudal obligations.

Source: James Harvey Robinson, *Readings in European History*, vol. 1 (Boston: Ginn & Company, 1904), 178–180.

*How the Count of Flanders received the homage of his vassals (1127):*

Through the whole remaining part of the day those who had been previously **enfeoffed** by the most pious Count Charles did homage to the [new] count, taking up now again their fiefs and offices and whatever they had before rightfully and legitimately obtained. On Thursday, the seventh of April, homages were again made to the count, being completed in the following order of faith and security.

First they did their homage thus. The count asked the vassal if he were willing to become completely his man, and the other replied, "I am willing"; and with hands clasped, placed between the hands of the count, they were bound together by a kiss. Secondly, he who had done homage gave his fealty to the representative of the count in these words, "I promise on my faith that I will in future be faithful to Count William, and will observe my homage to him completely against all persons, in good faith and without deceit." And, thirdly, he took his oath to this upon the relics of the saints. Afterward the count, with a little rod which he held in his hand, gave investitures to all who by this agreement had given their security and accompanying oath.

*Pons of Mont-Saint-Jean becomes the man of the Countess of Champagne (1219):*

I, Pons of Mont-Saint-Jean, make known to all, both present and future, that since I have long been the man of my beloved Lady Blanche, countess of Champagne, for twenty pounds assigned to the fair at Bar, and since later both the countess and my dear lord have added other twenty pounds assigned to the same fair and gave me three hundred pounds in cash,— I swore by the saints that I would in good faith aid them and their heirs with my people and fortifications. If necessary I will fight especially against Erard of Brienne and Philippa his wife, and against Adelaide, queen of Cyprus, and her heirs, and against all who would aid them; except that should the said countess or count or their people be against Milo of Noyers, my sister's husband, in his castle of Noyers or elsewhere in his lands, neither I nor my people shall be held to go thither. If, however, the said Milo or his people set upon the countess or the count or their people, we shall be held to defend them and their lands with all our might.

It is also to be known that my heir who shall hold Charniacum shall also have the fief above mentioned of forty pounds.

That all this shall be held valid, I corroborate what has here been written with the impression of my seal. Done in the year of grace 1219, in the month of June.

**Enfeoffed:** Invested with an estate, or "fief".

---

▶ Working with Sources

1. Why are religious terms invoked so often in these documents in order to solidify the relationships between lords and vassals?

2. Did feudal contracts with women differ from those with men?

SOURCE 11.3

# Peter Abelard, *The Story of My Misfortunes*

## ca. 1132

One of the most brilliant professors and theologians of the European Middle Ages, Peter Abelard (1070–1142) became a star performer in the academic art of "dialectic." His abilities also earned him many enemies. When he turned his attention to the thorny subject of the Trinity, one of the principal elements of Christian belief, Abelard incurred the wrath of powerful members of the institutional church, of which he, as a professor, was also a part. In his autobiography, *The Story of My Misfortunes*, Abelard detailed the episodes of envy, backbiting, and stupidity that dogged him throughout his life. He also recalled his affair with Heloise (d. 1163), his former pupil and intellectual equal. The letters they exchanged survive as some of the most passionate and beautiful documents of the period.

It so happened that at the outset I devoted myself to analysing the basis of our faith through illustrations based on human understanding, and I wrote for my students a certain tract on the unity and trinity of God. This I did because they were always seeking for rational and philosophical explanations, asking rather for reasons they could understand than for mere words, saying that it was futile to utter words which the intellect could not possibly follow, that nothing could be believed unless it could first be understood, and that it was absurd for any one to preach to others a thing which neither he himself nor those whom he sought to teach could comprehend. Our Lord Himself maintained this same thing when He said: "They are blind leaders of the blind" (Matthew, xv, 14).

Now, a great many people saw and read this tract, and it became exceedingly popular, its clearness appealing particularly to all who sought information on this subject. And since the questions involved are generally considered the most difficult of all, their complexity is taken as the measure of the subtlety of him who succeeds in answering them. As a result, my rivals became furiously angry, and summoned a council to take action against me, the chief instigators therein being my two intriguing enemies of former days, Alberic and Lotulphe.

. . .

On one occasion Alberic, accompanied by some of his students, came to me for the purpose of intimidating me, and, after a few bland words, said that he was amazed at something he had found in my book, to the effect that, although God had begotten God, I denied that God had begotten Himself, since there was only one God. I answered unhesitatingly: "I can give you an explanation of this if you wish

Source: *The Story of My Misfortunes: The Autobiography of Peter Abélard*, trans. Henry Adams Bellows (New York: Macmillan, 1922), 36–44.

it." "Nay," he replied, "I care nothing for human explanation or reasoning in such matters, but only for the words of authority." "Very well," I said; "turn the pages of my book and you will find the authority likewise." The book was at hand, for he had brought it with him. I turned to the passage I had in mind, which he had either not discovered or else passed over as containing nothing injurious to me. And it was God's will that I quickly found what I sought. This was the following sentence, under the heading "Augustine, On the Trinity, Book I": "Whosoever believes that it is within the power of God to beget Himself is sorely in error; this power is not in God, neither is it in any created thing, spiritual or corporeal. For there is nothing that can give birth to itself."

When those of his followers who were present heard this, they were amazed and much embarrassed.

. . .

Straightway upon my summons I went to the council, and there, without further examination or debate, did they compel me with my own hand to cast that memorable book of mine into the flames.

▶ **Working with Sources**

1. **Explain the positions of Abelard and Alberic concerning "logic" and "faith" in this regard.**

2. **How does Abelard turn the tables on Alberic in his line of reasoning?**

## SOURCE 11.4

# Giovanni Boccaccio, *The Decameron*, "Putting the Devil Back in Hell"

ca. 1350

A Latin scholar, poet, and biographer, Boccaccio (1313–1375) is most famous today as the author of the *Decameron*. This compilation of 100 tales, by turns serious, bawdy, and irreverent, purports to be a rendition of the stories told over the course of 10 days by 10 young men and women who had fled Florence to escape the Black Death. Many of the tales are based on older legends, and they frequently reflect the humor of the common people of the era, often at the expense of their spiritual and social betters. Religious authorities were frequent targets of this sort of satire, reflecting their ubiquitous presence in the lives of medieval Europeans, as well as, perhaps, a deep undercurrent of resentment regarding their privileges.

Source: Giovanni Boccaccio, "Putting the Devil Back in Hell" (3.10), from *The Decameron: Selected Tales / Decameron: Novelle scelte*, trans. Stanley Appelbaum (Mineola, NY: Dover, 2000), 87–93.

. . . And so, coming to the facts, I say that in the city of Gafsa in Tunisia there was once a very rich man who, among other children, had a beautiful and genteel daughter named Alibec. She, not being a Christian, but hearing many Christians who lived in the city praising the Christian religion and the service of God, asked one of them one day how God could be served in the easiest way. This man replied that God was best served by those who fled worldly things, like those men who had gone into the lonely deserts of the Thebaid.

[Alibec goes into the desert, seeking out a willing hermit, and finally arrives at the door of a man who is willing to help her.]

. . . She reached the cell of a young hermit, a very devout and kind person named Rustico, and asked him the same thing she had asked the others.

. . .

First feeling his way with certain questions, he learned that she had never slept with a man and was just as naïve as she looked. And so he planned a way to have her submit to his pleasure under the pretext of serving God. First he told her at length that the devil was the enemy of God; then he gave her to understand that the service most pleasing to God was putting the devil back in hell, to which place God had condemned him.

The girl asked him how that was done, and Rustico replied: "You'll soon know; to make it happen, do what you see me doing." And he began to take off the few garments he was wearing until he was stark naked; and the girl did the same. Then he knelt down as if he were going to pray, and he made her do the same, facing him.

As they knelt there, Rustico's desire flared up more than ever at the sight of her great beauty, and there ensued the resurrection of the flesh. Seeing that and wondering at it, Alibec said: "Rustico, what's that thing I see on you sticking out like that? I don't have one."

"My daughter," said Rustico, "that's the devil I told you about. And now look: he's giving me terrible discomfort, so that I can hardly stand it."

Then the girl said: "Praised be God, for I see that I'm better off than you, because I don't have that devil!"

Rustico said: "It's true, but you have something else that I don't have, and you have it in place of this."

Alibec said: "What is it?"

Rustico replied: "You have hell, and, believe me, I think God has sent you here to save my soul, because, whenever this devil causes me this distress, if you want to take pity on me and let me put him back in hell, you will give me the greatest relief, and you're doing God the greatest pleasure and service—if you've really come to this area for that purpose, as you say."

The girl replied in good faith: "Oh, Father, since I have hell, let it be whenever you like."

Then Rustico said: "Bless you, daughter! Let's go put him back so he'll leave me in peace."

Saying that, he led the girl to one of their pallets and taught her how to position herself to imprison that being who was accursed of God.

. . .

After a fire destroys much of Gafsa, Alibec is the only surviving heir to her father's property, and she is married to a young man named Neerbal.

But, being asked by the ladies what she had done to serve God in the

# Chapter 12 600–1600 CE

# Contrasting Patterns in India and China

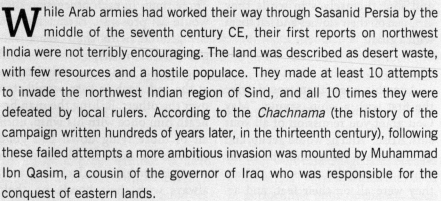

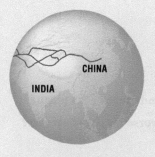

**W**hile Arab armies had worked their way through Sasanid Persia by the middle of the seventh century CE, their first reports on northwest India were not terribly encouraging. The land was described as desert waste, with few resources and a hostile populace. They made at least 10 attempts to invade the northwest Indian region of Sind, and all 10 times they were defeated by local rulers. According to the *Chachnama* (the history of the campaign written hundreds of years later, in the thirteenth century), following these failed attempts a more ambitious invasion was mounted by Muhammad Ibn Qasim, a cousin of the governor of Iraq who was responsible for the conquest of eastern lands.

Ibn Qasim's army pursued the move into India with brutal efficiency. Wearing coats of chain-mail armor and equipped with siege machinery for hurling projectiles and battering down walls, they decimated the major cities, executed most of the defenders, and extracted plunder and slaves before moving in to completely occupy the area in 711. Though Ibn Qasim's rule in the wake of his violent conquest was considered relatively moderate, the *Chachnama* claims that he met his death through a spectacular episode of duplicity concocted by his new subjects.

When the daughters of Dihar, the ruler of the conquered city of Dehal (Karachi in modern Pakistan), were taken back to the governor of Iraq as tribute,

*ABOVE: Mongol archers depicted in the* Jami al-Tawarika, *a fourteenth-century history of the world written by the Persian scholar Rashid al-Din Tabid (1247–1318).*

they accused Ibn Qasim of making sexual advances toward them. The governor immediately ordered his cousin Ibn Qasim to be sewn up in a stifling raw leather sheath and transported home. This torturous mode of transport was meant to inflict maximal suffering, and, indeed, the heat and lack of room for breathing soon did their work. Ibn Qasim died 2 days into the journey, and when his putrefied body was shown to the women who had accused him, they proudly admitted to their deception and revenge on their conqueror.

---

Though the reliability of the *Chachnama*'s account is questionable, it has come to symbolize the dramatic clash of cultural and religious outlooks that has marked the history of the Indian subcontinent ever since. In this contested area between radically different religious civilizations, the Hindu vision of Islam has remained one of ruthless conquest and purposeful disregard for long-established religious traditions. Muslims, on the other hand, have tended to view Hindus as despised infidels for whom no act of treachery is out of bounds. Such competing visions, despite periodic efforts to find compromise, have created over the centuries a pattern of *syncretic* social and political formation (a pattern in which attempts are made to reconcile two different traditions with little or no common ground). In this case, the two cultures actually coexist with considerable hostility toward one another. Despite extensive interaction, neither side has adopted much from the other; in fact, the dominant pattern has been that each has used the differences of the other to define its own religious civilization more consciously and distinctly.

The case of China provides a useful contrast. Here, despite a pervasive belief among officials and scholars of the Song dynasty (960–1279) that the fall of the previous dynasty, the Tang, had come about in large part because of the influence of the "foreign" religion of Buddhism, there were no mass persecutions or forced conversions. While Song Confucian scholars tended to lecture their audiences about "unseemly" Buddhist "superstitions," they also borrowed from Buddhist cosmological perspectives and Daoist beliefs to create a pattern of *synthetic* social and political formation (a pattern in which the most durable opposing elements merge together into a compatible whole). The result was a coherent Chinese religious civilization for the next 1,000 years, based on Neo-Confucianism, incorporating the fused body of Daoist and Buddhist religious traditions, and Confucian ethics.

# India: The Clash of Cultures

As we saw in Chapter 8, the early centuries of the Common Era saw the maturing of two large divisions among the multiple varieties of religious and cultural experience of India. The first was the rise and spread of Buddhism out of northern India into central Asia via the Silk Road and on to China and ultimately to Korea, Japan, and Vietnam. Along the way, the main branches of the various Buddhist schools were created—Theravada and Mahayana—and their scriptural foundations solidified.

## Seeing Patterns

▶ How did interactions between Muslims and Hindus in India lead to religious syncretism?

▶ What steps were taken by Hindus and Muslims to lessen the conflicts between the two rival religious traditions?

▶ How was the Tang dynasty in China different from its predecessors and successors?

▶ How effectively did the religious and philosophical traditions of Buddhism, Confucianism, and Daoism blend together in creating Neo-Confucianism? Where did they clash?

More important for the long term of Indian history, however, was that the efforts of the Guptas during India's "golden age" from the fourth to the sixth centuries CE helped in the maturation of the vast variety of religious practices that we know as "Hinduism." For it was Hinduism, rather than Buddhism, that would dominate Indian cultural and religious life until Islam ultimately established itself in the north. In the south and some areas of the north, however, Hinduism remained the dominant religious tradition down to the present day. Hence, India was transformed from a Hindu religious civilization into a frontier between the competing religious civilizations of Islam and Hinduism.

Following the collapse of India's "golden age" during the Gupta era, India experienced nearly 1,000 years of repeated attempts to establish unification of the subcontinent. None of these were effectual, however, owing not only to internal division and conflict among local rulers but also to different circumstances in the northern and southern parts of the vast region. Adding to the confusion were conflicting religious policies on the part of native Hindus and invading Muslims, which although producing something like a synthesis were nevertheless fully resolved.

## Buddhist and Hindu India after the Guptas

By the 500s CE, the last Gupta monarchs were under increasing pressure from a branch of the central Asian Huns pressing on their borders. Following the old invasion routes through the Khyber Pass into northern India, the Huns established themselves in the Punjab and adjacent regions and soon settled there to create new states as the Gupta lands shrank and finally dissolved.

**Harsha Vardhana**     One relatively stable regime that achieved a certain degree of power in the north following the Guptas was that of Harsha Vardhana (r. 606–647). Like Ashoka, Harsha is one of the few Indian monarchs about whom we know a good deal. The *Life of Harsha*, by the poet Bana, and the account of the famous Chinese Buddhist pilgrim Xuan Zang (see Chapter 9), who traveled throughout India from 630 to 644, offer a number of insights into Harsha's reign.

When Xuan Zang met Harsha in his capital at Kanauj on the Ganges River, he discovered that the ruler was a devout Buddhist. Xuan Zang's account notes the degree to which Buddhism had once permeated the land, despite the favoritism shown by the Guptas earlier toward Hinduism. It was also clear, however, that many Buddhist monasteries were now abandoned or in disrepair. Precipitated by the new devotional strains of Hinduism, the decline of Buddhism on the subcontinent as a whole was well advanced.

Still, Xuan Zang found Harsha's kingdom well run, wealthy, justly administered, and in many ways a model state. The state, however, barely outlived its ruler. The middle years of Harsha's reign saw the new power of the Arabs

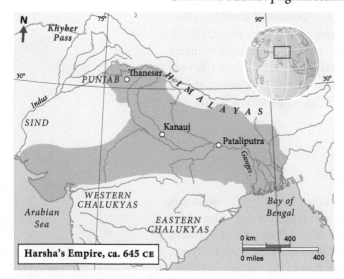

MAP 12.1 **Harsha's Empire, ca. 645 CE.**

probing the borders of Sind, the arid plain to the east of the Indus River, in advance of their full conquest in 711. Meanwhile, following Harsha's reign, northern India was once again divided into regional kingdoms (see Map 12.1).

**The Hindu States of the South** In the interim, the political center of the subcontinent had shifted south. By the latter part of the ninth century, a Chola [KO-luh] state based in Tanjore [tan-JO-ray] had concluded its long and bitter contest with the Pallavis. In 897 they captured Kanchipuram [kan-chih-POOR-um], advanced into the Pandya kingdom in the southern tip of the peninsula, and captured their capital at Madurai. In the next century, the

**Rajarajeshwara Temple, Tanjore, India.** This early-eleventh-century Hindu temple is the largest in all of India and one of the most beautiful. It was richly endowed with spoils taken from Chola conquests.

Cholas conquered Kerala, invaded Sri Lanka, and launched campaigns aimed at expanding their control of the trade with southeast Asia. The Cholas then advanced northward, allying themselves with the eastern Chalukyas in 1030. In the west, however, the revived western Chalukyas absorbed the Rashtakutras in 970 and repeatedly fought the Cholas to a standstill.

In the meantime, the development of the clove trade of the Molucca Islands (in what is now Indonesia) vastly increased the strategic value of the area, which the Indian-influenced Sumatran state of Srivijaya attempted to exploit in the tenth and eleventh centuries. In response to the exorbitant rates and threats of piracy Srivijaya posed, the Cholas sent a maritime expedition in 1025 that smashed its major ports and reduced its power for a time. In this context, the coming of the Arabs to India resulted in a broadening of the subcontinent's position in world trade. Along the western ports of India, Arab merchants continued to ply their trade much as before. Despite the newfound religious antagonisms, caravan traffic also continued much as before, and India became the bottom leg of a triangle of trade that spanned Eurasia (see Map 12.2).

**Vijayanagar** A new Hindu state emerged in 1336 with the founding of the city of Vijayanagar ("City of Victory"). The last in the two-millennium pattern of states ruled by god-kings, the new state was deemed fabulously wealthy by visitors to its capital, including the first Portuguese traders in the sixteenth century. From the City of Victory, the rulers presided over a political arrangement that, like the Gupta Empire, some scholars have described as feudal as it absorbed the remnants of the older southern kingdoms. Local leaders collected taxes and provided men and provisions for the army, while retaining considerable autonomy within their own realms.

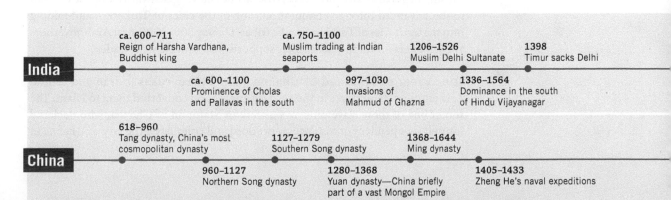

**India**

**ca. 600–711** Reign of Harsha Vardhana, Buddhist king

**ca. 600–1100** Prominence of Cholas and Pallavas in the south

**ca. 750–1100** Muslim trading at Indian seaports

**997–1030** Invasions of Mahmud of Ghazna

**1206–1526** Muslim Delhi Sultanate

**1336–1564** Dominance in the south of Hindu Vijayanagar

**1398** Timur sacks Delhi

**China**

**618–960** Tang dynasty, China's most cosmopolitan dynasty

**960–1127** Northern Song dynasty

**1127–1279** Southern Song dynasty

**1280–1368** Yuan dynasty—China briefly part of a vast Mongol Empire

**1368–1644** Ming dynasty

**1405–1433** Zheng He's naval expeditions

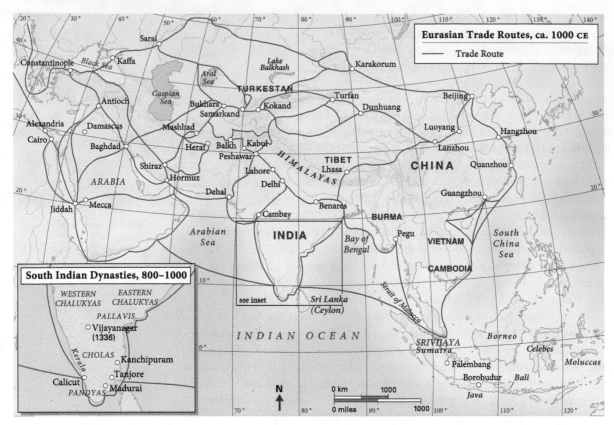

MAP 12.2 **Eurasian Trade Routes, ca. 1000 CE.**

For more than 200 years the state of Vijayanagar withstood penetration by the various Islamic sultanates of the north. In 1564, however, their huge armies were decimated by a regional coalition of northern Muslim sultanates whose forces were equipped with the newest technologies—cannon and small arms. The city of Vijayanagar was abandoned, and for the next several centuries local leaders ruled independently in different areas of the peninsula.

## Islam in India, 711–1398

As we have seen in the opening vignette, conquering Arabs incorporated much of modern Afghanistan, Pakistan, and some parts of northwest India into their empire during the early 700s. But for several centuries the rest of India experienced contact with the religion of Islam more peacefully through maritime trade conducted by Muslim merchants. In central Asia, Arab armies moving eastward along the caravan routes advanced through conquest, settling in the cities of Turkestan and raiding into the territories of Turkic nomadic tribes. During 700–1000, first Arab governors and later Persian autonomous rulers supported a profitable slave trade.

**The Career of Mahmud of Ghazna**   The Persian rulers in Iran and central Asia enrolled these slaves in their palace guards and converted them to Islam. The son of one of these slave officers was Sultan Mahmud of Ghazna, who declared himself independent of his Persian overlord and conquered the city of Ghazna in

Afghanistan. In 997 Mahmud embarked on a career of expansion lasting three decades, until his death in 1030. His tactical brilliance and utter ruthlessness have left his name both revered and reviled in Muslim and Hindu circles ever since.

Early in his career, Mahmud conquered an immense territory comprising part of Iran as well as Afghanistan and Turkestan. The wealth he extracted from this empire turned Ghazna into an opulent city and left the door open for the next round of expeditions into the old Ganges River states.

The Northern Sultanates    Mahmud and his successors, the Ghaznavids, ruled for nearly two centuries. The provinces of their empire, however, were too disparate—ranging from the central Asian desert to the rain forests of northern India—to cohere. A Persian ruler subject to the Ghaznavids, Muhammad of Ghur, declared his independence and conquered most Ghaznavid lands. In 1192, he defeated the Rajputs, considered Hindu India's most ferocious warriors, allegedly killing 100,000 soldiers. Striking deep into northern India, Muhammad set up a Muslim state at Delhi. He subsequently lost his territories in the north, but the Indian state he had set up endured (1181–1526) under the name of the Sultanate of Delhi. The founders of this state were, like many state builders we have seen in Islamic history, Turkic generals of slave origin who seized power after the death of Muhammad. Their successors were Turkic and Afghan dynasties who ruled until the invasion of Babur, the Mongol-descended founder of the Mughal Empire of India in 1526 (see Map 12.3).

**Qutb Minaret, Delhi.**
The sense of the northern Indian sultanates being a sanctuary for Muslims from other locales translated into efforts on the part of rulers to outperform their counterparts. The wealth of the area allowed them the resources with which to build a number of spectacular structures. The Qutb Minaret, built next to Delhi's first mosque, is said to still be the world's largest minaret, requiring the efforts of two rulers before being finished by the Tughluq sultan Feroz Shah (d. 1388).

The Delhi Sultanate successfully weathered an attempted invasion by Genghis Khan in 1222, whose military campaigns had so devastated the lands of southwest Asia and central Europe. Among the more colorful rulers of the Delhi Sultanate was the female sultan Raziya (r. 1236–1240), who seized the throne from her dissolute brother and, in an even more provocative move, dispensed with the veil required of Muslim women and wore male attire on the battlefield. During her short reign, she pressed south and east to Bengal and settled Muslim refugees from Mongol-controlled lands within her own domains.

The renewed Mongol expansion which led to the sack of Baghdad and the destruction of the Abbasid caliphate in 1258 was accompanied by raids along the Delhi Sultanate's borders. Out of this unsettled period came the long reign of Balban, who exercised power informally in Delhi for 20 years before ruling in his own right from 1266 through 1287. Balban's iron hand in suppressing potential rivals resulted in a succession struggle at his death, and a new set of sultans, the Khalijis, came to power in 1290. Like nearly all of their predecessors, the Khalijis soon expanded into southern India, where they acquired loot and established a short-lived overlordship.

After a brief period of turmoil came the accession of the Tughluq rulers in 1320, who held power until 1413. Perhaps the most controversial ruler of the line was Muhammad ibn Tughluq (d. 1351), named by his detractors "Muhammad the Bloody." Discontent over high taxes, debased coinage, famine, and ruthless atrocities against his enemies was prevalent during his reign. Such acts, however,

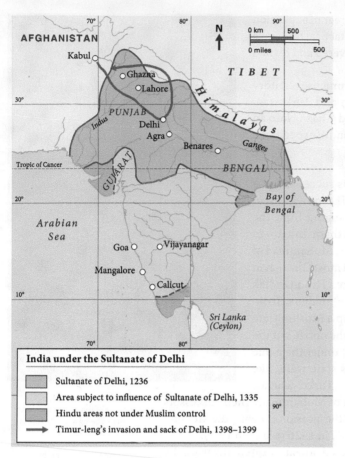

India under the Sultanate of Delhi

- Sultanate of Delhi, 1236
- Area subject to influence of Sultanate of Delhi, 1335
- Hindu areas not under Muslim control
- → Timur-leng's invasion and sack of Delhi, 1398–1399

MAP 12.3 **India under the Sultanate of Delhi.**

seemed to contradict his considerably more peaceful personal attainments. By all accounts he was highly educated, a renowned poet and calligrapher, and humble and chaste in his behavior at court. Regardless of the ultimate effects of his rule, by the time of his death at mid-century, powerful forces were once again gathering to the north. Within a few decades they would bring about the end of Tughluq rule and alter the region's politics for generations to come.

## Toward the Mughal Era, 1398–1450

In 1398, one of the last great invasions of central Asian nomads, that of Timur (r. 1370–1405) descended on northern India and southwest Asia (see Chapter 20). Though himself a Muslim, Timur did not spare the Muslim capital of Delhi. Though the wave of violence accompanying his conquests quickly subsided, his invasion had broken the power of the Tughluqs. Two smaller sultanates, those of the Sayyids (1414–1451) and the Lodis (1451–1526), held the area around Delhi. Once again, northern India had moved into a period of political disorder. The coming of the Mughals in 1526 would usher in another period of both stability and imperial aspirations.

**Economics in Islamic India**     India's rich economy generated repeated political problems. It continually attracted invasions by outsiders eager to take advantage of its wealth. While scholars have long debated whether the first Arab and Turkic incursions into India were motivated primarily by religious or economic reasons or a combination of the two, the vast wealth accumulated as a result provided ample justification for continuing them. Like the constantly feuding southern states of the subcontinent, the turnover of goods acquired through raids and warfare helped finance the economies of the emerging northern Muslim sultanates. Even after these states became financially stable, the attraction of the wealth of the southern states resulted in frequent expeditions against them for financial gain.

The northern sultanates also supported their economies through heavy taxation. In addition to the *jizya* tax on nonbelievers, Ala-ud-din of the Tughluqs, for example, instituted a 50 percent land tax, taxes on the ownership of milk cows, and a household tax. Beyond this, he embarked on an ambitious campaign to institute wage and price controls on a dizzying array of occupations and commodities in order to keep food prices low and urban granaries full. In this, Ala-ud-din was surpassed in zeal by the notorious Muhammad "the Bloody" Tughluq, who had one tax offender flayed alive, his skin stuffed and mounted, and his remains served as a meal to his unfortunate relatives.

Muhammad also instituted price controls and attempted to stabilize the currency by minting new gold coins, debasing silver ones, and manufacturing bronze tokens for use as temporary currency, measures ultimately abandoned as disruptive to the economy. Despite the sultans' constant need for money, however, Muslim prohibitions against **usury** kept banking and capital firmly in the hands of Hindus, Buddhists, and *Parsees* (descendants of Zoroastrian emigrants from Persia).

**Muslims and Caste** The role of Islam in calling the faithful together as equals tended to appeal to those most discontented with the caste system. Islam's minority status in India, however, meant that it was never possible to carve out an Islamic state within the sultanates in the same fashion as had been the case in other parts of the Muslim sphere.

Over time, a certain amount of cross-cultural compromise was reluctantly granted by both sides. Nearly all Hindu and Muslim sects were eventually allowed to practice to some degree, with the dress and markings distinguishing different castes allowed to continue. Muslim repugnance toward Hindu nakedness—as in the case of devotees of certain gods and the working attire of some of the lower castes—as well as discomfort with Hindu concepts of religious sexuality, gradually became less overt. At the same time, Hindus in some areas adopted the Muslim practice of veiling women.

**The Sikhs** Despite their profoundly different worldviews, traditions, and practices, by the fifteenth century the unique position of the Muslim sultanates of northern India as havens for refugees from the ravages of the Mongols, as well as for Sufis (practitioners of Islamic mysticism) and Muslim dissidents, provided a rare opportunity for interchange between Muslim and Hindu sects. Starting with the poet Kabir (1440–1518), the commonalities of the ecstatic, mystical experience of communion with the absolute shared alike by Hindu and Muslim devotional sects was the subject of repeated attempts to find common ground between the two faiths.

The climax of this movement came with the guru ("teacher") Nanak (1469–1539), who founded the faith of **Sikhism**, *sikh* meaning "disciple," which also emphasized a direct emotional experience with the divine. Combining elements of Hinduism and Islam, the Sikhs, due to religious persecution in the seventeenth century, eventually became more of a fighting faith, a stance that, even to the present, has served to continually place them at odds with various Indian governments.

While Sikhism at first appeared to be a step toward reconciliation between Islam and Hinduism, it in fact became the exception that proved the rule of their competition. Indeed, both Hindus and Muslims opposed the Sikhs, and they were persecuted a number of times under the Mughals. India thus remained a syncretic religious and cultural society among the world's religious civilizations. The experience of China, on the other hand, would be far less traumatic.

**Usury:** For Christians, the sin of lending money at high rates of interest; for Muslims, that of charging any interest at all on money loaned.

**Sikhism:** Indian religion founded by Guru Nanak that combines elements of Hindu and Muslim traditions.

# Interactions and Adaptations: From Buddhism to Neo-Confucian Synthesis in China

The Tang dynasty (618–907) marked the completion of the reconstitution of the Chinese empire begun under the Sui. At its height, the influence of Buddhism at the imperial court, especially with the famous Empress Wu, made China a Buddhist empire. Since the Han, China's ideology had been based on the ethics of Confucianism combined with the imperial structure inherited from the Qin (see Chapter 9). By the mid-600s this ideology of statehood had fused with Mahayana Buddhism to give China for the first time an overtly religious civilization. China thus dramatically joined the ranks of Hindu India (soon to be split by Islam), the growing spread of the Islamic caliphates, the Christian eastern Roman Empire, and the developing states of western Christian Europe as polities dominated by a universal religion. Such states would dominate world history until the European Enlightenment and Industrial Revolution created an entirely new type of society.

But the Tang, with their connections to the larger Buddhist cultural sphere, ultimately fell. The dynasty of their successors, the Song (960–1279), has often been seen as the beginning of China's early modern period, supported by the world's largest and most productive agrarian state. The political system that marked China from this period until the twentieth century, however, was in part derived from a departure from Buddhism, which was blamed for the downfall of the Tang. Instead, the new synthesis of official beliefs blended the ideas of three ethical-religious schools—Confucianism, Daoism, and Buddhism—to create a system called "Neo-Confucianism." Unlike India's competing religions, Neo-Confucianism in China had no real religious competitors inside or outside the empire, and its debates centered instead on interpretations and approaches to understanding its core teachings—not on the teachings themselves.

## Creating a Religious Civilization under the Tang

As we saw at the end of Chapter 9, the installation by Li Shimin of his father on the throne in 618 saw the founding of the Tang. His dismissal of his father in 627 saw it begin in earnest. For the next 150 years, the dynasty expanded its reach deep into central Asia and made incursions into Korea and Vietnam until its shape resembled a dumbbell, bulging at both ends connected with the narrow territory adjacent to the Silk Road.

**Expansion and Consolidation**   Determined to complete the consolidation begun under the Sui and expand the empire, the Tang led military expeditions into central Asia. The Tang reestablished rule in Korea and opened diplomatic relations with Japan, which in 645 announced the *Taika* (Great Reform)—a wholesale adoption of Tang imperial institutions, Buddhism, Confucian bureaucracy, record keeping, and even architecture. The Tang Empire's position as the eastern terminus of the Silk Road; its enhanced maritime trade with India, Japan, southeast Asia, the Middle East, and even Africa; and its integration of Buddhist culture led to China's first extensive encounter with the major agrarian–urban societies to the west. During the seventh century, Muslim conquests in southwest Asia brought China into contact with the rapidly expanding Arab Empire. In 674, members of the Sasanian Persian royal house fled the advancing Arabs to the Tang capital at Chang'an, bringing in their wake communities of merchants who established a taste among the Tang elites for Arab, Persian, and central Asian goods and cultural forms.

With the Tang Empire expanding, trade booming, and the bureaucracy well staffed and run, the Tang capital of Chang'an (the present city of Xi'an) grew into perhaps the largest city in the world, with its core comparable in size to Baghdad or Constantinople in the same era and as many as 2 million people living in its metropolitan area. Its streets, official buildings and residences, and south-facing imperial palace dominating the center became the model for urban planning throughout eastern Asia (see Map 12.4). The city included areas set aside for traders of many nationalities; even today one of the Xi'an's attractions is its Muslim market.

**The Examination System** The Tang refined the bureaucratic structure pioneered by the Han into a form that, with only minor alterations, survived into the twentieth century. The most noteworthy aspect of the Tang bureaucratic structure was the introduction of an examination system for entry into government service. Because the exams were open to a relatively large portion of the male population, state service ensured a degree of social mobility based on merit rather than birth. The initial entry-level tests, based on knowledge of the Confucian classics and, for most of the Tang era, Buddhist and Daoist texts, were open to men of all classes except merchants, artisans, and convicted criminals. The few who passed the initial, district-level tests could sit for provincial exams and, if successful, would be eligible for minor posts. Individuals who passed the metropolitan tests, usually held every 3 years in the capital, were eligible for national service. Other reforms undertaken by the Tang included the creation of a board of censors to check arbitrary behavior among officials, the obligation of lower officials to report the infractions of those above them, and the practice of rotating official posts to prevent individuals from developing local power bases.

**Prosperity and Its Discontents** As the prosperity of the Tang dynasty grew, many of the problems of uneven growth that had plagued the Han dynasty began to reassert themselves. For example, as the center of population continued to move south, the northern regions languished in relative poverty, while the capital grew economically isolated. The agriculturally productive subtropical areas south of the Yangzi now yielded about 90 percent of the empire's taxed grain and contained as much as 70 percent of the population. Moreover, as maritime trade grew and ports increased in size and number, the connecting infrastructure of roads, courier stations, and especially canals required ever more investment and attention. This was a particularly acute problem in the case of communication with the capital. As an administrative center and trade crossroads, the capital city of Chang'an had ballooned to a size that was now unsustainable without constant grain shipments from the south, while its isolation made it particularly vulnerable to attack. Thus, even before the Tang, work on the Grand Canal, connecting the Yangzi and Yellow Rivers, had been pushed forward to enhance water-based transport in the north.

Tang efforts to control military outposts along the Silk Road, with its lucrative trade and Buddhist shrines, brought the empire into conflict with Arab expansion by the early eighth century. Despite some early successes, Tang armies suffered a

**Camel with Musicians.** Music played an important role in Tang China and was enjoyed privately as well as on public occasions. This brightly colored glazed earthenware sculpture, dated to 723 CE, shows three musicians riding a Bactrian (two-humped) camel. Their long coats, facial hair, and hats indicate that they are from central Asia; indeed, the lute held by one of the figures is an instrument that was introduced to China from central Asia in the second century CE.

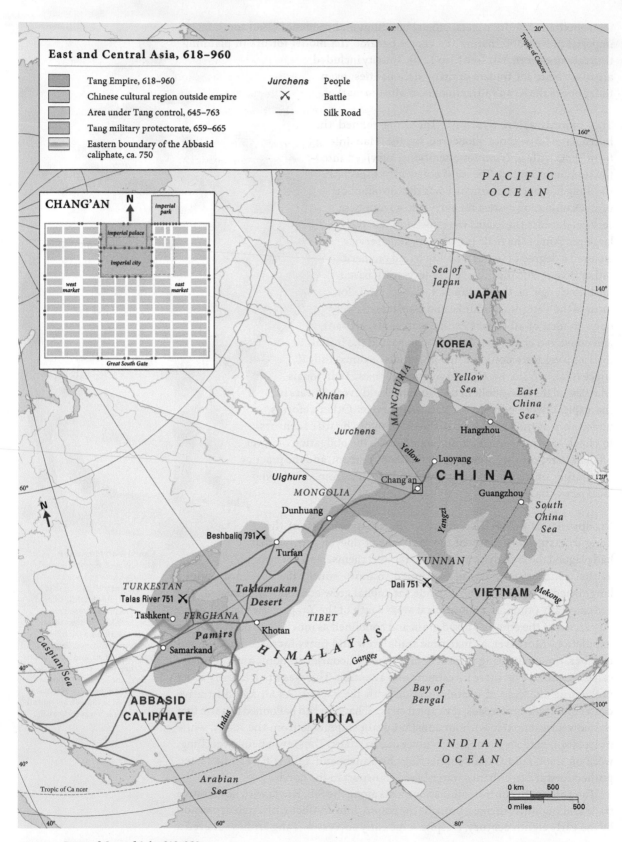

**East and Central Asia, 618–960**

- Tang Empire, 618–960
- Chinese cultural region outside empire
- Area under Tang control, 645–763
- Tang military protectorate, 659–665
- Eastern boundary of the Abbasid caliphate, ca. 750

*Jurchens* — People
✕ — Battle
— Silk Road

**CHANG'AN**

N ↑

imperial park

imperial palace

imperial city

west market

east market

Great South Gate

PACIFIC OCEAN

Sea of Japan

JAPAN

KOREA

MANCHURIA

Yellow Sea

East China Sea

Khitan

Jurchens

Hangzhou

*Yellow*

Luoyang

CHINA

Chang'an

Guangzhou

South China Sea

*Uighurs*

MONGOLIA

Dunhuang

*Yangzi*

YUNNAN

Beshbaliq 791 ✕

Turfan

Dali 751 ✕

VIETNAM

*Mekong*

TURKESTAN

Talas River 751 ✕

Taklamakan Desert

TIBET

Tashkent

FERGHANA

Pamirs

Khotan

HIMALAYAS

*Ganges*

Samarkand

Caspian Sea

ABBASID CALIPHATE

*Indus*

INDIA

Bay of Bengal

INDIAN OCEAN

Tropic of Cancer

Arabian Sea

0 km 500
0 miles 500

MAP 12.4 **East and Central Asia, 618–960.**

decisive defeat by Arab forces. That this loss followed a series of setbacks at the hands of the Tibetans from 745 to 750 and border uprisings in Manchuria, Korea, and the southern province of Yunnan helped spark a general revolt. From 755 to 762 a rebellion initiated by the Tang commander An Lushan (703–757) devastated large sections of the empire and resulted in heavy land taxes after its suppression. As with the later Han, the dynasty was now in a downward spiral, from which recovery would prove increasingly difficult.

For the next century and a half some economic and political recovery did in fact occur, but the problems of rebuilding and revenue loss persisted, accompanied by the questioning of a number of the premises of the regime, particularly by the Confucians. For example, Confucians criticized Buddhism for being patronized and subsidized by the Tang court. They were particularly critical of its "foreign" ideas and practices, such as monasticism, celibacy, and personal enlightenment, which contradicted the Confucian standards of filial piety, family life, and public service. At the same time, Buddhist monasteries, which paid no taxes, were tempting targets for an increasingly cash-strapped government. In 845, despite Tang sponsorship of Buddhism, the government forcibly seized all Buddhist holdings, although followers were allowed to continue their religious practices. Even with renewed campaigns against border peoples and other attempts at reinvigorating the empire, sporadic civil war continued for the remainder of the century, leading to the collapse of the Tang dynasty in 906. Following this collapse, China again entered a period of disunity as regional states battled for ultimate control. None of these states would be victorious until the emergence of the Song in 960.

**Cosmopolitan Commerce**   From the capital in Chang'an, merchants, monks, pilgrims, diplomats, and travelers made their way along the Silk Road, while Chinese, Indian, and Arab ships plied the seas as far away as Africa. The compass, invented by Chinese fortune-tellers and adapted for use in keeping to a constant direction at sea, now guided ships throughout the Indian Ocean and southeast Asia. In the Chinese versions of this instrument, however, the needle pointed south—the preferred direction of good fortune and architectural orientation. Drawn by lucrative opportunities, colonies of Chinese merchants could be found throughout the Indian Ocean and southeast Asia.

Among the export items most coveted by foreign merchants were tea and silk. Initially brought to China from southeast Asia, tea quickly established itself as the beverage of choice during the Tang and vied with silk for supremacy as a cash crop during the Song. Tea had a profound effect on the overall health of the population in China, Vietnam, Korea, Japan, and central Asia. The boiling of the water makes it potable, while the tea itself contains healthful properties. Moreover, its caffeine prompted alertness—an aid to monks in meditation. Tea production, particularly in the region near the city of Hangzhou, became a major industry and for hundreds of years remained China's most lucrative export item.

The influence of foreigners in art and artifact, fashion, taste, music, and dance marks a radical departure in many respects from the more demure Chinese styles that came before and after. For example, the Persian-influenced costumes of Tang dancers—with their daring and distinctive bare midriffs and transparent tops and trousers—were celebrated at the court in Chang'an but scandalized the

**Empress Wu.** Mistress of Emperor Gaozong, Wu Zetian declared herself empress dowager after his death in 684 and founded the Zhou dynasty in 690. She is the only woman in Chinese history until Empress Dowager Cixi at the turn of the twentieth century to exercise so much power.

**Empress dowager:** In monarchical or imperial systems in which succession is normally through the male line, the widow of the ruler.

"I will not spoil it [life] by any labor or care. / so saying, I was drunk all the day, / lying helpless at the porch in front of my door."

—Li Bo

more modest sensibilities of later centuries. Indeed, the period saw a number of controversial trends regarding the role and deportment of women. As exemplified in the person of the famous Empress Wu (r. 690–705), China's first **empress dowager**, women occasionally exercised considerable authority in political affairs during this period (see "Against the Grain," p. 370).

**Tang Poetry**   Tang poetry, especially the compressed "regulated verse" of eight five-character lines and the terse four-line "cut-off line" poems, attempts to suggest powerful emotions or themes in minimalist fashion. For example, the deep Confucian sensibilities of the Tang poet Du Fu (ca. 721–770) are often detectable in his emotionally charged poems such as "Mourning Chen Tao." Li Bai (or Li Bo, 701–762), his friend, was in many ways his opposite in both the way he lived his life and the emotions he sought to stir. Carefree, witty, a lover of wine and women—according to legend, Li Bai drowned after a drunken challenge to "embrace the moon" reflected in the water—his poetry evokes happier moments but frequently conveys them as fleeting and bittersweet. Wang Wei [wahng way] (ca. 699–759) was a third renowned Tang poet. Of him it was later said that "in every one of his poems is a painting, and in every painting a poem."

For all the accomplishments of the Tang, however, the role of Buddhism as a privileged religion left the dynasty open to severe criticism. With the coming of the Song, China would become a religious civilization in which its people reemphasized the indigenous traditions of Confucianism and Daoism, with elements of Buddhism on a more reduced level.

## The Song and Yuan Dynasties, 960–1368

During the Song dynasty, China achieved in many ways its greatest degree of sophistication in terms of material culture, technology, ideas, economics, and the amenities of urban living. Its short-lived incorporation into the huge empire of the Mongols opened the country to renewed influence from neighboring peoples and helped to spread Chinese influence westward, most famously through the accounts of the travelers Marco Polo and Ibn Battuta. Finally, the new synthesis of Neo-Confucianism would carry China as a religious civilization into the twentieth century.

**Reforms of Wang Anshi**   Like the Tang, the Song instituted a strong central government based on merit rather than heredity. The Song, however, broadened the eligibility of those seeking to take the civil service exams, and with increased opportunities to join the government service, a huge and increasingly unwieldy bureaucratic system emerged.

The need for administrative reform spurred the official Wang Anshi ([wahng ahn-SHR] 1021–1086) to propose a series of initiatives designed to increase state control over the economy and reduce the power of local interests. Wang proposed state licensing of both agricultural and commercial enterprises, the abolition of forced labor, and the creation of government pawnshops to loan money at reduced rates. He also urged cutting the number of bureaucratic positions in order to lessen the power of local officials and clan heads. Opposition to these proposed reforms, however, forced Wang from office in 1076.

In addition to internal problems, such as the financial strain of maintaining a huge bureaucracy, the Song faced external problems. Because the Tang had lost much of northern China, including the Silk Road, to nomadic groups, Song lands from the start were substantially smaller than those of the Tang. Although the Song spent a great deal of treasure and energy to maintain a professional army of more than 1.5 million as well as a formidable navy, this massive but ponderous force ultimately proved ineffective against the expert militaries of invading nomadic groups using swiftness to their advantage. The Song also tried careful diplomacy and bribery to maintain China's dominance. Such efforts, however, were unable to keep the northern part of the empire from falling to the nomadic Jurchens in 1127. Forced to abandon their capital at Kaifeng on the Grand Canal just south of the Yellow River, the Song created a new capital at Linan, the modern city of Hangzhou (see Map 12.5).

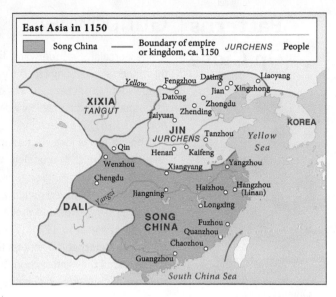

MAP **12.5  East Asia in 1150.**

The decreased size of the Song Empire resulted in a more southern-oriented and urbanized economy. The new capital at Hangzhou [hahng jo], described by Marco Polo as the most beautiful city in the world, may also have been the largest, with a population estimated at 1.5 million. Despite the bureaucracy's disdain for the merchant and artisan classes, the state had always recognized the potential of commerce to generate revenue through import, export, tariffs, and taxes. Thus, while attempting to bring the largest enterprises under state control, the government pursued measures to facilitate trade, such as printing the world's first paper notes, minting coins, and curbing usury. These practices, combined with an excellent system of roads and canals, fostered the development of an internal Chinese market. The Song conducted a lively overseas trade, and Chinese merchants established colonies in major ports throughout southeast Asia and the Indian Ocean.

**The Mongol Conquest**     Commercial success, however, could not save the Song from invasion by neighboring nomadic peoples. For centuries, disparate groups of nomadic Mongols had lived in tribes and clans in eastern central Asia. There was no real push to unite these groups until the rise to power of the Mongol leader Temujin (ca. 1162–1227). Combining military prowess with diplomatic strategy, Temujin united the various Mongol groups into one confederation in 1206. Temujin gave himself the title Genghis Khan ("Universal Ruler") of the united Mongol confederation.

# Gunpowder

If fine porcelain, lacquerware, landscape painting, poetry, and calligraphy marked the refined side of Song life, the most momentous invention to emerge from the era was gunpowder. The substance was originally used as a medicine for skin irritations until its propensity to burn rapidly was established. The early Chinese term for gunpowder, *huoyao* (火药) "fire medicine," preserves this sense of its use.

Though it was long packed into bamboo tubes to create fireworks ignited during religious festivals, it is unclear when the first weapons employing gunpowder were used. By the Southern Song, however, the Chinese army and navy had a wide array of weapons that utilized gunpowder either as a propellant or as an explosive. The use of "fire arrows"—rockets mounted to arrow shafts—was recorded during a battle with the Mongols in 1232. The Song navy launched missiles and even employed ships with detachable sections filled with explosives with which to ram other ships. By the end of the century, primitive cannon were also employed as well as gunpowder satchels to blow open city gates and fortifications.

The widespread use of gunpowder weapons by the Song against the Mongols was a powerful inducement to the invaders to adopt them for themselves. Indeed, toward the end of the war, the Mongols increasingly employed explosives in their siege operations against Chinese walled cities. They also used them in the 1270s and 1290s during their failed invasions of Japan. The need for these weapons pushed their dispersion throughout the Mongol holdings and beyond.

**Korean Rocket Launcher.**
Adapting Mongol and Chinese military technology, the Koreans repelled a Japanese invasion in 1592 with *hwacha*, mobile rocket launchers that were used with great effect against both enemy land forces and ships.

Following confederation, the Mongols launched a half-century of steady encroachment on northern China. The Mongols had several enormous advantages over the infantry-based armies of their opponents:

- their skill at horsemanship and archery
- their unsurpassed ability to fire arrows at pursuers while galloping away from them at full speed
- their repeatedly successful tactics of feigned retreat.

Genghis Khan's grandson Khubilai Khan [KOO-bleh con] (1215–1294) resumed the Mongol offensive in southern China after the Song unwisely attempted to enlist Mongol aid against the Jurchens. In 1267 he moved his capital from Karakorum to Khanbaligh, called by the Chinese "Dadu"—the future city of Beijing—and steadily ground down the Song remnant. Hangzhou fell to the Mongols in 1276; the death of the young Song emperor in 1279 as he attempted to flee by sea brought the dynasty to an end.

**The Yuan Dynasty**    In 1280 Khubilai Khan proclaimed the Yuan dynasty. This short-lived dynasty pulled China into an empire spanning all of Eurasia from Korea to the interior of Poland and probing as far as Hungary, Java, and Japan. Like their predecessors in the Northern Wei and Sui dynasties, however, the Mongols found themselves adapting to Chinese culture in order to administer the

It is difficult to overestimate the importance of gunpowder in human affairs. The next round of empires, the Ottomans, Safavids, and Mughals, made its use in warfare so central to their efforts that historians often refer to them as "the gunpowder empires." Its use in sixteenth-century Japan was so important in battle that the Tokugawa Shogunate banned it for two centuries once peace had been established. But it was among the states of Europe that these weapons achieved their highest levels of development over the following centuries. Incessant warfare among the European states and against the Ottomans fueled the development of bigger and deadlier cannon and lighter and more accurate small arms. The use of these weapons helped speed the decline of the heavily armed and armored mounted knight and brought on the age of the infantry armed with muskets as "the queen of battles." By the end of the eighteenth century, even though muskets and artillery were technologically more or less the same the world over, a high degree of drill among bayonet-equipped grenadiers gave European armies an edge against the Ottomans, Mughals, and Africans.

## Questions

- How do gunpowder's origins as a medicine complicate the way we typically view technological and cultural adaptations?

- What would have been the consequence for world history if the military uses of gunpowder had never been discovered?

densely populated and complex society they had wrested from the Song. Thus, while some senior Song bureaucrats resigned from the new Mongol government in protest, most carried on with their posts, and the examination system begun under the Han dynasty was finally reinstated in 1315.

Now that China was part of a much larger empire, its culture was widely diffused throughout Eurasia. In addition, China was open to a variety of foreign goods, ideas, and travelers. Paper money, gunpowder, coal, the compass, and dozens of other important Chinese innovations circulated more widely than ever, while emissaries and missionaries from the developing states of Europe traveled east to the Chinese capital city of Khanbaligh [con-beh-LYE]. The two most famous travel accounts of the era, those of the Venetian Marco Polo (1254–1324) and Ibn Battuta of Tangier (1304–1369), who lived and traveled throughout the Mongol Empire, are testaments to the powerful impact of Mongol rule in facilitating travel over such a vast area. Indeed, it was during the brief rule of the Mongols that the European image of China as a fairyland of exotica, fabulous wealth, and wondrous inventions was firmly set (see Map 12.6).

**Khubilai Khan as the First Yuan Emperor, Shizu (Shih-tzu).**

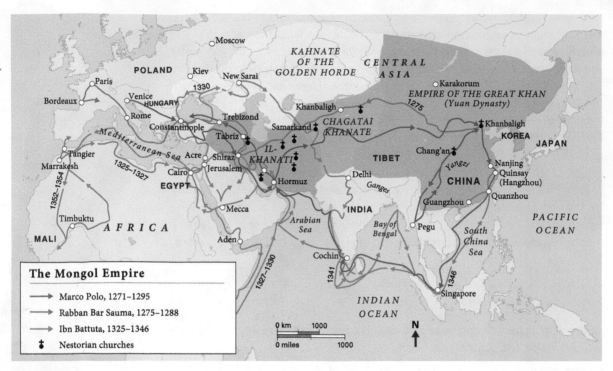

MAP **12.6** **The Mongol Empire.**

For Chinese historians, however, the Yuan period is almost universally regarded as one of imperial China's darkest times. Although the Mongols quickly restored order, administered the empire effectively, and allowed a relative tolerance of religious practice and expression, the Yuan period was seen as an oppressive time of large standing armies, withdrawal from service of many Chinese officials, forced labor, and heavy taxes. Compounding the intensity of these conditions was perhaps the single worst disaster of the fourteenth century, the bubonic plague, as we saw in Chapter 11.

By mid-century, all of these factors contributed to outbreaks of rebellion in China. Moreover, the Mongol Empire spanning Eurasia had now begun to dissolve into a series of increasingly squabbling regional states. By 1368, a coalition led by the soldier–Buddhist monk Zhu Yuanzhang [JOO yuwen-JAHNG] (1328–1398) had driven the Mongols from the capital at Khanbaligh and proclaimed a new dynastic line, the Ming. A final measure of revenge came when the last Mongol pretender to the throne was driven into the sea—just as the last Song emperor had been by the Mongols.

## The Ming to 1450: The Quest for Stability

The "Pig Emperor," as Zhu was sometimes derisively called because of his ungainly features, took the reign name of "Hongwu" and spent much of his rule driving the remaining Mongols out of his empire. Under Hongwu's leadership, Chinese politics and customs were restored and a powerful centralized government was put into place. This new imperial state that Hongwu and his successors created would, with minor modifications, see China into the twentieth century.

**The Grand Secretariat** Hongwu sought to streamline this newly reconstituted bureaucracy by concentrating power and governmental functions around the emperor, a practice that had been common during the Qin, Han, and Tang dynasties. Thus, one of his first steps in reshaping the government was to create the Grand Secretariat, a select group of senior officials who served as an advisory board for the emperor on all imperial matters; it remained at the apex of imperial Chinese power into the twentieth century. With a powerful, centralized government in place, Ming emperors now had a base from which to take measures to protect the empire from incursions by Mongols and other nomadic groups in the north. One step to protect against invasion was taken in 1421, when the capital of the empire was moved from Nanjing in the south to the old site of Khanbaligh, now renamed Beijing ("Northern Capital"), so that a strong Chinese presence in the region would discourage invasion. Further safeguards against invasion included the upgrading of the fortifications along the Great Wall.

**Population Recovery** While the country fortified its borders and reinstated political systems that had been dismantled by the Mongols, it also had to contend with a sharp drop in population due to warfare and the lingering effects of the bubonic plague that ravaged the country in the 1340s. The population rebound, however, did not assume significant proportions until it was aided by the introduction of a number of new food crops in the sixteenth and seventeenth centuries, which boosted agricultural productivity.

With the coming of new food and cash crops from the Americas by way of Spanish and Portuguese merchants, including potatoes, sweet potatoes, maize (corn), peanuts, and tobacco, the country's population grew from a low of perhaps 60 million at the end of the Yuan period to an estimated 150 million in 1600. The efficiency of Chinese agriculture and the consequent growth of the empire's immense internal trade contributed to another doubling of the population, to perhaps 300 million by 1800.

**The Interlude of Naval Power** Thanks to the foundation laid by Hongwu [hoong-WOO], the dynasty's third emperor, Yongle [young-LUH], inherited a state in 1403 that was already on its way to recovering its economic dynamism. Taking advantage of this increasing prosperity, and fearful of potential usurpers, he ordered China's first and last great naval expeditions. These voyages, sent out from 1405 to 1433 under the command of his childhood friend and imperial eunuch Zheng He [jung huh] (1371–1435), were perhaps the most remarkable feats of their day.

**Chinese Treasure Ship Compared to Columbus's *Santa Maria*.** Over 400 feet in length, the largest of Zheng He's treasure ships was nearly five times as long as the ships Columbus used to sail across the Atlantic.

The vast fleets that Zheng commanded were the largest amphibious forces the world would see until the twentieth century. With a length of over 400 feet, the largest of Zheng's "treasure ships," as they were called, was more than four times that of Columbus's *Santa Maria* and many times its bulk and was accompanied by a diverse array of smaller vessels that carried cargo, supplies, and troops. There were even tankers that carried fresh water for the fleet, while the larger ships grew fresh fruits and vegetables on their aft decks. Zheng's ships also carried a formidable arsenal of cannon, bombs, rockets, and other weaponry and a force of nearly 30,000 men. In addition, they featured such technological innovations as watertight compartments, sternpost rudders, magnetic compasses, and paper maps.

The first voyages were expeditionary forces aimed largely at overawing any nearby foreign powers that might be harboring pretenders to Yongle's throne. As the realization set in that these foreign threats were nonexistent, the voyages became focused on trade and exploration and ranged farther and farther afield, ultimately covering the Indian Ocean, the Persian Gulf, and the East African coast. Along the way they planted or reestablished contact with Chinese merchants in south and southeast Asia. Of particular interest were the first direct Chinese contacts with the Swahili-speaking states of East Africa. In one famous exchange of gifts, the king of Malindi (modern Kenya) sent Yongle a giraffe, which found the emperor among the awestruck admirers of the creature at the imperial court. Even today one can still see the stone markers left by the Chinese along the East African coast where their ships landed (see Map 12.7).

Although Zheng He's explorations firmly established Chinese predominance in naval technology and power, Yongle's successors put an end to the expeditions. The reasons for this abrupt

> "We have traversed . . . immense water spaces . . . and we have set eyes on barbarian regions far away . . . traversing those savage waves as if we were treading a public thoroughfare."
>
> —Zheng He

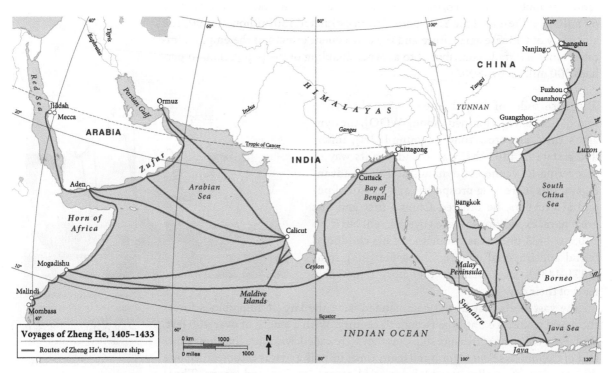

MAP **12.7** **Voyages of Zheng He, 1405–1433.**

turnabout were both political and strategic. By the 1430s the Mongols, having regrouped after their defeats, were again threatening the northern frontiers. The huge expense of the voyages and the realization that there were no significant naval rivals were convincing reasons to discontinue them in the face of the Mongol threat. In addition, the Confucian officials, always suspicious of the profit motive, argued that maritime trade was not useful to the overall welfare of the empire.

**Toward the Ming Decline**    The activist style of Hongwu and Yongle proved to be the exception rather than the rule during the nearly three centuries of Ming rule. As had so often been the case in Chinese history, a degree of weakness at the center of power encouraged probes of the frontier by nomadic peoples on the empire's periphery, a condition neatly summarized by the Chinese proverb "Disorder within, disaster without." A disconcerting foretaste of this occurred in 1449, when the emperor was taken prisoner by the Mongols following the defeat of his expeditionary force. Through most of the sixteenth century, a succession of weak emperors would erode the stability of the reformed Ming imperial system, which had been based on enhancing the emperor's power. To compensate for the chronic weakness at the center, power was increasingly diffused throughout the system. Over time, much of it was acquired by the grand secretaries and provincial governors, while at the village-level magistrates and village headmen assumed the bulk of power and responsibility.

## Society, Family, and Gender

With the refinement of the examination system and the elaboration of the bureaucracy during the Song, which was renewed during the Ming, the key point of intersection between the people and the government was the district magistrate. While magistrates occupied the lowest official rung of the bureaucracy, they wielded considerable power at the local level and constituted the entry-level position for the majority of those called to service. Some experience at the magistrate's level was considered essential for ambitious officials, and the wide-ranging skills developed during one's district tenure often proved indispensable for advancement to the higher levels of the bureaucracy.

**The Magistrate**    The position of magistrate brought with it enormous responsibility. Even in rural areas, the magistrate might have charge of 100,000 people—and in urban areas perhaps 250,000. Assisted by a small group of clerks and secretaries, messengers, and constables, he supervised all aspects of local government: collecting taxes, policing and security, investigating and prosecuting crimes, settling legal disputes, sentencing and overseeing punishments—including executions—presiding over all official ceremonies, conducting the local Confucian examinations, and setting an exemplary moral example for his constituents. The magistrate's responsibilities and powers were so all-encompassing that he was referred to as "father and mother to the people."

**The Scholar-Gentry and Rural Society**    While China boasted some of the world's largest cities, more than 85 percent of the country remained rural during the period from the Song to the Ming. At the top of the local structures of power and influence were the *scholar-gentry*. As a class, they were by definition the educated and included all ranks of degree holders, whether in or out of office, and their families.

Scholar-gentry membership was in theory open to most males and their families, though in practice it seldom exceeded 1–2 percent of the population in most areas of the empire. The chief qualification was attainment of at least the lowest official degree, *shengyuan* [SHUNG-yu-enn], which enabled the bearer to attend a government-sponsored academy for further study and draw a small stipend. The demands of memorizing the classical canon and learning to write in the rigid essay format required for the exams, however, were such that the wealthy had a distinct advantage given their leisure time, access to tutors, and the connections required to pass the exams. Still, there were enough poor boys who succeeded through hard work and the sacrifices of their families and neighbors to provide a surprising degree of mobility within the system.

Since prestige within the scholar-gentry derived from education even more than wealth, it was not uncommon for individuals to purchase degrees, though technically they were barred from doing so in the upper three categories. Thus, there was considerable snobbery among the upper gentry of advanced degree holders and officials toward the lower gentry. This was reinforced by an array of **sumptuary laws** and a court-directed protocol of buttons worn on the hats of officials signifying to which of the nine official grades—each with an upper and a lower rank—they belonged.

**Sumptuary laws:** Regulations mandating or restricting the wearing of certain clothes or insignia among different classes of people.

In keeping with their role as the informal administrative apparatus of the magistrate, the scholar-gentry enjoyed a number of privileges as well as responsibilities. At the same time, their position as community leaders and their grounding in Confucian ethics frequently placed them in tension with the official bureaucracy, especially when local interests appeared at odds with regional or imperial ones. Along with the district magistrate, they presided over all ceremonies at temples, and those holding the highest ranks led all clan ceremonies. In addition, the scholar-gentry mingled with the official authorities more or less as social equals; in the case of those in between appointments to high office, they frequently outranked the local magistrate.

Local government relied to an extraordinary degree on the cooperation of the gentry and people with the magistrates, subprefects, and prefects in order to function. Because the presiding officials were moved so frequently, the gentry represented a consistent network of people to carry out the day-to-day work of government. They took very seriously the Confucian injunction to remonstrate with officials, especially when their complaints coincided with local interests. Thus, they could—and did—rally the people to subvert the policies of unpopular magistrates. Moreover, as influential men themselves—and often officials with national connections—they could force the resignation of officials and sometimes even bring about changes in regional or imperial policy.

**Village and Family Life**    The tendency toward greater centralization under the Ming also reverberated within the structures of Chinese village life. While much of local custom and social relations among the peasants still revolved around family, clan, and lineage—with the scholar-gentry setting the pace—new institutions perfected under the Ming had a lasting impact into the twentieth century.

Originally conceived during the Song dynasty, the *baojia* system of village organization called for families to register all members and be grouped into clusters of 10. One family in each cluster was then assigned responsibility for the others. Each group of responsible families would then be grouped into 10, and a member would be selected from them to be responsible for the group of 100 households, and so on up to the 1,000-household level. The system was especially important in that it allowed the authorities to bypass potential gentry resistance to government directives and guaranteed a network of informers at all levels of rural life.

**Peasant Women's Lives**    Despite China's technological prowess and the introduction of new strains of rice during the Song period that propelled a surge in population, the patterns of work and the overall rhythms of peasant life changed little from the Song through the Ming. The tools available to the vast majority of cultivators, as later depicted in the seventeenth-century technology manual *Tiangong Kaiwu* (*The Works of Nature and Man*), had remained fundamentally unchanged from their prototypes of the preceding centuries. The very simplicity and efficiency of such tools in such a labor-rich environment encouraged their continued use.

Tensions in the older patterns of village life tended to be magnified during times of stress in the lives of women and girls. On the one hand, the education of upper-class women tended increasingly toward making them more marriageable. Study of proper Confucian etiquette (as outlined in Ban Zhao's *Admonitions for Women*, discussed in Chapter 9), light verse, and a heavy dose of filial piety occupied a large portion of their curriculum. The custom of painful **foot binding** originated during the Song, gained ground during the Ming, and continued until it was banned by the People's Republic of China after 1949. **Female infanticide** also rose markedly in rural areas during times of famine or other social stress. As in previous periods, rural girls were frequently sold into servitude or prostitution by financially pressed families.

## Perceptions of Perfection: Intellectual, Scientific, and Cultural Life

The period from the Tang to the Ming was marked by unsurpassed technological prowess. Indeed, according to the leading scholar of China's record of innovation, Joseph Needham, China remained the world's leading producer of new inventions until roughly 1500. So striking is this record, and so suddenly does it subside after this time, that historians sometimes refer to the problem of why it took place as "the Needham question." One possible answer may be that the Chinese felt that they had achieved a degree of perfection in so many areas that, like their great naval expeditions, there was simply no pressing need to advance them further. Within a few hundred years, however, the momentum of technological innovation had shifted decisively to the small, feuding states of Europe.

**The Neo-Confucian Synthesis**    The long period of the intermingling of Confucianism with Buddhist, Daoist, and other traditions of thought forced an

**Foot binding:** The practice of tightly wrapping the feet of young girls in order to break and reset the bones to compress the feet to about one-third of their normal size. Mothers generally did this to their daughters to make them more marriageable, since tiny feet were considered the epitome of female beauty.

**Female infanticide:** The killing of girl babies.

extensive reformulation of its core concepts by the Song period. During the twelfth century, this reformulation matured into Neo-Confucianism, which combined the moral core of Confucian ethics with a new emphasis on speculative philosophy borrowed from Buddhist and Daoist thinkers.

Neo-Confucianism holds that one cannot sit passively and wait for enlightenment, as the Buddhists do, but must actively "seek truth through facts" in order to understand correctly the relationships of form and substance as they govern the constitution of the totality of the universe, or "supreme ultimate."

Exploration of the physical universe undertaken in this spirit is thus the ultimate act of Confucian self-cultivation in that one apprehends the Way (*Dao*) on every level. This vision of Neo-Confucianism was propounded by the Cheng [chehng] brothers, Hao [how] (1032–1085) and Yi [yee] (1033–1107), and perfected by Zhu Xi [joo SHEE] (ca. 1129–1200), generally recognized as the leading Neo-Confucian thinker.

Zhu Xi's speculative Neo-Confucianism lost favor somewhat during a Buddhist revival of sorts during the Ming, in favor of the more direct ethical action favored by Wang Yangming [wahng yahn-MING] (1472–1529). For Wang, as for Zhu Xi, truth, whether in terms of epistemology or ethics, was unitary. He believed that all people carry within them an "original mind" in which rests an intuitive sense of the fundamental order of the universe. It is out of this instinct toward the right that one investigates the physical and moral universe in order to refine one's conclusions.

Wang's other area of emphasis was the unity of knowledge and action. While everyone has the spark of intuition, he argued, true understanding is inseparable from active pursuit and cultivation of that spark. Moreover, the sage must act in the world as his knowledge becomes increasingly refined, both to be a moral example to others and to complete his own self-cultivation.

**Technological Peaks**   In many respects, the notion of perfectibility woven through Song and Ming philosophy presented itself in the scientific and technical realms as well. A number of previous innovations were refined and, in some cases, brought to highly developed states. In a great many other cases, however, high points were achieved early on and continued substantially unchanged. For example, Zheng He's ships, with their dazzling array of innovative features in the fifteenth century, remained unsurpassed triumphs of Chinese naval architecture until the mid-nineteenth century, when the empire's first steamships were launched from Western-style dockyards. While new firearms were introduced in the seventeenth and eighteenth centuries, they came in part by way of Jesuit missionaries from Europe and remained essentially unchanged until the 1840s—yet another revealing pattern of core innovation (gunpowder weapons) reintroduced in improved form from the periphery.

From the Tang through the Southern Song, China was the site of an unprecedented number of technological innovations that would have a profound effect inside and outside the empire. The horse collar, moldboard plow, wheelbarrow, advanced iron casting, compass, gunpowder, porcelain, and paper diffused widely throughout Eurasia and the Indian Ocean basin. By the height of the Song period, tea, sugar, silk, porcelain, paper, and cotton cloth had all become major industries, and China dominated—in some cases, monopolized—production and distribution

**Song Porcelain.** Porcelain reached its full maturity during the Song dynasty, and objects from that period are highly coveted even today. This celadon (sea green, sometimes with a delicate crackle glaze) ewer with a double phoenix head and peony decorations dates from the Northern Song (960–1127).

of all of them. An increasingly sophisticated infrastructure of commercial credit, printed paper money, and insurance for merchant houses and their agents supported and secured China's vast network of industry and trade.

**Porcelain and Literature**  As we can see, many of the technical advances that took place revolved around luxury items. Most notable in this regard was the development of true porcelain. Following centuries of experimentation with kaolin clays, glazing mixes, and extremely high firing temperatures, Song craftspeople hit upon the formula for creating the world's most celebrated ceramics. Elegant white and celadon (a shade of green) porcelain vessels were manufactured in great numbers, and the surviving examples of Song wares today are among the world's most precious art treasures. Techniques for using distinctive blue cobalt oxide pigments were originally introduced from Iraq in the ninth century and were being utilized by Song and Ming potters to brighten their porcelain ware. Government-sponsored and government-run kilns, notably at the Jingdezhen works in Jiangxi Province, allowed for unprecedented volume and quality control.

The growing wealth, leisure, and literacy of the scholar-gentry and urban classes also created an increased demand for popular literature. The novel as a literary genre first made its appearance in China during the Yuan period but emerged as a form of mass entertainment only in the sixteenth century. Written in a rapidly evolving combination of classical and colloquial language, the swash-buckling adventures of the multiauthored *Water Margin* (or *All Men Are Brothers*) and the tale of family intrigue and woe of Cao Xueqin's [sow shew-eh-cheen] *The Dream of the Red Chamber* captured the imaginations of seventeenth- and eighteenth-century readers.

# Putting It All Together

The experiences of India and China during the period from the seventh through the fifteenth centuries provide us with several important areas of comparison. The first is in the realm of political continuity. India was subject to a succession of governments set up by invaders from the north and west, while the kingdoms to the south jock-eyed for power among themselves and for power over the Indian-influenced states of southeast Asia. While there was considerable cultural and religious continuity in the south, the north was alternately dominated by the Hinduism of the late Gupta period, the revived Buddhism of the seventh century, and ultimately by Islam. In the end, none of these claimed full dominance, though Islam remained the religion of the rulers after the twelfth century.

In the case of China, despite the Mongol invasion and political domination of China during the fourteenth century, the basic political structure changed relatively little and reemerged with greater centralization than ever during the Ming dynasty. Culturally, the Mongols' influence on China was negligible; moreover, the Mongols increasingly were compelled to make themselves culturally "Chinese" in order to rule, despite their concerted efforts to maintain their ethnic autonomy. Through it all, not only did Chinese leadership in technical innovation in so many fields keep up its former pace, but the brief incorporation into the Mongol Empire helped to greatly facilitate other cultures' interaction with and adaptation to Chinese advances.

The most dramatic difference, however, came in the realm of interaction with and adaptation to religion. India, from the time of Mahmud of Ghazna, never completely adapted itself to Islam—a situation that continues to the present day. Thus, northern India became a *syncretic* area—an area in which the world-views of rival religious civilizations confronted each other but were not signifi-cantly adopted or adapted by the other. Instead, Hindus and Muslims attempted to coexist with each other. Even notable attempts to bridge the gulf between Hindus and Muslims, such as Sikhism, were not successful in attaining wide-spread acceptance.

In China, however, the dominant political structures of empire and the cul-tural assumptions of Confucianism not only resisted Mongol attempts to circum-vent them but in the end were largely adopted by the conquerors. Unlike the Muslim conquerors in India, the Mongols did not adhere to a powerfully articu-lated universal religion. In fact, they proved receptive to several of the religious traditions they encountered in their conquests: Islam, Buddhism, and Nestorian Christianity all gained Mongol adherents. Even before this, however, in marked contrast to India's encounter with Islam, the very real tensions between Buddhism and Confucianism in China resulted not in persecution of the Buddhists but in

Confucian thinkers borrowing their approaches to speculative philosophy and creating an expanded synthetic ideology, Neo-Confucianism.

Thus, until the nineteenth century, these religious and cultural trends would continue. India, dominated by the Muslim Mughals in the north and increasingly by the British from the eighteenth century on, would struggle to reconcile and balance the tensions of syncretism. The British, quick to sense these tensions, increasingly exploited them in their strategy of "divide and rule." The Chinese, firm in the belief that all outsiders could ultimately "become Chinese," continued to pursue this policy through the same period. Ultimately, both empires would be reduced by the British and their fellow European powers, whose centuries-long rise was shortly to begin.

▶ For additional resources, including maps, primary sources, visuals, and quizzes, please go to www.oup.com/us/vonsivers. Please see the Further Resources section at the back of the book for additional readings and suggested websites.

# Against the Grain

# Empress Wu

The Tang ruler Wu Zetian, or Empress Wu (r. 690–705), exemplified her era's contradictory trends toward both greater restrictiveness and wider latitude in personal behavior. The daughter of a public works official, she spent a brief period at court as a servant to the empress. Disillusioned by life in the capital and drawn to the austerities of Buddhism, she joined a women's monastery, only to return to the palace when her beauty piqued the interest of an imperial prince. Seeing the opportunities this opening presented, she exploited them ably and ruthlessly.

Like Cleopatra in Egypt, hostile chroniclers in subsequent dynasties attributed much of her success to her sexual exploits, though the records also note that she was well educated, shrewd in her dealings with ministers, and a polished hand at employing imperial spectacle. In 684, after the death of her husband, who had become the emperor, she ruled as empress dowager and as regent for her son. In reality, however, she held all the actual power. A devout Buddhist, she declared Buddhism the state religion. She maneuvered to rule in her own right, and in 690, she inaugurated the new Zhou dynasty. The final step came in 693, when she took the Buddhist title Divine Empress Who Rules the Universe.

Though she was an able ruler according to the Tang official histories, the act of creating her own dynasty and new titles for herself was considered usurpation by many of her subjects, and a resistance soon followed. In the eyes of many influential Tang leaders, Wu's blatant empowering of Buddhists and Daoists over Confucians was deplorable. As a result, scurrilous accusations were laid against Wu, including allegations of executing and torturing of her opponents; she was even charged with the murder of her own child in her quest to achieve political power. Unlike many other Chinese rulers, however, she was able to stifle revolts and to preserve the continuity of the dynasty, only succumbing to natural causes in 705.

Following the Confucian backlash of the Song era, no woman in imperial China would wield this kind of power again until the reign of the empress dowager Cixi in the late nineteenth and early twentieth centuries. Even today, however, Wu remains a controversial figure; while she is widely celebrated in China as an early feminist role model, she is also seen as an ambitious, cruel, and self-serving schemer.

- In what ways does Empress Wu appear as a classic nonconformist?

- In what ways does Empress Wu resemble other ambitious women in history?

# Thinking Through Patterns

▶ **How did interactions between Muslims and Hindus in India lead to religious syncretism?**

In contemplating this question, we must consider what the fundamental beliefs of these two religious traditions were and what kinds of changes take place as religions move from one place to another and interact with other long-established beliefs. For Hindus, this is somewhat difficult, because Hinduism encompasses many different religious assumptions. Moreover, it has a long tradition of trying to fit newly arrived belief systems into its own traditions. This is where the clash with Islam is most evident. Islam teaches that there is no God but God (Allah); Hinduism would place Allah next to its other gods, which Muslims find intolerable. This fundamental clash of views makes any compromise difficult. But Muslim leaders find that they simply cannot coerce their Hindu subjects, who vastly outnumber them, to accept the new religion by force. They must therefore find ways to lessen its impact while holding true to the strictures of Islam. Thus, some leniency must be given, or rule becomes impossible, but each side keeps its distance from the other for fear of giving up core values. Thus, they coexist, albeit very uneasily.

Some compromises were made along the way to lessen conflict between the major traditions. Muslim rulers routinely had to suspend their insistence on governing by strict Islamic law and let the Hindu majority govern itself according to its own traditions. In some cases, Hindu women even adopted the veil, like their Muslim counterparts. The most spectacular steps were the founding of new religious traditions incorporating both Hindu and Muslim elements—Sikhism, for example, and, as we will see in Chapter 19, the Mughal ruler Akbar's attempt at a synthetic religion.

▶ **What steps were taken by Hindus and Muslims to lessen the conflicts between the two rival religious traditions?**

▶ **How was the Tang dynasty in China different from its predecessors and successors?**

As we saw, the Tang was China's most cosmopolitan dynasty, and this alone made it quite different from its predecessors. But why was it so cosmopolitan? Here, a large part of the answer must be seen in the widespread practice of Buddhism. China was now integrated into a Buddhist cultural sphere that allowed a greatly enhanced circulation of ideas and goods. Thus, China's rulers knew a good deal more about their neighbors than ever before and through Buddhism shared a community of religious interest with them. The reaction to Buddhism as a "foreign" faith in the Song period made China turn more inward; consequently, its larger ties with the Buddhist world deteriorated, never to reach Tang-level connections again.

The longevity and diversity of Neo-Confucianism over time suggest that the blending was quite effective. It represented a synthesis in which ethics and epistemology—Confucian, humanist-based morality coupled with the speculative ventures of Daoists and Buddhists—created a complete, self-sustaining system. In this, it parallels attempts by contemporary Christian and Muslim thinkers to marry faith and reason into an all-encompassing system designed to provide a means to answer both concrete and speculative questions.

▶ **How effectively did the religious and philosophical traditions of Buddhism, Confucianism, and Daoism blend together in creating Neo-Confucianism? Where did they clash?**

# Patterns of Evidence: Sources for Chapter 12

## SOURCE 12.1

## The *Chachnamah*

### ca. 1200

Composed in Arabic and translated into Persian in the twelfth and thirteenth centuries, the *Chachnamah* details the Arab conquest of the Sind (a province corresponding to northwest India and Pakistan) in the eighth century. The work details the campaign led by Muhammad Ibn Qasim, which was the most successful of the many attempts by Muslims to conquer the region. In this history of the campaign, Ibn Qasim is both a conquering hero and a defender of Islam, subduing non-Muslims and imposing new religious values in his wake.

**A description of the battle.**

Hazlí states that, in that army of the Arabs there was a brave soldier by name Háris son of Marrah. He was at the head of a column of one thousand fully armed warriors. He had three brave slaves with him, one of whom he retained to bear his arms, and the other two he appointed as officers in the army, each being made the leader of 500 men. When they arrived at Makrán the news was carried to Kíkánán, where the people prepared for battle and commenced fighting. They were about 20,000 men. (Nevertheless) the army of Islám attacked them and overpowered them, and seeing no other help, the natives retreated to the gates of the town. But when the Arab army left the battle-field and marched after the residents of Kíkánán, the latter came down to obstruct their progress. The Arab army made an onset, with their war cry of "Alláhu Akbar" (God is great) and from the left and the right the cliffs echoed the cry of "Alláhu Akbar." When the infidels of Kíkánán heard those cries they were much frightened, and some of them surrendered and accepted Islám and the rest fled away, and from that time up to our day, on the anniversary of that battle, cries of "Alláhu Akbar" are heard from the mountain.

They had already completed this victory when they received the sad news of the martyrdom of His

Source: *The Chachnamah: An Ancient History of Sind*, trans. Mirza Kalichbeg Fredunbeg, available online at http://persian.packhum.org/persian/main?url=pf%3Ffile%3D12701030%26ct%3D0.

Highness the Commander of the Faithful, Alí son of Abí Tálib, (on whom be peace). They, therefore, turned back, and when they arrived at Makrán, they learnt that Muáwiyeh son of Abísafiyán had become the Khalífah.

. . .

### A tradition.

It is related by Abul Hasan, who heard it from Hazlí, and Hazlí from Muslim son of Muhárib son of Muslim son of Ziyád, that when Muáwiyeh despatched the expedition of 4,000 men under Abdulláh son of Sawád, no one had to kindle fire in his camp, as they had carried abundant provisions for the journey, ready made for use. It was only on a single night that fire-light was perceived in the camp, and, on enquiry being made, it was found that a pregnant woman had been confined and fire was urgently required. Abdulláh gave her permission and she gave a merry banquet, and for three days continually entertained the whole army (with fresh-cooked food).

When Abdulláh arrived at Kíkánán, the enemy made an assault on him, but the army of Islám routed them, and secured plenty of booty. The people of Kíkánán assembled in large numbers, and occupied the mountain passes. The battle now raged furiously and Abdulláh son of Sawád found it necessary to keep his men in their ranks, by making a stand himself with a party of selected men, fully armed; and he appealed to the hearts of others in the following words: "O children of the Prophet's companions, do not turn your faces from the infidels, so that your faith may remain free from any flaw and you acquire the honour of martyrdom." Hearing these words his men assembled round the standard of Abdulláh, and one of these men, who belonged to the family of Abdul Kais, came out with a challenge to a single fight. Instantly the chief of the enemy's forces engaged with him. The example of this hero was followed by another Yásar son of Sawád. The chief was killed, but the army of Kíkánán made a general assault, by which the army of Islám was ultimately put to flight. The whole mountainous region now became alive with fighting men and the Musalmans beat a (hasty) retreat, and came back to Makrán.

### A tradition.

Abul Hasan relates that he heard Hátim son of Kutai-bíah Sahlí say: "That day I myself was in the army when the son of Sawád fought with his youthful adversary, and his friends advanced in the same manner, and killed many men of the enemy's side. After a hard fight they at last fell martyrs and I stripped the dead bodies of the enemy, and found a hundred signet rings."

. . .

### Safyán son of U'r dí appointed to carry on the religious war in Hind.

It is related by Hazlí who heard it from Tibuí son of Músá, who again heard it from his father, that on Abdulláh son of Sawád being martyred, he appointed Sinán son of Salmah as his successor. Soon afterwards Muáwiyeh wrote to Ziyád, (the then governor of Irák) to select a proper person for the holy wars in Hind.

When he received the letter, Ziyád nominated Ahnaf son of Kais, who was liked by all, and was the pride of the Faithful. Ahnaf forthwith went to Makrán, where he remained for a period of two years, and after two years and one month he was removed from that post.

▶ **Working with Sources**

1. To what extent is this conflict envisioned as a "religious war"?

2. Why does the document concern itself with successions of political power?

## SOURCE 12.2

# Harsha Vardhana, *The Lady of the Jewel Necklace*

### ca. 640 CE

Harsha Vardhana, one of the better-known monarchs of India, controlled a wide swath of territory in the northern subcontinent between 606 and 647. Harsha was visited during his reign by the Chinese Buddhist pilgrim Xuan Zang, who described his court and government, and the poet Bana wrote a biography of the king called the *Harshacarita*. However, Harsha himself also wrote at least three plays, two of which were dedicated to the Hindu god Shiva and incorporated actual incidents from his court. While the plays are ostensibly fictional, the scene below draws on a real event, reported by Xuan Zang, in which Harsha saved an image of Buddha from a fire that had broken out in his palace. His plays reflect the cosmopolitan and religiously eclectic nature of his court, as well as his view of the status of the advisors and women in his orbit.

KING: (*arising in haste*) What? A fire in the women's quarters? Oh no! What if Queen Vásava·datta has been burnt! Oh, my dear Vásava·datta!

VÁSAVA·DATTA: Help, my husband, help!

KING: Oh! Why, in my extreme haste and confusion, I didn't notice the queen even though she was standing right here beside me. Courage, my queen, courage!

VÁSAVA·DATTA: My husband, I didn't speak for my own sake. But

Source: Harsha Vardhana, *The Lady of the Jewel Necklace*, trans. Wendy Doniger (New York: NYU Press, 2006), 259–265.

Ságarika may die, for in my cruelty I had her chained up here. Save her, please, my husband.

KING: What? Ságarika may die, my queen? I will go!

VASU·BHUTI: Your majesty, why should you go the way of a moth for no real reason?

BABHRÁVYA: Your majesty, what Vasu·bhuti said is right.

JESTER: (*grabbing the King by his shirt*) My friend, don't do anything so rash!

KING: (*freeing his shirt*) You idiot! Ságarika may die! Why is the breath of life still in me even now? (*He mimes rushing into the fire and being overcome by smoke.*)

> Stop, fire, stop! Give up
>    this unbroken wave of
>       smoke!
> Why do you brandish on high
>    this circling mass of flames?
> If I wasn't burnt up by the fire
>    of separation from
>       my dear one,
> that blazed like the doomsday
>    fire, what can you do to me?

VÁSAVA·DATTA: Since my husband has unhesitatingly done this because of what I said—miserably unlucky woman that I am—I, too, will follow my husband.

JESTER: (*walking around and standing in front of her*) I, too, ma'am, will be your pathfinder.

VASU·BHUTI: Why, the king of Vatsa has already entered the fire! Then it is proper that I, too, who saw the princess die, should offer myself as an oblation into the fire here.

BABHRÁVYA: Your majesty, why jeopardize the race descended from Bharata for no good reason? But what's the use of idle talk? I too will act in accordance with my devotion.

> *All mime entering the fire.*
> *Enter Ságarika, in chains.*

SÁGARIKA: (*looking in all directions*) Oh no! The fire is blazing up on all sides! (*thinking, with satisfaction*) Fortunately, the fire, carrier of oblations, will put an end to my suffering today.

KING: Ságarika is here near the fire! I'll help her right away. (*approaching her in haste*) My dear, how can you remain so self-possessed even now in this haste and confusion?

SÁGARIKA: (*seeing the King, to herself*) Why, it's my husband! When I see him, my love of life comes back again. (*aloud*) Save me, your majesty! Save me!

KING: Don't be afraid, my timid one:

. . .

> Clearly the fire does not really
>    burn you,
>    even though it has caught you,
> for your touch now, darling,
>    takes away
>    even my burning anguish.

. . .

VÁSAVA·DATTA: (*touching the KING's body, with joy*) Thank goodness, my husband's body is unhurt.

KING: This is Babhrávya—

BABHRÁVYA: We've been brought back to life, your majesty.

KING: —and this Vasu·bhuti!—

VASU·BHUTI: Total victory to the great king!

▶ **Working with Sources**

1. **What does the play suggest about Harsha's vision of the ideal relationship between a king and his courtiers?**

2. **Why was Harsha so careful with stage directions? Did he intend the work to be performed, and how?**

## SOURCE 12.3

# Poetry of the Tang Dynasty

**ca. 750 CE**

The Tang period (618–960) witnessed a renaissance of poetry, oftentimes compressing vivid natural imagery and poignant emotion into short pieces of only a few verses. The poetry of Li Bo (or Li Bai, 701–762) was particularly influential in the West when his verses on drinking and the pleasures of life were rendered in translation. However, there is also a strong undercurrent of pacifism, drawing on Confucian philosophy, in Tang poetry, and the poems below address war and its consequences. A poem by Du Fu (ca. 721–770), who was also Li Bo's friend, reflects the same sentiment.

**Du Fu, "A Drawing of a Horse by General Cao at Secretary Wei Feng's House"**

Throughout this dynasty no one
  had painted horses
Likethemaster-spirit,PrinceJiangdu—
And then to General Cao through
  his thirty years of fame
The world's gaze turned, for royal
  steeds.
He painted the late Emperor's lumi-
  nous white horse.
For ten days the thunder flew over
  Dragon Lake,
And a pink-agate plate was sent him
  from the palace—
The talk of the court-ladies, the
  marvel of all eyes.
The General danced, receiving it in
  his honoured home

After this rare gift, followed rapidly
  fine silks
From many of the nobles, request-
  ing that his art
Lend a new lustre to their screens.
. . . First came the curly-maned
  horse of Emperor Taizong,
Then, for the Guos, a lion-spotted
  horse. . . .
But now in this painting I see two
  horses,
A sobering sight for whosoever
  knew them.
They are war-horses. Either could
  face ten thousand.
They make the white silk stretch
  away into a vast desert.
And the seven others with them are
  almost as noble

Source: "A Drawing of a Horse by General Cao at Secretary Wei Feng's House" adapted from http://www.shigeku.com/xlib/lingshidao/hanshi/dufu.htm, Li Bo poem adapted from *Bright Moon, White Clouds: Selected Poems of Li Po*, ed. and trans. J. P. Seaton (Boston: Shambhala, 2012), 113–115.

Mist and snow are moving across a
   cold sky,
And hoofs are cleaving snow-drifts
   under great trees-
With here a group of officers and
   there a group of servants.
See how these nine horses all vie
   with one another—
The high clear glance, the deep firm
   breath.
. . . Who understands distinction?
   Who really cares for art?
You, Wei Feng, have followed Cao,
   Zhidun preceded him.
. . . I remember when the late
   Emperor came toward his
   Summer Palace,
The procession, in green-feathered
   rows, swept from the eastern sky—
Thirty thousand horses, prancing,
   galloping,
Fashioned, every one of them, like
   the horses in this picture. . . .
But now the Imperial Ghost receives
   secret jade from the River God,
For the Emperor hunts crocodiles
   no longer by the streams.
Where you see his Great Gold
   Tomb, you may hear among the
   pines
A bird grieving in the wind that the
   Emperor's horses are gone.

## Li Bo, from *Bright Moon, White Clouds*

*Moon over the Pass*
Bright moon suddenly up from
   beyond Heaven Mountain,
where it had lain hid in the dark,
   endless sea of clouds.

The long winds came down tens of
   thousands of miles,
from the north to blow through
   Jade Gate Pass.
Here Han troops climbed the road
   to Paideng Mountain,
because the barbarians wanted our
   Great Dark Sea in the desert.
Of all who stood upon that ancient
   field,
I've never heard one returned.
Armed sojourners, they gazed
   hopelessly
homeward over barren ground,
their hearts gone home: read the
   bitter faces.
In home's many mansions, facing
   *this* same moon:
the wives and loved ones also
sigh and see clear, in the mind's eye,
   yet can't let go.

*War South of the Wall*
Last year, war:
at the Sang-gan's source.
This year, war:
along the Tsung-ho Road
Our whole army washed weapons
   in the Tiao chih Sea,
and set horse to graze on the grass
   that grew in patches
underneath the snows of the T'ian
   Shan Range.
Three thousand miles of battles,
three armies exhausted, withering
   away, *grown old* . . .
The Huns farm these battlefields for
   bones:
since the time of the Ancients,
   nothing to see

but bleached bones on yellow
  sands, their fields.
Ch'in built the Wall to keep them
  out.
Han fed the beacon fires to burn
  unceasing,
yet the War went on:
war, wasteland: men dying there.
The horses of the conquered neigh-
  ing skyward, mourning.
Vultures feed on man guts.

With flesh in their beaks they fly up,
  fly up to hang those guts in the
  withered branches.
Soldiers die, blood splashes brush
  and grass.
Generals?
Is all this done in vain? You know
  that soldiers
are the direst of instruments. The
  wise make use of them
only when there is no other way.

▶ **Working with Sources**

1. **What does this poetry suggest about the Confucian and Daoist conceptions of war and its consequences?**

2. **How do the poems reflect on the preservation of historical memory in monuments and paintings?**

## SOURCE 12.4

# Marco Polo, "Khubilai Khan at War"

### ca. 1290

**M**arco Polo (1254–1324) was a member of a clan of Venetian merchants, who had been active in trade in the Middle East for some decades. Polo claims to have accompanied his father and uncle on an extensive trade and diplomatic excursion to China in 1271, and in this account he describes the voyage as well as the people and places he has seen. He further claims to have lived 17 years in China and to have met with, and even served as an official for, Khubilai Khan (1215–1294), Genghis Khan's grandson. While some historians have suggested that the account may not be reliable, it demonstrates, at the very least, Western curiosity about Asia and the catalyst of trade in driving some Europeans into hitherto unknown parts of the world.

Source: Marco Polo, *The Travels of Marco Polo*, trans. Ronald Latham (Harmondsworth, UK: Penguin, 1958), 115–118.

When the Great Khan had mustered the mere handful of men of which I have spoken, he consulted his astrologers to learn whether he would defeat his enemies and bring his affairs to a happy issue. They assured him that he would deal with his enemies as he pleased. Thereupon he set out with all his forces and went on until after twenty days they came to a great plain where Nayan lay with all his forces, who were not less than 400,000 horsemen. They arrived early in the morning and caught the enemy completely unawares; the Great Khan had had all the roads so carefully watched that no one could come or go without being intercepted, and had thus ensured that the enemy had no suspicion of their approach. Indeed, when they arrived Nayan was in his tent, dallying in bed with his wife, to whom he was greatly attached.

What more shall I say? When the day of battle dawned, the Great Khan suddenly appeared on a mound that rose from the plain where Nayan's forces were bivouacked. They were quite at their ease, like men who had not the faintest suspicion that anyone was approaching with hostile intent. Indeed they felt so secure that they had posted no sentries round their camp and sent out no patrols to van or rear. And suddenly there was the Great Khan on the hill I have mentioned. He stood on the top of a wooden tower, full of crossbowmen and archers, which was carried by four elephants wearing stout leather armour draped with cloths of silk and gold. Above his head flew his banner with the emblem of the sun and moon, so high that it could be clearly seen on every side.

. . .

When Nayan and his men saw the troops of the Great Khan surrounding their camp, they were utterly taken aback. They rushed to arms, arrayed themselves in haste, and formed their ranks in due order.

. . .

So loud was the shouting and the clash of armies that you could not have heard the thunder of heaven. You must know that Nayan was a baptized Christian and in this battle he had the cross of Christ on his standard.

What need to make a long story of it? Enough that this was the most hazardous fight and the most fiercely contested that ever was seen. Never in our time were so many men engaged on one battlefield, especially so many horsemen. So many died on either side that it was a marvel to behold. The battle raged from daybreak till noon, and for a long time its issue hung in the balance; Nayan's followers were so devoted to him, for he was an open-handed master, that they were ready to die rather than turn their backs. But in the end the victory fell to the Great Khan. When Nayan and his men saw that they could hold out no longer, they took to flight. But this availed them nothing; for Nayan was taken prisoner, and all his barons and his men surrendered to the Great Khan.

When the Great Khan learnt that Nayan was a prisoner, he commanded that he should be put to death. And this was how it was done. He was wrapped up tightly in a carpet and then dragged about so violently, this way and that, that he died. Their object in choosing this mode of death was so that the blood of the imperial lineage might not be spilt upon the earth, and that sun and air might not witness it.

▶ **Working with Sources**

1. How did the Great Khan employ elements of "psychological warfare" on the battlefield?

2. Does Marco Polo seem to have felt sympathy for the defeat of a fellow Christian by the non-Christian Khan? Why not?

## SOURCE 12.5

# Model of a Ming ship in the flotilla of Zheng He

**ca. 1420**

Between 1405 and 1433, a series of naval expeditions were sent out by Yongle, the third emperor of the Ming Dynasty, under the command of the remarkable Zheng He (1371–1435). The largest of Zheng's ships were over 400 feet long and were thus more than four times the length of Christopher Columbus's *Santa Maria*. His voyages took Zheng to the coasts of southeast Asia, Indonesia, India, Arabia, and East Africa. In 2010, marine archaeologists attempted to find remains of one of Zheng's ships off the coast of Kenya, near Malindi, a site Zheng visited in 1418. This photograph shows a model of one of Zheng's ships, compared with a model of the *Santa Maria*. The model is displayed in a shopping mall in Dubai, United Arab Emirates.

▶ Working
with Sources

1. What does the greater size of Zheng He's ships compared to the ones Columbus used say about the imperial ambitions of Ming China in the fifteenth century?

2. Why might this ship be of interest to shoppers in Dubai?

Source: © Liu Liqun/Chinastock.

# Chapter **13** 550–1500 CE
# Religious Civilizations Interacting
## KOREA, JAPAN, AND VIETNAM

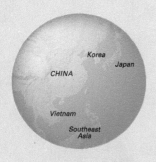

The brushstrokes flowed across the fine rice paper, as they had thousands of times since she began carefully practicing them as a young girl. For Murasaki Shikibu (ca. 973–1025), the daughter of a minor noble in the court at Heian-Kyo in central Japan, the words that now came so effortlessly had become her refuge from the rigid routine of palace life, where a woman's every move was carefully prescribed. The court women of Heian Japan (794–1185 CE), in their thick, stiff winter kimonos, their teeth blackened and faces powdered white to enhance their beauty, were carefully monitored by palace chamberlains and commented on by court gossips. Some of the women, like Murasaki's older contemporary Sei Shonagon, responded to this restricted life with savage wit and scathing commentary, skewering its pretentions in her scandalous *Pillow Book*.

Murasaki's literary interests, however, took a somewhat different turn. Though trained in *kanji*, the literary Chinese that functioned as Japan's first written language, her private writings, as were those of the handful of other literate Japanese women, were written in the simpler *kana* script based on a **syllabary** of sounds in the Japanese spoken language. Like Sei's, her work also centered on court life. But her subject was the adventures, loves, trials, and triumphs of a fictional prince named Genji. When it was finished, she had created in her *Genji Monagatori*, the *Tale of Genji* (ca. 1000), what scholars have

*ABOVE*: Detail from twelfth-century Japanese scroll depicting *The Tale of Genji*.

since recognized as the world's first novel. It remains even today Japan's most popular work of fiction and one of the world's great literary masterpieces.

The story of Murasaki, the court women of Heian-Kyo—the city we know today as Kyoto—and eleventh-century Japan more generally all help to illustrate the patterns of world history featured in this book.

---

In the sixth century CE, Chinese writing, culture, thought, and Buddhism arrived simultaneously in Japan and were swiftly adopted by the ambitious Japanese state of Yamato. Sensing that power and prestige would grow from adapting China's centralized imperial institutions to Japanese conditions, Yamato leaders thoroughly remade their state along these lines over the next two centuries. But in many ways, as we shall see, the suitability of these institutions to Japan's clan-based society was at best uneven.

The tensions in state formation, both large and small, created by this situation were noticeable as well in Korea and Vietnam, also in the process of interaction and adaptation to Chinese institutions. Like the Japanese, the Koreans and Vietnamese would go on to create their own writing systems while retaining Chinese as a literary language. They would also struggle, like the Japanese and Chinese, to balance the differing traditions of Buddhism with the practical elements of Confucian government. The dynamism within these tensions would allow each to ultimately make imported Chinese culture their own as they followed their own distinct courses of state formation: Korea and Vietnam, often struggling under China's political shadow, and Japan, clinging fiercely to its independence and protected by the intervening Sea of Japan.

# Korea to 1450: Innovation from Above

Like the influence of the Greek-Hellenistic and Roman worlds, that of imperial China became widespread throughout east, northeast, and southeast Asia. Chinese writing, literature, law, government, and thought, as well as imported religions such as Buddhism, shaped local social, cultural, and religious customs and practices. But as these imports were often imposed from the top down, they met frequent resistance at the village and clan levels. Thus, tensions between elites and locals continually played out in the assorted Korean kingdoms against a backdrop of invasion and collaboration. From the beginning these societies asserted their political independence from the Chinese. However, their position on or near the Chinese border, the role of the Korean kingdoms as havens for refugees, and the continual pressures of potential invasion provided a conduit for the spread of Chinese innovations—even to the islands of Japan. For the Koreans themselves, shifting relations with China provided both unity and disarray in the struggles of different kingdoms for dominance.

## People and Place: The Korean Environment

The terrain of the Korean peninsula resembles in many ways that of the adjacent region of Manchuria. The north is mountainous, marked by the Nangnim and Hamyong ranges running northeast to southwest, with the Taebaek chain

**Syllabary:** A system of written symbols representing the sounds of syllables, rather than individual consonants and vowels.

373

**Altaic:** In linguistics, the family of languages descended from that spoken by inhabitants of the region of the Altai Mountains in central Asia. Examples include the Turkish languages, Mongolian, and Manchu.

**Striated:** Having thin lines or bands.

"She He [the name of a Chinese commander] achieved distinction through treachery and became the cause of the bloodshed. Yang Pu . . . met with hardship and blame; regretting his failure to win distinction. . . . He [Yang Pu] sought for it this time but instead aroused suspicion. Xun Zhi contended for glory, but he and Gongsun Sui suffered execution. Both armies disgraced themselves and none of their leaders were enfeoffed as marquises."

—*Records of the Grand Historian*, 115

running north and south along the coast facing the Sea of Japan. The Amnokkang, better known as the Yalu River, and the Kangnam Mountains form the present dividing line with Manchuria, but Korean kingdoms have at times extended far beyond them into modern China's northeast. The areas south of the modern city of Seoul are somewhat flatter, but the entire peninsula is generally hilly, and agriculture has historically been concentrated in the river floodplains and coastal alluvial flats.

**Climate and Agriculture**    The climate of Korea is continental in the north but influenced by the monsoon system in the south. As in northern China, summer and winter temperatures tend to be extreme, with distinct rainy (summer) and dry (winter) seasons. Because of the configuration of the mountains and the peninsula's position along the northern perimeter of the monsoon, annual rainfall amounts differ widely: from average lows of 30 inches in the northeast to 60–70 inches in the southwest. Like the western side of the Japanese islands, however, Korea is largely blocked by Japanese mountain ranges from the moderating effects of the Japan Current.

The difficulties of the terrain and the ever-present possibility of drought have rendered the challenges of the region similar to those facing agriculturalists in northern China, with crops such as millet and wheat dominating and rice farming catching on only much later in the south, where rainfall and the terracing of hillsides made it feasible (see Map 13.1).

**Ethnic Origins**    The ethnic origins of the Koreans are still obscure, though the slim archaeological and linguistic evidence seems to point to a central Asian homeland and links to the **Altaic**-speaking peoples. In this way, the modern Korean language may be distantly related to such languages as Mongolian, Manchu, and possibly Japanese. East and northeast Asia, as we have seen, was home to some of the world's first pottery, though the potter's wheel did not arrive in the area for millennia. In the case of the Korean peninsula, potsherds dating from 4000 BCE have been uncovered in **striated** styles not unlike the Jomon wares of Japan, which some scholars have suggested points to an early period of interaction or perhaps even a common ancestry.

## Conquest and Competition: History and Politics to 1598

Though developments in northern China have long had a bearing on events on the Korean peninsula, the first Korean state predated any such influence. Zhou Chinese annals contain apparent references to the kingdom of Choson—"The Land of the Morning Calm." Choson seems to have extended deep into southern Manchuria, with its capital located on the site of the modern city of Pyongyang. It is believed to have been founded sometime after 1000 BCE. In the absence of a written Korean language, however, no indigenous records exist of its early years.

**The "Three Kingdoms"**    Such Chinese cultural influences as the use of written language appear to have been present in the region even before the first attempt at invasion under the Qin (221–206 BCE). By 108 BCE, their successors, the Han, briefly succeeded in bringing much of the peninsula under their sway. It is from this period that the first written records of exchanges with such outlying peoples as the Koreans, Japanese, and Vietnamese find their way into Han histories. As related in Sima Qian's *Records of the Grand Historian*, the Han quest to pursue the conquest of "Chaoxian" (Choson) was rife with chaos and mismanagement.

Long before this, however, Chinese agricultural techniques and implements, methods of bronze and iron smelting, and a wide variety of other technologies found their way to Choson and beyond. Early contacts between Choson and the Zhou Chinese states from the ninth century BCE on saw the arrival of bronze tools, coins, and weapons. By the fifth century BCE, the technology of iron smelting was also firmly established on the Korean peninsula.

Following the Han conquests, a more systematic Chinese transformation was attempted. The Han incorporated approximately two-thirds of the peninsula into their empire and took over Pyongyang as their regional capital. They also encouraged Chinese settlement in the newly acquired territories in order to help ensure loyalty. One of the indirect effects of the conquest was a steady stream of refugees into the unoccupied regions of the south and to the small tribal societies of Japan. This constant traffic back and forth across the narrow, 100-mile strait separating the Japanese islands from the

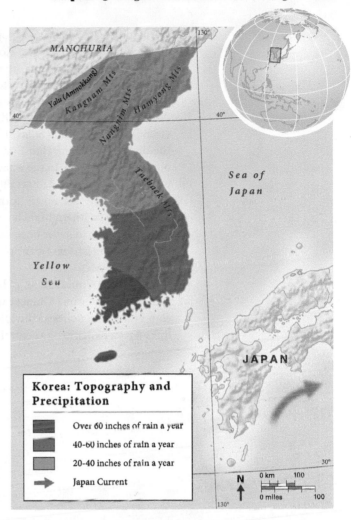

**Korea: Topography and Precipitation**

- Over 60 inches of rain a year
- 40–60 inches of rain a year
- 20–40 inches of rain a year
- Japan Current

MAP 13.1 **Korea: Topography and Precipitation.**

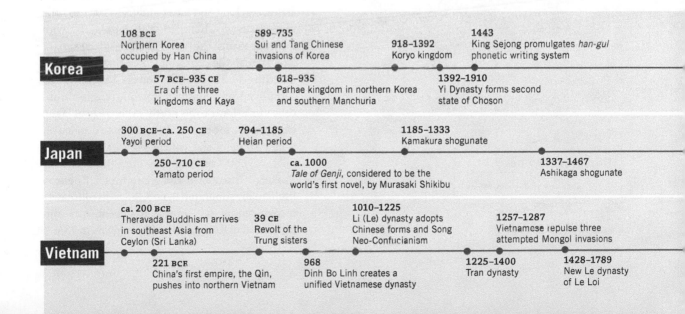

mainland created a transient population of colonists in both places and greatly facilitated cultural exchanges. Koreans became established as important actors in early Japanese history, and with the founding of the small Japanese holding of *Kaya* (Gaya) in 42 CE, Japanese territorial claims were established on the peninsula.

At the same time, the foundations had been laid for the so-called Three Kingdoms of Korea: *Koguryo* [go-GUR-yo] (37 BCE–668 CE), *Paekche* [BAAK-chih] (18 BCE–660 CE), and *Silla* [Si-lah] (57 BCE–935 CE). By the fourth century CE, the dissolution of the Han Empire encouraged the Koreans to push the Chinese out of the peninsula. In the wake of their retreat, the three rival kingdoms began a process of intrigue and intermittent war among themselves for dominance. Koguryo, in the extreme north, formed the largest state as the Chinese evacuated, moving into southern Manchuria in the absence of any strong rivals. In the south, the areas that had never been under Chinese control had a history of close ties to the developing Japanese clan powers and, consequently, tended to be more outward-looking (see Map 13.2).

In 372 the Chinese state of Jin began sending Buddhist missionaries to Koguryo. With them came Chinese writing and literature—and, significantly, Confucian ethics and political thought. In 427, Koguryo remade itself along Chinese lines. From Pyongyang a central Confucian bureaucracy was set up, examinations were instituted, and a reconstituted land tax and conscription system were installed.

Meanwhile, the two southern kingdoms fought continually to stave off domination by their northern rival. Paekche's maritime contacts with south China aided the spread of Buddhism there, as did, to some degree, its wars with Koguryo from 364 to 371. Buddhism had also come to Silla, but Chinese political institutions did not take the same form there as elsewhere. A clan-based, autocratic monarchy, Silla adopted a Chinese-style bureaucracy but retained its system of hereditary ranks, leaving power largely in the hands of warrior aristocrats.

The power struggle among the peninsular states was long and bitter and from time to time also involved China. In 550, Silla allied with Paekche against the renewed expansionist aims of Koguryo, in the course of which Kaya was eliminated in 562. The reunification of China under the short-lived Sui dynasty in 589 soon resulted in another invasion of the north. After several Tang campaigns were repulsed, the Chinese decided on a new strategy and concluded an alliance with Silla in 660, spelling the immediate end of Paekche. Threatened along two fronts, Koguryo itself finally submitted in 668. Silla was ultimately recognized by the Chinese as a client state controlling all of Korea south of Pyongyang in 735.

**Korea, ca. 500 CE**

—— Boundary of kingdom, 500 CE

MAP 13.2 **Korea, ca. 500 CE.**

**Pulguksa Temple.** Buddhism put down strong roots in Silla after its introduction in the fourth century. The Pulguksa temple was first built in Kyongjiu, the Silla capital, in 535 as part of the state Buddhist school. The stone pagodas were built in the ninth century under the auspices of the new Son school, better known by its Japanese name, Zen.

**Korea to the Mid-Fifteenth Century**    By the middle of the eighth century, Silla was in decline. In 780 the king was assassinated, and revolts led by various pretenders threatened to leave the country unstable for some time to come. Among the most restive members of Silla society were the merchants, who, like their counterparts in China, were aware of their growing economic power, though sensitive to the fear and contempt in which they were held by the Confucian-influenced aristocracy and bureaucrats.

MAP **13.3  Korea under the Koryo, 936–1392.**

One such merchant, Wong Kon (d. 943), subdued the crumbling kingdom and reconstituted it as Koryo—from which comes the name "Korea." The Chinese imperial model of state formation proved attractive to Wong, who, after the practice of Chinese emperors, was accorded a posthumous reign name, Taejo. He moved the capital to Kaesong, where he laid out a city in the grid pattern of the Tang capital of Chang'an and adopted Chinese-style bureaucratic and tax systems, with military and labor conscription. Koryo even built its own version of the Great Wall near the Yalu River as a barrier to the nomadic peoples to the north (see Map 13.3).

By the middle of the thirteenth century, Koryo, like much of the rest of Asia, had begun to feel the power of Mongol expansion. In 1231, with rockets, bombs, and assorted other new military items acquired from their victories over the Chinese, Mongol forces laid siege to Kaesong. The fall of the city inaugurated four

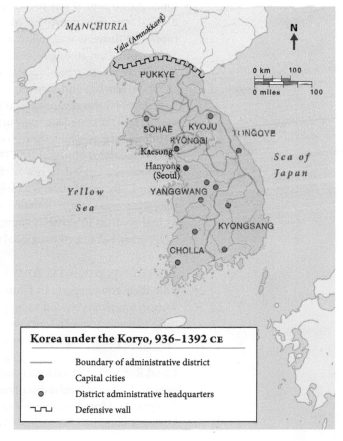

**Korea under the Koryo, 936–1392 CE**

| | |
|---|---|
| —— | Boundary of administrative district |
| ● | Capital cities |
| ● | District administrative headquarters |
| ⊓⊔ | Defensive wall |

decades of irregular warfare against the occupiers and forced the withdrawal of the government to the south. The Mongols' imperial ambitions prompted the deportation of perhaps 250,000 Koreans as slave laborers to other parts of the Mongol Empire, beginning in 1254. After the Koryo court finally capitulated in 1259, the Mongols intermarried and assimilated to Korean culture. As in most of the occupied areas of Eurasia, the advantages brought by Mongol unity in terms of easier travel and transport and increased public works were eclipsed in Korea by the cruelty of the conquest itself, the widespread perception of misrule, and oppressive taxation.

In 1368, the Mongol Yuan dynasty in China was overthrown by the forces of the soldier-monk Zhu Yuanzhi, who inaugurated the Ming dynasty (1368–1644). As had nearly every previous dynasty, the Ming laid plans to invade Korea. In 1388 the Korean leader Yi Song-gye made the strategic decision not to resist the Ming but moved against the Korean court instead, founding the Yi dynasty in 1392 and resurrecting the name of Choson for the new state. The Yi proved to be Korea's final imperial dynasty, ruling until the peninsula was annexed by Japan in 1910. The Yi concluded an agreement with China that formed the heart of what is often, though somewhat erroneously, referred to as the Ming "tribute system" (see Chapter 21).

Meanwhile, the Yi polity once again adapted to Chinese-style institutions. The highly centralized governmental structure of the Ming was echoed in Choson, and the adoption of Neo-Confucianism slowly began to drive out older local customs. A new capital was set up on the site of present-day Seoul, and the state was divided into eight provinces. Within each of these, the Chinese model of prefectures and districts was followed. A uniform law code was later promulgated in 1485, calling for, among other things, a permanent hereditary class structure. The Confucian exam structure was also broadened to include a two-tiered official class, the *yongban* and *chongin*.

Yet, for all the advantages created by the new class structure, old cleavages in many cases remained and new unanticipated ones soon developed. As a means of stabilizing the *yongban* class (and, so it was assumed, society as a whole), the Yi rulers made large land grants to the great officials of the kingdom. These landholders, however, tended to use such grants to amass more and more local power. Unlike Chinese officials, who were moved from place to place to avoid just this, they tended to remain in their own territories, where they could use a host of informal controls to resist attempts from the throne to rein in their excesses. Over time, many became like regional rulers.

## Economy, Society, and Family

Like their counterparts in China, rulers and government officials in the various Korean kingdoms tended to be preoccupied with recurrent problems of landlordism and tenancy, land reform, and maintenance of local infrastructures—especially in wet rice-producing areas—and alleviating want during times of shortage.

Land Reform    At various times, therefore, those under Chinese influence proposed schemes of land redistribution based on the Chinese "well-field" model (see Chapter 4). More ambitious was the *chongjon* system of Silla, begun in 722. Following a combination of Buddhist and Confucian precepts and with an eye to local custom, the *chongjon* system mandated a government-sponsored distribution of land, with taxes paid in kind. Additionally, peasants were instructed to develop specialized cash crops or engage in small-craft manufacture. A prime example was the planting of mulberry trees as food for silkworms and the development of **sericulture**.

**Sericulture:** Raising silkworms in order to obtain raw silk.

Under the Yi dynasty of Choson, the implanting of Neo-Confucian values in the countryside as well as among elites became a prime consideration. For example, a new system of land tenure was made part of a more general stabilizing of all classes. Peasant rents were fixed at half the crop, and a hierarchy of village headmen, bureaucrats, and magistrates similar to the Chinese system was set up to collect taxes, settle disputes, and dispense justice.

As noted previously, the institution of Chinese systems in Korea tended to attract the elites more than the peasant and artisan classes. Their spotty success in taking root tended in many ways to aggravate societal tensions, despite the governmental efficiencies they created. One factor in this was a repeated attempt on the part of the bureaucracy to enhance its power at the expense of the merchant and artisan classes. In the countryside, power remained in the hands of the landholder aristocracy, which tended to ensure that the peasants would be bound to them in a fashion not unlike the serfdom of their European contemporaries.

**Neo-Confucian Influence**     Particularly in the cities, the high level of Song Chinese–influenced material culture was increasingly evident. Interregional trade was brisk, and Korea's position at the center of the east Asian Buddhist world made it a trade and pilgrimage crossroads. Korean artisans became highly proficient in the new technologies of porcelain making and book printing; many of the oldest Chinese, Korean, and Japanese works extant were printed by Korean publishers.

Under the Yi, the Confucian exams became more open, though the new arrangement called for two official classes, the *yongban*, or scholar-gentry, drawn from high civil and military officials, and the *chungin*, or minor officials. Below these were the *yangmin*, commoners of different professions as well as peasants and serfs, while the lowest group, the *chonmin*, consisted of bond slaves, laborers, and prostitutes.

Though approximating the class structure in China, the new system was more like the composite one created in Heian Japan. As in Japan, it proved a troublesome fit, particularly in remote rural areas. Though the Confucian exams theoretically allowed for some degree of social mobility, they tended to be monopolized by the *yongban*. The institution of hereditary classes, intended to create a stable and harmonious social structure, instead concentrated wealth in the hands of the rural gentry, who often lacked a proper Confucian sense of the official responsibilities of their positions. In many places, the older patterns of aristocratic local power simply continued with only cosmetic changes. Thus, by the sixteenth century, the divide between the wealthy, educated, sophisticated capital and large provincial cities and the tradition-bound countryside was steadily increasing.

**Women and Society**     Until the arrival of Confucian institutions in the Korean countryside, local village life, as in Vietnam and Japan, tended toward more egalitarian structures, especially between men and women, than would later be the

**Matrilocal:** Living with the family of the bride.

case. In Korea, this egalitarianism retained a remarkable vitality in the face of Neo-Confucian precepts. Even today, there is far less of the traditional emphasis on filial piety and patriarchal custom than in China. Until the sixteenth and seventeenth centuries, for example, bilateral and **matrilocal** marriage patterns tended to be the norm. As in Japan and Vietnam, the communal and meticulous nature of rice agriculture tended to lessen the division between "male" and "female" work roles and made women and girls more equal partners in local rural society. Women's property and inheritance rights, far more expansive than in Confucian China, also reflected this.

Under the Neo-Confucian reforms of the Yi, however, some of these practices began to change. The idea of strictly delineated gender roles, of men dominating in the "outer" world and women being preeminent in the "inner" world of the home—long a staple among the urban elites and official classes—now became a cornerstone of moral training in rural academies and in the home.

## Religion, Culture, and Intellectual Life

As with many peoples of north and central Asia, early Korean religion appears to have been animistic. One could appeal to the spirits through shamans or animals believed to have certain powers. Like Shinto in Japan, these beliefs continued at the local level for many hundreds of years after the introduction of more formalized systems. The invasion of the Han brought the Chinese concepts of heaven, earth, and humankind along with the imperial rituals associated with them. Of more long-term importance, however, was the introduction of Buddhism to the Three Kingdoms during the fourth century CE.

**Buddhism, Printing, and Literacy**   All the Korean kings seized to varying degrees on the combination of Buddhism, Han Confucian political and moral philosophy, and their supporting institutions as a way to enhance the material and ethical foundation of their states. In Silla, for example, the court pursued a course of striving for Buddhist "perfection." It patronized a popular Buddhist-Confucian society, Hwarang—the "Flower of Youth Corps"—that helped to build the 210-foot Hwang Nyonsu temple in 645. Others sponsored mammoth publication projects of Buddhist works: Koryo produced a version of the *Tripitaka* printed on 80,000 hand-carved wood blocks as an act of piety and supplication during the war with the Mongols. All of this tended to expand the relatively high level of functional literacy in written Chinese among Korean elites. As a result, twelfth-century Korea developed into one of the world's handful of centers of printing and publishing due in large part to the demand for Buddhist works. By the 1100s as well, publishers were employing what may have been the world's first movable, cast metallic type (see "Patterns Up Close: Printing").

*Han-gul:* Korean phonetic script, introduced in the middle of the fifteenth century.

Korea's leading role in world literacy in the preindustrial era received a further boost during the reign of King Sejong (r. 1418–1450). Here, the development of the Korean phonetic script *han-gul*, like the use of *kana* in Japan, made the introduction of writing much simpler and closer to the vernacular than literary Chinese. Like the *kana* system in Japan, *han-gul* helped the spread of literacy in a far more efficient manner than had been the case with literary Chinese. Yet, like *kana* in Japan, it also tended to create a two-tiered system of literacy: Chinese tended to remain the written medium of choice among the highly educated and largely male elites, while *han-gul* became the written language of the commoners and, increasingly, women. One of the best examples of this is the anonymous, autobiographical *Memoirs of Lady Hyegong*, written in the eighteenth century. Such divisions notwithstanding, however, the explosion of vernacular literature—satires on *yongban* manners, social criticism, fiction, advice manuals for a variety of tasks—all contributed to Korea attaining, with Japan, some of the highest levels of functional literacy in the preindustrial world.

| Vowels / Consonants | ㅏ [a] | ㅑ [ya] | ㅓ [ŏ] | ㅕ [yŏ] | ㅗ [o] | ㅛ [yo] | ㅜ [u] | ㅠ [yu] | ㅡ [ŭ] | ㅣ [i] |
|---|---|---|---|---|---|---|---|---|---|---|
| ㄱ [k,g] | 가 | 갸 | 거 | 겨 | 고 | 교 | 구 | 규 | 그 | 기 |
| ㄴ [n] | 나 | 냐 | 너 | 녀 | 노 | 뇨 | 누 | 뉴 | 느 | 니 |
| ㄷ [t,d] | 다 | 댜 | 더 | 뎌 | 도 | 됴 | 두 | 듀 | 드 | 디 |
| ㄹ [r,l] | 라 | 랴 | 러 | 려 | 로 | 료 | 루 | 류 | 르 | 리 |
| ㅁ [m] | 마 | 먀 | 머 | 며 | 모 | 묘 | 무 | 뮤 | 므 | 미 |
| ㅂ [p,b] | 바 | 뱌 | 버 | 벼 | 보 | 뵤 | 부 | 뷰 | 브 | 비 |
| ㅅ¹ [s,sh] | 사 | 샤 | 서 | 셔 | 소 | 쇼 | 수 | 슈 | 스 | 시 |
| ㅇ² | 아 | 야 | 어 | 여 | 오 | 요 | 우 | 유 | 으 | 이 |
| ㅈ [ch,j] | 자 | 쟈 | 저 | 져 | 조 | 죠 | 주 | 쥬 | 즈 | 지 |
| ㅊ [ch'] | 차 | 챠 | 처 | 쳐 | 초 | 쵸 | 추 | 츄 | 츠 | 치 |
| ㅋ [k'] | 카 | 캬 | 커 | 켜 | 코 | 쿄 | 쿠 | 큐 | 크 | 키 |
| ㅌ [t'] | 타 | 탸 | 터 | 텨 | 토 | 툐 | 투 | 튜 | 트 | 티 |
| ㅍ [p'] | 파 | 퍄 | 퍼 | 펴 | 포 | 표 | 푸 | 퓨 | 프 | 피 |
| ㅎ [h] | 하 | 햐 | 허 | 혀 | 호 | 효 | 후 | 휴 | 흐 | 히 |

**The Conventions and Alphabet of *Han-gul*.** As originally given by King Sejong in his 1446 *Hunmin chong-um* ("Proper Sounds to Instruct the People"), *han-gul* contained 28 syllables. These have now been reduced to 24, with five double consonants and the additional vowels shown. The ease of learning the system is such that Korea has one of the highest levels of literacy in the world.

# Japan to 1450: Selective Interaction and Adaptation

Of all the places we have examined in east and south Asia thus far, Japan raises the most exciting questions about the effects of relative isolation. Like Britain in its "splendid isolation," Japan's geographical position allowed it to selectively interact with and adapt to continental innovations, experimenting, refining, and occasionally abandoning them as needed. Indeed, having never experienced a successful invasion, Japan's acculturation was almost completely voluntary, a characteristic unique among the societies of Eurasia.

## The Island Refuge

Japan's four main islands, Honshu, Hokkaido, Kyushu, and Shikoku, are varied in climate. The northernmost island of Hokkaido has cold, snowy winters and relatively cool summers; the central island of Honshu, bisected roughly north to south by substantial mountain ranges, has a temperate to subtropical climate on the eastern side—where it is moderated by the Japan Current—and a colder, more continental climate to the west of the mountains on the side facing Korea and northeastern China. The small southern island of Shikoku and the southernmost island of Kyushu have an abundance of warm, moist weather and are largely governed by the Pacific monsoon system (see Map 13.4).

**The Limitations of the Land**    The formation of Japan's islands from volcanic activity means that only about one-fifth of the territory has historically been arable. In the narrow plains and valleys, however, the majority of which are on the temperate Pacific side of the mountains, the soil is mineral-rich and the rainfall abundant. But the islanders from early on have also had to face the limitations of the land in supporting a steadily growing population. Like the Korean peninsula, the ruggedness of the land tended to force its people to live in politically isolated, culturally united communities. Thus, communication by water was often the most convenient method, both among the Japanese home islands and across the 100 mile strait to southern Korea.

## Adaptation at Arm's Length: History and Politics

Like the first peoples to inhabit the Korean peninsula, the origins of the Japanese are obscure. Two distinct groups appear to have migrated to the islands from the Asian mainland via Ice Age land bridges, perhaps 10,000–20,000 years ago. Their

# Printing

While the invention of the printing press and movable type is widely recognized as having revolutionized the intellectual life of early modern Europe, it is equally true that these developments seven centuries earlier in east Asia had a similar effect. Yet, in many respects, the consequences of these innovations were different because of the requirements of the languages and the technical media with which printers in China, Korea, Japan, and Vietnam worked. As in other places, the cultural patterns of handwriting and calligraphy as artistic skills necessary for elites to cultivate in order to complete their aesthetic and moral development also hampered the spread of printing to some degree. Yet, for all these differences, by the fourteenth century, the societies of east Asia still achieved the highest preindustrial literacy rates in the world. These would be unmatched in Europe until centuries after the use of printing had become widespread there.

By the fall of the Han dynasty in 220 CE, we have the earliest remnant examples of woodblock printing. Printers carved single- or double-page blocks of text on book-sized boards, inked them, and pressed the cloth or paper pages on them to get their copies. The boards could then be shaved down and carved again as needed. By the eighth century the Chinese had also begun to experiment with copper movable type inserted vertically into standardized rows in a system very much like the one Gutenberg devised centuries later. But, ironically, these presses remained more curiosities than practical devices for printing a variety of documents. Here, the chief problem was the nature of the Chinese

**The Korean Printing Industry.**
Because of its position as the northern crossroads of the Buddhist and Chinese literary world, Korea was a major center of printing. Printing with carved wooden blocks had been developed during the eighth century, and large publishers and academies kept great numbers of them on hand. The most famous was this storehouse, which still preserves the 80,000 blocks of the *Tripitaka,* carved between 1237 and 1257.

descendants, the Utari, are today regarded as Japan's aboriginal peoples and referred to by the Japanese as *Ainu,* the "hairy ones," or in early imperial times as *Emishi.* Their physical features, tribal hunting society, and language mark them as distinct from the later arrivals. Details of their religious practices have led some anthropologists to link them to the peoples of central Asia, Siberia, and the Americas.

The later inhabitants may have originally come from the peoples who migrated into southeast Asia, Indonesia, and eventually the central Pacific. They may also have been descended from later Polynesian travelers and later migrants from the Asian mainland. Linguistic evidence suggests a very tenuous connection to Korean and even to the Altaic language family. Japan's long linguistic isolation, however, renders its ultimate origins obscure at the present time.

**Jomon and Yayoi**   Japan's prehistory, which lasted from ca. 10,000 BCE down to 300 BCE, has been designated by archaeologists as the Jomon period. While pottery fragments at some sites have been dated to as early as 14,500 BCE, the most distinctive artifacts are of somewhat more recent vintage: lightly fired clay vessels marked with a unique horizontal herringbone pattern and often fanciful decorations, clay female figurines called *dogu,* and phallic symbols called *bo.* Others include a wide assortment of **microlith** items: arrowheads, spear points, tools made of bone and antler, and nets and fishhooks. **Matriarchal** and

**Microlith:** A very small blade made of flaked stone and used as a tool, especially in the Mesolithic era.

**Matriarchal:** A social system in which the mother is head of the family.

**Matrilineal:** Relating to, based on, or tracing ancestral descent through the maternal line.

written language—and, at this time, the written languages of Korea, Japan, and Vietnam as well. Unlike the English alphabet with its 26 letters, literary Chinese has thousands of different characters. It was simply impractical for typesetters to cast adequate supplies of even the most common characters, organize them, and sort through them to compose the text to be copied. It was far less work to just carve the text blocks from scratch, especially of popular works that would be widely copied and circulated.

In this case, one of the chief catalysts for printing was the growing popularity of Buddhism throughout east Asia. As would be the case centuries later with the spread of religious tracts during the Protestant Reformation, the desire of Buddhists to read scriptures and the openness of the various schools to all classes proved a stimulus to literacy, though in practical terms only those with considerable leisure could master the literary Chinese of the scriptures. Still, by the fourteenth century, the pattern of woodblock printing as a major industry in east Asia, with printing centers in the major cities of China, Japan, and Korea, has been seen by a variety of scholars as one of the hallmarks of early modernity centuries before that term is applied to Europe.

## Questions

- How did the innovation of woodblock printing facilitate the spread of Buddhism throughout east Asia?

- What does the use of *han-gul* script in Korea say about the relationship between literacy and state formation?

matrilineal clans appear to have dominated society, clustered mostly near the sea or slightly inland. Because game was increasingly limited on the islands, fishing and harvesting seaweed were the major forms of subsistence. As among the American peoples of the Pacific Northwest, the bounty of the sea and forests enabled substantial settled village life to develop in the absence of an early agricultural revolution.

During the final half-millennium before the Common Era, increased intercommunication among Japanese, Koreans, and some members of the Late Zhou Chinese coastal states laid the groundwork not only for the introduction of agriculture to the Japanese islands but for an almost simultaneous Bronze Age as well. During the last centuries of the Jomon period, it appears that some of the grain crops of northern Asia (such as millet) found their way to the islands. During a 600-year period designated Yayoi (300 BCE–300 CE), imported and domestically manufactured bronze and iron articles appeared. The fertile plains of southern Honshu and Kyushu also saw the cultivation of northern Eurasian vegetables and fruits and, most significantly, rice. The swiftness of these changes was in part because of the dislocations resulting from the creation of China's first empire in 221 BCE and the influx of Korean refugees in the wake of the initial Chinese invasion of Korea.

**Jomon Jar and Yamato Sharinseki Disk.** The distinctive herringbone pattern and flared top mark this pottery as Middle Jomon, perhaps 5,000–6,000 years old. The disk made of finely worked steatite was taken from a third-century CE *kofun* burial mound in central Japan. It may be related as a religious object to similar kinds of ornaments found in China.

MAP 13.4 **Japan: Topography and Climate.**

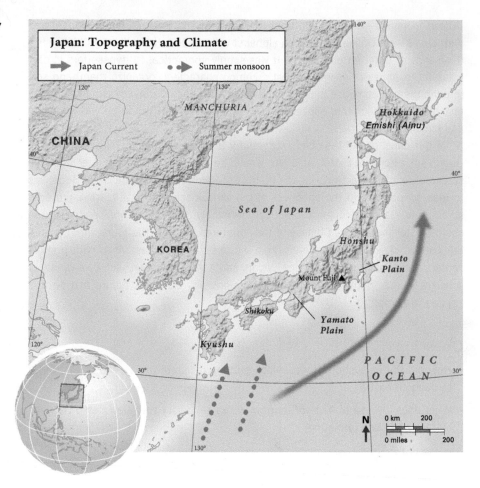

As it had in other areas of Asia, the rice revolution not only allowed the development of larger populations in Japan but also demanded them for efficient cultivation. The movement away from fishing and gathering combined with the efficiency of metal tools and weapons also fostered state formation among the larger and more powerful clans, or *uji*. The role of the new technologies is witnessed by the items included even now in the imperial regalia at the Shrine of Ise in southern Honshu: a jewel, a bronze mirror, and an iron sword, all of which date from about 260 CE. Thus, sometime after 250 CE, Japan's first fully evolved state, Yamato, centered on the Kanto Plain near modern Tokyo, emerged and quickly expanded, absorbing its weaker rivals on Honshu. Japan's first monumental architecture, enormous burial mounds called *kofun,* date from this period.

**Toward the Imperial Order**   While the nature of rulership in Japan is still obscured by myth, the earliest written records describing the islands were composed by Chinese chroniclers in 57 CE. In 297 CE, we have the first mention of the Yamato state, though, characteristically, the writers considered their subjects scarcely civilized.

Although there had been steady diplomatic and cultural contact back and forth across the Sea of Japan from the first century CE, a particularly high level was reached during the later sixth century CE. In 552, tradition has it that Buddhism was introduced to the islands from Paekche. With it came the Chinese writing system and written works of every description. A decade later, in 562, the Korean kingdom of Silla eliminated the Japanese colony of Kaya on the peninsula, precipitating a new flow of refugees to Japan. As we have seen, the years from 589 into the early seventh century saw the rise of the Sui and Tang dynasties in China, resulting in yet more Chinese attempts to dominate the Korean kingdoms, and pushing the level of emigration to new levels.

The impact of these events on Yamato cannot be overstated. The growing power of China and Silla helped prompt the Soga *uji*'s Empress Suiko (r. 592–628) and her nephew, Prince Shotoku (ca. 573–621), to connect Yamato more firmly to the mainland and its conceptions of politics, culture, literature, and, ultimately, the imperial system itself. A few signposts along the way include the adoption of Buddhism as a state religion (594), the adoption of the Chinese lunar calendar for state record keeping (604), and the adoption of the prince's 17-article constitution modeled on Confucian and Buddhist precepts (604).

> "The ministers and officials of the state should make proper behavior their first principle, for if the superiors do not behave properly, the inferiors are disorderly; if inferiors behave improperly offenses will naturally result. Therefore when lord and vassal behave with propriety, the distinctions of rank are not confused; when the people behave properly the Government will be in good order."
>
> —The Constitution of Prince Shotoku, Article 4

But perhaps the most far-reaching changes came later in the century, with the *Taika*, or Great Reform, of 645. The systematic remaking of the Yamato regime along Chinese lines in the wake of the *Taika* marks the beginning of the imperial Japanese state—that is, of a kingdom bent on expansion over multiple political groups and clans. Among other things, Soga clan control of the court was overturned, and Fujiwara No-Kamatari, who emerged as adviser to the new emperor, Tenchi, ushered in a connection between his family and the imperial court that continued into the twentieth century. In less than a century the first Chinese-style imperial histories, the *Kojiki* (712) and *Nihongi* (720), were composed; the concept of the Mandate of Heaven was adopted to justify the overthrow of the Sogas; the emperor as the center of a hierarchical system of government run through a rigorously selected bureaucracy was institutionalized; and a census, uniform taxation on land and produce, and systems of conscription and labor service were enacted. The edicts mandating these changes were promulgated as the Taiho Code of 702, which remained the basis of Japanese law until the late nineteenth century.

Yamato's spiritual roots in Shinto, with its connection to the rhythms of nature and renewal, had dictated that the seat of the state be frequently moved. Even today, the sacred shrine at Ise is disassembled and rebuilt every 20 years. Because of the requirements of a far larger and more sophisticated system of government, however, it was decided that a permanent capital be built. The first site selected, at Nara, saw the creation in 710 of a close replica of the Tang capital at Chang'an, down to the axial boulevards, grids of streets, and propitious placement of temples and government buildings. In 794, a larger capital was completed nearby along the same lines called Heian-kyo, the future city of Kyoto. The era of imperial rule from this capital, which lasted until 1185, is thus often referred to as the "Heian" period (see Map 13.5).

**Heian Japan**   As the imperial order penetrated all the Japanese home islands except Hokkaido and the widespread adoption of Buddhist culture connected

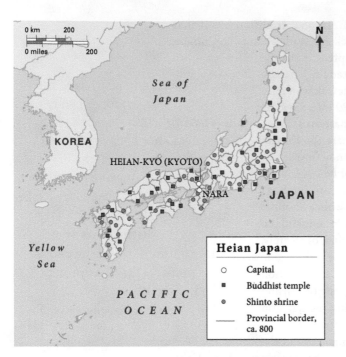

MAP **13.5  Heian Japan.**

Japan to an enormous, interconnected economic and cultural Asian sphere, Heian Japan increasingly became a land of contrasts, with local rumblings of discontent never far below the surface. For the elites of the capital and provincial administrative centers, life was not unlike that of their counterparts in Korea, Vietnam, or even China itself. The spread of literacy at the top and the common currency of Confucianism, Chinese literature, and the various Buddhist schools helped these elites see themselves as part of a cosmopolitan world, as did frequent travel for trade and pilgrimage. The latest fashions in poetry, literature, fine arts, calligraphy, music, and (to a lesser extent) clothing all found their way to court and beyond.

For the members of the new classes into which the vast majority of Japan's people had now been placed (peasants, artisans, and merchants—with Buddhist monks occupying an increasingly significant position in the hierarchy), many of the changes had been disruptive at best. Perhaps most tellingly, power, and soon military strength, was diffusing from the court and capital out into the countryside. This was particularly true in more remote regions where the most aggressive *uji* had assembled forces in support of their battles with the Emeshi. The bureaucracy, a tenuous institution at best during the Heian period, became weaker as the local *uji* began to reassert power. This was given a considerable push in the wake of a virulent smallpox epidemic (735–737), during which the population may have been reduced by as much as one-third.

Despite court attempts to create a Chinese-style "well-field" system, tenancy became a chronic problem. In many cases, the *shoen*, or clan estates, were given tax-exempt status because of their military contributions. The estates of Buddhist monasteries were similarly exempt and provided social services and refuge for outcasts, in effect becoming shadow societies of their own. By the late eleventh century, perhaps half of the land in the empire had become exempt from taxes. As the countryside became more self-sufficient, the capital became more isolated—and more reliant on local military cooperation.

In addition, the court itself was often divided by factional disputes, spurred by the practice of emperors abdicating but staying on as regents or advisers. Three decades of civil war between factions supporting the claims of the Taira clan and those pledged to the Minamoto, or Genji, finally ended in 1185 with the defeat of the Taira. Shortly thereafter, Minamoto Yoritomo was given the title Sei-i-tai **Shogun** (the "Great Barbarian-Suppressing General"), and the period of the **Shogunates** was inaugurated, lasting until 1867.

**Shogun:** The chief military official of Japan. The office was hereditary under the Tokugawa family from 1603 until 1867.

**Shogunate:** The government, rule, or office of a shogun.

**Japan under the Shoguns**  Though the emperor at Kyoto theoretically remained in charge with the shogun as his deputy, the arrangement in fact hastened

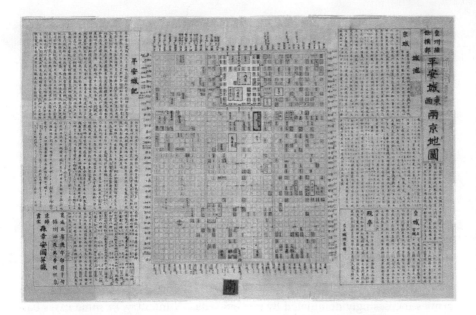

**Plan of the Capital at Heian-kyo (Kyoto).** The desire to copy the grandeur of Tang institutions extended even to city planning for the eighth-century Japanese court. The capital city at Heian was a faithful copy of the plan of the Tang capital of Chang'an, at the time one of the world's largest cities. The city grid was strictly laid out on a north–south axis, with the most important structures like the imperial palace placed in the northern section and their courtyards and main gates all facing south, the most propitious direction, indicated by the Chinese character highlighted in red at the bottom of the page, meaning "south." The placement of gardens and outlying structures was also carefully calculated according to Chinese notions of *feng shui* geomancy regarding trees, hills, and water.

the drain of power from the capital. Because of its parallels to the political and social order in Europe at the time, the term "feudal" has sometimes been applied to this period. As we saw in Zhou China, however, such similarities should not be pushed too far. In order to restore order in the hotbed of Taira opposition, Yoritomo set up his headquarters at Kamakura, several hundred miles from Kyoto, beginning an interval known as the Kamakura shogunate, 1185–1333. The court itself remained the center of religious and ceremonial life as well as a forum for intrigue, but the real center of power now resided at the shogun's headquarters. Meanwhile, in 1274, the Mongols launched the first of two major attempts to invade Japan. Their first armada was defeated handily, while in 1281 a much larger second fleet was smashed by a typhoon, known ever after by the Japanese as *kamikaze*, the "divine wind." Though the country was briefly roused to common action in the face of this threat, the dissipation of imperial power for the most part continued unabated.

Court life became even more ossified and formalized, while emperors very occasionally led unsuccessful attempts to reassert their own power. The most ambitious of these was the revolt by Emperor Go-Daigo in 1333. Securing the support of the powerful leader Ashikaga Takauji [ah-shee-KAH-gah tah kah-OO-jee], Go-Daigo's faction was crippled when the opportunistic Ashikaga switched sides twice during the conflict. Ashikaga finally placed his own candidate on the throne, drove Go-Daigo into exile, and moved his headquarters to the Muromachi [moo-roe-MA-chee] district in northern Kyoto. For the first time in nearly 200 years, the seats of political and cultural influence were reunited in the same city (see Map 13.6). Even more important for the future of Japanese aesthetics and cultural institutions, the refinements of court life were now available to the warrior classes. There thus was born the union of *bu* and *bun*, the "dual way" of the sword and writing brush. The patronage of the *daimyo*, or regional lords, and their retainers, the **samurai**, ensured steady development

**Samurai:** A Japanese warrior who was a member of the feudal military aristocracy.

of the Chinese-inspired arts of painting, poetry, and calligraphy, while the introduction of Zen and tea in the twelfth century forged an armature of discipline in both the martial and courtly arts that helped to foster the preservation of both for centuries to come.

While the aesthetic refinement of the warrior classes proceeded, the size and scope of warfare itself grew larger and ever more deadly. Like the codes of chivalry current in Europe at this time, *daimyo* and samurai prided themselves on acting according to a strict system of loyalty and honor, *bushido*, the "Way of the Warrior." A samurai was expected to be not just expert with sword and writing brush but unswervingly loyal to his *daimyo* to the point of death. Indeed, the tradition of *seppuku* or *hara-kiri*—ritual suicide—developed originally as a way to show one's "sincerity" and disdain for death and capture on the battlefield. One was also expected to show honor and respect to one's opponents, and tales abound from the period of warriors perfuming their helmets and decorating themselves so that whoever killed them would have a tolerable aesthetic experience amidst the gore of the battlefield.

By the fifteenth century, however, these personal touches were giving way to armies increasingly dominated by massed ranks of infantry, in some cases ballooning into the hundreds of thousands of men. By the middle of the following century, the adoption of firearms and accompanying advances in fortification made Japan perhaps the most heavily armed country on earth. The fluidity of the military situation had major social consequences as well, and by the middle of the sixteenth century it was increasingly possible for commoners to rise through the ranks and become commanders and even *daimyo*.

MAP **13.6** **Japan, ca. 1350.**

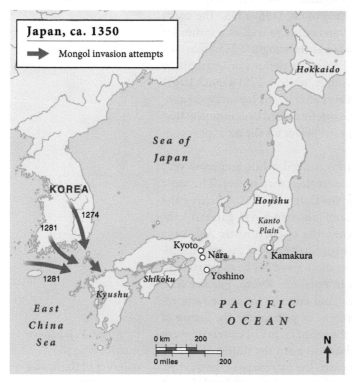

One important reason for these conditions was the chronic instability of the Ashikaga Shogunate. The position was never intended to be hereditary and was always the subject of *daimyo* intrigue both in Kyoto, where manipulation of the emperor was vital in order to achieve favor, and in the countryside, where power had become increasingly concentrated. In 1467, factional struggles would finally erupt into all-out war for 10 years, the effects of which would last more than a century.

## Economy, Society, and Family

The real beginning of the diversification of Japan's economy came with the Yayoi period, beginning around 300 BCE. As the early Japanese communities adopted wet rice and vegetable agriculture they gained the ability to sustain a sedentary population, which would prove crucial for assimilating new technologies and allowing the concentration of power for state formation.

The limited amount of arable land also meant that the populations of the few large open areas like the Kanto Plain were in an advantageous position to subdue their less numerous neighbors. In addition, they were better able to adopt technologies like bronze and iron making, silk weaving, and so forth that required an increasingly complex infrastructure. By the high point of the Yamato period, therefore, one finds Chinese accounts describing an economy that seems to resemble that of the Chinese or Korean countryside, with the majority of inhabitants engaged in agriculture and identifiable merchant and artisan classes coming into view.

**The New Economy**    The introduction of Chinese writing, concepts of law, and Buddhism during the sixth century allows historians to view in far greater detail the workings of Japanese economics. By this point, nearly every domesticated plant and animal from the mainland suitable to the environment had been introduced to Japan; and the productivity of the island's agriculture would soon approach levels comparable to those in China and Korea. Like its counterparts on the mainland, the Yamato court and its successors at Nara and Heian-kyo attempted to regulate economic activity in the form of land and produce taxes, taxes on trade, monopolies on strategic commodities, and requisitions of labor for infrastructural projects.

Yet almost from the beginning, as we noted earlier, these efforts at centralization were only partially effective. The larger *uji*, whose power had theoretically been cut by the creation of a state bureaucracy, got around the problem by supplying many of the officials for the new body. They took advantage of government incentives to reclaim land from the wilderness and the Ainu. By such means the large *shoen* and monastery estates with their tax exemptions tended to acquire regional political and military power.

Such multiple centers also produced an increase in and decentralization of trade. The period from 1250 to 1450 saw cycles of expansion in overseas commerce, with colonies of Japanese merchants—and often Japanese pirates—operating in the Philippines, Java, and Malacca as well as Korea and China. Through their wares, the *daimyo* and samurai became increasingly sophisticated connoisseurs of luxury goods such as silks, jade, porcelain, lacquerware, rare woods, and books and paper. As the early ports, market towns, regional capitals, and, by the sixteenth century, castle towns, grew, Japanese craftspeople became adept at imitating and refining Chinese crafts, in some cases surpassing the quality of the originals. Moreover, a growing and increasingly diverse middle class of merchants, artisans, actors, dancers, **sake** brewers, ship builders, and others organized into trade guilds (*za*) all partook of such luxury items. The increased demand for capital among them spurred a monetization of the economy and the beginnings of banking and credit systems.

**Advances in Agriculture**    Most of this would not have been possible without dramatic increases in food production. The period from 1250 to 1600 saw a vast increase in both intensive cultivation of Japan's limited arable land and the introduction of a host of new crops to multiply its productivity. As it had throughout east Asia, the widespread use of fast-ripening Champa rice strains

**Japanese *Daimyo* Armor.** This extraordinarily well-preserved torso armor and helmet is believed to date from the fourteenth century and may have belonged to the shogun Ashikaga Takauji (r. 1338–1358). The helmet is bronzed iron, while the cuirass is made of thousands of overlapping iron and lacquered leather scales held together in horizontal rows by means of rivets. The combination made for effective protection against swords and arrows while allowing considerable freedom of movement.

**Sake:** Traditional alcoholic drink brewed from rice.

from southeast Asia in southern Honshu, Kyushu, and Shikoku vastly enhanced stocks of this staple. In Kyushu it allowed three crops a year; in other areas, the wet paddy fields it required allowed dry raised beds for vegetables to be made from the soil taken out of the paddies. At the same time the introduction of the Chinese "dragon pump" (see Chapter 9) allowed for easy, small-scale irrigation. Finally, a triple-cropping system consisting of buckwheat in winter, wheat in spring, and rice during the monsoon, with vegetables grown on the raised beds in between fields, allowed an average family to sustain itself on only a few acres of land.

If one factors in the use of terracing and dry rice cultivation in more marginal areas and the introduction of oranges, grapes, and tea, the leaps in population seem almost inevitable. From an estimated population of about 5 million in 1100 a doubling occurred, perhaps as early as 1300; by 1450 it was on its way to doubling again.

**Family Structure**   As in Korea, the earliest social structures of Japan appear to have been matrilocal and, most likely, matriarchal. *Uji* before the sixth century were organized around female lineages, and the first Chinese accounts mention semimythical figures such as Queen Pimiko. With the coming of Chinese institutions, however, this changed radically at the uppermost levels and more gradually below. As we have seen, during the early importation of Chinese influences in the sixth and seventh centuries, women at the top could still wield considerable political power, as witnessed by Empress Suiko of the Soga clan. By the height of the power of the Heian court, Confucian patriarchal institutions had made a great deal of headway in Japan but were moderated somewhat by the pervasive influence of Buddhism and Shinto. Thus, aristocratic women controlled property, though they increasingly tended to wield political power through men. They were sequestered at court and forced into a highly refined and regulated ritual life, yet they created their own highly influential cultural world. Women like Murasaki Shikibu and Sei Shonagon (ca. 965–1025) set the standards for literary and aesthetic appreciation for generations to come in the *Tale of Genji* and *The Pillow Book*, respectively.

Outside the court, the moderating institution for commoners, and particularly women, was the Buddhist monastery. As in China and Korea, the monasteries provided havens for women and men who did not marry or had fled bad marriages. They provided enough education to allow reading the sutras, thus helping to increase literacy. They also provided important avenues of political power as large landholders, innkeepers, peacekeepers, and advisers.

As in China and Korea, however, the family life of commoners was mostly governed by a mix of Confucian filial piety, local clan relations, and the desire to improve the family's position through marriage. As in China, girls came to be considered expendable because they would move in with their husband's family. Arranged marriages were the norm, and by way of forcing such issues, rape, kidnapping, and family vendettas were all too common. A woman who would not consent to such a marriage, for example, could evade it only if she fled to a monastery before the groom's relatives caught up with her. Failure to escape could result in a beating or even murder. Such informal sanctions eventually gave way under the Tokugawa shogunate to strictly regulated Neo-Confucian family codes enforced by the shogun's local officials.

## Religion, Culture, and Intellectual Life

The foundations of Japan's original religion, Shinto, go far back into remote antiquity. Some scholars have used the word "vitalism"—akin to African spiritual practices and shamanism in Siberia and the Americas—to describe its common features: a deep-seated belief in the power of *kami*—spirits of divinities, beings living and departed, nature as a whole, and even inanimate objects like mountains and streams. Reverence for these forces extended early on to fertility and earthly vitality.

The importance of ritual vitality was reinforced by a tremendous emphasis on ritual purity—as Chinese observers recorded nearly 2,000 years ago, the Japanese seemed to bathe constantly—and waterfalls were enormously popular as places of ritual ablution and even miracle working. On the other hand, death and corruption were things to be separated from as much as possible—hence the practice of distancing shrines from burial mounds.

**The Way of the Gods**   Shinto means "the way of the gods," and Japanese mythology recognized a staggering array of deities. Chief among these were Izanagi and Izanami, whose initial sexual act created the Japanese home islands, as well as Amaterasu, the sun goddess, considered the ancestor of Japan's emperors, purportedly starting with Jimmu in 660 BCE. Until the emperor Hirohito officially renounced his divinity at the end of World War II, every Japanese emperor was considered a god in the Shinto pantheon by believers.

Although it had undoubtedly arrived some time before, the customary dating of the introduction of Buddhism to Japan is 552 CE, when the king of Paekche sent a collection of Buddhist scriptures as a present to Yamato. The new religion soon became well established among Japanese elites, and after four decades of struggle with the Shinto establishment at court, Buddhism had become the state religion of Yamato in 594. Both religious traditions, however, were ultimately able to coexist and, to some extent, fuse. The ability of Buddhism to adapt the cosmologies of other traditions to its core beliefs, along with its reverence for nature, emphasis on the transcendental, and lack of a priestly hierarchy, made it an easy fit for Shinto. For their part, Shinto believers could add the bodhisattvas and other Buddhist entities to the list of *kami*. Coupled with an already great admiration for things Chinese in Japan, such accommodations facilitated the spread of the religion.

Most of the schools of Buddhism established in Japan had first become popular in China. The first to establish itself at Nara was the Hosso school, based on the newly recovered texts brought back by the Chinese monk Xuan Zang from India. This was shortly displaced by the highly influential Tendai (from the Chinese Tiantai) school and the Shingon sect, which dominated the imperial court for most of the Heian period.

As noted in Chapter 9, for Tendai followers, the most important scripture was the Lotus Sutra, which includes the key revelation that all beings possess a "Buddha nature" and, hence, the potential for salvation. Esoteric Buddhism, on the other hand, placed more emphasis on scriptural study and aesthetics. For both, the degree to which one can grasp the central truth varies according to the capacity of the individual to study and contemplate it, but it is in theory open to all at some level. The popular devotional schools of Buddhism also came to Japan during the eighth and ninth centuries. Their simplicity and optimism—simply bowing repeatedly and calling on Amida Buddha with a sincere heart in order to be saved (*nembutsu*)—and the hope for a place in the Pure Land, or Western Paradise, ensured widespread adherence. Even today, it remains the most popular of the Japanese Buddhist schools.

Though neither achieved widespread popularity, two other Buddhist schools deserve mention because of their influence. The first is a wholly Japanese development. Nichiren (1222–1282) advocated a Japan-centered, patriotic form of Buddhism. Japan, he believed, because of its unique history and centrality in the Buddhist world, had become the repository of "true" Buddhism in the present decadent age and must be defended at all cost, a view that he believed was confirmed by the miraculous Japanese deliverance from the Mongols.

Perhaps more influential was the practice of Zen. Again, the Chinese origins of this movement, known as *chan*, were introduced in Chapter 12. Arriving in Japan

**The Miracles of Kannon.** Amida Buddhism was the most popular school throughout east Asia, and the most popular figure of the many bodhisattvas was Kannon (Guanyin in China). On this long hand scroll dated to 1257, Kannon saves her followers from assorted tribulations: Here, she appears to two men set upon by soldiers or brigands.

in the twelfth century, it spread among the *daimyo* and samurai, who had the discipline to pursue its rigors. Zen seeks to achieve *satori*, a flash of enlightenment signaling the recovery of one's Buddha nature. Everyone's path to this is different, so one must follow the instructions of an experienced master rather than engage in prolonged scriptural study. Zen practitioners seek to open themselves to enlightenment by lowly, repetitive tasks, contemplating paradoxes (koans) and, in some schools, sitting in meditation (*zazen*).

All of these practices can be useful to a warrior. Endless drilling with bow and arrow or sword to the point that the use of each weapon becomes instinctive certainly refines one's martial talents. Such an approach is equally useful in painting, poetry, and calligraphy, where a distinct Zen style of spontaneous, minimalist art suggesting the true inner nature of subject and artist is still a vital area of Japanese aesthetics today.

One final area in which Zen permeated the life of the warrior classes was in the use of tea. Introduced from China by the Zen monk Eisai (1141–1215), tea drinking in Japan became widely adopted as an aid to discipline and meditation among monks in the twelfth century. Soon, however, it became quite popular among the upper classes, and its presentation was ultimately refined into the ritual of the tea ceremony. Here, inside the teahouse where all were equal, under the movements prescribed by the sixteenth-century tea master Sen-no Rikyu (1522–1591), host and guest were to approach their encounter as if they were sharing their last moments together on earth. Since the ceremony was a popular preparation for battle among *daimyo* and samurai, this was often the case.

Forging a Japanese Culture    With the importation of Chinese political theory to Japan came an understanding of the importance of histories and record keeping. Thus, the first Chinese-influenced Japanese histories, the *Nihongi* (*Chronicles of Japan*) and *Kojiki* (*Records of Ancient Matters*), made their appearance during the early eighth century. At about the same time, the first collection of Japanese poetry published in Chinese, the *Man'yoshu* (*The Ten Thousand Leaves*) appeared in 760. This work, however, also illustrated the problems inherent in using Chinese logograms as a method of rendering Japanese sounds.

The *Man'yoshu* uses one-syllable Chinese characters picked for their similarity to Japanese sounds and strings them together into Japanese words. If one can follow the *sounds* of the words, one can grasp the meaning of the poems; if, however, one attempts to read them based on the *meaning* of the characters, they become gibberish. This fundamental problem was solved by devising the *kana* syllabary, a system of 50 symbols that form the building blocks of Japanese words. By the late ninth century, a kind of social divide had arisen—as it did later with *han-gul* in Korea—between predominantly male, Buddhist, elite users of literary Chinese and literate women and members of the lower elites who favored the convenience of the *kana* system. As in China and Korea, the technology of printing greatly spurred the circulation of these works and over the centuries helped push functional literacy to some of the highest premodern levels in the world.

In addition to the development of the 31-syllable *tanka* poetry form, perhaps the most important literary developments to come from the use of *kana* were the novel and the prose diary. The former, as we have seen, is credited to Murasaki

Shikibu, whose *Tale of Genji* is often considered the world's first novel. A skilled diarist as well, Murasaki was a tutor to the powerful courtier Fujiwara Michinaga, and she put all of her acute observations of the subtleties of court life into *Genji*. Seclusion for court women fostered a considerable amount of self-analysis, and one sees in Murasaki's writing a tension between Buddhist ideas and the requirements of place, name, reputation, and hierarchy at court. Similarly, her older contemporary Sei Shonagon, in her *Pillow Book*, sets an almost modern tone in her astute, funny, and sometimes spiteful categories of likes and dislikes at court.

# Vietnam: Human Agency and State Building

For much of the twentieth century, the history of southeast Asia was written according to the cultural divisions separating the areas influenced by China from those influenced by India. In the 1960s, however, this concept of a derivative "Indo-Chinese" history was challenged by scholars, who emphasized the similarities of the lived experience of the common people on both sides of the cultural divide. Of equal importance in this new approach was the *agency* of the people in question: their taking of the initiative in deciding matters of acculturation, political systems, and so forth. Our focus on the patterns of interactions and adaptations here is to explore the agency of people in their acceptance and rejection of certain influences and innovations.

## The Setting and Neolithic Cultures

The topography of southeast Asia as a whole is similar from the borders of Assam in India to the Mekong delta in the south of what is now Vietnam. Divided by several major river systems—the Irawaddy, Salween, and Mekong—running roughly north to south, and by the Red River, running northwest to southeast through Hanoi and meeting the Gulf of Tonkin at Haiphong, the region is divided into watersheds separated by low to medium mountain ranges running generally parallel to them. Even today much of the region is heavily forested, with abundant rainfall supplied by the summer monsoon, which acts as the region's principal climatic regulator. The river valleys and coastal plains are believed to have supplied the wild ancestors of the first rice plants, as well as some of the world's first domesticated fowl sometime after 8000 BCE (see Map 13.7).

The Neolithic revolution appears to have taken place in southeast Asia at about the same time as it did in southwest Asia. This Hoabinhian culture was characterized by the cultivation of root crops, millet, and rice and by about 6000 BCE saw the domestication of pigs and chickens. By 4500 BCE, the Dongsan cultures had emerged, marked shortly after by some of humankind's earliest bronze artifacts. The origins of these peoples are still obscure, with contemporary speculation centering on a homeland perhaps in southern China. Out of the fertile subtropical and tropical regions in which they settled, it is believed that the basics of wet rice agriculture and the domestication of chickens and pigs may well have diffused north into China and perhaps west to northern India.

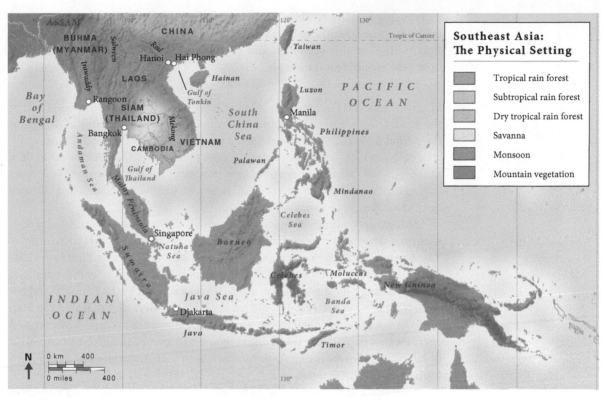

MAP **13.7 Southeast Asia: The Physical Setting.**

**Village Society and Buddhism**    The earliest records of the peoples and states in the region are likewise fragmentary. Late Zhou Chinese references frequently mention the state of Yue, but its southern borders appear to have been fluid and probably included parts of the modern provinces of Guangdong and Guangxi and perhaps the northern part of Vietnam. Once more, the social structure suggests a village-based agricultural system in which women enjoyed far more equality than would later be the case. Villages and clans were often bilateral or matrilineal and matrilocal. Men paid a **bride-price** to the families of their wives, and divorce for either spouse appears to have been relatively easy. As in other places in east Asia during the first millennium BCE, women occupied roles as officials, diplomats, merchants, and small-business operators. The area also became one of the first outposts of Theravada Buddhism outside India through the efforts of missionaries from Ceylon (Sri Lanka) in the second century BCE. It would come to be the majority religion in the region for the next 2,000 years.

**Bride-price:** Amount negotiated between the family of the groom and the family of the bride to be paid by the former to the latter in some marriage traditions, as compensation for the loss of her labor.

**The "Far South": History and Politics to 1450**    With the unification of China under the Qin in 221 BCE, Yue was incorporated into the First Emperor's new state. Thus began a prolonged period of Chinese occupation and local resistance in the area, ultimately lasting over 1,000 years. As in Korea, the occupation brought with it a cultural invasion, including the full spectrum of Chinese writing, political ideas, and cultural preferences. Like their counterparts in Korea and Japan as well, the new Vietnamese literate elites were incorporated into the increasingly far-flung world of Chinese civilization and the Buddhist cultural and religious sphere. Southeast Asia's geographical position in the center of the maritime portion of this economic and cultural sphere encouraged a considerable openness to outside influences.

**Sinicization and Resistance**   On the other hand, the repeated invasions from the north also encouraged a Vietnamese ethnic identity. The collapse of the Qin in the period 206–202 BCE encouraged a rebellion against the local Chinese officials of "Nam Viet"—the Vietnamese name for the Chinese *Nanyue* ("Far South"), as the Qin had called their new southern province. The Han emperor Wudi reoccupied northern Vietnam in 111 BCE, however, and swiftly reimposed Chinese institutions on the region.

Han attempts at sinicization raised tensions between the new Chinese-influenced elites and those who thus far had managed to retain their cultural independence. The situation was sufficiently volatile that in 39 BCE another rebellion began that to this day is commemorated as helping to form the modern Vietnamese national identity. Trung Trac, the widow of a local leader executed by the Chinese, and her sister Trung Nhi (both ca. 12–43) led their local militia and defeated the Han garrison, sparking a general revolt. The Chinese shortly regrouped, however, and overpowered the forces of the Trung sisters, who drowned themselves rather than be taken alive. For the next millennium, northern Vietnam would be firmly within the imperial Chinese orbit.

In the three and a half centuries following the breakup of the Han Empire in 220 CE, the region was able to gain a degree of political autonomy, but the power of Vietnam's sinicized elites continued to ensure their cultural loyalty to China. The growing regional power of the north allowed it to expand into the more Indian-influenced Buddhist kingdoms to the south. With the reunification of China under the Sui and Tang, the drive for Chinese political control of the region was taken up again, and the north was soon fully reincorporated into imperial China. During the political chaos following the fall of the Tang, however, the long-awaited opportunity for independence arrived again.

**Independence**   Dinh Bo Linh, the first emperor of Vietnam, solidified his control of the region in 968. Though politically independent of China, Vietnam's new Li dynasty (1010–1225), long immersed in Chinese notions of Confucianism and statecraft, swiftly instituted Song-style institutions and created its own bureaucracy. Continuing what by now was a long-established pattern of expansion, the Li systematically pushed south during their two centuries of control.

With the fall of the Li dynasty, the Tran dynasty (1225–1400) soon faced the potent threat of the Mongols, who in 1280 would subdue the southern Song in China and form the Yuan dynasty. The first Mongol attempt at invasion, in 1257, was mounted as the Mongols were busily reducing the last strongholds of the southern Song. Once this was accomplished, the attempt was renewed in 1285 and again in 1287. The unsuitability of Mongol strategy and tactics and the stubborn resistance of the Vietnamese ultimately prevented further Mongol expansion and allowed the Tran to keep the dynasty intact.

**Cultural and Political Conflict**    Even during the height of the Mongol threat, the Tran continued to push southward. Much of this drive was aimed at the state of Champa—the home of the fast-growing rice strains that would do so much to increase east Asian populations. Champa itself had ambitions to achieve regional dominance. Centuries before, in the complex interplay of political and cultural rivalries marking the region, the Vietnamese had expanded at the expense of Champa. Champa and the Khmers, heavily influenced by India, had briefly united to subdue another Indian-influenced state, the trading kingdom of Funan, in the 600s. Now a reconstituted Champa represented not just a strong political threat but, as a Sanskrit, Hindu, and Theravada Buddhist state, a cultural rival as well. In the resulting war, the new Le dynasty of Dai Viet ("Great Viet"), founded in 1428 by Le Loi, decisively broke the power of the Chams in 1471. The remnants of their state were incorporated into Vietnam in 1720 (see Map 13.8).

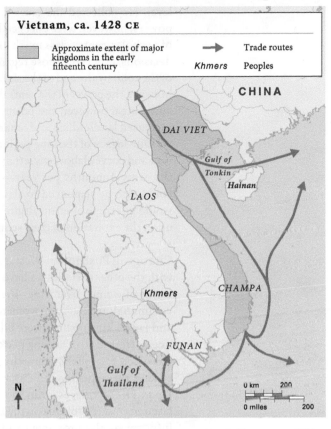

MAP **13.8** **Vietnam, ca. 1428.**

## Economy, Society, and Family

Since the Neolithic domestication of rice, Vietnam has been one of the world centers of wet rice cultivation. Perhaps 300 strains of rice were cultivated in northern Vietnam by the mid-fifteenth century, with yields running as high as 25 bushels per acre. Roughly 90 percent of the people were engaged in agriculture, a figure consistent with other east Asian agrarian-based societies. Like them, too, the rhythms of the agricultural year were governed by the monsoon cycle. During the long rainy season of the summer, rice, vegetables, and commercial crops such as hemp would be cultivated.

As in southern China and Japan, families could be sustained on relatively small amounts of land and required few complex tools beyond the treadle-powered "dragon pump" or a hand-cranked winnowing machine (see Chapter 9). Along with draft animals like water buffalo, these would often be held communally by clans within the *xa*, or village. Villages commonly consisted of raised, thatch-roofed dwellings, surrounded by a bamboo fence and centered on a shrine to the ancestral spirits.

**Politics, Labor, and Trade**    Two key political institutions kept order and acted as checks upon each other. The village headman, the *xa troung*, was elected but had to be approved by the imperial court, which, like its Chinese counterpart, ruled through a Confucian bureaucracy of provincial governors, prefects, and magistrates. The magistrate and his staff were the last official layer above the *xa troung*, so the headman had considerable power and responsibility at the local level. He collected the taxes and dues and sat with a council of notables. His powers, however, were checked by the council itself, which consisted of members of a scholar-gentry class much like that in China and who had to share in all major decisions, especially those regarding the use of communal land, about 20 percent of the total by the end of the sixteenth century. Thus, there was a balanced tension between the power of the central government and local interests. As in both China and Korea, however, the power of the local council often resulted in periods of increased landlordism and tenancy.

One legacy of the long period of Chinese occupation was the use of conscription and corvée labor by Vietnamese dynasties. Peasants were required to serve in the army 4 months per year—indefinitely during national emergencies. They could also be sentenced to slave labor for various offenses. In many cases, they would be sent to open up virgin land for agriculture, which would be theirs to keep upon the expiration of their sentences.

**Changing Position of Women**   One pattern of history the Vietnamese shared with the other societies we have examined in this chapter is that of changes in the status of women over time. The nature of the agricultural work undertaken was communal, and men and women tended to work in the fields together. As in Korea and Japan, kinship lines were bilateral—traced through either spouse—or matrilineal. Here again, the long period of Chinese influence and Neo-Confucian emphasis on filial piety, hierarchy, and sharply separate roles for men and women eroded this equality somewhat, though much less markedly than in Korea or Japan. In the villages, or in the ports and market cities, women commonly exercised prominent roles as merchants, entrepreneurs, and craftspeople. This was reinforced by the prominence of the different Mahayana schools of Buddhism. Once more, as in China, Korea, and Japan, the role of the monastery for both men and women allowed a place for, and gave an education to, those who for whatever reason were on society's fringes. Buddhist nuns and abbesses thus wielded considerable power, though their positions were often at odds with the Confucian precepts of the elites. Still, women's rights to divorce and property ownership were upheld in the Neo-Confucian law code of 1460.

## Religion, Culture, and Intellectual Life
Just as the Vietnamese struggled to maintain their political independence, they continually labored to develop their own cultural distinctiveness. While the porous border region with southern China and geographical and ethnic ties to other southeast Asian peoples ensured a constant flow of influences, not all were readily absorbed, and some were played against each other.

**Mahayana Buddhism**   Among the most important of these influences was that of religion. Whether the practice of ancestor veneration arrived with the Chinese or whether it was present before is as yet unsettled. Nearly all villages even into the twentieth century, however, had a shrine for a founding ancestor or famous headman where periodic ceremonies honoring him would take place. As in Korea, the coming of the Han emperor Wudi's armies in the

**Temple of Literature, Hanoi.** The independent Vietnamese states, beginning with Dai Viet in 939, instituted Chinese-style examinations for their civil service. The Temple of Literature was the first national academy for Confucian training, founded in 1076. This building was the examination hall for those testing for the equivalent of the Chinese *jinshi*, or metropolitan degrees. The large Chinese characters, read right to left, carry the motto "A Pattern for Emulation Through the Ages."

second century BCE brought the imperial system of the Son of Heaven as intermediary between heaven and earth. At about the same time, however, Theravada was being established in the Indianized ports of southeast Asia and became the first branch of Buddhism to be established there. Thus, as the Han retreat from the north allowed some political breathing space, the barest beginnings of Mahayana began to come into the area as well. For several hundred years, though, Indian-influenced Theravada dominated the religious and cultural life of Vietnam. Buddhist stupas were erected and the austere, mendicant, saffron-robed monks held sway in northern Vietnam, as they still do in much of southeast Asia.

The Tang occupation brought a large infusion of Mahayana influence with its vibrant art motifs, temples, and monasteries as well as the entire spectrum of Confucian and Daoist ideas. While Mahayana became the dominant division from this time on, the Vietnamese at the local level tended to pursue a synthesis of all of these systems in their beliefs. As in China, this collection was often referred to as *tam giao*, after the Chinese *san jiao*—"the three religions."

Similarly, the Vietnamese court sought to reconcile the differences among the systems by promulgating edicts on their compatibility. Indeed, some emperors sought to take a leading role in developing a unique strain of Vietnamese Buddhism. The later emperor Minh Mang (r. 1820–1841), for example, advocated combining the opposites of "abstention" from the world and "participation" in it.

**Chu Nom**     During the fifteenth-century consolidation of Dai Viet, the Le dynasty undertook a thoroughgoing sinicization of the country, in much the same way as under the Yi in Korea. Chinese law codes and even dress were adopted. As in Korea and Japan, Chinese-style histories were also compiled and court-sponsored literary projects of various sorts commissioned. Yet here again, the literary language favored by the court for such projects continued to be the Chinese of the elites who had the time and means to undertake its study. As in Korea and Japan, an attempt was made to develop a vernacular writing system, in this case sometime during the tenth century. Called *chu nom* ("southern characters"), the new script combined existing Chinese characters picked for the similarity of their sounds to Vietnamese words with newly invented Chinese-style characters for meaning. It was similar in this respect to the formation of many complex Chinese characters but would in theory be easier to use as a tool for literacy. However, it never had the widespread circulation of *han-gul* or *kana* in Korea or Japan.

## Putting It All Together

While there are a great many commonalities among the patterns of state formation and religious interaction among the states along the outer ring of Chinese influence, each responded to that influence in its own way. From the beginning, each state sought to maintain its political independence, though all acculturated to some degree to Chinese models. Yet here it should be stressed that the relative attractiveness of those models was largely related to their usefulness in state building. That is, while the Koreans and Vietnamese struggled to throw off the Chinese political yoke, the systems and values of the invaders also gave powerful tools to the invaded, allowing them to organize their new regimes after they had won independence. In a sense, the invaders had provided a ready-made package of laws, moral codes, and social organization for the new states but also came with moderating institutions like Mahayana Buddhism. They were therefore equipped with a wide range of options to adopt or discard as the situation demanded. In that sense, the cultural intrusion was far more successful than the political one.

In the case of Japan, since the early Yamato state did not have Chinese traditions imposed on it from the outside, its leaders could afford to be more selective in what to adopt. However, the wholesale adoption of Chinese institutions proceeded even more quickly in Japan than on the mainland. Part of this may be attributed to the growing sense of the power that such institutions could provide to a government; part of it may also have been a growing sense on the part of the Japanese that states on the mainland based on these institutions were a potential threat. In essence, they felt they had to join them to avoid being beaten by them.

By the end of the fifteenth century, all three of these states were in the process of consolidating civilizations based to varying degrees on Chinese models and prominently included Neo-Confucianism and Buddhism among their governing traditions. They may therefore be considered part of the dominant trend toward the formation of religious civilizations, a pattern we have emphasized in Part 3 of this volume. However, given the specific adaptations to local conditions, the three states were quite different from each other and from China. Even at the most signified level of governmental organization, the Japanese role of *daimyo* as feudal lords and samurai as retainers, to cite just one example, would have been unthinkable in China, Vietnam, or Korea. Yet all four of these countries, faced with varying degrees of dislocation, foreign intrusion, or rebellion, would seek similar solutions to solve these problems.

▶ For additional resources, including maps, primary sources, visuals, and quizzes, please go to www.oup.com/us/vonsivers. Please see the Further Resources section at the back of the book for additional readings and suggested websites.

## Against the Grain

# Zen and Bushido

One seemingly counterintuitive development in the political and religious history of Japan is the marriage of a sect of Buddhism—an avowedly pacifistic belief system—to the warrior nobility of Japan, the *daimyo*, and their retainers, the samurai. As we have seen, there were in fact two sects, Zen and Nichiren Buddhism, that had martial associations. But Nichiren Buddhism was centered on a kind of "Japanism" peculiar to Nichiren himself, and had its greatest influence during the time of grave national crisis precipitated by the Mongol invasions. Zen exercised a much deeper and longer-lasting effect, becoming the central religious practice of the warrior classes. The adoption by warriors of a pacifistic creed is not unique to Japan—one need only consider the history of Christianity to see some broad parallels. But Christianity, as the state religion of Rome and its successor empires and kingdoms, was the only approved religion for all classes. Zen was one of many competing variants of Buddhism available to Japanese warriors. So how does one account for its appeal?

Perhaps we may view it this way: While the overall tenets of Buddhism teach respect for all sentient beings, the duties of a warrior might induce one to extend the ideal of "nonattachment" to a state of indifference toward one's own life or death—and by extension to that of others. Moreover, the rigors of Zen training and practice are not unlike that of military training in some important respects: breaking down the ego by performing endless humbling tasks, being remade by strict discipline and constant repetition, and finally achieving a new "self" as a result of the long and rigorous training process. There is also an invaluable element of elitism in becoming one of the few who achieve the highest levels, though those who do reach them are expected to be extraordinarily humble in their bearing. Zen thus provides a carefully balanced harmony of opposites—the strict discipline to fight without regard for one's own safety on the battlefield, and in the process to transcend the self, reaching a state in which one is able to apprehend through extreme "mindfulness" the ultimate insights that bring the flash of enlightenment—*satori*. This condition of disciplined mindfulness extended to the aesthetic arts of poetry, painting, and calligraphy, providing the basis for yet another unity of opposites: the dual way of the sword and the writing brush unique to Japan.

- Are there other religions in Japan (such as Shinto) that might work equally well for warriors? Why?

- Is Japan unique in adapting a pacifistic religion for use by warrior classes? Can you think of ways that, for example, Christian warriors adapted their beliefs to support their profession?

# Thinking Through Patterns

▶ **How was the history of Korea affected by its relations with China? With Japan?**

The most obvious and dramatic way the various Korean kingdoms were affected by China was through conquest. Chinese culture and institutions were firmly planted in Korea during the Qin, Han, Sui, and Tang eras. In many respects this also prompted the Korean kingdoms to assert their political independence and to be discriminating about which Chinese institutions to adopt. Thus, Neo-Confucianism was adopted because of its use as a state-supporting ideology. Chinese writing, though quite useful as the means of acquiring the literature of China, ultimately yielded to the *han-gul* system as more convenient and user-friendly.

In the case of Japan, Korea's position was as a cultural intermediary and as a mainland target for conquest. Thus, during certain periods, Korea's status as a buffer between the two regional powers made its position precarious.

In addition to the Bronze Age elements of wet rice cultivation and bronze implements—which moved Japan ultimately toward agrarian–urban society—the cultural elements, beginning with the Chinese writing system, were the most influential. With the writing system came ideas of government, ethics, philosophy, literature, and, of course, Buddhism. Unlike Korea and Vietnam, Japan acquired all of these more or less voluntarily and had the leisure to adopt them according to its own needs, rather than have them imposed by conquest.

▶ **Which important elements of Chinese culture were adapted by the Japanese for their own purposes? What advantages did Vietnam have over Korea and Japan in this regard?**

▶ **Which Japanese adaptations of Chinese institutions did not work well in Japan? Why?**

While the Chinese writing system gave Japan a ready-made literature, the language itself was not well suited to the Japanese vernacular. Thus, by the 800–900s it had to be supplemented with the *kana* systems. But more serious was the less-than-perfect fit of the Chinese governmental structures with Japan's still clan based society. Here, the cleavages developing during the Heian period would cause the social breakdown that resulted in the era of the shoguns, lasting until 1867.

Like Japan and Korea, much of Vietnam was influenced by the importation of Chinese culture, including Buddhism, the imperial system, and Confucianism. Like Korea, and unlike Japan, Vietnam suffered centuries of Chinese invasion and occupation. But Vietnam, positioned on the border with the Indianized states of southeast Asia, also was influenced by Indian culture in its southern and western areas, causing interactions and adaptations that did not take place in the other states inside the Chinese sphere of cultural and political influence.

▶ **In what ways was the experience of Vietnam similar to that of Japan and Korea? How was it different?**

# Patterns of Evidence: Sources for Chapter 13

## SOURCE 13.1

# Murasaki Shikibu, *The Tale of Genji*

### ca. 1000

The daughter of a minor noble in the court at Heian-Kyo in central Japan, Murasaki Shikibu (ca. 973–1025) created Japan's most popular work of fiction and one of the world's great literary masterpieces. *The Tale of Genji* (*Genji Monagatori*) is composed of acute observations of the subtleties of court life, and Murasaki focused particularly on the lives of women at court. Although the tale is ostensibly fictional, it reflects the era in which it was written, as the novelist strove to make the action in it plausible to the reader. In the process, she also crafted a compelling and compulsively readable story.

**Lord Fugen:** A bodhisattva closely associated with the Lotus Sutra.

When he [Genji] returned to His Excellency's residence, sleep eluded him. Images of her [the Rokujō Haven, his love interest] as he had known her down the years ran through his mind, and he wondered in vain regret why she had taken such offense at each of his casual diversions, undertaken while he complacently assumed that she would eventually change her mind about him, and why she had persisted to the end in disliking him so. It seemed like a dream now to be wearing gray, and the thought that her gray would have been still darker if she had outlived him prompted,

> I may do no more, and the mourning I now wear is a shallow gray,
> but my tears upon my sleeves
> have gathered in deep pools.

He went on to call the Buddha's Name, looking more beautiful than ever, and his discreet chanting of the scripture passage, "O **Lord Fugen** who seest all the manifest universe," outdid the most practiced monk's. The sight of his little son would start fresh tears for "the grasses of remembering" and yet without this reminder of her. . . . The thought gave him some comfort.

. . .

He now held the world and its ways, so distasteful already, in unqualified aversion, and he thought that without this fresh tie he would certainly assume the guise to which he aspired, except that every time his mind took this turn, he would straightaway start thinking how much his young lady in the west wing must miss him. He still felt a void

Source: Murasaki Shikibu, *The Tale of Genji*, trans. Royall Tyler (Harmondsworth, UK: Penguin, 2001), "Heart-to-Heart" (Aoi), 178–179.

beside him, however closely his women might gather around him while he lay at night alone in his curtained bed. Often he lay wakeful, murmuring, "Is autumn the time to lose one's love?" and listening, sick at heart, to the priests, whom he had chosen for their voices, calling the name of the Buddha Amida.

Oh, how sadly the wind moans as autumn passes! he thought as for once he lay alone and sleepless into a foggy dawn, but then a letter arrived on deep blue-gray paper, tied to chrysanthemums just now beginning to open and placed beside him by a messenger who left without a word. The delightful effect pleased him, and he noted that the writing was the Haven's.

> "Have you understood my silence? The sad news I hear, that a life can pass so soon, brings tears to my eyes, but my thoughts go first of all to the sleeves of the bereaved. My heart is so full, you know, beneath this sky."

Her writing is more beautiful than ever! He could hardly put it down, but her pretense of innocence repelled him. Still, he had not the heart to withhold an answer, and he hated to imagine the damage to her name if he should do so. Perhaps the lady he had lost had indeed been destined somehow to meet this end, but why should he have seen and heard the cause so clearly? Yes, he was bitter, and despite himself he did not think that he could ever feel the same about the Haven again.

After long hesitation, since the Ise Priestess's purification might well present another difficulty, he decided that it would be cruel not to answer a letter so pointedly sent, and he wrote on mauve-gray paper, "My own silence has indeed lasted too long, but although I have thought of you, I knew that in this time of mourning you would understand."

▶ **Working with Sources**

1. **What view of Japanese court life in the Heian period is revealed in this passage? How do the requirements of place, name, reputation, and hierarchy create tension for Genji?**

2. **What does the passage suggest about the religious beliefs and syncretism of Japanese society in this period?**

## SOURCE 13.2

# *Haedong kosŭng chŏn,* on Buddhism in Korea

**ca. 1215**

The *Lives of Eminent Korean Monks* is a compilation of biographies of Buddhist monks from the Three Kingdoms period of Korean history (first century BCE through the tenth century CE). It promotes Buddhist piety by stressing the (often supernatural) deeds of these monks, and it is also a valuable source for Korean history. In spite of its importance, the work was long thought lost until portions of it were found at a Buddhist temple in the early twentieth century. This passage of the *Lives* deals with the introduction of Buddhism as the national faith of the Silla Kingdom in 527 CE, under King Pŏpkong.

The monk Pŏpkong was the twenty-third king of Silla, Pŏphŭng [514–540]. His secular name was Wŏnjong; he was the first son of King Chijŭng [500–514] and Lady Yŏnje. He was seven feet tall. Generous, he loved the people, and they in turn regarded him as a saint or a sage. Millions of people, therefore, placed confidence in him. In the third year [516] a dragon appeared in the Willow Well. In the fourth year [517] the Ministry of War was established, and in the seventh year [520] laws and statutes were promulgated together with the official vestments. After his enthronement, whenever the king attempted to spread Buddhism his ministers opposed him with much dispute. He felt frustrated, but, remembering Ado's devout vow, he summoned all his officials and said to them: "Our august ancestor, King Mich'u, together with Ado, propagated Buddhism, but he died before great merits were accumulated. That the knowledge of the wonderful transformation of Śākyamuni should be prevented from spreading makes me very sad. We think we ought to erect monasteries and recast images to continue our ancestor's fervor. What do you think?" Minister Kongal and others remonstrated with the king, saying, "In recent years the crops have been scarce, and the people are restless. Besides, because of frequent border raids from the neighboring state, our soldiers are still engaged in battle. How can we exhort our people to erect a useless building at this time?" The king, depressed at the lack of faith among his subordinates, sighed, saying, "We, lacking moral power, are unworthy of succeeding to the throne. The yin and the yang are disharmonious and the people ill at ease; therefore you opposed my idea and did not want to follow. Who can enlighten the strayed people by the wonderful dharma?" For some time no one answered.

In the fourteenth year [527] the Grand Secretary Pak Yŏmch'ok (Ich'adon or Kŏch'adon), then twenty-six years old, was an upright man. With a heart that was sincere and deep, he advanced resolutely for the righteous cause. Out of willingness to help the king fulfill his noble vow, he secretly memorialized the throne: "If Your Majesty desires to establish Buddhism, may I ask Your Majesty to pass a false decree to this officer that the king desires to initiate Buddhist activities? Once the ministers learn of this, they will undoubtedly remonstrate. Your Majesty, declaring that no such decree has been given, will then ask who has forged the royal order. They will ask Your Majesty to punish my crime, and if their request is granted, they will submit to Your Majesty's will."

The king said, "Since they are bigoted and haughty, we fear they will not be satisfied even with your execution."

Source: "Pŭpkong Declares Buddhism the National Faith," in Peter H. Lee, ed. *Sourcebook of Korean Civilization*, vol. 1, From Early Times to the Sixteenth Century (New York: Columbia University Press, 1993), 75–77.

Yŏmch'ok replied, "Even the deities venerate the religion of the Great Sage. If an officer as unworthy as myself is killed for its cause, miracles must happen between heaven and earth. If so, who then will dare to remain bigoted and haughty?" The king answered, "Our basic wish is to further the advantageous and remove the disadvantageous. But now we have to injure a loyal subject. Is this not sorrowful?" Yŏmch'ok replied, "Sacrificing his life in order to accomplish goodness is the great principle of the official. Moreover, if it means the eternal brightness of the Buddha Sun and the perpetual solidarity of the kingdom, the day of my death will be the year of my birth." The king, greatly moved, praised Yŏmch'ok and said, "Though you are a commoner, your mind harbors thoughts worthy of brocaded and embroidered robes." Thereupon the king and Yŏmch'ok vowed to be true to each other.

Afterward a royal decree was issued, ordering the erection of a monastery in the Forest of the Heavenly Mirror, and officials in charge began construction. The court officials, as expected, denounced it and expostulated with the king. The king remarked, "We did not issue such an order." Thereupon Yŏmch'ok spoke out, "Indeed, I did this purposely, for if we practice Buddhism the whole country will become prosperous and peaceful. As long as it is good for the administration of the realm, what wrong can there be in forging a decree?" Thereupon, the king called a meeting and asked the opinion of the officials. All of them remarked, "These days monks bare their heads and wear strange garments. Their discourses are wrong and in violation of the Norm. If we unthinkingly follow their proposals, there may be cause for regret. We dare not obey Your Majesty's order, even if we are threatened with death." Yŏmch'ok spoke with indignation, saying, "All of you are wrong, for there must be an unusual personage before there can be an unusual undertaking. I have heard that the teaching of Buddhism is profound and arcane. We must practice it. How can a sparrow know the great ambition of a swan?" The king said, "The will of the majority is firm and unalterable. You are the only one who takes a different view. I cannot follow two recommendations at the same time." He then ordered the execution of Yŏmch'ok.

▶ **Working with Sources**

1. **What does Yŏmch'ok's plan reveal about resistance to Buddhism in Korea in the sixth century—and about the role of an advisor to the Korean king in the period?**

2. **What seems to have been the role of self-sacrifice in the establishment of Buddhism in Korea?**

## SOURCE 13.3

# Nihongi (Chronicles of Japan)

## ca. 720 CE

The *Nihongi* (*Nihon Shoki*) is the first official history of Japan. It draws on numerous sources, including Chinese histories, clan histories, and the accounts of religious authorities. While it parallels the *Kojiki* in describing the ancient and mythological origins of Japan, it continues the narrative far beyond the *Kojiki* into the recent past, specifically the reign of the Empress Jitō (686–697). This particular story concerns the eleventh emperor of Japan, Suinin, but it differs from the *Kojiki* in certain key details, and probably reflects the values of the eighth century rather than its ostensible setting (the first century CE).

Fourth year, autumn, Ninth Month, twenty-third day. The empress's elder maternal brother, Prince Sahobiko, plotted treason and tried to endanger the state. He watched for an occasion when the empress was enjoying her leisure and addressed her as follows: "Whom do you love best—your elder brother or your husband?"

At this, the empress, ignorant of his object in making this inquiry, immediately answered, saying: "I love my elder brother." Then he enticed the empress by saying: "If one serves a man by beauty, when the beauty fades, his affection will cease.... I beg you, therefore, to slay the emperor for me." So he took a dagger and, giving it to the empress, said: "Put on this dagger with your garments, and when the emperor goes to sleep, stab him in the neck and kill him."

. . .

Fifth year, winter, Tenth Month, first day. The emperor proceeded to Kume, where he dwelled in Takamiya. Now the emperor took his noon-day nap with the empress's knees as his pillow. Up to this time the empress had done nothing but thought vainly to herself: "This would be the time to do what the prince, my elder brother, plotted." And she wept tears which fell on the emperor's face.

The emperor woke and addressed the empress, saying: "Today we have had a dream. A small brocade-color snake coiled itself around our neck and a great rain arose from Saho, which coming here wet our faces. What does this portend?" At this the empress, knowing that she could not conceal the plot, in fear and awe bowed to the earth and informed the emperor fully of the circumstances of the prince's, her elder brother's, treason.

. . .

Then the emperor addressed the empress, saying: "This is not your crime," and raising a force from the neighboring district, he commanded Yatsunada, the remote ancestor of the Kimi of Kōzuke, to slay Sahobiko. Now Sahobiko withstood him with an army, and, hastily piling up rice stalks, made a castle, which was so solid that it could not be breached. This is what was called a "rice castle." A month passed, and yet it did not surrender.

The empress grieved at this, saying: "Even though I am empress, with what countenance can I preside over the empire, after bringing to ruin the prince, my elder brother?" Accordingly, she took in her arms the imperial prince Homutsu-wake and entered the rice castle of the prince, her elder brother. The emperor increased his

Source: "The Empress and Her Brother Prince Sahobiko," from *Traditional Japanese Literature: An Anthology, Beginnings to 1600*, ed. Haruo Shirane (New York: Columbia University Press, 2007), 47–49.

army still more and, having surrounded the castle on all sides, proclaimed to those inside, saying: "Send forth quickly the empress and the imperial prince." But they would not send them out. So General Yatsunada set fire to the castle. Then the empress, taking in her bosom the imperial child, crossed the castle and came out.

Immediately she sought the emperor saying: "The reason why your handmaiden at first fled into her elder brother's castle was in the hope that her elder brother might be absolved from guilt for the sake of her and her child. But now he has not been absolved, and I know that I am guilty. Shall I have my hands tied behind my back? There is nothing left but for me to strangle myself. But even though I,

your handmaiden, die, I cannot bear to forget the favor shown me by the emperor. I pray, therefore, that the empress's palace, which I had charge of, may be granted to consorts for you. In the land of Tanba there are five ladies, all of virtuous minds, the daughters of the prince, who is Michi no Ushi of Tanba. Let them be placed in the side courts to complete the number of the consort chambers." To this the emperor agreed. Then the fire blazed up, and the castle was destroyed. All the troops ran away, and Sahobiko and his younger sister died together inside the castle. Thereupon the emperor commended the good service of General Yatsunada and granted him the name of Yamato-hi-muke-hiko Yatsunada.

▶ **Working with Sources**

1. Contrast the emperor's reactions to his wife in the two episodes. What do these differences reveal about Japanese culture?

2. What does the document suggest about women's familial roles and expectations for their behavior?

## SOURCE 13.4

# P'i Jih-hsiu, "Three Poems of Shame"

ca. 003 CE

Because there are very few sources of information on the history of Vietnam before the Li dynasty (1010–1225), Chinese dynastic histories and Chinese poetry are indispensable sources. They are valuable even when, as in this case, they were composed by those on the other side of conflict with Vietnamese insurgents. P'i Jih-hsiu was a prominent Tang poet of the late ninth century, and he was particularly drawn to the Mencian notion that the people have the right to revolt if their country is being mismanaged.

Source: Keith Weller Taylor, *The Birth of Vietnam* (Berkeley: University of California Press, 1983), 345–346.

While traveling through the country in 865, he stopped in the city of Hsü, from which 2,000 men had been drafted for the Tang army and sent to fight Nan-chao in Vietnam. These soldiers were probably lost when Nan-chao defeated the Chinese forces in Vietnam in early 863, and news of their defeat apparently reached Hsü while Jih-hsiu was there.

The south was neglected, officials
were not selected,
Causing the overthrow of our
Giao-chi,
Which, for three or four successive
years,
Has drifted away, bringing disgrace
to the empire.
The timid yield readily in battle;
The warlike revel in their weapons.
Soldiers fill the empire,
Battle leaders accumulate treasure;
Exactions reduce the common
people to misery,
In order to distribute the wages of
valiant men.
Brave Hsü-ch'ang warriors,
Their loyalty and daring brought
honor to their families;
They went with the wind of myriad
galloping horses,
They ceased in a river of flesh.
Yesterday morning the defeated
troops returned;
There is weeping at a thousand
gates and ten thousand hearths.
The sound of wailing echoes
through the village streets;

Resentment spreads over the
mountains and valleys.
Who can listen to wardrums in the
daytime,
And not suffer the sight of metal
arrowheads?
I have a plan for victory,
Though irregular and considered
worthless by others.
I store it in my mind and heart;
I am ashamed to see the families of
the Hsü warriors.
I lament those thoughtless ones,
Who simply follow the steps of
their ancestors.
My family does not produce grain
for the army;
I am not familiar with military
affairs.
Yet I wear the same kind of clothing
as the Hsü warriors,
And I eat the same kind of food as
the Hsü warriors.
Now I know that the teachings of
the Ancients
Are already enough to shelter me.
To whose shame is this song sung?
The Ying River flows far and green.

▶ Working with Sources

1. **Can this poem be compared with other T'ang poetry regarding pacifism and war?**

2. **What does the poem indicate about the growth of a national identity and culture in Vietnam?**

## SOURCE 13.5

# Copper head of Bodhisattva Avalokiteshvara, Vietnam

**eighth–ninth century CE**

This head, crafted from copper alloy, is all that remains of an impressive image found in central Vietnam. It depicts the Avalokiteshvara, the embodiment of Buddhist compassion, and the Amitabha Buddha is perched on the crown. It points to the emergence of a pan–southeast Asian bodhisattva type in the eighth and ninth centuries, as well as to the superb metal-casting skills of artisans in the Cham territories of Vietnam.

▶ **Working with Sources**

1. **How does the image reveal the phenomenon of "religious civilizations interacting" and the emergence of an international Buddhist culture in Southeast Asia?**

2. **What does the head suggest about the social structure of Vietnam in this period?**

Source: Thierry Ollivier. © RMN-Grand Palais/
Art Resource, NY

# Chapter 14 600–1450 CE

# Patterns of State Formation in Africa

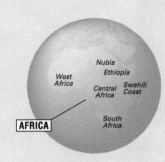

According to local tradition, the founder of the gold-trading kingdom of ancient Ghana (ca. 400–1200) in West Africa was Dinga. He was a descendant of Bilal, the Ethiopian whom, according to tradition, the Prophet Muhammad chose as the first *muezzin*, or crier who calls the Muslim faithful to prayer. When Dinga arrived from Arabia to the Sahel, the east–west belt of steppe south of the Sahara Desert in West Africa, he asked a many-headed snake at a well for water. The snake refused, and Dinga subdued her through magic to receive his drink. After marrying the snake's three daughters, he fathered three sons, the eldest of whom was a half-human, half-serpent being who went to live underground. The two younger sons were still growing when their father left to return to Arabia.

The second son grew into an inconsiderate man who mistreated his father's old servant. The third son turned into a much kinder person, giving the same servant his leftovers. Years later, Dinga, nearly blind, felt his end coming and summoned his two sons to give them their respective heritages. The elderly servant, who had never forgotten the kindness of the younger son, persuaded the youngest son to go first, disguised as his older brother, to receive the lion's share of Dinga's estate. Indeed, the father bestowed his power of magic as

*ABOVE:* **Detail from the *Catalan Atlas* (1375), showing Mansa Musa, the king of Mali, on his throne.**

well as the kingdom on the youngest son, while the older son received the more modest power of rain making.

The two sons struck a deal whereby Ghana would receive enough rain and gold as long as its people would sacrifice a virgin and a colt every year. After many years of human and animal sacrifices, a Wagadu man and admirer of a virgin about to be sacrificed slew the snake brother. As he was dying, the snake brother cursed the people of Wagadu, which lost its abundance of rain and gold. A parched and impoverished Ghana fell to its enemies.

This story gives us a glimpse of the main pattern underlying the history of sub-Saharan Africa between 600 and 1450. In this period, rulers converted to Islam and incorporated its beliefs and practices into their traditional **African spirituality**.

While the Eurasian and North African pattern during 600–1450 was that of the formation of religious civilizations that contained commonwealths of states, the pattern of sub-Saharan Africa in the same period was that of religious kingdom and empire formation. In the northeast of sub-Saharan Africa, kingdoms had already adapted to Christianity prior to 600, and the new kingdoms of Nubia and Ethiopia continued the Christian heritage, with Ethiopia assuming imperial dimensions. In West Africa, Mali, the successor of ancient Ghana, adapted to Islamic imperial traditions and became a multilinguistic, multiethnic, and multireligious empire. On Africa's east coast, a set of small Islamic merchant states emerged, the Swahili port cities, under either kings or councils of notables. Finally, in the interior of central and southern Africa, indigenous kingdoms rose on the basis of the African tradition of magic-empowered authority, descended from the naturalist spiritual heritage.

## Christians and Muslims in the Northeast

During 600–1250, Nubia was a Christian kingdom along the middle Nile in the Sahara and sub-Saharan steppe, built on agriculture and trade between tropical Africa and the Middle East. Ethiopia, Nubia's neighbor in the highlands to the southeast, was similarly Christian but, unlike Nubia, was initially a collection of decentralized chiefdoms. When one of the chiefs eventually centralized rule in 1137, the new kingdom of Ethiopia unified the highlands, sent missionaries to the southern provinces to convert non-Christian Africans, and battled the Muslims in the lowlands on the Red Sea coast in the name of a Christian crusade. Both Nubia and Ethiopia were fascinating cases of sub-Saharan polities adopting patterns of state formation from the Middle East into their African heritage: They adapted to Middle Eastern plow agriculture and Christianity, while long retaining African traditions of decentralization.

### Nubia in the Middle Nile Valley
About a century after the end of the kingdom of Meroë, sometime around 350 (see Chapter 6), small Nubian successor states dominated the middle Nile valley

## Seeing Patterns

▶ What patterns of adaptation did the Christian kingdoms of northeast Africa demonstrate in their interactions with the civilizations of the Middle East and eastern Mediterranean?

▶ What were the responses of Africans to Muslim merchants who connected them with the trading zone of the Indian Ocean and Mediterranean? As these Africans adapted to Islam, which forms of political organization did they adopt?

▶ In what ways did the economic and political transformations on the East African coast and West Africa affect developments in the interior?

**African spirituality:** The experience of and/or belief in the presence of a life substance or spirit shared by all living beings and things in nature. People or ancestors, therefore, could influence each other, positively or negatively. A human or animal mask allowed a person to assume a different identity.

from north to south. In the course of the mid-500s, these states converted to Coptic Christianity and subsequently united into a single kingdom. Open to trade with the then rising empire of the Arab Umayyads, Nubia experienced a gradual ascendancy of Arab merchants to dominance in Nubian commerce. Eventually, the enhanced position of these merchants led to Muslim political control: In 1276, the Egyptian Mamluks defeated the Christian king of Nubia and installed a puppet regime. By around 1450 Christianity in Nubia had largely given way to Islam.

**The Rise of Christian Kingdoms in Nubia**    Meroë's power ended as a result of deforestation near the capital and nomadic attacks against its northern provinces. The nomads had adapted to the use of the camel in the early centuries of the Common Era, which allowed them to carry out swift long-distance raids over vast tracts of inhospitable territory. Indeed, the use of the camel created a transportation revolution in the Sahara in general and opened up new routes for commerce and invasion. One immediate result of this was that a new ruling class of Nubians arose in the middle Nile valley during the 400s. Nubian chiefs and their followers established three small kingdoms along the middle Nile that prospered in large part as the result of the rapid spread of the animal-driven waterwheel (*saqiya* [SAH-qee-ya]) invented in Egypt in the first century CE. Water could now be lifted into channels all year round, even at some distance from the river, for the purpose of planting two annual grain crops. Archaeological evidence points to a substantial increase in the number of villages in the region as a result of this innovation.

In the 500s, Egyptian missionaries converted the Nubians to Christianity. Pagan temples became churches, and new churches and monasteries were built, ultimately in nearly every village. Kings and members of the ruling class sponsored these Christian institutions. As did their contemporaries in the Mediterranean and Middle East, the Nubian rulers appreciated the unifying effect of a single state religion over the multiplicity of local temple cults.

Barely Christianized, Nubia now had to withstand an invasion of Arabs from Egypt. After the establishment of the Arab emirate of Syria, Iraq, and Egypt (see Chapter 10), the new governors in Egypt organized military campaigns into neighboring countries. In 652, one of these campaigns penetrated deep into Nubia. The Arab military used siege engines and caused considerable damage to one of the Nubian capitals. But an army of Nubian archers, long famous for their skill with bow and arrow, defeated the Arabs, forcing them to retreat. In a subsequent agreement, the two sides formally recognized each other, made a pact, and drew up a schedule of future friendly exchanges among their respective rulers. Later Muslim historians reinterpreted this pact, ignoring the defeat and presenting it as a treaty of submission to Islamic hegemony. Such differing interpretations notwithstanding, the pact endured and blocked the advance of Islam into East Africa for 600 years.

**Royal Power and Governance**    At the turn of the 700s, a "great king" emerged who unified the three Nubian kingdoms. Power remained largely decentralized, however, with a dozen vassal rulers and an appointed—later hereditary—official called an "eparch." This official governed the northern subkingdom and was responsible for its defense against Egypt. The Coptic patriarch of Alexandria appointed the bishops, who, therefore, were independent from the kings, in marked contrast to Catholic Europe in the contemporary early Middle Ages, where the kings appointed church officials (see Chapter 11).

In terms of financial administration, archaeologists have so far discovered no evidence of a kingdom-wide taxation system. The dozen vassal rulers were probably powerful landlords who might have sent presents to the great king as tokens of their position. As in Europe, abbots of monasteries were also landlords, endowed with royal grants of villages, where peasant farmers paid rent. Monasteries, however, were not numerous, given the limited fertile land on the Nile banks, in contrast to Ethiopia, western Europe, and Byzantium. Most likely, in the vicinity of the great king's residence some basic fiscal mechanisms existed whereby village headmen delivered taxes in kind. Another, perhaps even the principal, source of income for the kings and eparchs was long-distance trade, which they controlled. In this respect, the Christian great kings of Nubia were similar to their Islamic counterparts in eastern and western Africa.

**Agriculture**   The farmland of the Nubian villages consisted of small strips of arable land on the up-to-2-mile-wide fertile banks of the Nile. The annual summer floods between June and September inundated these strips, leaving them covered with rich sediment. In a few places, a wider valley or low-level islands in the river allowed for the farming of additional fields. Palm orchards helped to anchor the silt, and stone walls and jetties built into the Nile captured additional amounts of alluvial soil. As the floods receded in fall, villagers grew sorghum, millet, barley, wheat, and cotton with the help of plows pulled by oxen.

Higher fields away from the banks, which required waterwheels for irrigation, were planted during the winter with pulses, okra, melons, and other garden crops for spring harvesting. In the spring, farmers planted second crops on both the banks and higher elevations. Vineyards became more important as the kingdoms evolved, and wine was consumed by villagers in taverns as well as by priests and monks in daily religious services. Farmers also planted limited amounts of alfalfa for the feeding of cattle and donkeys. Sheep and goats fed on the stubble of grain fields and on scrubland, while pigs ate household remnants. Arabic written sources report the necessity of occasional food transports during local famines on the Nile, but generally the Nubian villages were self-supporting.

**Long-Distance Trade**   The pact of 652 between the Arabs and Nubia included clauses concerning the trade of Egyptian cloth, pottery, iron utensils, leather goods, and wine for ivory and slaves. The latter two items came from the tropical

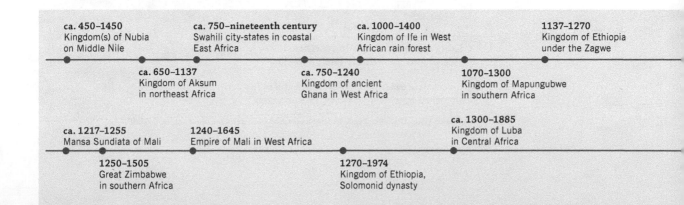

| ca. 450–1450 Kingdom(s) of Nubia on Middle Nile | ca. 750–nineteenth century Swahili city-states in coastal East Africa | ca. 1000–1400 Kingdom of Ife in West African rain forest | 1137–1270 Kingdom of Ethiopia under the Zagwe |
| --- | --- | --- | --- |

ca. 650–1137
Kingdom of Aksum
in northeast Africa

ca. 750–1240
Kingdom of ancient
Ghana in West Africa

1070–1300
Kingdom of Mapungubwe
in southern Africa

ca. 1300–1885
Kingdom of Luba
in Central Africa

ca. 1217–1255
Mansa Sundiata of Mali

1240–1645
Empire of Mali in West Africa

1250–1505
Great Zimbabwe
in southern Africa

1270–1974
Kingdom of Ethiopia,
Solomonid dynasty

territories on the White Nile, though nothing is known about how Nubian merchants and slave-raiding troops operated in these territories. Whatever the specifics of the Nubian activities along the White Nile, the kings taxed the merchant caravans at various resting places along the way.

In the period between 800 and 1200, the long-distance trade attracted Muslim merchants and craftspeople from beyond Aswan to the northern province of the Nubian kingdom, where they settled in a number of villages and possibly built mosques. A ruling in the mid-800s by an Egyptian Muslim judge (recognized by Nubia) allowed the Muslims in Nubia to acquire private property. A money economy then emerged, based on Islamic gold dinars. Muslim merchants also settled along the Red Sea coast, especially once the North African Fatimid caliphs had conquered Egypt in 969. To compete with the Iraqi Abbasid caliphs on the Persian Gulf, the Fatimids developed maritime trade with India through the Red Sea. Both of these trade avenues would bolster the commerce of the entire Mediterranean region and even reach to far-off western Europe (see Map 14.1).

**From Christian to Islamic Nubia**    In the mid-1000s, to secure their hold on the Red Sea, Egyptian rulers resettled nomadic migrants from Arabia to Upper Egypt. Unfortunately for Nubia, these migrants and their neighbors began raiding the kingdom in the 1100s. The local rulers in northern Nubia, principal defenders against the raids, gained in power vis-à-vis the Nubian kings. Perhaps as a

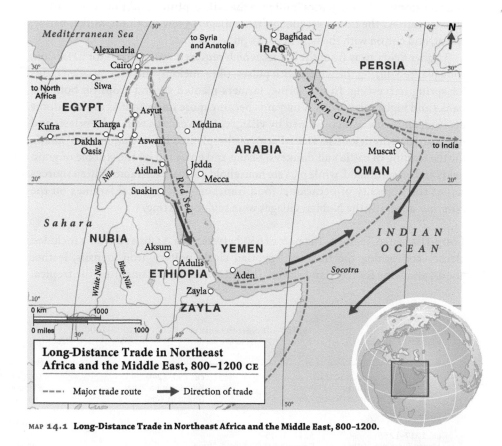

MAP 14.1  **Long-Distance Trade in Northeast Africa and the Middle East, 800–1200.**

consequence, dynastic rivalries broke out, and in the 1200s both usurpers and pretenders to the throne appealed to Egypt for support. The Mamluks, who governed Egypt at this time (1250–1517), responded to the appeals with enthusiasm, including Nubia in their anti-Christian holy war efforts. They propagated the reinterpreted pact of 652 as a treaty requiring regular tributes, particularly the delivery of slaves, from Nubia. In 1276, they conquered Nubia, installed a Christian vassal king, and levied the *jizya* head tax, which non-Muslims in Islamic lands had to pay. In due time, the Christian dynasty gave way to Muslim rulers; and in 1365, after a new wave of Arab nomadic incursions, the Nubian kingdom ceased to exist altogether.

Viewed in retrospect, through interaction with the Roman Empire Nubia adapted itself to the Christian institutions of sacred kingship. A specifically Nubian pattern of political formation emerged that resembled the feudal practices (see Chapter 11) of many other places around the world. In this pattern, kings acted as representatives of God on earth but lacked the resources to govern with the help of centralized institutions. Instead, they relied on the support of federated chiefs, who functioned much like vassals.

The kings were also not strong enough to incorporate the clerical hierarchy into their states, so the patriarch of Alexandria never lost control over the appointment of Nubian bishops—unlike the pope in his struggles during the high Middle Ages with the Holy Roman emperors over lay investiture. Nubian churches were outposts of the Egyptian **Coptic** Church rather than indigenous institutions with their own hierarchy intertwined with the Nubian royal dynasty. Had the Nubian Church been a "national church" like those we will examine in Europe (see Chapter 17), it might have been in a better position to resist Islamization once Muslim rulers took over.

## Ethiopia in the Eastern Highlands

After the Christian kingdom of Aksum had lost Yemen to the Sasanid Persians in 570 and had exhausted the timber resources around its capital in the 600s, it shriveled to a chiefdom. However, in cooperation with the Coptic Church, Aksum continued to represent the church's mission to convert the southern highland Africans. Eventually, new dynasties arose and renewed the mission, among which the Solomonids and their Christian Crusades were the most successful. In Ethiopia, the adaptation to Christianity was more thorough than in Nubia. The Ethiopians embarked on a pattern of forming an African Christian civilization, including the Judeo-Christian symbolism of Zion and Christian law.

**Christianity in the Highlands** The kings of Aksum and the patriarch of the Coptic Church abandoned the capital perhaps as early as the mid-600s and reestablished themselves in a modest chiefdom with better agrarian resources farther south. They continued to trade ivory, ostrich feathers, musk, and myrrh for linen and cotton textiles as well as spices on the Red Sea but no longer issued coins. When Muslim rulers in Egypt in the late 800s occupied ports on the west coast of the Red Sea and expanded trade with India and East Africa, Aksum became a partner in this trade. In addition to these goods, it sold slaves captured in raids in the lowlands to the south. The main effort of the small Aksum kings was directed toward campaigning southward, taking priests and settlers with them to convert

**Coptic Christianity:** A branch of Christianity centered in Egypt that emphasizes the sole divine nature of Jesus, in contrast to Catholic western and Orthodox eastern Christianities, in which the divine and human nature of Jesus are declared to be indivisible.

and pacify the defeated highland Africans. A monastery, founded in the late 800s some 200 miles southwest of Aksum, became the main center for sending out missionaries to the south. Reduced as it was, Aksum continued to be a factor in highland politics.

Quite dramatically, however, in the 970s the Africans subjected to conversion struck back. A mysterious queen, Gudit (Judith), led several destructive campaigns in which churches and monasteries were burned, towns destroyed, and thousands of people killed or enslaved. The situation was so chaotic that the patriarch of Alexandria refused to appoint the customary metropolitan bishop from Egypt to the country. Scholars, scouring the scant evidence to identify the area of this queen's origin, have determined that she might have been from the recently Christianized parts of the highlands. After her regime of terror of a purported 40 years, a remnant of the Aksumite kingdom recovered and survived modestly for another century, but little is known about its kings and nothing about the extent of their rule.

**State and Church under the Zagwe Kings**    Political stability eventually returned to the highlands with the foundation of the Zagwe dynasty (1137–1270), centered on a Christianized province some 300 miles south of Aksum. To its neighbors, the Zagwe kingdom was known as Ethiopia or Abyssinia, names rooted in the Hebrew and Christian Bibles. The Zagwe kings laid the foundation for a return to dominant royal power and continued the Aksumite tradition of church sponsorship and missionary work in the south.

A first step toward reunification was the request of an early king in the mid-twelfth century to his metropolitan bishop to appoint seven additional bishops. The idea was that this nucleus of an Ethiopian episcopate would later grow to the 10 members required for a vote of independence from the patriarch of Alexandria. The king, however, did not get far with his attempt to create an independent Ethiopian Church. After lengthy negotiations with the patriarchs of Egypt and

**Church of St. George, Lalibela, Ethiopia.** Stonemasons cut this church and its interior from the surrounding rock formation. This and 10 other churches, built in the early 1200s, are part of a pilgrimage center created in the image of the Holy Land in Palestine.

Syria and the Muslim ruler of Egypt, the Egyptian sultan refused the split. The Muslims were not about to relinquish the indirect leverage they possessed in Ethiopia through their political control over the patriarchs in Egypt. Had Ethiopia succeeded, the significant development of a "national church" would have occurred—just the opposite of the situation in Europe at that time, where the pope wrested control of the church from the kings during the investiture controversy.

Church sponsorship expressed itself in the construction of 11 remarkably innovative structures carved out from subterranean rock during the early 1200s, called the Lalibela churches. The kings arranged the churches in two groups, separated by a stream named the Yordanos, after the biblical Jordan River. The policy of the Zagwe dynasty was the recreation of Zion, perhaps in succession to Jerusalem, which the Muslims reconquered in 1187 from the western European crusaders. Accordingly, the dynasty used these churches for elaborate annual masses and processions during Holy Week. The Lalibela monoliths are unique in the history of Christian church construction and have no parallels elsewhere.

Under the Zagwe kings, the conversion of the peoples in the central and southern highlands to Christianity resumed. In addition, the kings encouraged the colonization of the land with Christian settlers from the north. These settlers introduced the plow and cereal agriculture, adding them to the existing hoe and tuber crops (ensete, taro, and yam). The central and southern highlands were geographically much larger than those in the north and offered ample opportunities for the establishment of new villages, fields, and pastures. With its fertile volcanic soil, southern Ethiopia became one of the most productive agricultural regions of sub-Saharan Africa.

The political system that emerged in the center and south was an extension of what Aksum had pioneered in the north. Under a king ruling by divine right, Ethiopia was a confederation of provincial lords, some of whom also used royal titles. These lords lived in villages among their farmers and collected rents, consisting of grain, pulses, and cattle. Legally, ownership of the land was vested in families and had the status of inalienable property, with the family lords holding the right to collect rents.

**The Solomonid Dynasty**   Once Christians from the north had settled as farmers in the central highlands and had converted the locals to Christianity, they shifted the focus of their missionary efforts southward. In 1270, a new dynasty of kings, the Solomonids, emerged some 300 miles south of Aksum, in the region of today's capital of Ethiopia, Addis Ababa. These new kings claimed descent from the Aksumite kings and sponsored the composition of an elaborate foundation narrative, the *Kebra Negast*, which legitimized the Solomonid dynasty until its fall in 1974.

According to this narrative, the kings of Aksum were not only the descendants of a union between the queen of Sheba and the Israelite king Solomon but also the heirs to the Israelite Ark of the Covenant after the destruction of the First Temple by the Neo-Babylonians. The Ethiopians thus appropriated the biblical heritage more thoroughly than any eastern or western European Christian peoples did. The religious heritage of the Solomonids still lives on in Ethiopia. Outside Africa, this heritage has been embraced by the *Rastafarians*—Afrocentric Christians who form a small minority in Jamaica and who have found many

MAP 14.2 **The Ethiopian Highlands, ca. 1450.**

admirers, some perhaps more because of the popular reggae music of Bob Marley (1945–1981) than its doctrines.

**Ethiopian Christians and Coastal Muslims**
During the 1300s and most of the 1400s, Ethiopia was a powerful kingdom. The kings continued to depend on the collaboration of their provincial lords, but they also commanded a sizeable mercenary army of their own. With this army, they extended their authority over small principalities of Christians, traditional Africans, and Muslims in the southern highlands and Rift Valley, as well as Muslim sultanates along the Red Sea coast.

This extension began with the conquests of King Amda Seyon (r. 1314–1344), who in effect doubled the kingdom's territory. An unknown priest accompanied the king on his campaigns, which he related to posterity in vivid prose and with great detail in *The Glorious Victories of Amda Seyon*, one of the earliest written histories in sub-Saharan Africa. A century after the Mamluks had eradicated the crusader kingdom of Jerusalem in the Middle East (1291), Solomonid Ethiopia was carrying on the Christian holy war in sub-Saharan Africa (see Map 14.2).

"Now be ready to fight for Christ, as it is said in the *Book of Canons*, 'slay the infidels and renegades with the sword of iron, and draw the sword in behalf of the perfect faith.'"

—Amda Seyon

Foremost among the Muslim sultanates along the Red Sea coast, which came under Ethiopian authority, were Ifat (1285–1415) and its successor state Adal (1415–1555) on the west coast of the Red Sea, at its entrance to the Indian Ocean. Both relied principally on trade, linking East Africa via the Rift Valley with the India–Mediterranean sea lane. Only the sultanate of Zayla, near modern Djibouti, and a few other places along the coast had sufficient water from wells to allow for a modest garden agriculture. The steppe lowlands farther away from the coast were too dry to support more than widely dispersed populations of camel nomads, who supplied animals and guides to the trade caravans and soldiers to the wars of the sultans against Ethiopia. Urban dwellers, nomads, and pastoralists astride the trade route through the Rift Valley had converted to Islam gradually in the centuries after 800 when autonomous Muslim rulers in Egypt began the expansion of trade via the Red Sea with India and East Africa.

The Ethiopian kings were ruthless in their efforts to subdue the sultans. But the kings' crusading image notwithstanding, they were also pragmatic enough to exempt Muslim merchants and pastoralists from the church's missionary efforts in the south of the kingdoms. Similarly, the kings had little choice but to tolerate the sultans of Ifat and Adal as Muslim vassals. Ethiopia became de facto a multiethnic, multilinguistic, and multireligious empire in which the kings limited the church's conversion efforts.

Legally, however, the kings continued to emphasize their Christian identity, adopting in the mid-1400s a Christianized version of Roman law, *the Law of the*

Kings (*Fetha Nagast*), from the Egyptian Copts. The law brought with it an intriguing history. According to Islamic law, Christians in Islamic civilization were entitled to self-rule, and for this purpose, the Coptic Church in Egypt adopted portions of Justinian's code and resolutions of church councils for its governance. In the mid-1300s, an Egyptian Copt compiled these law books and resolutions into a single codex governing church affairs, civil law, and criminal law, translated from Greek into Arabic. The Ethiopian translator added a section on kingship, and as such, *the Law of the Kings* remained the law of the land until 1930, when the Ethiopian emperor Haile Selassie issued the first modern constitution.

The reinvigorated Ethiopian kingdom of the Solomonids was keenly interested in establishing contacts with western Christianity, wishing especially for the dispatch of craftspeople (and receiving a few). A first embassy of 30 members traveled in 1297–1312 to visit the popes. A churchman in Genoa reported on these visitors, identifying their king for the first time with the mythical Prester John, a great Christian ruler in the "east" expected to come to the aid of the crusaders in recovering Jerusalem and the Holy Land. Previously, Prester John had been considered to be an Indian priest-king, commander of a huge army; but now after the loss of the Holy Land in 1291, Ethiopia appeared as a better hope for an ally than the more distant India.

# Adaptation to Islam: City-States and Kingdoms in East and Southern Africa

During the period 600–1450, the Swahili people emerged as an indigenous African population of Muslims. They formed a society with common features but were divided into dozens of city-states along a 2,000-mile stretch of the African east coast, from today's Somalia in the north to Mozambique in the south. The Swahilis' most common feature was their function as merchant middlemen between the interior of East Africa and the Middle East as well as India. In the interior, increasing agricultural resources and trade with the Swahilis encouraged the expansion of chiefdoms but not yet the rise of kingdoms, except in the far south, in the middle Limpopo valley, and on the Zimbabwean plateau, where local people mined gold. Here, beginning around 1075, towns, cities, and kingdoms arose, the best known of which was Great Zimbabwe (ca. 1250–1505).

## The Swahili City-States on the East African Coast

Dissenting Arabs, driven by the centralizing caliphs to the margins of the Arab Empire in the Middle East, were the first to establish trade contacts in the 700s with Bantu-speaking villagers in coastal East Africa. In the following centuries, these villagers adapted themselves to long-distance trade and Islamic civilization. They evolved into an urban society of kings, **patricians**, religious scholars, sailors, fishermen, and farmers based in small port cities. The kings and patricians were consumers of luxury goods brought to them by Middle Eastern and Indian merchants. As sellers of goods manufactured in their cities to the populations of the interior, the patricians acquired goods from the interior, which the Muslim merchants from overseas took back home. Thus, the Swahilis were brokers in a complex system of exchanges among the people around the Indian Ocean.

**Patrician:** Term used in this chapter to denote Muslims in Swahili society claiming Middle Eastern descent and, by virtue of profiting from long-distance trade with the countries around the Indian Ocean, either ascending to the throne of their cities as kings or governing their cities in councils, together with other patricians.

**Swahili Beginnings**    The East African coast follows a fairly straight line from the northeast to the southwest, with few bays and natural harbors. For the most part, the coast is low, in most places rising only gradually. Many small rivers open into the Indian Ocean, and their estuaries provide some room for anchorage. Only the Zambezi River in the south was large enough to allow longer-range water traffic and the building of inland towns. Islands, reefs, and mangrove swamps were numerous and limited the construction and use of large vessels among the Swahilis. Under the influence of the monsoons blowing from the southwest from April to September, the northern half of the East African coast—from today's northern Tanzania to southern Somalia—receives most of its annual rain during the summer. These monsoon winds supported sailing with the wind to the Middle East and India. The opposite direction of the winter monsoons facilitated the return voyages. The southern half of the coast, from northern Tanzania to Mozambique, has rainy winters and no reliable seasonal winds, making sailing conditions less predictable. Accordingly, the southern half was less settled than the northern part.

The main ethnic group in the interior of sub-Saharan Africa was that of the Bantus, who had migrated to central, eastern, and southern Africa from roughly 600 BCE to 600 CE (see Chapter 6). The Bantus possessed a diversified agriculture and a wide variety of iron implements. In the mid-700s CE, a cultural differentiation between the Bantus of the interior and the east coast began to emerge. Archaeological remnants from Shanga, near today's Somali–Kenyan border, indicate the existence of a small wooden Islamic congregation hall, holding perhaps 25 people, and Muslim burials with an orientation toward Mecca. Small silver coins with Islamic inscriptions similar to Yemeni coins of the same period but minted in Shanga have also been found. The coastal population thus adapted to Islam, while the hinterland remained wedded to traditional African spirituality.

The earliest Muslim merchants in East Africa were Khariji dissidents from the Middle East. These Muslims were sectarians who opposed the emergence of a centralized empire, whose caliphs were actively shaping the emergent Islamic state religion. The caliphs pursued them relentlessly, pushing them into political insignificance in far-away provinces, such as Oman at the mouth of the Persian Gulf and oases in the North African Sahara. Given the agricultural limitations in these regions, the Kharijis took to trade, in both East and West Africa.

Early on, the Kharijis were mostly interested in slaves, who were in great demand in the Islamic empire. Merchants in Basra, the main port for the Indian Ocean trade, invested their profits in the purchase of marshland around the mouth of the Tigris–Euphrates Rivers and in the acquisition of slaves from East Africa to clear this land for the planting of rice and sugarcane. From 868 to 883, a revolt among these slaves disrupted the Abbasid Empire's entire trade through the Persian Gulf with India, East Africa, and China. When the caliphs finally succeeded in suppressing the revolt, large-scale agricultural slavery in the region ended. Black slave imports from East as well as West Africa continued on a smaller scale, however, primarily for domestic purposes.

**Adapting to Islam**    After the Kharijis lost their edge in the trade, mainstream Muslim merchants from the heartland of the Islamic empire traveled with textiles, glazed pottery, and glassware to East Africa to purchase luxury goods, such as ivory, hardwoods, and skins. One of the heartland cities was Shiraz, the capital of the Shiite dynasty of the Buyids (945–1055) in Iran. Their prestige appears to have surpassed that of the Kharijis, since wealthy Swahili merchant families associated themselves with them, claiming Shirazi descent. Members of these families migrated from the northern Swahili city of Shanga southward and founded new trading centers as far away as the Comoros Islands.

After 1050, mainstream Islam, with its mixture of Sunnism and mysticism, rose in prestige. *Sharifian* descent—that is, the possession of a genealogy going back to the Prophet Muhammad—began to rival Shirazi descent among the coastal elites. Leading Islamic families claiming Shirazi or Sharifian descent thus assumed dominant positions in the Swahili cities, from Mogadishu in the north to Chibuene (in Mozambique) in the south.

**Urbanism**    Swahili urbanism along the East African coast encompassed several hundred towns and about two dozen city-states of up to 10,000 inhabitants, either on the mainland or on islands off the coast (see Map 14.3). The mark of many cities was the central open space containing the Friday mosque for the congregational noon prayer, the main city well, and tombs of Islamic saints. Around the mosque and usually facing the sea were the densely built inner cities of the patricians. In the less densely settled outskirts, nonpatricians from overseas or the interior and manumitted slaves earned their living as craftspeople. On the perimeter were cemeteries, pastures, brushland, and mangrove swamps.

Separate commoner towns housed fishermen, boat builders, and sailors. Their families grew vegetables and fruits in their gardens and sold the surplus in the nearby patrician cities. Further inland lived various non-Muslim client populations who traded meat and food staples, primarily sorghum, to the cities. Cities, towns, and inland people thus formed loosely organized city-states under the leadership of the patricians.

**Governance**    In the period 600–1450, the Swahili city-states were governed by kings and/or councils of patrician elders. Mainland cities, such as Mogadishu, Gede, and Malindi, were more vulnerable to occasionally hostile hinterland people and, therefore, more dependent on inland alliances than cities located on islands, such as Lamu, Paté, Pemba, or Zanzibar. Both hinterland and inland populations were trade partners whom the Swahili patrician merchants or their agents—usually slaves—visited but among whom they did not settle. The merchants did not establish mosques in the interior, and the interior population did not convert to Islam, nor did holy men venture into non-Islamic territories to establish retreats or pilgrimage centers.

In the absence of Islam as a common bond, the office of chieftainship as the traditional African institution binding lineage federations together served to express the communality of the cities and surrounding rural peoples. The mainland kings were Muslims from leading Shirazi or Sharifian patrician families, but in the dealings with their non-Muslim allies they acted more like traditional chiefs. By contrast, the patrician councils in the island cities—often clusters of several cities, commoner towns, and villages—had no inland allies and at times even dispensed with kings.

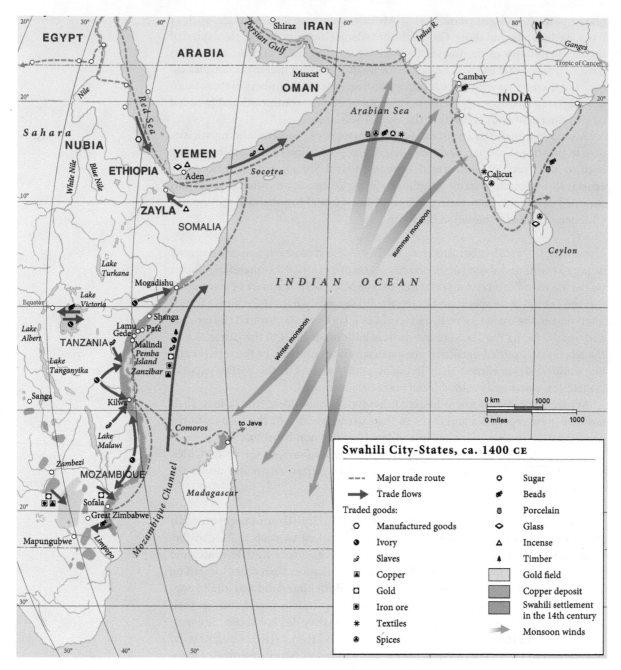

MAP **14.3 Swahili City-States, ca. 1400.**

The Swahili city- or port states were considerably smaller than the Christian or Islamic kingdoms of Nubia, Ethiopia, and southern, central, and western Africa. Nevertheless, the patricians' regalia clearly expressed the same royal aspirations. The Moroccan Muslim traveler Ibn Battuta (1304–1369) visited Mogadishu in 1331 and left a detailed description of the African-spiritual and Islamic royal customs as displayed by Sheikh Abu Bakr, who claimed Yemeni Sharifian descent. Every Friday, so Ibn Battuta writes, the king attended the noon prayer in his enclosed space in the mosque. Afterward, in a procession led by royal musicians (playing large drums, trumpets, and wind instruments), the king, judge, officials, and military commanders walked through town to the audience hall of the palace. The most important royal prerogative was the minting of coins, made of copper or gold. Given, however, that power on the Swahili coast was based on commercial, and not landed, wealth from which to collect taxes, in administrative practice the kings were never more than firsts among equals in the patriciate.

Another prominent visitor was Zheng He, the admiral whom the Ming emperors entrusted with an Indian Ocean expedition and who in 1405 explored among other areas the Swahili coast (see Chapter 12). Wherever he landed along the coast, he presented his hosts with gold, silver, porcelain, and silk. In return, the Swahili rulers and merchants presented the visitors with the exotic tropical animals (as seen in the image below) they often bought from their contacts in the African interior. Zheng He followed maritime routes well traveled in previous centuries, and even though his journey was more for the purpose of displaying Ming power after the Mongol interlude, it can be seen as falling within the pattern of routine merchant journeys across the Indian Ocean and the South China Sea.

## Traditional Kingdoms in Southern and Central Africa

The first region in the interior where a pattern of increasing wealth and population density became visible during the period 600–1505 was southern Africa, on and around the Zimbabwean plateau. Here, the original foragers of the vast grasslands

**Gift of a Lion by a Swahili Merchant.** This painting, which dates from the Ming Dynasty (1368–1648), depicts the exchanges between East Africa and the Ming court in China.

were in the process of adapting to the Bantu culture arriving from the north, which included the influx of herders and farmers discussed in Chapter 6. Chiefs became powerful on the basis of large herds of cattle. Later, by trading first ivory and then also gold to coastal Swahili merchants, the chiefs initiated a pattern of political formation, building cities and kingdoms, such as Mapungubwe and Great Zimbabwe. Adapting their new economic power to indigenous traditions, these kings assumed the same exalted status which we encountered in the cases of Christian Nubia and Ethiopia.

**The Kingdom of Mapungubwe**   In the course of the 700s, hunters increasingly went after elephants for their ivory. Khariji Swahili merchants from the north had founded the coastal town of Chibuene for the purpose of buying ivory, in return for textiles, glass beads, glazed pottery, and glass bottles. These items, being storable goods, added to the wealth accumulated by chiefs. Thus, the ivory trade marked the beginning of the southern African hinterland being incorporated into Swahili long-distance trade.

When chiefs acquired cattle and imported goods from the coast, the first towns arose in the interior. Larger towns with around 1,500 inhabitants followed during the next few centuries, culminating with Mapungubwe [mah-poon-GOOB-way], the capital of the first full-fledged kingdom (1070–1300), with some 5,000 inhabitants. In the early 900s, villagers to the north, on the Zimbabwean plateau, began to mine gold, which for the next four centuries was the major export item from Swahili cities to the Middle East and India. Workshops for the manufacture of ivory and gold figurines in the Limpopo towns testify to the emergence of an indigenous demand for the products of specialized craftspeople. When Mapungubwe arose as an urban-centered kingdom, the southern African interior not only was integrated into the Swahili Indian Ocean trade but also developed the crucial urban and royal mark of an urban craftspeople class who did not practice agriculture and cattle herding.

Excavations in Mapungubwe and ethnographic studies have yielded important insights into the institution of southern African kingship. The king resided on a hill that had previously been used chiefly for rainmaking ceremonies. He was in ritual seclusion from the commoners, who lived in the town at the foot of the hill. The hill also contained residences for a few senior wives. The remainder of the wives resided in villages outside Mapungubwe, where they were married to allies and clients of the kings. The graves of the royal cemetery contained large numbers of gold and glass beads, a bowl made of gold leaf, and shards of Chinese dishes. Seclusion and an elaborate set of regalia thus marked the king of Mapungubwe.

**Golden Rhinoceros.** This golden rhinoceros was found among the items of the royal dynasty of Mapungubwe, signifying the power and magic of the kings. The kingdom was organized around the mining and trading of gold with the Swahili cities and, from there, with the Islamic Middle East.

Court rituals also emphasized the exalted position of the king. The king was in charge of rainmaking ceremonies and harvest feasts, but the actual rituals were conducted by the diviner. Of forager descent and often itinerant, diviners were experts in spirituality, experienced in dealing with the realm of the benevolent and evil spirits. Although royal power was associated with spiritual authority, there was an institutional division between the king's power over life and death and the diviner's authority to summon the spirits. Thus, African kingship shared the pattern of rulership development encountered also in Eurasia and the Americas: Royal power was legitimate only if combined with spiritual or divine authority.

**The Kingdom of Great Zimbabwe**    The kingdom of Great Zimbabwe (1250–1505) (Shona *ziimba remabwe* or *ziimba rebwe*—"the great house built of stone boulders") represents the culmination of the southern African kingdoms (see Map 14.4). Initially a tributary state of Mapungubwe, Great Zimbabwe emerged as a kingdom in its own right when the cooling and drying trend in the climate, which in Eurasia signaled the end of the early medieval agricultural expansion, made agriculture in the relatively dry Limpopo valley more difficult. Inhabitants abandoned Mapungubwe in the second half of the 1200s, with evidence of some royalty migrating north to Great Zimbabwe, which was more humid.

**Great Zimbabwe, Passageway.** The boy, visible at the end of the curve, provides an idea of the massive urban structures erected under the kings. The stone masons were highly specialized crafts-people, who constructed walls that have outlasted the demise of the Zimbabwe kingdom in the middle of the fifteenth century.

Great Zimbabwe was located at the southern end of the arc of rock surfaces on the Zimbabwean plateau where gold was found. Granite for the construction of stone walls could be quarried easily, using heat from fires to split off layers of rock. Regular building blocks from these layers could be dressed with less effort than in Mapungubwe. At its height, the capital encompassed 18,000 inhabitants and was the seat of a kingdom extending northward across the Zimbabwean plateau. Most settlements in the kingdom were dedicated to gold mining and trading, but a few practiced different trades, such as iron mining and salt panning. The primary sources of income, however, were cattle and grain.

Today, three main archaeological complexes remain of the capital. The first is a hill with a walled palace, accessible through a staircase. Two other complexes at a distance of half a mile to the south are the Western and Central Valley Walled Enclosures. The best-known structure is the so-called Great Enclosure within the Western Enclosure complex, an imposing 36-feet-high circular wall built of closely fitting blocks of granite. The royal palace precinct contained buildings similar to those in Mapungubwe. In the enclosures, some of the better-preserved ruins indicate that they once were buildings with solid stone walls, with plastered and perhaps even painted surfaces inside. Some residences were connected with walls which formed courtyards or narrow passageways. All enclosures were once densely packed with houses, presumably occupied by the kings and/or the ruling classes. Commoners lived in the space between the hill and around the two enclosures, occupying simple thatched huts built with timber and plastered with clay.

The kingdom of Great Zimbabwe ended around 1505 when Swahili merchants replaced the initial southern Limpopo trade route with the shorter northern Zambezi route. A Chinese porcelain dish bearing this date was found in a burned and collapsed structure in the compound, though it appears that portions of Great Zimbabwe were still inhabited for some time. Thus, there was some overlap between the decline of Zimbabwe and the rise of the new trade route.

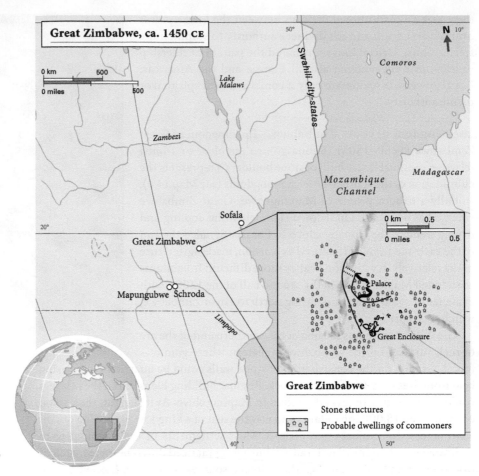

MAP 14.4  **Great Zimbabwe, ca. 1450.**

## Central African Chiefdoms and Kingdoms

The central African rain forest and savanna, although more sparsely settled than the other parts of Africa during 600–1450, nevertheless participated in the general pattern of increased agricultural production and population expansion. In a number of places, especially the Congo Basin, favorable agricultural conditions supported the formation of chiefdoms which evolved into kingdoms. One savanna site, the Lake Upemba depression in the south of today's Democratic Republic of the Congo, was the home of the Luba people, who founded a kingdom based on a diversified agriculture and regional trade sometime in the period between 1000 and 1300 (see Map 14.5).

**Luba Origins**   Archaeologists date the earliest evidence for the existence of permanent agricultural and fishing settlements around Lake Upemba to the period around 800. They found these settlements between the lakes, marshes, and rivers of one of the tributaries of the Congo River. Apart from fish, the villagers also relied on sorghum, millet, chickens, goats, and sheep for their sustenance. Locally produced iron and salt added to the resources. Hunting groups cut across the village lineages and formed the nucleus, around 1000, for the emergence of chiefs who were recognizable in their graves through copper ornaments. Copper had to be acquired through regional trade with the west, and its value made it the metal preferred for jewelry, as in many other parts of Africa.

Luba oral tradition reaches back to the period between 1000 and 1300. The founding myth appears to refer to a process whereby two chiefs, each claiming his own source of legitimacy, were competing for the unification of the villages. As in many other African foundation stories, the true founder is conceived of as a suffering, disadvantaged hero who has to go against multiple enemies before becoming a successful founder king. In the traditions of Africa, as in those of many other parts of the world, exalted kingship was unacceptable unless rooted in humble beginnings.

Similar to the kings of Zimbabwe, Luba kings possessed magic powers, which entitled only descendants from their bloodline to succeed to the throne. The chieftains of other clans, although holding court offices and meeting in council to assist in the administration, were excluded from the succession. The royal clan maintained a small military force, sufficient to collect tributes from outlying villages but not large enough to destroy any of the chieftainships. A stable balance was established between the king and the chieftains, making Luba the model for subsequent kingdoms in the savanna of central Africa. The Luba kingdom itself survived until the beginning of Belgian colonialism at the end of the nineteenth century.

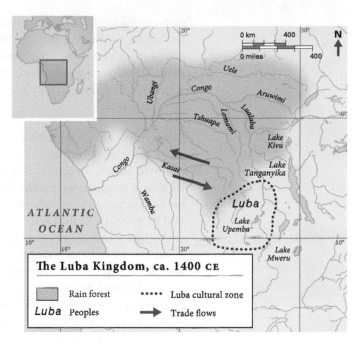

MAP 14.5 **The Luba Kingdom, ca. 1400.**

# Cultural Encounters: West African Traditions and Islam

A pattern of regional trade, urbanization, and chiefdom formation was also characteristic for the Sahel and savanna of West Africa from the middle of the first millennium CE onward. Around 600, chiefs became kings when they unified their clans, conquered some neighbors from whom they collected tributes, and arranged alliances with others. Like their later African colleagues in the eastern half of Africa, they claimed to possess magic powers and adopted royal customs of seclusion. Two kingdoms, ancient Ghana and Mali, followed each other in the period 600–1450. Their royal–military ruling clans benefited from trans-Saharan trade with Islamic civilization and gradually converted to Islam, while the general population of herders, farmers, miners, smiths, and other craftspeople remained faithful to their African religious traditions.

## The Kingdom of Ancient Ghana

Ancient Ghana emerged in the 600s as the strongest group of chiefdoms in the Sahel and savanna between the Niger inland delta in the east and the Senegal valley in the west. It advanced to the status of a kingdom after 750, when it became the center for trade across the Sahara with the North African Islamic states. Thanks to this trade, the kingdom was dominant in the Sahel for half a millennium. In the 1100s, however, drought and provincial unrest weakened Ghana. The kingdom gave way in 1240 to Mali, an empire which began its rise in the upper Niger rain forest and savanna.

**Formation of Ancient Ghana**   As discussed in Chapter 6, a long period of progressive desertification (3000–300 BCE) had driven the inhabitants of the southern Sahara southward into what became the Sahel, a belt of steppe, grassland, and marginal agriculture. They had domesticated millet and bred cattle herds in Saharan villages shortly before the desiccation began. During the period 600 BCE–600 CE, the climate stabilized, and millet agriculture, cattle herding, and village formation expanded across the Sahel and northern savanna from Lake Chad in the east to the Senegal valley in the west. In some places, as in the inland delta of the Niger, where irrigation was possible, villages were clustering. Jenné-jeno emerged around 300 as a city surrounded by a collection of villages. The city was a center of regional trade for iron and gold from the upper Niger and Senegal valleys and copper from the Sahara, in return for urban manufactures, such as textiles, leather goods, metal implements, and utensils. The people who populated the Sahel were ethnically Soninke, speaking a Niger-Congo language, like the majority of West Africans.

After 300, the regional trade became a long-distance trade. Thanks to the arrival of the Arabian camel among the Berbers of North Africa and the northern Sahara, it became possible to travel through the desert. Long-distance merchants from the cities of Roman North Africa made contact with Soninke merchants in the Sahel, some 3 months away by camel caravan. They exchanged Roman manufactures, such as glassware, cloth, and ceramics, plus Saharan copper and salt for gold. Berber miners in the central Sahara quarried salt from deposits left by dried-up prehistoric lakes. Cowrie shells, imported by Rome from the Indian Ocean and exported to West Africa, attest to trade connections even farther than the Mediterranean.

It took some time, however, for the initially infrequent trans-Saharan exchanges to intensify and become regular. Only after the loss of their gold mines in northwestern Iberia to Germanic migrants did the Romans regularize the trans-Saharan trade, beginning in the mid-500s. The regularization had a profound effect in the Sahel. In the 600s, Soninke chiefs on the western outskirts of the inland Niger delta, enriched by the profits from the Saharan trade, equipped their followers with arms, such as swords and lances. Riding on small West African horses immune to the diseases carried by the tsetse fly, they subjugated more distantly related Soninke groups in the Sahel between the Niger and Senegal valleys. In the mid-700s, one of the chiefs proclaimed himself king in Wagadu, a city in the Sahel northwest of the inland delta, and founded the kingdom of ancient Ghana (as distinguished from the modern state of Ghana).

As told in the founding myth at the beginning of this chapter, Dinga was the first mythical king. His kingdom, so it was foretold, was destined to rule the Sahel, dominate the gold trade, and benefit from abundant rain as long as its subjects sacrificed a virgin and a colt every year to its well-dwelling patron snake. Modern scholars would say that ancient Ghana lasted through the wet period of the first millennium (300–1100) and eventually succumbed to its successor, Mali, when it could not adapt in the Sahel to the emerging dry period (1100–1500).

**From Roman to Islamic Trade**   Ancient Ghana received its gold from Bambuk, a region in the rain forest at the western edge of the kingdom. Villagers on a left-bank tributary of the middle Senegal River panned and mined the metal during the dry season, and Soninke merchants transported it by donkey and bullock some 500 miles east to Wagadu. The Bambuk gold fields occupied a no-man's-land between the kingdom of ancient Ghana and the chiefdom of Takrur on the lower Senegal. The two polities left the villagers to their own devices, since neither possessed the technical and administrative means to organize or even control the panning and mining operations. Soninke merchants went no farther than nearby towns, from which they conducted their trading activities with the villagers.

> "On every donkey-load of salt when it is brought into the country [from Bambuk] their king levies one golden dinar and two dinars when it is sent out [across the Sahara]."
>
> —Abu Ubayd al-Bakri

Romanized Berbers gave way to Islamized Berbers in the trans-Saharan trade after about 750. As was the case in Swahili East Africa, Khariji merchants pushed by the emerging Islamic empire into the outer provinces were the first Muslims to travel to the African interior. According to an eleventh-century Arabic source, Wagadu was a twin city, with its merchant and royal halves several miles apart. If Wagadu can be identified with the partially excavated ruins of Koumbi-Saleh on the southern border of today's Mauritania—an identification still disputed among scholars— the merchant city had a dozen mosques, a market place, and residences. Several thousand inhabitants called it their home.

The royal city consisted of a domed palace and other domed buildings, including a courthouse and the homes of the king's treasurer, translator, and other ministers. A grove surrounded the palace area, containing the royal prison and the dwellings of the priests and diviners, as well as the tombs of ancestral kings. In contrast to their Swahili colleagues, the kings of Ghana avoided a combination of traditional kingship with Islam. Even though they benefited from including Muslims in their administration, they were not about to surrender their exalted, magical royal authority over life and death to the supremacy of Islamic law.

**From African Spirituality to Islam in the Ruling Class**   While the kings of Ghana had reasons to hold on to traditional African spirituality, the Soninke merchants gradually converted to Islam. Business with the North African and Middle Eastern merchants was easier to transact if everyone adhered to the same ethics and laws. By the early 1000s, the merchants in the trading towns near the Bambuk villages were Muslims, and the adjacent state of Takrur had also become Islamic. The sectarian Khariji Islam gave way to mainstream Sunnism, which rose to dominance in the Islamic world after 1050. In North Africa, the proponents of Sunnism were the Almoravids, southern Moroccan Berbers who spearheaded a movement that evolved into a short-lived empire in Morocco, the western Sahara, and Islamic Spain.

Perhaps under the pressure of the Almoravids, in the early 1100s the kings of Ghana followed their merchants by also converting to Islam. The Sahel and savanna villagers, however, remained wedded to their African spirituality. As a result, Ghana now resembled the states on the Swahili coast and their hinterlands, where only the rulers and merchants were Muslim. In addition to the villagers, a number of allied Soninke chiefs remained faithful to traditional spirituality; and during the second half of the 1100s the cohesion of the kingdom began to soften. In 1180, the founding clan of ancient Ghana ceded power to another clan, which established a new dynasty in Wagadu and adopted a policy of conquest of the southern savanna. For the next half century Ghana was an imperial power, trading gold not only from the Senegal River in the west but also from newly developed fields in the rain forest on the upper Niger and Black Volta Rivers (see Map 14.6).

## The Empire of Mali

The opening of new gold fields in the rain forest exposed hitherto marginal peoples to the influence of long-distance trade, royal rule, and Islam. One of these peoples, the Malinke (variant terms Manden, Mandinka), followed the by-now-familiar pattern of rallying around an inspiring chief who, as a conqueror, laid the foundations for an expanding polity. By uniting both savanna and Sahel peoples, the Malinke built the empire of Mali, a polity of many ethnic, linguistic, and religious groups. At its height, Mali stretched from the Atlantic to the Niger bend and from the Sahara to the rain forest.

**Increased Trade**    Mali was the beneficiary of a significantly increased demand for gold in the Islamic realm on the other side of the Sahara. In addition to the existing Islamic mints, Christian mints began to stamp gold coins. The king of Castile in Spain was the first, in 1173, and by the mid-1200s Italian city-states had followed suit. In response to this increased demand, merchants encouraged the aforementioned opening of new gold fields in the savanna and rain forest of the upper Niger and its tributaries.

The people in this region were Malinke villagers who spoke a language related to that of the Soninke in the north but who were ethnically distinct. In the course of the 1000s, these villagers had acculturated to ancient Ghana, which they recognized as overlord. Living in dozens of chiefdoms, the Malinke also encompassed hunter groups, apart from the chiefdoms, which formed the basis for ambitious leaders seeking to unify the Malinke. When the new dynasty of Ghana conquered much of the Malinke lands at the end of the 1100s, resistance led by the hunters against the new rulers rose quickly. In a rebellion in 1230–1235, the Malinke not only liberated themselves but went on to conquer ancient Ghana.

**Oral traditions:** Myths, tales, and stories (e.g., the foundation myth of Wagadu) handed down from generation to generation.

The leader of the conquest was the inspiring hero Sundiata (also spelled Sunjata or Sundjata, ca. 1217–1255). He and his adventures were at the center of an **oral tradition**, with traveling bards telling stories which they handed down from generation to generation and told and retold publicly in villages. In the nineteenth and twentieth centuries, anthropologists recorded these traditions and made them available in translation. At the head of a cavalry force borrowed from a chiefdom in the Sahel, Sundiata defeated ancient Ghana in 1235 and founded the empire of Mali, with its capital, Niani, on an upper Niger tributary in modern Guinea.

**The Malian Empire**    Mali was the first enduring empire in sub-Saharan Africa, lasting officially for over four centuries (1235–1645). At its height in the early

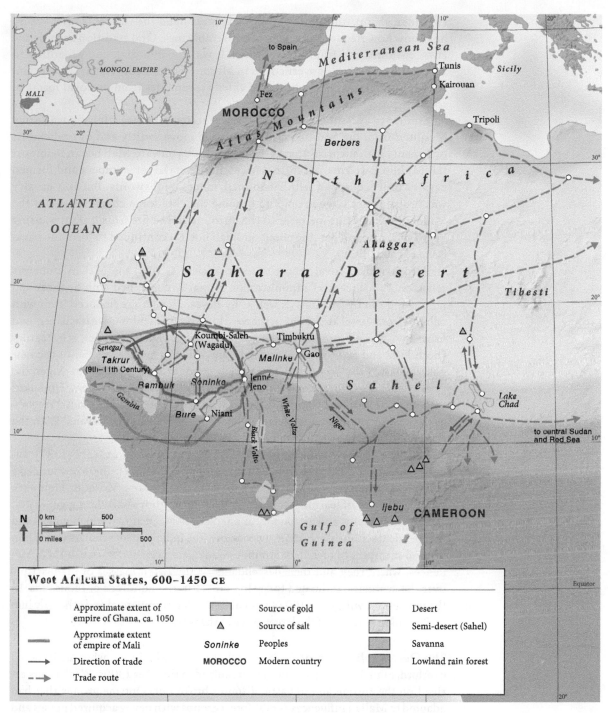

MAP 14.6 **West African States, 600–1450.**

1300s, Mali encompassed most of the West African Sahel, large parts of the savanna, and the gold fields in the rain forest—a territory surpassed only by that of the contemporary Mongol Empire. At the core of the empire were privileged Malinke clans whose kings and chiefs formed an alliance and met in an assembly

(Malinke *gbara*), under the emperors who assumed the title of *mansa*. We do not know how frequently or long this assembly met. Oral tradition records the laws, customs, and traditions of which it was the guardian and according to which the empire was governed. As in Mesopotamia, Vedic India, Greece, and Rome, Mali preserved traditions of chiefly assemblies from preroyal forms of social organization.

Similar to ancient Ghana, Mali's power rested on a large, horseborne army recruited from the Soninke clans that could move swiftly and overwhelm its opponents with surprise attacks. From the 1300s onward Mali began to import tall Middle Eastern and North African horses in larger numbers and formed cavalry units equipped with chain mail, lances, and swords. But this cavalry was probably not large enough to become the elite force characteristic of the Middle East and Europe prior to the introduction of firearms. Infantry, using bow and arrow and moving about on small horses, continued to form the backbone of the military.

Also like their royal predecessors in ancient Ghana, the Malian emperors relied on a small central administration primarily concerned with finances and justice and run by Muslims as well as by slaves. The empire financed itself with tributes from vassal kingdoms in the Sahel and river chiefdoms with villagers and fishermen, as well as taxes on the commerce of gold, iron, copper, salt, textiles (both local and foreign), leather goods, and other manufactures. Since the new gold fields and the capital of Niani were located on a tributary of the Niger, the rulers relied on water transport downriver to the cities of Jenné-jeno, Timbuktu (founded in 1100), and Gao. In the mid-1300s, these three cities replaced Wagadu as the main transshipment centers of goods for the Saharan caravans. With the rise of Mali, the trans-Saharan trade shifted eastward.

In 1324, the most famous ruler of Mali, Mansa Musa (r. ca. 1312–1337), annexed the city of Timbuktu from its Touareg Berber founders. There he founded a college (Arabic *madrasa*) and library, part of the Sankoré Mosque. Timbuktu became a center of learning, focused on Islamic law but also offering geometry, algebra, geography, and astronomy as ancillary fields of study, which judges and independent scholars were required to know. The independent scholars were often well-off members of merchant families. Many kept private libraries in their residences, where they and their descendants accumulated masses of manuscripts over the centuries, estimated today to number in the hundreds of thousands. In the mid-1400s, with some 100,000 inhabitants, the commercial and scholarly hub of Timbuktu was one of the larger cities in the world.

**The Decentralization of Mali**    Timbuktu flourished even while its imperial overlord, Mali, became more loosely organized in the later 1300s. Weak rulers arrived on the throne and dynastic disputes broke out. Outside groups that had adapted to Malian influences—rain-forest groups with newly acquired horses and Touareg nomads from the desert—attacked from the south and north. As a result, some of the subjugated provinces in the Sahel began to break away and established independent kingdoms. More generally, even though Mali had exploited the weakening of ancient Ghana at the onset of the dry period after 1100, the deepening of the drought conditions eventually caught up with Mali as well. By 1450, Mali had shrunk to a kingdom in the savanna.

# Rain-Forest Kingdoms

As discussed in earlier chapters, the West African rain forest was a 200-mile-wide strip of tropical vegetation stretching from modern Guinea above the southwestern corner of West Africa to Cameroon on the bend to central Africa, where it transitions to the Congo rain forest. In the earlier period of 600 BCE to 600 CE, savanna peoples with iron implements had entered the rain forest and founded villages in clearings, farming oil palms, yams, and bananas. As elsewhere in Africa, the result was a pattern of political formation which included village clusters, chiefdoms, and kingdoms with urban centers and sophisticated crafts, such as bronze casting in Nigeria.

**The Sankoré Mosque of Timbuktu, Mali.** The mosque evolved in the fourteenth century into a large university with a library housing hundreds of thousands of manuscripts. A preservation program under UN auspices seeks to restore and preserve these manuscripts today

**The Kingdom of Ife**   The earliest village cluster to urbanize was that of Ife [EE-fay], west of the Niger delta, in 500 CE, the spiritual center of the Yoruba ethnic group and its oral traditions. By 1000 it was a kingdom with a walled capital, which enclosed a palace, groves, shrines, stone-built residences, and craft workshops for pottery, textiles, and glassware (especially beads). Courtyards and passageways in the city were paved with terra-cotta, to remain passable during the rainy season. One highly developed art was sculpting, in terra-cotta, copper, or bronze, documenting Ife's urban achievements.

**Sungbo's Eredo**   Ife set the example for several further chiefdoms to advance to the threshold of kingdoms between 1000 and 1450. One of them toward the north was Oyo, which (thanks to the adoption of a cavalry force) expanded from the rain forest northward toward the edge of the savanna. It arose as a trade center for the exchange of palm oil kernels and kola nuts (a mild narcotic containing caffeine) in return for Mediterranean manufactures and Sahel horses, through first Ghanaian and then Malian merchants. In the other chiefdoms, leaders mobilized villagers for the construction of earthworks, including Sungbo's Eredo, which astound even today with their size and scope. One of these chiefdoms, Ijebu, encompassed a capital and villages on a territory of 22 square miles, surrounded by a combined moat and rampart up to 70 feet deep/high and 100 miles long. In nearby Benin, smaller earthworks around villages collectively added up to 10,000 miles and became the nucleus for an important kingdom in 1440. In both Ijebu and Benin, the moats and ramparts cut through the hard, iron-saturated soil, rivers, and swamps, requiring centuries of hard labor with nothing more than iron shovels.

Scholars are still undecided over the purpose of these constructions: Did they protect against enemies and elephants, were they boundary markers for ancestral lands and their spirits, or did they facilitate the collection of tolls? Perhaps they were intended to do all three. Equally difficult is the explanation for the phenomenon of collective labor: How were chiefs able to motivate workers to contribute their voluntary efforts? Evidently they were, as they were also in the Americas and Pacific, where followers built huge temples or rolled heavy stone sculptures across distances. Authority without power, buttressed by ancestral pedigree and spirituality, can thus be seen as a powerful motivator to take on great tasks and validate the institutions it represents.

# The Sculptures of Ife

Sculptures, figures, and figurines in Africa followed a pattern that was shared early on with Eurasia and, during the periods of 600 BCE–600 CE and 600–1450 CE, also with Australia, the Pacific, and parts of the Americas. Broadly speaking, forager, village, and pastoral societies developing in the direction of chiefdoms, but not yet kingdoms, preserved traditional ancestor cults within their African spirituality.

As lineages evolved, the memory of the generations between the founder and living people blurred so that the in-between ancestors became an anonymous collective. The spirits of the ancestors in the invisible world, therefore, were conceived as being collectively present, to be consulted, nourished through sacrifices, cajoled, etc. One could "trap" them in sculptures, figures, and figurines, which emphasized the head, believed to be the seat of the spirit, at the expense of the torso and limbs, which were indicated in rudimentary fashion. Even the heads were generally fashioned in abstract, geometrically simplified ways, corresponding to the collective nature of the ancestors. These artifacts, therefore, were not "primitive," even though they are still today often described as such. Their style was generic because the collective of the ancestors was generic.

When societies reached levels of wealth and complexity that led to the emergence of kingdoms, kings became exceptional persons, endowed with ancestral magic (in Africa) or a transcendent divine mandate (in Eurasia) to exercise power, not merely chiefly authority. Generic ancestor "traps" would not do: Artists had to apply the techniques of naturalistic representation so that the kings would recognize themselves in them. Of course, after a while sculptures turned into generic

(*a*) **Guardian Figure, Bakota Area, Gabon, Nineteenth–Twentieth Century.** The abstract Bakota figure, above, with its generic geometric elements, represents the collective lineage spirit; the much more realistic Nigerian figure on the next page represents royalty who wished to be remembered individually.

# Putting It All Together

Africa in the period 600–1450 displayed patterns of political and cultural development that included creative adaptation of African spirituality to the monotheisms of Christianity and Islam and indigenous kingdom formation. Depending on regional conditions and the degree of integration into Eurasian long-distance trade, peoples in the different parts of sub-Saharan Africa mixed the two cultural heritages of Christianity and Islam in a variety of ways. The Nile valley and northeastern highlands, long adapted to the Mediterranean prior to 600, incorporated Christianity into their local traditions. They adopted the Christian institutional division between kingship and church, in which kingship was a sacred office but subject to Christian law and ethics. The church, for its part, was an autonomous, hierarchical body. As in post-1000 Christian western Europe, the Nubian and Ethiopian churches were subject to a distant religious authority.

Coastal East and West Africa adopted Islam, which arrived through merchants, not soldiers or missionaries. In eastern Africa, Islam took root among the coastal people and did not penetrate inland. In western Africa, only merchants and kings converted but did so across the interior. Thus, Africans adapted to Christianity and Islam during 600–1450 in very different ways.

In the same period, African kingship was a new institution with roots in the traditions of chieftainship in villages and village clusters. The kings emphasized their likenesses again, as they did in Mesopotamia and Egypt, since kingship became an ordinary institution with undistinguished kings not worth remembering (a).

The Ife terra-cotta, copper, and bronze royal heads stem from that short, experimental, and highly innovative time period of about 200 years (1100–1300) when kingship was new in Ife. The naturalism of these figures is striking, especially when one takes into consideration that Christian and Muslim figurative art during the same period was still "primitive," in the sense of being hieratic—that is, it typically represented standardized ideas about how biblical and prophetic figures should look so that their God-pleasing nature was immediately recognizable. The stripes on the faces of some Ife figures (b) are believed to represent *scarifications*, or scars marking the passage from youth to adulthood or distinguishing one lineage from another, as practiced in parts of Africa.

## Questions

- How does the history of African sculpture, such as those from Ife, provide evidence for studying the patterns of state building in this period?

- Why does material culture play such an important dimension in understanding the African past?

(b) Ife Shrine Head, Terra-Cotta, Nigeria, ca. 1200.

royal powers over life and death but also continued to claim the traditional chiefly powers of spirituality and magic. As Christians or Muslims, they paid at least lip service to the divine laws to which they were subject. In southern and central Africa, kingship arose from its African context without modification by Christian or Islamic law, and it is important to emphasize that Africa needed neither Christianity nor Islam to embark on its own distinctive pattern of kingdom formation.

During 600–1450, however, this pattern clearly remained an exception amid the sub-Saharan population, the majority of which remained "stateless," to use an expression in common use among historians of Africa. This population, organized in farming villages or herder camps, possessed chiefs, often with slave retinues, but did not unite into larger polities or trade farther away than regionally for locally unavailable metals and salt. It also had specialized craftspeople forming villages, such as smiths or leather workers. The silent presence of this unrecorded majority of stateless Africans should always be kept in mind, alongside the kingdoms and empires, in seeking to understand Africa's significance in world history during this period.

▶ For additional resources, including maps, primary sources, visuals, and quizzes, please go to www.oup.com/us/vonsivers. Please see the Further Resources section at the back of the book for additional readings and suggested websites.

## Against the Grain

# Sundiata's Rise to Power

The Sundiata epic is the story of a disadvantaged hero who rises in spite of the most hostile environment imaginable. It begins with a king's sister: Insulted by not receiving her fair share of a meal during a royal feast, she turns herself into a forest buffalo and devastates the fields of the kingdom's villages. Hunters from the neighboring kingdom of the Malinke slay her. As forest people, they know how to deal with the dangerous spirits of the wilderness (such as buffaloes). The king rewards them with an ugly hunchback woman, heir of the buffalo spirit's forest powers. The reward is in fulfillment of a prophecy according to which the Malinke king has to find an ugly hunchback to give him a successor. But a jealous co-wife casts a spell, and Sundiata, the successor, is born a cripple, walking on all fours. During puberty, thanks to the inheritance of his mother's forest powers, Sundiata stands up, uproots a tree, and becomes a physically superior man—a true hunter.

But the king's co-wife does not give up and forces Sundiata into exile. Her son, succeeding to the throne, is unable to withstand conquest by another neighboring king. As a former blacksmith, this king is endowed with forest powers. He uses them for malevolent purposes, tyrannizing the Malinke. In despair, the Malinke recall Sundiata from exile. The tyrant king and Sundiata fight each other in titanic battles. In the end, Sundiata prevails because his beautiful sister sacrifices her honor. During a night in the tyrant's chamber she discovers his dark secret: A cock's spur attached to an arrow can break his invulnerability. Shooting one such arrow, Sundiata achieves his final victory and creates the empire of Mali.

Traditional West African spirituality is built on the conceptualization of a world created by a remote god, in which civilization and nature mingle. Accordingly, existence is embedded in pairs of opposing but complementary elements, such as village/forest, civilization/wilderness, order/chaos, safety/danger, village farmer/forest hunter or blacksmith, man/woman, beauty/ugliness, invisible (masked) village spirits/visible forest spirits, etc. These pairs are skillfully woven into the epic, suggesting that figures marginal to village life, such as hunters or blacksmiths, can cut across the established social order with its jealousies and intrigues and tap into the wild, creative, benevolent (or evil) forces of nature, and found new kingdoms and empires.

- What are the similarities and differences between the epics of Sundiata and Homer (Chapter 7)?

- Compare the messages of the Epic of Sundiata and Machiavelli's *The Prince* (Chapter 17). In what ways are they comparable, even if separated by time and region?

# Thinking Through Patterns

▶ **What patterns of adaptation did the Christian kingdoms of northeast Africa demonstrate in their interactions with the civilizations of the Middle East and eastern Mediterranean?**

In the period 600–1450, the northeast of sub-Saharan Africa was firmly drawn into the orbit of eastern Christian and Islamic civilizations, without, however, fully adapting their formative patterns. Perhaps the most extensive adaptation occurred in the sphere of trade, where the Christian kingdoms became the providers of luxury goods, such as ivory, skins, and hardwoods from tropical Africa to the Middle East and eastern Mediterranean, in return for manufactures, Indian spices, and Chinese silks. Beginning in 1250 in the Nilotic kingdom of Nubia, the expansionist regime of the Muslim Mamluks in Egypt put the African Christians on the defensive. By 1450 the middle Nile region was Islamized. In contrast, an expansionist Christian Ethiopia put Muslims on the coast of the Red Sea on the defensive and Christianized the pagan southern highlands.

The inclusion of the East African coast and sub-Saharan West Africa into the Muslim Indian Ocean and Mediterranean trading zone resulted in the rise of small coastal Swahili states and two large West African polities: the kingdom of ancient Ghana and the empire of Mali. Muslim mariners and merchants interacted with Islamized local African rulers and merchants to exchange Middle Eastern textiles, leather goods, and metal wares for ivory, gold, slaves, skins, and hardwoods. African rulers and merchants obtained their African goods from pagan miners and hunters in the African interior outside their states. Adaptation to Islamic religious civilization was a phenomenon limited to the ruling classes and associated merchant circles.

▶ **What were the responses of Africans to Muslim merchants who connected them with the trading zone of the Indian Ocean and Mediterranean? As these Africans adapted to Islam, which forms of political organization did they adopt?**

▶ **In what ways did the economic and political transformations on the east African coast and West Africa affect developments in the interior?**

The adaptation of coastal East Africa to Islamic religious civilization had an indirect effect on the interior in the region of southern Africa. Here, chiefs in Zimbabwe attached themselves to the Swahili trade network and used the wealth from this trade for the transformation of their chiefdoms into kingdoms. Impressive masonry constructions serving as centers for incipient administrative structures testify to the ability of kings to transform chiefly authority into royal military power. The East and West African expansion of trade under the impact of Islam may have also indirectly led to a population increase in the interior of Africa. Such an increase became noticeable toward the 1300s, especially in the Congo basin, where the Luba kingdom was the first to emerge.

# Patterns of Evidence: Sources for Chapter 14

## SOURCE 14.1

## *The Fetha Nagast*, Ethiopia

**Fifteenth century**

In the medieval period Ethiopia became a multiethnic, multilingual, and multireligious state in which the kings limited the Church's conversion efforts. Nevertheless, the kings continued to emphasize their Christian identity, and this factor is reflected in their adoption and endorsement of the Fetha Nagast, or Law of the Kings, in the mid-fifteenth century. This legal code had originally been written in Arabic by a Coptic Christian in Egypt, probably in the mid-thirteenth century. While living under Muslim rule, the Copts were allowed to adopt portions of Justinian's law code and the resolutions of church councils for their own governance. Translated from Greek, and with many Biblical passages added, the code connected Egyptian Christians to their Byzantine, Roman, and Judeo-Christian heritage, founding the basis of law squarely in that tradition. The Ethiopian monarchs had the Arabic source translated into Ge'ez (the state language of Ethiopia at the time), and the translator added a section on kingship, a portion of which is offered below. The Law of the Kings remained the law in Ethiopia until 1930, when Emperor Haile Selassie I issued the country's first modern constitution.

### CHAPTER XLIV
### KINGS

*Section I.*

**TH.** The king you appoint must be one of your brethren. It is not proper for you to appoint over yourself an alien and an infidel, lest he multiply horses, women, gold and silver [to himself]. And when he sits on the throne of his kingdom, some priests shall write for him the Divine Book, so that he may keep it by his side and read it throughout his life, in order to learn the fear of God, his Creator, to observe his commandments, and to practice them, lest his heart become proud [and feel contempt] for his brethren. He must never swerve either to the right or to the left from what has been laid down in the Law, so that his days and his sons' days may be prolonged in his kingdom [Deuteronomy 17:15f], and his faith in God may be perfect. **EB 9**. Because of faith the walls of Jericho were pulled down, when the sons of Israel marched around them for seven days. Because

Source: Excerpt from *The Fetha Nagast*, trans. Paulos Tzadua, ed. Peter L. Strauss (Durham, NC: Carolina Academic Press, 2009), 271–273.

of faith, Gideon and Barak and Samson and Jephtha and David defeated the kings, served the cause of justice, found what they hoped for, were victors in war, and defeated the army of the enemy [Hebrews 11:30, 32f]. **RSTA 54.** And if the king becomes a heretic, from that moment he is no longer a king, but a rebel.

### Section II.

Our Lord said in the Gospel: "Give to the king what is the king's and to God what is God's [Matthew 22:21]." And Apostle Paul said in his letter to the Romans: "Every one of you must be submissive to the authority of your ruler, since a ruler is appointed only by God. And God has appointed all these rulers...." [Romans 13:1f].

St. John Chrysostom, in his explanation of this passage, has said: The Apostle had already shown [this] in his other letters, commanding the [lesser] chiefs to give due obedience to the higher chiefs, as the servant must obey the master. This the Apostle did, showing that Our Lord did not abrogate all the laws by His precepts, but confirmed them. And his saying: "Every soul" is because every man must conform himself to this; and his saying: "A ruler is appointed only by God," means that God has provided for the appointment of judges and rulers to take place, so that the world may become beautifully calm. And for that reason He has established the ruler, since equality of forces causes many wars. And God in His wisdom has established many kinds of authority, such as that of a man in respect to woman, the father in respect to the son, the old in respect to the young, the master in respect to the slave, the teacher in respect to the disciple, and, more so, the chief in respect to the one who is placed under him. The Lord acted in the same manner with the body, [creating] the head and placing the other parts under it; he also did thus with other animals, such as bees, *raza*, ants, antelopes, eagles, buffaloes, and all kinds of fish—every one has its chief, and when there is no authority there is confusion and lack of order. And his words: "Since he is God's minister calling thee to good and beautiful things," mean that he will lead you daily in your obedience to God. His punishments will be directed against those who rebel against God, murderers, fornicators, thieves, and wrongdoers; but his favors go to the obedient, who obey the Highest—Whose name be praised!—to those who despite the world and to those who do works of perfection and are righteous.

. . .

### Section III.

**MAK 37.** Let the king give honor to the order of the clergy, as Constantine, elected, faithful, and righteous king, and those who were after him did. Let him give from his wealth to each of them, according to their rank. First of all he shall give to the bishops, then to the priests, next, to the deacons, and then to those who are below them. He shall exempt them from tribute, presents, and the other things to be given to the rulers. Let him assign something to the churches for the maintenance of widows, orphans, and the poor, so that they may entreat God to strengthen the true faith with belief in the Holy Trinity, so that the day of the Christians' king may be long.

. . .

### Section IV.

The king shall judge with equity in the middle of his people. He shall not be partial, either toward himself or toward the others, toward his son, his relatives, his friends, or the alien in any way

**Raza:** A type of bird.

which brings about injustice. And it is written in reference to kings: "The honored king loves justice, but the unjust king loves evil and injustice, to the ruin of his soul." And Solomon the wise has said: "To increase justice and save the oppressed is better than the offering and sacrifices" [Proverbs 21:3].

Do not take the wealth of anyone by violence; do not buy from him by force, either openly or by trick, in order not to be afflicted by God in this world and in the future. In this world, as befell the King Ahab and his wife Jezebel, when Naboth refused to sell him his vineyard and Jezebel schemed to kill him and took the vineyard; God smote Ahab and made his race perish; and next to him he smote Jezebel, and the dogs ate her in the aforesaid vineyard [2 Kings 21]. As for the future world, the Apostle said: "Wrong-doers and apostates shall not inherit God's Kingdom" [1 Corinthians 6:9].

▶ Working with Sources

1. **How does the author of this portion of the Fetha Nagast use Biblical passages and historical comparisons to accentuate his points? Why?**

2. **What is the king's primary obligation to his people? Under what conditions could he lose his power?**

## SOURCE 14.2

# Ibn Battuta on Mali, from the *Rihla*

### ca. 1354

One of the great world travelers of all time, Ibn Battuta was an educated Moroccan who journeyed throughout Africa, the Middle East, Persia, and Asia. In 1354, at age 50, Ibn Battuta dictated an account of his travels, the *Rihla* (the *Journey*), to Ibn Juzayy, a court secretary in Morocco. Both men therefore had a role to play in shaping the narrative.

I set out on the 1st Muharram of the year seven hundred and fifty-three (18 February, 1352 CE) with a caravan including amongst others a number of the merchants of Sijilmasa [present-day Morocco/Algerian frontier region]. After twenty-five days we reached Taghaza, an unattractive village, with the curious feature that its houses and mosques are built of blocks of salt, roofed with camel skins. There are no trees there, nothing but sand. In the sand is a salt mine; they dig for the salt, and find it in thick slabs, lying one on top of the other, as though they had been tool-squared and laid under the surface of the earth. A camel will carry two of these slabs. No one lives at Taghaza except the slaves of the Masufa tribe, who dig for the salt; they

Source: Ibn Battuta, "Mali," from *Travels in Asia and Africa, 1325–1354*, trans. and ed. H. A. R. Gibb (New York: Robert M. McBride, 1929), 323–327, 329–330.

subsist on dates imported from Dara and Sijilmasa, camel's flesh, and millet imported from the Negro-lands. The Negroes come up from their country and take away the salt from there. At Walata a load of salt brings eight to ten mithqals; in the town of Mali it sells for twenty to thirty, and sometimes as much as forty. The Negroes use salt as a medium of exchange, just as gold and silver is used elsewhere; they cut it up into pieces and buy and sell with it. The business done at Taghaza, for all its meanness, amounts to an enormous figure in terms of hundredweights of gold dust. . . .

Thus we reached the town of Walata after a journey of two months to a day. Walata is the northern most province of the Negroes, and the Sultan's representative there was one Farba Husayn, Farba meaning deputy (in their language). . . .

It was an excessively hot place, and boasts a few small date-palms, in the shade of which they sow watermelons. Its water comes from underground water beds at that point, and there is plenty of mutton to be had. The garments of the inhabitants, most of whom belong to the Masufa tribe, are of fine Egyptian fabrics. Their women are of surpassing beauty, and are shown more respect than the men. The state of affairs amongst these people is indeed extraordinary. Their men show no sign of jealousy whatever; no one claims descent from his father, but on the contrary from his mother's brother. A person's heirs are his sister's sons, not his own sons. This is a thing which I have seen nowhere in the world except among the Indians of Malabar. But those are heathens; these people are Muslims, punctilious in observing the hours of prayer, studying books of law, and memorizing the Koran. Yet their women show no bashfulness before men and do not veil themselves, though they are assiduous in attending prayers. Any man who wishes to marry one of them may do so, they do not travel with their husbands. . . .

The women have their "friends" and "companions" amongst the men outside their own families, and the men in the same way have "companions" amongst the women of other families. A man may go into his house and find his wife entertaining her "companion," but he takes not objection to it. One day at Walata I went into the **qadi's** house, after asking his permission to enter, and found with a young woman of remarkable beauty. When I saw her I was shocked and turned to go out, but she laughed at me, instead of being overcome by shame, and the quadi said to me, "Why are you going out? She is my companion." I was amazed at their conduct, for he was a theologian and a pilgrim to boot. I was told that he had asked the sultan's permission to make the pilgrimage that year with his "companion" (whether this one or not I cannot say) but the sultan would not grant it.

. . . On feast-days, after Dugha [interpreter] has finished his display, the poets come in. Each of them is inside a figure resembling a thrush, made of feathers, and provided with a wooden head with a red beak, to look like a thrush's head. They stand in front of the sultan in this ridiculous make-up and recite their poems. I was told that their poetry is a kind of sermonizing in which they say to the sultan: "This pempi [throne] which you occupy was that whereon sat this king and that king, and such were this one's noble actions and such and such the other's. So do you too do good deeds whose memory will outlive you." After that the chief of the poets mounts the steps

*Qadi:* A Muslim judge.

of the pempi and lays hid head on the sultan's lap, then climbs to the top of the pempi and lays his head on first on the sultan's right shoulder and then on his left, speaking all the while in their tongue, and finally he comes down again. I was told that this practice is a very old custom amongst them prior to the introduction of Islam, and they have kept it up.

. . . The Negroes possess some admirable qualities. They are seldom unjust, and have a greater abhorrence of injustice than any other people. The sultan shows no mercy to anyone who is guilty of the least act of it. There is a complete security in their country. Neither traveler nor inhabitant in it has anything to fear from robbers or men of violence. They do not confiscate the property of any white man [Arab trader] who dies in their country, even if it be accounted wealth. On the contrary, they give it into the charge of some trustworthy person among the whites, until the rightful heir takes possession of it. They are careful to observe the hours of prayer, and assiduous in attending them in congregations, and in bringing up their children to them. On Fridays, if a man does not go early to the mosque, he cannot find a corner to pray in, on account of the crowd. It is a custom of theirs to send each man his boy (to the mosque) with his prayer-mat; the boy spreads it out for his master in a place befitting him and remains on it (until his master comes to the mosque). The pray-mats are made of the leaves of a tree resembling a date-palm, but without fruit.

Another of their good qualities is their habit of wearing clean white garments on Fridays. Even if a man has nothing but an old worn shirt, he washes it and cleans it, and wears it at the Friday service. Yet another is their zeal for learning the Koran by heart. They put their children in chains if they show any backwardness in memorizing it, and they are not set free until they have it by heart. I visited the qadi in his house on the day of the festival. His children were chained up, so I said to him, "Will you not let them loose?" He replied, "I shall not do so until they learn the Koran by heart." Among their bad qualities are the following. The women servants, slave-girls, and young girls go about in front of everyone naked, without a stitch of clothing on them. Women go into the sultan's presence naked and without coverings, and his daughters also go about naked. Then there is the custom of their putting dust and ashes on their heads as a mark of respect, and the grotesque ceremonies we have described when the poets recite their verses.

▶ **Working with Sources**

1. Why does Ibn Battuta remark so often on the lack of generosity on the part of the sultan of Mali?

2. Ibn Battuta offers many details about the material culture of Mali. What does his description reveal about the interactions between Mali and other cultures? How do they interact?

SOURCE 14.3

# Golden Bracelets from the "Lost City" of Mapungubwe, South Africa

**Thirteenth century**

The archaeological site of Mapungubwe, first discovered and excavated in the 1930s, spans the borders of present-day South Africa, Zimbabwe, and Botswana. It was one of the most powerful African Iron Age states, dominating southern Africa from 1070 to 1300 and establishing trade contacts with the Middle East and India. The source of its influence was the gold mined in the territory, fashioned into objects, and then exported far beyond the borders of the kingdom.

▶ **Working with Sources**

1. How do these items crafted from gold illustrate the sophistication of Mapungubwe culture, as well as its desire to display wealth?

2. Might these particular items have been related to the social structure of Mapungubwe, and particularly to the role of royal wives?

SOURCE 14.4

# 'Abd al-'Azīz al-Bakrī, *Description of West Africa*

**1068**

Al-Bakrī was born in Spain, and it appears that he never left that country. However, he collected information from people he met who had traveled to the Sahara and the Sudan, and he published his findings in a work called *The Book of Routes and Realms* (*Kitāb al-masālik wa-'l-mamālik*).

Source: 14.3: University of Pretoria Museums, South Africa, Mapungubwe Collection, copyright University of Pretoria. 14.4: 'Abd al-'Azīz al-Bakrī, "Ghāna and the Customs of Its Inhabitants," trans. J. F. P. Hopkins, in N. Levtzion and J. F. P. Hopkins, *Corpus of Early Arabic Sources for West African History* (Cambridge, UK: Cambridge University Press, 1981), 79–81.

Al-Bakrī, who died in 1094, was famous for his curiosity about the geography, languages, and natural landscape of places he had not himself visited. The greater part of his major book is still unpublished, but the following section provides insight into the changing religious landscape in Ghana in the early eleventh century.

### GHĀNA AND THE CUSTOMS OF ITS INHABITANTS

Ghāna is a title given to their kings; the name of the region is Awkār, and their king today, namely in the year 460/1067–8, is Tunkā Manīn. He ascended the throne in 455/ 1063. The name of his predecessor was Basī and he became their ruler at the age of 85. He led a praiseworthy life on account of his love of justice and friendship for the Muslims. At the end of his life he became blind, but he concealed this from his subjects and pretended that he could see. When something was put before him he said: "This is good" or "This is bad." His ministers deceived the people by indicating to the king in cryptic words what he should say, so that the commoners could not understand.

. . .

The city of Ghāna consists of two towns situated on a plain. One of these towns, which is inhabited by Muslims, is large and possesses twelve mosques, in one of which they assemble for the Friday prayer. There are salaried imams and muezzins, as well as jurists and scholars. In the environs are wells with sweet water, from which they drink and with which they grow vegetables. The king's town is six miles distant from this one and bears the name of Al-Ghāba. Between these two towns there are continuous habitations. The houses of the inhabitants are of stone and acacia (*sunt*) wood. The king has a palace and a number of domed dwellings all surrounded with an enclosure like a city wall (*sūr*). In the king's town, and not far from his court of justice, is a mosque where the Muslims who arrive at his court (*yafid 'alayh*) pray. Around the king's town are domed buildings and groves and thickets where the sorcerers of these people, men in charge of the religious cult, live. In them too are their idols and the tombs of their kings. These woods are guarded and none may enter them and know what is there. In them also are the king's prisons. If somebody is imprisoned there no news of him is ever heard. The king's interpreters, the official in charge of his treasury and the majority of his ministers are Muslims. Among the people who follow the king's religion only he and his heir apparent (who is the son of his sister) may wear sewn clothes. All other people wear robes of cotton, silk, or brocade, according to their means. All of them shave their beards, and women shave their heads.

. . .

When the people who profess the same religion as the king approach him they fall on their knees and sprinkle dust on their heads, for this is their way of greeting him. As for the Muslims, they greet him only by clapping their hands.

Their religion is paganism and the worship of idols (*dakākīr*). When their king dies they construct over the place where his tomb will be an enormous dome of *sāj* [acacia?] wood. Then they bring him on a bed covered with a few carpets and cushions and place him beside the dome. At his side they place his ornaments, his weapons, and the vessels from which he used to eat and drink, filled with various kinds of food and beverages. They place there too the men who used to serve his meals. They close the door of the dome and cover it with mats and furnishings. Then the people assemble, who heap earth upon it until it becomes like a big hillock and dig a ditch around it until the mound can be reached at only one place.

▶ **Working with Sources**

1. Is there anything surprising, at least in al-Bakrī's description, in the reinforcement of royal authority in Ghana?

2. How was the religious balance between Muslims and non-Muslims maintained in this kingdom, and why?

## SOURCE 14.5

# Walls and moats at Sungbo's Eredo, Nigeria

**ca. 1000–1450**

The chiefdom of Ijebu encompassed a capital and villages on a territory of 22 square miles, surrounded by a deep moat and towering rampart almost 100 miles long. The iron-saturated soil would have made the construction process very difficult, especially since the labor was achieved with nothing more than iron shovels. This drawing illustrates what archaeologists believe to have been the arrangement of a typical cross section of this structure. It is named for Bilikisu Sungbo, a mythical priestess-queen who was credited with ordering the construction of the moat and rampart.

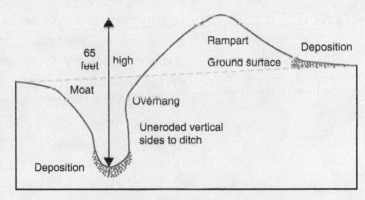

▶ **Working with Sources**

1. Was this moat and rampart constructed for defensive purposes, or for some other reason? How do the size and extent of walls and moats of Ijebu compare with defensive structures created by other civilizations in the period before 1500 CE?

2. What does the existence of this edifice reveal about the use of collective labor in Ijebu in this period?

Source: By Nyame Akuma, 1998.

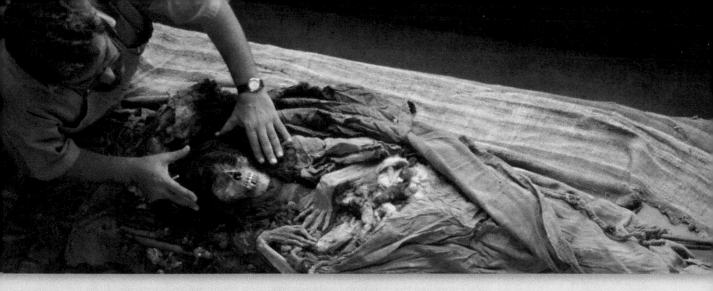

# Chapter **15** 600–1550 CE

# The Rise of Empires in the Americas

J ust outside Lima, in a sandy and dry ravine 3 miles to the east of the city, is the shantytown of Túpac Amaru, named after the last Inca ruler, who died in 1572. People fleeing the Maoist Shining Path guerillas in the highlands southeast of Lima settled here during the 1980s. Archaeologists had known for years that the site was an ancient burial place called Puruchuco (Quechua "Feathered Helmet") but could not prevent the influx of settlers. By the late 1990s, the temporary shantytown had become an established settlement with masonry houses, streets, and a school. Dwellers were anxious to acquire title to their properties, introduce urban services and utilities, and clean up ground contaminated in many places by raw sewage. However, residents realized that archaeologists had to be called in before the shantytown could be officially recognized. Túpac Amaru was facing an increasingly familiar dilemma in the developing world, pitting modern needs against the wish to know the past through discovering and (if possible) preserving its last traces.

During emergency excavations from 1999 to 2001, the archaeologist Guillermo Cock, together with Túpac Amaru residents hired as field assistants, unearthed one of the most astounding treasures in the history of American archaeology. The team discovered some 2,200 mummies, most of them bundled up in blankets and perfectly preserved with their hair, skin,

*ABOVE:* **One of 2,200 mummies from the Inca period (1438–1533) excavated in Túpac Amaru, Peru.**

eyes, and genitals intact. Many bundles also contained rich burial gifts, including jewelry, corn, potatoes, peanuts, peppers, and coca leaves. Forty bundles had false heads made of cotton cloth, some topped with wigs, making the bundles look like oversized persons.

Scholars hope that in a few years, when all of the mummies have been unwrapped, answers can be given as to the social characteristics of the buried people. Were they members of an Inca colony planted into one of the empire's provinces? Or were they locals under their own lord, recognizing Inca overlordship? Were they specialized laborers, such as weavers, who produced cloth tributes for the Incas? Were children and women sacrificed to accompany the cotton king in his journey to the afterlife? Had assimilation between the conquerors and conquered begun? These questions are difficult to answer as so much about the Inca Empire that ruled the Andes from 1438 to 1533 remains unknown. Yet the questions are exciting precisely because they could not have been posed prior to the discovery of these mummies.

The Inca Empire and its contemporary the Aztec Empire (1427–1521) grew out of political, economic, and cultural patterns that began to form around 600 CE in Mesoamerica and the Andes (see Chapter 5). At that time, kingdoms had emerged out of chiefdoms in two small areas of Mesoamerica, the southern Yucatán Peninsula and the Mexican Basin. After 600, kingdom formation became more general across Mesoamerica and arose for the first time in the Andes. These kingdoms were states with military ruling classes that used new types of weapons and could conquer larger territories than was possible prior to the 600s. Military competition prepared the way for the origin of empires—multireligious, multilinguistic, and multiethnic states encompassing many thousands of square miles. Even though empires arrived later in the Americas than in Eurasia, they demonstrate that humans, once they had adopted agriculture, followed remarkably similar patterns of social and political formation across the world.

## The Legacy of Teotihuacán and the Toltecs in Mesoamerica

As discussed in Chapter 5, the city-state of Teotihuacán had dominated northern Mesoamerica from 200 BCE to the late 500s CE. It fell into ruin probably as the result of an internal uprising against an overbearing ruling class. After its collapse, the surrounding towns and villages, as well as half a dozen other cities in and around the Mexican Basin, perpetuated the cultural legacy of Teotihuacán for centuries. Employing this legacy, the conquering state of the Toltecs unified a major part of the region for a short period from 900 to 1180. At the same time, after an internal crisis, the southern Maya kingdoms on the Yucatán Peninsula reached their late flowering, together with the northern state of Chichén Itzá.

## Seeing Patterns

▶ Within the patterns of state formation basic to the Americas, which types of states emerged in Mesoamerica and the Andes during the period 600–1550? What characterized these states?

▶ Why did the Tiwanaku and Wari states have ruling classes but no dynasties and central bureaucracies? How were these patterns expressed in the territorial organization of these states?

▶ What patterns of urban life characterized the cities of Tenochtitlán and Cuzco, the capitals of the Aztec and Inca Empires? In which ways were these cities similar to those of Eurasia and Africa?

## Militarism in the Mexican Basin

After the ruling class of Teotihuacán disintegrated at the end of the sixth century, the newly independent local lords and their supporters in the small successor states of Mesoamerica continued Teotihuacán's cultural heritage. This heritage was defined by Teotihuacán's temple style, ceramics, textiles, and religious customs, especially the cult of the feathered serpent god Quetzalcoatl [ket-sal-COA]. The Toltecs, migrants from the north, militarized the Teotihuacán legacy and transformed it into a program of conquest.

**Ceremonial Centers and Chiefdoms**　In the three centuries after the end of the city-state of Teotihuacán, the local population declined from some 200,000 to about 30,000. Although largely ruined, the ceremonial center continued to attract pilgrims, but other places around the Mexican Basin and beyond rose in importance. The semiarid region to the northwest of the valley had an extensive mining industry, with many mine shafts extending a mile or more into the mountains. The region produced gemstones such as greenstone, turquoise, hematite, and cinnabar. Independent after 600, inhabitants built ceremonial centers and small states of their own, trading their gemstones to their neighbors in all directions.

To the north were the Pueblo cultures in today's southwestern United States. These cultures were based on sophisticated irrigated farming systems and are known for their distinctive painted pottery styles. They flourished between 700 and 1500 in the canyons of what are today the states of New Mexico, Arizona, southwestern Colorado, and southeastern Utah. In turn, these cultures might have been in contact with the Mississippi cultures, among which the ceremonial center and city of Cahokia (650–1400) near modern St. Louis is the best-known site. An obsidian scraper from the Pachuca region north of the Mexican Basin found in Spiro Mounds, Oklahoma, attests to at least occasional contacts between Mesoamerica and the Mississippi culture (see Map 15.1).

In western Mesoamerica, ceremonial centers and chiefdoms flourished on the basis of metallurgy, which arrived through Ecuadoran seaborne merchants ca. 600–800. The Ecuadorans received their copper from Peru, in return for seashells found in the warm waters off their coast as well as farther north. Copper, too soft for agricultural implements or military weapons, served mostly in households and as jewelry for the rich.

In the south, a number of small, fortified hilltop states flourished in the post-Teotihuacán period. Their inhabitants built moats and ramparts to protect these states. More than in other Mesoamerican states, the southern ruling classes were embroiled in fierce wars during 600–900, images of which are depicted in stone reliefs of gruesome battle scenes.

**The Toltec Conquering State**　Early after the collapse of Teotihuacán, craftspeople and farmers migrated some 60 miles north to Tula, a place on a ridge in the highlands watered by two tributaries of a river flowing into the Gulf of Mexico. They founded a small ceremonial center and town with workshops known for the high quality of the scrapers, knives, and spear points fabricated from the local Pachuca obsidian. Around 900, new migrants arrived from northwest Mexico as well as the Gulf Coast. The northerners spoke Nahuatl [NA-hua], the language of the later Aztecs, who considered Tula their ancestral city.

MAP 15.1 **North America and Mesoamerica, ca. 1100.**

The integration of the new arrivals was apparently not peaceful, since it re-sulted in the abandonment of the temple and the departure of a defeated party of Tulans. This abandonment may well have been enshrined in the myth of Tolpiltzin, a priest-king of the feathered serpent god Quetzalcoatl, who after his departure to the east would one day return to restore the cult to its rightful center. Later, Spaniards used the myth to justify their rule in the Americas (see Chapter 18).

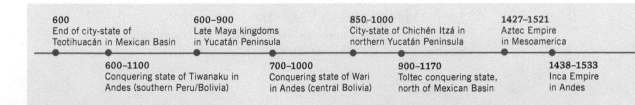

| 600 | 600–900 | 850–1000 | 1427–1521 |
|---|---|---|---|
| End of city-state of Teotihuacán in Mexican Basin | Late Maya kingdoms in Yucatán Peninsula | City-state of Chichén Itzá in northern Yucatán Peninsula | Aztec Empire in Mesoamerica |

| 600–1100 | 700–1000 | 900–1170 | 1438–1533 |
|---|---|---|---|
| Conquering state of Tiwanaku in Andes (southern Peru/Bolivia) | Conquering state of Wari in Andes (central Bolivia) | Toltec conquering state, north of Mexican Basin | Inca Empire in Andes |

The new Tula of 900 developed quickly into a large city with a new temple, 60,000 urban dwellers, and perhaps another 60,000 farmers on surrounding lands. It was the first city-centered state to give pictorial prominence to the sacrifice of captured warriors. As it evolved, Tula became the capital of the conquering state of the Toltecs, which imprinted its warrior culture on large parts of Mesoamerica from around 900 to 1180 (see Map 15.1).

The Toltecs introduced two innovations in weaponry that improved the effectiveness of hand-to-hand combat. First, there was the new weapon of a short (1.5-foot) sword made of hardwood with inlaid obsidian edges, which could slash as well as crush, in contrast to the obsidian-spiked clubs that had been the primary weapons in earlier times. Second, warriors wore obsidian daggers with wooden handles inside a band on the left arm, replacing simpler obsidian blades, which were difficult to use as they had no handles. Traditional dart throwers and slings for stone projectiles completed the offensive armament of the warriors.

The Toltec army of 13,000–26,000 soldiers was sufficiently large to engage in battles of conquest within an area of 4 days' march (roughly 40 miles) away from Tula. Any target beyond this range was beyond their capabilities, given the logistics of armor, weapons, food rations, narrow dirt roads, and uneven terrain—and, of course, Toltecs did not have the benefit of wheeled vehicles. Thus, the only way of projecting power beyond the range of 40 miles was to establish colonies and to have troops accompany traders, each of which could then supply themselves by foraging or through trade along the way. As a result, the Toltec state projected its power through the prestige of its large military, rather than through a full-scale administrative scheme with the imposition of governors, tributes, and taxes.

**Trade**    Apart from demonstrating military might, the Toltecs pursued the establishment of a large trade network. Merchants parlayed Tula's obsidian production into a trade network that radiated southward into the cacao, vanilla, and bird-feather production centers of Chiapas and Guatemala; to the north into gemstone mining regions; and westward into centers of metal mining. Metallurgy advanced around 1200 with the development of the technology of bronze casting. Bronze axes were stronger and more useful for working with wood than copper axes. Bronze bells produced a greater variety of sounds than those of copper. As ornamental objects, both were trade goods highly prized by the elites in Tula.

**The Late Toltec Era**    Toltec military power declined in the course of the twelfth century when the taxable grain yield around the city diminished, because of either prolonged droughts or a depletion of the topsoil on the terraces, or a combination of the two. Sometime around 1180, a new wave of foraging peoples from the northwest invaded, attacking with bows and arrows and using hit-and-run tactics against Toltec communication lines. The disruptions caused an internal revolt, which brought down the ceremonial center and its palaces. By 1200, Tula was a city with a burned-out center, like Teotihuacán six centuries earlier, and Mesoamerica relapsed into a period of small-state coexistence like that of the pre-600 period.

## Late Maya States in Yucatán

Teotihuacán's demise at the end of the sixth century was paralleled by a realignment of the balance of power among the Maya kingdoms in the southern Yucatán lowlands of Mesoamerica. This realignment, accompanied by extensive warfare, was resolved by around 650. A period of late flowering spanned the next two centuries, followed by a shift of power from the southern to the northern part of the peninsula.

**The Southern Kingdoms** At its height during the fourth and fifth centuries, Teotihuacán in the Mexican Basin had interjected itself into the delicate balance of power existing among the Maya kingdoms of southern Yucatán. Alliances among the states shifted, and prolonged wars of conquest racked the lowlands, destroying several older states. A dozen new kingdoms emerged and established a new balance of power among themselves. After a lengthy hiatus, Maya culture entered its final period (650–900).

The most striking phenomenon of the final period in the southern, rain forest–covered lowlands and adjacent highlands were massive new programs of agricultural expansion and ceremonial monument construction. Agriculture was expanded again through cutting down the rain forest on hillsides and terracing the hills for soil retention. The largest kingdoms grew to 50,000–60,000 inhabitants and reached astounding rural population densities of about 1,000 persons per square mile. (In comparison, England's most densely populated counties just prior to its agricultural expansion after 1700 were Middlesex and Surrey, with 221 and 207 persons per square mile, respectively.) Although the late Maya states were geographically small, they were administratively the most centralized polities ever created in indigenous American history.

The late Maya states did not last long. In spite of all efforts, the usually torrential downpours of the rainy season gradually washed the topsoil from the newly built hillside terraces. The topsoil, accumulating as alluvium in the flatlands, was initially quite fertile, but from around 800 onward it became more and more depleted of nutrients. In addition, in many wetlands, farmers found it difficult to prevent clay from forming over the alluvium and hardening in the process. Malnutrition resulting from the shrinking agricultural surface began to reduce the labor force. Ruling classes had to make do with fewer workers and smaller agricultural surpluses. In the end, even the ruling classes suffered, with members killing each other for what remained of these surpluses. By about 900, the Maya kingdoms in southern Yucatán had shriveled to the size of chiefdoms with small towns and villages.

**Chichén Itzá in the North** A few small Maya states on the periphery survived. The most prominent among them was Chichén Itzá [chee-CHEN eat-SA] in the northern lowlands, which flourished from about 850 to 1000. At first glance the region would appear to be less than hospitable to a successful state. The climate in the north was much drier than that in the south. The surface was rocky or covered with thin topsoil, supporting mostly grass, scrub vegetation, and isolated forests. In many places, where the soil was too saline, agriculture was impossible, and the production of salt was the only source of income. There were no rivers, but many sinkholes in the porous limestone underneath the soil held water. Countless cisterns to hold additional amounts of water for year-round use were cut into the limestone and plastered to prevent seepage. This water, carried in jars to the surface, supported an intensive garden agriculture, productive enough to sustain entire towns and city-states.

**Chacmool (Offering Table) at the Entrance to the Temple of Warriors, Chichén Itzá.** Chacmools originated here and spread to numerous places in Mesoamerica, as far north as Tenochtitlán and Tula. Offerings to the gods included food, tobacco, feathers, and incense. Offerings might have included also human sacrifices. The table in the form of a prostrate human figure is in itself symbolic of sacrifice.

Chichén Itzá was founded during the phase of renewed urbanization in 650. It was built near two major sinkholes and several salt flats. The population was composed of local Maya as well as the Maya-speaking Chontal from the Gulf Coast farther west. Groups among these people engaged in long-distance trade, both overland and in boats along the coast. Since trade in the most lucrative goods (such as cacao, vanilla, jade, copper, bronze, turquoise, and obsidian) required contact with people well outside even the farthest political reach of either Teotihuacán or Tula, merchants (*pochtecas* [potsh-TAY-cas]) traveled in armed caravans. These merchant groups enjoyed considerable freedom and even sponsorship by the ruling classes of the states of Mesoamerica.

Chontal traders adopted Toltec culture, and when they based themselves in Chichén Itzá around 850 they superimposed their adopted culture over that of the original Maya. How the city was ruled is only vaguely understood, but there is some evidence that there were two partially integrated ruling factions, possibly descended from the Chontal and local Maya, sharing in the governance of the city. At the very end of the period of Teotihuacán, Maya, and Toltec cultural expansion, the three cultural traditions finally merged on the Yucatán Peninsula in only one geographically marginal place. This merger, however, did not last long; already around 1000 the ruling-class factions left the city-state for unknown reasons. As a result, the city-state diminished in size and power to town level.

## The Legacy of Tiwanaku and Wari in the Andes

Mesoamerica and the Andes, from the time of chiefdom formation in 2500 BCE in Caral-Supé onward, shared the tradition of regional temple pilgrimages. In the Andes, the chiefdoms remained mostly coastal, with some inland extensions along valleys of the Andes. Around 600 CE, the two conquering states of Tiwanaku in the highlands of what are today southern Peru and Bolivia and Wari in central Peru emerged. Both states encompassed tens of thousands of inhabitants and represented a major step in the formation of larger, militarily organized polities.

### The Expanding State of Tiwanaku

Tiwanaku was a political and cultural power center in the south-central Andes during the period 600–1100. It began as a ceremonial center with surrounding villages and gradually developed into a state dominating the region around Lake Titicaca. At its apogee it was an expanding state, planting colonies in regions far from the lake and conveying its culture through trade to peoples even beyond the colonies.

**Agriculture on the High Plain**  The Andes consist of two parallel mountain chains stretching along the west coast of South America. For the most part, these chains are close together, divided by small plains, valleys, and lower mountains. In southeastern Peru and western Bolivia an intermountain plain, 12,500 feet above sea level, extends as wide as 125 miles. At its northern end lies Lake Titicaca, subdivided into a larger and deeper northern basin and a smaller, shallower, swampy, and reed-covered southern basin. Five major and 20 smaller rivers coming from the eastern Andes chain feed Lake Titicaca, which has one outlet at its southern end, a river flowing into Lake Poopó [po-POH], a salt lake 150 miles south. The Lake Titicaca region, located above the tree line, receives winter rains sufficient for agriculture and grazing, whereas the southern plain around Lake Poopó is too dry to sustain more than steppes.

**Tiwanaku, Kalassaya Gate.** Within the Temple of the Sun, this gate is aligned with the sun's equinoxes and was used for festive rituals. Note the precise stone work, which the Incas later developed further.

In spite of its elevation, the region around Lake Titicaca offered nearly everything necessary for an advanced urbanization process. The lake's freshwater supported fish and resources such as reeds from the swamps, which served for the construction of boats and roofs. Corn flourished only in the lower elevations of the Andes and had to be imported, together with the corn-derived *chicha*, a beer-like drink. Instead of corn, the food staples were potatoes and quinoa. The grasslands of the upper hills served as pastures for llama and alpaca herds. Llamas were used as transportation animals, and alpacas provided wool. The meat of both animals—preserved for winter through drying—was a major protein source. Although frost was an ever-present danger in Tiwanaku, nutrition was quite diversified.

Farmers grew their crops on hillside terraces, where runoff water could be channeled, or on raised fields close to the lake. The raised-field system, which farmers had adopted through interaction with the peoples of the Maya lowlands, consisted of a grid of narrow strips of earth, separated from each other by channels. Mud from the channels, heaped onto the strips, replenished their fertility. A wooden foot plow, perhaps with a bronze blade, seems to have been the main farming implement, although hard archaeological proof is still elusive. By 500, the combined sustenance from fishing, hunting, farming, and herding supported dozens of villages and, by 700, the city of Tiwanaku and its 20,000 inhabitants.

Coordinated with the calendar as well as life-cycle events (such as initiation rituals), ceremonial feasts brought together elite lineages and clients, or ordinary craftspeople and villagers. Elites and clients cohered through **reciprocity**—that is, communal labor for the construction of the ceremonial centers and elaborate feasting, in which elite wealth was expended for the ceremonial leveling of status differences. Until shortly before the end of the state, it does not appear that this reciprocity gave way to more forcible ways of allocating labor through conscription or taxation.

**Reciprocity:** In its basic form, an informal agreement among people according to which a gift or an invitation has to be returned after a reasonable amount of time; in the pre-Columbian Americas, an arrangement of feasts instead of taxes shared by ruling classes and subjects in a state.

**Expansion and Colonization**  Like Tiwanaku, the core region around the southern basin of Lake Titicaca housed a set of related but competing elite–client hierarchies. Ruling clans with intermediate leaders and ordinary farmers in the villages comprised a state capable of imposing military power beyond the center. But counterbalancing clans at the head of similar hierarchies prevented the rise of dynasties that would command permanent, unified central administrations and military forces.

The projection of power over the northern lake, therefore, was not primarily of a military nature: The prevalent form of Tiwanaku authority was the outstanding prestige of its ceremonial center. This center attracted pilgrims not merely from the northern lake but also from more distant regions. Pilgrims partaking in Tiwanaku feasting ceremonies can be considered extensions of the reciprocity and clientage system of the ruling classes and, hence, of Tiwanaku power.

But there were also armed trading caravans and the foundation of colonies in the western valleys of the Andes, where military force played a role. Merchants accompanied by warriors and llama drivers crossed multiple polities in order to exchange textiles and ceramics for basalt cores in the south, metal ingots and obsidian cores in the north, and coca leaves and other psychotropic substances in the east, often hundreds of miles away. Settler colonies were additional forms of power projection, especially those established in the Moquegua [mow-KAY-gah] valley 200 miles, or 10–12 days of walking, to the west. Here, at some 2,800 feet above sea level, Tiwanaku emigrants established villages, which sent their corn or beer to the capital in return for salt, as well as stone and obsidian tools. Although overall less militarily inclined than the Mesoamerican states of the same time period, Tiwanaku wielded a visible influence over southern Peru (see Map 15.2).

## The Expanding City-State of Wari

Little is known about early settlements in central Peru, some 450 miles, or 3–4 weeks of foot travel, north from Tiwanaku. The state of Wari emerged around 600 from a number of small polities organized around ceremonial centers. Expansion to the south put Wari into direct contact with Tiwanaku. The two states came to some form of mutual accommodation, and it appears that neither embarked on an outright conquest of the other. Their military postures remained limited to their regional spheres of influence.

**Origins and Expansion**    Wari was centered on the Ayacucho valley, a narrow plain in the highlands of northern Peru. Here, the land between the two chains of the Andes is mountainous, interspersed with valleys and rivers flowing to the Pacific or the Amazon. The elevation of 8,000 feet in the Ayacucho valley allowed for the cultivation of potatoes as well as corn and cotton. In the course of the seventh century, Wari grew into a city of 30,000 inhabitants and brought a number of neighboring cities under its control. It also pushed for an enlargement of the agricultural base through the expansion of terrace farming. Like Tiwanaku, Wari eventually became the center of a developed urbanism and a diversified agriculture.

In addition to maintaining control over the cities in its vicinity, Wari employed architects who constructed new towns. These planned centers included plazas, housing for laborers, and halls for feasting. Outside the core area, Wari elites established colonies between 100 and 450 miles away. It appears that Wari exercised much stronger political control over the elites of its core region than Tiwanaku and was more active in founding colonies.

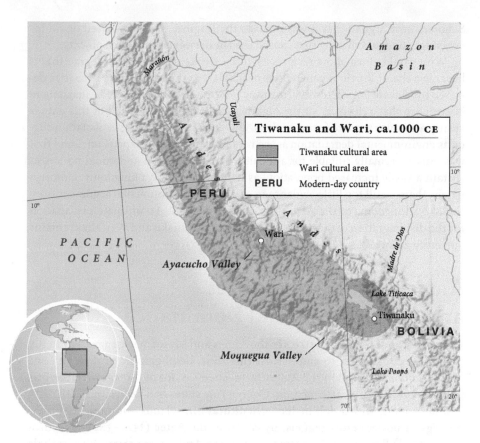

MAP 15.2 **Tiwanaku and Wari, ca. 1000.**

**The Wari–Tiwanaku Frontier**    Early on, Wari established a colony upstream in the Moquegua valley near southern Peru's west coast, some 100 miles southeast. The settlers built extensive terraces and canals together with protective walls and settlements on mountain peaks. This building activity coincided with the establishment by Tiwanaku of downstream farming colonies. It is possible that there was considerable tension with Tiwanaku during the initial period (650–800) over the division of water between the two colonies. But during 800–1000 the two agricultural communities developed closer ties, with indications that the two local elites engaged in a peaceful sharing of the water resources and common feasting activities. Very likely, the Moquegua valley was politically so far on the periphery of both states that neither had the means to impose itself on the other.

In its evolution, Wari was an expanding state very similar to Tiwanaku. Both were governed by elite clans under leaders who derived their strength from reciprocal patron–client organizations binding leaders to farmers and craftspeople. Extensive feasts strengthened the bond. Something must have happened to erode this bond, however, since there is evidence of increased internal tension after 950 in the two states. Groups arose which defaced sculptures, destroyed portals, and burned down edifices. Somehow, crowds previously happy to uphold elite control in return for participation in the lavish feasts provided by the elites must have become angry at these elites, their ceremonies, and the temple sculptures.

Scholars have argued that it was perhaps the fragility of power based on an increasingly unequal sharing that caused the rift between elites and subjects.

Why would elites allow reciprocity to be weakened to such a degree that it became a sham? Previous generations of scholars argued that climatic change deprived the elites of the wherewithal to throw large feasts. In the case of Tiwanaku there is evidence that a drought hit the high plain beginning in 1040, but this date is clearly a century too late for an explanation. A more convincing explanation suggests environmental degradation as the result of agricultural expansion. Land that was only marginally suitable for agriculture was exhausted and could no longer sustain a vastly increased population, as with the late Maya kingdoms. Unfortunately, there is still too little evidence to extend the environmental argument from the Maya kingdoms to the Andes highland and sierra. An ultimate explanation for the disintegration of the expanding states of Tiwanaku and Wari thus remains currently elusive.

# American Empires: Aztec and Inca Origins and Dominance

Expanding and conquering states in the Andes and Mesoamerica gave way in the early fifteenth century to empires. At this time, demographic growth and the evolution of militarism in the Americas reached a point of transition to the pattern of imperial political formation. Conquering states had been cities with ceremonial centers, which dominated agricultural hinterlands and projected their prestige or power across regions. By contrast, the Aztec (1427–1521) and Inca (1438–1533) Empires in Mesoamerica and the Andes were states with capitals and ceremonial centers, vastly larger tributary hinterlands, and armies capable of engaging in campaigns at distances twice (or more) as far as previous states could. As in Eurasia, they were centralized multireligious, multiethnic, and multilinguistic polities: empires in every sense of the word.

## The Aztec Empire of Mesoamerica

Forming part of the Uto-Aztecan–speaking group of Native Americans originating in the Great Basin of the American Southwest, the ancestors of the Aztecs entered Mexico at an unknown time as migrants in search of a better life. They found this life eventually as conquerors of the Mexican Basin, the site of today's Mexico City (after the drainage of most of the valley). In the course of the fifteenth century they conquered an empire that eventually encompassed Mesoamerica from the Pacific to the Gulf of Mexico and from the middle of modern northern Mexico to the Isthmus of Panama.

**Settlement in the Mexican Valley**  Once arrived in northern Mexico, the Aztecs traced their beginnings to a founding myth. According to this myth, the first Aztec was one of seven brothers born on an island in a lake or in a mountain cave 150 leagues (450 miles) northwest of the Mexican Basin. The distance, recorded by Spaniards in the sixteenth century, can be interpreted as corresponding to a mountain in the modern state of Guanajuato [goo-wa-na-hoo-WA-to]. This Aztec ancestor and his descendants migrated south as foragers dressed in skins and lacking agriculture and urban civilization. Their hunter–warrior patron god Huitzilpochtli [hoo-it-zil-POSHT-lee] guided them to a promised land of plenty.

After settling for a while in Tula (claimed later as a place of heritage), their god urged the foragers to move on to the Mexican Basin. Here, an eagle perched on a cactus commanded the Aztecs to settle and build a temple to their god. In this temple, they were to nourish him with the sacrificial blood of humans captured in war. Like many peoples in Eurasia as well as the contemporary Incas, the Aztecs contrasted their later empire and its glory with a myth of humble beginnings and long periods of wandering toward an eventual promised land.

The historical record in the Mexican Basin becomes clearer in the fourteenth century. In the course of this period, the Aztecs appeared as clients of two Toltec-descended overlords in states on the southwestern shore. Here, they created the two islands of Tenochtitlán [te-notsh-tit-LAN] and Tlatelolco [tla-te-LOL-co], founded a city with a ceremonial center on Tenochtitlán, engaged in farming and rendered military service to their overlords. Thanks to successes on the battlefield, Aztec leaders were able to marry into the elites of the neighboring city-states and gained the right to have their own ruler ("speaker," *tlatloani* [tla-tlo-AH-nee]) presiding over a council of leading members of the elite and priests. Toward the end of the fourteenth century, an emerging Aztec elite was firmly integrated with the ruling classes of many of the two dozen or so city-states in and around the valley.

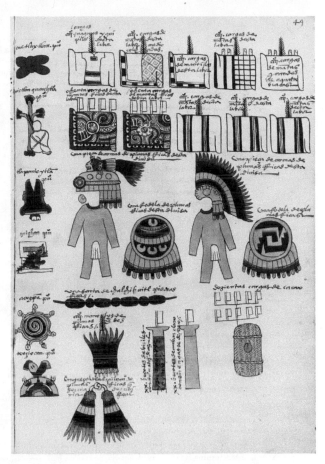

**List of Tributes Owed to the Aztecs.** The list includes quantities of cotton and wool textiles, clothes, headgear with feathers, and basketry. The Aztecs did not continue the complex syllabic script of the Maya but used instead images, including persons with speech bubbles, for communication. Spanish administrators and monks who copied the Aztec manuscripts added their own explanations to keep track of Native American tributes.

**The Rise of the Empire**    After a successful rebellion in 1428 of a triple alliance among the Aztec city state of Tenochtitlán and two other vassal states against the reigning city-state in the Mexican Basin the Aztec leader Itzcóatl [its-CO-aw] (r. 1428–1440) emerged as the dominant figure. Itzcóatl and his three successors, together with the rulers of the two allied states, expanded their city-states on the two islands and the shore through conquests into a full-fledged empire. Tenochtitlán, on one of the islands, became the capital of what became an empire that consisted of a set of six "inner provinces" in the Mexican Basin. Local elites were left in place, but they were required to attend ceremonies in Tenochtitlán, bring and receive gifts, leave their sons as hostages, and intermarry with the elites of the triple alliance. Commoner farmers outside the cities had to provide tributes in the form of foodstuffs and labor services, making the imperial core self-sufficient.

After the middle of the fifteenth century, the triple alliance conquered a set of 55 city-states outside the valley as "outer provinces." It created an imperial polity from the Pacific to the Gulf, from Tarasco, 200 miles to the northwest, to Oaxaca, over 500 miles to the south (see Map 15.3). This state was now far more centralized than the preceding Teotihuacán and Toltec city-states. In this empire, local ruling families with their ceremonial centers and gods were generally left in place,

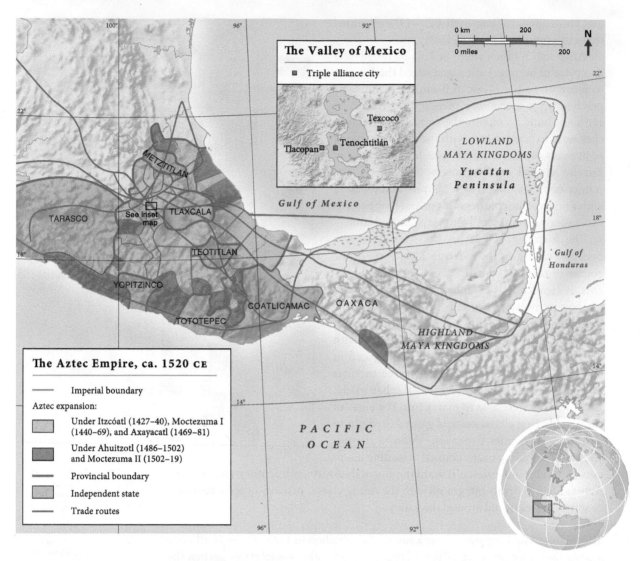

MAP 15.3 **The Aztec Empire, ca. 1520.**

but commoners had to produce tributes in the form of raw materials or lightweight processed and manufactured goods.

In some provinces, Aztec governors replaced the rulers; in most others, Aztec tribute collectors (supported by troops) held local rulers in check and supervised the transportation of the tributes by porters to the valley. Reciprocity, once of central importance in Mesoamerica, continued on a grand scale but was now clearly subordinate to military considerations.

The resulting multiethnic, multireligious, and multilinguistic empire of eventually some 19 million inhabitants was still a work in progress in the early sixteenth century when the Spanish arrived. Right in the middle of the empire, just 50 miles east of the Mexican Basin, the large state of Tlaxcala [tlash-KAH-lah], Nahuatl-speaking like the Aztecs, held out in opposition, together with multiple enemy states on the periphery. Although the ruling elites of the triple alliance did everything to expand, even inviting enemy rulers to their festivities in order to secure their loyalty through gestures of reciprocity, pockets of anti-Aztec states survived and eventually became crucial allies of the Spanish, providing the latter's tiny military forces with a critical mass of fighters.

Some outer provinces possessed strategic importance, with Aztec colonies implanted to prepare for eventual conquest of remaining enemies outside the empire. The most relentlessly pursued policy of continued expansion of Aztec central control was the threat of warfare, for the purpose of capturing rebels or enemies as prisoners of war to be sacrificed to the gods in the ceremonial centers. This fear-inducing tactic—or "power propaganda"—was an integral innovation in the imperialism of the Aztecs.

**Aztec Weapons.** Aztec weapons were well-crafted hardwood implements with serrated obsidian edges, capable of cutting through metal, including iron. As slashing weapons they were highly effective in close combat.

**The Military Forces** The triple alliance ruled a Nahuatl-speaking population of some 1.5 million inhabitants in the core provinces of the Mexican Basin. This number yielded a maximum of a quarter of a million potential soldiers, taking into consideration that most soldiers were farmers with agricultural obligations. From this large number of adult males, the Aztecs assembled units of 8,000 troops each, which they increased as the need arose. Initially, the army was recruited from among the elite of the Aztecs and their allies. But toward the middle of the fifteenth century, Aztec rulers set up a military school system for the sons of the elite plus those commoners who were to become priests. A parallel school system for the sons of commoners, aged 15–20 years, also included military training. After graduation, recruits began as porters, carrying supplies for the combat troops—an Aztec innovation which considerably enlarged the marching range of armies on campaign. Soldiers rose in the army hierarchy on the basis of merit, particularly as demonstrated by their success in the capture of enemies for future sacrifice.

The Aztecs inherited the weaponry and armor of the Toltecs but also made some important innovations. The bow and arrow, which arrived from northwest Mexico at the end of Toltec rule, became a standard weapon in Aztec armies. In addition, perhaps as late as the fifteenth century, the Aztecs developed the three-foot obsidian-spiked broadsword, derived from the Toltec short sword, in order to enhance the latter's slashing force. As a result, clubs, maces, and axes declined in importance in the Aztec arsenal. Thrusting spears, dart throwers, and slings continued to be used as standard weapons. Body armor, consisting of quilted, sleeveless cotton shirts, thick cotton helmets, and round wooden or cane shields, was adopted from the Toltecs. With the arrival of the Aztecs, the Americas had acquired the heaviest infantry weaponry in their history, reflective of the intensity of militarism in their society—a militarism which was also typical of the earlier empires of the beginning Iron Age in the Middle East.

"When a child was born, his parents would put him into the Calmécac [elite school] or in the Telpochcalli [commoner school], that is, they would promise the child as a gift [to the patron divinity], . . . that he would become a priest . . . or . . . become a warrior."

*—Florentine Codex*

## The Inca Empire of the Andes

After the disintegration of Tiwanaku and Wari around 1100, the central Andes returned to the traditional politics of local chiefdoms in small city-states with ceremonial centers and agricultural hinterlands. The best-known city-state was Chimú on the Peruvian coast, with its capital of Chan Chan numbering

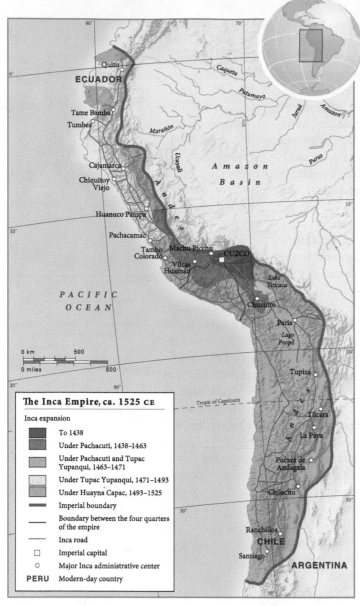

MAP 15.4 **The Inca Empire, ca. 1525.**

The Inca Empire, ca. 1525 CE

Inca expansion

- To 1438
- Under Pachacuti, 1438–1463
- Under Pachacuti and Tupac Yupanqui, 1463–1471
- Under Tupac Yupanqui, 1471–1493
- Under Huayna Capac, 1493–1525
- Imperial boundary
- Boundary between the four quarters of the empire
- Inca road
- □ Imperial capital
- ○ Major Inca administrative center
- **PERU** Modern-day country

30,000 inhabitants. Tiwanaku cultural traditions, however, remained dominant and were expressed in religious ceremonies, textile motifs, and ceramic styles.

Given the fierce competition among the pilgrimage centers, insecurity was rampant during the period 1100–1400, with particular influence granted to charismatic military leaders who could project military force and pacify the land. After a gestation period during the fourteenth century, the southern Peruvian city-state of Cuzco with its Inca elite emerged in the early fifteenth century at the head of a highly militaristic conquering polity. Within another century, the Incas had established an empire, called Tawantinsuyu [ta-wan-tin-SOO-yuh] (Quechua "Four Regions"), symbolizing its geographical expanse. It stretched from Ecuador in the north to central Chile in the south, with extensions into the tropical upper Amazon region and western Argentinean steppes (see Map 15.4).

As in the case of the Aztecs, the founding myth of the Incas involves a cave, an island, and a promised land of rich agriculture. In one version, the creator god Viracocha [vee-rah-KO-chah] summoned four brothers and four sisters from caves seven leagues (21 miles) from Cuzco to the south, pairing them as couples and promising them a land of plenty. They would find this land when a golden rod, to be used on their wanderings, would get stuck in the soil. Alternatively, the sun god Inti [IN-tee] did the pairing of the couples on an island in Lake Titicaca and thereby bestowed the glory of Tiwanaku on them, before sending them with the golden rod to their promised land. Cuzco, where the rod plunged into the fertile soil, was settled land, however, and a war ensued in which the Incas drove out the existing farmers.

In the fourteenth century, Cuzco became a serious contender in the city-state competition. Like Wari, Cuzco was located at a highland elevation of 11,300 feet between the two Andes chains of southern Peru, roughly one-third of the way from Lake Titicaca north to Wari. Eight rulers (*curacas* [koo-RA-kas]) are said to have succeeded each other in the consolidation of Cuzco as a regional power. Although their names are recorded, events are hazy and dates are missing altogether. Firm historical terrain is reached with the ninth ruler, Pachacuti (r. 1438–1471). The history of the Incas from 1438 onwards is known much better, primarily because of the memories of the grandchildren of the fifteenth-century Inca conquerors, recorded by the Spanish who defeated them in their conquest.

**Imperial Expansion** The system of reciprocity that characterized earlier Mesoamerican and Andean history continued under the Incas but was also, as in the case of Aztecs, decisively cast in the mold of power-enforced unilateralism. *Ayllu* [AY-yoo], the Quechua term for a household with an ancestral lineage, implied mutual obligations among groups of households, neighborhoods, villages, and city-states. To negotiate these obligations, Inca society—from households to provinces—was divided into two halves with roughly equal reciprocities. At the elite level, there were two sets of reciprocities, the first within two main branches of the elite and the second between the two branches of the elite and the subjects. The most important social expression of reciprocity remained the feast. In the Incan Empire, the state collected considerably more from the subject *ayllus* than Tiwanaku and Wari had done, but whether it returned comparable amounts through feasts and celebrations was a matter of contention, often leading to armed rebellion.

The earliest conquests under Pachacuti were toward the near south around Lake Titicaca, as well as the agriculturally rich lands north of the former Wari state. Thereafter, in the later fifteenth century, the Incas expanded 1,300 miles northward to southern Ecuador and 1,500 miles southward to Chile. The final provinces, added in the early sixteenth century, were in northern Ecuador as well as on the eastern slopes of the Andes, from the upper Amazon to western Argentina. The capital, Cuzco, which counted some 100,000 inhabitants in the early sixteenth century, was laid out in a cross-shaped grid of four streets leading out into the suburbs. Symbolically, as indicated by the empire's Quechua name, the capital reached out to the four regions of the empire—coast, north, south, and Amazon rain forest.

**Administration** Ethnic Inca governors administered the four regions, which were subdivided into a total of some 80 provinces, each again with an Inca subgovernor. Most provinces were composites of former city-states, which remained under their local elites but had to accept a unique decimal system of population organization imposed by the Inca rulers. According to this system, members of the local elites commanded 10,000, 1,000, 100, and 10 household, or *ayllu*, heads for the purpose of recruiting the manpower for the *mit'a* [MIT-ah] ("to take a turn," in reference to service obligations rotating among the subjects). The services, which subjects owed the empire as a form of taxes, were in farming, herding, manufacturing, military service, and portage. In its structure it was not unlike the Ming and Qing Chinese systems of local organization called *baojia* (see Chapter 12).

The *mit'a* was perhaps the single most important innovation the Incas contributed to the history of the Americas. In contrast to the Aztecs, who shipped taxes in kind to their capital by boat, the Incas had no efficient means of transportation for long distances. The only way to make use of the taxes in kind was to store them locally. The Incas built tens of thousands of storehouses everywhere in their empire, requiring subjects to deliver a portion of their harvests, animal products, and domestically produced goods under *mit'a* obligations to the nearest storehouse in their vicinity. These supplies were available to officials and troops and enabled the Incas to conduct military campaigns far from Cuzco without the need for foraging among local farmers. In addition, it was through the *mit'a* that quotas of laborers were raised for the construction of inns, roads, ceremonial centers, palaces, terraces, and irrigation canals, often far away from the urban center. Finally, *mit'a* provided laborers for mines, quarries, state and temple farms, and colonies. No form of labor or service went untaxed.

To keep track of *mit'a* obligations, officials passed bundles of knotted cord (*quipú*, or *khipu* [KEE-poo], "knot") upward from level to level in the imperial administration. The numbers of knots on each cord in the bundles contained information on population figures and service obligations. As discussed in Chapter 5, the use of quipús was widespread in the Andes long before the Inca and can be considered as the Andean equivalent of a communication system. The only innovation contributed by the Incas seems to have been the massive scale on which these cord bundles were generated and employed. Some 700 have been preserved. Unfortunately, all modern attempts to decipher them have so far failed, and thus it is impossible to accurately outline the full picture of Inca service allocations.

**Inca Roads.** Inca roads were paths reserved for runners and the military. They were built on beds of rocks and rubble and connected strategic points in the most direct line possible.

**Military Organization**   Perhaps the most important *mit'a* obligation which subject households owed to the Inca in the conquest phase of the empire was the service of young, able-bodied men in the military. Married men 25–30 years old were foot soldiers, often accompanied by wives and children; unmarried men 18–25 years of age served as porters or messengers. As in the Aztec Empire, administrators made sure that enough laborers remained in the villages to take care of their other obligations of farming, herding, transporting, and manufacturing. Sources report armies in the range of 35,000–140,000. Intermediate commanders came from the local and regional elites, and the top commanders were members of the two upper and lower Inca ruling elites.

Inca weaponry was comparable to that of the Aztecs, consisting of bows and arrows, dart throwers, slings, clubs with spiked bronze heads, wooden broadswords, bronze axes, and bronze-tipped javelins. Using Bolivian tin, Inca smiths were able to make a much harder and more useful bronze than was possible with earlier techniques. The Incas lacked the Aztec obsidian-serrated swords but used a snare (which the Aztecs did not possess) with attached stone or bronze weights to entangle the enemy's legs. Protective armor consisted of quilted cotton shirts, copper breastplates, cane helmets, and shields. These types of weapons and armor were widely found among the Incas and their enemies. The advantage enjoyed by the Incas resulted from the sheer massiveness of their weapons and supplies, procured from craftspeople through the *mit'a* and stored in strategically located armories.

During the second half of the fifteenth century the Incas turned from conquest to consolidation. Faced at that time with a number of rebellions, they deemphasized the decimal draft and recruited longer-serving troops from among a smaller number of select, trusted peoples. These troops garrisoned the forts distributed throughout the empire. They also were part of the settler colonies implanted in rebellious provinces and in border regions. The fiercest resistance came from the people of the former Tiwanaku state and from the northeast Peruvian provinces, areas with long state traditions of their own. Since elite infighting also became more pronounced toward the end of the fifteenth century, personal guards recruited from non-Inca populations and numbering up to 7,000 soldiers accompanied many leading ruling-class members. The professionalization of the Inca army, however, lagged behind that of the Aztecs, since the Incas did not have military academies open to their subjects.

**Communications**   Although they lacked the military professionalization of the Aztecs, the Incas created an imperial communication and logistics structure that was unparalleled in the Americas. Early on, the Incas systematically improved on the road network that they inherited from Tiwanaku, Wari, and other states. Two parallel trunk roads extended from Cuzco nearly the entire length of the empire in both southerly and northerly directions. One followed the coast and western slopes of the western Andes chain; the other led through the mountain lands, valleys, and high plains between the western and eastern Andes chains. In numerous places, additional highways connected the two trunk roads. Suspension bridges made of thick ropes crossed gorges, while rafts were used for crossing rivers. The roads, 3–12 feet wide, crossed the terrain as directly as possible, often requiring extensive grounding, paving, staircasing, and tunneling. In many places, the 25,000-mile road network still exists today, attesting to the engineering prowess of the Incas.

The roads were reserved for troops, officials, and runners carrying messages. For their convenience, every 15 miles, or at the end of a slow 1-day journey, an inn provided accommodation. Larger armies stopped at barracks-like constructions or pitched tents on select campgrounds. Like the Romans, and despite the fact that they did not have wheeled transport, the Incas were well aware of how crucial paved and well-supplied roads were for infantry soldiers.

# Imperial Society and Culture

As Mesoamerica and the Andes entered their imperial age, cosmopolitan capitals with monumental ceremonial centers and palaces emerged. The sizes of both capitals and monuments were visual expressions of the exalted power that the rulers claimed. Almost daily ceremonies and rituals, accompanied by feasts, further underscored the authority of rulers. These ceremonies and rituals expressed the American spiritual and polytheistic heritage but were modified to impress on enemies and subjects alike the irresistible might of the empires.

## Imperial Capitals: Tenochtitlán and Cuzco

In the fifteenth century, the Aztec and Inca capitals were among the largest cities of the world, encompassing between 100,000 and 200,000 inhabitants. Both cities maintained their high degree of urbanism through a complex command system of labor, services, and goods. Although their monumental architecture followed different artistic traditions, both emphasized platforms and sanctuaries atop large pyramid-like structures as symbols of elevated power as well as closeness to the astral gods, especially those associated with the sun and Venus.

**Tenochtitlán as an Urban Metropolis**    More than half of the approximately 1.5 million people living during the fifteenth century in the Mexican Basin were urban dwellers, including elites, priests, administrators, military officers, merchants, traders, craftspeople, messengers, servants, and laborers. Such an extraordinary concentration of urban citizens was unique in the agrarian world prior to the industrialization of Europe (beginning around 1800), when cities usually held no more than 10 percent of the total population (see Map 15.5).

The center of Tenochtitlán, on the southern island, was a large platform where the Aztec settlers had driven pilings into marshy ground and heaped rocks and rubble. In an enclosure on this platform were the main pyramid, with temples to the Aztec gods on top, and a series of smaller ceremonial centers. Adjacent to this on the platform were a food market and a series of

**Aqueduct from the Western Hills to Tenochtitlán.** This aqueduct, still standing today, provided fresh water to the palace and mansions of the center of the island, to be used as drinking water and for washing.

palaces of the ruling elite, which included guest quarters, administrative offices, storage facilities for tributes, kitchens, the high court for the elite and the court of appeals for commoners, the low court for civil cases, workshops for craftspeople, the prison, and councils for teachers and the military. Large numbers of Aztecs and visitors assembled each day to pay respect to the ruler and to trade in the market in preparation for assemblies and feasts.

In 1473, the southern island was merged with the northern island to form a single unit. At the center of the northern island was a platform that contained the principal market of the combined islands. This daily market attracted as many as 40,000 farmers, craftspeople, traders, porters, and laborers on the main market day. The sophistication of the market was comparable to that of any market in Eurasia during the fifteenth century.

A number of causeways crossed the capital and linked it with the lakeshore. People also traveled inside the city on a number of main and branch canals. Dikes with sluices on the east side regulated both the water level and the salinity of the lake around the islands. The runoff during the summer rainy season from the southwestern mountains provided freshwater to dilute the lake's salinity, and the eastern dikes kept out salt water from the rest of the lake. Potable water arrived from the shore via an aqueduct on one of the western causeways. This aqueduct served mostly the ceremonial center and palace precinct, but branches brought potable water to a number of elite residences nearby as well. Professional water carriers took fresh water to commoners in the various quarters of the city; professional waste removers collected human waste from urban residences and took it to farmers for fertilizer. In short, Tenochtitlán possessed a fully developed urban infrastructure.

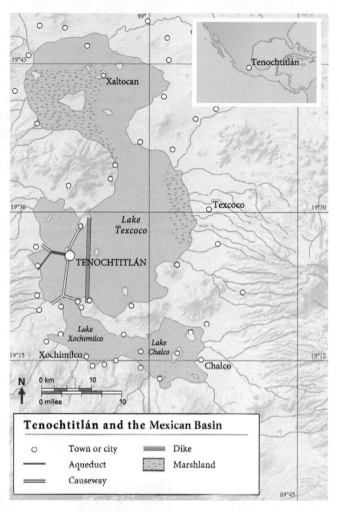

MAP 15.5 **Tenochtitlán and the Mexican Basin.**

The two city centers—the pyramid and palaces in the south and the market in the north—were surrounded by dozens of residential city quarters. Built on a layer of firm ground, many of these quarters were inhabited by craftspeople of a shared profession, who practiced their crafts in their residences. As discussed earlier in this chapter, merchants occupied a privileged position between the elite and the commoners. As militarily trained organizers of large caravans of porters, the merchants also provided the Aztec capital with luxury goods. Depending on their social rank, craftspeople occupied residences of larger or smaller size, usually grouped into compounds of related families. The rooms of the houses surrounded a central patio on which most of the household activities took place—an architectural preference common to Mesoamerica and the Andes, as well as the Middle East and Mediterranean.

Residents of quarters farther away from the center were farmers. In these quarters, making up nearly two-thirds of Tenochtitlán's surface, families engaged in intensive farming. Here, a grid of canals encased small, rectangular islands devoted to housing compounds and/or farming. People moved within these barrios by boat. Since the Mexican Basin received year-round rains that were often

*Chinampas*: Mesoamerican agricultural practice by which farmers grew crops upon small, human-made islands in Lake Texcoco.

insufficient for dry farming, a raised-field system prevailed, whereby farmers dredged the canals, heaped the fertile mud on top of the rectangular islands, called **chinampas,** and added water from the canals and waste from their households or brought by boat from the urban neighborhoods. In contrast to the luxurious palaces of the elite, housing for farmers consisted of plastered huts made of cane, wood, and reeds. As in all agrarian societies, farmers—subject to high taxes or rents—were among the poorest folk.

On the surface of the *chinampas*, farmers grew corn, beans, squash, amaranth, and peppers. These seed plants were supplemented by *maguey* [mag-AY], a large succulent agave. This evergreen plant grew in poor soils; had a large root system, which helped in stabilizing the ground; and produced fiber useful for weaving and pulp useful for making *pulque* [POOL-kay], a fermented drink. To plant these crops in the soft soil, a digging stick, slightly broadened at one end, was sufficient. Regular watering made multicropping of seed plants possible. Trees, planted at the edges, protected the *chinampas* against water erosion.

Ownership of the *chinampas* was vested in clans, which, under neighborhood leaders, were responsible for the allocation of land and adjudication of disputes as well as the payment of taxes in kind to the elite. But there were also members of the elite who, as absentee owners, possessed estates and employed managers to collect rents from the farmers. Whether there was a trend from taxes to rents (that is, from a central tax authority to a decentralized landowner class) is unknown. Given the high productivity of raised-field farming, which was similar to that of the Eurasian agrarian–urban centers, such a trend would not have been surprising.

**Cuzco as a Ceremonial-Administrative City**  The site of the Inca city of Cuzco was an elongated triangle formed by the confluence of two rivers. At one

**Cuzco Stone Masonry.** Inspired by the masonry of the people of Tiwanaku, the Inca built imposing structures with much larger blocks of limestone or granite. To cut the blocks, masons used copper and bronze chisels, making use of natural fissures in the stone.

end, opposite the confluence, was a hill with a number of structures, including the imperial armory and a temple dedicated to the sun god. Enormous, zigzagging walls followed the contours of the hill. The walls were built with stone blocks weighing up to 100 tons and cut so precisely that no mortar was needed, a technique which the Incas adopted from Tiwanaku.

Below, on the plain leading to the confluence, the city was laid out in a grid pattern. The residents of the city, all belonging to the upper and lower Inca ruling class, lived in adobe houses arranged in a block-and-courtyard pattern similar to that of Wari. Several squares and temples within the city served as ceremonial centers. One plaza contained a platform, with the imperial throne and a pillar placed symbolically atop what the Incas considered the earth's center or navel. The Coricancha [co-ri-CAN-tsha], the city's main temple, stood near the confluence of the rivers. This temple was a walled compound comprising six buildings set around a courtyard. Chambers in these buildings contained the Inca gods and goddesses as well as the divine statues or sacred objects confiscated from the provinces. Each year priests of the empire's ceremonial centers sent one such sacred object to the Coricancha, to demonstrate their obedience to the central Inca temple (see Map 15.6).

Across the rivers, in separate suburbs, were settlements for commoners with markets and storehouses. They were surrounded by fields, terraces, and irrigation canals. In the fields, interspersed stone pillars and shrines were aligned on sight lines radiating from the Coricancha, tying the countryside closely to the urban center. These alignments were reminiscent of the Nazca lines drawn half a millennium earlier in southern Peru (Chapter 9). Farther away were imperial estates with unfree laborers from outside the *mit'a* system and its reciprocal feasting. In contrast to the Aztec elite, which allowed meritorious generals to rise in the hierarchy, the Inca elite remained exclusionary, allowing no commoners to reside in Cuzco.

## Power and Its Cultural Expressions

Ruling elites, as repeatedly emphasized in this chapter, put a strong emphasis on displaying their power during the period 600–1500. This was particularly true with the Aztecs and Incas during the fifteenth century. Among these displays were human sacrifices, mausoleums, and mummy burials. Although all three involved changes in social relations, these changes were accommodated in the existing overall religious culture.

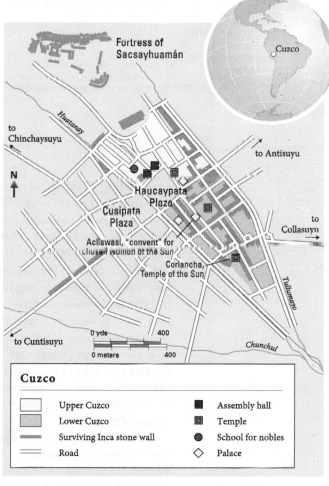

MAP **15.6 Cuzco.**

# Patterns Up Close

## Human Sacrifice and Propaganda

In the first millennium CE, Mesoamerica and the Andes evolved from their early religious spirituality to polytheism. The spiritual heritage, however, remained a strong undercurrent. Both American regions engaged in human as well as animal and agricultural sacrifices. Rulers appeased the gods also through self-sacrifice—that is, the piercing of tongue and penis, as was the case among the Olmecs (1400–400 BCE) and Mayas (600 BCE–900 CE). The feathered serpent god Quetzalcoatl was the Mesoamerican deity of self-sacrifice, revered in the city-states of Teotihuacán (200 BCE–570 CE) and Tula (ca. 900 CE). Under the Toltecs and the Aztecs, this god receded into the background, in favor of warrior gods such as Tezcatlipoca and Huitzilpochtli. The survival of traditional blood rituals within polytheism was a pattern that distinguished the early American empires from their Eurasian counterparts.

Whether human sacrifices were prolific under Aztec and Inca imperialism is questionable. About the same number of human victims were excavated at the Feathered Serpent Temple of Teotihuacán and at the Templo Mayor of Tenochtitlán: 137 versus 126 skeletons. These numbers are minuscule in comparison to the impression created

52.

**Human Sacrifice.** Human sacrifice among the pre-Columbian Mesoamericans and Andeans was based on the concept of a shared life spirit or mind, symbolized by the life substance of blood. In the American spiritual-polytheistic conceptualization, the gods sacrificed their blood, or themselves altogether, during creation; rulers pierced their earlobes, tongues, or penises for blood sacrifices; and war captives lost their lives when their hearts were sacrificed.

**Inca Ruling Class Gender Relations** The ruling classes in the Inca Empire displayed their power in several ways. Among the examples were the "Houses of Chosen Women" in Cuzco and provincial colonies. The greatest honor for Inca girls was to enter at age 10–12 into the service of these houses. An inspector from Cuzco made regular visits to the villages of the empire to select attractive young girls for the service. The girls were marched to the capital or the colonies, where they were divided according to beauty, skills, and social standing. These houses had female instructors who provided the girls with a 4-year education in cooking, beer making, weaving, and officiating in the rituals and ceremonies of the Inca religion. After their graduation, the young women became virgin temple priestesses, were given in marriage to non-Incas honored for service to the ruler, or became palace servants, musicians, or concubines of the Inca elite. The collection of this girl tribute was separate from the reciprocity system. As such, it was an act of assigning gender roles in an emerging social hierarchy defined by power inequalities.

Traditionally, gender roles were less strictly divided than in Eurasia. The horticultural form of agriculture in Mesoamerica and the Andes gave males fewer opportunities to accumulate wealth and power than plow agriculture did in Eurasia. Hoes and foot plows distinguished men and women from each other less than plows and teams of oxen or horses did. Nevertheless, it comes as no surprise that

by the Spanish conquerors and encourage doubts about the magnitude of human sacrifices in temple ceremonies. It appears that even though the Aztec and Inca ruling classes were focused on war, the ritual of human sacrifice was not as pervasive as has been widely assumed.

Could it be that there was no significant increase in human sacrifice under the Aztecs and Incas, as the self-serving Spanish conquerors alleged? Were there perhaps, instead, imperial propaganda machines in the Aztec and Inca Empires, employed in the service of conquest and consolidation—similar to those of the Assyrians and Mongols in Eurasia—who sought to intimidate their enemies? In this case, the Aztec and Inca Empires would not be exceptional barbaric aberrations in world history. Instead, they would be but two typical examples of the general world-historical pattern of competitive militaristic states during the early agrarian era using propaganda to further their imperial power.

## Questions

- In examining the question of whether empires such as the Inca and the Aztec employed human sacrifice for propaganda purposes, can this practice be considered an adaptation that evolved out of earlier rituals, such as royal bloodletting?

- If the Aztec and the Inca did indeed employ human sacrifice for propaganda purposes, what does this say about the ability of these two empires to use cultural and religious practices to consolidate their power?

the gradual agrarian–urban diversification of society, even if it was slower in the Americas than in Eurasia, proceeded along similar paths of increasing male power concentration in villages, ceremonial centers, temple cities, conquering states, and empires. Emphasizing gender differences, therefore, should be viewed as a characteristic phenomenon arising in imperial contexts.

**Inca Mummy Veneration**   Other houses in Cuzco were ghostly residences in which scores of attendants and servants catered to what were believed to be the earthly needs of deceased, mummified Inca emperors and their principal wives. During the mummification process attendants removed the cadaver's internal organs, placed them in special containers, and desiccated the bodies until they were completely mummified. Servants dressed the mummies (*mallquis* [MAY-kees]) in their finest clothing and placed them back into their residences amid their possessions, as if they had never died. The mummies received daily meals and were carried around by their retinues for visits to their mummified relatives. On special occasions, mummies were lined up according to rank on Cuzco's main plaza to participate in ceremonies and processions. In this way, they remained fully integrated into the daily life of the elite.

> "We order that everyone bury their deceased in a chamber [*pucullo*, stone tomb], that the dead not be buried in their houses and that the deceased's spindle, dining service, food, drink, and garments be buried with them."
>
> —Ordinances of the Inca, recorded by Felipe Guaman Poma de Ayala

"Ghost residences" with mummies can be considered an outgrowth of the old Andean custom of mummification. This custom was widely practiced among the elites of the ceremonial centers, who, however, generally placed their ancestors in temple tombs, shrines, or caves. Mummies were also buried in cemeteries, sometimes collectively in bundles with false heads made of cotton. Preserving the living spaces of the deceased obviously required considerable wealth—wealth provided only by imperial regimes for their elites.

As a general phenomenon in Andean society, of course, mummies were a crucial ingredient in the religious heritage, in which strong spiritual elements survived underneath the polytheistic overlay of astral gods. In the spiritual tradition, body and spirit cohabit more or less loosely. In a trance, a diviner's mind can travel, enter the minds of other people and animals, or make room for other people's minds. Similarly, in death a person's spirit, while no longer in the body, remains nearby and therefore still needs daily nourishment in order not to be driven away. Hence, even though non-Incan Andean societies removed the dead from their daily living spaces, descendants had to visit tombs regularly with food and beer or provide buried mummies with ample victuals.

The expenses for the upkeep of the mummy households were the responsibility of the deceased emperor's bloodline, headed by a surviving brother. As heirs of the emperor's estate, the members of the bloodline formed a powerful clan within the ruling class. The new emperor was excluded from this estate and had to acquire his own new one in the course of his rule, a mechanism evidently designed to intensify his imperial ambitions for conquest. In the early sixteenth century, however, when it became logistically difficult to expand much beyond the enormous territory already accumulated in the Andes, this ingenious mechanism of keeping the upper and lower rungs of the ruling class united became counterproductive. Emperors lacking resources had to contend with brothers richly endowed with inherited wealth and ready to engage in dynastic warfare—as actually occurred shortly before the arrival of the Spanish (1529–1532).

## Putting It All Together

During the short time of their existence, the Aztec and Inca Empires unleashed extraordinary creative energies. Sculptors, painters, and (after the arrival of the Spanish) writers recorded the traditions as well as the innovations of the fifteenth century. Aztec painters produced codices, or illustrated manuscripts, that present the divine pantheons, myths, calendars, ceremonial activities, chants, poetry, and administrative activities of their societies in exquisite and colorful detail. They fashioned these codices using bark paper, smoothing it with plaster, and connecting the pages accordion-style. Today, a handful of these codices survive, preserved in Mexican and European libraries.

The Aztec and Inca Empires were polities that illustrate how humans not in contact with the rest of the world and living within an environment that was different from Eurasia and Africa in many respects developed patterns of innovation that were remarkably similar. On the basis of an agriculture that eventually produced ample surpluses, humans made the same choices as their cousins in Eurasia and Africa. Specifically, in the period 600–1500, they created temple-centered city-states, just like their Sumerian and Hindu counterparts. Their military states were not unlike the Chinese warring states. And, finally, their empires—although just beginning to flourish in the Bronze Age—were comparable to those of the New Kingdom Egyptians or Assyrians. The Americas had their own unique variations of these larger historical patterns, to be sure; but they nevertheless displayed the same humanity as found elsewhere.

▶ For additional resources, including maps, primary sources, visuals, and quizzes, please go to www.oup.com/us/vonsivers. Please see the Further Resources section at the back of the book for additional readings and suggested websites.

## Against the Grain

# Amazon Rain Forest Civilizations

For many years, prevailing scholarly opinion held that the vast Amazonian river basin, covered by dense rain forest, was too inhospitable to allow for more than small numbers of widely dispersed foragers to subsist. Even farmers, living in more densely populated villages, could not possibly have founded complex, stratified societies. Slash-and-burn agriculture, the common form of farming on poor tropical soils even today, by definition prevented the advance of urban life: After exhausting the soil in a given area, whole villages had to pack up and move.

Beginning in the 1990s, however, a few scholars realized that this belief was erroneous. Modern farmers, increasingly encroaching on the rain forest, made these scholars aware of two hitherto neglected features. First, these farmers often advanced into stretches of forest and savanna on top of what is called in Portuguese *terra preta*—black soil so fertile that it did not require fertilizers for years. Second, as they slashed and burned the rain forest and savanna with their modern tools, they exposed monumental earthworks that had previously escaped attention under the cover of vegetation. The two features were actually connected. *Terra preta* was the result of centuries of patient soil enrichment by indigenous people who were also the builders of the earthworks. Instead of slashing and burning, these people had engaged in "slashing and charring"—that is, turning the trees into longer-lasting nutrient-rich charcoal rather than less fertile and quickly depleted ash.

Since the early 2000s, scholars have documented large-scale settlements in areas along the southern tributaries to the Amazon, describing large village clusters with central plazas, fortification walls, bridges, causeways, and waterworks. One such cluster is located on the upper Xingu, a tributary of the lower Amazon. A set of two clusters is situated near the upper reaches of the Purus, a tributary of the upper Amazon. One occupies a fertile flood plain, the other the less fertile highlands further away from the river. In the Purus region, researchers employing aerial photography revealed a huge area home to perhaps 60,000 inhabitants during a period around the late thirteenth century. This area is adjacent to the farthest northeastern extension of the Inca Empire into the Amazon, with fortresses being excavated by Finnish teams. Thus, when the Incas expanded into the rain forest, they clearly did so to incorporate flourishing, advanced societies into their empire. Thanks to scholars who challenged the orthodoxy of the "empty rain forest," we are rediscovering the Amazonian past.

- Which is more important: to save the rain forest or uncover its archaeological past? Can the two objectives be combined?

- Compare the Amazonian earthworks to those of Benin in Africa during the same period (Chapter 14). Which similarities and differences can you discover?

# Thinking Through Patterns

▶ **Within the patterns of state formation basic to the Americas, which types of states emerged in Meso- america and the Andes during the period 600–1550? What characterized these states?**

The basic pattern of state formation in the Americas was similar to that of Eurasia and Africa. Historically, it began with the transition from foraging to agriculture and settled village life. As the population increased, villages under elders became chiefdoms, which in turn became city-states with temples. As in Eurasia and Africa, American city-states often became conquering states, beginning with the Maya king- doms and Teotihuacán. Both, however, remained small. Military states, in which ruling classes sought to expand territories, such as Tula and, to a lesser degree, Tiwanaku and Wari, were characteristic for the early part of the period 600–1550. The succes- sors of these—the Aztec and Inca Empires—were multiethnic, multilinguistic, and multireligious polities that dominated Mesoamerica and the Andes for about a century, before the Spanish conquest brought them to a premature end.

The states of Tiwanaku and Wari had more or less cohesive ruling classes but no dynasties of rulers and centralized bureaucracies. These ruling classes and their subjects—corn and potato farmers—were integrated with each other through systems of reciprocity—that is, military protection in return for foodstuffs. They customarily renewed the bonds of reciprocity in common feasts. After one or two centuries, how- ever, tensions arose, either between stronger and weaker branches of the ruling classes or between rulers and subjects over questions of obligations and justice. When these tensions erupted into internal warfare, the states disintegrated, often in conjunction with environmental degradation and climate change.

▶ **Why did the Tiwanaku and Wari states have ruling classes but no dynas- ties and central bureaucracies? How were these patterns expressed in the ter- ritorial organization of these states?**

▶ **What patterns of urban life charac- terized the cities of Tenochtitlán and Cuzco, the capitals of the Aztec and Inca Empires? In which ways were these cities similar to those of Eurasia and Africa?**

Tenochtitlán and Cuzco, the capitals of the Aztec and Inca Empires, were two urban centers organized around temples and associated residences of the ruling dynasties and their priestly classes. They also contained large city quarters inhabited by craftspeople specializing in the production of woven textiles, pottery, leather goods, and weapons. Large central markets provided for the exchange of foodstuffs, crafts, and imported luxury goods. Armed caravans of merchants and porters transported the luxury goods, such as cacao, feathers, obsidian, and turquoise, across hundreds of miles. Tenochtitlán had an aqueduct for the supply of drinking water, and Cuzco was traversed by a river. Both capitals had agricultural suburbs in which farmers used irrigation for the production of the basic food staples.

# Patterns of Evidence: Sources for Chapter 15

## SOURCE 15.1

## The Temple of the Jaguars, Chichén Itzá

**ca. 850–1000 CE**

Chichén Itzá was founded during a period of renewed urbanization in the Mayan states around 650, and a remarkable state flourished in its vicinity between 850 and 1000. The population was composed of local Maya, as well as Maya-speaking peoples from the Gulf of Mexico coast. It owed its prosperity to long-distance trade, both overland and in boats along the coast. Around 1000, the ruling-class factions abandoned Chichén Itzá for unknown reasons, and the city-state dwindled in size to the level of a town.

Source: Dreamstime/©Alexandre Fagundes De Fagundes (top); Shutterstock/Danilo Ascione (bottom).

▶ **Working with Sources**

1. What does the construction of this monument suggest about the social structure of Chichén Itzá at its height?

2. What might have been the significance of the jaguars? Why would the temple have been decorated in such an elaborate fashion?

SOURCE 15.2

# Skeletons in a Wari royal tomb site, El Castillo de Huarmey, Peru

## ca. 600–1000 CE

In 2013, 63 skeletons were discovered in a tomb at El Castillo de Huarmey, about 175 miles north of Lima, in what would seem to be the first imperial tomb of the Wari culture discovered in modern times. Most of the bodies were female, and wrapped in bundles in a seated position typical of Wari burials. Three of the women appear to have been Wari queens, as they were buried with gold and silver jewelry and brilliantly painted ceramics. However, six of the skeletons were not wrapped in the textiles, but instead positioned on top of the burials. Archaeologists have concluded that these people may have been sacrificed for the benefit of the others.

Source: REUTERS/Enrique Castro-Mendivil.

▶ **Working with Sources**

1. **How do the burial practices of Wari culture compare with those of other civilizations in Mesoamerica and the Andes?**

2. **What might this tomb suggest about the roles and expectations of women in Wari culture?**

## SOURCE 15.3

# Bernal Díaz, *The Conquest of New Spain*

### ca. 1568

In the course of the fifteenth century, the Aztecs established an empire centered in the Mexican Basin (surrounding present-day Mexico City, after the drainage of most of the valley) but encompassing Mesoamerica from the Pacific to the Gulf of Mexico. The resulting state, far more centralized than the preceding Teotihuacán and Toltec city-states, commanded a large extent of territory and thrived on the trade in raw materials that were brought in from both coasts of their empire. Bernal Díaz, born in 1492 in Spain, would join the Spaniards in the "conquest" of Mexico, but he also left behind vivid eyewitness accounts of occupied Aztec society in the sixteenth century. Among them is this description of the market in Tlatelolco, one of the central cities at the heart of Aztec imperial power.

Our Captain and those of us who had horses went to Tlatelolco mounted, and the majority of our men were fully equipped. On reaching the market-place, escorted by the many **Caciques** whom Montezuma had assigned to us, we were astounded at the great number of people and the quantities of merchandise, and at the orderliness and good arrangements that prevailed, for we had never seen such a thing before. The chieftains who accompanied us pointed everything out. Every kind of merchandise was kept separate and had its fixed place marked for it.

Let us begin with the dealers in gold, silver, and precious stones, feathers, cloaks, and embroidered goods, and male and female slaves who are also sold there. They bring as many slaves to be sold in that market as the Portuguese bring Negroes from Guinea. Some are brought there attached to long poles by means of collars round their necks to prevent them from escaping, but others are left loose. Next there were those who sold coarser cloth, and cotton goods and fabrics made of twisted thread, and there were chocolate merchants with their chocolate. In this way you

**Caciques:** Nobles.

Source: Bernal Díaz del Castillo, *The Conquest of New Spain*, trans. J. M. Cohen (Baltimore: Penguin, 1963), 232–234.

could see every kind of merchandise to be found anywhere in New Spain, laid out in the same way as goods are laid out in my own district of Medina del Campo, a centre for fairs, where each line of stalls has its own particular sort. So it was in this great market. There were those who sold sisal cloth and ropes and the sandals they wear on their feet, which are made from the same plant. All these were kept in one part of the market, in the place assigned to them, and in another part were skins of tigers and lions, otters, jackals, and deer, badgers, mountain cats, and other wild animals, some tanned and some untanned, and other classes of merchandise.

. . .

Then there were the sellers of pitch-pine for torches, and other things of that kind, and I must also mention, with all apologies, that they sold many canoe-loads of human excrement, which they keep in the creeks near the market. This was for the manufacture of salt and the curing of skins, which they say cannot be done without it. I know that many gentlemen will laugh at this, but I assure them it is true. I may add that on all the roads they have shelters made of reeds or straw or grass so that they can retire when they wish to do so, and purge their bowels unseen by passers-by, and also in order that their excrement shall not be lost.

But why waste so many words on the goods in their great market?

If I describe everything in detail I shall never be done. Paper, which in Mexico they call *amal*, and some reeds that smell of liquid amber, and are full of tobacco, and yellow ointments and other such things, are sold in a separate part. Much cochineal is for sale too, under the arcades of that market, and there are many sellers of herbs and other such things. They have a building there also in which three judges sit, and there are officials like constables who examine the merchandise. I am forgetting the sellers of salt and the makers of flint knives, and how they split them off the stone itself, and the fisherwomen and the men who sell small cakes made from a sort of weed which they get out of the great lake, which curdles and forms a kind of bread which tastes rather like cheese. They sell axes too, made of bronze and copper and tin, and gourds and brightly painted wooden jars.

We went on to the great *cue*, and as we approached its wide courts, before leaving the market-place itself, we saw many more merchants who, so I was told, brought gold to sell in grains, just as they extract it from the mines. This gold is placed in the thin quills of the large geese of that country, which are so white as to be transparent. They used to reckon their accounts with one another by the length and thickness of these little quills, how much so many cloaks or so many gourds of chocolate or so many slaves were worth, or anything else they were bartering.

**Cue:** Temple.

▶ **Working with Sources**

1. How and why does Díaz use comparisons from other markets while describing the one in Tlatelolco?

2. What do the specific elements of this market suggest about the importance of trade and commerce in pre-Columbian Mexico?

## SOURCE 15.4

# Pedro Cieza de León on Incan roads

### 1541–1547

The Incas created an imperial communications and logistics infrastructure that was unparalleled in the Americas, with two highways extending to the north and south from Cuzco nearly the entire length of the empire. The roads, which were up to 12 feet wide, crossed the terrain as directly as possible, which clearly required a tremendous labor force to create. In many places, even today, the 25,000-mile road network still exists. Pedro Cieza de León was born in Spain in 1520 and undoubtedly traveled along the extensive, and still-functional, Roman road system of his native land as a child. When he arrived in the New World at the age of 13, he was captivated and impressed by the civilizations that the Spanish were supplanting. In 1541, he began writing his account of the Incas, tracing their heritage and government for the benefit of those who would never see the territory he did—or travel the roads that made his observations possible.

### CHAPTER 42 (ii.xv)

*Of how the buildings for the Lord-Incas were constructed, and the highways to travel through the kingdom [of Peru].*

One of the things that most took my attention when I was observing and setting down the things of this kingdom was how and in what way the great, splendid highways we see throughout it could be built, and the number of men that must have been required, and what tools and instruments they used to level the mountains and cut through the rock to make them as broad and good as they are. For it seems to me that if the Emperor were to desire another highway built like the one from Quito to Cuzco, or that which goes from Cuzco to Chile, truly I do not believe he could do it, with all his power and the men at his disposal, unless he followed the method the Incas employed. For if it were a question of a road fifty leagues long, or a hundred, or two hundred, we can assume that, however rough the land, it would not be too difficult, working hard, to do it. But there were so long, one of them more than 1100 leagues, over mountains so rough and dismaying that in certain places one could not see bottom, and some of the sierras so sheer and barren that the road had to be cut through the living rock to keep it level and the right width. All this they did with fire and picks.

. . .

When a Lord-Inca had decided on the building of one of these famous highways, no great provisioning or levies or anything else was needed except for the Lord-Inca to say, let this be done. The inspectors then went through the provinces, laying out the route and assigning Indians from one end to the other to the building of the

Source: Pedro Cieza de León, *The Incas*, trans. Harriet de Onis, ed. Victor Wolfgang von Hagen (Norman: University of Oklahoma Press, 1959), 135–137.

road. In this way, from one boundary of the province to the other, at its expense and with its Indians, it was built as laid out, in a short time; and the others did the same, and, if necessary, a great stretch of the road was built at the same time, or all of it. When they came to the barren places, the Indians of the lands nearest by came with victuals and tools to do the work, and all was done with little effort and joyfully, because they were not oppressed in any way, nor did the Incas put overseers to watch them.

Aside from these, great fine highways were built, like that which runs through the valley of Xaquixahuana, and comes out of the city of Cuzco and goes by the town of Muhina. There were many of these highways all over the kingdom, both in the highlands and the plains. Of all, four are considered the main highways, and they are those which start from the city of Cuzco, at the square, like a crossroads, and go to the different provinces of the kingdom. As these monarchs held such a high opinion of themselves, when they set out on one of these roads, the royal person with the necessary guard took one [road], and the rest of the people another. So great was their pride that when one of them died, his heir, if he had to travel to a distant place, built his road larger and broader than that of his predecessor, but this was only if this Lord-Inca set out on some conquest, or [performed] some act so noteworthy that it could be said the road built for him was longer.

▶ **Working with Sources**

1. How were the Incas' roads a manifestation of royal power, at least in Cieza de León's estimation?

2. What technical challenges faced the Incan road builders, and how did they overcome them?

## SOURCE 15.5

# Garcilaso de la Vega, "The Walls and Gates of Cuzco"

### 1609–1616

The Incan city of Cuzco was an elongated triangle formed by the confluence of two rivers. At one end, enormous, zigzagging walls followed the contours of a steep hill. The walls were built with stone blocks weighing up to 100 tons and cut so precisely that no mortar was needed. The ruins of the walls were still visible after the Spanish siege of 1536 (as they are today),

Source: Garcilaso de la Vega, *Royal Commentaries of the Incas and General History of Peru*, trans. Harold V. Livermore (Austin: University of Texas Press, 1966), vol. 1, 463–468.

and they were a marvel to Garcilaso de la Vega, when he viewed them in the mid-sixteenth century. Garcilaso was born in 1539, the decade of the conquest of Peru, to a Spanish conqueror and a Native American princess, a second cousin of the last two Inca rulers. As a young man, Garcilaso left his native Peru never to return. Toward the end of his life he retired to a secluded Spanish village, where he wrote his general history of the Incas. He was particularly proud of the monumental achievements of his Incan relatives, and of the power that their construction projects represented.

## CHAPTER XXVII

*The fortress of Cuzco; the size of its stones.*

The Inca kings of Peru made marvelous buildings, fortresses, temples, royal palaces, gardens, storehouses, roads, and other constructions of great excellence, as can be seen even today from their remaining ruins, though the whole building can scarcely be judged from the mere foundations.

The greatest and most splendid building erected to show the power and majesty of the Incas was the fortress of Cuzco, the grandeur of which would be incredible to anyone who had not seen it, and even those who have seen it and considered it with attention imagine, and even believe, that it was made by enchantment, the handiwork of demons, rather than of men. Indeed the multiplicity of stones, large and small, of which the three **circumvallations** are composed (and they are more like rocks than stones) makes one wonder how they could have been quarried, for the Indians had neither iron nor steel to work them with. And the question of how they were conveyed to the site is no less difficult a problem, since they had no oxen and could not make wagons: nor would oxen and wagons have sufficed to carry them. They were in fact heaved by main force with the aid of thick cables. The roads by which they were brought were not

flat, but rough mountainsides with steep slopes, up and down which the rocks were dragged by human effort alone.

. . .

## CHAPTER XXVIII

*The three circumvallations, the most remarkable part of the work.*

On the other side, opposite this wall, there is a large level space. From this direction the ascent to the top of the hill is a gradual one up which an enemy could advance in order of battle. The Incas therefore made three concentric walls on the slopes, each of which would be more than two hundred fathoms long. They are in the shape of a half moon, for they close together at the ends to meet the other wall of smooth masonry on the side facing the city. The first of these three walls best exhibits the might of the Incas, for although all three are of the same workmanship, it is the most impressive and has the largest stones, making the whole construction seem incredible to anyone who has not seen it, and giving an impression of awe to the careful observer who ponders on the size and number of the stones and the limited resources of the natives for cutting and working them and setting them in their places.

. . .

**Circumvallations:**
Walls built around
the city.

Almost in the middle of each wall there was a gate, and these gates were each shut with a stone as high and as thick as the wall itself which could be raised and lowered. The first of these was called Tiupuncu, "gate of sand," since the plain is rather sandy or gravelly at this point: *tiu* is "sand," or "a sandy place," and *puncu*, "gate, door." The second is called Acahuana Puncu, after the master mason, whose name was Acahuana, the syllable *ca* being pronounced deep down in the throat. The third is Viracocha Puncu, dedicated to the god Viracocha, the phantom we have referred to at length, who appeared to Prince Viracocha Inca and fore-warned him of the rising of the Chancas, as a result of which he was regarded at the defender and second founder of Cuzco, and therefore given this gate with the request that he should guard it and defend the fortress as he had guarded the city and the whole empire in the past.

▶ **Working with Sources**

1. Why did the Incas feel the need to fortify Cuzco so heavily, and would these preparations have been successful in typical battle situations?

2. What aspect of the city's walls most arouses Garcilaso's admiration and wonder, and why?

# Chapter 16 1450–1650

# The Western European Overseas Expansion and Ottoman–Habsburg Struggle

**A**l-Hasan Ibn Muhammad al-Wazzan (ca. 1494–1550) was born into a family of bureaucrats in Muslim Granada soon after the Christian conquest of this kingdom in southern Iberia in 1492. Unwilling to convert to Christianity, Hasan's family emigrated to Muslim Morocco around 1499–1500 and settled in the city of Fez. Here, Hasan received a good education in religion, law, logic, and the sciences. After completing his studies, he entered the administration of the Moroccan sultan, traveling to sub-Saharan Africa and the Middle East on diplomatic missions.

In 1517, as he was returning home from a mission to Istanbul, Christian **corsairs** kidnapped him from his ship. Like their Muslim counterparts, these corsairs roamed the Mediterranean to capture unsuspecting travelers, whom they then held for ransom or sold into slavery. For a handsome sum of money, they turned the cultivated Hasan over to Pope Leo X (1513–1521), who ordered Hasan to convert to Christianity and baptized him with his own family name, Giovanni Leone di Medici. Hasan became known in Rome as Leo Africanus ("Leo the African"), in

ABOVE: *An Officer in the Army of Charles V Buys the Freedom of two Christian Women from their Muslim Captor.* **Painting by Jan Cornelisz Vermeyen (ca. 1500–1559); he accompanied Emperor Charles V on his victorious campaign against Muslim Tunis in 1535.**

reference to his travels in sub-Saharan Africa. He stayed for 10 years in Italy, initially at the papal court and later as an independent scholar in Rome. During this time, he taught Arabic to Roman clergymen, compiled an Arabic–Hebrew–Latin dictionary, and wrote an essay on famous Arabs. His most memorable and enduring work was a travelogue, first composed in Arabic and later translated into Italian, *Description of Africa*, which was for many years the sole source of information about sub-Saharan Africa in the western Christian world.

After 1527, however, life became difficult in Rome. In this year, Charles V (r. 1516–1558), king of Spain and emperor of the Holy Roman Empire of Germany, invaded Italy and sacked the city. Hasan survived the sack of Rome but departed for Tunis sometime after 1531, seeking a better life in Muslim North Africa. Unfortunately, all traces of Hasan after his departure from Rome are lost. It is possible that he perished in 1535 when Charles V attacked and occupied Tunis (1535–1574), although it is generally assumed that he lived there until around 1550.

The world in which Hasan lived and traveled was a Muslim–Christian world composed of the Middle East, North Africa, and Europe. Muslims on the Iberian Peninsula and in the Balkans bracketed this world, with the western Christians in the center. Although Muslims and Christians traveled in much of this world more or less freely—as merchants, mapmakers, adventurers, mercenaries, or corsairs—the two religious civilizations were locked in a pattern of fierce competition. During 800–1050, the Muslims justified their conquests as holy wars (*jihads*), and during 1050–1300 the Christians retaliated with their Crusades and the reconquest of Iberia.

By the fifteenth century, the Christians saw their liberation of Iberia and North Africa from Muslim rule and circumnavigation of the Muslims in the Mediterranean as stepping stones toward rebuilding the crusader kingdom of Jerusalem, which had been lost to the Muslims in 1291. Searching for a route that would take them around Africa, they hoped to defeat the Muslims in Jerusalem with an attack from the east. Driven at least in part by this search, the Christians discovered the continents of the Americas. For their part, the Muslims sought to conquer eastern and central Europe while simultaneously shoring up their defense of North Africa and driving the Portuguese out of the Indian Ocean. After a hiatus of several centuries—when commonwealths of states had characterized western Christian and Islamic civilizations—imperial polities reemerged, in the form of the Ottoman and Habsburg Empires vying for world rule.

# The Muslim–Christian Competition in the East and West, 1450–1600

After a long period during which the Christian kings in Iberia found tributes by the Muslim emirs more profitable than war, in the second half of the fifteenth

## Seeing Patterns

▶ What patterns characterized Christian and Muslim competition in the period 1300–1600? Which elements distinguished them from each other, and which elements were similar? How did the pattern change over time?

▶ How did centralizing states in the Middle East and Europe function in the period 1450–1600? How did economics, military power, and imperial objectives interact to create the centralizing state?

▶ Which patterns did cultural expressions follow in the Habsburg and Ottoman Empires? Why did the ruling classes of these empires sponsor these expressions?

**Corsairs:** In the context of this chapter, Muslim or Christian pirates who boarded ships, confiscated the cargoes, and held the crews and travelers for ransom; they were nominally under the authority of the Ottoman sultan or the pope in Rome but operated independently.

century the kings resumed the *Reconquista*. During the same time period, the small principality of the Ottomans took advantage of Mongol and Byzantine weakness to conquer lands in both Anatolia and the Balkans. After the Muslim conquest of Constantinople in 1453 and the western Christian conquest of Granada in 1492, the path was open for the emergence of the Ottoman and Habsburg Empires.

## Iberian Christian Expansion, 1415–1498

During a revival of anti-Muslim Crusade passions in the fourteenth century, Portugal resumed its *Reconquista* policies by expanding to North Africa in 1415. Looking for a way to circumnavigate the Muslims, collect West African gold, and reach the Indian spice coast, Portuguese sailors and traders established fortified harbors along the African coastline. Castile and Aragon, not to be left behind, conquered Granada in 1492, occupied ports in North Africa, and sent Columbus to discover an alternate route to what the Portuguese were seeking. Although Columbus's discovery of America did not yield Indian spices, he delivered a new continent to the rulers of Castile and Aragon (see Map 16.1).

**Maritime Explorations**　Portugal's resumption of the *Reconquista* had its roots in its mastery of Atlantic seafaring. In 1277–1281, mariners of the Italian city-state of Genoa pioneered commerce by sea between the Mediterranean and northwestern Europe. One port on the route was Lisbon, where Portuguese shipwrights and their Genoese teachers teamed up to develop new ships suited for the stormy Atlantic seas. In the early fifteenth century they developed the *caravel*, a small ship with high, upward-extending fore and aft sides, a stern rudder, and square as well as triangular lateen sails. With their new ships, the Portuguese became important traders between England and the Mediterranean countries.

The sea trade stimulated an exploration of the eastern Atlantic. By the early fifteenth century, the Portuguese had discovered the uninhabited islands of the Azores and Madeira, while the Castilians, building their own caravels, began a century-long conquest of the Canary Islands. Here, the indigenous, still Neolithic Berber inhabitants, the Guanches, put up a fierce resistance. But settlers, with the backing of Venetian investors, carved out colonies on conquered parcels of land, on which they enslaved the Guanches to work in sugarcane plantations. They thus adopted the sugarcane plantation system from the eastern Mediterranean, where it had Byzantine and Crusader roots on the island of Cyprus, as discussed in greater detail in Chapter 18, and made it an Atlantic one.

**Apocalyptic Expectations**　Parallel with the Atlantic explorations, Iberian Christians began to rethink their relationship with the Muslims on the peninsula. The loss of the crusader kingdom in Palestine to the Muslim Mamluks in 1291 was an event that stirred deep feelings of guilt among the western Christians. Efforts to dispatch military expeditions to reconquer Jerusalem failed, however, mostly because rulers in Europe—busy centralizing their realms—were now more interested in warring against each other for territorial gain. The failure did not dampen spiritual revivals, however, especially among the monks of the Franciscan and **military orders** of Iberia. These monks, often well connected with the Iberian

**Military orders:** Ever since the early 1100s, the papacy encouraged the formation of monastic fighting orders, such as the Hospitalers and Templars, to combat the Muslims in the crusader kingdom of Jerusalem; similar *Reconquista* orders, such as the Order of Santiago and the Order of Christ, emerged in Iberia to eliminate Muslim rule.

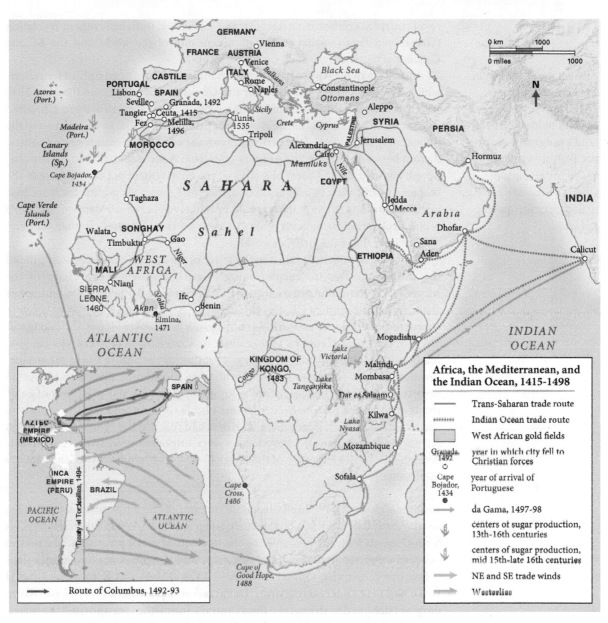

MAP **16.1** **Africa, the Mediterranean, and the Indian Ocean, 1415–1498.**

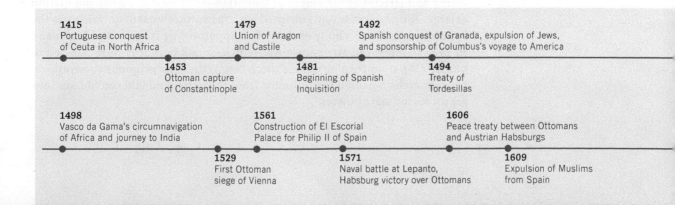

| 1415 | 1479 | 1492 |
|------|------|------|
| Portuguese conquest of Ceuta in North Africa | Union of Aragon and Castile | Spanish conquest of Granada, expulsion of Jews, and sponsorship of Columbus's voyage to America |

| 1453 | 1481 | 1494 |
|------|------|------|
| Ottoman capture of Constantinople | Beginning of Spanish Inquisition | Treaty of Tordesillas |

| 1498 | 1561 | 1606 |
|------|------|------|
| Vasco da Gama's circumnavigation of Africa and journey to India | Construction of El Escorial Palace for Philip II of Spain | Peace treaty between Ottomans and Austrian Habsburgs |

| 1529 | 1571 | 1609 |
|------|------|------|
| First Ottoman siege of Vienna | Naval battle at Lepanto, Habsburg victory over Ottomans | Expulsion of Muslims from Spain |

royal courts as confessors, preachers, and educators, were believers in revelation (Greek *apokalypsis*)—that is, the imminent end of the world and the Second Coming of Christ.

**Apocalypse:** In Greek, "revelation"—that is, unveiling the events at the end of history, before God's judgment; during the 1400s, expectation of the imminence of Christ's Second Coming, with precursors paving the way.

According to the **Apocalypse**, Christ's return could happen only in Jerusalem, which, therefore, made it urgent for the Christians to reconquer the city. They widely believed that they would be aided by Prester John, an alleged Christian ruler at the head of an immense army from Ethiopia or India. In the context of the intense religious fervor of the period, Christians as well as Muslims saw no contradiction between religion and military conquest. A providential God, so they believed, justified the conquest of lands and the enslavement of the conquered. The religious justification of military action, therefore, was not a pretext for more base material interests (though these would be a likely effect of such conquests) but a proud declaration by believers that God was on their side to help them convert and conquer the non-Christian world.

In Portugal, political claims in the guise of apocalyptic expectations guided the military orders in "reconquering" Ceuta, a northern port city of the Moroccan sultans. The orders argued that prior to the Berber–Arab conquest of the early eighth century CE, Ceuta had been Christian and that it was therefore lawful to undertake its capture. Accordingly, a fleet under Henry the Navigator (1394–1460) took Ceuta in 1415, capturing a huge stock of West African gold ready to be minted as money. Henry, a brother of the ruling Portuguese king, saw himself as a precursor in the unfolding of apocalyptic events and invested huge resources into the search for the *Rio de Oro*, the West African "river of gold" thought to be the place where Muslims obtained their gold. By the middle of the fifteenth century, Portuguese mariners had reached the "gold coast" of West Africa (today's Ghana), where local rulers imported gold from the interior Akan fields, near a tributary of the Niger River—the "gold river" of the Muslim merchants.

**Reforms in Castile**    The Portuguese renewal of the *Reconquista* stimulated a similar revival in Castile. For a century and a half, Castile had collected tributes from Granada instead of completing the reconquest of the peninsula. The revival occurred after the dynastic union of Castile and Aragon–Catalonia under their respective monarchs, Queen Isabella (r. 1474–1504) and King Ferdinand II (r. 1479–1516). The two monarchs embarked on a political and religious reform program designed to strengthen their central administrations and used the reconquest ideology to help speed up the reforms.

Among the political reforms was the recruitment of urban militias and judges, both under royal supervision, to check the military and judicial powers of the aristocracy. Religious reform focused on improved education for the clergy and stricter enforcement of Christian doctrine among the population at large. The new institution entrusted with the enforcement of doctrine was the Spanish Inquisition, a body of clergy first appointed by Isabella and Ferdinand in 1481 to ferret out any people whose beliefs and practices were deemed to violate Christian theology and church law. With their religious innovations, the monarchs regained the initiative from the popes and laid the foundations for increased state power.

**The Conquest of Granada**    The *Reconquista* culminated in a 10-year campaign (1482–1492), now fought with cannons on both sides. In the end, Granada fell into Christian hands because the Ottomans, still consolidating their power in the Balkans, sent only a naval commander who stationed himself in North Africa and harassed Iberian ships. The Mamluks of Egypt, less powerful than the Ottomans, sent an embassy to Granada that made a feeble threat of retribution against Christians in Egypt and Syria. Abandoned by the Muslim powers, the last emir of Granada negotiated terms for an honorable surrender. According to these terms, Muslims who chose to stay as subjects of the Castilian crown were permitted to do so, practicing their faith in their own mosques.

The treaty did not apply to the Jews of Granada, however, who were forced either to convert to Christianity or emigrate. In the 1300s, anti-Jewish preaching by the Catholic clergy and riots by Christians against Jews in Seville had substantially reduced the Jewish population of some 300,000 at its peak (ca. 1050) to a mere 80,000 in 1492. Of this remainder, a majority emigrated in 1492 to Portugal and the Ottoman Empire, strengthening the urban population of the latter with their commercial and crafts skills. Portugal adopted its own expulsion decree in 1497. Thus, the nearly millennium-and-a-half-long Jewish presence in Sefarad, as Spain was called in Hebrew, ended, with an expulsion designed to strengthen the Christian unity of Iberia.

After the expulsion of the Jews, it did not take long for the Christians to violate the Muslim treaty of surrender. The church engaged in forced conversions, the burning of Arabic books, and transformations of mosques into churches, triggering an uprising of Muslims in Granada (1499–1500). Christian troops crushed the uprising, and Isabella and Ferdinand used it as an excuse to abrogate the treaty of surrender. In one province after another during the early sixteenth century, Muslims were forced to convert, disperse to other provinces, or emigrate.

**Columbus's Journey to the Caribbean**    At the peak of their royal power in early 1492, Isabella and Ferdinand seized a golden opportunity to catch up quickly with the Portuguese in the Atlantic. They authorized the seasoned mariner Christopher Columbus (1451–1506) to build two caravels and a larger carrack and sail westward across the Atlantic. Columbus promised to reach India ahead of the Portuguese, who were attempting to find a route to India by sailing around Africa. The two monarchs pledged money for the construction of ships from Castilian and Aragonese Crusade levies collected from the Muslims.

In September, Columbus and his mariners departed from the Castilian Canary Islands, catching the favorable South Atlantic easterlies. After a voyage of a little over a month, Columbus landed on one of the Bahaman islands. From there he explored a number of Caribbean islands, mistakenly assuming that he was close to the Indian subcontinent. After a stay of 3 months, he left a small colony of settlers behind and returned to Iberia with seven captured Caribbean islanders and a small quantity of gold.

Columbus was a self-educated explorer. Through voracious but indiscriminate reading, he had accumulated substantial knowledge of such diverse subjects as geography, cartography, the Crusades, and the Apocalypse. On the basis of this reading (and his own faulty calculations), he insisted that the ocean stretching between western Europe and eastern Asia was relatively narrow. Furthermore, he fervently believed that God had made him the forerunner of an Iberian apocalyptic world ruler who would recapture Jerusalem from the Muslims just prior to the Second Coming of Christ.

For many years, Columbus had peddled his idea about reaching India (and subsequently Jerusalem) from the east at the Portuguese court. The Portuguese, however, while sharing Columbus's apocalyptic fervor, dismissed his Atlantic Ocean calculations as fantasies. Even in Castile, where Columbus went after his rejection in Portugal, it took several years and the victory over Granada before Queen Isabella finally listened to him. Significantly, it was at the height of their success at Granada in 1492 that Isabella and Ferdinand seized their chance to beat the Portuguese to Asia. Although disappointed by the meager returns of Columbus's first and subsequent voyages, Isabella and Ferdinand were delighted to have acquired new islands in the Caribbean, in addition to the Canaries. In one blow they had drawn even with Portugal.

**Vasco da Gama's Journey to India**    Portugal redoubled its efforts after 1492 to discover the way to India around Africa. In 1498, the king appointed an important court official and member of the crusading Order of Santiago, Vasco da Gama (ca. 1469–1524), to command four caravels for the journey to India. Da Gama, an experienced mariner, made good use of the accumulated Portuguese knowledge of seafaring in the Atlantic and guidance by Arab sailors in the Indian Ocean. After a journey of 6 months, the ships arrived in Calicut, the main spice trade center on the Indian west coast.

The first Portuguese mariner sent ashore by da Gama in Calicut encountered two North African Muslims, who addressed him in Castilian Spanish and Genoese Italian: "The Devil take you! What brought you here?" The mariner replied:

> "We [da Gama and his crew] were so amazed at this that we heard him [the mariner] speak and we could not believe it—that there could be anyone so far away from Portugal who could understand our speech."
> —Álvaro Velho

"We came to seek Christians and spices." When da Gama went inland to see the ruler of Calicut, he was optimistic that he had indeed found what he had come for. Ignorant of Hinduism, he mistook the Indian religion for the Christianity of Prester John. Similarly ignorant of the conventions of the India trade, he offered woolen textiles and metal goods in exchange for pepper, cinnamon, and cloves. The Muslim and Hindu merchants were uninterested in these goods designed for the African market and demanded gold or silver, which the Portuguese had only in small amounts. Rumors spread about the Muslims plotting with the Hindus against the apparently penniless Christian intruders. Prudently, da Gama lifted anchor and returned home with small quantities of spices.

After these modest beginnings, however, within a short time Portugal had mastered the India trade. The Portuguese crown organized regular journeys around Africa, and when Portuguese mariners on one such journey—taking a far western route in the Atlantic—landed in northeast Brazil they claimed it for their expanding commercial network. During the early sixteenth century, the Portuguese India fleets brought considerable amounts of spices from India back to Portugal, threatening the profits of the Egyptian and Venetian merchants who had hitherto dominated the trade. Prester John, of course, was never found, and the project of retaking Jerusalem receded into the background.

# Rise of the Ottomans and Struggle with the Habsburgs for Dominance, 1300–1609

While Muslim rule disappeared in the late fifteenth century from the Iberian Peninsula, the opposite was happening in the Balkans. Here, the Ottoman Turks spearheaded the expansion of Islamic rule over Christians. By the late sixteenth century, when the East–West conflict between the Habsburgs and Ottomans reached its peak, entire generations of Croats, Germans, and Italians lived in mortal fear of the "terrible Turk" who might conquer all of Christian Europe.

**Late Byzantium and Ottoman Origins**    The rise of the Ottomans was closely related to the decline of Byzantium. The emperors of Byzantium had been able to reclaim their "empire" in 1261 from its Latin rulers and Venetian troops by allying themselves with the Genoese. This empire, which during the early fourteenth century included Greece and a few domains in western Anatolia, was no more than a midsize kingdom with modest agricultural resources. But it was still a valuable trading hub, thanks to Constantinople's strategic position as a market linking the Mediterranean with Slavic kingdoms in the Balkans and the Ukrainian–Russian principality of Kiev. Thanks to its commercial wealth, Byzantium experienced a cultural revival, which at its height featured the lively scholarly debate over Plato and Aristotle that exerted a profound influence on the western Renaissance in Italy (see Chapter 10).

Inevitably, however, both Balkan Slavs and Anatolian Turks appropriated Byzantine provinces in the late thirteenth century, further reducing the empire. One of the lost provinces was Bithynia, across the Bosporus in Anatolia. Here, in 1299, the Turkish warlord Osman (1299–1326) gathered his clan and a motley assembly of Islamic holy warriors (Turkish *gazis*, including a local saint and his followers), as well as adventurers (including renegade Byzantines) and declared himself an independent ruler. Osman and a number of other Turkish lords in the region were nominally subject to the Seljuks, the Turkish dynasty which had conquered Anatolia from the Byzantines two centuries earlier but by the early 1300s had disintegrated.

During the first half of the fourteenth century, Osman and his successors emerged as the most powerful emirs by conquering further Anatolian provinces from Byzantium. The Moroccan Abu Abdallah Ibn Battuta (1304–1369), famous for his journeys through the Islamic world, Africa, and China, passed through western Anatolia and Constantinople during the 1330s, visiting several Turkish principalities. He was duly impressed by the rising power of the Ottomans, noting approvingly that they manned nearly 100 forts and castles and maintained pressure on the eastern Christian infidels. In 1354, the Ottomans gained their first European foothold on a peninsula about 100 miles southwest of Constantinople. Thereafter, it seemed only a matter of time before the Ottomans would conquer Constantinople.

Through a skillful mixture of military defense, tribute payments, and dynastic marriages of princesses with Osman's descendants, however, the Byzantine emperors salvaged their rule for another century. They were also helped by Timur the Great

"We journeyed next to Bursa [the capital of the Ottomans, conquered in 1326 from Byzantium], a great city with fine bazaars, surrounded by orchards and springs. Outside it are two thermal establishments, one for men and the other for women to which patients come."

—Ibn Battuta

**Siege of Constantinople, 1453.**
Note the soldiers on the left pulling boats on rollers and wheels over the Galata hillside. With this maneuver, Sultan Mehmet II was able to circumvent the chain stretched across the entrance to the Golden Horn (in place of the anachronistic bridge in the image). This allowed him to speed up his conquest of Constantinople by forcing the defenders to spread their forces thinly over the entire length of the walls.

part of the Byzantine defenses was the central section of the western walls, where it was relatively easy to tunnel into the soil underneath. Here, Mehmet stationed his heaviest guns to bombard the masonry and had his sappers undermine the foundations of the walls.

Another weak section was on the northeastern side, along the harbor in the Golden Horn, where the walls were low. Here, the Byzantines had blocked off the entrance to the Golden Horn with a huge chain. In a brilliant tactical move, Mehmet circumvented the chain. He had troops drag ships on rollers over a hillside into the harbor. The soldiers massed on these ships were ready to disembark and assault the walls with the help of ladders. On the first sign of cracks in the northeastern walls, the Ottoman besiegers stormed the city. The last Byzantine emperor, Constantine XI, perished in the general massacre and pillage which followed the Ottoman occupation of the city.

Mehmet quickly repopulated Constantinople ("Istanbul" in Turkish, from Greek "to the city," *istin polin*) and appointed a new patriarch at the head of the eastern Christians, to whom he promised full protection as his subjects. In quick succession, he ordered the construction of the Topkapı Palace (1459), the transfer of the administration from Edirne (which had been the capital since 1365) to Istanbul, and the resumption of expansion in the Balkans, where he succeeded in forcing the majority of rulers into submitting to vassal status. One of the Balkan lords resisting the sultan was Vlad III Dracul of Wallachia, who according to tradition in 1461–1462 impaled a contingent of Ottoman troops sent against him on sharpened tree trunks. Mehmet replaced Vlad with his more compliant brother, but the memory of the impalements lived on to inspire vampire folktales and, eventually, in 1897, the famous Gothic horror novel *Dracula*.

Mehmet's ongoing conquests eventually brought him to the Adriatic Sea, where one of his generals occupied Otranto on the heel of the Italian peninsula. The Ottomans were poised to launch a full-scale invasion of Italy from Otranto, when the sultan died unexpectedly. His successor evacuated Otranto, preferring to consolidate the Ottoman Empire in the Middle East, North Africa, and the Balkans before reconsidering an invasion of central and western Europe.

**Imperial Apogee**   Between 1500 and 1600 the Ottoman sultans succeeded magnificently in the consolidation of their empire. In 1514, with superior cavalry and infantry forces, cannons, and muskets, the Ottomans defeated the Persian Safavids in Iran, who had risen in 1501 to form a rival Shiite empire in opposition to the Sunni Ottomans. In the southern Middle East, intermittent tensions between the Ottomans and the Mamluk Turks in Egypt, Syria, and eastern Arabia gave way to open war in 1517. The Ottomans, again due to superior firepower, defeated the Mamluks and took control of western Arabia, including the holy pilgrimage city of Mecca. A year later, in 1518, Sultan Süleyman I, "the Magnificent" (r. 1520–1566), appointed a naval commander to drive the Spanish from a series of fortifications and cities in North Africa, which the latter had conquered in the name of the *Reconquista* in the 1490s and early 1500s.

In the Balkans, the Ottomans completed their conquests of Serbia and Hungary with the annexation of Belgrade and Buda (now part of Budapest) as well as a brief siege of Vienna in 1529, begun too late in the year and eventually stopped by the approaching winter. By the second half of the sixteenth century, when the submission of most of Hungary had been secured, the Ottoman Empire was a vast multiethnic and multireligious state of some 15 million inhabitants extending from Algeria in the Maghreb to Yemen in Arabia and from Upper Egypt to the Balkans and the northern shores of the Black Sea (see Map 16.2).

**Morocco and Persia**    In the period of 1450–1600, the two large empires of the Ottomans and Indian Mughals dominated Islamic civilization. Two smaller and more short-lived realms existed in Morocco and Persia, ruled by the Saadid (1509–1659) and Safavid (1501–1722) dynasties, respectively. The Saadid sultans defended themselves successfully against the Ottoman expansion and liberated themselves from the Portuguese occupation of Morocco's Atlantic ports which had followed the conquest of Ceuta in 1415. In 1591, after their liberation, the Saadids sent a firearm-equipped army to West Africa in order to revive the gold trade, which had dwindled to a trickle after the Portuguese arrival in Ghana. The army succeeded in destroying the West African empire of Songhay but failed to revive the gold trade. Moroccan army officers assumed power in Timbuktu, and their descendants, the Ruma, became provincial lords independent of Morocco. The Saadids, unable to improve their finances, split into provincial realms. The still-reigning Alaouite dynasty of Moroccan kings replaced them in 1659.

**Vlad Dracul next to Impaled Ottoman Soldiers.** The woodcut depicts the alleged impalement of 1,000 Ottoman soldiers sent against Vlad Dracul, prior to Sultan Mehmet II leading a victorious campaign into Wallachia and removing Dracul from power. Dracul's cannibalism, suggested in the image, is not confirmed by historical sources.

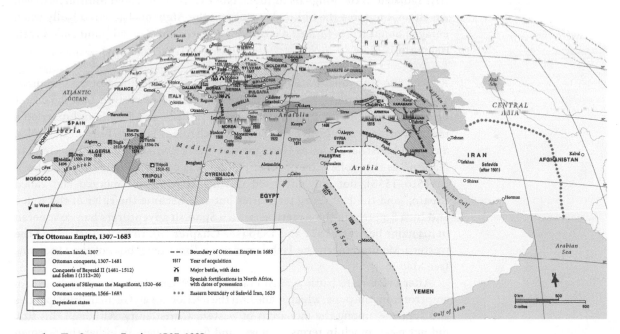

MAP **16.2 The Ottoman Empire, 1307–1683.**

The Safavids grew in the mid-1400s from a Kurdish mystical brotherhood in northwestern Iran into a Shiite warrior organization (similar to the Sunni one participating in the early Ottoman expansion) that carried out raids against Christians in the Caucasus. In 1501, the leadership of the brotherhood put forward the 14-year-old Ismail as the Hidden Twelfth Imam. According to Shiite doctrine, the Hidden Imam, or Messiah, was expected to arrive and establish a Muslim apocalyptic realm of justice at the end of time, before God's Last Judgment. This realm would replace the "unjust" Sunni Ottoman Empire. The Ottomans countered the Safavid challenge in 1514 with the Battle of Chaldiran, where they crushed the underprepared Safavids with their superior cannon and musket firepower. After his humiliating defeat, Ismail dropped his claim to messianic status, and his successors assumed the more modest title of king (Persian *shah*) as the head of state, quite similar in many respects to that of the Ottomans.

Learning from their defeat, the Safavids recruited a standing firearm-equipped army from among young Christians on lands conquered in the Caucasus. They held fast to Shiism, thereby continuing their opposition to the Sunni Ottomans, and supported the formation of a clerical hierarchy, which made this form of Islam dominant in Iran. As sponsors of construction projects, the Safavids greatly improved urbanism in the country. After moving the capital from Tabriz to the centrally located Isfahan in 1590, they built an imposing palace, administration, and mosque complex in the city. In a suburb they settled a large colony of Armenians, who held the monopoly in the production of Caspian Sea silk, a high-quality export product which the Dutch—successors of the Portuguese in the Indian Ocean trade—distributed in Europe.

As patrons of the arts, the shahs revived the ancient traditions of Persian culture to such heights that even the archrival Ottomans felt compelled to adopt Persian manners, literature, and architectural styles. Persian royal culture similarly radiated to the Mughals in India. Not everyone accepted Shiism, however. An attempt to force the Shiite doctrines on the Afghanis backfired badly when enraged Sunni tribes formed a coalition, defeated the Safavids, and ended their regime in 1722.

**Rise of the Habsburgs**    Parallel to the rise and development of the Ottomans and Safavids, Castile–Aragon on the Iberian Peninsula evolved into the center of a vast empire of its own. A daughter of Isabella and Ferdinand married a member of the Habsburg dynastic family, which ruled Flanders, Burgundy, Naples, Sicily, and Austria, as well as Germany (the "Holy Roman Empire of the German Nation," as this collection of principalities was called). Their son, Charles V (r. 1516–1558), not only inherited Castile–Aragon, now merged and called "Spain," and the Habsburg territories but also became the ruler of the Aztec and Inca Empires in the Americas, which Spanish adventurers had conquered in his name between 1521 and 1536 (see Chapter 18). In both Austria and the western Mediterranean the Habsburgs were direct neighbors of the Ottomans (see Map 16.3).

After a victorious battle against France in 1519, Charles V also won the title of emperor from the pope, which made him the overlord of all German principalities and supreme among the monarchs of western Christianity. Although this title did not mean much in terms of power and financial gain in either the German

MAP 16.3 **Europe and the Mediterranean, ca. 1560.**

principalities or western Christianity as a whole, it made him the titular political head of western Christianity and thereby the direct counterpart of Sultan Süleyman in the struggle for dominance in the Christian–Muslim world of Europe, the Middle East, and northern Africa. Both the Habsburgs and the Ottomans renewed the traditional Islamic–Christian imperialism which had characterized the period 600–950 and which had been replaced by the Muslim and Christian commonwealths of 950–1450.

**Habsburg Distractions**   Charles V faced a daunting task in his effort to prevent the Ottomans from advancing against the Christians in the Balkans and Mediterranean. Multiple problems in his European territories diverted his attention and forced him to spend far less time than he wanted on what Christians in most parts of Europe perceived as a pervasive Ottoman–Muslim threat. During the first three decades of the sixteenth century, revolts in Iberia, the Protestant Reformation in the German states, and renewed war with France for control of Burgundy and Italy commanded Charles's attention.

The emperor's distractions increased further in 1534 when, in an attempt to drive the Habsburgs out of Italy, France forged an alliance with the Ottomans. This alliance horrified western Europe. It demonstrated, however, that the Ottomans, on account of their military advances against the Christians in eastern Europe and the western Mediterranean, had become a crucial player in European politics. As fierce as the struggle between Muslims and Christians for dominance was, when the French king found himself squeezed on both sides of his kingdom by his archrival, Charles V, the Ottomans became his natural allies.

**Habsburg and Ottoman Losses**    All these diversions seriously strained Habsburg resources against the Ottomans, who pressed relentlessly ahead on the two fronts of the Balkans and North Africa. Although Charles V deputized his younger brother Ferdinand I to the duchy of Austria in 1521 to shore up the Balkan defenses, he was able to send him significant numbers of troops only once. After a series of dramatic defeats, Austria had to pay the Ottomans tribute and, eventually, even sign a humiliating truce (1562). On the western Mediterranean front, the Habsburgs did not do well either. Even though Charles V campaigned several times in person, most garrisons on the coast of Algeria, Tunisia, and Tripoli were too exposed to withstand the Ottoman onslaught by sea and by land. In 1556, at the end of Charles V's reign, only two of eight Habsburg garrisons had survived.

A third frontier of the Muslim–Christian struggle for dominance was the Indian Ocean. After Vasco da Gama had returned from India in 1498, the Portuguese kings invested major resources into breaking into the Muslim-dominated Indian Ocean trade. In response, the Ottomans made great efforts to protect existing Muslim commercial interests in the Indian Ocean. They blocked Portuguese military support for Ethiopia and strengthened their ally and main pepper supplier, the sultan of Aceh on the Indonesian island of Sumatra, by providing him with troops and weapons. War on land and on sea, directly and by proxy, raged in the Indian Ocean through most of the sixteenth century.

In the long run, the Portuguese were successful in destroying the Ottoman fleets sent against them, but smaller convoys of Ottoman galleys continued to harass Portuguese shipping interests. As new research on the Ottoman "age of exploration" in the Indian Ocean has demonstrated, by 1570 the Muslims traded again as much via the Red Sea route to the Mediterranean as the Portuguese did by circumnavigating Africa. In addition, the Ottomans benefited from the trade of a new commodity—coffee, produced in Ethiopia and Yemen. Portugal (under Spanish rule 1580–1640) reduced its unsustainably large military presence in the Indian Ocean, followed by the Ottomans, which allowed the Netherlands in the early seventeenth century to overtake both Portugal and the Ottoman Empire in the Indian Ocean spice trade (see Map 16.4).

**Habsburg–Ottoman Balance**    In the 1550s, Charles V despaired of being able to ever master the many challenges posed by the Ottomans as well as by France and

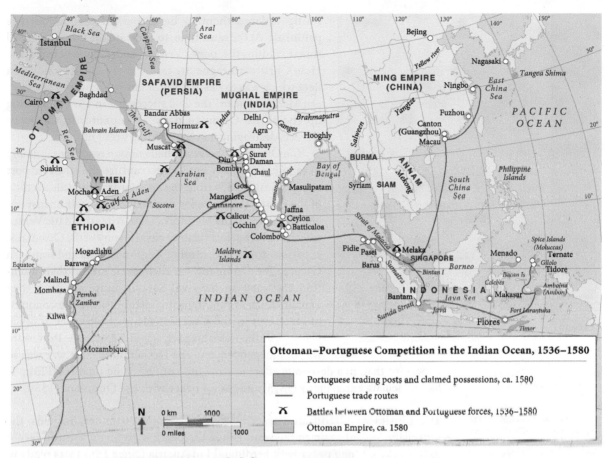

MAP 16.4 **Ottoman–Portuguese Competition in the Indian Ocean, 1536–1580.**

the Protestants. He decided that the only way to ensure the continuation of Habsburg power would be a division of his western and eastern territories. Accordingly, he bestowed Spain, Naples, the Netherlands, and the Americas on his son Philip II (r. 1556–1598). The Habsburg possessions of Austria, Bohemia, and the remnant of Hungary not lost to the Ottomans, as well as the Holy Roman Empire (Germany), went to his brother Ferdinand I (r. 1558–1564). Charles hoped that his son and brother would cooperate and help each other militarily against the Ottomans.

When Philip took over the Spanish throne, he realized, to his concern, that most of the Habsburg military was stationed outside Spain, leaving that country vulnerable to attack. As the Ottomans had recently conquered most Spanish strongholds in North Africa, a Muslim invasion of Spain was a distinct possibility. Fearful of morisco support for an Ottoman invasion of Spain, Philip's administration and the Inquisition renewed their decrees of conversion which had lain dormant for half a century.

This sparked a massive revolt among the moriscos of Granada in 1568–1570, supported by Ottoman soldiers and Moroccan arms. Philip was able to suppress the revolt only after recourse to troops and firearms from Italy. To break up the dangerously large concentrations of Granadan moriscos in the south of Spain,

**Paolo Veronese, *Battle of Lepanto*, altar painting with four saints beseeching the Virgin Mary to grant victory to the Christians (ca. 1572).** In the sixteenth century, the entire Mediterranean, from Gibraltar to Cyprus, was a naval battleground between Christians and Muslims. The Battle of Lepanto was the first major sea battle in world history to be decided by firepower: Even though Christian forces had slightly fewer ships, they had more, and heavier, artillery pieces. At the end of the battle "the sea was entirely covered, not just with masts, spars, oars, and broken wood, but with an innumerable quantity of blood that turned the water as red as blood."

Philip ordered them to be dispersed throughout the peninsula. At the same time, to alleviate the Ottoman naval threat, Philip, the pope, Venice, and Genoa formed the Holy Christian League. Its task was the construction of a fleet which was to destroy Ottoman sea power in the eastern Mediterranean. The fleet succeeded in 1571 in bottling up the entire Ottoman navy at Lepanto, in Ottoman Greece, destroying it in the ensuing firefight.

The Ottomans, however, had enough resources not only to rebuild their navy but also to capture the strategic port city of Tunis in 1574 from the Spaniards. With this evening of the scores, the two sides decided to end their unsustainable naval war in the Mediterranean. After this date, Venice was the only (but formidable) naval enemy of the Ottomans, at various times in control of Aegean islands and southern Greece. The Ottomans, for their part, turned their attention eastward, to the rival Safavid Empire, where they exploited a period of dynastic instability for the conquest of territories in the Caucasus (1578–1590). The staunch Catholic Philip II, for his part, was faced with the Protestant war of independence in the Netherlands. This war was so expensive that, in a desperate effort to straighten out his state finances, Philip II had to declare bankruptcy (1575) and sue for peace with the Ottomans (1580).

**The Limits of Ottoman Power**   After their victory over the Safavids, the Ottomans looked again to the west. While the peace with Spain was too recent to be broken, a long peace with Ferdinand I in Austria (since 1562) was ready to collapse. A series of raids and counter-raids at the Austrian and Transylvanian borders had inflamed tempers, and in 1593 the Ottomans went on the attack. Austria, however, was no longer the weak state it had been a generation earlier. Had it not been for a lack of support from the Transylvanian and Hungarian Protestants, who preferred the sultan to the Catholic emperor as overlord, the Austrians might have actually prevailed over the Ottomans.

However, thanks to the Protestants' support, the Ottomans drew even on the battlefield with the Austrians. In 1606, the Ottomans and Austrian Habsburgs made peace again. With minor modifications in favor of the Austrians, the two sides returned to their earlier borders. The Austrians made one more tribute payment and then let their obligation lapse. Officially, the Ottomans conceded nothing, but in practical terms Austria was no longer a vassal state.

**Expulsion of the Moriscos**   In the western Mediterranean, the peace between the Ottomans and Spanish Habsburgs held. But Philip and his successors remained aware of the possibility of renewed Ottoman aid to the Iberian Muslims, called *moriscos* ("little Moors"). Even though they had been scattered across the peninsula after 1570, the moriscos continued to resist conversion. Among Castilians, an intense debate began about the apparent impossibility of assimilating them to Catholicism in order to create a religiously unified state. The church advocated the expulsion of the moriscos, arguing that the allegedly high Muslim birthrate in a population of 7.5 million (mostly rural) Spaniards was a serious threat.

Fierce resistance against the proposed expulsion, however, rose among the Christian landowners in the southeastern province of Valencia. These landowners benefited greatly from the farming skills of the estimated 250,000 morisco tenant farmers who worked their irrigated rice and sugarcane estates. Weighing the potential Ottoman threat against the possibility of economic damage, the government decided in 1580 in favor of expulsion. Clearly, they valued Christian unity against the Ottomans more than the prosperity of a few hundred landowners in Valencia.

It took until 1609, however, before a compensation deal with the landowners in Valencia was worked out. In the following 5 years, some 300,000 moriscos were forcibly expelled from Spain, under often appalling circumstances: They had to leave all their possessions behind, including money and jewelry, taking only whatever clothes and household utensils they could carry. As in the case of the Jews a century earlier, Spain's loss was the Ottoman Empire's gain, this time mostly in the form of skilled irrigation farmers.

**Expulsion of the Moriscos (secret Muslims) from Spain, 1609–1614.** The Moriscos had to leave all their valuables behind, carrying only their barest belongings and watched closely by soldiers, as seen in this etching.

# The Centralizing State: Origins and Interactions

The major technological change that occurred in the Middle East and Europe during 1250–1350 was the growing use of firearms. It took until the mid-1400s, however, before cannons and muskets were technically effective and reliable enough to make a difference in warfare. At this time, a pattern emerged whereby rulers created centralized states to finance their strategic shift to firearm-bearing infantries. They resumed the policy of conquest and imperialism, which had lain dormant during the preceding period, when the religious civilizations of Islam and Christianity had evolved into commonwealths of many competing realms. Both the Ottomans and the Habsburgs raised immense amounts of cash in silver and gold to spend on cannons, muskets, and ships for achieving world rule.

### State Transformation, Money, and Firearms

In the early stages of their realms, the kings of Iberia (1150–1400) and the Ottoman sultans (1300–1400), with little cash on hand, compensated military commanders for their service in battle with parcels of conquered land, or land grants. That land, farmed by villagers, generated rental income in kind for the officers. Once the Iberian and Ottoman rulers had conquered cities and gained control over long-distance trade, however, patterns changed. Rulers began collecting taxes in cash, with which they paid regiments of personal guards to supplement the army of land-grant officers and their retainers. They created the centralizing state, forerunner of the absolutist state of the early seventeenth century.

**Money economy:**
Form of economic
organization in which
mutual obligations
are settled through
monetary exchanges;
in contrast, a system of
land grants obliges the
landholders to provide
military service, without
payment, to the grantee
(sultan or king).

**Janissaries:** Centrally
paid infantry soldiers
recruited among the
Christian population
of the Ottoman Empire.

**The Land-Grant System** When the Ottoman *beys*, or military lords, embarked on their conquests in the early 1300s, they created personal domains on the choice lands they had conquered. Here, they took rents in kind from the resident villagers to finance their small dynastic households. Their comrades in arms, such as members of their clan or adherents (many of whom were holy warriors and/or adventurers), received other conquered lands, from which they also collected rents. As the Ottomans conquered Byzantine cities, first in Anatolia and then, in the second half of the 1300s, in the Balkans, they gained access to the **money economy**. They collected taxes in coins from the markets and tollbooths at city gates where foods and crafts goods were exchanged, as well as from the Christians and Jews subject to the head tax. The taxes helped in adding luxuries to the households of the Ottoman beys and enabling them to build palaces.

As a consequence of the full conquest of the southern Balkans by the Ottoman Empire in the fifteenth and sixteenth centuries, both the land-grant system and the money economy expanded exponentially. An entire military ruling class of grant holders emerged, forming the backbone of the early Ottoman army and administration. The grant holders were cavalrymen who lived with their households of retainers in the villages and towns of the interior of Anatolia and the Balkans.

**Boy Levy (*devşirme*) in a Christian Village.** This miniature graphically depicts the trauma of conscription, including the wailing of the village women and the assembly of boys waiting to be taken away by implacable representatives of the sultan.

Most of the time, they were away on campaign with the sultans, leaving managers in charge of the collection of rents from the villagers on their lands. At the conclusion of the period of rapid growth of the Ottoman Empire in the early years of the sixteenth century, the landed ruling class of cavalrymen numbered some 80,000, constituting a vast reserve of warriors for the mobilization of troops each summer.

**The Janissaries** An early indicator of the significance of the money economy in the Ottoman Empire was the military institution of the **Janissaries**—troops which received salaries from the central treasury. This institution probably appeared during the second half of the fourteenth century and is first documented in 1395. It was based on a practice (called *devşirme* [dev-SHIR-me]) of conscripting young boys, which palace officers carried out irregularly every few years among the empire's Christian population. For this purpose, the palace officers traveled to Christian villages, towns, and cities in the Balkans, Greece, and Anatolia. At each occasion, they selected boys between the ages of 6 and 16 and marched them off to Istanbul, where they were converted to Islam and trained as future soldiers and administrators. The boys and young men then entered the central system of palace slaves under the direct orders of the sultan and his viziers or ministers.

The *devşirme* contradicted Islamic law, which forbade the enslavement of "peoples of the Book" (Jews, Christians, and Zoroastrians). Its existence, therefore, documents the extent to which the sultans reasserted the Roman–Sasanid–Arab imperial traditions of the ruler making doctrine and law. Ruling by divine grace, the Ottomans were makers of their own law, called *kanun* (from Greek *kanon*). Muslim religious scholars, who had assumed the role of guardians of law and doctrine during the preceding commonwealth period of Islamic civilization (950–1300), had no choice but to accept sultanic imperialism and seek to adapt it to the Sharia as best they could.

Toward the first half of the fifteenth century, the sultans equipped their Janissaries with cannons and matchlock muskets. According to reports in Arabic chronicles, firearms first appeared around 1250 in the Middle East, probably coming from China. When the Janissaries received them, firearms had therefore undergone some 150 years of experimentation and development in the Middle East and North Africa. Even though the cannons and muskets were still far from being decisive in battle, they had become sophisticated enough to make a difference. By the mid-1400s, gigantic siege cannons and slow but reliable matchlock muskets were the standard equipment of Ottoman and other armies. The sultans relied on large numbers of indigenous, rather than European, gunsmiths, as new research in Ottoman archives has revealed.

**Revenues and Money**    The maintenance of a salaried standing army of infantry soldiers and a central administration to provide the fiscal foundation would have been impossible without precious metals. Therefore, the Ottoman imperial expansion was driven by the need to acquire mineral deposits. During the fifteenth century the Ottomans captured the rich silver, lead, and iron mines of Serbia and Bosnia. Together with Anatolian copper, iron, and silver mines conquered earlier, the Balkan mines made the Ottomans the owners of the largest precious metal production centers prior to the Habsburg acquisition of the Mexican and Andean mines in the mid-1500s.

The sultans left the Balkan mining and smelting operations in the hands of preconquest Christian entrepreneurs from the autonomous Adriatic coastal city-state of Ragusa or Dubrovnik. These entrepreneurs were integrated into the Ottoman imperial money economy as tax farmers obliged to buy their right of operation from the government in return for reimbursing themselves from the mining and smelting profits. **Tax farming** was the preferred method of producing cash revenues for the central administration. The holders of tax farms delivered the profits from the production of metals, salt, saltpeter, and other minerals to the state, minus the commission they were entitled to subtract for themselves. They also collected the head tax—payable in money—from the Jews and Christians and the profits from the sale of the agricultural dues from state domains. Thus, tax farmers were crucial members of the ruling class, responsible for the cash flow in the state.

The right to mint silver into the basic coin of the empire was similarly part of the tax-farm regime, as were the market, city gate, and port duties. The tax-farm regime, of course, was crucially dependent on a strong sultan or chief minister, the grand vizier. Without close supervision, this regime could easily deteriorate into a state of decentralization, something which indeed eventually happened in the Ottoman Empire on a large scale, although not before the eighteenth century.

**Devşirme:** The levy on boys in the Ottoman Empire; that is, the obligation of the Christian population to contribute adolescent males to the military and administrative classes.

**Tax farming:** Governmental auction of the right to collect taxes in a district. The tax farmer advanced these taxes to the treasury and retained a commission.

**Ottoman Siege of a Christian Fortress.** By the middle of the fifteenth century, cannons had revolutionized warfare. Niccolò Machiavelli, ever attuned to new developments, noted in 1519 that "no wall exists, however thick, that artillery cannot destroy in a few days." Machiavelli could have been commenting on the Ottomans, who were masters of siege warfare. Sultan Mehmet II, the conqueror of Constantinople in 1453, founded the Imperial Cannon Foundry shortly thereafter; it would go on to make some of the biggest cannons of the period.

**Süleyman's Central State**    The centralizing state of the Ottomans reached its apogee under Sultan Süleyman I, "the Magnificent." At the beginning of the sultan's reign, the amount of money available for expenditures was twice that of half a century earlier. By the end of his reign, this amount had again doubled. With this money, the sultan financed a massive expansion of the military and bureaucracy. Palace, military, and bureaucracy formed a centralized state, the purpose of which was to project power and cultural splendor toward its predominantly rural subjects in the interior as well as Christian enemies outside the empire.

The bureaucrats were recruited from two population groups. Most top ministers and officers in the fifteenth and sixteenth centuries came from the *devşirme* among the Christians. The conscripted boys learned Turkish, received an Islamic education, and underwent intensive firearm and (for some) horsemanship training, in preparation for salaried service in the Janissary army or administration.

The empire's other recruits came from colleges in Istanbul and provincial cities to which the Muslim population of the empire had access. Colleges were institutions through which ambitious villagers far from major urban centers could gain upward mobility. Graduates with law degrees found employment in the bureaucracy or as judges in the villages, towns, and cities. Muslims of Christian parentage made up the top layer of the elite, while Muslims of Islamic descent occupied the middle ranks.

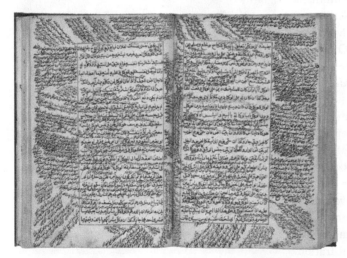

**Ottoman Law Book.** Covering the entire range of human activity—from spiritual matters, family relations, and inheritances to business transactions and crimes—the *Multaqa al-abhur* (*The Confluence of the Currents*) was completed in 1517 and remained for hundreds of years the authoritative source for many of the laws in the Ottoman Empire. It was written in Arabic by the legal scholar Ibrahim al-Halabi; later commentators added annotations in the margins and within the body of the text itself.

Under Süleyman, the Janissaries comprised about 18,000 soldiers, divided into 11,000 musket-equipped troopers, a cavalry of 5,000, and 2,000 gunners who formed the artillery regiments. Most were stationed in barracks in and near the Topkapı Palace in Istanbul, ready to go on campaign at the sultan's command. Other Janissaries provided service in provincial cities and border fortresses. For his campaigns, the sultan added levies from among the cavalry troops in the towns and villages of the empire.

Typical campaigns involved 70,000 soldiers and required sophisticated logistics. All wages, gunpowder, and weapons and the majority of the foodstuffs were carried on wagons and barges, since soldiers were not permitted to provision themselves from the belongings of the villagers, whether friend or foe. Although the state collected heavy taxes, it had a strong interest in not destroying the productivity of the villagers.

**Charles V's Centralizing State**    The centralizing state began in Iberia with the political and fiscal reforms of Isabella and Ferdinand and reached its mature phase under Charles V. From the late fifteenth century onward, Castile and Aragon shared many fiscal characteristics with those of the Ottomans. The Spanish monarchs derived cash advances from tax farmers, who organized the production and sale of minerals and salt. From other tax farmers, they received advances on the taxes collected in money from the movement of goods in and out of ports, cities, and markets, as well as on taxes collected in kind from independent farmers and converted through sale on urban markets. In addition, Muslims paid head taxes in cash. Most of the money taxes were also enforced in Flanders, Burgundy, Naples, Sicily, and Austria, after Iberia's incorporation into the Habsburg domain in 1516. Together, these taxes were more substantial than those of Spain, especially in highly urbanized Flanders, where the percentage of the urban population was about twice that of Spain.

From 1521 to 1536, the Spanish crown enlarged its money income by the one-fifth share to which it was entitled from looted Aztec and Inca gold and silver treasures. Charles V used these treasures to finance his expedition against Tunis. Thereafter, he collected a one-quarter share from the silver mines in the Americas that were brought into production beginning in 1545. Full production in the mines was not reached until the second half of the sixteenth century, but already under Charles V Habsburg imperial revenues doubled, reaching about the same level as those of the Ottomans. Thus, at the height of their struggle for dominance in the Muslim–Christian world, the Habsburgs and the Ottomans expended roughly the same amounts of resources to hurl against each other in the form of troops, cannons, muskets, and war galleys.

In one significant respect, however, the two empires differed. The cavalry ruling class of the Ottoman Empire was nonhereditary. Although land-grant holdings went in practice from father to son and then grandson, their holders had no recourse to the law if the sultans decided to replace them. By contrast, ever since the first half of the thirteenth century, when the Iberian kings were still lacking appreciable monetary resources, their landholders possessed a legal right to inheritance. The landholders met more or less regularly in parliaments (Spanish *cortes*), where they could enforce their property rights against the kings through majority decisions. When Isabella and Ferdinand embarked on state centralization, they had to wrestle with a powerful, landed aristocracy that had taken over royal jurisdiction and tax prerogatives (especially market taxes) on their often vast lands, including cities as well as towns and villages. The two monarchs took back much of the jurisdiction but were unable to do much about the taxes, thus failing in one crucial respect in their centralization effort. Although Habsburg Spain relied on precious metals as heavily as the Ottoman Empire did, it was in the end less centralized than that of the Ottomans.

The Habsburgs sought to overcome their lack of power over the aristocracy and the weakness of their Spanish tax base by squeezing as much as they could out of the Italian and Flemish cities and the American colonies. But in the long run their finances remained precarious, plentiful in some years but sparse in others. Relatively few Spanish aristocrats bothered to fulfill their traditional obligation to unpaid military service. Others who did serve forced the kings to pay them like mercenaries. As a result, in the administration and especially in the military, the kings hired as many Italians, Flemings, and Germans as possible. At times, they even had to deploy them to Spain in order to maintain peace there. Most of these foreigners were foot soldiers, equipped with muskets.

The Ottoman and Habsburg patterns of centralized state formation bore similarities to patterns in the Roman and Arab Empires half a millennium earlier. At that time, however, the scale was more modest, given that the precious metals from West Africa and the Americas were not yet part of the trade network.

In addition, earlier empires did not yet possess firearms, requiring an expensive infrastructure of charcoal and metal production, gunsmithing, saltpeter mining, and gunpowder manufacture. Thanks to firearms, the centralizing states of the period after 1450 were much more potent enterprises. They were established polities, evolving into absolutist and eventually national states.

# Imperial Courts, Urban Festivities, and the Arts

Ottoman and Habsburg rulers set aside a portion of revenues to project the splendor and glory of their states to subjects at home as well as enemies abroad. They commissioned the building of palaces, mosques, and churches and sponsored public festivities. Since the administrators, nobility, tax farmers, and merchants had considerable funds, they also patronized writers, artists, and architects. Although Christian and Muslim artists and artisans belonged to different religious and cultural traditions and expressed themselves through different media, their artistic achievements were inspired by the same impulse: to glorify their states through religious expression.

## The Ottoman Empire: Palaces, Festivities, and the Arts

The Ottomans built palaces and celebrated public feasts to demonstrate their imperial power and wealth. In Ottoman Islamic civilization, however, there were no traditions of official public art. The exception was architecture, where a veritable explosion of mosque construction occurred during the sixteenth century. Refined pictorial artistry, in the form of portraits, book illustrations, and miniatures, was found only inside the privacy of the Ottoman palace and wealthy administrative households. As in Habsburg Spain, theater and music enjoyed much support on the popular level, in defiance of official religious restrictions against these forms of entertainment.

**The Topkapı Palace**   When the Ottoman sultans conquered the Byzantine capital Constantinople in 1453, they acquired one of the great cities of the world. Although richly endowed with Roman monuments and churches, it was dilapidated and depopulated when the Ottomans took over. The sultans initiated large construction projects, such as covered markets, and populated the city with craftspeople and traders drawn from both the Asian and European sides of their empire. By 1600 Istanbul was again an imposing metropolis with close to half a million inhabitants, easily the largest city in Europe at that time.

One of the construction projects was a new palace for the sultans, the Topkapı Sarayı, or "Palace of the Gun Gate," begun in 1459. The Topkapı was a veritable minicity, with three courtyards, formal gardens, and forested hunting grounds. It also included the main administrative school for the training of imperial bureaucrats, barracks for the standing troops of the Janissaries, an armory, a hospital, and—most important—the living quarters, or harem, for the ruling family. Subjects were permitted access only through the first courtyard— reserved for imperial festivities—to submit their petitions to the sultan's council of ministers.

The institution of the harem rose to prominence toward the end of the reign of Süleyman. At that time, sultans no longer pursued marriage alliances with neighboring Islamic rulers. Instead, they chose slave concubines for the procreation of children, preferably boys. Concubines were usually from the Caucasus or other frontier regions, often Christian, and, since they were slaves, deprived of family attachments. A concubine who bore a son to the reigning sultan acquired privileges, such as influence on decisions made by the central administration.

The head eunuch of the harem guard evolved into a powerful intermediary for all manner of small and large diplomatic and military decisions between the sultan's mother, who was confined to the harem, and the ministers or generals she sought to influence. In addition, the sultan's mother arranged marriages of her daughters to members of the council of ministers and other high-ranking officials. In the strong patriarchal order of the Ottoman Empire, it might come as a surprise to see women exercise such power, but this power evidently had its roots in the tutelage exercised by mothers over sons who were potential future sultans.

**Imperial Hall, Topkapı Palace.** The Ottomans never forgot their nomadic roots. Topkapı Palace, completed in 1479 and expanded and redecorated several times, resembles in many ways a vast encampment, with a series of enclosed courtyards. At the center of the palace complex were the harem and the private apartments of the sultan, which included the Imperial Hall, where the sultan would receive members of his family and closest advisors.

**Public Festivities**    As in Habsburg Spain, feasts and celebrations were events that displayed the state's largesse and benevolence. Typical festivities were the Feast of Breaking the Fast, which came at the end of the fasting month of Ramadan, and the Feast of Sacrifice, which took place a month and a half later at the end of the Meccan pilgrimage. Festive processions and fairs welcomed the return of the Meccan pilgrimage caravan. Other feasts were connected with the birthday of the Prophet Muhammad and his journey to heaven and hell. Muslims believed that the Prophet's birth was accompanied by miracles and that the angel Gabriel accompanied him on his journey, showing him the joys of heaven and the horrors of hell. Processions with banners, music, and communal meals commemorated the birthdays of local Muslim saints in many cities and towns. As in Christian Spain, these feasts attracted large crowds.

Wrestlers, ram handlers, and horsemen performed in the Hippodrome, the stadium for public festivities. Elimination matches in wrestling determined the eventual champion. Ram handlers spurred their animals to gore one another with their horns. Horsemen stood upright on horses, galloping toward a mound, which they had to hit with a javelin. At the harbor of the Golden Horn, tightrope artists stood high above the water, balancing themselves on cables stretched between the masts of ships, as they performed juggling feats. Fireworks—featuring a variety of effects, noises, and colors—completed the circumcision festival in the evening. Court painters recorded the procession and performance scenes in picture albums. The sultans incorporated these albums into their libraries, together with history books recording in word and image their military victories against the Habsburgs.

**Popular Theater**    The evenings of the fasting month of Ramadan were filled with festive meals and a special form of entertainment, the Karagöz ("Black Eye")

**Ottoman Festivities, 1720.**
The sultan watches from a kiosk on the shore of the Golden Horn as artists perform high-wire acts, musicians and dancers perform from rowboats offshore, and high officials and foreign dignitaries view the festivities from a galleon.

shadow theater. This form of theater came from Egypt, although it probably had Javanese–Chinese roots. The actors in the Karagöz theater used figures cut from thin, transparent leather, painted in primary colors, and fashioned with movable jaws and limbs. With brightly burning lamps behind them, actors manipulated the figures against a cloth screen. The audience was seated on the other side of the screen, following the plays with rapt attention (or not).

Among boys, a performance of the Karagöz theater accompanied the ritual of circumcision, a rite of passage from the ancient Near East adopted in Islamic civilization. The custom called for boys between the ages of 6 and 12 to be circumcised. Circumcision signified the passage from the nurturing care of the mother to the educational discipline of the father. Groups of newly circumcised boys were placed in beds from which they watched the Karagöz plays.

**Mosque Architecture**   During the sixteenth century, the extraordinarily prolific architect Sinan (ca. 1492–1588) filled Istanbul and the earlier Ottoman capital Edirne with a number of imperial mosques, defined by their characteristic slender minarets. According to his autobiography, Sinan designed more than 300 religious and secular buildings, from mosques, colleges, and hospitals to aqueducts and bridges. Sultan Süleyman, wealthy officials, and private donors provided the funds. Sinan was able to hire as many as 25,000 laborers, enabling him to build most of his mosques in six years or less.

**Selimiye and Hagia Sophia.**
The architect Sinan elegantly melded the eight, comparatively thin, columns inside the mosque (*a*) with the surrounding walls and allowed for a maximum of light to enter the building. In addition, light enters through the dome (*b*). Compare this mosque with the much more heavily built, late-Roman-founded Hagia Sophia (*c*).

Sinan described the Shehzade and Süleymaniye mosques in Istanbul and the Selimiye mosque in Edirne as his apprentice, journeyman, and master achievements. All three followed the central dome-over-a-square concept of the Hagia Sophia, which in turn is built in the tradition of Persian and Roman dome architecture. His primary, and most original, contribution to the history of architecture was the replacement of the highly visible and massive four exterior buttresses, which marked the square ground plan of the Hagia Sophia, with up to eight slender pillars as hidden internal supports of the dome. His intention with each of these mosques was not massive monumentality but elegant spaciousness, giving the skylines of Istanbul and Edirne their unmistakable identity.

## The Spanish Habsburg Empire: Popular Festivities and the Arts

The centrality of Catholicism gave the culture of the Habsburg Empire a strongly religious coloration. Both state-sponsored spectacles and popular festivities displayed devotion to the Catholic faith. More secular tendencies, however, began to appear as well, if only because new forms of literature and theater emerged outside the religious sphere as a result of the Renaissance. Originating in Italy and the Netherlands, Renaissance aesthetics emphasized pre-Christian Greek and Roman heritages, which had not been available to medieval Christian artists.

**Capital and Palace**  The Habsburgs focused relatively late on creating the typical symbols of state power and splendor—that is, a capital city and a palace. Most Spaniards lived in the northern third and along the southern and eastern rims of the Iberian Peninsula, leaving the inhospitable central high plateau, the Meseta, thinly inhabited. Catholicism was the majority religion by the sixteenth century and a powerful unifying force, but there were strong linguistic differences among the provinces of the Iberian Peninsula. Charles V resided for a while in a palace in Granada next door to the formerly Muslim Alhambra palace. Built in an Italian Renaissance-derived style and appearing overwhelming and bombastic in comparison to the outwardly unprepossessing Alhambra, Granada was too Moorish and, geographically, too far away in the south for more than a few Spanish subjects to be properly awed.

Only a few places in the river valleys traversing the Meseta were suited for the location of a central palace and administration. Philip II eventually found such a place near the city of Madrid (built on Roman-Visigothic foundations), which in the early sixteenth century had some 12,000 inhabitants. There, he had his royal architect in chief and sculptor Juan Bautista de Toledo (ca. 1515–1567), a student of Michelangelo, build the imposing Renaissance-style palace and monastery complex of El Escorial (1563–1584).

As a result, Madrid became the seat of the administration and later of the court. A large central square and broad avenue were cut across the narrow alleys of the old city, which had once been a Muslim provincial capital. People of all classes gathered in the square and avenue, to participate in public festivities and learn the latest news "about the intentions of the Grand Turk, revolutions in the Netherlands, the state of things in Italy, and the latest discoveries made in the Indies," as the writer Antonio de Liñán y Verdugo remarked in a work published in 1620.

Like its Italian paradigm, the architecture of the Spanish Renaissance emphasized the Roman imperial style—itself derived from the Greeks—with long friezes, round arches, freestanding columns, and rotunda-based domes. With this style, Spanish architects departed from the preceding Gothic, stressing horizontal extension rather than height and plain rather than relief or ornament-filled surfaces.

**Christian State Festivities**    Given the close association between the state and the church, the Spanish crown expressed its glory through the observance of feast days of the Christian calendar. Christmas, Easter, Pentecost, Trinity Sunday, Corpus Christi, and the birthdays of numerous saints were the occasion for processions and/or **passion plays**, during which urban residents affirmed the purity of their Catholic faith. Throngs lined the streets or marched in procession, praying, singing, weeping, and exclaiming. During Holy Week, the week preceding Easter, Catholics—wearing white robes, tall white or black pointed hats, and veils over their faces—marched through the streets, carrying heavy crosses or shouldering wooden platforms with statues of Jesus and Mary. A variety of religious lay groups or confraternities competed to build the most elaborately decorated platforms. Members of flagellant confraternities whipped themselves. The physical rigors of the Holy Week processions were collective reenactments of Jesus' suffering on the Cross.

**Passion play:** Dramatic representation of the trial, suffering, and death of Jesus Christ; passion plays are still an integral part of Holy Week in many Catholic countries today.

By contrast, the Corpus Christi (Latin, meaning "body of Christ") processions that took place on the Sunday after Trinity Sunday (several weeks after Easter) were joyous celebrations. Central to these processions was a platform with a canopy covering the consecrated host (bread believed to have been transfigured into the body of Jesus). Marchers dressed as giants, serpents, dragons, devils, angels, patriarchs, and saints participated in jostling and pushing contests. Others wore masks, played music, performed dances, and enacted scenes from the Bible. Being part of the crowd in the Corpus Christi processions meant partaking in a joyful anticipation of salvation.

**The Auto-da-Fé**    The investigation or proceeding of faith (Portuguese *auto-da-fé*, "act of faith") was a show trial in which the state, through the Spanish Inquisition, judged a person's commitment to Catholicism. Inquisitional trials were intended to display the all-important unity and purity of the Catholic Reformation. The Inquisition employed thousands of state-appointed church officials to investigate anonymous denunciations of individuals failing to conform to the prescribed doctrines and liturgy of the Catholic faith.

Suspected offenders, such as Jewish or Muslim converts to Catholicism or perceived deviants from Catholicism, had to appear before one of the 15 tribunals distributed throughout the country. In secret trials, officials determined the degree of the offense and the appropriate punishment. These trials often employed torture, such as stretching the accused on the rack, suspending them with weights, crushing hands and feet in an apparatus called "the boot," and burning them with firebrands. In contrast to the wide perception of the Inquisition as marked by pervasive cruelties, however, scholarship has emphasized that in the great majority of cases the punishments were minor, or the investigations did not lead to convictions.

**Popular Festivities**    *Jousts* (mock combats between contestants mounted on horseback) were secular, primarily aristocratic events, also frequently connected with dynastic occurrences. The contestants, colorfully costumed as Muslims, Turks, and Christians, rode their horses into the city square accompanied by trumpets and drums and led their horses through a precise and complex series of movements. At the height of the spectacle, contestants divided into groups of three or four at each end of the square. At a signal, they galloped at full speed past each other, hurling their javelins at one another while protecting themselves with their shields. The joust evolved eventually into exhibitions of dressage ("training"), cultivated by the Austrian Habsburgs, who in 1572 founded the Spanish Court Riding School in Vienna.

Bullfights, also fought on horseback, often followed the jousts. Fighting wild animals, including bulls, in spectacles was originally a Roman custom that had evolved from older bovine sacrifices in temples around the Mediterranean. During the Middle Ages, bullfights were aristocratic pastimes that drew spectators from local estates. Bullfighters, armed with detachable metal points on 3-foot-long spears, tackled several bulls in a town square, together with footmen who sought to distract the bulls by waving red capes at them. The bullfighter who stuck the largest number of points into the shoulders of the bull was the winner.

**Theater and Literature**    The dramatic enactments of biblical scenes in the passion plays and Corpus Christi processions were the origin of a new phenomenon in Italy and Spain, the secular theater. During earlier centuries, traveling troupes had often performed on wagons after processions. Stationary theaters with stages, main floors, balconies, and boxes appeared in the main cities of Spain during the sixteenth century. A performance typically began with a musical prelude and a prologue describing the piece, followed by the three acts of a drama or comedy. Brief sketches, humorous or earnest, filled the breaks. Plays dealt with betrayed or unrequited love, honor, justice, or peasant–nobility conflicts. Many

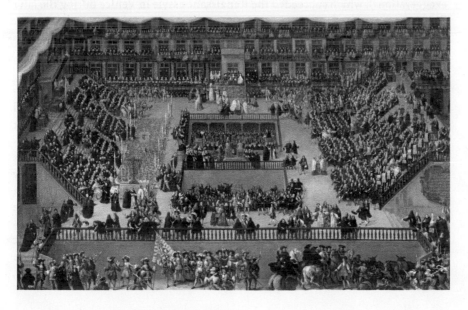

**Auto-da-Fé, Madrid.** This detail from a painting showing a huge assembly in the Plaza Mayor, Madrid, in 1683, captures the drama and spectacle of the auto-da-fé. In the center, below a raised platform, the accused stand in the docket waiting for their convictions to be pronounced; ecclesiastical and civil authorities follow the proceedings from huge grandstands set up for the event. On the left, an outdoor altar is visible—the celebration of Mass was a common feature of the auto-da-fé, which would often last for several hours.

**El Greco, *View of Toledo*, ca. 1610–1614.** The painting, now in the Metropolitan Museum of Art in New York City, illustrates El Greco's predilection for color contrasts and dramatic motion. Baroque and Mannerist painters rarely depicted landscapes, and this particular landscape is represented in eerie green, gray, and blue colors, giving the impression of a city enveloped in a mysterious natural or perhaps spiritual force.

were hugely successful, enjoying the attendance or even sponsorship of courtiers, magistrates, and merchants.

An important writer of the period was Miguel de Cervantes (1547–1616), who wrote his masterpiece, *Don Quixote*, in the new literary form of the novel. Don Quixote describes the adventures of a poverty-stricken knight and his attendant, the peasant Sancho Panza, as they wander around Spain searching for the life of bygone *Reconquista* chivalry. Their journey includes many hilarious escapades during which they run into the reality of the early modern centralizing state dominated by monetary concerns. Cervantes confronts the vanished virtues of knighthood with the novel values of the life with money.

**Painters** The outstanding painter of Spain during Philip II's reign was El Greco (Domenikos Theotokopoulos, ca. 1546–1614), a native of the island of Crete. After early training in Crete as a painter of eastern Christian icons, El Greco went to Venice for further studies. In 1577, the Catholic hierarchy hired him to paint the altarpieces of a church in Toledo, the city in central Spain that was one of the residences of the kings prior to the construction of El Escorial in Madrid. El Greco's works reflect the spirit of Spanish Catholicism, with its emphasis on strict obedience to traditional faith and fervent personal piety. His characteristic style features elongated, pale figures surrounded by vibrant colors and represents a variation of the so-called mannerist style (with its perspective exaggerations), which succeeded the Renaissance style in Venice during the later sixteenth century.

# Putting It All Together

The Ottoman–Habsburg struggle can be seen as another chapter in the long history of competition that began when the Achaemenid Persian Empire expanded into the Mediterranean and was resisted by the Greeks in the middle of the first millennium BCE. Although India and China were frequently subjected to incursions from central Asia, neither of the two had to compete for long with any of its neighbors. Sooner or later the central Asians either retreated or were absorbed by their victims. The Ottomans' brief experience with Timur was on the same order. But the Middle East and Europe were always connected, and this chapter, once more, draws attention to this connectedness.

There were obvious religious and cultural differences between the Islamic and western Christian civilizations as they encountered each other during the Ottoman–Habsburg period. But their commonalities are equally, if not more, interesting. Most importantly, both Ottomans and Habsburgs were representatives of the return to imperialism, and in the pursuit of their imperial goals, both adopted the policy of the centralizing state with its firearm infantries and pervasive urban money economy. Both found it crucial to their existence to project their glory to the population at large and to sponsor artistic expression. In the long run, however, the imperial ambitions of the Ottomans and Habsburgs exceeded their ability to raise cash. Although firearms and a monetized urban economy made them different from previous empires, they were as unstable as all their imperial predecessors. Eventually, around 1600, they reached the limits of their conquests.

▶ For additional resources, including maps, primary sources, visuals, and quizzes, please go to www.oup.com/us/vonsivers. Please see the Further Resources section at the back of the book for additional readings and suggested websites.

## Against the Grain
# Tilting at Windmills

Cervantes's *The Ingenious Gentleman Don Quixote of La Mancha* was an instant hit in the Spanish-speaking literary world of the early 1600s and contributed to the rise of the novel as a characteristic European form of literary expression. As stated in his preface, Cervantes composed his novel in opposition to the dominant literary conventions of his time, to "ridicule the absurdity of those books of chivalry, which have, as it were, fascinated the eyes and judgement of the world, and in particular of the vulgar."

Every episode in this novel, from the literary frame to its most famous story, Don Quixote's joust against windmills he believes to be fantastic giants, is cast in the forms of gentle, hilarious, or biting parodies of one or another absurdity in society. The frame is provided by the fictional figure of Cide Hamete Benengeli, a purportedly perfidious Muslim and historian who might or might not have been lying when he chronicled the lives of the knight Don Quixote and his squire Sancho Panza in the 74 episodes of the novel. Don Quixote's joust, or "tilting," against windmills has become a powerful metaphor for rebelling against the often overpowering conventions of society.

*Don Quixote* is today acclaimed as the second most printed text after the Bible. Over the past four centuries, each generation has interpreted the text anew. Revolutionary France saw Don Quixote as a doomed visionary; German Romantics, as a hero destined to fail; Communists, as an anti-capitalist rebel before his time; and secular progressives, as an unconventional hero at the dawn of modern free society. For Karl Marx, Don Quixote was the hidalgo who yearned for a return to the feudal aristocracy of the past which in his time was becoming a pleasure aristocracy, enjoying its useless life at the royal court and imitated later by the bourgeoisie. Sigmund Freud enjoyed reading and rereading *Don Quixote* throughout his life, looking at the knight-errant as "tragic in his helplessness while the plot is unraveled." In our own time, Don Quixote became the quintessential postmodern figure; in the words of Michel Foucault, his "truth is not in the relation of the words to the world but in that slender and constant relation woven between themselves as verbal signs. The hollow fiction of epic exploits has become the representative power of language. Words have swallowed up their own nature as signs." As a tragic or comic figure, Don Quixote continues to be the irresistible symbol of opposition.

- What explains the lasting literary success of Don Quixote?

- Why has the phrase "tilting at windmills" undergone a change of meaning from the original "fighting imaginary foes" to "taking on a situation against all seeming evidence" in our own time?

# Thinking Through Patterns

▶ **What patterns characterized the Christian and Muslim imperial competition in the period 1300–1600? Which elements distinguished them from each other, and which elements were similar? How did the pattern change over time?**

In 1300, the Ottomans renewed the Arab-Islamic tradition of jihad against the eastern Christian empire of Byzantium, conquering the Balkans and eventually defeating the empire with the conquest of Constantinople in 1453. They also carried the war into the western Mediterranean and Indian Ocean. In western Christian Iberia, the rekindling of the reconquest after the lull of the thirteenth and fourteenth centuries was more successful. Invigorated by a merging of the concepts of the Crusade and the *Reconquista*, the Iberians expanded overseas to circumvent the Muslims and trade for Indian spices directly. The so-called Age of Exploration, during which western Christians traveled to and settled in overseas lands, is deeply rooted in the Western traditions of war against Islamic civilization.

In the mid-1400s, the Middle East and Europe returned to the pattern of imperial state formation after a lull of several centuries, during which states had competed against each other within their respective commonwealths. The element which fueled this return was gunpowder weaponry. The use of cannons and handheld firearms became widespread during this time but required major financial outlays on the part of the states. The Ottomans and Habsburgs were the states with the most resources, and the Ottomans even assembled the first standing armies. To pay the musket-equipped soldiers, huge amounts of silver were necessary. The two empires became states based on a money economy: Bureaucracies maintained centralized departments that regulated the collection of taxes and the payroll of soldiers.

▶ **How did the centralizing state in the Middle East and Europe function in the period 1450–1600? How did economics, military power, and imperial objectives interact to create the centralizing state?**

▶ **Which patterns did cultural expressions follow in the Habsburg and Ottoman Empires? Why did the ruling classes of these empires sponsor these expressions?**

The rulers of these empires were concerned to portray themselves, their military, and their bureaucracies as highly successful and just. The state had to be as visible and benevolent as possible. Rulers, therefore, were builders of palaces, churches, or mosques. They celebrated religious and secular festivities with great pomp and encouraged ministers and the nobility to do likewise. In the imperial capitals, they patronized architects, artists, and writers, resulting in a veritable explosion of intellectual and artistic creativity. In this regard, the Ottomans and the Habsburgs followed similar patterns of cultural expression.

# Patterns of Evidence: Sources for Chapter 16

## SOURCE 16.1

# Christopher Columbus,
# *The Book of Prophecies*

### 1501–1502

**A**lthough he is more famous for his voyages—and for the richly detailed accounts he made of them—Columbus (1451–1506) also composed a book of prophetic revelations toward the end of his life, entitled *El Libro de las Profecias*. Written after his third voyage to the Americas, the book traced the development of God's plans for the end of the world, which could be hastened along, particularly by a swift and decisive move to reclaim Jerusalem from Muslim control. When Jerusalem was once more restored to Christian sovereignty, Columbus predicted, Jesus could return to earth, and all of the events foreseen in the Book of Revelation (and in various medieval revelations, as well) could unfold. It is helpful to place the plans for Columbus's original voyage in 1492 against the backdrop of his religious beliefs, as he encourages Ferdinand and Isabella to take their rightful place in God's mystical plan—as well as in Columbus's own cartographic charts.

*Letter from the Admiral to the King and Queen [Ferdinand and Isabella]*

. . .

Most exalted rulers: At a very early age I began sailing the sea and have continued until now. This profession creates a curiosity about the secrets of the world. I have been a sailor for forty years, and I have personally sailed to all the known regions. I have had commerce and conversation with knowledgeable people of the clergy and the laity. Latins and Greeks, Jews and Moors, and with many others of different religions. Our Lord has favored my occupation and has given me an intelligent mind. He has endowed me with a great talent for seamanship; sufficient ability in astrology, geometry, and arithmetic; and the mental and physical dexterity required to draw spherical maps of cities, rivers and mountains, islands and ports, with everything in its proper place.

During this time I have studied all kinds of texts: cosmography, histories, chronicles, philosophy, and other disciplines. Through these writings,

Source: Christopher Columbus, *The Book of Prophecies*, ed. Roberto Rusconi, trans. Blair Sullivan (Berkeley: University of California Press, 1997), vol. 3, 67–69, 75–77.

the hand of Our Lord opened my mind to the possibility of sailing to the Indies and gave me the will to attempt the voyage. With this burning ambition I came to your Highnesses. Everyone who heard about my enterprise rejected it with laughter and ridicule. Neither all the sciences that I mentioned previously nor citations drawn from them were of any help to me. Only Your Highnesses had faith and perseverance. Who could doubt that this flash of understanding was the work of the Holy Spirit, as well as my own? The Holy Spirit illuminated his holy and sacred Scripture, encouraging me in a very strong and clear voice from the forty-four books of the Old Testament, the four evangelists, and twenty-three epistles from the blessed apostles, urging me to proceed. Continually, without ceasing a moment, they insisted that I go on. Our Lord wished to make something clearly miraculous of this voyage to the Indies in order to encourage me and others about the holy temple.

. . .

Most of the prophecies of holy Scripture have already been fulfilled. The Scriptures say this and the Holy Church loudly and unceasingly is saying it, and no other witness is necessary. I will, however, speak of one prophecy in particular because it bears on my argument and gives me support and happiness whenever I think about it.

I have greatly sinned. Yet, every time that I have asked, I have been covered by the mercy and compassion of Our Lord. I have found the sweetest consolation in throwing off all my cares in order to contemplate his marvelous presence.

I have already said that for the voyage to the Indies neither intelligence nor mathematics nor world maps were of any use to me; it was the fulfillment of Isaiah's prophecy. This is what I want to record here in order to remind Your Highnesses and so that you can take pleasure from the things I am going to tell you about Jerusalem on the basis of the same authority. If you have faith in this enterprise, you will certainly have the victory.

. . .

I said above that much that has been prophesied remains to be fulfilled, and I say that these are the world's great events, and I say that a sign of this is the acceleration of Our Lord's activities in this world. I know this from the recent preaching of the gospel in so many lands.

The Calabrian abbot Joachim said that whoever was to rebuild the temple on Mount Zion would come from Spain.

The cardinal Pierre d'Ailly wrote at length about the end of the religion of Mohammed and the coming of the Antichrist in his treatise *De concordia astronomicae veritatis et narrationis historicae* [*On the agreement between astronomical truth and historical narrative*]; he discusses, particularly in the last nine chapters, what many astronomers have said about the ten revolutions of Saturn.

▶ **Working with Sources**

1. How does Columbus appeal to the "crusading" goals of Ferdinand and Isabella, and why?

2. Would this appeal have found favor with the monarchs, given their other actions in Spain in 1492?

## SOURCE 16.2

# Thomas the Eparch and Joshua Diplovatatzes, "The Fall of Constantinople"

## 1453

The siege and conquest of Constantinople by the Ottoman Turks under Mehmet II (r. 1451–1481) was one of the turning points of world history. Unfolding over two months between April 5 and May 29, 1453, the siege exposed the inability of the Byzantine emperor Constantine XI to withstand a sustained and massive attack. Outnumbering the defenders 11 to 1, the Ottomans battered Constantinople's walls with heavy cannons and took advantage of the natural weaknesses of the city's geography. This account, told by two survivors and (self-proclaimed) eyewitnesses to the siege and its aftermath, details some of the specific stages of the defeat—and the suffering for Christians that came as a result.

When the Turk then drew near to Pera in the fortified zone, he seized all the boats he could find and bound them to each other so as to form a bridge which permitted the combatants to fight on the water just as they did on land. The Turks had with them thousands of ladders which they placed against the walls, right at the place which they had fired [their cannon] and breached the wall, just as they did at the cemetery of St. Sebold. The Genoese handled this breach; they wanted to protect it with their ships because they had so many. In the army of the Turk the order had been given fifteen days before the attack that each soldier would carry a ladder, whether he was fighting on land or sea. There also arrived galleys full of armed men: it seemed that they were Genoese and that they had come to aid the besieged, but in fact they were Turks and they were slipping into the gates. Just as this was becoming less worrisome and the city seemed secure, there arrived under the flag of the Genoese several ships which repelled the Turks with great losses.

At dawn on Monday, 29 May, they began an attack that lasted all night until Tuesday evening and they conquered the city. The commander of the Genoese, who was leading the defense of the breach, pretended to be

Source: trans. William L. North from the Italian version in A. Pertusi, ed., *La Caduta di Constantinopoli: Le testimonianze dei contemporanei* (Milan: Mondadori, 1976), 234–239, available online at https://apps.carleton.edu/curricular/mars/assets/Thomas_the_Eparch_and_Joshua_Diplovatatzes_for_MARS_website.pdf.

wounded and abandoned his battle station, taking with him all his people. When the Turks realized this, they slipped in through the breach. When the emperor of the Greeks saw this, he exclaimed in a loud voice: "My God, I have been betrayed!" and he suddenly appeared with his people, exhorting the others to stand firm and defend themselves. But then the gate was opened and the crush of people became such that the emperor himself and his [men] were killed by the Turks and the traitors.

Then the Turks ran to the Hagia Sophia, and all those whom they had imprisoned there, they killed in the first heat of rage. Those whom they found later, they bound with a cord around their neck and their hands tied behind their backs and led them out of the city. When the Turk learned that the emperor had been killed in Constantinople, he captured the Grand Duke who was governing in the emperor's stead and had the Grand Duke's son beheaded and then the Grand Duke himself. Then he seized one of the Grand Duke's daughters who was quite beautiful and made her lie on the great altar of Hagia Sophia with a crucifix under her head and then raped her. Then the most brutish of the Turks seized the finest noble women, virgins, and nuns of the city and violated them in the presence of the Greeks and in sacrilege of Christianity. Then

they destroyed all the sacred objects and the bodies of the saints and burned everything they found, save for the cross, the nail, and the clothing of Christ: no one knows where these relics ended up, no one has found them. They also wanted to desecrate the image of the Virgin of St. Luke by stabbing six hundred people in front of it, one after another, like madmen. Then they took prisoner those who fell into their hands, tied them with a rope around the neck and calculated the value of each one. Women had to redeem themselves with their own bodies, men by fornicating with their hands or some other means. Whoever was able to pay the assessed amount could remain in his faith and whoever refused had to die. The Turk who had become governor of Constantinople, named Suleiman in German, occupied the temple of Hagia Sophia to practice his faith there. For three days the Turks sacked and pillaged the city, and each kept whatever he found— people and goods—and did with them whatever he wished.

. . .

All this was made known by Thomas the Eparch, a count of Constantinople, and Joshua Diplovatatzes. Thutros of Constantinople translated their Greek into "welisch" and Dumita Exswinnilwacz and Matheus Hack of Utrecht translated their welisch into German.

▶ **Working with Sources**

1. What does this account suggest about the preparedness of the Turks for the sack of Constantinople—and the lack of preparation on the part of the Byzantine defenders?

2. What details indicate that the taking of Constantinople was seen as a "religious" war on the Ottoman side?

## SOURCE 16.3

# Evliya Çelebi, "A Procession of Artisans at Istanbul"

## ca. 1638

**B**orn on the Golden Horn and raised in the Sultan's palace in Istanbul, Çelebi traveled throughout Ottoman domains between 1640 and 1680. He published an account of his travels and experiences as the *Seyahatname*, or *Book of Travels*. In the first of his 10 books in the document, Çelebi provides a lengthy description of Istanbul around the year 1638, including a panoramic view of 1,100 artisan and craft guilds. The numbers and diversity of trades represented underscore the extent of Ottoman commerce—as well as the pride of place each of the city's working people claimed as their due.

*The numbers in brackets refer to the order of listing in this chapter.*

### I: Ship-captains [7] vs. Saddlers [30]

Following the bakers [6], the saddlers wished to pass, but the ship-captains and sea-merchants raised a great fuss. When Sultan Murad got wind of the matter, he consulted with the ulema and the guild shaikhs. They all agreed that it made sense for the ship-captains to proceed after the bakers, because it was they who transported the wheat, and the bakers were dependent on them, and also because Noah was their patron saint.

*Comment: the saddlers do not reappear until much later, between the tanners [29] and the shoemakers [31].*

. . .

### III: Egyptian Merchants [9] vs. Butchers [10]

Following the procession of these Mediterranean Sea captains, the butchers were supposed to pass, according to imperial decree. But all the great Egyptian merchants, including the dealers in rice, hemp, Egyptian reed mats, coffee and sugar gathered together and began quarreling with the butchers. Finally they went before the sultan and said: "My padishah, our galleons are charged with transporting rice, lentils, coffee and hemp. They cannot do without us, nor we without them. Why should these bloody and tricky butchers come between us? Plagues have arisen from cities where they shed their blood, and for fear of this their stalls and shambles in other countries are outside of the city walls. They are a bloody and filthy band of ill-omen. We, on the other hand, always make Istanbul plentiful and cheap with grains of all sorts."

Now the butchers' eyes went bloodshot. "My padishah," they said, "Our patron saint is Butcher Cömerd and our occupation is with sheep, an animal which the Creator has made

Source: Robert Dankoff, *An Ottoman Mentality: The World of Evliya Çelebi*, 2nd ed. (Leiden, the Netherlands: Brill, 2006), 86–89.

the object of mercy, and whose flesh He has made lawful food for the strengthening of His servants' bodies. Bread and meat are mentioned as the foremost of God's gifts to mankind: with a small portion of meat, a poor man can subsist for five or six days. We make our living with such a lawful trade, and are known for our generosity (cömerdlik). It is we who make Istanbul plentiful and cheap. As for these merchants and dealers and profiteers: concerning them the Koran says (2:275), 'God has made selling lawful and profiteering unlawful'. They are such a despised group that after bringing their goods from Egypt they store it in magazines in order to create a shortage, thus causing public harm through their hoarding.

. . .

"Egyptian sugar? But in the Koran the rivers of paradise are praised as being made 'of pure honey' (47:15). Now we have honey from Turkey, Athens, Wallachia, Moldavia, each with seventy distinct qualities. Furthermore, if my padishah wished, thousands of quintals of sugar could be produced in Alanya, Antalya, Silifke, Tarsus, Adana, Payas, Antakya, Aleppo, Damascus, Sidon, Beyrut, Tripoli and other such provinces— enough to make it plentiful and cheap throughout the world—so why do we need your sugar?

"As for coffee: it is an innovation; it prevents sleep; it dulls the generative powers; and coffee houses are dens of sedition. When roasted it is burnt; and in the legal compilations known as *Bezzaziye* and *Tatarhaniye* we have the dictum that 'Whatever is carbonized is absolutely forbidden'—this holds even for burnt bread. Spiced sherbet, pure milk, tea, fennel, salep, and almond-cream—all these are more wholesome than coffee."

. . .

To these objections of the butchers, the Egyptian merchants replied:

. . . "It is true that Turkey has no need of sugar and hemp, and that European sugar is also very fine. But tell us this, O band of butchers: what benefit and return do you offer to the public treasury?"

The butchers had nothing to say to this, and the Egyptian merchants continued: "My padishah, the goods arriving in our galleons provide the public treasury an annual revenue of 11,000 purses from customs dues. As a matter of justice ('adalet ederseñiz) we ought to have precedence in the Muhammadan procession, and the butchers ought to come after us." The şeyhülislam Yahya Efendi and Mu'id Ahmed Efendi cited the hadith, "The best of men is he who is useful to mankind," and the sultan gave the Egyptian merchants a noble rescript authorizing them to go first, and the butchers to go second.

▶ **Working with Sources**

1. Why did the order in which they appeared in the procession matter so much to these particular groups?

2. How did appeals to the Quran accentuate or diminish their case to be placed ahead in the procession?

## SOURCE 16.4

# Ogier Ghiselin de Busbecq, "The Court of Suleiman the Magnificent"

**1581**

Ghiselin (1522–1592) was a Flemish ambassador who represented the Austrian Habsburgs at the court of Suleiman the Magnificent (1520–1566) in Istanbul. In 1581, he published an account of his time among the Ottomans as *Itinera Constantinopolitanum et Amasianum* (*Travels in Constantinople and Asia Minor*). In this segment of his travel narrative, he draws attention to the personal habits and behaviors of a contemporary emperor—one who saw himself as the heir to the Romans as well as to the other monarchs who had held Constantinople/Istanbul.

The Sultan was seated on a very low ottoman, not more than a foot from the ground, which was covered with a quantity of costly rugs and cushions of exquisite workmanship; near him lay his bow and arrows. His air, as I said, was by no means gracious, and his face wore a stern, though dignified, expression. On entering we were separately conducted into the royal presence by the chamberlains, who grasped our arms. . . . After having gone through a pretense of kissing his hand, we were conducted backwards to the wall opposite his seat, care being taken that we should never turn our backs on him. The Sultan then listened to what I had to say; but the language I held was not at all to his taste, for the demands of his Majesty breathed a spirit of independence and dignity . . . and so he made no answer beyond saying in a tetchy way, "Giusel, giusel," i.e. well, well . . .

. . .

I was greatly struck with the silence and order that prevailed in this great crowd. There were no cries, no hum of voices, the usual accompaniments of a motley gathering, neither was there any jostling; without the slightest disturbance each man took his proper place according to his rank. The Agas, as they call their chiefs, were seated, to wit, generals, colonels (*bimbashi*), and captains (*soubashi*). Men of a lower position stood. The most interesting sight in this assembly was a body of several thousand Janissaries, who were drawn up in a long line apart from the rest; their array was so steady and motionless that, being at a little distance, it was some time before I could make up my mind as to whether they were human beings or statues; at last I received a hint to salute them, and saw all their heads bending at the same moment to return my bow.

. . .

Source: Wayne S. Vucinich, *The Ottoman Empire: Its Record and Legacy* (Princeton, NJ: Van Nostrand, 1965), 127–129.

When the cavalry had ridden past, they were followed by a long procession of Janissaries, but few of whom carried any arms except their regular weapon, the musket. They were dressed in uniforms of almost the same shape and colour, so that you might recognize them to be the slaves. . . . There is only one thing in which they are extravagant, viz., plumes, head-dresses, etc., and veterans who formed the rear guard were specially distinguished by ornaments of this kind. The plumes which they insert in their frontlets might well be mistaken for a walking forest.

▶ **Working with Sources**

1. Why were order and discipline apparently so important at Suleiman's court?

2. Why might Ghiselin have found the Janissaries so particularly impressive?

## SOURCE 16.5

# Janissary Musket

### ca. 1750–1800

The Janissaries constitute the most famous and centralized of the Ottomans' military institutions. A feared and respected military force, the Janissaries were Christian-born males who had been seized from their homes as boys, converted to Islam, and then trained as future soldiers and administrators for the Turks. Under the direct orders of the sultan and his viziers, the Janissaries were equipped with the latest military innovations. In the early fifteenth century, these units received cannons and matchlock muskets. The muskets continued their evolution in the Janissaries' hands, becoming standard equipment for Ottoman and other armies.

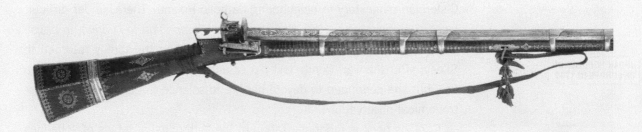

▶ **Working with Sources**

1. What does the elaborate decoration of this musket suggest about its psychological as well as its practical effects?

2. Was this firearm likely to have been produced by indigenous, rather than European, gunsmiths? Why or why not?

# Chapter 17 1450–1750

# The Renaissance, New Sciences, and Religious Wars in Europe

**URBAN POPULATION OF EUROPE IN 1700**

London · Amsterdam
Paris ·
Naples ·

- Over 30%
- 25-30%
- 10-15%
- 5-10%
- 1-5%
- 0-1%
- · city with population over 200,000

Though less celebrated than many of her male contemporaries, one of the most remarkable scientific minds of the seventeenth century was Maria Cunitz (ca. 1607–1664). Under the tutorship of her father, a physician, she became accomplished in six languages (Hebrew, Greek, Latin, Italian, French, and Polish), the humanities, and the sciences. For a number of years, while the Thirty Years' War (1618–1648) raged in Germany and her home province of Silesia, Cunitz and her Protestant family sought refuge in a Cistercian monastery in neighboring Catholic Poland. There, under difficult living conditions, she wrote *Urania propitia* (*Companion to Urania*), in praise of the Greek muse and patron of astronomy. When the family returned to Silesia after the war, Cunitz lost her scientific papers and instruments in a fire, but she continued to devote her life to science through her careful astronomical observations.

Cunitz's book is a popularization of the astronomical tables of Johannes Kepler (1571–1630), the major scientific innovator remembered today for his discovery of the elliptical trajectories of the planets. Cunitz's book makes corrections in Kepler's tables and offers simplified calculations of star positions. Writing in both Latin and German, she published it privately in 1650. It was generally well received, although there were a few detractors who

*ABOVE: Telescopic drawing of the moon by Galileo Galilei (1564–1642), showing the moon as a solid body—an observation that led him to argue that the earth was not unique.*

found it hard to believe that a woman could succeed in the sciences. Whatever injustice was done to her during her lifetime, today the scientific community has made amends. A crater on Venus has been named after her, and a statue of her stands in the town where she grew up.

Cunitz lived in a time when western Christianity had entered the age of early global interaction, from 1450 until 1750. During most of this time, Europe remained institutionally similar to the other parts of the world, especially the Middle East, India, China, and Japan. Rulers throughout Eurasia governed by divine grace. All large states followed patterns of political centralization. Their urban populations were nowhere more than 40 percent, and their economies depended on the productivity of agriculture. As research on China, the Middle East, and India during 1450–1750 has shown, there was no "great divergence" in the patterns of political organization, social formation, and economic production between western Christianity and the other religious civilizations until around 1750.

Culturally, however, northwestern Europe began to move in a different direction from Islamic, Hindu, Neo-Confucian, and Buddhist civilizations after 1500. New developments in the sciences and philosophy in England, France, the Netherlands, and parts of Germany initiated new cultural patterns for which there was no equivalent in the other parts of Eurasia, including southern Europe. As significant as these patterns were, for almost the entire span of time between 1500 and 1750 the new mathematized sciences remained limited to a few hundred and later to a few thousand educated persons, largely outside the ruling classes. Their ideas and outlooks diverged substantially from those represented by the Catholic and Protestant ruling classes and resulted frequently in tensions or, in a few cases, even repression of scientists by the authorities. The new scientific and intellectual culture broadened into a mass movement only after 1750. The subsequent Industrial Revolution of modernity was rooted in this movement.

___

The European Renaissance, Baroque, and New Sciences formed a cultural sequence that broke with much that had been inherited from medieval times. It began with the appropriation of the Greek and Roman cultural heritage, allegedly absent from the Middle Ages, by a small educated elite. In their enthusiasm for all things Greek and Roman, however, the members of this elite overestimated the extent of their break from the Middle Ages. In today's view from a greater distance, we think of this break as far less radical, with much in culture remaining unchanged. Many centuries were needed before the new cultural pattern initiated by Renaissance, Baroque, and the New Sciences became a general phenomenon.

▶ What were the reasons for the cultural change that began in Europe with the Renaissance around 1400? In which ways were the subsequent patterns of cultural change different from those in the other religious civilizations of Eurasia?

▶ When and how did the mathematization of the sciences begin, and how did it gain popularity in northwestern Europe? Why is the popularization of the sciences important for understanding the period 1500–1750?

▶ What were the patterns of centralized state formation and transformation in the period 1400–1750? How did the Protestant Reformation and religious wars modify these patterns?

Similarly, the political and social changes of the period 1400–1750 have to be balanced against the inherited continuities. The rise of firearm-equipped armies of foot soldiers was a new phenomenon, but the use of these infantries by rulers to further increase their centralizing powers was an inheritance from the Middle Ages. The idea of a religious return to the roots of Christianity, pursued by the leaders of the Protestant Reformation, can also be traced back to the Middle Ages. When rulers used the Reformation for their centralizing ambitions, however, the ensuing religious wars became a new phenomenon. Overall, the seeds of an eventual departure of western Christianity from the general patterns of agrarian–urban society were planted around 1500. But for a long time thereafter these seeds remained largely underground, and the "great divergence" from the agrarian–urban patterns of Islamic, Hindu, and Chinese civilizations began only after 1750.

# Cultural Transformations: Renaissance, Baroque, and New Sciences

**Renaissance:** "Rebirth" of culture based on new publications and translations of Greek, Hellenistic, and Roman authors whose writings were previously unknown in western Christianity.

The **Renaissance** was a period of cultural transformation which in the fifteenth century followed the scholastic Middle Ages in western Christianity. In many ways, the Renaissance was an outgrowth of scholasticism, but its thinkers and artists saw themselves as having broken away from scholastic precepts. They considered their period a time of "rebirth" (which is the literal meaning of "renaissance" in French). During this period they were powerfully influenced by the writings of Greek and Hellenistic-Roman authors who had been unknown during the scholastic age. In the sixteenth century, the Renaissance gave way to the Baroque in the arts and the **New Sciences**. Thus, the Renaissance was just the first of a sequence of periods of cultural transformation following each other in rapid succession.

**New Sciences:** Mathematized sciences, such as physics, introduced in the 1500s.

## The Renaissance and Baroque Arts

Beginning around 1400 in Italy and spreading later through northwestern Europe, an outpouring of learning, scholarship, and art came from theologians, philosophers, writers, painters, architects, and musical composers. These thinkers and artists benefited from Greek and Hellenistic-Roman texts which scholars had discovered recently in mostly eastern Christian archives in Byzantium. In addition, in the early fifteenth century Byzantine scholars from Constantinople arrived in Italy with further newly rediscovered texts, which had a profound impact. The emerging cultures of the Renaissance and Baroque were creative adaptations of those Greek and Hellenistic-Roman writings to the cultural heritage of western Christianity. Out of this vibrant mixture arose the overarching concept of **humanism**.

**Humanism:** Intellectual movement focusing on human culture, in such fields as philosophy, philology, and literature, and based on the corpus of Greek and Roman texts.

**New Manuscripts and Printing**    Eastern Christian Byzantium experienced a cultural revival between its recovery in 1261 from the Latin interlude and its collapse in 1453 when the Muslim Ottomans conquered Constantinople. During this revival, for example, scholars engaged in a vigorous debate about the compatibility of Plato and Aristotle with each other. The debate made Italian scholars fully aware of how much of Greek literature was still absent from western Christianity. For example, at the time they possessed just two of Plato's 44 dialogues. Italians invited about a dozen eastern Christian scholars, who brought manuscripts to Florence, Rome, and Venice to translate and teach. Their students became fluent in Greek and translated Hesiod and Homer, some Greek tragedies and comedies, Plato and the Neo-Platonists, the remaining works of Aristotle, Hellenistic scientific texts, and the Greek church fathers. Western Christianity had finally absorbed the ancient heritage.

The work of translation was helped by the development of a more rounded, simplified Latin script, which replaced the angled, dense Gothic script used since the 1150s. In addition, the costly vellum (scraped leather) writing material on which many manuscripts had been laboriously written was replaced by cheaper paper, which had been introduced from Islamic Spain in the early twelfth century and had become common in the rest of Europe by 1400. Experimentation in the 1430s with movable metal typeface resulted in the innovation of the printing press. A half century later, with more than 1,000 printers all over Europe and more than 8 million books in the hands of readers, a veritable printing revolution had taken place in Europe.

**Philology and Political Theory** The flood of new manuscripts and the renewed examination of existing manuscripts in libraries encouraged the study of Greek, Latin, and Hebrew philology. Scholars trained in these languages edited critical texts based on multiple manuscripts. The best known among these philologists was the Dutchman Desiderius Erasmus (1466–1536), who published an edition of the Greek and Latin New Testaments in 1516. Critical textual research, which became central to subsequent scholarship, can trace its foundations to the Renaissance.

Another type of critical stance emerged as a central element in political thought. In *The Prince*, Niccolò Machiavelli (1469–1527) reflected on the ruthless political competition among the princes of Europe for dominance over his hopelessly disunited native Italy. What Italy needed in his own generation, Machiavelli argued, was a unifier who possessed what Aristotle discussed in Book 5 of his *Politics*, namely a person of intuitive strength, valor, or indomitable spirit (Italian, *virtù*) to take the proper steps—subtle or brutal—when political success was to be achieved. Many Renaissance scholars preferred Plato, but Machiavelli remained faithful to Aristotle, the superior political realist—an Aristotle held in high esteem centuries later by the American founding fathers.

**Bookseller.** By 1600, the increase in literacy levels combined with widespread printing of books, pamphlets, and tracts had made people like this itinerant bookseller in Italy a commonplace sight throughout much of Europe.

| | | | | |
|---|---|---|---|---|
| **1506–1558** Reign of King Charles V of Spain | **1517** Martin Luther posts his 95 theses; beginning of Protestant Reformation | **1561** Beginning of Catholic Reformation | **1565–1620** Dutch Protestant war of liberation from Spain | **1589–1610** Reign of King Henry IV of France |
| **1514** First formulation of the heliocentric solar system by Nicolaus Copernicus | | **1524–1525** German Peasants' War | **1562–1598** French war of religion | **1571–1630** Johannes Kepler, discoverer of the elliptical paths of the planets |
| **1556–1598** Reign of King Philip II of Spain, the Netherlands, and the Americas | **1618–1648** Thirty Years' War in Germany | **1643–1715** King Louis XIV of France | **1688** "Glorious Revolution" in England | **1740–1786** Frederick II, builder of the centralizing state of Prussia |
| **1604** Galileo Galilei's first formulation of the mathematical law of falling bodies | | **1642–1661** English Civil War and Puritan Republic | **1687** Isaac Newton unifies physics and astronomy | **1690** Denis Papin's first steam engine |

"But the duke [of Milan, Francesco Sforza, 1401–1466] possessed such indomitable spirit [*virtù*] and so much ability, he was so well aware that men must either be won over or else destroyed, and had such a sound basis for his power, which he had established in such a short period, that he would have overcome all of the difficulties if he had not had those two armies on top of him, or if he had been in good health."

—Machiavelli

**The Renaissance Arts**    In Italy, the reception of the new texts of the fifteenth century was paralleled by a new artistic way of looking at the Roman past and the natural world. The first artists to adopt this perspective were the sculptor Donatello (ca. 1386–1466) and the architect Filippo Brunelleschi (1377–1446), who received their inspiration from Roman imperial statues and ruins. The artistic triumvirate of the high Italian Renaissance was composed of Leonardo da Vinci (1452–1519), Michelangelo (1475–1564), and Raphael (1483–1520). Inspired by the Italian creative outburst, the Renaissance flourished also in Germany, the Netherlands, and France, making it a Europe-wide phenomenon.

The earliest musical composers of the Renaissance in the first half of the fifteenth century were Platonists, who considered music a part of a well-rounded education. The difficulty, however, was that the music of the Greeks or Romans was completely unknown. A partial solution for this difficulty was found through emphasizing the relationship between the word—that is, rhetoric—and music. In the sixteenth century this emphasis coincided with the Protestant and Catholic demand for liturgical music, such as hymns, masses, and *madrigals* (verses sung by unaccompanied voices). A pioneer of this music was the Italian composer Giovanni Pierluigi da Palestrina (ca. 1525–1594), who represented Renaissance music at its most exquisite.

The theater was a relatively late expression of the Renaissance. The popular mystery, passion, and morality plays from the centuries prior to 1400 continued in Catholic countries. In Italy, in the course of the fifteenth century, the *commedia dell'arte* (a secular popular theater) emerged, often using masked actors in plays of forbidden love, jealousy, and adultery. In England during the sixteenth century the popular traveling theater troupes became stationary and professional, attracting playwrights who composed more elaborate plays. Sponsored by the aristocracy and the Elizabethan court, playwrights wrote hundreds of scripts—some 600 are still extant—beginning in the 1580s. The best known among these playwrights was William Shakespeare (1564–1616), who also acted in his tragedies and comedies.

**The Baroque Arts**    The Renaissance gave way around 1600 to the Baroque, which dominated the arts until about 1750. Two factors influenced its emergence. First, the Protestant Reformation, Catholic Reformation, and religious wars changed the nature of patronage, on which architects, painters, and musicians depended. Many Protestant churches, opposed to imagery as incompatible with their view of early Christianity, did not sponsor artists for the adornment of their buildings with religious art. Wealthy urban merchants, often Protestant, stepped into the breach but avoided paintings with religious themes, preferring instead secular portraits, still lifes, village scenes, and landscapes.

Second, the predilection for Renaissance measurement, balance, and restraint gave way in both Catholic and Protestant regions to greater spontaneity and dramatic effect. Even more pronounced was the parallel shift in church and palace architecture to a "baroque" voluptuousness of forms and decorations, exemplified by Bavarian and Austrian Catholic churches, the Versailles Palace, and

**Renaissance Art.** Brunelleschi's cupola for the cathedral of Florence, completed in 1436, was one of the greatest achievements of the early Renaissance (*a*). Raphael's *School of Athens* (1509–1510) depicts some 50 philosophers and scientists, with Plato (in red tunic) and Aristotle (blue) in the center of the painting (*b*). Peter Brueghel's *The Harvesters* (1565) shows peasants taking a lunch break (*c*).

St. Paul's Cathedral in London, all completed between 1670 and 1750. Baroque music, benefitting from ample church and palace patronage and exemplified by the Italian Antonio Vivaldi (1678–1741) and the German Johann Sebastian Bach (1685–1750), experienced a veritable explosion of unrestrained exploration.

## The New Sciences

Eastern Christian scholars invited from Byzantium to Florence in Italy during the first half of the fifteenth century brought with them Hellenistic scientific treatises, which aroused great interest among Italian Renaissance scholars. Battle lines were drawn between those scholars who continued to adhere to the Aristotelian-scholastic scientific method, even though this method had undergone significant changes during the 1300s, and scholars (such as Copernicus) who were more interested in newly translated mathematical, astronomical, and geographical texts. Eventually, in the 1600s, two scientific pioneers—Galileo and Newton—abandoned much of the *qualitative* scientific method of Aristotelian scholasticism in favor of the *mathematized* science of physics. In the eighteenth century, Newton's unified astronomical-physical-based science of a mechanical, deterministic universe became the foundation for the development of modern scientific–industrial society.

**Copernicus's Incipient New Science**   According to Aristotle, nature was composed of the four elements of (in ascending order of lightness) earth, water, air, and fire. In astronomical terms, he thought that these elements formed distinct layers, together shaping the world. In geographical terms, however, it was obvious to Aristotle that not all earth was submerged by water. He knew that Europe, Asia, and Africa formed a contiguous land mass of continents above water. Aristotle did not resolve the contradiction in his writings, but subsequent medieval scholars sought to find a resolution. They developed the theory of the "floating apple," whereby they assumed that most of earth was submerged, and a minimal protruding amount—the three continents—was surrounded everywhere by water.

During the Renaissance, the *Geography*, written by the Hellenistic cosmographer Ptolemy (see Chapter 5), became available from Constantinople (a Latin translation was printed in 1477). This important work proposed the geographical concept of a globe composed of a single sphere of intermingled earth and water. When Nicolaus Copernicus (1473–1543) appeared on the scene, scholars were still grappling with these competing theories of the floating apple and the intermingled earth-water spheres.

Copernicus was born in Torun, a German-founded city which had come under Polish rule a few years before his birth. He began his studies at the University of Kraków, the only eastern European school to offer courses in astronomy. During the years 1495–1504, he continued his studies—of canon law, medicine, geography, cosmography, and astrology—at Italian universities. In 1500 he briefly taught mathematics in Rome and perhaps read Greek astronomical texts translated from Arabic in the library of the Vatican. Eventually, Copernicus graduated with a degree in canon law and took up an administrative position at the cathedral of Torun, which allowed him time to pursue astronomical research.

Sometime between 1507 and 1514 Copernicus realized that the discovery of the Americas in 1492 provided a decisive empirical proof for the theory of the world as a single earth-water sphere. During this time, it is likely that he saw the new world map by the German cartographer Martin Waldseemüller (ca. 1470–1520), which made him aware of the existence of the Americas as hitherto unknown inhabited lands on the other side of the world. Much more land protruded from the water and was not limited to the interconnected land mass of Eurasia-Africa, than had been previously assumed in the floating-apple theory.

"To these regions [Eurasia-Africa], moreover, should be added the islands discovered in our time under the rulers of Spain and Portugal, and especially America, named after the ship's captain who found them. On account of their still undisclosed size they are thought to be a second group of inhabited countries."

—Copernicus

As a result, this theory became questionable. Copernicus firmly espoused the Ptolemaic theory of the single intermingled water-earth sphere with mountainous protrusions. A globe with well-distributed water and land masses is a perfect body that moves in perfect circular paths, so he argued further, and formulated his hypothesis, according to which the earth is a body that performs the same motions as the other bodies in the planetary system. The discovery of the Americas, therefore, can be considered as the empirical trigger that convinced Copernicus of the correctness of his trigonometric calculations, which removed the earth from the center of the planetary system and made it revolve around the sun.

**Galileo's Mathematical Physics**   During the near century between the births of Copernicus and Galileo Galilei (1564–1642), mathematics—with its two branches of Greek geometry and Arabic algebra—improved considerably. Euclid's *Elements*, badly translated from Arabic in the late twelfth century, with a garbled definition of proportions, was retranslated correctly from the original Greek in 1543. Shortly thereafter, the new translation in 1544 of a text on floating and descending

**Waldseemüller's 1507 World Map.** The German mapmaker Martin Waldseemüller (ca. 1470–1520) was the first western Christian to draw a world map which included the newly discovered Americas. He gave them the name "America" after the Italian explorer Amerigo Vespucci (1454–1512), who was the first to state that the Americas were a separate land mass, unconnected to Asia. The single copy of Waldseemüller's map still extant is among the holdings of the US Library of Congress.

bodies by the Hellenistic scholar Archimedes (287–212 BCE) attracted intense scholarly attention. The text, unknown to the Arabs, had been translated from the Greek in the thirteenth century but subsequently remained unappreciated, on account of its incompatibility with the then-prevailing Aristotelian scholasticism.

What was required for a scholar critical of scholastic traditions was to combine geometry, algebra, and Archimedean physics. In 1604, that scholar appeared in the person of Galileo, when he formulated his famous mathematical "law of falling bodies." It is true that this law had been foreshadowed by the reflections of scholastic scholars at the University of Oxford's Merton College and the University of Paris in the 1300s. But these earlier scholars reflected on the logical and/or geometric properties of motion only "according to imagination." Galileo was the scholar who systematically combined imagination with empirical research and experimentation and thereby became the founder of what we now call the (mathematized) New Sciences.

**Running Afoul of the Church**     Galileo was not only a physicist but also a first-rate astronomer, one of the first to use a telescope, which had been recently invented in Flanders. On the basis of his astronomical work, in 1610 he received a richly endowed appointment as chief mathematician and philosopher at the court of the Medici, the ruling family of Florence. But his increasing fame also attracted the enmity of the Catholic Church.

As a proponent of Copernican heliocentrism, Galileo seemed to contradict the passage in the Hebrew Bible where God recognized the motion of the sun around the earth. (In Joshua 10:12–13, he stopped the sun's revolution for a day, in order to allow the Israelites to win a critical battle against the Amorites.) In contrast to the more tolerant pope at the time of Copernicus, the Roman Inquisition favored a strictly literal interpretation of this passage, which implied that God had halted the sun's motion. In 1632 Galileo found himself condemned to house arrest and forced to make a public repudiation of heliocentrism.

The condemnation of Galileo had a chilling effect on scientists in the southern European countries where the Catholic Reformation was dominant (see p. 503). Prudent patrons reduced their stipends to scientists, and scientific research subsequently declined. During the seventeenth century, interest in the New Sciences shifted increasingly to France, Germany, the Netherlands, and England. In these countries, no single church authority, of either the Catholic or the Protestant variety, was sufficiently dominant to enforce the literal understanding of scripture. As a result, these countries produced numerous mathematicians, astronomers, physicists, and inventors, Catholic as well as Protestant. The New Scientists in northern Europe had a certain liberty that their southern colleagues lacked. It was this relative intellectual freedom, not any great sympathy on the part of religious authorities for the New Sciences, which allowed the latter to flourish, especially in the Netherlands and England.

**Iberian Natural Sciences**    The shift of New Sciences research to northwestern Europe notwithstanding, southern European countries such as Spain were well situated to make substantial scientific contributions, even if not in the New Sciences. Hundreds of botanists, geographers, ethnographers, physicians, and metallurgists fanned out across the new colonies to take advantage of what their northern colleagues in the New Sciences could not do: They researched the new plants, diseases, peoples, and mineral resources of the New World, Africa, and Asia with the traditional descriptive and qualitative methods of the natural sciences and accumulated a voluminous amount of knowledge. For long periods, the Habsburg monarch kept the manuscripts with this knowledge under wraps, fearful that his colonial competitors would benefit from them—hence it was only through recent research efforts that the Iberian contributions to the sciences in the 1500s and 1600s have become more widely known.

**Isaac Newton's Mechanics**    In the middle of the English struggles between the Protestants and the Catholic/Catholicizing Stuart monarchs, Isaac Newton (1643–1727) brought the New Sciences of Copernicus and Galileo to their culmination. As a professor at the University of Cambridge, he worked in the fields of mathematics, optics, astronomy, physics, alchemy, and theology. His primary early contribution was calculus, a new field in mathematics, which he developed at the same time as the German philosopher Gottfried Wilhelm Leibniz (1646–1716). Later in his career, Newton unified the fields of physics and astronomy, establishing the so-called Newtonian synthesis. His *Mathematical Principles of Natural Philosophy*, published in 1687, was the towering achievement of the New Sciences. It established a deterministic universe following mathematical rules and formed the basis of science until the early twentieth century, when Albert Einstein's relativity theory superseded Newtonianism.

## The New Sciences and Their Social Impact

Scientists in the seventeenth century were in close communication with each other. They met in scientific societies or residential salons. Popularizers introduced an increasingly large public to the New Sciences. Scientists carried out experiments with constantly improved scientific instruments, such as telescopes, microscopes, thermometers, and barometers. Experience with barometers led technically versatile scientists and engineers to experiment with vacuum chambers and cylinders operating with condensing steam. Experimentation culminated with the invention of the steam engine in England in 1712.

**New Science Societies**   When the Catholic Reformation drove the New Sciences to northwestern Europe, the Italian-style academies gave way to chartered scientific societies, such as the Royal Society of London (1660) and the Paris Academy of Sciences (1666). Other countries, like Prussia, Russia, and Sweden, soon followed suit. These societies employed staffs of administrators, co-opted scientists as fellows, held regular discussion meetings, challenged their fellows to answer scientific questions, awarded prizes, and organized field trips and expeditions. They also published transactions, correspondences, and monographs. Many societies attracted thousands of members—famous pioneers, obscure amateurs, technically proficient tinkerers, theoretical mathematicians, daring experimenters, and flighty dreamers—representing an important cross section of seventeenth-century urban society in northwest Europe (see Map 17.1).

Other popularizers were textbook authors and itinerant lecturers who addressed audiences of middle-class amateurs, instrument makers, and specialized craftspeople, especially in England and the Netherlands. Many lecturers toured coffeehouses, urban residences, country estates, and provincial schools. Coffeehouses allowed the literate urban public to meet, read the daily newspapers (first appearing in the early seventeenth century), and exchange ideas. Coffee, introduced from Ethiopia and Yemen via the Ottoman Empire in the sixteenth century, was the preferred nonalcoholic social drink before the arrival of tea in the later eighteenth century. Male urban literacy is estimated to have exceeded 50 percent in England and the Netherlands during this period, although it remained considerably lower in France, Germany, and Italy.

Some lecturers were veritable entrepreneurs of the speaking circuit, teaching a kind of "Newtonianism lite" for ladies and gentlemen with little time or patience for serious study. Other lecturers set up subscriptions for month-long courses. Wealthy businessmen endowed public lectures and supported increasingly elaborate experiments and expensive laboratory equipment. In the first half of the eighteenth century, the New Science triumphed in northwestern Europe among a large, scientifically and technically interested public of experimenters, engineers, instrument makers, artisans, business people, and lay folk.

**Women, Social Salons, and the New Science**   Women formed a significant part of this public. In the fields of mathematics and astronomy, Sophie Brahe (1556–1643), sister of the Danish astronomer Tycho Brahe (1546–1601), and Maria Cunitz (see chapter-opening vignette) were the first to make contributions to the new astronomy of Copernicus and Kepler. According to estimates, in the second half of the seventeenth century some 14 percent of German astronomers were women. A dozen particularly prominent female astronomers practiced their science privately in Germany, Poland, the Netherlands, France, and England.

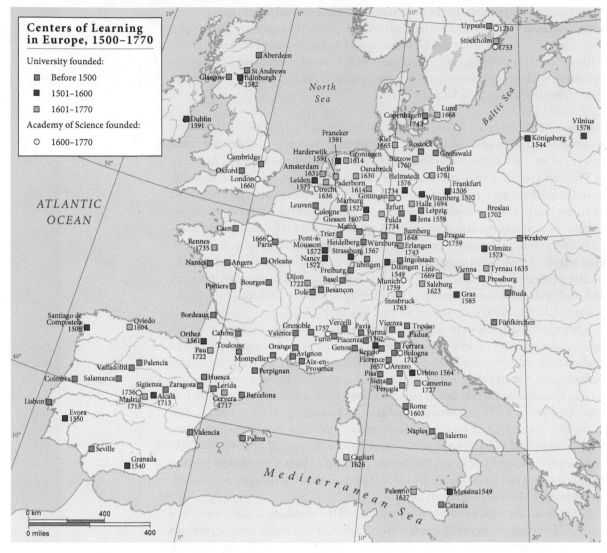

MAP **17.1 Centers of Learning in Europe, 1500–1770.**

Another institution which helped in the popularization of the New Sciences was the salon. As the well-furnished, elegant living room of an urban residence, the salon was both a domestic chamber and a semipublic meeting place for the urban social elite to engage in conversations, presentations, and experiments. The culture of the salon emerged first in Paris sometime after the closure of the court-centered Palace Academy in the 1580s. Since the Catholic French universities remained committed to Aristotelian scholasticism, the emerging stratum of educated urban aristocrats and middle-class professionals turned to the salons as places to inform themselves about new scientific developments. Furthermore, French universities as well as scientific academies refused to admit women, in contrast to Italian and German institutions. The French salon, therefore, became a bastion of well-placed and respected female scholars.

One outstanding example of French salon science was Gabrielle-Emilie du Châtelet (1706–1749). In her youth, Châtelet fulfilled her marital duties to her

husband, the Marquis of Châtelet. She had three children before turning to the sciences. In one of the Paris
salons she met François Marie Arouet, known as Voltaire
(1694–1778), the eighteenth-century Enlightenment
writer, skeptic, satirist, and amateur Newtonian. Châtelet
and Voltaire became intimate companions under the
benevolent eyes of the Marquis at the family estate in
Lorraine in northeastern France. Although Voltaire
published prolifically, Châtelet eventually outstripped
him both in research and scientific understanding. Her
lasting achievement was the translation of Newton's
*Mathematical Principles* into French, published in 1759.

**Discovery of the Vacuum**   Among the important
scientific instruments of the day were telescopes, microscopes, and thermometers. It was the barometer,
however, that was the crucial instrument for the exploration of the properties of the vacuum and condensing
steam, eventually leading to the invention of the steam
engine. The scientist laying the groundwork for the
construction of the barometer was Evangelista Torricelli
(1608–1647), a mathematician and assistant of Galileo.
In collaboration with Florentine engineers, he experimented with mercury-filled glass tubes, demonstrating
the existence of atmospheric pressure by the air and of
vacuums in the tubes.

**New Scientist.** Maria Cunitz is
honored today with a sculpture
in Świdnica, Poland, where she
grew up.

A few years later, the French mathematician and philosopher Blaise Pascal
(1623–1662) had his brother-in-law haul a mercury barometer up a mountain to
demonstrate lower air pressures at higher altitudes. Soon thereafter, scientists discovered the connection between changing atmospheric pressures and the weather,
laying the foundations for weather forecasting. The discovery of the vacuum, the
existence of which Aristotle had held to be impossible, made a deep impression on
the scientific community in the seventeenth century and was an important step
toward the practical application of the New Sciences to mechanical engineering
in the eighteenth century.

**The Steam Engine**   The French Huguenot scientist and engineer Denis Papin
(ca. 1647–1712) took the first crucial step from the vacuum chamber to the steam
engine. In 1690, when he was a court engineer and professor in Germany, Papin
constructed a cylinder with a piston. Weights, via a cord and two pulleys, held the
piston at the top of the cylinder. When heated, water in the bottom of the cylinder
turned into steam. When subsequently cooled through the injection of water, the
steam condensed, forcing the piston down and lifting the weights up. Papin spent
his last years (1707–1712) in London, where the Royal Society of London held
discussions of his papers, thereby alerting engineers, craftspeople, and entrepreneurs in England to the steam engine as a labor-saving machine. In 1712, the mechanic Thomas Newcomen built the first steam engine to pump water from coal
mine shafts.

**Vacuum Power.** In 1672, the mayor of Magdeburg, the New Scientist Otto von Guericke, demonstrated the experiment that made him a pioneer in the understanding of the physical properties of the vacuum. In the presence of German emperor Ferdinand III, two teams of horses were unable to pull the two sealed hemispheres apart. Guericke had created a vacuum by pumping out the air from the two sealed copper spheres.

Altogether, it took a little over a century, from 1604 (Galileo) to 1712 (Newcomen), for Europeans to apply the New Sciences to engineering—that is, the construction of the steam engine. Had it not been for the New Sciences, this engine—based on contracting steam—would not have been invented. (Hero of Alexandria, who invented steam-driven machines in the first century CE, made use of the expanding force of steam.) Prior to 1600, mechanical inventions—such as the wheel, the compass, the stern rudder, and the firearm—were constructed by anonymous tinkerers with a good commonsense understanding of nature. In 1700, engineers had to have at least a basic understanding of mathematics and such abstract physical phenomena as inertia, gravity, vacuums, and condensing steam if they wanted to build a steam engine or other complex machinery.

## The New Sciences: Philosophical Interpretations

The New Sciences engendered a pattern of radically new intellectual, religious, and political thinking, which evolved in the course of the seventeenth and early eighteenth centuries. This thought was largely incompatible with the inherited medieval scholasticism. It eventually evolved into a powerful instrument of critique of Christian doctrine and the constitutional order of the absolutist states. Initially, the new philosophical interpretations were confined to a few thinkers, but through the new concept of the social contract in the course of the 1700s they became a potent political force.

**Descartes's New Philosophy**    After the replacement of qualitative with mathematical physics, brought about by Galileo with his law of descending bodies, the question arose whether Aristotelian philosophy and Catholic theology were still adequate for the understanding of reality. New Scientists perceived the need to start philosophizing and theologizing from scratch. The first major New Scientist who, in his own judgment, started a radical reconsideration of philosophy from the ground up was the Frenchman René Descartes (1596–1650). He earned a degree in law, traveling widely after graduation. In the service of the Dutch and Bavarian courts, he bore witness to the beginning of the Thirty Years' War and its atrocities committed in the name of religious doctrines. During the war, he spent two decades in the Netherlands, studying and teaching the New Sciences.

His principal innovation in mathematics was the discovery that geometry could be converted through algebra into analytic geometry.

Descartes was shocked by the condemnation of Galileo and decided to abandon all traditional propositions and doctrines of the church as well as Aristotelianism. Realizing that his common sense (that is, the five senses of seeing, hearing, touching, smelling, and tasting) was unreliable, he determined that the only reliable body of knowledge was thought, especially mathematical thought. As a person capable of thought, he concluded—bypassing his unreliable senses—that he existed: "I think, therefore I am" (*cogito ergo sum*). A further conclusion from this argument was that he was composed of two radically different substances, a material substance consisting of his body (that is, his senses) and another, immaterial substance consisting of his thinking mind. According to Descartes, body and mind, although joined through consciousness, belonged to two profoundly different realms of reality.

**Variations on Descartes's New Philosophy**   Descartes's radical distinction between body and mind stimulated a lively debate, not only among a growing circle of philosophers of the New Sciences. Was this distinction only conceptual while reality was experienced as a unified whole? If the dualism was real as well as conceptual, which substance was more fundamental, sensual bodily experience or mental activity, as the creator of the concepts of experience? The answers of three philosophers—Baruch Spinoza, Thomas Hobbes, and John Locke—stood out in the 1600s. They set the course for two major directions of philosophy during the so-called Enlightenment of the 1700s (see Chapter 23), one Continental European and the other Anglo-American.

For Baruch Spinoza (1632–1677), Descartes's distinction between body and mind was to be understood only in a conceptual sense. In our daily experience we do not encounter either bodies or minds but persons endowed with both together. He therefore abandoned Descartes's distinction and developed a complicated philosophical system that sought to integrate Galilean nature with the ideas of God, the Good in ethics, and the Just in politics into a unified whole. The Jewish community of Amsterdam, into which he had been born, excommunicated him for heresy, since he seemed to make God immanent to the world. But he enjoyed a high esteem among fellow philosophers on the continent who appreciated his effort to moderate Descartes's radical mind/body distinction.

Both Thomas Hobbes (1588–1679) and John Locke (1632–1704) not only accepted Descartes's radical distinction; they furthermore made the body the fundamental reality and the mind a dependent function. Consequently, they focused on the bodily passions, not reason, as the principal human character trait. For Hobbes, the violent passions of aggression and fear were constitutive of human nature. He speculated that individuals in the primordial state of nature were engaged in a "war of all against all." To survive, they forged a social contract in which they transferred all power to a sovereign. Hobbes's famous book *Leviathan* (1651) can be read as a political theory of absolute rule, but his ideas of a social contract and transfer of power nevertheless imply a sprinkling of constitutionalism.

Locke, who lived through the less violent phases of the English religious wars, focused on the more benign bodily passion of acquisitiveness. Primordial individuals, so he argued, engaged as equals in a social contract for the purpose of erecting

# Mapping the World

The world—its shape, its size, its orientation—has been rendered so thoroughly knowable by modern technology that we fail to appreciate how long it took to map the planet scientifically.

In 1400, no accurate map of the world existed anywhere on the planet. Prior to the first Portuguese sailing expeditions down the west coast of Africa in the 1420s and 1430s, mariners all over the world relied upon local knowledge of winds, waves, and stars to navigate. The Portuguese were the first to use science to sail, adapting highly sophisticated scholarship in trigonometry, astronomy, and solar timekeeping developed in previous centuries by Jewish and Muslim scientists in Iberia.

Crucial to this novel approach was latitude. Mathematically challenging, fixing exact latitude required precise calculations of the daily changes in the path of the sun relative to the earth and determination of the exact height of the sun. The invention of the nautical astrolabe in 1497 by the Jewish scientist Abraham Zacuto aided this process tremendously. Determining longitude was also important, and Jewish scientists in Portugal adapted a method based on the pioneering work of the Islamic astronomer al-Biruni (973–1048).

Although primarily resting upon achievements in astronomical observation and measurement in the Jewish and Islamic scientific traditions, the new maps of the fifteenth century also drew upon an innovation from another part of the world: the

a government that protected their properties and, more generally, established a civil society governed by law. With Hobbes and Locke a line of new thought came to its conclusion, leading from Galileo's mathematized physics and Descartes's two substances to the ideas of absolutism as well as democratic constitutionalism.

# Centralizing States and Religious Upheavals

The pattern of the centralizing state transforming the institutional structures of society was characteristic not only of the Ottoman and Habsburg Empires during 1450–1750, as we have seen in Chapter 16, but also of other countries of Europe, the Middle East, and India. The financial requirements for sustaining such a state required everywhere a reorganization of the relationship between rulers, ruling classes, and regional as well as local forces. The Protestant Reformation and religious wars slowed the pattern of central state formation, but once the religious fervor died down, two types of states emerged: the French, Russian, and Prussian landed centralizing state and the Dutch and English naval centralizing state.

## The Rise of Centralized Kingdoms

The shift from feudal mounted and armored knights to firearm-equipped professional infantries led to the emergence of states whose rulers sought to strengthen the power of their administrations. Rulers sought to centralize state power, collect

compass. Originating in China, the compass was first widely used as a navigational instrument by Muslim sailors during the twelfth century. In the thirteenth century, mapmakers in the Mediterranean began to include compasses on portolans, or nautical charts, enabling sailors to follow their direction on a map.

With an accurate science for fixing latitude and improved knowledge for longitude (determining precise longitude would not be achieved until 1774 with the invention of the marine chronometer), the science of cartography was transformed in the fifteenth and sixteenth centuries. Any place on earth could be mapped mathematically in relation to any other place, and the direction in which one place lay in relation to another could be plotted using compass lines. By 1500 mapmakers could locate any newly discovered place in the world on a map, no matter how remote.

**Portolan by Pedro Reinel.** Drawn in 1504 by the great Portuguese cartographer Pedro Reinel (ca. 1462–ca. 1542), this nautical chart (portolan) shows compass lines and is the earliest known map to include lines of latitude.

## Questions

- How were adaptations from various cultural traditions essential to the transformation of cartography in the fifteenth and sixteenth centuries?

- How are developments in cartography in this time period an example of the shift from descriptive science to mathematical science?

higher taxes to subsidize their infantries, and curb the decentralizing forces of the nobility, cities, and other local institutions. Not all autonomous units (such as city-states, city-leagues, and religious orders dating to the previous period, 600–1450) were able to survive the race to centralization. A winnowing process occurred during 1450–1550, which left a few territorially coherent kingdoms in control of European politics.

**The Demographic Curve**   Following the demographic disaster of the Black Death in 1348 and its many subsequent cycles, the population of the European states expanded again after 1470. It reached its pre-1348 levels around 1550, with some 85 million inhabitants (not counting the Spanish Habsburg and Ottoman Empires). The population continued to grow until about 1600 (90 million), when it entered a half century of stagnation during the coldest and wettest period in recorded history, the Little Ice Age (1550–1750).

During 1650–1750, the population rose slowly at a moderate rate from 105 to 140 million. In 1750, France (28 million) and Russia (21 million) were the most populous countries, followed by Germany (18 million), Italy (15 million), Poland (13 million), England (7 million), and the Netherlands and Sweden (2 million each). While the population figures of the individual countries for the most part bore little resemblance to their political importance during 1450–1750, as we shall see, the overall figures for Europe demonstrate that western Christianity had risen by 1750 to the status of demographic equivalence to the two leading religious civilizations of India (155 million) and China (225 million).

**A Heritage of Decentralization**   Bracketed between the two empires of the Ottomans and Habsburgs at either geographical end, western Christian Europe during the second half of the fifteenth century was a quilt of numerous independent or autonomous units, including the nascent centralizing kingdoms of France and England, the Hanseatic League of trading cities, the territory ruled by the Catholic crusading order of Teutonic Knights, and the small kingdoms of Denmark, Sweden, Norway, Poland–Lithuania, Bohemia, and Hungary. It furthermore comprised the principalities and cities of Germany, the duchy of Burgundy, the Alpine republic of Switzerland, and the city-states of Italy. At the northeastern periphery was the Grand Duchy of Moscow, representing eastern Christianity after the fall of Byzantium to the Ottomans in 1453. In this quilt, the majority of units competed vigorously with each other, seeking either to exploit the new possibilities which armies of mercenaries with firearms gave them or to survive as best as possible with just a handful of mercenaries.

**Table 17.1 Victims of State Centralization in Europe, 1450–1600.**

- Duchy of Burgundy, absorbed by France, 1477
- City-states Milan, Naples, taken by France 1499–1501
- Rest of Italy, except Venice, taken by Spain, 1550s
- Kingdoms of Bohemia and rump Hungary taken by Austrian Habsburgs, 1526; majority of Hungary to the Ottoman Empire
- Calais, last toehold of England on continent, to France, 1558
- Hanseatic League of ports in northern Europe, centered on the Free Cities of Lübeck and Hamburg, de facto dissolved 1669
- Duchy of Prussia lost by Teutonic Order to the kingdom of Poland, 1525; Prussia as fief of the kingdom of Poland, under its own dynasty of the Hohenzollern
- Prussia united with Brandenburg, 1618; Hohenzollerns as Polish vassals in Prussia and Habsburg vassals in Brandenburg
- Sweden independent from Denmark, 1523

**Military and Administrative Capacities**   In the course of the sixteenth century, some kingdoms turned their mercenary troops into standing armies and stationed them in star-shaped forts. These forts were a fifteenth-century Italian innovation that made walls more resistant to artillery fire and trapped attackers in cross fires. Sweden introduced the line infantry in the mid-seventeenth century. In this formation, three-deep lines of musketeers advanced on a broad front toward the enemy, with the front line firing, stepping back to reload, and making room for the next line to step forward and repeat the actions. Since the line formation required extensive peacetime drills and maneuvers, the regimental system came into use. Soldiers formed permanent regiments and wore standardized, multicolored uniforms.

The French-invented flintlock gradually replaced the matchlock musket during 1620–1630, the advantage being that the flint produced a spark more quickly than the wick fuse. Similarly, during 1660–1700 the French introduced and gradually improved the bayonet—a sharp knife fixed to the end of the muzzle. With the appearance of the bayonet, pikemen, equipped with thrusting spears-cum-battle-axes for the protection of musketeers in hand-to-hand combat, were

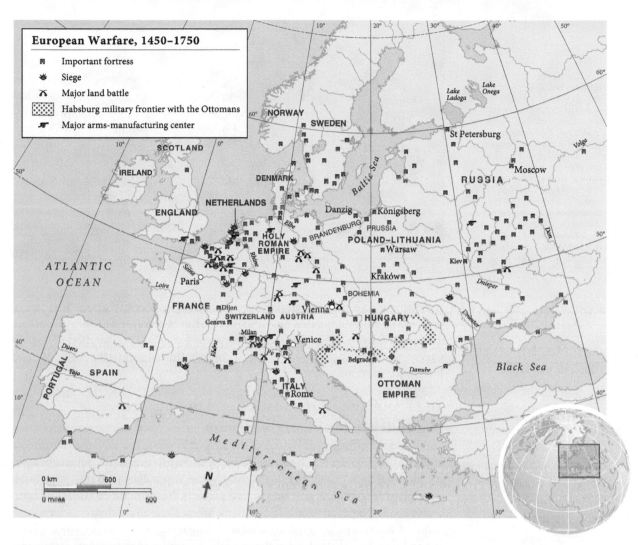

MAP 17.2 **European Warfare, 1450–1750.**

phased out. By 1750, armies in the larger European countries were both more uniform in their armaments and larger, increasing from a few thousand to tens of thousands of soldiers (see Map 17.2).

The military forces devoured copious amounts of tax money. Accordingly, taxes expanded substantially during the period 1450–1550. But rulers could not raise land, head, and commerce taxes without the formal (in assemblies) or informal (based on customs and traditions) assent of the ruling classes and cities. Similarly, villagers voted with their feet when taxes became too oppressive. The taxation limits were reached in most European countries in the mid-sixteenth century, and for the next two centuries rulers could raise additional finances only to the detriment of their previously acquired central powers, such as by borrowing from merchants and selling offices. The Netherlands was an exception. Only there did the urban population rise from 10 to 40 percent, willing to pay higher taxes on expanded urban manufactures and commercial suburban farming. The Dutch

**Musketeers.** These pictures from an English illustrated drill manual demonstrate the steps by which a seventeenth-century musketeer "makes ready" his weapon, typically in less than 30 seconds. In battle, a sergeant would stand alongside each company of musketeers, organizing its movements and volley fire. Once a rank of musketeers had discharged its weapons, it would move out of the way for another rank to fire. If combat was joined at close quarters, the musketeers would use their rifle butts as clubs.

government also derived substantial revenues from charters granted to armed overseas trading companies. Given the severe limits on revenue-raising measures in most of Europe, the eighteenth century saw a general deterioration of state finances, which eventually became major contributing factors to the American and French Revolutions.

## The Protestant Reformation, State Churches, and Independent Congregations

Parallel to the growing centralism of the kings, the popes restored the central role of the Vatican in the church hierarchy, after the devastating Great Schism of competing papal lines (1305–1415). Outwardly, the popes displayed this restoration through expensive Vatican construction projects that aroused considerable criticism outside Rome, especially in Germany, where the leading clergy under a weak emperor was more strongly identified with Rome than elsewhere. Growing literacy and lay religiosity helped in the growth of a profound theological dissatisfaction, which exploded in the **Protestant Reformation**. The Reformation began as an antipapal movement of reform in the early sixteenth century that demanded a return to the simplicity of early Christianity. The movement quickly engulfed the kingdoms and divided their ruling classes and populations alike. Vicious religious wars were the consequence. Although these wars eventually subsided, the divisions were never healed completely and mark the culture of many areas in Europe even today.

**Protestant Reformation:** Broad movement to reform the Roman Catholic Church, the beginnings of which are usually associated with Martin Luther.

**Background to the Reformation**   Several religious and political changes in the fifteenth century led to the Protestant Reformation. One important religious shift was the growth of popular theology, a consequence of the introduction of the printing press (1454/1455) and the distribution of printed materials. A flood of devotional tracts, often read aloud to congregations of illiterate believers, catered to the spiritual interests of ordinary people. Many Christians attended Mass daily, confessed, and did penance for their sins. Wealthy Christians endowed saint cults, charitable institutions, or confraternities devoted to the organization of processions and passion plays. Poor people formed lay groups or studied scripture on their own and devoted themselves to the simple life of the early Christians. More Europeans than in previous centuries had a basic, though mostly literal, understanding of Christianity.

An important political change in the fifteenth century was an increasing inability for the popes, powerful in Rome, to appoint archbishops and bishops outside Italy. The kings of France, Spain, England, and Sweden were busy transforming their kingdoms into centralized states, in which they reduced the influence of the popes. Only in Germany, where the powers of the emperor and the rulers in the various principalities canceled each other out, was the influence of the popes still strong. What remained to the popes was the right to collect a variety of dues in the kingdoms of Europe. They used these dues to finance their expensive and, in the eyes of many, luxuriously worldly administration and court in Rome, from which they engaged in European politics. One of the dues was the sale of **indulgences**, which, in popular understanding, were tickets to heaven. Many contemporary observers found the discrepancy between declining papal power and the remaining financial privileges disturbing and demanded reforms.

**Indulgence:** Partial remission of sins after payment of a fine or presentation of a donation. Remission would mean the forgiveness of sins by the Church, but the sinner still remained responsible for his or her sins before God.

**Luther's Reformation**   One such observer was Martin Luther (1483–1546), an Augustinian monk, ordained priest, and New Testament professor in northeastern Germany. Luther was imbued with deep personal piety and confessed his sins daily, doing extensive penance. After a particularly egregious sale of indulgences in his area, in 1517 he wrote his archbishop a letter with 95 theses in which he condemned the indulgences and other matters as contrary to scripture. Friends translated the theses from Latin into German and made them public. What was to become the Protestant Reformation had begun.

News of Luther's public protest traveled quickly across Europe. Sales of indulgences fell off sharply. In a series of writings, Luther spelled out the details of the church reform he envisaged. One reform proposal was the elevation of original New Testament scripture over tradition—that is, over canon law and papal decisions. Salvation was to be by faith alone; good works were irrelevant. Another reform was the declaration of the priesthood of all Christians, doing away with the privileged position of the clergy as mediators between God and believers who could forgive sins. A third reform was a call to German princes to begin church reform in their own lands through their power over clerical appointments, even if the Habsburg emperor was opposed. Finally, by translating the Bible into German, Luther made the full sacred text available to all who, by reading or listening, wanted to rely solely on scripture as the source of their faith. Luther's Bible was a monument of the emerging literary German language. A forceful and clear writer in his translation and own publications, Luther fully explicated the basics of Protestantism.

**Reaction to Luther's Demands**   Both emperor and pope failed in their efforts to arrest Luther and suppress his call for church reform. The duke of Saxony was successful in protecting the reformer from seizure. Emperor Charles V, a devout Catholic, considered Castile's successful church reform of half a century earlier to be fully sufficient. In his mind, Luther's demands for church reform were to be resisted. Two other pressing concerns, however, diverted the emperor's attention.

**Anti-Catholic Propaganda.**
This anonymous woodcut of 1520 by a German satirist depicts the devil (complete with wings and clawed feet) sitting on a letter of indulgence and holding a money collection box. The devil's mouth is filled with sinners who presumably bought letters of indulgence in good faith, thinking they had been absolved of their sins.

First, the Ottoman-led Islamic threat, in eastern Europe and the western Mediterranean, had to be met with decisive action. Second, his rivalry with the French king precluded the formation of a common Catholic front against Luther. Enthusiastic villagers and townspeople in Germany exploited Charles's divided attention and abandoned both Catholicism and secular obedience. A savage civil war, called the Peasants' War, engulfed Germany from 1524 to 1525, killing perhaps as many as 100,000 people.

Luther and other prominent reformers were horrified by the carnage. They drew up church ordinances that regulated preaching, church services, administrative councils, education, charity, and consistories for handling disciplinary matters. In Saxony, the duke endorsed this order in 1528. He thereby created the model of Lutheran Protestantism as a state religion, in which the rulers were protectors and supervisors of the churches in their territories. A decade later, Saxony was fully Lutheran.

A minority of about half a dozen German princes and the kings of Denmark and Sweden followed suit. In England, Protestants gained strength in the wake of the break with Rome by Henry VIII (r. 1509–1547) and his assumption of church leadership in his kingdom (1534). Although remaining Catholic, he surrounded himself with religious reformers and proclaimed an Anglican state church whose creed and rites combined elements of Catholicism and Protestantism. In Switzerland, several cantons adopted the religious reforms of Huldrych Zwingli (1484–1531). In Scotland, the reforms of John Knox (1514–1572) became the foundation for the state church. Thus, most of northern Europe followed a pattern of alliances between Protestant reformers and the state (see Map 17.3).

**Calvinism in Geneva and France** In France, as in England, the king controlled all church appointments. King Francis I, however, did not take the final step toward the creation of an independent state church. Since he competed with Charles V of the Habsburg Empire for dominance over the papacy in Italy, he had to appear especially loyal and devout. When a few Protestants in France went public with their demands for church reform, Francis I gave them the stark choice of exile or burning at the stake.

One reformer who chose exile was the French lawyer John Calvin (Jean Cauvin, 1509–1564). During his exile, he passed at one point (in 1536) through Geneva, where a French friend of his beseeched him to help him in preaching the faith. Calvin relented and began a stormy and at one point interrupted career as the city's religious reformer. Geneva's city council—not yet part of Switzerland and under the nominal rule of the duke of Savoy (himself under the nominal rule of the Habsburgs)—was unsure about which path of reform to embrace. It took Calvin well into the 1550s before his form of Protestantism prevailed in the city.

As expressed in Calvin's central work, *Institutes of the Christian Religion* (1536), and numerous other writings, a crucial doctrine of Calvin's was *predestination*. According to this doctrine, God has "predestined" each human prior to birth for

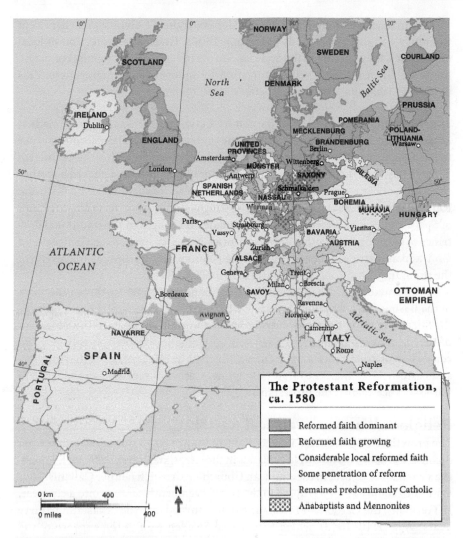

MAP 17.3 **The Protestant Reformation, ca. 1580.**

heaven or hell. Believers could only hope, through faith alone, that sometime during a life of moral living they would receive a glimpse of their fate. In contrast to Luther, however, Calvin made the enforcement of morality through a formal code, administered by local authorities, part of his version of Protestantism.

Interestingly, this code did not prohibit the taking of interest on loans. While Luther as well as the Catholic Church, in accordance with scripture, condemned all interest as usury, Calvin considered a few percentage points to be entirely justifiable. The strong condemnation of interest on loans in the Hebrew Bible was rooted in the precariousness of Palestinian rain-fed agriculture: Several years of drought could drive farmers into total dependence on landlords if the latter demanded interest on loans. By placing moneylending into the increasingly urban context of the 1500s, Calvin displayed a greater sense of economic reality than Luther. Acquiring wealth with the help of money and thereby perhaps gaining a glimpse of one's fate became one of the hallmarks of Calvinism. Wealth began to become respectable in Christian society.

Calvin died in his Genevan exile, but Geneva-trained Calvinist preachers went to France and the Netherlands in the mid-1500s. Under the protection of local magistrates, they organized the first clandestine independent Calvinist congregations. Calvinist religious self-organization by independent congregations thus became a viable alternative to Lutheran state religion.

**The Catholic Reformation**    The rivalry between Spain and France made it initially difficult for the popes to tackle the problem of Catholic reforms in order to meet the Protestant challenge. When they finally called together the Council of Trent (1545–1563), they abolished payment for indulgences and phased out other church practices considered to be corrupt. These actions launched the **Catholic Reformation**, an effort to gain back dissenting Catholics. Supported by the kings of Spain and France, however, the popes made no changes to the traditional doctrines of faith together with good works, priestly mediation between believer and God, and monasticism. They even tightened church control through the revival of the papal Inquisition and a new Index of Prohibited Books.

**Catholic Reformation:** Reaffirmation of Catholic papal supremacy and the doctrine of faith together with works as preparatory to salvation; such practices as absenteeism (bishops in Rome instead of their bishoprics) and pluralism (bishops and abbots holding multiple appointments) were abolished.

To counterbalance these punitive institutions, the popes furthered the work of the Basque priest Ignatius Loyola (1491–1556). At the head of the new order of the Society of Jesus, or Jesuits, Loyola devoted himself tirelessly to the education of the clergy, establishment of a network of Catholic schools and colleges, and conversion of Protestants as well as non-Christians by missionaries to the Americas and eastern Asia. Thanks to Jesuit discipline, Catholics regained a semblance of self-assurance against the Protestants.

## Religious Wars and Political Restoration

The growth of Calvinism led to a civil war in France and a war of liberation from Spanish Catholic rule in the Netherlands in the later sixteenth century. In England, the slow pace of reform in the Anglican Church, with which neither Calvinists nor Catholics could identify, erupted in the early seventeenth century into a civil war. In Germany, the Catholic–Protestant struggle turned into the devastating Thirty Years' War (1618–1648), which France and Sweden won at the expense of the Habsburgs. On the religious level, western Christians grudgingly accepted denominational toleration; on the political level, the centralizing states evolved into polities based on absolutism, tempered by provincial and local administrative practices.

**Civil War in France**    During the mid-1500s, Calvinism in France grew to about 1,200 congregations, mostly in the western cities of the kingdom, where literate merchants and craftspeople catering to trade overseas were receptive to Protestant publications. Calvinism was essentially an urban denomination, and peasants did not join in large numbers. Some 2 million, or 10 percent of the total population of 18.5 million, were Huguenots, as the Protestants were called in France. They continued to be persecuted, but given their numbers, it was impossible for the government to imprison and execute them all. In 1571, they even met in a kingdom-wide synod, where they ratified their congregational church order. They posed a formidable challenge to French Catholicism.

In many cities, relations between Huguenots and Catholics were uneasy. From time to time, groups of agitators crashed each other's church services. The arrival of a child king to the French throne in 1560 was an open invitation to escalate hostilities. In vain, the queen mother, Catherine de' Medici (1519–1589), who acted as the king's regent, sought to rein in the passions. The first three rounds of war ended with the victorious Huguenots achieving full freedom of religious practice and self-government in four western cities. In this new situation, she arranged in 1572 for the marriage of her daughter to King Henry III of Navarre (later King Henry IV of France, 1589–1610), a Protestant of the Bourbon family in southwestern France. Henry had risen to the leadership of the Huguenots a few years earlier, but he detested the fanaticism that surrounded him.

The prospect of a Huguenot king drove the Catholic aristocracy into a renewed frenzy of religious persecution. On St. Bartholomew's Day (August 24, 1572), just 6 days after the wedding of the future Henry IV, they perpetrated a wholesale slaughter of thousands of Huguenots. This massacre, in response to the assassination of a French admiral, occurred with the apparent connivance of the queen. For over a decade and a half, civil war raged, in which Spain aided the Catholics and Henry enrolled German and Swiss Protestant mercenaries.

A turning point came only in 1589 when Henry of Navarre became King Henry IV. Surviving nearly three dozen plots against his life, the new king needed 9 years and two conversions to Catholicism—"Paris is well worth a Mass," he is supposed to have quipped—before he was able to calm the religious fanaticism among the majority of French people. With the Edict of Nantes in 1598, he decreed freedom of religion for Protestants. A number of staunch Catholic adherents were deeply offended by the edict as well as the alleged antipapal policies of Henry IV. The king fell victim to an assassin in 1610. Catholic resentment continued until 1685, when King Louis XIV revoked the edict and triggered a large-scale emigration of Huguenots to the Netherlands, Germany, and England. At last, France was Catholic again.

**Dutch War of Independence** In the Netherlands, the Spanish overlords were even more determined to keep the country Catholic than the French monarchs prior to Henry IV. When Charles V resigned in 1556 (effective 1558), his son Philip II (r. 1556–1598) became king of Spain and the Netherlands, consisting of the French-speaking regions of Wallonia in the south and the Dutch-speaking regions of Flanders and Holland in the north. Like his father, Philip was a staunch supporter of the Catholic Reformation. He asked the Jesuits and the Inquisition to aggressively persecute the Calvinists. For better effect, Philip subdivided the bishoprics into smaller units and recruited clergymen in place of members of the nobility.

In response, in 1565 the nobility and Calvinist congregations rose in revolt. They dismantled the bishoprics and cleansed the churches of images and sculptures, thereby triggering what was to become a Protestant war of Dutch liberation from Catholic Spanish overlordship (1565–1620). Philip retaliated by sending in an army that succeeded in suppressing the liberation movement. He reimposed Catholicism, and executed thousands of rebels, many of them members of the Dutch aristocracy.

Remnants of the rebellion struggled on and, in 1579, renewed the war of liberation in three of the 17 northern provinces making up the Netherlands. Later joined by four more provinces, the people in these breakaway regions called themselves members of the "United Provinces of the Dutch Republic." Spain refused to recognize the republic and kept fighting until acute Spanish financial difficulties prompted the truce of 1609–1621. Although drawn into fighting again during the Thirty Years' War, the Netherlands gained its full independence in 1648.

At the head of the Dutch republic was a governor (*stadhouder*) from the House of Orange-Nassau, one of the leading aristocratic families of the Netherlands. The representative body, with which the *stadhouder* governed, was the States General, and the privileged religious body was the Calvinist Dutch Reformed Church. About 20 percent of the population of 1 million was Calvinist, double the percentage in France and England. But there were also sizeable groups of Catholics and other Protestants. Among the latter, the Anabaptists and Mennonites (characterized by the doctrines of adult baptism and pacifism, respectively) were prominent. The Netherlands was also a haven for Jews, who had originally arrived there after their expulsion from Spain and Portugal in 1492–1498 (see above, on Baruch Spinoza, p. 507). Gradually, the Dutch accepted each other's doctrinal differences, and the Netherlands became a model of religious tolerance.

**Civil War in England**    As in the Netherlands, the prevalent form of Protestantism in England was Calvinism. During the sixteenth century, the Calvinists numbered about 10 percent in a kingdom in which the Anglican Church encompassed the vast majority of subjects in a total population of 7 million. English Catholics, who refused to recognize the king as the head of the Anglican Church, numbered 3 percent. The percentage of Calvinists was the same as in France before 1685, but the partially reformed Anglican Church was able to hold them in check. The Calvinists were, furthermore, a fractious group, encompassing moderate and radical tendencies that neutralized each other. Among the radicals were the Puritans, who demanded the abolition of the Anglican clerical hierarchy and a new church order of independent congregations. In the early seventeenth century, when Anglican Church reform slowed under the Catholic successors of Elizabeth I (r. 1558–1603), the Puritan cause began to acquire traction. Realizing that these Stuart successors and their bishops were immovable, some Puritans emigrated to North America rather than continue to chafe under the Anglican yoke. Other Puritans began to agitate openly.

Along with their efforts to restrain would-be reformers, the Stuart kings were busy building their version of the centralized state. They collected taxes without the approval of Parliament. Many members resented being bypassed since Parliament was the constitutional cosovereign of the kingdom. A slight majority in the House of Commons was Puritan, and the stalled church reform added to their resentment. Eventually, when all tax resources were exhausted, the king, Charles I (r. 1625–1649), had to call Parliament back together. Mutual resentment was so deep, however, that the two sides were unable to make any decisions on either financial or religious matters. The standoff erupted into civil war, leading to the king's execution and ending the monarchy.

Despite the brutal fate of Charles I, the English civil war of 1642–1651 was generally less vicious than that in France. Nevertheless, because of widespread pillage and destruction of crops and houses, the indirect effects of the war for the population of thousands of villages were severe. The New Model Army, a professional body of 22,000 troops raised by the Puritan-dominated Parliament against the king, caused further upheavals by cleansing villages of their "frivolous" seasonal festivals, deeply rooted in local pagan traditions and featuring pranks, games, dances, drunkenness, and free-wheeling behavior. A republican theocracy emerged, with preachers enforcing Calvinist morality among the population.

**Republic, Restoration, and Revolution**   The ruler of this theocracy, Oliver Cromwell (r. 1649–1658), was a Puritan member of the lower nobility (the gentry) and a commander in the New Model Army. After dissolving Parliament, Cromwell handpicked a new parliament but ruled for the most part without its consent. Since both Scotland and Ireland had opposed the Puritans in the civil war, Cromwell waged a savage war of submission against the Scottish Presbyterians (Calvinists organized in a state church) and Irish Catholics. The Dutch and Spanish, also opponents of the Puritans in the Civil War, were defeated in naval wars that substantially increased English shipping power in the Atlantic. But fear among the gentry in Parliament of a permanent centralized state led to a refusal of further financial subsidies for the army. After Cromwell's death in 1658, it took just 3 years to restore the Stuart monarchy and the Anglican state church to their previous places.

The recalled Stuart kings, however, resumed the policies of centralization and Catholicism. As before, the kings called Parliament together only sparingly and raised funds without its authorization. But their standing army of 30,000, partially stationed near London, was intended more to intimidate the parliamentarians than to actually wage war. In 1687, the king even espoused a major plan of reform, as new research has shown. In the "Glorious Revolution" of 1688, the defiant Parliament, dominated since the Restoration by mostly Anglican gentry, seized the initiative for reform and deposed the Catholic king, James II (r. 1685–1688). It feared that the recent birth of a royal son threatened the succession of the king's daughter by his first marriage, Mary, a Protestant married to William of Nassau-Orange, the *stadhouder* of the Netherlands. It offered the throne to William and Mary as joint monarchs, and the Stuarts went into exile in France.

**The Thirty Years' War in Germany**   As religious tensions were mounting in England during the early seventeenth century, similar tensions erupted into a full-blown war in Germany, bringing about the second such conflagration in a century, the Thirty Years' War. As we saw earlier, even though the rulers of the German principalities had made either Catholicism or Protestantism their state religion, minorities were tolerated or even admitted to offices. The Jesuit-educated Ferdinand II (r. 1619–1637), ruler of the Holy Roman Empire, however, refused to appoint Protestants in majority-Protestant Bohemia, of which the Habsburgs were kings since 1526. In response, Protestant leaders in 1618 renounced Ferdinand's authority and made the Calvinist prince of the Palatinate in the Rhineland their new king. With these events in Protestant Bohemia, open hostilities between the religious denominations began in Germany.

In a first round of war (1619–1630), Ferdinand and the Catholic princes suppressed the Bohemian rebellion and slowly advanced toward northern Germany, capturing territories for reconversion to Catholicism. When the Danish king intervened in favor of Lutheranism (1625–1629), he was crushed, and the Protestant cause seemed to be doomed. In 1630, however, the Lutheran king

**Centralizing States at War.** German imperial troops besiege Swedish troops in the northern German city of Stralsund in 1628. The etching shows typical features of the centralizing state, from top to bottom: galleon-style warships (successors of the caravel); a star-shaped fort (an Italian innovation) designed to withstand artillery barrages; the medieval walls of the city; musket-equipped infantry troops; field cannons; and the colorful Baroque uniforms worn by the musketeers of the period.

Gustavus II Adolphus (r. 1611–1632) of Sweden intervened. The king's main goal was the creation of a Swedish-Lutheran centralized state around the Baltic Sea, a project begun before the Thirty Years' War. By aiding the German Lutherans, he hoped to consolidate or even increase his predominance in the region. Louis XIII (r. 1610–1643) of France granted Sweden financial subsidies, since he was concerned that Ferdinand's victories would further strengthen the Habsburg Spanish–Flemish–Austrian–German–Italian grip around France. With the politically motivated alliance between Sweden and France, the German Catholic–Protestant war turned into a war for state dominance in Europe.

At first, the Swedes were successful, advancing victoriously as far as Bavaria in the south. But when Gustavus fell unexpectedly in battle, Ferdinand II—fearful that the Swedish ally France would enter the war—decided to compromise with the Protestant princes of Germany. In the peace of 1635, the two sides agreed to a return to the prewar territorial division between Catholic and Protestant princes in northern Germany. But the French entered the war anyway. During the next 13 years, French armies sought to cut the Habsburg supply lines from Italy to the Netherlands by occupying Habsburg Alsace. Swedish armies, exploiting the French successes against the Habsburgs, fought their way back into Germany. In the end, the Austrian–German Habsburgs, pressured on two sides, agreed in October 1648 to the Peace of Westphalia.

The agreement provided for religious freedom in Germany and ceded territories in Alsace to France and the southern side of the Baltic Sea to Sweden. It granted territorial integrity to all European powers. The Spanish Habsburgs continued their war against France until 1659, when they also bowed to superior French strength, giving up parts of Flanders and northeastern Spain. In the Caribbean, Spain also lost territories to France, the Netherlands, and England, accelerating the decline of Spain's overseas power. France emerged as the strongest country in Europe, and the Spanish-dominated Caribbean became an area of open power rivalry (see Map 17.4).

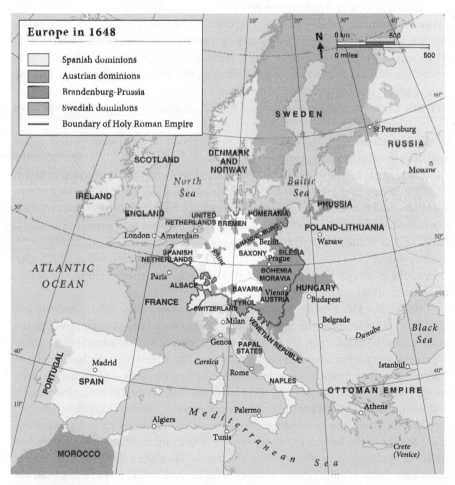

MAP **17.4 Europe in 1648.**

**Absolutism in France?**    During its period of greatest political dominance, France came under the rule of its longest-reigning monarch, King Louis XIV (1643–1715). He was of small stature—for which he compensated with high-heeled shoes—but his hardy constitution and strong self-discipline helped him to dominate even the most grueling meetings with his advisors. He enjoyed pomp and circumstance and built Versailles—his gigantic palace and gardens near Paris, populated with 10,000 courtiers, attendants, and servants—into a site of almost continuous feasting, entertainment, and intrigue. It was here that Louis, the "Sun King," beamed benevolently with his "absolute" divine mandate upon his aristocracy and commoners alike.

Versailles played an important role in Louis's efforts to undercut the power of the nobility. Anyone with any aspirations of attracting the king's attention had to come to the palace to attend him. By keeping both friends and potential enemies close by and forcing them to spend lavishly to keep up with the fashions inspired by the king and vie for his attention, he was able, like the Tokugawa shoguns in Edo, Japan, to bypass them administratively and rule through central bureaucratic institutions.

**Absolutism:** Theory of the state in which the unlimited power of the king, ruling under God's divine mandate, was emphasized. In practice, it was neutralized by the nobility and provincial and local communities.

In practice, the French **absolutism** of Louis XIV and his eighteenth-century successors, as well as absolutism in other European countries, was a complex mixture of centralized and decentralized forces. On the one hand, after the end of the religious wars in 1648, mercenary armies under autonomous dukes and counts disappeared from the European scene, replaced by permanent armies or navies under the central command of royal or princely dynasties. The kings also no longer called their respective assemblies of nobles and notables together to have new taxes approved (in France from 1614 to 1789), and thus, many of the nobility's tax privileges disappeared.

On the other hand, the kings of the seventeenth century were acutely aware that true absolutism was possible only if centrally salaried employees collected taxes. It was physically impossible, however, to transport tax revenues, in the form of silver money and grain, from the provinces to the capital, pay the central bureaucrats, and then cart the remaining money back to the provinces to pay salaried tax collectors there. A centrally paid bureaucracy would have required a central bank with provincial branches, using paper money. The failed experiment with such a bank in Paris from 1714 to 1720 demonstrates one such effort to find a solution to the central salarization problem. The bank's short life demonstrates that absolute central control was beyond the powers of the kings.

Instead, the kings had to rely on subcontracting out most offices and the collection of most taxes to the highest bidders, who then helped themselves to the collection of their incomes. Under Louis XIV, a total of 46,000 administrative jobs were available for purchase in Paris and the provinces. Anyone who had money or borrowed it from financiers was encouraged to buy an office—from the old aristocracy of the "sword" receiving rents from the farmers on their rural estates to ordinary merchants' sons with law degrees borrowing money from their fathers.

Once in office, the government often forced these officers to grant additional loans to the crown. To retain their loyalty, the government rewarded them with first picks for retaining their offices within the family. They were also privileged to buy landed estates or acquire titles of nobility to the secondary (and less prestigious) tier of the "nobility of the robe" (as opposed to the first-tier "nobility of the sword," which by the seventeenth century was demilitarized). With this system of offering offices and titles for sale, the king sought to bind the financial interests of the two nobilities to those of his own.

About the only way for Louis XIV to keep a semblance of a watchful eye on the officeholders was to send salaried, itinerant *intendants* around the provinces to ensure that collecting taxes, rendering justice, and policing functioned properly within the allowable limits of the "venality of office," as the subcontracting system was called. Louis XIV had roughly one intendant for each province. About half of the provinces had *parlements*—appointed assemblies for the ratification of decrees from Paris—whose officeholders, drawn from the local noble, clerical, and commoner classes, frequently resisted the intendants. The Paris *parlement* even refused to accept royal writs carried by the intendants.

In later years, when Louis XIV was less successful in his many wars against the rival Habsburgs and Protestant Dutch than previously, the crown overspent and had to borrow heavily with little regard for the future. Louis's successors in the second half of the eighteenth century were saddled with crippling debts. French-inspired European "absolutism" was thus in practice a careful (or not so careful) balancing act between the forces of centralization and decentralization in the states of Europe.

**The Rise of Russia**  Although France's absolutism was more theory than practice, its glorious ideological embodiment in the Versailles of Louis XIV spawned adaptations across Europe. These adaptations were most visible in eastern Europe, which was populated more thinly and had far fewer towns and cities. Since rulers in those areas did not have a large reservoir of urban commoners to aid them as administrators in building the centralized state, they had to make do with the landowning aristocracy. As a result, rulers and aristocracy connived to finance

**A World Turned Upside Down.** In this popular satirical woodcut of 1766, based on a similar woodcut from the early 1700s, the mice are capturing and burying the cat: In other words, Peter the Great has turned the world upside down with his reforms.

state centralization through an increased exploitation of the farmers in the villages: In the 1600s, their legal status deteriorated, their tax liabilities increased continuously, and they became serfs.

In Russia, Tsar Peter I, "the Great" (r. 1682–1725), of the eastern Christian Romanov dynasty, was a towering figure who singlehandedly sought to establish the French-type centralized state during his lifetime. At nearly 7 feet tall, Peter was an imposing, energetic ruler, controllable only by his second wife (and former mistress) Catherine, a warmhearted woman and beloved tsarina. Peter invited western European soldiers, mariners, administrators, craftspeople, scholars, and artists into his service and succeeded within just a few years in building a disciplined army and imposing navy. He built ports on the Baltic Sea and established the new capital of St. Petersburg, distinguished by many very beautiful palaces and official buildings.

A typical example among the thousands invited to Russia by the tsar was Peter von Sivers, a Danish mariner (and ancestor of one of the coauthors of the book) who rose to the position of admiral in the Baltic fleet that broke Swedish dominance in northern Europe. Since the tsar was not able to pay these advisors salaries (any more than Louis XIV could pay salaries to advisors to the French court), he gave many western guests estates with serfs in the Baltic provinces and Finland, conquered from Sweden, and made them aristocrats in his retinue.

The Russian military was completely reorganized by the tsar. After an early rebellion, Peter savagely decimated the inherited firearm regiments and made them part of a new army recruited from the traditional Russian landed nobility. Both classes of soldiers received education at military schools and academies and were required to provide lifelong service. In order to make his soldiers look more urban, Peter decreed that they shave their traditional beards and wear European uniforms or clothes. Every twentieth peasant household had to deliver one foot soldier to conscription. A census was taken to facilitate the shift from the inherited household tax on the villagers to a new capitation tax collected by military officers. In the process, the remaining free farmers outside the estate system of the aristocracy found themselves classified and taxed as serfs, unfree to leave their villages. The result of Peter's reforms was a powerful, expansionary centralizing state that played an increasingly important role among European kingdoms during the eighteenth century (see Map 17.5).

**The Rise of Prussia**   Similar to Russia, the principality of Prussia-Brandenburg was underurbanized. It had furthermore suffered destruction and depopulation during the Thirty Years' War. When the Lutheran Hohenzollern monarchs embarked on the construction of a centralized state in the later seventeenth century, they first broke the tax privileges of the landowning aristocracy in the estates general and raised taxes themselves. As in Russia, farmers who worked on estates held by landlords were serfs. Since there were few urban middle-class merchants and professionals, the kings enrolled members of the landlord aristocracy in the army and civilian administration.

Elevated by the Habsburg Holy Roman emperor from the status of dukes to that of kings in 1701, the Hohenzollern rulers systematically enlarged the army, employing it during peacetime for drainage and canal projects as well as palace construction in Berlin, the capital. Under Frederick II, "the Great" (1740–1786),

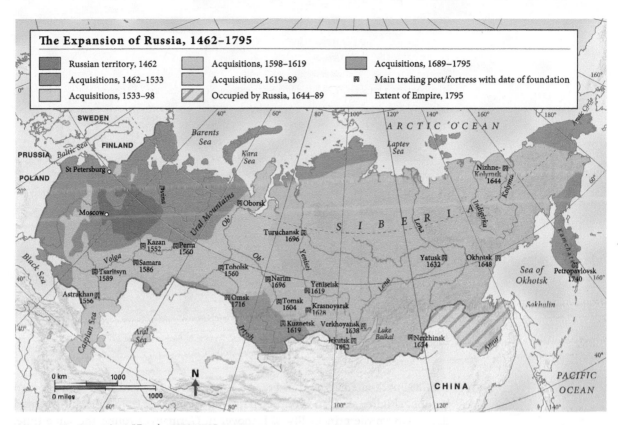

MAP 17.5 **The Expansion of Russia, 1462–1795.**

Prussia pursued an aggressive foreign policy, capturing Silesia from the Habsburgs in a military campaign. Frederick also expended major efforts to attracting immigrants, intensifying agriculture, and establishing manufacturing enterprises. Prussia emerged as a serious competitor of the Habsburgs in the Holy Roman Empire of Germany.

**English Constitutionalism**    In contrast to Prussia, France, Spain, Austria, and other European states, England had since 1450 a political system ruled by a king or a queen, with a parliament composed of the aristocracy as well as representatives of towns and cities. Only in England did the interests of the nobility and the urban merchants gradually converge. Rulers on the European continent financed their early centralizing states through raising indirect taxes on sales, commerce, imports, and exports, affecting cities more than noble estates. In England, the cities allied with the aristocracy in resisting indirect tax increases and forcing the throne to use the less ample revenues of its royal estates to pay soldiers. Efforts of the Stuart kings to create a centralized land-based state based on firearm infantries failed. Instead, the ruling class preferred to build a centralized naval state. After the Glorious Revolution of 1688, England became the dominant power on the world's oceans.

After its victory over the Stuart kings, Parliament consolidated its financial powers through the creation of the Bank of England in 1694, two decades before a

**Prussian Military Discipline.** The Prussian line infantry made full use in the mid-1700s of flintlock muskets, bayonets, and drilling.

similar but ill-fated attempt in France. When first Mary and then William died without children, England continued in 1714 with a king from a distantly related dynasty from the principality of Hanover in Germany. Around the same time, England and Scotland united, creating the United Kingdom. Parliament collected higher taxes than France and, through its bank, was able to keep its debt service low during the early 1700s. The navy grew twice as large as that of France and was staffed by a well-salaried, disciplined military, while the few land troops, deemed superfluous, were mostly low-paid Hessian-German mercenaries. A rudimentary two-party system of two aristocracy–merchant alliances came into being. The two parties were known as the Whigs and the Tories, the former more parliamentarian and the latter more royalist, with the Whigs in power for most of the first half of the eighteenth century.

## Putting It All Together

Prior to 1500, all religious civilizations possessed sophisticated mathematics and practiced variations of qualitative sciences, such as astrology, geography, alchemy, and medicine. The one exception was trigonometry-based astronomy in Islamic, Hindu, and Christian religious civilizations, pioneered by the Hellenistic scholar Ptolemy (Chapter 5). Physics became the second mathematical science in the early 1500s, but only in western Christianity. This transformation of the sciences, however, had no practical (that is, engineering) consequences prior to the invention of the steam engine in the 1700s and the subsequent industrialization of England in the 1800s. Furthermore, the mathematization of physics did little to influence the continued prevalence of qualitative description as the methodology of the other sciences. Astrology, chemistry, and medicine continued with what we regard today as outmoded qualitative theories well into the nineteenth century.

Most importantly, the rise of the New Sciences should not be confused with the vast political, social, economic, and cultural changes, called "modernity" after 1800, which propelled the West on its trajectory of world dominance. Although the West began to acquire its specific scientific and philosophical identity with the introduction of the mathematical sciences in the 100-year span between Copernicus and Galileo, the impact of these sciences on the world became felt only after 1800 when it was applied to industry. Once this application gathered momentum, in the nineteenth century, Asia and Africa had no choice but to adapt to modern science and industrialization.

▶ For additional resources, including maps, primary sources, visuals, and quizzes, please go to www.oup.com/us/vonsivers. Please see the Further Resources section at the back of the book for additional readings and suggested websites.

## Against the Grain

# The Digger Movement

I n April 1649, toward the end of the English Civil War and just three months after the execution of King Charles I, a group of 70 mostly landless farmers and day laborers occupied "common" (public) land near Walton, Surrey (about 25 miles south of London), to establish a colony. As the farmers and laborers dug up the soil and sowed the ground with parsnips, carrots, and beans, they came to be called the "Diggers."

Driven off by enraged small landowners who benefited greatly from the use of common land for grazing sheep and cutting timber, a much-reduced group of colonists moved on to common land in nearby Cobham in August 1649. After some delay, this time it was the gentry with their manor rights to the common land who destroyed the Diggers' cottages and fields in the winter of 1650. The Diggers, although ultimately unsuccessful, made a much-publicized statement that public land was "the treasure of all people" and should not be reserved for the benefit of anyone, be they gentry or even small property owners—a bold demand which ran counter to the rapidly increasing privatization of land and commercialization of agriculture.

The leader of the group was Gerrard Winstanley (1609–1670), an embittered former cloth merchant in London who had to abandon his trade in 1643 after he became insolvent. He struggled to regain his solvency in the countryside of Surrey, at one point working as a grazier of cattle. Parts of Surrey had suffered substantial hardship during the Civil War, having been forced to provision and quarter troops. In a flurry of pamphlets between 1648 and 1650 Winstanley explained the motives and goals of the Diggers most eloquently, displaying a remarkable familiarity with local affairs. In addition, he had a superb ability to make these affairs relevant, in the religious idiom of Protestantism, for England as a whole. He was the first to clearly identify the problem of the rising numbers of rural landless laborers victimized by the increasing commercialization of agriculture in England—a labor force that continued to increase until the industrializing cities of the later 1700s eventually absorbed them.

- **Was Winstanley hopelessly utopian in his efforts to establish farmer communities on common land in England?**

- **How have other figures in world history sympathized with the lot of poor and landless farmers and attempted reform (or revolution) on their behalf?**

# Thinking Through Patterns

▶ **What were the reasons for the cultural changes that began in Europe around 1450? In which ways were the patterns of cultural changes during 1450–1750 different from those in the other religious civilizations of Eurasia?**

Located far from the traditional agrarian–urban centers of Eurasia, western Christianity repeatedly adapted its culture (particularly theological, philosophical, scientific, and artistic forms of expression) in response to outside stimuli coming from Islamic and eastern Christian civilizations. Without these stimuli, the Renaissance, Baroque, New Science, and Enlightenment would not have developed. In contrast, the Middle East, Byzantium, India, and China, originating firmly within the traditional agrarian–urban centers, received far fewer outside stimuli prior to the scientific–industrial age. Scholars and thinkers in these religious civilizations did not feel the same pressure to change their cultural heritage as their colleagues in western Christianity did.

The discovery of the two new continents of the Americas prompted Nicolaus Copernicus to reject Aristotle's astronomical theory of spheres and to posit a sun-centered planetary system. Copernicus's new approach to science continued with Galileo Galilei's discovery of the mathematical law of falling bodies in physics and was completed when Isaac Newton unified physics and astronomy. The New Sciences became popular in educated urban circles in northwestern Europe, where Catholic and Protestant church authorities were largely divided. In southern Europe, where the Catholic Reformation was powerful and rejected Galileo, the adoption of the New Sciences occurred more slowly. As scientists in northwestern Europe discovered, the New Sciences possessed practical applicability: After studying the proportics of condensing steam and the vacuum, scientists and mechanics began experimenting with steam engines, which served as the principal catalysts for the launching of the scientific–industrial age.

▶ **When and how did the New Sciences begin, and how did they gain popularity in northwestern European society? Why is the popularization of the New Sciences important for understanding the period 1450–1750?**

▶ **What were the patterns of centralized state formation and transformation in the period 1450–1750? How did the Protestant Reformation and religious wars modify these patterns?**

European kingdoms, such as France, Sweden, and Prussia, expanded their powers of taxation to the detriment of the nobility. With the accumulated funds, they hired and salaried mercenary infantries equipped with firearms, using them to conquer land from their neighbors. The religious wars of the 1500s and 1600s strengthened centralization efforts and hastened the demise of the nobility as an obstacle to the centralized state. In England, Parliament blocked the Stuart kings from building a landed central state and instead pursued the construction of a naval state, which succeeded a similar one built by the Netherlands in 1688.

# Patterns of Evidence: Sources for Chapter 17

## SOURCE 17.1

# Examination of Lady Jane Grey, London

### 1554

Jane Grey, the granddaughter of Henry VIII's sister Mary, was born in 1537, the same year as Edward VI, the only surviving son of the king who had sought a male heir so desperately. Jane, who like Edward was raised in the Protestant religion Henry had introduced to England, proved a diligent and intellectually gifted teenager. In spite of her youth and gender, Jane corresponded with Protestant authorities on the Continent, but fast-moving events in England precluded further study. When Edward died without an heir in 1553, the throne passed, by prearranged agreement, to his fiercely Catholic half-sister Mary.

However, in order to forestall a Catholic successor—and the dramatic rollback of the Protestant reforms instituted by Henry's and Edward's Church of England—Jane's relatives proclaimed her queen. Her rule lasted a mere nine days. She was imprisoned in the Tower of London by Mary, who was then forced to consider whether Jane's execution was warranted. Shortly before Jane's death, at age 16, Queen Mary sent her own chaplain, Master Feckenham (sometimes rendered as "Fecknam") to try to reconcile Jane to the Catholic faith. The results of this attempt were triumphantly recorded in John Foxe's *Acts and Monuments*, published after the Protestant Queen Elizabeth had triumphed over Mary and the Catholics. Although the conversation recorded here is not a trial transcript—and is a highly partisan account—it does distill some of the central issues that divided Catholics and Protestants in an extremely chaotic and violent period.

FECKNAM: "I am here come to you at this present, sent from the queen [Mary] and her council, to instruct you in the true doctrine of the right faith: although I have so great confidence in you, that I shall have, I trust, little need to travail with you much therein."

Source: "The Examination of Lady Jane Grey (1554)," from Denis R. Janz, ed., *A Reformation Reader: Primary Texts with Introductions*, 2nd ed. (Minneapolis, MN: Fortress, 2008), 360–362, taken from *The Acts and Monuments of John Foxe* (London: Seeleys, 1859), 415–417.

JANE: "Forsooth, I heartily thank the queen's highness, which is not unmindful of her humble subject: and I hope, likewise, that you no less will do your duty therein both truly and faithfully, according to that you were sent for."

. . .

FECKNAM: "How many sacraments are there?"

JANE: "Two: the one the sacrament of baptism, and the other the sacrament of the Lord's Supper."

FECKNAM: "No, there are seven."

JANE: "By what Scripture find you that?"

FECKNAM: "Well, we will talk of that hereafter. But what is signified by your two sacraments?"

JANE: "By the sacrament of baptism I am washed with water and re-generated by the Spirit, and that washing is a token to me that I am the child of God. The sacrament of the Lord's Supper, offered unto me, is a sure seal and testimony that I am, by the blood of Christ, which he shed for me on the cross, made partaker of the everlasting kingdom."

FECKNAM: "Why? What do you re-ceive in that sacrament? Do you not receive the very body and blood of Christ?"

JANE: "No, surely, I do not so believe. I think that at the supper I neither receive flesh nor blood, but bread and wine: which bread when it is broken, and the wine when it is drunken, put me in remembrance how that for my sins the body of Christ was broken, and his blood shed on the cross; and with that bread and wine I receive the benefits that come by the breaking of his body, and shedding of his blood, for our sins on the cross."

FECKNAM: "Why, doth not Christ speak these words, 'Take, eat, this is my body?' Require you any plainer words? Doth he not say, it is his body?"

JANE: "I grant, he saith so; and so he saith, 'I am the vine, I am the door'; but he is never the more for that, the door or the vine. Doth not St. Paul say, 'He calleth things that are not, as though they were?' God forbid that I should say, that I eat the very natural body and blood of Christ: for then either I should pluck away my redemp-tion, or else there were two bodies, or two Christs. One body was tormented on the cross, and if they did eat another body, then had he two bodies: or if his body were eaten, then was it not broken upon the cross; or if it were broken upon the cross, it was not eaten of his disciples."

. . .

With these and like such per-suasions he would have had her lean to the [Catholic] church, but it would not be. There were many more things whereof they rea-soned, but these were the chiefest.

After this, Fecknam took his leave, saying, that he was sorry for her: "For I am sure," quoth he, "that we two shall never meet."

JANE: "True it is," said she, "that we shall never meet, except God turn your heart; for I am assured, unless you repent and turn to God, you are in an evil case. And I pray God, in the bowels of his mercy, to send you his Holy Spirit; for he hath given you his great gift of utterance, if it please him also to open the eyes of your heart."

▶ **Working with Sources**

1. **What does this source reveal about the religious education of young people in the extended royal household during the final years of Henry VIII and the reign of Edward VI?**

2. **How does the literal interpretation of the Bible enter into this discussion, and why?**

## SOURCE 17.2

# Sebastian Castellio, *Concerning Whether Heretics Should Be Persecuted*

### 1554

In October 1553, the extraordinarily gifted Spanish scientist Michael Servetus was executed with the approval and the strong support of John Calvin and his followers in Geneva. The charge was heresy, specifically for denying the existence of the Trinity and the divinity of Christ, and the method of execution—burning at the stake—elicited commentary and protest from across Europe. One of the fullest and most sophisticated protests against this execution was issued by Sebastian Castellio, a professor of Greek language and New Testament theology in the Swiss city of Basel. His book *De Haereticis* is a collection of opinions, drawn from Christian writers, from both before and after the Protestant Reformation and across 15 centuries. It is more than an academic exercise, however, as this dedication of the Latin work to a German noble demonstrates.

**Turks:** Muslims.

From the Dedication of the book to Duke Christoph of Württemberg:

. . . And just as the **Turks** disagree with the Christians as to the person of Christ, and the Jews with both the Turks and the Christians, and the one condemns the other and holds him for a heretic, so Christians disagree with Christians on many points with regard to the teaching of Christ, and condemn one another and hold each other for heretics. Great controversies and debates occur as to baptism, the Lord's Supper, the invocation of the saints, justification, free will, and other obscure questions, so that Catholics, Lutherans, Zwinglians, Anabaptists, monks, and others condemn and persecute one another more cruelly than the Turks do the Christians. These dissensions arise solely from ignorance of the truth, for if these matters were so obvious and evident as that there is but one God, all Christians would

Source: Sebastian Castellio, *Concerning Heretics, Whether They Are to Be Persecuted and How They Are to Be Treated, A Collection of the Opinions of Learned Men Both Ancient and Modern*, trans. Roland H. Bainton, (New York: Octagon, 1965), 132–134.

agree among themselves on these points as readily as all nations confess that God is one.

What, then is to be done in such great contentions? We should follow the counsel of Paul, "Let not him that eateth despise him that eateth not . . . To his own master he standeth or falleth" [Romans 14:3–4]. Let not the Jews or Turks condemn the Christians, nor let the Christians condemn the Jews or Turks, but rather teach and win them by true religion and justice, and let us, who are Christians, not condemn one another, but, if we are wiser than they, let us also be better and more merciful. This is certain that the better a man knows the truth, the less is he inclined to condemn, as appears in the case of Christ and the apostles. But he who lightly condemns others shows thereby that he knows nothing precisely, because he cannot bear others, for to know is to know how to put into practice. He who does not know how to act mercifully and kindly does not know the nature of mercy and kindness, just as he who cannot blush does not know the nature of shame.

If we were to conduct ourselves in this fashion we should be able to dwell together in concord. Even though in some matters we disagreed, yet should we consent together and forbear one another in love, which is the bond of peace, until we arrive at the unity of the faith [Ephesians 4:2–3]. But now, when we strive with hate and persecutions we go from bad to worse. Nor are we mindful of our office, since we are wholly taken up with condemnation, and the Gospel because of us is made a reproach unto the heathen [Ezekiel 22:4], for when they see us attacking one another with the fury of beasts, and the weak oppressed by the strong, these heathen feel horror and detestation for the Gospel, as if it made men such, and they abominate even Christ himself, as if he commanded men to do such things. We rather degenerate into Turks and Jews than convert them into Christians. Who would wish to be a Christian, when he saw that those who confessed the name of Christ were destroyed by Christians themselves with fire, water, and the sword without mercy and more cruelly treated than brigands and murderers? Who would not think Christ a **Moloch**, or some such god, if he wished that men should be immolated to him and burned alive? Who would wish to serve Christ on condition that a difference of opinion on a controversial point with those in authority would be punished by burning alive at the command of Christ himself more cruelly than in the bull of **Phalaris**, even though from the midst of the flames he should call with a loud voice upon Christ, and should cry out that he believed in Him? Imagine Christ, the judge of all, present. Imagine Him pronouncing the sentence and applying the torch. Who would not hold Christ for a Satan? What more could Satan do than burn those who call upon the name of Christ?

**Moloch:** A Phoenician deity who, according to the Bible, demanded the sacrifice of human children.

**Phalaris:** Tyrant in pre-Christian Sicily who burned victims alive in a giant bronze bull.

▶ **Working with Sources**

1. Was Castellio minimizing the significant theological disputes that had arisen as a result of the Reformation? Were his objections directly applicable to the Servetus case?

2. What did Castellio see as the practical, as well as the theological, consequences of burning those perceived to be "heretics"? Is he convincing on this point?

## SOURCE 17.3

# Duc de Saint-Simon, "The Daily Habits of Louis XIV at Versailles"

### ca. 1715

A minor noble at Louis XIV's court at Versailles, Louis de Rouvroy, the duc de Saint-Simon (1675–1755), would achieve lasting fame after his death with the publication of his copious, frank, and witty observations of the court. While resident at Versailles for brief periods after 1702 until the king's death in 1715, Saint-Simon paid particular attention to the maneuverings of his fellow aristocrats. He managed to garner the resentment of many of them, especially the king's illegitimate children, "the Bastards," who held a prominent place at court. His accounts of the daily routine of life at Versailles, and the central position of the king who had famously declared, "L'état, c'est moi!," are often applied today to spectacles that can also be described as at once grand and a little absurd.

At eight o'clock the chief valet de chambre on duty, who alone had slept in the royal chamber, and who had dressed himself, awoke the King. The chief physician, the chief surgeon, and the nurse (as long as she lived), entered at the same time. The latter kissed the King; the others rubbed and often changed his shirt, because he was in the habit of sweating a great deal. At the quarter [hour], the grand chamberlain was called (or, in his absence, the first gentleman of the chamber), and those who had, what was called the *grandes entrées*. The chamberlain (or chief gentleman) drew back the curtains which had been closed again, and presented the holy water from the vase, at the head of the bed. These gentlemen stayed but a moment, and that was the time to speak to the King, if any one had anything to ask of him; in which case the rest stood aside. When, contrary to custom, nobody had aught to say, they were there but for a few moments. He who had opened the curtains and presented the holy water, presented also a prayer-book. Then all passed into the cabinet of the council. A very short religious service being over, the King called, they re-entered. The same officer gave him his dressing-gown; immediately after, other privileged courtiers entered, and then everybody, in time to find the King putting on his shoes and stockings, for he did almost everything himself and with address and grace. Every other day we saw him shave himself; and he had a little short wig

Source: *Memoirs of the Duc de Saint-Simon*, trans. Bayle St. John, ed. W. H. Lewis (New York: Macmillan, 1964), 140–141, 144–145.

in which he always appeared, even in bed, and on medicine days. He often spoke of the chase, and sometimes said a word to somebody. No toilette table was near him; he had simply a mirror held before him.

As soon as he was dressed, he prayed to God, at the side of his bed, where all the clergy present knelt, the cardinals without cushions, all the laity remaining standing; and the captain of the guards came to the balustrade during the prayer, after which the King passed into his cabinet.

He found there, or was followed by all who had the entrée, a very numerous company, for it included everybody in any office. He gave orders to each for the day; thus within half a quarter of an hour it was known what he meant to do; and then all this crowd left directly. The bastards, a few favourites, and the valets alone were left. It was then a good opportunity for talking with the King; for example, about plans of gardens and buildings; and conversation lasted more or less according to the person engaged in it.

. . .

At ten o'clock his supper was served. The captain of the guard announced this to him. A quarter of an hour after the King came to supper, and from the ante-chamber of Madame de Maintenon [his principal mistress] to the table again, any one spoke to him who wished. This supper was always on a grand scale, the royal household (that is, the sons and daughters of France), at table, and a large number of courtiers and ladies present, sitting or standing, and on the evening before the journey to Marly all those ladies who wished to take part in it. That was called presenting yourself for Marly. Men asked in the morning, simply saying to the King, "Sire, Marly." In later years, the King grew tired of this, and a valet wrote up in the gallery the names of those who asked. The ladies continued to present themselves.

. . .

The King, wishing to retire, went and fed his dogs; then said good night, passed into his chamber to the **ruelle** of his bed, where he said his prayers, as in the morning, then undressed. He said good night with an inclination of the head, and whilst everybody was leaving the room stood at the corner of the mantelpiece, where he gave the order to the colonel of the guards alone. Then commenced what was called the *petit coucher*, at which only the specially privileged remained. That was short. They did not leave until he got into bed. It was a moment to speak to him.

**Ruelle:** The "little path" between a bed and the wall.

▶ Working with Sources

1. Why does Saint-Simon pay particular attention to moments of the day during which a courtier could speak directly with the king?

2. What does the combination of religious and secular pursuits in the king's daily habits suggest about life at his court?

## SOURCE 17.4

# Giorgio Vasari, *The Life of Michelangelo Buonarroti*

## 1550

Trained as a painter, architect, and goldsmith, Giorgio Vasari (1511–1574) practiced various artistic trades, but is most renowned today as the first art historian. His *Lives of the Most Eminent Painters, Sculptors, and Architects*, first published in 1550, is the principal source of information about the most prominent artists of the European Renaissance. Having studied under the great artist Michelangelo Buonarroti (1475–1564), Vasari was particularly keen to tell this story. In these scenes from his biography of Michelangelo, Vasari draws attention to his master's early training, as well as the prominent roles Lorenzo il Magnifico de' Medici and ancient sculpture played in his artistic development.

In those days Lorenzo de' Medici the Magnificent kept Bertoldo the sculptor in his garden near Piazza San Marco, not so much as the custodian or guardian of the many beautiful antiquities he had collected and assembled there at great expense, but rather because he wished above all else to create a school for excellent painters and sculptors . . . Thus, Domenico [Ghirlandaio] gave him some of his best young men, including among others Michelangelo and Francesco Granacci; and when they went to the garden, they found that Torrigiani, a young man of the Torrigiani family, was there working on some clay figures in the round that Bertoldo had given him to do.

After Michelangelo saw these figures, he made some himself to rival those of Torrigiani, so that Lorenzo, seeing his high spirit, always had great expectations for him, and, encouraged after only a few days, Michelangelo began copying with a piece of marble the antique head of an old and wrinkled faun with a damaged nose and a laughing mouth, which he found there. Although Michelangelo had never before touched marble or chisels, the imitation turned out so well that Lorenzo was astonished, and when Lorenzo saw that Michelangelo, following his own fantasy rather than the antique head, had carved its mouth open to give it a tongue and to make all its teeth visible, this lord, laughing with pleasure as was his custom, said to him: "But you should have known that old men never have all their teeth and that some of them are always missing." In that simplicity of his, it seemed to Michelangelo, who loved and feared this lord, that Lorenzo was correct; and as soon as Lorenzo left, he immediately broke a tooth on the head and dug out the gum in such a way that it seemed the tooth had fallen out, and anxiously awaited

Source: Giorgio Vasari, *The Lives of the Artists*, trans. Julia Conaway Bondanella and Peter Bondanella, (New York: Oxford University Press, 1998), 418–420; 427–428.

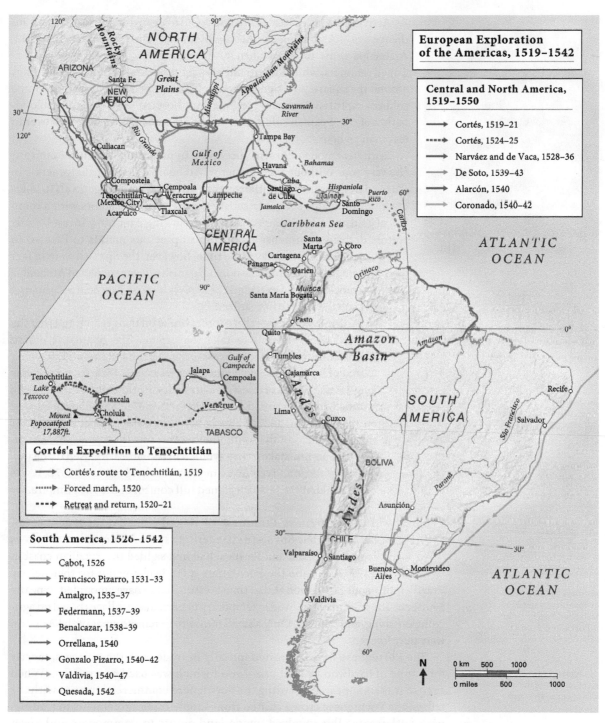

**European Exploration of the Americas, 1519–1542**

**Central and North America, 1519–1550**

→ Cortés, 1519–21
┈┈▸ Cortés, 1524–25
→ Narváez and de Vaca, 1528–36
→ De Soto, 1539–43
→ Alarcón, 1540
→ Coronado, 1540–42

**Cortés's Expedition to Tenochtitlán**

→ Cortés's route to Tenochtitlán, 1519
┈┈▸ Forced march, 1520
━━▸ Retreat and return, 1520–21

**South America, 1526–1542**

→ Cabot, 1526
→ Francisco Pizarro, 1531–33
→ Amalgro, 1535–37
→ Federmann, 1537–39
→ Benalcazar, 1538–39
→ Orrellana, 1540
→ Gonzalo Pizarro, 1540–42
→ Valdivia, 1540–47
→ Quesada, 1542

MAP **18.1** **The European Exploration of the Americas, 1519–1542.**

between two surviving sons. Atahualpa, in the north, sent his army south to the capital, Cuzco, where it defeated his half-brother, Huáscar. When Pizarro entered the Inca Empire, Atahualpa was encamped with an army of 40,000 men near the northern town of Cajamarca, on his way south to Cuzco to install himself as emperor.

ATAHUALLPA. INCA XIIII.

**Conquest by Surprise.**
The Spanish conqueror Francisco Pizarro captured Emperor Atahualpa (top) in an ambush. Atahualpa promised a roomful of gold in return for his release, but the Spaniards collected the gold and murdered Atahualpa (bottom) before generals of the Inca army could organize an armed resistance.

Arriving at Cajamarca, Pizarro succeeded in arranging an unarmed audience with Atahualpa in the town square. On November 16, 1532, Atahualpa came to this audience, surrounded by several thousand unarmed retainers, while Pizarro hid his soldiers in and behind the buildings around the square. At a signal, these soldiers rushed into the square. Some soldiers captured Atahualpa to hold him hostage. In the ensuing bloodbath, not one Spanish soldier was killed. The whole massacre was over in less than an hour.

With his ambush, Pizarro succeeded in paralyzing the Inca Empire at the very top. Without their emperor, Atahualpa, none of the generals in Cuzco dared to seize the initiative. Instead of ordering his generals to liberate him, Atahualpa sought to satisfy the greed of his captors with a room full of gold and silver as ransom. In the following 2 months, Inca administrators delivered immense quantities of precious metals to Pizarro in Cajamarca. During the same time, however, the Spanish were in fear of being attacked from the north. Spanish officers subjected Atahualpa to a mock trial and executed the hapless king on July 26, 1533, hoping to keep the Incas disorganized.

And indeed, the northern forces broke off their march and thereby allowed the Spaniards to take the capital. The Spaniards did so against minimal resistance, massacring the inhabitants and stripping Cuzco of its immense gold and silver treasures. Pizarro did not stay long in the now worthless, isolated city in the Andes. In 1535 he founded a new capital, Lima, which was more conveniently located on the coast and about halfway between Cajamarca and Cuzco. At this time, Incas in the south finally overcame their paralysis. Learning from past mistakes, they avoided mass battles, focused on deadly guerilla strikes, and rebuilt a kingdom that held out until 1572. It was only then that the Spanish gained full control of the Inca Empire.

**The Portuguese Conquest of Brazil**    The Portuguese were not far behind the Spaniards in their pursuit of conquest. Navigators from both Spain and Portugal had first sighted the Brazilian coast in 1499–1500, and the Portuguese quickly claimed it for themselves. Brazil's indigenous population at that time is estimated to have amounted to nearly 5 million. The great majority lived in temporary or permanent villages based on agriculture, fishing, and hunting. Only a small minority in remote areas of the Amazon were pure foragers.

The Portuguese were interested initially in trade with the villagers, mostly for a type of hardwood called brazilwood which was used as a red dye. When French traders appeared, ignoring the Portuguese commercial treaties with the tribes, the Portuguese crown shifted from simple trade agreements to trading-post settlements. This involved giving land grants to commoners and lower noblemen with the obligation to build fortified coastal villages for settlers and to engage in agriculture and friendly trade. By the mid-sixteenth century, a handful of these villages became successful, their inhabitants intermarrying with the surrounding indigenous chieftain families and establishing sugarcane plantations.

**Explanations for the Spanish Success**    The slow progression of the Portuguese in Brazil is readily understood. But the stupendous victories of handfuls of Spaniards over huge empires with millions of inhabitants and large cities defy easy explanation. Five factors invite consideration.

First, and most important, the conquistadors went straight to the top of the imperial pyramid. The emperors and their courts expected diplomatic deference from inferiors, among whom they included the minuscule band of Spaniards. Confronted, instead, with a calculated combination of arrogance and brutality, the emperors and courts were thrown off balance by the Spaniards, who ruthlessly exploited their opportunity. As the emperors were removed from the top level, the administration immediately below them fell into paralysis, unable to seize the initiative and respond in a timely fashion.

Second, both the Aztec and Inca Empires were relatively recent creations in which there were individuals and groups who contested the hierarchical power structure. The conquistadors either found allies among the subject populations or encountered a divided leadership. In either case, they were able to exploit divisions in the empires.

**Brazil in 1519.** This early map is fairly accurate for the northern coast but increasingly less accurate as one moves south. First explorations of the south by both Portuguese and Spanish mariners date to 1513–1516. Ferdinand Magellan passed through several places along the southern coast on his journey around the world in 1520–1521. The scenes on the map depict Native Americans cutting and collecting brazilwood, the source of a red dye much in demand by the Portuguese during the early period of colonization.

Third, European-introduced diseases, traveling with or ahead of the conquerors, took a devastating toll. In both empires, smallpox hit at critical moments during or right before the Spanish invasions, causing major disruptions.

Fourth, thanks to horses and superior European steel weapons and armor, primarily pikes, swords, and breast plates, small numbers of Spaniards were able to hold large numbers of attacking Aztecs and Incas at bay in hand-to-hand combat. Contrary to widespread belief, cannons and matchlock muskets were less important, since they were useless in close encounters. Firearms were still too slow and inaccurate to be decisive.

A fifth factor, indigenous religion, was probably of least significance. According to some now-outdated interpretations, Moctezuma was immobilized by his belief in a prophecy that he would have to relinquish his power to the savior Quetzalcoatl returning from his mythical city of Tlapallan on the east coast (see Chapter 15). Modern scholarship provides convincing reasons, however, to declare this prophecy a postconquest legend, circulated by Cortés both to flatter Charles V and to aggrandize himself as the predicted savior figure bringing Christianity.

## The Establishment of Colonial Institutions

The Spanish crown established administrative hierarchies in the Americas, similar to those of the Aztecs and Incas, with governors at the top of the hierarchy and descending through lower ranks of functionaries. A small degree of

**Spanish Steel.** The *Lienzo de Tlaxcala*, from the middle part of the sixteenth century, is our best visual source for the conquest of Mexico. In this scene, Malinche, protected by a shield, directs the battle on the causeway leading to Tenochtitlán. The two Spanish soldiers behind her, one fully armored, brandish steel swords, which were more effective than the obsidian blades carried by the Aztec defenders (one of whom is dressed in leopard skins), shown on the left.

**Creoles:** American-born descendants of European, primarily Iberian, immigrants.

settler autonomy was permitted through town and city councils, but the crown was determined to make the Americas a territorial extension of the European pattern of centralized state formation. Several hundred thousand settlers (including Alonso Ortíz) found a new life in the Americas, mostly as urban craftspeople, administrators, and professionals. By the early seventeenth century, a powerful elite of Spanish who had been born in America, called **Creoles** (Spanish *criollos*, Portuguese *crioulos*, natives) was in place, first to assist and later to replace most of the administrators sent from Spain in the governance of the Americas (see Map 18.2).

**From Conquest to Colonialism**    The unimaginable riches of Cortés and Pizarro inspired numerous further expeditions. Adventurers struck out with small bands of followers into Central and North America, Chile, and the Amazon. Their expeditions, however, yielded only modest amounts of gold and earned more from selling captured Native Americans into slavery. In the north, expeditions penetrated as far as Arizona, New Mexico, Texas, Oklahoma, Kansas, and Florida but encountered only villagers and the relatively poor Pueblo towns. No new golden kingdoms (the mythical El Dorado, or "golden city") beyond the Aztec and Inca Empires were discovered in the Americas.

In the mid-sixteenth century, easy looting was replaced by a search for the mines from where the precious metals came. In northern Mexico, Native Americans led a group of soldiers and missionaries in 1547 to a number of rich silver mines. In addition, explorers discovered silver in Bolivia (1545) and northern Mexico (1556), gold in Chile (1552), and mercury in Peru (1563). The conquistadors shifted from looting to the exploitation of Native American labor in mines and in agriculture.

In a small number of areas, indigenous peoples resisted incorporation into the Spanish colonies. Notably, in southern Chile the Mapuche repulsed all attempts by the Spanish to subdue them. They had already prevented the Incas from expanding their empire to the southern tip of the continent. Initially, in 1550–1553 the Spanish succeeded in establishing a number of forts and opening a gold mine. But in campaign after campaign they failed to gain more than a border strip with an adjacent no-man's-land. In 1612 they agreed to a temporary peace which left the majority of the Mapuche independent.

Another Native American people who successfully resisted the Spanish conquest were the Asháninka in the Peruvian rain forest. Located along the Eno River, one of the headwater tributaries of the Amazon, they were the first standing in the way of the Spanish attempts to extend their dominance from Peru eastward. The Asháninka exploited hillside salt veins in their region and were traders of goods between the Andes and the rain forest. Although Jesuits and later Franciscans established missions among the Asháninka in the 1600s, they failed to make many converts. It was only in 1737 that the Spanish finally built a fort in the region—a first step toward projecting colonial power into the rain forest.

**Bureaucratic Efficiency**    During the first two generations after the conquest, Spain maintained an efficient colonial administration, which delivered between

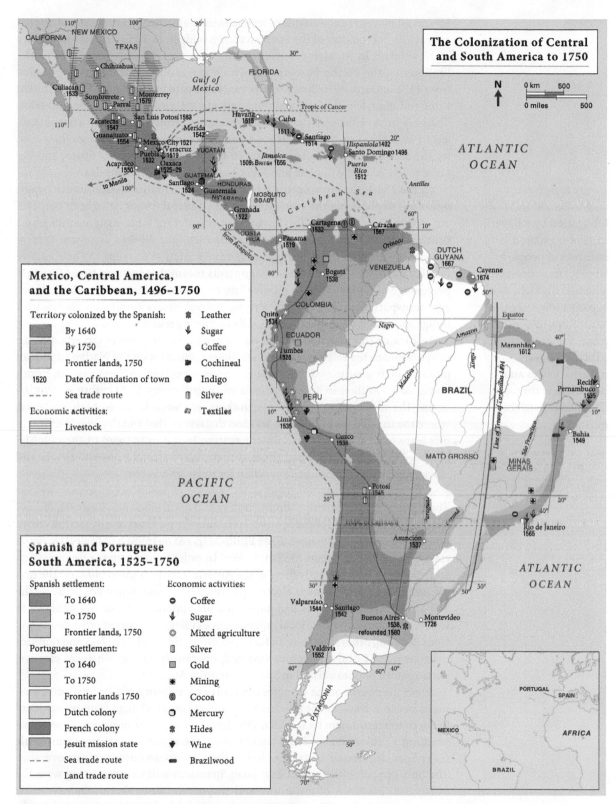

MAP 18.2 **The Colonization of Central and South America to 1750.**

50 and 60 percent of the colonies' revenues to Spain. These revenues contributed as much as one-quarter of the Spanish crown budget. In addition, the viceroyalty of New Spain in Mexico remitted another 25 percent of its revenues to the Philippines, the Pacific province for which it was administratively responsible from 1571 onward. As in Spain, settlers in New Spain had to pay up to 40 different taxes and dues, levied on imports and exports, internal trade, mining, and sales. The only income tax was the tithe to the church, which the administration collected and, at times, used for its own budgetary purposes. Altogether, however, for the settlers the tax level was lower in the New World than in Spain, and the same was true for the English and French colonies in North America.

**Labor assignment (*repartimiento*):** Obligation by villagers to send stipulated numbers of people as laborers to a contractor, who had the right to exploit a mine or other labor-intensive enterprise; the contractors paid the laborers minimal wages and bound them through debt peonage to their businesses.

In the 1540s the government introduced rotating **labor assignments** (*repartimientos*) to phase out the *encomiendas* that powerful owners sought to perpetuate within their families. This institution of rotating labor assignments was a continuation of the *mit'a* system, which the Incas had devised as a form of taxation, in the absence of money and easy transportation of crops in their empire (see Chapter 15). Rotating labor assignments meant that for fixed times a certain percentage of villagers had to provide labor to the state for road building, drainage, transportation, and mining. Private entrepreneurs could also contract for indigenous labor assignments, especially in mining regions.

In Mexico the *repartimiento* fell out of use in the first half of the seventeenth century due to the toll of recurring smallpox epidemics on the Native American population. It is estimated that the indigenous population in the Americas, from a height of 54 million in 1550, declined to 10 million by 1700 before recovering again. The replacement for the lost workers was wage labor. In highland Peru, where the indigenous population was less densely settled and the effects of smallpox were less severe, the assignment system lasted to the end of the colonial period. Wage labor expanded there as well. Wages for Native Americans and blacks remained everywhere lower than for those for Creoles.

**The Rise of the Creoles**   Administrative and fiscal efficiency, however, did not last very long. The wars of the Spanish Habsburg Empire cost more than the crown was able to collect in revenues. King Philip II (r. 1556–1598) had to declare bankruptcy four times between 1557 and 1596. In order to make up the financial deficit, the crown began to sell offices in the Americas to the highest bidders. The first offices put on the block were elective positions in the municipal councils. By the end of the century, Creoles had purchased life appointments in city councils as well as positions as scribes, local judges, police chiefs, directors of processions and festivities, and other sinecures. In these positions, they collected fees and rents for their services. Local oligarchies emerged, effectively ending whatever elective, participatory politics existed in Spanish colonial America.

Over the course of the seventeenth century a majority of administrative positions became available for purchase. The effects of the change from recruitment by merit to recruitment by wealth on the functioning of the bureaucracy were far-reaching. Creoles advanced on a broad front in the administrative positions, while fewer Spaniards found it attractive to buy their American positions from overseas. The only opportunities which European Spaniards still found enticing were the nearly 300 positions of governors and inspectors, since these jobs gave their owners the right to subject the Native Americans to forced purchases of goods, yielding huge profits. For the most part, wealthy Spanish merchants delegated junior partners to these highly lucrative activities. By 1700, the consequences of the Spanish crown selling most of its American administrative offices were a decline in the competence of office holders, the emergence of a Creole elite able to bend the Spanish administration increasingly to its will, and a decentralization of the decision-making processes.

**Northwest European Interference**    As Spain's administrative grip on the Americas weakened during the seventeenth century, the need to defend the continents militarily against European interlopers arose. At the beginning, there were European privateers, holding royal charters, who harassed Spanish silver shipments and ports in the Caribbean. In the early seventeenth century, the French, English, and Dutch governments sent ships to occupy the smaller Caribbean islands not claimed by Spain. Privateer and contraband traders stationed on these islands engaged in further raiding and pillaging, severely damaging Spain's monopoly of shipping between Europe and the Caribbean.

Conquests of Spanish islands followed in the second half of the century. England captured Jamaica in 1655, and France colonized western Hispaniola (Saint-Domingue) in 1665, making it one of their most profitable sugar-producing colonies. Along the Pacific coast, depredations continued into the middle of the eighteenth century. Here, the galleons of the annual Acapulco–Manila fleet carrying silver from Mexico to China and returning with Chinese silks, porcelain, and lacquerware were the targets of English privateers. Over the course of the seventeenth century, Spain allocated one-half to two-thirds of its American revenues to the increasingly difficult defense of its annual treasure fleets and Caribbean possessions.

**Bourbon Reforms**    After the death of the last, childless Habsburg king of Spain in 1700, the new French-descended dynasty of the Bourbons made major efforts to regain control over their American possessions. They had to begin from a discouragingly weak position as nearly 90 percent of all goods traded from Europe to the Americas were of non-Spanish origin. Fortunately, population increases among the settlers as well as the Native Americans (after having overcome their horrific losses to disease) offered opportunities to Spanish manufacturers and merchants. After several false starts, in the middle of the eighteenth century the Bourbon reform program began to show results.

The reforms aimed at improved naval connections and administrative control between the mother country and the colonies. The monopolistic annual armed silver fleet was greatly reduced. Instead, the government authorized more frequent single sailings at different times of the year. Newly formed Spanish companies, receiving exclusive rights at specific ports, succeeded in reducing contraband trade. Elections took place again for municipal councils. Spanish-born salaried officials replaced scores of Creole tax and office farmers. The original two viceroyalties were subdivided into four, to improve administrative control. The sale of tobacco and brandy became state monopolies. Silver mining and cotton textile manufacturing were expanded. By the second half of the eighteenth century, Spain had regained a measure of control over its colonies.

As a result, government revenues rose substantially. Tax receipts increased more than twofold, even taking into account the inflation of the late eighteenth century. In the end, however, the reforms remained incomplete. Since the Spanish economy was not also reformed, in terms of expanding crafts production and urbanization, the changes did not diminish the English and French dominance of the import market by much. Spain failed to produce textiles, metalwares, and household goods at competitive prices for the colonies; thus the level of English and French exports to the Americas remained high.

**Early Portuguese Colonialism**    In contrast to the Spanish Americas, the Portuguese overseas province of Brazil remained initially confined to a broad coastal strip, which developed only slowly during the sixteenth century. The first governor-general, whose rank was equivalent to a Spanish viceroy, arrived in 1549. He and his successors were members of the high aristocracy, but their positions were salaried and subject to term limits. As the colony grew, the crown created a council in the capital of Lisbon for all Brazilian appointments and established a high court for all judicial affairs in Bahia in northern Brazil. Commoners with law degrees filled the nonmilitary colonial positions. In the early seventeenth century, however, offices became as open to purchase as in the Spanish colonies, although not on the city council level, where a complex indirect electoral process survived.

Jesuits converted the Native Americans, whom they transported to Jesuit-administered villages. Colonial cities and Jesuits repeatedly clashed over the slave raids of the "pioneers" (*bandeirantes*) in village territories. The bandeirantes came mostly from São Paulo in the south and roamed the interior in search of human prey. Native American slaves were in demand on the wheat farms and cattle ranches of São Paulo as well as the sugar plantations of the northeast. Although the Portuguese crown and church had, like the Spanish, forbidden the enslavement of Native Americans, the bandeirantes exploited a loophole. The law was interpreted as allowing the enslavement of Native Americans who resisted conversion to Christianity. For a long time, Lisbon and the Jesuits were powerless against this flagrantly self-interested interpretation.

**Expansion into the Interior**    In the middle of the seventeenth century, the Jesuits and Native Americans finally succeeded in pushing many bandeirantes west and north, where they switched from slave raiding to prospecting for gold. In the far north, however, the raids continued until 1680, when the Portuguese administration finally prevailed and ended Native American slavery, almost a century and a half after Spain. Ironically, it was mostly thanks to the "pioneer" raids for slaves that Brazil expanded westward, to assume the borders it has today.

As a result of gold discoveries in Minas Gerais in 1690 by bandeirantes, the European immigrant population increased rapidly, from 1 to 2 million during the 1700s. Minas Gerais, located north of Rio de Janeiro, was the first inland region of the colony to attract settlers. By contrast, as a result of smallpox epidemics beginning in the 1650s in the Brazilian interior, the Native American population declined massively, not to expand again until the end of the eighteenth century. To replace the lost labor, Brazilians imported slaves from Africa, at first to work in the sugar plantations and, after 1690, in the mines, where their numbers increased to two-thirds of the labor force. In contrast to Spanish mines, Brazilian mines were surface operations requiring only minimal equipment outlays. Most blacks worked with pickaxes and shovels. The peak of the gold boom came in the 1750s, when the importance of gold was second only to that of sugar among Brazilian exports to Europe.

Early in the gold boom, the crown created the new Ministry of the Navy and Overseas Territories, which greatly expanded the administrative structure in Brazil. It established 14 regions and a second high court in Rio de Janeiro, which replaced Bahia as the capital in 1736. The ministry in Lisbon ended the sale of offices, increased the efficiency of tax collection, and encouraged Brazilian textile manufacturing to render the province more independent from English imports. By the mid-1700s, Brazil was a flourishing overseas colony of Portugal, producing brazilwood, sugar, gold, tobacco, cacao, and vanilla for export.

**North American Settlements**  Efforts at settlement in the less hospitable North America in the sixteenth century were unsuccessful. Only in the early part of the seventeenth century did French, English, and Dutch merchant investors succeed in establishing small communities of settlers on the northeastern coast, who grew their own food on land purchased from the local Native American villagers. These settlements were Jamestown (founded in 1607

**Mine Workers.** The discovery of gold and diamonds in Minas Gerais led to a boom, but did little to contribute to the long-term health of the Brazilian economy. With the Native American population decimated by disease, African slaves performed the backbreaking work.

in today's Virginia), Quebec (1608, Canada), Plymouth and Boston (1620 and 1630, respectively, in today's Massachusetts), and New Amsterdam (1625, today's New York). Subsistence agriculture and fur, however, were meager ingredients if the settlements were to prosper. The northerly settlements struggled through the seventeenth century, sustained either by Catholic missionary efforts or by the Protestant enthusiasm of the Puritans who had escaped persecution in England. Southern places like Jamestown survived because they adopted tobacco, a warm-weather plant, as a cash crop for export to Europe. In contrast to Mexico and Peru, the North American settlements were not followed—at least not at first—by territorial conquests (see Map 18.3).

**Native Americans**  European arrivals in North America soon began supplementing agriculture with trade. They exchanged metal and glass wares, beads, and seashells for furs, especially beaver pelts, with the Native American groups of the interior. The more these groups came into contact with the European traders, however, the more dramatic the demographic impact of the trade on them was: Smallpox, already a menace during the 1500s in North America, became devastating as contacts intensified. In New England, for example, of the ca. 144,000 estimated Native Americans in 1600, fewer than 15,000 remained in 1620.

The introduction of guns contributed an additional lethal factor to trading arrangements, as English, French, and Dutch traders provided their favorite Native

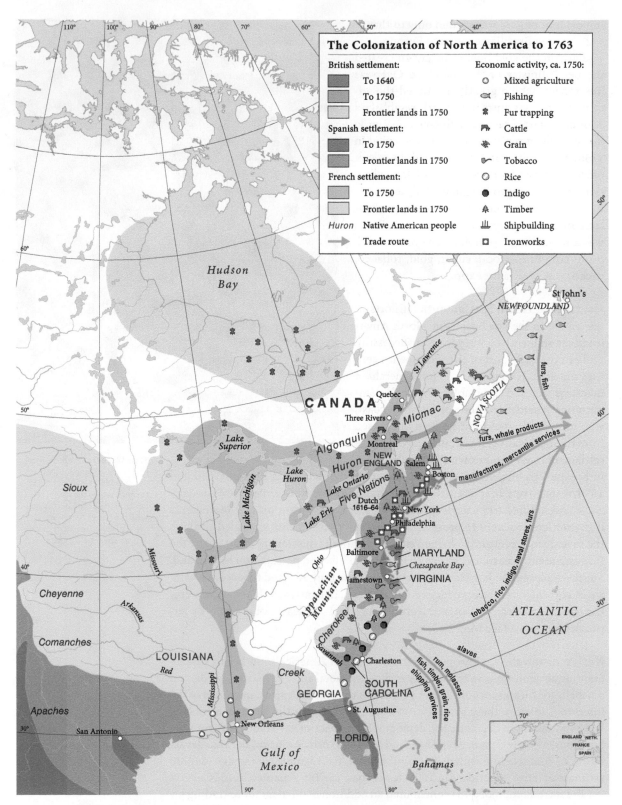

**The Colonization of North America to 1763**

British settlement:
- To 1640
- To 1750
- Frontier lands in 1750

Spanish settlement:
- To 1750
- Frontier lands in 1750

French settlement:
- To 1750
- Frontier lands in 1750

*Huron* — Native American people

→ Trade route

Economic activity, ca. 1750:
- Mixed agriculture
- Fishing
- Fur trapping
- Cattle
- Grain
- Tobacco
- Rice
- Indigo
- Timber
- Shipbuilding
- Ironworks

*Hudson Bay*

St John's
NEWFOUNDLAND

CANADA
Quebec
Three Rivers
*St Lawrence*
Micmac
NOVA SCOTIA

Lake Superior
Algonquin
Montreal
NEW ENGLAND
Salem
Boston

Lake Huron
Huron
Lake Ontario
Five Nations
Lake Erie
Dutch 1616–64
New York
Philadelphia

Sioux

Lake Michigan

Missouri

Cheyenne
*Ohio*
Baltimore
MARYLAND
*Chesapeake Bay*

Arkansas
Appalachian Mountains
Jamestown
VIRGINIA

Comanches

Cherokee

LOUISIANA
*Red*
Savannah
Creek
Charleston
SOUTH CAROLINA
GEORGIA

Apaches
*Mississippi*
St. Augustine

San Antonio
New Orleans
FLORIDA

*Gulf of Mexico*

ATLANTIC OCEAN

furs, fish
furs, whale products
manufactures, mercantile services
tobacco, rice, indigo, naval stores, furs
slaves
rum, molasses
fish, timber, grain, rice
shipping services

*Bahamas*

ENGLAND  NETH.
FRANCE
SPAIN

**MAP 18.3 The Colonization of North America to 1763.**

American trading partners with flintlocks, in order to increase the yield of furs. As a result, in the course of the 1600s the Iroquois in the northeast were able to organize themselves into a heavily armed and independent-minded federation, capable of inflicting heavy losses on rival groups as well as on European traders and settlers.

Further south, in Virginia, the Jamestown settlers encountered the Powhatan confederacy. These Native Americans, living in some 200 well-fortified, palisaded villages, dominated the region between the Chesapeake Bay and the Appalachian Mountains. Initially, the Powhatan supplied Jamestown with foodstuffs and sought to integrate the settlement into their confederation. When this attempt at integration failed, however, benevolence turned to hostility, and the confederacy raided Jamestown twice in an attempt to rid their region of foreign settlers. But the latter were able to turn the tables and defeat the Powhatan in 1646, thereafter occupying their lands and reducing them to small scattered remnants. Pocahontas, the daughter of the Powhatan chief at the time of the foundation of Jamestown, was captured during one of the raids, converted to Christianity, and lived in England for a number of years as the wife of a returning settler. The decline of the Powhatan in the later 1600s allowed English settlers to move westward, in contrast to New England in the north, where the Iroquois, although allied with the English against the French, blocked any western expansion.

The Iroquois were fiercely determined to maintain their dominance of the fur trade and wrought havoc among the Native American groups living between New England and the Great Lakes. In the course of the second half of the 1600s they drove many smaller groups westward into the Great Lakes region and Mississippi plains, where these groups settled as refugees. French officials and Jesuit missionaries sought to create some sort of alliance with the refugee peoples, to counterbalance the powerful Iroquois to the east. Many Native Americans converted to Christianity, creating a Creole Christianity similar to that of the Africans of Kongo and the Mexicans after the Spanish conquest of the Aztecs.

Major population movements also occurred further west on the Great Plains, where the Apaches arrived from the Great Basin in the Rockies. They had captured horses which had escaped during the Pueblo uprising of 1680–1695 against Spain. The Comanches, who arrived at the same time also from the west and on horses, had, in addition, acquired firearms and around 1725 began their expansion at the expense of the Apaches. The Sioux from the northern forests and the Cheyenne from the Great Basin added to the mix of federations on the Great Plains in the early 1700s. At this time, the great transformation of the Native Americans in the center of North America into horse breeders and horsemen warriors began. Smallpox epidemics did not reach the Plains until the mid-1700s while in the east the ravages of this epidemic had weakened the Iroquois so much that they concluded a peace with the French in 1701.

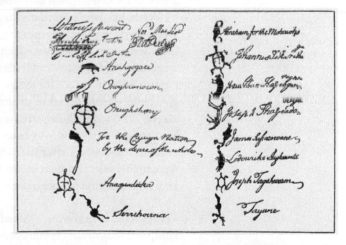

**Land Sale.** Signatures of the leaders of the Iroquois federation on a treaty with Thomas and Richard Penn in 1736. By the terms of this treaty the Iroquois sold land to the founders of the English colony of Pennsylvania. The leaders of the six nations that made up the Iroquois federation (Mohawk, Oneida, Onondaga, Cayuga, Seneca, and Tuscarora) signed with their pictograms. The names were added later.

**French Canada**   The involvement of the French in the Great Lakes region with refugees fleeing from the Iroquois was part of a program of expansion into the center of North America, begun in 1663. The governor of Quebec had dispatched explorers, fur traders, and missionaries not only into the Great Lakes region but also the Mississippi valley. The French government then sent farmers, craftspeople, and young single women from France with government-issued agricultural implements and livestock to establish settlements. The most successful settlement was in the subtropical district at the mouth of the Mississippi, called "La Louisiane," where some 300 settlers with 4,000 African slaves founded sugar plantations. Immigration was restricted to French subjects and excluded Protestants. Given these restrictions, Louisiana received only some 30,000 settlers by 1750, in contrast to English North America, with nearly 1.2 million settlers by the same time.

**Colonial Assemblies**   As immigration to New England picked up, the merchant companies in Europe, which had financed the journeys of the settlers, were initially responsible for the administration of about a dozen settlement colonies. The first settlers to demand participation in the colonial administration were Virginian tobacco growers with interests in the European trade. In 1619 they deputized delegates from their villages to meet as the House of Burgesses. They thereby created an early popular assembly in North America, assisting their governor in running the colony. The other English colonies soon followed suit, creating their own assemblies. In contrast to Spain and Portugal, England— racked by its internal Anglican–Puritan conflict—was initially uninvolved in the governance of the overseas territories.

When England eventually stepped in and took the governance of the colonies away from the charter merchants and companies in the second half of the seventeenth century, it faced entrenched settler assemblies, especially in New England. Only in New Amsterdam, conquered from the Dutch in 1664–1674 and renamed "New York," did the governor initially rule without an assembly. Many governors were deputies of wealthy aristocrats who never traveled to America but stayed in London. These governors were powerless to prevent the assemblies from appropriating rights to levy taxes and making appointments. The assemblies thus modeled themselves after Parliament in London. As in England, these assemblies were highly select bodies that excluded poorer settlers, who did not meet the property requirements to vote or stand for elections.

**Territorial Expansion**   Steady immigration, also from the European mainland, encouraged land speculators in the British colonies to cast their sights beyond the Appalachian Mountains. (According to historical convention, the English are called "British" after the English–Scottish union in 1707.) In 1749, the Ohio Company of Virginia received a royal permit to develop land, together with a protective fort, south of the Ohio River. The French, however, also claimed the Ohio valley, considering it a part of their Canada–Mississippi–Louisiana territory. A few years later, tensions over the valley erupted into open hostility. Initially, the local encounters went badly for the Virginian militia and British army. In 1755, however, the British and French broadened their clash into a worldwide war for dominance in the colonies and Europe, the Seven Years' War of 1756–1763.

**The Seven Years' War**  Both France and Great Britain borrowed heavily to pour resources into the war. England had the superior navy and France the superior army. Since the British navy succeeded in choking off French supplies to its increasingly isolated land troops, Britain won the war overseas. In Europe, Britain's failure to supply the troops of its ally Prussia against the Austrian–French alliance caused the war on that front to end in a draw. Overseas, the British gained most of the French holdings in India, several islands in the Caribbean, all of Canada, and all the land east of the Mississippi. The war costs and land swaps, however, proved to be unmanageable for both the vanquished and the victor. The unpaid debts became the root cause of the American, French, and Haitian constitutional revolutions that began 13 years later. Those revolutions, along with the emerging industrialization of Great Britain, signaled the beginning of the modern scientific–industrial age in world history.

# The Making of American Societies: Origins and Transformations

The patterns which made the Americas an extension of Europe emerged gradually and displayed characteristics specific to each region. On the one hand, there was the slow transfer of the plants and animals native to each continent, called the **Columbian Exchange** (see "Patterns Up Close"). On the other hand, Spain and Portugal adopted different strategies of mineral and agricultural exploitation. In spite of these different strategies, however, the settler societies of the two countries in the end displayed similar characteristics.

**Columbian Exchange:** Exchange of plants, animals, and diseases between the Americas and the rest of the world.

## Exploitation of Mineral and Tropical Resources

The pattern of European expansion into subtropical and tropical lands began with the Spanish colonization of the Caribbean islands. When the Spanish crown ran out of gold in the Caribbean, it exported silver from Mexico and Peru in great quantities to finance a centralizing state that could compete with the Ottomans and European kings. By contrast, Portugal's colony of Brazil did not at first mine for precious metals, and consequently the Portuguese crown pioneered the growing of sugar on plantations. Mining would be developed later. The North American colonies of England and France had, in comparison, little native industry at first. By moving farther south, however, they adopted the plantation system for indigo and rice and thus joined their Spanish and Portuguese predecessors in exploiting the subtropical–tropical agricultural potential of the Americas.

**Silver Mines**  When the interest of the Spaniards turned from looting to the exploitation of mineral resources, two main mining centers emerged: Potosí in southeastern Peru (today Bolivia) and Zacatecas and Guanajuato in northern Mexico. For the first 200 years after its founding in 1545, Potosí produced over half of the silver of Spanish America. In the eighteenth century, Zacatecas and Guanajuato jumped ahead of Potosí, churning out almost three times as much of the precious metal. During the same century, gold mining in Colombia and Chile rose to importance as well, making the mining of precious metals the most important economic activity in the Americas.

**The Silver Mountain of Potosí.**
Note the patios in the left foreground and the water-driven crushing mill in the center, which ground the silver-bearing ore into a fine sand that then was moistened, caked, amalgamated with mercury, and dried on the patio. The mine workers' insect-like shapes reinforce the dehumanizing effects of their labor.

function was to feed and protect Havana, the collection point for Mexican and Peruvian silver and the port from where the annual Spanish fleet shipped the American silver across the Atlantic.

A second region, Argentina and Paraguay, was colonized as a bulwark to prevent the Portuguese and Dutch from cutting across the southern end of the continent and accessing Peruvian silver. Once established, the two colonies produced wheat, cattle, mules, horses, cotton, textiles, and tallow to feed and supply the miners in Potosí. The subtropical crop of cotton, produced by small farmers, played a role in Europe's extension into warm-weather agriculture only toward the end of the colonial period.

A third colonial region, Venezuela, began as a grain and cattle supply base for Cartagena, the port for the shipment of Colombian gold, and Panama and Portobelo, ports for the transshipment of Peruvian silver from the Pacific to Havana. Its cocoa and tobacco exports flourished only after the Dutch established themselves in 1624 in the southern Caribbean and provided the shipping. Thus, three major regions of the Spanish overseas empire in the Americas were mostly peripheral as agricultural producers during the sixteenth century. Only after the middle of the century did they begin to specialize in tropical agricultural goods, and they were exporters only in the eighteenth century. By that time, the Dutch and English provided more and more shipping in the place of the Spanish.

**Wheat Farming and Cattle Ranching**   To support the mining centers and administrative cities, the Spanish colonial government encouraged the development of agricultural estates (*haciendas*). These estates first emerged when conquistadors used their *encomienda* rights to round up Native American labor to produce subsistence crops. Native American tenant farmers were forced to grow wheat and raise cattle, pigs, sheep, and goats for the conquerors, who were now agricultural entrepreneurs. In the latter part of the sixteenth century, the land grants gave way to rotating forced labor as well as wage labor. Owners established their residences and built dwellings for tenant farmers on their estates. A land-owner class emerged.

Like the conquistadors before, a majority of landowners produced wheat and animals for sale to urban and mining centers. Cities purchased wheat and maintained granaries in order to provide for urban dwellers in times of harvest failure. Entrepreneurs received commissions to provide slaughterhouses with regular supplies of animals. As the Native American population declined in the seventeenth century and the church helped in consolidating the remaining population in large villages, additional land became available for the establishment of estates. From 1631 onward, authorities granted Spanish settler families the right to maintain their estates undivided from generation to generation. Through donations, the church also acquired considerable agricultural lands. Secular and clerical land-owning interests supported a powerful upper social stratum of Creoles from the eighteenth century onward.

**Plantations and Gold Mining in Brazil**   Brazil's economic activities began with brazilwood, followed by sugar plantations, before gold mining rose to prominence in the eighteenth century. A crisis hit sugar production in 1680–1700, mostly as a result of the Dutch beginning production of sugar in the Antilles. It was at that time that the gold of Minas Gerais, in the interior of Brazil, was discovered.

Gold-mining operations in Brazil during the eighteenth century were considerably less capital-intensive than the silver mines in Spanish America. Most miners were relatively small operators with sieves, pickaxes, and a few black slaves as unskilled laborers. Many entrepreneurs were indebted for their slaves to absentee capitalists, with whom they shared the profits. Since prospecting took place on the land of Native Americans, bloody encounters were frequent. Most entrepreneurs were ruthless frontiersmen who exploited their slaves and took no chances with the indigenous people. Brazil produced a total of 1,000 tons of gold in the eighteenth century, a welcome bonanza for Portugal at a time of low agricultural prices. Overall, minerals were just as valuable for the Portuguese as they were for the Spanish.

**Plantations in Spanish and English America**   The expansion of plantation farming in the Spanish colonies was a result of the Bourbon reforms. Although sugar, tobacco, and rice had been introduced early into the Caribbean and southern Mexico, it was only in the expanded plantation system of the eighteenth century that these crops (plus indigo, cacao, and cactuses as host plants for cochineal) were produced on a large scale for export to Europe. The owners of plantations did not need expensive machinery and invested instead in African slave labor, with the result that the slave trade hit full stride, beginning around 1750.

English North American settlements in Virginia and Carolina exported tobacco and rice beginning in the 1660s. Georgia was the thirteenth British colony, founded in 1733 as a bulwark against Spanish Florida and a haven for poor Europeans. In 1750 it joined southern Carolina as a major plantation colony and rice and indigo producer. In the eighteenth century, even New England finally had its own export crop, in the form of timber for shipbuilding and charcoal production in Great Britain, at the amazing rate of 250 million board-feet per year by the start of the nineteenth century. These timber exports illustrate an important new factor appearing in the Americas in the eighteenth century. Apart from the cheap production of precious metals and warm-weather crops, the American extension of Europe became increasingly important as a replacement for dwindling fuel resources across much of northern Europe. Altogether, it was thanks to the Americas that cold and rainy Europe rose successfully into the ranks of the wealthy, climatically balanced, and populated Indian and Chinese empires.

## Social Strata, Castes, and Ethnic Groups
The population of settlers in the New World consisted primarily of Europeans who came from a continent that had barely emerged from its population losses to

the Black Death. Although population numbers were rising again in the sixteenth century, Europe did not have masses of emigrants to the Americas to spare. Given the small settler population of the Americas, the temptation to develop a system of forced labor in agriculture and mining was irresistible. Since the Native Americans and African slaves pressed into labor were ethnically so completely different from the Europeans, however, a social system evolved in which the latter two not only were economically underprivileged but also made up the ethnically nonintegrated lowest rungs of the social ladder. A pattern of legal and customary discrimination evolved which, even though partially vitiated by the rise of ethnically mixed groups, prevented the integration of American ethnicities into settler society.

**The Social Elite**    The heirs of the Spanish conquistadors and estate owners— farmers, ranchers, and planters—maintained city residences and employed managers on their agricultural properties. In Brazil, cities emerged more slowly, and for a long time estate owners maintained their manor houses as small urban islands. Estate owners mixed with the Madrid- and Lisbon-appointed administrators and, during the seventeenth century, intermarried with them, creating the top tier of settler society known as Creoles, some 4 percent of the population. In a wider sense, the tier included also merchants, professionals, clerks, militia officers, and the clergy. They formed a relatively closed society in which descent, intermarriage, landed property, and a government position counted more than money and education.

"And now the Indians of that town [Tejupan, southern Mexico] appeared before me and reported that the time of the contract [with the Spaniards] was finished and that they wished to raise silk on their own for the profit and usefulness that [the industry] would bring them."

—Petition by Native Americans, 1543

In the seventeenth and eighteenth centuries, the estate owners farmed predominantly with Native American forced labor. They produced grain and/or cattle, legumes, sheep, and pigs for local urban markets or mining towns. In contrast to the black slave plantation estates of the Caribbean and coastal regions of Spanish and Portuguese America, these farming estates did not export their goods to Europe. From the beginning of colonialism, furthermore, Madrid and Lisbon discouraged estate owners, as well as farmers in general, from producing olive oil, wine, or silk, to protect their home production.

As local producers with little competition, farming and ranching estate owners did not feel market pressures. Since they lived for the most part in the cities, they exploited their estates with minimal investments and usually drew profits of less than 5 percent of annual revenues. They were often heavily indebted, and as a result there was often more glitter than substance among the landowning Creoles.

**Lower Creoles**    The second tier of Creole society consisted of people like Alonzo Ortíz, the tanner introduced at the beginning of this chapter. Even though of second rank, they were privileged European settlers who, as craftspeople and traders, theoretically worked with their hands. In practice, many of them were owner-operators who employed Native Americans and/or black slaves as apprentices and journeymen. Many invested in small plots of land in the vicinity of their cities, striving to rise into the ranks of the landowning Creoles.

Wealthy weavers ran textile manufactures mostly concentrated in the cities of Mexico, Peru, Paraguay, and Argentina. In some of these manufactures, up to

**Textile Production.** Immigrants from Spain (like Alonso Ortíz, discussed at the beginning of the chapter), maintained workshops (*obrajes*) as tanners, weavers, carpenters, or wheelwrights. As craftspeople producing simple but affordable goods for the poor, they remained competitive throughout the colonial period, in spite of increasingly large textile, utensil, and furniture imports from Europe. At the same time, indigenous textile production by native women continued as in the preconquest period, albeit under the constraints of labor services imposed by officials or clergy, as shown in these examples.

300 Native American and black workers produced cheap, coarse woolens and a variety of cottons on dozens of looms. Men were the weavers and women the spinners—in contrast to the pre-Columbian period, when textile manufacture was entirely a woman's job. On a smaller scale, manufactures also existed for pottery and leather goods. On the whole, the urban manufacturing activities of the popular people, serving the poor in local markets, remained vibrant until well into the nineteenth century, in spite of massive European imports.

**Mestizos and Mulattoes**   The mixed European–Native American and European–African population had the collective name of "caste" (*casta*), or ethnic group. The term originated in the desire of the Iberian and Creole settlers to draw distinctions among degrees of mixture in order to counterbalance as much as possible the masses of Native Americans and Africans, especially from the eighteenth century onward. The two most important castes were the *mestizos* (Spanish), or *mestiços* (Portuguese), who had Iberian fathers and Native American mothers, and *mulatos*, who had Iberian fathers and black mothers. By 1800 the castas as a whole formed the third largest population category in Latin America (20 percent), after Native Americans (40 percent) and Creoles (30 percent). In Brazil, black freedmen and mulattoes were numerically even with Creoles (28 percent each), after black slaves (38 percent) and before Native Americans (6 percent in the settled provinces outside Amazonia). In both Spanish and Portuguese America, there was also a small percentage of people descended from Native American and black unions. Thus, most of the intermediate population groups were sizeable, playing important neutralizing roles in colonial society, as they had one foot in both the Creole and subordinate social strata (see Figure 18.1).

As such neutralizing elements, mestizos and mulattoes filled lower levels of the bureaucracy and the lay hierarchy in the church. They held skilled and supervisory positions in mines and on estates. In addition, in the armed forces mulattoes

**Race, Class, and Gender in Colonial Mexico.** An outraged mulatta defends herself against an aggressive Creole, with a fearful child clinging to the woman's skirt.

dominated the ranks of enlisted men; in the defense militias, they even held officer ranks. In Brazil, many mulattoes and black freedmen were farmers. Much of the craft production was in their hands. A wide array of laws existed to keep mestizos and mulattoes in their peculiarly intermediate social and political positions.

**Women**    The roles played by women depended strongly on their social position. Well-appointed elite Creole households followed the Mediterranean tradition of secluding women from men. Within the confines of the household, elite women were persons of means and influence. They were the owners of substantial dowries and legally stipulated grooms' gifts. Often, they actively managed the investment of their assets. Outside their confines, however, even elite women lost all protection. Crimes of passion, committed by honor-obsessed fathers or husbands, went unpunished. Husbands and fathers who did not resort to violence nevertheless did not need witnesses to obtain court judgments to banish daughters or wives to convents for alleged lapses in chastity. Thus, even elite women were bound by definite limits set by a patriarchal society.

On the lower rungs of society, be it popular Creole, mestizo, mulatto, or Native American, gender separation was much less prevalent. After all, everyone in the family had to work in order to make ends meet. Men, women, and children shared labor in the fields and workshops. Girls or wives took in clothes to wash or went out to work as domestics in wealthy households. Older women dominated retail in market stalls. As in elite society, wives tended to outlive husbands. In addition, working families with few assets suffered abandonment by males. Women headed one-third of all households in Mexico City, according to an 1811 census. Among black slaves in the region of São Paulo, 70 percent of women were without formal ties to the men who fathered their children. Thus, the most pronounced division in colonial society was that of a patriarchy among the Creoles and a slave society dominated by women, with frequently absent men—an unbridgeable division that persists today.

**Figure 18.1 Ethnic Composition of Latin America, ca. 1800.**

- 10%
- 5%
- 40%
- 30%
- 15%

- ■ American Indian
- ■ Mestizo
- ■ Creole
- ■ Mulatto
- ■ African

**Native Americans**    In the immediate aftermath of the conquest, Native Americans could be found at all levels of the social scale. Some were completely marginalized in remote corners of the American continents. Others acculturated into the ranks of the working poor in the silver mines or textile manufactures.

**Illustration from an Indian Land Record.** The Spaniards almost completely wiped out the Aztec archives after the conquest of Mexico; surviving examples of Indian manuscripts are thus extremely rare. Although the example shown here, made from the bark of a fig tree, claims to date from the early 1500s, it is part of the so-called Techialoyan land records created in the seventeenth century to substantiate native land claims. These "títulos primordiales," as they were called, were essentially municipal histories that documented in text and pictures local accounts of important events and territorial boundaries.

A few even formed an educated Aztec or Inca propertied upper class, exercising administrative functions in Spanish civil service. Social distinctions, however, disappeared rapidly during the first 150 years of Spanish colonialism. Smallpox reduced the Native American population by nearly 80 percent. Diseases were more virulent in humid, tropical parts of the continent than in deserts, and the epidemics took a far greater toll on dense, settled populations than they did on dispersed forager bands in dry regions. In the Caribbean and on the Brazilian coast, Native Americans disappeared almost completely; in central and southern Mexico, their population shrank by two-thirds. It was only in the twentieth century that population figures reached the preconquest level again in most parts of Latin America.

Apart from European diseases, the native forager and agrarian Native Americans in the Amazon, Orinoco, and Maracaibo rain forests were the least affected by European colonials during the period 1500–1800. Not only were their lands economically the least promising, but they also defended those lands successfully with blowguns, poison darts, and bow and arrow. In many cold and hot arid or semiarid regions, such as Patagonia, southern Chile, the Argentine grasslands (*pampas*), the Paraguayan salt marshes and deserts, and northern Mexican mountains and steppes, the situation was similar. In these lands, the seminomadic Native Americans quickly adopted the European horse and became highly mobile warrior peoples in defense of their mostly independent territories.

The villagers of Mexico, Yucatán, Guatemala, Colombia, Ecuador, and Peru had fewer choices. When smallpox reduced their numbers in the second half of the sixteenth century, state and church authorities razed many villages and concentrated the survivors in *pueblos de indios*. Initially, the Native Americans put up strong resistance against these resettlements, by repeatedly returning to their destroyed old settlements. From the middle of the seventeenth century, however, the pueblos were fully functional, self-administering units, with councils (*cabildos*), churches, schools, communal lands, and family parcels.

The councils were important institutions of legal training and social mobility for ordinary Native Americans. Initially, the traditional "noble" chiefly families descending from the preconquest Aztec and Inca ruling classes were in control as administrators. The many village functions, however, for which the *cabildos* were responsible allowed commoners to move up into auxiliary roles. In some of these roles, they had opportunities to learn the system and acquire modest wealth. Settlers constantly complained about insubordinate Native Americans pursuing lawsuits in the courts. Native American villages were closed to settlers, and the only outsiders admitted were Catholic priests. Contact with the Spanish world remained minimal, and acculturation went little beyond official conversion to Catholicism. Village notaries and scribes were instrumental in preserving Nahuatl in Mexico and Quechua in Peru, making them into functional, written languages. Thus, even in the heartlands of Spanish America, Native American adaptation to the rulers remained limited.

Unfortunately, however, tremendous demographic losses made the Native Americans in the pueblos vulnerable to the loss of their land. Estate owners expanded their holdings, legally and illegally, in spite of the heroic litigation efforts of the villages opposed to this expansion. When the population rebounded, many estates had grown to immense sizes. Villages began to run out of land for their inhabitants. Increasing numbers of Native Americans had to rent land from estate owners or find work on estates as farmhands. They became estranged from their villages, fell into debt peonage, and entered the ranks of the working poor in the countryside or city, bearing the full brunt of colonial inequities.

**New England Society**    For a long time in the early modern period, the small family farm, where everyone had to work to eke out a precarious living, remained the norm for the majority of New England's population. Family members specializing in construction, carpentry, spinning, weaving, or iron works continued to be restricted to small perimeters around their villages and towns. An acute lack of money and cheap means of transportation hampered the development of market networks in the interior well into the 1770s. The situation was better in the agriculturally more favored colonies in the Mid-Atlantic, especially in Pennsylvania. Here, farmers were able to produce marketable quantities of wheat and legumes for urban markets. The number of plantations in the south rose steadily, demanding increasing numbers of slaves (from 28,000 in 1700 to 575,000 in 1776), although world market fluctuations left planters vulnerable. Except for boom periods in the plantation sector, the rural areas remained largely poor.

Real changes occurred during the early eighteenth century in the urban regions. Large port cities emerged which shipped in textiles and ironwares from Europe in return for timber at relatively cheap rates. The most important were Philadelphia (28,000 inhabitants), New York (25,000), Boston (16,000), and Newport, Rhode Island (11,000). A wealthy merchant class formed, spawning urban strata of professionals (such as lawyers, teachers, and newspaper journalists). Primary school education was provided by municipal public schools as well as some churches, and evening schools for craftspeople existed in some measure. By the middle of the eighteenth century a majority of men could read and write, although female literacy was minimal. Finally, in contrast to Latin America, social ranks in New England were less elaborate.

## The Adaptation of the Americas to European Culture

European settlers brought two distinct cultures to the Americas. In the Mid-Atlantic, Caribbean, and Central and South America, they brought with them the Catholic Reformation, a culture and perspective that resisted the New Science of Galileo and the Enlightenment thought of Locke until the late eighteenth century. In the northeast, colonists implanted dissident Protestantism as well as the Anglicanism of Great Britain. The rising number of adherents of the New Science and Enlightenment in northwestern Europe had also a parallel in North America. Settlers and their locally born offspring were proud of their respective cultures, which, even though provincial, were dominant in what they prejudicially viewed as a less civilized, if not barbaric, Native American environment.

**Catholic Missionary Work** From the beginning, Spanish and Portuguese monarchs relied heavily on the Catholic Church for their rule in the new American provinces. The pope granted them patronage over the organization and all appointments on the new continents. A strong motive driving many in the church as well as society at large was the belief in the imminent Second Coming of Jesus. This belief was one inspiration for the original Atlantic expansion (see Chapter 16). When the Aztec and Inca Empires fell, members of the Franciscan order, the main proponents of the belief in the imminence of the Second Coming, interpreted it as a sign of the urgent duty to convert the Native Americans to Christianity. If Jesus' kingdom was soon to come, according to this interpretation, all humans in the Americas should be Christians.

Thousands of Franciscan, Dominican, and other preaching monks, later followed by the Jesuits, fanned out among the Native Americans. They baptized them, introduced the sacraments (Eucharist, baptism, confession, confirmation, marriage, last rites, and priesthood), and taught them basic theological concepts of Christianity. The missionaries learned native languages, translated the catechism and New Testament into those languages, and taught the children of the ruling native families how to read and write. Thanks to their genuine efforts to understand the Native Americans on their own terms, a good deal of preconquest Native American culture was recorded without too much distortion.

The role and function of saints as mediators between humans and God formed one element of Catholic Christianity to which Native Americans acculturated early. Good works as God-pleasing human efforts to gain salvation in the afterlife formed another. The veneration of images of the Virgin Mary and pilgrimages to the chapels and churches where they were kept constituted a third element. The best-known example of the last element is Our Lady of Guadalupe, near Mexico City, who in 1531 appeared in a vision to a Native American in the place where the native goddess Tonantzin used to be venerated. On the other hand, the Spanish Inquisition also operated in the Spanish and Portuguese colonies, seeking to limit the degree to which Catholicism and traditional religion mingled. The church treaded a fine line between enforcement of doctrine and leniency toward what it determined were lax or heretical believers.

**Education and the Arts** The Catholic Reformation expressed itself also in the organization of education. The Franciscans and Dominicans had offered general

**Spanish Cruelty to Incas.**
Felipe Guamán Poma de Ayala, a Peruvian claiming noble Inca descent, was a colonial administrator, well educated and an ardent Christian. He is remembered today as a biting critic of the colonial administration and the clergy, whom he accused of mistreating and exploiting the Andean population, as in this colored wood print.

education to the children of settlers early on and, in colleges, trained graduates for missionary work. The first New World universities, such as Santo Domingo (1538), Mexico City, and Lima (both 1553), taught theology, church law, and Native American languages. Under the impact of the Jesuits, universities broadened the curriculum, offering degrees also in secular law, Aristotelian philosophy, the natural sciences, and medicine. Although the universities did not admit the New Sciences and Enlightenment of northwestern Europe into their curriculum, there was nevertheless considerable scientific research on tropical diseases, plants, and animals as a counterbalance. The vast extent of this research, long kept secret by the Spanish and Portuguese monarchs from their European competitors, is becoming gradually known only now.

Furthermore, missionary monks collected and recorded Native American manuscripts and oral traditions, such as the Aztec *Anales de Tula* and the Maya *Popol Vuh*. Others wrote histories and ethnographies of the Taíno, Aztec, Maya, Inca, and Tupí peoples. Bartolomé de las Casas, Toribio Motolonía de Benavente, Bernardino de Sahagún, Diego de Landa, Bernabé Cobo, and Manoel da Nóbrega are merely a handful of noteworthy authors who wrote about the Native Americans. Many labored for years, worked with legions of informers, and produced monumental tomes.

A number of Native American and mestizo chroniclers, historians, and commentators on the early modern state and society are similarly noteworthy. Muñoz Camargo was a Tlaxcaltecan; Fernando de Alva Ixtlixóchitl and Fernando Alvarado Tezózomoc were Mexican mestizos; and Juan de Santa Cruz Pachacuti Yamqui and Felipe Inca Garcilaso de la Vega were Peruvian mestizos, all writing on their native regions. Felipe Guamán Poma de Ayala (ca. 1535–1616), a native Peruvian, is of particular interest. He accompanied his 800-page manuscript, entitled (in English translation) *The First New Chronicle and Good Government*, with some 400 drawings of daily-life activities in the Peruvian villages. These drawings provide us with invaluable cultural details, which would be difficult to render in writing. Unfortunately, King Philip II of Spain, a relentless proponent of the Catholic Reformation, took a dim view of authors writing on Native American society and history. In 1577 he forbade the publication of all manuscripts dealing with what he called idolatry and superstition. Many manuscripts lay hidden in archives and did not see the light of day until modern times.

**Protestantism in New England**    From the start, religious diversity was a defining cultural trait of English settlements in North America. The spectrum of Christian denominations ranged from a host of English and continental European versions of Protestantism to Anglicanism and a minority of Catholics. As if this spectrum had not been sufficiently broad, dissenters frequently split from the existing denominations, moved into new territory, and founded new settlements. Religiosity was a major characteristic of the early settlers.

An early example of religious splintering was the rise of an antinomian ("anti-law") group within Puritan-dominated Massachusetts. The Puritans dominant in this colony generally recognized the authority of the Anglican Church but strove to move it toward Protestantism from within. The preachers and settlers represented in the General Court, as their assembly was called, were committed to the Calvinist balance between "inner" personal grace obtained from God and "outer" works according to the law. The antinomian group, however, digging deep into early traditions in Christianity, advocated an exclusive commitment to inner grace through spiritual perfection.

Their leader was Anne Hutchinson, an early and tireless proponent of women's rights and an inspiring preacher. She was accused of arguing that she could recognize those believers in Calvinist Protestantism who were predestined for salvation and that these believers would be saved even if they had sinned. After a power struggle with the deeply misogynistic magistrates opposed to influential women, the General Court prevailed and forced the antinomians to move to Rhode Island in 1638.

The example is noteworthy because it led to the founding of Harvard College in 1636 by the General Court. Harvard was the first institution of higher learning in North America, devoted to teaching the "correct" balanced Calvinist Protestantism. Later, the college functioned as the main center for training the colony's ministers in Puritan theology and morality, although it was not affiliated with any specific denomination.

**The New Sciences in the New World.** This painting by Samuel Collings, *The Magnetic Dispensary* (1790), shows how men and women, of lay background, participated in scientific experiments in the English colonies of North America, similar to educated middle-class people in western Europe at the same time.

**New Sciences Research**  As discussed in Chapter 17, the New Sciences had found their most hospitable home in northwestern Europe by default. The rivalry between Protestantism and Catholicism had left enough of an authority-free space for the New Sciences to flourish. Under similar circumstances—intense rivalry among denominations—English North America also proved hospitable to the New Sciences. An early practitioner was Benjamin Franklin (1706–1790), who began his career as a printer, journalist, and newspaper editor. Franklin founded the University of Pennsylvania (1740), the first secular university in North America, and the American Philosophical Society (1743), the first scientific society. This hospitality for the New Sciences in North America was quite in contrast to Latin America, where a uniform Catholic Reformation prevented its rise.

**Witch Hunts**  In the last decade of the seventeenth century, a high level of religious intensity and rivalry was at the root of a witchcraft frenzy which seized New England. The belief in witchcraft was the survival on the popular level of the ancient concept of a shared mind or spirit that allows people to influence each other, either positively or negatively. Witches, male and female, were persons exerting a negative influence, or black magic, on their victims. In medieval Europe, the church had kept witchcraft out of sight, but in the wake of Protestantism and the many challenges to church authority it had become more visible. In the North American colonies, with no overarching religious authority, the visibility of witchcraft was particularly high.

**Witch Trial.** In the course of the 1600s, in the relatively autonomous English colonies of North America, more persons were accused, tried, and convicted of witchcraft than anywhere else. Of the 140 persons coming to trial between 1620 and 1725, 86 percent were women. Three witch panics are recorded: Bermuda, 1651; Hartford, Connecticut, 1652–1665; and Salem, Massachusetts, 1692–1693. This anonymous American woodcut of the early 1600s shows one method to try someone for witchcraft: swim or float if guilty, or sink if innocent.

The one case where this sensitivity erupted into hysteria was that of Salem, Massachusetts. Here, the excitement erupted in 1692 with Tituba, a Native American slave from Barbados who worked in the household of a pastor. Tituba practiced voodoo, the West African–originated, part-African and part-Christian religious practice of influencing others. When a young daughter and niece in the pastor's household suffered from convulsions, mass rioting broke out, in which 20 women accused of being witches were executed, although Tituba, ironically, survived. A new governor finally calmed the passions and restored order.

**Revivalism**  Religious fervor expressed itself also in periodic Protestant renewal movements, among which the "Great Awakening" of the 1730s and 1740s was the most important. The main impulse for this revivalist movement came from the brothers John and Charles Wesley, two Methodist preachers in England who toured Georgia in 1735. Preachers from other denominations joined, all exhorting Protestants to literally "start anew" in their relationship with God. Fire-and-brimstone sermons rained down on the pews, reminding the faithful of the absolute sovereignty of God, the depravity of humans, predestination to hell and heaven, the inner experience of election, and salvation by God's grace alone. Thus, revivalism, recurring with great regularity to the present, became a potent force in Protestant America, at opposing purposes with secular founding-father constitutionalism.

## Putting It All Together

During the period 1500–1800 the contours of a new pattern in which the Americas formed a resource-rich and warm-weather extension of Europe took shape. During this time, China and India continued to be the most populous and wealthiest agrarian–urban regions of the world. Scholars have estimated China's share of the world economy during this period as comprising 40 percent. India probably did not lag far behind. In 1500, Europe was barely an upstart, forced to defend itself against the push of the Ottoman Empire into eastern Europe and the western Mediterranean. But its successful conquest of Iberia from the Muslims led to the discovery of the Americas. Possession of the Americas made Europe similar to China and India in that it now encompassed, in addition to its northerly cold climates, subtropical and tropical regions which produced rich cash crops as well as precious metals. Over the course of 300 years, with the help of its American extension, Europe narrowed the gap between itself and China and India, although it was only after the beginning of industrialization, around 1800, that it eventually was able to close this gap.

Narrowing the gap, of course, was not a conscious policy in Europe. Quite the contrary, because of fierce competition both with the Ottoman Empire and internally, much of the wealth Europe gained in the Americas, especially silver, was wasted on warfare. The centralizing state, created in part to support war, ran into insurmountable budgetary barriers, which forced Spain into several state bankruptcies. Even mercantilism, a logical extension of the centralizing state, had limited effects. Its centerpiece, state support for the export of manufactures to the American colonies, functioned unevenly. The Spanish and Portuguese governments, with weak urban infrastructures and low manufacturing capabilities, especially in textiles, were unable to enforce this state-supported trade until the eighteenth century and even then only in very limited ways. France and especially England practiced mercantilism more successfully but were able to do so in the Americas only from the late seventeenth century onward, when their plantation systems began to take shape. Although the American extension of Europe had the potential of making Europe self-sufficient, this potential was realized only partially during the colonial period.

A fierce debate has raged over the question of the degree of wealth the Americas added to Europe. On the one hand, considerable quantitative research has established that the British slave trade for sugar plantations added at best 1 percent to the British gross domestic product (GDP). The profits from the production of sugar on the English island of Jamaica may have added another 4 percent to the British GDP. Without doubt, private slave-trading and sugar-producing enterprises were at times immensely profitable to individuals and groups, not to mention the mining of silver through forced labor. In the larger picture, however, these profits were considerably smaller if one takes into account the immense waste of revenues on military ventures—hence, the doubts raised by scholars today about large gains made by Europe through its American colonial acquisitions.

On the other hand, the European extension to the Americas was clearly a momentous event in world history. It might have produced dubious overall profits for Europe, but it definitely encouraged the parting of ways between Europe and Asia and Africa, once a new scientific–industrial society began to emerge around 1800.

▶ For additional resources, including maps, primary sources, visuals, and quizzes, please go to www.oup.com/us/vonsivers. Please see the Further Resources section at the back of the book for additional readings and suggested websites.

## Against the Grain

# Juana Inés de la Cruz

**I** n the wake of the Protestant and Catholic Reformations of the 1500s, it was no longer unusual for European women to pursue higher education. In the considerably more conservative Latin American colonies of Spain, Juana Inés de la Cruz (1651–1695) was less fortunate, even though her fame as the intellectually most brilliant figure of the seventeenth century in the colonies endured.

De la Cruz was the illegitimate child of a Spanish immigrant father and a Creole mother. She grew up on the hacienda of her maternal grandfather, in whose library she secretly studied Latin, Greek, and Nahuatl, and also composed her first poems. Unable as a woman to be admitted to the university in Mexico City, de la Cruz nevertheless was fortunate to receive further education from the wife of the vice regent of New Spain. In order to continue her studies and eschewing married life in the ruling class, in 1668 she entered a convent. Here, she continued to study and write hundreds of poems, comedies, religious dramas, and theological texts. Her seminars with courtiers and scholarly visitors were a major attraction in Mexico City.

In 1688, however, she lost her protection at court with the departure of her vice-regal supporters for Spain. Her superior, the archbishop of Mexico, was an open misogynist, and even though her confessor and the bishop of Puebla were admirers, their admiration had limits. A crisis came in 1690 when the bishop of Puebla published de la Cruz's critique of a famous sermon of 1650 by the Portuguese Jesuit António Vieira on Jesus' act of washing his disciples' feet, together with his own critique of de la Cruz. The complex theological arguments addressed the question of whether the foot washing was an inversion of the master/slave (Vieira) or master/servant (de la Cruz) relationship—a theological question unresolved in the Gospels, as well as among the Christian churches in the subsequent centuries. De la Cruz viewed Vieira's interpretation as more hierarchical/male and her own interpretation as more humble/female.

A year later, in 1691, de la Cruz wrote a highly spirited, lengthy riposte to the bishop's apparently well-meaning advice to her in his critique to be more conscious of her status as a woman. Her message was clear: Even though women had to be silent in church, as St. Paul had taught, neither study nor writing were prohibited for women. Before the church could censor her, in 1693 Juana Inés de la Cruz stopped writing. She died two years later.

- Why were the Latin American colonies more socially conservative than Europe?

- Was de la Cruz right to stop her correspondence with the Mexican clergy in 1693?

# Thinking Through Patterns

▶ **What is the significance of western Europeans acquiring the Americas as a warm-weather extension of their northern continent?**

In their role as supplementary subtropical and tropical extensions of Europe, the Americas exerted considerable impact on Europe's changing position in the world. First, Europe acquired large quantities of precious metals, which its two largest competitors, India and China, lacked. Second, with its new access to warm-weather agricultural products, Europe rose to a position of agrarian autonomy similar to that of India and China. In terms of resources, compared with the principal religious civilizations of India and China, Europe grew between 1550 and 1800 from a position of inferiority to one of near parity.

Because the numbers of Europeans who emigrated to the Americas was low for most of the colonial period—just 300,000 Spaniards left for the New World between 1500 and 1800—they never exceeded the numbers of Native Americans or African slaves. The result was a highly privileged settler society that held superior positions on the top rung of the social hierarchy. In principle, given an initially large indigenous population, labor was cheap and should have become more expensive as diseases reduced the Native Americans. In fact, labor always remained cheap, in part because of the politically supported institution of forced labor and in part because of racial prejudice.

▶ **What was the main pattern of social development in colonial America during the period 1500–1800?**

▶ **Why and how did European settlers in South and North America strive for self-government, and how successful were they in achieving their goals?**

Two contrasting patterns characterized the way in which European colonies were governed. The Spanish and Portuguese crowns, primarily interested in extracting minerals and warm-weather products from the colonies, had a strong interest in exercising as much centralized control over their possessions in the Americas as they could. In contrast, the British crown granted self-government to the North American colonies from the start, in part because the colonies were initially far less important economically and in part because of a long tradition of self-rule at home. Nevertheless, even though Latin American settlers achieved only partial self-rule in their towns and cities, they destroyed central rule indirectly through the purchase of offices. After financial reforms, Spain and Portugal reestablished a degree of central rule through the appointment of officers from the home countries.

# Patterns of Evidence:
# Sources for Chapter 18

## SOURCE 18.1

## Hernán Cortés, *Second Letter from Mexico to Emperor Charles V*

### 1522

With a handful of untrained and poorly equipped soldiers, Hernán Cortés overthrew the powerful Aztec civilization between 1519 and 1520. Born in Spain around 1485, Cortés decided to inform the king of Spain (and Holy Roman emperor) Charles V of his achievements, in a series of written updates. Despite their ostensible purpose, these "letters" were designed for more than the edification and delight of the emperor. Like Julius Caesar's dispatches from the Gallic Wars of the 50s BCE—in which at least one million Gauls were killed and another million enslaved—these accounts were designed for broad public consumption. Each letter was sent to Spain as soon as it was ready, and it seems likely that Cortés's father, Martín, arranged for their immediate publication. Over the course of these five published letters, although Cortés developed a persona for himself as a conquering hero and agent of imperial power, he also exposed the ruthlessness and brutality of his "conquest" of Mexico.

From henceforth they offered themselves as vassals of Your Sacred Majesty and swore to remain so always and to serve and assist in all things that Your Highness commanded them. A notary set all this down through the interpreters which I had. Still I determined to go with them; on the one hand, so as not to show weakness and, on the other, because I hoped to conduct my business with Mutezuma from that city because it bordered on his territory, as I have said, and on the road between the two there is free travel and no frontier restrictions.

When the people of Tascalteca saw my determination it distressed them considerably, and they told me many times that I was mistaken, but since they were vassals of Your Sacred Majesty and my friends they would go with me to assist me in whatever might happen. Although I opposed this and asked them not to come, as it

Source: Hernán Cortés, *Letters from Mexico*, ed. and trans. Anthony Pagden (New Haven, CT: Yale University Press, 1986), 72–74.

was unnecessary, they followed me with some 100,000 men, all well armed for war, and came within two leagues of the city. After much persuasion on my part they returned, though there remained in my company some five or six thousand of them. That night I slept in a ditch, hoping to divest myself of these people in case they caused trouble in the city, and because it was already late enough and I did not want to enter too late. The following morning, they came out of the city to greet me with many trumpets and drums, including many persons whom they regard as priests in their temples, dressed in traditional vestments and singing after their fashion, as they do in the temples. With such ceremony they led us into the city and gave us very good quarters, where all those in my company were most comfortable. There they brought us food, though not sufficient.

. . .

During the three days I remained in that city they fed us worse each day, and the lords and principal persons of the city came only rarely to see and speak with me. And being somewhat disturbed by this, my interpreter, who is an Indian woman from Putunchan, which is the great river of which I spoke to Your Majesty in the first letter, was told by another Indian woman and a native of this city that very close by many of Mutezuma's men were gathered, and that the people of the city had sent away their women and children and all their belongings, and were about to fall on us and kill

us all; and that if she wished to escape she should go with her and she would shelter her. All this she told to Gerónimo de Aguilar, an interpreter whom I acquired in Yucatán, of whom I have also written to Your Highness; and he informed me. I then seized one of the natives of this city who was passing by and took him aside secretly and questioned him; and he confirmed what the woman and the natives of Tascalteca had told me. Because of this and because of the signs I had observed, I decided to forestall an attack, and I sent for some of the chiefs of the city, saying that I wished to speak with them. I put them in a room and meanwhile warned our men to be prepared, when a harquebus was fired, to fall on the many Indians who were outside our quarters and on those who were inside. And so it was done, that after I had put the chiefs in the room, I left them bound up and rode away and had the harquebus fired, and we fought so hard that in two hours more than three thousand men were killed.

. . .

After fifteen or twenty days which I remained there the city and the land were so pacified and full of people that it seemed as if no one were missing from it, and their markets and trade were carried on as before. I then restored the friendly relations between this city of Curultecal and Tascalteca, which had existed in the recent past, before Mutezuma had attracted them to his friendship with gifts and made them enemies of the others.

▶ **Working with Sources**

1. Does Cortés offer a justification for his treatment of the people of Tascalteca? Why or why not?

2. What were the risks associated with Cortés's reliance on translators as he conquered the natives of Mexico?

## SOURCE 18.2

# Marina de San Miguel's Confessions before the Inquisition, Mexico City

### 1598–1599

The Inquisition was well established in Spain at the time of Cortés's conquest in the 1520s. A tribunal of the Holy Office of the Inquisition came in the conquistadors' wake, ultimately established at Mexico City in 1571 with authority to regulate Catholic morality throughout "New Spain." Most of the Inquisition trials concerned petty breaches of religious conduct, but others dealt with the much more serious crime of heresy. In November 1598, the Inquisition became alarmed about the rise of a group who believed that the Day of Judgment was at hand. Among the group denounced to the Holy Office was Marina de San Miguel, a Spanish-born woman who held a high status due to her mystical visions. Her confessions, offered between November 1598 and January 1599, reveal the degree to which confessions of "deviance" could be extorted from a victim. In March 1601, Marina was stripped naked to the waist and paraded upon a mule. Forced to confess her errors, she was sentenced to 100 lashes with a whip.

### First Confession

In the city of Mexico, Friday, November 20, 1598. The Lord Inquisitor *licenciado* don Alonso de Peralta in his morning audience ordered that a woman be brought before him from one of the secret prisons of this Holy Office. Being present, she swore an oath *en forma devida de derecho* under which she promised to tell the truth here in this audience and in all the others that might be held until the determination of her case, and to keep secret everything that she might see or believe or that might be talked about with her or that might happen concerning this her case.

. . .

She was asked if she knows, presumes, or suspects the cause for her arrest and imprisonment in the prisons of the Holy Office. . . . The inquisitor said that with her illness she must have imagined it. And she says that she wants to go over her memory so that she can tell the truth about everything that she might remember.

With this the audience ceased, because it was past eleven. The above was read and she approved it and signed it. And she was ordered to return to her cell, very admonished to examine her memory as she was offered to do.

. . .

### Third Confession

In the city of Mexico, Tuesday, November 24, 1598. . . .

She said that what she has remembered is that in the course of her life

Source: Jacqueline Holler, "The Spiritual and Physical Ecstasies of a Sixteenth-Century Beata: Marina de San Miguel Confesses Before the Mexican Inquisition," in Richard Boyer and Geoffrey Spurling, eds., *Colonial Lives: Documents on Latin American History, 1550–1850* (New York: Oxford University Press, 2000), 79–98.

some spiritual things have happened to her, which she has talked about to some people. And she believes that they have been the cause of her imprisonment, because they were scandalized by what she told them.

. . .

And then she opened her eyes and began to shake and get up from the bench on which she was seated, saying, "My love, help me God, how strongly you have given me this." And among these words she said to the Lord Inquisitor that when she is given these trances, she should be shaken vigorously to awaken her from her deep dream. Then she returned to being as though sleeping. The inquisitor called her by her name and she did not respond, nor the second time. And the third time she opened her eyes and made faces, and made signs with her hands to her mouth.

. . .

### Sixth Confession

In the city of Mexico, Monday, January 25, 1599. . . .

She said that it's like this. . . . She has been condemned to hell, because for fifteen years she has had a sensual temptation of the flesh, which makes her perform dishonest acts with her own hands on her shameful parts. She came to pollution [orgasm] saying dishonest words that provoke lust, calling by their dishonest names many dirty and lascivious things. She was tempted to this by the devil, who appeared to her internally in the form of an Angel of Light, who told her that she should do these things, because they were no sin. This was to make her abandon her scruples. And the devil appeared to her in the form of Christ our Redeemer, in such a way that she might uncover her breasts and have carnal union with him. And thus, for fifteen years, she has had carnal union occasionally from month to month, or every two months. And if it had been more she would accuse herself of that too, because she is only trying to save her soul, with no regard to honor or the world. And the carnal act that the devil as Angel of Light and in the form of Christ had with her was the same as if she had had it with a man. And he kissed her, and she enjoyed it, and she felt a great ardor in her whole body, with particular delight and pleasure.

. . .

### Eighth Confession

In the city of Mexico, Wednesday, January 27, 1599. . . .

But all the times she had the copulation with the devil in the form of Christ she doubted whether it was the devil or not, from which doubts one can infer that she did not believe as firmly as she ought to have that such things could not possibly be from Christ. In this she should urgently discharge her conscience. . . .

[After the *Ninth Confession:*]

In the city of Mexico, Tuesday, Day of the Purification of our Lady, February 2, 1599, the Lord Inquisitor in his afternoon audience ordered Marina de San Miguel brought before him. And once present she was told that if she has remembered anything in her case she should say it, and the truth, under the oath that she has made.

She said no. . . .

▶ **Working with Sources**

1. **What does this document indicate about the working methods of the Inquisition (and their "successes") in Mexico in the 1590s?**

2. **Does the Inquisition seem to have been more concerned about Marina's sexuality than her mystical experiences?**

## SOURCE 18.3

# Nahuatl Land Sale Documents, Mexico

### ca. 1610s

After the conquest of the Aztec imperial capital of Tenochtitlan, Spaniards turned their attention to the productive farmland in the surrounding countryside, which was inhabited by Nahuatl-speaking native people. By the late sixteenth century, Spaniards began to expand rapidly into this territory. They acquired estates in a variety of ways, from royal grants to open seizure of property. Nevertheless, the purchase of plots of land from individual Nahuas was also common—although sometimes the sellers came to regret the transaction and petitioned higher authorities for redress of their grievances.

**Altepetl:** City-state.

**Teopixqui:** Priest, in Nahuatl.

**Tlaxilacalli:** Subunit of an *altepetl*.

Here in the *altepetl* Santo Domingo Mixcoac, Marquesado del Valle, on the first day of July of the year 1612, I, Joaquín de San Francisco, and my wife, Juana Feliciana, citizens here in the *altepetl* of Santa María Purificación Tlilhuacan, sell to Dr. Diego de León Plaza, *teopixqui*, one field and house that we have in the *tlaxilacalli* Tlilhuacan next to the house of Juan Bautista, Spaniard. Where we are is right in the middle of [in between] their houses. And now we receive [the money] in person. The reason we sell it is that we have no children to whom it might belong. For there is another land and house, but [the land] here we can no longer [work] because it is really in the middle of [land belonging to] Spaniards. [The land] is not *tributario*, for my father, named Juan Altamirano, and my mother, María Catalina, really left it to me. And now I give it to [the doctor] very voluntarily. And now he is personally giving me 130 pesos. Both my wife and I receive it in person before the witnesses. And the tribute will be remedied with [the price]; it will pay it. The land [upon which tribute is owed] is at Colonanco. It is adjacent to the land of Miguel de Santiago and Lucas Pérez. And the witnesses [are] Antonio de Fuentes and señora Inés de Vera and Juana de Vera, Spanish women (and the Nahuas) Juan Josef, Gabriel Francisco, María, Mariana, and Sebastián Juan. And because we do not know how to write, I, Joaquín [de San] Francisco, and my wife asked a witness to set down [a signature] on our behalf [along with the notary?] Juan Vázquez, Spaniard. Witnesses, Antonio de Fuentes, [etc.] Before me, Matías Valeriano, notary. And both of them, he and his wife [Joaquín de San Francisco and Juana Feliciana], received the 140 pesos each three

Source: Rebecca Horn, "Spaniards in the Nahua Countryside: Dr. Diego de León Plaza and Nahuatl Land Sale Documents (Mexico, Early Seventeenth Century), in Richard Boyer and Geoffrey Spurling, eds., *Colonial Lives: Documents on Latin American History, 1550–1850* (New York: Oxford University Press, 2000), 102–103, 108–109.

months, [presumably paid in installments?] before the witnesses who were mentioned. Before me, Matías Valeriano, notary.

. . .

[Letter of complaint to the authorities of Santo Domino Mixcoac, on the behalf of a group of Nahuas, undated:]

We are citizens here in Santo Domingo Mixcoac. We state that we found out that Paula and Juana and María and Catalina and Inés and Anastacia complain about the *teniente* before you [the *corregidor, gobernador, regidores,* etc.]. It is Antonio de Fuentes whom they are accusing because they say he mistreats them. [They say] he robs [people's land].

. . .

And now [the] Spaniard Napolles disputes with the *teniente*. And Napolles goes around to each house exerting pressure on, forcing many people [to say "get rid of the *teniente*"]. [He says:] "Let there be no officer of the justice. I will help you expel the *teniente* because we will be happy if there

is no officer of the law on your land." Napolles, Spaniard, keeps a woman at his house and he is forcing her. For this reason [the authorities] arrested him for concubinage. They gave him a fine about which he became very angry and they arrested him. He stole four pigs, the property of a person named Francisco Hernández, Spaniard, and because of that they arrested him. He was scorched [burned] for their relatives accuse them.

. . .

And so now with great concern and with bowing down we implore you [the *corregidor, gobernador,* and *regidores,* etc.] and we ask for justice. Everyone knows how [the blacks and *mestizos*] mistreat us. They don't go to confession. They are already a little afraid and are already living a little better. And we ask for justice. Let them be punished. We who ask it are Juan Joseph, Francisco de San Juan, and Francisco Juan.

**Teniente:** Lieutenant.

▶ **Working with Sources**

1. Why do the documents incorporate Nahuatl terms at some times but not at others?

2. How do the documents illustrate the various levels of justice available to native people and to "Spaniards"?

## SOURCE 18.4

# *The Jesuit Relations,* French North America

### 1649

*The Jesuit Relations* are the most important documents attesting to the encounter between Europeans and native North Americans in the seventeenth century. These annual reports of French missionaries from the Society of Jesus document the conversions—or attempted conversions—of the various indigenous peoples in what is today the St. Lawrence River basin and the Great Lakes region. When they arrived on the banks of the St. Lawrence in 1625, French Jesuits were entering a continent still very much under control of First Nations peoples, who were divided by their own ethnic and linguistic differences. Even the catch-all terms "Huron" and "Iroquois" masked their nature as confederacies, composed of several distinct nations, who had joined together prior to the arrival of Europeans.

When the Jesuits made headway with one group, they usually lost initiative with the group's rivals—and sometimes found themselves in the midst of a conflict that they could barely understand or appreciate. This section of the *Relations* concerns the torture and murder of Jean Brébeuf, who had lived among the Hurons at various points from the 1620s through the 1640s, observing their culture and systematically attempting to convert them to Catholicism. However, when an Iroquois raiding party invaded his settlement, the depth of the Hurons' Christian commitment—and his own—would be tested.

The sixteenth day of March in the present year, 1649, marked the beginning of our misfortunes—if an event, which no doubt has been the salvation of many of God's elect, can be called a misfortune.

The Iroquois, enemies of the Hurons, arrived by night at the frontier of this country. They numbered about a thousand men, well furnished with weapons, most of them carrying firearms obtained from their allies, the Dutch. We had no knowledge of their approach, although they had started from their country in the autumn, hunting in the forests throughout the winter, and had made a difficult journey of nearly two hundred leagues over the snow in order to take us by surprise. By night, they reconnoitered the condition of the first place upon which they had designs. It was surrounded by a pine stockade fifteen or sixteen feet in height, and a deep ditch with which nature had strongly fortified this place on three sides. There remained only a small space that was weaker than the others.

It was at this weak point that the enemy made a breach at daybreak, but so secretly and promptly that he was master of the place before anyone could mount a defense. All were then sleeping deeply, and they had no time to recognize the danger. Thus this village was taken, almost without striking a blow and with only ten Iroquois killed. Part of the Hurons—men, women, and children—were massacred then and there, while the others were made captives and were reserved for cruelties more terrible than death.

. . .

The enemy did not stop there, but followed up his victory, and before sunrise he appeared in arms to attack the town of St. Louis, which was fortified with a fairly good stockade. Most

Source: Paul Ragueneau, "Relation of 1648–49,"
in Allan Greer, ed., *The Jesuit Relations: Natives and
Missionaries in Seventeenth-Century North America*
(Boston: Bedford/St. Martin's, 2000), 112–115.

of the women and the children had just gone from it upon hearing the news which had arrived regarding the approach of the Iroquois. The people of greatest courage, about eighty persons, being resolved to defend themselves well, courageously repulsed the first and the second assaults, killing about thirty of the enemy's boldest men, in addition to many wounded. But finally, the larger number prevailed, as the Iroquois used their hatchets to undermine the palisade of stakes and opened a passage for themselves through some considerable breaches.

About nine o'clock in the morning, we perceived from our house at St. Marie the fire which was consuming the cabins of that town, where the enemy, after entering victoriously, had reduced everything to desolation. They cast into the flames the old, the sick, the children who had not been able to escape, and all those who, being too severely wounded, could not have followed them into captivity. At the sight of those flames, and by the color of the smoke which issued from them, we understood sufficiently what was happening, for this town of St. Louis was no more than a league distant from us. Two Christians who escaped the fire arrived about this time and confirmed this.

In this town of St. Louis were at that time two of our fathers, Father Jean de Brébeuf and Father Gabriel Lalemant, who had charge of a cluster of five towns. These formed but one of the eleven missions of which we have spoken above, and we call it the mission of St. Ignace.

Some Christians had begged the fathers to preserve their lives for the glory of God, which would have been as easy for them as for the more than five hundred persons who went away at the first alarm, for there was more than enough time to reach a place of safety. But their zeal could not permit such a thing, and the salvation of their flock was dearer to them than the love of their own lives. They employed the moments left to them as the most previous which they had ever had in the world, and through the heat of the battle their hearts were on fire for the salvation of souls. One was at the breach, baptizing the **catechumens**, and the other was giving absolution to the **neophytes**. Both of them urged the Christians to die in the sentiments of piety with which they consoled them in their miseries. Never was their faith more alive, nor their love for their good fathers and pastors more keenly felt.

An infidel, seeing the desperate situation, spoke of taking flight, but a Christian named Etienne Annaotaha, the most esteemed in the country for his courage and his exploits against the enemy, would never allow it. "What!" he said. "Could we ever abandon these two good fathers, who have exposed their lives for us? Their love for our salvation will be the cause of their death, for there is no longer time for them to flee across the snows. Let us then die with them, and we shall go together to heaven." This man had made a general confession a few days previously, having had a presentiment of the danger awaiting him and saying that he wished that death should find him disposed for Heaven. And indeed he, as well as many other Christians, had abandoned themselves to fervor in a manner so extraordinary that we shall never be sufficiently able to bless the guidance of God over so many predestinated souls. His divine providence continues lovingly to guide them in death as in life.

**Catechumens:** Native converts who had not yet been baptized.

**Neophytes:** Recently baptized Christians.

▶ **Working
with Sources**

1. How well do the Jesuits seem to have understood the conflicts among native peoples in this region?

2. How was Ragueneau's reporting of the battle designed to highlight the "success" of the mission, despite an apparent setback?

## SOURCE 18.5

# The Salem Witch Trials, British North America

## 1692

The witch hunt that took place in Salem, Massachusetts, in 1692 has been frequently (if sensationally) depicted in modern films and plays. But a reading of the extant documents used in the trial of the supposed witches provides a more nuanced insight into the process of denunciation, conviction, and execution that unfolded in this persecution, which was among the last in the Western world. Although the Salem witch hunt resulted in the conviction of 30 and the execution of 19, the total number of persons who had been formally accused reached 164. Doubts about the guilt of those executed eventually led to a reconsideration of the procedures used in the trial, and the governor of the colony abruptly suspended the trials in the autumn of 1692. In spite of the admission by some of the Salem jurors that they had been mistaken, the judgments passed on seven of the convicted were not reversed until 2001.

Samuel Gray of Salem, aged about 42 years, testifieth and saith that about fourteen years ago, he going to bed well one [a.m.] one Lord's Day at night, and after he had been asleep some time, he awakened and looking up, saw the house light as if a candle or candles were lighted in it and the door locked, and that little fire there was raked up. He did then see a woman standing between the cradle in the room and the bedside and seemed to look upon him. So he did rise up in his bed and it vanished or disappeared. Then he went to the door and found it locked, and unlocking and opening the door, he went to the entry door and looked out and then again did see the same woman he had a little before seen in the room and in the same garb she was in before. Then he said to her, "What in the name of God do you come for?" Then she vanished away, so he locked the door again and went to bed, and between sleeping and waking he felt something come to his mouth or lips cold, and thereupon started and looked up again and did see the same

Source: Brian P. Levack, ed., *The Witchcraft Sourcebook* (New York: Routledge, 2004), 225–226, 228–229.

woman with some thing between both her hands holding before his mouth upon which she moved. And the child in the cradle gave a great screech out as if it was greatly hurt and she disappeared, and taking the child up could not quiet it in some hours from which time the child that was before a very lively, thriving child did pine away and was never well, although it lived some months after, yet in a sad condition and so died. Some time after within a week or less he did see the same woman in the same garb and clothes that appeared to him as aforesaid, and although he knew not her nor her name before, yet both by the countenance and garb doth testify that it was the same woman that they now call Bridget Bishop, alias Oliver, of Salem. Sworn Salem, May 30th 1692.

. . .

The deposition of Joseph Ring at Salisbury, aged 27 years, being sworn, saith that about the latter end of September last, being in the wood with his brother Jarvis Ring hewing of timber, his brother went home with his team and left this deponent alone to finish the hewing of the piece for him for his brother to carry when he came again. But as soon as his brother was gone there came to this deponent the appearance of Thomas Hardy of the great island of Puscataway, and by some impulse he was forced to follow him to the house of Benovy Tucker, which was deserted and about a half a mile from the place he was at work in, and in that house did appear Susannah Martin of Amesbury and the aforesaid Hardy and another female person which the deponent did not know. There they

had a good fire and drink—it seemed to be cider. There continued most part of the night, [the] said Martin being then in her natural shape and talking as if she used to. But towards the morning the said Martin went from the fire, made a noise, and turned into the shape of a black hog and went away, and so did the other. Two persons go away, and this deponent was strangely carried away also, and the first place he knew was by Samuel Woods' house in Amesbury.

. . .

The deposition of Thomas Putnam, aged 40 years and [Edward Putnam] aged 38 years, who testify and say that we have been conversant with the afflicted persons or the most of them, as namely Mary Walcott, Mercy Lewes, Elizabeth Hubbard, Abigail Williams, Sarah Bibber and Ann Putnam junior and have often heard the aforementioned persons complain of Susannah Martin of Amesbery [sic] torturing them, and we have seen the marks of several bites and pinches which they say Susannah Martin did hurt them with, and also on the second day of May 1692, being the day of the examination of Susannah Martin, the aforenamed persons were most grievously tortured during the time of her examination, for upon a glance of her eyes they were struck down or almost choked and upon the motion of her finger we took notes they were afflicted, and if she did but clench her hands or hold her head aside the afflicted persons aforementioned were most grievously tortured, complaining of Susannah Martin for hurting them.

▶ **Working with Sources**

1. What do these documents suggest about the (supposed) powers of witches, especially in terms of acting at a distance upon their victims?

2. Although all of the witnesses in this set of documents were men, do they reveal something about the connection between witchcraft accusations and gender?

# Chapter 19 1450–1800

# African Kingdoms, the Atlantic Slave Trade, and the Origins of Black America

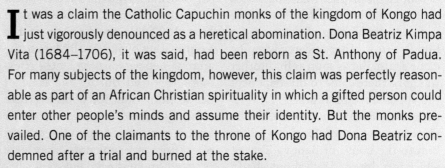

I t was a claim the Catholic Capuchin monks of the kingdom of Kongo had just vigorously denounced as a heretical abomination. Dona Beatriz Kimpa Vita (1684–1706), it was said, had been reborn as St. Anthony of Padua. For many subjects of the kingdom, however, this claim was perfectly reasonable as part of an African Christian spirituality in which a gifted person could enter other people's minds and assume their identity. But the monks prevailed. One of the claimants to the throne of Kongo had Dona Beatriz condemned after a trial and burned at the stake.

Dona Beatriz had been intellectually precocious. In her childhood, her family had her initiated in a *kimpasi* enclosure as a *nganga marinda* (a Kikongo word derived from "knowledge" or "skill"). Such enclosures at the edges of towns and cities had become common and contained altars with crosses and censers (for burning incense). They also, however, included statues believed to be capable of recognizing evildoers, animal claws to grab them, horns to mark the line between the worlds of nature and the spirit, and animal tails as symbols of power. In her initiation ceremony, the head woman of the enclosure put the young Dona Beatriz into a trance that enabled her to

THE ATLANTIC
WORLD,
1500–1800

*ABOVE*: In this watercolor by Capuchin monk Antonio Cavazzi (1621–1678), a European monk and Kongo natives participate in a religious procession.

recognize and repel all the troubling forces that might disturb a person or the community. The people in Kongo were very much aware, however, that not all *ngangas* were benevolent. Some *ngangas* were thought to misuse their spiritual powers and engage in witchcraft. For the missionary Capuchin monks, preaching the Catholic Reformation, all *ngangas* were seen as witches. Whether the young Dona Beatriz was intimidated by their denunciations or not, she followed the church's rulings, renounced her initiation, married, and pursued the domestic life of any other young woman in Kongo society.

But Dona Beatriz's spiritual path did not end here. In 1704, she again underwent a series of deep religious transformations in which she "died," only to be reborn as St. Anthony of Padua (1195–1231), a Portuguese Franciscan monk and one of the patron saints of Portugal. Devotees of the saint believe he blesses marriages and helps people find lost items. With her new saintly and male identity, more powerful than her earlier one as a *nganga*, Dona Beatriz preached a novel and inspiring vision: She was God's providential figure, arrived to restore the Catholic faith and reunify the kingdom of Kongo, both of which she saw as having been torn asunder during nearly half a century of dynastic disunity and civil war (1665–1709).

After her spiritual rebirth, Dona Beatriz immediately went to Pedro IV, king of Kongo (r. 1695–1718), and his Capuchin ally, the chief missionary Bernardo da Gallo, and accused them of being laggards in their efforts to restore the faith and unity of the kingdom. Pedro, perhaps impressed with her claims and the potential power at her command, temporized in his response. Bernardo, however, subjected Dona Beatriz to an angry interrogation about her faith and alleged saintly possession. In a startling and, for Bernardo, alarming parallel to Martin Luther's arguments nearly two centuries before, Beatriz countered with a remarkable attack on the Catholic cornerstone of sacraments. Intention or faith alone, she argued, not the sacraments of the church, would bring salvation. Unlike Luther, however, Dona Beatriz did not derive her convictions from the letters of St. Paul in the New Testament but from her *nganga* initiation: Here, good intentions distinguished the inspired preacher from the witch.

Unable to arrive at a plan of action, the king and Bernardo let Beatriz go. In a journey reminiscent of that of Joan of Arc, she led a growing crowd of followers to the ruined capital of Kongo, M'banza (called São Salvador by the Portuguese). There, she trained "little Anthonies" as missionaries to convert the Kongolese to her new Antonian-African Christianity. Under the protection of a rival of the king, Beatriz was at the pinnacle of her spiritual power when everything unraveled. Though married, she gave birth to a child conceived with one of her followers. She did so secretly at her ancestral home

## Seeing Patterns

▶ **What was the pattern of kingdom and empire formation in Africa during the period 1500–1800?**

▶ **How did patterns of plantation slavery evolve in the Atlantic and the Americas?**

▶ **What are the historic roots from which modern racism evolved?**

in King Pedro's territory, evidently in a deep crisis over her spiritual mission. Allies of the king discovered the lovers by accident and arrested them. They brought them before Pedro, who, in the meantime, had decided to reject Beatriz's challenge and silence her. After a state trial—the church stayed out of the proceedings—Beatriz, her companion, and the baby were executed by the favored means of punishing heretics—burning at the stake.

The story of Dona Beatriz illustrates a major pattern discussed in this chapter: the process by which many Africans adapted their religious heritage to the challenge of European Christianity. Europeans arrived on the western coast of Africa in the fifteenth century as both missionaries and merchants—at times also as slave traders and slave raiders. Africans responded with gold, goods, and their own adaptive forms of Christianity, as well as efforts—as in Kongo, Angola, and Benin—to limit the slave trade in accordance with their own political interests. Elsewhere, however, Africans also exploited and adapted indigenous systems of household, agricultural, administrative, and military slavery to reap voluminous profits from the developing Atlantic human traffic. The unprecedented massive transfer of African slaves to the plantations and mines of the Americas brought to those continents a vast and complex array of peoples from foragers and herders to villagers and city dwellers, representing a wide variety of religious experiences—including those of both Islam and Christianity. In many cases, their cultures would not only survive in the Americas under extraordinarily difficult circumstances but become foundational in the new societies being created there.

## African States and the Slave Trade

In the north of sub-Saharan Africa the pattern of Islamic and Christian dynastic state formation that had been ongoing for centuries continued to dominate herder and village societies in the period 1500–1800. An invasion by Muslim forces from Morocco during the sixteenth century, however, ended the trend toward empire building and strengthened the forces of decentralization. By contrast, in the savanna and Great Lakes regions of central Africa, improved agricultural wealth and intensified regional trade helped perpetuate the kingdom formation already under way. An important set of institutions in the chiefdoms and states of Africa was slavery, though its form and character were far different from the chattel slavery that would characterize the Americas. When the Europeans inserted themselves into these systems, they profoundly altered them to benefit their own interests in the production of warm-weather cash crops on American plantations. The implications of the new trade provided both enormous opportunities and horrific challenges for African traders and local leaders. As the Mediterranean slave trade had for Venetian, Genoese, and North African traffickers, the growing Atlantic slave trade appealed to some West African rulers as a path to enhanced wealth and power, and they enriched themselves through warfare, raids, and trading. More often, however, rulers tried by various means to resist what ultimately became the greatest forced migration in human history.

## The End of Empires in the North and the Rise of States in the Center

The Eurasian empires with universal ambitions of the premodern world united peoples of many different religions, languages, and ethnic affiliations. Mali (1240–1460) was the first African empire that was similar to the empires of Eurasia in this respect. Mali's successor state, the focus of this section, was the even larger Songhay Empire (1460–1591). Though vast, it lasted only a short time.

**Origins of the Songhay**    Songhay was initially a tributary state of Mali. It was centered on the city of Gao downstream on the Niger River from the agricultural center of Jenné-jeno and the commercial and scholarly center of Timbuktu. Gao's origins dated to 850, when it emerged as the end point of the eastern trans-Saharan route from Tunisia and Algeria, parallel to the more heavily traveled western route from Morocco. Gao was located at the northern end of the Songhay Empire, near the Niger Bend, and was inhabited by the Songhay, an ethnic grouping composed of herders, villagers, and fishermen.

The Songhay were ethnically distinct from the Soninke of the kingdom of ancient Ghana and the Malinke of the Mali Empire further west. Their homeland was located to the east and southeast of the Niger Bend. At the end of the eleventh century, the leading clans of the Songhay, profiting from the trans-Saharan trade, converted to Islam. Two centuries later the warriors among them assumed positions of leadership as vassals of the *mansa*, or emperor, of Mali.

**The Songhay Empire**    The Songhay began their imperial expansion in the mid-1400s, toward the end of the dry period in West Africa (1100–1500), during which control of the steppe region was sometimes difficult to maintain. Mali, which had its center in the much wetter savanna, lost its northern outpost, Timbuktu, to the Songhay in 1469. In the following decades, Mali slowly retreated southwestward. Eventually, it became a minor vassal of the Songhay. At its height, the Songhay Empire stretched from Hausaland in the savanna southeast of Gao all the way westward to the Atlantic coast (see Map 19.1).

As in the previous centuries in ancient Ghana and Mali, the decisive difference that elevated the Songhay emperors (*askiyas*) above their vassals was their taxation of the gold trade. The gold fields of the Upper Niger, Senegal, and Black Volta Rivers in the southern rain forest were outside the empire, but merchant clans, often accompanied by troop detachments, transported the gold to Timbuktu and Gao. Here, North African merchants exchanged their Mediterranean manufactures and salt for gold, slaves, and kola nuts. Agents of the *askiyas* in these cities

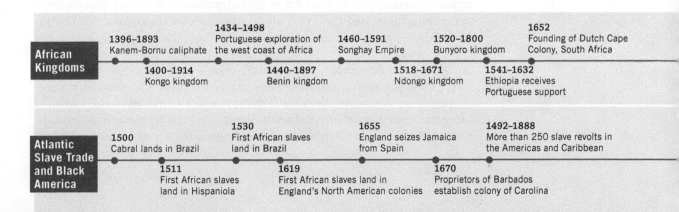

| | | 1434–1498 | | | | 1652 |
|---|---|---|---|---|---|---|
| | 1396–1893 | Portuguese exploration of | 1460–1591 | 1520–1800 | | Founding of Dutch Cape |
| **African Kingdoms** | Kanem-Bornu caliphate | the west coast of Africa | Songhay Empire | Bunyoro kingdom | | Colony, South Africa |
| | 1400–1914 | 1440–1897 | | 1518–1671 | 1541–1632 | |
| | Kongo kingdom | Benin kingdom | | Ndongo kingdom | Ethiopia receives Portuguese support | |

| | | 1530 | | 1655 | | 1492–1888 |
|---|---|---|---|---|---|---|
| | 1500 | First African slaves | | England seizes Jamaica | | More than 250 slave revolts in |
| **Atlantic Slave Trade and Black America** | Cabral lands in Brazil | land in Brazil | | from Spain | | the Americas and Caribbean |
| | 1511 | 1619 | | 1670 | | |
| | First African slaves land in Hispaniola | First African slaves land in England's North American colonies | | Proprietors of Barbados establish colony of Carolina | | |

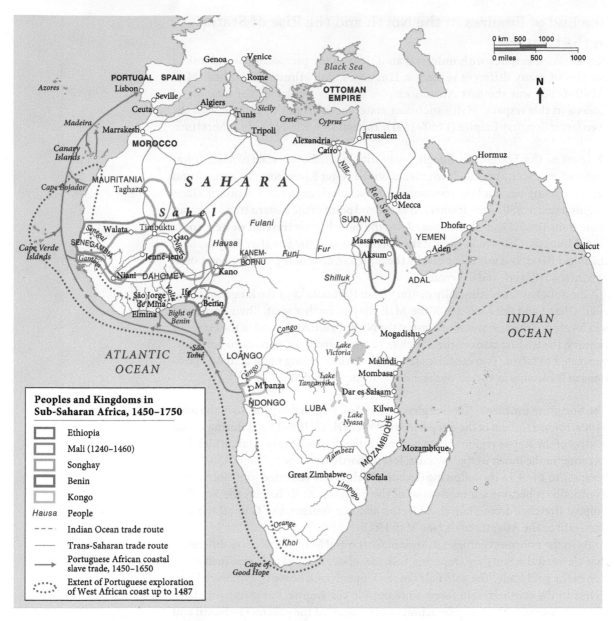

**Peoples and Kingdoms in
Sub-Saharan Africa, 1450–1750**

☐  Ethiopia
☐  Mali (1240–1460)
☐  Songhay
☐  Benin
☐  Kongo
*Hausa*  People
- - - -  Indian Ocean trade route
———  Trans-Saharan trade route
→  Portuguese African coastal
   slave trade, 1450–1650
·····  Extent of Portuguese exploration
   of West African coast up to 1487

MAP **19.1  Peoples and Kingdoms in Sub-Saharan Africa, 1450–1750.**

collected market taxes in the form of gold. Agricultural taxes and tributes supported kingdoms; long-distance trade was needed in addition for an empire to come into being.

**Songhay's Sudden End**    After the initial conquests, the Songhay Empire had little time to consolidate its territory on a more peaceful footing. After just over a century of dominance, the Songhay Empire came to a sudden end in 1591 when a Moroccan force invaded from the north. The invasion was prompted by Moroccan sultans who had successfully driven the Portuguese from their Atlantic coast but were concerned about the flourishing Portuguese trade for gold on the West African coast. They therefore decided to find and occupy the West African gold fields in the rain forest, thus depriving the Portuguese of their supply.

However, after defeating Songhay, they were unable to march any farther, lacking necessary logistical support from Morocco through the Sahara. Although the officers initially turned the Niger delta and bend into a Moroccan province, within a generation they assimilated into the West African royal clans. As a result, imperial politics in West Africa disintegrated, together with much of the trans-Saharan gold trade, which was siphoned off by the Portuguese on what became known as the Gold Coast (modern Ghana).

**The Eastern Sahel and Savanna**   The steppes between Songhay in the west and Ethiopia in the northeastern highlands near the Red Sea also were home to Islamic regimes governing moderate to large territories. Kanem-Bornu (1396–1893) was a long-lived Islamic realm, calling itself a caliphate, but with a majority of subjects following local African religious traditions. Located in both the steppe and savanna, it was based on a slave and ivory trade with the Mediterranean and on agriculture and fishing for its internal organization on the south side of Lake Chad. Kanem-Bornu's imperial frontier was in the southwest, where it waged long intermittent wars with the savanna kingdoms of Hausaland.

The Hausa kingdoms, numbering about half a dozen, had formed during the height of the Mali-dominated trans-Saharan trade as southeastern extensions of this trade into rain-forest Africa. Although they were under frequent attack by Songhay and Kanem-Bornu during the period 1500–1800, the Hausa kingdoms enjoyed periods of independence during which many of the ruling clans converted to Islam. Like their northern neighbors, they maintained cavalry forces, which—apart from military purposes—served to protect the caravans of the traders. In addition to taxing these traders, the Hausa kings collected dues from the villagers. Craftspeople produced pottery, iron implements and utensils, cotton cloth, basketry, leather goods, and iron weapons. Miners and smiths smelted and forged copper, iron, and steel. Although more agricultural in orientation, the Hausa kingdoms closely resembled their northern neighbors in the steppe.

Farther east, in the steppe between Lake Chad and the Nile, the Fur and the Funj, cattle-breeding clan-lineage federations, converted fully to Islam, from the royal clans down to the commoners. In contrast, in West Africa only the dynasties and merchants became Muslim. Their leaders adopted the title "sultan" and became increasingly Arabized in the period 1500–1800, while Christianity along the upper Nile disappeared completely.

**South Central Africa**   On the southern side of the rain forest, the eastern part of the southern savanna and the Great Lakes area in central Africa remained outside the reach of the slave trade. As a result, their populations continued to grow. Large numbers of farmer and cattle herder groups, organized in chiefdoms, inhabited these regions. In the eastern savanna, the kingdom of Luba emerged before 1500, while others followed at various intervals thereafter.

A steady increase in regional trade for copper, iron, salt, dried fish, beads, cloth, and palm oil enabled chieftain clans to consolidate their rule and enlarge their holdings into kingdoms. Living in enclosures and surrounded by "courts," or dense ruling-class settlements, kings maintained agricultural domains worked by slaves. Villages nearby delivered tribute in the form of foodstuffs. From the mid-seventeenth century onward, the American-origin staples corn and cassava (manioc) broadened the food supply. Tributaries at some distance delivered prestige goods, especially copper and ironware, as well as beads. At times, the kings mobilized thousands of workers to build moats and earthworks around their courts, which became centers of incipient urbanization processes.

The Great Lakes region, to the north, south, and west of Lake Victoria, was a highly fertile eastward extension of the southern savanna supporting two annual crops of sorghum and sesame, as well as banana groves and herds of cattle. Traders distributed salt, iron, and dried fish. Agriculture, cattle breeding, and trade supported intense political competition in the region. Small agricultural–mercantile kingdoms shared the region, but sometime in the sixteenth century cattle breeders—the Luo, relatives of the Shilluk—arrived from southern Sudan and shook up the existing political and social structures. Pronounced disparities in cattle ownership emerged on the rich pasture lands. Cattle lords, bolstered by their new wealth and status, rose as competitors of the kings.

North of Lake Victoria, the Bunyoro kingdom, based on agriculture and regional trade, held the cattle lords at bay, while on the south side of the lake the cattle lords created new small kingdoms. After a while cattle breeders and farmers settled into more or less unequal relations of mutual dependence. Under the colonial system in the nineteenth century, these unequal relations froze into a caste system in which the minority Tutsi cattle breeders were continually at odds with the majority Hutu farmers. (The tensions in this social situation were part of a combination of factors that ultimately led to the mass killings and genocide committed by the Hutus against the Tutsis in the modern state of Rwanda in 1993–1994.) Farther south the pre-1500 tradition of gold-mining kingdoms, such as Great Zimbabwe, continued. But here the interaction of Africa with Portugal set the kingdoms on a different historical trajectory.

## Portugal's Explorations along the African Coast and Contacts with Ethiopia

The Portuguese expansion into North Africa and the exploration of the African coast were outgrowths of both the *Reconquista* and crusading impulses. Mixed in with these religious motives was the practical necessity of financing the journeys of exploration through profits from trade. The combination of the two guided Portugal within a single century around the African continent to India. Along the coast, the Portuguese established forts as points of protection for their merchants. In Ethiopia they supported the Christian kingdom there with military aid, providing protection against the Ottomans in Yemen, just across the Red Sea.

**Chartered Explorations in West Africa**    Henry the Navigator (1394–1460), brother of the ruling king, a principal figure of the Portuguese *Reconquista* and chief embodiment of the crusading zeal, occupied the Moroccan port of Ceuta in 1415. He claimed that Ceuta had been Christian prior to the Berber-Arab conquest and subsequent Islamization of Iberia. He also wished to renew crusading for the reconquest of Jerusalem, lost to the Muslims in 1291. But the merchant wing of the Lisbon court was wary of the military expenditures. During the fifteenth century, campaigns for the military occupation of other cities of Morocco, mostly along the Atlantic coast, alternated with voyages financed by Portuguese groups of merchants and aristocrats for commerce along the West African coast.

In 1434, mariners discovered that ships could overcome adverse currents and winds and return from the West African coast by sailing out into the Atlantic, setting course for the newly discovered islands of the Canaries, Madeira, and Azores, before turning east toward Lisbon. It was the impossibility of returning along the coast from the southern part of West Africa that had doomed all previous efforts. Sailors either had to return by land, via the Sahara to the Mediterranean, or they disappeared without a trace. Thus, sailing south in the Atlantic and developing a route by which to return was a decisive step toward circumnavigating the continent.

Between 1434 and 1472, through a combination of royally chartered, merchant-financed voyages, as well as public state-organized expeditions, Portuguese mariners explored the coast as far east as the Bight of Benin. Trade items included European woolens and linens, which were exchanged for gold, cottons, and Guinea pepper. Small numbers of African slaves were included early on as trade items, mostly through purchases from chieftains and kings. Several uninhabited tropical islands off the coast were discovered during this time, and the Portuguese used slaves for the establishment of sugar plantations on them. They shipped other slaves to Europe for domestic employment, adding to the long-standing Mediterranean and trans-Saharan practice of household slavery.

**Portugal and Ethiopia**    By the second half of the fifteenth century, private merchant interests focused on developing trade in West Africa provided few incentives for further explorations. It required the military wing of the Portuguese court to revive crusading. From 1483 through 1486 the king organized state expeditions for further expansion from the Bight of Benin south to the Congo River. Here, mariners sailed upstream in hopes of linking up with Prester John (see Chapter 16), a mythical Christian king believed to live in Ethiopia or India who could help Portugal in the reconquest of Jerusalem. Instead of Prester John, the Portuguese mariners encountered the ruler of the powerful kingdom of Kongo, who converted to Christianity and established close relations with Portugal.

A few years later, after Christopher Columbus had sailed to the Americas for Castile–Aragon in 1492, the Portuguese crown continued the search for a way to Ethiopia or India, a route presumed to lie around the southern tip of Africa. Eventually, Vasco da Gama circumnavigated the southern tip, established trade outposts in Swahili city-states of East Africa, and reached India in 1498. From this point Portuguese development of the Indian spice trade grew in importance.

The Portuguese discovered in the early sixteenth century that the Ethiopian kingdom was extremely weak in the face of the aggressive Muslim sultanate of Adal, on the Red Sea to the east. Until the end of the fifteenth century, Ethiopia had been a powerful Coptic Christian kingdom in the highlands of northeastern Africa. Its people practiced a productive plow-based agriculture for wheat and teff (a local grain), and its kings controlled a rich trade of gold, ivory, animal skins, and slaves from the southern Sudan through the Rift Valley to the Red Sea. Possession of a Red Sea port for this trade, however, was a bone of contention between Ethiopia and Adal during the first half of the sixteenth century.

**Prester John.** The legend of Prester John, a Christian ruler whose lost kingdom in northeast Africa, surrounded by Muslims and pagans, captivated the European imagination from the twelfth through the seventeenth centuries. Purportedly a descendant of one of the Three Magi, Prester John (or Presbyter John) presided over a realm full of riches and fabulous creatures.

A Christian incursion into Muslim territory in 1529 triggered a response by Adal in the form of a furiously destructive Muslim holy war. Ethiopia would have been destroyed in this war had it not been for the timely arrival in 1541 of a Portuguese fleet with artillery and musketeers. For its part, Adal received Ottoman Muslim artillery and musketeer support from Yemen, but 2 years later, after several fierce battles, the Christians prevailed.

Ethiopia paid a high price for its victory, however. Adal Muslim power was destroyed, but in its place, the Ottomans took over the entire west coast of the Red Sea, mostly in order to keep out Portugal. Non-Christian cattle breeders from the southwest occupied the Rift Valley, which separated the northern and southern Ethiopian highlands and had been depopulated during the Christian–Muslim wars. Cut off by the newcomers, Christians in the southern highlands were left to their own devices, surviving in small states. Small numbers of Portuguese stayed in Ethiopia, with Jesuit missionaries threatening to dominate the Ethiopian church, which had long followed its own traditions, as well as the kings. In 1632 the Ethiopian king expelled the Jesuits and consolidated the kingdom as a shrunken power within much smaller borders.

Initially, Ethiopian culture continued to be active under a strong court, expressed mostly through theological writings and iconic paintings. But from about 1700 Ethiopia decentralized into provincial lordships with little interest in their cultural heritage. Only in the mid-nineteenth century, in response to the Western challenge, did the kings take back their power from the provincial lords.

## Coastal Africa and the Atlantic Slave Trade

After Portuguese mariners had circumnavigated Africa, they initially focused on developing their spice trade with India. Gradually, however, they also built their Atlantic slave trade, which took off in the early seventeenth century, to be followed by mariner-merchants from other European countries. To understand the pattern underlying the slave trade from 1500–1800 it is crucial to be aware of the importance of slavery within the African historical context. Different kinds of

*(a)* Elmina as it appeared in a European etching from 1562.    *(b)* Outer defensive walls.

**Elmina.** This town in present-day Ghana was, along with the village of São Jorge da Mina, the first Portuguese fortified trading post on the African coast, from 1482 until it passed to the Dutch in 1637. Merchants used it for storing the goods they traded and for protection in case of conflicts with Africans. It was staffed by a governor and 20–60 soldiers along with a priest, surgeon, apothecary, and a variety of craftspeople. Throughout the first half of the sixteenth century Elmina was also the center of Portuguese slaving activities.

slavery existed in a number of regions in Africa. In many places, a form of slavery existed in the place of land ownership. The more slaves a household, clan leader, chief, or king owned, to work at home or in the fields, the wealthier he was. This form of **household slavery** was the most common variety.

**Trade Forts**   Early on, in the 1440s, Portuguese mariners raided the West African coast in the region defined by the Senegal and Gambia Rivers—Senegambia—for slaves. But they suffered losses since the performance and reliability of their muskets was not yet superior to the precisely aimed poisoned arrows of the Africans. Furthermore, dwelling in a rain forest with its many rivers opening to the coast, West Africans possessed a well-developed tradition of boat building and coastal navigation. Boats hollowed out from tree trunks could hold as many as 50 warriors. These warriors paddled swiftly through the estuaries and mangrove swamps along the coast and picked off the mariners from their caravels if they approached the coast in a hostile manner. The Portuguese thus learned to set foot on the beach in a less threatening way and began what developed into a lucrative coastal fort trade in a variety of items, including slaves.

Through treaties with local African leaders, Portugal acquired the right to build posts or forts from which to trade. Africans involved in trade in these regions produced a variety of items that were soon in demand in Europe. They wove colorful cotton cloth and wore it by the yard. A particular kind of bark or leaf cloth from central West Africa was at times highly sought in Portugal and the Caribbean. For a long time, Senegambian mats were preferred as bedcovers in Europe. In many places, Africans smelted iron and forged steel that was of higher quality than that of iron-poor Portugal.

Trade, as in most other parts in the world during the period 1500–1800, was for expensive luxury goods, not ordinary articles of daily life. Merchants had to be able to achieve high profits while carrying comparatively little to weigh them down. African rulers purchased luxuries in order to engage in conspicuous consumption, fashion display, and lavish gift giving—all ways to enhance their status and cement power relations. They sold slaves to the Europeans in a similar fashion, as luxuries in return for luxuries. Thus, scarcity raised demand on both sides in their respective quest for luxury items.

**Household slavery:** African chiefs and kings maintained large households of retainers, such as administrators, soldiers, domestics, craftspeople, and farmers; many among these were slaves, acquired through raids and wars but also as a form of punishment for infractions of royal, chiefly, or clan law.

**Portuguese Traders.** This brass plaque, from about the middle of the sixteenth century, decorated the palace of the Benin *obo* and shows two Portuguese traders. The fact they are holding hands suggests that they could be father and son.

**African Slavery**   Sub-Saharan Africa—with few long rivers and immense equatorial rain forests—was a vast region with enormous hurdles to a shift in patterns from local self-sufficiency to exchange agriculture and urbanization. Inland exchanges of food for manufactured goods over distances greater than 20 miles were for the most part prohibitively expensive. Human portage or donkey transport, the only available forms of moving goods, were limited to highly valuable merchandise, such as salt, copper, and iron. Everything else was manufactured within self-sufficient households, such as pottery, textiles, mats, basketry, utensils, implements, leather goods, and weapons, alongside a full range of agricultural goods.

Such self-sufficiency required large households. In villages with limited outside trade, the polygamous household with the largest number of males and females employed at home and in the fields was the wealthiest. To increase his wealth further, a household master often raided neighboring villages and acquired captives, to be enslaved and put to work inside and outside the household. Not surprisingly, therefore, slave raiding and household slavery were general features in sub-Saharan African societies, though some peoples like the San of southern Africa lacked the institution altogether. The more stratified slaveholding societies were—with chiefly or royal institutions such as central administrations, armies, and juridical and fiscal offices—the more slaves rose into positions of responsibility and, frequently, autonomy. This was especially the case in the large empires like Mali and Songhay, where a variety of institutions of servitude existed outside of the category of household slaves. Thus, as in a number of societies outside of Africa, the varieties of slavery in sub-Saharan Africa tended to be highly complex and flexible in structure and function.

**Limited Slave Trade from Benin**   When Portugal began the slave trade to supply labor for its sugar plantations on West African offshore islands, African chiefs and kings had to evaluate the comparative value of slaves for their households or for sale. The kingdom of Benin in the rain-forest region west of the Niger delta was an early example of this calculation. The ruler Ewuare (r. 1440–1473) was the first to rise to dominance over chiefs (*azuma*) and assume the title of king (*obo*). Through conquests in all directions, Ewuare acquired large numbers of slaves who were employed in his army and for the construction of extensive earthworks protecting the capital, Benin City.

Early trade contacts between Portuguese mariners and Benin intensified when the successor of Ewuare granted permission to build a fort on the coast in 1487. But the king kept the exchange of palm oil, ivory, woolens, beads, pepper, and slaves for guns, powder, metalware, salt, and cottons under close control. A generation later, when the kings prohibited the sale of male slaves, the Portuguese promptly abandoned their fort. Later, a compromise was reached whereby a limited number of slaves were traded, perhaps some 30 percent of the total trade volume between Portugal and Benin, in return for firearms. The kingdom admitted missionaries and members of the dynasty acculturated to the Portuguese, making Benin increasingly economically diversified and culturally complex.

Slave exports remained restricted during the following two centuries, when Benin was a strong, centralized state. Under subsequent weak kings, decentralization set in. Provincial chiefs began to compete with each other, requiring increased numbers of firearms. To buy more weapons, toward the end of the seventeenth century a weak Benin palace lifted the restrictions on the slave trade. Even more weapons were purchased and slaves were sold during a civil war in the first half of the eighteenth century. But the kingdom reunified, and the palace never lost complete control over Benin's trade with the Portuguese and, from the mid-seventeenth century onward, Dutch and British merchants. Compared to the slave trade farther west on the West African coast, the large centralized kingdom of Benin with its high internal demand for slave labor remained a modest exporter of slaves and thus retained a considerable degree of autonomy and agency.

**The Kingdom of Kongo**    Farther south, on the central West African coast, the Portuguese established trade relations with several coastal kingdoms, among which Kongo and Ndongo were the most important. These kingdoms were located south of the Congo River, with rain forest to the north and savanna to the south. Kongo, the oldest and most centralized kingdom in the region, emerged about 1400, or a century before the arrival of the Portuguese. Its capital, M'banza (São Salvador), was 20 miles inland in the fertile highlands. With 60,000 inhabitants in the sixteenth century, its size was comparable to such European cities as London, Amsterdam, Moscow, and Rome at the time. M'banza also contained a large palace population and a royal domain, where slaves farmed sorghum, millet, and corn.

Within a radius of some 20 miles, the kings governed a region of about 300,000 independent villagers directly. To defend their rule, they relied on a standing army of 5,000 troops, including 500 musketeers, in the sixteenth century. They appointed members of the royal family as governors, who were entitled to rents but were also obliged to deliver taxes in kind to the palace. In addition, the kings collected a head tax in the form of cowrie shells, an indication that farmers engaged in a limited form of trading their agricultural surplus on markets in the capital to obtain the shells for the tax. This region of direct rule was marked by a unified law and administration. Royal appointees traveled around to represent the royal writ. Farther away, vassal kings, called dukes (Portuguese *duque*), governed and sent tribute or gifts to the capital. They sometimes rebelled and broke away; thus, the territory of Kongo, similar to that of Songhay, shifted constantly in size.

The kings of Kongo converted to Christianity early and sent members of the ruling family to Portugal for their education. Portuguese missionaries converted the court and a number of provincial chiefs. Among the ruling class, many read and wrote Portuguese and Latin fluently, impressing European aristocrats with their comportment whenever they went on missions. Muslim ethnic stereotypes against "reddish" Christians and Christian stereotypes and patronizing attitudes against dark Muslims, called *moros*, and, by extension, black people from sub-Saharan Africa had existed for a long time in Iberia and expressed themselves in Portugal's dealings with Kongo.

Kongolese royalty wore Portuguese dress, listened to church music and hymns, and drank wine imported from the Canaries. Lay assistants converted many urban and villager commoners to Catholicism, and schoolmasters instructed children at churches and chapels. The result was an African Creole culture, in which the veneration of territorial and ancestral spirits was combined with Catholicism. As the story of Dona Beatriz Kimpa Vita demonstrates, this Creole culture should not be viewed as a simple copy of European culture. Instead, as with the Creole cultures of the Americas, it was a creative adaptation of traditions: in this case, of Portuguese Catholicism to the indigenous African spiritual and cultural heritage, in the same way that East and West Africa adapted to Coptic Christianity or Islam and represented genuine variations of African culture.

Kongo began to sell slaves to Portuguese traders as early as 1502 for labor on the sugar plantations of the island of São Tomé. By the mid-1500s, the kings permitted the export of a few thousand slaves a year. But Portugal wanted more slaves, and in 1571 the crusader king Sebastião I (r. 1557–1578), who renewed Henry the Navigator's devotion to territorial conquest, chartered a member of the aristocracy with creating a colony in the adjacent kingdom of Ndongo for the mining of salt and silver by slaves. At first, this holder of the charter assisted the king of Ndongo in defeating rebels; but when his colonial aims became clear, the king turned against him, and a full-scale Portuguese war of conquest and for slaves erupted.

In this war, which lasted with short interruptions from 1579 to 1657, the Portuguese allied themselves with Ibangala bands. The Ibangala were a large group of loosely organized, fierce warriors from the eastern outreaches of Kongo and Ndongo into central Africa who raided in both kingdoms for slaves. Their propaganda as well as their swift campaigns threw the population into fear and turmoil. Tales of cannibalism and the forcible recruitment of child soldiers spread by word of mouth. The Ibangala reputation for fierceness was enhanced by their consumption of large quantities of palm wine and imported Portuguese wine from the Canaries, the latter received from traders in payment for slaves. Together, a few hundred Portuguese musketeers and tens of thousands of Ibangalas raided the kingdoms of Ndongo and Kongo for slaves, often capturing as many as 15,000 a year.

The war reduced the resourceful Queen Nzinga (r. 1624–1663) of Ndongo to a guerilla fighter. In the end, thanks to an alliance with some Ibangalas, she recreated a kingdom, greatly reduced in size, that also engaged in the slave trade. The widening conflict also spilled over into Kongo, where Portuguese and allied Ibangala troops exploited a long civil war (1665–1709) and enslaved even Catholic and Antonian Christians. The war expanded further when new entrants onto the scene, the Dutch West India Company, mistakenly assumed that the small numbers of Portuguese troops would be no match in a quick conquest for the coastal forts. Thanks to Brazilian help, however, Portugal was able to drive out the Dutch. The latter decided to return to a more peaceful trade for slaves from other fortified strongholds on the African west coast.

**The Dutch in South Africa**    In 1652, the Dutch built a fort on the South African coast to supply fresh water and food to ships traveling around the Cape of Good Hope. Employees of the company, working on time contracts, grew wheat on

**Kongolese Cross of St. Anthony.** Considered an emblem of spiritual authority and power, the Christian cross was integrated into Kongo ancestral cults and burial rituals and was believed to contain magical protective properties. In Antonianism, the religious reform movement launched by Dona Beatriz, or Kimpa Vita, in 1704, St. Anthony of Padua, a thirteenth-century Portuguese-born saint, became known as Toni Malau, or "Anthony of Good Fortune," and was the patron of the movement. His image was widely incorporated into religious objects and personal items, such as this cross.

**Queen Nzinga.** In this contemporary engraving, Queen Nzinga is shown conducting negotiations with the Portuguese in 1622. She sits on a slave's back to avoid having to stand in the presence of a person beneath her rank.

small lots and bought cattle from the Khoi, local cattle breeders. A few wealthy landowners imported the first black slaves in 1658, from Dahomey, on the West African coast, to convert the original Dutch smallholdings into larger wheat and grape plantations. Gradually, a culturally Dutch settler society emerged, which included Protestants fleeing religious persecution in France and Germany.

The majority of these settlers were urban craftspeople and traders, while most of the actual farmers employed slaves from Mozambique, the island of Madagascar, and even as far away as Indonesia, the epicenter of Dutch colonial ambitions in the East Indies. Around 1750, there were about 10,000 *Boers* (Dutch for "farmer") in the Cape Colony, easily outnumbered by slaves. Through relentless land expansion into the interior, ranchers destroyed the Khoi, forcing their absorption into other local groups. The Boers governed themselves, following the model of Dutch representative institutions. Their descendants, who called themselves "Afrikaners," would one day fight the Zulu for land and the British for independence and create the system of apartheid in South Africa. Today, they share political power and a troubled political legacy with their black African countrymen.

# American Plantation Slavery and Atlantic Mercantilism

The patterns of African slavery were quite different from the patterns of American plantation slavery. While European slave traders exploited existing African slave systems, the American plantation slave system had its roots in the eastern Christian religious civilization of Byzantium. There, the Roman institution of agricultural estate slavery survived, in both law and practice. Imperial estates on the Mediterranean islands of Cyprus and Crete employed Muslim prisoners as well as captives from the Russian steppes as slaves for the cultivation of such labor-intensive crops as wine and olive oil. After 1191, when crusaders conquered Cyprus from Byzantium, crusader landlords and Venetian and Genoese merchants expanded into sugar production, which had been introduced in the eastern Mediterranean by Arabs in the period 800–1000. Two and a half centuries later, Venetians, Spaniards, and Portuguese established slave-based sugarcane plantations on the islands of Madeira, the Canaries, and São Tomé off the West African coast.

### The Special Case of Plantation Slavery in the Americas

**Plantation slavery:** Economic system in which slave labor was used to grow cash crops such as sugarcane, tobacco, and cotton on large estates.

In examining the rise and perpetuation for more than three centuries of the patterns of American **plantation slavery**, a number of questions arise: How many Africans were forcibly taken from Africa to the Americas? Who were they, and who were the people who exploited their labor? What institutions were created to capture, transport, supply, and work slaves? What did the labor of the African slaves help to build? And, perhaps most of all, why did this system develop the way it did—and last so long?

**Numbers**    The enslavement of Africans for labor in the Western Hemisphere constituted the largest human migration—voluntary or involuntary—in world history before the later nineteenth century. Though it is estimated that millions of Africans had earlier been taken into servitude in the Muslim world from the eighth to the fourteenth century, their numbers are dwarfed by those shipped across the Atlantic from the fifteenth through the early nineteenth century.

While the figures have been hotly debated by scholars and activists over recent decades, the latest estimates put the numbers of Africans shipped out of Africa at around 12.5 million—more than twice the number taken in the so-called Oriental slave trade to the Middle East and Indian Ocean basin during the period 700–1400. Nearly half of these slaves, 5.8 million, went to Brazil. While historical demographers and other scholars try to determine how many slaves died in the process of being transferred to the African coast after their initial capture and how many more perished at sea, their conclusions are at present only tentative. However, most estimates place the numbers of slaves lost during these transfers at another 1.4 million, or 12 percent, with a total of 11 million reaching the American shores. These figures, it should be noted, exclude the numbers killed in the African slave raids and wars themselves, which will probably never be precisely known (see Map 19.2).

**Chattel:** Literally, an item of moveable personal property; chattel slavery is the reduction of the status of the slave to an item of personal property of the owner, to dispose of as he or she sees fit.

**Chattel Slavery**    By the mid-eighteenth century African slaves everywhere in the New World had been reduced to the status of **chattel**. The perfect expression of this condition may be found in the famous Dred Scott decision, handed down by the US Supreme Court a century later, in 1857. In the court's opinion, the chief justice, Roger B. Taney, forcefully stated that black African slaves "had no rights which a white man was bound to respect."

Within this statement we see another qualitatively different element from earlier kinds of slavery: what came to be known as the "color line." While color was sometimes not the determining factor in the early years of American slavery, it had very much come to be that by the eighteenth century. The equation of blackness with slavery prompted assumptions over time of African inferiority and

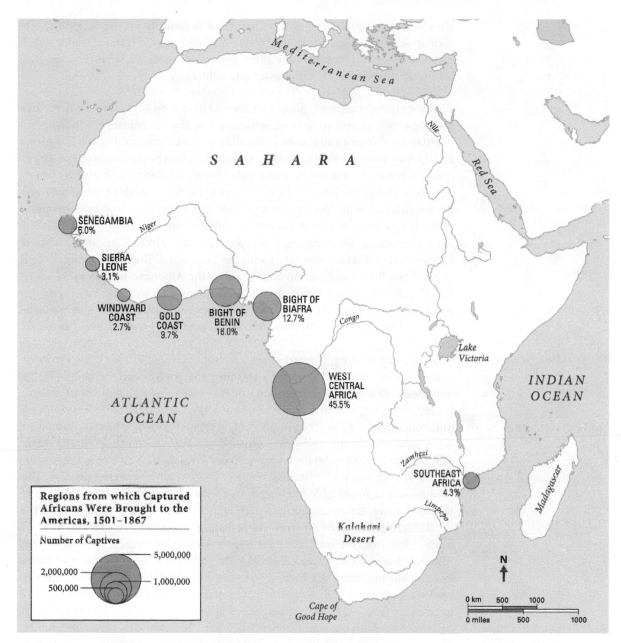

MAP 19.2 **Regions from which Captured Africans Were Brought to the Americas, 1501–1867.**

created the basis for the modern expression of the phenomenon of racism, a problem that has plagued all societies touched by the institutions of African slavery to this day.

Historians have long debated the role of present-day sensibilities and issues in the study of the past. The practice of looking at the past through the lens of the present is called **presentism**. Of course, everyone brings his or her own views and biases along when studying history. Historians, however, consciously try to distance themselves from these while attempting to empathetically enter the past.

**Presentism:** A bias toward present-day attitudes, especially in the interpretation of history.

Nowhere is this problem more evident than in looking for the origins of the plantation system and African slavery. Here, the origins are certainly modest and distant in time and present many alternatives. But, above all, what those origins led to remains repellent to our present sensibilities.

**Caribbean Plantations** Soon after the first European voyages to the Americas and the establishment of Spanish settlements in the Caribbean, the indigenous population of Taínos and Caribs all but disappeared, decimated by the European smallpox against which the native peoples were helpless. Beginning in the sixteenth century, Native Americans on the mainland were similarly decimated by smallpox. To replenish the labor force, as early as 1511, the Spanish crown authorized the importation of 50 African slaves for gold mining on the island of Hispaniola. In the following decades thousands more followed for work on newly established sugar plantations. The Africans, at this point primarily from Senegambia, shared a similar set of disease immunities with the Europeans. They were acclimated to tropical conditions and had no home base in the American islands to which to flee. For their European overlords, this made them ideal workers. Indeed, by the late sixteenth century African slaves outnumbered Europeans in the Spanish-controlled islands and in Mexico and Peru, where they were primarily involved in mining.

Apart from mining, plantation work for sugar production is among the most arduous forms of labor. Sugarcane leaves have sharp edges and the mature stalks must be cut down with *machetes*—long, heavy knives. The stalks are then bundled, loaded into a cart, and carried to a mill. The early mills utilized horizontal rotating millstones (later versions used stone or metal rollers) turned by human, animal, or water power. Once the stalks were crushed and their juice extracted, the waste was used as food for animals, or occasionally for slaves. The refining process involved boiling successive batches of juice, itself a hot and taxing process. The charred animal bones added to the refining were often supplemented by those of deceased slaves, thus contributing a particularly sinister element to the process.

The average slave field hand on a sugar plantation was estimated to live just 5 or 6 years. Early on, the workforce was largely male, which meant that there were relatively few children to replenish the slave population. With the price of slaves low and the mortality rate high, it was economically more desirable to literally work slaves to death and buy more than to make the extra investments necessary to cultivate families. Not surprisingly, revolts, work slowdowns, and sabotage of equipment and cargoes were frequent, with punishments being severe and public. Slaves were flogged and branded for minor infractions and maimed, castrated, hanged, burned, and sometimes dismembered for more severe crimes.

**Mercantilism: Political theory according to which the wealth derived from the mining of silver and gold and the production of agricultural commodities should be restricted to each country's market, with as little as possible expended on imports from another country.**

**Mercantilism in Action in the Caribbean** With the decline of Spanish power and the rise of the North Atlantic maritime states during the seventeenth century, a profound shift of the political balance in the Caribbean took place. Portugal, Spain, the Netherlands, Great Britain, and France all followed a similar path to enrichment that came to be known as **mercantilism**—that is, when the wealth of the state depends on having the maximum amount of gold and silver in its treasury. Thus, states should keep their economies blocked off from competitors and import as little and export as much as possible. Colonies were seen as vital

**Grinding sugarcane.** The steps in the making of refined sugar were elaborate and backbreaking. In the center, a wagon brings the harvested cane in from the fields, while slaves in the foreground sort the stalks under the watchful eyes of an overseer. The wind-powered mill uses rollers to crush the cane and extract its juice for boiling.

to this economic system, because they supplied raw materials to the European homeland and provided safe markets for goods manufactured in the home country.

It followed that one way to enhance your riches was to capture those of your rivals. Thus, from the late sixteenth through the early eighteenth centuries, the navies of the Dutch, English, French, Spanish, and Portuguese all attacked each other's shipping interests and maritime colonies. The Spanish, with their lucrative treasure fleets from Acapulco and through the Caribbean along the Spanish Main, were the favorite targets of all. Moreover, all of these governments issued "letters of marque" allowing warships owned by individuals or companies called **privateers** to prey on the shipping of rival powers for a share in the prize money they obtained. Not surprisingly, a number of individuals also went into this business for themselves as pirates.

The growing trade in plantation commodities from the Caribbean compelled Spain's European competitors to oust the Spanish from their valuable sugar islands. Thus, the rising naval power of England seized Jamaica from Spain in 1655. France, by the mid-seventeenth century the premier continental European power, followed a decade later in seizing the western part of Hispaniola, which came to be called Saint-Domingue.

This process was accompanied by two developments that enhanced the mercantilist economics of both powers. First, English and French as well as Dutch merchants became involved in the African slave trade, usurping the Portuguese near-monopoly on the traffic. The second was that the growing demand for molasses (a syrup that is a by-product of sugar refining) and the even greater popularity of its fermented and distilled end product, rum, pushed both sugar planting and slavery to heights that would not reach their peak until after 1750. As we will see in more detail, sugar, slaves, molasses, and rum form the vital legs of the famous triangular trade that sustained the Atlantic economic system.

**Privateers:** Individuals or ships granted permission to attack enemy shipping and to keep a percentage of the prize money the captured ships brought at auction; in practice, privateers were often indistinguishable from pirates.

**Indentured laborers:** Poor workers enrolled in European states with an obligation to work in the Americas for 5–7 years in return for their prepaid passage across the Atlantic.

"The Negroes are so wilful and loth to leave their own country, that they have often leap'd out of the canoes . . . into the sea, and kept under water until they were drowned. . . . They have a more dreadful apprehension of Barbadoes than we can have of hell."

—Thomas Phillips, "The Voyage of the Ship *Hannibal* of London," 1693

The human toll, however, was appalling. Barbados, for example, was settled initially in 1627 by English planters, who grew tobacco, cotton, indigo, and ginger, employing English and Irish **indentured laborers**. In 1640, however, planters switched to the more profitable sugarcane. English and Irish indentured laborers now proved so unwilling to leave their home countries for Barbados that law courts in the home ports resorted to convicting them on trumped-up charges and sentencing them to "transportation." Many others were tricked or seized by press-gangs and sent there. So great was the mortality of their African counterparts that they had to be shipped to the sugar islands at a rate of two to one in order to keep the population from declining.

**The Sugar Empire: Brazil** The Portuguese first planted sugarcane as a crop in Brazil in the 1530s, well before Caribbean planters began to grow it and a generation after the original trade in brazilwood (a red dye) was established. Portuguese colonists turned to the production of sugar because, unlike their counterparts in the Caribbean, Mexico, and Peru, they did not find any gold or silver. Like the Spanish, the Portuguese crown repeatedly issued edicts to the colonists to refrain from enslaving indigenous people for work on the sugar plantations; these edicts, however, were widely ignored. In addition, in the 1530s, the Portuguese trading network on the central African coast began to supply the colony with African slaves. By the end of the century, a dramatic rise in demand for sugar in Europe increased the importation of African slaves, of which the Portuguese carefully cultivated their carrying monopoly. The insatiable demand of the sugar industry for slaves received a further boost in 1680 when enslavement of Indians was finally abolished, and in 1690 the discovery of gold in Minas Gerais, in the interior, led to a gold boom and increased demand for labor even more. Brazil ultimately became the final destination of nearly half of all the slaves transported to the Americas. Indeed, Brazil went on to be the largest slave state in the world, with about two-fifths of its entire population consisting of people of African descent, and was the last country in the Americas to give up the institution, in 1888 (see Map 19.3).

## Slavery in British North America

Modern historians have identified a plantation zone which, in 1750, extended unbroken from the Chesapeake Bay in England's North American colonies to Brazil, embracing the entire Caribbean. This zone represented a pattern unprecedented in world history. No system of cash cropping had ever extended over so much territory or brought so much profit to its owners and investors. It created the largest demand for human labor yet seen, which after 1700 was satisfied almost exclusively through the African slave trade. As we noted in the beginning of this section, this in turn created a nearly immutable color line that defined a permanent underclass and identified blackness with slavery and inferiority. Though it was eventually destined to die out in the northernmost British and French possessions as well as the northern United States, legal slavery at one time extended far beyond the plantation zone into what is now Canada.

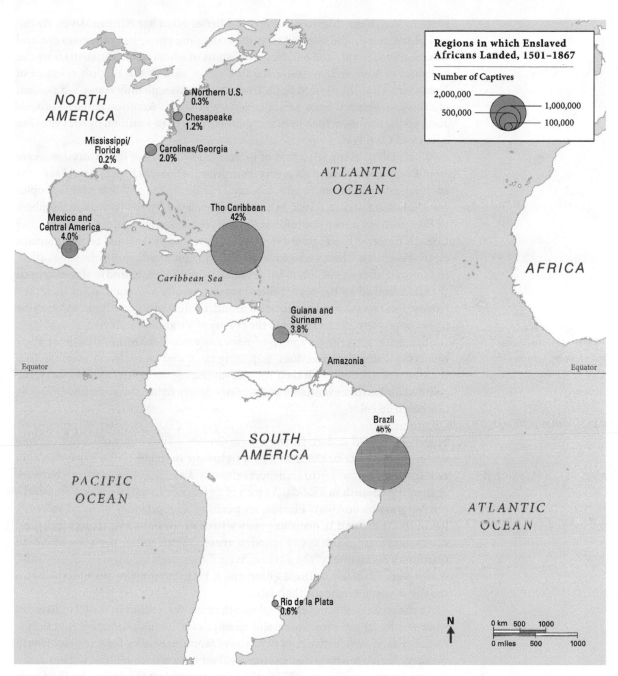

MAP 19.3 **Regions in which Enslaved Africans Landed, 1501–1867.**

**The "Sot Weed" Enterprise**    As we saw in preceding chapters, the first permanent English settlements in the Americas were the for-profit enterprise at Jamestown
in 1607 and the religious "errand in the wilderness" of the initial settlements in
Massachusetts from 1620 on. Both would soon count Africans among them,
though their descendants in Jamestown would be by far the more economically
important. In August of 1619 a Dutch privateer surprised a Portuguese slaver en

route to Vera Cruz, Mexico, and relieved her of 60 of her African slaves. By the end of the month, the ship put in at the struggling enterprise of Jamestown and disembarked "twenty and odd Negroes," some of whom were Christians from the kingdom of Kongo. These were the first slaves sold in the English colonies of North America. They would be far from the last. Though only about 3–5 percent of the slaves shipped from Africa ended up in North America, through procreation on the continent their numbers grew to more than 4 million by the eve of the American Civil War.

Their labor, along with that of increasing numbers of indentured workers from Europe, was needed for a new enterprise that, it was hoped, would save the colonial enterprise from failure: tobacco. The Powhatan and other local peoples grew tobacco for themselves, but it was considered by the increasing numbers of European smokers to be inferior to the varieties grown in the Caribbean. The English, however, had acquired some of the Caribbean plants and begun intensive cultivation in the Chesapeake Bay region of this "sot weed," as it came to be called. Indentured labor was widely used, but those workers were bound to stay only until they had worked off the cost of their passage, usually 5–7 years. After that, they worked for wages or acquired their own land. Under these conditions, slaves came to be the preferred labor source in the colony of Virginia.

**Manumission:** The process by which slaves are legally given freedom.

Though a surprising number of Africans earned **manumission** from their owners, gaining their freedom, acquiring land, and on occasion even starting their own plantations with their own slaves during the seventeenth century, the colonial authorities eventually passed laws firmly fixing the slave underclass as one based on color.

**Sugar, Rice, and Indigo in the Lower South**    The colony of Carolina came under the purview of the Lords Proprietors in Barbados, who began sending settlers in 1670 as a way to transport religious dissenters and to form a bulwark against the Spanish in Florida. As part of a vast pine forest running from southern Virginia to northern Florida, its position as a provider of naval stores—pitch, tar, rosin, and turpentine—as well as tall, straight tree trunks for ships' masts, was vital in the age of wooden vessels. Even today, the state of North Carolina's nickname is "the Tarheel State." Although indentured laborers and slaves were involved in these enterprises, plantation crops were destined to see the largest demand for their labor.

In the seventeenth and early eighteenth centuries, settlers in the Carolinas ran what was by far the most successful attempt ever to enslave Native Americans. As many as 50,000 Native American slaves labored there by the early eighteenth century. Native resistance to slaving resulted in war between the settlers and a Native American alliance in 1715–1717 that almost lost the colony for the Lords Proprietors. The settlers, angry with what they considered the mismanagement of the Lords Proprietors, appealed to the crown, and South Carolina was split off in 1719 and set up as a royal colony shortly thereafter. Deprived of Native Americans for slaves, the colonies began to import large numbers of West African slaves as the Dutch dominance of the trade gave way to the British. This initial wave of slave immigration ultimately grew to a point that made South Carolina the only North American colony, and later state, in which African Americans outnumbered those of European descent.

In addition, South Carolina produced many of the same plantation commodities as Brazil and the Caribbean (such as sugarcane, molasses, and rice), along with one vitally important new addition: indigo, which was destined to become the colony's most important cash crop until the cotton boom of the nineteenth century.

The dark blue dye produced from the tropical plant *Indigofera tinctoria* had been grown extensively throughout Asia, the ancient Mediterranean, and North and West Africa. A similar American species, *Indigofera suffruticosa*, had long been in use in Mexico and Central America. Maritime countries with Indian and East Asian connections imported vast quantities of it into Europe, while the Spanish began to cultivate the American variety. Sales in northern Europe were initially hampered because there indigo competed with the local production of dyes made from the woad plant. Restrictions on imports were gradually lifted, and

TO BE SOLD on board the Ship *Bance-Island*, on tuesday the 6th of *May* next, at *Ashley-Ferry*, a choice cargo of about 250 fine healthy NEGROES, just arrived from the Windward & Rice Coast. —The utmost care has already been taken, and shall be continued, to keep them free from the least danger of being infected with the SMALL-POX, no boat having been on board, and all other communication with people from *Charles-Town* prevented.
Austin, Laurens, & Appleby.

*N. B.* Full one Half of the above Negroes have had the SMALL-POX in their own Country.

**Advertisement for a Slave Auction.** In this notice from 1766, potential slave buyers in Charleston, South Carolina, are informed of the time and place for the sale of a "choice cargo" of recently arrived Africans. As Charleston was undergoing a smallpox epidemic at the time, potential customers are reassured that the captives are healthy and likely to be immune to the disease.

South Carolina entered an indigo boom starting in the 1740s. The burgeoning need for labor in planting, stripping the leaves, fermenting, cleaning, draining, scraping, and molding the residue into balls or blocks—all accompanied by a considerable stench—drove the slave trade even further.

The last new English possession in southern North America prior to 1750 was Georgia. The southern regions of what was to become the colony of Georgia had been claimed by the Spanish as early as 1526 as part of their exploration of Florida and the Gulf Coast. Attempts by the French to found a colony near Port Royal, South Carolina, and Fort Caroline (near present-day Jacksonville) in the 1560s were ultimately undone. With the expansion of the English presence in the seventeenth century and the French concentrating on their vast claims in Canada and the Mississippi valley, the territory between Carolina and the Spanish fort at St. Augustine became increasingly disputed.

Into this situation stepped James Oglethorpe (1696–1785), the only founder of an English colony in North America who lived to see it become part of the United States. Oglethorpe's vision was to set up a colony for England's poor, debtors (who would otherwise be imprisoned), and dispossessed. He obtained a royal charter for his idea and in 1733 landed with his first band of settlers at the site of the modern city of Savannah. After buying land from the local Native Americans, he began to develop the colony as a free area in which slavery was banned. The Spanish attempted to claim Georgia in 1742 but were repulsed. Pressed by settlers bringing their slaves in from South Carolina, Georgia's ban on slave labor was soon rescinded. By the end of Oglethorpe's life, which he spent in retirement in England, Georgia had developed its own slave-based plantation economy, producing rice, sugar, indigo, and, on the Sea Islands along the coast, a fine, long-fiber variety of cotton, which proved to be a harbinger of the commodity that would ensure slavery's survival in the United States until 1865.

## The Fatal Triangle: The Economic Patterns of the Atlantic Slave Trade

As mentioned, the European countries that successively dominated the transportation of slaves from the West African coast moved steadily northward in a pattern that paralleled their naval and merchant marine power. That is, during the fifteenth and sixteenth centuries, Portugal had an effective monopoly on the trade from outposts in Senegambia, Elmina, and Ndongo. The success of Dutch and English privateers encouraged more concerted economic warfare and, with it, the seizure by the Dutch of Elmina in 1637. Now it was the Dutch who became the principal slave carriers, part of a pattern of aggressive colonizing that made the Netherlands the world's richest country in per capita terms through much of the seventeenth century. The rise of England's naval power at the expense of the Dutch and the fading of the Spanish and Portuguese naval presence allowed the English—and, to a lesser extent, the French—to dominate the slave trade. By the mid-eighteenth century, as the trade approached its height, it had become the base upon which the world's most lucrative economic triangle was constructed (see Map 19.4).

MAP 19.4  **The North Atlantic System, ca. 1750.**

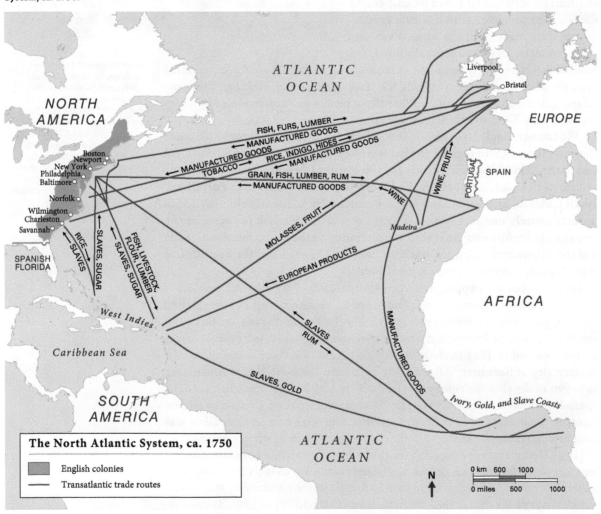

**Rum, Guns, and Slaves**    As we have seen, England's colonies in the Americas, especially those in the Caribbean, were by the eighteenth century producing valuable crops, including sugar, tobacco, cotton, and indigo, for export to the Old World. Tobacco was raised mainly in England's North American colonies, along with some cotton for export to England, though at this point England still imported most of its cotton from India. So profitable were these exports that, in keeping with the policy of mercantilism, the crown passed a series of acts in 1651 and 1660 that produced even greater profits for merchants in the motherland. The Navigation Acts required that all goods imported to England from American colonies had to be transported only on English ships, thereby guaranteeing a virtual monopoly on transatlantic trade.

British merchants acquired enormous profits through their colonial trading practices, particularly with the Atlantic colonies. We are afforded a good example of how this worked through an analysis of the **Atlantic system**, or the "triangular trade." In general terms, British ships would leave home ports in either their North American colonies or Britain with goods of various kinds, then travel to ports along the western coast of Africa, where these goods would be exchanged for African slaves; these ships would then sail across the Atlantic, where slaves would be exchanged for goods produced in western Atlantic colonies; and finally, these goods would be carried back to the home port.

One common pattern consisted of the following stages: An English ship loaded with New England rum would sail from Europe to the western coast of Africa, where the rum would be exchanged for a cargo of slaves; laden with slaves, the ship would then sail westward across the Atlantic to sugar colonies in the Caribbean, where the slaves would be exchanged for a cargo of molasses; the ship would sail to New England, where the molasses would be processed into rum. A variant pattern consisted of British ships leaving their home ports—increasingly Liverpool and Bristol, the ports that benefited most dramatically from the slave trade— loaded with manufactured goods, such as guns, knives, textiles, and assorted household wares. They would sail to the western coast of Africa, where these goods would be exchanged for a cargo of slaves, then sail westward across the Atlantic to the British colony of Virginia, where their human cargo would be exchanged for tobacco; they would then sail eastward across the Atlantic to their home ports in Britain, where the tobacco would be unloaded and then sold to British and European merchants.

**Atlantic system:** Economic system in which European ships would exchange goods for slaves in West Africa and slaves would then be brought to America and exchanged for goods that would be carried back to the home port.

**The Middle Passage**    Following capture in Africa, prisoners were usually marched to slave markets and embarkation ports roped, chained, or ganged together by forked tree limbs. Slave lots were then wholesaled to middlemen or auctioned directly to foreign factors. From this point they would be imprisoned in fortified slave pens called "barracoons" until the next ship bound for their sale destination arrived. But it was on the voyage from Africa to the Americas, the infamous "Middle Passage," that the full horror of the slave's condition was most fully demonstrated.

Because the profits involved in transportation were so high for captains, officers, and even crewmen, they constantly experimented with ways to pack the maximum number of human beings into the holds of their ships. Because a certain percentage of mortality was expected during a voyage that lasted from a few weeks to

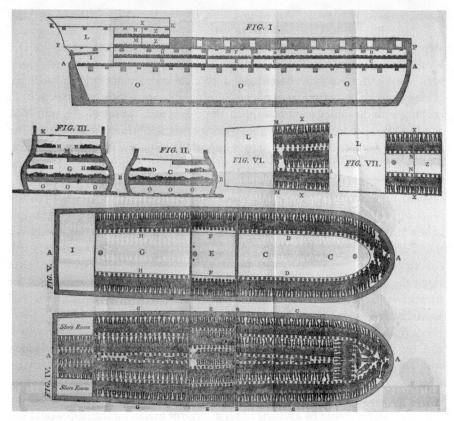

**Plan of a Slave Ship, 1789.** This image, based on the *Brooks*, a Liverpool slave ship, was one of the first to document the horrors of the slave trade. It shows the captives laid like sardines below deck. In such conditions slaves perished at the rate of 10–30 percent during the Middle Passage. The engraving was widely distributed by British abolitionists, who eventually succeeded in banning the trade in 1807.

nearly 2 months, some ship captains favored "tight packing"—deliberate over-crowding on the assumption that a few more captives might survive than on a ship with fewer captives but a higher rate of survival. On the other hand, some captains favored the "loose pack" method, with the assumption that a higher number would survive if given marginally more room. In either case, conditions were abominable.

Due to well-founded fears of slave mutiny, the holds of slave ships were locked and barred and the hatchways and vents covered with iron gratings. The slaves were chained to tiny bunks arranged in tiers configured to maximize the space of the hold. Food was minimal, usually corn mush, and sanitation nonexistent. Small groups of captives would be brought up on deck on a rotating basis to be haphaz-ardly washed of their vomit and feces with buckets of frigid ocean water thrown at them by the crew. They would then be "danced" for minimal exercise and sent back down, and the next group would be brought up. The dead, sick, and resistant would simply be thrown overboard. The ship and crew were also well armed to fight off mutineers and attacks by competitors or pirates. On landing at their des-tination, the slaves were again barracooned, cleaned up, and given better meals pending their auction to individual buyers. In the process somewhere between 10 and 30 percent of them died en route.

# Culture and Identity in the African Diaspora

The original meaning of the term "diaspora" referred to the dispersal of the Jews around the Roman Empire after their revolt of the first century CE was put down. Scholars now use the term more generally for the wide dispersal by forced or voluntary migration of any large group. In the case of the **African diaspora**, in which Africans moved to nearly all parts of the Americas primarily through the slave trade, the story is far too varied and complex for us to do more than note some general patterns related to culture and identity.

**African diaspora:** Dispersal of African peoples throughout the world, particularly the Americas, as part of the transatlantic slave trade.

## A New Society: Creolization of the Early Atlantic World

As discussed earlier in this chapter, one of the effects of the Portuguese implantation on African coasts through trade forts and colonies was the adaptation of coastal African societies to western Christianity and Portuguese culture. These societies were highly diverse. Some were clan- or lineage-based and welcomed trade with outsiders; others were militarily oriented and saw the new arrivals as unwelcome competitors; still others were kingdoms, some of which cooperated intermittently or permanently with the Portuguese and later with the Dutch, English, and French. Depending on the type or intensity of interaction, African Creole cultures emerged—that is, cultures in which some adaptation to Catholicism occurred and in which Africans appropriated certain outside cultural elements into their own heritage.

In earlier scholarship this creolization was often described as resulting in certain elements of an alien, colonizing culture uneasily grafted onto "genuine" Africanness. As in the case of Dona Beatriz and the rise of a Kongolese Catholicism, however, Creole culture has to be seen as an "authentic" phenomenon in its own right. This is similarly true for black Creole cultures in the Americas. Africans arrived with either their own local spiritual traditions or as Christians and Muslims, since foreign and indigenous slave raiders penetrating inland Africa made no religious distinctions among their victims. Either way, African slaves adapted to their plantation life through creolization or, as African Christian or Muslim Creoles, through further creolization, a process that expressed itself in distinct languages or dialects as well as synthetic (or hybrid) religious customs. Adaptation was thus not simple imitation but a creative transformation of cultural elements to fit the new conditions of a life of forced labor abroad.

Recent scholarship suggests that a key formative element in the development of culture and identity of Africans in the Americas lay in the influence of the central African Creoles from Kongo and Ndongo (today's Congo and Angola) up to the middle of the seventeenth century. The Christianity of some believers and its later variants helped to nurture this religion among Africans in the new lands, especially when it was reinforced by the religious practices of the slave owners. The mix of language and terms for a multitude of objects similarly gave the early arrivals a certain degree of agency and skill in navigating the institutions of slavery as they were being established.

An example of a Creole language that has survived for centuries is Gullah, used by the isolated slave communities along the coastal islands of South Carolina and

# Voodoo and Other New World Slave Religions

**Altar and Shrine from the Interior of the Historic Voodoo Museum in New Orleans.**

One prominent pattern of world history that we have seen a number of times already is the way indigenous elements work to shape the identity of imported religions as they are taken up by their new believers. Buddhism in China and Japan, for example, adopted elements from Daoism and Chinese folk beliefs as well as spirits and demons from Shinto. Christianity added Roman and Germanic elements to its calendar of holidays, architecture, and cult of saints. Islam in Iran and India and Christianity in Africa underwent similar processes. In Kongo, for example, the African Christian cult of St. Anthony merged Portuguese Catholic and Kongolese spiritual traditions into a new church. This trend of interaction continues today, where we find the African Christian churches among the fastest growing in the world and increasingly sending clergy and missionaries to Europe and the United States.

In the Americas three main strains of this kind of interaction and adaptation of imported and indigenous traditions developed over time and are still widely practiced today: Santeria is found primarily in Cuba and among the Spanish-speaking Africans of the Caribbean but is now also in the larger cities of North America with communities of Caribbean immigrants; vodoun, usually written as "voodoo," developed in Haiti

Georgia and still spoken by their descendants today. In Haiti, Creole (*Kreyòl*) is not only the daily spoken language but one also used in the media and in literary works. (French is recognized as the other national language, especially in law and official pronouncements.) Creole cultures thus typically involve not only the phenomenon of adaptation but also multiple identities—in language, religion, and culture.

**Music and Food**    It can justifiably be said that the roots of most popular music in the Americas may be found in Africa. Regardless of where they came from in Africa, slaves brought with them a wide variety of musical instruments, songs, and chants, all of which contributed to shaping the musical tastes of their owners and society at large. The widespread use of rhythmic drumming and dance in African celebrations, funerals, and even coded communications has come down to us today as the basis for music as diverse as Brazilian samba, Cuban and Dominican rumba and meringue, New Orleans jazz, and American blues, rock and roll, soul, and hip-hop. It is difficult to imagine American country and western music, or bluegrass, without the modern

and old Saint-Domingue and is widely practiced among African-descended French speakers around the Caribbean and in areas of Louisiana; and the adherents of Candomblé are mostly confined to Brazil.

All three are syncretic religions composed of elements that appear disconnected to outsiders but which practitioners see as part of an integrated whole. They intermingle Roman Catholic saints with West African natural and ancestral spirits and gods, see spiritual power as resident in natural things, and incorporate images of objects to represent a person or thing whose power the believer wants to tap or disperse (as in the use of so-called voodoo dolls). They also hold that proper ritual and sacrifices by priests and priestesses can tune into the spirits of the natural world. In some cases, they see these practices as curing sicknesses and raising the dead—the source of the famous "zombie" legends. Such innovations allowed the slaves to create a religious and cultural space in which they carved out autonomy from their masters—indeed, in which they *were* the masters. They also provided a kind of alternate set of beliefs which could be invoked alongside more mainstream Christian practices. In a real sense, they provided a precious degree of freedom for people who had almost no other form of it.

**Mami Wata.** Both a protector and a seducer, Mami Wata is an important spirit figure throughout much of Africa and the African Atlantic. She is usually portrayed as a mermaid, a snake charmer, or a combination of both. She embodies the essential, sacred nature of water, across which so many African Americans traveled in their diaspora.

## Questions

- How do black Christianity and voodoo religion show the new patterns of origins, interaction, and adoption that emerged after 1500?

- Can you think of more recent examples of syncretic religions? If so, which ones? Why are they syncretic?

descendant of a West African stringed instrument we know today as the banjo. The chants of field hands, rhyming contests, and gospel music contributed mightily to many of these genres.

Like music, cuisine passed easily across institutional barriers. Here, the dishes that most Americans consider "southern" have in many cases deep African roots. The first rice brought to the Carolinas was a variety native to the Niger inland delta in West Africa. Africans brought with them the knowledge of setting up and running an entire rice-based food system, which was established in the Carolina lowlands and Gulf Coast. The yam, the staple of West African diets, also made its way to the Americas. The heart of Louisiana Creole cooking, including rich and spicy gumbos, "dirty rice," jambalaya, and other dishes, comes from the use of the African vegetable okra and a heady mixture of African, American, and Asian spices along with rice.

**Plantation Life and Resistance**    Although nineteenth-century apologists for slavery frequently portrayed life under it as tranquil, the system was in fact one of constant real and implied violence.

**Slave Culture.** This ca. 1790 painting from Beaufort, South Carolina, shows the vibrancy of African American culture in the face of great hardship. Note the banjo, whose origins lie in West Africa and which would have a great impact on the development of American music.

"I hold that in the present state of civilization, where two races of different origin, and distinguished by color . . . are brought together, the relation now existing in the slaveholding states between the two, is, instead of an evil, a good— a positive good."

—Senator John C. Calhoun

Most slaves reconciled themselves to their condition and navigated it as best they could, but the reminders of their status were constantly around them. Obviously, those who endured the Middle Passage had violence thrust upon them immediately upon capture. Even those born into slavery, however, lived in squalid shacks or cabins; ate inadequate rations, perhaps supplemented with vegetables they were allowed to grow themselves; and spent most of their waking hours at labor.

Those working as house servants had a somewhat easier life than field hands. In some cases, they were the primary guardians, midwives, wet nurses, and even confidants of their masters' families. Often, there was considerable expressed affection between the household slaves and the master's family. But more often, this was tempered by the knowledge that they or their family members could be sold at any time, that infractions would be severely punished, and that they would be treated as unruly, temperamental children at best.

As we saw earlier, field hands led a far harder and shorter life. The price of slavery for the master was eternal vigilance; his nightmare was slave revolt. Over the years a variety of methods were developed to keep slaves in line and at their work. Overseers ran the work schedules and supervised punishments; drivers kept slaves at their work with a long bullwhip in hand to beat the slow or hesitant. Slaves leaving plantations on errands had to carry passes, and elaborate precautions were taken to discourage escape or even unauthorized visits to neighboring plantations. In the Carolinas, for example, owners spread tar on fence rails so that slaves attempting to climb or vault them would be marked for easy detection. Runaways were pursued with relentless determination by trackers with bloodhounds and flogged, branded, maimed, or castrated when returned.

**Punishing Slave Revolts.** John Gabriel Stedman (1744–1797) was a British–Dutch soldier and writer whose years in Surinam, on the northern coast of South America, were recorded in *The Narrative of a Five Year Expedition against the Revolted Negroes of Surinam* (1796). With its graphic depictions of slavery it became an important tract in the abolitionist cause. In this illustration, *A Negro Hung Alive by the Ribs to a Gallows*, engraved by the famous artist and Romantic poet William Blake (1757–1827), Stedman shows a rebel who was hung by his ribs for two days as punishment for his crimes. Masters routinely cut off the noses of their slaves, burnt them alive, and whipped them to death with impunity.

Given these conditions, slave behaviors designed to try to manage their work on their own terms or to get back at their owners were frequent. Slaves staged work slowdowns, feigned illnesses, sabotaged tools and equipment, or pretended not to understand how to perform certain tasks. Kitchen slaves would sometimes spit or urinate into soups or gravies. Despite the risks involved, runaways were quite common. Later, in the United States in the 1850s, enforcement of the Fugitive Slave Act would be a prime factor driving the country toward civil war.

Despite all their precautions, slave owners throughout the Americas constantly faced the prospect of slave insurrection. By some estimates, there were more than 250 slave uprisings involving 10 or more slaves during the four centuries of Atlantic slavery. In some cases, these rebellions were successful enough for the slaves to create their own isolated settlements where they could, for a time, live in freedom. These escapees were called *Maroons*. Three of the more successful

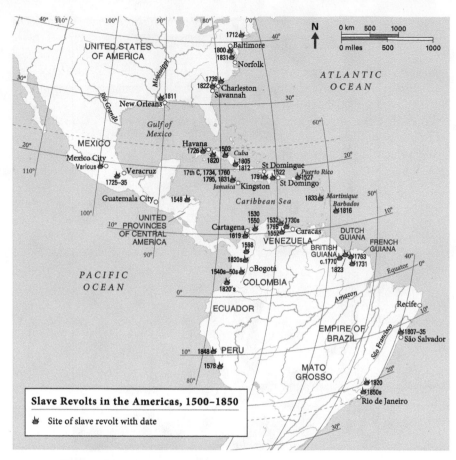

MAP **19.5**  **Slave Revolts in the Americas, 1500–1850.**

Maroon settlements existed in Jamaica, Colombia, and Surinam. In Brazil, slaves developed their own system of weaponless martial arts called *capoeira*, in which fighters walk on their hands and use their legs to strike. Map 19.5 lists some of the larger slave insurrections from 1500 to 1850.

# Putting It All Together

Portugal, the Netherlands, England, France, and Spain built up a fully evolved pattern of trading for plantation slaves on the Atlantic coast of Africa in the course of the sixteenth and seventeenth centuries. The trade took off toward the end of the sixteenth century, with 28,000 slaves annually, and by 1700 it had reached 80,000 annually, where it stayed until the early nineteenth century, when the slave trade was abolished. As for the patterns of state formation in Africa, on the whole, the more powerful a kingdom was, the fewer slaves it sold, given its own labor requirements. Conversely, the more conducive the circumstances were to the collapse of chiefly or royal rule and the emergence of raider societies such as the Imbangala, Ashante, or Dahomey, the more damaging the impact was on a given population.

Thus, no global judgment is possible. Undoubtedly, in some regions of western and central Africa the effects were grave, while in others, often directly adjacent, the impact was less decisive. Nonetheless, the period marked a profound transformation, with many areas depopulated by the slave trade, some enhanced through the trade and the introduction of new food crops like maize and cassava, and others undergoing creolization to some degree.

The interaction and adaptation patterns of Europeans and Africans in Africa and Europeans, Africans, and Native Americans in the Caribbean and Americas over the course of three centuries (1500–1800) created not just a new, two-hemisphere world system of trade but a new kind of society as well. The Atlantic slave trade was the foundation on which the mass production of cash crops and commodities, the first world pattern of its kind, was brought into being. This economic sphere was by far the richest of its kind in the world, but with it came the creation of an enduring social underclass and the foundation of modern racism.

Yet even as early as the 1750s, one finds the origins of the abolition movement—the international movement to end first the slave trade and ultimately slavery itself. Among the leaders of Europe's Enlightenment, thinkers were already calling for the end of the trade and institution. Within a few decades, works like the memoirs of the former slave and abolitionist Olaudah Equiano (ca. 1745–1797) would push the movement forward, as would the work of England's William Wilberforce (1759–1833), who actually lived to see the outlawing of the trade and of English slavery itself. Elsewhere, it would take a revolution, as in Haiti, or a civil war, as in the United States, for abolition to occur. In the Atlantic world, slavery finally ended in Brazil in 1888. But it persists informally in India, Africa, and the Middle East even today.

▶ For additional resources, including maps, primary sources, visuals, and quizzes, please go to www.oup.com/us/vonsivers. Please see the Further Resources section at the back of the book for additional readings and suggested websites.

## Against the Grain

# Oglethorpe's Free Colony

Set against the backdrop of both expanding colonial slavery and the hardening of the so-called color line, James Oglethorpe's dream of a colony of Georgia in which both slavery and rum were to be banned, and where the colonists were to consist of the "worthy poor" freed from the threat of debtor's prison, would appear to defy the patterns of the times. Oglethorpe, as a young member of the House of Commons, was appalled at the conditions of London prisons, and perhaps even more by the practice of imprisoning debtors and forcing them to pay for their own upkeep while incarcerated. Appointed to a parliamentary committee investigating the situation, he developed a scheme that he hoped would solve several problems plaguing English society: growing indebtedness on the part of the working poor and the jobless; rampant alcoholism fueled by cheap rum and gin; and migration to cities by the landless.

His solution was to found a colony as a haven for those most afflicted by these ills. He bought land at fair prices from the Creek people, ensured that skilled craftsmen and laborers were among the initial settlers, and laid out what became the city of Savannah in a design that called for houses with ample lots, a 45-acre farm outside the city for self-sufficiency, and numerous common areas and squares to create close-knit neighborhoods. To ensure that the labor of the immigrants would be valued, slavery was strictly forbidden, as was the slave-produced product of rum. While scholars differ on whether he was a true abolitionist, he did declare slavery to be "immoral" and felt that it violated English law.

As we saw in this chapter, however, his visionary aims ultimately ran aground on the shoals of the colony's position on the border with Spanish Florida. With Oglethorpe's retirement to England in 1750, his fellow trustees returned control of the colony to the British crown, and the ban on slavery was rescinded. The invention of the cotton gin in the 1790s began a process by which that commodity would become the most valuable export in the world and the bulwark of the US economy. And as cotton became king, the slave state of Georgia would be at the epicenter of its expansion.

- Why were institutions of slavery so prevalent in so many places in the world?

- Even though many people found slavery to be immoral on humanitarian and even economic grounds, the institution persisted for centuries in the Atlantic world. Why do you think it proved so difficult to dismantle?

# Thinking Through Patterns

▶ **On what was the pattern of kingdom and empire formation in Africa based during the period 1500–1800?**

What is remarkable about Africa during these 300 years is that it continued its pattern of kingdom and empire formation and actually did so on an accelerated pace, on the basis of increased intra-African trade. The half-dozen examples analyzed in this chapter could be applied to another dozen states. In the interior of Africa the pattern continued in spite of the demographic effects (in whatever form they had in specific regions) of the Atlantic slave trade.

The pattern of plantation production evolved over several centuries before it was transplanted to the islands of the Atlantic and the Caribbean as well as the Americas. It was above all a system for growing labor-intensive cash crops—indigo, sugar, tobacco—that relied increasingly on African slave labor. By 1800, the demand for plantation commodities by Europeans and the guns, textiles, rum, and other manufactured goods that Africans took in trade for slaves swelled the system to huge proportions. In turn, the mercantilist economics of western Europe regulated the trade within an efficient, tightly controlled, triangular system.

The gradual domination of African slavery in the Americas and Caribbean over other kinds of servitude created a pattern of racism, in which blackness was permanently associated with slavery. As the economics of slavery became entrenched, the participants in the system answered the criticism of slavery on moral grounds by claiming that black Africans were inherently inferior and thus deserved to be enslaved. The argument was essentially circular: They were enslaved because they were inferior, and they were inferior because they were slaves.

▶ **How did the patterns of slave trade and plantation slavery evolve in the Atlantic and the Americas?**

▶ **What are the historic roots from which modern racism evolved?**

In North America, long after slavery was abolished, these attitudes were preserved in law and custom in many places and reinforced during the colonization of Africa in the nineteenth century and in the practice of segregation in the United States. In Latin America—although racism is no less pervasive—racial views are more subtle. People describing themselves as *mulato*, *sambo*, or *pardo* have had a better chance to be recognized as members of their own distinct ethnic groups than in the United States, where until recently the census classified people simply as either black or Caucasian. The 2010 census form, however, expanded its choices to 14 racial categories and allowed people to check multiple boxes. Clearly, the complexities of race and ethnicity in the Americas are continuing to evolve.

# Patterns of Evidence: Sources for Chapter 19

## SOURCE 19.1

## Abd al-Rahman al-Saadi on the scholars of Timbuktu

**ca. 1655**

**B**orn in Timbuktu in 1596, Abd al-Rahman al-Saadi wrote, in Arabic, a chronicle entitled *Tarikh al-Sudan* (*History of the Sudan*). The document addresses the political, cultural, and religious history of the Songhay state in the fifteenth and sixteenth centuries, and it also offers detailed accounts of various states in the Niger River valley into al-Saadi's own day. Al-Saadi was particularly interested in the impact of Islamic thought and culture on the African kingdoms, as the following excerpt demonstrates. The document was discovered by a German explorer in the 1850s during his visit to Timbuktu.

**Hizb:** Segment.

**Badal:** Fifth rank in the Sufi hierarchy.

This is an account of some of the scholars and holymen who dwelt in Timbuktu generation after generation—may God Most High have mercy on them, and be pleased with them, and bring us the benefit of their *baraka* in both abodes—and of some of their virtues and noteworthy accomplishments. In this regard, it is sufficient to repeat what the trustworthy shaykhs have said, on the authority of the righteous and virtuous Friend of God, locus of manifestations of divine grace and wondrous acts, the jurist *Qāḍī* Muhammad al-Kābarī—may God Most High have mercy on him. He said: "I was the contemporary of righteous folk of Sankore, who were equaled in their righteousness only by the Companions of the Messenger of God—may God bless him and grant him peace and be pleased with all of them."

Among them were (1) the jurist al-Hājj, grandfather of *Qāḍī* 'Abd al-Rahmān b. Abī Bakr b. al-Hājj. He held the post of *qāḍī* during the last days of Malian rule, and was the first person to institute recitation of half a *hizb* of the Qur'ān for teaching purposes in the Sankore mosque after both the mid-afternoon and the evening worship. He and his brother Sayyid Ibrāhīm the jurist left Bīru to settle in Bangu. His tomb there is a well-known shrine, and it is said he is a **badal**. The following account is related on the authority of our virtuous and ascetic shaykh, the jurist al-Amīn b. Ahmad, who said, "In his day the

---

Source: Abd al-Rahman al-Saadi, *Timbuktu and the Songhay Empire*, trans. John Hunwick (Leiden, the Netherlands: Brill, 2003), 38–40.

Sultan of Mossi came campaigning as far as Bangu, and people went out to fight him. It so happened that a group of people were sitting with al-Hājj at that moment, and he uttered something over [a dish of] millet and told them to eat it. They all did so except for one man, who was his son-in-law, and he declined to do so because of their relationship by marriage. Then the holy man said to them, "Go off and fight. Their arrows will do you no harm." All of them escaped harm except for the man who did not eat, and he was killed in that battle. The Sultan of Mossi and his army were defeated and driven off, having gained nothing from the people of Bangu, thanks to the *baraka* of that sayyid.

From him is descended the Friend of God the Most High the jurist Ibrāhīm, son of the Friend of God Most High, the jurist *Qāḍī* ʿUmar who lived in Yindubuʿu, both of whom were righteous servants of God. It was Askiya *al-hājj* Muhammad who appointed ʿUmar *qāḍī* of that place. From time to time one of his sister's sons used to visit Timbuktu, and the jurist *Qāḍī* Mahmūd complained to Askiya *al-hājj* Muhammad that this man was slandering them to the people of Yindubuʿu. When the Askiya visited Tila the jurist *Qāḍī* ʿUmar came with a group of men from Yindubuʿu to pay him a courtesy call. The Askiya inquired after his sister's son, so ʿUmar presented him to him. The Askiya said, "You are the one who was been sowing discord between the jurist Mahmūd and your maternal uncle." The *qāḍī* was annoyed, and retorted, "You, who appointed one *qāḍī* in Timbuktu and another in Yindubuʿu, are the one sowing discord." Then he got up angrily and went off to the waterfront, saying to his companions, "Let us go off and cross the river and be on our way." When they got there, he wanted to cross it, but they said, "It is not yet time for the ferry. Be patient until it comes." He replied, "What if it does not come?" They realised that he was prepared to cross the river without a boat. So they restrained him and sat him down until the ferry came, and they all crossed over together—may God have mercy on them and bring us benefit through them. Amen!

▶ **Working with Sources**

1. Why did the scholars and holy men of Timbuktu draw a visitor's attention?

2. Are there indications in this document of a culture that was still fusing Islamic and non-Islamic traditions together?

## SOURCE 19.2

# Letter of Nzinga Mbemba (Afonso I) of Kongo to the King of Portugal

### 1526

A Portuguese sailor came into contact with the Kingdom of Kongo, which occupied a vast territory along the Congo River in central Africa, in 1483. When he returned in 1491, he was accompanied by Portuguese priests and

Portuguese products, and in the same year the Kongolese king and his son were baptized as Catholics. When the son succeeded his father in 1506, he took the Christian name Afonso and promoted the introduction of European culture and religion within his kingdom. His son Henrique was educated in Portugal and became a Catholic bishop. However, Afonso's kingdom began to deteriorate in subsequent decades, as the Portuguese made further inroads into his territory, pursuing ruthless commercial practices and trading in slaves captured in his dominions. In 1526, the king sent desperate letters to King João III of Portugal, urging him to control his own subjects and to respect the alliance—and the common Catholic faith—that bound the Europeans and the Africans.

Sir, Your Highness should know how our Kingdom is being lost in so many ways that it is convenient to provide for the necessary remedy, since this is caused by the excessive freedom given by your agents and officials to the men and merchants who are allowed to come to this Kingdom to set up shops with goods and many things which have been prohibited by us, and which they spread throughout our Kingdoms and Domains in such an abundance that many of our vassals, whom we had in obedience, do not comply because they have the things in greater abundance than we ourselves; and it was with these things that we had them content and subjected under our vassalage and jurisdiction, so it is doing a great harm not only to the service of God, but the security and peace of our Kingdoms and State as well.

And we cannot reckon how great the damage is, since the mentioned merchants are taking every day our natives, sons of the land and the sons of our noblemen and vassals and our relatives, because the thieves and men of bad conscience grab them wishing to have the things and wares of this Kingdom which they are ambitious of; they grab them and get them to be sold; and so great, Sir, is the corruption and licentiousness that our country is being completely depopulated, and Your Highness should not agree with this nor accept it as in your service. And to avoid it we need from those (your) Kingdoms no more than some priests and a few people to reach in schools, and no other goods except wine and flour for the holy sacrament. That is why we beg of Your Highness to help and assist us in this matter, commanding your factors that they should not send here either merchants or wares, because it is our will that in these Kingdoms there should not be any trade of slaves nor outlet for them. Concerning what is referred [to] above, again we beg of Your Highness to agree with it, since otherwise we cannot remedy such an obvious damage. Pray Our Lord in His mercy to have Your Highness under His guard and let you do forever the things of His service. I kiss your hands many times. . . .

(At our town of Kongo, written on the sixth day of July in 1526.)

Moreover, Sir, in our Kingdoms there is another great inconvenience which is of little service to God, and this is that many of our people, keenly desirous as they are of the wares and

Source: https://www2.stetson.edu/secure/history/hy10430/afonso.html

things of your Kingdoms, which are brought here by your people, and in order to satisfy their voracious appetite, seize many of our people, freed and exempt men, and very often it happens that they kidnap even noblemen and the sons of noblemen, and our relatives, and take them to be sold to the white men who are in our Kingdoms; and for this purpose they have concealed them; and others are brought during the night so that they might not be recognized.

And as soon as they are taken by the white men they are immediately ironed and branded with fire, and when they are carried to be embarked, if they are caught by our guards' men the whites allege that they have bought them but they cannot say from whom, so that it is our duty to do justice and to restore to the freemen their freedom, but it cannot be done if your subjects feel offended, as they claim to be.

And to avoid such a great evil we passed a law so that any white man living in our Kingdoms and wanting to purchase goods in any way should first inform three of our noblemen and officials of our court whom we rely upon in this matter, and these are Dom Pedro Manipanza and Dom Manuel Manissaba, our chief usher, and Goncalo Pires our chief freighter, who should investigate if the mentioned goods are captives or free men, and if cleared by them there will be no further doubt nor embargo for them to be taken and embarked. But if the white men do not comply with it they will lose the aforementioned goods. And if we do them this favor and concession it is for the part Your Highness has in it, since we know that it is in your service too that these goods are taken from our Kingdom, otherwise we should not consent to this....

(date of letter, October 18, 1526)

▶ **Working with Sources**

1. What do these documents indicate about the intersections of international commerce and the slave trade?

2. In what terms does King Afonso issue his protest to the Portuguese king, and why?

## SOURCE 19.3

# Documents concerning the slave ship *Sally*, Rhode Island

## 1765

Rhode Islanders were the principal American slave traders during the eighteenth century, during which a total of approximately 1,000 slave-trading voyages set out from the colony to Africa. The "triangular trade" between the Atlantic seaboard, the Caribbean, and West Africa was the main source of great wealth for many families in this small British settlement.

Source: John Carter Brown Library. http://cds.library
.brown.edu/projects/sally/documents.html

Among these families was that of John Brown, whose donation to a struggling college in Providence would lead to the renaming of the institution in his honor. Aware of their university's explicit connection to the profitable and lethal slave trade, archivists at Brown University have attempted to tell the full story of voyages like that of the *Sally*. In the excerpts that follow, lines from the ship's log are annotated with details of the events they describe; italicized text is transcribed directly from the log.

Log Book From the Slave Ship *Sally*.

### December 11, 1764: At James Fort, on the River Gambia

By early December, the Sally had arrived at James Fort, the primary British slave "factory" on Africa's Windward Coast. Located fifteen miles from the mouth of the Gambia River, James Fort was the collection point for slaves coming down from the interior, and British and North American ships routinely stopped there to acquire provisions and slaves. On December 11, Hopkins purchased thirteen Africans from Governor Debatt, the British official who ran the fort, in exchange for 1,200 gallons of rum and sundry stores.

### June 8, 1765: "Woman Slave hanged her Self between Decks"

While most slave ships worked their way along the coast, the Sally appears to have remained largely in one place, apparently at a small British slave "factory" near the mouth of the River Grande, in what is today Guinea-Bissau. Hopkins traded rum with passing slave ships, acquiring manufactured goods like cloth, iron bars, and guns, which he then used to acquire slaves. On June 8, 1765, he purchased his 108th captive. That same day, an enslaved woman committed suicide. She was the second captive to die on the ship.

Newport July 17, 1765
Sir

*Having heard by Capt Morris that you had Lost all your Hands in the River Basa I came down here, last Evening on purpose to Take Some method to suply the misfortune as much as Possable, by the Two Vessels Just about sailing from this place Capt Briggs & Capt Moor but Receiving your Letter of ye 15th May this morning which giving us Such favourable accounts of your Circumstance from what we had heard Quite aleviates our Misfortune and prevents dewing any thing further than Writing you by these opertunitys principaly to Inform you that (Notwithstanding our first orders to you & our Letter to Barbadoes of ye 4th Ultimo advising you to go to South Carolina,) that the market there is Surpriseingly Glutted with Slaves So that it will not by any means do to go there Therefore Recomend if you Can get £20 Sterling for your Well Slaves Land at Barbadoes to sell there . . . and Lay out ye Neet proceed in 30 hogshead Rum 8 or 10 hogshead Sugar & 3 or 4 Baggs of Cotton the remainder in full Weight money or Good Bills but money full Weight is 5 percent better for us than bills and proceed home, without giving yourself any further trouble about Loading with Salt But if your Slaves Should be in good order and you Cannot get that proceed to Jamaica and there Dispose of them for ye same of pay & proceed home, but Notwithstanding what we here advise if you think any other port in the Westindes will Do better Considering all ye Risque, you are At full Liberty to go and Inshort do by Vessel & Cargo in that Respect as if She wass your own all friends and particularly your family is Well*
M

2

*Burroughs is this morning gone to Providence in order to Carry your Letter to Mrs Hopkins. you may depend. . . . Friends nor money shall not be Wanting to make the Insurance you Wish for to your Wife whose Letter Mr Burrows opend in order to Relieve the aprehentions of his father & family from ye Maloncholy Tale Brought by Capt Morris*
*I am for Self & Co. your Assured Frend*
MB
*Copy Letter*
*to Capt Esek*
*Hopkins July*
*1765*

## July 17, 1765: The Browns receive word from Hopkins

In June, 1765, after months with no news from the Sally, the Browns received reports that the ship and crew had been lost. Those rumors were contradicted on July 17, when a letter belatedly arrived from Hopkins, safe on the River Grande. Though Hopkins reported the loss of one crewman and substantial loss of his cargo through leakage, the Browns were elated. Your letter "Quite Aleviates our Misfortune," they wrote.

## August 20, 1765: The Sally embarks for the Americas

On August 20, 1765, more than nine months after his arrival on the African coast, Hopkins acquired his 196th and final captive. Nineteen Africans had already died on the ship. A twentieth captive, a "woman all Most dead," was left behind as a present for Anthony, the ship's "Linguister," or translator. At least twenty-one Africans had been sold to other slave traders on the coast, bringing the Sally's "cargo" to about 155 people.

## August 28, 1765: "Slaves Rose on us was obliged fire on them and Destroyed 8"

Four more Africans died in the first week of the Sally's return voyage. On August 28, desperate captives staged an insurrection, which Hopkins and the crew violently suppressed. Eight Africans died immediately, and two others later succumbed to their wounds. According to Hopkins, the captives were "so Desperited" after the failed insurrection that "Some Drowned them Selves Some Starved and Others Sickened & Dyed."

**October, 1765: The Sally arrives in the West Indies**

The Sally reached the West Indies in early October, 1765, after a transatlantic passage of about seven weeks. After a brief layover in Barbados, the ship proceeded to Antigua, where Hopkins wrote to the Browns, alerting them to the scope of the disaster. Sixty-eight Africans had perished during the passage, and twenty more died in

the days immediately following the ship's arrival, bringing the death toll to 108. A 109th captive would later die en route to Providence.

**November 16, 1765: "Sales of Negroes at Public Vendue"**

When they dispatched the Sally, the Brown brothers instructed Hopkins to return to Providence with four or five "likely lads" for the family's use. The rest of the Sally survivors were auctioned in Antigua. Sickly and emaciated, they commanded extremely low prices at auction. The last two dozen survivors were auctioned in Antigua on November 16, selling, in one case, for less than £5, scarcely a tenth of the value of a "prime slave."

▶ **Working with Sources**

1. How do these documents illuminate the economic and market forces that were bound up in the transatlantic slave trade?

2. What were the practical consequences of viewing human slaves as a commercial product?

## SOURCE 19.4

# *The Interesting Narrative of the Life of Olaudah Equiano*

### 1789

This autobiography of a slave who would emerge as a leading voice in the abolitionist cause has been enormously significant for understanding Atlantic slavery. Equiano claimed to have been born a prince among the Igbo people of modern Nigeria around 1745, kidnapped as a child, and transported across the ocean to the West Indies and Virginia. Named by his first

Source: Henry Louis Gates, Jr., ed., *The Classic Slave Narratives* (New York: Mentor, 1987), 99–100, 102–103.

(of several) masters after the sixteenth-century king Gustav I of Sweden, "Gustavus Vas[s]a" would travel throughout the southern American colonies and the Caribbean, always longing to achieve his freedom. Shaming his Quaker master into honoring a promise, Equiano was freed in 1765, but he continued to suffer the indignities and risks attending a free black man living in a slave society. His published memoir was designed to galvanize antislavery forces, and his work elicited sufficient sympathy and respect to contribute to the abolition of the British slave trade (though not slavery itself) in 1807.

We set sail once more for Montserrat, and arrived there safe; but much out of humour with our friend, the silversmith. When we had unladen the vessel, and I had sold my venture, finding myself master of about forty-seven pounds, I consulted my true friend, the Captain, how I should proceed in offering my master the money for my freedom. He told me to come on a certain morning, when he and my master would be at breakfast together. Accordingly, on that morning I went, and met the Captain there, as he had appointed. When I went in I made my obeisance to my master, and with my money in my hand, and many fears in my heart, I prayed him to be as good as his offer to me, when he was pleased to promise me my freedom as soon as I could purchase it. This speech seemed to confound him; he began to recoil; and my heart that instant sunk within me. "What," said he, "give you your freedom? Why, where did you get the money? Have you got forty pounds sterling?" "Yes, sir," I answered. "How did you get it?" replied he. I told him, "very honestly." The Captain then said he knew I got the money very honestly and with much industry, and that I was particularly careful. On which my master replied, I got money much faster than he did; and said he would not have made me the promise which he did, had he thought I should have got the money so soon. "Come, come," said my worthy Captain, clapping my master on the back. "Come, Robert, (which was his name) I think you must let him have his freedom. You have laid your money out very well; you have received good interest for it all this time, and here is now the principal at last. I know Gustavus has earned you more than a hundred a year, and he will still save you money, as he will not leave you. Come, Robert, take the money." My master then said, he would not be worse than his promise; and, taking the money, told me to go to the Secretary at the Register Office, and get my manumission drawn up.

These words of my master were like a voice from heaven to me: in an instant all my trepidation was turned into unutterable bliss, and I most reverently bowed myself with gratitude, unable to express my feelings, but by the overflowing of my eyes, and a heart replete with thanks to God; while my true and worthy friend, the Captain, congratulated us both with a peculiar degree of heartfelt pleasure.

. . .

During our stay at this place [Savannah, Georgia], one evening a slave belonging to Mr. Read, a merchant of Savannah, came near our vessel, and began to use me very ill. I entreated him, with all the patience of which I was master, to desist, as I knew there was little or no law for a free negro here. But the fellow, instead of taking my advice, persevered in his insults, and even struck me. At this I lost all temper, and fell on him, and beat him soundly. The next morning his master came to our vessel, as we lay alongside the wharf, and desired me to come ashore that he might have me flogged all round the town, for beating his negro slave! I told him he had insulted me, and had given the provocation by first striking me. I had also told my Captain the whole affair that morning, and desired him to go along with me to Mr. Read, to prevent bad consequences; but he said that it did not signify, and if Mr. Read said any thing he would make matters up, and desired me to go to work, which I accordingly did.

The Captain being on board when Mr. Read came and applied to him to deliver me up, he said he knew nothing of the matter, I was a free man. I was astonished and frightened at this, and thought I had better keep where I was, than go ashore and be flogged round the town, without judge or jury. I therefore refused to stir; and Mr. Read went away, swearing he would bring all the constables in the town, for he would

have me out of the vessel. When he was gone, I thought his threat might prove too true to my sorrow; and I was confirmed in this belief, as well by the many instances I had seen of the treatment of free negroes, as from a fact that had happened within my own knowledge here a short time before.

There was a free black man, a carpenter, that I knew, who for asking a gentleman that he had worked for, for the money he had earned, was put into gaol; and afterwards this oppressed man was sent from Georgia, with false accusations, of an intention to set the gentleman's house on fire, and run away with his slaves. I was therefore much embarrassed, and very apprehensive of a flogging at least. I dreaded, of all things, the thoughts of being stripped, as I never in my life had the marks of any violence of that kind. At that instant a rage seized my soul, and for a little I determined to resist the first man that should attempt to lay violent hands on me, or basely use me without a trial; for I would sooner die like a free man, than suffer myself to be scourged, by the hands of ruffians, and my blood drawn like a slave.

▶ **Working with Sources**

1. **What did being free mean to Equiano? Was he disappointed in his change of status?**

2. **What role does the captain play in the narrative at this point?**

## SOURCE 19.5

# Casta paintings, Mexico

**Eighteenth century**

Some of the most remarkable visual records of colonial Mexico are the series of paintings called "casta" paintings, illustrating every racial combination of Spanish, mestizo, black, Native American, and other types thought possible in the New Spain of the eighteenth and early nineteenth centuries. Casta paintings were always created in a series, and each picture usually contains a male–female couple and at least one child. Occasionally more than one child and even other animal or human figures are depicted. At the top or bottom of the painting is an inscription that explains the racial mix shown in the image. At least 50 groups of these paintings have been identified, although very few survive today in complete series.

▶ **Working with Sources**

1. How do the inscription and the image work together, and what was the entire painting meant to convey?

2. Analyze the clothing styles depicted in the painting; do these clothes provide any indication of a "reality" that may appear in the work?

Source: De Espanol y Negra, Mulato (From Spaniard and Black, Mulatto), attributed to Jose de Alcibar, c. 1760. Denver Art Museum: Collection of Frederick and Jan Mayer. Photo (c)James O. Milmoe

# Chapter 20 1400–1750

# The Mughal Empire

## MUSLIM RULERS AND HINDU SUBJECTS

June 17, 1631, could hardly have been a less auspicious day for the family of the Mughal emperor Shah Jahan. Though he ruled over the most powerful empire in India's history and commanded unprecedented wealth, the emperor's beloved wife, Mumtaz Mahal, had just died in giving birth to their fourteenth child. The royal family was naturally plunged into mourning, a grief conveyed by the following lines read at the announcement of her death:

> The world is a paradise full of delights,
>
> Yet also a rose bush filled with thorns;
>
> He who picks the rose of happiness
>
> Has his heart pierced by a thorn.

Shah Jahan himself, however, plumbed far greater depths of depression. His beard turned gray, and it was said that he wept for nearly 2 years afterward. Indeed, his eyes grew so weak from his tears that he needed to wear glasses to read his daily correspondence. Inconsolable for months on end, he finally resolved to build a magnificent tomb complex for Mumtaz Mahal over her burial site along the Jumna (or Yamuna) River near the giant fortress at Agra. At a time when monumental building projects were the order of the day for Mughal rulers, this tomb, with its balance of deceptively simple lines,

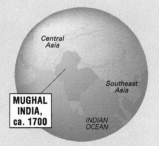

MUGHAL
INDIA,
ca. 1700

*ABOVE:* **The Taj Mahal (1631–1653), a magnificent architectural synthesis of Hindu and Muslim influences and Persian classicism.**

harmony of proportion, and technical skill, would become the most recognized symbol of India throughout the world: the Taj Mahal.

Beyond its architectural elegance, however, the Taj Mahal also conveys a great deal of information about the circumstances of Mughal rule in India, particularly about the syncretism of Muslim rulers and Hindu subjects we first saw in Chapter 12. Like their predecessors, the Mughals discovered the difficulties of being an ethnic and religious minority ruling a huge and diverse population. By Shah Jahan's time, moreover, religious revival was sweeping Islamic India and earlier Mughal rulers were subject to criticism about their laxity in ruling according to Islamic law and the accommodations they had made with India's other religious communities. Shah Jahan therefore devoted himself anew to a study of the Quran and resolved to rule insofar as it was possible according to Islamic precepts. Over the coming decades, such policy changes would raise tensions between Hindus and Muslims.

## Seeing Patterns

▶ What were the strengths and weaknesses of Mughal rule?

▶ What was the Mughal policy toward religious accommodation? How did it change over time?

▶ What factors account for the Mughal decline during the eighteenth century?

The gleaming white stone dome and minarets of Shah Jahan's architectural masterpiece are the centerpiece of a much larger complex that is, in fact, a vision of the entrance to paradise recreated on earth. The complex is, as one scholar put it, a vast **allegory** of Allah's judgment in paradise on the day of the resurrection. In the end, Mughal ambition to create an empire as the earthly expression of this vision lent itself to that empire's ultimate decline. The constant drive to bring the remaining independent Indian states under Mughal control continually strained imperial resources. Dynastic succession almost always resulted in internal wars fought by rival claimants to the Mughal mantle. By the eighteenth century, prolonged rebellion and the growing power of the East India companies of the European powers would conspire to send the dynasty into a downward spiral from which it never recovered. But its most visible symbol, the Taj Mahal—literally the "Crown Palace"—remains the emblem of India's peak as a syncretic religious civilization in the modern period.

**Allegory:** A literary, poetic, dramatic, pictorial, or architectural device in which the parts have symbolic value in depicting the meaning of the whole.

## History and Political Life of the Mughals

Though we have noted previously that relations between Muslims and India's other religions were *syncretic*—that despite attempts to integrate them more thoroughly into India's larger religious mosaic, they coexisted, sometimes on difficult or hostile terms, but remained largely separate from the other traditions. Yet the political and social systems created by the Mughals were in many respects a successful *synthesis*. That is, the Mughals brought with them a tradition that blended the practices of what social scientists call an "extraction state"—one that supplies itself by conquest and plunder—with several centuries of ruling more settled areas. This legacy would guide them as they struggled with a set of problems similar to those faced by rulers in other areas in creating an empire centered on one religion. Aided in their conquests by the new military technologies of cannon and small firearms, the Mughals created a flexible bureaucracy with a strict hierarchy of ranks and sophisticated separation of powers but with ultimate power concentrated in the hands of the emperors. Like those of the Chinese and Ottomans, the system was easily expanded into newly conquered areas, gave considerable free rein to the ambitious, and weathered all the major political storms it encountered until its decline during the eighteenth century.

## From Samarkand to Hindustan

As we have seen in earlier chapters, the rise to prominence of speakers of Turkic languages of the Altaic group had taken place over the course of many centuries. From at least the time of the Huns, these groups regularly coalesced into potent raiding and fighting forces, often putting together short-lived states such as those of the Toba in fifth- and sixth-century China, the Uighurs in the eighth and ninth centuries, and, most importantly, the Mongols in the twelfth and thirteenth centuries. But the Mongol Empire, the largest in world history, soon fell apart, and in its wake the central Asian heartland of the Turkic peoples—roughly speaking, from the Sea of Azov to the western reaches of present-day Mongolia—evolved into a patchwork of smaller states, many of whose rulers claimed descent from Genghis Khan. With the ousting of the Mongol Yuan dynasty from China in 1368, the eastern regions of this vast territory were thrown into further disarray, which set the stage for another movement toward consolidation.

**The Empire of Timur**    Aided by the ease of travel within the Mongol Empire, Islam had by the fourteenth century become the dominant religion among the central Asian Turkic peoples. By this time some of the Turkic groups, like the Seljuks and the Ottomans, had long since moved into the eastern Mediterranean region and Anatolia. In the interior of central Asia, however, the memory of the accomplishments of the Mongol Empire among the inhabitants of Chaghatay— the area given to Genghis Khan's son of that name—was still fresh. Their desire for a new Mongol Empire, now coupled with Islam, created opportunities for military action to unite the settled and nomadic tribes of Chaghatay. The result by the end of the fourteenth century was the stunning rise of Temur Gurgan (r. 1370–1405), more widely known by a variation of the Persian rendering of his name, Timur-i Lang, as Timur the Lame, or Tamerlane.

> "I am not a man of blood; and God is my witness that in all my wars I have never been the aggressor, and that my enemies have always been the authors of their own calamity."
>
> —Timur-i Lang

What little is known about Timur's early years has been clouded by the mystique he cultivated as a ruler, which continued to grow long after his death. Though he came close to matching the conquests of Genghis Khan, his forebearers were not direct descendants of the conqueror. He therefore devised genealogies connecting him to the dominant Mongol lines to give him legitimacy as a ruler, and he even found a direct descendant of Genghis Khan to use as a figurehead for his regime. He also portrayed himself as a man whose destiny was guided by God from humble beginnings to world domination.

From 1382, when he secured the region of his homeland around the capital, the Silk Road trading center of Samarkand, until his death in 1405, Timur ranged widely through western central Asia, Afghanistan, northern India, Iran, Anatolia, and the eastern Mediterranean lands (see Map 20.1). Like his model, Genghis Khan, he proved surprisingly liberal in his treatment of certain cities that surrendered peacefully. Many more times, however, he reduced besieged cities to rubble, slaughtered the inhabitants, and erected pyramids of skulls as a warning to others to submit. "Your sins must be great indeed for God to send me to punish you," he would tell his unfortunate opponents.

At the time of his death in 1405, Timur was contemplating the invasion of Ming China. This, however, never came to pass, and Timur's empire, like that of Genghis Khan, did not long outlast him. As it fell apart, the various Chaghatay peoples largely resumed their local feuds, once again leaving the way open for a strong military force to impose order.

**Babur and the Timurid Line in India**    By the beginning of the sixteenth century, the region from Samarkand south into the Punjab in northern India had largely become the province of feuding Turkic tribes and clans of Afghan fighters, many of whom had migrated south to serve with the Lodi sultans of India. Into this volatile environment was born Zahir ud-Din Muhammad Babur (1483–1530, r. 1526–1530), more commonly known as simply Babur (though the Turkic *babur* means "lion," Zahir's nickname was from the Persian *babr* for "leopard" or "tiger") in 1483. Babur's claims to legitimate rule were considerable: His father was a direct descendant of Timur, while his mother claimed the lineage of Genghis Khan.

At 14, Babur conquered Samarkand, though he was soon forced out by a competing tribe. Like Timur and Genghis Khan, his accomplishments as a youthful prodigy led him to believe that God had provided him with a special destiny to fulfill. This belief sustained him during the next several years when, out of favor with certain powerful relatives, he roamed the border regions seeking an opportunity to return to power.

In 1504, accompanied on a campaign by his strong-willed mother, Babur moved into Afghanistan, captured Kabul, and went on to raid points farther south over the following decade. By 1519, he stepped up his raids into northern India with a view to subjugating and ruling it. After 7 more years of campaigning, this goal was achieved. In 1526, Babur's army of approximately 12,000 met the forces of Sultan Ibrahim Lodi, whose army boasted perhaps 100,000 men and 1,000 elephants, at Panipat, near Delhi. Though the sultan enjoyed such vast numerical superiority, Babur's forces employed the new technologies of matchlock muskets and field cannon to devastating effect. In the end, the Lodi sultan was killed, along with many of the Afghan tribal chiefs whose forces made up the bulk of his army, and Babur's way was now clear to consolidate his new Indian territories.

**Area Subjugated by Timur-i Lang, 1360–1405**

☐ Area under Timur-i Lang's control, 1405

MAP **20.1** **Area Subjugated by Timur-i Lang, 1360–1405.**

| 1336–1405 | 1542–1605 | 1618–1707 | 1739 |
|---|---|---|---|
| Timur (Tamerlane), founder of Timurid line of rulers | Akbar, most innovative of Mughal rulers | Aurangzeb, last powerful Mughal ruler | Invasion by Persians; looting of Delhi; taking of Peacock Throne |

| 1483–1530 | 1627–1657 | 1707–1858 |
|---|---|---|
| Babur, founder of Timurid line in India—the Mughals | Shah Jahan, builder of the Taj Mahal | Ebbing of Mughal power in India; rise of British influence |

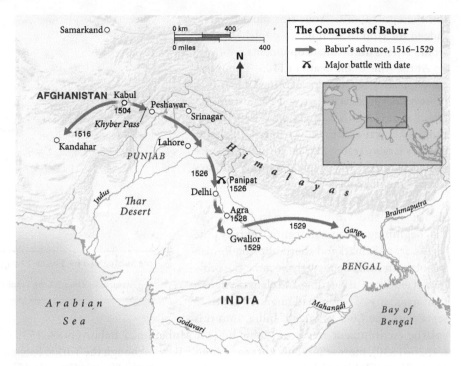

**Institutionalization:** The creation of a regular system for previously improvised or ad hoc activities or things, such as law codes to replace local customs.

MAP 20.2 **The Conquests of Babur.**

**Portrait of Babur.** This imagined portrait of Babur was done about 60 years after his death. He is shown receiving representatives of the Uzbeks of central Asia and the Rajputs of India in an audience dated December 18, 1528.

Victory at Panipat was swiftly followed by conquest of the Lodi capital of Agra and further success over the Hindu Rajputs in 1528. On the eve of his death in December 1530, Babur controlled an enormous swath of territory extending from Samarkand in the north to Gwalior in India in the south (see Map 20.2). For Babur and his successors, their ruling family would always be the "House of Timur," prompting historians to sometimes refer to the line as the Timurids. Because of their claims to the legacy of Genghis Khan, however, they would be better known to the world as the Mughals (from "Mongols").

**Loss and Recovery of Empire**    As had been the case so many times in the past with other newly conquered empires, the House of Timur's new rulers were now faced with the problem of consolidating, organizing, and administering Babur's vast domain. Like Timur before him, Babur had given comparatively little thought to the arts of peace. Now it fell upon his son Humayun (r. 1530–1556) to create a state. Unfortunately, Humayun's interests were aimed more toward Islamic Sufi mysticism, poetry, astrology, and at times wine and opium than they were toward responsible leadership. Though chroniclers have generally been critical of him for losing much of Babur's legacy, he tapped a considerable reservoir of courage and determination to ultimately win it back.

A chronic problem for the long-term health of the dynasty was the **institutionalization** of traditional nomadic succession practices among the Mughal rulers. Though only one son was designated as the ruler's successor, the others were given substantial territories to govern within the empire, a situation that frequently led to conflict. In addition to such ongoing family difficulties, Humayun faced various hostile military forces still active in unconquered areas of northern India and Afghanistan. An Afghan leader named Sher Khan Sur managed to unite many of these forces and invaded the extreme eastern region of Bengal. Twice routed, Humayun fled to Persia in 1540, where, utterly humiliated, he was forced to convert to Shia Islam in a desperate bid to court the favor of the Safavid ruler, Shah Tahmasp. As distasteful as this was for him as a Sunni Muslim, he now at least had Persian backing and proceeded to move into Afghanistan and, ultimately, to Delhi. By 1555, after 15 years of exile and fighting, the dynasty was restored. For Humayun, however, the peace brought only a brief respite. In a final irony for this bookish man, he fell from the roof terrace of his palace library and died in January 1556.

**Regency:** The setting up of a guardian for an underage or incapacitated monarch to rule in his or her stead.

**Consolidation and Expansion**    Because of the difficulties involved in Humayun's own accession to the throne, his death was kept secret for several weeks, while the court worked out plans for a **regency** for the emperor's son, 14-year-old Jalal ud-Din Akbar (r. 1556–1605). His military education began quickly as Humayun's old enemy, Sher Khan Sur, sent an army to attack Delhi in 1557. In a close fight, Mughal forces finally carried the day. Over the next year and a half, they secured the eastern, southern, and western flanks of their lands, bringing them conclusively into the Mughal fold and again anchoring Islam in the former areas of its influence—"Hindustan."

Upon finally seizing power in a palace coup, Akbar plunged into renewed campaigning in quest of more territory. Along the way, he seemed at once determined to master all India by any military means necessary yet also intolerant of cruelties practiced by his subordinates in his name. Akbar abhorred religious violence of any kind and spent much of his rule attempting to reconcile the different religious traditions of his empire. In the end his attempts, though remarkably farsighted, would prove futile and earn him the enmity of many of his fellow Muslims, who felt he had become an unbeliever.

As a warrior Akbar was far more successful. Through the 1560s, aided by capable military advisors, Mughal armies continued to push the boundaries of the empire west, south, and east. In 1562 they subdued Malwa and in 1564 Gondwana; in 1568, the great Rajput fortress of Chitor fell. This string of victories continued into the next decade, with the long-sought conquest of Gujarat taking place in 1573. Turning eastward, Akbar set his sights on Bengal, which, along with the neighboring regions of Bihar and Orissa, fell to the Mughals by the mid-1570s. They remained, however, volatile and hostile to Mughal occupation. Both Muslim and Hindu princes in the region continued their campaigns of resistance into the following decades (see Map 20.3).

In the meantime, resistance and rebellion periodically plagued other areas of the empire. In central Asia, as early as 1564, a rebellion of Uzbek Mughal allies required a skilled combination of violence and diplomacy to defuse. At the same time, revolts in Malwa and Gujarat required reconquest of those territories. In order to keep the old Islamic heartland of northern India—Hindustan—under

**Humayun Being Received by the Persian Shah Tahmasp.** This gouache rendering of a pivotal moment in Mughal dynastic history is from a painting on a wall at Chel Soloun in Isfahan. Although all seems cordial between the two men and Humayun was treated well by the Shah, a number of accounts claim that he was threatened with execution if he did not covert to Shia Islam.

firm Mughal control, the Mughals built fortresses at strategic points throughout their inner domains as well as along the frontier. Among the most important of these were Allahabad, Lahore (in modern Pakistan), Ajmer (the Amber Fort in Jaipur), and the largest—the famous Red Fort in Delhi.

**The New City**   In addition to fielding large armies—one European observer estimated that the army he accompanied on one of Akbar's campaigns surpassed 100,000—and huge, expensive forts, the immense revenues of the Mughal lands allowed other monumental projects to be undertaken. In an effort to show solidarity with his non-Muslim subjects, Akbar had married a Hindu Rajput princess named Manmati. Manmati had twins, who tragically died, and a distraught Akbar sought advice from a famous Sufi holy man named Salim Chishti. Salim told Akbar that he would ultimately have a son. When that son—named Salim in honor of the holy man—was born, Akbar began to build a city on the site of Salim Chishti's village of Sikri. Fatehpur Sikri, as the new city was known when it was completed in 1571, was built from the same red sandstone as the great fort at Agra, 26 miles away. Akbar's instincts for design and dynastic propaganda were

**Visions of Akbar.** A depiction of Akbar from ca. 1630 (*above*) shows him in all of his religious glory: surrounded by a luminous halo, surmounted by angels glorifying him and holding his crown, and graced with the holiness to make the lion lie down with the heifer.

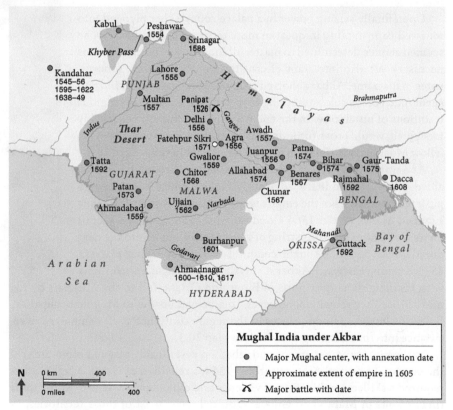

MAP **20.3  Mughal India under Akbar.**

everywhere evident within the city. At its center was the mosque, which housed the tomb of Salim Chishti and became an object of veneration and pilgrimage for Indian Sufis. Despite its amenities, however, the city was untenable in the long run and ultimately abandoned because there was simply not enough available water to sustain the population.

## The Summer and Autumn of Empire

In a way, the saga of Fatehpur Sikri runs parallel to Mughal fortunes over the next century. The military accomplishments of the dynasty are in many ways spectacular, but they were eventually worn down by internal rebellion and succession struggles; the immense fortunes of the rulers were ultimately squeezed by the needs of defense and of ostentation to demonstrate power; and new economic and, ultimately, military competitors arrived on the scene with the coming of the Europeans.

**The Revolt of the Sons**   In 1585, Akbar left Fatehpur Sikri with his army for Lahore, which he would make his temporary capital for most of the rest of his life. Once again, the Afghan princes were chafing under Mughal domination and intriguing with the Uzbeks and Safavid Persians to wrest local control for themselves. For Akbar, as for his predecessors, it was vital to maintain a hold over these areas because of their historical connection to the Chaghatay and the need to keep control of the essential Silk Road trade. Now the key city of Kandahar, in modern Afghanistan, was in Safavid hands, disrupting Mughal control of the trade. For the next 13 years, Akbar and his generals fought a long, stubborn war to subdue the Afghans and roll back the Safavids. Though his forces were defeated on several occasions, in the end the Mughals acquired Sind and Kashmir, subdued for a time the region of Swat, and, with the defection of a Safavid commander, occupied Kandahar. By 1598, the regions in question were secure enough for Akbar to move back to Agra.

In 1600, Akbar embarked on his last great campaign against the remaining free Muslim sultanates of central India. These were reduced within a year, but Akbar was now faced with a domestic crisis. His son Salim launched a coup and occupied the fort at Agra. Salim declared himself emperor, raised his own army,

**Salim Chishti's Tomb at Fatehpur Sikri.** The tomb of the Sufi mystic Salim Chishti shows the sense of restrained flamboyance that marks the mature Mughal architectural style. The Chishtis had long been revered by India's Sufis, and Salim's simple, elegant tomb, with its domed sarcophagus, multihued marble, and Quranic inscriptions, quickly became a favorite pilgrimage site. Surrounding it is one of the red sandstone courtyards of Akbar's Fatehpur Sikri.

and even had coins struck with his name on them. In the end, one of Akbar's wives and a group of court women were able to reconcile Akbar and Salim. Salim was confined within the palace amid intrigues that threatened to bypass him as heir in favor of his own son, Khusrau. In the end, however, he retained his position, and upon Akbar's death on October 25, 1605, Salim acceded to the throne as Jahangir (r. 1605–1627).

**Renewed Expansion of the "War State"**    As if to underscore the dynasty's continual problems with orderly succession, Jahangir's son Khusrau left the palace, quickly put a small army together, and marched on Lahore. When negotiations with his son went nowhere, Jahangir's forces swiftly defeated the insurgents. To impart to his son a special horror at what he had done, Khusrau was made to watch his comrades put to death by impalement—a punishment also used by the Ottomans and the famous Vlad "the Impaler" Dracula (Chapter 16). Sharpened posts were driven through their midsections and planted in the ground so that they would die slow, agonizing deaths suspended in the air. The doomed soldiers were made to salute Khusrau, who was forced to ride among them in a macabre military review. Undeterred, Khusrau rebelled again, and on failing this time, was blinded and imprisoned for his efforts.

As one scholar writes, "Under Jahangir the empire continued to be a war state attuned to aggressive conquest and territorial expansion." This now meant pushing south into the Deccan and periodically resecuring Afghanistan and its adjacent regions. A move into Bengal, however, foreshadowed a major clash with a very different kind of enemy: the Shan people of southeast Asia called the Ahoms. Southeast Asia was where the expanding cultural and political influence of China met that of Hindu and Buddhist India. In the case of the Ahoms, the territory in question was in the vicinity of Assam, along the Brahmaputra River to the north of Burma and Thailand. Though they had recently converted to Hinduism, the Ahoms had no caste system and drew upon a legacy of self-confident expansion that the Mughals had not encountered before in their opponents. With little fixed territory to defend because of their mobility, the Ahoms proved the most stubborn enemies the empire had yet encountered. Year after year, Jahangir's armies labored to secure the northeastern territories only to have the Ahoms bounce back and mount fresh offensives against them. Though both sides employed troops armed with matchlocks and cannon, neither side could obtain a clear tactical edge, and their wars dragged on for decades.

More culturally and psychologically threatening to the Mughals was their relationship with the empire to their west, Safavid Persia. Both sides constantly jockeyed for position against each other and periodically went to war. There was also intense religious rivalry, with the predominantly Sunni Mughals and Shiite Safavid Persians each denouncing the other as heretical unbelievers. For the Mughals, moreover, it was particularly galling that they owed the survival of their dynasty in part to the Persian shah Tahmasp, who had given aid to Humayun—forcing him to convert to Shiism in return.

In addition, among the sizeable number of Persians and Shiites within the Mughal elites there was a pronounced feeling that Persian culture, language, and literature were superior to those of the Turks and Muslim India as a whole. In some respects, both Persians and "Persianized" Indians saw Muslim India as a

kind of cultural colonial outpost, in much the same way that Chinese sophisti-
cates viewed the high cultures of Japan, Korea, and Vietnam. This made for a complex set of relations between the two empires, with both vying for power in
religious and cultural terms as much as in the political and military realm.

**New Directions in Religious Politics**   After Jahangir died of a fever in
October 1627, his oldest son, Khurram, outmaneuvered his younger brother for
the throne and reigned as Shah Jahan (r. 1627–1657). His rule coincided with perhaps the high point of Mughal cultural power and prestige, as reflected in its iconic
building, the Taj Mahal. However, his record is less spectacular
in political and military terms. In this case, the Mughal obsession
with controlling the northern trade routes coincided with the need
to take back the long-contested great fort at Kandahar, once again
in Persian hands. Thus, Shah Jahan spent much of his reign on the
ultimately fruitless drive to finally subdue the northwest.

> "Nothing resulted from this expedition except the shedding of blood, the killing of thirty to forty thousand people, and the expenditure of thirty-five million rupees."
>
> —Sadiq

As we noted earlier, the reign of Akbar and, to a considerable
extent, that of Jahangir had marked a time of extraordinary religious tolerance. The attraction of both men to the Sufi school of Salim Chishti,
with its mystical leanings and parallels with similar Hindu movements, created a
favorable emotional environment for religious pluralism. It also made Muslims,
for whom strict adherence to Sunni doctrine was necessary to guard against undue
Persian Shia influence, apprehensive. Others, noting the ability of Hindus to incorporate the gods and beliefs of other faiths into their own, feared that the ruling
Muslim minority might ultimately be assimilated into the Hindu majority.

With Shah Jahan, however, we see a definite turn toward a more legalistic tradition. Under the influence of this trend among leading Sunni theologians, Shah
Jahan began to block construction and repair of non-Muslim religious buildings,
instituted more direct state support for Islamic festivals, and furnished lavish subsidies for Muslim pilgrims to Mecca. The old ideal of a unified Muslim world governed by Quranic law steadily gained ground at the Mughal court and would see
its greatest champion in Shah Jahan's son Aurangzeb. In the meantime, the trend
lent itself to the creation of a new capital, Shajahanabad Delhi, just south of Delhi,
complete with the largest mosque, college (madrasa), and hospital complex in
India and, of course, the Taj Mahal at Agra.

**The Pinnacle of Power**   The ascendancy of Aurangzeb (r. 1658–1707) was
marked yet again by the now all-too-familiar pattern of princely infighting. In this
case it was brought on by the extended illness of Shah Jahan in 1657. A four-way
struggle broke out among the sons of Shah Jahan and his beloved Mumtaz Mahal.
Although Shah Jahan soon recovered, he returned to Agra broken and depressed,
while his sons fought bitterly for control. By 1661 three had been defeated and
killed, leaving Aurangzeb in control of the empire. Shah Jahan lived on in captivity until 1666.

Aurangzeb's long rule, despite its violent birth, seemed to begin auspiciously
enough. Renewing the Mughal bid to expand into the northeastern areas controlled by the Ahoms, his armies fought them to a standstill in the early 1660s and
made them Mughal clients. When Mughal control of the area around Kabul and
the Khyber Pass was threatened by a revolt of local tribesmen, Aurangzeb fought

# Patterns Up Close | Akbar's Attempt at Religious Synthesis

Like their predecessors, the Mughals as Muslim rulers in India were faced with an immense array of diverse, and sometimes antagonistic, religious and cultural traditions. Amid this "religious syncretism," as we have termed it, Akbar's innovation within the world-historical pattern of religious civilizations was to create a new religion that would encompass these traditions and bind his followers directly to him as emperor and religious leader: to create an Indian "religious synthesis."

Already graced with a larger-than-life reputation for charisma and openness, he was also resistant to the strictures of Sunni Islam or any other organized religion. As a boy, he was condemned by his tutors as uneducable because he remained unable to read or write. Some scholars have suggested that he was dyslexic. Perhaps because of this, he developed an extraordinary memory for literature and poetry. Some have also suggested that his illiteracy was in emulation of the stories of the early prophets, who found illumination directly from God. In any case, his tastes within Islam centered on Sufi mysticism, which had a long tradition of tolerance and eclecticism. This openness encouraged him to study the mystical traditions of the Hindus, Parsis (Zoroastrian immigrants from Persia), and Christians. After establishing himself at Fatehpur Sikri, he sponsored regular Thursday-night theological debates, mostly among Muslim scholars but gradually including Hindus, Parsis, and in 1578 Catholic missionaries. He honored many of the cultural traditions of India's various religions as well: He wore his hair long under his turban like the Sikhs and

**Akbar Presiding Over a Religious Debate.** Akbar's distaste for religious orthodoxy manifested itself most dramatically in his conducting regularly held debates among theologians from many of India's faiths. Here, a discussion is taking place with two Jesuit missionaries, Fathers Rudolph Aquaviva and Francis Henriquez (dressed in black) in 1578. Interestingly, the priests had unfettered access to Akbar, were free to preach, and even gave instruction to members of Akbar's family at his request.

several stubborn campaigns to retain control of the region and bought off other potentially troublesome groups with lavish gifts.

With these campaigns, the political power of the Mughals reached perhaps its greatest extent. But the period also marked a watershed in at least two respects. First, it saw the opening of decades-long wars with the Hindu Marathas, in which the empire's cohesion was steadily eroded. In addition, the various trading companies of the British, French, and Dutch expanded their own fortified outposts in Indian ports outside Mughal domains. As Mughal power was sapped by the revolts of the eighteenth century, the companies' armed forces became important players in regional politics.

The other watershed was Aurangzeb's bid for a more effective "Islamification" of Mughal India. Aurangzeb's vision for the empire was rule by Islamic Sharia law. As an Islamic state, connected to the larger commonwealth of Islamic states,

some Hindus, coined emblems of the sun to honor the Parsis, and kept paintings of the Virgin Mary as a nod to the Christians.

During one particularly lavish and bloody hunting party in 1578, he had a sudden, intense mystical experience. Like Ashoka so long before him—of whom Akbar was completely unaware— he was now appalled by the destruction and waste in which he had participated. Out of this experience and his religious consultations, he gradually developed a personal philosophy he called *sulh-i kull*—"at peace with all." While this did not end his military campaigns, which he saw as ordained by God, it did push him to develop a new religion he called *din-i ilahi* (divine faith). Akbar shrewdly directed the movement at key courtiers, nobles, and those aspiring to gain favor from the regime. He devised elaborate rituals in which adherents swore loyalty to him not only as emperor but as the enlightened religious master of the new sect. Borrowing heavily from Sufi mysticism, Persian court protocols, Zoroastrian sun and fire veneration, and even Muslim- and Christian-influenced spiritualism, he sought to at once limit the power of Sunni Islamic clerics and draw followers of other religions to what he taught was a "higher" realm, one that embraced all religions and provided the elect with secret insights into their ultimate truths.

In the end, however, despite its creative merging of the needs of state and religion to overcome what had been considered deep religious and cultural divisions, Akbar's attempt must be counted as a failure. While some Hindu and Muslim courtiers embraced *din-i ilahi* enthusiastically for its perceived religious truths, many did so for opportunistic reasons, and it was roundly condemned by most Sunni theologians. And while Akbar's personal magnetism was able to hold the sect together during his lifetime, his successors not only repudiated it but swung increasingly in the direction of stricter Sunni Islam.

## Questions

- How does Akbar's attempt at religious syncretism demonstrate the pattern of origins–innovations–adaptations that informs the approach of this book?
- Why was Akbar's attempt to create a new divine faith doomed to failure?

he believed that Mughal rule should be primarily for the benefit of Muslims. This was an almost complete repudiation of his great-grandfather Akbar's vision of religious transcendence. While Aurangzeb stopped short of forcible conversion, he did offer multiple inducements to bring unbelievers into the faith. Elites who converted to Islam were given lavish gifts and preferential assignments, while those who did not convert found themselves isolated from the seat of power. Discriminatory taxes were also levied on unbelievers, including a new tax on Hindu pilgrims. Zealous Muslim judges in various cities prompted protests from Hindus regarding their rulings. Moving a step beyond the actions of Shah Jahan, Aurangzeb ordered the demolition of dozens of Hindu temples that had not been constructed or repaired according to state-approved provisions. The most unpopular measure, however, was the reimposition of the hated *jizya* tax on unbelievers, which had been abolished by Akbar.

The new religious policies also created problems in dealing with self-governing, non-Muslim groups within the empire. The legacy of distrust of the Mughals among the Sikhs, who blended Hindu and Muslim traditions, was enhanced by Aurangzeb's heavy-handed attempts to intervene in the selection of a new Sikh guru, or religious leader, and by the destruction of some Sikh temples. When the Sikhs did not choose the candidate Aurangzeb favored, the emperor arrested the other candidate for allegedly converting Muslims and had him executed. His son and successor, Gobind Singh, would later lead a full-blown Sikh revolt.

**The Maratha Revolt** Notwithstanding these internal problems, Aurangzeb's military prowess netted him key areas that had long eluded Mughal efforts: Bijapur, Golconda, and much of the Maratha lands of the Deccan region of south central India. Yet even here, the preconditions were already in place for a rebellion that would sap the strength of the empire for generations.

The Hindu Marathas, like the inhabitants of many regions bordering Mughal India, had evolved working relationships with the old Muslim sultanates that, over time, were annexed by the Timurids. For the earlier Mughal rulers, it was often enough for these small states to remit tribute and, on occasion, supply troops in order to retain their autonomy. For Aurangzeb, however, commitment to a more robust and legalistic Islam also meant political expansion of the Mughal state. This was justified on the religious grounds that the sultanates to the south had drifted from correct observance of Quranic law, that it was permissible to confiscate the lands of unbelievers, and that unbelievers would more likely convert if guided by proper Muslim rulers. Hence, Aurangzeb spent much of the last two decades of his life campaigning to bring central India under his sway.

Despite the tenacity of Maratha resistance, Aurangzeb's carrot-and-stick strategy—supporting pro-Mughal factions among the Maratha leaders, lavishing money and gifts on Maratha converts and deserters, and fielding large armies to attack Maratha fortifications—was successful. In the early 1690s 11 Maratha strongholds fell to his forces. Yet prolonged fighting, with the emperor staying in the field year after year, also led to problems at court and in the interior of the empire.

The demands of constant campaigning reduced the flow of money and goods from south to north and east to west across central India. Moreover, by the early eighteenth century, the Maratha frontier, far from being steadily worn down, was actually expanding into Mughal areas. The Marathas had set up their own administrative system with its own forts and tax base and encouraged raids on Mughal caravans and pack trains. By the time of Aurangzeb's death in 1707, the Marathas were noticeably expanding their sway at Mughal expense. With the weakening of the Mughal interior, Persia took the opportunity to settle scores. The Persians sent an expeditionary force that sacked Delhi in 1739 and carried off Shah Jahan's fabled Peacock Throne—from this time forward associated with the monarchs of Persia and Iran, rather than with India and the Mughals.

**The East India Companies** Within a dozen years of Vasco da Gama's first voyage to India in 1498, armed Portuguese merchant ships seized the port of Goa in 1510. Portugal's pioneering efforts in capturing the spice trade and setting up fortified bases from which to conduct business were swiftly imitated by other

European maritime countries. For the English, Dutch, and French, these enterprises were conducted by royally chartered companies, which were given a monopoly over their country's trade within a certain region. Because these companies were operating thousands of miles from home in areas that were often politically chaotic, they acted much like independent states. They maintained fortified warehouses, their armed merchant ships functioned as naval forces, and they assembled their own mercenary armies.

Throughout the seventeenth century English, French, and Dutch enterprises largely supplanted Portuguese influence in the region, while the location of their trading ports outside Mughal lands allowed them considerable freedom. European naval prowess had by this time also surpassed that of any of the Indian states, and European ships controlled the sea-lanes to Indian ports. Thus, the companies grew richer and more powerful and increasingly found themselves involved in local politics. For the English, the acquisition of Bombay (Mumbai) from Portugal in the 1660s gave the company a superb harbor. In 1690, after unwisely becoming involved in a struggle with Aurangzeb, British traders were pushed down the Hugli (also Hoogli or Hooghly) River in Bengal and began building a new trading station called Calcutta (not to be confused with the port of Calicut, on the west coast of India). By 1750, the power of the Dutch in India had been eclipsed by that of the British and French East India Companies. With the victory of the British East India Company commander, Robert Clive, at Plassey over the French forces in 1757 came British domination of Bengal and, by century's end, much of northern India.

**The Dutch Trading Post at Hugli, 1665.** The mid-seventeenth century was the high point of Dutch influence and trade in Asia, and the Dutch East India Company was one of the most powerful entities in the region. This fortified outpost on the Hugli River was typical of European trading establishments in the region during the late sixteenth and most of the seventeenth century. By the end of the century, however, the Dutch would be supplanted on the Hugli by their archrivals, the English, who would establish their own base, which would swiftly grow into the great trading center of Calcutta.

## Administration, Society, and Economics

One of the large patterns characteristic of the period under consideration in this section is a pronounced trend toward centralization. In a way, this phenomenon is not surprising, since the creation of states and empires requires power at the center to hold the state together, ensure consistent governance, provide for revenues, and maintain defense. What is noteworthy, however, is that in widely separate regions throughout Eurasia a variety of states concurrently reached a point where their governments, with armies now aided by firearms, made concerted efforts to focus more power than ever at the center. As part of this trend toward the development of centralizing states, some form of enforcement of approved religion or belief system legitimating the rulers was also present. As we saw in the Ottoman and Habsburg Empires in Chapter 16 and in seventeenth-century France and other European countries in Chapter 17, the trend was toward what came to be called "absolutism," with vast powers concentrated in the person of the monarch. In China and Japan, as we will see in Chapter 21, it meant additional powers concentrated in the hands of the emperor (China) and shogun (Japan). For Mughal

India, the system that attempted to coordinate and balance so many disparate and often hostile elements of society is sometimes called "autocratic centralism." While never as effective as the Chinese bureaucratic system or as tightly regulated as absolutist France, its policies and demands stretched into the lives of its inhabitants in often unexpected ways.

## Mansabdars and Bureaucracy

As we saw earlier, Babur and his successors found themselves forced to govern a largely settled, farming and city-dwelling society, whose traditions, habits, and (for the majority) religious affiliations were different from their own. While not unfamiliar with settled societies, the nomadic Timurids initially felt more comfortable in adapting their own institutions to their new situation and then grafting them onto the existing political and social structures. The result was a series of hybrid institutions that, given the tensions within Indian society, worked remarkably well when the empire was guided by relatively tolerant rulers but became increasingly problematic under more dogmatic ones.

**Political Structure**    The main early challenge faced by the Timurids was how to create a uniform administrative structure that did not rely on the unusual gifts of a particular ruler. It was the problem of moving from what social scientists call "charismatic leadership" (in which loyalty is invested in a leader because of his personal qualities) to "rational-legal" leadership (in which the institution itself commands primary respect and loyalty). Thus, Akbar created four principal ministries: one for army and military matters; one for taxation and revenue; one for legal and religious affairs; and one for the royal household.

Under the broad central powers of these ministries, things functioned much the same on the provincial and local levels. The provincial governors held political and military power and were responsible directly to the emperor. In order to prevent their having too much power, however, the fiscal responsibility for both the civil and military affairs of the provinces was in the hands of officers who reported to the finance minister. Thus, arbitrary or rebellious behavior could, in theory at least, be checked by the separation of financial control.

**Administrative Personnel**    One key problem faced by the Mughals was similar to that confronting the French king Louis XIV and the Tokugawa shoguns in Japan during the following century—that is, how to impose a centralized administrative system on a state whose nobles were used to wielding power themselves. In all three cases, the solutions were remarkably similar. For the Mughals, India's vast diversity of peoples and patchwork of small states offered a large pool of potential noble recruits, and the competition among the ambitious for imperial favor was intense. The Timurid rulers were careful to avoid overt favoritism toward particular ethnic, or even religious, groups; and though most of their recruited nobility were Sunni Muslims, Hindus and even Shiite Muslims were also represented.

The primary criteria—as one would expect in a centralizing state—were military and administrative skills. An elaborate, graded system of official ranks was created in which the recipients, called *mansabdars*, were awarded grants of land and the revenues those working the land generated. In turn the mansabdars were responsible for remitting the correct taxes and, above a certain rank, for furnishing men and materiel for the army. Standards for horses, weapons, and physical qualities for soldiers, to which recruiters were expected to adhere, were established by the central government. The positions in the provincial governments and state ministries were filled by candidates from this new mansabdar elite chosen by the court. Thus, although the nobles retained considerable power in their own regions, they owed their positions to the court and had no hope of political advancement if they did not get court preferment.

## The Mughals and Early Modern Economics

Mughal India had a vigorous trade and manufacturing economy, though, as with all agrarian-based societies, land issues and agriculture occupied the greatest part of the population. Unlike the societies of China, Japan, Korea, and Vietnam, which were influenced to a greater or lesser degree by Neo-Confucian ideas that regarded commerce as vaguely disreputable, Hindu, Muslim, Buddhist, and Jain traditions reserved an honored place for commerce and those who conducted it. Thus, Mughal economic interests routinely revolved around keeping the flow of goods moving around the empire, maintaining a vigorous import and export trade, and, as we have seen, safeguarding access to the Silk Road routes.

**Agriculture and Rural Life**    The basic administrative unit of rural India at the time of the Mughals was the *pargana*, a unit comprising an area usually containing a town and from a dozen to about 100 villages. It was in the pargana that the lowest levels of officialdom had met the network of clan and caste leaders of the villages under both the Hindu rajas and the Muslim sultans before the Timurids, and this pattern continued over the coming centuries. But because the earliest years of the Mughals were marked by conquest and plunder, and later by an administrative apparatus that contented itself with taxation and defense at the local level, life in the villages tended to go on much as it had before the conquest. Thus, the chief duties of the *zamindars*, as the local chiefs and headmen were called, were to channel the expansive and competitive energies among local clans, castes, and ethnic and religious groups into activities the Mughals considered productive. In border areas especially, this frequently involved clearing forests for farmland, harvesting tropical woods and products for market, and often driving off bands of foragers from the forests and hills.

Agricultural expansion went hand in hand with systematic integration of the rural and urban economies. One enormous obstacle facing the Mughals, which had faced previous regimes, was efficiency and equity in rural taxation. Grain and other agricultural commodities provided the bulk of Indian tax revenues, but vast differences in regional soil conditions, climate, and productivity made uniform tax rates extremely difficult to enforce. During Akbar's reign, therefore, massive surveys of local conditions were conducted to monitor harvests and grain prices over 10-year periods. These were then compiled into data tables used by local officials to calculate expected harvests and tax obligations. Imperial and local officials would sign agreements as to grain amounts to meet tax obligations over a set period. These obligations, like the Chinese "single-whip" system (see Chapter 21), would then be paid in silver or copper coin in four installments.

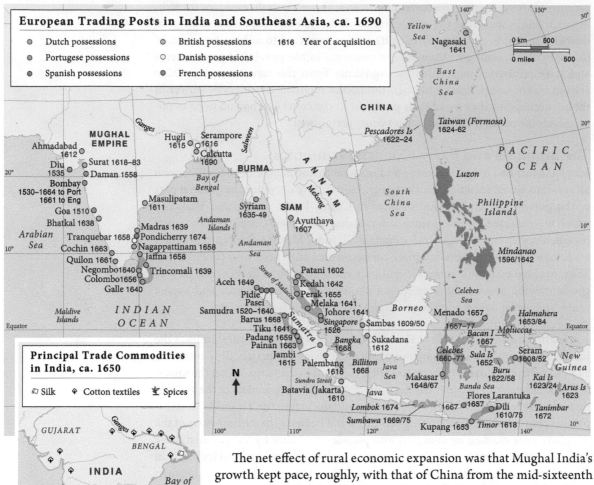

**European Trading Posts in India and Southeast Asia, ca. 1690**

- Dutch possessions
- Portugese possessions
- Spanish possessions
- British possessions
- Danish possessions
- French possessions

1616 Year of acquisition

**Principal Trade Commodities in India, ca. 1650**

🕮 Silk    ✦ Cotton textiles    ⚓ Spices

MAP 20.4 **European Trading Posts in India and Southeast Asia, ca. 1690.**

The net effect of rural economic expansion was that Mughal India's growth kept pace, roughly, with that of China from the mid-sixteenth century to the beginning of the nineteenth. Expansion in Bengal and northeast India of wet rice cultivation and the introduction of American crops such as maize and potatoes in dryer areas allowed for a population increase from about 150 million in 1600 to 200 million in 1800. Moreover, acreage under cultivation increased by perhaps as much as one-third over this same period. Preferential tax rates on tobacco, indigo, sugarcane, cotton, pepper, ginger, and opium ensured that supplies of these coveted trade items would be secure. India began a burgeoning silk industry during this time as well. Thus, revenues more than doubled between Akbar's and Aurangzeb's reigns, to about 333.5 million rupees a year, while the increase in population meant that the per capita tax burden actually went down.

**International Trade** India had been the center of Indian Ocean trade for nearly two millennia before the rise of the Mughals, but the advent of the world trading systems being created by the Atlantic maritime states added a vastly expanded dimension to this commerce. The intense and growing competition among the English, Dutch, and French East India Companies meant that Indian commodities were now being shipped globally, while imports of American silver and food and cash crops were growing annually. By the mid-seventeenth century, the Dutch and British dominated maritime trade in Indian spices. Between 1621 and 1670, for example, Indian exports of pepper to Europe doubled to 13.5 million pounds. An often added bonus was Indian saltpeter, a vital component of gunpowder, used as ships' ballast (see Map 20.4).

Perhaps of even more long-term importance, however, was the growth of India's textile trade. Here, French access to Bengali silk contributed immensely to French leadership in European silk products, while Indian indigo supplied European needs for this dye until slave production of it in the Americas lowered its cost still further. Most momentous of all, though, was the rapid rise of Indian cotton exports. Lighter and more comfortable than wool or linen, Indian cotton *calicoes* (named for Indian port of Calicut) proved immensely popular for underwear and summer clothing. Indeed, the familiar term "pajamas" comes from the Hindi word *pajama*, the lightweight summer garments worn in India and popularized as sleepwear in Europe.

## Society, Family, and Gender

Though the majority of the material in this chapter describes the activities of the Muslim Timurids in Indian history and society, it must be kept in mind that the vast majority of people in all areas of India were Hindus rather than Muslims. Thus, although the laws and customs of the areas controlled by the Mughals had a considerable effect on all members of Indian society, most of the everyday lives of Indians at the pargana, village, clan, and family levels went on much as it had before the arrival of the Mughals—or, for that matter, before the arrival of Islam.

**Caste, Clan, and Village**    As we saw in earlier chapters, the ties of family, clan, and caste were the most important for the majority of Indians (most of whom were Hindu), particularly in rural society, which comprised perhaps 90 percent of the subcontinent's population. Even after the reimposition of the tax on unbelievers by Aurangzeb and the restrictions on the building and rehabilitating of Hindu temples, Hindu life at the local level went on much as it had before. Indeed, many new converts to Islam retained their caste and clan affiliations, especially in areas in which caste affiliation was determined by language, village designation, or profession.

For rural Indian society, however, even in areas under Muslim control for centuries, religious and cultural tensions as well as local friction with central authority were present. Thus, during the reign of Akbar, whose tolerant rule eased tensions somewhat, clan archives are relatively quiet; in contrast, during Aurangzeb's long rule and periods of internal conflict, these same archives bristle with militia drives and petitions for redress of assorted grievances. In areas only marginally under Mughal control, clan councils offered resources for potential rebels.

**Family and Gender**    For the Indian elites outside the areas of Mughal control, family life of the higher castes went on largely as it had from the time of the Guptas. The "twice-born" Hindus of the brahman varna went through lengthy training and apprenticeship in the household of a trusted guru in preparation for their roles as religious and societal leaders through their various stages of life. Women, who

**Jahangir's Influential Wife, the Former Persian Princess Nur Jahan, in Her Silk Gauze Inner-Court Dress.**

in the pursuit of dharma it was said are "worthy of worship," nevertheless spent most of their lives in seclusion. Whether among the highest castes or the lowest, their primary duties still included the running of the household and childrearing. Among the elites, where education in literature, poetry, and basic mathematics was also available to certain women, maintaining the household accounts, supervising servants, as well as education in the arts of living and loving as depicted in the *Kama Sutra* were also considered part of a wife's proper knowledge. In all cases, however, as in China, the "inner" world of the household and the "outer" world of business, politics, warfare, and so on were clearly defined by gender. In rural areas, the lives and work of peasant families, though generally guided by traditional gender roles, were more flexible in that large collective tasks such as planting and harvesting required the participation of both men and women.

The conquests of the Mughals brought with them a somewhat different temperament among their elites. The nomadic Turkic peoples of the Asian steppes, with their reliance on mobility and herding and organization around small groups of fiercely independent families and clans, had not developed the elaborate class, caste, and gender hierarchies of their settled neighbors. Women could, and often did, exercise a far greater degree of power and influence than even among the Hindu, Sikh, or Muslim elites in India.

Even after the conversion of these nomadic peoples to Islam, this tradition of female independence continued among the Timurids. As we saw earlier, for example, Babur's mother played a vital role in his rise to power, and emperors' wives, like Mumtaz Mahal, exercised a considerable degree of control in the imperial household. Moreover, since marriages played a vital role in cementing diplomatic and internal relations, women exercised a good deal of influence in terms of the extension of imperial power. Nur Jahan (d. 1645), the striking Persian princess married to Jahangir, played a leading role in court politics and in mediation during the succession wars at the end of Jahangir's reign. Indeed, Jahangir turned the running of the empire over to her on several occasions, stating that he felt quite secure with it in her capable hands.

As the Mughals assimilated local Muslim elites, the court quickly set up the harem as an institution of seclusion and protection for court women. Yet within the harem, women enjoyed considerable freedom, constructed their own hierarchies among the imperial wives and their attendants, and celebrated their own holidays and ceremonies largely insulated from the influence of men. It was in many respects a kind of alternative women's society, in which a distinct system of values was instilled in daughters and, crucially, women newly married into the household. For these women, navigating the harem's social relationships was of supreme importance, since the inner harmony of the court—and sometimes human lives—depended on it.

# Science, Religion, and the Arts

While the advancement of science and technology in Mughal India did not match the pace set during the scientific revolution in western Europe, there were none-theless several noteworthy developments in weaponry, mathematics, and astron-omy. In terms of religion, as we have seen, the great theological differences between Hindus and Muslims persisted—and with the reign of Aurangzeb increased. Again, however, the tendency of Hinduism to assimilate other traditions and the relative compatibility of Islamic Sufi practices with other mystical traditions did sometimes decrease tensions. This, of course, was most dramatically seen with Akbar's efforts at bridging the religious gaps of his empire. Finally, one could say that where attempts at reconciling religions failed, language, literature, art, and architecture often succeeded and left a brilliant legacy of cultural synthesis.

## Science and Technology

As they had done for centuries already, Muslim scholars in India drew upon the rich scientific history of the subcontinent and merged it with their efforts at pre-serving, commenting on, and transmitting the ancient Greco-Roman and Persian achievements. Among the most important developments in this regard, as we have seen in other chapters, was the spreading of the Indian decimal number system and the use of zero as a placeholder in mathematical computations. This had already had a profound effect on the development of European science, which forever after referred to that system as "Arabic numerals." Among the develop-ments that directly fostered the rise of Muslim empires, none was more important than the rapid development of gunpowder weapons.

**New Directions in Firearms in the Gunpowder Empires**   The spread of firearms from China and the shift in emphasis among weapons developers from rockets to tubular weapons firing projectiles is an extraordinarily complex subject and one littered with claims and counterclaims for the ultimate sources of par-ticular innovations. We can say, however, that by the beginning of the sixteenth century, the armies of the major European kingdoms, Ming China, Ottoman Turkey, and Persia had all become accustomed to employing cannons and explo-sive charges for besieging fortresses, were developing more convenient and effect-ive small arms for their infantries, and were beginning to employ lighter, more portable cannons as field guns for pitched battles. The use of these weapons became so pervasive and the changes that accompanied them so important that scholars often refer to the states of the Mughals, Persians, and Ottomans as the **gunpowder empires**.

Given the desire on the part of all armies to expand their firepower, it is not surprising that a gifted engineer, astronomer, and philosopher named Fathullah Shirazi (ca. 1580) came up with a design for a multibarreled gun—similar to one designed by Leonardo da Vinci—for Akbar's armies. In this case, 12–16 light can-nons were mounted side by side on a gun carriage and fired by the operator in quick succession.

**Gunpowder empires:** Muslim-ruled empires of the Ottomans, Safavids, and Mughals that used cannons and small arms in their military campaigns, 1450–1750.

**Mathematics and Astronomy**   India's long history of mathematical innova-tion merged with Muslim work on astronomical observation to make impressive

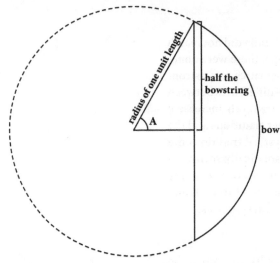

**Origins of the Trigonometric Sine of an Angle as Described by Indian Mathematicians.** Indian mathematicians did pioneering work in all of the areas of mathematics, particularly arithmetic and geometry. Hindu geometers knew of the trigonometric sine of an angle from at least the eighth century CE, if not earlier. In the early ninth century, the great Arabic mathematician al-Khwarizmi described the sine of an angle in his treatise on "Hindu" numbers, which was subsequently translated into Latin in the twelfth century. Through a series of mistranslations from one language to another, the original Sanskrit word for sine, *jya-ardha* ("half the bowstring"), ended up being rendered as "sinus" in Latin and other European languages—the modern sine.

advances in celestial calculation. A century before Akbar, Indian mathematicians had pushed their calculations of the value of pi to nine decimal places and expanded their facility with trigonometry to the point where some of the fundamental concepts of infinite series and calculus had been worked out.

Like other agrarian peoples reliant on an accurate calendar for the yearly agricultural and ceremonial cycle, Mughal rulers had a vital interest in knowing when unusual celestial phenomena such as comets, eclipses, and meteor showers were due and in having explanations for them ready at hand. Using extremely fine calculations and careful observation, the astronomers of the Kerala school, active from the fourteenth to the sixteenth centuries, had calculated elliptical orbits for the visible planets a century in advance of Johannes Kepler and suggested systems of planetary orbits similar to those of both Tycho Brahe and Copernicus (Chapter 17).

## Religion: In Search of Balance

As scholars have often noted, Indian Islam went through relatively open, inclusive, and Sufi-oriented cycles—most notably in this chapter during the reigns of Babur, Humayun, and Akbar—and phases in which a more rigorous attention to orthodox Sunni practices and the desire to connect with Muslim communities beyond India prevailed, such as during the reigns of Jahangir, Shah Jahan, and especially Aurangzeb. These periods, as we have already seen, had a profound effect on the relations of minority Muslim rulers with non-Muslim subjects. But they also played an important role in mandating which forms of Islam would be most influential in Mughal India and the relations of the Mughals with the Muslims of other regions.

**The Position of Non-Muslims in Mughal India**    As we have seen in earlier chapters, despite profound theological differences between the monotheism of Islam and the profuse polytheism of popular Hindu religious traditions, there was a degree of attraction between the adherents of the two religions. As was the case with mystical and devotional sects of both, they saw a commonality in their ways of encountering the profound mysteries of faith. Thus, Akbar's grounding in Islamic Sufi mysticism made him interested in and receptive to Hindu mystical traditions. For their part, in addition to the mystical elements of Islam—in any case accessible only to a relative few—far more Hindus of the lower castes were attracted to the equality before God of all Islamic believers. Thus, like Buddhism before it, Islam promised emancipation from the restrictions of the caste system and a shared brotherhood of believers without regard for ethnicity, race, job, or social position.

More generally, however, the religious divisions remained difficult to reconcile. From the time of the first occupation of territories by Muslim armies in the seventh century, nonbelievers had been granted the legal status of protected peoples (Chapter 10). That is, they were allowed to worship as they pleased and govern according to their own religious laws. There were also inducements and penalties aimed at conversion to Islam. Unbelievers were subject to the *jizya* and pilgrimage taxes, and they suffered job discrimination in official circles, all of which disappeared once they converted. For their part, Hindus considered Muslims to be ritually unclean (*mleccha*), and upper-caste members underwent elaborate purification rites after coming into contact with them.

Yet the presence of a vastly larger Hindu population also meant that considerable accommodation had to be made by the rulers in order to run the empire effectively and even more to maintain order at the local level. Akbar, as we noted earlier, banned the discriminatory taxes on unbelievers. In addition, the financial skills of Hindus and Jains were increasingly sought by the court, and their status rose further when Akbar made a Hindu his finance minister and employed Hindu court astrologers. Perhaps of even more symbolic and political importance was the habit of Mughal rulers of occasionally marrying Hindu women.

The position of Christians was similar. They, along with Jews, were considered "people of the Book" and therefore protected but still subject to the same taxes and impediments before the reign of Akbar. While the position of Christian missionaries in Mughal lands was often precarious, the reverence with which Muslims regarded the biblical prophets and Jesus also helped to smooth diplomatic relations at court. Akbar invited Jesuits to his debates, and paintings of Christian religious figures, especially the Virgin Mary, can be found in Mughal depictions of court life.

Yet this period of relative religious openness peaked with Akbar, and the pendulum soon began to swing back with increasing speed. Mughal receptiveness of Islamic mysticism and other religions, as most dramatically displayed by Akbar's new *din-i ilahi* religion, offended more orthodox Sunni Muslims. Their influence was felt at court during the reign of Jahangir and especially during that of Shah Jahan, who merged love and piety in the form of the Taj Mahal. It reached its zenith during Aurangzeb's reign. As Mughal lands stretched to their greatest extent, the austere Aurangzeb reimposed the taxes on unbelievers and purged many Hindus from his court.

**Islamic Developments**   While the vast majority of India's Muslims remained adherents of the Sunni branch of Islam and Hanafi school of interpretation of Islamic law, there were also several noteworthy developments in other areas. First, as we have noted several times already, there was an influential Shiite presence in India. For centuries, Shiites had migrated into Hindu areas of southern India, where, despite being a notable minority, they generally escaped the discrimination at the hands of Sunnis characteristic of the north. In addition, Mughal relations with Safavid Persia, where Shia Islam was the official state religion, meant a certain influence on the Mughal court was unavoidable. Hence, Akbar studied mystical elements of Shiism, while Jahangir married the Safavid princess Nur Jahan, probably the most powerful woman of the Mughal period.

One branch of Shiism that attained considerable influence despite its small numbers was that of the Ismailis. Like a number of Muslim mystical brotherhoods, the Ismailis, originally refugees from the fall of the Fatimid caliphate, blended Shiite mysticism with practices borrowed from the devotional (*bhakti*) cults of Hinduism. During Aurangzeb's reign they were suppressed as part of his general drive to bring Indian Islam more in accordance with Islamic law. They survived and later prospered, however, and in the twentieth century, their leader, the Aga Khan, was one of the world's wealthiest men.

## Literature and Art

The Mughal period was one of India's most prolific in terms of its profusion of literary genres. Moreover, literature, art, and architecture were the areas in which India's rich multicultural environment produced its most arrestingly synthetic works. In translation projects, classical Persian works, poetry in nearly all of India's languages, and even treatises on law and theology, Indian writers borrowed freely and frequently from each other. In painting, realistic portraits of personages and dramatic contemporary and historical scenes were recorded; and of course the great buildings of the era remain for many the "authentic" symbols of India.

**New Literary Directions**   As they had been for centuries in Islamic India, Arabic and Persian remained the principal literary languages. The use of both, however, was considerably enlivened by the introduction of the latest wave of Turkic terms by the Chaghatay–Turkic Mughals. Chaghatay itself remained in use among the elites until the nineteenth century, while many of its loan words, along with a considerable Persian and Arabic vocabulary, were grafted onto the base of Sanskrit to form the modern languages of Hindi and Urdu. Regional languages, such as Kashmiri and Bengali, also rose to prominence for both literary and general use.

Ironically, one of the catalysts for the explosion of literary work from the mid-sixteenth to the mid-seventeenth centuries came from the Mughals' most humiliating period. The exile of Humayun to Persia in the 1540s coincided with the Persian Shah Tahmasp embarking on a program of self-denial and abstinence in response to criticism about the worldliness of his court. Writers, painters, and poets who suddenly found themselves out of favor at the Persian court attached themselves to Humayun. They followed him to India, where their talents enlivened the arts already developing there. Their classical Arab and Persian verse forms were ultimately adopted into Urdu, as seen in the classical verse forms of *qasida* and *mathnavi*. By the following century, these forms had matured with the verses of Qudsi and Abu Talib Kalim (d. 1602), whose verses were considered models of adept compression of emotion.

> "Life's tragedy lasts but two days.
>    I'll tell you what these two are for;
>    One day, to attach the heart to this and that;
>    One day, to detach it again."
> —Abu Talib Kalim

Though Sunni scholarship languished somewhat under Akbar, Sufi works proliferated, many borrowing concepts and terminology from non-Islamic sources. The most famous of these was Muhammad Ghauth Gwaliori's *The Five Jewels*, which tapped sources from Hindu and Muslim astrology and Jewish Kabbala traditions, as well as Sufi mysticism. By Aurangzeb's reign, the pendulum had swung back to the more Mecca-centered, prophetic, and exclusive strain in Indian Islam. Thus, the works tended to be more often treatises on Islamic law, interpretation of *hadith*—the traditions of the Prophet—and Sunni works on science and philosophy.

**Art and Painting**   One of the more interesting aspects of Islam as practiced by the Mughals—as well as the Safavid Persians and Ottomans—is that the injunctions against depicting human beings in art were often widely ignored in the inner chambers and private rooms of the court. Of course, during Aurangzeb's long reign, there was a marked drop in artistic output because of his much stricter interpretation of proper Islamic behavior.

Not surprisingly, Akbar had a direct hand in the creation of what is considered to be the first painting in the "Mughal style"—a combination of the extreme delicacy of Persian miniature work with the vibrant colors and taste for bold themes of Hindu painters. Akbar inherited two of the master painters who accompanied Humayun from Persia, and the contact they acquired with Hindu works under Akbar's patronage resulted in hundreds of Mughal **gouache** works, including the colossal illustrated *Hamzanama* of 1570. The Persian tradition of miniature painting flourished under the Mughals. Illustrations of Muslim and Hindu religious themes and epics were perennial favorites, as were numerous depictions of imperial *durbars*—receptions requiring noble attendance at court. These usually included authentic portraits of key individuals and provide scholars with important clues as to the identities of courtiers and dignitaries. Mughal artists often passed their skills on within their families over generations and represented an important subset of members at the imperial court and among the entourages of regional elites.

By the end of the sixteenth century, a new influence was beginning to affect Mughal art: Europeans. The realistic approach of European artists and their use of perspective began to be felt at the courts of Akbar and Jahangir. One prominent female artist, Nadira Banu, specialized in producing Flemish-style works. Some took European paintings and added Mughal touches—flatter backgrounds, gold leaf, and mosques in the distance. The period of Akbar's religious experiments also prompted an unparalleled interest among Mughal painters in Christian religious figures. Depictions of Christ from the gospels and from Muslim tales were popular fare, as were angels; even more so was the figure of the Virgin, a picture of whom even appears in a portrait of Jahangir. It was perhaps the most dramatic meeting of cultural influences since the era of the Gandharan Buddhas that were fashioned in the style of the Greek god Apollo.

**The *Hamzanama* (Book of Hamza).** Akbar so enjoyed the *Hamzanama*, a heroic romance about the legendary adventures of the Prophet Mohammad's uncle Amir Hamza, that he commissioned an illustrated version in 1562. This painting from Akbar's version shows the prophet Elijah rescuing Hamza's nephew Prince Nur ad-Dahr.

**Gouache:** Watercolors with a gum base.

Architecture    Nowhere was the Mughal style more in evidence than in the construction of tombs and mausoleums. The most prominent of these, the Taj Mahal, was introduced in the opening to this chapter and needs little additional discussion. The ethereal lightness of so colossal a construction and the perfection of its layout make it the most distinctive construction of its kind. Europeans sometimes assumed that its architects were influenced by French or Italian artistic trends, though this remains a subject of debate. The chief architect, Ustad Ahmad Lahori (d. 1649), also designed the famous Red Fort of Shah Jahan's city, Shahjahanabad.

During the high point of Mughal wealth and power, several Mughal emperors built entire cities. By far the most famous of these, as we have previously seen, was Akbar's Fatehpur Sikri. Indeed, as an idealized tribute to the inclusive Sufi master Salim Chishti, with architectural influences from Hindu and Muslim sources, materials from all over India, and a quote from Jesus, as handed down in Islamic lore, over its gateway—"The world is but a bridge; cross over it but build no house upon it"—it does indeed reflect Akbar's vision of what his realm should be. Not to be outdone, of course, Shah Jahan created his own city complex at Delhi, Shahjahanabad.

As one would expect, just as they were integral to the tomb complexes of the Mughals, mosques would be among the empire's most important constructions. Many were built as shrines at holy sites or to mark significant events in the lives of holy men or martyrs. Once again, a distinctive style emerged in which the basic form of the dome symbolically covering the world and the slender arrow of the minaret pointing heavenward interacted with central Asian, Persian, and even Hindu architectural influences. The largest Mughal mosques, like the Friday Delhi Mosque (Jama Masjid) in Shahjahanabad and Aurangzeb's huge Badshahi Mosque in Lahore, contain immense courtyards, surrounded by cloisters leading to small rooms for intimate gatherings, domed areas for men and women, and distinctive minarets with fluted columns and bell-shaped roofs. One mosque in Burhanpur built by Shah Jahan even has Sanskrit translations of Quranic verses in it. As scholars have noted, the location of many of the largest mosques, like those of some European cathedrals, is adjacent to government buildings and forts in order to demonstrate the seamless connections of these religious civilizations.

## Putting It All Together

The rise of the Turkic central Asian peoples to prominence and power, from the borders of successive Chinese dynasties to Anatolia and the domains of the Ottomans, and with the Timurids or Mughals in India, is one of the most dramatic sagas of world history. In India, this latest group of outside conquerors faced what might be called the "great question" of the subcontinent: how to create a viable state out of so many long-standing religious traditions, many of which are in direct opposition to each other. Even before the coming of Islam, rulers such as Ashoka felt the need to use transcendent concepts, such as dharma, to try to bridge cultural and religious gaps. The Guptas, for their part, tried to use state-supported Hinduism. With the arrival of Islam, a new religion that stood in opposition to the older Hindu pattern of assimilation of gods and favored instead the conquest and conversion of opponents, a divide was created, which persists to this day. It should be remembered that, as recent scholarship has shown, even within these dramatically opposed religious traditions, much more accommodation than previously supposed took place. The later development of Sikhism, as another attempt at a syncretic bridge across India's religious divide, both added to attempts at greater tolerance and at times contributed to religious tensions.

Against this backdrop the accomplishments of the Mughals must be weighed as significant in terms of statecraft and artistic and cultural achievement, and perhaps less so in religious areas. At its height, Mughal India was the most populous, wealthy, politically powerful, and economically vibrant empire in the world next to China. It thus allowed the Mughal rulers unprecedented wealth and financed the proliferation of monumental architecture that became forever identified with India: the Red Fort, Fatehpur Sikri, and, above all, the Taj Mahal.

Yet, for all its wealth and power, the Mughal dynasty was plagued by problems that ultimately proved insoluble. The old nomadic succession practices of the Timurids repeatedly led to palace revolts by potential heirs. These wars in turn encouraged conflict with internal and external enemies who sensed weakness at the core of the regime. Protracted conflicts in Afghanistan, with Safavid Persia, and in Bengal also bled this centralized state of resources. Finally, the Maratha wars slowly wore down even the semblance of unity among the rulers following Aurangzeb.

But perhaps an equally important factor in the ultimate dissolution of the empire was that of Hindu–Muslim syncretism. Here, we have two of the world's great religions interacting with each other in prolonged and profound ways, with the added complication of Muslim rulers and Muslims in general being a minority among the subcontinent's people. Despite the flexibility of the early rulers in trying to deemphasize the more oppressive elements of Islamic rule in Hindu India— most dramatically, Akbar through his effort to create an entirely new religion— the attempt at a stricter orthodoxy under Aurangzeb hardened Hindu–Muslim and Sikh divisions for centuries to come.

Throughout the period, one other factor loomed larger day by day as the dynasty went into decline. The well-financed and well-armed trading companies of the Europeans, increasingly adept at reading Indian politics, gradually moved into positions of regional power. By 1750, they were on the cusp of changing the political situation completely. Indeed, the seeds that had been planted by 1750 would soon be reaped as the first great clash of mature religious civilizations with the new industrially based societies. By 1920, all of these religious civilizations would be gone.

▶ For additional resources, including maps, primary sources, visuals, and quizzes, please go to www.oup.com/us/vonsivers. Please see the Further Resources section at the back of the book for additional readings and suggested websites.

## Against the Grain

# Sikhism in Transition

As we saw in Chapter 13, the example of Zen Buddhism affords an example of a pacifistic religious tradition that was taken up by warrior classes. In some respects, Sikhism underwent a similar transformation, though not as thoroughgoing as that of Zen, and one that took place for very different reasons. As we remember from Chapter 12, the Sikhs had started from an avowedly peaceful premise: that the tension, and even all-out warfare, between Hindus and Muslims must somehow be transcended. Influenced by poets and mystics like Kabir and Guru Nanak, and drawing upon the emotional connections experienced by Muslim Sufis and Hindu Bhakti devotees who proclaimed that "there is no Hindu; there is no Musselman [Muslim]," the Sikhs had emerged during the sixteenth century as an entirely new religious movement.

Yet, far from providing a model for the two contending religions to emulate, Sikhs were viewed with suspicion by both. Although they attracted enough of a following to remain vital to the present day, their attempts at transcendence were viewed in much the same light as Akbar's attempts at a new religious synthesis were. Though they were awarded the city of Amritsar, the Golden Temple of which became their religious center, Mughal repression of the Sikhs under Aurangzeb in the seventeenth century provoked a prolonged rebellion, which turned them into a fierce fighting faith in self-defense. The Sikhs established control of most of the Punjab region during the eighteenth-century decline of the Mughals. During the days of British control, the reputation of the Sikhs as fierce fighters prompted the British to employ them as colonial troops and policemen throughout their empire. Even after independence, smoldering disputes between the government and Sikhs urging local autonomy for Punjab led to the assassination of Indian prime minister Indira Gandhi in retaliation for a government operation to forcibly remove a Sikh splinter group from the Golden Temple in 1984.

- **Why would both Hindus and Muslims express hostility toward a religion that claims to want to transcend the differences between them? Did the Sikhs appear to have any alternatives to becoming a fighting faith in order to ensure their survival?**

- **Why does it seem that, on the whole, what we have termed "religious civilizations" have difficulty tolerating different religious traditions within their domains? Does loyalty to a state require loyalty to its approved religion(s) as well? Why?**

# Thinking Through Patterns

▶ **What were the strengths and weaknesses of Mughal rule?**

The weaknesses are probably more obvious than the strengths at first glance. Two things are immediately apparent: first, the position of the Mughals as an ethnic and religious minority ruling a vastly larger majority population and, second, the conflict-prone succession practices of the older central Asian Turkic leaders. The minority position of the Mughals aggravated long-existing tensions between Hindu subjects and Muslim rulers in India, of which the Mughals were to be the last line. In an age of religious civilizations, where some kind of unity of religion was the ideal, this put considerable strains on the Mughals as rulers—as it did the Ottomans in predominantly Christian lands and Catholics and Protestants in Europe. Central Asian Turkic succession practices almost always guaranteed conflict when it was time for a new ruler to accede the throne. Nearly every Mughal successor during this period ended up having to fight factions and family to gain the empire.

In some respects the strengths of Mughal rule developed in reaction to these problems. Babur and Akbar, in particular, were extraordinarily tolerant rulers in terms of religion. When later rulers like Aurangzeb returned to strict Sunni Islamic policies, it prompted resistance, especially among Hindus. Also, while Mughal rulers were never able to completely free themselves from succession struggles, they succeeded in setting up a well-run fiscal–military state with the mansabdar system, largely undercutting old local and regional loyalties and tying the new loyalty to the state. Like France, the Ottomans, and the Confucian states of eastern Asia, the development of bureaucratic forms was an important earmark of the early modern era.

As we noted, Mughal rulers faced the problem confronted by nearly all "religious civilizations": Religious orthodoxy was seen, in theory, as a vital element of loyalty to the state. But for the Mughals, as for previous Muslim rulers in India, the desire for strict adherence to Muslim law was always tempered by the problem of Islam being a minority religion in India. Here, as we saw, the early Mughal rulers—Babur, Humayun, Akbar—were far less tied to strict Sunni Islam than their successors. Thus, their way

▶ **What was the Mughal policy toward religious accommodation? How did it change over time?**

of ruling was to uphold Sunni Islam as the approved state religion but to scrupulously refrain from forcing Muslim practices on other religious groups. Akbar went so far as to create a new religion and held Thursday-night discussions with leaders of other religions to find ways to satisfy the desires of all. With Shah Jahan, however, the reaction building among reform-minded Sunni Muslims to this liberalization turned into enforcing more strict practices, which peaked during the long reign of Aurangzeb. By the end of Aurangzeb's reign the Sikhs were near revolt and the long Hindu Maratha revolt was in full swing. But even during this period, local religious customs remained largely intact and, indeed, often thrived.

▶ **What factors account for the Mughal decline during the eighteenth century?**

At the beginning and for much of the eighteenth century, Mughal India was the second richest and most prosperous empire in the world, after China. But by 1750 it was already in pronounced decline. A large part of this was due to rebellions by the Sikhs, Rajputs, and especially the Marathas that raged off and on through the century. By the 1750s as well, the European trading companies with their small but well-trained armies were becoming locally powerful. Here, the great milestone would take place during the Seven Years' War (1756–1763), when the British East India Company eliminated its French competitors and in essence took over the rule of Bengal from its headquarters in Calcutta. Within 100 years it would take over all of India.

## SOURCE 20.2

# Muhammad Dara Shikuh, *The Mingling of Two Oceans*

### ca. 1650s

The eldest son of Shah Jahan, the fifth Mughal emperor, Dara Shikuh was defeated by his younger brother in a struggle for power in 1658. The victorious brother, Muhiuddin, ruled as the Emperor Aurangzeb, and he had Dara declared, by a court of nobles and clergy, an apostate from Islam and assassinated in 1659. Dara left behind a remarkable series of writings, advocating an enlightened program of harmonizing the various, bitterly opposed religions of the subcontinent. He had developed friendships with Sikhs, followed a Persian mystic, and completed a translation of 50 Upanishads from their original Sanskrit into Persian in 1657. His most famous work, the *Majma-ul-Bahrain* (*The Mingling of Two Oceans*), addressed the overlapping ideas of Hindu and Muslim mysticism. His attempt to combine the traditions into a coherent whole may have been rejected by his fervently Muslim brother, but he also represents a strain of ecumenical thought within the Mughal Empire.

### X. Discourse on the Vision of God (*Rūyat*).

The Indian monotheists call the Vision of God, *Sāchātkār*, that is, to see God with the (ordinary) eyes of the forehead. Know that the Vision of God, either by the Prophets, may peace be on them, or by the perfect divines, may their souls be sanctified, whether in this or the next world and whether with the outer or the inner eyes, cannot be doubted or disputed; and the "men of the Book" (*ahl-i-kitāb*), the perfect divines and the seers of all religions— whether they are believers in the Kur'ān, the Vedas, the Book of David or the Old and the New Testaments— have a (common) faith in this respect. Now, one who disbelieves the beholding of God is a thoughtless and sightless member of his community, the reason being: if the Holy Self is

Omnipotent, how can He not have the potency to manifest himself? This matter has been explained very clearly by the 'Ulamā of the Sunnī Sect. But, if it is said, that (even) the Pure Self (*dhāt-i-baht*) can be beheld, it is an impossibility; for the Pure Self is elegant and undetermined, and, as He cannot be determined, He is manifest in the veil of elegance only, and as such cannot be beheld, and such beholding is an impossibility. And the suggestion that He can be beheld in the next and not in this world, is groundless, for if He is Omnipotent, He is potent to manifest Himself in any manner, anywhere and at any time He likes. (I hold) that one who cannot behold Him here (i.e., in this world) will hardly behold Him there (i.e. in the next world); as He has said in the Holy verse: "And whoever is blind in

---

Source: Muhammad Dara Shikuh, *The Mingling of Two Oceans*, trans. and ed. M. Mafuz ul-Haq (Calcutta: Asiatic Society of Bengal, 1929), 50–53.

this, he shall (also) be blind in the hereafter" [Qur'an 17:72].

The *Mu'tazila* and the *Shī'a* doctors, who are opposed to *rūyat* (Beholding), have committed a great blunder in this matter, for had they only denied the capability of beholding the Pure Self, there would have been some justification, but their denial of all forms of *rūyat* is a great mistake; the reason being that most of the Prophets and perfect divines have beheld God with their ordinary eyes and have heard His Holy words without any intermediary and, now, when they are, by all means, capable of hearing the words of God, why should they not be capable of beholding Him? Verily, they must be so; and, just as it is obligatory to have faith in God, the Angels, the (revealed) Books, the Prophets, the Destiny, the Good and the Evil, and the Holy Places, etc., so it is obligatory and incumbent to have faith in *rūyat*.

. . .

Now, the beholding of God is of five kinds: first, in dream with the eyes of heart; secondly, beholding Him with the ordinary eyes; thirdly, beholding Him in an intermediate state of sleep and wakefulness, which is a special kind of Selflessness;

fourthly, (beholding Him) in (a stage of) special determination; fifthly, beholding the One Self in the multitudinous determinations of the internal and external worlds. In such a way beheld our Prophet, may peace be on him, whose "self" had disappeared from the midst and the beholder and the beheld had merged in one and his sleep, wakefulness and selflessness looked as one and his internal and the external eyes had become one unified whole—such is the state of perfect *rūyat*, which is not confined either to this or the next world and is possible everywhere and at every period.

### XI. Discourse on the Names of God, the Most High (*Asmāi Allāh Ta'ālā*).

Know that the names of God, the Most High, are numberless and beyond comprehension. In the language of the Indian divines, the Absolute, the Pure, the Hidden of the hidden and the Necessary Self is known as *asan, tirgun, nirankār, niranjan, sat* and *chit*. If knowledge is attributed to Him, the Indian divines designate Him as *chitan*, while the Muslims call Him 'Alīm (Knowing).

▶ **Working with Sources**

1. To what extent, and in what specific ways, did Dara Shikuh represent an ecumenical spirit with respect to Islam and other religions?

2. How does Dara Shikuh anticipate and address the objections of others within the Muslim community?

## SOURCE 20.3

# Edicts of Aurangzeb

**1666–1679**

When he became emperor in 1658, Aurangzeb attempted a radical "Islamification" of Mughal India, imposing a strict interpretation of Sharia law and implementing reforms that he thought would benefit Muslims more than adherents of other religions. Repudiating his great-grandfather

Akbar's vision of religious transcendence and harmony but stopping short of forcible conversion, Aurangzeb offered incentives to non-Muslims to convert, destroyed many of their temples, and reimposed the hated *jizya* tax. This tax on Hindus had been abolished by Akbar in 1564, and its reinstatement by Aurangzeb in 1679 triggered mass protests and violent reactions from authorities in many cities. Revolts among Sikhs and among Hindus left the Mughal Empire weakened and in decline by the time of Aurangzeb's death in 1707. An excerpt from his proscriptions is offered below.

**Exhibit No. 6: Keshava Rai Temple. "Even to look at a temple is a sin for a Musalman," Aurangzeb. Umurat-i-Hazur Kishwar-Kashai Julus (R.Yr.) 9, Rabi II 24 / 13 October 1666.**

'It was reported to the Emperor (Aurangzeb) that in the temple of Keshava Rai at Mathura, there is a stone railing presented by Bishukoh (one without dignity i.e. Prince Dara, Aurangzeb's elder brother). On hearing of it, the Emperor observed, "In the religion of the Musalmans it is improper even to look at a temple and this Bishukoh has installed this kathra (barrier railing). Such an act is totally unbecoming of a Musalman. This railing should be removed (forthwith)." His Majesty ordered Abdun Nabi Khan to go and remove the kathra, which is in the middle of the temple. The Khan went and removed it. After doing it he had audience. He informed that the idol of Keshava Rai is in the inner chamber. The railing presented by Dara was in front of the chamber and, formerly, it was of wood. Inside the kathra used to stand the sevakas of the shrine (pujaris etc.) and outside it stood the people (khalq)'.

**Exhibit No. 7: Demolition of Kalka's Temple - I. Siyah Waqa'i- Darbar Regnal Year 10, Rabi I, 23 / 3 September 1667.**

'The asylum of Shariat (Shariat Panah) Qazi Abdul Muqaram has sent this arzi to the sublime Court: a man known to him told him that the Hindus gather in large numbers at Kalka's temple near Barahapule (near Delhi); a large crowd of the Hindus is seen here. Likewise, large crowds are seen at (the mazars) of Khwaja Muinuddin, Shah Madar and Salar Masud Ghazi. This amounts to bid'at (heresy) and deserves consideration. Whatever orders are required should be issued.

Saiyid Faulad Khan was thereupon ordered (by the Emperor) to send one hundred beldars to demolish the Kalka temple and other temples in its neighbourhood which were in the Faujdari of the Khan himself; these men were to reach there post haste, and finish the work without a halt'.

**Exhibit No. 8: Demolition of Kalka Temple II. Siyah Akhbarat-i-Darbar-i-Mu'alla Julus 10, Rabi II 3 / 12 September 1667.**

'Saiyad Faulad Khan reported that in compliance with the orders, beldars were sent to demolish the Kalka temple which task they have done. During the course of the demolition, a Brahmin drew out a sword, killed a

Source: http://www.aurangzeb.info/2008/06/exhibit-no_7171.html.

bystander and then turned back and attacked the Saiyad also. The Brahmin was arrested'.

### Exhibit No. 16: Reimposition of Jizyah by Aurangzeb. (2nd April 1679)

'As all the aims of the religious Emperor were directed to the spreading of the law of Islam and the overthrow of the practices of the infidels, he issued orders to the high diwani officers that from Wednesday, the 2nd April 1679 / 1st Rabi I, in obedience to the Quranic injunction, "till they pay commutation money (Jizyah) with the hand in humility," and in agreement with the canonical tradition, Jizyah should be collected from the infidels (zimmis) of the capital and the provinces. Many of the honest scholars of the time were appointed to discharge the work (of collecting Jizyah). May God actuate him (Emperor Aurangzeb) to do that which He loves and is pleased with, and make his future life better than the present'.

▶ **Working with Sources**

1. How did the legacy of Akbar's and Dara's ecumenism influence Aurangzeb's policies?

2. What was the stated purpose of the reimposition of financial penalties on non-Muslims? Was this policy likely to have the effect he intended?

## SOURCE 20.4

# Muhammad Ghawth Gwaliori, *The Five Jewels*

ca. 1526

In sixteenth-century Hindustan, the Sufi mystic Muhammad Ghawth Gwaliori claimed to have experienced an astounding ascension through multiple heavenly spheres up to the throne of God. This intensely personal experience, which he underwent in his 20s, occurred within a volatile political and social context. Born around 1501, Ghawth left home at age 12 to further his religious education and to undertake a series of mystic initiations that prepared him for his ascension in 1526. Ghawth lived during the rule of Humayun, when Mughal control was still tentative, and Akbar was still a young man. After his mystical experiences made him famous, Ghawth was seen as a spiritual support for the Mughal regime. When Humayun fell from power in 1540, Ghawth was persecuted by a group of Afghan warlords who followed a more orthodox form of Islam and attacked the reality—as well as the political implications—of his mystical experiences.

Source: Excerpts from Scott A. Kugle, "Heaven's Witness: The Uses and Abuses of Muhammad Ghawth's Mystical Ascension," *Journal of Islamic Studies* 14 (2003): 17–20.

We reached the limit of the fourth heavenly sphere; the sphere split open; the stars waned like glowing crescents. I passed up into the heaven. The spirits of all the prophets came forward to greet me. They all shook my hand joyfully, along with the angels of that sphere. They praised me and their faces lit up, saying, "We have been waiting for so long, asking the Lord when you would be passing by this way. On the day that the Prophet ascended along this route, there were with him some saints, and you were one of them. However, at that time, you were in the form of pure spirit. In contrast, this time you are fully attached to your body! This is a completely new and different spectacle." They stood around amazed at my appearance. I ascended with ʿAlī and Abū Bakr, until we neared the limit of the fifth heavenly sphere.

. . .

The fourth heaven split open; the stars flared up, blazing brightly. I ascended into the fifth heavenly sphere. Such wondrous and strange things came into sight while all the angels of that sphere came forward into my presence. They carried in their hands pages, like those of a book. I asked, "What are these pages?" They answered, "These are the registers of Might which will consume the people consigned to the flames. They haven't been displayed yet or made public, but they record all the people's deeds." I asked, "Where are the people of the flames?" They invited me to come this way in order to see. When I came forward, I saw a chamber formed from the purest substance of Divine wrath. In it, there were many beings sitting, all in the shape of women. One woman among them was explaining clearly the meaning of Divine unity [tawhīd]. I asked, "Who is that woman who is teaching so eloquently?" They answered, "That is the mother of all humankind, Eve!"

I rushed forward to greet her and pay my respects, and asked her, "Why have you, a true Muslim, appeared in the midst of all the people who are overcome by Divine wrath?" Eve replied, "We are the most comprehensive, most perfect and most beautiful of all the manifestations of the Divine. We are called 'the People of Divine Might' who are the manifestation of Allah's attribute of utter singularity." I requested Eve to explain this to me further; she said, "The authority of Allah's beauty is delegated to the prophets, and that authority has already come to its full completion long ago and its delegation is now over. Then the saints were raised up and were given authority. To the saints was delegated the authority of Allah's beauty mixed with Allah's might. Now listen, these women whom you see here are the messengers who will be sent to the people punished in hell fire. They are called 'the People of Divine Might.' They each wish to raise people up from the fires of hell into the realm of pure Divine might. The Prophet himself revealed this from the inner world when he said, 'Women are the emissaries of Satan.'"

. . .

The heaven split open and we ascended into it. The essences both lofty and lowly appeared before me. I hesitated there, thinking that, if I don't understand the appearance of these essences, I will have no way to advance religious knowledge and intuitive knowledge [ʿilm-i dīnī o ʿilm-i ladūnī]. My thoughts inclined to find out what religious knowledge really looked like. At that moment, Jesus spoke to me, saying, "Have you ever seen the four Imams [who fashioned the structure of Islamic law]?" I answered, "No." Jesus directed me to look at a certain place in the vastness; there I saw the four Imams standing together, each disputing with the others, saying, "No, no, the certain truth is this, not that." I thought to myself, if this is the outer knowledge of religion, then what is the inner knowledge of intuition? The thought simply flashed in my mind, but I didn't say anything to that effect. Just then, all the Divine names of Allah emerged, each in the particular dimension of its knowability, from the realm of the primal archetypes. Each took a distinct shape, giving rise to the whole multitude of perceptible and existent forms. I could see the continuity between the Divine names and all the created forms that arose from their various natures. I could see the universe contained within the relation between the Divine names that prepared the universe for its worldly existence.

▶ **Working with Sources**

1. What do the inclusion of Ali, Eve, and Jesus in Ghawth's mystical vision suggest about religious culture in sixteenth-century Hindustan?

2. What might one learn from Ghawth's vision about the Sufi view of gender and the roles of women?

## SOURCE 20.5

# Calico textile

## ca. 1806

Calico was a fine printed cotton cloth first imported to England from Calicut, on the western shore of the subcontinent, by the British East India Company. A domestic manufacture of calico-inspired textiles followed, as English artisans attempted to mimic the bright colors, careful weaving, and intricate designs of Indian cloth. This example commemorates Vice Admiral Lord Nelson, a British naval hero of the Napoleonic Wars and the American War of Independence. Nelson, who died in the Battle of Trafalgar in 1805, was buried in St. Paul's Cathedral after an elaborate funeral service.

▶ **Working with Sources**

1. What specific elements are incorporated into this commemorative calico, and how are they symbolic of Nelson's military career?

2. How were the interests of the British East Indies Company furthered by internal conflict on the subcontinent in the seventeenth and eighteenth centuries?

Source: National Maritime Museum, London.

# Chapter 21 1500–1800
# Regulating the "Inner" and "Outer" Domains

## CHINA AND JAPAN

CHINA AND JAPAN, 1500–1800

The time seemed right for a letter home. In only 2 weeks the Japanese invasion force had captured the Korean capital of Seoul, and the skill and firepower of the Japanese warriors seemed to let them brush their opponents aside at will. The Japanese commander, Toyotomi Hideyoshi, was a battle-hardened commoner who had risen through the ranks of his patron, Oda Nobunaga, as Oda fought to unite Japan before his assassination in 1582. Now, a decade later, Hideyoshi, as he was still known (as a commoner he had no surname and had only been given the family name Toyotomi by the imperial court in 1586) had embarked on an audacious campaign to extend his power to the Asian mainland. Six years before, he had written his mother that he contemplated nothing less than the conquest of China. Now seemed like a good time to inform her that his goal might actually be within his grasp.

As if in an eerie foreshadowing of another Korean conflict to come centuries later, however, the Japanese soon faced a massive Chinese and Korean counterattack and became mired in a bloody stalemate, their guns and tactics barely enough to compensate for the determination and numbers of their

*ABOVE:* This scene, one of 15 from the handscroll painting *A Visit to the Yoshiwara* by Hishikawa Mononobu (ca. 1625–1694), depicts the "floating world" of Tokugawa Japan.

enemies. After 4 more years of negotiation punctuated by bitter fighting, Hideyoshi finally withdrew to Japan. One final invasion attempt of Korea in 1597 collapsed when his death the following year set off a bloody struggle for succession, which ultimately placed in power the Tokugawa family, who would go on to rule Japan for more than 250 years.

Hideyoshi's dream of conquering China was, in a sense, a quest to claim the wellsprings of Japanese civilization as well. The episode brought together the politics, cultures, and fortunes of three of the four fiercely independent realms that together wove the primary strands of an east Asian pattern of history. The fourth, Vietnam, while not involved in this particular struggle, had been subject to similar pressures of Chinese cultural and political diffusion for eighteen centuries. The rise of Japanese power represents a vitally important pattern of world history, which we have seen in other areas, such as the Mediterranean and the expanding kingdoms of Europe: A state on the periphery absorbs innovation from a cultural center, in this case China, and then becomes a vital center itself. And like the other states in the region, Japan had absorbed the structures of "religious civilizations," as we have termed them—in this case, the philosophical system of Neo-Confucianism.

Of equal importance, Hideyoshi's invasion was made possible in part by the arrival of a new factor: the appearance of the first Europeans in the region. While their arrival in the sixteenth century provided only the smallest inkling of the reversals of fortune to come, by the middle of the nineteenth century their presence would create a crisis of power and acculturation for all of east Asia. For Japan, the industrializing West would then become a new center from which to draw innovation. For the present, however, European intrusions provided powerful incentives for both China and Japan to turn inward to safeguard their own security and stability.

## Late Ming and Qing China to 1750

Proclaimed as a new dynasty in 1368, the Ming in its early years appears to have followed the familiar pattern of the "dynastic cycle" of previous dynasties. Having driven out the Mongol remnant, the Hongwu emperor and his immediate successors consolidated their rule, elevated the Confucian bureaucracy to its former place, and set up an administrative structure more focused on the person of the emperor than in previous dynasties. In 1382, the Grand Secretariat was created as the top governmental board below the emperor. Under the Grand Secretariat were the six boards, the governors and governors-general of the provinces, and lower-level officials of various degrees down to the district magistrate.

In this section we will also take up the question of China's retreat from its greatest period of maritime expansion in the early 1400s—and sudden withdrawal to concentrate on domestic matters. Why such an abrupt change in policy? What factors led to the ultimate decline of the Ming dynasty and the rise to power of the Manchus, a bordering nomadic people who drove out the Ming and created China's last imperial dynasty, the Qing [ching]? By what means did the Manchus

## Seeing Patterns

▶ Why did late Ming and early Qing China look inward after such a successful period of overseas exploration?

▶ How do the goals of social stability drive the policies of agrarian states? How does the history of China and Japan in this period show these policies in action?

▶ In what ways did contact with the maritime states of Europe alter the patterns of trade and politics in eastern Asia?

▶ How did Neo-Confucianism in China differ from that of Tokugawa Japan?

create a state in which, despite being a tiny ruling minority, they held their grip on power into the twentieth century? Finally, what faint hints of the dynasty's problems appeared during its time of greatest power in the mid-eighteenth century?

## From Expansion to Exclusion

During the late fourteenth and early fifteenth centuries, while China was rebuilding from the war to drive out the Mongols, the more pressing problems of land distribution and tenancy had abated somewhat. As in Europe, the depopulation of some areas from fighting and banditry and the lingering effects of the Black Death (which had reduced China's population from perhaps 100 million to about 60 million) had raised the value of labor, depressed the price of land, and increased the proportional amount of money in circulation. While the problems of land tenure would recur, another period of relief from their full effects soon came, albeit indirectly, from the creation of overseas empires by the Portuguese and the Spanish in the sixteenth century. The resulting Columbian Exchange saw the circulation of a number of new food crops on a global scale that had a substantial impact on the world's agricultural productivity (see Chapter 18).

New Food Crops   In addition to new, higher-yielding rice strains from southeast Asia, the Chinese began to cultivate sugarcane, indigo, potatoes, sweet potatoes, maize (corn), peanuts, and tobacco that came from Africa and the Americas by way of the Spanish in the Philippines and the Portuguese at Macau. Corn and potatoes, versatile crops suitable for cultivation in a variety of marginal environments, accounted for a considerable increase in the arable land within China. Peanuts, sugarcane, indigo, and tobacco quickly established themselves as important cash crops.

Aided by the productivity of these new crops, China's population grew from its low of perhaps 60 million at the beginning of the Ming period to an estimated 150 million by 1600. There was also a marked growth in urbanism as market towns and regional transshipment points multiplied. The efficiency of Chinese agriculture, the continued incorporation of marginal and border lands into production, and the refinement of the empire's immense internal trade all contributed to another doubling of the population to perhaps 300 million by 1800. This accelerating growth began China's movement toward what some historical demographers have called a *high-level equilibrium trap*—a condition in which the land has reached its maximum potential for feeding an increasing population; that population then (barring radical improvements in crops or technology) becomes slowly squeezed into impoverishment (see Map 21.1).

China and the World Commercial Revolution   China's rapid recovery, particularly as the sixteenth century brought new crops from the Americas, placed the late Ming and Qing Empires in the center of an increasingly extensive and complex worldwide commercial revolution (see "Patterns Up Close: The 'China' Trade"). The competition for markets among the emerging maritime Atlantic states of Europe pushed them to develop ever-widening trade networks in the Indian and Pacific Oceans, along the African coast, and in the Americas. In all of these regions (except the Americas) they faced stiff competition from local traders long involved in regional networks, particularly in the Indian Ocean, among the many ports of what is now Indonesia.

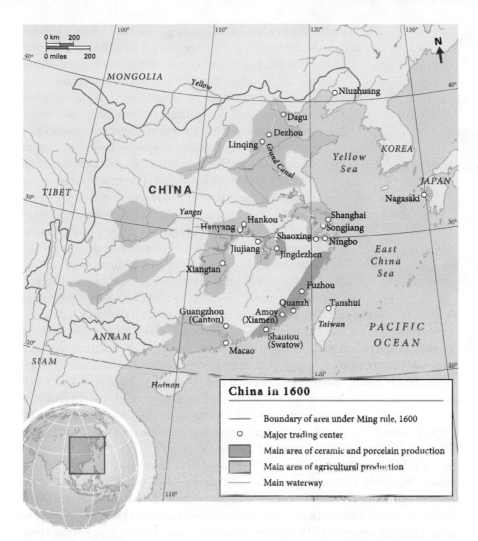

MAP **21.1  China in 1600.**

Among the European states, commercial, political, and religious competition resulted in policies of mercantilism (see Chapters 17, 18, and 19) in which countries strove to control sources of raw materials and markets. Similarly, China and Japan (by the early seventeenth century) sought to tightly control imports, regulate the export trade, and keep potentially subversive foreign influences in check.

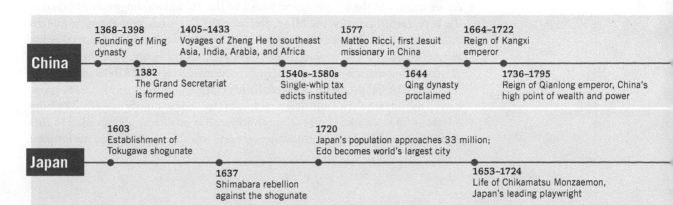

**China**

**1368–1398**
Founding of Ming dynasty

**1405–1433**
Voyages of Zheng He to southeast Asia, India, Arabia, and Africa

**1577**
Matteo Ricci, first Jesuit missionary in China

**1664–1722**
Reign of Kangxi emperor

**1382**
The Grand Secretariat is formed

**1540s–1580s**
Single-whip tax edicts instituted

**1644**
Qing dynasty proclaimed

**1736–1795**
Reign of Qianlong emperor, China's high point of wealth and power

**Japan**

**1603**
Establishment of Tokugawa shogunate

**1720**
Japan's population approaches 33 million; Edo becomes world's largest city

**1637**
Shimabara rebellion against the shogunate

**1653–1724**
Life of Chikamatsu Monzaemon, Japan's leading playwright

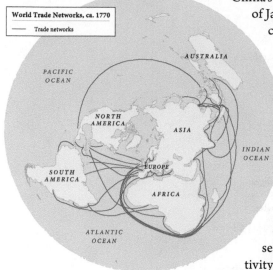

World Trade Networks, ca. 1770
——  Trade networks

PACIFIC
OCEAN

AUSTRALIA

NORTH
AMERICA

ASIA

INDIAN
OCEAN

EUROPE

SOUTH
AMERICA

AFRICA

ATLANTIC
OCEAN

MAP 21.2  **World Trade Networks, ca. 1770.**

China's immense production of luxury goods, the seclusion policies of Japan and Korea, and the huge and growing demand for porcelain, tea, silk, paper, and cotton textiles made the Chinese empire the world's dominant economic engine until the productive capacity of the Industrial Revolution vaulted Great Britain into that position in the nineteenth century. Indeed, recent work by world historians has shown how extensively China's economy powered that of Eurasia and much of the rest of the world before what Kenneth Pomeranz has called "the great divergence" of Western economic ascendancy (see Map 21.2).

In the midst of this growth, the government took steps to simplify the system of land taxation. *Corvée* labor—the required contribution of labor as a form of tax—was effectively abolished. As in previous regimes, land was assessed and classified according to its use and relative productivity. Land taxes were then combined into a single bill, payable in silver by installments over the course of the year: the so-called single-whip tax system. The installment plan allowed peasants to remain relatively solvent during planting season when their resources were depleted, thus reducing the need to borrow at high rates from moneylenders at crucial times of the yearly cycle. Significantly, the requirement that the payment be in silver also played a crucial role in the increasing monetization of the economy. This was aided considerably by the increasing amounts of silver entering the Chinese economy by means of the Manila trade. Merchants from south China exchanged spices and Chinese luxury goods such as porcelain (see Patterns Up Close below) in Manila for Spanish silver from the Americas. Manila thus became a vital axis around which the trade economies of three continents revolved. Though ultimately eclipsed in trade share and economic importance with the rise of the Canton system in the eighteenth century, Spanish (and later Mexican) silver continued to be the preferred medium of exchange for Chinese merchants for more than three centuries.

**Regulating the Outer Barbarians**    By the late fifteenth century, Ming China had made considerable progress toward establishing the peace and stability long sought by Chinese regimes. In addition to the practical requirements of defending the historic avenues of invasion in China's remote interior, the view of the empire cultivated by China's elites placed it at the center of a world order defined by Neo-Confucian philosophy and supported by a host of Chinese cultural assumptions. As we will see in the following sections, like the Tokugawa shogunate in Japan in the seventeenth century, the Ming, and later the Qing, had come to view foreign influence as less "civilized" and far too often injurious to established social order. Hence, successive rulers placed severe restrictions on maritime trade and conceived of diplomatic relations primarily in commercial terms. "All the world is one family," imperial proclamations routinely claimed, and the emperor was conceived as the father, in Confucian terms, of this world-family system. "Tribute missions," a term sometimes (though somewhat misleadingly) applied to this diplomatic–commercial relationship, were sent from Korea, Vietnam, the Ryukyu

Islands, and occasionally Japan to pay periodic ceremonial visits to the emperor, who then bestowed presents on the envoys and granted them permission to trade in China. This arrangement worked reasonably well within the long-standing hierarchy of the Confucian cultural sphere. By the late eighteenth century, however, it came into direct conflict with the more egalitarian system of international trade and diplomacy that had evolved in the West.

**The Ming in Decline**    Despite the increased attention directed at the Mongol resurgence of the 1440s, periodic rebellions in the north and northwest punctuated the late fifteenth and sixteenth centuries. The huge commitment of Chinese troops in Korea against the forces of the Japanese leader Hideyoshi during his attempted invasion of Korea and China from 1592 to 1598 weakened the dynasty further during a crucial period that saw the rise of another regional power: the Manchus. By the turn of the seventeenth century, under the leadership of Nurhachi (r. 1616–1626) and Abahai (r. 1636–1643), the Manchus, an Altaic speaking nomadic people inhabiting the northeastern section of the Ming domain, had become the prime military force of the area, and dissident Chinese sought them as allies. In 1642, the Chinese general Wu Sangui invited the Manchu leader Dorgon to cross the Great Wall where it approaches the sea at Shanhaiguan. For the Chinese, this event would come to carry the same sense of finality as Caesar's crossing of the Rubicon: The Manchus soon captured Beijing and declared the founding of a new regime, the Qing, or "pure," dynasty. Like the defeated remnant of the Nationalist regime in 1949, some Ming loyalists fled to the island of Taiwan, where they expelled the Dutch (who had established a trading base there) and held on until succumbing to Qing forces in 1683.

**Manchu Bannermen, Canton, ca. 1872.** Until the twentieth century, the Qing maintained garrisons of Manchu soldiers organized under the old "banner system" in all of China's major cities. The bannermen lived in their own quarter, often in reduced circumstances, as a check on the local Chinese population. Significantly, in terms of China's difficulties with Western imperialism in the later nineteenth century, the group pictured here was part of the guard of the British consul.

## The Spring and Summer of Power: The Qing to 1750

Like the Toba and Mongols before them, the Manchus now found themselves in the position of having to "dismount and rule." A good deal of preparation for this had already taken place within the borderland state they had created for themselves—for a time, successfully isolated by the Ming—on the Liaodong Peninsula of south Manchuria. Long exposure to Chinese culture and Confucian administrative practices provided models that soon proved adaptable by Manchu leaders within the larger environment of China proper.

**The Banner System**    The **banner system**, under which the Manchus were organized for military and tax purposes, was also expanded under the Qing to provide for segregated Manchu elites and garrisons in major cities and towns. Under the banner system, the Manchu state had been divided into eight major military and ethnic (Manchu, Han Chinese, and Mongolian) divisions, each represented by a distinctive banner. Within each division, companies were formed of 300 fighters recruited from families represented by that banner. Originally devised for a

**Banner system:** The organizational system of the Manchus for military and taxation purposes; there were eight banners under which all military houses were arranged, and each was further divided into blocks of families required to furnish units of 300 soldiers to the Manchu government.

# Patterns Up Close | The "China" Trade

Ming and Qing China may be said to be at the heart of two innovations of enormous importance to the patterns of world history. The first is one that we have tracked through all of the chapters in this book pertaining to China: the technical and aesthetic development of ceramics, culminating in the creation of true porcelain during the Song period (960–1279). The early Ming period saw the elaboration of the use of kaolin white clays with what are called "flux" materials—minerals, metals, and compounds—that can fuse with the clay under extremely high temperatures to form durable glazes and striking artistic features. Thus, the Song and Yuan periods were characterized by pure white and celadon green wares, some with a purposely created "crackle" glaze on them, while by the Ming period, highly distinctive blue and white ware—the result of employing pigments with cobalt oxide imported from the areas around modern Iran and Iraq—set the world standard for elegance.

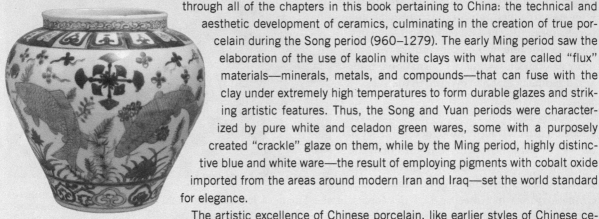

**Porcelain Vase, Ming Period.** Porcelain ware of the Song and Ming periods is among the most coveted Chinese art objects even today. Here we have a Ming vase showing characteristically vibrant colors and a degree of technical perfection indicative of the best Chinese pottery works, such as Jingdezhen. The motif of the grass carp on the vase is symbolic of endurance and perseverance, and thus associated with the god of literature and scholarship.

The artistic excellence of Chinese porcelain, like earlier styles of Chinese ceramics, spawned imitations throughout the Chinese periphery. By 1500, porcelain works in Korea, Japan, and Vietnam supplied a burgeoning market both at home and throughout east and southeast Asia. While these regional manufacturers for the most part followed the designs of the Chinese imperial works at Jingdezhen, some, especially the Japanese ceramicist Chojiro, preferred highly rustic, rough-hewn earthenware designs with glazes that formed spontaneous designs as the pieces were fired—the famous raku ware. Thus, there was already a highly developed regional market for what was, at the time, arguably the world's most highly developed technology.

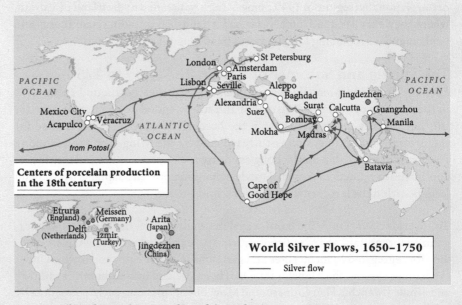

**Centers of porcelain production in the 18th century**

Etruria (England)  Meissen (Germany)
Delft (Netherlands)  Izmir (Turkey)  Arita (Japan)
Jingdezhen (China)

**World Silver Flows, 1650–1750**
—— Silver flow

MAP 21.3 **Silver Flows and Centers of Porcelain Production.**

The period from 1500 to the mid-nineteenth century brings us to the second great innovation in which China was the driving force: the world market for porcelain. China's wares had found customers for centuries in nearly every corner of Eurasia and North and East Africa. Shipwrecks have been found in the Straits of Malacca laden with Ming porcelain; traders in the Swahili cities along the East African coast were avid collectors, while Africans farther inland decorated their graves with Chinese bowls. All stops on the Silk Road had their precious supplies of porcelain, while the Ottoman Turks did their best to copy the blue and white Ming wares in their own factories at Izmir.

Before the sixteenth century, a trickle of Ming porcelain also made its way to Europe. With the establishment of the first European trade empires, however, the demand for porcelain skyrocketed. Portuguese, Spanish, and later Dutch, French, English, and (after 1784) American merchants all sought porcelain in ever-increasing amounts. From 1500 to 1800 it was arguably the single most important commodity in the unfolding world commercial revolution. While estimates vary, economic historians have suggested that between one-third to one-half of all the silver produced in the Americas during this time went to pay for porcelain. Incoming ships often used the bulk cargoes of porcelain as ballast, and foreign merchants sent custom orders to their Chinese counterparts for Chinese-style wares designed for use at Western tables. Such was the prominence of this "export porcelain" in the furnishings of period homes that scarcely any family of means was without it (see Map 21.3).

With the prominence of mercantilist theory and protectionism toward home markets during the seventeenth and eighteenth centuries, it is not surprising that foreign manufacturers sought to break the Chinese monopoly. During Tokugawa times, the Japanese, for example, forced a group of Korean potters to labor at the famous Arita works to turn out Sino–Korean designs; the Dutch marketed delftware as an attempt to copy Chinese "blue willow" porcelain. It was not until German experimenters in Saxony happened upon a workable formula for hard-paste porcelain—after years of trial and error, even melting down Chinese wares for analysis—that their facility at Meissen began to produce true porcelain in 1710. Josiah Wedgwood set up his own porcelain factory in 1759 in England. But Chinese manufacturers would still drive the market until the end of the nineteenth century. And fine porcelain would forever carry the generic name of "china" regardless of its origins.

**Porcelain Candlestick for the Export Market, Qing Period.** By the early 1700s, luxury exports from China such as porcelain, lacquerware, and, of course, tea had become important staples of European maritime trade. Export porcelain—either items made to order by Chinese porcelain works for overseas buyers or generic ones made to suit European and colonial tastes—had become such a big business that cheaper pieces were sometimes actually used as ship's ballast on the homeward voyages. Shown here is a candlestick for use in a European home with Chinese motifs of vessels at the top. The cobalt blue color is characteristic of the Ming and Qing designs.

## Questions

- How does the development of porcelain serve as an example of Chinese leadership in technical innovation during the premodern and early modern periods?

- How did the emergence of a global trading network after 1500 affect both the demand for porcelain and its impact on consumer tastes?

mobile warrior people, the system eventually became the chief administrative tool of the Manchu leadership. It was now introduced into China in such a way as to establish the Manchus as a hereditary warrior class occupying its own sections of major Chinese cities. The Han, or ethnic Chinese, forces were organized into their own "Armies of the Green Standard," so named for the color of the flags they carried.

**Minority Rule**   Always conscious of their position as a ruling minority in China, with their numbers comprising only about 2 percent of the population, the Manchus, like the Mongols before them, sought to walk a fine line between administrative and cultural adaptation and the kind of complete assimilation that had characterized previous invaders. Thus, under what is sometimes termed the Sino–Manchu **dyarchy**, Chinese and Manchus were scrupulously recruited in equal numbers for high administrative posts; Manchu quotas in the examination system were instituted; edicts and memorials were issued in both Chinese and Manchu; Qing emperors sought to control the empire's high culture; and, of course, Manchu "bannermen" of the various garrisons were kept in their own special quarters in the towns and cities. In addition, the Manchu conqueror Dorgon instituted the infamous "queue edict" in 1645: All males, regardless of ethnicity, were required on pain of death to adopt the Manchu hairstyle of a shaved forehead and long pigtail in the back—the queue—as the outward sign of loyalty to the new order. This hairstyle can be seen in early photographs taken of Chinese men until the Qing dynasty fell in 1912. As a darkly whimsical saying put it, "Keep the hair, lose the head; keep the head, lose the hair."

The results, however, were bloody and long-lasting. The queue edict provoked revolts in several cities, and the casualties caused by its suppression may have numbered in the hundreds of thousands. For the remainder of the Qing era, rebels and protestors routinely cut their queues as the first order of business; during China's Taiping Rebellion (1851–1864), perhaps the bloodiest civil war in human history, insurgents were known as "the long-haired rebels" for their immediate abandonment of the Qing hairstyle.

**Creating the New Order**   Though the Qing kept the centralized imperial system of the Ming largely intact, while importing the banner system as a kind of Manchu parallel administrative apparatus, they also made one significant addition to the uppermost level of the bureaucracy. While retaining the Ming Grand Secretariat, the emperor Kangxi's successor, Yongzheng, set up an ad hoc inner advisory body called the Grand Council in 1733. Over the succeeding decades the Grand Council became the supreme inner advisory group to the emperor, while the Grand Secretariat was relegated to handling less crucial "outer" matters of policy making and implementation.

For much of the seventeenth century, however, the pacification of the empire remained the primary task. Under the able leadership of Nurhachi's great-grandson the Kangxi Emperor (r. 1661–1722), the difficult subjugation of the south was concluded, the Revolt of the Three Feudatories (1673–1681) ultimately crushed, and the naval stronghold of the Ming pretender called Koxinga by the Dutch captured on Taiwan in 1683.

As had been the case in past dynasties, the Qing sought to safeguard the borders of the empire by bringing peoples on the periphery into the imperial system

**Dyarchy:** A system of administration consisting of two equal or parallel parts.

through a judicious application of the carrot and the stick, or, as it was known to generations of Chinese strategists, the "loose rein" and "using barbarians to check barbarians." In practical terms, this meant a final reckoning with the Mongols in the 1720s by means of improved cannon and small arms, along with bribes and presents to friendly chieftains, and the intervention of the Qing in religious disputes regarding Tibetan Buddhism, which had also been adopted by a number of the Mongol groups. Toward this end, the Qing established a protectorate over Tibet in 1727, with the Dalai Lama ruling as the approved temporal and religious leader. To cement the relationship further, the emperor built a replica of a Tibetan stupa just outside the Manchu quarter in Beijing and a model of the Dalai Lama's Potala Palace at the emperor's summer retreat in Jehol [ych-HOLE].

**Tibetan Stupa and Temple, Beijing.** This marble *chorten*, the Tibetan version of the Buddhist stupa, or reliquary, was built by the Qianlong emperor for the visit of the Panchen Lama in 1779, in part to cement the new Sino-Tibetan relationship growing from the establishment of a Qing protectorate over Tibet.

**The Qianlong Emperor**   With the traditional threats from the borders now quashed, the reign of the Qianlong [chien-LUNG] emperor, from 1736 to 1795, marked both the high point and the beginning of the decline of the Qing dynasty—and of imperial China itself. The period witnessed China's expansion to its greatest size during the imperial era. This was accompanied by a doubling of its population to perhaps 300 million by 1800. By almost any measure, its internal economy dwarfed that of any other country and equaled or surpassed that of Europe as a whole until the Industrial Revolution was well under way.

The Qing army, though perhaps already eclipsed in terms of efficiency and weaponry by the leading nations of Europe, was still many times larger than that of any potential competitor. Moreover, Qianlong wielded this power successfully a number of times during his reign, with expeditions against pirates and rebels on Taiwan and in punitive campaigns against Vietnam, Nepal, and Burma between 1766 and 1792 (see Map 21.4). During his long life, he also tried, with limited success, to take up the writing brush of a scholar and connoisseur, creating the collection of art that is today the core of the National Palace Museum's holdings on Taiwan. Under his direction, the state sponsored monumental literary enterprises on a scale still awesome to contemplate today. Based on the small but steady stream of information on the Qing empire circulating around Europe, it seemed to some that the Chinese had solved a number of the problems of good government and might provide practical models of statecraft for Europeans to emulate.

**Early European Contacts**   Ironically, it was precisely at the time that China abandoned its oceanic expeditions that tiny Portugal on the Atlantic coast surmounted its first big hurdle in pursuit of what would become a worldwide maritime trade empire (see Chapters 16, 18, 19). By the 1440s, Portuguese navigators had rounded the bulge of West Africa and opened commercial relations with the coastal kingdoms there. Scarcely a decade after Vasco da Gama arrived in Calicut in 1498, the first Portuguese ships appeared in Chinese waters. By 1557, these *Folangqi*—the Chinese transliteration of "Franks," a generic term for Europeans transmitted

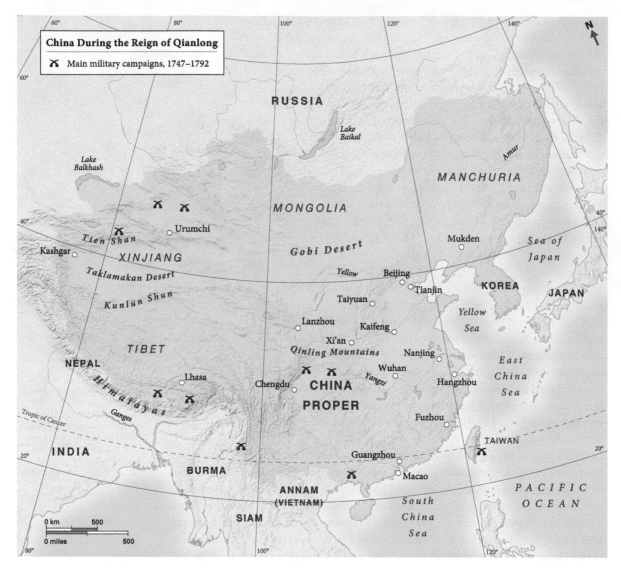

**China During the Reign of Qianlong**

✕ Main military campaigns, 1747–1792

MAP 21.4 **China during the Reign of Qianlong.**

by the Arabs to Malacca, where it was transformed into *Ferenghi* [fa-REN-gee]—had wrested the first European colony from the Chinese at Macau. It was destined to be the longest-lived European colony as well, remaining under Portuguese control until 1999. From this point on, through merchants and missionaries, the contacts would frequently be profitable—and, sometimes, disastrous. Ultimately, they provided some of the most far-reaching interactions of world history.

**Missionaries** The arrival of the first European merchants in east Asia was followed shortly by that of the first Catholic missionaries. Although the crusading impulse was still very much alive in Christian dealings with Muslim merchants in the Indies, Christian missionaries (at first from the Franciscan and Dominican orders and later from the Jesuits) were quick to realize the vast potential for religious conversions in China and Japan. The various missionary orders set up headquarters in Malacca, and in 1549 the Franciscan Francis Xavier landed in Japan. The endemic conflict among the *daimyo* (regional warlords) of Japan helped create a demand for Western goods, especially firearms, and the association of these with Christianity allowed considerable progress to be made in gaining conversions. China, however, required a vastly different strategy.

Wary of potentially disruptive foreign influences, the Ming at first refused entry to missionaries. Once admitted, the Franciscans and Dominicans, with their limited training in Chinese language and culture, made little headway. Additionally, their efforts were largely aimed at seeking conversions among the poor, which won them scant respect or influence among China's elite. The Jesuits, however, tried a different tack. Led by Matteo Ricci (1552–1610) and his successors Adam Schall von Bell (1591–1666) and Ferdinand Verbiest (1623–1688), they immersed themselves in the classical language and high culture of the empire and gained recognition through their expertise in mathematics, astronomy, military science, and other European learning sought by the imperial court. Jesuit

**Matteo Ricci and Li Paul.** The cross-cultural possibilities of sixteenth- and seventeenth-century Sino–Western contact were perhaps best exemplified by the activities of the Jesuit Matteo Ricci (1552–1610). Ricci predicated his mission in China on a respectful study of the language and classical canon of the empire coupled with a thorough knowledge of the new mathematics and astronomy of the West. Here, he is pictured with one of his most prominent converts, a literatus and veteran of the war against the Japanese in Korea, Li Yingshi. Upon his conversion in 1602, Li took the Christian name of Paul.

advisors served the last Ming emperors as court astronomers and military engineers and successfully made the transition to the new dynasty. The high point of their influence was reached during the reign of the Qing Kangxi Emperor. With Schall as the official court astronomer and mathematician and an entire European-style observatory set up in Beijing, Kangxi actively considered conversion to Catholicism.

The papacy, however, had long considered Jesuit liturgical and doctrinal adaptations to local sensibilities problematic. In the case of China, competition among the three orders for converts and disturbing reports from the Franciscans and Dominicans regarding the Jesuits' alleged tolerance of their converts' continued veneration of Confucius and maintenance of ancestral shrines set off the "rites controversy." This was worsened in the eyes of the papacy by the Jesuits' acquiescence to the use of tea and rice for the Eucharist instead of bread and wine. After several decades of intermittent discussion, Kangxi's successor, Yongzheng, banned the order's activities in China in 1724. Christianity and missionary activity were thus driven underground, though the Qing would retain a Jesuit court astronomer into the nineteenth century.

**The Canton Trade**   While China's commerce with the maritime Atlantic states grew rapidly in the eighteenth century, the Europeans had not yet been fully incorporated into the Qing diplomatic system. A century before, the expansion of

**Canton Factories, ca. 1800.**
Under the "Canton system" begun in 1699, all maritime trade with the Europeans was tightly controlled and conducted through the single port of Canton, or Guangzhou. Foreign merchants were not allowed to reside within the walled city, so they constructed their own facilities along the Pearl River waterfront. Though it kept profits high for the concerned parties, the restrictiveness of the system caused nineteenth-century merchants and diplomats to push the Chinese to open more ports to trade, which proved to be a major sticking point in Sino–Western relations.

**Factory:** Here, the place where various "factors" (merchants, agents, etc.) gathered to conduct business.

Russia into Siberia and the region around the Amur River had prompted the Qing to negotiate the Treaty of Nerchinsk in 1689. Under its terms, negotiated with Kangxi's Jesuit advisors acting as interpreters and go-betweens, the Russians agreed to abandon their last forts along the Amur and were given rights to continue their lucrative caravan trade in the interior. Formal borders were established in Manchuria, and the first attempts at settling claims to the central Asian regions of Ili and Kuldja were made. Significantly, Russian envoys were also permitted to reside in Beijing but in a residence like those used by the temporary envoys of tribute missions.

The situation among the European traders attempting to enter Chinese seaports, however, was quite different. The British East India Company, having established its base at Calcutta in 1690, soon sought to expand its operations to China. At the same time, the Qing, fresh from capturing the last Ming bastion on Taiwan and worried about Ming loyalists in other areas, sought to control contact with foreign and overseas Chinese traders as much as possible, while keeping their lucrative export trade at a sustainable level. Their solution, implemented in 1699, was to permit overseas trade only at the southern port of Guangzhou [GWAHNG-joe], more widely known as Canton. The local merchants' guild, or *cohong* (in pinyin, *gonghang*), was granted a monopoly on the trade and was supervised by a special official from the imperial Board of Revenue. Much like the Tokugawa in seventeenth-century Japan, the Qing permitted only a small number of foreigners, mostly traders from the English, French, and Dutch East India Companies, to reside at the port. They were confined to a small compound of foreign "**factories**," were not permitted inside the city walls, and could not bring their wives or families along. Even small violations of the regulations could result in a suspension of trading privileges, and all infractions and disputes were judged according to Chinese law. Finally, since foreign affairs under these circumstances were considered a dimension of trade, all diplomatic issues were settled by local officials in Canton.

The eighteenth century proved to be a boom time for all involved in the Canton trade, and the British in particular increasingly viewed it as a valuable part of their growing commercial power. While the spread of tea drinking through Europe and its colonies meant that tea rapidly grew to challenge porcelain for trade supremacy, silk also grew in importance, as well as lacquerware, wicker and rattan furniture, and dozens of other local specialties increasingly targeted at the export market. After 1784, the United States joined the trade; but despite the growing American presence, it was the British East India Company that dominated the Canton factories. Both the cohong and foreign chartered companies carefully guarded their respective monopolies, and the system worked reasonably well in keeping competition low and profits high on all sides.

## Village and Family Life

Just as the effort toward greater control and centralization was visible in the government and economy of China during the Ming and Qing, it also reverberated within the structures of Chinese village life. While much of local custom and social relations among the peasants still revolved around family, clan, and lineage—with the scholar-gentry setting the pace—new institutions perfected under the Ming and Qing had a lasting impact into the twentieth century.

**Organizing the Countryside**    During the sixteenth century, the administrative restructuring related to the consolidation of the tax system into the single-whip arrangement led to the creation of the *lijia* system. All families were placed into officially designated *li*, or "villages," for tax purposes; 10 households made up a *jia*, and 100 households composed a *li*, whose headmen, appointed by the magistrate, were responsible for keeping tax records and labor dues.

While the lijia system was geared primarily toward more efficient tax collection and record keeping, the *baojia* (Chapter 12) system functioned as a more far-reaching means of government surveillance and control. The baojia system required families to register all members **and** be organized into units of 10 families, with one family in each unit assuming responsibility for the other nine. Each of these responsible families was arranged in groups of 10, and a member of each was selected to be responsible for that group of 100 households, and so on up to the *bao*, or 1,000-household level. Baojia representatives at each level were to be chosen by the families in the group. These representatives were to report to the magistrate on the doings of their respective groups and held accountable for the group's behavior.

**Glimpses of Rural Life**    As with other agrarian–urban empires, much of what little we know about Chinese peasant life comes to us through literary sources. Most of these were compiled by the scholar-gentry, though starting in the seventeenth century a small but influential number of chronicles were also produced by Westerners traveling in China. Based on these accounts, some generalizations can be made about rural and family life in Ming and Qing times.

First, while the introduction of new crops during the period had brought more marginal land under cultivation, allowed for a huge increase in the population, and helped lend momentum to the trend toward more commercialization of

**Chinese Commercial Enterprises.** The growing volume and profits of the export trade encouraged further development and specialization of long-standing Chinese domestic industries during the eighteenth and nineteenth centuries. Moneychangers known as *shroffs* (*a*), were involved in testing the quality of silver taken from foreign concerns in exchange for Chinese goods. A worker and overseer demonstrate the operation of a silk reeling machine (*b*). Women worked to sort tea; in this photograph (*c*), packing chests for tea are stacked behind the sorters. The hairstyle of the men in these photos—shaved forehead with long braid called a queue—was mandatory for all Chinese males as a sign of submission to the Qing.

agriculture, the work, technology, and overall rhythms of peasant life had changed little over the centuries.

Second, as with gathering political tensions, some early signs of economic stress were already present toward the end of Qianlong's reign. Chief among these was the problem of absentee landlordism. This would grow increasingly acute as the vitality of the commercial networks and market towns of central and southern China increased and the gentry were drawn away from the countryside by urban opportunities and amenities. In addition, successful tea, cotton, silk, and luxury goods traders frequently retained their compounds in the cities while buying land and degrees and becoming scholar-gentry, further increasing the incidence of absenteeism in the countryside. During the next century, with the dislocations of the Opium Wars, the Taiping Rebellion, and the foreign treaty ports, the problem of absentee landlordism greatly accelerated.

Third, as we have seen before, pressures on patterns of village life tended to be magnified in the lives of women and girls. Elite women were routinely educated to be as marriageable as possible. Study of proper Confucian decorum, writing model essays, chanting poetry, and developing a firm grasp of the *Xiaojing* (*Classic of Filial Piety*) were central to their lessons. As noted earlier, women were expected to be modest and obedient and were usually separated from and subordinate to men. Marriage and property laws were set up to reinforce these qualities. In addition to the emphasis placed on mourning by both sexes, widows were expected to remain single and be subordinate to their oldest sons. As also noted previously, the custom of foot binding had long since become institutionalized, though in some areas—among southern China's Hakka minority, for example—it never caught on. The sale of infant girls and, in extreme cases, female infanticide rose markedly in rural areas during times of war, famine, or other social stresses. It should be remembered, however, that, as in previous Chinese dynasties, the dominance of women over the "inner realm" of the family remained largely complete, though this realm was never considered equal in importance to the outer sphere of men's activities.

## Science, Culture, and Intellectual Life

As we saw in Chapter 12, the Ming dynasty in many ways marked the high point as well as the beginning of the decline of China's preeminent place as a world technological innovator. One area in which this became painfully evident by the eighteenth and nineteenth centuries was in military matters.

**Superpower** The Ming at their height have been described by some Chinese scholars as a military superpower. Perhaps most important in this regard was that the ascendancy of the Ming in 1368 marked the beginning of what one historian has called a "military revolution" in the use of firearms. The first use of metal gun barrels in the late thirteenth century spurred the rapid development of both

**Observatory in Beijing.** One of the ways the Jesuits were able to gain favor at the imperial courts of two successive dynasties was through the New Sciences of the West. Jesuit mathematicians, technical advisors, mapmakers, and astronomers found an eager reception among their Chinese counterparts, the fruits of which included armillary spheres (pictured on the left and right foreground) and the celestial globe (center). The instruments were cast by Chinese artisans to the specifications of the Jesuit court mathematician Ferdinand Verbiest in the 1680s.

cannon and small arms—so much so that by the mid-fifteenth century the Ming arsenal at Junqiju [JWUN-chee-joo] was producing thousands of cannon, hand-guns, and "fire lances" every year. By one estimate, in 1450 over half of the Ming frontier military units had cannon and one-third of all troops carried firearms. As early as the 1390s large shipborne cannon were already being installed in naval vessels. Indeed, court historians of the late Ming credited nearly all the military successes of the dynasty to the superiority of their firearms.

By the Qing period, however, following the pacification of the realm, the need for constant improvement of arms was seen as increasingly costly and unnecessary. While marginal improvements were made in the **matchlock** firing mechanisms of Chinese small arms, such improvements as were made in larger guns were largely directed by European missionary advisors to the throne.

**Matchlock:** An early type of gun in which the gunpowder charge is ignited by a burning taper (the "match") attached to the trigger mechanism.

**Science and Literature** In geography, mathematics, and astronomy a fruitful exchange was inaugurated between European Jesuit missionaries and a small but influential group of Chinese officials in the seventeenth and eighteenth centuries. The most lasting legacy of this meeting was the European-style observatory in Beijing and a number of new maps of the world based on sixteenth- and seventeenth-century explorations. Unfortunately, by the nineteenth century these were all but forgotten, and the inadequacy of the geographical knowledge of Chinese officials in policy-making positions was soon all too apparent.

As in seventeenth-century France, the centralizing tendency of the government of China led to the exercise of considerable control in the cultural realm through patronage, monopoly, and licensing. As Manchus, the Kangxi, Yongzheng, and Qianlong emperors strove to validate their reigns by being patrons of the arts and aspiring to high levels of connoisseurship and cultivation of the best of the literati. As in other centralizing realms, they not only set the tone in matters of aesthetics but also used mammoth cultural projects to direct the energies of scholars and officials into approved areas. At the same time, they sought to quash unorthodox views through lack of support and, more directly, through literary inquisitions. Kangxi, for example, sponsored the compilation of a huge dictionary of approved definitions of Chinese characters—still considered a primary reference work today. Under his direction, the commentaries and interpretations of Neo-Confucianism championed by the Song philosopher Zhu Xi became the approved versions. Kangxi's 13 sacred edicts, embodying maxims distilled in part from Zhu Xi's thought, became the official Qing creed from 1670 on. Anxious to legitimize themselves as culturally "Chinese," Kangxi and Qianlong sponsored huge encyclopedia projects. Qianlong's effort, at 36,000 volumes, was perhaps the most ambitious undertaking of its kind ever attempted.

**Neo-Confucian Philosophy** While the urge to orthodoxy pervaded both dynasties, considerable intellectual ferment was also brewing beneath the surface of the official world. As we saw in Chapter 12, in the sixteenth century the first major new directions in Neo-Confucianism were being explored by Wang Yangming (1472–1529). While Wang's school remained a popular one, his emphasis on intuition, on a kind of enlightenment open to all, and, more and more, on a unity of opposites embracing different religious and philosophical traditions placed his more radical followers increasingly on the fringes of intellectual life. In addition, the Qing victory ushered in an era of soul-searching among Chinese literati and a wholesale questioning of the systems that had failed in the face of foreign conquest.

Two of the most important later figures in Qing philosophy were Huang Zongxi [hwang zung-SHEE] (1610–1695) and Gu Yanwu [goo yen-WOO] (1613–1682). Both men's lives spanned the Qing conquest, and like many of their fellow officials, both men concluded that the collapse of the old order was in part due to a retreat from practical politics and too much indulgence in the excesses of the radicals of the Wang Yangming school. With a group of like-minded scholars, they based themselves at the Donglin Academy, founded in 1604. There, they devoted themselves to reconstituting an activist Confucianism based on rigorous self-cultivation and on remonstrating with officials and even the court. One outgrowth of this development, which shares interesting parallels with the critical textual scholarship of the European Renaissance, was the so-called Han learning movement. Convinced that centuries of Buddhism, religious Daoism, and Confucian commentaries of questionable value had diverted Confucianism from the intent of the sages, Han learning sought to recover the original meaning of classic Confucian works through exacting textual scholarship and systematic philology, or historical linguistics. The movement, though always on the fringe of approved official activities, peaked in the eighteenth century and successfully uncovered a number of fraudulent texts, while setting the tone for critical textual analysis during the remainder of the imperial era.

**The Arts and Popular Culture**   Although China's artists and writers clung to an amateur ideal of the "three excellences" of poetry, painting, and calligraphy, increasing official patronage ensured that approved schools and genres of art would be maintained at a consistent, if not inspired, level of quality. Here, the Qianlong emperor was perhaps the most influential force. Motivated in part by a lifelong quest to master the fine arts, he collected thousands of paintings—to which he added, in the tradition of Chinese connoisseurs, his own colophons—rare manuscripts, jade, porcelain, lacquerware, and other objets d'art. Because the force of imperial patronage was directed at conserving past models rather than creating new ones, the period is not noteworthy for stylistic innovation. One interesting exception to this, however, was the work of the Jesuit painter Giuseppe Castiglione (1688–1766). Castiglione's access to Qianlong resulted in a number of portraits of the emperor and court in a style that merged traditional Chinese subjects and media with Western perspective and technique. Evidence of this synthesis can also be seen in the Italianate and Versailles-inspired architecture at the emperor's Summer Palace just outside of Beijing.

**Local Custom and Religion**   Chinese cities and villages were populated by storytellers, corner poets, spirit mediums, diviners, and a variety of other sorts of entertainers. While village social life revolved principally around clan and family functions, popular culture was also dominated by Daoism, Buddhism, and older

"The great man regards Heaven and earth and the myriad things as one body. He regards the world as one family and the country as one person. Even the mind of the small man is no different. Only he himself makes it small.'"

—Wang Yangming, *Inquiry on the Great Learning*

**Qianlong Emperor (1736–1795).** One of the more interesting cross-cultural interactions during the early Qing period was that inspired by the Jesuit missionary Giuseppe Castiglione (1688–1766). Trained as an architect and painter, Castiglione (Chinese name Lang Shining) arrived in Beijing in 1715 and served as court painter to emperors Kangxi, Yongzheng, and Qianlong. He influenced Chinese painters in the use of Western perspective and also absorbed Chinese techniques of portraiture and landscape painting. Here, the young Qianlong emperor is shown in his imperial regalia—including his robes of imperial yellow with dragon motifs—but with an authentically detailed face gazing confidently at the viewer.

traditions of local worship, all with their own temples, shrines, and festivals. The oldest beliefs of the countryside involving ancestral spirits, "hungry ghosts" (roaming spirits of those not properly cared for in death), fairies, and demons were enhanced over the centuries by a rich infusion of tales of Daoist adepts and "immortals," *yijing* diviners, Buddhist bodhisattvas, and underworld demons. Popular stories incorporating all of these, like *A Journey to the West*, continued to be popular fare for the literate as well as for storytellers and street performers.

One of the richest glimpses into local society comes from Pu Songling's (1640–1715) *Strange Tales from the "Make-Do" Studio*, sometimes rendered in English as *Strange Tales from a Chinese Studio*. Though considered a master stylist among his circle of friends, Pu never progressed beyond the provincial-level examinations and spent most of his life in genteel poverty. He traveled extensively, collecting folktales, accounts of local curiosities, and especially stories of the supernatural. His stories are available to us today thanks to the foresight of his grandson, who published them in 1740. In Pu's world, "fox-fairies" appear as beautiful women, men are transformed into tigers, the young are duped into degenerate behavior—with predictable consequences—and crooked mediums and storytellers take advantage of the unwary.

# The Long War and Longer Peace: Japan, 1450–1750

As we recall from Chapter 13, the struggles by court factions in Japan's capital of Heian-Kyo (Kyoto) had ultimately resulted in the creation of the office of the *shogun*, the chief military officer of the realm, in 1185. Actual executive power gradually receded from the emperor's hands, however, into the shogun's, and by the fourteenth century the emperor had become in reality the puppet of his first officer. As we also saw, a fundamental shift occurred with the attempt by Emperor Go-Daigo to reassert his prerogatives in 1333. When his one-time supporter Ashikaga Takauji expelled him and set up his headquarters in the capital, power and prestige were pressed together once again, with profound political and cultural consequences for Japan. Courtly elegance insinuated itself into the brutal world of the warrior, while power, intrigue, and ultimately a prolonged and debilitating civil war would ravage the capital until it ended with Japan's unification.

The price of unification, however, was high. As we saw in the opening vignette of this chapter, the first of Japan's unifiers, Oda Nobunaga, was assassinated for his efforts; the invasions of Korea undertaken by his successor Hideyoshi resulted in the loss of hundreds of thousands of lives. The final custodians of Japanese unification, the Tokugawa family, created a system over several generations that they hoped would preserve Japan forever in a state of unity and seclusion. Yet over the two and a half centuries of the Tokugawa peace, forces were building that would allow Japan to vault into the modern world with unprecedented speed in the late nineteenth century.

## The Struggle for Unification

As we have seen, the fundamental instability of the Ashikaga regime lent itself to the continual contesting for the shogun's office among the more powerful daimyo, or regional warlords. In 1467, these factional battles finally erupted into a devastating civil war that would last off and on for more than a century. The opening phase of this struggle, the Onin War, lasted 10 years and devastated the city of Kyoto, while leaving the imperial court barely functional and the shogunate in tatters. With no real center of power, a bitter struggle of all against all among the daimyos continued into the 1570s.

**Oda Nobunaga and Toyotomi Hideyoshi**   For the Japanese, the period was called *Gekokujo*, or "those below toppling those above." By the mid-sixteenth century, a handful of daimyo began the painful process of consolidating their power and securing allies. One important factor in deciding the outcome of these wars was the result of intrusion from the outside. By the 1540s, the first Portuguese and Spanish merchants and missionaries had arrived in southern Japan. One daimyo who was quick to use the newcomers and their improved small arms to his advantage was Oda Nobunaga, the son of a small landholder who had risen through the ranks to command. Oda employed newly converted Christian musketeers to secure the area around Kyoto and had largely succeeded in unifying the country when he was assassinated in 1582. His second in command, Hideyoshi, whom we met in the opening of this chapter, was another commoner who had risen through the ranks. Now he assumed Oda's mantle and systematically brought the remaining daimyo under his sway over the next nine years.

Hideyoshi viewed a foreign adventure at this point as an excellent way to cement the loyalties of the newly subdued daimyo. In addition, the army he had put together—battle-hardened, well trained, with perhaps the largest number of guns of any force in the world at the time—might prove dangerous to disband. Hence, as early as 1586 he announced his grandiose plans to conquer China itself. Thus, in 1592 he set out with a massive expeditionary force, which at its peak numbered over 200,000 men. Though his supply lines were harassed unmercifully by the Korean naval forces in their well-armored "turtle ships," the Japanese made good progress up the peninsula until massive Chinese counterattacks slowly eroded their gains and decimated large stretches of Korea.

Hideyoshi's adventure ended when he turned homeward to Japan with the remnants of his army in 1596. His stature as a commander and force of personality kept his coalition of daimyo together until his death during his troubled second Korean campaign in 1598.

The coalition then broke in two, and a civil war began between Tokugawa Ieyasu, the charismatic leader of the eastern coalition of daimyos, and their western counterparts. In the fall of 1600, the back of the western coalition was broken by the Tokugawa victory at the Battle of Sekigahara, near Kyoto. Ieyasu, who claimed

**Toyotomi Hideyoshi (1536–1598).** Portraits of Japanese daimyo and shoguns tend to position them in similar ways, looking to the front left, with stiff, heavily starched official robes that reflect their austerity and dignity. In this 1601 portrait, done several years after his death, Hideyoshi is shown in a typical pose, with the signs of his adopted family and imperial crests around the canopy to denote his role of imperial guardian.

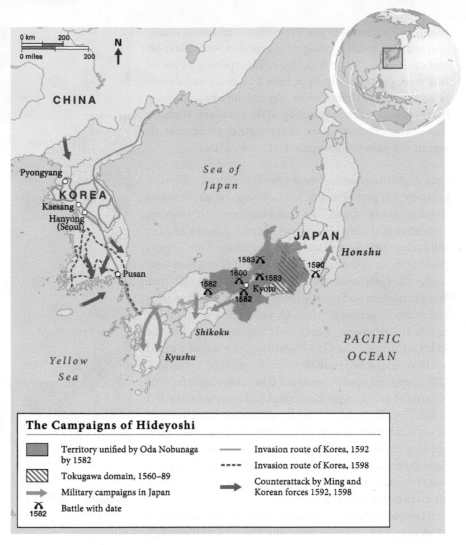

MAP 21.5 **The Campaigns of Hideyoshi.**

The Campaigns of Hideyoshi

Territory unified by Oda Nobunaga by 1582

Tokugawa domain, 1560–89

Military campaigns in Japan

1582 Battle with date

Invasion route of Korea, 1592

Invasion route of Korea, 1598

Counterattack by Ming and Korean forces 1592, 1598

"Don't let my soldiers become spirits in a foreign land."

—Toyotomi Hideyoshi to his commanders shortly before his death

to be a descendant of the Minamoto clan, the original shoguns, laid claim to the office and was officially invested with it in 1603. His accession marked the beginning of Japan's most peaceful, most secluded, and perhaps most thoroughly regulated and policed interval in its long history. Breaking precedent, the Tokugawas would create a hereditary shogunate, organized along Chinese Neo-Confucian models of morality and government, that would last until 1867 (see Map 21.5).

### The Tokugawa *Bakufu* to 1750

The realm that Tokugawa Ieyasu (1542–1616) had won at the Battle of Sekigahara was one that had been scarred by seemingly endless warfare and social disruption. The daimyo and samurai, their armies as large as hundreds of thousands of soldiers in some cases, employed some of the most advanced military technology in the world, but their depredations had broken old loyalties and alliances. The intrusion of European missionaries and merchants, along with their converts and agents, contributed to the social ferment. The brief interlude of unity behind Hideyoshi's continental adventures had thoroughly unraveled and, indeed, had been a contributing cause of the civil war that had brought Ieyasu to power.

Ieyasu's assumption of the shogunate in 1603 thus began a process of unparalleled centralization and stabilization in Japan that would last until 1867. Initially, however, seclusion did not figure among its principles. In fact, under the direction of European advisors, Ieyasu and his son Hidetada (1579–1632) laid plans to build a powerful naval and merchant fleet during their first decade of rule. Seclusion did not emerge as the shogunate's policy until the 1630s. The most pressing order of business was to erect a system within which to place all the daimyo that would at once reward the loyal and keep a watchful eye on the defeated.

**"Tent Government"**    The system devised under the Tokugawa *bakufu* ("tent government," referring to the shogun's official status as the emperor's mobile deputy) was called *sankin kotai*, the "rule of alternate attendance." An inner ring of daimyo holdings was annexed by the Tokugawa family and administered by their retainers. All daimyo were then given either *fudai*, or "inner" domains, if they had been allies of the Tokugawa, or *tozama*, "outer" domains, if they had ultimately surrendered to Ieyasu's eastern coalition. The shogunate placed its new headquarters in the Tokugawa castle in Edo, the future city of Tokyo. In order to ensure their loyalty, all outer daimyo were required to reside in the capital in alternate years and return to their domains during the off years. Members of their families were required to stay as permanent hostages in Edo. Daimyo were also required to bring their most important retainers and their households with them during their stays. Almost from the beginning, therefore, the main roads to Edo, most famously the Tokaido, were the scene of constant daimyo processions. Like the great pilgrimage routes of Islam, Buddhism, and Christianity, these roads spurred enormous commerce and the creation of an array of services to meet the needs of the constant traffic. And like the French nobility a few decades later at Versailles, the daimyo found both their power and their purses increasingly depleted.

**Freezing Society**    In turning the office of shogun over to his son Hidetada in 1605, Ieyasu made it legally hereditary for the first time. With the possibility of revolt always just under the surface, Ieyasu stayed on as regent and pursued further measures to enhance the stability of the regime. Under his grandson Iemitsu (1604–1651), most of the characteristic Tokugawa policies in this regard became institutionalized. The shogunate declared that, like in the jati system in India, the members of the officially recognized classes in Japan—daimyo, samurai, peasants, artisans, merchants—and their descendants would be required to stay in those classes forever. The Tokugawa adopted Neo-Confucianism as the governing ideology, thus joining the commonwealth of Confucian "religious civilizations" in the region, and its long-established precepts of filial piety, models of ethical behavior, and unswerving loyalty to the government were incorporated into the new law codes.

Significant differences, however, separated the practice of this system in Japan from similar, concurrent systems in China, Korea, and Vietnam. In China and Vietnam, a civil service had long been in place, complete with a graded system of examinations from which the best candidates would be drawn for duty. The situation in Japan was closer to that of Korea, in which the *Yangban* were already a hereditary aristocracy in the countryside and so monopolized the official classes. Japan, though, differed even further because the samurai and daimyo were now not just a hereditary class of officials but a military aristocracy as well. Not only was the low position traditionally given to the military in Chinese Confucianism totally reversed, but the daimyo and samurai had absolute, unquestioned power of life and death over all commoners. Like their counterparts in China, they were expected to have mastered the classics and the refined arts of painting, poetry, and calligraphy. But official reports and popular literature are full of accounts of samurai cutting down hapless peasants who failed to bow quickly enough to daimyo processions or who committed other infractions, no matter how trivial.

**Giving Up the Gun**    In order to ensure that the samurai class would be free from any serious challenge, the government required them to practice the time-honored skills of swordsmanship, archery, and other forms of individual martial arts. But the rapid development of firearms and their pervasive presence in the realm remained a threat to any class whose skills were built entirely around hand-

to-hand combat. Thus, in a way perhaps unique among the world's nations, the Tokugawa literally "gave up the gun." Tokugawa police conducted searches for forbidden weapons among commoners and destroyed almost the entire stock of the nation's firearms. A few museum pieces were kept as curiosities, as were the bronze cannon in some of the Tokugawa seaside forts. Thus, weapons that had been among the most advanced in the world when they were cast in the 1600s were the ones that confronted the first foreign ships nearly 250 years later in 1853.

As the shogunate strove to impose peace on the daimyo and bring stability to the populace, it became increasingly anxious to weed out disruptive influences. In addition to the unsettling potential of the country's guns, therefore, they began to restrict the movements of foreigners, particularly missionaries. From the earliest days of European arrivals in Japan, subjects of competing countries and religions had brought their quarrels with them, often involving Japanese as allies or objects of intrigue. The influence of the missionaries on the growing numbers of Japanese Christians—perhaps 200,000 by the 1630s—was especially worrisome to those intent on firmly establishing Neo-Confucian beliefs and rituals among the commoners.

**Christian Martyrs.** Beginning in 1617 and culminating in the suppression of a rebellion by impoverished Christian peasants in 1637–1638, missionaries and their converts to the foreign faith were brutally persecuted by the Tokugawa. Wholesale massacres and even crucifixions along the main roads were not uncommon, or, as in this engraving, hanging criminals—in this case Jesuits—upside down and setting them on fire.

Moreover, the bitter duel between Catholic and Protestant missionaries and merchants carried its own set of problems for social stability, especially in the ports, where the majority of such activities tended to take place.

**Tokugawa Seclusion**    Ultimately, therefore, missionaries were ordered to leave the country, followed by their merchants. The English and Spanish withdrew in the 1620s, while the Portuguese stayed until 1639. Ultimately, only the Dutch, Koreans, and Chinese were allowed to remain, in small, limited numbers and subject to the pleasure of the shogunate. Further, in 1635 it was ruled that Japanese subjects would be forbidden to leave the islands and that no oceangoing ships were to be built. Any Japanese who left would be considered traitors and executed upon return. Like the Canton system later in Qing China, foreign merchants would be permitted only in designated areas in port cities and could not bring their families with them. The only Europeans permitted to stay, the Dutch, were chosen because they appeared to be the least affected by the religious bickering that characterized their European counterparts. They were, however, restricted to a tiny island called Dejima (also known as Deshima) built on a landfill in Nagasaki harbor. In return for the privilege, they were required to make yearly reports in person to the shogun's ministers on world events. Over time, the collections of these reports found a small but willing readership among educated and cultured Japanese. This "Dutch learning" and the accounts of Chinese and Korean observers formed the basis of the Japanese view of the outside world for over two centuries. Like European learning in Korea and Vietnam, it also provided useful examples for reformers to use in critiquing Neo-Confucian society.

**Trampling the Crucifix**    Much less tolerance was shown to Japan's Christian community. Dissatisfaction with the new Tokugawa strictures provoked a rebellion at Shimabara just outside Nagasaki in 1637 by Christian converts and disaffected samurai. As the revolt was suppressed, many of those facing the prospect of capture and execution by the Tokugawa flung themselves into the volcanic hot springs nearby. Those who were captured were subjected to what their captors understood to be appropriate European-style punishment: Instead of being burned at the stake, they were clustered together and roasted to death inside a wide ring of fire. Subsequently, remaining missionaries were sometimes crucified upside down, while suspected converts were given an opportunity to "trample the crucifix" to show they had discarded the new faith. Those who refused to convert back to

**Dutch Ships in Nagasaki Harbor.** This detail from a 1764 map shows Dutch and Japanese ships in Nagasaki harbor. The Japanese ships are dwarfed by the much larger Dutch sailing vessels. The small fan-shaped area connected to the town of Nagasaki was the only place where the Dutch were allowed to disembark and trade. They were forbidden to cross the causeway into the city itself.

approved faiths were imprisoned or executed. In the end, perhaps 37,000 people were killed. For all their attempts at suppressing the religion, however, tens of thousands continued to practice in secret until Christianity was declared legal again during the reign of Emperor Meiji (r. 1867–1912). Though foreign ships would occasionally attempt to call at Japanese ports, by the eighteenth century Europeans generally steered clear of the islands. As we will see in Chapter 24, however, by the middle decade of the nineteenth century the opening of more ports in China for trade, the growth of the whaling industry, and the quest for gold in California would all conspire to change this situation forever.

## Growth and Stagnation: Economy and Society

While a number of the processes begun under earlier shogunates continued during the seventeenth and eighteenth centuries, their pace quickened immensely. Perhaps most dramatically, by 1750, Japan had become the most urbanized society on earth. Edo itself reached a million people, making it arguably the world's largest city. Osaka and Kyoto were both approaching 400,000, and perhaps as much as 10 percent of Japan's population lived in cities with populations above 10,000 (see Map 21.6). In a way, such explosive growth is even more remarkable given that the Tokugawa placed strict curbs on travel within their realms. Commoners, for example, were not to leave their home districts without permission from the local authorities. On the other hand, as we have seen, the law of alternate attendance ensured an immense and growing traffic in and out of the major cities along the major routes into Edo. The vast array of services required to support that traffic aided urban and suburban growth and had the effect of spreading the wealth down to the urban merchants, artisans, entertainers, bathhouse proprietors, and even refuse collectors.

**Population, Food, and Commerce**   Perhaps a more direct cause of this urbanization may be found in the growth of the population as a whole. By various estimates, Japan may have had as many as 33 million people in 1720. The efficiency of small-scale, intensive rice and vegetable farming, aided by easy-to-operate, simple machines such as the Chinese-style "climbing stair" or "dragon wheel" pump made Japanese agriculture the most efficient in the preindustrial world. Such efficiencies would create one of the most densely populated rural landscapes in the world even into the twentieth century.

As we have noted, various Tokugawa policies aimed at stabilizing the country politically and socially had the unanticipated effect of spurring the economy. A number of factors contributed to this in addition to the forced movement of the daimyo and their retinues in alternate years. The Tokugawa tax structure set quotas of rice for each village, rather than for individuals, and left the individual daimyos responsible for remitting these to the capital. Thus, an immense traffic in bulk rice further spurred the carrying trade along the roads and in the coastal waters. In addition to guaranteeing provisions for the cities, the need to convert rice to cash for the treasury contributed greatly to building a banking and credit infrastructure. Indeed, the practice of merchant bankers advancing credit to wholesalers against anticipated rice crops created what some scholars have called an early kind of futures market. The progress of the famous Mitsui *zaibatsu*, or cartel, of the nineteenth and twentieth centuries followed such a route, its members starting

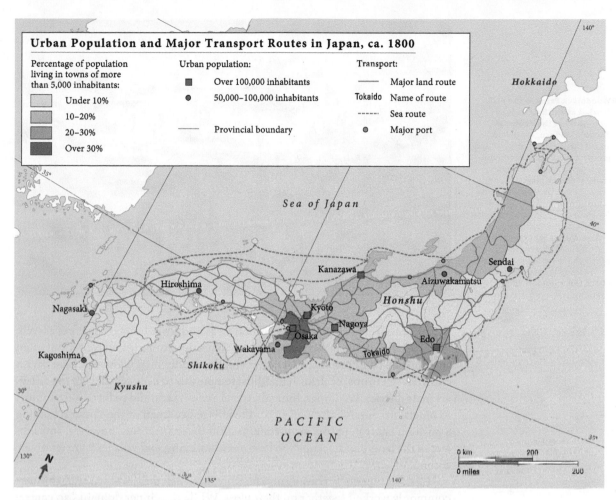

### Urban Population and Major Transport Routes in Japan, ca. 1800

Percentage of population living in towns of more than 5,000 inhabitants:
- Under 10%
- 10–20%
- 20–30%
- Over 30%

Urban population:
- ■ Over 100,000 inhabitants
- ● 50,000–100,000 inhabitants
- —— Provincial boundary

Transport:
- —— Major land route
- Tokaido  Name of route
- ------  Sea route
- ● Major port

MAP 21.6  Urban Population and Major Transport Routes in Japan, ca. 1800

in 1670 as dry goods merchants and gradually moving into the position of bankers for the shogunate.

The tastes of the three largest cities—Edo, with its high concentration of the wealthy and well-connected; Kyoto, with its large retinue of the imperial household; and Osaka, the chief port—created a huge demand for ever more sophisticated consumer goods and services. Such enterprises as sake brewing, wholesaling dried and prepared foods, running bathhouses, and managing large studios of artisans all became booming businesses. Even the import and export trades, slowed to a relative trickle by government regulations, proved quite lucrative for the few engaged in them. Books, porcelains, lacquerware, and objets d'art were exchanged for Japanese hard currency. Indeed, the vibrancy of Japanese urban life and a burgeoning middle class created what scholars have sometimes called the "democratization of taste." That is, what was once the strict province of the court, daimyo, and samurai was now widely available to anyone who had the money and interest to afford it. Moreover, the new moneyed classes were also creating new directions in the arts and entertainment.

**Woodblock Print of the Fish Market at the East Side of Nihonbashi (The Bridge of Japan).** The Tokugawa period, with its long interlude of peace and prosperity, was Japan's first great age of urban life. The constant traffic of daimyo progressions along the main roads and the large coasting trade along the Inland Sea ensured a growing middle class of artisans, tradespeople, and merchants. The capital, Edo, had ballooned to over a million people on the eve of the American intrusion; and the bustle of the capital is illustrated in this panel depicting a famous fish market.

**Rural Transformations**    Life in rural areas underwent certain changes as well. As they had with the military houses, the Tokugawa promulgated Neo-Confucian rules for the comportment of families and their individual members. Like parish churches in Europe, each local Buddhist temple was to keep registers of the villagers in its district. Weddings, funerals, travel, rents, taxes, and so forth were subject to official permission through either the village headman or the samurai holding a position equivalent to a magistrate. Within these strictures, however, and subject to the hereditary occupation laws, families, clans, and villages were relatively autonomous.

This was especially true of rural families, in which men, women, and children commonly worked together on their plots. While the "inner domain," so central to Neo-Confucian thought as the strict province of women, retained a good deal of that character, there were also many areas that mitigated it. Men, for example, routinely helped in the everyday tasks of childrearing. As late as the 1860s, foreign observers reported watching rural groups of men minding infants while their wives were engaged in some collective task. Women in cities and larger villages routinely ran businesses, especially those involved in entertainment. Indeed, the women of the famous geisha houses, owned and run by women, were renowned for their skills, education, wit, and refinement. Even on a more humble level, women ran bathhouses, taverns, restaurants, and retail establishments of all sorts. Interestingly, by the eighteenth century, merchants increasingly utilized the spinning and weaving talents of rural and semirural women in parceling out the various steps in textile manufacturing to them—a Japanese version of the English "putting out system."

**The Samurai in Peacetime**    As time went by, the position of the samurai in rural society changed as well. Though he was expected to hone his military skills, his role as an official and Neo-Confucian role model gradually became paramount. Samurai existed on stipends, either directly from the Tokugawa or from their local daimyo. These, however, were no guarantee of prosperity, and by the later eighteenth century the samurai living in genteel poverty had become something of a popular stereotype. In many areas, they functioned as schoolmasters and founded village academies in the local temples for the teaching of practical literacy and correct moral behavior. By the mid-nineteenth century Japan may have had the world's highest level of functional literacy. As in Korea, this proved important in popularizing new crops or agricultural techniques.

By the middle of the eighteenth century there were signs of tension among the aims of the government in ensuring peace and stability, the dynamism of the internal economy, and the boom in population. Like China a century later, some scholars contend that Japan had approached the limit of the ability of the land to support its people. In fact, Japan's population remained remarkably steady from the middle of the eighteenth century to the latter nineteenth. Repeated signs of creeping rural impoverishment and social unrest manifested themselves, however, and were often noted by commentators. Inflation in commodity prices ran ahead of efforts to increase domain revenues, squeezing those on fixed incomes and stipends. Efforts to keep rural families small enough to subsist on their plots led to an increasing frequency of infanticide. Compounding such problems were large-scale famines in 1782 and 1830. By the early nineteenth century, there was an increasing perception that the government was gradually losing its ability to care for the populace.

## Hothousing "Japaneseness": Culture, Science, and Intellectual Life

As with so many elements of Japanese cultural history, existing genres of art—major styles of painting, poetry, and calligraphy—continued to flourish among the daimyo and samurai, while exerting an increasing pull on the tastes of the new middle classes. Indeed, Zen-influenced **monochrome** painting, the ideals of the tea ceremony championed by Sen Rikyu, the austere Noh theater, and the abstract principles of interior design and landscape gardening were carefully preserved and popularized until they became universally recognized as "Japanese."

**New Theater Traditions**  Traditional cultural elements coexisted with new forms, with some adapting aspects of these earlier arts and others conceived as mass entertainment. Among the former was the development of *bunraku*, the elaborate puppet theater still popular in Japan today. Bunraku puppets, perhaps one-third life size, generally took three puppeteers to manipulate. Their highly facile movements and facial expressions staged against a black backdrop to conceal their handlers readily allowed the audience to suspend disbelief and proved a highly effective way to popularize the older Noh plays. But renowned playwrights soon wrote special works for these theaters as well. The most revered was Chikamatsu Monzaemon [chick-ah-MAT-soo mon-ZAE-mon] (1653–1724), who skillfully transferred the tragically noble sentiments of the best Noh works into contemporary themes. The fatal tension between love and social obligation, for example, made his *Love Suicide at Sonezaki* wildly popular with Edo audiences. His most famous work, *The Forty-Seven Ronin*, written in 1706, is based on a 1703 incident in which the daimyo of 47 samurai was killed by a political opponent, leaving them as *ronin*—masterless. Out of loyalty to their dead daimyo the ronin kill his assassin in full knowledge that their lives will then be forfeit to the authorities, a price they stoically go on to pay.

Monochrome: Single-color; in east Asian painting, a very austere style popular in the fourteenth and fifteenth centuries, particularly among Zen-influenced artists.

Originally written for bunraku, *The Forty-Seven Ronin* was adapted a few decades later as a work for *kabuki*, the other great mass entertainment art of Tokugawa Japan. Because kabuki was originally a satirical and explicitly bawdy form of theater, the government banned women from appearing in it, hoping to sever its association with prostitution. Female impersonators as actors continued its risqué reputation, however, while more serious works also drew immense crowds to the pleasure districts, to which the theaters were by law segregated. Kabuki remained by far the most popular Japanese mass entertainment, and interestingly, given the medium's off-color reputation, *The Forty-Seven Ronin* remained the most frequently performed play throughout the Tokugawa period.

"Summer grass;
Great warriors;
Remains of dreams"

夏草や
兵どもが
夢の跡

　　—Basho

The era also marked the golden age of the powerfully brief poetic form of *haiku*, the most famous practitioner of which was the renowned Matsuo Basho (1644–1694). As a poet he used a dozen pen names; he took "Basho" from the banana plant he especially liked in his yard. In poems like "Old Battlefield" the 17-syllable couplets compressed unbearable emotion and release in a way that has made them a treasured form in Japan and, more recently, in much of the world.

The visual arts found new forms of expression through the widespread use of fine woodblock printing, which allowed popular works to be widely duplicated. The new genre was called *ukiyo-e*, "pictures of the floating world," a reference to the pleasure quarters on the edge of the cities that furnished many of its subjects. Though largely scorned by the upper classes, it remained the most popular form of advertising, portraiture, and news distribution until the end of the nineteenth century, when it began to be supplanted by photography. During Tokugawa times, one of the most famous practitioners of the art was Kitagawa Utamaro (1753–1806), whose studies of women became forever associated with Japanese perceptions of female beauty. In the works of Katsushika Hokusai (1760–1849) and Ando Hiroshige (1797–1858) scenes like Hokusai's *Thirty-Six Views of Mt. Fuji*, or, like Utamaro's work, gentle snowfalls on temples, formed many of the first popular images that nineteenth-century Westerners had of Japan.

**Two Courtesans.** During the late seventeenth century, the new genre of *ukiyo-e*, "pictures of the floating world," developed and remained popular through the nineteenth century. Finely wrought woodblock prints in both monochrome and color, they take their name from the pleasure districts whose people and scenes were favorite subjects. This work is from a series by the noted artist Kitagawa Utamaro (ca. 1753–1806) on famous courtesans of the "Southern District," part of the Shinagawa section of Edo.

# Putting It All Together

During the late Ming and early Qing periods, imperial China achieved social and political stability and developed the world's largest economy. Yet, by the second part of the eighteenth century, internal problems were already germinating that would come to the surface in succeeding decades. In the following century, these initial cracks in the empire's structure would continue to grow and have a profound impact on China's fortunes.

The arrival of large numbers of foreign traders who brought with them the new technologies of the first scientific–industrial societies, combined with China's profound self-confidence in its own culture and institutions, added more pressure to an already volatile internal situation and ultimately created an unprecedented challenge for China. Over the coming decades, Chinese expectations of being able to civilize and assimilate all comers would dissolve, along with the hope that a renewed faithfulness to Confucian fundamentals would produce the leaders necessary to navigate such perilous times. But at the halfway mark of the eighteenth century, the Chinese still expected that they would successfully regulate the "inner" and "outer" domains of their empire and keep pernicious foreign influences at arm's length.

Ravaged by a century of warfare and foreign intrusion, Japan also sought to regulate its inner and outer domains and minimize outside influences. As with China, however, the stability perfected by the Tokugawa shogunate in the seventeenth and eighteenth centuries would be increasingly threatened in the nineteenth by the growing commercial power of the Europeans and Americans. Before the nineteenth century was finished, China would be rent by the bloodiest civil war in human history, while Japan would experience its own civil war and, in its aftermath, install a unified government under an emperor for the first time since the twelfth century. In the final years of the nineteenth century, Japan would once again invade Korea to attack China—this time with very different results. In the process, the historical relationship of more than two millennia between the two countries would be altered forever.

▶ For additional resources, including maps, primary sources, visuals, and quizzes, please go to www.oup.com/us/vonsivers. Please see the Further Resources section at the back of the book for additional readings and suggested websites.

## Against the Grain

# Seclusion's Exceptions

Despite Japan's *sakoku* (closed country) policies of seclusion during the Tokugawa era, scholars have long understood that the country was more porous than popularly supposed. This was of course most true for Chinese and Korean merchants doing business in Japan. Formal relations of a sort with Korea on a more or less equal footing were maintained by the Tokugawa through the lord of the Tsushima *han*, or feudal domain, who also maintained a trading post in the Korean port of Pusan. Korean vessels, like those of the Chinese, were permitted to put in at Nagasaki, and Korean goods were in high enough demand that the shogunate's attempts to curtail silver exports were generally waived for Korean trade. Moreover, more than a dozen Korean trade missions traveled to the shogun's court during the Tokugawa period.

No official exchanges with Chinese representatives took place either in Edo or Beijing, since neither side wanted to be seen as the junior partner in the Neo-Confucian hierarchy of diplomacy by the so-called tribute mission system. In addition to the predominance of Chinese ships at Nagasaki, however, both Chinese and Japanese merchants took advantage of a loophole in the sovereignty of the Ryukyu Islands to trade there. China and Japan both insisted that the islands were their protectorate, though the Japanese domain of Satsuma had captured Okinawa in 1609. The leaders in Okinawa, however, sent trade and tribute missions to both China and the Japan in order to safeguard their freedom of action, thus keeping the conduit for trade semiofficially open for both sides.

The Dutch remained the European exceptions. In part, this was a condition they had helped engineer themselves: They had continually warned the Tokugawa about the sinister religious intentions of their Iberian competitors, suggesting that the Dutch alone should handle Japan's European trade. Indeed, though the volume of China's trade in Japan was many times larger, it was the Dutch who retained yearly access to the shogunate. Though their power and influence in European markets ebbed considerably during the eighteenth and early nineteenth centuries, their influence among the small but intellectually vital circle of Japanese scholars and leaders engaged in *rangaku*—"Dutch learning"—remained strong right up to the time of the coming of Perry's "Black Ships" in 1853. Thus, as one scholar of Japan has put it, "The Nagasaki door was always ajar and sometimes wide open."

- While the attempts by China, Korea, and Japan to keep out foreign influences may strike us as impractical, many nations today still seek to limit foreign influences, particularly in the realm of culture. What are the advantages and disadvantages of such policies? Are they inevitably self-defeating?

- Were the policies of turning inward among these agrarian–urban societies part of larger historical patterns at work during this time? Why or why not?

# Thinking Through Patterns

▶ **Why did late Ming and early Qing China look inward after such a successful period of overseas exploration?**

In some respects the problem is similar to that faced by planners for defense spending in nations today: Why maintain huge, expensive systems when there are no enemies against which to use them? While the commercial prospects for China's fleets grew in prominence, maritime trade was simply not essential to the Chinese economy at that point. Moreover, urgent defense preparations were needed in the overland north against the resurgent Mongols. It is important to remember that the discontinuing of the fleets seems like a mistake in hindsight because of what happened to China hundreds of years later due to a lack of adequate naval defenses. At the time, however, these measures seemed both rational and appropriate to the Chinese and outside observers.

One almost universal pattern of world history among agrarian states is that their governments adopt policies aimed at promoting social stability. The reason for this is that, in short, nearly everything depends on having reliable harvests. Given the agricultural techniques and technology of preindustrial societies, the majority of the population must be engaged in food production to ensure sufficient surpluses to feed the nonproducing classes. If such a society places a premium on change and social mobility, it risks chronic manpower shortages and insufficient harvests. Thus, social classes—whether in feudal Europe, India, China, or Japan—are carefully delineated, and the state directs its policies toward eliminating social upheaval.

▶ **How do the goals of social stability drive the policies of agrarian states? How does the history of China and Japan in this period show these policies in action?**

▶ **In what ways did contact with the maritime states of Europe alter the patterns of trade and politics in eastern Asia?**

In both China and Japan, these connections resulted in severe restrictions on maritime trade: the Canton system in China and the seclusion policies of the Tokugawa in Japan. Earlier, the Chinese emperor had welcomed Jesuit missionaries for their expertise in mathematics and science and even considered conversion to Catholicism. But the backlash against "subversive" influence induced the Qing to drive Christianity underground. In Japan such contact had earlier injected European influences into Japan's civil wars, and the reaction against this was Tokugawa seclusion.

The fundamental difference was that Japan was a military society, which adopted the forms and structures of Neo-Confucianism to make the daimyo and samurai into officials. They therefore were expected to maintain this civil role as bureaucrats but also to stand ready to fight if need be. The low esteem in which the military was held in China was just the inverse of that of the martial elites of Japan. Another key difference was that officials in China were selected on the basis of competitive examinations, thus creating some social mobility. In Japan, the social classes were frozen and no exams were offered for potential officials.

▶ **How did Neo-Confucianism in China differ from that of Tokugawa Japan?**

China in 1583, the Jesuit Matteo Ricci (1552–1610) encouraged his followers to immerse themselves in the language and to become conversant with the rich traditions of Chinese literature. He also came to be respected by, and especially helpful to, the emperor, as he offered his expertise in the sciences and mathematics to the imperial court. With a European Jesuit (Adam Schall von Bell) as the official court astronomer to Kangxi, there were reports that the Emperor himself considered converting to Catholicism. Nevertheless, not every encounter between Chinese and Europeans went so smoothly, as the following anecdote from Ricci's diary reveals.

Of late they [the Chinese] had become quite disturbed by the coming of the Portuguese, and particularly so because they can do nothing about it, due to the great profit reaped from Portuguese traders by the public treasury and by certain influential merchants. Without referring to the public treasury or to the merchants who come from every other province, they complain that the foreign commerce raises the price of all commodities and that outsiders are the only ones to profit from it. As an expression of their contempt for Europeans, when the Portuguese first arrived they were called foreign devils, and this name is still in common use among the Cantonese.

The citizens of Sciauquin have their own particular reasons for hating the strangers. They are afraid that the Portuguese merchants will get into the interior of the realm with the missionaries, and their fears are not without some foundation. The frequent visits of the Fathers to the town of Macao and their growing intimacy with the Governor have already aroused their antipathy. There is nothing that stirs them up like a wide-spreading slander, and they had a good one in the story that the tower which had been built at such great expense, and with so much labor, was erected at the request of the foreign priests. This probably had its origin in the fact that the tower was completed while the Fathers were building their mission houses. This false rumor had such an effect that the people called it the Tower of the Foreigners instead of The Flowery Tower, as it was named. As a result of the animosity which grew out of this incident, when they realized that they could not drive out the Mission, as they wanted to, they took to insulting the missionaries whenever an occasion occurred or they could trump up a reason for doing so. It was quite annoying and dangerous to be made a continual target for stones hurled from the tower, when people came there every day to play games, the purpose for which these towers are built. Not a stone was thrown at the Mission House from the high tower nearby that missed its roof as a target. These showers of stones were heaviest when they knew that there were only one or two of the servants at home. Another silly reason for their taking offense was that the doors of our house, which were kept open for inspection while it was being built, were now kept closed according to the rule of our Society. What they wanted to do was to use the house as they did their temples of idols, which are always left wide open and are often the scenes of uncouth frivolity.

It happened one day, when their insolence became really unbearable, that one of our servants ran out and seized a boy, who had been throwing stones at the house, and dragging him inside threatened to bring him to court. Attracted by the shrieking of the boy, several men, who were known in the neighborhood, ran into the house to intercede for the culprit, and Father Ricci ordered that he be allowed to depart without further ado. Here was a good pretext for a major calumny, and two of the neighbors who disliked the Fathers went into conference with a bogus relative of the boy, who knew something about court procedure. Then they trumped up a story that the boy had been seized by the Fathers and hidden in their house for three days, that he had been given a certain drug, well known to the Chinese, which prevented him from crying out, and that the purpose of it all was to smuggle him back to Macao, where they could sell him into slavery. The two men were to be called in as witnesses.

. . .

[A trial takes place before the Governor, and he hears the "witnesses" to the crime.]

. . .

Finally, in order to save the Father present from any embarrassment, he [the Governor] declared him [Ricci] wholly innocent and . . . his next move was to summon the three members of the building commission, who were at the tower on the day the incident occurred. The plaintiff requested that he call in the neighbors also, the real authors of the charge, who had a full knowledge of all its details. The Governor dismissed the multitude and, as he was leaving, he forbade the Father to leave the court. In the meantime, and in deep humiliation, the Father betook himself to prayer, commending his cause and its solution to God, to the Blessed Mother and to the Saints.

. . .

Then he [the Governor] told the missionary and his interpreter and the three Commissioners that he had heard enough of this affair, and that they might return to their homes and their business.

. . .

On the following day the Governor sent a solemn document to be posted at the main entrance of the Mission House. This notice, after explaining that the foreigners were living here with permission of the Viceroy, stated that certain unprincipled persons, contrary to right and reason, were known to have molested the strangers living herein, wherefore: he, the Governor, strictly forbade under severest penalty that anyone from now on should dare to cause them further molestation.

▶ **Working with Sources**

1. What seems to have been Ricci's attitude toward Chinese customs and religious practices?
2. To what extent did trade rights and religious goals intersect in this setting? What was in the immediate and long-term interests of the Chinese "hosts" of the mission?

dynasty, swaying the myriad races of the globe, extends the same benevolence towards all. Your England is not the only nation trading at Canton. If other nations, following your bad example, wrongfully importune my ear with further impossible requests, how will it be possible for me to treat them with easy indulgence? Nevertheless, I do not forget the lonely remoteness of your island, cut off from the world by intervening wastes of sea, nor do I overlook your excusable ignorance of the usages of our Celestial Empire. I have consequently commanded my Ministers to enlighten your Ambassador on the subject, and have ordered the departure of the mission. But I have doubts that, after your Envoy's return he may fail to acquaint you with my view in detail or that he may be lacking in lucidity, so that I shall now proceed . . . to issue my mandate on each question separately. In this way you will, I trust, comprehend my meaning. . . .

. . .

(7) Regarding your nation's worship of the Lord of Heaven, it is the same religion as that of other European nations. Ever since the beginning of history, sage Emperors and wise rulers have bestowed on China a moral system and inculcated a code, which from time immemorial has been religiously observed by the myriads of my subjects. There has been no hankering after heterodox doctrines. Even the European (missionary) officials in my capital are forbidden to hold intercourse with Chinese subjects; they are restricted within the limits of their appointed residences, and may not go about propagating their religion. The distinction between Chinese and barbarian is most strict, and your Ambassador's request that barbarians shall be given full liberty to disseminate their religion is utterly unreasonable.

It may be, O King, that the above proposals have been wantonly made by your Ambassador on his own responsibility, or peradventure you yourself are ignorant of our dynastic regulations and had no intention of transgressing them when you expressed these wild ideas and hopes. . . . If, after the receipt of this explicit decree, you lightly give ear to the representations of your subordinates and allow your barbarian merchants to proceed to Chêkiang and Tientsin, with the object of landing and trading there, the ordinances of my Celestial Empire are strict in the extreme, and the local officials, both civil and military, are bound reverently to obey the law of the land. Should your vessels touch the shore, your merchants will assuredly never be permitted to land or to reside there, but will be subject to instant expulsion. In that event your barbarian merchants will have had a long journey for nothing.

▶ **Working with Sources**

1. **How did Qianlong attempt to keep China and Great Britain on an equal footing, and in what specific regards?**

2. **How effectively does the emperor balance courtesy and warning in his letter?**

## SOURCE 21.4

# Chikamatsu Monzaemon, *Goban Taiheiki*

### 1710

This one-act puppet play is one of the first fictionalized (though only thinly disguised) treatments of a famous event that occurred in Tokugawa Japan in 1701–1703. The historical incident began with a knife attack by the daimyo (feudal lord) Asano Naganori on an imperial official named Kira Yoshinaka. Whatever the justice of the provocation, Asano had committed a serious breach in conduct and was forced to pay the most severe penalty. Even though Kira had suffered only a minor wound to his face, Asano was commanded to commit *seppuku*, ritual suicide. When he did so, his 47 samurai vassals were left leaderless (*rōnin*), but they swore to avenge Asano's memory by killing Kira.

In January 1703, the 47 rōnin entered Kira's home, chasing him and killing several of his retainers and wounding others, including Kira's grandson. When they finally trapped and overcame Kira, the rōnin cut off his head and brought it to their master's grave. However, they then decided to turn themselves in to the authorities and commit *seppuku* themselves, true to their code until the bitter end. In order to elude the censors, Chikamatsu altered the names, condensed some of the main details, and offered a judge that was more sympathetic to the rōnin cause. The essential story would reemerge repeatedly in popular culture (both Japanese and non Japanese) down to the present day.

NARRATOR: Just then someone announces that the messenger from the shogun, Hatakeyama Sakyō no Dayū, has come. The puffed-up samurai are cowed and prostrate themselves to the left and right of the gate. The doors are opened from inside and Hatakeyama meets face to face with the old priest.

HATAKEYAMA: "Last night the retainers of En'ya Hangan forced their way into the mansion of Kō no Moronao in order to take revenge on the enemy of their lord, and killed him. As samurai, this has earned them both merit and praise. But they showed no respect for the fact that the shogun's palace was in the vicinity and disturbed the peace of Kamakura. It is the shogun's decision that these men be placed in the charge of Niki and Ishidō,

Source: Jacqueline Miller, "A Chronicle of Great Peace Played Out on a Chessboard: Chikamatsu Monzaemon's *Goban Taiheiki*," *Harvard Journal of Asiatic Studies* 46 (1986): 221–267, 263–267.

and he orders that today they all cut open their bellies in front of the grave of En'ya. He also grants the head of Moronao to his only son, Moroyasu, and orders you to deliver it to him."

NARRATOR: The head priest accepts the written decree. He prepares a container for the head and sees to it that the arrangements are properly carried out.

HATAKEYAMA: "Let a member of Lord Moroyasu's household who has some semblance of respectability receive the head."

NARRATOR: At this, a chief retainer, Misumi no Gunji, announces his name in an imposing fashion, but there seems to be little honor for him when he returns with heavy heart, bearing the head of his useless master. Told that they ought to begin their preparations right away, the priests place En'ya's shrine in the center. They then place tatami mats to the right and left and spread white sand in front to soak up the blood that will be spilled. Behind they draw a white curtain and set out cushions covered in white silk. And on footed trays they place the knives for the suicides of the more than forty men.

Samurai throughout Kamakura pay solemn visits to the shrines, praying to the tutelary gods of warriors that they themselves, as military men, will be favored with the same good fortune. Poets write sheaves of verse about grief, and litterateurs search for rhymes to express their sorrow. Everyone, regardless of rank, age or sex, regrets this parting and they jostle each other in their haste to gather at the Kōmyōji. There, the scene in front of the gates resembles a fair.

Now the time has come—it is noon. As the moment of death approaches, the official observer, the Lord of Nagoya in Bizen, arrives at the Kōmyōji. Then, beginning with those who will act as seconds, all the officials, including the recording clerks and supervisors, accept their respective commissions and take their places on this formal occasion.

. . .

LORD OF NAGOYA: "The shogun declares that the forty and more retainers of En'ya Hangan, in avenging their late lord by killing Kō no Moronao, committed an act of unprecedented loyalty, with each man worth a thousand. He is deeply impressed and would like to save their lives, but they erred in taking up arms in this age of great peace and by troubling the shogun's direct vassal. The government has no choice but to order them to commit seppuku. Under strong officers there are no weak soldiers. Your loyalty has reminded him of the benevolence of En'ya Hangan while he was alive. There is no doubt about the claim to succession of En'ya's only son, Takeōmaro, and the shogun decrees that he shall govern the two provinces of Izumo and Hōki. Go to the underworld and report this to your lord with gratitude. Now quickly cut your bellies!"

NARRATOR: He announces this in a loud voice, and the men lower their heads, weeping or laughing in their joy. One by one they remove their sleeveless overrobes. Yuranosuke takes the knife and stabs himself in the left side. As he does so, Rikiya, too, stabs himself. One by one they all stab themselves and, having done so, pull the blade across. At the same time and in the same place, sitting to the right and left of their master's grave, they have all cut their bellies, for the bond over three lives is strong. Finally all have been beheaded by their seconds, and the temple quickly becomes a graveyard. The *rōnin* leave their names on stones that will stand for ages to come. The foundation of the success of their lord's descendants and house, their prosperity and unbounded good fortune, lies in those honest hearts filled with loyalty and filial spirit. They conformed to the laws of both heaven and earth, and the gods and buddhas graciously watched over them.

▶ **Working with Sources**

1. **Why does the court official express sympathy for the rōnin and still persist in enforcing the sentence against them?**

2. **Is Chikamatsu's admiration for the actions of the rōnin justified by the historical reality of the period and original circumstances?**

## SOURCE 21.5

# Honda Toshiaki, "Secret Plan for Managing the Country"

### 1798

Drawing on the conclusions of his "Western" education, Japanese economist Honda Toshiaki (1749–1821) advocated a three-pronged plan of action to level the playing field between the Tokugawa shogunate and European powers. Having studied mathematics as a young man, Honda learned the Dutch language and studied Dutch medicine, astronomy, and military science. The choice of Dutch was fortuitous, since these were the only Europeans permitted to remain in Japan after 1639. Nevertheless, it was the prowess of these particular Europeans in shipping and trade, dependent on a scientific and mathematical knowledge of navigation, that most interested Honda. This section of his "Secret Plan" addresses the need for the emperor to control ships and shipping in order to ensure Japanese prosperity.

Source: Ryusaku Tsunoda, William Theodore de Bary, and Donald Keene eds., *Sources of Japanese Tradition* (New York: Columbia University Press, 1964), vol. 2, 51–53.

As long as there are no government-owned ships and the merchants have complete control over transport and trade, the economic conditions of the samurai and farmers grow steadily worse. In years when the harvest is bad and people die of starvation, the farmers perish in greater numbers than any other class. Fields are abandoned and food production is still further reduced. There is then insufficient food for the nation and much suffering. Then the people will grow restive and numerous criminals will have to be punished. In this way citizens will be lost to the state. Since its citizens are a country's most important possession, it cannot afford to lose even one, and it is therefore most unfortunate that any should be sentenced to death. It is entirely the fault of the ruler if the life of even a single subject is thereby lost.

. . .

Some daimyo have now ceased to pay their retainers their basic stipends. These men have had half their property confiscated by the daimyo as well, and hate them so much that they find it impossible to contain their ever accumulating resentment. They finally leave their clan and become bandits. They wander lawlessly over the entire country, plotting with the natives who live on the shore, and thus entering a career of piracy. As they become ever more entrenched in their banditry one sees growing a tendency to revert to olden times.

It is because of the danger of such occurrences that in Europe a king governs his subjects with solicitude. It is considered to be the appointed duty of a king to save his people from hunger and cold by shipping and trading. This is the reason why there are no bandits in Europe. Such measures are especially applicable to Japan, which is a maritime nation, and it is obvious that transport and trade are essential functions of the government.

Ships which are at present engaged in transport do not leave coastal waters and put out to sea. They always have to skirt along the shore, and can navigate only by using as landmarks mountains or islands within visible range. Sometimes, as it inevitably happens, they are blown out to sea by a storm and lose their way. Then, when they are so far away from their familiar landmarks that they can no longer discern them, they drift about with no knowledge of their location. This is because they are ignorant of astronomy and mathematics, and because they do not possess the rules of navigation. Countless ships are thereby lost every year. Not only does this represent an enormous annual waste of produce, but valuable subjects also perish. If the methods of navigation were developed, the loss at sea of rice and other food products would be reduced, thus effecting a great saving. This would not only increase the wealth of the nation, but would help stabilize the prices of rice and other produce throughout Japan. The people, finding that they are treated equally irrespective of occupation and that the methods of government are fair, would no longer harbor any resentment, but would raise their voices in unison to pray for the prosperity of the rulers. By saving the lives of those subjects who would otherwise be lost at sea every year, we shall also be able to make up for our past shame, and will keep foreign nations from learning about weak spots in the institutions of Japan from Japanese sailors shipwrecked on their shores. Because of these and numerous other benefits to be derived from shipping, I have termed it the third imperative need.

▶ Working
with Sources

1. How does Toshiaki use comparisons to European practices to solidify his case regarding imperial control of shipping?

2. How does he envision the ideal relationship between the emperor and his people? What should be the emperor's central principle in ruling?

# PART FIVE

# The Origins of Modernity

## 1750–1900

**W**hat we have termed "modernity" in this section may be said to have begun roughly around 1800 in western Europe and may be characterized as the product of what historian Eric Hobsbawm (1917–2012) called the "twin revolutions" of the late eighteenth century. One of these was the new political landscape brought into being by the trio of constitutional revolutions in North America, France, and Haiti, which dealt a telling blow to the concept of traditional monarchial rule by divine right and introduced popular sovereignty as the new justification for political power. The other was the Industrial Revolution, which began in England with the introduction of steam-driven machine–produced textiles and other goods. Scientific–industrial modernity, with its developing constellation of values marked by experimentation; political, social, and technological progress; social mobility; and secularism, was thus set on a path to displacing the older agrarian–urban order of religious civilizations that had been characterized by hierarchy, natural order, and divinely ordained law and morality. This transition is, in fact, still ongoing. Although the old agrarian–urban political order has been almost universally superseded, its values still contend with those of modernity in many parts of the world today.

## The Origins of Modernity

The political and industrial revolutions that define modernity have intellectual roots reaching back to the 1500s. As scholars increasingly recognize, the discovery of the Americas, as well as the Copernican revolution in astronomy, provided powerful incentives for the introduction of new patterns of science and political philosophy. For more than two centuries, however, these ideas remained the province of only a small intellectual elite.

## Political and Industrial Revolutions

By the 1700s, however, adherents of the new science and philosophy among urban, educated administrators and professionals in northwestern Europe had grown in numbers and began to become influential in society. In Britain, the *theory* of the social contract entered into the *practice* of constitutionalism following the Glorious

**1765**
James Watt perfects the steam engine

**1776–1804**
American, French, and Haitian revolutions

**1798–1801**
Napoleon's occupation of Egypt

**1815**
Congress of Vienna

**1832**
Greece wins independence from the Ottomans

**1839–1876**
Tanzimat reforms in the Ottoman Empire

**1848**
Karl Marx and Friedrich Engels publish *The Communist Manifesto*

**1853–1854**
Commodore Perry opens trade and diplomatic relations with Japan

Revolution of 1688. Both were vastly expanded by thinkers during the eighteenth-century Enlightenment and helped to inspire the American, French, and Haitian Revolutions. These were narrow revolutions in the sense of ending monarchial-aristocratic rule—courageous revolts during still deeply religious times. Nonetheless, this era set the emancipation of humanity from the confining traditions of the past as a goal to be achieved. And in the case of Haiti, the idea that "all men are created equal," emblazoned earlier in the American Declaration of Independence and echoed in the French Declaration of the Rights of Man, formed the basis of a successful slave rebellion against revolutionary France itself.

The Industrial Revolution, beginning around 1800 in Great Britain, was a socially transformative and self-sustaining sequence of technical inventions and their commercial applications. Britain industrialized during the first half of the 1800s through steam-driven iron foundries, textile factories, overland transportation, and ocean travel. In a second wave, Germany and the United States industrialized, with the introduction of chemicals, electricity, and motorcars into the factory system. The two waves of industrialization created an unequal class system, with a citizenry composed of both landed aristocrats—fading in power as the old agrarian–urban order decayed—and a new, dynamic urban middle class amassing political and economic power. But the equally new phenomenon of the industrial working class, bidding for political, social, and economic equality, added a volatile social factor to the mix as its members sought to make good on the promises of the constitutional revolutions.

## Resistance and Adaptation to the Western Challenge

The twin political–industrial revolutions in Europe were a major factor in the mid-nineteenth-century expansion of the existing seaborne European empires in Asia and Africa. Postrevolutionary France renewed its competition with Britain, and both later used "gunboat diplomacy" to establish favorable commercial conditions and trade outposts. From here, these two European nations, and others, proceeded to compete in imperial conquests for what they now considered to be strategically important territories across the globe.

The traditional agrarian and religious empires and states of Asia and Africa responded to the increasingly superior military power of the European maritime empires and the United States during the 1800s with both resistance and adaptation. Resisting with traditional armies and weapons, however, became more difficult as the 1800s unfolded and the industrial development of the West spawned new and sophisticated weaponry. "Adaptation," as it occurred under the duress of imperialism, was a creative process in which the states under challenge selected generic elements from the constitutional and industrial revolutions that had made the West powerful and attempted to harmonize them with their inherited traditions.

# Thinking Like a World Historian

▶ What were the origins of the "twin revolutions" of the late eighteenth century? How did they combine to create what we call "modernity"?

▶ Why were the values of scientific–industrial society opposed to the older agrarian–urban order? Why does this conflict still persist in many parts of the world today?

▶ What patterns of resistance and adaptation characterized the responses of traditional agrarian and religious empires to European military power and expansion?

| 1857 Sepoy Mutiny, India | 1868–1912 Reign of Emperor Meiji, Japan | 1878–1885 Independence of Serbia, Montenegro, Romania, and Bulgaria | 1888 End of slavery, Brazil | 1894–1895 Sino-Japanese War | 1904–1905 Russo-Japanese War |
|---|---|---|---|---|---|

| | 1861 Emancipation of serfs in Russian Empire | 1869 Opening of Suez Canal | 1884 Hiram Maxim invents the first fully automatic machine gun | 1900 Boxer Rebellion | 1905 Albert Einstein publishes theory of relativity | 1908 "Young Turks" rise to power in Ottoman Empire |
|---|---|---|---|---|---|---|

# Chapter 22 1750–1871

# Patterns of Nation-States and Culture in the Atlantic World

When the French Revolution broke out in 1789, a young Caribbean mulatto named Vincent Ogé (ca. 1755–1791) was in France on business. His extended family of free light-skinned blacks owned a coffee plantation and a commercial business with black slaves on Saint-Domingue [SAN-dow-MANG] (modern Haiti). Caught up in the excitement of 1789, Ogé embraced the French revolutionary principles of liberty, equality, and fraternity with great enthusiasm and quickly became an adherent of French constitutional nationalism: The former absolute monarchy in France was swiftly reorganized to incorporate a written constitution and an elected National Assembly. As part of the general atmosphere of emancipation so prevalent during the early part of the revolution, he joined the antislavery Society of the Friends of Blacks in Paris and demanded that French constitutionalism be extended to Saint-Domingue.

**THE NORTH ATLANTIC, 1750–1880**

In a short time the society's efforts appeared to bear fruit. In March 1790, the National Assembly granted self-administration to the colonies, and Ogé returned to Saint-Domingue full of hope that he would be able to participate as a free citizen in the island's governance. But the governor stubbornly refused to admit mulattoes as citizens of the new order. Ogé and a group of friends therefore joined a band of 250–300 freedmen and took up arms to

ABOVE: Thousands of Polish soldiers joined Napoleon's forces sent to Haiti in 1802, depicted here in *Battle on Santo Domingo* by Polish painter January Sucholdoski (1797–1875).

carve out a stronghold for themselves in the north of the island by arresting plantation owners and occupying their properties. One plantation owner later testified that the rebels looted and killed during their uprising but that Ogé himself was a man of honor who treated his prisoners fairly and even left him in the possession of his personal arms.

After only a few weeks of fighting, however, government troops pushed the rebels into the Spanish eastern part of the island. Ogé and his followers surrendered after being guaranteed their safety. But the Spanish governor betrayed his prisoners, turning them over to the French. After a trial for insurrection in February 1791, Ogé and 19 followers were condemned to death. Ogé suffered particularly barbaric tortures before expiring: Executioners strapped him spread-eagle on a wagon wheel and systematically broke his bones with an iron bar until he was dead.

---

The Ogé insurrection was a prelude of the Haitian Revolution, which began in August 1791 as a rebellion against discrimination and culminated with the achievement of independence under a black government in 1804. It was the third of the great constitutional-nationalist revolutions—after the American and French Revolutions—that inaugurated, with the Industrial Revolution, the modern period of world history. The new pattern of constitutional nation formation encouraged other peoples who possessed a cultural but not political unity to strive for their own ethnolinguistic nation-states. Italians and Germans united in their own states and Irish, Scots, and Welsh strove for autonomy within the United Kingdom.

The political ferment which led to the three constitutional revolutions was part of a larger cultural ferment called the Enlightenment. The rising urban middle classes of professionals, officials, and entrepreneurs embraced the New Sciences and their philosophical interpretations, which not only provided the intellectual ammunition for the revolutions but also stimulated entirely new forms of cultural creativity in the movements of romanticism and realism.

## Origins of the Nation-State, 1750–1815

The Glorious Revolution of 1688 in England (Great Britain after 1707) bestowed rights and duties on English subjects who had never enjoyed them before. In this revolution, for the first time in Europe, the traditional divine rights of a monarch were curbed. A century later, the innovative ideas of *subjects* becoming *citizens* with constitutionally guaranteed rights and duties and of Parliament representing the citizens spread from Great Britain to North America, France, and Haiti. Beyond the Glorious Revolution, however, the American, French, and Haitian Revolutions were more radical in the sense that they rejected the British compromise of royal and parliamentary power and led to republican, middle-class or liberated slave nation-states without traditional divine-right monarchies.

## Seeing Patterns

▶ How did the pattern of constitutional nationalism, emerging from the American and French Revolutions, affect the course of events in the Western world during the first half of the nineteenth century?

▶ In what ways did ethnolinguistic nationalism differ from constitutional nationalism, and what was its influence on the formation of nation-states in the second half of the nineteenth century?

▶ What were the reactions among thinkers and artists to the developing pattern of nation-state formation? How did they define the intellectual-artistic movements of romanticism and realism?

# The American, French, and Haitian Revolutions

The American and French Revolutions were outgrowths of the Seven Years' War, in which Great Britain and France fought for the dominance of their respective seaborne empires in the world. The governments of both kingdoms went deeply into debt to wage the war. They owed this debt to their wealthy subjects, many of whom were landowners and administrators forming the ruling class. To pay back the debt, the kings had to go to all of their subjects and raise their taxes. The incongruence of monarchs holding the mass of their subjects responsible for their debts to a few wealthy subjects was apparent to a large number of people, who therefore formulated political principles of reform and, ultimately, revolution. Once the revolutions were under way, the American and French revolutionary principles of freedom and equality had repercussions in the wider Atlantic world, first in Haiti and ultimately the Latin American colonies of Spain and Portugal (Chapter 27).

**Conditions for Revolution in North America**  When Britain won the Seven Years' War, it acquired France's trade forts in India as well as French possessions in Canada and the Ohio–Mississippi River valley. France turned what remained of Louisiana over to its ally Spain (which had lost Florida to Britain) and retreated entirely from the continent of North America. But the British victory and territorial gains came at the price of a huge debt: The payment of the interest alone devoured most of the country's regular annual budget. Taxes had to be raised domestically as well as overseas, and in order to do so the government had to strengthen its administrative hand in an empire that had grown haphazardly and, in North America, without much oversight.

By 1763, the 13 North American colonies had experienced both rapid demographic and powerful economic growth. Opening lands beyond the Appalachian Mountains into the Ohio valley would relieve a growing population pressure on the strip of land along the Atlantic coast that the colonies occupied. Environmental degradation, through overplanting and deforestation, had increased the landless population and contributed to the presence of growing numbers of poor people in the burgeoning cities of Philadelphia, Boston, and New York.

The occupation of new land across the Appalachians, on the other hand, increased the administrative challenges for the British. They had to employ large numbers of standing troops to protect not only the settlers from the hostility of the Native Americans but also the Native Americans from aggression by settlers. Grain, timber, and tobacco exports had made the colonies rich prior to 1763, but the war boom inevitably gave way to a postwar bust. While new land created new opportunities, the economic slump created hardships (see Map 22.1).

In view of the complicated political and economic situation in the North American colonies, the British government failed to devise a clear plan for strengthening its administrative as well as taxing powers. It was particularly inept with the imposition of new taxes intended to help in the reduction of the national debt. In 1765, it introduced the Stamp Act, forcing everyone to pay a tax on the use of paper, whether for legal documents, newspapers, or even playing cards. The tax was to be used for the upkeep of the standing troops, many of which were withdrawn from the Ohio valley and ordered to be quartered in the colonies for the enforcement of the increased taxes.

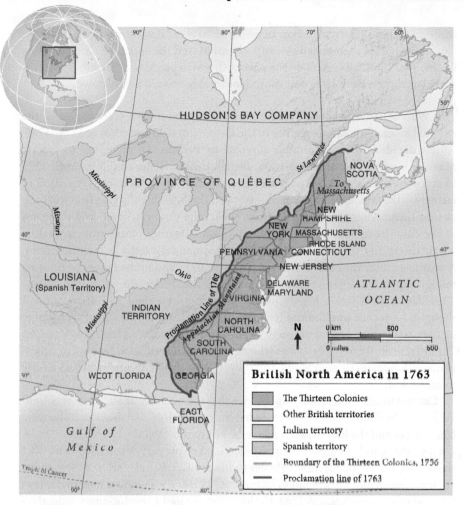

MAP 22.1 **British North America in 1763.**

**Countdown to War** A firestorm of protest against the Stamp Act broke out among the urban lower-middle ranks of shopkeepers, small merchants, mechanics, and printers, who organized themselves in groups such as the Daughters of Liberty and Sons of Liberty. The Daughters declared a highly successful boycott of British goods and promoted the production of homespun textiles. In Boston, one of the flashpoints of unrest, the British administration offended colonists of the upper urban class when it dissolved the Massachusetts Assembly for opposing the tax. The British Parliament withdrew the Stamp Act in 1766 when exports fell, but replaced it with indirect taxes on a variety of commodities. Although these taxes were less visible, there were still levied without the colonies' consent.

The one indirect tax which aroused particular anger among the American colonists was the tea tax. This tax was actually a subsidy to keep the near-bankrupt East India Company afloat and had nothing to do either with America or Britain's debt. In 1773 the colonists protested the tax with the symbolic dumping of a

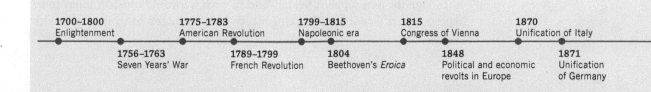

| 1700–1800 | | 1775–1783 | | 1799–1815 | | 1815 | | 1870 | |
| Enlightenment | | American Revolution | | Napoleonic era | | Congress of Vienna | | Unification of Italy | |
| | 1756–1763 | | 1789–1799 | | 1804 | | 1848 | | 1871 |
| | Seven Years' War | | French Revolution | | Beethoven's *Eroica* | | Political and economic revolts in Europe | | Unification of Germany |

cargo of tea into Boston Harbor. In response to this "Boston Tea Party," Britain closed the harbor, demanded restitution, and passed the so-called Coercive Acts (called the "Intolerable Acts" in the colonies), which put Massachusetts into effective bankruptcy. Both sides now moved inexorably toward a showdown.

**The War of Independence**   To countermand the British Coercive Acts, the colonial assemblies came together in the Continental Association of 1774–1776, which decided on an economic boycott of Britain. In an effort to isolate Massachusetts from the Association, British troops ventured out in April 1775 to seize an assumed cache of arms and ammunition in Concord. A militia of farmers—the famous "minutemen"—stopped the British, inflicting heavy casualties on them. After this clash of forces, war broke out in earnest, and delegates of the colonies appointed George Washington, a former officer from a wealthy Virginian family of tobacco planters, as commander of the colonists' troops. A year later, after the mobilization of popular forces and in the hope of garnering foreign support, delegates of the colonies issued the Declaration of Independence. This declaration was a highly literate document steeped in Enlightenment thought. Its author was Thomas Jefferson, like Washington the son of a Virginian planter, with an advanced university education that included the New Sciences. The great majority of the delegates who signed were also educated men of means— planters, landowners, merchants, and lawyers. The urban middle class was clearly in command.

Central to the declaration was the idea that the equality of all "men" was "self-evident." The declaration tacitly excluded the one-fifth of all Americans who were black slaves and the half who were women, not to mention the Native Americans. On the other hand, the signers also excluded Locke's property ownership from what they considered to be the most valuable rights of citizens and rendered these rights as "life, liberty, and the pursuit of happiness." When the colonists eventually won the War of Independence in 1783, the founders created a revolutionary federal republic with a Congress that was more representative of its citizens than the Parliament in Great Britain but still excluded a substantial proportion of inhabitants.

**The Early United States**   The new republic's initial years were fraught with organizational difficulties. The governing document, the Articles of Confederation, granted so much power to the individual states that they operated de facto like separate countries. In 1787, a constitutional convention came together in Philadelphia to create a far more effective federal constitution. Careful to add checks and balances in the form of a bicameral legislature and separation of powers into legislative, executive, and judicial branches, the new constitution seemed to embody many of the ideals of the Enlightenment—including a set of 10 initial amendments: the Bill of Rights. Though still imperfect—particularly in sidestepping the contentious issue of slavery—it provided a model for nearly all the world's constitutions that followed. A later commentator praised it as "a machine that would go of itself"; another, more critical one called its checks and balances "a harmonious system of mutual frustration." In 1789, under the new system, George Washington was elected the first president of the United States.

Though the new republic fell far short of what we would consider today to be "representative"—until 1820 voting rights were restricted to white males with property—its abolition of the divine right of monarchial rule and its replacement by the sovereignty of the people was for most people a previously unimaginable reversal of the natural order of things. In this respect, the American and French Revolutions signaled the inauguration of a new pattern of state formation and the advent of modernity.

**Conditions for the French Revolution**  King Louis XVI (r. 1774–1792) and the French government had watched the American War of Independence with great sympathy, hoping for an opportunity to avenge the kingdom's defeat in the Seven Years' War. France supplied the Americans with money, arms, and officers, and in 1778–1779, in alliance with Spain, waged war on Great Britain. The French–Spanish entry into the war forced Britain into an impossible defense of its entire colonial empire. Although mounting a creditable military effort, Britain conceded defeat in 1783 in the hope of escaping with minimal territorial losses, apart from the North American colonies. Indeed, in the peace negotiations France and Spain made few territorial gains. The French government furthermore had to begin exorbitant payments—much higher than what Britain faced after the Seven Years' War—on the interest for the loans to carry out the war. Crippling debt, which the French government was ultimately unable to pay, played a large role in establishing the preconditions underlying the outbreak of the French Revolution.

As in America, the French population had increased sharply during the 1700s. Food production could barely keep up, and inflation increased. As new scholarship has shown, the rural economy responded to the rising demand, though with difficulty, and in the region of Paris, production for the market was highly profitable. Furthermore, colonial trade with the Caribbean colonies boomed. Had it not been for the debt, the government would have been well-financed: It collected direct taxes as well as monies from compulsory loans and the sale of titles and offices to a large upper stratum of ordinary people of means—merchants, lawyers, and administrators. These people were deeply invested in the regime, buying themselves into the ranks of the aristocracy and benefiting from administrative offices handling the kingdom's tax revenue. Although claiming to be the absolute authority, the king in reality shared power and wealth with a large ruling class of old and new aristocrats as well as aspiring ordinary urban people of wealth.

In 1781, suspicions arose about the solvency of the regime when the finance minister quit. He had kept the extent of the subsidies for the American revolutionaries a government secret. But the government continued to borrow, even though bad weather leading to two poor harvests in 1786–1787 diminished tax revenues. The hardship caused by these two years became crucial for the eventual revolution in 1789: Without reserves in grain and animals, the peasants suffered severe famine and grew increasingly angry when government imports intended to help ended up in the hands of profiteers and hoarders.

By 1788, the government was unable to make payments on short-term loans and had to hand out promissory notes, with bankruptcy looming in the background. As in Britain in the 1760s, a reform of the tax system became unavoidable. At first, the king sought to initiate this reform with the help of a council of appointed notables. When this failed, he held general elections for a popular assembly to meet in Versailles (called the Estates-General, last convened in 1614). Voters, defined as males over 25 who were French and paid taxes, met in constituent meetings in their districts across France, according to their "estate" as clergy, aristocrats, or commoners. Peasants met in large numbers in the "third estate," or commoner meetings; but the deputies they elected to meet in Paris were overwhelmingly administrators, lawyers, doctors, academics, businessmen, and debt holders. At the request of the king, the deputies composed petitions in which they listed their grievances about taxes, waste, luxury at court, and ministerial "despotism" to form the basis for the reform legislation.

The most famous among the petitions was the pamphlet of the priest Emmanuel-Joseph Sieyès [see-YES], entitled *What Is the Third Estate?* Sieyès was elected as a commoner from Paris and became one of the leading intellectual figures in the revolution. In his pamphlet he put forward the revolutionary idea that the French nation of 25 million *was* the third estate, while the other two estates, totaling 200,000 members, were no more than a tiny fraction. The third estate, embodying Rousseau's idea of the "general will" of the nation, should alone form a "national assembly" and translate this general will into a constitution, fiscal reform, and the abolition of aristocratic privileges.

Amid widespread unrest and rioting among peasants in many places in France and workers in Paris, the third estate now outmaneuvered the other estates and the king. In June 1789 it seceded from the Estates-General and declared itself the National Assembly. Pressured by the pro-aristocracy faction at court, the king issued a veiled threat: If the Assembly would not accept his reform proposals, he said, "I alone should consider myself their [the people's] representative." The king then reinforced his troops in and around Paris and Versailles and dismissed his popular finance minister, who had brought some famine relief in spring. Parisians, afraid of an imminent military occupation of the city, swarmed through the streets on July 14, 1789. They provisioned themselves with arms and gunpowder from arsenals, gunsmith shops, and the Bastille, the royal fortress and prison inside Paris, which they stormed.

**Three Phases of the Revolution**    The French Revolution, unfolding from 1789 to 1799, went through the three phases of constitutional monarchy (1789–1792), radical republicanism (1792–1795), and military consolidation (1795–1799). The first phase began with the "great fear" of near anarchy, which reigned during July and August 1789. People in the provinces, mostly peasants, chased many of their aristocratic and commoner landlords from their estates. Paris, too, remained in an uproar, since food supplies, in spite of a good harvest, remained spotty. Agitation climaxed in October when thousands of working women, many with arms, marched from Paris to Versailles, forcing the king to move to Paris and concern himself directly with their plight. No longer threatened by the king, the National Assembly issued the Declaration of the Rights of Man and of the Citizen (1789), subjected the Catholic Church to French civil law (1790), established a constitutional monarchy (1791), and issued laws ending the unequal taxes of the Old Regime (1792)—four major reforms carried out in the spirit of constitutional nationalism.

The second phase of the revolution (1792–1795), the period of radical republicanism, began when the revolutionaries found themselves unable to establish a stable constitutional regime. After the king tried unsuccessfully to flee Paris with his unpopular Austrian-born, Habsburg wife, Marie-Antoinette, to a monarchist

stronghold in eastern France in the summer of 1791, Austria and Prussia threatened to intervene if the king and queen were harmed. Patriotic feelings were aroused, and the idea of preventive war gained adherents. In April 1792 the government declared war on its eastern neighbors, to which many aristocratic families had fled.

Events quickly escalated, with republicans deposing the king and holding elections for a new assembly, the National Convention, to draw up a constitution. In the following year, the republicans executed the royal couple and created a conscript army, to regain control of the borders. Fears of plots from outside France as well as among the revolutionaries led to the formation of the Committee of Public Safety. This committee, the executive organ of the National Convention, ruthlessly eliminated some 30,000 real and suspected "reactionaries" during its "Reign of Terror," making mockery of the Revolution's Declaration of the Rights of Man and universal male suffrage.

The Revolution entered its third phase (1795–1799) after the army had succeeded in securing the borders at the end of 1793. A growing revulsion at the Reign of Terror led to the emasculation of the Committee of Public Safety and its eventual replacement by the Directory in November 1795. A new constitution and bicameral legislature were created, but political and financial stability remained elusive. The Directory depended increasingly on the army to survive. What was originally an untrained conscript army of able-bodied male civilians had become highly professionalized during two years of constant warfare and was the only stable institution in France.

Within the army, a brash young brigadier general named Napoleon Bonaparte (1769–1821), of minor aristocratic Corsican descent, was the most promising commander. From 1796 to 1798 Napoleon scored major victories against the Austrians in northern Italy and invaded Egypt, which he occupied in preparation for an invasion of British India. But, thwarted by a pursuing British fleet, he returned to France and overthrew the ineffective Directory in November 1799, thus ending the Revolution.

**The French Revolution.** After the storming of the Bastille (top left), the French Revolution gained momentum when Parisian women marched to Versailles, demanding that the king reside in Paris and end the famine there (top right). The inevitability of a republic became clear when the king and queen were captured after they attempted to flee (bottom left).

# The Guillotine

It is estimated that during the period of the Terror (June 1793–July 1794) the guillotine was responsible for around 1,000 executions in Paris alone and for perhaps as many as 30,000 throughout France. This iconic symbol of grisly public executions is attended by many myths. Among these is the idea that the guillotine was invented by—and took its name from—one Dr. Guillotin solely for the purpose of speeding up executions of perceived enemies of the republic during the infamous Reign of Terror. Neither of these notions is true, however. Indeed, the actual train of events is far more compelling—and ironic.

Far from appearing for the first time during the French Revolution, the first known model of a "decapitation machine" is probably the Halifax Gibbet, in use in England from around 1300 until 1650. Another model, the Scottish Maiden, was derived from the Halifax Gibbet and used in 150 executions from 1565 until 1708. It was subsequently turned over to a museum in Edinburgh in 1797 and may have earlier served as a model for the French machine.

When and how did the instrument first appear in France? Ironically, it came as an indirect result of efforts to end the death penalty. During the early days of the revolution the National Assembly pondered the abolition of the death penalty in France altogether. On October 10, 1789, the Assembly was addressed by Dr. Joseph Ignace Guillotin (1738–1814), founder of the French Academy of Medicine and a staunch opponent of capital punishment, who urged the assembly to at the very least find "a machine that beheads painlessly," if they could not ultimately agree to stop executions altogether. Toward this end Guillotin presented sketches of the kind

**The Execution of Marie-Antoinette.** During the radical republican period of the French Revolution, the Committee of Public Safety had Queen Marie-Antoinette condemned to death for treason after a show trial. She was executed on October 16, 1793, 9 months after the execution of her husband, Louis XVI.

**Revival of Empire**    Once in power, Napoleon embarked on sweeping domestic reforms that, taken together, curtailed much of the revolutionary fervor and restored order and stability in France. His crowning achievement was the reform of the French legal system, promulgated in the Civil Code of 1804, which in theory established the equality of all male citizens before the law but in reality imposed restrictions on many revolutionary freedoms. In 1804 Napoleon sealed his power by crowning himself emperor of the French. Secure in his authority at home, he now struck out on a lengthy campaign of conquest in Europe. Victory followed upon victory from 1805 to 1810, resulting in the French domination of most of Continental Europe.

The goal was the construction of an Enlightenment-influenced but newly aristocratic European empire, land-based and in the tradition of the Habsburgs, Ottomans, and Russians (see Map 22.3). With this empire, he planned to form a

of machine he had in mind, but his initial design was rejected, followed by a second rejection on December 1 of the same year. In 1791 the Assembly finally agreed to retain the death penalty, noting that "every person condemned to the death penalty shall have his head severed." But instead of adopting Dr. Guillotin's design, the Assembly accepted a model designed by Dr. Antoine Louis, secretary of the Academy of Surgery; Dr. Louis then turned to a German engineer, Tobias Schmidt, who constructed the first version of the "painless" decapitation machine. It was not until April 25, 1792, that the guillotine, nicknamed "Louisette" after Dr. Louis, claimed its first victim. It is not clear when the name was changed to "guillotine" (the final "e" was added later), but historians speculate that Dr. Guillotin's early advocacy of quick and painless executions was a major factor. As for Dr. Guillotin himself, the crowning irony was that, after fighting a losing battle with the government to change the name of the machine because of embarrassment to his family, he changed his own name and retreated to the obscurity he had come to crave.

**Execution by Guillotine in France, 1929.** An Enlightenment innovation, the guillotine was intended to execute humans swiftly and humanely. But the mass executions of the French Revolution turned the guillotine into a symbol of barbarism. It was not until 1977 that France executed its last criminal by guillotine. Today, most countries subscribe to the belief that even criminals have inalienable human rights, the most basic being the right to live.

## Questions

- Can the guillotine be viewed as a practical adaptation of Enlightenment ideas? If so, how?

- Why do societies like France in the late eighteenth century debate the means they use to execute prisoners? What are the criteria by which one form of execution is considered more humane than others?

Continental counterweight to the maritime British Empire that was unchallengeable in the Atlantic and Indian Oceans. The failure of Napoleon's Russian campaign in 1812, however, marked the beginning of the end of Napoleon's grand scheme. An alliance of Great Britain, Austria, Prussia, and Russia ended Napoleon's empire in 1815 and inaugurated the restoration of the pre–French Revolution regimes in Europe.

**Conditions for the Haitian Revolution** French Saint-Domingue was one of the richest European colonies, based on plantations that produced vast amounts of sugar, indigo, coffee, and cotton for export to the Old World. At the time of the French Revolution, the colony produced nearly half of the world's sugar and coffee. Originally, it had been a Spanish possession. But as Spain's power slipped during the seventeenth and eighteenth centuries, France took advantage of the

**Punishment of a slave on the estate of Charles Balthazar Julien Févret de Saint-Mémin.** This watercolor vividly depicts the vast differences between the slave strapped to a frame and the completely unconcerned estate owner on horseback. During the uprising of 1791 slaves occupied the great majority of estates, ended slavery, and drove their owners into exile. Saint-Mémin, whose mother was Creole, waited for a decade in the United States for the return of his estate before giving up and returning to France.

situation and established its colony on the western part of the island. In the following century, settlers enjoyed French mercantilist protectionism for splendid profits from their slave plantations.

In the second half of the 1700s, some 30,000 white settlers, 28,000 mulattos (holding about one-third of the slaves), and about 500,000 black plantation and household slaves formed an extremely unequal colonial society. Similarly extreme inequalities existed only in Brazil and Jamaica. When France, like Britain and Spain after the Seven Years' War, tightened colonial controls, the French administrators in Haiti were afraid that the white and mulatto plantation owners would form a united resistance. In order to split the two, they introduced increasingly racist measures to deprive the mulattos of their privileges. It was this increasing split which created the conditions for Vincent Ogé's uprising discussed in the vignette of this chapter and eventually for the slave rebellion once the French Revolution itself was under way.

**Revolt of the Slaves**    After the failure of Ogé's uprising, resentment continued to simmer among the mulattos in the south as well as the black slaves in the north of Haiti. Resentment turned into fury when the white settler Provincial Assembly refused any concessions even though the French revolutionary National Constituent Assembly in May 1791 granted citizen rights to mulattos whose parents were free. Aware of the by now open hostility between the mulattos and whites, slaves seized the opportunity for their own rebellion in August 1791. The leaders of the slaves were overseers, coachmen, or managers on plantations who called the slaves under their authority to arms. Almost simultaneously, but with little coordination, the mulattos of the south rose in rebellion as well. Within weeks, the slave and mulatto rebellion had 100,000 followers and encompassed the entire northern and southern provinces of the colony. The settlers were well armed but suffered heavy losses under the onslaught of overwhelming numbers.

With the rebellion taking an increasingly severe toll on the economy, the Assembly in Paris sent commissioners and troops in November 1791 and April 1792 to reestablish order. Neither commission made much headway, largely because of the unrelenting hostility of the whites, especially lower-class whites in urban centers. In their desperation to gain support, even from the blacks, the second commission made the momentous decision in August 1793 to abolish slavery. This decision, however, failed to rally the black military leaders who had allied themselves with the Spanish, rulers of the eastern half of Santo Domingo. Revolutionary France was embroiled in war against Spain and Britain since early 1793, and the latter had invaded Haiti in the summer of 1793. Spain and Britain looked like inevitable victors, and the commissioners' emancipation declaration appeared to have been too little too late.

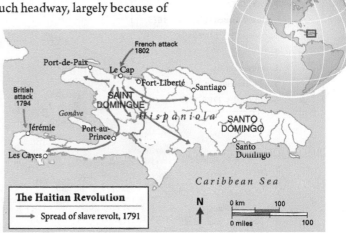

MAP **22.2** **The Haitian Revolution.**

Both invasions stalled, however, largely because of the impact of tropical diseases catching up with the British occupation forces (1793–1797). A by now sympathetic Assembly in Paris confirmed the emancipation declaration in February 1794, and the French position on the island began to improve. In May 1794, a shrewd black rebel leader from the north, François-Dominique Toussaint Louverture (ca. 1743–1803), decided that the tide was turning. He left the Spanish with his 4,000 troops and joined the French, whose numbers had dwindled to a few thousand (see Map 22.2). Toussaint, grandson of a vassal king (*onlo*) in Benin, West Africa, had obtained his freedom in the 1770s. For a short period he had leased a coffee farm with a number of slaves, but after financial difficulties he went back to the plantations of his former owner as a coachman. Upon his return to the French in 1794, he accommodated himself with the mulatto faction of the rebellion in the south. In the following years, the northern blacks and southern mulattos transformed the rebellion into a full-fledged revolution.

**Nation-State Building**   During the violent events of 1791–1794, many plantation owners had fled the colony. The former slaves carved out plots for themselves on deserted plantations and grew subsistence crops for their families. Toussaint remained committed to the plantation system, however, in order to supply revenues for his state-building ambitions. He dispatched his officers to the countryside to force former slaves to resume production, with moderate success. In 1801, Toussaint was sufficiently powerful to assume the governorship of Saint-Domingue from the French officials in a soft coup and proclaim a constitution that incorporated the basic principles of French constitutional nationalism. By this time, the civil administration was reasonably functional again, and efforts were under way to build local courts and schools to broaden the revolution.

But Toussaint still had to reckon with Atlantic politics. Napoleon Bonaparte, in control of France since 1799, was determined to rebuild the French overseas empire. In Egypt (perhaps with plans to continue to India) he was thwarted by the British, but in the Americas he was successful in purchasing Louisiana from Spain

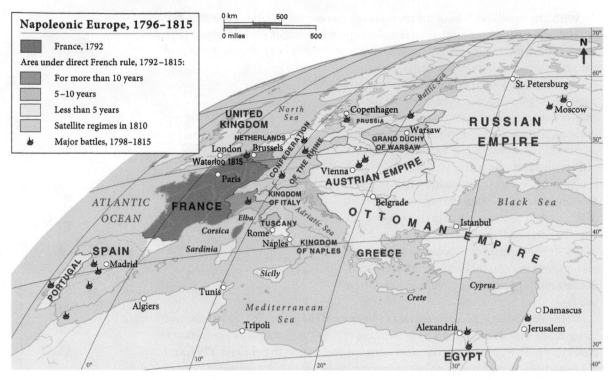

**Napoleonic Europe, 1796–1815**

- France, 1792

Area under direct French rule, 1792–1815:

- For more than 10 years
- 5–10 years
- Less than 5 years
- Satellite regimes in 1810
- Major battles, 1798–1815

MAP 22.3  **Napoleonic Europe, 1796–1815.**

in 1800 (ceded after the Seven Years' War of 1758–1763). With the defeat of Austria in 1802, Napoleon was able to get its ally Britain to recognize the French Republic and make peace. Immediately, Napoleon dispatched troops to Saint-Domingue to add the colony to Louisiana and revive the French Atlantic empire. Toussaint was well prepared for the invasion, but when the French landed in February 1802 several of his officers surrendered without a fight. As the French advanced into the island against declining resistance, one general, Jean-Jacques Dessalines, betrayed Toussaint to the French in June 1802. After his arrest, Toussaint was sent to France, where he died in April 1803. The revolution seemed to be finished.

Jean-Jacques Dessalines (r. 1802–1806) was a former slave from northern Haiti who, as a roofer, was of higher rank than the plantation slaves. Toussaint had made him the point man for the repair of the plantation system but without giving him the preferential role that he thought he deserved. Seemingly obedient to the French, Dessalines waited for the dreaded yellow fever to take its toll among the invaders. When more than two-thirds of the French forces were dead by the summer of 1802, Napoleon realized that his Atlantic dream was unrealizable. He sold Louisiana to the United States in April 1803 and withdrew the remnants of his troops from Saint-Domingue in November 1803. On January 1, 1804, Dessalines assumed power and declared the colony's independence.

Subsequently, he made himself emperor, to counter Napoleon, and renamed the country Haiti, its supposed original Taíno name. When he changed the constitution in favor of autocratic rule, he provoked a conspiracy against him, which culminated in his assassination in 1806. In the aftermath, the state split into an autocratically ruled black north with a state-run plantation economy and a more democratic mulatto south with privatized economy of small farms (1806–1821).

Of the three revolutions resulting in the new form of the republican nation-state based on a constitution, that of Haiti is clearly the one that realized the Enlightenment principles of liberty, equality, and fraternity most fully. By demonstrating the power of the new ideology of constitutional nationalism, it inaugurated a new pattern of state formation in world history not only among the new white and colored urban middle classes but also among the uprooted black African underclass of slaves.

# Enlightenment Culture: Radicalism and Moderation

The American, French, and Haitian Revolutions were embedded in the culture of the **Enlightenment** (ca. 1700–1800). The origins of this culture lay in the new mathematized sciences, which inspired a number of thinkers, such as Descartes, Spinoza, Hobbes, and Locke, to create new philosophical interpretations (see Chapter 17). The radical interpretation was materialism, according to which all of reality consisted of matter and Descartes's separate substance of mind or reason could either be dispensed with or be explained as a byproduct of matter. Moderates held on to Descartes's mind or reason as a separate substance, struggling to explain its presence in reality. The radical Enlightenment tradition evolved primarily in France, most prominently among the so-called Encyclopedists, who were materialists and agnostics or even atheists. The moderate tradition found adherents in Germany, where the Enlightenment mingled with ethnolinguist awareness.

**Enlightenment:** European intellectual movement (1700–1800) growing out of the New Sciences and based largely on Descartes's concept of reality consisting of the two separate substances of matter and mind.

## The Enlightenment and Its Many Expressions

Energetic writers popularized the new, science-derived philosophy in eighteenth-century France, Holland, England and Germany. Thousands subscribed to Enlightenment-themed books, pamphlets, and newspapers and attended academies, salons, and lectures. The audiences were still a minority, however, even among the growing middle class of urban administrators, professionals, merchants, and landowners, not to mention the 80 percent of the population engaged in the crafts and in farming. But their voices as radical or moderate "progressives" opposing tradition-bound ministers, aristocrats, and clergy became measurably louder.

It was the late eighteenth-century generation of this vociferous minority that was central to the revolutions in America and France and—a minority within the minority—in the French slave colony Haiti. They translated their New Sciences–derived conception of reality into such "self-evident" ideals as life, liberty, equality, social contract, property, representation, nation, popular sovereignty, and constitution. In the wider, more broadly conceived culture of the Enlightenment, they fashioned new forms of expression in the arts and thereby made the Enlightenment a broad movement.

**Denis Diderot and the *Encyclopédie***   The idea to bring together all the new knowledge accumulated since the Renaissance and the advent of the New Sciences in an alphabetically organized encyclopedia appeared first in England in 1728. A French publisher decided in 1751 to have it translated. But under the editorship of Denis Diderot (1713–1784) and (until 1759) Jean le Rond d'Alembert (1717–1783) it became a massively expanded work in its own right. Both poured all their energy into writing entries and soliciting contributions from the "republic of letters," as the French Enlightenment thinkers were called.

Many entries dealt with delicate subjects, such as science, industry, commerce, freedom of thought, slavery, and religious tolerance, sometimes edited by the cautious publisher without Diderot's knowledge. Publication itself was not easy, since the Catholic Church and the French crown banned the project as subversive for several years and forced it to continue in secret. But the roughly 4,000 subscribers received their twenty-eighth and last volume in 1772, ready and able to assimilate everything modern, urbane gentlemen and gentlewomen should know.

**Philosophy and Morality**    Jean-Jacques Rousseau (1712–1778), in contrast to his atheist Enlightenment colleagues of the *Encyclopédie*, was a firm believer in the religious morality of the masses. The son of a cultivated and music-loving Geneva watchmaker, Rousseau was philosophically moderate, even if emotionally fragile and at times given to paranoia. To the consternation of the radicals in France, he espoused in his *Social Contract* (1762) the notion that humans had suffered a steady decline from their "natural" state ever since civilization began and imposed its own arbitrary authority on them. The radicals held that even though humans had lost their natural state of freedom and equality and had come under arbitrary authority, they were experiencing a steady progress of civilization toward ever-improving degrees of freedom and equality. Rousseau did share with his former friends a low opinion of the absolutist French regime, of which he ran afoul just as much as they did. But he had little faith in such concepts as popular sovereignty, elections, and electoral reforms that they propagated. Instead, he believed that people, rallying in a nation, should express their unity directly through a "general will," a sort of direct democracy—more applicable to his native city of Geneva than a large nation like France.

**Philosophy and the Categorical Imperative**    Immanuel Kant (1724–1804), a much more disciplined philosopher than Rousseau, was a firm believer in the progress of civilization and history, as expressed in his *Perpetual Peace* (1795). In fact, he quite immodestly thought of himself as having performed a second "Copernican turn" in modernity with his two main books, *Critique of Pure Reason* and *Critique of Practical Reason* (1781–1787). Like all Enlightenment thinkers, Kant took his departure from Descartes. But he rejected the materialist turn of Locke and the radical French Enlightenment. Even though he admitted that sensory or bodily experience was primary, he insisted that this experience could be understood only through the categories of the mind or reason which were not found in experience. Reason transcended experience.

In contrast to Rousseau with his traditional Christian ethics, Kant sought to build morality on transcendent reason. He came to the conclusion, therefore, that this morality had to be erected on the basis of the *categorical imperative*: to act in such a way that the principle of your action can be a principle for anyone's action.

This highly abstract principle later entered modern thought as the basis for human rights, with their claim to universality, as in the Charter of the United Nations (1945).

**Economic Liberalism**　The Enlightenment also saw the birth of the academic discipline of economics. French and British thinkers who were appalled by the inefficient administration of finances, taxes, and trade by the regimes in their countries found the official pursuit of mercantilism wanting. As discussed in previous chapters, mercantilism was the effort to import as little as possible, except from the warm-weather colonies, and develop domestic crafts so as to export manufactured goods in exchange for the commodities of the colonies. Opposed to mercantilist state control in France, the so-called physiocrats argued that individual freedom and equality should be the principles of the economy. The state should reduce taxes and other means of control to a minimum so that entrepreneurism in the general population could flourish. It should adopt a policy of *laissez-faire* [les-say-FAIR]—that is, "hands-off."

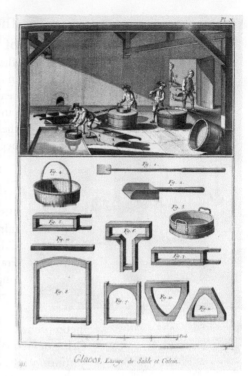

The Scottish economist Adam Smith (1723–1790), who spent some time in Paris and was familiar with many of the physiocrats, developed a British version of laissez-faire economics. In his *Inquiry into the Nature and Causes of the Wealth of Nations* (1776) Smith argued that if the market were largely left to its own devices, without many state regulations and restrictions, it would regulate itself through the forces of supply and demand, appropriate prices, and so forth. It would then move in the direction of increasing efficiency as if guided by "an unseen hand." Smith became the founding father of modern economics, whose ideas are still regularly invoked today.

**The *Encyclopédie*.** Denis Diderot's massive work promoted practical, applied science, such as this illustration showing glassmaking.

**Literature and Music**　As in the other fields of modern cultural expression, the Enlightenment also inspired writers and composers. Noteworthy among them were Johann Wolfgang von Goethe (1749–1832) and Wolfgang Amadeus Mozart (1756–1791), sons of a lawyer and a court musician, respectively. Among Goethe's numerous poems, novels, plays, and even scientific works (on color) was his drama *Faust* about an ambitious scientific experimenter who sells his soul to the devil to acquire mastery of nature. Faust became a metaphor for modernity—for the technicians and engineers whose dominance of natural forces runs roughshod over environmental concerns. Mozart was a child prodigy who composed an astounding number of symphonies, operas, and chamber music pieces. One of his best-known operas is *The Magic Flute*, a work displaying the influence of the Freemasons, a fraternal association popular in Enlightenment Europe devoted to "liberty, fraternity, and equality"—principles which the French Revolution borrowed as its motto.

The imperial turn of the French Revolution under Napoleon may be said to have effectively ended the Enlightenment. A few years later, with the fall of Napoleon and the restoration of monarchies, the European kings actively worked to rescind its effects, and in the face of overwhelming power, the Enlightenment constitutionalists went either silent or underground.

**Grimm's Fairy Tales.** Perhaps the most famous collection of folktales in the Western tradition, *Children's and Household Stories* (1812) was assembled by Wilhelm and Jakob Grimm as a way to preserve their country's cultural commonality and to rekindle in their countrymen an appreciation for their Germanic roots. The stories they collected, such as "Rapunzel," shown in this illustration, were brought together through fieldwork and by peasant women who would visit the brothers Grimm and recite stories that awoke "thoughts of the heart."

## The Other Enlightenment: The Ideology of Ethnolinguistic Nationalism

The constitutional nationalists who led the revolutions of 1776–1804 in America, France, and Haiti proclaimed universal human rights in centuries-old monarchical states that had evolved into overseas empires. Ethnic descent or linguistic affiliations did not play a part in their revolutionary actions. After 1815, however, these affiliations began to play increasingly important roles.

**Constitutional versus Ethnic Nationalism** In North America, prior to the revolution the great majority of the constitutional nationalists were "British," which meant that they were Englishmen, with minorities from among the Irish, Welsh, and Scots. These minorities did not express their ethnolinguistic autonomy until the later 1800s. France was a similarly old monarchy at the heart of an Atlantic empire. A grammatically complex "high" French spoken in the Paris region set the national linguistic standard, while some of the provincial dialects spoken by nearly half of the population were mutually incomprehensible. The other half spoke no French at all and were ethnically either Celtic or German. These two minorities did not emphasize any ethnolinguistic autonomy in the 1700s, and—in contrast to Britain—not even in the 1800s.

Overseas Haiti presents the remarkable case of a rebellion in favor of the French metropolitan constitutional nationalism which transformed itself gradually into a revolutionary ethnolinguistic nationalism. After the Haitians achieved their independence, they elevated their West/Central African ethnic heritage and spoken language, Kreyòl, into their national identity, deemphasizing their French constitutional heritage.

**German Cultural Nationalism** In contrast to Great Britain and France, Germany was politically fragmented during the 1700s. Even though it had always possessed a central ruling institution, its imperial, rather than royal, constitution made for a much higher degree of political decentralization than in the English and French kingdoms. In addition, many Germans in eastern Europe were widely dispersed among people with different cultural and even religious heritages, such as Czechs, Slovaks, Hungarians, Poles, and Russians. Educated Germans, such as urban professionals, administrators, and educators, clearly shared a common culture wherever they lived, but in the absence of a strong central state, this culture was largely nonpolitical.

A central figure in articulating the commonly shared culture into an ethnolinguistic ideology was Johann Gottfried Herder (1744–1803). Herder's father was an elementary school teacher and Lutheran church warden in eastern Germany. At college, Herder studied with Kant but also with others under whose influence he became familiar with Pietism, a Lutheran version of the medieval Catholic mystical tradition. Employed first as a preacher and then as an administrator at assorted courts in central Germany, he published widely as a literary critic and was on close terms with Goethe and other German Enlightenment figures. In his writings, such as *On the Origin of Language* (1772), Herder sought to meld the diffuse cultural heritage into a more or less coherent ideology of Germanness combined with the Enlightenment. This ideology, so he hoped, would be preached not only to the educated but to the people in general through school curricula, history, and the arts.

The Herder-inspired ethnolinguistic version of the Enlightenment received a major boost during the French Revolution. Many Germans began to realize that any adoption of French constitutional nationalism made sense only in a politically united Germany. Before any unification plan could mature, however, Napoleon ended the French Revolution, declared himself emperor, and proceeded to defeat Prussia and Austria. With this, he aroused patriotic passions for liberation from French rule and hopes for a unified Germany under a consti-tutional government. Times seemed to be ripe for the realization of political unification on the basis of a combined constitutional and ethnolinguistic nationalism.

> "Thus was the German nation [*Volk*] placed—sufficiently united within itself by a common language and a common way of thinking and sharply enough severed from other peoples."
>
> —Johann Gottlieb Fichte, 1808

# The Growth of the Nation-State, 1815–1871

Napoleon's defeat in Russia in 1812 and the Congress in Vienna of 1815 were the principal occasions for rulers to turn back the clock in Europe. Monarchies and aristocracies reappeared throughout the continent, and the restored kings allowed only for the barest minimum of popular representation in parliaments. By contrast, in Anglo-America, the supremacy of constitutionalism was unchallenged during the 1800s. Here, a pattern of increasing citizen participation in the constitutional process manifested itself, although not without challenges, which culminated in the American Civil War.

## Restoration Monarchies, 1815–1848

For a full generation, monarchists in Europe sought to return to the politics of absolutism. This return required repression and elaborate political manipulation to keep the now-identifiable middle class of public employees, professionals, school-teachers, and factory entrepreneurs away from meaningful political participation. A "Concert of Europe" emerged in which rulers avoided intervention in the domestic politics of fellow monarchs, except in cases of internal unrest.

**The Congress of Vienna**   European leaders met in 1815 at Vienna after the fall of Napoleon in an effort to restore order to a war-torn continent. The driving principle at the session was monarchical conservatism, articulated mainly by Prince Klemens von Metternich (1773–1859), Austria's prime minister. An opponent of constitutional nationalism, Metternich was determined to resist the aspirations of the still-struggling middle classes outside France, which he regarded with contempt.

To accomplish his objective of reinstituting kings and emperors ruling by divine grace, Metternich had the Congress hammer

> "We see this intermediary [middle] class abandon itself with a blind fury and animosity . . . applying itself to the task of persuading kings that their rights are confined to sitting upon a throne, while those of the people are to govern, and to attack all that centuries have bequeathed as holy and worthy of man's respect."
>
> —Klemens von Metternich, 1820

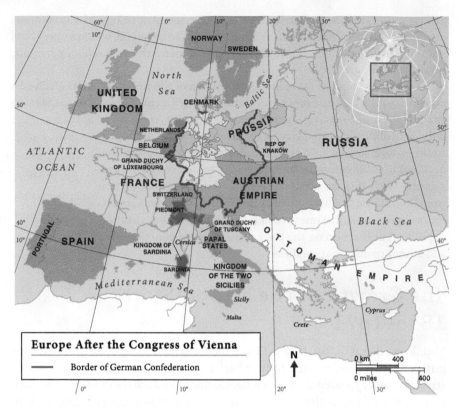

MAP 22.4 **Europe after the Congress of Vienna.**

out two principles: legitimacy and balance of power. The principle of legitimacy was conceived as a way to both recognize exclusive monarchial rule in Europe and to reestablish the borders of France as they were in 1789. The principle of the balance of power involved a basic policy of preventing any one state from rising to dominance over any other. Members agreed to convene at regular intervals in the future in what they called the "Concert," so as to ensure peace and tranquility in Europe. What is remarkable about this is that, with only minor exceptions, this policy of the balance of power remained intact down to 1914 (see Map 22.4).

As successful as the implementation of these two principles was, the solution devised for the German territories—now no longer with an overall ruler since the Holy Roman Empire was dissolved in 1806—was less satisfactory. The Congress of Vienna created an unwieldy and weak confederation of 39 German states, including the empire of Austria and the kingdoms of Prussia, Denmark, and the Netherlands. Prussia and Austria promptly embarked on a collision course over dominance in the confederation, with Prussia keeping the initiative and creating a customs union in 1834. Prussia's main purpose in this was to find outlets for its rising industrial and commercial interests in the northern German Ruhr region. Constitutionalist and republican Germans disliked the confederation as well, since they had no meaningful voice in it. Thus, by resolving the overall issue of coexistence among the German states, but not of their fragmentation, the Congress was only partially successful.

**Further Revolutions in France**    In keeping with the principle of legitimacy, the Congress restored the French Bourbon monarchy with the coronation of King Louis XVIII (r. 1814–1824), a brother of Louis XVI. Louis, even though determined to restore full absolutist powers, was indecisive as to which republican institutions to abolish first. Playing for time, he tolerated the "White Terror," during which the returning aristocracy and other royalists pursued revenge for their sufferings during the revolution. When Louis died in 1824 the conservatives succeeded in putting Charles X (1824–1830), a second brother of Louis XVI, on the throne. Charles took the extreme course of restoring the property of the aristocracy lost during the revolution and reestablishing the crown's ties to the Catholic Church.

Republican reaction to Charles's restoration policy was swift. In two elections, the republicans won a majority and overthrew the king. But they stopped short of abolishing the monarchy and elevated Louis-Philippe (1830–1848), son of a pro-republican duke who had been guillotined and had fought in the republican guards during 1789–1792, to the throne. Under this "bourgeois king," as he was sometimes caricatured, however, rising income gaps in the middle class as well as difficult living conditions among the nascent industrial working class led to new tensions. In the ensuing revolution of 1848, in which thousands of workers perished, the adherents of restoration and republicanism attempted another compromise: Louis-Philippe went into exile, and the parliament elected Louis-Napoleon Bonaparte (r. 1848–1852; self-declared emperor 1852–1870), a nephew of the former emperor, as president.

**Rebellion.** Following the successful revolution of 1848 that ended the monarchy of Louis-Philippe in France, similar uprisings broke out across Europe. This image shows the Berlin Alexander Square barricades of March 1848.

**Uprisings across Europe**    After the revolution in Paris, uprisings occurred in the spring of 1848 in cities such as Berlin, Vienna, Prague, Budapest, Palermo, and Milan, as well as in three Irish counties. In Prussia the king seemingly bowed to pressure from revolutionaries and promised constitutional reforms. In Austria, hit by uprisings in multiple cities and by multiple nationalities, both the emperor and Metternich, the driving forces of 1815, resigned. The successors, with Russian help, slowly regained military control over the Italians, Czechs, and Hungarians, as well as his own Austrians.

In the German Confederation, also hit by uprisings, moderate and republican delegates convened a constitutional assembly in Frankfurt in May 1848. This assembly elaborated the basic law for a new, unified state for German speakers and elected a provisional government. The new hard-line Austrian emperor, however, refused to let go of his non-German subjects. Therefore, the constitution joined only the German Federation and Prussia (also with non-German minorities) into a unitary state, with the provision for a future addition of German-speaking Austria. Against strong resistance by republicans, the delegates offered the Prussian king a new hereditary imperial crown in the name of the German people. But the king, unwilling to accept the principle of popular sovereignty, refused the crown "of clay." This refusal turned the tide against the Frankfurt Assembly. Moderate delegates departed, and radical ones instigated revolts. Prussian troops stepped in and relieved a group of grateful regional monarchs of their insurrectionists. By July 1849, the provisional Frankfurt government had come to an end and Germany's constitutional experiment was over.

**Ethnolinguistic Nationalism in Italy**    Italy was as fragmented politically as Germany, but unlike Germany it was also largely under foreign domination. Austria controlled the north directly and the center indirectly through relatives from the house of Habsburg. The monarchy of Piedmont in the northwest, the Papal States in the center, and the kingdom of Naples and Sicily (the "Two Sicilies") were independent but administratively and financially weak. After the Metternich restoration, the Italian dynasties had made concessions to constitutionalists, but Austria repressed uprisings in 1820–1821 and 1831–1832 without granting liberties. The republican Carbonari inspired both uprisings; they were members of the crafts guild of charcoal burners who had formed Enlightenment fraternities similar to the Freemasons during the eighteenth century. After their decisive defeat in 1831, the remnants formed the Young Italy movement.

Realistic second-generation politicians of the Restoration recognized that the middle-class ethnolinguistic nationalism coming to the fore in 1848 was a potent force that could be harnessed. By remobilizing this force in the 1860s, they would be able to end state fragmentation and make Italy and Germany serious players in the European Concert. These politicians were more sympathetic to French-style constitutionalism than the Restoration politicians but still opposed to republicanism. Their pursuit of realpolitik—exploitation of political opportunities—resulted in 1870–1871 in the transformations of the Italian kingdom of Piedmont and the German Empire of Prussia into the nation-states of Italy and Germany.

The Italian politician who did the most to realize Italy's unification was the prime minister of Piedmont-Sardinia, Count Camillo di Cavour (1810–1861).

Cavour was the scion of an old aristocratic family in northwestern Italy with training as a military officer. While in the army, he read widely among French and British political philosophers and became a constitutional nationalist. A supporter of Adam Smith's liberal trade economics, he imported South American guano fertilizer and grew cash crops, like sugar beets, on his estate. As prime minister he was the driving force behind the development of railroads, first in Piedmont and later in Italy. With the backing of his similarly liberal-minded king, Victor Emanuel II (r. 1849–1878), he began the Italian unification process under decidedly trying circumstances. Through adroit maneuvering, he was able to arrange for a favorable plebiscite in north-central Tuscany and Emilia in 1859, gaining these two regions from Austria for Piedmont. A year later Cavour occupied the Papal States and accepted the offer of Giuseppe Garibaldi (1807–1882) to add adjoining Naples and Sicily to a now nearly unified Italy.

Garibaldi, a mariner from Nice in the northwest (present-day France), was a Carbonaro and Young Italy republican nationalist with a colorful career as a freedom fighter not only in Italy but also in Brazil and Uruguay. Dressed in his trademark red gaucho shirt with poncho and sombrero, the inspiring Garibaldi attracted large numbers of volunteers wherever he went to fight. Cavour died shortly afterward and did not live to see Piedmont transform itself into Italy in 1870, when it gained Venice from Austria and Rome from France in the wake of the Prussian–Austrian war of 1866. But he clearly was the power politician who laid the decisive groundwork.

**Bismarck and Germany**    In contrast to Italy, neither King Wilhelm I (r. 1861–1888) nor his chancellor (prime minister) Otto von Bismarck (in office 1862–1890) in Prussia had deep sympathies for constitutionalism. By combining their antipathies and forming a coalition of convenience, they succeeded in keeping the constitutionalists in the Prussian parliament in check. But they realized they could dip into the ethnolinguistic nationalism that had poured forth in 1848, using it for power politics: realpolitik.

Bismarck was a Prussian aristocrat with a legal education rather than a military career. He was multilingual, widely read, and experienced in the diplomacy of the European Concert. He realized that Prussia, a weak player in the Concert, had a chance for greater influence only if the kingdom could absorb the German Federation. For Prussia to do so, Bismarck argued, it had to progress from talk about unification, as in Frankfurt, to military action, using "blood and iron." From the time of his appointment to 1871, he systematically maneuvered Prussia into an internationally favorable position for the coup that would eventually bring unification: war with France.

First, he exploited a succession crisis in Denmark for a combined Prussian–Austrian campaign to annex Denmark's southern province of Schleswig-Holstein in 1865. Then, when Austria objected to the terms of annexation, he declared war on Austria (1866). After Prussia won, Bismarck dissolved the German Confederation and annexed several German principalities. In France, Louis-Napoleon Bonaparte

**Giuseppe Garibaldi.** Garibaldi was an Italian nationalist who, in collaboration with Count Cavour, prime minister of the kingdom of Piedmont, contributed decisively to the unification of Italy. Garibaldi and his "Red Shirts" were able to seize Sicily and Naples from its Bourbon-descended monarch in 1860. He then unified his conquests with the constitutional kingdom of Piedmont to form the nucleus of Italy, which was fully unified a decade later.

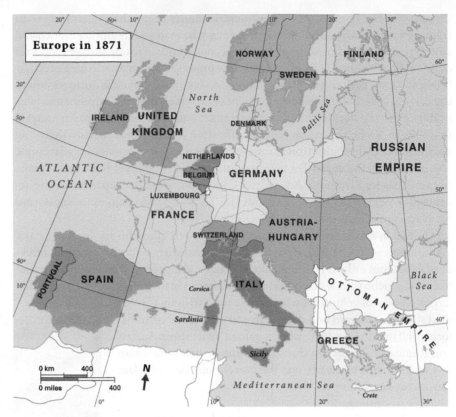

MAP 22.5 **Europe in 1871.**

was greatly concerned about the rising power of Prussia. He had carried out a coup d'état in 1852, ending the Second Republic and declaring himself emperor—an act that prompted the readily quotable Karl Marx to claim that "history always repeats itself, the first time as tragedy, the second time as farce." A distraction on his eastern flank was not at all what Emperor Napoleon III desired.

But he carelessly undermined his own position. First, he prevented a relative of King Wilhelm from succeeding to the throne of Spain after it fell vacant. But when he demanded additional assurances that Prussia would not put forward candidates for any other thrones in the future, the canny Bismarck outmaneuvered him. He advised King Wilhelm to refuse the demand and edited the refusal in such a way as to make it insulting to the French. France then declared war on Prussia but was defeated (1870). Now Bismarck had the upper hand that he had been diligently working to gain. He used it to annex Alsace-Lorraine from the French, carried out the final unification of Germany, and elevated the new state to the status of empire in 1871 (see Map 22.5).

## Nation-State Building in Anglo-America, 1783–1900

After the independence of the United States in 1783, both the United States and Great Britain were free to pursue their versions of constitutional nation-state development. The old and new monarchies and ethnolinguistic movements which complicated nation-state formation in central Europe did not affect the United States, giving rise instead to a long tradition among American historians of claiming American "exceptionalism." While it is indeed true that the growth of the United States in the 1800s followed its own trajectory, there is also no question that the underlying pattern of modern nation-state formation was not unlike that of the other two constitutional nations, France and Great Britain: Neither was much affected by ethnolinguistic nationalism (although Britain was more than France, as we shall see below).

**The United States**   During the first half of the nineteenth century the newly independent North American states not only prospered but also began a rapid westward expansion. As this process unfolded, toward 1850 it became increasingly apparent that sectional differences were developing in the process. Whereas the North developed an industrial and market-driven agricultural economy, the South remained primarily agrarian, relying heavily upon the production of cotton for its economic vitality. Even more, the South relied upon vast numbers of slaves to work the fields of the cotton plantations. Cotton was the main fiber for the industrial production of textiles, and it not only defined the wealth of the plantation owners but led them to see chattel slavery as the only viable means to keep the "cotton kingdom" prosperous. In defense of its stance, the South increasingly relied upon the notion of states' rights in opposition to federal control. With the acquisition of new territory extending to the Pacific coast after the war with Mexico from 1846 to 1848 and the push of settlement beyond the Mississippi, the vital question of which of the new territories would become "free states" and "slave states" resulted in increasing tensions between North and South.

The result was an attempt by a number of southern states to secede and form a new union, the Confederate States of America. When the new administration of President Abraham Lincoln attempted to suppress this movement, the disastrous American Civil War (1861–1865) ensued. Resulting in an enormous loss of life— more than 600,000 combatants on both sides were killed—the Civil War finally ended with a northern victory in 1865. There were several major results of the conflict, not least of which was an enhanced unification of the country during the occupation of the southern states. Here, federal troops enforced the policies of the Reconstruction (1865–1877). First, Lincoln's concept of the primacy of national government over individual assertions of states' rights was now guaranteed. Second, slavery was abolished and slaves were granted full citizenship. Third, the rebuilding of the country and opening of the west resulted in a period of remarkable growth, facilitated especially by the expansion of a national network of railroads. By 1900, about 200,000 miles of uniform-gauge track crisscrossed the country, and the United States was on its way to becoming the world's predominant industrial power (see Map 22.6).

The price of reintegrating the old South into the new order was the end of Reconstruction and the reversion over the course of two generations to an imposition of de facto peonage on its black citizens. Indeed, between 1877 and 1914 state legislatures in the South systematically stripped African Americans of voting rights by means of poll taxes and literacy tests and imposed formal and informal segregation in social and public accommodations. These were enforced by law and all too often by lynchings and other forms of violence. In order to accommodate the sensibilities of white southerners regarding race, most northern policy and opinion makers gradually backed away from the views espoused by the champions

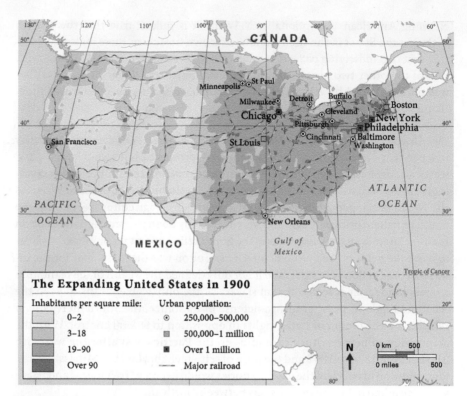

MAP 22.6 **The Expanding United States in 1900.**

of racial equality during Reconstruction and gave tacit acquiescence to southern efforts to maintain white hegemony. The drive for full civil rights would thus occupy a sizeable share of American domestic policy debates throughout the twentieth century.

**Native Americans**    While blacks made uneven advances during the 1800s, Native Americans suffered unmitigated disasters. When the Louisiana Purchase in 1803 (see above, p. 671) nearly doubled the size of the United States, politicians quickly conceived of the idea of moving Native Americans from their eastern homelands to the new territories. For their part, Native Americans realized that only a large-scale unification would help them to stay put, especially in the South (Georgia, Alabama, and Florida) and the Midwest (Ohio, Indiana) where white settler encroachment was strong after independence.

In the Midwest, Tecumseh (1768–1812) and his brother Tenskwatawa (1775–1836) renewed the prophecies of unification that had been in circulation since the mid-1700s. Tecumseh traveled widely between the Midwest and South, seeking to forge a Native American resistance federation. Tenskwatawa, claiming his authority from visions of the Master of Life, the spirit of spirits in the world, preached that Native Americans needed to reject white culture and return to traditional life. In Tippecanoe, a newly founded town in Indiana, thousands of followers from a variety of nations came together, but suffered a severe defeat at the hands of US troops in 1812. The defeat ended the dream of Native American unity.

In the South, discriminatory legislation and brutal assaults by the states made it more and more difficult for Native American nations to survive on their lands. With the declared intention of helping these nations against the states, in 1830 the federal government issued the Indian Removal Act. In fact, however, this act only deepened the sufferings of the Native Americans: A quarter never made it on the "Trail of Tears" to their designated new homeland Oklahoma, dying on the way from disease and deprivation. The survivors settled and reconstructed their agriculture, schools, and councils as best as they could, having to accommodate the regular arrival of newly displaced Native Americans from the east in the subsequent decades.

**Two Girls of the Hopi Nation with Their Characteristic Hairstyles and Blankets.** The Hopi live in the American Southwest, today's Arizona. They are best known as sophisticated farmers in adobe pueblos, some of which were built into the rock walls of canyons. In 1680, the Hopi rebelled for a dozen years against Spanish missionaries and colonists in their midst, achieving a degree of autonomy as a result. The United States organized the nation in 1882 into the Hopi Reservation.

**Destruction of the Buffalo Herds**   By mid-century, white ranchers and miners began to encroach on the lands farther west of the Mississippi, and beyond Missouri, already a state in 1821. Again, the federal government passed a law supposedly protecting the Native Americans of the Plains from increasingly bloody clashes with advancing whites by creating "reservations" (1851). The obligation, especially for such free-roaming groups as the Sioux and Apache, to stay on reservations rather than to hunt freely was a first aggravation. Further affronts came through the Homestead Act (1862), the construction of the transcontinental railroad (1863–1869), and the rapid appearance of towns and cities along the railroad corridors. The worst injury was the destruction of the gigantic herds of buffalo (bison), the hunting of which formed the principal livelihood of the Native Americans on the Plains.

Within a mere two decades (1865–1884), some 10–15 million animals were slaughtered until fewer than 1,000 remained. Research in the early 2000s has demonstrated that new chemical methods developed in 1871 in Britain and Germany made the tanning of the thick buffalo skin feasible for high-quality shoe leather and industrial belting, greatly stimulating the hunt for hides. In the American Indian Wars (1862–1890), the Native Americans defended their homelands tenaciously but ultimately in vain. Once more, visionaries sought to unify the various groups through the Ghost Dance, enacting a prophecy of the return of the buffalo herds and the disappearance of the whites. Their last stand was at Wounded Knee Creek, South Dakota, in December 1890. Defeated and demoralized by 1900, under a quarter million Native Americans (down from 600,000 in 1800) found themselves on 310 reservations on 2.3 percent of American soil.

**Reform Measures**   As in other Western nation-states, rapid industrialization produced social and labor unrest in the United States, resulting in the reforming initiatives of the Progressive era, which extended from 1890 to 1914. Although the later nineteenth century is referred to as the Gilded Age, epitomized by the staggering wealth of industrial tycoons like Andrew Carnegie (1835–1919) and John D. Rockefeller (1839–1937), all was not well beneath the surface. Big business had grown to such an extent that in the early 1900s a few hundred firms controlled two-fifths of all American manufacturing. The "trust buster" president, Theodore

Roosevelt (r. 1901–1909), and Congress ended the monopolies of many firms, Rockefeller's Standard Oil among them, which had to divide itself into 30 smaller companies. A new Department of Commerce and Labor (1903) and the Pure Food and Drug and Meat Inspection Acts (1906) helped the hard-pressed workers and consumers. With the Federal Reserve Act (1913) and the Federal Trade Commission Act (1914) Congress created an overall framework for the supervision of the financial and business sectors. As many people at the time realized, a free market prospered only with at least a minimum of regulations.

**Great Britain**   The pattern of constitutional nation-state construction that Britain followed in the eighteenth and nineteenth centuries was gradual and uninterrupted by wars. Challenges did not come from a civil war but from the rise of ethnolinguistic nationalisms outside the English core. The first signs of Irish nationalism, based not only in ethnic and linguistic but also religious traditions, appeared after the Great Famine of 1845–1849. Rural production and land issues were the main points of contention, leading to demands for home rule or even independence. A Protestant landlord class still controlled most of the land, which was farmed by Catholic tenant farmers. During the worldwide Long Depression of 1873–1896 Irish farmers received low prices for their crops but no reductions in rent. A "land war" (mass protests against tenant evictions) ensued which the British Army sought to quell. This eventually led in 1898 to local self-rule for the Irish and in 1903–1909 to land reform.

Scotland, traditionally divided between the Highlands and Lowlands, developed an ethnolinguistic sense of its identity only slowly. The development began on the level of folklore, with the revival of Scottish dress and music (clan tartans, kilts, and bagpipes). More serious issues came to the fore in 1853 when the Scots, upset by what their perception that the British government paid more attention to Ireland, founded an association for the vindication of Scottish rights. But they had to wait until 1885, when the British Liberal Party wrested power from the conservative Tories, thanks to the support of Irish members of Parliament. With the creation of the position of a secretary for Scotland, the nationalists found their first recognition.

Welsh nationalism arose in the context of industrialization and the development of a Welsh working class, which organized uprisings in the 1830s. Religious issues, mostly related to opposition to the Church of England among nonconformists (e.g., Methodists, Quakers, and Presbyterians), and education issues surrounding the so-called Treachery of the Blue Books added to the unrest. A governmental report of 1847, bound in blue covers, found that education in Wales was substandard: Sunday schools were the only schools offering education in Welsh, while regular schools used English as the language of instruction for children who spoke only Welsh. Both issues were the focus of most Welsh nationalist agitation in the second half of the 1800s, and it was not until 1925, with the foundation of the Party of Wales, that Welsh nationalism became a force of its own.

While ethnolinguistic nationalisms arose around the English core, Parliament, the guardian of British constitutional nationalism, undertook major legal reforms of its constitutional order in the course of the 1800s. As industrialization progressed, both Liberals and Tories took cognizance of the growing middle and working classes. The Great Reform Bill of 1832 shifted seats from southern districts to the more populated and industrialized center and north. The repeal of the Corn Laws in 1846 liberated imports and made grain cheaper, and the Second Reform Act of 1867 extended the franchise to larger numbers of working-class voters. The end result was not only that Britain escaped the revolutions of 1848 but also that the British electorate was largely united during the Victorian period (1837–1901) in its support for British imperialism around the globe.

## Romanticism and Realism: Philosophical and Artistic Expression to 1850

Parallel to the evolution of the patterns of constitutional and ethnolinguistic nationalism, the two movements of romanticism and realism patterned the evolution of culture on both sides of the Atlantic. Romanticism was an outgrowth of strains in the Enlightenment in which the independence of the mind from matter was emphasized. Taking their cue from Rousseau and Kant, romantics emphasized unrestrained individual creativity and spontaneity for the expression of their feelings. As industrialization progressed, however, a growing sense of realism concerning material conditions set in, expressing itself in the arts by greater social awareness.

### Romanticism

Inspired by the Enlightenment and the revolutions, a number of philosophers, writers, composers, and painters of the period of **romanticism** in the early 1800s drew the conclusion that humans possessed a fullness of freedom to remake themselves. To them, the mind was entirely independent, creating new aesthetic categories out of its own powers. Not all thinkers and artists went this far, but for romantics creativity became absolute. Indeed, the stereotype of the bohemian creative "genius" crossing new imaginative thresholds became firmly implanted in the public imagination during this time.

**Romanticism:** Intellectual and artistic movement that emphasized emotion and imagination over reason and sought the sublime in nature.

**Philosophers and Artists**   The one philosopher who, building on Kant, postulated the complete freedom of mind or spirit was Georg Wilhelm Friedrich Hegel (1770–1831). The most systematic of the so-called idealist philosophers in Germany, Hegel asserted that all thought proceeded dialectically from the "transcendental ego" to its opposite, matter, and from there to the spiritualized synthesis of nature. This **dialectic** permeates his entire system of philosophy.

Even more than philosophy, music became the medium for expressing the creative genius. The German Ludwig van Beethoven (1770–1827) and the Frenchman Hector Berlioz (1803–1869) pioneered the new genre of program music, with the *Pastoral Symphony* (Symphony no. 6) and the *Symphonie phantastique*, respectively, emphasizing passion and emotional intensity and the freedom of the musical spirit over traditional form. From among the emerging middle class, eager to develop their romantic sensibilities and play music at home, a veritable explosion of composers erupted during the first half of the 1800s. Often composing at a furious rate, these musicians were also virtuosi on the violin or piano, playing their own new musical forms and traveling on concert circuits all across Europe.

**Dialectic:** The investigation of truth by discussion; in Hegel's thought, the belief that a higher truth is comprehended by a continuous unification of opposites.

The medium of painting also lent itself to the expression of romantic feelings of passion and the mind's overflowing imaginative aesthetics. Not surprisingly, the proliferation of romantic painters numbered in the hundreds. The common feature of these painters was that they departed from the established academic practices and styles. They either let nature dictate the direction and extent of their absorption into it or expressed their personal impressions forcefully with new, dramatic topics.

As in the other art forms, romanticism in literature appears in heroines or heroes and their passions and sentiments. In the still late-Enlightenment-informed prose of the British author Jane Austen (1775–1817), witty and educated urbane society shapes the character and sensibilities of young women and prepares them for their reward, namely the love of the proper gentleman and marriage to him. A generation later, also in Britain, the three Brontë sisters, Charlotte (1816–1855), Emily (1818–1848), and Anne (1820–1849), published novels with equally complex plots but much greater emphasis on romantic passion on the one hand and character flaws or social ills on the other. The novels also contain mysterious, seemingly inexplicable happenings—artistic devices which the American Edgar Allan Poe (1809–1849) used more explicitly in his thematic Gothic stories and tales, such as "The Fall of the House of Usher" (1839).

## Realism

**Realism:** The belief that material reality exists independently of the people who observe it.

Toward the middle of the 1800s, many artists and writers shifted their focus from the romanticism of the self and its aesthetic or moral sentiments to the **realism** of the middle classes whose constitutionalist dreams had been smothered by the repression of the revolutions of 1848. In philosophy, thinkers identified stages leading progressively to the rise of middle classes and industrialism. And in literature, the complex and tangled relationships that characterized the plots of the romantics continued, but now set in the more prosaic urban world of factories and working classes.

**Philosophy of History**    Toward the middle of the 1800s, the French thinker Auguste Comte (1798–1857) composed a six-volume work entitled *The Positive Philosophy* (1830–1842). In it he arranged world history into the three successive stages of the theological, metaphysical, and scientific. In his view, the scientific advances of the sciences had all but eclipsed the metaphysical stage and had ushered in the last, scientific era. For Comte this was a sign of Europe's progress and a "positive" stage. His philosophy, labeled "positivism," exerted a major influence in Europe as well as in Latin America. Comte further argued that the only sure way of arriving at truth was based on scientific facts and knowledge of the world acquired through the senses. In Comte's view, the laws governing human behavior could be ascertained with the same degree of precision as the laws of nature: a utopian ideology still with us today.

**Prose Literature**    Realistic writers of fiction moved away from personal sentiments to realistic scenes as they were encountered in middle-class society. New aesthetic experimentations ensued so that the ordinary could be a heightened reflection of the new "reality" of life in the industrial age. William Makepeace Thackeray (1811–1863) in England, for example, was a supreme satirist, as

(a)

(b)

**Romantic Art.** Romantic painters expressed an absorbing, encompassing nature in their art. Note the barely recognizable steam-powered train in this painting (*a*) by J. M. W. Turner, *Rain, Steam, and Speed: The Great Western Railway* (1844). Romantic painters also depicted dramatic or exotic scenes relating to revolutions or foreign lands, such as the languid harem in *The Women of Algiers in Their Apartment* (1834) by Eugène Delacroix (*b*).

displayed in *Vanity Fair*, a book on bourgeois human foibles and peccadilloes. His compatriot Charles Dickens (1812–1870) had a similar focus but centered on working- and lower-middle-class characters in his many novels. The English-woman George Eliot, born Mary Ann Evans (1819–1880), was politically oriented,

**Realism.** The documentary power of photography spurred the new impulses of realism that emerged around 1850. The photograph here shows the execution of hostages in the Commune of Paris in the spring of 1871 shortly before its final defeat by troops of the provisional French national government. One of the executed hostages was Georges Darboy, archbishop of Paris, a critic of the pope and strong patriot who cared for the wounded of the war against Prussia in 1870.

ASSASSINAT DES OTAGES À LA PRISON DE LA ROQUETTE LE 24 MAI 1871
Mr Darboy    Bonjean    Duguerry    Ducoudray    Clere    Allard

placing small-town social relations within the context of concrete political events in Great Britain, as in *Middlemarch* (1874). Gustave Flaubert (1821–1880) in France experimented with a variety of styles, among which those featuring extremely precise and unadorned descriptions of objects and situations are perhaps the most important (*Madame Bovary*, 1857). Henry James (1843–1916), an American living in Britain, in his self-declared masterpiece, *The Ambassadors* (1903), explored the psychological complexities of individuals whose entwined lives crossed both sides of the Atlantic. In the end, realism, with its individuals firmly anchored in the new class society of the 1800s, moved far from the freedom and exuberance celebrated by the romantics.

# Putting It All Together

Though the pattern of nation-state building in Europe and North America was relatively slow and, in places, painful, it has become the dominant mode of political organization in the world today. As we will see in subsequent chapters, the aftermath of World War I and the decolonization movement following World War II gave a tremendous boost to the process of nation-state formation around the world. Here, the legacy of European colonialism both planted these ideas among the colonized and, by supplying the Enlightenment ideas of revolution and the radical remaking of society, gave them the ideological means of achieving their own liberation from foreign rule. In both cases, the aspirations of peoples to "nationhood" followed older European models as the colonies were either granted independence or fought to gain it from declining empires. But, in many respects, their efforts mirrored the difficulties of the first constitutional and ethnolinguistic nation-states.

Take the example of the United States. Though it achieved world economic leadership by 1914, it had faced an early constitutional crisis, endured a prolonged sectional struggle in which slavery marred the constitutional order for almost three-quarters of a century, fought a bloody civil war for national unification that very nearly destroyed it, and remained united in part by acquiescing in practices of overt segregation and discrimination against the 10 percent of its population that was of African descent. Or take the case of France. Its people adopted constitutional nationalism in 1789, but the monarchy it seemingly replaced bounced back three times. Thus, even in the later nineteenth century, Abraham Lincoln's resolution that "government of the people, by the people, for the people shall not perish from the earth" was still far from guaranteed.

Yet another example is the case of Germany, where ethnolinguistic nationalism diluted the straightforward enthusiasm for the constitution and the symbols accompanying it. Historians continue to argue over whether Germany, and by extension other central and eastern European nations, took a special route (*Sonderweg*) to constitutional normality or whether the path was the same except that the pace slowed at critical times. In retrospect, it is impossible to say which of the speed bumps on the way toward the nation-state—slavery/racism, residual monarchism, or the twentieth-century experiments of communism and supremacist nationalism—were responsible for the longest delay. In Part 6 we will consider all of these developments in more detail.

▶ For additional resources, including maps, primary sources, visuals, and quizzes, please go to www.oup.com/us/vonsivers. Please see the Further Resources section at the back of the book for additional readings and suggested websites.

## Against the Grain

# Defying the Third Republic

Republican and socialist Parisians despised the new conservative Third Republic of France, which was dominated by two monarchist factions. They considered it defeatist against the Prussians who had been victorious in the war of 1870. After two failed protests, the final trigger for an outright revolution was the government's attempt, on March 18, 1871, to collect some 400 guns under the command of the Parisian National Guard. The attempt turned into a fiasco. The number of horses to pull the hundreds of cannons away was insufficient, and the troops fraternized with the crowds who swarmed around the cannons, offering flowers and food to the soldiers. In the melee, however, several government soldiers and two generals were killed (the latter probably by army deserters in Paris, not guardsmen). Seizing the opportunity, the central committee of the National Guard declared its independence and held elections on the basis of male suffrage for a communal council on March 26 (Commune of Paris: March 18 to May 28, 1871).

The council of mostly workers and craftsmen plus a strong contingent of professionals issued a flurry of new laws. All deputies were under binding mandates and could be recalled anytime. As a commune of a desired universal republic, Paris considered all foreigners as equals. France itself was to become a federation of communes. Abandoned factories and workshops were to be directed by workers' councils. Church properties were confiscated, and the separation of church and state was declared. Under the auspices of the women-run Union of Women for the Defense of Paris and the Care of the Injured, measures for equal pay and pensions for retired survivors, regardless of marital status, were envisaged. The official symbol of the Commune was the red flag of the radical French Revolution of 1792, not the republican tricolor. In short, as Haiti had done in 1794, the Commune pushed equality much further than the American and French revolutions had ever done, frightening the middle classes to their core.

The Commune had no chance of survival against the superior troops of the Third Republic. It was bloodily repressed, although with far fewer victims, according to new documentation analyzed in 2012. The total of communards killed is now estimated to be at most 7,400. The symbolical significance of the Commune, however, was immense: Socialists and communists made it the mythical dawn of world revolution, working class dictatorship, and the eventual withering away of the (national) state in the utopia of a classless society.

- **Did the members of the Commune of Paris opponents run counter to the pattern of nation-state formation in the nineteenth century, and if so, how did they want to replace it?**

- **Did the ideas of small communities and opposition to centralized national governments retain their attraction in the twentieth and twenty-first centuries? If yes, which examples come to mind and for which reasons?**

# Thinking Through Patterns

▶ **How did the pattern of constitutional nationalism, emerging from the American and French Revolutions, affect the course of events in the Western world during the first half of the nineteenth century?**

Constitutional nationalism emerged as a result of the success of American and French revolutionaries in overthrowing absolute rule. The constitutional revolutionaries replaced the loyalty of subjects to a monarch with that of free and equal citizens to the national constitution. This form of nationalism called for unity among the citizens regardless of ethnic, linguistic, or religious identity. In the United States, this nationalism had to overcome a conservative adherence to slavery in the South before it gained general recognition after the end of the Civil War. In France, republican nationalists battled conservative monarchists for nearly a century before they were able to finally defeat them in the Third Republic.

Constitutional nationalists emphasized the principles of freedom, equality, constitution, rule of law, elections, and representative assembly regardless of ethnicity, language, or religion. However, nationalists in areas of Europe lacking centralized monarchies sought to first unify what they identified as dispersed members of their nation through ideologies that emphasized common origin, centuries of collective history, and shared literary, artistic, and religious traditions. In these ethnolinguistic (and sometimes religious) ideologies constitutional principles were secondary. Only once unification in a nation-state was achieved would the form of government—monarchist, constitutional-monarchist, republican—then be chosen.

▶ **In what ways did ethnolinguistic nationalism differ from constitutional nationalism, and what was its influence on the formation of nation-states in the second half of the nineteenth century?**

▶ **What were the reactions among thinkers and artists to the developing pattern of nation-state formation? How did they define the intellectual-artistic movements of romanticism and realism?**

Philosophers and artists in the romantic period put a strong emphasis on individual creativity. They either viewed this creativity as an upwelling of impulses and sentiments pouring forth with little intellectual control or, conversely, considered their creativity to be the result of an absolute or transcendent mind working through them as individuals. By the 1850s, with the rise of the middle class, individual creativity gave way to a greater awareness, called "realism," of the social environment with its class structure and industrial characteristics.

▶ **Working with Sources**

1. To what extent does the declaration mix specific provisions and general principles of human rights?
2. How does the document aim to uphold the "common utility"? How is the "public necessity" to be determined?

## SOURCE 22.2

# Olympe de Gouges, *The Declaration of the Rights of Woman*

### September 1791

Women were not included among the new officeholders of Revolutionary France, nor were they members of the National Assembly, which supposedly represented all members of the country's Third Estate. An immediate question arose concerning the extent to which the benefits of the Revolution should be extended to females (as well as to slaves throughout France's global empire). Some men did advocate the extension of these rights and privileges, but women also took action in their own cause. Among these was the "Cercle Social" (Social Circle), a group of female activists who coordinated their publishing activities on behalf of women and their own goals in the developing Revolution.

One of the leaders of this group was Marie Gouze (1748–1793), who, under her pen name "Olympe de Gouges," attacked both the institution of slavery and the oppression of women in 1791. A playwright, pamphleteer, and political activist, de Gouges published this thoughtful meditation on what the National Assembly should declare concerning "the rights of woman" (as opposed merely to "the rights of man"). Other members of the Social Circle were arrested as the Revolution entered its radical phase, but Olympe de Gouges was executed by guillotine in November 1793.

To be decreed by the National Assembly in its last sessions or by the next legislature.

**Preamble**

Mothers, daughters, sisters, female representatives of the nation ask to be constituted as a national assembly. Considering that ignorance, neglect, or contempt for the rights of woman are the sole causes of public misfortunes and governmental corruption, they have resolved to set forth in a

Source: Lynn Hunt, ed. and trans., *The French Revolution and Human Rights: A Brief Documentary History* (Boston: Bedford St. Martin's, 1996), 124–126.

solemn declaration the natural, inalienable, and sacred rights of woman: so that by being constantly present to all the members of the social body this declaration may always remind them of their rights and duties; so that by being liable at every moment to comparison with the aim of any and all political institutions the acts of women's and men's powers may be the more fully respected; and so that by being founded henceforward on simple and incontestable principles the demands of the citizenesses may always tend toward maintaining the constitution, good morals, and the general welfare.

In consequence, the sex that is superior in beauty as in courage, needed in maternal sufferings, recognizes and declares, in the presence and under the auspices of the Supreme Being, the following rights of woman and the citizeness.

1. Woman is born free and remains equal to man in rights. Social distinctions may be based only on common utility.

2. The purpose of all political association is the preservation of the natural and imprescriptible rights of woman and man. These rights are liberty, property, security, and especially resistance to oppression.

3. The principle of all sovereignty rests essentially in the nation, which is but the reuniting of woman and man. No body and no individual may exercise authority which does not emanate expressly from the nation.

4. Liberty and justice consist in restoring all that belongs to another; hence the exercise of the natural rights of woman has no other limits than those that the perpetual tyranny of man opposes

to them; these limits must be reformed according to the laws of nature and reason.

5. The laws of nature and reason prohibit all actions which are injurious to society. No hindrance should be put in the way of anything not prohibited by these wise and divine laws, nor may anyone be forced to do what they do not require.

6. The law should be the expression of the general will. All citizenesses and citizens should take part, in person or by their representatives, in its formation. It must be the same for everyone. All citizenesses and citizens, being equal in its eyes, should be equally admissible to all public dignities, offices, and employments, according to their ability, and with no other distinction than that of their virtues and talents.

. . .

11. The free communication of thoughts and opinions is one of the most precious of the rights of woman, since this liberty assures the recognition of children by their fathers. Every citizeness may therefore say freely, I am the mother of your child; a barbarous prejudice [against unmarried women having children] should not force her to hide the truth, so long as responsibility is accepted for any abuse of this liberty in cases determined by the law [women are not allowed to lie about the paternity of their children].

12. The safeguard of the rights of woman and citizeness requires public powers. These powers are instituted for the advantage of all and not for the private benefit of those to whom they are entrusted.

13. For maintenance of public authority and for expenses of administration, taxation of women and men is equal; she takes part in all forced labor service, in all painful tasks; she must therefore have the same proportion in the distribution of places, employments, offices, dignities, and in industry.

14. The citizenesses and citizens have the right, by themselves or through their representatives, to have demonstrated to them the necessity of public taxes. The citizenesses can only agree to them upon admission of an equal division, not only in wealth, but also in the public administration, and to determine the means of apportionment, assessment, and collection, and the duration of the taxes.

. . .

17. Property belongs to both sexes whether united or separated; it is for each of them an inviolable and sacred right, and no one may be deprived of it as a true patrimony of nature, except when public necessity, certified by law, obviously requires it, and then on condition of a just compensation in advance.

▶ **Working with Sources**

1. What does de Gouges consider woman's "natural and reasonable" share in the "common" life of a society?

2. To what extent does biology determine the particular roles and sufferings of women? Are women (in de Gouges's context) to be considered the superior element of human society as a result?

## SOURCE 22.3

# Voltaire, "Torture," from the *Philosophical Dictionary*

**1769**

Voltaire (the pen name of François-Marie Arouet) epitomized the Enlightenment. His *Dictionnaire philosophique* (*Philosophical Dictionary*), the first edition of which appeared in 1764, distilled his thought on philosophical matters in what he self-deprecatingly called an "alphabetical abomination." Voltaire invariably found ways to deploy humor in the pursuit of serious moral, religious, and ethical truths, as the continued popularity of his "contes

Source: Voltaire, *Philosophical Dictionary*, ed. and trans. Theodore Besterman (Harmondsworth, UK: Penguin, 1972), 394–396.

philosophiques" (philosophical tales), including *Candide*, *Zadig*, and *Micro-mégas*, attests.

In this "dictionary," arranged alphabetically according to the entry's title (in French), Voltaire tackled matters like atheism, fanaticism, the soul, superstition, and tolerance. His tone is always light and witty, despite the weightiness of (and the violence associated with) the subject matter. Inspired by ongoing court cases and interrogation methods, Voltaire added the following miraculous little essay on the use (and, in some countries, disuse) of torture as a legal instrument to the 1769 version of the *Dictionary*. His satirical approach resonates today, as issues of what constitutes torture and how it ought to be applied continue to dominate our political discourse.

Although there are few articles on jurisprudence in these respectable alphabetical reflections, a word must nevertheless be said about torture, otherwise named the question. It is a strange way to question one. Yet it was not invented by the merely curious. It would appear that this part of our legislation owes its first origin to a highwayman. Most of these gentlemen are still in the habit of squeezing thumbs, burning the feet of those who refuse to tell them where they have put their money, and questioning them by means of other torments.

The conquerors, having succeeded these thieves, found this invention of the greatest utility. They put it into practice when they suspected that some vile plot was being hatched against them, as, for instance, that of being free, a crime of divine and human lèse-majesté. The accomplices had to be known; and to arrive at this knowledge those who were suspected were made to suffer a thousand deaths, because according to the jurisprudence of these first heroes anyone suspected of having had so much as a disrespectful thought about them was worthy of death. And once a man has thus deserved death it matters little whether appalling torments are added for a few days or even several weeks. All this even had something of the divine about it. Providence sometimes tortures us by means of the stone, gravel, gout, scurvy, leprosy, pox great and small, griping of the bowels, nervous convulsions, and other executants of the vengeance of providence.

Now since the first despots were images of divinity, as all their courtiers freely admitted, they imitated it so far as they could.

. . .

The grave magistrate who has bought for a little money the right to conduct these experiments on his fellow creatures tells his wife at dinner what happened during the morning. The first time her ladyship is revolted, the second time she acquires a taste for it, for after all women are curious, and then the first thing she says to him when he comes home in his robes is: "My angel, did you give anyone the question today?"

The French, who are considered to be a very humane people, I do not know why, are astonished that the English, who have had the inhumanity to take the whole of Canada from us [in 1760 and ratified in 1763, as a result of the Seven Years' War], have renounced the pleasure of applying the question.

. . .

In 1700 the Russians were regarded as barbarians. We are now only in 1769, and an **empress** has just given this vast state laws that would have done honour to Minor, to Numa, and to Solon if they had had enough intelligence to compose them. The most remarkable of them is universal toleration, the second is the abolition of torture. Justice and humanity guided her pen, she has reformed everything. Woe to a nation which, long civilized, is still led by atrocious ancient practices! "Why should we change our jurisprudence?" it asks. "Europe uses our cooks, our tailors, our wig-makers; therefore our laws are good."

**Empress:** Catherine the Great.

▶ **Working with Sources**

1. Does Voltaire make a convincing case that the use of torture results from excessive curiosity and a warped desire to inflict suffering?

2. How does he ridicule the continuation of "ancient" practices into modern times, and how does this essay reflect the values of the philosophical Enlightenment?

## SOURCE 22.4

# Edmund Burke, *Reflections on the Revolution in France*

### 1790

**B**orn in Dublin to a Protestant father and a Catholic mother, Edmund Burke (1729–1797) struggled to build a political career in Georgian England. Having established a reputation for brilliant thinking and speaking, he entered Parliament in 1766. One of his principal causes in the 1760s and 1770s was the defense of the American colonists in their conflict with the mother country. Burke opposed the English government's position that England was sovereign over the colonies and could tax the colonists as she saw fit. By contrast, Burke insisted that a "right" was not an abstract principle and that policy should be guided by actual circumstances. When the French Revolution began in 1789, Burke surprised some of his political

Source: Edmund Burke, *Reflections on the Revolution in France*, ed. Thomas H. D. Mahoney (Indianapolis: Liberal Arts, 1955), 66, 68–69, 70–71, 73–74.

allies by speaking against it, mainly because he believed that "reason" and "rights" were not absolute principles that justified violent change. His statement against the extremes of revolution, published in November 1790, became the basis for a form of political ideology known as conservatism.

It is no wonder, therefore, that with these ideas of everything in their constitution and government at home, either in church or state, as illegitimate and usurped, or at best as a vain mockery, they look abroad with an eager and passionate enthusiasm. Whilst they are possessed by these notions, it is vain to talk to them of the practice of their ancestors, the fundamental laws of their country, the fixed form of a constitution whose merits are confirmed by the solid test of long experience and an increasing public strength and national prosperity. They despise experience as the wisdom of unlettered men; and as for the rest, they have wrought underground a mine that will blow up, at one grand explosion, all examples of antiquity, all precedents, charters, and acts of parliament. They have "the rights of men." Against these there can be no prescription, against these no agreement is binding; these admit no temperament and no compromise, anything withheld from their full demand is so much of fraud and injustice. Against these their rights of men let no government look for security in the length of its continuance, or in the justice and lenity of its administration.

...

Government is not made in virtue of natural rights, which may and do exist in total independence of it, and exist in much greater clearness and in a much greater degree of abstract perfection; but their abstract perfection is their practical defect. By having

a right to everything they want everything. Government is a contrivance of human wisdom to provide for human wants. Men have a right that these wants should be provided for by this wisdom. Among these wants is to be reckoned the want, out of civil society, of a sufficient restraint upon their passions. Society requires not only that the passions of individuals should be subjected, but that even in the mass and body, as well as in the individuals, the inclinations of men should frequently be thwarted, their will controlled, and their passions brought into subjection. This can only be done *by a power out of themselves*, and not, in the exercise of its function, subject to that will and to those passions which it is its office to bridle and subdue. In this sense the restraints on men, as well as their liberties, are to be reckoned among their rights. But as the liberties and the restrictions vary with times and circumstances and admit to infinite modifications, they cannot be settled upon any abstract rule; and nothing is so foolish as to discuss them upon that principle.

...

The pretended rights of these theorists are all extremes; and in proportion as they are metaphysically true, they are morally and politically false. The rights of men are in a sort of *middle*, incapable of definition, but not impossible to be discerned. The rights of men in governments are their advantages; and these are often in balances between differences of good, in

and oppression? What is that of England? Do not its own inhabitants say, It is a market where every man has his price, and where corruption is common traffic, at the expense of a deluded people? No wonder, then, that the French Revolution is traduced.

Had it confined itself merely to the destruction of flagrant despotism, perhaps Mr. Burke and some others had been silent. Their cry now is, "It is gone too far": that is, it has gone too far for them. It stares corruption in the face, and the venal tribe are all alarmed. Their fear discovers itself in their outrage, and they are but publishing the groans of a wounded vice.

But from such opposition, the French Revolution, instead of suffering, receives an homage. The more it is struck, the more sparks it will emit; and the fear is, it will not be struck enough. It has nothing to dread from attacks: Truth has given it an establishment; and Time will record it with a name as lasting as its own.

Having now traced the progress of the French Revolution through most of its principal stages, from its commencement, to the taking of the Bastille, and its establishment by the Declaration of Rights, I will close the subject with the energetic apostrophe of M. de Lafayette—May this great monument, raised to Liberty, serve as a lesson to the oppressor, and an example to the oppressed!

...

From the Revolutions of America and France, and the symptoms that have appeared in other countries, it is evident that the opinion of the world is changed with respect to systems of government, and that revolutions

are not within the compass of political calculations. The progress of time and circumstances, which men assign to the accomplishment of great changes, is too mechanical to measure the force of the mind, and the rapidity of reflection, by which revolutions are generated. All the old governments have received a shock from those that already appear, and which were once more improbable, and are a greater subject of wonder, than a general revolution in Europe would be now.

When we survey the wretched condition of man under the monarchical and hereditary systems of government, dragged from his home by one power, or driven by another, and impoverished by taxes more than by enemies, it becomes evident that those systems are bad, and that a general revolution in the principle and construction of governments is necessary.

What is government more than the management of the affairs of a nation? It is not, and from its nature cannot be, the property of any particular man or family, but of the whole community, at whose expense it is supported; and though by force or contrivance it has been usurped into an inheritance, the usurpation cannot alter the right of things. Sovereignty, as a matter of right, appertains to the nation only, and not to any individual; and a nation has at all times an inherent indefeasible right to abolish any form of government it finds inconvenient, and establish such as accords with its interest, disposition, and happiness. The romantic and barbarous distinction of [making] men into kings and subjects, though it may suit the condition of courtiers, cannot that of citizens; and is exploded by the principle upon which governments are now founded. Every citizen is a member of the sovereignty, and, as such, can acknowledge no personal subjection; and his obedience can be only to the laws.

▶ Working with Sources

1. How does Paine defend the Revolution against the charge of "extremism," as levied by Burke and others?

2. Why does Paine think it dangerous to romanticize kings and queens?

# Chapter 23 1790–1917
# Creoles and Caudillos

## LATIN AMERICA IN THE NINETEENTH CENTURY

Among the leaders of the Latin American wars of independence (1810–1826) from Spain, a woman named Juana Azurduy de Padilla (1781–1862) stands out for her bravery. Azurduy was a mestiza military commander in what are today the countries of Bolivia and Argentina. Her father was a Creole landowner near the city of Chuquisaca [choo-kee-SA-ca], and her mother was a Quechua-speaking Amerindian. Sent by her parents to a convent for her education and perhaps the life of a nun, Azurduy preferred the stories of heroic women warrior saints to a more sedate life of contemplation. After she completed her schooling, she married Manuel Ascencio Padilla, the son of a Creole landowner in Upper Peru, a military man in his youth and a law student after that. Together, the two enthusiastically joined the cause of independence in 1810, creating a mini republic (*republiquita*) in the mountains.

Here, Azurduy learned swordsmanship, firearms handling, and logistics for fighting guerilla wars. Well versed in Quechua and Aymara, Azurduy and Ascencio recruited some 6,000 locals, armed with the traditional Inca arms of clubs and slings. Azurduy, adored by these locals as Mother Earth (*pachamamba*), and Ascencio with their men joined in 1813 an expeditionary force of independence fighters from Buenos Aires. This force suffered a crushing defeat, however, at the hands of royal troops sent by the vice-regent

LATIN AMERICA AND THE CARIBBEAN

*ABOVE: Amerindian laundry women in Rio de Janeiro, 1835.*

of Peru. In an effort to recover, Azurduy borrowed a training manual and drilled what she called her "Loyal Battalion" for ambushes and quick retreats. But under the relentless pressure of the viceregal troops, the battalion suffered a constant loss of men, including her husband in 1816. Azurduy had no choice but to retreat to what is today northwestern Argentina, where she was incorporated as a lieutenant colonel in the regular independence army, in recognition of her bravery.

In 1825 Upper Peru finally gained its independence, under the name of Bolivia (in honor of the Venezuelan independence leader Simón Bolívar). Azurduy returned from Argentina to retire in her birthplace, renamed Sucre, after the first president of Bolivia. Four of her children had died of malaria, and only her daughter Lisa remained of her family. When Azurduy died in 1862 she was largely forgotten, but in the early 1900s Bolivians remembered her again and named a town near her birthplace after her.

---

The story of Juana Azurduy highlights important elements in the wars of independence in Latin America. Much more than in the United States, these wars as well as the subsequent creation of republican constitutions were the work not only of European American settlers but also of Amerindians, mestizos, black freedmen, and black slaves. In the United States, only a smattering of Native and African Americans participated in the wars, while independence in Mexico, Colombia, Bolivia, Peru, and Chile would be unthinkable without the prominent participation of Native and/or African Americans. Finally, the fact that a woman was able to buck patriarchal conventions in the early 1800s and rise in the ranks of the military demonstrates the power of the revolutionary ideas of liberty and of the republican and constitutional nation-state—a power that still inspires today.

## Independence, Constitutionalism, and Landed Elites

In Latin America, the eighteenth-century Enlightenment was far less an intellectual incubator of independence and constitutionalism than in North America. In a few places, notably New Granada (today Colombia, Venezuela, Ecuador, and Panama), there was actually some limited awareness of the New Sciences and social contract theories. But the American and French revolutions had a limited intellectual impact, and the Haitian slave revolution raised apprehension among Creoles. Although the struggle for independence was clearly another chapter in the history of the revolutionary wars of independence since 1776, its prehistory was much shorter.

This is not to say that there were not tensions between the Spanish or Portuguese reforming administrators of the second half of the 1700s and the Creoles who had to accept the reforms, or that there were not indigenous rebellions against the

## Seeing Patterns

▶ Which factors in the complex ethnic and social structures of Latin America were responsible for the emergence of authoritarian politicians, or caudillos?

▶ After achieving independence, why did Latin American countries opt for a continuation of mineral and agricultural commodity exports?

▶ How do the social and economic structures of this period continue to affect the course of Latin America today?

reforming colonial regimes, notably among the Guajira in Colombia (1769) and the Quechua and Aymara in Peru (1780–1781). But the catalyst for people of all ranks and even races to come together for the cause of independence from Spain and eventually nation-state republicanism in Latin America was Napoleon's occupation of Spain and Portugal (1807–1814). The occupation confronted Creoles, mestizos, Amerindians, mulattoes, and African American slaves with the choice of continued loyalty to the deposed absolutist Bourbon dynasty or full republican independence, notably after the collapse of Napoleon's regime in Iberia. (In Brazil, the monarch declared independence in the place of the nation in 1822.) Thus the constitutional crisis of the colonial regime itself made a decision about the constitutional future of Latin America unavoidable.

## Independence and Southern and Western South American Politics

Independence movements in the far south of South America began in June 1810. Under the guise of loyalty to the deposed Fernando VII of Spain, Creoles in Buenos Aires seized the initiative to establish a junta rejecting the viceregal Spanish authorities. By contrast, Creoles in the Andes avoided declarations of loyalty to Napoleon but supported the existing colonial administration, even after 1814 when fresh Spanish troops arrived. The figure who eventually broke the logjam between the two sides of pro- and anti-Spanish Creole parties in 1816–1822 was José de San Martín, one of the heroes of Latin American independence.

**Independence in Argentina**    The viceroyalty of La Plata, comprising the modern countries of Argentina, Uruguay, Paraguay, and Bolivia, was the youngest of Spain's colonial units. In the course of the Bourbon reforms, Spain had separated it in 1776 from the viceroyalty of Peru, where declining silver exports diminished the importance of the port of Lima. La Plata, with the rising port of Buenos Aires, had grown through contraband trade with Great Britain, and the Bourbon reformers wanted to redirect its trade more firmly back to Spain. Buenos Aires was so important to the British, however, that they occupied Buenos Aires in 1806–1807, until Spanish colonial forces drove them out again.

Creoles in La Plata had far fewer Amerindians, African slaves, mestizos, and mulattoes to deal with—or fear—than in any of the other viceroyalties. But in 1810, when the first independence movements formed, there was a clear distinction between the pro-independence Creoles of Buenos Aires, or *porteños*, and the Creoles of the *pampas* (grasslands of the temperate interior of Argentina and Uruguay) and the subtropical plains and hills of Paraguay, who favored continued colonialism. The latter were either royalists or strove for independence separate from La Plata.

Uruguay, furthermore, was initially claimed by Brazil and eventually achieved its own independence only in 1828. Upper Peru, or modern Bolivia, with its high-elevation plains, lowland Amazon basin rain forest, large Native American population, and Potosí silver mines, was heavily defended by colonial and Spanish troops. Given these various urban–rural and geographical circumstances, the porteño independence fighters achieved only a standstill during the initial period of 1810–1816, as mentioned in the vignette at the beginning of the chapter.

The breakthrough for independence eventually came via an experienced military figure, the highly popular José de San Martín (ca. 1778–1850). San Martín was a Creole from northeastern Argentina. His father, an immigrant from Spain, was a military officer and administrator of a Jesuit-founded Native American mission district. The son, educated from an early age in a Spanish military academy, began service in the porteño independence movement in 1812, where he distinguished himself in the Argentine struggle for independence.

During his service, San Martín realized that ultimate success in the struggle for independence in the south would require the liberation of the Andes provinces. Accordingly, he trained the Army of the Andes, which included large numbers of mulatto and black volunteers. With this army, he crossed the mountains to Chile in 1818, liberating the country from royalist forces. With the help of a newly established navy composed of ships acquired from the United States and Britain, he conquered Lima in Peru. However, San Martín was defied by the local Creoles when he sought to introduce social reforms, such as an end to the Native American tribute system, the *mit'a*, and the emancipation of the children of African slaves. When he was also unable to dislodge Spanish troops from Peru, he left for Argentina to complete the fight for independence against the royalist Creoles and Spanish troops. The capture of Peru was left to Simón Bolívar, the second liberation hero of South America (see below, p. 700).

**Independent Peru** Peru's independence came following the defeat of Spanish forces in 1824–1826. As with the other new states in South America, it took decades for Peru, Chile, and Bolivia to work out territorial disputes. The most serious of these by far was the War of the Pacific from 1879 to 1884, resulting in a victorious Chile annexing Peruvian and Bolivian lands. Most devastating for Peru was the destruction that Chilean troops wrought in southern Peru. The economy, which had made modest progress by using nitrate exports in the form of guano to fund railroad building and mining, was only painfully rebuilt after the destructions of war. Political stability for several decades returned under the presidency of Nicolás de Piérola, who introduced a number of belated reforms during his terms (1879–1881 and 1895–1899). As the presidency from this time until the 1920s was held by men from the upper landowning Creole class, it is sometimes called the period of the "Aristocratic Republic."

**Caudillos and Oligarchic Rule** During the later 1820s the independence junta in Buenos Aires solidified into an oligarchy of the city's landowning Creole elite, but the vast, largely undeveloped areas of the pampas with their small floating population of Amerindians and Creole *gauchos*, or cowboys, remained largely outside the new state. A war with Brazil drained the country of much of its manpower and resources. The political circles in Buenos Aires began to solidify around those favoring a central government to conduct a strong foreign policy and exercise control over the provinces, which—by contrast—advocated a looser federal

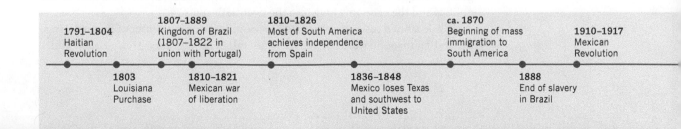

| 1791–1804 Haitian Revolution | 1807–1889 Kingdom of Brazil (1807–1822 in union with Portugal) | 1810–1826 Most of South America achieves independence from Spain | ca. 1870 Beginning of mass immigration to South America | 1910–1917 Mexican Revolution |
|---|---|---|---|---|
| 1803 Louisiana Purchase | 1810–1821 Mexican war of liberation | | 1836–1848 Mexico loses Texas and southwest to United States | 1888 End of slavery in Brazil |

**Fiercely Independent Gauchos, around 1900.** Gauchos, shown here sharpening their long knives (*facónes*), were recognizable by their ponchos or wool blankets which doubled as winter coats and saddle cloths. As in North America, they were expert riders, calf ropers, and—with their dogs shown in front—cattle herders.

**Caudillo:** Political-military leader with authoritarian tendencies.

system. By the 1830s these unsettled conditions gave rise to the first of many Argentine **caudillos**, Juan Manuel de Rosas (in office 1829–1852).

De Rosas was descended from a wealthy Creole ranching family and tended to identify with the gauchos. But he saw himself as a champion of national unity rather than one who sought to limit the role of the government in regional affairs. After becoming governor of Buenos Aires in 1829, he systematically extended his personal influence (*personalismo*) over his fellow governors until he was named caudillo in 1835, imposing a severe and fundamentally conservative brand of autocratic rule on the country.

Ultimately, his centralism and appetite for expansion contributed to his downfall. Fiercely opposed to British annexation of the Malvinas Islands—or Falklands, as the British called them—though frustrated by not being able to reverse it, he unwisely intervened in a civil war in Uruguay in 1843. His popularity flagged as the war dragged on for 9 years. Finally, the unsuccessful war, coupled with his unwillingness to lend his support to a constitution favorable to the provinces, led to his ouster in 1852.

**The Settling of the Pampas** The victor was a provincial governor named Justo José de Urquisa, who became the new caudillo. Urquisa swiftly extricated Argentina from Uruguay, defeated an army of de Rosas loyalists, and successfully sponsored a constitutional convention in 1853, lessening political centralism. In 1854 he was elected president, and it seemed for the moment that Argentina was on the road to a more open, representative government. But the presidency remained the property of a small Creole oligarchy from the provincial landowning elite. Not surprisingly, renewed conflict broke out over the issue of a centralized regime versus a projected new federal arrangement. In 1861, the forces of Buenos Aires defeated Urquisa's provincial forces and the country was reunited, with Buenos Aires as the national capital.

In the following years, many of the same forces that were shaping the North American West were also actively transforming the pampas. Encouraged by the government, European immigrants streamed into the country. The land was opened to settlement, driving the gauchos from their independent existence into becoming hired hands. The railroad was spurring settlement, and the remaining Amerindians were driven south to Patagonia or exterminated. In contrast to the homesteading policies in the United States, however, the pampas were divided up into huge estates (*estancias*) of tens of thousands of acres, aided by the introduction of barbed wire to fence in the ranges. The old system of rounding up essentially wild livestock and driving it to market now gave way to the ranching of cattle, sheep, and goats. As in other areas of South America, the new landed Creole elite dominated politics and the economy long into the twentieth century.

While landed interests continued to prevail, the urban center of Buenos Aires, expanding through waves of Spanish and Italian immigrants, grew restless under the rotating presidency that characterized the period of 1880–1900. Spurred by the development of radical politics in Europe, especially versions of Marxism and socialism, two major urban opposition parties took shape in the 1890s: the Radical Party and the Socialists. As the influence of these parties grew, electoral reforms were forced on an unwilling landed oligarchy. In 1912, universal male suffrage was passed, and voting by secret ballot was established. By 1916, the closed oligarchy was at last cracked open by the arrival of a new president, Hipólito Yrigoyen (1916–1922, 1928–1930). He relied for support mostly on an urban constituency, which dominated politics in the early twentieth century.

## Independence and Development in Northern South America

Compared to the viceroyalty of La Plata (Argentina), the viceroyalty of New Granada in northern South America, with today's countries of Venezuela, Colombia, Ecuador, and Panama, had far fewer Creoles. For its struggle for independence to succeed, leaders had to seek support from the *pardos*, as the majority population of free black and mulatto craftspeople in the cities was called. Independence eventually came through the building of strong armies from these diverse elements, mostly by Simón Bolívar, the liberator of northern South America. After independence, however, the Creoles quickly moved to dissolve their coalitions with the lower classes and embraced the caudillo politics that were also practiced in other parts of South America.

**Creoles and Pardos**    In contrast to Mexico, with its relatively large Creole and mestizo populations in the cities and countryside, New Granada's Creole population was small in relation to mestizos and pardos. The latter constituted over half of the urban and two-thirds of the rural people. In 1810, the New Granadans created *juntas*, or committees, among which the junta of Cartagena was the most important, and drove the colonial Spaniards from their administrative positions. Initially, the Creole-led juntas agreed on the equality of all ethnicities and worked on constitutions that provided for elections by all free men. But they were also suspicious of each other, denouncing their allegedly aristocratic, nondemocratic aspirations.

In 1811, cooperation broke down and the pardos assumed power in a coup. The Creoles struck back a year later when they declared the First Republic of Cartagena. Their power was limited by the pardo-dominated militias, however, and in a compromise they agreed on the continuation of full voting rights. In the long run, during the 1800s, this revolutionary achievement did not last, and the Creoles established oligarchic rule.

**Bolívar the Liberator**    The junta of Cartagena, together with other juntas, formed the federation of the United Provinces of New Granada in 1811, with a weak executive unable to prevent squabbling among the juntas or even defend their independence. The Spanish king, Fernando VII, after returning to the throne in 1813, was determined to reestablish colonial control by dispatching armies to Latin America. The largest forces, comprising some 10,000 troops, landed in the United Provinces in 1814, taking Cartagena after a siege, and resurrected the viceroyalty of New Granada.

**Simón Bolívar Liberating Slaves in Colombia.** As a Creole growing up on his father's cacao plantation, worked by slaves, Bolívar was intimately familiar with slavery. But his exile in post-revolutionary Haiti 1814–1816 demonstrated to him that slavery was incompatible not only with the principles of the American and French Revolutions but also with the revolutions in Spanish America, of which he was one of the main leaders.

The eventual liberator of northern South America from renewed Spanish rule in 1819 was Simón Bolívar (1783–1830). Bolívar was born in Venezuela, into a wealthy Creole family; it owned cacao plantations worked by African slaves and was engaged in colonial trade. Although lacking a formal education, thanks to his tutor Bolívar was familiar with Enlightenment literature. In 1799, he visited Spain, where he met his future wife, and he later returned to Europe after her death. In 1804, he was deeply impressed when he watched the lavish spectacle of Napoleon crowning himself emperor in Paris. These European visits instilled in Bolívar a lasting admiration for European ideals of liberty and popular sovereignty, and he longed to create a constitutional republic in his homeland.

In 1810, as in Cartagena, Venezuelan cities formed Creole-led juntas with pardo participation. A young Bolívar participated in the congress of juntas that declared outright independence for Venezuela in 1812, against the resistance of royalists who remained faithful to Fernando VII. A civil war ensued, which made Bolívar's tenure in Venezuela insecure and, after the arrival of the Spanish expeditionary force of 1814, impossible. He went into exile first to British Jamaica and then to revolutionary Haiti. In 1816 Bolívar returned from exile to Venezuela with a military force, partly supplied by Haiti. After some initial difficulties, he succeeded in defeating the Spanish troops. In 1822, he assumed the presidency of "Gran Colombia," an independent republic comprising the later states of Colombia, Venezuela, Ecuador, and Panama.

**The Bolívar–San Martín Encounter**    After their defeat in Gran Colombia, Spanish troops continued to occupy Peru in the Andes, where an independence movement supported by Argentina—including Juana Azurduy, discussed in the opening vignette of this chapter—was active but had made little progress against Spanish and royalist Creole troops. In the face of this situation, the Argentinean liberator José de San Martín (discussed above) and Bolívar met in 1822 to deliberate on how to drive the Spanish from Peru and to shape the future of an independent Latin America.

As for fighting Spain, they agreed that Bolívar was in a better geographical position than San Martín to send military forces to Peru. But even with these forces the task of attacking the Spanish was daunting for Bolívar. The troops were unaccustomed to high-altitude fighting and were hindered as much by mountain sickness as by enemy resistance. After two years of fighting, one of Bolívar's lieutenants finally got the better of the fiercely resisting Spanish. Two years later, in 1826, Spanish colonialism in Latin America finally ended when the last troops surrendered on an island off the Chilean coast.

The content of the discussion for the future of Latin America between San Martín and Bolívar never became public and has remained a bone of contention among historians. San Martín, bitterly disappointed by endless disputes among liberal constitutionalists and royalists, federalists and centralists, as well as Creole elitists and mestizo, pardo, and mulatto populists, favored monarchical rule to bring stability to Latin America. Bolívar preferred republicanism and Creole oligarchical rule. Both sought limited mestizo and pardo collaboration, especially in their armies. Apart from their awareness of the need for ethnic and racial integration, there was not much common ground between the two independence leaders.

San Martín's sudden withdrawal from the Andes after the meeting and his subsequent resignation from politics, however, can be taken as an indication of his realization that the chances for a South American monarchy were small indeed. Bolívar, also acutely aware of the multiple cleavages in Latin American politics, more realistically envisioned the future of Latin America as that of relatively small independent republics, held together by strong, lifelong presidencies and hereditary senates. He actually implemented this vision in the 1825 constitution of independent Upper Peru, renamed Bolivia after him.

> "Without envy, San Martín accepted that Bolívar, with whom he shared the glory of liberating half a world, would wear the laurels of victory, and he even recognized the modest inferiority of his own accomplishments, although he was morally and militarily the better man."
>
> —Bartolomé Mitre, 1882

Ironically, in his own country of Gran Colombia Bolívar was denied the role of strong president. Although he made himself a caudillo, he was unable to coax recalcitrant politicians into an agreement on a constitution for Gran Colombia similar to that of Bolivia. Eventually, in 1830 Bolívar resigned, dying shortly afterward of tuberculosis. In 1831 Gran Colombia divided into its component parts of Colombia, Venezuela, Ecuador, and (later) Panama.

**Caudillo Rule**    Independent Venezuela, as perhaps the poorest and most underpopulated of northern South America's newly independent countries, became the politically most turbulent Latin American republic. In Carácas, the capital, caudillos from the landowning Creole families displaced each other at a rapid rate. By one estimate, there were 41 presidencies and 30 insurrections in the period of 1830–1899. Although many of the presidents sought foreign financial support for development, little was accomplished and much of the money went into the private coffers of the leaders. The main issue that kept rival factions at odds was federalism versus tighter central control, with at least one all-out war being fought over the issue during the 1860s.

Venezuela's neighboring countries followed a similar pattern of caudillo politics. Though enjoying longer periods of stability, Colombia—the name adopted in 1861 to replace that of New Granada—also saw a continuing struggle between federalists and centralizers, with each side seeking the support of the Catholic Church. From 1899 until 1902, the two sides fought the War of a Thousand Days, leaving the country sufficiently weak for Panamanian rebels to establish an independent state of Panama in 1903, supported by the United States.

After independence, the administration of Theodore Roosevelt (1901–1909) swiftly concluded a treaty with the new country. In this treaty, the United States was to take control of a 10-mile-wide strip bisecting the narrow isthmus for the completion of the construction of the Panama Canal. A French consortium had begun gigantic earth-moving work in 1879 but was constantly behind schedule, as a result of landslides, flooding, tropical diseases, and engineering disputes, and went bankrupt in 1888. The government-sponsored construction took only seven years (1904–1911), but at the cost of appalling conditions for the Caribbean

**Land and Liberty.** This enormous mural by Diego Rivera (1886–1957), in the National Palace in Mexico City, shows Father Hidalgo above the Mexican eagle, flanked by other independence fighters. Above them are Emiliano Zapata and Pancho Villa, the heroes of the Revolution of 1910, holding a banner, "Tierra y Libertad." The other parts of the mural show historical scenes from the Spanish conquest to the twentieth century.

(African American) and European (Spanish) workers, who received half of the wages of their American counterparts on the railroad carrying the spoils.

## Independence and Political Development in the North: Mexico

In contrast to the central Spanish colony of New Granada with its substantial black and mulatto populations and relatively few Amerindians, New Spain (Mexico) had few inhabitants of African descent and large numbers of indigenous Americans. Therefore, from the beginning of the independence struggle mestizos and Amerindians had prominent and ongoing roles in the political development of the nineteenth century. As in the other two regions, however, conservative landowning Creoles were for most of the time dominant in the political process. Only toward the end of the 1800s did urban white, mestizo, and Amerindian residents acquire a voice. Landless rural laborers entered the political stage in the early twentieth century, during the Mexican Revolution.

**The Mexican Uprising**   In New Spain (modern Mexico), Miguel Hidalgo y Costilla (1753–1811), the son of a Creole hacienda estate administrator and his Creole wife, launched a movement for independence from Spain in 1810. A churchman since his youth, Hidalgo was broadly educated, well versed in Enlightenment literature, conversant in Nahuatl, and on the margins of strict Catholicism. As a young adult, he became a parish priest and devoted himself to creating employment opportunities for Amerindians in a province southeast of Mexico City.

In 1808, Hidalgo participated in a conspiracy of Creoles, some of them members of the military, to overthrow a group of Spanish colonial military officers who had staged a successful coup d'état against the civilian colonial administration of New Spain in 1808. Just before being discovered, the conspiracy launched a popular rebellion in 1810, declaring itself in favor of Fernando VII, the Spanish king deposed by Napoleon, whom the members considered to be the legitimate ruler.

Under the leadership of Hidalgo, tens of thousands of poor Creoles, mestizos, and Amerindians, who had suffered in a recent drought, marched on Guanajuato (in south-central Mexico), indiscriminately looting and killing both Spaniards and Creoles. Initially, they were successful in defeating the Spanish troops marching against them. When Hidalgo, shocked by the violence, called off an attack on Mexico City, however, the rebellion began to sputter and was eventually defeated in 1811. Loyal Spanish forces ultimately captured and executed Hidalgo.

**War of Independence**   After the defeat, associates of Hidalgo carried on in several southwestern provinces of Mexico but failed to make a comeback in the heartland around Mexico City, where royalists intent on preserving the union between Spain and Mexico remained supreme. In 1813, the pro-independence nationalist rebels adopted a program for independence that envisioned a constitutional government, abolished slavery, and declared all native-born inhabitants of New Spain "Americans," without regard to ethnic differences. A year later they promulgated a constitution providing for a strong legislature and a weak executive. Both program and constitution, however, still awaited the conclusion of the civil war between nationalists and royalists for their implementation.

The war ended in 1821 with Mexico's independence, based on a compromise between the nationalist Vicente Guerrero (1782–1831) and the royalist Agustín de Iturbide (1783–1824). Both leaders came from wealthy landowning families, although the Guerreros also owned transportation enterprises and gunsmithies. Guerrero's father was a mestizo, his mother an African slave; Iturbide was a Creole of Basque gentry descent who insisted—against some doubts—that his mother was also Creole. According to the compromise, Mexico was to become an independent constitutional "empire," give full citizenship rights to all inhabitants regardless of race and ethnicity, and adhere to Catholicism.

Iturbide became Mexico's first ruler, with the title "emperor," but abdicated in 1823 when his prolandowner policies and continued tolerance of slavery provoked a military uprising. By that time, Mexico was no longer an empire; already in 1821, El Salvador, Nicaragua, Costa Rica, and Honduras had declared their independence. With a new constitution in 1824, Mexico became a republic. For eight months in 1829, the liberation hero Guerrero was the republic's second president. During his short tenure he officially abolished slavery, before losing both his office and his life in another military uprising. As in other parts of Latin America during the period of early independence, politics remained unstable, pitting federalists and centralists against each other. Centralists eventually triumphed and, for a long period under Santa Anna, maintained authoritarian rule until 1857.

**Revolutionary Women.** Women, such as these *soldaderas* taking rifle practice, played many significant roles in the Mexican Revolution, 1910–1920.

**Northern Mexico and the Comanches**   Initially, Mexico had a number of advantages as an independent nation. It had abundant natural resources, and its nominal northern territories—Texas, New Mexico, and California—contained much valuable pasture and agricultural land. These territories were inhabited by numerous Native American peoples, among whom the Comanches were the most powerful. Originally from the Great Basin, they had migrated to the Colorado plains around the Arkansas River in the 1600s. Here, they acquired horses after the Pueblo Revolt (1680) against Spain. As migrants, they adopted more readily to the opportunities offered through horse breeding and contraband firearms than other, more settled Native American peoples.

In the course of the mid-1700s, they built a 400-mile-wide empire from the Arkansas River to just north of San Antonio. They raided regularly into New Mexico and maintained a flourishing trade of horses, cattle, bison hides, and enslaved war

captives, including blacks, on their borders. In the last decades of Spanish rule, colonial reformers, intent on creating a northern buffer zone to protect their silver mines, dispatched troops to check the Comanche expansion. But during the war of Mexican independence, Comanche raids resumed and wiped out the recent gains.

**Northern Immigration** To diminish the endemic insecurity in the northern borderlands resulting from the Comanches, beginning in the early 1820s Mexico supported immigration from the United States. It sold land to settlers on generous terms and allowed them to be largely self-governing as long as taxes were duly paid. At the same time, the United States entered a protracted period of growth. Settlement of the rich agricultural areas of

**Highly Mobile Comanches.**
The Comanches, having acquired horses and muskets, became the most efficient bison hunters prior to white Americans moving in with modern breechloaders. Living in tents, as shown here in a late nineteenth century photograph, the highly mobile Comanches maintained a militarily powerful trading and raiding empire on the southwestern plains (1700–1875).

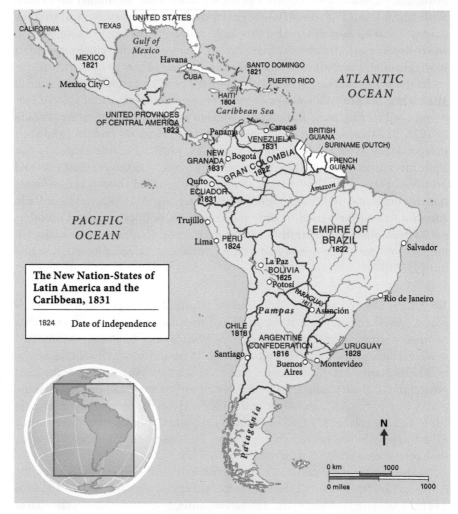

MAP **23.1** The New Nation-States of Latin America and the Caribbean, 1831.

the formerly French Ohio and Mississippi valleys moved with astonishing speed. The new demand for American cotton in British and American factories drove a frenetic expansion into Alabama, Mississippi, Louisiana, and Arkansas. Cotton exhausted the soil quickly, and the availability of cheap land made it more efficient to abandon the depleted lands and keep pushing the realm of "King Cotton" ever westward.

Many US citizens emigrated to Mexico to take advantage of its generous land policy and autonomy. The Mexican province of Texas was particularly attractive, especially to southerners, because of its nearness to the settled southern states and its suitability for cotton cultivation. While Mexico had outlawed slavery, most slave owners who migrated to Texas ignored these restrictions. The increasingly blatant violation of the antislavery laws and the swelling numbers of immigrants seeking opportunity in Texas came to alarm the Mexican national government by the 1830s.

**The US–Mexico War**   In 1836, the Mexican president Antonio López Santa Anna led some 4,000 troops against the militias maintained by the Texans. At first, these troops were successful, decimating Texan militiamen and US volunteers defending the Alamo, a fort near San Antonio. But then Texan forces defeated Santa Anna, and the state declared its independence (1836). Mexico refused to recognize Texas, and nine years later Texas opted for the security of union with the United States. It had also settled with the Comanches for an end to the raiding which had wrought havoc in western Texas.

When the United States declared war on Mexico over a Texas border dispute in the following year (1846), the other northern territories of Mexico had suffered such debilitating devastations from Comanche raids that the government found it impossible to build strong defenses against the US invasion. Within two years, Santa Anna's troops were defeated and Mexico was forced to give up over half of its territory (everything north of the Rio Grande and Gila Rivers), in return for 18 million dollars as part of a previous purchase offer and the Mexican state debt, as well as a promise of protection from future Comanche raids (see Map 23.2).

**The French Interlude in Mexico**   After the crushing losses of land to the United States, Santa Anna eventually fell from power, and in 1855 liberals gained the upper hand. They introduced a new constitution in 1857 which reaffirmed federalism, guaranteed individual liberties, and separated church and state. The conservatives in Mexico detested this new constitution and waged the "Reform War" (1857–1861) to abolish it. They lost, and the liberals elected Benito Juárez (1861–1864) president, the first Amerindian to accede to the office.

MAP 23.2 **Mexico's Loss of Territory to the United States, 1824–1854.**

Map legend:
**Mexico, 1824–1854**
- Boundary of Mexico, 1824
- Texas, independent republic 1836–45, 1845 to US
- Ceded 1845, 1850
- Ceded by Treaty of Guadalupe Hidalgo, 1848
- Ceded 1853 (Gadsden Purchase)
- Mexico, 1854

As soon as he was in office, however, he discovered that the war had drained Mexico's financial reserves, obliging him to suspend payment on the state debt. International reaction was swift, with British, Spanish, and France forces seizing the customs house in the port city of Veracruz, making a mockery of the US Monroe Doctrine of 1823, which had been inspired by the Latin American independence wars. According to the doctrine, no foreign intervention would be tolerated again in the Americas. For four decades the doctrine had been remarkably successful at deterring the European powers, largely because it suited British trade policy as well. Mexico had easily beaten back two invasion attempts by small expeditionary forces, one from Spain in 1829 and another from France in 1838. Not wishing to violate the pan-American opposition to European intervention with a prolonged occupation, Britain and Spain withdrew their forces quickly.

> "With good reason the public now feels that constitutions are born and die, that governments succeed each other, that codes are enlarged and made intricate, that pronouncements and plans come and go, and that after so many mutations and upheavals, so much inquietude and so many sacrifices, nothing positive has been done for the people."
>
> —Ponciano Arriaga, "Father of the 1857 Constitution"

The French, however, stayed, exploiting the inability of the United States to intervene as a result of the outbreak of the Civil War. Louis-Napoleon III Bonaparte, nephew of Napoleon and self-declared emperor (r. 1852–1870), was determined to return France to imperial glory overseas. He seized on the issue of suspended debt payments and, with an eye on the Mexican silver mines, set in motion an ambitious plan of imposing a pliable ruler in the country. In 1862, he provided military backing to the Austrian prince Maximilian, well liked by Mexican conservatives, who installed himself as the emperor of Mexico (1864–1867).

With the defeat of the Confederate states in the US Civil War in April 1865, however, Maximilian's position became precarious. The Union army was ballooning to over a million men, many of whom had just been sent to Texas to suppress

*The Execution of Emperor Maximilian of Mexico, June 19, 1867.* Édouard Manet has been characterized as the "inventor of modernity," not only for his technique but for the way he portrayed events, even significant political events, in a calm and composed manner. The soldiers who dispatch the hapless emperor come across as cool and professional—what they are doing is all in a day's work.

the last Confederate holdouts. In 1866, after some discreet aid from the US government, an uprising broke out in Mexico. With Maximilian cut off from any hope of quick support from France, liberal forces defeated and captured him, executing him by firing squad in 1867.

**Díaz's Long Peace**    A period of relative peace arrived at last with the withdrawal of most US government troops from Texas at the end of Reconstruction—ending the potential threat of invasion or border incursions—and the rise of Mexico's next caudillo, Porfirio Díaz (in office 1876–1880 and 1884–1911). Díaz's lengthy hold on power allowed a degree of conservative stability to settle over Mexico's turbulent politics. Moreover, the period also coincided with the defeat of the last Amerindians north of the border and the settlement and development of the American West.

In addition, Díaz, like his contemporary President José Balmaceda (1886–1891) of Chile, was the first to favor infrastructural and industrial development. The two realized that mineral and agricultural exports made their countries too dependent on the world market with its periodic depressions, such as the Long Depression of 1873–1896. The basic infrastructure of Mexico's rail, telegraph, and telephone systems were laid during this time; textile factories and some basic heavy industries were set up; oil was produced in quantity; and modest agricultural improvements were made. Overall, the economy expanded by 6 percent annually during the Porfiriato, as the period of Díaz's government was called.

Much of Díaz's conservative stability was built on the faction of Creole landowners with whom Díaz had come to power. This faction had grown through the addition of groups of technocrat administrators (*científicos*), financiers, land speculators, and industrialists. As in all ruling classes, personal connections and mutual promotions provided the glue for cohesiveness; but what characterized the Porfiriato regime in addition was the undisguised desire for self-enrichment while disregarding the law and even resorting to physical violence. Critics of the regime were arrested, beaten, and sent to exile on the Yucatán peninsula as the Porfiriato became increasingly repressive.

The number of critics rose steadily, however, in tandem with the growth of cities and the urban middle classes of professionals (journalists, lawyers, doctors, teachers, small businessmen, accountants, etc.). They found themselves excluded from economic or even political participation. Meeting in liberal clubs, they demanded a return to the constitution of 1857. Critics also arose among the working classes (miners, railroad and streetcar workers, textile and steel workers, and some craftsmen) who found themselves prohibited from forming trade unions and carrying out strikes, although there were nevertheless frequent strikes in the textile factories. In the early 1900s, an aging Díaz and his septuagenarian *científicos* faced an increasingly restless urban population.

The countryside, where the large majority of Mexicans still lived and worked, was just as restless. Ever since colonial times, there was a profound division between Creole estate (*hacienda*) owners, as well as mestizo and Amerindian rurals (that is, people farming or working on the estates and peasants in their own villages). For most of the 1800s, the economy of the countryside had been typified by self-sufficiency: Nearly everything was produced and consumed there, as transportation costs were prohibitive.

But with the construction of the railroad system under Díaz, the transportation costs of sending a ton of cotton from the provinces to Mexico City sank from $63 to $3. Now the hacienda landlords could produce crops for the market and, accordingly, gobbled up acres of farmland by the millions from villagers who could not show legal titles to the land. Even if villagers did legally own the land, corrupt lawyers outmaneuvered them. The wealthiest landlord was Luis Terrazas, with 50 haciendas totaling nearly 7 million acres, mostly in the northern state of Chihuahua. Asked whether he was *from* Chihuahua, Terrazas was reported to have said, "*I am* Chihuahua!"

**The Early Mexican Revolution**    Middle-class discontent was the first to manifest itself in the elections of 1910, which Díaz had to hold according to the constitution. As before, this election had once more been manipulated in favor of Díaz. But the president, currying the favor of a fawning US journalist, had declared in 1908 that he would like to have an opposition party in Mexico. For a short time, liberals in the country were greatly encouraged, and they found a surprisingly popular candidate.

This candidate was Francisco Madero (1873–1913), the dissident son of a wealthy Creole landowner family who was deeply committed to the social justice proclaimed in the 1857 constitution. Madero refused to recognize the election and called on the middle classes, working classes, and peasants to rise up against the tyrant Díaz. The call was couched in cautious terms, making the case for a return to the constitutional revolution of the early 1800s. But by mentioning also the right of workers to organize in trade unions and of peasants to receive their own plots of land, he inevitably opened the floodgates for a full social and economic revolution.

Among the first to respond was Pancho Villa (1878–1923), a muleteer-cum-cattle rustler asked by a motley of miners, ranch hands, cowboys, and military colonists to lead them in their rebellion in the northern state of Chihuahua. Another rebel leader was Emiliano Zapata (1879–1919), head of a village in the state of Morelos in south-central Mexico, who had begun with his *campesinos* (tenant farmers, laborers, and village peasants) to occupy sugar plantations and distribute plantation land to them. Victories of Villa in the north and Zapata as close as 20 miles from Mexico City against federal troops persuaded Díaz to step down in May 1911 and leave for exile in France.

Madero was sworn in as the new president. But soon into his tenure it became clear that his vision for a constitutional revolution was incompatible with the social and economic revolutions pursued by Zapata and Villa. Madero sent federal troops against Zapata to force an end to his land distributions. Compromising and pacific, Madero was increasingly driven into the arms of Porfiriato officers who, supported by the US government, were nervous about the events in Mexico. The officers had no use for Madero, however, and deposed and executed him in February 1913.

**Emiliano Zapata and Fellow Revolutionaries in Mexico City, June 4, 1911.** Shortly after the fall of Díaz, his opponents Madero, Villa, and Zapata (seated, second from left) entered Mexico City in triumph, to celebrate the end of the regime of Díaz. But already by June 8, Zapata and Madero disagreed on the issue of land reform. The moderate Madero wanted to halt it; Zapata wanted to continue it in his state of Morelos. This disagreement, among other internal rifts in the revolutionary camp, was responsible for the revolution dragging on to 1920.

The Later Revolution    During the subsequent 15 months, power in Mexico was disputed between Porfiriato reactionaries in Mexico City and the Constitutionalists (those faithful to the liberal constitution of 1857) in the wealthy states of the north, along the US border. Many of the Constitutionalists were from the urban middle classes whose ambitions had been thwarted during Díaz's regime. They were opposed to land distribution, but they needed more troops to overthrow the reactionaries. Constitutionalists, Pancho Villa, and Emiliano Zapata, therefore, forged an alliance that made Venustiano Carranza (1859–1920), from a wealthy but liberal Creole family, their leader. Together, they ended the reactionary regime in Mexico City in July 1914.

Once in power, the Constitutionalists dissolved the reactionary federal army but then broke apart over the issue of land reform. The antireform minority left Mexico City and retreated to Veracruz on the east coast to reorganize itself. Villa and Zapata, at the head of the pro-reform majority, entered Mexico City. But they were too committed to the continuing land reforms in their respective northern and south-central states to form a functional central government. By default, the working classes and their union representatives began to assume their own role in the revolution. They decided to support Álvaro Obregón (1880–1928), a rising commander among the Constitutionalists from the northern state of Sonora, where he had been a commercial farmer and businessman opposed to Díaz. After the departure of Villa and Zapata for their home states, Obregón entered Mexico City in February 1915.

Although the Constitutionalists had overcome the reactionary Creole landowner interests, they were deeply divided between a policy of a constitutional revolution under a strong central government with a modest land and labor reform program and a policy of agrarian revolutions in autonomous states. The supporters of the constitutional revolution gained the initiative when Obregón succeeded in driving Villa in the north from power. Carranza followed by having Zapata eliminated by treachery.

Carranza, in office as president of Mexico from 1915 to 1920, systematically removed a host of minor agrarian revolutionaries from their states and villages and ended all land distributions. But Obregón, more sympathetic to labor and land reform (albeit guided from the top and carried out in moderation), successfully challenged Carranza for the presidency in the next elections. With the support of the Constitutional army he forced Carranza to surrender and ended the Mexican Revolution late in 1920.

All constitutional revolutions of 1776–1826 in Europe and the Americas were works in progress, because they proclaimed universal liberty, equality, and brotherhood without initially granting it to all inhabitants of the nation. In Mexico, as in the other Latin American nation-states, only the estate-owning Creole oligarchy embodied the nation in the years after 1826. The Mexican Revolution expanded the constitutional process to the urban middle class, workers, farmers, and villagers. It did so because it also brought about real social and economic gains for men and women other than the landowners. All this happened at the tremendous human cost of one million victims, but as complex as the events of 1910–1920 were, they made the Mexican nation much more cohesive than it had been a century earlier.

## Brazil: From Kingdom to Republic

During the late colonial period, Brazil underwent the same centralizing administrative, fiscal, and trade reforms as the Spanish possessions. These reforms were resented as much by the Brazilian planters and urban Creoles (Portuguese *crioulos*) as by their Spanish counterparts, but their fear of rebellion among the huge population of black slaves held them back from openly demanding independence. As it happened, independence arrived without bloody internecine wars, through the relocation of the monarchy from Portugal to Brazil in the wake of Napoleon's invasion of Iberia in 1807. Brazil had since become an empire, and when the second emperor, Dom Pedro II (r. 1831–1889), under pressure from Britain, finally abolished slavery in 1888, the politically abandoned plantation oligarchy avenged itself by deposing him and switching to a republican regime under the military in 1889. Given the enormous size of the country, as well as the split of the Creole oligarchy into groups with mining, sugar, and coffee interests, the regime became solidly federal, making it difficult for caudillos to succeed and eventually allowing for the rise of civilian presidents.

**Relocation of the Dynasty**   Portugal's royal family fled the country in advance of Napoleon's armies in 1807. Escorted by British ships, they took refuge in Brazil and elevated the colony to the status of a coequal kingdom in union with Portugal but governed from Brazil after Napoleon's defeat in 1815. The arrival of some 15,000 Portuguese together with the dynasty, however, created resentment among the Brazilian Creoles, sharpening the traditional tension between Creoles and Portuguese-born reformers. A crisis point was reached in 1820 when rebels in Portugal adopted a liberal constitution, which demanded the return of Brazil to colonial status as well as the transfer of the dynasty back to Portugal. The reigning king went back but left his son, Pedro I (r. 1822–1831), behind in Brazil. On the advice of both his father and courtiers, Pedro uttered in 1822 his famous *"Fico"* ("I remain"), and proclaimed, "Independence or death!" thereby making Brazil an independent kingdom.

**Pedro I's Authoritarianism**   On acceding to the throne, Pedro declared Brazil an empire because of its size and diversity. His rule at the head of the Creole landowner ruling class, however, shared many of the same characteristics as that of the early caudillos in the Spanish-speaking South American countries. In addition, like the restoration monarchs of Europe in the early 1800s, he firmly adhered to his belief in divine right, which was incompatible with more than token constitutionalism. Consequently, he rejected an attempt by the landed oligarchy to introduce limited monarchical rule. Instead, he issued his own constitution in 1823, which concentrated most powers in his hands, as well as a council of state, with a weak lifetime senate and a legislative chamber based on severely limited voting rights. Since he also reserved for himself the nomination and dismissal of ministers, the dissolution of the chamber, and, above all, the appointment of provincial governors, his rule was far too authoritarian even for the conservative planter elite.

In reaction, in 1824 six northeastern provinces attempted to secede. They proclaimed the republican Federation of the Equator and, somewhat illogically, demanded more central government support for the traditional northern sugar and cotton plantations, neglected by a rising emphasis on south-central coffee plantations. Increased British patrols in the Atlantic to suppress the slave trade had increased the price for slaves. The sugar planters could ill afford the increased prices, but the expanding coffee market enabled its planters to pay (see "Patterns Up Close").

Given the close ties between Britain and Brazil, Pedro found it difficult to resist mounting British demands for the abolition of slavery. As a result, early signs of alienation between the crown and the Creole planter elite crept in. It also did not help that Pedro supported the open immigration to Brazil of skilled foreigners from Europe, as well as foreign loans and investments for development. As the sources document, Pedro's policy was directed at increasing the number of whites in order to decrease the proportion of blacks and Amerindians.

By contrast, the plantation elites were primarily interested in acquiring servile labor and control of the courts to ensure severe punishments for infractions by slaves. They voiced their opposition to internal improvements, like railroads, for fear of disrupting the stability of the plantation system. Ultimately, a succession crisis in Portugal in 1830 led to a conservative revolt against Pedro. In 1831, he lost his nerve and abdicated, sailing back to Portugal. He left the throne to his 5-year-old son, Pedro II (r. 1831–1889), who required a regent. The landowning elite exploited the opportunity of the temporarily weak monarchy by renewing its demands for federalism.

**The Federalist Interlude**    After lengthy debates, in 1834 the government granted the provinces their own legislative assemblies with strong tax and budget powers, effectively strengthening the provincial landholding elites with their various regional interests. It also abolished the council of state but created a national guard to suppress slave revolts and urban mobs. This mixed bag of reforms was too much for some provinces. The most dangerous revolt against the reforms was that of 1835 in Rio Grande do Sul, a southern province dominated by cattle owners who did not own many slaves and commanded military forces composed of gauchos. These owners established an independent republic that attracted many domestic and foreign radicals opposed to slavery, including Giuseppe Garibaldi, the Italian nationalist who played a crucial role in the unification of Italy. In reaction to the coexistence of a now weak and decentralized monarchy and an antislavery republic offering refuge to runaways on Brazilian soil, the centralists reasserted themselves. In 1840 they proclaimed the 14-year-old Pedro II king and curbed the powers of the provincial assemblies. In 1845 they negotiated a return of Rio Grande do Sul to Brazil.

**The End of Slavery**    The 1830s and 1840s coincided with a transition in Brazil from sugar to coffee as a major export commodity on the world market. The old sugar plantation elite lost clout, and a newer coffee planter oligarchy ascended to prominence. Both needed slaves, and as long as the crown did not seriously seek to fulfill its promises of 1831 to the British to curb the importation of slaves, there was no more than unease about the mutual dependence of the king and the oligarchy on the continued existence of slave labor. But when the British in 1849 authorized warships to enter Brazilian waters to intercept slave ships, the importation of slaves virtually ceased, causing a serious labor shortage. Sugar, cotton, and coffee plantation owners began to think of ridding themselves of a monarchy that was unable to maintain the flow of slaves from overseas.

# Slave Rebellions in Cuba and Brazil

Blacks had gained little from the American and French Revolutions, and the pattern of brutal exploitation continued in many parts of the Americas. Not surprisingly, therefore, blacks sought to emulate the example of Haiti's successful slave revolt during the first half of the 1800s. However, none of the subsequent Haiti-inspired revolts were any more successful against the well-prepared authorities than previous revolts had been in the 1700s, as a look at rebellions in Cuba and Brazil during the first half of the nineteenth century shows.

In Cuba, the decline of sugar production in Haiti during the revolution encouraged a rapid expansion of plantations and the importation of African slaves. As previously in Haiti, a relatively diversified eighteenth-century society of whites, free mulattoes, and blacks, as well as urban and rural black slaves, was transformed into a heavily African-born plantation slave society, forming a large majority in many rural districts. The black freedman José Antonio Aponte (ca. 1756–1812),

**Slave Revolt Aboard Ship.** Rebellions aboard ship, such as the famous 1839 mutiny aboard the *Amistad* shown here, were common occurrences. The Amistad was engaged in intra-American slave trafficking, and the slaves overpowered the crew shortly after embarkation in Cuba. After protracted legal negotiations, the slaves were eventually freed and returned to Africa.

In the 1860s and 1870s, antimonarchy agitation gathered speed. Brazilians, especially professionals and intellectuals in the cities, became sensitive to their country being isolated in the world on the issue of slavery. After the United States emancipated slaves in 1863, the Spanish colonies of Puerto Rico and Cuba followed suit by ending slavery for all elderly slaves and newborn children. Brazil was now left as the only unreformed slaveholding country in the Western Hemisphere.

In the following decade and a half, the antislavery chorus increased in volume. While the government introduced a few cosmetic changes, it fell to the provinces to take more serious steps. Planters, who began to see the demise of the system on the horizon, encouraged their provinces to increase the flow of foreign immigrants, to be employed as wage labor on the coffee plantations. The political situation neared the point of anarchy in 1885, with mass flights of slaves from

a militiaman and head of the Yoruba confraternity (*cabilde*) in Havana, led an abortive revolt in 1812 that drew support from both sectors. In the subsequent revolts of 1825, 1835, and 1843, the urban element was less evident. Authorities and planters, heavily invested in new industrial equipment for sugar production and railroads, and exhausted by the unending sequence of uprisings, unleashed a campaign of sweeping arrests of free blacks and mulattoes that cut the urban–rural link once and for all.

Brazil, like Cuba, also benefited from the collapse of sugar production on Haiti in the 1790s and the first half of the 1800s. It expanded its plantation sector, particularly in the province of Bahia, and imported large numbers of slaves from Africa. But here distrust divided those born in Africa from Brazilian-born slaves, freedmen, and mulattoes. Many freedmen and mulattoes served in the militias that the authorities used to suppress the revolts. Furthermore, in contrast to the narrow island of Cuba, plantation slaves could run away more easily to independent settlements (called *quilombos*) in the wide-open Brazilian interior, from where revolts were more easily organized than in cities or on plantations. In fact, no fewer than a dozen quilombo revolts extending into plantations occurred in Bahia during 1807–1828, revolts which the militias found difficult to crush, having to march into often remote areas.

Two urban revolts of the period were remarkable for their exceptional mix of insurgents, unparalleled in Cuba or elsewhere in Latin America. The first was the Tailor's Rebellion of 1798 in Salvador, Bahia's capital. Freedmen, mulattoes, and white craftspeople cooperated in the name of freedom and equally against the Creole oligarchy. The second was the Muslim uprising of 1835, also in Bahia, organized by African-born freedmen as well as slaves with Islamic clerical educations that they had received in West Africa before their enslavement.

## Questions

- Do the slave rebellions in Cuba and Brazil in the early nineteenth century confirm or complicate the pattern of slave revolutions that was manifested first in Haiti?

- What role did geography play in the success or failure of a revolution?

plantations and armed clashes to keep them there. Only in 1888 did the central government finally end slavery.

**The Coffee Boom**     Predictably, given the grip of the planter elite on the labor force, little changed in social relations after the abolition of slavery. The coffee growers, enjoying high international coffee prices and the benefits of infrastructure improvements through railroads and telegraph lines since the 1850s, could afford low-wage hired labor. The now-free blacks received no land, education, or urban jobs, scraping by with low wages on the coffee and sugar plantations. Economically, however, after freeing itself from the burdens of slavery, Brazil expanded its economy in the 5 years following 1888 as much as in the 70 years of slavery since independence.

The monarchy, having dragged its feet for half a century on the slavery issue, was thoroughly discredited among the landowners and their military offshoot, the officer corps. By the 1880s, officers were also drawn from professional and intellectual urban circles. Increasingly, they subscribed to the ideology of *positivism* coming from France, which celebrated the idea of secular scientific and technological progress (see Chapter 22). Positivists, almost by definition, were liberal and republican in political orientation. In 1889, a revolt in the military supported by the Creole plantation oligarchy resulted in the abolition of the monarchy and proclamation of a republic, with practically no resistance from any quarter.

Two political tendencies emerged in the constituent assembly 2 years after the proclamation of the republic. The coffee interests of the south-central states favored federalism, with the right of the provinces to collect export taxes and maintain militias. The urban professional and intellectual interests, especially lawyers, supported a strong presidency with control over tariffs and import taxes as well as powers to use the federal military against provinces in cases of national emergency. The two tendencies resulted in a compromise with a tilt toward federalism, which produced provincial caudillos on the one hand but also regularly elected presidents on the other.

Following this tilt, in the 1890s the government was strongly supportive of agricultural commodity exports. Coffee, rubber, and sugar exports yielded high profits and taxes until 1896, when overproduction of coffee resulted in diminishing returns. The state of São Paulo then regulated the sale of coffee on the world market through a state purchase scheme, which brought some stabilization to coffee production. At the same time and continuing into the early twentieth century (and without much state or central government support), immigrants and foreign investors laid the foundation for **import-substitution industrialization**, beginning with textile and food-processing factories. The comparative advantage afforded by commodity exports had run its course by the late 1800s and early 1900s and now had to be supplemented with industrialization.

**Import-substitution industrialization:** The practice by which countries protect their economies by setting high tariffs and construct factories for the production of consumer goods (textiles, furniture, shoes, followed later by appliances, automobiles, electronics) and/or capital goods (steel, chemicals, machinery).

# Latin American Society and Economy in the Nineteenth Century

Independence meant both disruptions and continuities in the economy just as much as in politics (discussed in the first half of this chapter). In Spanish America, four colonial regions broke apart into what were eventually 21 independent republics, organized around the pattern of constitutional nationalism. Trade with Europe was thus radically altered. What continued were deep divisions between the small landowning elites and the urban masses of officials, professionals, craftspeople, and laborers. Although many members of the elites and urban middle and lower classes had collaborated in the drive for independence, afterward the Creole landowning elite made participation of the urban classes in the constitutional process increasingly difficult. Correspondingly, when trade with Europe resumed, this elite was primarily interested in the export of mineral and agricultural commodities, from which it reaped the most benefits (see Map 23.3).

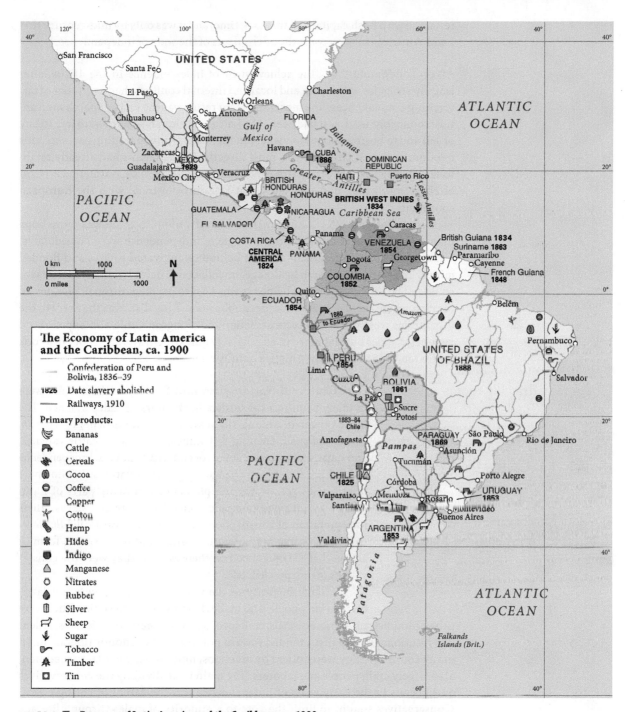

MAP 23.3 **The Economy of Latin America and the Caribbean, ca. 1900.**

## Rebuilding Societies and Economies

Reconstruction in the independent Spanish-speaking republics and the Brazilian monarchy took several decades. Mercantilist trade was gone, replaced by free trade on the world market. Production in the mines and on the estates had to be restarted with fresh capital. All this took time, and it was only by mid-century that Latin America had overcome the after-effects of the wars of independence.

**After Independence** The achievement of independence in the 1820s, after lengthy struggles with Spain and local and internal conflicts, had a number of far-reaching consequences. The most important result was the end of Spain's mercantilist monopoly, weak as it had been. The Latin American republics were free to buy or sell and to borrow money anywhere in the world. Among trading partners, this freedom benefited Great Britain most directly. Its merchants had already established themselves in several Latin American cities during the Continental boycott of Napoleon, which had shut out Great Britain from trade with the European continent.

Initially, however, for Latin Americans the freedom to trade was more hope than reality. Dislocations from the struggle of independence were considerable. Capital had fled the continent and left behind uncultivated estates and flooded mines. The Catholic Church held huge, uncollectable debts. In many areas taxes could not be collected. Troops helped themselves to payment through plunder. In Mexico, where the struggle between republicans and royalists was the fiercest, the disruptions were worst and reconstruction took longest. Chile also experienced violent struggles but stabilized itself relatively quickly. On average, though, it took until around 1850 for Latin America to fully recover.

"There were drawing rooms where only those [Creoles] with certain surnames could enter and which were closed to those who had only the power of money; there were families before which one knelt with respect, awe, and adulation. The daughter of one of these said in Europe, 'In my country I am like a princess.'"

—Jorge Basadre, 1946

**Constitutional Nationalism and Society** The Creoles were in many countries the leaders in the wars of independence. The most powerful among them were large landowners—that is, owners of grain-farming self-sufficiency estates, cattle ranches, and sugar, indigo, cacao, coffee, or cotton plantations. Independence did not produce much change in agrarian relations: Landowners of self-sufficient estates and plantations in many parts of Latin America continued to employ tenant farmers and slaves. Their interpretation of constitutionalism tended toward *caudillismo*— that is, the same kind of authoritarian and paternalistic form of action that they practiced on their estates. They were the conservatives of independence.

The large majority of the Creoles, however, were not landowners but people who made their money in the cities. They were urban administrators, professionals, craftspeople, and laborers. Their leaders, ardent constitutional nationalists, tended toward political and economic liberalism. In many countries they were joined by mestizos, mulattoes, and black freedmen, also largely craftspeople and laborers. The main issue dividing the conservatives and liberals in the early years of independence was the extent of voting rights: Conservatives sought to limit the vote to a minority of males through literacy and property requirements, while liberals wanted to extend it to all males. No influential group at this point considered extending voting rights to women.

**Political Divisions** Once independence was won, distrust between the two groups with very different property interests set in, and the political consensus fell apart. Accordingly, landed constitutional conservatives restricted voting rights, to the detriment of the urban constitutional liberals. The exceptions were Argentina and, for a time during the mid-nineteenth century, Peru: The former had few mestizos and mulattoes but a relatively large urban Creole population that gained the upper hand, and the latter had large numbers of urban mestizos and Amerindians who could not be ignored. Nevertheless, even if liberal constitutionalism was submerged for periods of time under caudillo authoritarianism in the mid-1800s, the expansion of constitutionalism from the landowning oligarchy to larger segments of the population remained a permanent fixture in the minds of many, especially intellectuals and political activists in cities. It was this early presence of constitutionalism in the wider population which distinguished Latin America from the Ottoman Empire, Russia, China, and Japan and made its constitutional process similar to the United States and France.

**Split over State–Church Relations**  Among the many issues over which conservatives and liberals split, the relationship between state and church was the deepest. Initially, given the more or less close collaboration between conservatives and liberals during the struggle for independence, Catholicism remained the national religion for all. Accordingly, education and extensive property remained under church control, as guaranteed by the constitutions.

But the new republics ended the powers of the Inquisition and claimed the right of *patronato*—that is, of naming bishops. At the behest of Spain, however, the pope left bishoprics empty rather than agreeing to this new form of lay investiture. In fact, Rome would not even recognize the independence of the Latin American nations until the mid-1830s. The conflict was aggravated by the church's focus on its institutional rather than pastoral role. The Catholic clergy provided little guidance later on during the 1800s when rapid urbanization and industrial modernity were crying out for spiritual reorientation. At the same time, papal pronouncements made plain the church's hostility toward the developing capitalist industrial order.

This hostility of the church was thus one of the factors that in the mid 1800s contributed to a swing back to liberalism, beginning with Colombia in 1849. Many countries adopted a formal separation between church and state and introduced secular educational systems. But the state–church issue remained bitter, especially in Mexico, Guatemala, Ecuador, and Venezuela, where it was often at the center of political shifts between liberals and conservatives. In Colombia, for example, it even led to a complete reversal of liberal trends in the mid-1880s, with the reintroduction of Catholicism as the state religion.

**Economic Recovery**  Given the shifts of leadership between conservatism and liberalism during the period of recovery after independence (ca. 1820–1850), the reconstruction of a coherent fiscal system to support the governments was difficult to accomplish. For example, governments often resorted to taxation of trade, even if this interfered with declared policies of free trade. The yields on tariffs and export taxes, however, were inevitably low and made the financing of strong central governments difficult. Consequently, maneuvering for the most productive mix of the two taxes trumped official pronouncements in favor of free trade and often eroded confidence among trade partners.

This maneuvering had little effect on the domestic economy—self-sufficiency agriculture and urban crafts production—which represented the great bulk of economic activities in Latin America. Grain production on large estates and small farms, especially in Brazil, where gold production declined in late colonial times, had escaped the turbulence of the independence-war and recovery periods relatively unscathed. Land remained plentiful, and the main bottleneck continued to be labor. The distribution of marketable surpluses declined, however, given the new internal borders in Latin America with their accompanying tariffs and export taxes. Self-sufficiency agriculture, and local economies relying on it, thus remained largely unchanged throughout the 1800s.

The crafts workshops, especially for textiles, suffered from the arrival of cheap British factory-produced cottons, which represented the majority of imports by the mid-1800s. Their impact, however, remained relatively limited, mostly to the coasts, since in the absence of railroads transportation costs to the interior were prohibitively expensive. Only Mexico encouraged the financing of machine-driven textile factories, but the failure of its state bank in 1842—from issuing too many loans— ended this policy for a number of decades. On the one hand, there was a definite awareness in most countries of the benefits of factories, using domestic resources, and linking the self-sufficiency agricultural sector to modern industrial development. On the other hand, its necessity in the face of traditional opposition was not demonstrated until later in the nineteenth century.

## Export-Led Growth

The pursuit of a policy of commodity exports—export-led growth—from about 1850 led to rises in the standard of living for many Latin Americans. The industrializing countries in Europe and North America were voracious consumers of the minerals that Latin America had in abundance, as well as of its tropical agricultural products. More could have been sold, had there not been a chronic labor shortage.

**Raw Materials and Cash Crops**   Mining and agricultural cash crop production recovered gradually, so that by the 1850s nearly all Latin American governments had adopted export-led economic growth as their basic policy. This was about all the conservatives and liberals were able to agree on, since land distribution to poor farmers and a system of income taxes were beyond any consensus. Mexican and Peruvian silver production, the mainstay of the colonial mercantilist economy, became strong again, although the British adoption of the gold standard in 1821 imposed limits on silver exports. Peru found a partial replacement for silver with guano, which was mined and exported for use as an organic fertilizer and as a source of nitrates for explosives. Chile hit the jackpot with guano, nitrate, and copper exports, of crucial importance during the chemical- and electricity-driven second Industrial Revolution in Germany and the United States.

In other Latin American countries, tropical and subtropical cash crops defined export-led economic growth during the mid-1800s. In Brazil, Colombia, and Costa Rica, labor-intensive coffee growing redefined the agricultural sector. In Argentina, the production of jerked (dried) beef, similarly labor-intensive, refashioned the ranching economy. The main importers of this beef were regions in the Americas where plantation slavery continued into the second half of the 1800s, especially the United States, Brazil, and Cuba. The latter, which remained a Spanish colony until 1895, profited from the relocation of sugarcane plantations from the mainland and

Caribbean islands after the British outlawing of the slave trade (1807) and slavery itself (1834) as well as the Latin American wars of independence (1810–1826).

In the long run, however, like silver, cane sugar had a limited future, given the rise of beet sugar production in Europe. Minerals and cash crops were excellent for export-led economic growth, especially if they required secondary activities such as the processing of meat or the use of mining machinery. But competition on the world market increased during the 1800s, and thus there was ultimately a ceiling, which was reached in the 1890s.

**Broadening of Exports**    With their eyes increasingly focused on exports, Latin American governments responded quickly to the increased market opportunities resulting from the Industrial Revolution in Great Britain, the European continent, and the United States. Peru broadened its mineral exports with copper, Bolivia with tin, and Chile with nitrates. Brazil and Peru added rubber, Argentina and Uruguay wool, and Mexico *henequen* (a fiber for ropes and sacks) to its traditional exports. Luxuries from tropical Latin America, like coffee, cacao (for chocolate bars, invented in 1847), vanilla, and bananas, joined sugar after 1850 in becoming affordable mass consumer items in the industrialized countries. Argentina, with investments in refrigeration made by Britain, added frozen meat to this list in 1883. This commodity diversification met not only the broadened demand of the second Industrial Revolution, with its need for chemicals and electricity, but also the demand for consumer goods among the newly affluent middle classes.

Since the choice among minerals and crops was limited, however, most nations remained wedded to one commodity only (50 percent of exports or more). Only two, Argentina and Peru, were able to diversify (exports of less than 25 percent for the leading commodity). They were more successful at distributing their exports over the four main industrial markets of Great Britain, Germany, France, and the United States. On the eve of World War I the United States had grown to be the most important trading partner in 11 of the 21 Latin American countries. Given its own endowments and under the conditions of world trade in the second half of the nineteenth century, the continent's trade was relatively well diversified.

The prices of all Latin American commodities fluctuated substantially during the second half of the nineteenth century, in contrast to the imported manufactured goods (primarily textiles, metal utensils, and implements), which became cheaper over time. In fact, Brazil's government was so concerned about fluctuating coffee prices in the 1890s that it introduced the Taubaté coffee valorization scheme in 1906. As the largest producer, it regulated the amount of coffee offered on the world market, carefully adjusting production to keep market prices relatively stable in much the same way that oil-producing countries would later do with petroleum.

Since coffee trees need 5 years to mature, Brazil was largely successful with its scheme until World War I, when global conditions changed. An American oligopoly (the United and Standard Fruit Companies) in control of banana production in Central America from the 1890s controlled prices similarly. A careful investigation of commodity prices by economic historians has resulted in the conclusion that, in spite of all fluctuations, commodity prices rose overall during 1850–1914.

**Rising Living Standards**    From all evidence, in the period from the middle of the 1800s to the eve of World War I, Latin American governments can be judged as having been successful with their choice of export-led growth as their consensus policy. Living standards rose, as measured in gross domestic product (GDP). At various times during 1850–1900, between five and eight Latin American countries kept pace with the living standards in the industrialized countries. Argentina and Chile were the most consistent leaders throughout the period. Thus, although many politicians were aware that at some point their countries would have to industrialize in addition to relying on commodity export growth, they can perhaps be forgiven for keeping their faith in exports as the engine for improved living standards right up to World War I.

**Labor and Immigrants**    As in the industrialized countries, the profitability of exports was achieved through low wages. Together with the rest of the world, Latin America experienced high population increases during the 1800s. The population grew sevenfold, to 74 million, although it remained small in comparison to the populations of Europe, which doubled to 408 million, and Africa and Asia, which each grew by one-third to 113 and 947 million, respectively. The increases were not large enough to alter the favorable land–person ratio, so it is not surprising that the high demand for labor continued during the 1800s. This demand, of course, was the reason the institution of forced labor—revolving labor duties (*mit'a*) among Amerindians in the Andes and slavery—had come into existence in the first place.

Not surprisingly, *mit'a* and slavery continued during the 1800s, liberal constitutionalism notwithstanding, in a number of countries. Even where forced labor was abolished early, moreover, low wages continued. One would have expected wages to rise rapidly, given the continuing conditions of labor shortage and land availability. Mine operators and landowners, however, were reluctant to raise wages

**Dining Hall for Recently Arrived Immigrants, Buenos Aires.** Immigrants, all male, and more than likely all Spanish and Italian, rub shoulders sometime around 1900 in a dining hall in Buenos Aires set up for newly arrived immigrants. By 1914, 20 percent each of the population of Argentina had been born in Spain and Italy.

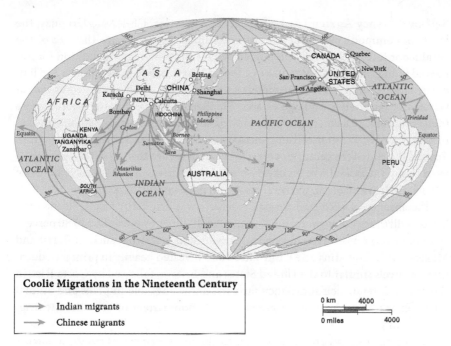

**Coolie Migrations in the Nineteenth Century**

→ Indian migrants

→ Chinese migrants

0 km    4000
0 miles    4000

MAP 23.4 **Non-Western Migrations in the Nineteenth Century.**

because they feared for the competitiveness of their commodities on the world market. They could get away with low wages because of ethnic discrimination: Racism trumped market conditions. Nevertheless, on occasion labor shortages were so severe and European immigration so insufficient that governments resorted to measures of selective mass immigration, in order to enlarge the labor pool.

Typical examples of selective immigration were *coolies* (from Urdu *kuli*, hireling)—that is, indentured laborers recruited from India and China on 5- or 10-year contracts working off the costs of their transportation. During 1847–1874, nearly half a million East Indians traveled to various European colonies in the Caribbean. Similarly, 235,000 Chinese came to Peru, Cuba, and Costa Rica, working in guano pits and silver mines, on sugar and cotton plantations, and later on railroads. If the experience of five Caribbean islands can be taken as a guide, only about 10 percent of the coolies returned home. Coolie migration to Latin America, therefore, can be described as a major part of the pattern of massive migration streams across the world that typified the nineteenth century (see Map 23.4).

Immigration to Latin America from Europe was less controlled, more regular, and on a much bigger scale. In Argentina, Uruguay, Brazil, and Chile, Italians and Spaniards settled in large numbers from around 1870 on. In Argentina, nearly one-third of the population consisted of immigrants, a share much higher than at any time in the United States. The Italian population of Argentina numbered close to 1 million by the turn of the century. Most immigrants settled in cities, and Buenos Aires became the first city on the continent with more than a million people. Only here did a semiregular labor market develop, with rising urban and rural wages prior to World War I. Elsewhere in Latin America, governments, beholden to large landowners, feared the rise of cities with immigrant laborers who did not share their interests. They, therefore, opposed mass immigration.

**Self-Sufficiency Agriculture**    Except for Argentina, Chile, and Uruguay, the levels of commodity exports did not rise sufficiently to reduce the size of the rural labor force engaged in self-sufficiency farming—a major condition for improved living standards. On the eve of World War I, between two-thirds and half of the laborers in most Latin American countries were still employed as tenant farmers or farmhands on large estates. Smaller numbers of these laborers were indigenous village farmers who owned their small farmsteads. Their contribution to the national GDP in Brazil and Mexico, for example, was less than one-quarter. Toward the end of the century, observers began to realize that export-led growth—even though it looked like an effective economic driver—did not have much of a transformative effect on the rural masses in most countries.

The absence of such transformative effects was especially visible in the high levels of illiteracy among rural inhabitants. Adult illiteracy rates of up to 80 percent were not uncommon, even in relatively diversified countries, such as Brazil and Mexico. Only Argentina and Chile after 1860 invested heavily in primary education, on levels similar to the United States and Britain, followed by Costa Rica in the 1890s. Literate self-sufficiency farmers, knowledgeable in plant and animal selection as well as fertilizers, were practically nonexistent prior to the Mexican Revolution.

Governments paid greater attention to the improvement of rural infrastructures from about 1870 onward, with the development of railroads. Almost everywhere, they looked to direct foreign investment, given the low-yielding and highly regressive trade taxes on which the relatively slim central domestic revenues depended. The foreign investors or consortiums built these railroads primarily for the transportation of commodities to ports. Many self-sufficiency farmers and even landlords, therefore, received little encouragement to produce more food staples for urban markets inland. Argentina and Chile, followed by Costa Rica and Uruguay, built the most railroads. Correspondingly, with fertilizers and better implements available via railroads, corn yields quintupled in Argentina. Conversely, these yields changed little in Mexico outside the railroad corridors concentrated in the north and center. Overall, the Latin American railroad network represented only about one-fifth to one-third of that in other Western developing settler countries, such as Australia, Canada, and New Zealand.

**Mexican Textile Factory.** Cocolapam in the state of Veracruz was the site of the first Mexican cotton textile factory, founded in 1836 by Lucas Alamán, a Mexican government minister and investment banker. Its machinery, imported from Great Britain, was water-driven. The textiles it produced remained inferior to imports, but they were cheap and satisfied the needs of most Mexicans.

**Factories**    Until about 1870, the handicrafts sector met the demands of the rural and low-earning urban populations. It produced cheap, low-quality textiles, shoes, soap, candles, tools, implements, cutlery, and horse tack. As is well known, this sector failed in most parts of the world during the 1800s or 1900s to mechanize itself and establish a modern factory system. Latin America was no exception. Most crafts shops were based on family labor, with a high degree of self-exploitation, unconnected to the landowning elite and deemed too small by lending banks. There was no path from workshops to factories.

However, even entrepreneurial investors interested in building factories for the manufacture of yarn or textiles were hampered in their efforts. They had little chance of success prior to the appearance of public utilities in the 1880s, providing water during the dry season and electricity as an energy source, in the absence of high-quality coal in most parts of Latin America. Even then, the risk of engaging in manufacturing, requiring long-term strategies with no or low profits, was so great that the typical founders of factories were not Creoles but European immigrants.

In Argentina and Chile these immigrants labored hard during their first years after arrival and saved the start-up capital necessary to launch small but modern textile, food-processing, and beverage factories. Argentina, Chile, Mexico, and Peru made the greatest advances toward factory industrialization, producing import-substituting consumer goods to the tune of 50–80 percent. Prior to World War I, the only country that took the step from consumer goods to capital goods (goods for building and equipping factories) was Mexico. This occurred with the foundation of the Fundidora Iron and Steel Mill in 1910 in Monterrey, which, however, was unprofitable for a long time. Full capital goods industrialization had to await the postwar period.

## Culture, Family, and the Status of Women

Economic growth and urbanization added considerably to the growth of constitutional-nationalist modernity in Latin America. But the absence of industrialization until the end of the nineteenth century slowed the transformation of society and its cultural institutions. The law and custom represented by the Catholic Church remained pervasive. In the second half of the nineteenth century, however, with the diversification of the urban population, the idea of separating church and state gained adherents, with some major legal consequences for social institutions.

**Role of the Church**   In most countries, repeated attempts by governments after independence to reduce the role of the Catholic Church in society remained unsuccessful. The church resisted the efforts of the constitutional nationalists to carry out land expropriations and to separate state and church in social legislation. In a number of civil codes women's rights in inheritance and property control improved, but overall husbands retained their patriarchal rights over their families. Typically, they were entitled to the control over the family budget, contractual engagements, choice of husbands for their daughters (up to age 25 in some countries), or residence of unmarried daughters (at home, up to age 30). Only from the middle of the nineteenth century did the influence of the Catholic Church diminish sufficiently to allow legislation for secular marriages and divorce in a number of countries. Catholicism remained doctrinally unchanged.

**Family Relations**   As it also developed in the Euro-American Victorian world, on the cultural level there was a popular ideal in nineteenth-century Latin America of nuclear-family domesticity. But, as research has also shown, in both places this was often honored more in the breach than the observance. That is to say, in Mexico and South America, despite the long-standing proverb *El hombre en la calle, la mujer en la casa* ("Men in the street, women in the home"), it was often the case that the two spheres were intermingled. In urban areas, women frequently ran shops, managed markets, were proprietors of *cantinas*, and performed a host of skilled and unskilled jobs, particularly in the textile and food trades. In rural areas, farm work on small holdings and peonages was often shared by men and women, though a number of individual tasks—plowing, for example—were most frequently done by men.

As in Europe and North America, too, there was a remarkably high level of widowhood and spinsterhood. In areas where the predominant form of employment was dangerous—mining, for example—the incidence of widowhood was very high. Widows often could not or chose not to remarry, especially if they had relatives to fall back on or were left an income. The stereotype of the stern patriarchal husband was also pervasive enough so that many middle-class women, often to the consternation of their families, chose not to marry at all.

Both of these conditions were common enough so that by one estimate one-third of all the households in Mexico City in the early nineteenth century were headed by women. Widows were entitled to their dowries and half of the community property, while boys and girls received equal portions of the inheritance. Thus, despite society's pressures to marry and raise children, many women did not marry or, after becoming widowed, remained single. In this sense, they achieved a considerable degree of autonomy in a male-dominated society. Thus social realities and legal rights diverged in early independent Latin America, even before legal reform.

**The Visual and Literary Arts**    To try to encapsulate the culture and arts of more than a continent—and one so vast and diverse as Latin America—is far beyond the scope of this textbook. Suffice it to say that the trend in nineteenth-century culture under the aegis of Spanish and Portuguese influences after independence was toward "indigenization": Much like the way the United States attempted during this time to break away from European art and literary influences, a similar movement pervaded the Latin American world. Along with attempts to form national and regional styles of their own, many countries also engaged in art as a nation-building exercise—artistic and literary celebrations of new national heroes or famous historic events through portraiture and landscape painting. Finally, there were also periodic engagements with the popular or folk arts of Amerindian peoples, mulattoes, mestizos, and Africans in celebration of regional uniqueness.

Literature to some extent paralleled the trajectory of the other arts. In the later eighteenth and early nineteenth centuries, an indigenous style developed, called *criollo*, for its inception and popularity in the Creole class. Literature often turned to themes befitting countries trying to establish themselves as nations with distinct historic pasts and great future potential. In some cases, critique of the present was the order of the day. Artists had a keen eye for a society caught between the specific kind of preindustrial tradition and modernity that characterized the Spanish- and Portuguese-speaking countries of the Americas during the nineteenth century.

# Putting It All Together

The term "banana republic" appeared for the first time in 1904. The American humorist O. Henry (1862–1910) coined it to represent politically unstable and economically poor Latin American countries, governed by small elites and relying on tropical exports, such as bananas. O. Henry had spent several years at the end of the nineteenth century in Honduras, hiding from US authorities. Thus, he knew whereof he spoke.

Today, political stability is much greater; but many parts of Latin America are still poor and underindustrialized. Consequently, the expression "banana republic" still resonates. Were Latin American elites, therefore, wrong to engage in a pattern of export-led growth through mineral and agricultural commodities? And did they collude with elites in the industrial countries to maneuver the continent into permanent dependence on the latter? Indeed, an entire generation of scholars in the second half of the twentieth century answered the question in the affirmative and wrote the history of the 1800s in gloomy and condemnatory tones. They called their analysis "dependency theory."

Contemporary historians are less certain about many of these conclusions. They compare Latin America not with the United States or western Europe but with the settler colonies of South Africa, Australia, and New Zealand or the old empires of the Middle East and Asia. In these comparisons, Latin America did very well and was not any more dependent on the industrializing countries than the latter were on Latin America.

Dependence increased only at the very end of the 1800s when industrial countries like the United States and Britain began to make significant capital investments. It was then that foreign companies, such as those that owned railroads in Nicaragua and Honduras, succeeded in exploiting and controlling production and export. The question we may need to ask then is not why Latin America failed to industrialize in the 1800s but, rather, whether Latin America, selecting from the available choices, made the right decision when it opted for export-led growth up to about 1890. Did such a choice represent a "third way" toward economic growth, separate from industrial capitalism and tenacious attempts to keep economies closed off from the vagaries of world trade? Perhaps it did.

▶ For additional resources, including maps, primary sources, visuals, and quizzes, please go to www.oup.com/us/vonsivers. Please see the Further Resources section at the back of the book for additional readings and suggested websites.

# Against the Grain

# Early Industrialization in Chile?

In the early 1880s, Chilean businessmen began to discuss the idea of moving away from exclusive reliance on the export of coal and copper, as world market prices for those commodities fluctuated widely, and encouraging the turn to industrialization. They founded the Society for the Stimulation of Manufacturing in 1883, with the purpose of building factories for the transformation of raw materials into finished goods. Their ideas turned into a concrete governmental program under the presidency of José Manuel Balmaceda Fernández (1886–1891), who in 1888 created a ministry for industry and public works. Balmaceda, a black sheep of Chile's conservative Creole class, had strong liberal-constitutionalist convictions and was acutely aware of Chile's changing economic and social conditions in the last quarter of the century.

Chile had experienced a substantial population increase, from 2 to 2.5 million during 1875–1885. The urban population had grown even faster, rising from half to two-thirds the size of the rural population during the same time. Farmers and farmhands were particularly drawn to the mining cities in the newly acquired north (as the result of Chile winning the War of the Pacific during 1879–1884 against Peru and Bolivia), with its nitrate deposits. Other cities had grown near the existing coal and copper mines further south. Santiago, Valparaíso, and Concepción had evolved into major urban centers. Although farming still supported the majority of Chileans, urban employments had risen greatly in numbers and importance.

Balmaceda's new ministry for industry and public works engaged in a massive investment program in education, railroads, ports, armaments, and naval ships, financed with the revenue from mining exports, including the northern nitrates. Keeping at least a portion of these nitrates in the country and making them the foundation for a chemical industry became a newly envisaged option. The second Industrial Revolution had begun during the 1860s in Germany and the United States on the basis of nitrates, crucial for the production of sulfuric acid, which, in turn, was used for the production of glass, soap, bleach, paper, dyes, pottery, and nitroglycerin—all transformative industries absorbing large numbers of the urban population of unskilled and skilled laborers.

Unfortunately, Balmaceda's energetic program of import-substitution industrialization fell apart as soon as 1891, without any outside imperialist British or other foreign intervention. Perhaps Balmaceda's investment program was too much, introduced too fast. Favoritism in appointments and corruption among office holders aroused opposition not only among the conservative Creole landowners but also among dissident liberals who disliked Balmaceda's imperious style. The opposition unleashed a civil war, in which Balmaceda was deposed. With Balmaceda's suicide the incipient indigenous industrialization program ended, apparently still too weak against the dominant policy of export-led economic growth based on mineral extraction.

- Why and how does rapid urbanization create the demand for industrialization?

- Was Balmaceda too progressive for the Chilean Creole class? Should he have attempted a different course?

# Thinking Through Patterns

▶ **Which factors in the complex ethnic and social structures of Latin America were responsible for the emergence of authoritarian politicians, or caudillos?**

Similar to the United States and France, which also underwent revolutions in the late 1700s and early 1800s, Latin America's independence movements (1810–1824) did not extend the constitutional revolution beyond a small number of property owners who inhabited the highest levels of the social strata. The dominant class of large landlords and plantation owners was conservative and did not favor land reform for the benefit of small farmers. Urban professionals and craftspeople, divided in many places by ethnicity, did not share common interests that allowed them to provide an effective opposition to the landed class. Landowning and plantation interests thus protected themselves through authoritarian caudillo politics and sought to keep the opposition weak.

In colonial times, Latin America was the warm-weather extension of Europe, sending its mineral and agricultural commodities to Europe. When it acquired its independence and Europe industrialized during the 1800s, these commodities became even more important, and the continent opted for a pattern of export-led development. This meant the systematic increase of mineral and agricultural commodity exports, with rising living standards not only for those who profited directly from the exports but also for many in the urban centers. Even with rising living standards it became clear by the turn of the century that a supplementary policy of industrialization had to be pursued.

▶ **Why did Latin American countries, after achieving independence, opt for a continuation of mineral and agricultural commodity exports?**

▶ **How do the social and economic structures of this period continue to affect the course of Latin America today?**

Many countries in Latin America are barely richer than they were in the 1800s. Even though industry, mineral and commodity exports, and services expanded in urban centers in the early part of the twentieth century, poor farmers with low incomes continued to be a drag on development. This phenomenon still characterizes many parts of Latin America today.

# Patterns of Evidence: Sources for Chapter 23

## SOURCE 23.1

## Memoirs of General Antonio López de Santa Anna

### 1872

Santa Anna (1794–1876) is recognized today by Americans, and especially by Texans, primarily for his successful siege of the Alamo in March 1836. However, he also epitomized the caudillo type in nineteenth-century Mexico, dominating his country's political life and weathering a series of highs and lows throughout his long career. Although he served as president for 11 nonconsecutive terms (some of only a few months) over a period of 22 years, Santa Anna is more famous for his military achievements and losses—including some extraordinary adventures. For example, in an 1838 battle against the French at Veracruz, Santa Anna's leg was shattered during a cannon volley. The leg was amputated and buried with full military honors. Exiled multiple times, to Cuba, Jamaica, Colombia, and even the United States, Santa Anna devoted his final years to compiling his memoirs, an excerpt of which is translated below. This passage details his turbulent political career—at least from his perspective—in the early 1840s.

Sixty-two days after my foot had been amputated, Gen. Guadalupe Victoria called on me at the instigation of the government. He informed me that a revolution was threatening, and that the government desired me to take [Anastasio] Bustamante's place as temporary president in this time of trial. How well the people knew me! They knew I would never desert my principles and would always be on hand when my country needed me!

I was carried to the capital on a litter. Although my trip was made with extreme care, the hardships of the journey and the change of climate weakened me. However, despite my poor health, I assumed the office of president immediately. The tasks involved completely overwhelmed me,

Source: Antonio López de Santa Anna, *The Eagle: The Autobiography of Santa Anna*, ed. and trans. Ann Fears Crawford (Austin, TX: Pemberton, 1967), 65–69, as excerpted in James A. Wood and John Charles Chasteen, *Problems in Modern Latin American History: Sources and Interpretations*, 3rd ed. (Lanham, MD: Rowman & Littlefield, 2009), 79–81.

but I pulled through. The government forces triumphed throughout the country. Gen. Gabriel Valencia captured and executed the hope of the revolution, José A. Mejia, in the vicinity of the town of Acajeta. The dreaded threat of revolution died, and peace was restored.

Bustamante once again took up the reins of government, and I retired to [my estate] to complete my recovery. However, Bustamante's loss of prestige with the people caused his government to fail. In the town of Guadalajara, in the early months of 1841, arrangements were made for Bustamante to abdicate and for the reform of the Constitution of 1824. In Tacubaya, a council of generals agreed upon basic ground rules to help bring about these reforms, and once again I assumed the office of provisional president. . . .

In order to conform to public opinion, I called together a group of prominent citizens from all states in the nation to instigate needed reforms. This group drew up *The Principles of Political Organization* on June 12, 1844. This constitution was circulated by the government, and each of the states accepted and ratified it without dissension.

In September 1844, my beloved wife died. Greater sorrow I had never known! General of Division Valentín Canalizo substituted for me while I devoted myself to family matters.

During the first session under our new Constitution, I was duly elected president and called to the capital to administer the customary oath. The election saddened me even more. My deep melancholy drove me to abhor the glamorous life of the capital and to prefer a life of solitude. I resigned the noble office to which I had been called, but the public intruded upon my privacy, pleading that I return. My friends, with the greatest of good faith, also begged me to resume my office. Their pleas led me to sacrifice myself to the public good. I withdrew my resignation.

Near the end of October, General [Mariano] Paredes rebelled against the government in Guadalajara. When the news was communicated to me by the government, they ordered me to take the troops quartered in Jalapa and march to the capital. I instantly obeyed the orders. Paredes had been relieved of his command of the Capital District due to excesses of intoxication while he was commanding his troops. He bore a grudge and was determined to take revenge. In our country one spark was sufficient to set aflame a revolution.

I was marching toward Guadalajara under orders, when I received the news of an upheaval in the capital. The situation seemed serious, and I halted my advance. Details of the revolt in the capital arrived soon after my halt. The messenger read me the following infamous words:

> The majority of Congress openly favor the Paredes revolution. The government, in self-defense or wishing to avoid revolution, has issued a decree by which the sessions of Congress have been suspended. This decree has served as a pretext for General José J. Herrera to join the revolt. Rioters have torn down the bronze bust of President Santa Anna that stood in the Plaza del Mercado. They have also taken his amputated foot from the cemetery of Santa Paula and proceeded to drag it through the streets to the sounds of savage laughter.

I interrupted the narrator, exclaiming "Stop! I don't wish to hear any more! Almighty God! A member of my body, lost in the service of my country, dragged from the funeral urn, broken into bits to be made sport of in such a barbaric manner!" In that moment of grief and frenzy, I decided to leave my native country, object of my dreams and of my illusions, for all time.

▶ **Working with Sources**

1. How were Santa Anna's personal setbacks interwoven with his political career in this period, at least in his recollection?

2. What does Santa Anna's memoir reveal about the presumed indispensability of the caudillo, and the connection between his physical body and his political power?

## SOURCE 23.2

# Simón Bolívar, "The Jamaica Letter"

### September 6, 1815

Simón Bolívar (1783–1830), the eventual liberator of northern South America from Spanish control, was born in Venezuela but profoundly influenced by the culture of peninsular Spain and the European Enlightenment. He visited Spain in 1799, and traveled to Paris to witness Napoleon's coronation as emperor in 1804. Bolívar aspired to bring the values of the Enlightenment, and particularly the notions of liberty and popular sovereignty, to his homeland. Having declared an independent Venezuela in 1812, he was driven into exile in British Jamaica with the landing of a Spanish expeditionary force in 1815. In 1816, he returned with a military force and assumed the presidency of "Gran Colombia" in 1822. The following letter is renowned for its expression of Bolívar's ambitions, at a time when the outcome of "liberation" from Spain seemed uncertain.

Kingston, Jamaica, September 6, 1815. My dear Sir:
I hasten to reply to the letter of the 29th ultimo which you had the honor of sending me and which I received with the greatest satisfaction.

. . .

With what a feeling of gratitude I read that passage in your letter in which you say to me: "I hope that the success which then followed Spanish arms may now turn in favor of their adversaries, the badly oppressed people of South America." I take this hope as a prediction, if it is justice that determines man's contests. Success will crown our efforts, because the destiny of America has been irrevocably

Source: *Selected Writings of Bolívar*, trans. Lewis Bertrand (New York: Colonial, 1951), as edited in: http://faculty.smu.edu/bakewell/BAKEWELL/texts/jamaica-letter.html.

decided; the tie that bound her to Spain has been severed. Only a concept maintained that tie and kept the parts of that immense monarchy together. That which formerly bound them now divides them. The hatred that the Peninsula has inspired in us is greater than the ocean between us. It would be easier to have the two continents meet than to reconcile the spirits of the two countries. The habit of obedience; a community of interest, of understanding, of religion; mutual goodwill; a tender regard for the birthplace and good name of our forefathers; in short, all that gave rise to our hopes, came to us from Spain. As a result there was a born principle of affinity that seemed eternal, notwithstanding the misbehavior of our rulers which weakened that sympathy, or, rather, that bond enforced by the domination of their rule. At present the contrary attitude persists: we are threatened with the fear of death, dishonor, and every harm; there is nothing we have not suffered at the hands of that unnatural stepmother—Spain. The veil has been torn asunder. We have already seen the light, and it is not our desire to be thrust back into darkness. The chains have been broken; we have been freed, and now our enemies seek to enslave us anew. For this reason America fights desperately, and seldom has desperation failed to achieve victory.

Because successes have been partial and spasmodic, we must not lose faith. In some regions the Independents triumph, while in others the tyrants have the advantage. What is the end result? Is not the entire New World in motion, armed for defense? We have but to look around us on this hemisphere to witness a simultaneous struggle at every point.

. . .

This picture represents, on a military map, an area of 2,000 longitudinal and 900 latitudinal leagues at its greatest point, wherein 16,000,000 Americans either defend their rights or suffer repression at the hands of Spain, which, although once the world's greatest empire, is now too weak, with what little is left her, to rule the new hemisphere or even to maintain herself in the old. And shall Europe, the civilized, the merchant, the lover of liberty allow an aged serpent, bent only on satisfying its venomous rage, devour the fairest part of our globe? What! Is Europe deaf to the clamor of her own interests? Has she no eyes to see justice? Has she grown so hardened as to become insensible? The more I ponder these questions, the more I am confused. I am led to think that America's disappearance is desired; but this is impossible because all Europe is not Spain. What madness for our enemy to hope to reconquer America when she has no navy, no funds, and almost no soldiers! Those troops which she has are scarcely adequate to keep her own people in a state of forced obedience and to defend herself from her neighbors. On the other hand, can that nation carry on the exclusive commerce of one-half the world when it lacks manufactures, agricultural products, crafts and sciences, and even a policy? Assume that this mad venture were successful, and further assume that pacification ensued, would not the sons of the Americans of today, together with the sons of the European *reconquistadores* twenty years hence, conceive the same patriotic designs that are now being fought for?

. . .

More than anyone, I desire to see America fashioned into the greatest nation in the world, greatest not so much by virtue of her area and wealth as by her freedom and glory. Although I seek perfection for the government of my country, I cannot persuade myself that the New World can, at the moment, be organized as a great republic. Since it is impossible, I dare not desire it; yet much less do I desire to have all America a monarchy because this plan is not only impracticable but also impossible. Wrongs now existing could not be righted, and our emancipation would be fruitless. The American states need the care of paternal governments to heal the sores and wounds of despotism and war. The parent country, for example, might be Mexico, the only country fitted for the position by her intrinsic strength, and without such power there can be no parent country. Let us assume it were to be the Isthmus of Panamá, the most central point of this vast continent. Would not all parts continue in their lethargy and even in their present disorder? For a single government to infuse life into the New World; to put into use all the resources for public prosperity; to improve, educate, and perfect the New World, that government would have to possess the authority of a god, much less the knowledge and virtues of mankind.

. . .

It is a grandiose idea to think of consolidating the New World into a single nation, united by pacts into a single bond. It is reasoned that, as these parts have a common origin, language, customs, and religion, they ought to have a single government to permit the newly formed states to unite in a confederation. But this is not possible. Actually, America is separated by climatic differences, geographic diversity, conflicting interests, and dissimilar characteristics. How beautiful it would be if the Isthmus of Panamá could be for us what the Isthmus of Corinth was for the Greeks! Would to God that some day we may have the good fortune to convene there an august assembly of representatives of republics, kingdoms, and empires to deliberate upon the high interests of peace and war with the nations of the other three-quarters of the globe. This type of organization may come to pass in some happier period of our regeneration. But any other plan, such as that of Abbé St. Pierre, who in laudable delirium conceived the idea of assembling a European congress to decide the fate and interests of those nations, would be meaningless.

Among the popular and representative systems, I do not favor the federal system. It is over-perfect, and it demands political virtues and talents far superior to our own. For the same reason I reject a monarchy that is part aristocracy and part democracy, although with such a government England has achieved much fortune and splendor. Since it is not possible for us to select the most perfect and complete form of government, let us avoid falling into demagogic anarchy or monocratic tyranny. These opposite extremes would only wreck us on similar reefs of misfortune and dishonor; hence, we must seek a mean between them. I say: Do not adopt the best system of government, but the one that is most likely to succeed.

▶ **Working with Sources**

1. How does Bolívar's advice combine practical suggestions with idealistic principles?
2. To what extent does Bolívar believe the revolt to have been triggered by Spain's refusal to live up to its own best principles?

## SOURCE 23.3

# Domingo Faustino Sarmiento, *Travels in the United States in 1847*

1849

The journalist and eventual Argentine president Sarmiento (1811–1888) is most famous today for his novel *Facundo: Civilization and Barbarism* (1845), a sharp and daring satire of the caudillo Juán Manuel de Rosas. His indictment of Rosas, thinly disguised as the biography of another brutal dictator (called Juán Facundo Quiroga), was written while Sarmiento was an exile from the regime. Representing the government of Chile, Sarmiento traveled throughout Europe, North Africa, and North America, observing local political and social conditions closely and comparing them with what he knew of Argentine society. The result is a fascinating travelogue of his impressions of and reactions to the people of the United States, with vivid descriptions of many of its manmade and natural wonders. Nevertheless, his hopes for his native Argentina were never very far from the foreground, as this excerpt reveals.

The fatal error of the Spanish colonization of South America, the deep wound which has condemned present generations to inertia and backwardness, was in the system of land distribution. In Chile, great concessions of land, measuring from one hill to another and from the side of a river to the banks of an arroyo, were given to the conquistadors. The captains established earldoms for themselves, while their soldiers, fathers of the sharecropper, that worker without land who multiplies without increasing the number of his buildings, sheltered themselves in the shade of their improvised roofs. The passion to occupy lands in the name of the king drove men to dominion over entire districts, which put great distances between landowners so that after three centuries the intervening land

Source: Domingo Faustino Sarmiento, *Travels in the United States in 1847*, trans. Michael Aaron Rockland (Princeton, NJ: Princeton University Press, 1970), 164–166.

dimension. It was then placed in a small leather pouch, which was sewn shut. In many cases, besides the paper, other ingredients appeared in those charms. A police scribe described the contents of one amulet as follows:

> Little bundles or leather pouches were opened at this time by cutting them at the seams with a penknife. Inside were found several pieces of insignificant things such as cotton wrapped in a little powder [sic], others with tiny scraps of garbage, and little sacks with some seashells inside. Inside one of the leather pouches was a piece of paper with Arabic letters written on it.

The "insignificant" substances referred to here likely included sand moistened beforehand in some sort of holy water, perhaps water used by some renowned and pious alufá or water used to wash the tablets on which Malês wrote their religious texts. In the latter case, this water could also be drunk, since the ink was made of burnt rice; such a drink was believed to seal the body against outside harm. Some of the amulets were made of West African fabric; leather was used more often, since it provided better protection for both the sacred words and the other charms. There is a remarkable similarity between the Bahian Malê talismans and those still in use in black Africa, although the Bahian amulet seems to have had more "pagan" ingredients. According to Vincent Monteil, "In general the Islamic Talisman is a leather case, sewn together and containing a piece of stiff cardboard . . . and inside this is a folded piece of paper on which are written phrases in praise of God and cabalistic symbols—that is, Arabic letters, pentacles, and the like." Kabbalistic drawings such as the ones mentioned here were found in several amulets confiscated in 1835.

The Magrebian Arabic in the Malê amulets found on the bodies of dead rebels or in Muslims' houses has been studied and translated by Vincent Monteil and Rolf Reichert. Reichert took stock of twelve amulets, some of which contained kabbalistic shapes. . . .

The magic in the Islamic texts and drawings worked as protection against various threats. The Africans arrested in 1835 said little about their magic, and when they did say something, they avoided linking it to the revolt. However, besides their obvious political function, these amulets were especially designed to control daily life. A freedman named Silvestre José Antônio, a merchant, was arrested with five amulets in his case. He declared they "were prayers to save [him] from any unfortunate happenstance in his travels through the Recôncavo." Whether in Africa or in Brazil, a good Muslim merchant never traveled without a considerable number of protecting charms. A booklet of Islamic prayers could also work to protect its holder against evil spells. It was for that reason that a freedman named Pedro Pinto asked a literate Malê to make one for him, so he could "be free from wagging tongues." Pedro, by the way, was not a Malê.

. . .

Even so, one Malê fisherman made a good living from amulet making. According to one witness, Antônio, a Hausa slave residing in Itapagipe, "wrote prayers in his language and sold them to his partners making 4 *patacas* [1,280 réis] a day doing that." When he was arrested, a writing quill was found in his room: "Asked . . . by the justice [of the peace] why he kept such a quill, the same slave answered that he kept it so as to write things having to do with his Nation. He was then asked to write and he made a few scribbles with the phoney quill and the justice asked . . . what he had written. He answered that what he had written was the name of the 'Hail Mary.'" This Islamic-Christian melding does not seem to have impressed the justice of the peace. Antônio calmly went on telling his questioners that "when he was a young boy in his homeland, he went to school," and there he had learned Arabic so as to write "prayers according to the schism of his homeland."

▶ **Working with Sources**

1. How did the Malês use the written word to resist authority, and why did they use the Arabic language?

2. What do the documents created by the slaveholders and their supporting institutions reveal about the power of written sources as well?

## SOURCE 23.5

# Photograph of a Chinese coolie, Peru

### 1881

Chinese migration to Latin America was a major part of the pattern of mass migration streams across the world that typified the nineteenth century. "Coolies" (from the Urdu word *kuli*, or "hireling") were indentured laborers recruited from India and China on 5- or 10-year contracts, who were forced to work to pay off the cost of their transportation. Roughly 235,000 Chinese came to Peru, Cuba, and Costa Rica, working in guano pits and silver mines, on sugar and cotton plantations, and later on railroads. Such work contracts were little better than slavery, and oftentimes were accompanied by institutions familiar from enslavement itself. This photograph, published in a Chilean army newspaper, depicts a Chinese coolie who is being liberated by an invading Chilean army in 1881.

▶ **Working with Sources**

1. Look closely at the man's feet and ankles. What might have been attached to him, and why?

2. How might this image have been deployed for propaganda purposes by the invading Chilean army?

Source: http://commons.wikimedia.org/wiki/
File:Enslaved_Chinese_coolie_in_Peru_1881.jpg.

# Chapter **24** 1750–1910

# The Challenge of Modernity

## EAST ASIA

In Asia, our two countries, China and Japan, are the closest neighbors, and more-over have the same [written] language. How could we be enemies? Now for the time being we are fighting each other, but eventually we should work for perma-nent friendship . . . so that our Asiatic yellow race will not be encroached upon by the white race of Europe.

So commented the Chinese statesman Li Hongzhang to his Japanese counterpart, Ito Hirobumi, as they discussed terms to end the Sino–Japanese War in the Japanese town of Shimonoseki in the spring of 1895. For Li it was the culmination of more than three decades of frustration as China's most powerful advocate of *self-strengthening*—using new foreign technologies and concepts to preserve China's Confucian society in the face of European and American intrusion. During Li's lifetime such intrusions had come with alarming frequency. Now, at 71, he was forced to go to Japan to sue for peace as Japanese troops occupied Korea and southern Manchuria. To add injury to insult, he had just narrowly survived being shot in the face by a Japanese fanatic while en route to the peace talks.

For Ito, one of the architects of Japan's astonishing rise to power, the vic-tory over China was tinged with sadness and puzzlement as he responded: "Ten years ago when I was at Tientsin [Tianjin], I talked about reform with [you]. . . . Why is it that up to now not a single thing has been changed or

ABOVE: A Japanese print (1895) depicting negotiations held in the Japanese town of Shimonoseki to end the Sino–Japanese War.

reformed? This I deeply regret." This feeling was shared by Li, whose reply betrays a weary bitterness at China's deteriorating position: "At that time when I heard you . . . I was overcome with admiration . . . [at] your having vigorously changed your customs in Japan so as to reach the present stage. Affairs in my country have been so confined by tradition that I could not accomplish what I desired. . . . I am ashamed of having excessive wishes and lacking the power to fulfill them."

The significance of this rueful exchange was not lost on the other countries with interests in east Asia, who viewed the war's outcome with a mixture of fascination and alarm. Japan's surprisingly complete victory over China was cited as proof that it was now ready to join the ranks of the great powers. It also upset a shaky balance of power that was dependent on China's feeble Qing dynasty not collapsing altogether. Now Japan had dramatically raised the stakes. In addition to imposing a crippling indemnity on the Qing, reducing Korea to a client state, and annexing the island of Taiwan, the new Treaty of Shimonoseki called for the occupation by Japan of Manchuria's Liaodong Peninsula, which guarded the approaches to Beijing.

For Russia, France, and Germany, who saw their own interests threatened by this move, it was time to act. In what became known as the Triple Intervention, they threatened Japan with joint action if it did not abandon its claims to Liaodong. Unable to take on all three powers, the Japanese bitterly acquiesced. They grew more bitter the following year when the Qing secretly leased the territory to Russia in a desperate attempt to counter Japanese expansion. For the Japanese, this began a decade-long state of tension with Russia that would culminate in the Russo–Japanese War of 1904–1905. For the other powers in east Asia, it began a "race for concessions" in China that stopped just short of dismembering the empire.

For the Chinese, however, it marked the most dramatic and humiliating role reversal of the past 1,500 years. China had always viewed Japan in Confucian terms as a younger brother. Like Korea and Vietnam, Japan was considered to be on the cultural periphery of the Chinese world, acculturating to Chinese institutions and following Chinese examples in those things considered "civilized." Now, after barely a generation of exposure to Euro-American influence, Japan had eclipsed China as a military power and threatened to extend its sway throughout the region.

The new order in east Asia brought about by the Sino–Japanese War underscores the larger effects of one of the most momentous patterns of world history: the phenomenon of imperialism growing from the innovations that created scientific–industrial society—one of the foundations of modernity

## Seeing Patterns

▶ What was the impact of Western imperialism on the "regulated societies" of China and Japan?

▶ Why did European empire building in Asia have such dramatically different effects on China and Japan?

▶ How have historians seen the nature of these outside forces and their influences in east Asia?

that we have examined in this part of the text. As we began to see in the previous two chapters, in less than a century, European countries and their offshoots—and now Japan—expanded their power so rapidly and completely that on the eve of World War I in 1914 more than 85 percent of the world's people were under their control or influence. How were a very few countries like Japan able to resist and adapt to the broad forces of modernity, while China struggled to cope with its effects through most of the nineteenth and twentieth centuries?

# China and Japan in the Age of Imperialism

As we saw in Chapter 21, the reign of the Qing emperor Qianlong (r. 1736–1795) marked perhaps the high point of China's power in the early modern world and the period in which the first hints appeared of trouble to come. Some of the problems facing the Qing began to emerge within a year after Qianlong stepped down from the throne in 1795. A Buddhist sect called the White Lotus sparked a rebellion, which took years to suppress while at the same time highlighting the limitations of the Manchu bannermen as a military force. Less obvious, but perhaps more debilitating for the agrarian imperial order as a whole, were the new directions in economics. China was steadily drawn into the emerging European global commercial system, but the increasing forces of free trade were eroding its established systems of exchange control. Specifically, China's efforts to retain close control over its export trade in luxury goods coupled with efforts to eradicate the lucrative but illegal opium trade created a crisis with Great Britain in the summer of 1839. This crisis led to the First Opium War, China's first military encounter with the industrializing West.

## China and Maritime Trade, 1750–1839

By the 1790s, with the China trade at record levels and the French Revolution making European trade increasingly problematic, the British government sought to establish diplomatic relations with the Qing. In the summer of 1793, they dispatched Lord George Macartney, an experienced diplomat and colonial governor, to Beijing with a sizeable entourage and boatloads of presents. His mission was twofold: to persuade the Qianlong emperor to allow the stationing of diplomatic personnel in the Chinese capital and create a system for the separate handling of ordinary commercial matters and diplomacy along the lines of European practices. Qianlong, however, politely but firmly rebuffed Macartney's attempts to establish a British embassy, observing that China really had "no need of your country's ingenious manufactures." A second British mission in 1816 met with similar results.

The Imbalance of Trade?    One important reason that Europeans and Americans were anxious to bring the Chinese into their diplomatic system was the widespread perception that China was benefiting from a huge trade imbalance. Though recent scholarship has shown that China's economy actually supported much of the interconnected Eurasian commercial system, contemporary merchants and political economists were convinced that China's control of trade functioned in the same way as European mercantilism. Thus, they believed that the money paid to Chinese merchants essentially stayed in the "closed" economy of the Qing Empire, draining the West of its stocks of silver. However, as Qianlong's reply to Macartney noted, European merchants offered little that the Chinese needed or wanted.

Thus, by the end of the eighteenth century, European and American traders had become increasingly anxious to find something that Chinese merchants would buy in sufficient quantities to stem the flow of Western silver into China. By the beginning of the nineteenth century, a growing number of merchants were clandestinely turning to a lucrative new commodity, with tragic consequences. When tobacco was introduced into China from the Americas, the innovation of smoking quickly spread. In southwestern China, tribesmen living in remote mountain villages began combining small quantities of powdered opium with tobacco. The Dutch, who briefly maintained bases on Taiwan, also introduced the practice there, from which it spread gradually to the maritime provinces of south China. Disturbed by the growing use of opium beyond normal medicinal practice in the area, the Qing banned the smoking of the substance as early as 1729. For the rest of the century opium use remained a strictly local problem in China's south.

**Smugglers, Pirates, and "Foreign Mud"**  By the end of the eighteenth century, the British East India Company's territory in Bengal had come to include the area around Patna, historically a center of medicinal opium production. While company traders were strictly prohibited from carrying opium to China as contraband, an increasing number of noncompany merchants willing to take the risk discovered that they could circumvent Chinese regulations and sell small quantities of the drug for a tidy profit. Initially, their customers were the wealthy of Canton society; and the exotic "foreign mud," as opium was nicknamed, soon became a favorite local diversion. With success came increased demand, and by the early decades of the nineteenth century, an elaborate illicit system of delivery had been set up along the south China coast. Heavily armed ships unloaded their cargo of opium on small, sparsely inhabited offshore islands, from which Chinese middlemen picked up the drug and made their rounds on the mainland (see Map 24.1). The ever-rising profits from this illegal enterprise encouraged piracy and lawlessness along the coast, and the opium trade soon became a major irritant in relations between China and the West.

The relationship that the British East India Company and the government-licensed Chinese merchant guild, or *cohong*, had so carefully developed over the previous century was now being rapidly undermined by the new commerce.

**China**

1736–1795
Reign of Qianlong emperor

1793
Macartney mission to Beijing

1839–1842
First Opium War with Great Britain

1851–1864
Taiping Rebellion

1860–1895
Self-strengthening era

1894–1895
Sino–Japanese War

1898
"Hundred days" of reform; emperor placed under house arrest

1900
Boxer Rebellion

**Japan**

1853–1854
Perry mission opens trade and diplomatic relations with Japan

1863–1867
Restoration War

1868–1912
Reign of Emperor Meiji

1899–1902
Japan abrogates unequal treaties and negotiates alliance with Great Britain

1900
Seiyukai (Constitutional Government Party) founded

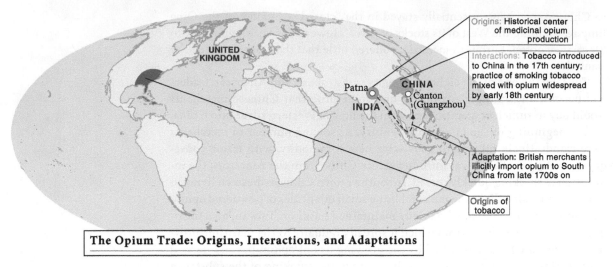

UNITED
KINGDOM

Patna    **CHINA**
            ○Canton
**INDIA**   (Guangzhou)

Origins: Historical center
of medicinal opium
production

Interactions: Tobacco introduced
to China in the 17th century;
practice of smoking tobacco
mixed with opium widespread
by early 18th century

Adaptation: British merchants
illicitly import opium to South
China from late 1700s on

Origins of
tobacco

**The Opium Trade: Origins, Interactions, and Adaptations**

MAP 24.1 **The Opium Trade: Origins, Interactions, Adaptations.**

Moreover, growing free-trade agitation in England put an end to the East India Company's monopoly on the China trade in 1833. With the monopoly lifted, the number of entrepreneurs seeking quick riches in the opium trade exploded. With wealth came power, and in the foreign trading "factories" in Canton, newcomers engaged in the opium trade vied for prestige with older firms involved in legitimate goods.

The push for legitimacy among the opium merchants coincided with an aggressive attempt by Westerners to force China to open additional trading ports for legal items. Chinese authorities, however, viewed this Western assertiveness as driven primarily by opium and Christian evangelism. The East India Company itself was now fatally compromised as well, since an estimated one-quarter of its revenues in India were directly tied to opium production.

Far worse, however, were the effects on the ordinary inhabitants of south China. The huge rise in availability and consequent plunge in prices increased opium usage to catastrophic levels. Its power to suppress pain and hunger made it attractive to the poor engaged in physical labor, though the dreamlike state it induced often made it dangerous to work under its influence. Its addictive properties led people to seek it even at the expense of food, thus creating a health crisis for tens of thousands, made infinitely worse by the drug's notoriously difficult withdrawal symptoms.

"Let us ask, where is your conscience? I have heard that the smoking of opium is very strictly forbidden by your country. . . . Since it is not permitted to do harm to your own country, then even less should you let it be passed on to the harm of other countries—how much less to China!"

—Lin Zexu, "A Letter to the English Ruler"

**Commissioner Lin Zexu** Matters came to a head in the spring of 1839. The Daoguang emperor sent Lin Zexu (1785–1850), a widely respected official with a reputation for courage and honesty, to Canton as an imperial commissioner. Lin, charged with cutting off the opium trade at its source, was given wide-ranging powers to deal with both Chinese and foreign traffickers. In addition to setting up facilities for the recovery of addicts, he demanded that all foreign merchants surrender their opium stocks and sign a pledge that they would not, under penalty of death,

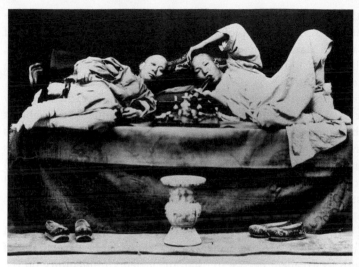

**Chinese Opium Smoker.** This photograph, taken in the early 1870s, shows the pervasiveness of the opium habit among ordinary Chinese. These men are smoking in the back room of a restaurant, a common practice, even here in British-controlled Hong Kong.

**Commissioner Lin Destroys the Opium.** This drawing depicts Lin Zexu "burning" 20,000 chests of opium surrendered by the foreign merchants. In fact, however, he did not actually the burn the drug, but mixed it with water, salt, and lime and flushed it through sluiceways out to sea. The mixture created clouds of fumes, which misled some onlookers into believing it had been burned. The legend was perpetuated by depictions like this one in a 1000 Canton newspaper as part of a series called "Portraits of the Achievements of Our Dynasty's Illustrious Officials."

deal in the drug anymore. He even wrote a letter to the young Queen Victoria in which he lectured her on the morality of the opium trade.

When the foreign community balked at surrendering the goods, Lin blockaded the port and withdrew all Chinese personnel from Western firms. His determined stance finally ended the stalemate, and the dealers eventually surrendered 20,000 chests of opium, with most also signing the pledge. Lin then publicly treated the opium with lime and water and flushed the resulting slurry into the sea. Following Lin's actions, however, the dealers appealed to the British government for compensation.

The British government decided to use the incident to settle the long-standing diplomatic impasse with the Qing over foreign representation and open ports. In a show of force, the British sent a fleet of warships to Canton to demand reparations for the destroyed opium, pressure the Qing to establish diplomatic relations, and open more ports. In sad contrast to the days four centuries earlier when Zheng He commanded his great fleets, the Chinese now had no real naval forces to contest the British. What vessels they had were modestly armed with seventeenth-century cannon and used for customs collection. The British fleet, on the other hand, was the most powerful in the world and in a high state of readiness. When negotiations broke down, a small Chinese squadron sailed out to confront the British men-o'-war. The British ships sank a number of the junks and easily scattered the Chinese squadron. Such inauspicious circumstances marked the beginning of the First Opium War (1839–1842) and, with it, a long, painful century of foreign intrusion, domination, and ultimately revolution for China.

## The Opium Wars and the Treaty Port Era
The hostilities that began in the fall of 1839 between China and Great Britain exposed the growing gap between the military capabilities of industrializing

countries and those, like China, whose armed forces had fallen into disuse. The military had never been an honored profession in China, and the consequences of maintaining scattered Manchu banner garrisons, discouraging militia recruiting, and underfunding the Chinese regular forces (Armies of the Green Standard) were immediately evident.

Over the next 2 years, with a brief truce called in 1841, the British methodically attacked and occupied ports along the Chinese coast from Canton to Shanghai at the mouth of the Yangzi River, for the most part without serious opposition. As the British planned to move north to put pressure on Beijing, Chinese officials opened negotiations in August 1842. The resulting Treaty of Nanjing (Nanking) marked the first of the century's "unequal treaties" that would be imposed throughout east Asia by European powers.

**The Treaty of Nanjing**    Curiously, the treaty ending the First Opium War did not mention opium. In the final agreement, the British claimed the island of Hong Kong, with its excellent deep-water harbor; levied an indemnity on the Chinese to pay the costs of the war; and forced the Chinese to open the ports of Shanghai, Ningbo, Fuzhou, and Xiamen (Amoy), in addition to Canton. The Chinese were also confronted with British insistence on **nontariff autonomy**: By treaty they could now charge no more than a 5 percent tariff on British goods. The British also imposed the policy of **extraterritoriality** in the newly open ports: British subjects who violated Chinese laws would be tried and punished by British consuls.

Over the next several years, the Chinese signed similar treaties with France and the United States. An important addition in these later treaties was the *most-favored nation* clause: Any new concessions granted to one country automatically reverted to those who by treaty were "most-favored nations." Thus, the time-honored Chinese diplomatic strategy of "using barbarians to check barbarians" was dealt a near-fatal blow (see Map 24.2).

**Nontariff autonomy:** The loss by a country of its right to set its own tariffs.

**Extraterritoriality:** The immunity of a country's nationals from the laws of their host country.

**Steam Power Comes to China.** The new technologies of the Industrial Revolution were on painful display in China in 1840 as the British gunboat HMS *Nemesis* took on provincial warships down the river from Canton. The *Nemesis* featured an armored hull put together in detachable sections, shallow draft and steam-powered paddle wheel propulsion for river fighting, and a large pivot gun to take on shore batteries. Its power and versatility convinced Lin Zexu and a growing number of Chinese officials over the coming decades that China needed, at the very least, the same kinds of "strong ships and effective cannon" if they were to defend their coasts and rivers. By the 1860s the first attempts at such craft were finally under way.

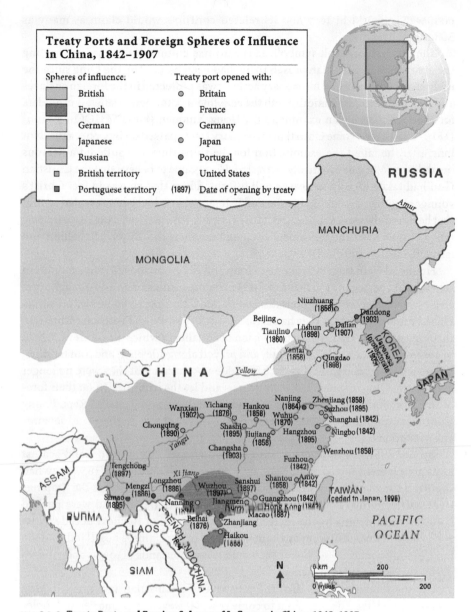

**Treaty Ports and Foreign Spheres of Influence in China, 1842–1907**

Spheres of influence:

- British
- French
- German
- Japanese
- Russian
- British territory
- Portuguese territory

Treaty port opened with:

- Britain
- France
- Germany
- Japan
- Portugal
- United States
- (1897) Date of opening by treaty

MAP 24.2  **Treaty Ports and Foreign Spheres of Influence in China, 1842–1907.**

**The Taiping Movement, 1851–1864**   In addition to the spread of the opium trade to the newly opened ports, long-established trade routes for more licit items swiftly shifted from Guangzhou to more convenient outlets. The growth of Shanghai was especially important in this regard because it served the Yangzi River, the greatest highway through China's heartland. Coastal trade also increased, while Hong Kong grew as the primary point of opium transfer to small smuggling vessels. The swiftness of all of these changes and their accompanying economic dislocation, along with smoldering discontent at the inability of the Qing government to resist foreign demands, made south China particularly volatile. In 1851 the region exploded in rebellion. Before it was over, this largest civil war in world history and its related conflicts would claim as many as 30 million lives.

The catalyst for revolt symbolized the diverse cultural influences penetrating the area. Though Christian proselytizing had been banned by the Qing since the early eighteenth century, missionary activity was protected in the foreign enclaves and now increased dramatically with the enactment of the new treaties. A candidate for the local Confucian examinations, Hong Xiuquan [hung SHIOO-chwahn] (1813–1864), read some Christian missionary tracts passed on by a colleague. Not long after, he failed the examination for the third time and suffered a nervous breakdown. When he eventually recovered, Hong came to believe that the Christian God had taken him up to heaven and informed him that he was in fact Christ's younger brother. Hong told his startled listeners that it had been revealed to him that he must now work to bring about the Heavenly Kingdom of Great Peace (*taiping tianguo*) on earth. The movement became known as the Taiping Rebellion and lasted from 1851 until 1864.

Hounded from their community, Hong and his group moved into a mountain stronghold and began to gather followers from the disillusioned and unemployed, anti-Manchu elements, religious dissidents, and fellow members of south China's Hakka minority. By 1851 they had created a society based on Protestant Christian theology, Chinese traditions, and a vision of equality in which all goods were held in common; women worked, fought, and prayed alongside men; and foot binding, opium smoking, and gambling were forbidden. As a sign that they were no longer loyal to the Qing, the men cut their queues and let the hair grow in on their foreheads, prompting the Qing to refer to them as "the long-haired rebels." Repudiating Confucian tradition, the rebels targeted the scholar-gentry in their land seizures and executions.

By late 1851, the movement had gathered enough strength to stand against local government forces and began an advance to the north. By 1853 they had captured the city of Nanjing and made it their capital. That winter the Taipings were narrowly thwarted from driving the Qing from Beijing and were pushed back to central China by the revived imperial forces. For the next decade, however, Hong's movement would remain in control of the Chinese heartland, and the long, bloody contest to subdue them would leave thousands of towns and villages devastated for decades to come.

For the foreigners in China, the prospect of a Christian movement taking power seemed like a dream about to come true. However, missionaries and diplomats gradually became less sure of the movement's aims. On the one hand, Hong and his advisors talked about instituting Western-style administrative reforms and building a modern industrial base—things Western well-wishers had continually urged on Chinese officials. On the other hand, a powerful Taiping China might repudiate the unequal treaties and throw the new trade arrangements into disarray. Thus, the foreign powers in the end grudgingly elected to continue recognizing the Qing as China's legitimate rulers (see Map 24.3).

**The Second Opium War, 1856–1860** At the height of the rebellion in 1856, a new dispute arose between the Qing and the British and French. After 4 years of intermittent fighting, this conflict produced the next round of "unequal treaties" that greatly expanded foreign interests and control in the empire. Britain,

France, and the United States all felt by the mid-1850s that the vastly expanded trade in China—and now Japan—called for the opening of still more ports, an end to Qing prohibitions on missionary activity, and diplomatic relations along Western lines.

The catalyst came in late 1856. A Chinese customs patrol in Canton hauled down the British flag on the *Arrow*, a Chinese vessel whose registry had been falsified to take advantage of British trading privileges. The British used this purported insult to their flag as an opportunity to force treaty revision. The French, who considered themselves the protectors of Catholic missionaries and their converts, saw an excellent opening to pressure China on the missionary issue and so joined the British.

The war itself was fought intermittently in a highly localized fashion. The British seized the walled city of Canton, captured the governor-general of the region's two provinces, and sent him into exile in India. But by 1857 the Great Rebellion in India consumed British attention, while in China negotiations dragged on intermittently and the Qing remained preoccupied with the Taipings. In 1858 the Qing court refused a draft treaty. Returning in 1860 with a large expeditionary force, British and French troops advanced to Beijing, drove the emperor from the city, and burned and looted his summer palace. The final treaty stipulated that a dozen ports be opened to foreign trade, that opium be recognized as a legal commodity, that extraterritoriality be expanded, and that foreign embassies be set up in the capital. A newly created Chinese board, the Zongli Yamen, was to handle Qing foreign relations, and the Chinese were invited to send their own ambassadors abroad.

MAP 24.3 **The Taiping Rebellion, 1851–1864.**

**Self-Strengtheners.** Two of the key figures in China's self-strengthening movement were Zeng Guofan (left) and Li Hongzhang (right). The two men began working together during the last years of the Taiping Rebellion, both having formed and led militia armies in their home provinces of Hunan (Zeng) and Anhui (Li). Both men also pioneered the use of modern weapons by their troops. After Zeng's death in 1872, Li emerged as the most active proponent of self-strengthening and China's most powerful official.

## Patterns Up Close

# Interaction and Adaptation: "Self-Strengthening" and "Western Science and Eastern Ethics"

Most of the important technical innovations taking place in China and Japan during the late eighteenth and early nineteenth centuries came from outside east Asia. This, of course, is not surprising, since the scientific and industrial revolutions were largely focused on developing labor-saving machinery and weaponry and improving the speed and efficiency of transportation—matters of lesser priority in these labor-rich societies. Confronted by the expansive, newly industrialized countries of Europe and America, their possible responses were largely confined to what might be called the "three Rs"—reaction, reform, and revolution. Perhaps most interesting in this regard is the middle path of reform taken by both countries in attempting to create a synthesis of tried-and-true Confucian social structures and what were considered to be the best of the new technologies and institutions.

As we have seen in past chapters, Chinese philosophical concepts tended toward the desire for correlation and the reconciliation of opposites. In this tradition, *ti* and *yong*, or "essence" and "function/application," became the two key terms in the popular self-strengthening formulation *Zhongxue wei ti; Xixue wei yong* ("Chinese studies for the essence; Western studies for the practical application"). Thus, Chinese thinkers were able to accommodate the need for new foreign technologies within historically and philosophically acceptable terminology.

**Interaction and Adaptation in China and Japan.** Weapons on display at the Nanjing Arsenal in 1868 include an early Gatling-type rotary machine gun and a pyramid of round explosive shells (a), while an 1890 lithograph of a Japanese seamstress (b) shows the delicate balance between "essence" and "function" that Japan has tried to maintain since the middle of the nineteenth century. The woman is attired in Western dress, and she works a Western-style sewing machine. Has the "function" degraded the essence of what she is doing? It is a question that many in Japan still ask today.

**Self-Strengthening** Chinese officials, desperate to roll back the foreign threat and suppress the Taipings, favored a diverse array of strategies. Few advocated simply fighting the foreigners with whatever means were at hand. Most, like the emperor's brother Prince Gong, felt that over time these new peoples would be assimilated to Chinese norms, like invaders and border peoples of the past. In the meantime, however, they should be "soothed and pacified," but not unconditionally. As the prince later remarked to the British ambassador, "Take away your opium and your missionaries and you will be welcome."

Similarly, the Japanese, also schooled in Neo-Confucianism, were able to justify an even more thoroughgoing transformation of society by means of the balanced formula they called "Western science and Eastern ethics."

However, the two sides of the concept were not evenly balanced. As with many Neo-Confucian formulae, the "essence" and "ethics" elements were considered to be primary and the method of implementation—"function"—secondary. Thus, their proponents could argue that their chief aim was the preservation of the fundamentals of Confucian society while remaining flexible about the appropriate means of attaining their goals. Opponents, however, argued that the formula could—and eventually would—be reversed: that "function" would eventually degrade the "essence." Here, they pointed to the alleged Westernization of students sent abroad and the wearing of Western clothes in Japan as examples of the dangers of this approach.

Yet in both countries, one can argue that this has remained a favored approach, even through war and revolution. Though societal and generational tensions over "tradition" and "modernity" have been present for nearly a century and a half in Japan, the Japanese have made foreign technologies and institutions their own, while retaining some of their most cherished Shinto and Buddhist practices alongside social customs still tinged with Neo-Confucianism. Similarly, in China, since the beginning of the Four Modernizations in 1978, coupling technological and institutional modernization with an effort to rediscover and preserve what is considered to be the best of traditional Chinese civilization has been the dominant approach. Thus, the present regime pursues a policy of "socialism with Chinese characteristics" and supports the founding of Confucius Institutes alongside computer factories—all in the service of creating what the Communist Party calls "the harmonious society."

## Questions

- How were the Chinese and Japanese adaptations to Western innovations similar? How were they different? What do these similarities and differences say about the cultures of these two countries?

- Do you believe that, over the course of time, the "function" of foreign innovations has degraded the "essence" in China and Japan?

In order to do this, however, China needed to be able to halt further encroachments by the Western powers. Toward this end, a growing number of prominent officials advocated a policy that came to be called "self-strengthening." During the 1860s, the two most prominent were Li Hongzhang (1823–1901) and his senior colleague Zeng Guofan (1811–1872). Both men had distinguished themselves as Confucian scholars and as leaders of militia armies during the Taiping years. In 1864, their combined forces finally captured the Taiping capital at Nanjing and forced the suicide of Hong Xiuquan, bringing the movement to an end.

Like a number of leaders during these desperate times, Li and Zeng were also distinguished by the flexibility of their thinking and, increasingly, by their growing familiarity with the new weapons and techniques brought to China by foreign forces. By the end of the rebellion, they had begun to move toward a strategy of what a later slogan called "Chinese studies for the essence; Western studies for practical application." In the 1860s and early 1870s they sponsored a foreign language and technical school, modern arsenals and factories at Nanjing and Jiangnan (Kiangnan), a modern navy yard at Fuzhou, initiatives to send Chinese students to the United States and Europe, a modern shipping concern, and the first moves toward sending representatives abroad.

## Toward Revolution: Reform and Reaction to 1900

While China's efforts at self-strengthening seemed promising to contemporaries during the 1870s, signs of their underlying weakness were already emerging. As we have seen, the architect of many of these efforts, Li Hongzhang, was all too aware of the political constraints he faced. With the ascension of the infant Guangxu as emperor in 1874 came the regency of Empress Dowager Cixi. Desperate to preserve Manchu power, Cixi constantly manipulated factions at court and among the high officials to avoid concentration of power in any particular area. Such maneuverings, sometimes favoring Li's colleagues and as often opposing them, severely hampered the long-term health of many self-strengthening measures. In addition, the new programs were costly, usually requiring foreign experts, and China's finances were continually strained by the artificially low treaty tariffs and the obligation to pay old indemnities.

**China and Imperialism in Southeast Asia and Korea**    By the 1880s foreign tensions exposed more problems. France had been steadily encroaching upon southeast Asia since the late 1850s. By the early 1890s rising tensions surrounding the Korean court and intrigues by Japanese and Chinese agents involving various factions threatened war. Japan sent a force which they claimed to be "diplomatic"; troops of a Chinese counterforce were killed when a Japanese warship sunk their transport. By the fall of 1894, both sides were sending troops and naval forces to Korea, and a full-scale war over the fate of Korea and northeast Asia was under way.

**The Sino–Japanese War**    As we noted at the beginning of this chapter, the war between China and Japan over control of Korea graphically exposed the problems of China's self-strengthening efforts. China's arms procurement, for example, was not carried out under a centralized program, as Japan's was. The result was that different Chinese military units were armed with a wide variety of noninterchangeable weapons and ammunition, making it difficult for them to support each other. China's rebuilt fleet, though impressive in size and armament, faced similar problems.

While many of the land battles were hotly contested, superior organization and morale enabled the Japanese to drive steadily through Korea. A second force landed in southern Manchuria to secure the territory around the approaches to Beijing, while Japanese naval forces reduced the fortress across from it at Weihaiwei. By spring 1895, after some preliminary negotiations, Li made his humiliating trip

(a)

(b)

**Scenes from the Sino–Japanese War.** News accounts of the Sino–Japanese War aroused great interest and an unprecedented wave of nationalism in Japan. They also marked the last extensive use of *ukiyo-e* woodblock printing in the news media, as the technology of reproducing photos in newspapers was introduced to Japan shortly after the conflict. Because few of≈the artists actually traveled with the troops, the great majority of these works came from reporters' dispatches and the artists' imaginations. In these representative samples from the assault on Pyongyang showing the use of the new technology of the electric searchlight to illuminate an enemy fort (a), the pride in Japan's modernization and the disdain for China's "backwardness" are all too evident. Note the almost demon-like faces and garish uniforms of the Chinese as they are invariably depicted as being killed or cowering before the Japanese; note, too, the modern, Western uniforms and beards and mustaches of the Japanese (b),

to Shimonoseki and was forced to agree to Japan's terms. The severity of the provisions, especially the annexation of Taiwan, the control of Korea, and, temporarily at least, the seizure of Liaodong, signaled to the Western powers in east Asia that China was now weak enough to have to acquiesce to massive economic and territorial demands.

Thus, a "race for concessions" began in which France demanded economic and territorial rights in south China adjacent to Indochina, Great Britain did the same in the Yangzi River valley, Russia and Japan made demands in the north for rights in Manchuria, and a newcomer, Germany, demanded naval bases and rights at Qingdao [ching-DOW] (Tsingtao) on the Shandong Peninsula. China's total dismemberment was avoided in 1899 when John Hay, the US secretary of state, circulated a note with British backing suggesting that all powers refrain from securing exclusive concessions and instead maintain an "open door" for all to trade in China.

**The Hundred Days of Reform**   Amid this growing foreign crisis, the aftermath of the war produced a domestic crisis as well. The terms of the Shimonoseki

742    **Part 5**  The Origins of Modernity

**EN CHINE**
Le gâteau des Rois et... des Empereurs

**Dismembering China.** The weakness of the Qing during the final years of the nineteenth century prompted the so-called race for concessions among the imperial powers in east Asia. In this French cartoon, China is depicted as a cake around which caricatures of the monarchs and national symbols of the various powers sit with their knives poised arguing over who should get the best pieces. A desperate Chinese official—perhaps Li Hongzhang himself—with his long fingernails and flapping queue, holds up his hands imploring them to stop. The French caption says, "In China: The cake of kings and emperors."

treaty had prompted patriotic demonstrations in Beijing and raised levels of discussion about reform to new levels of urgency. A group of younger officials headed by Kang Youwei (1858–1927) petitioned Emperor Guangxu, now ruling in his own right, to implement a list of widespread reforms, many modeled on those recently enacted in Japan. Guangxu issued a flurry of edicts from June through September 1898, attempting to completely revamp China's government and many of its leading institutions. Resistance to this "hundred days' reform" program, however, was extensive, and much of it was centered on the emperor's aunt, the empress dowager. With support from her inner circle at court, she had the young emperor placed under house arrest and rounded up and executed those of Kang's supporters who could be found. Kang and his junior colleague, the writer and political theorist Liang Qichao [leeahng chee-CHOW] (1873–1929), managed to escape to the treaty ports. For the next decade they traveled to overseas Chinese communities attempting to gather support for their Constitutional Monarchy Party.

**The Boxer Rebellion and War**  The turmoil set off by the "race for concessions" among the imperial powers was particularly intense in north China, where the ambitions of Russia, Japan, and Germany clashed. The increased activity of German missionaries on the Shandong Peninsula sparked renewed antiforeign sentiment, increasingly perpetrated by a Chinese group calling itself the Society of the Harmonious Fists. This group was anti-Qing as well as antiforeign, and the members' ritual exercises and name prompted the foreign community to refer to them as the "Boxers." By late 1899 the Boxers were regularly provoking the foreign and Christian communities, hoping that foreign governments would pressure the Qing to suppress the movement, thereby fomenting a larger rebellion against the Qing.

In the spring of 1900 matters came to a crisis when Boxers assassinated the German ambassador. The Germans demanded that the Qing crush the movement, pay a huge indemnity, and erect a statue to their ambassador as a public apology. In the midst of this crisis, the empress dowager, who had been negotiating in secret with the Boxers, declared war on all the foreign powers in China and openly threw the court's support behind the movement. The result was civil war across northern China, as Boxer units hunted down missionaries and Chinese Christians, many Chinese army units aided the Boxers in attacking foreigners, and the foreign diplomatic quarter in Beijing was besieged.

The foreign governments quickly put together a multinational relief force led by the Germans and British and largely manned by the Japanese but including

units of nearly all the countries with interests in China. By August they had fought
their way to the capital and chased the imperial court nearly to Xi'an. Amid considerable carnage in the mopping up of Boxer sympathizers, Li Hongzhang, in his
last official duty before his death, was commissioned to negotiate an end to the
conflict for the court. With Qing power utterly routed, the foreign governments
were able to impose the most severe "unequal treaty" yet: They extracted the right
to post troops in major Chinese cities, demanded the total suppression of any
antiforeign movements, and received such a huge indemnity that China had to
borrow money from foreign banks in order to service the interest on the loan. One
positive outcome of the Boxer Protocols of 1901 was that the United States agreed
to return its share of the indemnity money to China on the condition that it would
be used to send Chinese students to study in American institutions. This resulted
in considerable goodwill toward the United States; indeed, in subsequent decades
a significant portion of Chinese leaders were educated in the United States.

## In Search of Security through Empire:
## Japan in the Meiji Era

As we have just seen, the close of the nineteenth century saw Japan looming larger
and larger as China's chief threat. Yet they both faced similar pressures and, as
Li Hongzhang observed, shared a common culture and in many ways a common
cause. How, then, was Japan, with only a fraction of China's population and resources, able not only to survive in the face of foreign pressure but join the imperial powers itself?

**The Decline of Tokugawa Seclusion**   Though the eighteenth century saw occasional attempts by foreign ships to put in at Japanese ports, Europeans generally

寅六十戈

提督ペルリ肖像

**"Blue-eyed Barbarians."** The Japanese commonly referred to Westerners as "blue-eyed barbarians." In this sketch, part of a long series that artists made after Commodore Perry's four heavily armed steamships sailed into Tokyo Bay in July 1853, Perry's son Oliver, who served as his father's personal secretary, is portrayed as jowly and slightly demonic looking.

**Coolies:** Poor migrant laborers from China and India who performed menial work in other parts of the world in the nineteenth century.

honored Japan's seclusion policies. Moreover, since all maritime trade with China took ships along a southerly route to Canton, the opportunity to go to Japan seldom presented itself. By the first decades of the nineteenth century, however, the situation was changing. The vastly expanded legitimate trade with China and the development of the opium trade increased the volume of shipping closer to Japanese waters. Moreover, the rapid growth of the whaling industry in the northern Pacific increasingly brought European and American ships into waters adjacent to Japan. From their perspective, the need for establishing relations for the disposition of shipwreck survivors and perhaps trade was therefore becoming ever more urgent.

By the 1840s the pressure to establish relations with the Tokugawa shogunate became even more intense for the Western powers with interests in China. The treaty ports created in the wake of the First Opium War included Shanghai, which was rapidly becoming east Asia's chief commercial enclave. Because of its geographical position, major shipping routes to Shanghai now ran directly adjacent to southern Japan. Moreover, the Mexican-American War (1846–1848) (see Chapter 23) brought the Pacific coast of North America under the control of the United States. At the same time, the discovery of gold in California made San Francisco the premier port for all American transpacific trade. In addition, increasing numbers of Chinese sought passage to the gold fields and the promise of employment in the American West, while the infamous **"coolie** trade" continually increased human traffic to Cuba and Peru. Plans to open steamship service along the great circle route from San Francisco to Shanghai, and the need for coaling stations to supply it, now threatened to place Japan squarely in the path of maritime traffic.

**The Coming of the "Black Ships"** The Tokugawa were well aware of the humiliation of the Qing at the hands of the British in 1842 and watched nervously as foreign commerce mounted in the Chinese treaty ports. As pressure increased on Japan to open its ports, divided counsels plagued the shogunate. The influential Mito School, long exposed to "Dutch learning" (see Chapter 21), feared the growing military and technological power of the Europeans and Americans and advocated a military response to any attempt at opening the country. Others looking at the situation in China felt that negotiation was the only possible way for Japan to avoid invasion.

The Americans, taking the lead in seeking diplomatic and commercial relations, put together a fleet of their newest and most powerful warships, which arrived in Japan in July 1853. Their commander, Matthew C. Perry, assembled multiracial and multiethnic crews in order to impress his Japanese hosts with the reach and power of the United States. Anxious to awe them as well with the new technologies available, he brought along as presents a telegraph set and a model railroad, both of which proved immediately popular with the Japanese. When negotiations flagged, the shogun's men gleefully amused themselves aboard the miniature train, smacking the engine and its operator with their fans to make it go faster.

On Perry's return trip in 1854 with even more of the "black ships," as the Japanese dubbed them, the Treaty of Kanagawa was signed, Japan's first with an outside power. Like China, Japan had now entered the treaty port era.

**"Honor the Emperor and Expel the Barbarian!"**   The widely differing attitudes toward foreign contact expressed within the shogunate were reflected among the daimyo and samurai as well. The treaty with the Americans, and the rapid conclusion of treaties with other foreigners, tended to reinforce antiforeignism among many of the warrior elite, while emphasizing the weakness of the Tokugawa to resist further demands. Moreover, the new cultural contacts taking place in treaty ports like Yokohama and Nagasaki hardened positions and raised tensions further. Many samurai felt that dramatic gestures were called for to rouse the country to action. Hence, as with the Boxers later in China, they attacked foreigners and even assassinated Tokugawa officials in an effort to precipitate antiforeign conflict. By 1863, a movement aimed at driving out the Tokugawa and restoring imperial rule had coalesced around the samurai of two southern domains, Satsuma and Choshu. Taking the slogan *Sonno joi* ("Honor the emperor, expel the barbarian") members of this "Satcho" (*Satsuma* and *Choshu*) clique challenged the shogunate and fought the smoldering Restoration War, which by the end of 1867 forced the Tokugawa to capitulate. In short order, the new regime moved to the Tokugawa capital of Edo and renamed it Tokyo (Eastern Capital).

The new emperor, 15-year-old Mutsuhito, took the reign name of Meiji (Enlightened Rule) and quickly moved to make good on its promise. As proof that the new regime would adopt progressive measures, in April 1868 the throne issued a "charter oath" in which the new emperor renounced the restrictive measures of the past. A constitution was also promulgated, which spelled out in more detail how the new government was to be set up.

**Creating a Nation-State**   While the Tokugawa had created an efficient warrior bureaucracy based on Neo-Confucianism, Japan was still dominated by regional loyalties and fealty to the daimyo of one's *han*, or feudal domain. The foreign threat and restoration of the emperor provided the opportunity as well as the necessity to forge a more thoroughgoing national unification. Thus, the new government quickly set about dismantling the feudal han and replacing them with a centralized provincial structure; the daimyo were replaced by governors, and the samurai were disbanded, given stipends, and encouraged to form business enterprises or to teach. In their place, a new conscript army modeled after that of Germany was created, and a navy modeled on Great Britain's was established. In addition, the new order was to be held together by a national system of compulsory education in which loyalty to the emperor and state was carefully nurtured at every level.

**Emperor Meiji.** A number of portraits and photographs of Emperor Meiji were done during his lifetime, particularly in his twenties and thirties. Here, in a portrait probably done in the late 1870s or early 1880s, he is shown as a vigorous and decisive man at the height of his powers. Note the European style military uniform and Van Dyke beard of the kind frequently sported by Western monarchs and leaders.

The 1870s also marked the flourishing of government-managed social experimentation. Like the Chinese "self-strengtheners," Japanese senior advisors to the emperor, or *genro* [GEN-row, with a hard g], sought to use new foreign technologies and institutions to strengthen the state against further foreign intrusion. Japan's planners, however, proved more systematic and determined in their efforts and, unlike their Chinese counterparts, had the full backing of the imperial court. Thus, Japan's proclaimed goals of using "Western science and Eastern ethics" in the service of "civilization and enlightenment" were seen as the primary tools in reaching eventual equality with the Western imperial powers and rolling back Japan's unequal treaties.

**Creating an Empire**    As we saw earlier in this chapter, rising tensions between Japan and China over the disposition of Korea ultimately led to the Sino–Japanese War of 1894–1895. The issue was temporarily held in abeyance by the Treaty of Tianjin of 1885, but continuing difficulties arising from the instability of the

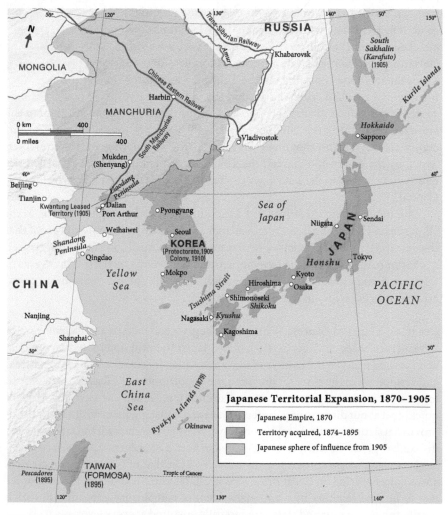

MAP **24.4  Japanese Territorial Expansion, 1870–1905.**

Korean government, feuding pro-Chinese and pro-Japanese factions within it, and the *Tonghak*, or "Eastern learning," movement, kept the region a volatile one. Combining elements of Confucianism, Buddhism, and a pronounced strain of antiforeignism, Tonghak-led peasant rebellions had erupted in 1810 and 1860. Though the rebellion had been suppressed in the 1860s, the forced opening of Korea to trade in the following decade and the constant intrigues of the Qing and the Japanese surrounding the Yi court in succeeding decades brought about the movement's revival in the 1890s.

As we have seen, Japan's successful showing in the war surprised and alarmed the Western powers in the region. The Triple Intervention, in which Russia, Germany, and France forced Japan to return the Liaodong Peninsula to China, only to have the Chinese lease it to Russia the following year, put that empire on a collision course with Japanese aspirations on the Asian mainland. Japan's control of Korea made it intensely interested in acquiring concessions in Manchuria. For Russia, it was vital to build rail links from the Trans-Siberian Railway to their new outposts of Port Arthur and Dairen (Dalian) in Liaodong and to extend the line across Manchuria to Vladivostok on the Pacific. As the twentieth century began, the Russians pressured the Chinese into allowing them the rights to build the Chinese Eastern Railway across Manchuria and the South Manchurian Railway to Port Arthur, with a vital junction at Mukden, known today as Shenyang. Japan and Russia would shortly fight a war that would secure Japan's dominant position in northeast Asia and begin a long train of events that would end in revolution for Russia (see Map 24.4).

# Economics and Society in Late Qing China

The century and a half from 1750 to 1900 marked the structural, cultural, and economic decline of the great agrarian empires. Nowhere was this more evident than in Qing China. By 1900, China's treasury was bankrupt; its finances increasingly were controlled by foreign concerns; its export trade was outstripped by European and Japanese competitors; its domestic markets turned to factory-produced foreign commodities; and its land, ravaged by war, eroded by declining productivity, and squeezed by the world's largest population, grew less and less capable of sustaining its society.

## The Seeds of Modernity and the New Economic Order

As we have seen a number of times in this chapter, the economic policies of late imperial China were increasingly at odds with those of the industrializing and commercially expanding West. For Chinese thinkers, this was considered sound in both ideological and economic terms. Confucianism held that agriculture was China's primary concern; that the values of humanity, loyalty, and filial piety were tied to agrarian society; and that the values of the merchant—particularly the drive for profit—were in direct opposition to these agrarian values. As the nineteenth century advanced, the opium trade provided ample evidence to Confucian officials of the correctness of this stance.

While opium was the great entering wedge, the building pressures on China and other regulated societies to lower their barriers to legitimate trade and the steps taken by those countries exerting the pressure to safeguard their own markets had equally severe long-term effects. Briefly, China was squeezed both ways in terms of trade. That is, the unequal treaties imposed artificially low tariff rates on the empire, making it increasingly difficult to protect its markets; at the same time, trading nations in the West increased tariffs on their own imports and, in some cases, developed their own substitutes for Chinese products.

**Self-Strengthening and Economics**    The programs to improve China's economics and trade were set up as "government-sponsored/merchant-operated" enterprises. Amid the halting attempts at government-sponsored innovation, however, other economic forces at work would also have a profound effect on China's later economic development. The first was that in the treaty ports themselves the economic climate created by the Western powers for their own benefit exposed much of China's urban population to aspects of modern industrial and commercial society. A substantial class of Chinese people who made a living mediating between Westerners and Chinese interests had developed by the end of the nineteenth century.

The other long-term process at work was the growing influx and popularity of European, Japanese, and American consumer goods diffused from the treaty ports to the interior. While foreign curiosities had been popular with Chinese elites since the eighteenth century, Qing efforts to safeguard domestic markets through the Canton system and internal transit taxes had been steadily beaten down. By the end of the nineteenth century, foreign machine-made cotton cloth dominated the Chinese interior; John D. Rockefeller's Standard Oil Company was giving away kerosene lamps to market their fuel; the British–American Tobacco Company had established its products in the empire; and even the Japanese invention of the rickshaw had become a popular mode of transport in China's cities. With the Qing finally committed to railroad and telegraph construction and modern deep mining and with China's commercial ports resembling more and more those of their foreign counterparts, the seeds of economic modernity had been at least fitfully planted.

**Rural Economics and Society**    While about 80–85 percent of China's population remained rural, the old structures of the empire's peasant-based society were slowly beginning to crumble. As we saw during the Taiping era, tensions among peasants, village headmen, scholar-gentry, and local officials were never far from the surface. Landlordism, especially the growing incidence of absentee landlordism, exacerbated these tensions. Living on the edge of poverty in many areas, with old trade routes and handicrafts disrupted by the treaty ports, many peasants saw in the Taipings, the Nian, and other local rebellions a desperate way to change their situations. But in the end, the radical ideologies and ruthlessness of the rebels disillusioned the peasantry, while in many places their poverty increased due to the immense destruction caused by rebel clashes and the flight of many wealthy scholar-gentry to the treaty ports. As a result, by the beginning of the twentieth century, absentee landlordism had become an increasingly acute problem. As some scholars have noted, the land problems of China—and their parallels in India and the Ottoman Empire—were an important impediment to an effective response to the scientific–industrial challenge of Europe and America.

**Social Trends**    While changes were certainly noticeable in the family, in relationships between men and women, and in the level of confidence the Chinese

**Chinese Family, ca. 1873.** While the later nineteenth century marked changes on a number of fronts, the centrality of the family and its Confucian hierarchy remained largely intact. In the portrait here of the Yang family of Beijing, the father and eldest son occupy the places of honor under the central window of the ground floor, while the wives, concubines, infants, and servants are arrayed on the upper veranda. In most cases, the seclusion of such wealthy women was nearly complete. The photographer reported, however, that these women frequently moistened their fingertips and rubbed them on the paper windowpanes to make them transparent so they could secretly watch events outside.

displayed in the Confucian system—particularly among urban Chinese—the durability of long-standing traditions is probably far more striking. As we have seen in every chapter on China, the family remained the central Chinese institution. Within it, the father continued to be the most powerful figure, and the Confucian ideal of hierarchical relationships between husband and wife, father and son, and elder brother and younger brother remained in force. Daughters, though most often treated with affection, were also considered a net drain on family resources because they would marry outside the family. Thus, the education they received was generally aimed at fostering the skills the family of their husbands-to-be would consider valuable—cooking, sewing, running a household, and perhaps singing and poetry. It was also desirable for girls to acquire enough literacy to read such classics as *Admonitions for Women*, the *Classic of Filial Piety*, and other guides to proper behavior. But the proverbial wisdom remained that "a woman with talent is without virtue." Hence, the daughters of the wealthy were kept secluded in the home, and most—with the exception of the Manchus and certain minorities like south China's Hakkas—continued the practice of foot binding.

## Culture, Arts, and Science
Though the late Qing period is often seen by scholars as one more concerned with cataloging and preserving older literary works than innovation, there was nevertheless considerable invigoration due to foreign influences toward the end of the

dynasty. Indeed, one could say that the era begins with one of China's great literary masterpieces and ends with China's first modern writers pointing toward a vernacular-language literary renaissance starting around 1915. Reversing the trend of thousands of years, the most significant Chinese developments in science and technology were those arriving from the West as products of the Industrial Revolution and the new kind of society emerging there.

*The Dream of the Red Chamber*    Though the novel during Ming and Qing times was not considered high literature by Chinese scholars, the form, as with Europeans in the eighteenth and nineteenth centuries, proved immensely popular. During the mid-eighteenth century, what many consider to be China's greatest novel, *Hong Lou Meng* (*The Dream of the Red Chamber*), was written by the shadowy Cao Xueqin [sow shway-CHIN] (ca. 1715–ca. 1764). The novel, which chronicles the decline and fall of a powerful family, is seen by some scholars as a loose autobiography of Cao's own family and a thinly veiled account of events in the early days of the Qing. In fact, the novel has been so closely studied and analyzed that in China there is an entire field called "red studies" or "redology" (*hong xue*) devoted to examination of the work.

Poetry, Travel Accounts, and Newspapers    China's increasing need to understand new threats as well as opportunities prompted publication of a great number of atlases, gazetteers of foreign lands, and eyewitness travel accounts. Many of the early attempts at compiling information about foreign countries were copies of Western works. The most significant of these were the *Illustrated Gazetteer of the Maritime Countries* of 1844 by Wei Yuan (1794–1856) and the *Record of the World* of 1848 by Xu Jiyu (1795–1873). These accounts, especially Xu's, formed the backbone of what Chinese officials knew about the outside world until the first eyewitness accounts of travelers and diplomats began to arrive in the late 1860s.

Though hundreds of thousands of Chinese had emigrated to various parts of the world by the mid-1860s, it was only in 1866 that the first authorized officials began to visit foreign countries and not until 1876 that diplomats began to take up their posts in foreign capitals and ports. All of these men, however, were required to keep official journals of their experiences for use by the government and/or for publication, and by the later part of the century China began to acquire a far more complete sense of what the outside world was like. The journals of the diplomats Zhang Deyi (1847–1919) and Guo Songtao (1818–1891) were particularly significant in this regard.

The popular newspaper also emerged in the treaty ports and eventually in most Chinese cities during this time. For centuries newsletters tracking official doings at the capital had been circulated among the elites. However, the 1860s saw the first popular Chinese-language papers, the most prominent of which was *Shenbao*. By the turn of the century, Liang Qichao (1873–1929) had emerged as China's most influential journalist and scholar, having started and edited five newspapers, each heavily influenced by his views on reform. Such publications and the growing numbers of journals and popular magazines, many started by missionaries anxious to use science and Western material culture as a vehicle for their work, were vitally important in the transfer of ideas between Chinese and foreigners.

**Science and Technology**    The most pressing need for China during the early nineteenth century was military technology. During the period between the two Opium Wars, Chinese officials attempted with some success to purchase guns and cannon from European and American manufacturers to bolster their coastal defenses. It was quickly apparent to the self-strengtheners, however, that China must understand the basic principles behind these revolutionary weapons and begin to manufacture them on its own. Moreover, this would be impossible to do unless the infrastructure was in place and such supporting industries as mining, railroads, and telegraphy were also established.

Despite the general animosity directed against them by Chinese officials, missionaries ironically were key players in transfers of science and technology. Unlike the Jesuit missionaries of the seventeenth century, Protestant missionaries in the nineteenth century directed their efforts at ordinary Chinese, but often did so by attracting them with the new advantages of science. Central to their efforts was the role of medical missionaries in setting up clinics and using their presence in the community to foster conversion. The missionary community was also active in popularizing developments in Western science and technology through journals like the *Globe Magazine*. By the latter part of the century, increasing numbers of Chinese scholars were becoming involved in the study of foreign subjects, going abroad for education, and in the translation of Western works into Chinese. The Chinese mathematician Li Shanlan (1810–1882), for example, collaborated with Shanghai missionaries in translating works on algebra, calculus, and analytical geometry. Later, Liang Qichao and Yan Fu (1854–1921) studied and translated a wide range of foreign scientific and social science works.

Thus, while China had not yet completed its move to the new scientific–industrial society, the momentum had already begun to build among the empire's intellectual leaders. Even so, nearly all agreed that the future would not lie in slavish imitation of the West. In the meantime, however, the example of Japan confronted them only a short distance away.

# Zaibatsu and Political Parties: Economics and Society in Meiji Japan

Scholars of Japan's economic history have often pointed out that the commercial environment developing through the Tokugawa period was well suited to the nurturing of capitalism and industrialism in the nineteenth century. As we saw in Chapter 21, for example, the imposition of the law of alternate attendance created a great deal of traffic to and from Edo as daimyo processions made their biannual trips to the capital. This guaranteed traffic supported numerous hostels, restaurants, stables, supply stores, theaters, and all the other commercial establishments necessary to maintain the travelers in safety and comfort. The infrastructure of the major roads also required constant tending and improvement, as did the port facilities for coastal shipping and fishing industries. Towns and cities along the routes also grew, as did the regionally specialized crafts and industries they supported. By 1850, for example, Edo had well over 1 million inhabitants, while Osaka and Kyoto both had about 375,000. Finally, commercial credit establishments, craft guilds, and large-scale industries in ceramics, sake brewing, fine arts, fishing, and coastal shipping—all intensified by being compressed into a relatively small area—had already regularized many of the institutions characteristic of the development of a modern economy.

## Commerce and Cartels

Perhaps because of the urgency of their situation following Perry's visits, the Japanese were quicker to go abroad to study the industrially advanced countries of Europe and the United States. In 1860, for example, they sent an embassy to America in which the participants—including the future journalist Fukuzawa Yukichi (1835–1901)—were expected to keep diaries of everything they saw. Even during the last days of the Tokugawa regime, Japanese entrepreneurs were already experimenting with Western steamships and production techniques.

**Cooperation and Capitalism**    When the Meiji government began its economic reforms, its overall strategy included elements that still mark Japanese policy today. The first was to make sure that ownership, insofar as possible, would remain in Japanese hands. The second was that, taking its cue from the success of the leading commercial nations of the West, Japan would develop its exports to the utmost while attempting to keep imports to a minimum. Japanese entrepreneurship also received an enormous boost from the cashing out of the samurai. While many of the former warriors found anything to do with commerce distasteful, some took to heart the government's injunction that starting economic enterprises was a patriotic duty. By the end of the century, Japan's industrial statistics were impressive by any standards: Coal production had increased to six times its 1860 base level, and iron, copper, and other mining industries expanded at a similar rate—but still could not keep pace with Japan's industrial needs. By the turn of the century Japan needed to import much of its raw material, a situation that has continued to this day.

Not surprisingly, families with long-standing connections to capital swiftly moved to unite their enterprises to gain market share. The Mitsui Company, for example, used its extensive brewing profits to fund a host of other enterprises, soon becoming one of Japan's largest industrial concerns. Similarly, the Mitsubishi Company expanded from coastal shipping to manufacturing—later creating military vehicles and aircraft during World War II as well as popular cars today. The encouragement of the government and the cooperation of social networks among elites in finance and industry led to the creation of a number of **cartels** called *zaibatsu*. By the end of the nineteenth century, the zaibatsu would control nearly all major Japanese industries.

**Cartel:** A group of domestic or international businesses that form a group to control or monopolize an industry.

**The Transportation and Communications Revolutions**    The rapid development of railroads and telegraphs was one of the most stunning transformations of the Meiji era. The Japanese pursued these devices with an enthusiasm scarcely paralleled anywhere else in the world at the time. By the mid-1870s Japan had in place a trunk railroad line along the main coastal road and several branches to major cities in the interior. Though Westerners found Japanese trains quaint—along with the custom of leaving one's clogs on the platform before boarding the cars—they were efficient and marked a trend for railroad building wherever the Japanese went. Similarly, telegraph—and, by the end of the century,

**Visions of the New Railroads.** The marvels of the new systems of railroads and telegraphs springing up in Japan provided practitioners of *ukiyo-e* woodblock art a host of new subjects to depict in the 1870s and 1880s. Here is one of a number of views of new stations, in this case, Ueno on the Ueno–Nakasendo–Tokyo Railway, with small commuter trains arriving and departing.

telephone—lines were swiftly strung between the major cities and towns, followed by undersea cables to the Asian mainland and North America. By 1895, Japan was estimated to have over 2,000 miles of private and government railroads in operation and over 4,000 miles of telegraph wires in place (see Map 24.5).

**The Meiji Constitution and Political Life**   While the charter oath and constitution of 1868 were instituted with considerable success, a debate had already begun among the genro concerning the liberalization of representative government in Japan. In 1881 the emperor approved a plan whereby Ito Hirobumi (1841–1909)

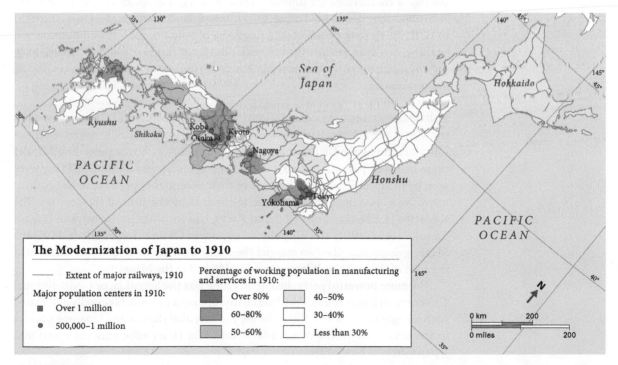

**The Modernization of Japan to 1910**

—— Extent of major railways, 1910

Major population centers in 1910:
- ▪ Over 1 million
- ● 500,000–1 million

Percentage of working population in manufacturing and services in 1910:
- Over 80%
- 60–80%
- 50–60%
- 40–50%
- 30–40%
- Less than 30%

MAP **24.5** **The Modernization of Japan to 1910.**

and several senior colleagues would launch a study of the constitutional governments of the United States, Great Britain, France, Germany, and other countries, to see what aspects of them might be suitable for Japan's needs. The Meiji Constitution, as it came to be called, was promulgated in 1889 and remained in force until it was supplanted by the constitution composed during the Allied occupation of Japan after World War II.

While borrowing elements from the US and British models, Ito's constitution drew most heavily from that of Germany. Much of it was also aimed at preserving the traditions of Japan's Confucian society that Ito and the genro most valued. Chief among these was the concept of *kokutai*, the "national polity." In this view, Japan was unique among nations because of its unbroken line of emperors and the singular familial and spiritual relationship between the emperor and his people. Thus, the Meiji Constitution is presented, in Ito's words, as "the gift of a benevolent and charitable emperor to the people of his country." The sovereignty of the country was placed in the person of the emperor as the embodiment of kokutai; the emperor's Privy Council, the army and navy, and the ministers of state were answerable directly to him. There was also a bicameral parliamentary body called the Diet, with an upper House of Peers and a lower House of Representatives. Like the House of Lords in Great Britain, Japan's House of Peers consisted of members of the nobility; the representatives were elected by the people. The primary purpose of the Diet in this arrangement was to vote on financing, deliberate on the everyday items of governance, and provide advice and consent to the Privy Council, Ministry of State, and Imperial Court.

As for the people themselves, 15 articles spelled out "the rights and duties of subjects." Duties included liability for taxes and service in the military, while the rights enumerated are similar to those found in European and American constitutions: the right to hold office, guarantees against search and seizure, the right to trial, the right to property, and freedoms of religion, speech, and petition. All of these, however, are qualified by such phrases as "unless provided by law," leaving the door open for the government to invoke extraordinary powers during national emergencies.

**Political Parties**    As constitutional government began to be implemented in the 1890s, the factional debates among senior advisors naturally began to attract followers among the Diet members and their supporters. In the preceding decades there had been political parties, but their membership was limited, and they were seen by many as illegitimate because of their potential opposition to the government. Now, two major parties came to the fore by the turn of the century. The Kenseito [KEN-say-toe], or Liberal Party, had its roots in the work of Itagaki Taisuke (1837–1919) and his political opponent Okuma Shigenobu [OH-ku-ma SHIH-geh-no-bu]. The two merged their followers but later split into factions at the turn of the century. It later was reestablished as the Minseito.

The more powerful party during this time was the Seiyukai, or Constitutional Government Party, founded by Ito and his followers in 1900. Generally associated with the government and the zaibatsu, the Seiyukai dominated Japanese politics in the era before World War I; after World War II, its adherents coalesced into Japan's present Liberal Democratic Party.

**Social Experiments** In addition to creating an industrial base and a constitutional government, Japan's rulers attempted to curb practices in Japan that were believed to offend foreign sensibilities as part of its program of "civilization and enlightenment." Bathhouses, for example, were now required to have separate entrances for men and women, and pleasure quarters were restricted in areas near foreign enclaves; meat eating was even encouraged in largely Buddhist Japan, resulting in the new dish *sukiyaki*. In the boldest experiment of all, the government mandated the use of Western dress for men and women, accompanied by a propaganda campaign depicting the advantages of this "modern" and "civilized" clothing. Criticism from a variety of quarters, however, including many Westerners, ultimately forced the government to relent and make the new dress optional.

In the same vein, traditional restrictions on women were altered. Though the home remained the primary domain for women, as it does even today, women were far more often seen in public. Concubines were now accorded the same rights as wives. Courtesans and prostitutes were no longer legally considered servants. Among elites, the fad of following all things Western established to some degree Victorian European standards of family decorum. More far-reaching, however, was the role of the new education system. Even before the Meiji Restoration, Japan had one of the highest levels of preindustrial literacy in the world— 40 percent for males and 15 percent for females. With the introduction of compulsory public education, literacy would become nearly universal, and the upsurge in specialized women's education created entire new avenues of employment for women.

This same trend toward emancipation was evident among the rural population. The formal class barriers between peasants and samurai were eliminated, though informal deference to elites continued. In addition, some barriers between ordinary Japanese and outcast groups, such as the Eta, were also reduced. During the latter part of the nineteenth century, aided by better transportation, improved crops, maximum utilization of marginal lands, and the opening up of Hokkaido for development, Japan became the most intensely farmed nation in the world. Japan's already well-developed fishing industry contributed mightily by introducing commercial fish-based fertilizers that boosted yields enormously. The result was that although Japan's population increased to 40 million by 1890, it was a net exporter of food until the turn of the century.

## "Enlightenment and Progress": Science, Culture, and the Arts

As we saw in Chapter 21, while the Tokugawa sought seclusion, they were by no means cut off entirely from developments in other nations. Of particular importance in this regard was the requirement imposed on the Dutch merchants at Deshima to make their annual reports to the Shogun on the state of the world. By the time of Commodore Perry's visit the accumulated amount of "Dutch learning" was impressive. Much of it consisted of notes on scientific and technical developments.

**Engaging "Western Science"** Nevertheless, at the time of their initial contact with the Western powers, the Tokugawa were stunned at the degree to which the accelerating technologies of the Industrial Revolution had armed their adversaries. During Perry's visits Japanese sketch artists frantically sought to capture the details of the ships' gun ports and cannon and the outward signs of their steam power. The Japanese were also immediately engaged with the notion of the railroad; just as quickly they sought to create oceangoing steamships. By 1860, they had built and manned steamers and insisted that their embassy to the United States travel aboard a ship the Japanese had built themselves.

The demand for industrial and military technology encouraged large numbers of Japanese to seek technical education. During the initial stages of the Meiji era, thousands of Japanese students studied in Europe and the United States, and the Japanese government and private concerns hired hundreds of foreign advisors to aid in science and technical training. By the 1880s a university system anchored by Tokyo Imperial University was offering courses in medicine, physics, chemistry, engineering, and geology, among other advanced disciplines. On the whole, however, the bulk of the nation's efforts went into the practical application of science to technology and agriculture in order to support the government's modernization efforts.

**Culture and the Arts**    As was the case a decade later in China, Japanese intellectuals eagerly absorbed copies of Western Enlightenment, philosophical, and social science works in translation. As was also true in China, journalism played a dominant role in disseminating information to the public. Here, Fukuzawa Yukichi, like Liang Qichao in China, held a central place both in fostering the growth of newspapers and in articulating the role of journalists in a modern society.

"In editing the paper [*Jiji-shimpo*] I encouraged the reporters to write bravely and freely. I have no objection to any severe criticism or extreme statements, but I warned them that they must limit their statements to what they would be willing to say to the victim face to face."

—Fukuzawa Yukichi

As with nearly all the arts in late nineteenth-century Japan, the novel was also heavily influenced by Western examples. In some respects, the culmination of this trend was *Kokoro*, by Natsume Soseki (1867–1916), published in 1914. Soseki utilizes the wrenching changes in Meiji Japan set against traditional and generational values to create the tension and ultimate tragic end of the central character in his work.

More traditional arts such as Noh and kabuki theater and *ukiyo-e* printing survived, but often in a somewhat altered state. Updated kabuki variations now featured contemporary themes and often had female actors playing female parts. In addition, European plays such as Ibsen's *A Doll's House* enjoyed considerable vogue. As for *ukiyo-e*, it remained the cheapest and most popular outlet for depictions of contemporary events until the development of newspaper photography. Especially telling in this regard are *ukiyo-e* artists' interpretations of the Sino–Japanese War.

# Putting It All Together

Scholars of China and Japan have long debated the reasons for the apparent success of Japan and failure of China. One school of thought sees the fundamental reasons growing from the respective cultural outlooks of the two countries.

China, it is argued, assumed that outsiders would simply be won over to Confucian norms and modes of behavior, because this is what China's historical experience had been for the last 2,000 years. When it became apparent that defensive measures were necessary, it was still assumed that China's superior culture would win out. Japan, on the other hand, because of its long history of cultural borrowing and its much smaller size, assumed a more urgent defensive posture. In addition, the Japanese had the advantage of watching events unfold in China before the danger reached their own shores. This allowed them to act in a more united and pragmatic fashion when resisting the Western threat.

Some historians, however, disagree with this analysis. They argue instead that the cultural differences between China and Japan were secondary in the face of the foreign threat. According to this school of thought, the primary cause of the radically different outcomes for China and Japan was that China was victimized by foreign imperialism much earlier and much more thoroughly than Japan. Once Japanese modernization efforts were under way, the Japanese won for themselves a breathing spell with which to keep imperialism at bay and ultimately fought their way into the great power club themselves.

▶ For additional resources, including maps, primary sources, visuals, and quizzes, please go to www.oup.com/us/vonsivers. Please see the Further Resources section at the back of the book for additional readings and suggested websites.

# Against the Grain

# Reacting to Modernity

One of the enduring patterns of world history has been the complexity of acculturation to innovation from outside—particularly if it is perceived to be forced. As scientific and industrial society developed and expanded its control and influence into the old agrarian–urban empires in the nineteenth century, the clashes, as we have seen, were particularly fierce, and all the more so, since societies like those of China or Japan felt themselves to be culturally superior to the invaders.

Not surprisingly, given the categories of choices we have outlined in this chapter's Patterns Up Close feature—reform, reaction, or revolution—many people in a variety of places in different parts of the world chose what we might term a "culturally fundamentalist" approach. That is, faced with a growing threat that seems increasingly insurmountable by the more conventional approaches of reform or resistance, they chose to take radical action by harkening back to a time when the virtues that first made their societies great prevailed. By bringing such virtues back into play, they believed they could restore the country's greatness. In almost every case this involved considerable invented nostalgia and often a charismatic messiah figure. To cite just a few examples of this phenomenon, the Taipings and Boxers in China, the Tonghaks in Korea, the followers of the Mahdi in the Sudan, the Ghost Dancers of the Native Americans in the United States, and the Samurai Rebellion in Japan all held out a kind of mystical view that proper prayers, ritual, and confidence in the rightness of their cause would win the day. In some cases, they believed that their ritual purity and correctness, along with certain sacred gestures or garments, made them invulnerable to the enemy's weapons. In the end, however, all of these movements were ultimately crushed by the modern or modernizing forces arrayed against them. Yet the bootless courage of their stands is often celebrated today— ironically by the representatives of the very societies that they sought to turn back.

- What factors make people turn to solutions during times of extreme stress that they wouldn't consider otherwise? Can you think of other instances in history where this phenomenon has taken place?

- Are there current movements you can think of that seem to fit this phenomenon? What stresses in their societies do you think are provoking such movements?

# Thinking Through Patterns

▶ **What was the impact of Western imperialism on the "regulated societies" of China and Japan?**

The impact of the intrusion of Great Britain, France, the United States, and later Germany and Russia forced both China and Japan into defensive postures. Both countries had sought to keep out what they considered subversive foreign influences after an earlier period of exposure to Western traders and missionaries. China had created a tightly controlled system of overseas trade based in Guangzhou (Canton); Japan allowed only the Dutch to trade with them. But the expansion of trade in both legitimate goods and opium and the need of the British for regularization of diplomatic practices pushed Britain and China into a cycle of war and "unequal treaties" under which China was at an increasing disadvantage. Japan, suddenly thrust into international commerce and diplomacy by the young United States, now sought to protect its borders without pushing the Western powers into seizing any of its territory.

China's long history of absorbing and acculturating outside invaders to Confucian norms encouraged its leaders to assume that the Westerners would be no different. Though many officials realized the qualitative difference between the industrializing Euro-American countries and invaders from the Chinese past, they were divided about what to do. Thus, attempts at reform were often undercut by political infighting at court and in the bureaucracy. The Taiping Rebellion also played a central role in further depleting China's strength and resources. As time went on, increasing Western control of China's ports and tariffs, absentee landlordism, and declining agricultural productivity also played a role.

▶ **Why did European empire building in Asia have such dramatically different effects on China and Japan?**

For Japan, after a decade of indecision about how to handle the foreign intrusion, a civil war ended in the dismantling of the shogunate and the unification of the country under Emperor Meiji. With remarkable unity born of a deep sense of urgency, Japan embarked upon a thoroughgoing reform program aimed at remaking the country along avowedly Western lines. The focus and consistency displayed by Meiji and his advisors avoided many of the problems China experienced, and Japan's late Tokugawa economics to some degree had predisposed the country toward a smoother transition into scientific–industrial society.

▶ **How have historians seen the nature of these outside forces and their influences in east Asia?**

Historians have long debated the relative weight that should be assigned to cultural and material reasons for the differing paths of China and Japan. China's long history as the region's cultural leader, some have argued, made it difficult for the empire to remake itself to face the Western challenge; Japan, on the other hand, has a long history of cultural borrowing and thus found it easier to borrow from the Euro-American world. Some historians have argued that China's earlier experience with imperialism hobbled the modernizing tendencies within the empire and kept it from responding; they argue that Japan had the advantage of being "opened" later and so could respond more effectively. Others have argued that Japan's tradition of military prowess played a role, and still others contend that China's more complete incorporation into the modern "world system" hampered its ability to respond more independently.

# Patterns of Evidence: Sources for Chapter 24

## SOURCE 24.1

## Lin Zexu's letter to Queen Victoria of Great Britain

### August 27, 1839

In March 1839, the Daoguang emperor sent Lin Zexu (1785–1850), a widely respected official with a reputation for courage and honesty, to Canton as an imperial commissioner, charged with the task of cutting off the opium trade—a trade which had proved extremely lucrative to British traders in the region. Lin confiscated vast opium stocks, ordered them destroyed, and made merchants sign an agreement that they would no longer sell the drug, on pain of death. British merchants appealed to their government for compensation—and for military action against Lin's agents. This effort culminated in the First Opium War (1839–1842). In the midst of his anti-opium efforts, however, Lin also attempted to shame Queen Victoria (whom he believed was at the center of governmental policy in Great Britain) into cutting off the opium trade that was causing so much damage to the Chinese people, even though it generated profits for the British.

His Majesty the Emperor comforts and cherishes foreigners as well as Chinese: he loves all the people in the world without discrimination. Whenever profit is found, he wishes to share it with all men; whenever harm appears, he likewise will eliminate it on behalf of all of mankind. His heart is in fact the heart of the whole universe.

Generally speaking, the succeeding rulers of your honorable country have been respectful and obedient. Time and again they have sent petitions to China, saying: "We are grateful to His Majesty the Emperor for the impartial and favorable treatment he has granted to the citizens of my country who have come to China to trade," etc. I am pleased to learn that you, as the ruler of your honorable country, are thoroughly familiar with the principle of righteousness and are grateful for the favor that His Majesty the Emperor has bestowed upon your subjects. Because of this fact, the

Source: *Chinese Repository*, Vol. 8 (February 1840), pp. 497–503; reprinted in William H. McNeil and Mitsuko Iriye, eds., *Modern Asia and Africa*, Readings in World History Vol. 9, (New York: Oxford University Press, 1971), pp. 111–118.

Celestial Empire, following its traditional policy of treating foreigners with kindness, has been doubly considerate towards the people from England. You have traded in China for almost 200 years, and as a result, your country has become wealthy and prosperous.

As this trade has lasted for a long time, there are bound to be unscrupulous as well as honest traders. Among the unscrupulous are those who bring opium to China to harm the Chinese; they succeed so well that this poison has spread far and wide in all the provinces. You, I hope, will certainly agree that people who pursue material gains to the great detriment of the welfare of others can be neither tolerated by Heaven nor endured by men. . . .

Your country is more than 60,000 *li* from China. The purpose of your ships in coming to China is to realize a large profit. Since this profit is realized in China and is in fact taken away from the Chinese people, how can foreigners return injury for the benefit they have received by sending this poison to harm their benefactors? They may not intend to harm others on purpose, but the fact remains that they are so obsessed with material gain that they have no concern whatever for the harm they can cause to others. Have they no conscience? I have heard that you strictly prohibit opium in your own country, indicating unmistakably that you know how harmful opium is. You do not wish opium to harm your own country, but you choose to bring that harm to other countries such as China. Why?

. . .

I have heard that the areas under your direct jurisdiction such as London, Scotland, and Ireland do not produce opium; it is produced instead in your Indian possessions such as Bengal, Madras, Bombay, Patna, and Malwa. In these possessions the English people not only plant opium poppies that stretch from one mountain to another but also open factories to manufacture this terrible drug. As months accumulate and years pass by, the poison they have produced increases in its wicked intensity, and its repugnant odor reaches as high as the sky. Heaven is furious with anger, and all the gods are moaning with pain! It is hereby suggested that you destroy and plow under all of these opium plants and grow food crops instead, while issuing an order to punish severely anyone who dares to plant opium poppies again. If you adopt this policy of love so as to produce good and exterminate evil, Heaven will protect you, and gods will bring you good fortune. Moreover, you will enjoy a long life and be rewarded with a multitude of children and grandchildren! In short, by taking this one measure, you can bring great happiness to others as well as yourself. Why do you not do it?

Li: Roughly 1/3 mile.

▶ **Working with Sources**

1. How does Lin contrast honorable with dishonorable trade? Is this "honor" bound up in the product itself?

2. What does Lin see as the responsibility of a monarch to his/her own subjects, as well as to the subjects of other monarchs?

## SOURCE 24.2

# Narrative of the British ship *Nemesis* during the First Opium War

**1845**

When hostilities broke out between China and Britain in 1839, the British fleet was the most powerful in the world and in a high state of readiness. The Chinese had no real naval forces to contest the British, but a small Chinese squadron sailed out to confront the British men-o'-war. The underfunded and frantically assembled Chinese navy could not stand up to armored steam gunboats like the *Nemesis*, whose heavy pivot gun dominated riverside batteries and allowed British expeditionary forces to land wherever they pleased. The British methodically attacked and occupied forces along the Chinese coast from Guangzhou to Shanghai, and the Treaty of Nanjing (1842) marked an end to hostilities. However, the "heroes" of the *Nemesis* continued to receive attention for their victory over the Chinese, and a book detailing the ship's voyages and military successes was rushed into print in 1845.

**CHAPTER XVI.**

Keshen, who had spent all his life either in large provincial capitals or in the imperial city itself, could have had little opportunity of learning anything either relating to foreign trade or foreign ships, still less was he acquainted with the "outer waters" along the coast of the empire.

After describing them to his imperial master, he boldly ventures his opinion, that the reputation of the fortifications of the Bocca Tigris, as a place of defence, have been much overrated, and he goes on to say—"It is, then, clear that we have no defences worthy to be called such. It is, in truth, the local character of the country,

that there is no important point of defence by which the whole may be maintained."

No wonder that such a declaration from a man who was also the third member of the imperial cabinet, taken, as it was, from personal observation, should have sounded unpalatable and even traitorous to the emperor's ear. But this was not all. Indeed, one might almost imagine that some European must have pointed out to him defects which his own unpractised and unaided eye could never have detected.

Lin [Zexu], on the other hand, had never dared to report to his master the full extent of the information which was given to him, though he was fully

Source: W. H. Bernard and W. D. Hall, *Narrative of the Voyages and Services of the Nemesis from 1840 to 1843, and of the Combined Naval and Military Operations in China: Comprising a Complete Account of the Colony of Hong-Kong and Remarks on the Character and Habits of the Chinese*, 2nd ed. (London: Henry Colburn, 1845), 149–152, available online at http://www.gutenberg.org/files/43669/43669-h/43669-h.htm.

prepared to adopt every advice which tended to obstruct the commerce of England, and impede an amicable settlement of the difficulties.

Such truths are always hard to bear, and harder to believe, and were consequently *not* believed, *because* they were true. But Keshen did his best to improve his weapons; he sent for a founder of cannon, who gave him a new model, and undertook to make some experimental pieces. Yet it did not escape Keshen that, even if he succeeded in casting good cannon, he could only do so as a preparation *for the future.* "They could not be ready," says he, "for the business we have now in hand. These are the proofs," he adds, "of the inefficiency of our military armament, which is such *that no reliance can be placed upon it.*"

He proceeded to say that it would be necessary to employ a naval as well as a land force to defend the Bogue, but then threw out a suspicion that the seamen were not to be depended on, for that "he had heard a report that, after the battle of Chuenpee, these men all went to their commander, or Tetuh, and demanded money of him, threatening that they would otherwise disperse; and he had, therefore, personally made inquiry into the matter, and found that the report was perfectly true, and, moreover, that the Tetuh, having no other remedy, (evidently the pay was in arrear,) was obliged to *pawn his own clothes and other things*, by which means he was enabled to give each of them a bonus of two dollars, and thus only could he get them to remain for a time at their posts."

Moreover, he added, "our ships of war are not large and strong, and it is difficult to mount heavy guns upon them. Hence it is evident that our force here, (he was writing at the Bogue,) as a guard and defence against the foreigners, is insufficient."

Keshen next remarked upon the character of the people of the province. "Your slave has found them ungrateful and avaricious. Of those who are actual traitors it is unnecessary to say anything. But the rest are accustomed to see the foreigners day by day, and intimacy has grown up between them." And he proceeds to contrast them very unfavourably with the people of Chusan, "who felt at once that the foreigners were of *another race.*"

. . .

The memorial containing Captain Elliot's demands was sent up to Pekin, together with this report, which was founded upon personal observation; and Keshen implored the emperor to look with pity upon "his black-haired flock, the people, and that he would be graciously pleased to accede to the requests made by the foreigners, and to grant them favours beyond measure. Thus," he added, "shall we lay the foundation for victory hereafter, by binding and curbing the foreigners now, while we *prepare* the means of cutting them off at some future period."

Keshen was a true Chinaman of the new school, (for there are new schools even in antique China,) and, in most respects, the very opposite of Lin. Sensible of the weakness of his country when matched with England, conscious of his inability to fight his enemy with success, he nevertheless hazarded the chance, when the *commands* of the emperor compelled him to aim the blow. He, however, did his utmost to gain time, and even endeavoured to impose upon Captain Elliot, and to hope against hope itself. After all that Keshen had said, the defence of the Bogue was conducted, as we shall now perceive, with more energy than might have been expected, and, indeed, with considerable spirit.

. . .

S24-8 **Patterns of Evidence:** Sources for Chapter 24

"civilization and enlightenment" were designed to put Japan on an equal footing with Western powers. The constitution itself, composed after a painstaking study of the constitutional governments of many Western countries, reflects this drive to "Westernize." Nonetheless, the document also contained various escape clauses, in case the power of the emperor was questioned too openly.

## Imperial Oath Sworn in the Sanctuary in the Imperial Palace (Tsuge-bumi)

We, the Successor to the prosperous Throne of Our Predecessors, do humbly and solemnly swear to the Imperial Founder of Our House and to Our other Imperial Ancestors that, in pursuance of a great policy co-extensive with the Heavens and with the Earth, We shall maintain and secure from decline the ancient form of government.

In consideration of the progressive tendency of the course of human affairs and in parallel with the advance of civilization, We deem it expedient, in order to give clearness and distinctness to the instructions bequeathed by the Imperial Founder of Our House and by Our other Imperial Ancestors, to establish fundamental laws formulated into express provisions of law, so that, on the one hand, Our Imperial posterity may possess an express guide for the course they are to follow, and that, on the other, Our subjects shall thereby be enabled to enjoy a wider range of action in giving Us their support, and that the observance of Our laws shall continue to the remotest ages of time. We will thereby to give greater firmness to the stability of Our country and to promote the welfare of all the people within the boundaries of Our dominions; and We now establish the Imperial House Law and the Constitution.

. . .

## CHAPTER I.
## THE EMPEROR

Article 1. The Empire of Japan shall be reigned over and governed by a line of Emperors unbroken for ages eternal.

Article 2. The Imperial Throne shall be succeeded to by Imperial male descendants, according to the provisions of the Imperial House Law.

Article 3. The Emperor is sacred and inviolable.

Article 4. The Emperor is the head of the Empire, combining in Himself the rights of sovereignty, and exercises them, according to the provisions of the present Constitution.

Article 5. The Emperor exercises the legislative power with the consent of the Imperial Diet.

Article 6. The Emperor gives sanction to laws, and orders them to be promulgated and executed.

. . .

## CHAPTER II.
## RIGHTS AND DUTIES OF SUBJECTS

Article 18. The conditions necessary for being a Japanese subject shall be determined by law.

Article 19. Japanese subjects may, according to qualifications determined in laws or ordinances, be appointed to civil or military or any other public offices equally.

Article 20. Japanese subjects are amenable to service in the Army or Navy, according to the provisions of law.

Article 21. Japanese subjects are amenable to the duty of paying taxes, according to the provisions of law.

Article 22. Japanese subjects shall have the liberty of abode and of changing the same within the limits of the law.

Article 23. No Japanese subject shall be arrested, detained, tried or punished, unless according to law.

Article 24. No Japanese subject shall be deprived of his right of being tried by the judges determined by law.

Article 25. Except in the cases provided for in the law, the house of no Japanese subject shall be entered or searched without his consent.

Article 26. Except in the cases mentioned in the law, the secrecy of the letters of every Japanese subject shall remain inviolate.

Article 27. The right of property of every Japanese subject shall remain inviolate. (2) Measures necessary to be taken for the public benefit shall be any provided for by law.

Article 28. Japanese subjects shall, within limits not prejudicial to peace and order, and not antagonistic to their duties as subjects, enjoy freedom of religious belief.

Article 29. Japanese subjects shall, within the limits of law, enjoy the liberty of speech, writing, publication, public meetings and associations.

Article 30. Japanese subjects may present petitions, by observing the proper forms of respect, and by complying with the rules specially provided for the same.

Article 31. The provisions contained in the present Chapter shall not affect the exercises of the powers appertaining to the Emperor, in times of war or in cases of a national emergency.

▶ **Working with Sources**

1. **What was the source of the emperor's power, according to this document?**

2. **To what extent could military considerations limit the rights and freedoms of Japanese citizens? Were these merely potential limitations?**

## SOURCE 24.5

# Natsume Soseki, *Kokoro*

1914

Like nearly all the arts in late-nineteenth-century Japan, the novel was also heavily influenced by Western examples. The culmination of this trend, in Meiji society generally, was *Kokoro*, published by Natsume Soseki (1867–1916) in 1914. Soseki, a lecturer in English literature at the Imperial University in Tokyo, depicts the wrenching changes in Meiji Japan and their effect on traditional and generational values, leading ultimately to the tragic end of the central character in the novel. *Kokoro* (the word means, roughly,

Source: Natsume Soseki, *Kokoro*, trans. Edwin McClellan (Washington, DC: Regnery, 1957), 108–110, 117–118, 120–122.

"the heart of things") was Soseki's best-known novel, and appeared two years after the death of Emperor Meiji. The excerpts below also touch on the real-life suicide of General Nogi, a hero of the Russo–Japanese War (1904–1905) who killed himself immediately after the death of the Meiji in 1912. The sense of honor that accompanied Nogi to his grave is thus at the heart of the novel, and Soseki's main theme may have been the ongoing interaction between Western-style reforms and traditional Japanese culture.

My father was the first to see the news of General Nogi's death in the paper.

"What a terrible thing!" he said. "What a terrible thing!"

We, who had not yet read the news, were startled by these exclamations.

"I really did think he had finally gone mad," said my brother later.

"I must say I was surprised too," agreed my brother-in-law.

About that time, the papers were so full of unusual news that we in the country waited impatiently for their arrival. I would read the news by my father's bedside, taking care not to disturb him, or, if I could not do this, I would quietly retire into my own room, and there read the paper from beginning to end. For a long time, the image of General Nogi in his uniform, and that of his wife dressed like a court lady, stayed with me.

The tragic news touched us like the bitter wind which awakens the trees and the grass sleeping in the remotest corners of the countryside. The incident was still fresh in our minds when, to my surprise, a telegram arrived from Sensei. In a place where dogs barked at the sight of a Western-style suit, the arrival of a telegram was a great event. My mother, to whom the telegram had been given, seemed to think it necessary to call me to a deserted part of the house before handing it to me. Needless to say, she looked quite startled.

"What is it?" she said, standing by while I opened it.

It was a simple message, saying that he would like to see me if possible, and would I come up? I cocked my head in puzzlement. My mother offered an explanation. "I am sure he wants to see you about a job," she said.

I thought that perhaps my mother was right. On the other hand, I could not quite believe that Sensei wanted to see me for that reason. At any rate, I, who had sent for my brother and brother-in-law, could hardly abandon my sick father and go to Tokyo. My mother and I decided that I should send Sensei a telegram saying that I could not come. I explained as briefly as possible that my father's condition was becoming more and more critical. I felt, however, that I owed him a fuller explanation. That same day, I wrote him a letter giving him the details. My mother, who was firmly convinced that Sensei had some post in mind for me, said in a tone filled with regret, "What a pity that this should have happened at such a time."

. . .

My father began to talk deliriously.

"Will General Nogi ever forgive me?" he would say. "How can I ever face him without shame? Yes, General, I will be with you very soon."

When he said such things, my mother would become a little frightened, and would ask us to gather around the bed. My father too, when he came out of his delirium, seemed to want everybody by his side so as not to feel lonely. He would want my mother most of all. He would look around the room and, if she was not there, he would be sure to ask, "Where is Omitsu?" Even when he did not say so, his eyes would ask the question. Often, I had to get up and find her. She would then leave her work, and enter the sickroom saying, "Is there anything you wish?" There were times when he would say nothing, and simply look at her. There were also times when he would say something quite unexpectedly gentle, such as: "I've given you a lot of trouble, haven't I, Omitsu?" And my mother's eyes would suddenly fill with tears. Afterwards, she would remember how different he used to be in the old days, and say, "Of course, he sounds rather helpless now, but he used to be quite frightening, I can tell you."

. . .

Almost violently, I tore open the tough paper which contained the letter. The letter had the appearance of a manuscript, with the characters neatly written between vertically ruled lines. I smoothed out the sheets which had been folded over twice for easier handling in the post.

I could not but wonder what it was that Sensei had written at such great length. I was, however, too much on edge to read the whole letter properly. My mind kept wandering back to the sickroom. I had the feeling that something would happen to my father before I could finish reading the letter. At least, I was sure that I would soon be called away by my brother, or my mother, or my uncle. In this unsettled state, I read the first page.

"You asked me once to tell you of my past. I did not have the courage then to do so. But now, I believe I am free of the bonds that prevented me from telling you the truth about myself. The freedom that I now have, however, is no more than an earthly, physical kind of freedom, which will not last forever. Unless I take advantage of it while I can, I shall never again have the opportunity of passing on to you what I have learned from my own experience, and my promise to you will have been broken. Circumstances having prevented me from telling you my story in person, I have decided to write it out for you."

I read thus far, and realized why it was that the letter was so long. That Sensei would not bother to write about my future career, I had more or less known from the very beginning. What really worried me was that Sensei, who hated to write at all, had taken the trouble to write such a long epistle. Why had he not waited, I asked myself, until I was once more in Tokyo?

I said to myself repeatedly, "He is free now, but he will never be free again," and tried desperately to understand what the words meant; then all of a sudden I became uneasy. I tried to read on further but, before I could do so, I heard my brother's voice calling me from the sickroom. Frightened, I stood up, and hurried along the corridor to where the others were gathered. I was prepared to learn that the end had come for my father.

▶ **Working with Sources**

1. In what specific ways does this excerpt reflect the incorporation of Western ideas and items into traditional Japanese society?

2. How does Soseki use the dying father and the teacher as metaphors for a young man's life in the Meiji period?

# Chapter 25 1683–1908

# Adaptation and Resistance

## THE OTTOMAN AND RUSSIAN EMPIRES

**Serfdom:** Legal and cultural institution in which peasants are bound to the land.

RUSSIA

Balkans

OTTOMAN EMPIRE

Persia

**RUSSIAN AND OTTOMAN EMPIRES, 1683–1908**

October 13, 1824, saw a most unusual event in Russia. On this date, Aleksander Nikitenko, born into serfdom, received his freedom at the age of 20 from his lord, a fabulously wealthy landowning count. Even more remarkable is the subsequent course of Nikitenko's life and career. After earning a university degree, he went on to become a professor of literature at St. Petersburg University, a member of the distinguished Academy of Sciences, and a censor in the Ministry of Education.

Beginning in 1818 at the age of 14, the precocious Nikitenko kept a diary, which provides insights into the role of serfdom in the Russian Empire. He writes that "when the inevitable happened," the errant serfs were turned over to a lackey in charge of meting out punishment in the form of flogging with birch rods: "Woe to the unfortunates who fell into [his] hands! He was a master and enthusiast of flogging, especially of girls, and they were terrified by the mere sight of him." Nikitenko's curse, Russian serfdom, was scarcely different from plantation slavery in the Americas or from untouchability in the Indian caste system. Slavery was also the common lot of many in the neighboring Ottoman Empire, where, though limited to households, it was no less demeaning. The end of serfdom in Russia would not come until 1861 and that of slavery in the Ottoman Empire not until 1890.

*ABOVE: Auction of Serfs (1910), a painting by Klavdiy Vasilievich Lebedev (1852–1916), shows a wealthy Russian family auctioning off its valuables—and its serfs.*

Serfdom and slavery were dramatic examples of the kinds of practices that the new Enlightenment constitutionalism, in theory at least, stood firmly against. As such, they were among the first of many challenges the world outside western Europe and North America faced from the West in the nineteenth century. Russia was an empire that had inherited Byzantine Christian civilization but had not adopted the New Sciences and their offspring, the twin revolutions of the Enlightenment and Industrial Revolution. For its part, the Ottoman Empire was heir to both Islamic and Byzantine traditions but also had not participated in the transition to the New Sciences, Enlightenment, and industrialization. Even though Enlightenment thought had produced and elaborated the political theories of the social contract and popular sovereignty, which were realized in the American, French, and Haitian Revolutions, shortly before the onset of the Industrial Revolution in Great Britain, it would be the campaigns of Napoleon in the early nineteenth century that sowed these ideas throughout Europe.

They also would cast these seeds on the initially unpromising soil of the Russian and Ottoman Empires. Napoleon's invasions of Ottoman Egypt in 1798 and Russia in 1812 drove home to their rulers that his new armies of mass conscripts, equipped with flintlock muskets and light, mobile artillery and drilled to fight in flexible formations, were superior to their own military forces. It became essential for the Ottomans and Russians, if they were to keep their independence, to update their armies and training and to respond somehow to the constitutional nationalism arising from the French Revolution and carried by Napoleon's armies, which now attracted rising numbers of adherents among their subjects.

At the same time, the two empires became mortal enemies: An expanding eastern (Orthodox) Christian Russia declared its goal to be conquest of the former eastern Christian capital Constantinople (Istanbul) and to drive a shrinking Ottoman Empire from Europe back into "Asia" (Asia Minor, or Anatolia). Since both empires were members of the Concert of Europe, their conflict involved the other European powers as well. These powers found themselves increasingly drawn into confrontation, culminating in the Crimean War of 1853–1856, that was only partially European and increasingly involved Russia and the Ottomans in Asia. For the monarchs, politicians, and diplomats focused after 1815 on the balance of power in western and central Europe, such a power struggle between the Russians and Ottomans held little interest: For them, this contest was "Oriental" and therefore alien.

It is important that we keep this partially non-Western identity of the Russian and Ottoman Empires in mind for this chapter: As forcefully as Russia asserted itself in the European Concert in the early years after 1815 and again at the end of the nineteenth century, it was in reality—despite its Christian character—not any more or less "European" than the increasingly harried Muslim Ottoman Empire. Indeed, as we will see, both empires had far more in common with each other, and to some degree with the empire of the Qing in China, than they did with the evolving nation-states of western Europe. Furthermore, their reactions to the challenges posed by the new nation-states paralleled each other to a degree not often appreciated by students and scholars studying them outside of a world context. Therefore, we consider them together here as their own case studies in the overall patterns of constitutionalism, nation-state formation, and the challenge of modernity.

## Seeing Patterns

▶ Which new models did the Ottomans adopt during the nineteenth century to adapt themselves to the Western challenge?

▶ How did the agrarian Ottoman and Russian Empires, both with large landholding ruling classes, respond to the western European industrial challenge during the 1800s?

▶ Why did large, well-established empires like the Russian and the Ottoman Empires struggle with the forces of modernity, while a small, secluded island nation like Japan seemed to adapt so quickly and successfully?

# Decentralization and Reforms in the Ottoman Empire

Prior to the Russian–Ottoman rivalry in the 1800s, the traditional enemies of the Ottomans were the Austrian Habsburgs. This enmity had reached its climax in the second half of the 1600s. The Habsburgs ultimately won but in the course of the 1700s were increasingly sidelined by the rise of Russia as a new, Orthodox Christian empire, whose rulers, the tsars, saw themselves as representatives of the "third Rome"—that is, Moscow as the successor of Rome and Constantinople. After consolidating itself on the fertile northeast European plains, Russia expanded eastward and southward, clashing with the Muslim Ottomans, conquerors of Constantinople. Because the Russians adapted themselves earlier than the Ottomans to new western European military tactics, the Ottomans found it increasingly difficult to defend themselves in the later 1700s. They sought to improve their defenses through military and constitutional–nationalist reforms in the mid-1800s but were only partly successful. Russia became the patron of nationalist movements among the Slavic populations in the European provinces of the Ottoman Empire. Although they strengthened themselves through reforms, the Ottomans were no match for the combined Russian–southern Slavic aggression. At the end of the Second Balkan War of 1913, they had lost nearly the entire European part of their empire to ethnic–nationalist liberation movements and were barely able to hang on to Istanbul (see Map 25.1).

## Ottoman Imperialism in the 1600s and 1700s

In the period from 1500 to 1700 the Ottoman Empire was the dominant political power in the Middle East and North Africa, flanked by the two lesser realms of Persia in the east and Morocco in the west. At that time, the main enemy of the Ottomans was not yet Russia but the Habsburg Empire in Spain, Germany, and Austria. The two were fighting each other on dual fronts, the Balkans in the east and North Africa in the western Mediterranean, each gaining and losing in the process and eventually establishing a more or less stable disengagement. It was during this disengagement period that Russia began its expansion southward at the increasing expense of the Ottomans.

**Demographic Considerations**   As with the other agrarian–urban regions of Asia and Europe, the Middle East had experienced a sustained recovery of population levels after the Black Death of the mid-1400s. This recovery came to an end around 1600, with 25 million inhabitants, though with slow increases reaching 27 million by 1700 and about 30 million by 1800. The population figures were thus smaller than those of the Habsburg countries, with 37 million in 1700 and 42 million in 1800. If one takes into consideration, however, that the Spanish Habsburg line died out in Spain in 1700 and the Austrian Habsburgs governed only indirectly in Germany, the resulting figure for the smaller territory in 1800 is a comparable 25 million. Russia, for its part, had population figures roughly comparable to those of the Ottoman Empire. As the Ottomans approached the era of the challenge of modernity, they formed part of a relatively sparsely populated eastern Europe and Middle East.

**From Conquests to Retreats**    At the end of the 1500s, after a long period of military showdowns, the Ottomans and Habsburgs were beset by problems of military overextension. Therefore, in 1606 they concluded a peace to gain time for recovery, during which the Ottomans recognized the Habsburgs for the first time as a de facto Christian power on the border of the Ottoman province of Hungary. The peace lasted until the end of the 1600s, when both were sufficiently recovered to renew their competition. The Ottoman recovery was based on the recruitment of the Janissary infantry from exclusively rural Christian boys and young, mostly urban Muslims. By shifting from the increasingly less important cavalry to their firearm-equipped infantry and artillery, the Ottoman army regained its edge.

In 1683 the Ottomans renewed their competition with the Habsburgs and marched with a giant force to their northwestern border. For a second time in their history, they laid siege to Vienna (the first siege was in 1529), the capital of the Austrian Habsburgs. But even though sappers and siege cannons succeeded in breaching the walls in several places, a Polish relief army allied with the Habsburgs arrived just in time to drive the besiegers, who had neglected to fortify their camp, into a retreat. The Habsburgs followed up on this retreat by seizing Hungary, Transylvania, and northern Serbia, thus making a third siege of Vienna impossible. In the peace of 1699, the Ottomans and Habsburgs finally agreed to recognize each other fully in the territories they possessed.

**Renewed Reforms**    During the war years of the later 1600s, the Janissary force had swollen to some 70,000 soldiers. In the end, however, only about 10,000 were on active duty. Since they were all on the payroll, and given renewed fiscal shortfalls, the money was often debased or in arrears, forcing them to earn a living as craftspeople. In short, the Janissary force was in the process of becoming a collection of crafts guilds on a kind of government welfare.

New reforms were clearly necessary. In the early 1700s the sultan's government cut the Janissary rolls by half and enlisted Anatolian farmers to supplement the active Janissaries. In order to increase revenues with which to pay the Janissaries, the reformers introduced the new institution of the lifetime tax farm, or **life lease**, for agricultural rents from village farmers. As in France, which developed a similar tax-farm regime at the time, the idea was to diminish the temptation—endemic among the annual tax farmers—to squeeze farmers dry so that they would flee from the countryside to the cities. Wealthy and high-ranking courtiers, officers, administrators, and Islamic clerics in Istanbul bought these life leases. Thus, here in the early 1700s was the beginning of a development parallel to similar developments in France and England, with efforts to organize a kind of capital market.

**Life lease:** Lifelong tax farm, awarded to a wealthy member of the ruling class, in return for advances to the central imperial treasury on the taxes to be collected from village farmers.

| 1683 | 1768–1774 | 1832 |
|---|---|---|
| Second Ottoman siege of Vienna | First Ottoman–Russian war | Greece secures independence from Ottomans |

| 1762–1796 | 1798–1801 | 1839–1876 |
|---|---|---|
| Catherine II of Russia | Napoleon's occupation of Egypt | Tanzimat reforms in Ottoman Empire |

| 1853–1856 | 1878–1885 | 1908 |
|---|---|---|
| Crimean War of Great Britain, France, and Ottoman Empire against Russia | Independence of Serbia, Montenegro, Romania, and Bulgaria | "Young Turks" rise to power in Ottoman Empire |

| 1861 | 1904–1905 |
|---|---|
| Emancipation of serfs in Russian Empire | Russo–Japanese War, followed by abortive Russian revolution |

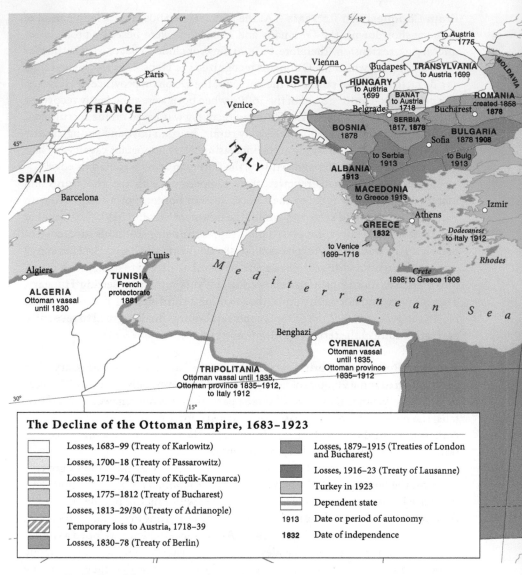

The following are labels on the map:

to Austria 1775
Vienna
Paris
Budapest
**TRANSYLVANIA** to Austria 1699
**MOLDAVIA**
**AUSTRIA**
**HUNGARY** to Austria 1699
**BANAT** to Austria 1718
**ROMANIA** created 1858 1878
Belgrade
Bucharest
**FRANCE**
Venice
**SERBIA** 1817, 1878
**BOSNIA** 1878
**BULGARIA** 1878 1908
Sofia
**ITALY**
to Serbia 1913
to Bulg 1913
**ALBANIA** 1913
**SPAIN**
Barcelona
**MACEDONIA** to Greece 1913
Izmir
Athens
**GREECE** 1832
*Dodecanese* to Italy 1912
to Venice 1699–1718
*Rhodes*
*Crete* 1898; to Greece 1908
Algiers
Tunis
**TUNISIA** French protectorate 1881
*Mediterranean Sea*
**ALGERIA** Ottoman vassal until 1830
Benghazi
**CYRENAICA** Ottoman vassal until 1835, Ottoman province 1835–1912
**TRIPOLITANIA** Ottoman vassal until 1835, Ottoman province 1835–1912, to Italy 1912

**The Decline of the Ottoman Empire, 1683–1923**

Losses, 1683–99 (Treaty of Karlowitz)
Losses, 1700–18 (Treaty of Passarowitz)
Losses, 1719–74 (Treaty of Küçük-Kaynarca)
Losses, 1775–1812 (Treaty of Bucharest)
Losses, 1813–29/30 (Treaty of Adrianople)
Temporary loss to Austria, 1718–39
Losses, 1830–78 (Treaty of Berlin)

Losses, 1879–1915 (Treaties of London and Bucharest)
Losses, 1916–23 (Treaty of Lausanne)
Turkey in 1923
Dependent state
1913    Date or period of autonomy
**1832**    Date of independence

MAP 25.1 **The Decline of the Ottoman Empire, 1683–1923.**

As a result of the reforms, in 1720, for the first time in a century and a half, the central budget was balanced again.

**Decentralization**    An accelerating transformation of cavalry-held lands into tax farms started a pattern of political decentralization in the Ottoman Empire. Agents responsible for the collection of taxes for their superiors succeeded in withholding increasing amounts from the treasury in Istanbul. By the mid-1700s, these agents were in positions of considerable provincial power as "notables" in the Balkans or "valley lords" in western Anatolia. Starved for funds, the sultan and central administration were no longer able to support a large standing army of infantry and cavalry in the capital.

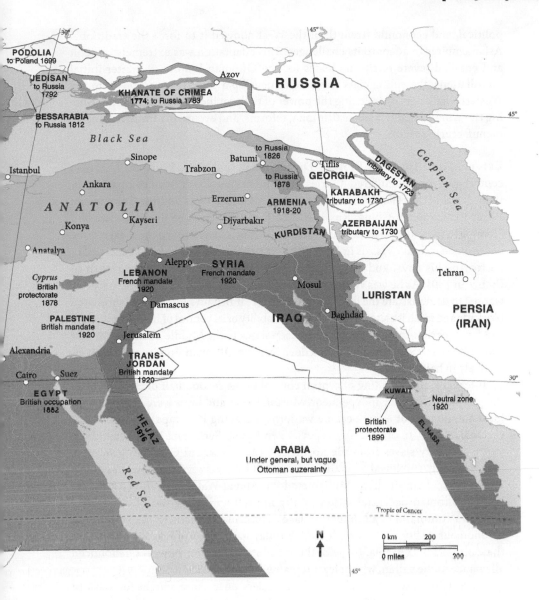

In 1768–1774 the notables and valley lords played a crucial role not only in financing a major war against Russia but also in recruiting troops—untrained and underarmed peasants—since the numbers of government forces in fighting order had shrunk to minimal levels. The war was the first in which the Russian tsars exploited Ottoman decentralization for a systematic expansion southward. When the sultan lost the war, he was at the mercy of these notables and lords in the provinces.

## The Western Challenge and Ottoman Responses

Soon after this Ottoman–Russian war, the Ottoman Empire began to face the challenge of Western modernity. As with China and Japan, the increasing military, political, and economic strength of the West allowed it to force the traditional Asian empires to adapt to its challenges. This adaptation was extremely difficult and entailed severe territorial losses for the Ottoman Empire. But after initial humiliations, the ruling class was able to develop a pattern of responses to the Western challenge, by reducing the power of the provincial magnates, modernizing the army, introducing constitutional reforms, and eventually transforming its manufacturing sector.

**External and Internal Blows**    During the period 1774–1808, the Ottoman central government suffered a series of humiliations which were comparable in their destabilizing effects to those in the later Opium Wars and the Taiping and Boxer Rebellions in China. Russia gained the north coast of the Black Sea and Georgia in the Caucasus. Napoleon invaded Egypt and destroyed the local regime of Ottoman military vassals in 1798. But a British fleet sent after him succeeded in destroying his navy, and a subsequent land campaign forced him to return to France in 1801. As he was victimizing the Ottoman Empire, Napoleon apparently wanted to demonstrate the ineffectiveness of Great Britain's European continental blockade and teach it a lesson about the vulnerability of its control of India. Napoleon's sudden imperialist venture produced a deep shock in the Middle East: For the first time a Western ruler had penetrated deep into the Ottoman Empire, cutting it effectively in half.

Internally, the lessening of central control in the second half of the 1700s left the provinces virtually independent. Most notables and lords were satisfied with local autonomy, but a few became warlords, engaging in campaigns to become regional leaders. In other cases, especially in Egypt, Syria, and Iraq, *Mamluks*— that is, military slaves from the northern Caucasus whom Ottoman governors had previously employed as auxiliaries in the military—seized power. In eastern Arabia, a local Sunni cleric, Muhammad ibn Abd al-Wahhab [wah-HAHB], exploited Ottoman decentralization to ally himself with the head of a powerful family in command of a number of oases, Ibn Saud [sa-OOD], to establish an autonomous polity in the desert, which today is the most powerful oil state in the world—Saudi Arabia. None of these ambitious leaders, however, renounced allegiance to the sultan, who at least remained a figurehead.

To reclaim power, the sultan and his viziers once more sought for ways to reform the empire. In 1792, they proclaimed a "new order," defined by a reorganization of the army with the creation of a new, separate artillery and flintlock musket corps of some 22,000 soldiers alongside the Janissaries. The ad hoc financing of the new order, however, came to haunt the reformers. During a severe fiscal crisis in 1807, auxiliary Janissaries, refusing to wear new uniforms, assassinated a new-order officer. Inept handling of this incident resulted in a full-scale revolt of Janissaries as well as religious scholars and students, costing the sultan his life and ushering in the dissolution of the new troops. In a counter-revolt, thanks to the timely arrival from northern Bulgaria of a Ukrainian-born notable with his private army, a new sultan came to power in 1808. As a price for his accession, the sultan had to agree to power sharing with the provincial lords.

**Renewed Difficulties**    After a dozen years of careful maneuvering, during which the sultan reconstituted the core of another new army and neutralized many notables and valley lords, he was able to crush the Janissaries in a bloody massacre (1826).

But the new corps was in no shape yet to provide the backbone for a sustained recentralization of the empire. New internal enemies arose, in the form of Greek ethnic nationalists, whom the Ottomans would have defeated had it not been for the military intervention of the European powers. As a result, Greece became independent in a war of liberation (1821–1832). It was the first country, prior to Italy and Germany, in which ethnic nationalism was an element in its foundation.

Russia, providing support for its fellow Orthodox Christian Greeks, acquired new territories from the Ottomans around the Black Sea. Several Balkan provinces achieved administrative autonomy. Algiers in North Africa was lost in 1830, falling to an invading French force. Worst of all, in 1831, the new Ottoman vassal in Egypt, the Albanian-born officer Muhammad Ali (r. 1805–1848), seeking greater influence within the empire, rose in rebellion. After occupying Syria (1831–1840), he would have conquered Istanbul had he not been stopped by Russian, British, and French intervention. Without the diplomacy of Great Britain, which carefully sought to balance the European powers after the end of the Napoleonic empire, the Ottoman Empire would not have survived the 1830s.

**Muhammad Ali.** Muhammad Ali transformed Egypt during the first half of the nineteenth century more thoroughly than the Ottoman overlord sultan could in his far-flung empire. He astutely realized that long-staple cotton, bred first in Egypt, could make Egypt a wealthy state in the beginning industrial transformation of the world.

**Life, Honor, and Property**   The cumulative effect of these setbacks was a realization among Ottoman administrators that only a serious effort at recentralization would save the empire. In 1839, with a change of sultans, the government issued the Rose Garden Edict, the first of three reform edicts, plus more specific additional ones in between, which are collectively known as **Tanzimat** ("Reorganizations"). In the Rose Garden Edict, the government bound itself to three basic principles: the guarantee of life, honor, and property of all subjects regardless of religion; the replacement of tax farms and life leases with an equitable tax system; and the introduction of a military conscription system, all in accordance with the Sharia, the compendium of Islamic morality and law. The edict carefully avoided a definition of the position of the Christians and Jews in the empire before the law, offering them the rights of life, honor, and property while maintaining their inequality vis-à-vis the Muslims proclaimed in Islamic law.

**Tanzimat:** Ottoman reforms inspired by constitutional nationalism in Europe, including the adoption of basic rights, a legal reform, and a land code.

The edict addressed the two fundamental problems of the empire (that is, taxes and the military), carefully emphasizing the Islamic justification. It also enumerated basic human rights, inspired by the American Declaration of Independence and the French Rights of Man. Here, we can see a first adaptation of the Ottoman Empire to the Western challenge: The Ottoman Empire adapted, at least in an initial and partial way, to constitutional nationalism, the outgrowth of Enlightenment thought.

**Further Reforms**   As these reforms were being implemented, a new European political initiative challenged the Ottoman Empire. The aggressively imperialistic Napoleon III (president 1848–1852, emperor 1852–1870), self-declared emperor of France, challenged the Russian tsar's claim to be the protector of the Christian holy places in Palestine, a claim which the Ottoman sultan had acceded to after his defeat in 1774. As we saw in Chapter 24, the French joined the British during the Second Opium War for much the same reason: protection of Catholics and French missionaries in China. While the French and Russian diplomats each sought to influence a vacillating sultan, the political situation turned increasingly tense. Through careful maneuvering, Ottoman diplomats were able to strengthen themselves in a coalition with Great Britain and France. In the Crimean War of 1853–1856 this coalition was victorious against an isolated Russia. It forced Russia in the subsequent peace to recognize the Ottoman Empire's right to full integrity, provided the latter would continue the reforms announced in 1839.

Accordingly, the sultan promulgated the "Fortunate Edict" of 1856, in which he clarified the question of equality left open in the earlier edict: Regardless of religion, all subjects had the right to education, employment, and administration of justice. A number of subsequent measures spelled out this right and the earlier edicts in greater detail. To begin with, the reformers reorganized the judiciary by establishing law courts for the application of newly introduced commercial, maritime, and criminal legal codes, based on European models. A further reform measure was the introduction of a system of secular schools, initially for males, from age 10 through high school. But a lack of funds delayed the building of this system, which at the end of the 1800s still lagged far behind the traditional religious primary schools and colleges as well as the more rapidly expanding Christian, Jewish, and foreign missionary schools.

A measure that worked out quite differently from what was intended was the Land Code of 1858. The code reaffirmed the sultan as the owner of all land unless subjects or religious foundations possessed title to specific parcels of private property. But it also confirmed all users of the sultan's land—that is, farmers who produced harvests on family plots as well as landowners collecting rents from the farmers of entire villages. Theoretically, the code subjected all users, family farmers as well as landowners, to taxation. But in practice the central administration had no money to appoint tax collectors (or even establish a land registry prior to 1908). It could not do without tax farmers, who still collected what they could get and transmitted to the government as little as they were able to get away with.

> "The land of an inhabited village cannot be given to one person independently in order to make a [family plot]."
>
> —The Ottoman Land Code

Highly uneven forms of landownership thus developed. Overall, tax yields remained as low as ever, improving only toward the end of the nineteenth century, long after the introduction of the Tanzimat. The much-needed land reform remained incomplete.

**Constitution and War**   Seen in the context of the centralization reforms in previous centuries, the Tanzimat decrees of 1839 and 1856 were little more than enactments of traditional policies. In the context of nineteenth-century constitutional nationalism, however, they appeared like autocratic dictates from above, lacking popular approval. In the 1860s, younger Tanzimat bureaucrats and journalists working for the first Ottoman newspapers, meeting in loose circles in Istanbul and Paris under the name of "Young Ottomans," became advocates for the introduction of a constitution as the crowning element of the Tanzimat, to end the autocracy of the sultan.

The idea of a constitution became reality in the midst of a deep crisis in which the empire found itself embroiled from 1873 to 1878. The crisis began when the Ottoman government defaulted on its foreign loans. In order to service the renegotiated loans, it had to increase taxes. This increase triggered ethnic–nationalist uprisings in Herzegovina, Bosnia, and Bulgaria in the Balkans in 1875 and 1876. The heavy-handed repression of these uprisings resulted in a political crisis, with a palace coup d'état by

**Ottoman Parliament.** The constitutional reforms (Tanzimat) of the Ottoman Empire culminated in elections for a parliament and two sessions, uniting deputies from a multiplicity of ethnic backgrounds (1876–1878). It met during the Russian–Ottoman War of 1877–1878, which the Ottomans lost. The newly installed Sultan Abdülhamit used the war as an excuse for ending constitutional rule and governing by decree.

the Young Ottomans, during which a new sultan, Abdülhamit II (r. 1876–1909), ascended the throne and a constitution was adopted. Finally, in this sequence of events, the Russians exploited the perceived political weakness of the new constitutional Ottoman regime for a new Russo–Ottoman war in support of the Balkan nationalist uprisings.

Amid a rapid advance of Russian troops against a crumbling Ottoman army, the Ottomans held elections for the constitutionally decreed parliament between December 1876 and January 1877. Provincial and county councils elected 130 deputies to meet for two sessions in Istanbul. With the invading Russian forces practically at the gates of Istanbul in February 1878, the deputies engaged in a spirited criticism of the government. Irritated, the sultan dismissed the parliament and ruled by decree.

A few months later, at the Congress of Berlin, the sultan had to accept the loss of two-thirds of the empire's European provinces. Montenegro, Serbia, Romania, and (after a delay of 7 years) Bulgaria gained their independence. Bosnia-Herzegovina and Cyprus, although still Ottoman, received an Austrian administration and a British administration, respectively. Sultan Abdülhamit never reconvened the parliament, and the empire reverted back to autocratic rule.

**Autocracy**   Sultan Abdülhamit surrounded himself with capable second-generation Tanzimat bureaucrats who did not have the constitutionalist leanings of the Young Ottomans. He had very little financial leeway, since the Public Debt Administration, imposed by the European powers in 1881, collected about one-third of the empire's income to pay for its accumulated foreign debt. Furthermore, the European price depression in the second half of the nineteenth century (1873–1896) was not favorable to foreign investments in the empire. Nevertheless, a few short-distance railroads connecting the fertile Anatolian valleys and their agricultural produce with Mediterranean ports were built thanks to French capital. A postal service and telegraph system connected all provinces, and steamship lines connected the ports. Once the depression was over, foreign investors enabled the government to build long-distance railroads across Anatolia. By the early 1900s, a basic communication infrastructure was in place in the Ottoman Empire.

Given his fiscal limits, the sultan was all the more active as a propagandist, burnishing his credentials as the pan-Islamic caliph of Muslims in Eurasia, from

Austrian Bosnia and Russian Asia to British India. He astutely sensed that the Balkan events of 1875/1876 and subsequent Congress of Berlin had been a watershed in European politics. The Concert of Europe, with its Britain-supported concept of a balance of power, was no more. It was being replaced by the beginning of an imperial rivalry between Germany and Great Britain. France, Austria-Hungary, and Russia played their own subsidiary imperial roles. Since France and Great Britain, furthermore, carried out their imperialism against the Ottoman Empire, with the conquests of Tunisia in 1881 and Egypt in 1882, respectively, Abdülhamit was particularly affected. His pan-Islamism was therefore a carefully executed effort to instill the fear of jihad in European politicians and their publics.

Although most of the Ottoman Balkan provinces had become independent nations by 1878, three ethnic–nationalist movements were still left inside the empire. Abdülhamit met them with an iron fist. The first movement consisted of Serb, Bulgarian, Vlah, and Greek nationalists agitating in Macedonia during 1893–1895. Without outside support, none of these feuding groups could impose itself on the province, and Ottoman troops were therefore able to repress them.

The next were the Armenians, who formed sizeable minorities in the six eastern provinces of Anatolia. Most Armenian farmers and craftspeople in these provinces were politically quiet but urban-based and secularized Armenian ethnic nationalists organized terrorist incidents. In reaction, the sultan armed Kurdish tribal units, which massacred thousands of Anatolian Armenian villagers from 1894 to 1896. Finally, the Ottomans met a revolt in Crete in 1897, in favor of union with Greece, with an invasion and defeat of Greece itself, which had to pay an indemnity. Europe, busy with its imperialist competition in Africa and Asia, had no time to help the remaining ethnic–nationalist movements of the Macedonians and Armenians in the Ottoman Empire.

In the later years of his rule, Abdülhamit increasingly failed to stem dissatisfaction with the lack of political freedom among the graduates of the elite administrative and military academies. As so often prior to revolts or revolutions, improved economic conditions—as they materialized after the end of the worldwide recession of 1893—stoked political ambitions to create a condition social scientists sometimes call a "revolution of rising expectations." In a pattern similar to that unfolding in Qing China at the same time, oppositional circles among Ottoman intellectuals abroad merged with secret junior officer groups in Macedonia and Thrace in 1907. Barely one step ahead of the sultan's secret service, the officers launched a coup d'état in 1908, which urban Ottomans generally received with great relief. The officers forced the sultan to reinstate the constitution of 1878 and, after elections, accept a new parliament.

**Decline of the Ottomans**    Emboldened by their success, leaders of the coup formed the Committee of Union and Progress (CUP), commonly referred to as the "Young Turks," and in 1909 they forcibly deposed Abdülhamit. The CUP then embarked on a policy of self-strengthening and modernization in order to create a new, Turkish national identity for the Ottoman Empire.

A series of unanticipated reactions to what was perceived as a reassertion of Ottoman power in the Balkans produced a sequence of cascading events that threatened to undermine the CUP and to bring down the empire. Austria-Hungary and Bulgaria formally annexed Bosnia-Herzegovina and northern Rumelia, respectively, in 1908. Albania revolted in 1910 and Italy invaded Tripolitania in 1911. In the following year Serbia, Montenegro, Bulgaria, and Greece collaborated in the First Balkan War, forcing Ottoman forces to retreat from the strategically important city of Erdine and to move back toward Istanbul. Fortunately for the CUP, the four victorious Balkan states were unable to agree on the division of the spoils. The Ottomans exploited the disagreements and retook Edirne, succeeding in a new peace settlement to push the imperial border westward into Thrace. Nevertheless, the overall losses were horrendous; the Ottoman Empire had now been driven out of Europe, ending more than half a millennium of rule in the Balkans.

**Economic Development**    While the empire was disintegrating politically, the economic situation improved. The main factor was the end of the depression of 1873–1896 and a renewed interest among European investors in creating industrial enterprises in the agrarian but export-oriented independent and colonial countries of the Middle East, Asia, and South America. When Abdülhamit II was at the peak of his power in the 1890s and early 1900s, investors perceived the Ottoman Empire as sufficiently stable for the creation of industrial enterprises.

The Ottoman Empire in the 1800s can be described as a state in which the traditional crafts-based textile industry initially suffered under the invasion of cheap industrially produced English cottons in the period 1820–1850. But a recovery took place in the second half of the 1800s, both in the crafts sector and in a newly mechanized small factory sector of textile manufacturing, producing cottons, woolens, silks, and rugs. This recovery was driven largely by domestic demand and investments, because the European price depression of 1873–1896 was not conducive to much inflow of foreign capital. Operating with low wages and even more low-paid female labor, domestic small-scale manufacturing was able to hold foreign factory-produced goods at bay.

Throughout the 1800s, the empire was also an exporter of agricultural commodities. But the recovery of domestic textile production demonstrates that the Ottomans did not succumb completely to the British free market system. When foreign investments resumed in the 1890s and early 1900s, there was a base on which industrialization could build, similar to conditions in the Netherlands, France, and Latin America when they industrialized.

## Iran's Effort to Cope with the Western Challenge

Iran (also called Persia, in recognition of its long heritage) had risen in the 1500s as the Shiite alternative to the Sunni Ottomans. The two dynasties of kings (*shahs*) who ruled Iran, the Safavids (1501–1722) and Qajars (1795–1925), nurtured a hierarchy of Shiite clerics who formed an autonomous religious institution in their state. While the Ottoman sultans always kept their leading Sunni religious leaders under firm control, the Iranian rulers had to respect a delicate balance of power with their Shiite leaders. Therefore, when Iran in the 1800s faced the Western challenges, reformers had to establish an alliance with the Shiite clerics to bring about constitutional reforms.

**Safavid and Qajar Kings**    The Safavid Empire was a less powerful state than that of the Ottomans. It comprised Shiite Iran, the Caucasus, Sunni Afghanistan,

# Patterns Up Close | Sunni and Shiite Islam

Like all revealed religions, Islam followed the pattern of splitting into multiple denominations. Revelation is centered on God, whose covenant with humans includes, among several theological teachings, the idea of providence. God's providence is contained in his promise of salvation in the future, on the Day of Judgment, both for the believers and for the world as a whole. How quickly and under whom this providential future prior to the Judgment unfolds, however, was a major source of conflict. Some of the fiercest theological debates raged around the providential future of Islam and have led to the foundation of the two major branches of Islam, Sunnism and Shiism.

During the formative period of Islam in the 800s and 900s, Muslims were deeply divided over the question of providential leadership. Was the leader of the Muslim community until the Day of Judgment a caliph (or representative) of the Prophet Muhammad and descended from the Quraysh, the dominant lineage of Mecca? Sunnis answered this question in the affirmative and regarded the caliphate as an institution guaranteeing the future of Islam until the Judgment in the distant future.

Shiites denied this answer and saw the future of Islam in a community led by the Imam (or leader), who was a descendant of Fatima and Ali, the daughter and cousin of Muhammad, respectively. Until 874, the

**Husayn, Comforting His Dying Son Ali Akbar.** In the early stage of the battle of Karbala, the Umayyad soldiers killed Ali Akbar, before Husayn himself was martyred. Processions and performances in remembrance of Karbala during the month of Muharram passed frequently by Shiite shrines which were embellished by local painters with frescoes showing imagined scenes of Karbala. This image, painted in 1905, is from the Imamzadeh Shah Zayd shrine in Isfahan, Iran.

eldest son in each generation was entitled to lead the Muslims, at which time the last Imam was believed to have entered "occultation"—that is, a state of concealment from where he would return as the Mahdi ("rightly guided leader") at the end of time, just before God's Judgment. In contrast to Sunni Islam, the Shiite Imam was believed to be endowed with divine inspiration, a special kind of inner knowledge received from God and shared with Muhammad but no other human. This inspiration made the Imams sinless and infallible, enabling them to pronounce authoritative interpretations of the Quran and Islamic Tradition. No Sunni caliph ever claimed inspiration, sinlessness, or infallibility.

Just before 900, a conflict broke out among the Shiites over the imminence of the Imam's return. A minority, the Ismailis, believed that the seventh Imam (in the line of descent from Fatima and Ali) would emerge from hiding already in the early 900s. Their returned Imam and Mahdi founded the Ismaili, or Fatimid, Empire in Tunisia, Egypt, and Syria. The majority, the Twelver Shiites, adhered to the belief that it would be the twelfth Imam who would return from occultation in the distant future. They were the founders of the Buyid dynasty of emirs in Iran and Iraq (934–1055) and, much later, of the Safavid dynasty in Iran (1501–1722). Both dynasties sponsored large establishments of jurists and religious scholars who created a body of traditions and legal interpretations which made Twelver Shiism comparable to legalism in Sunni Islam.

The particular legal school that came to dominate in Twelver Shiism was Usulism. It emerged in the second half of the 1700s and is still dominant in contemporary Iran. Its central characteristic is its emphasis on the special status of a small number of senior legal scholars (ayatollahs ["signs of God"], today about half a dozen in number) who are distinguished by their knowledge of the Quran and Islamic tradition, power of reason, and inspiration. This combination of special qualifications enables them to collectively interpret theology and law in an authoritative manner, binding for everyone, even in the absence of the Hidden Imam. Among Sunnis, anyone can acquire learning and practice interpretation, although traditionally theological schools also awarded, and still award, diplomas.

In a further interpretation, Ayatollah Ruhollah Khomeini (1902–1989), leader of the Islamic Revolution of Iran in 1979, expanded the religious guardianship of the jurist—that is, of all Shiite clerics with himself at the head—to include that of political rulership. Accordingly, Iran is a partially elective Islamic theocracy, governed by certified pious Shiites and the Shiite hierarchy of clerics, from mosque preachers and middle-ranking jurists ("proofs of Islam" or *hojjatalislams*) to ayatollahs. Sunnis do not have such a hierarchy and today not even a corporate clerical establishment.

In the history of Islamic civilization, Shiites were always a minority, today about 10–20 percent among the totality of Muslims. At times, therefore, they suffered persecution from the Sunnis. In order to survive, Shiites developed the theological concept of dissimulation (*taqiyya*), which allows Shiites to pretend that they are Sunnis. Even in places where they could live under their own authorities, however, they developed customs which celebrate their minority status, making Shiism a religion of sufferance. In annual processions in the month of Muharram Shiites reenact the martyrdom of two of Imam Ali's sons, Husayn and Abbas, who perished in 680 at Karbala, Iraq, with 71 followers in a desperate uprising against the Sunni caliph. Participants in these processions often flagellate themselves in their fervor for suffering. Today, the two mausoleums for Husayn and Abbas are important pilgrimage sites for Shiites, together with those of the other nine Imams. Nearby Najaf, the burial place of Imam Ali, is also the site of one of the leading Shiite seminaries for the training of Shiite clerics.

Although overall they constitute a minority, today Shiites are a majority in Iran and pluralities in Iraq and Lebanon, making them important political actors in the Middle East. Their importance has led to restlessness among Shiite minorities in Bahrain and eastern Saudi Arabia as well as major clashes between Sunnis and Shiites in Pakistan and Yemen (where the Shiites base themselves on the Fifth Imam). Thus, in present times relations between Sunnis and Shiites are shifting from the relative mutual tolerance of the 1800s and 1900s to increasing tension.

## Questions

- Which other revealed religions split into denominations, and over which issues?

- Which questions do rulers face when they declare themselves the returned Imam and Mahdi, as in the case of the founders of the Fatimid Empire in the early tenth century CE and the Safavid Empire in 1501?

**Isfahan, Naqsh-i Jahan Square.** At its southeastern end is the majestic Shah (today Imam) Mosque (1611–1629), a major example of the Iranian and Central Asian open courtyard mosque style.

and parts of Sunni central Asia. The Safavid kings, whose lands were limited in most provinces to oasis agriculture, were not wealthy enough to recruit a large firearm infantry to match the Janissaries. As a result, for most of the time the Ottomans were able to keep the Safavid rivalry at a manageable level, especially from the mid-1600s onward.

At this time, the Safavids ruled Iran from their newly founded capital of Isfahan in the center of the country, which they embellished with palaces and mosques. Safavid Iran was a major exporter of silk yarn and clothes, second in quality only to Chinese wares, and thus supplemented its limited agrarian revenues with an international trade in silk.

The Safavids were vulnerable not only to the military challenges of their Ottoman neighbors to the west but also to those of tribal federations in the Sunni provinces to the east. In Afghanistan, one of the two major Pashtu tribal federations revolted repeatedly against the efforts of the Safavids to convert them to Shiite Islam. Eventually, in 1722, this federation succeeded in conquering Iran and ending Safavid rule, at a time of advanced decentralization in the empire. The Afghanis, however, were unable to establish a stable new regime. Instead, provincial Iranian rulers reunified and even expanded the empire for short periods during the 1700s. Stabilization finally occurred in 1796, with the accession of the new Qajar dynasty.

The Qajars had been among the founding Shiite Turkic tribal federation of the Safavids, but in contrast to their brethren, they had no Shiite aspirations of their own. Instead, they paid respect to the clerical hierarchy that had become powerful in the aftermath of the Afghani conquest in the 1700s. The clerics supported themselves through their own independent revenues from landholdings in the vicinity of their mosques and colleges, and the Qajars were not powerful enough to interfere.

During the 1800s, two developments dominated Iran's historical evolution. First, like the Ottoman Empire, primarily agrarian Iran was subject to oscillating periods of decentralization and recentralization, following the decline or rise of tax revenues from the countryside. Second, the increasingly hierarchical and theologically rigid Shiite clerics were challenged by the popular, theologically less tradition-bound Babi movement. This movement, begun in 1844, rallied around a figure who claimed to be the promised returned Twelfth Imam or Mahdi with a new law superseding the body of legal interpretations of the Shiite clergy. A combination of Qajar troops and clerically organized mobs succeeded in suppressing this widespread movement, which subsequently evolved into the Baha'i faith.

The Qajars not only faced an unstable internal situation but also suffered from Russian imperialism. The declared Russian goal of liberating Constantinople implied the conquest of the central Asian Turkic sultanates as well as the north face of the Caucasus Mountains astride the land bridge between the Black and Caspian Seas. Accordingly, Russian armies sought to drive the Qajars from their Caucasus provinces. In response, the Qajar kings embarked on centralizing military and administrative reforms, which were similar to those of the Ottomans though less pervasive. In the absence of sizeable groups of reformers of their own and bowing to Russian pressures, they hired Russian officers to train a small corps of new troops, the Cossack Brigade. (The tsar, although bent on expanding into the Caucasus, did not want Iran to collapse and cease being a counterweight to the Ottomans.) Swedish advisors trained the police force, in an effort to improve civil peace. British subjects acquired economic concessions, such as monopolies on minerals and telegraph connections or the manufacture of tobacco. The increasing foreign influence in Iran aroused the ire of the conservative clerical hierarchy, and the kings had to withdraw the concessions. The Qajar ruling class was acutely aware of the Western challenge, but its reformist power vis-à-vis the clerical establishment was limited.

Perceptive Iranian constitutional nationalists from among the educated younger ruling class were less numerous than their Young Ottoman colleagues. They therefore founded a tactical alliance toward the end of the 1800s with conservative clerics and merchants. In 1906, after widespread revolts against tax increases to cover a lavish European trip by the shah, this alliance mounted a successful constitutional revolution, imposing parliamentary limits on the Qajar regime. The constitutional–nationalist alliance with the clerics was, however, inherently unstable, and parliamentary rule failed to become a reality. As World War I drew near, Iran reverted to autocratic rule by the shahs. Nevertheless, the memory of the abortive Constitutional Revolution of 1906 lived on, becoming decisive in the later twentieth century with the formation of the Islamic Republic in 1979 and the enactment of a hybrid Islamic–democratic constitution.

## Westernization, Reforms, and Industrialization in Russia

The Russian Empire that expanded during the 1800s southward at the expense of the Qajar and Ottoman Empires had arisen in 1547 as a tsardom in Moscow, succeeding the Byzantine eastern Christian "caesars" (from which the Russian term "tsar," or "czar," is derived). It was a relatively late empire, succeeding that of the Mongols; and it spanned eastern Europe as well as Asia. Given this geographical location at the eastern edge of Europe and outside western Christian civilization, Russia developed along an uneven pattern of relations with western Europe. Unlike the Qing, but like the Meiji and the Ottomans, Russia aspired to adapt western values and practices. Western culture became a force only around 1700 when the tsar Peter the Great (r. 1682–1725) became its advocate. The idea of constitutionalism arrived in the wake of the French Revolution and Napoleon's failed invasion of Russia (1812). But it remained weak and was diluted by pan-Slavic ethnic nationalism, an ideology whereby Russians sought unification with the Slavic peoples of the Balkans. Multiple small political groups competed with each other, with no single united reformist force emerging. These groups rose amid the social dislocations that followed the Russian industrialization effort at the end of the nineteenth century, but none was able to take over leadership in the abortive revolution following the disastrous defeat at the hands of a modernizing Japan in 1905. Although this uprising produced a weak Russian parliament, the Duma, the autocratic tsarist regime tottered on until collapsing under the unbearable strain of World War I.

## Russia and Westernization

The states of western Europe were, of course, aware of a large empire on their eastern flank but did not consider it fully European. Indeed, at a time when feudal practices were dying in western Europe, Russia under the Romanov dynasty *institutionalized* serfdom. Half a century earlier, Tsar Peter the Great went on a mission of investigation to western Europe and began a reform and urbanization process from the top, against an often-fierce resistance in both the ruling class and the population at large, to bring Russia more in line with the western European norms. His legacy was the new capital of St. Petersburg, extensive military reorganization, and concerted attempts to rein in the power of Russia's high nobility, the *boyars*. But another legacy was political and cultural resistance to any such measures coming from outside Russia, not unlike the cultural resistance that would plague Chinese reformers in the nineteenth century.

The German-born "enlightened despot" Tsarina Catherine II, "the Great" (r. 1762–1796), continued the reform process from the top; however, it was slow to trickle down. When the constitutional–nationalist revolutions broke out in the United States, France, and Haiti, the Russian Empire was an autocratic, fiscal–military state that had expanded in all directions.

**Catherine II's Reforms**    Catherine the Great, the dominant figure of tsarist Russia during the eighteenth century, was intellectually engaged with Enlightenment concepts that spread among the European courts. Rulers were to remain firmly committed to absolute rule but should also pursue administrative, judicial, and educational reforms in order to increase the welfare of their subjects. Her Enlightenment outlook made Catherine far ahead of the Russian aristocracy, not to mention the small urban educated upper strata, both of which were still much beholden to eastern Christian traditions.

As much an activist as Peter the Great but more subtle, the energetic Catherine pushed through a number of major reforms. Urban manufactures, especially of linen and woolen cloth, had greatly expanded in the early 1700s, and Catherine strengthened urban development with a provincial reform in 1775 and a town reform in 1785 that allowed local nonaristocratic participation. But in 1785 she also strengthened the aristocracy with a charter that exempted its members from the poll tax and increased their property rights, including the purchase of serfs. This was largely a measure to head off a repetition of the terrible peasant rebellions of 1762–1775, which had culminated with Pugachev's Cossack revolt, which had the effect of limiting Catherine's implementation of enlightened policies. Yet, in a reform of the educational system (1782), the government set up a free, mostly clergy-staffed educational system, from urban primary schools to high schools. Catherine's legal reform project, however, apart from a police ordinance issued in 1782, remained incomplete, and the codification and humanization of Russia's laws had to wait for another 80 years.

In foreign affairs, Catherine was determined to continue and even exceed Peter the Great's expansionism. She first undertook the dismemberment of the Kingdom of Poland, accomplished together with Prussia and the Austrian Habsburgs in three stages, from 1772 to 1795. Then, in two wars with the Ottoman Empire (1768–1792), Catherine waged a successful campaign to expand Russian power over the Tatars, a Turkic-speaking population of mixed ethnic descent that had succeeded the Mongols of the Golden Horde (ca. 1240–1502) in Crimea and adjacent northern Black Sea lands. Catherine's modernized infantry forces were successful in humbling the considerably larger but disorganized Ottoman army and navy. In the first war, Russia gained access to the Black Sea, ending the Tatar–Ottoman alliance and gaining free access for Russian ships to the Mediterranean. In the second war, Russia absorbed the Tatars within its imperial borders, which now advanced to the northern coast of the Black Sea.

## Russia in the Early Nineteenth Century

The ideas of the French Revolution made their first fleeting mark on Russia in the form of the Decembrist Revolt in 1825, several decades before they did in the Ottoman Empire. But since in the pattern of traditional empire formation the personality of the ruler still counted more than the continuity of the administration, the reign of the deeply monarchical Nicholas I for a generation in mid-1800s Russia meant that whatever the Decembrists had set in motion could only spread under the surface. Above ground, Nicholas pursued an aggressive foreign policy of expansion, in the tradition of Catherine the Great (see Map 25.2).

**Russia and the French Revolution**  In her old age, Catherine was aghast at the monarchical constitutionalism of the French Revolution, not to mention its republicanism and radicalism. In an abrupt about-face, her government had Voltaire's books burned and other Enlightenment books banned. The situation eased under Catherine's grandson, Alexander I (r. 1801–1825), who was educated in Enlightenment ideas. He initially showed inclinations toward constitutionalism, coaxed by his discreetly constitutionalist minister Mikhail Speranskii (1772–1839), but Napoleon's imperial designs interrupted any idea of implementation.

Russia emerged as a key power in efforts to undo Napoleon's takeover of Europe. In 1805 Russia joined Britain and Austria in the Third Coalition against France. After a long and initially humiliating war, Russia defeated Napoleon during his disastrous invasion of 1812. At the Congress of Vienna in 1815, Alexander assumed a prominent role in the negotiations for the territorial settlements and reestablishment of peace, advocating a "holy alliance" of monarchs to be its guarantors. As a result, Napoleon's Duchy of Warsaw became the Kingdom of Poland, with the Russian tsar as its king. In contrast to his monarchical colleagues in Europe, however, Alexander remained open to Enlightenment reforms, initiating the liberation of serfs in Russia's Baltic provinces, pursuing constitutional reform in Finland and Poland, and mapping out a new status for eastern Christianity. But Russia also experienced unrest, so Alexander gradually lost interest in the continuation of his reforms.

**Orthodoxy, Autocracy, and Nationality**  No sooner did Nicholas I (1825–1855) ascend the throne in 1825 than a bloody revolt broke out, led by a small number of Russian officers who had been exposed to the ideas of constitutional nationalism. Known as the Decembrist Revolt, the uprising was quickly suppressed and its leaders were hanged. Nevertheless, the revolt had a decided effect on the intelligentsia, who vowed to avenge tsarist repression. The revolt had few connections

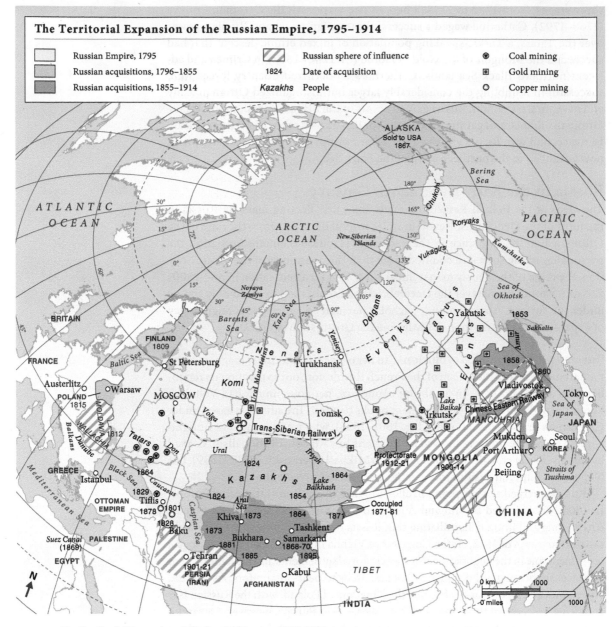

**The Territorial Expansion of the Russian Empire, 1795–1914**

| | | | |
|---|---|---|---|
| ☐ | Russian Empire, 1795 | ⬗ | Coal mining |
| ☐ | Russian acquisitions, 1796–1855 | ▣ | Gold mining |
| ☐ | Russian acquisitions, 1855–1914 | ○ | Copper mining |
| ▨ | Russian sphere of influence | | |
| 1824 | Date of acquisition | | |
| *Kazakhs* | People | | |

MAP 25.2 **The Territorial Expansion of the Russian Empire, 1795–1914.**

with civilians and was furthermore intellectually divided between federalists and unionists. The former serf Nikitenko, introduced at the beginning of this chapter, was fortunate to escape with his life from his contacts with Decembrists. Despite this relative lack of impact, the revolt represented the first antitsarist, constitutional-revolutionary movement and thus became a harbinger of things to come.

Determined to preclude any future constitutional revolts, in 1833 Nicholas implemented the doctrine known as "official nationality," aimed particularly at the suppression of constitutional movements sweeping the European continent in the early 1830s. According to this new formulation of tsarist policy, three fundamental concepts would in the future guide the government: *orthodoxy*, reaffirming the adherence to eastern Christianity and rejection of secularist notions originating in the Enlightenment; *autocracy*, meaning the absolute authority of the tsar; and *nationality*, or the equivalent of something like the "spirit" of Russian identity. In order to enforce these directives, Nicholas created a secret police agency known as the Third Section, which vigorously suppressed dissidence against the government in any form.

Nicholas also carried through on his conservative policies by joining other conservative European rulers in suppressing constitutional revolts. When a revolt in Poland in 1830 threatened to topple the viceroy (meaning ultimately the tsar himself as overlord), Nicholas intervened by suppressing it and abolishing the country's autonomy. Then, during the widespread agitation of revolutionary constitutional movements across Europe in 1848, Nicholas supported the Austrian emperor in suppressing the Hungarian nationalists. The failure of the attempted constitutional revolutions of 1848 was largely attributable to Nicholas's determined intervention.

In larger terms, Nicholas was determined to continue Russia's drive toward Constantinople (Istanbul). In the Russo–Ottoman War of 1828–1829 Russia succeeded in helping the Greeks achieve independence. With Russian help Serbia attained autonomy, while Moldavia and Wallachia—technically still within the Ottoman Empire—became protectorates of Russia. However, when Napoleon III of France in 1853 demanded recognition as protector of the Christians in Palestine under Ottoman rule, Russia did not fare as well. After Nicholas responded by insisting that the Ottomans honor their agreement with the Russian tsars as the actual protectors, the ensuing diplomatic wrangling ended in the outbreak of the Crimean War (1853–1856) between Britain, France, and the Ottoman Empire on one side and Russia, on the other.

Poor planning, missed opportunities, language barriers, and a lack of coordination between soldiers and officers plagued both sides in the Crimean War. One of the first products of the mid-nineteenth-century industrial weapons revolution, the French Minié ball, whose hollow expanding base allowed for ease of ramming in muzzle loading rifles, quadrupled the effective range of infantry weapons and vastly increased their accuracy. As they would a few years later during the American Civil War, armies fighting with increasingly obsolescent tactics would suffer fearful losses from these new weapons. French steam-powered and iron-hulled floating batteries inaugurated the age of ironclad navies. Telegraph lines permitted correspondents to send frontline reports to their London newspapers. And the nascent technology of photography was there to document the conflict. To lessen the sufferings of the wounded, doctors and nurses on both sides staffed field hospitals—including the English nurse Florence Nightingale (1820–1910), the founder of modern medical care on battlefields and the first prominent advocate of nursing as a profession for women. The new scientific–industrial age had manifested itself for the first time in war.

The Ottomans, still in the initial stages of their military reform, did not acquit themselves well, suffering from a weak officer corps and the absence of noncommissioned officers. They would have

"They came closer and closer. Suddenly, right across the line, our bugles sounded, followed by the booming of our cannon and the firing of our guns; the earth shook, there was a thunderous echo, and it was so dark from the gunsmoke that nothing could be seen. When it cleared we could see that the ground in front of us was covered with the bodies of the fallen French."

—Prokofii Podpalov, a Russian officer describing the Battle of Malakoff, September 1855

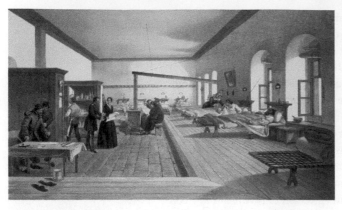

**Hospital Ward, Scutari, Ottoman Empire, 1856.** This airy, uncluttered, warm hospital room shows injured and recovering soldiers. Florence Nightingale is depicted in the middle ground, in conversation with an officer.

been defeated, had it not been for allied participation. The Russians did not perform well either, except for their navy with its superior shells. The Russian army suffered from overextending its battle lines on too many fronts, from the Danube and Crimea to the Caucasus. Thus, as far as the two imperial foes, the Russian and Ottoman Empires, were concerned, the war was a setback for both in their effort to meet the challenges of the West. Like their counterparts in China during the Second Opium War, also fought in the mid-1850s, however, they did receive a renewed taste of the state of the art in military technology and usage. This would mark many of the reform efforts of all three empires in the coming decades.

**The Golden Age**  During the period 1810–1853, in spite of periods of censorship and repression, Russia enjoyed an outburst of intellectual and cultural activity. Taken as a whole, this period was considered the golden age of Russian culture. Inspired by European romantics, a Russian intelligentsia—many of whom were Western-educated intellectuals predominantly from the ranks of the landowner nobility—met in the salons of Moscow and St. Petersburg, where they considered and debated issues related to religion and philosophy, as well as Russian history. A significant development was the appearance of literary journals, which introduced new literary forms as well as new ideas. Many of these ideas were potentially seditious, since they concerned ways to end the autocracy of the tsars and to reform serfdom. More important, the first stirrings of reform movements emanated from these circles—as illustrated below in Against the Grain.

## The Great Reforms

The Russian defeat in the Crimean War convinced the newly enthroned Alexander II (r. 1855–1881) of the need for reforms. Russia, so he believed, lost the war because of a technologically inferior army, a lack of infrastructure, and the unwillingness of the serf-owning aristocracy to shift from subsistence to market agriculture. He implemented major reforms, which, however, took time to produce the intended effects. Many Russians did not want to wait, and the empire entered a time of social destabilization, balanced abroad to a degree by successes against the Ottoman Empire.

**Russian Serfdom**  Serfdom in Russia varied according to factors including topography, economic status, and dispositions of landlords. Settlements were similar to medieval manorial villages, with dwellings clustered in the center, surrounded by arable fields. These were organized into *mirs*, or communes, which oversaw economic and legal affairs. Many Russian peasants lived near the subsistence level; dependent upon agriculture, economies fluctuated owing to frequent poor harvests and famines. Peasant dwellings were modest, consisting of small log houses covered by thatched roofs. Interiors featured a small stove for cooking and heating, along with wooden shelves that served as beds. Livestock were occasionally admitted as well. Most serfs had a small plot of land on which to grow vegetables, and they owned livestock of various sorts, including pigs, goats, sheep, and chickens. Diets consisted mainly of grains (mostly rye), meat, and dairy products, as well as foraged nuts, berries, fruits, and occasionally fish. Households consisted of husbands, wives, and children, and occasionally extended to nuclear families consisting of relatives and in-laws. Organized along patriarchal lines, families were dominated by husbands. Misogyny was common—a Russian folk saying translates as "A hen is not a bird and a woman is not a person"—as was wife beating. Nevertheless, Russian women were considered important helpmates in agricultural labors as well as in cooking and other household chores; and although accorded second-class status in Russian society, they were not without some legal rights.

**The Emancipation of Serfs**    Nicholas tackled serfdom first. In 1861, Alexander (the "tsar liberator") issued the Emancipation Edict, in which peasants were ostensibly freed from their bondage to their villages and their dues and labor services to the Russian landowning aristocracy. On the face of it, the edict ended the centuries-old system of serfdom, affecting some 50 million serfs. But the edict fell far short of liberating the peasantry for three key reasons. First, the decree of emancipation did not go into effect immediately but took 2 years to be fully enacted. Second, peasants were not given land titles directly; rather, the land was turned over to the control of local mirs, which then in turn allocated parcels to individual serfs. Finally, serfs had to redeem their new holdings by making annual payments to the state to pay back long-term government loans, the proceeds from which were then used to compensate the landowning nobility. Even worse, these payments were often higher than the former dues that serfs had owed the aristocracy. In effect, then, tens of millions of farmers remained mired in poverty-stricken agricultural self-sufficiency.

Following Western models, Alexander enacted further reforms. For example, in 1864 the administration of government at the local level was reorganized by the establishment of regional councils known as *zemstvos*. Each zemstvo was in reality controlled by the local aristocracy, although peasants had a say in their election. Whatever their drawbacks, it must be said that zemstvos made advances in education, health, and the maintenance of roads within their regions. Legal reforms were enacted shortly afterward; these provided all Russians access to courts, trial by jury, and especially the concept of equality before the law. Then, in 1874, a series of reforms aimed at modernizing the military and bringing it closer to Western standards was enacted. Among these was the reduction of active duty service in the military from 25 to 6 years, followed by several years of service in the reserves, along with an overall improvement in the quality of life in the ranks. Planned infrastructural reforms, however, remained limited by lack of funds. As in the Ottoman Empire, the reforms brought important changes to Russia, but in many cases, their effects would not be known until years later.

**Starving Russian Peasants.** Severe weather in 1890–1891 resulted in poor harvests, which in turn led to a period of famine during the 1890s. Russian peasants were especially hard hit by grain shortages and by the government's policy of exporting surpluses in order to boost the Russian economy. Here, peasants beg food from a horse-mounted soldier in St. Petersburg.

**Pan-Slavism:** Ideology that espoused the brotherhood of all Slavic peoples and gave Russia the mission to aid Slavs in the Balkans suffering from alleged Ottoman misrule.

**Pan-Slavism and Balkan Affairs** In the 1870s, conservative intellectuals broadened Tsar Nicholas's concept of the Russian nationality into the ideology of **pan-Slavism**.

Two issues contributed to mounting Russian pan-Slavic engagement in the Balkans. First, across the nineteenth century the Ottomans had been forced to relinquish control of large areas of their empire in the Balkans. Second, the increasingly popular appeal of ethnolinguistic nationalism in Europe—embodied in Italian unification in 1870, followed by German unification in 1871—strengthened the assertiveness of the Balkan nationalities. In 1875 Bosnia-Herzegovina revolted against the Ottomans, and the rebellion then spread to Bulgaria, Serbia, and Montenegro. What would happen if these provinces did in fact break away from the Ottoman Empire? Which of the European powers might then take them over and thus increase its presence in this vital region? Thus, the Balkans became an area of increasing attention for the leading powers, while at the same time resembling a powder keg ready to ignite.

**The Russo–Ottoman War** Encouraged by Russian popular support for pan-Slavism and sensing an opportunity to exploit rising anti-Ottoman sentiments among ethnic national movements in the Balkans, the tsar reopened the war front against the Ottomans in July 1877. The pretext was the Ottoman repression of uprisings in Bosnia-Herzegovina and Bulgaria, which had led to a declaration of war by neighboring Montenegro and Serbia in June 1876 and a call for Russian military aid. The Russians invaded across the Danube and by December had advanced as far as Rumelia. Serbia, claiming complete independence, and Bulgaria, under Russian tutelage, were now poised to gain control of Istanbul. The other European powers stood by, anxiously waiting to see whether Russia would advance on the Ottoman capital.

In 1878, alarmed over what appeared to be an imminent Russian occupation of Istanbul, Austria and Britain persuaded Germany to convene the Congress of Berlin. In order to preserve peace among the great powers and to diffuse rising tensions over this "eastern question," the congress decided to amputate from the Ottoman Empire most of its European provinces. For its part, Russia agreed to give up its designs on Istanbul in return for maintaining control over lands it had secured in the Caucasus Mountains. Serbia, Romania, and Montenegro became independent states. Austria acquired the right to "occupy and administer" the provinces of Bosnia and Herzegovina. There things stood for the rest of the nineteenth century, as the European powers began their imperial scramble, and Russia, forced to deal with renewed internal unrest, turned its attention away from the Balkans.

## Russian Industrialization

Following the assassination of Alexander II in 1881 by a leftist terrorist organization impatient for further reforms, the next Romanov tsars reaffirmed autocratic authority and exercised tight political control, harkening back to the policies of Nicholas I. They surrounded themselves with conservative advisors and buttressed their hold on absolute rule by connecting loyalty to the state with adherence to eastern Christianity. These tsarist policies provoked renewed calls for constitutional reforms and generated new movements opposed to the autocracy of the regime. At the same time, when the depression of 1873–1896 began to ease in the 1890s, the country enjoyed a surge in industrialization, aggravating the political and social contradictions in Russia.

**The Reassertion of Tsarist Authority**    In the face of increasing demands by constitutionalists and social reformers, Alexander III (r. 1881–1894) unleashed a broad program of "counter-reforms" in order to shore up autocratic control over the country. These actions turned Russia into a police state, in which political trials before military courts were commonplace. Revolutionaries, terrorists, and opponents among the intelligentsia were especially targeted for intimidation, exile, or even death. Outside Russia, Alexander insisted on a program of *Russification*, or forced assimilation to Russian culture, especially language, for Poles, Ukrainians, and the Muslim populations of central Asia. For the time being, the regime maintained its grip on power.

Nicholas II (r. 1894–1917), regarded by many contemporaries as a narrow-minded, unimaginative, and ultimately tragic figure, followed in his father's footsteps. Nicholas's paramount concern was loyalty not only to the state but also to the church. Any deviations were considered treasonous. He felt a special contempt for revolutionary groups and individuals, who therefore retaliated with increasingly strident demands for the overthrow of the tsarist government. In addition to continuing the repressive policies of his father, Nicholas held an enduring distrust of Russian Jews as unpatriotic, which climaxed in the pogroms of 1903–1906. These pogroms, repetitions of earlier ones in 1881–1884 following the assassination of Alexander II, triggered mass emigrations to the United States and smaller ones to Britain, South America, South Africa, and Palestine as Russian Jews sought to escape persecution.

**Industrialization**    Industrial development was as slow in Russia as it was in the Ottoman Empire, and for many of the same reasons. For one thing, the empire suffered from a poor transportation infrastructure. Although canal construction had started under Peter the Great, road construction did not follow until the early 1800s. Railroad construction was even slower, owing to the great distances in the empire that made large capital investments from abroad necessary. The first line, from St. Petersburg to Moscow, opened in 1851, but only a few thousand miles of track were laid until 1890 when the European depression of the previous three decades lifted. A major reason for the defeat in the Crimean War was the absence of railroad connections from Moscow to the Black Sea, forcing the army to rely on water transport and horse-drawn carts. Moreover, Russian railroads never adopted the standard gauge of their Western counterparts, necessitating costly and time-consuming changes of carriages and rolling stock at border crossings.

Among other factors driving the push toward accelerated industrialization was the dawning recognition of the regime that Russia was falling behind the industrialized nations of Europe in the race for economic—and thus political—global

**Aristocratic Splendor.** This oil painting of the wedding of Nicholas II and Alexandra in 1894, by the Danish painter Laurits Regner Tuxen (1853–1927), shows the rich glory of the Eastern Christian Church and the empire in ascendancy, with the couple's iconic art, ermine furs, veiled ladies in waiting, and decorated officers.

political influence. But the driving force in Russia's push for industrialization in the 1890s was the minister of finance, Sergei Witte (1849–1915, in office 1892–1903). His "Witte system" included an acceleration of heavy industrial output, the establishment of import tariffs, increased taxes on the peasantry, and conversion to the gold standard in order to stabilize the currency. Although historians debate the overall success of Witte's reforms, there is no question that Russia made tremendous progress in heavy industrialization during the late nineteenth century.

Witte's crowning achievement was the Trans-Siberian Railroad, built during 1891–1905 and connecting Moscow with Vladivostok on the Pacific coast. During Catherine's time, it took 3 years for communications to be sent to and from Vladivostok; now, the distance was covered in 8 days. Witte's objective was not only to make Russia more competitive but also to extend Russia's reach into Siberia with its rich agricultural and mineral resources, while at the same time extending Russia's influence in east Asia. Russia's policy of opening east Asia was the equivalent of Western imperialism in Asia and Africa and was designed to ensure that Russia enjoyed a share of the global race for empire.

**Industrialism and Society**   In the 1890s, British, French, and Belgian capital poured into the empire and helped in building railroads, mining ventures, iron smelters, and textile factories. It is estimated that during this decade Russia's industrial output increased at an annual rate of nearly 8 percent. Owing, however, to Russia's late start in industrializing, as well as to a lack of abundant reserves of financial capital, many of the factories were technologically inferior to those of the west.

In other ways social adjustments and changes similar to those experienced in industrialized cities in the west occurred in major Russian industrial centers. The populations of Moscow and St. Petersburg in the second half of the nineteenth century soared from around 250,000 to 1 million. And, like their western counterparts, industrialized urban centers consisted of overcrowded and unhealthy slums adjacent to factories.

Again, as in the west, industrialism spawned changes in social structures. Factories and mines employed a new class of workers. Their working conditions were oppressive, including 11 hours and more a day of manual labor in less-than-ideal circumstances. Mounting calls for reforms throughout the later nineteenth century led to the formation of several protest and socialist groups, all of whom contributed to the increasing pressures and chaos that would explode in the 1905 Revolution.

There was, however, one striking difference between the Russian and western industrial experiences. While it is true that the economic upturn in Russia produced a rising urban middle class, the numbers of wealthy factory owners, entrepreneurs, and merchants pales in comparison with the west. Many factors account for this disparity, but perhaps the most important was that many Russian manufacturing plants were controlled by western investors, and those that were not were under the supervision of the Russian government.

**The Russo–Japanese War**   The dramatic surge in industrialization, in conjunction with imperial ambitions in east Asia, brought Russia into conflict with Japan. As we saw in Chapter 24, with the Meiji Restoration in 1867–1868, Japan had embarked on a systematic program of modernization and industrialization. Like western Europe and Russia, it developed imperial ambitions in the 1890s, seeking to replace China as the dominant power in east Asia. To this end Japan provoked war with China and in the Sino–Japanese War (1894–1895) occupied Taiwan and the Liaodong Peninsula of Manchuria. Although Japan was successful in defeating China and replacing it as the protector of Korea, the European powers forced Japan to give up the Liaodong Peninsula in the Triple Intervention (1895), which was in turn leased to Russia the following year. Determined to continue Russian expansion in east Asia, Witte completed the construction of a railway spur from the Trans-Siberian Railroad through Manchuria to the warm-water fortress city of Port Arthur on the southern tip of Liaodong.

The construction of this spur was the final straw for Japan, whose imperial goals seemed suddenly threatened by Russian expansion. Already smarting from what they considered Russia's double-dealing in helping to engineer the Triple Intervention and leasing the naval base at Port Arthur from the Qing, in early 1904 Japanese naval forces suddenly attacked the Russian fleet moored at Port Arthur, destroying several of its ships and laying siege to the fortress. The Russian Baltic fleet, sent for relief, not only arrived too late to prevent the fall of Port Arthur but was destroyed in May 1905 by Japan when it tried to reach Vladivostok. In the peace settlement, Japan gained control of the Liaodong Peninsula and southern Manchuria, as well as increased influence over Korea, which it finally annexed in 1910.

## The Abortive Russian Revolution of 1905

In addition to Russia's mauling by the Japanese in the war of 1904–1905, a variety of factors coalesced in the early 1900s that sparked the first revolution against tsarist rule. One of these was a rising discontent among the peasantry, who continued to chafe under injustices such as the redemption payments for landownership. Another was the demand by factory workers for reform of working conditions: The workday ran to 11.5 hours and wages were pitifully low. Although the government had allowed for the formation of labor unions, their grievances fell on deaf ears. In response, workers in major manufacturing centers across the country, especially in St. Petersburg, mounted massive protests and occasional strikes.

**Revolutionary Parties**    The discontent among workers and peasants spurred calls for reforms, resulting in the creation of new political parties. One of these was the Social Democratic Labor Party, formed in 1898 by Vladimir Ilyich Lenin (1870–1924), a staunch adherent of Marxism (discussed in Chapter 26). This group sought support from workers, whom they urged to stage a socialist revolution by rising up and overthrowing the bourgeois capitalist tsarist government.

During its meeting in London in 1903 the Social Democratic Labor Party developed two competing factions. The more moderate group, the Mensheviks ("minority," though they were actually numerically in the majority), was willing to follow classical Marxism, which allowed for an evolutionary process from fully evolved capitalism to social revolution and then on to the eventual overthrow of capitalism and tsarist rule. The more radical faction, known as Bolsheviks ("majority"), led by Lenin, was unwilling to wait for the evolutionary process to unfold and instead called for revolution in the near term. In 1902 Lenin had sketched out his agenda in *What Is to Be Done?* which laid out the principal Bolshevik aims. Foremost among these was a demand for the overthrow of the tsar, which could be accomplished only by relying on a highly disciplined core of dedicated revolutionaries leading the masses, whom Lenin distrusted as unwieldy and potentially unreliable. Even after the split in the Social Democratic Labor Party, however, the Bolsheviks were still a long way away from the kind of elite "vanguard of the revolution" party Lenin envisaged.

**The Revolution of 1905**    Events moved toward a violent climax in the Revolution of 1905. Amid mounting calls for political and economic reforms during the early 1900s, two concurrent events in 1904 shook the government to its foundations. First, reports of the humiliating defeats during the ongoing Russo–Japanese War began to filter to the home front. These made apparent the government's mismanagement of the war. Second, in January 1905, 100,000 workers went on strike in St. Petersburg, resulting in massive disruptions and loss of life commemorated later by Lenin.

> "Today is the twelfth anniversary of 'Bloody Sunday,' . . . which is rightly regarded as the beginning of the Russian revolution."
>
> —Vladimir Lenin

Then, from September to October, workers in all the major industrial centers staged a general strike, which brought the country to a standstill. Finally forced to make concessions, Nicholas issued the "October Manifesto," in which he promised to establish a constitutional government. Among other things, the manifesto guaranteed individual civil liberties, universal suffrage, and the creation of a representative assembly, the Duma. During 1905–1907, however, Nicholas repudiated the concessions granted in the manifesto, especially an independent Duma, which remained a rubber-stamp parliament until Nicholas abdicated in 1917. Its momentum sapped, the revolution withered.

**Vladimir Yegorovich Makovsky (1846–1920),** *Death in the Snow* **(1905).** This dramatic oil painting of the crowd protesting against the tsarist regime during the abortive revolution of 1905 is one of the greatest Russian realist paintings. Makovsky was one of the founders of the Moscow Art School and continued to paint after the Russian Revolution of 1917.

The main reason for the failure of the revolution was the absence of a broadly based constitutionalism. Its replacement was small revolutionary parties which lacked popular backing. This failure of constitutionalism made the formation of broader reformist coalitions, perhaps even with military participation, as in the Ottoman Empire, impossible. The tsarist regime, though humbled by Japan, still had enough military resources to wear down the combination of small groups of Marxist revolutionaries and street demonstrators. Without sympathizers in the army, a determined tsarist regime was impossible to bring down. But like Qing China during these years, whatever belated reforms were initiated by the government would increasingly be seen as irrelevant. It was now felt that nothing short of changing the system would be effective. For both empires, the revolutionaries would now dominate the scene.

# Putting It All Together

Both the Ottoman and Russian Empires faced the initial Western military and constitutional challenges directly on their doorsteps, not from across the ocean, as China and Japan did. Of course, once military technology had undergone its own industrial transformation in Europe during the first half of the 1800s, China was no longer too far away for British steam-powered gunboats and rifled breech-loading weapons. The Ottoman Empire, as a mature empire struggling to regain its traditional centralism, fought largely defensive wars. Russia, still a young empire, expanded aggressively against the defensive Ottomans and its weaker Asian neighbors (except Japan), all the while suffering occasional military and diplomatic setbacks. India failed to master the Western military challenge altogether. China, the Ottoman Empire, and Qajar Iran survived at the price of diminished territories. The Western challenge was pervasive across the world.

Western constitutional nationalism was another powerful and corrosive pattern. The transformation of kingdoms or colonies into nations in which subjects would become citizens, regardless of language or dialect, social rank, or religion, was difficult enough in Europe. France, with its uneasy shifts between monarchy and republic during the 1800s, demonstrated this difficulty. In the Ottoman Empire, a wide gap existed between constitutional theory and practice, especially as far as religion was concerned. Russia, plagued by the reluctance of its aristocracy to give up serfdom even after emancipation, left its constitutionalists out in the cold. Japan created a constitutional state but, like Germany, left the great majority of real power in the hands of its emperor and his advisors. China's bid for a constitutional monarchy died once in 1898 and was never fully reborn before its revolution in 1911. Sultans, emperors, and kings knew well that none of their constitutions would fully satisfy the demands for liberty, equality, and fraternity.

To complicate matters for both the Ottoman and Russian Empires, in the second half of the 1800s, many members of the rising educated urban middle class deserted constitutional nationalism and turned to ethnic nationalism (in the Ottoman Empire) or pan-Slavism and Marxism (in the Russian Empire). By contrast, both the Ottoman and Russian Empires met the Western *industrial* challenge—cheap, factory-produced cotton textiles—without completely surrendering their markets. Once they were able to attract foreign capital for the construction of expensive railroads and factories at the end of the 1800s, they even started on their own paths to industrialization—the seemingly stable Russia faster than the apparently sick Ottoman Empire. In spite of wrenching transformations, the two were still empires in control of themselves when World War I broke out. Neither would survive the war. Instead, they would be transformed by the forces that had beset them throughout the nineteenth century: Turkey would become a modern, secular nation-state, though always running somewhat behind its European contemporaries in economic development. Inspired by the Revolution of 1905, and influenced by its tremendous losses in World War I, Russia would be transformed into the world's first Marxist state, pursue breakneck industrial and economic development at a tragic cost, and emerge after World War II as one of two "superpowers" with the United States.

▶ For additional resources, including maps, primary sources, visuals, and quizzes, please go to www.oup.com/us/vonsivers. Please see the Further Resources section at the back of the book for additional readings and suggested websites.

## Against the Grain

# Precursor to Lenin

As noted earlier in this chapter (pp. 780) Russia's humiliating defeat in the Crimean War inspired Alexander II to enact a series of reforms in order to advance Russia into the age of modernity. At the forefront was the Emancipation Edict, issued in 1861, which was touted as making vast improvements in the lives of Russia's peasantry. When it became apparent in the 1860s that reform measures fell far short of the mark, enhancing rather than limiting autocracy, radical and even terrorist political factions demanded more far-reaching reforms. In the vanguard was a group of Russian intelligentsia who spread their notions and ideas by widely circulating them in pamphlets and literary journals.

Of these activists, one of the most notable was Nikolai Chernyshevsky (1828–1889), who defied conventional approaches to Russia's problems. In Chernyshevsky's view, Alexander's reforms were either ineffective or wrong-headed from the start. As editor of the radical journal *Contemporary*, and inspired by western intellectuals like Hegel, Chernyshevsky wrote numerous critiques of moderate reforms, especially those advocated by liberals and intelligentsia. The only way to resolve the current status quo, according to Chernyshevsky, was through outright revolution, and the Russian peasantry was designated as the dynamo that would drive meaningful reforms. To this end Chernyshevsky advocated the formation of social collectives, or communes, based on the utopian models of Charles Fourier and others.

Chernyshevsky's writing finally resulted in his imprisonment in 1862. During this time he wrote the inflammatory novel *What Is to Be Done?*, frequently referred to as a "handbook of radicalism." In it, Chernyshevsky called for innovative actions and policies informed by socialist ideals, including women's liberation, and broad programs of social justice. Running as a subtle thread through the novel was an oblique call for outright revolution. As such, the book served as an inspiration for radical activists and terrorists during the 1870s and 1880s, and earned for Chernyshevsky the distinction of being labeled the first revolutionary socialist as well as both the inspiration for and forerunner of the 1905 revolution. Lenin was so impressed by Chernyshevsky's novel that he not only referred to it as one of the most influential books he had ever read—including those of Marx—but he also entitled his own manual of revolution *What Is to Be Done?*

- **In what ways does Chernyshevsky epitomize radical socialist ideas?**

- **How does Chernyshevsky compare to earlier contrarians like Thomas Paine and Joseph Sieyès?**

# Thinking Through Patterns

▶ **Which new models did the Ottomans adopt during the nineteenth century to adapt themselves to the Western challenge?**

The traditional model for reform in the Ottoman Empire was based on the Islamic concept of the divinely sanctioned, absolute authority of the sultan: Officials could be appointed or dismissed at will. The later history of the Ottoman Empire is significant in world history because it shows the *adaptation pattern* to the Western challenge, in this case the borrowing of constitutional nationalism and modern military technology from Europe.

As agrarian polities with large landowning classes collecting rents from tenant farmers or serfs, the Ottoman and Russian Empires found it difficult to respond to the European industrial challenge. Large foreign investments were necessary for the building of steelworks, factories, and railroads. Given the long economic recession of the last quarter of the 1800s, these investments—coming from France and Germany—went to an expanding Russia, more than the shrinking Ottoman Empire, as the safer bet.

▶ **How did the agrarian Ottoman and Russian Empires, both with large landholding ruling classes, respond to the western European industrial challenge during the 1800s?**

▶ **Why did large, well-established empires like the Russian and the Ottoman Empires struggle with the forces of modernity, while a small, secluded island nation like Japan seemed to adapt so quickly and successfully?**

This is in many respects a tantalizing question for world historians. Aside from philosophical debates about what actually constitutes "success," one avenue of inquiry is cultural: How receptive were the Russians and Ottomans—or the Qing, for that matter—to the ideas of the Enlightenment? The short answer must be "Not very." Even the most willing leaders in those empires risked alienating a host of entrenched interests by attempting the most modest reforms. They therefore walked a very fine political line in what they attempted, and they often found that the reforms disrupted traditional routines but left little or nothing to replace them with effectively. In addition, such large multiethnic empires as those of Russia and the Ottomans found it difficult to rally subjects around a distinct "nationality," since they encompassed so many divergent ones. In contrast, the Meiji reformers had the advantage of a unity derived from outside pressures. With the old shogunate gone, the emperor could formulate completely new institutions and count on the loyalty of subjects who had seen him as a semidivine figure. Moreover, the new regime immediately began creating an ideology of Japaneseness—a form of ethnic nationalism—and institutionalized it in education and national policy. There was, to be sure, opposition; but it was scattered, class-based, and not effective against the modern army and industrial power the new regime created. Japan's legacy of cultural borrowing may also have been an advantage, as well as a nascent capitalist system developing in the late Tokugawa era. Finally, the goal of using its progress toward "enlightenment and civilization" according to Western standards could be measured along the way, as were the power and prestige of its new programs.

# Patterns of Evidence: Sources for Chapter 25

## SOURCE 25.1

## Lady Mary Wortley Montagu, *Letters from the Levant*

**April 1, 1717**

Mary Wortley Montagu (1689–1762), who was born into the British aristocracy, sought out an acquaintance with the leading literary and scientific figures of her day and traveled with her husband to Constantinople while he was ambassador to the Ottoman emperor. Although her husband was recalled to England within a year, Lady Mary had endeavored to learn as much as possible about Turkish customs and behavior, especially those concerning women and children. She frequently had paintings made of herself (and her son) dressed in Turkish costume, and she considered it patriotic to import Turkish customs that she thought could benefit her fellow Englishmen. Her introduction of the Turkish practice of inoculation against smallpox drew the great admiration of Voltaire, who praised her intelligence and her willingness to learn from others in his *Letters Concerning the English Nation* (1733).

To the Countess of Mar [her sister], Adrianople, April 1, 1717.

. . .

Pray let me into more particulars, and I will try to awaken your gratitude, by giving you a full and true relation of the novelties of this place, none of which would surprise you more than a sight of my person, as I am now in my Turkish habit, though I believe you would be of my opinion, that is admirably becoming. I intend to send you my picture; in the mean time accept of it here.

The first part of my dress is a pair of drawers, very full, that reach to my shoes, and conceal the legs more modestly than your petticoats. They are of a thin rose-coloured damask, brocaded with silver flowers. My shoes are of white kid leather, embroidered with gold. Over this hangs my smock, of a fine white silk gauze, edged with embroidery. This smock has wide sleeves, hanging half-way down the arm, and is closed at the neck with a diamond button; but the shape and colour of the bosom

Source: Mary Wortley Montagu, *Letters from the Levant during the Embassy to Constantinople*, 1716–18 (New York, Arno, 1971), 124, 128–129, 146–148.

are very well to be distinguished through it.

. . .

Upon the whole, I look upon the Turkish women as the only free people in the empire; the very divan pays respect to them, and the grand signior himself, when a pasha is executed, never violates the privileges of the *harém*, (or women's apartment,) which remains untouched and entire to the widow. They are queens of their slaves, whom the husband has no permission so much as to look upon, except it be an old woman or two that his lady chooses. It is true their law permits them four wives; but there is no instance of a man of quality that makes use of this liberty, or of a woman of rank that would suffer it. When a husband happens to be inconstant, (as those things will happen,) he keeps his mistress in a house apart, and visits her as privately as he can, just as it is with you. Amongst all the great men here, I only know the *tefterdar*, (i.e. treasurer) that keeps a number of she slaves for his own use (that is, on his own side of the house; for a slave once given to serve a lady is entirely at her disposal,) and he is spoken of as a libertine, or what we should call a rake, and his wife will not see him, though she continues to live in his house.

Thus you see, dear sister, the manners of mankind do not differ so widely as our voyage writers would make us believe. Perhaps it would be more entertaining to add a few surprising customs of my own invention; but nothing seems to me so agreeable as truth, and I believe nothing so acceptable to you.

. . .

Letter to Mrs. S. C——[Sarah Chiswell], Adrianople, April 1 [1717].

. . .

*A propos* of distempers: I am going to tell you a thing that will make you wish yourself here. The small-pox, so fatal and so general amongst us, is here entirely harmless by the invention of *ingrafting*, which is the term they give it. There is a set of old women who make it their business to perform the operation every autumn, in the month of September, when the great heat is abated. People send to one another to know if any of their family has a mind to have the small-pox: they make parties for this purpose, and when they are met (commonly fifteen or sixteen together,) the old woman comes with a nutshell full of the matter of the best sort of small-pox, and asks what vein you please to have opened. She immediately rips open that you offer to her with a large needle (which gives you no more pain than a common scratch,) and puts into the vein as much matter as can lie upon the head of her needle, and after that binds up the little wound with a hollow bit of shell; and in this manner opens four or five veins. The Grecians have commonly the superstition of opening one in the middle of the forehead, one in each arm and one on the breast, to mark the sign of the cross; but this has a very ill effect, all these wounds leaving little scars, and is not done by those that are not superstitious, who choose to have them in the legs, or that part of the arm that is concealed. The children or young patients play together all the rest of the day, and are in perfect health to the eighth.

Then the fever begins to seize them, and they keep their beds two days, very seldom three. They have very rarely above twenty or thirty in their faces, which never mark; and in eight days' time they are as well as before their illness. Where they are wounded, there remain running sores during the distemper, which I do not doubt is a great relief to it. Every year thousands undergo this operation; and the French ambassador says pleasantly, that they take the small-pox here by way of diversion, as they take the waters in other countries. There is no example of any one that has died in it; and you may believe I am well satisfied of the safety of this experiment, since I intend to try it on my dear little son.

I am patriot enough to take pains to bring this useful invention into fashion in England; and I should not fail to write to some of our doctors very particularly about it, if I knew any one of them that I thought had virtue enough to destroy such a considerable branch of their revenue for the good of mankind. But that distemper is too beneficial to them, not to expose to all their resentment the hardy wight that should undertake to put an end to it.

▶ **Working with Sources**

1. **Was Montagu naïve about the role of women in Turkish society? Is she using the experiences of Turkish women principally as a foil for those of English women?**

2. **How does Montagu contrast "superstition" with "reasonable" behavior, and why?**

## SOURCE 25.2

# *Imperial Edict of the Rose Garden*

### November 3, 1839

With a change of Ottoman sultans in 1839, the government issued the Rose Garden Edict, the first of three reform edicts which are collectively known as the Tanzimat (reorganizations). With this edict, the government bound itself to basic principles with respect to relations between it and its subjects, and it carefully avoided a definition of the position of religious minorities in the empire. The document also enumerates basic human rights,

Source: Herbert J. Liebesny, *The Law of the Near and Middle East: Readings, Cases, and Materials* (Albany: State University of New York Press, 1975), 46–49.

drawing on ideas from the American and French revolutionary declarations of the eighteenth century. Accordingly, it reflects the adaptability of the Ottoman Empire to Western ideas, at least in the general context of the Tanzimat reforms.

### The Hatti-Sherif of Gülhane

All the world knows that in the first days of the Ottoman monarchy, the glorious precepts of the Qur'an and the laws of the Empire were always honored.

The Empire in consequence increased in strength and greatness, and all its subjects, without exception, had acquired the highest degree of ease and prosperity. In the last one hundred and fifty years a succession of accidents and divers causes have brought about a disregard for the sacred code of laws and the regulations flowing therefrom, and the former strength and prosperity have changed into weakness and poverty; an empire in fact loses all its stability as soon as it ceases to observe its laws.

These considerations are ever present in our mind and, from the day of our advent to the throne the thought of the public weal, of the improvement of the state of the provinces, and of relief to the [subject] peoples has not ceased wholly to engage it. If, therefore, the geographical position of the Ottoman provinces, the fertility of the soil, the aptitude and intelligence of the inhabitants are considered, the conviction will remain that by striving to find efficacious means, the result, which with the help of God we hope to attain, can be obtained within a few years. Full of confidence, therefore, in the help of the Most High and supported by the intercession of our Prophet, we deem it right to seek through new institutions to provide the provinces composing the Ottoman Empire with the benefit of a good administration.

These institutions must be principally carried out under three heads which are:

1. Guarantees insuring to our subjects perfect security of life, honor, and fortune.
2. A regular system of assessing and levying taxes.
3. An equally regular system for the levying of troops and the duration of their service.

. . .

From henceforth, therefore, the cause of every accused person shall be judged publicly, as our divine law requires, after inquiry and examination, and so long as a regular judgment shall not have been pronounced, no one can secretly or publicly put another to death by poison or in any other manner.

No one shall be allowed to attack the honor of any person whatever.

Each person shall possess his property of every kind and shall dispose of it in all freedom, without let or hindrance from any person whatever; thus, for example, the innocent heirs of a criminal shall not be deprived of their legal rights, and the property of the criminal shall not be confiscated. These imperial grants shall extend to all our subjects, of whatever religion or sect they may be; they shall enjoy them without exception. Perfect security is thus given to the inhabitants of our Empire in their lives, their honor, and their fortunes, as they are secured to them by the sacred text of our law.

As for the other points, as they must be settled with the assistance of enlightened opinions, our council of justice (increased by new members as shall be found necessary), to whom shall be joined, on certain days which we shall determine, our ministers and the notables of the Empire, shall assemble in order to frame laws regulating these matters concerning the security of life and fortune and the assessment of taxes. Each one in these assemblies shall freely express his ideas and give his advice.

. . .

As the object of these institutions is solely to revivify religion, government, the nation, and the Empire, we engage not to do anything which is contrary thereto.

In testimony of our promise we will, after having deposited these presents in the hall containing the glorious mantle of the Prophet, in the presence of all the *"ulama"* and the grandees of the Empire, make oath thereto in the name of God, and shall afterwards cause the oath to be taken by the *"ulama"* and grandees of the Empire.

▶ **Working with Sources**

1. **How are Islamic religious principles used to substantiate and reinforce the force of law in the Tanzimat era? Would this be applied to the adherents of *all* religions in the empire?**

2. **Were the declarations in this edict too vague to be workable? Are they deliberately vague?**

## SOURCE 25.3

# Writings of Bahá'u'lláh

### ca. 1880s

In 1844 a young merchant from Shiraz in Persia began to teach a new faith, and he was given the title of the Báb ("the Gate"). Preaching against the hypocrisy of Muslim religious leaders, he proclaimed the beginning of a new spiritual era. When he was arrested and executed in 1850, his work was continued by Mirza Husayn Ali, who was given the title Bahá'u'lláh ("the glory of God"). Despite arrest, exile, and other forms of persecution from governmental authorities, Bahá'u'lláh composed a series of revelations and meditations. He sent letters of proclamation (generally following the same template) to a host of Western leaders, including Queen Victoria, Pope Pius IX,

Source: *Gleanings from the Writings of Bahá'u'lláh*, trans. Shoghi Effendi (Wilmette, IL: Bahá'í Publishing Trust, 1952), 73–76, 79.

and even American presidents. The Bahá'í faith that resulted from his teachings was organized around the central principle that the human race is one and whole, and should be united in brotherhood. Needless to say, this message did not appeal to everyone in the nineteenth century.

XXX. God witnesseth that there is no God but Him, the Gracious, the Best-Beloved. All grace and bounty are His. To whomsoever He will He giveth whatsoever is His wish. He, verily, is the All-Powerful, the Almighty, the Help in Peril, the Self-Subsisting. We, verily, believe in Him Who, in the person of the Báb, hath been sent down by the Will of the one true God, the King of Kings, the All-Praised. We, moreover, swear fealty to the One Who, in the time of Mustaghath, is destined to be made manifest, as well as to those Who shall come after Him till the end that hath no end. We recognize in the manifestation of each one of them, whether outwardly or inwardly, the manifestation of none but God Himself, if ye be of those that comprehend. Every one of them is a mirror of God, reflecting naught else but His Self, His Beauty, His Might and Glory, if ye will understand.

. . .

XXXI. Contemplate with thine inward eye the chain of successive Revelations that hath linked the Manifestations of Adam with that of the Báb. I testify before God that each one of these Manifestations hath been sent down through the operation of the Divine Will and Purpose, that each hath been the bearer of a specific Message, that each hath been entrusted with a divinely-revealed Book and been commissioned to unravel the mysteries of a mighty Tablet. The measure of the Revelation with which every one of them hath been identified had been definitely fore-ordained.

. . .

XXXII. That which thou hast heard concerning Abraham, the Friend of the All-Merciful, is the truth, and no doubt is there about it. The Voice of God commanded Him to offer up Ishmael as a sacrifice, so that His steadfastness in the Faith of God and His detachment from all else but Him may be demonstrated unto men. The purpose of God, moreover, was to sacrifice him as a ransom for the sins and iniquities of all the peoples of the earth. This same honor, Jesus, the Son of Mary, besought the one true God, exalted be His name and glory, to confer upon Him. For the same reason was Husayn offered up as a sacrifice by Muhammad, the Apostle of God.

No man can ever claim to have comprehended the nature of the hidden and manifold grace of God; none can fathom His all-embracing mercy. Such hath been the perversity of men and their transgressions, so grievous have been the trials that have afflicted the Prophets of God and their chosen ones, that all mankind deserveth to be tormented and to perish. God's hidden and most loving providence, however, hath, through both visible and invisible agencies, protected and will continue to protect it from the penalty of its wickedness. Ponder this in thine heart, that the truth may be revealed unto thee, and be thou steadfast in His path.

. . .

The measure of the revelation of the Prophets of God in this world, however, must differ. Each and every one of them hath been the Bearer of a distinct Message, and hath been commissioned to reveal Himself through specific acts. It is for this reason that they appear to vary in their greatness. Their Revelation may be likened unto the light of the moon that sheddeth its radiance upon the earth. Though every time it appeareth, it revealeth a fresh measure of its brightness, yet its inherent splendor can never diminish, nor can its light suffer extinction.

It is clear and evident, therefore, that any apparent variation in the intensity of their light is not inherent in the light itself, but should rather be attributed to the varying receptivity of an ever-changing world. Every Prophet Whom the Almighty and Peerless Creator hath purposed to send to the peoples of the earth hath been entrusted with a Message, and charged to act in a manner that would best meet the requirements of the age in which He appeared.

▶ **Working with Sources**

1. **To what extent do documents like this reflect an ecumenical, all-embracing spirit among the Bahá'í?**

2. **Who would have found this attempt at religious synthesis worthy of suppression, and why?**

## SOURCE 25.4

# Tsar Alexander II's Abolition of Serfdom

**February 19, 1861**

The defeat of Russia in the Crimean War (1853–1856) convinced the newly enthroned Alexander II (r. 1855–1881) of the need for fundamental reforms in his country. The first institution he tackled was serfdom, and his Emancipation Edict (1861) ostensibly freed peasants from their bondage to the landowning aristocracy. Although the edict affected some 50 million serfs, it was not fully implemented. Peasants were not given land titles per se; the land was turned over to the control of local communities (*mirs*), which then allocated parcels to individual serfs. Moreover, they were forced to make annual payments to the government in the form of loans that would compensate the former landowners; the loan amounts were often higher than the dues aristocrats had demanded before emancipation.

Source: http://academic.shu.edu/russianhistory/index.php/Alexander_II,_Emancipation_Manifesto,_1861.

By the Grace of God WE, Alexander II, Emperor and Autocrat of All Russia, King of Poland, Grand Duke of Finland, etc., make known to all OUR faithful subjects: Called by Divine Providence and by the sacred right of inheritance to the Russian throne of OUR ancestors, WE vowed in OUR heart to respond to the mission which is entrusted to Us and to surround with OUR affection and OUR Imperial solicitude all OUR faithful subjects of every rank and condition, from the soldier who nobly defends the country to the humble artisan who works in industry; from the career official of the state to the plowman who tills the soil.

Examining the condition of classes and professions comprising the state, WE became convinced that the present state legislation favors the upper and middle classes, defines their obligations, rights, and privileges, but does not equally favor the serfs, so designated because in part from old laws and in part from custom they have been hereditarily subjected to the authority of landowners, who in turn were obligated to provide for their well being. Rights of nobles have been hitherto very broad and legally ill defined, because they stem from tradition, custom, and the good will of the noblemen. In most cases this has led to the establishment of good patriarchal relations based on the sincere, just concern and benevolence on the part of the nobles, and on affectionate submission on the part of the peasants. Because of the decline of the simplicity of morals, because of in the diversity of relations, because of the weakening of the direct paternal relationship of nobles toward the

peasants, and because noble rights fell sometimes into the hands of people exclusively concerned with their personal interests, good relations weakened. The way was opened for an arbitrariness burdensome for the peasants and detrimental to their welfare, causing them to be indifferent to the improvement of their own existence.

. . .

Having invoked Divine assistance, WE have resolved to execute this task.

On the basis of the above-mentioned new arrangements, the serfs will receive in time the full rights of free rural inhabitants.

The nobles, while retaining their property rights to all the lands belonging to them, grant the peasants perpetual use of their household plots in return for a specified obligation; and, to assure their livelihood as well as to guarantee fulfillment of their obligations toward time government, [the nobles] grant them a portion of arable land fixed by the said arrangements as well as other property.

While enjoying these land allotments, the peasants are obliged, return, to fulfill obligations to the noblemen fixed by the same arrangements. In this status, which is temporary, the peasants are temporarily bound.

At the same time, they are granted the right to purchase their household plots, and, with the consent of the nobles, they may acquire in full ownership the arable lands and other properties which are allotted them for permanent use. Following such acquisition of full ownership of land, the peasants will be freed from their obligations to the nobles for the land thus purchased and will become free peasant landowners.

. . .

WE also rely upon the zealous devotion of OUR nobility, to whom WE express OUR gratitude and that of the entire country as well, for the unselfish support it has given to the realization of OUR designs. Russia will not forget that the nobility, motivated by its respect for the dignity of man and its Christian love of its neighbor, has voluntarily renounced serfdom, and has laid the foundation of a new economic future for the peasants. WE also expect that it will continue to express further concern for the realization of the new arrangement in a spirit of peace and benevolence, and that each nobleman will bring to fruition on his estate the great civic act of time entire group by organizing the lives of his peasants and his household serfs on mutually advantageous terms, thereby setting for the rural population a good example of a punctual and conscientious execution of the state's requirements.

The examples of the generous concern of the nobles for the welfare of peasants, amid the gratitude of the latter for that concern, give Us the hope that a mutual understanding will solve most of the difficulties, which in some cases will be inevitable during the application of general rules to the diverse conditions on some estates, and that thereby the transition from the old order to time new will be facilitated, and that in the future mutual confidence will be strengthened, and a good understanding and a unanimous tendency towards the general good will evolve.

. . .

And now WE confidently expect that the freed serfs, on the eve of a new future which is opening to them, will appreciate and recognize the considerable sacrifices which the nobility has made on their behalf.

They should understand that by acquiring property and greater freedom to dispose of their possessions, they have an obligation to society and to themselves to live up to the letter of the new law by a loyal and judicious use of the rights which are now granted to them. However beneficial a law may be, it cannot make people happy if they do not themselves organize their happiness under protection of the law. Abundance is acquired only through hard work, wise use of strength and resources, strict economy, and above all, through an honest God-fearing life.

▶ **Working with Sources**

1. How does the "Tsar Liberator" attempt to use religion and morality to persuade nobles to benefit their peasants?

2. To what extent does the document limit peasants' rights? Why?

SOURCE 25.5

# Nikolai Chernyshevsky, *What Is to Be Done?*

## 1863

The novelist Nikolai Chernyshevsky (1828–1889) believed that even the emancipation of serfs was insufficient to reform Russian society, since its authoritarian and patriarchal institutions had rendered it unequal and backward by every measure. An educated elite had emerged in Russia in the mid-nineteenth century, and this group felt alienated both from the larger culture and the traditions of Russian society. Chernyshevsky advocated a top-to-bottom restructuring of Russia, and he was particularly drawn to the idea of liberating women from their subordination within the Russian family. Arrested on largely fabricated charges in 1862 and awaiting trial in St. Petersburg, Chernyshevsky produced his last significant and most influential work, the novel *What Is to Be Done?* In early 1864, he was convicted of subversion, and he spent the next eighteen years in prison or in exile in eastern Siberia. *What Is to Be Done?* offers a fascinating portrait of intelligent young people attempting to reform a society that seemed in desperate need of change.

When Rakhmetov came to Petersburg at the age of sixteen, he was an ordinary youth of somewhat above-average height and strength, but by no means remarkable. Out of any ten of his peers, two could probably have gotten the better of him. But in the middle of his seventeenth year he decided to acquire physical prowess and began to work hard at it. He took up gymnastics with considerable dedication. That was all right, but gymnastics can improve only the material available; one has to provide oneself with such material. And so, for a while, he spent several hours every day, twice as long as he practiced gymnastics, working at common labor that required physical strength. He carried water, chopped and hauled firewood, felled trees, cut stone, dug earth, and forged iron. He tried many different kinds of work and changed jobs frequently because with each job and every change, different muscles were being developed. He put himself on a boxer's diet. He began to nourish himself (precisely!) only on those things reputed to build physical strength—beefsteak most of all, almost raw; since that time he's continued on this regimen. About a

Source: Nikolai Chernyshevsky, *What Is to Be Done?*, trans. Michael R. Katz (Ithaca, NY: Cornell University Press, 1989), 278–279, 280–281, 283–284.

year after adopting this program, he set off on his travels and had even greater opportunities to devote himself to building physical strength. He worked as a plowman, carpenter, ferryman, and laborer at all sorts of healthful trades. Once he even worked as a barge hauler along the whole length of the Volga, from Dubovka to Rybinsk. If he'd told the captain of the barge and the crew that he wanted to work as a barge hauler, they'd have considered it the height of stupidity and would never have accepted him. So he went aboard as a passenger and became friendly with the crew and began to help them tow the boat. In a week he buckled himself into a harness, just like a real barge hauler. Soon they realized his strength and put him to the test: he outpulled three or four men, the sturdiest of his comrades. He was only twenty years old at the time, and his comrades on the barge christened him Nikitushka Lomov, in memory of their hero, who'd already departed the scene. The next summer he was traveling on a steamer. One of the many common folk on deck turned out to be one of his fellow workers from the barge the year before; that was how some students, his fellow travelers, learned about his nickname, Nikitushka Lomov. In fact he had acquired and, without skimping on time, had maintained enormous strength. "It's necessary," he used to say. "It inspires respect and love of the common people. It's useful and may come in handy someday."

. . .

However, in the making of such an extraordinary man, of course the principal element had to have been nature. For some time before he'd left the university and had set off for his own estate, and later on his journey through Russia, he'd already adopted a set of original principles to govern his material, moral, and spiritual life. When he returned to Petersburg, these principles had already developed into a complete system, which he followed faithfully. He said to himself, "I shall not drink one drop of wine. I shall not touch any women." But he was so passionate by nature! "Why on earth? Such extreme measures are unnecessary!" "They are necessary. We demand complete enjoyment of life for all people. Therefore, in our own lives we must demonstrate that we demand this not to satisfy our own passions, not for ourselves alone, but for man in general. We must show that we're speaking according to principles and not passions, according to convictions and not personal desires."

. . .

Gymnastics, physical labor to develop his strength, and reading were Rakhmetov's personal pursuits. Upon his return to Petersburg these activities occupied only about a quarter of his time. The remainder he devoted to matters of concern to others or to no one in particular, constantly maintaining the same rule he had for his reading: not to waste time over secondary matters or subsidiary people, to occupy himself only with things of fundamental importance, those that shape secondary matters and second rate people without their participation. For example, outside his circle he made the acquaintance only of those people who had some influence over others. Someone who wasn't an authority for other people couldn't even enter into conversation with Rakhmetov. He would say, "You'll excuse me, but I don't have the time," and would walk away. By the same token, no one could avoid becoming acquainted with Rakhmetov if the latter wanted it to happen. He simply appeared and declared what it was he required with the following prelude: "I wish to become acquainted with you. It's essential. If this isn't a good time, set another." He paid no attention whatever to your petty concerns, even if you were his closest acquaintance and were begging him to become involved in your predicament. "I haven't time," he would say and turn aside. But he did get involved in important matters, when in his own opinion it was necessary, even though no one desired it. "I must," he would say. The things he used to say and do on such occasions are beyond comprehension.

▶ Working
with Sources

1. How does Rakhmetov connect revolutionary activity with a direct and physical identification with the common people of Russia?

2. Is Rakhmetov's self-disciplined, ascetic lifestyle comparable to that of a medieval monk? Why might this have been the case?

# Chapter 26 1750–1914

# Industrialization and Its Discontents

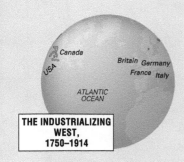

**THE INDUSTRIALIZING WEST, 1750–1914**

In the late summer of 1845, Mary Paul, age 15, made a life-altering decision. Having already realized just how limited her prospects were in the hardscrabble farm country of rural Vermont, she decided to head for Massachusetts and stake her future on a job in the newly expanding textile industry.

Exactly how that future would unfold can be seen in letters she wrote to her widowed father, Bela. Her correspondence reveals that the primary reason behind her dramatic decision was simply to earn steady wages, rather than rely on the uncertainties and drudgery of farm work. On September 13, 1845, Mary wrote for her father's consent to leave her nearby domestic job and seek employment in the booming mill town of Lowell, Massachusetts. On November 20, Mary wrote that she had already "found a place in a spinning room and the next morning [she] went to work." She continued, "I like very well have [sic] 50cts first payment increasing every payment as I get along in work. [I] have a first rate overseer and a very good boarding place." Shortly before Christmas, Mary reported that her wages had increased: "Last Tuesday we were paid. In all I had six dollars and sixty cents paid $4.68 for board. With the rest I got me a pair of rubbers and a pair of 50.cts shoes. Next payment I am to have a dollar a week beside my board." She then offered her father glimpses into her daily routine in the mill, one with which millions of

*ABOVE:* American photojournalist Lewis Hine (1874–1940) documented child labor, including these girls in a North Carolina textile mill in 1910.

workers around the world would soon grow quite familiar: "At 5 o'clock in the morning the bell rings for the folks to get up and get breakfast. At half past six it rings for the girls to get up and at seven they are called into the mill. At half past 12 we have dinner are called back again at one and stay till half past seven." Mary closes by pointing out, "I think that the factory is the best place for me and if any girl wants employment I advise them to come to Lowell."

———

Mary Paul's experiences, shared by thousands of other young, unmarried women in rural farming regions, signaled a momentous change in the patterns of American and world history. Like Great Britain and areas throughout northern Europe, the northeastern United States was now in the initial stages of what we have termed "scientific–industrial society." The agrarian–urban model, which had lasted for millennia on every inhabited continent except Australia, was now slowly giving way to a society based on machine-made goods, large-scale factories, regimented work hours, and wage labor. Moreover, the economies of the industrializing states would increasingly be dominated by capitalism. An ideology of progress (a legacy of the Enlightenment), backed by the acceleration of technology and science, constituted what we term the "challenge of modernity." That challenge was already being spread globally through innovations in transportation, communications, and weaponry produced by this Industrial Revolution.

# Origins and Growth of Industrialism, 1750–1914

Like the agricultural revolution of the Neolithic age, which resulted in humankind's transition from foragers to food producers and made urbanization possible, the Industrial Revolution forever altered the lives of tens of millions around the globe. Whether or not this movement was in fact a "revolution," however, is a matter of some debate. It is perhaps more accurate to say that the process of industrialization evolved gradually, originating in Britain in the eighteenth century, then spreading to the European continent and North America in the nineteenth century and subsequently around the globe, interacting with and adapting to local circumstances and cultures along the way. But there is no question that the transition from manual labor and natural sources of power to the implementation of mechanical forms of power and machine-driven production resulted in a vast increase in the production of goods, new modes of transportation, and new economic policies and business procedures.

## Early Industrialism, 1750–1870
The industrialization of western Europe began in Britain. As with all transformative events in history, however, a number of important questions arise: Why did the industrial movement begin in Britain? Why not, say, in China in the Song or Ming period? Why in the eighteenth century? Why in such areas as textiles, iron, mining, and transport? How did these changes become not only self-sustaining but also able to transform so many other manufacturing processes? And was this

## Seeing Patterns

▶ Where and when did the Industrial Revolution originate?

▶ What were some effects of industrialization on Western society? How did social patterns change?

▶ In what ways did industrialization contribute to innovations in technology? How did these technological advances contribute to Western imperialism in the late nineteenth century?

▶ What new directions in science, philosophy, religion, and the arts did industrialism generate? What kind of responses did it provoke?

process "inevitable," as some have claimed, or was it contingent on a myriad of complex interactions that we are still struggling to comprehend?

**Preconditions**    Although there are no simple answers to these questions, it is possible to cite several distinct conditions and advantages enjoyed by both Europe in general and Britain in particular. For one thing, unlike China, Europeans had earlier seen the rise to prominence of a prosperous and largely independent middle class consisting of merchants and manufacturers. In addition, Europe was unique among global civilizations in that it had experienced an earlier scientific revolution, essential for providing the technological foundation for the creation and application of machine technology to production.

Three key factors made Britain especially suitable for launching the industrial movement. First, Britain benefited from what some historians refer to as the "coal and colonies" theory. Large reserves of coal and iron ore, combined with the establishment of overseas colonies and subsequent global trading networks, provided a foundation for commercial expansion, which in turn created capital to fund new enterprises. Second, a thriving merchant class, empowered by the Glorious Revolution of 1688, grew in significance in the House of Commons of the British Parliament and supported legislation that promoted economic development. Finally, Britain developed a flourishing banking system: the Bank of England (founded in 1694) provided needed funds to entrepreneurs willing to make risky investments in new ventures.

Thanks to agricultural improvements, in part coming from the introduction of new crops from the Americas, Britain experienced a surge in population. Whereas in 1600 Britain's population was around 5 million, by 1700 it had nearly doubled to around 9 million. At the same time, a demographic shift in which displaced tenant farmers migrated to towns and cities caused a rapid increase in urban growth and created greater demand for food and consumer goods, such as textiles.

Indeed, the impact of these changes was especially notable in the textile industry. Although woolen cloth had long been the staple of the British textile industry, the introduction of new fabrics from Asia, such as silk and cotton, began to gain in popularity among consumers. Cotton's advantages of light weight and ease of cleaning resulted in a growing demand for the domestic production of affordable cotton clothing, or "calicoes." At first, the demand for finished cloth goods was satisfied by weavers working in the older, domestic cottage industries, a system known as "protoindustrialism." Due in large part to concerns for the woolen industry, however, Parliament enacted the protectionist Calico Acts of 1700 and 1720, which prohibited the importation of cotton goods from India. But this legislation had the unintended consequence of increasing domestic demand for English-made cotton textiles, which quickly outstripped available supplies. Given soaring demand, it was apparent that some sort of means was needed to speed up production.

**British Resources**    The impasse was resolved by a combination of factors peculiar to Britain at this time, which taken together made the use of machines more practical and cost-efficient than it might have been somewhere else. Since wages for workers in rural industries were high, the use of labor-saving machinery was increasingly seen as a means to help firms be profitable. By contrast, where wages were relatively low (such as in the Dutch Republic and France), there was no urgent need to develop more cost-effective means of production. At the same time, Britain's vast reserves of coal resulted in cheap energy.

Moreover, Britain was singularly fortunate in its social and cultural capital. The composition of British society in the seventeenth and eighteenth centuries was unusually attuned to what historians sometimes call the "Industrial Enlightenment." As discussed in Chapter 17, eighteenth-century Britain was at the center of the European scientific revolution, which was realized in a more widespread fashion in Britain than elsewhere. The majority of British inventors had interests in and ties to societies aligned with scientific aspects of the Enlightenment, which served as centers of discourse and exchange between leading scientists, inventors, experimenters, and mechanics.

**New Technologies and Sources of Power**    These factors produced an explosion of technological innovation in Britain. From 1700 to 1800 over 1,000 inventions were developed, most of which were related to the textile industry. Among the most prominent were the flying shuttle (1733), the spinning jenny (1764), the water frame (1769), and the spinning mule (1779). Each of these devices greatly increased the speed and quality of spinning or weaving; the mule combined both operations into one machine. The power loom (1787) then set the technological stage for full-scale machine production of textiles, gradually replacing manually operated looms. This in turn resulted in the decline of handicraftsmen, particularly hand weavers, whose livelihoods were threatened by the new power-driven looms. In desperation, handicrafters of all sorts mounted an organized and combined campaign to sabotage the increasing use of machines in textile factories (see "Against the Grain" on p. 820).

Even these improvements were not enough, however, to supply both domestic and colonial markets with sufficient quantities of textiles. What was needed in order to speed up production was some sort of reliable mechanical power to drive the looms. The solution was provided by the development of the steam engine, easily the most important—and iconic—innovation of the industrial era.

**The Factory System**    The growing dependence on large machinery, the necessity of transporting fuel and raw materials to centers of production, and the efficiency afforded by housing a multitude of machines under one roof necessitated the construction of large manufacturing buildings. These facilities were initially located near sources of running water in order to provide the power to run mechanical looms. The implementation of steam power to drive machinery allowed entrepreneurs to move mills and production centers away from water sources in rural areas to urban settings, where there were large pools of cheap labor. Another attraction of urban areas

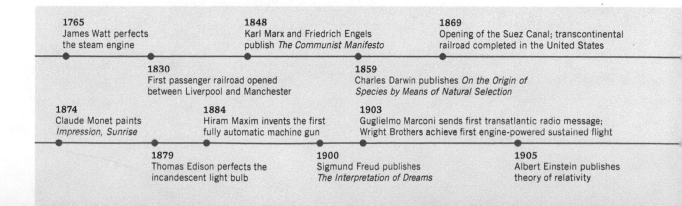

| 1765<br>James Watt perfects<br>the steam engine | 1848<br>Karl Marx and Friedrich Engels<br>publish *The Communist Manifesto* | 1869<br>Opening of the Suez Canal; transcontinental<br>railroad completed in the United States |
|---|---|---|

| | 1830<br>First passenger railroad opened<br>between Liverpool and Manchester | 1859<br>Charles Darwin publishes *On the Origin of<br>Species by Means of Natural Selection* |
|---|---|---|

| 1874<br>Claude Monet paints<br>*Impression, Sunrise* | 1884<br>Hiram Maxim invents the first<br>fully automatic machine gun | 1903<br>Guglielmo Marconi sends first transatlantic radio message;<br>Wright Brothers achieve first engine-powered sustained flight |
|---|---|---|

| | 1879<br>Thomas Edison perfects the<br>incandescent light bulb | 1900<br>Sigmund Freud publishes<br>*The Interpretation of Dreams* | 1905<br>Albert Einstein publishes<br>theory of relativity |
|---|---|---|---|

was their greater accessibility to roads, canals, and, later, railroads. Once established, these factories in their turn drew increasing numbers of workers, which contributed to urban population surges, particularly in the north and Midlands of England. By the 1830s over 1 million people drew wages from textile factories, and close to 25 percent of Britain's industrial production came from factories (see Map 26.1).

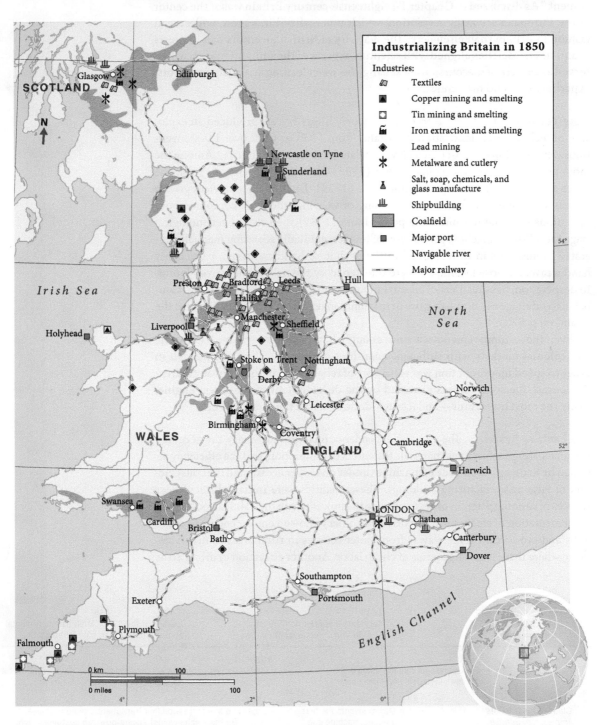

**Industrializing Britain in 1850**

Industries:

- Textiles
- Copper mining and smelting
- Tin mining and smelting
- Iron extraction and smelting
- Lead mining
- Metalware and cutlery
- Salt, soap, chemicals, and glass manufacture
- Shipbuilding
- Coalfield
- Major port
- Navigable river
- Major railway

**MAP 26.1  Industrializing Britain in 1850.**

**Global Commerce**   The application of machines to the production of textile manufactures resulted in Britain's increasingly important role in the development of intercontinental trade and commerce. Prior to the Industrial Revolution, India and China dominated global trade in textiles. But thanks to its vast holdings in American and Asia, combined with mercantilist policies, Britain had ready-made markets for the distribution and sale of its increased output of goods. Britain also benefited from slave labor in its former colonies, which kept the price of commodities like American cotton low. One result was growing demand among colonial markets for textile products, which in turn stimulated the necessity to step up production. Yet another consequence of the surge in the volume of textile production was that manufacturers were able to lower the prices of their goods, making them more competitive in global markets.

**Transportation**   While steam-powered factories provided much of the muscle of the Industrial Revolution, it was the steam railroad that captivated the imagination of the public. Its origins, like those of the earlier stationary pumping engines, began at the mines. For more than a century, miners had used track-mounted cars to pull loads of coal and iron out of mines. By the 1820s experiments were already under way to attach engines to moving carriages. Whereas in 1840 Great Britain counted only 1,800 miles of rail, by 1870 the figure had jumped nearly ninefold to 15,600 miles. Railroads vastly improved the shipping of coal and other bulk commodities and greatly enhanced the sale and distribution of manufactures of all kinds. The railroad itself developed into a self-sustaining industry, employing thousands in all sorts of related jobs and spurring further investment by wealthy entrepreneurs.

Although their impact was realized somewhat later, the application of steam to ships had far-reaching ramifications, especially in the second half of the nineteenth century. Credit for the first practical steam-powered riverboat goes to the American engineer and inventor Robert Fulton (1765–1815). Fulton's *Clermont*, constructed in 1807, plied the Hudson River from New York to Albany. English engineers were quick to copy Fulton's lead; by 1815 there were 10 steamboats hauling coal across the Clyde River in Scotland. During the 1820s and 1830s steamboats were in regular use on Europe's principal rivers. Steamboats also played a vital role in opening up the Great Lakes and the Ohio and Mississippi Rivers to commerce in the United States. By the 1830s and 1840s the British East India Company used iron-hulled steamers to facilitate maritime trade with its markets in India. Military uses soon followed.

## The Spread of Early Industrialism

By the 1830s, in Belgium, northern France, and the northern German states—all of which had coal reserves—conditions had grown more suitable for industrialization than earlier when wages were low. More settled political conditions after the Napoleonic Wars led to population increases, contributing to higher consumer demand. At the same time, larger urban areas provided greater pools of available workers for factories. Moreover, within these regions improved networks of roads, canals, and now railways facilitated the movement of both raw materials to industrial centers and manufactured goods to markets. In addition, governmental involvement greatly enhanced the investment climate; protective tariffs for manufactures and the gradual removal of internal toll restrictions, particularly in the northern German states, opened up the trading industry.

**The United States**    Industrialism was imported to the United States toward the end of the eighteenth century by Samuel Slater (1768–1835), a British engineer. Slater established the first water-powered textile factory in America, in Rhode Island in 1793. By 1825 factories in the northeastern section of the country were producing vast quantities of textile goods on mechanically powered looms.

After a brief interruption during the American Civil War—during which the majority of factories on both sides were engaged in producing munitions and war materiel—industrialization in America resumed at a greatly accelerated pace. As production data indicate, by 1870 America was producing far more spindles of cotton than Great Britain, and its production of iron ingots was swiftly catching up to that of British and European producers. By 1914 the United States had become the world's single largest industrial economy.

In addition to manufacturing, trade and commerce across the vast American continent were facilitated by a national network of railroads, which swiftly took over the carrying trade from the canal networks created in the early nineteenth century. Data for US rail construction show this astonishing growth: from 2,800 miles of rail in 1840 to about 35,000 miles by the conclusion of the Civil War—more than the rest of the world combined. By 1869 the first transcontinental railroad was joined with a final golden spike at Promontory Point, Utah, resulting in an astonishing total of 53,000 rail miles by 1870.

## Later Industrialism, 1871–1914

In many ways the next stage of industrialism, often referred to as "the second Industrial Revolution," grew out of the first phase. Perhaps the best measure of the difference in the two periods, however, is that while the first stage relied upon steam power, the second introduced several high-technology innovations that, taken together, altered the course not only of the Industrial Revolution but also of world history. Among the most significant were steel, electricity, and chemicals (see Map 26.2).

**New Materials: Steel**    An important element in the second Industrial Revolution was the increasing use of steel instead of iron. Refined techniques for making steel had existed for many hundreds of years in different parts of the world but were largely the province of highly skilled craftspeople such as swordsmiths. New technical advances, however, now made it possible to produce large quantities of high-grade yet *inexpensive* steel. Subsequent improvements in production in the 1860s and 1870s included the blast furnace and the open-hearth smelting method.

Following the conclusion of the Franco–Prussian war, Germany's annexation of the ore-rich regions of Alsace-Lorraine led to a dramatic increase in industrial production. Starting with almost no measurable steel production in the 1870s, Germany managed to catch up to British annual steel production in 1893 and then went on to surge far ahead: By 1914 its annual tonnage of steel was more than twice that of Britain. One advantage enjoyed by Germany was that it was able to model its new industrial facilities on those of its most modern competitors, saving substantial time and investment capital and resulting in newer and more efficient equipment and business methods. Yet another advantage was Germany's development of sophisticated scientific research capabilities at universities.

Industrialization also spread further afield during the second half of the nineteenth century. Aware of the growing power and influence of western European industrial powers, both Russia and Japan implemented economic reforms to compete on a more equal footing with the West. One factor in Russia's decision to convert from an agrarian to an industrial economy was their defeat by French and British forces in the Crimean War (1853–1856). Following the emancipation of serfs in 1861, Russia embarked on an ambitious plan to industrialize, as discussed in greater detail in Chapter 25. Stunned by the bold intrusion of the West into its waters by Commodore Matthew Perry in 1853, which led to the Meiji Constitution in 1868, Japan also adapted its economy to industrialism in order to keep pace with the West (see Chapter 24).

MAP 26.2 **The Industrialization of Europe by 1914.**

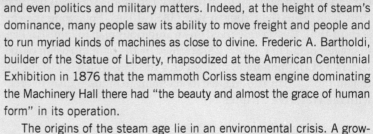

# Patterns Up Close

# "The Age of Steam"

More than any other innovation of the industrial age, the advent of practical steam power revolutionized manufacturing, transportation, communications, economics, and even politics and military matters. Indeed, at the height of steam's dominance, many people saw its ability to move freight and people and to run myriad kinds of machines as close to divine. Frederic A. Bartholdi, builder of the Statue of Liberty, rhapsodized at the American Centennial Exhibition in 1876 that the mammoth Corliss steam engine dominating the Machinery Hall there had "the beauty and almost the grace of human form" in its operation.

The origins of the steam age lie in an environmental crisis. A growing shortage of wood for fuel and charcoal making in Britain in the early 1700s forced manufacturers to turn to another fuel source: coal. As we have seen, Britain was blessed with vast amounts of coal, but getting to it was difficult because of a high water table: Mineshafts often flooded after only a few feet and had to be abandoned. Early methods of water extraction featured pumps operated by either human or animal power, but these were inefficient, expensive, and limited in power.

The first steam-driven piston engine based on experimentation with vacuum chambers and condensing steam came from the French Huguenot Denis Papin (1647–ca. 1712), who spent his later career in England. Thomas Savery (ca. 1650–1715), also taking up the idea of condensing steam and vacuum power, built a system of pipes employing the suction produced by this process dubbed the "Miner's Friend" that was able to extract water from shallow shafts but was useless for the deeper mines that were more common in rural Britain.

**Corliss Steam Engine.** A tribute to the new power of the steam engine was this huge power plant in the Machinery Hall of the American Centennial Exposition in 1876. The Corliss engine pictured here produced over 1,400 horsepower and drove nearly all the machines in the exhibition hall—with the distinct exception of those in the British display. Along with the arm of the Statue of Liberty, also on exhibition there, it became the most recognized symbol of America's first world's fair.

This drawback was partially addressed by Thomas Newcomen (1663–1729), who in 1712 vastly improved the efficiency of Papin's piston-and-cylinder design. Though over 100 Newcomen engines were in place throughout Britain and Europe at the time of Newcomen's death in 1729, a number of flaws still rendered them very slow and energy-inefficient. It remained for James Watt (1736–1819), a Scottish engineer, to make the final changes needed to create the prototype for fast engines sufficiently

The advantages of steel over iron were that it was lighter, harder, and more durable. Thus, it provided better rails for railroads and, increasingly, girders for the construction of high-rise buildings. Indeed, structural steel and steel-reinforced concrete made possible the construction of high-rise "skyscrapers," which by the turn of the century were soaring past the tallest masonry buildings. The switch from iron to steel construction of ships also marked a significant advance in steamship technology during the third quarter of the nineteenth century. Steel ships greatly improved the travel time between far-flung continents. By 1900, 95 percent of all commercial ocean liners were being constructed of steel. Steel also made possible stronger, faster, and roomier ships, while steel warships also proved far more durable in battle and set the tone for naval construction to this day.

efficient and versatile to drive factory machinery. Watt had been engaged in repairing Newcomen engines and quickly realized their limitations. His newly refined model, completed in 1765 and patented in 1769, was five times as efficient as Newcomen's engine and used 75 percent less coal.

After making several refinements Watt introduced a further improved model in 1783 that incorporated more advances. First, by injecting steam into both the top and bottom of the piston cylinder, its motion was converted to double action, making it more powerful and efficient. Second, through a system of "planetary gearing"—in which the piston shaft was connected by a circular gear to the hub of a flywheel—the back-and-forth rhythm of the piston was converted to smooth, rotary motion, suitable for driving machines in factories and mills. Watt's steam engines proved so popular that by 1790 they had replaced all of the Newcomen engines and by 1800 nearly 500 Watt engines were in operation in mines and factories.

Within a few decades, adaptations of this design were being used not just for stationary engines to run machinery but also to move vehicles along tracks and turn paddle wheels and screw propellers on boats—the first railroad engines and steamships. Both of these innovations soon provided the muscle and sinew of enhanced commerce and empire building among the newly industrializing nations. Indeed, by 1914, there was scarcely a place on the globe not accessible by either railroad or steamship. Although societies seeking to protect themselves from outside influence saw the railroad and steamer as forces of chaos, the web of railroad lines grew denser on every inhabited continent, and the continents themselves were connected by the tissue of shipping lines. Steam may indeed be said to be the power behind the creation of modern global society.

## Questions

- How is the innovation of steam power the culmination of a pattern that began with the rise of the New Sciences in western Europe in the sixteenth and seventeenth centuries?

- Does Frederic A. Bartholdi's statement in 1876 that the Corliss steam engine "had the beauty and almost the grace of the human form" reflect a romantic outlook? If so, how?

**Chemicals**   Advances were also made in the use of chemicals. Here, the most significant developments were initiated by academic scientists, whose work resulted in later advances in the chemical industry. In 1856 the first synthetic dye, mauveine, was created, which initiated the synthetic dyestuffs industry. The result of these advances was not only a wider array of textiles but also new chemical compounds important in the refinement of wood pulp products, ranging from cheaper paper in the 1870s to artificial silk, known as rayon. Later discoveries, such as the synthesizing of ammonia and its conversion to nitrate for use in fertilizers and explosives, were to have far-reaching effects during World War I. The invention of dynamite by the Swedish chemist and engineer Alfred Bernhard

Nobel (1833–1896) provided the means to blast through rock formations, resulting in great tunnels and massive excavation projects like the Panama Canal (1914). In yet another chemical advance, Charles Goodyear (1800–1860) invented a process in 1839 that produced vulcanized rubber, and celluloid—the first synthetic plastic—was developed in 1869. Other innovations in chemistry, ranging from pharmaceuticals and drugs like aspirin to soap products, contributed to improved health. By the early part of the twentieth century, these developments had led to a "hygiene revolution" among the industrialized countries.

**New Energies: Electricity and the Internal Combustion Engine**    Although electricity had been in use during the first period of industrialization, its development and application were greatly advanced after 1850, especially in the generation of electrical power. The first step came with Michael Faraday (1791–1867) patenting the electromagnetic generator in 1861. But large-scale electrical generation would require a number of other innovations before it became a reality. Perhaps the most important devices in this regard were developed by engineer Nikola Tesla (1856–1943). Among Tesla's inventions were the alternating current (AC), the Tesla Coil (1891) for the more efficient transmission of electricity, and a host of generators, motors, and transformers. In 1888 the introduction of Tesla's "electric induction engine" led to the widespread adoption of electricity-generating power plants throughout industrialized Europe.

Another key source of energy to power the industrial revolution was the internal combustion engine. When oil, or liquid petroleum, was commercially developed in the 1860s and 1870s, it was at first refined into kerosene and used for illumination. One of the by-products of this process, gasoline, however, soon revealed its potential as a new fuel source. The first experimental internal combustion engines utilizing the new fuel appeared in the 1860s. Their light weight relative to their power was superior to steam engines of comparable size, and the first practical attempts to use them in powering vehicles came along in the next decade.

Who invented the automobile? Although two Germans, Gottlieb Daimler (1834–1900) and Karl Benz (1844–1929), are usually credited with the invention, the first true automobile was invented by an unheralded Austrian mechanic and inventor named Siegfried Marcus (1831–1898). As early as 1864 Marcus harnessed his own experimental internal combustion engine to a cart, which moved under its own power for over 200 yards. Over the next several years Marcus tinkered with several gadgets and devices in order to perfect his self-propelled contraption. Among these were the carburetor, the magneto ignition, various gears, the clutch, a steering mechanism, and a braking system. All of these inventions were included in the first real combustion-engine automobile, which Marcus drove through the streets of Vienna in 1874.

Internal combustion engines were also applied to early attempts at sustained flight. In 1900 Ferdinand von Zeppelin (1838–1917) constructed a rigid airship—a *dirigible*—consisting of a fabric-covered aluminum frame that was kept aloft by the incorporation of bags filled with hydrogen gas and powered by two 16-horsepower engines. Zeppelin's airships thus became the ancestors of the blimps that even today still ply the airways. Perhaps more momentous was the marriage of the gasoline engine to the glider, thus creating the first airplanes. Though there were several claimants to this honor, the Wright brothers are usually credited with the first sustained engine-powered flight in Kitty Hawk, North Carolina, on December 17, 1903. By 1909, the first flight across the English Channel had been completed; in 1911 the first transcontinental airplane flight across the United States took place, though by taking 82 hours of flight time over a span of 2 months it could scarcely compete with railroad travel. Still, the potential of both the automobile and the airplane were to be starkly revealed within a few years during the Great War.

**The Communication Revolution**    Although electric telegraph messages were transmitted as early as the 1840s with the advent of the devices and code devised by Samuel F. B. Morse (1791–1872), it was only in the 1860s and 1870s that major continental landmasses were linked by submarine transoceanic cables. The first successful link from Britain to India was installed in 1865. The first transatlantic cable, from Britain to America, was laid as early as 1858, though it was only in 1866 that the cable was deemed operationally successful. By the latter part of the nineteenth century, telegraphic communication was a worldwide phenomenon, which has been likened to the Internet in its impact on human contact. This was vastly augmented with the telephone, invented by Alexander Graham Bell (1847–1922) in 1876, which made voice communication possible by wire.

But perhaps most revolutionary of all was the advent of wireless communication. The theoretical groundwork for this had been laid by James Clerk Maxwell (1831–1879), a Scottish physicist researching the theoretical properties of electromagnetism, and Heinrich Rudolf Hertz (1857–1894). In 1885 Hertz—whose name was later given to the unit of measurement for radio wave cycles—discovered that electromagnetic radiation actually produces unseen waves that emanate through the universe. In the later 1890s, Guglielmo Marconi (1874–1937) developed a device using these radio waves generated by electric sparks controlled by a telegraph key to send and receive messages over several miles. By 1903 Marconi had enhanced the power and range of the device enough to send the first transatlantic radio message, from Cape Cod in the United States to Cornwall in England. The "wireless telegraph" was quickly adopted by ships for reliable communication at sea. Subsequent improvements, such as the development of the vacuum tube amplifier and oscillator, resulted in greater power and reliability and, within a few years, the ability to transmit sound wirelessly.

**The Weapons Revolution**    The advances in chemistry and explosives, metallurgy, and machine tooling during the second half of the nineteenth century also contributed to a vastly enhanced lethality among weapons. Earlier advances from the 1830s to the early 1860s (including the percussion cap, the conical bullet, the revolver, and the rifled musket) provided the base for of the development of ever more sophisticated firearms. Breech-loading weapons, in their infancy during the early 1860s, rapidly came of age with the advent of the brass cartridge. By 1865, a number of manufacturers were marketing repeating rifles, some of whose designs, like the famous Winchester lever-action models, are still popular today. Rifles designed by the German firms of Krupp and Mauser pioneered the bolt-action, magazine, and clip-fed rifles that remained the staple of infantry weapons through two world wars.

Artillery went through a similar transformation. Breech-loading artillery, made possible by precision machining of breech locks and the introduction of metallic cartridges for artillery shells, made loading and firing large guns far more efficient.

By the early 1880s the invention of the recoil cylinder—a spring or hydraulic device like an automobile shock absorber—to cushion the force of the gun's recoil eliminated the necessity of reaiming the piece after every shot. Field artillery could now be anchored, aimed, and fired continuously with enhanced accuracy: It had become "rapid-fire artillery." Its effectiveness was enhanced further by the new explosives like guncotton, dynamite, and later TNT, for use in its shells. Another innovation in this regard was the development of smokeless powder, or *cordite*, which, in addition to eliminating much of the battlefield smoke generated by black powder, was three times more powerful as a propellant. Thus, the range and accuracy of small arms and artillery were pushed even further.

By far, the most significant—and lethal—advance in weaponry during the later nineteenth century, however, was the invention of the machine gun, the deadliest weapon ever developed. Though many quick-firing weapons had been developed with varying degrees of success during these years—the most famous being the Gatling Gun (1861)—the first fully automatic machine gun was conceived by Hiram Maxim (1840–1916), an American inventor and dabbler in electricity.

> "In 1882 I was in Vienna . . . [an acquaintance] said: . . . 'If you want to make a pile of money, invent something that will enable these Europeans to cut each others' throats with greater facility.'"
>
> —Hiram Maxim

By the outbreak of World War I, every major army in the world was equipping itself with Maxim's guns, now manufactured in licensed factories in Europe and the United States. Perhaps more than any other single weapon, the machine gun made the western front in Europe from 1914 to 1918 the most devastating killing field in human history. In his memoirs, Maxim notes somewhat ruefully that he was applauded more highly for inventing his "killing machine" than for inventing a steam inhaler for those suffering from bronchitis.

**Hiram Maxim.** In this 1900 photo, the proud inventor of the machine gun looks on with self-satisfied pride as Albert Edward, Prince of Wales (the future King Edward VII), experiences for himself the awesome firepower of Maxim's "little daisy of a gun." In 1885 Maxim put on a similar demonstration for Lord Wolseley, commander in chief of the British Army. The British War Office adopted the gun 3 years later. The lethal power of the machine gun was first put to use in Africa at the Battle of Omdurman in 1898, where 20,000 Sudanese cavalrymen were slaughtered in fruitless charges against a line of 20 Maxim guns.

# The Social and Economic Impact of Industrialism, 1750–1914

All of these changes in modes of production, particularly the emergence of the factory system, resulted in wholesale transformations in the daily lives of millions around the globe. Along with new networks of transportation and communication, new materials, and new sources of energy, the industrialized nations underwent significant changes in how they viewed politics, social institutions, and economic relationships during this time.

## Demographic Changes

Changes in the demographics of industrialized nations followed the development of new industries. Perhaps most significantly, the populations of these countries grew at unprecedented rates and became increasingly urbanized. Indeed, Great Britain became by the latter half of the nineteenth century the first country to have more urban dwellers than rural inhabitants. This trend would continue among the industrialized nations through the twentieth century.

**Population Surge and Urbanization**    As data from 1700 to around 1914 reveal, the industrialized nations experienced a significant population explosion (see Map 26.3). Advances in industrial production, expansion of factories, and improved agriculture during the first Industrial Revolution combined to produce increasing opportunities for jobs as well as more plentiful and nutritious food in order to sustain a larger population. In the second Industrial Revolution scientific advances in medicine, including drugs and vaccinations, along with notions of sanitation, contributed to a declining mortality rate. For example, the population of Britain grew from around 9 million in 1700 to around 20 million in 1850. Then from 1871 to 1914 Britain's population soared from 31 million to nearly 50 million. Other industrialized states experienced similar population increases; in Germany, for example, the population grew from around 41 million in 1871 to 58 million in 1914.

More revealing than overall population figures is the shift of populations from rural to urban areas. For example, in Great Britain in 1800 around 60 percent of the population lived in rural areas. By 1850, however, about 50 percent of the population lived in cities. In numerical terms, the population of London amounted to around 1 million in 1800, but by 1850 that figure had more than doubled to around 2.5 million. Moreover, in 1801 only 21 cities in Europe (including London) could boast of populations over 100,000. By 1850, this had doubled to 42. Significant in this respect was the appearance of new industrial and commercial centers such as Manchester, Liverpool, Birmingham, and Glasgow, as well as vast increases in the size of older capital cities such as Paris, Berlin, and St. Petersburg.

**European Migrations**    Another social change during the industrial era concerns overseas emigrations of Europeans. In part, this movement was sparked by the dramatic rise in population in industrialized areas of Europe. Another contributing factor, however, was the desire to escape the grinding poverty of underdeveloped regions of Europe—particularly Ireland and southeast Europe—in order to seek better opportunities in developing industrial parts of America. In

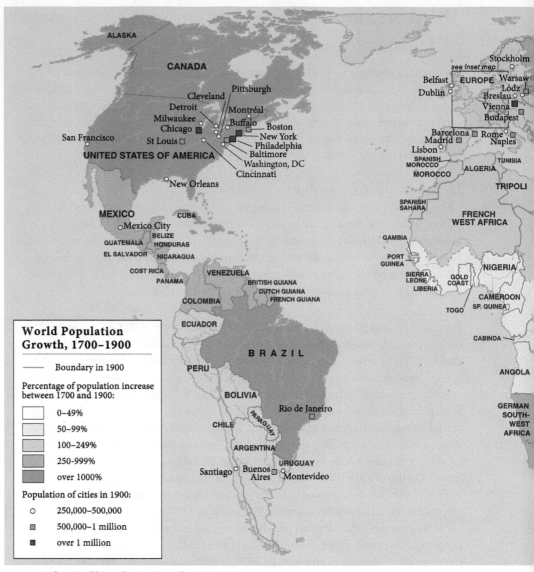

MAP 26.3  **World Population Growth, 1700–1900.**

addition, advances in transportation made it easier for Europeans to emigrate. In all, some 60 million Europeans left for other parts of the world (North and South America, Australia, and Asiatic Russia) between 1800 and 1914. Of these, the majority emigrated to the United States and Canada (see Map 26.4).

## Industrial Society

Industrialization led to significant changes in the hierarchy of social ranks. Although the elites continued to enjoy their privileged status, the "new money" of the rising middle classes began to eclipse "old money" in terms of social status and influence. The increasing importance of capitalism and commerce, and with it the accumulation of significant wealth, greatly enhanced the status and influence of the upper echelons

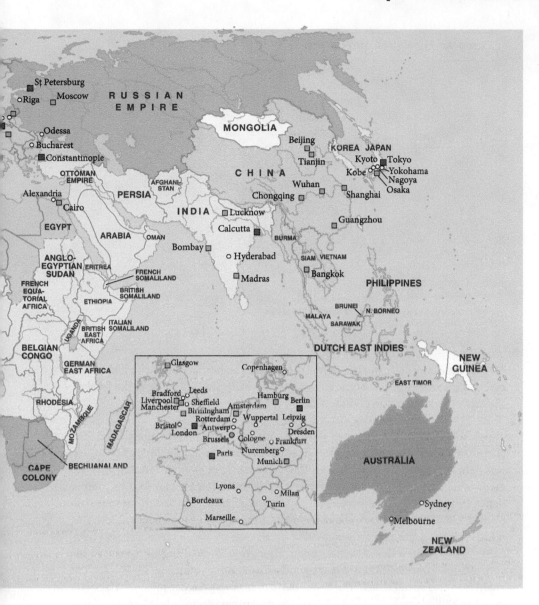

of the middle class, or bourgeoisie. No longer were status and power determined solely by aristocratic birth or privilege. The principal alteration in the social hierarchy, however, was the appearance of a new rank: the working class. For the first time, the advent of industrialism created the concept of "class consciousness," or growing awareness of, and emphasis on, social standing determined by occupation and income.

**The Upper Classes**    At the top of the European social scene, members of the landed aristocracy were joined by the new urban elites. Together, they constituted only 5 percent of the total population. These urban elites were the extremely rich factory owners, bankers, and merchants who had made personal fortunes from industrial pursuits. Although a tiny minority, they managed to control almost

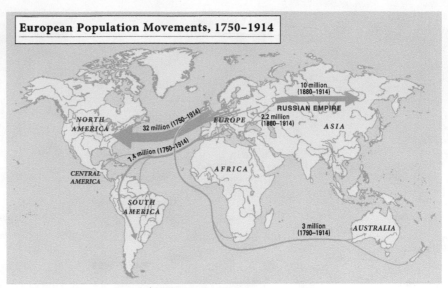

MAP 26.4 **European Population Movements, 1750–1914.**

40 percent of Europe's wealth. Below these were the bourgeoisie, who had either married into the highest social rank or whose wealth was not quite at the level of the aristocrats and urban elites.

**The Middle Classes**    A notch down from the upper classes were the middle classes, who constituted around 15 percent of Europe's total population. This rank was peopled mostly by professionals (lawyers, physicians), high-ranking government officials, and prosperous businessmen and merchants, who rose to prominence in the new age thanks largely to their acquisition of cash. Distinguished from the landed aristocracy above them and from the working classes below, the middle classes were themselves divided by a sense of class consciousness. They enjoyed better lifestyles in terms of education, fine homes, and as measured by conspicuous consumption of luxury goods. The lower middle class was itself divided into two social strata. The upper tier was made up for the most part by artisans and skilled workers in factories, mines, and other places, while beneath them were unskilled workers, tradespeople, and handcrafters.

It was the middle class, particularly concerned with "respectability," which set the cultural and moral tone for the second half of the nineteenth century. Impropriety and sexual scandal were not to be tolerated; indeed, in 1867 the English parliament passed the Obscene Publications Bill in an attempt to crack down on pornographic literature. They set themselves apart from the elites above, and especially from those below, by emphasizing what they considered their respectability, frugality, and industry. Determined to succeed at all costs, the industrial middle classes eagerly consumed numerous "self-help" books, of which the most famous was Samuel Smiles's *Self-Help* (1859). The book went through several editions in subsequent years, and emerged as the most popular of the self-help books in Victorian England.

**The Working Class**   Urban factory workers were distinguished from farmers and workers in rural areas by their daily routine regulated by the factory time clock and by selling their labor in return for cash wages. Among the working classes, divisions existed between skilled and unskilled workers, largely determined by familiarity with the intricacies of industrial machinery and its maintenance.

**Woman and Children Coal Putters, Mid and East Lothian, Scotland ca. 1848.** Women and children (some as young as 5 or 6 years old) worked long hours in terrible conditions in underground mines. Here, a woman and two children, known as "putters," struggle to push a wagon of coal to the surface. Other children, called "trappers," maintained airflow in the tunnels by operating ventilation doors.

Typical working conditions in British textile mills in the early 1800s were deplorable. Without traditional protective guilds or associations, workers were at the mercy of factory owners. The factory clock and the pace of factory machinery determined the day's work, which was repetitive, dirty, and dangerous. Even young children—some as young as 7 years old—worked in factories, some alongside their parents as family units and others who had been orphaned or turned over to local parishes by parents who could no longer provide for their care. Working long hours—12- to 14-hour days were common in the early 1800s—children were constantly urged to speed up production and severely disciplined for "idling." Indeed, they were commonly beaten for falling asleep and to keep them from falling into the machinery, which, because of the lack of protection from its moving parts, could easily maim or kill them. In fact, until the 1840s in Britain, the majority of "hands," or factory workers, were women and children, who, by virtue of their inexperience and expendability, could be paid less than their male counterparts.

Conditions were often even worse in the mines. Children frequently began work in mines as early as age 6 or 7, most often as "trappers," responsible for opening and shutting ventilation doors in mineshafts. Because of their small size, children were put to work "hurrying," or lugging newly dug coal along long, low underground passageways for conveyance to the surface. Girls were especially victimized in underground mines, where they not only had to drag heavy coal-filled carts by chains fixed to leather belts around their waists but also were frequently sexually abused by their supervisors.

**Factory Towns**   Because industrial cities expanded close to factories and mills, conditions there were as grim as within the factories themselves. Clouds of coal smoke blackened buildings, acidified the rain and soil, and caused respiratory ailments among the citizens, prompting the poet William Blake's famous allusion to "dark Satanic Mills." In addition to the acrid smell of coal, a variety of other stenches assaulted the nostrils of the inhabitants. Piles of coal ash and clinker, pungent waste materials from coking or from gas works, and vile outpourings from tanneries and dye works combined with household waste, sewage, and horse manure. With the population exploding and only rudimentary waste disposal and access to clean water, diseases like cholera, typhus, and tuberculosis were rampant.

Adding to the miseries of the inhabitants of factory towns were their wretched living conditions. The working classes lived in

"In one of these courts there stands . . . a privy without a door, so dirty that the inhabitants can pass . . . only by passing through foul pools of stagnant urine and excrement."

—Friedrich Engels

**Working-Class Tenements in English Industrial Cities.** In this engraving, entitled *Over London by Rail*, the celebrated engraver Gustave Doré (1832–1883) depicts the overcrowded and squalid living conditions in working-class tenements during the early years of the Industrial Revolution. Notice the long rows of houses separated by walls and arranged in back-to-back fashion. Notice also the stretched lines for drying clothes, as well as the large number of occupants in each outdoor area.

crowded tenements consisting of row after row of shoddily built houses packed together in narrow, dark streets. One social activist, Friedrich Engels (1820–1895), the son of a wealthy mill owner and later collaborator with Karl Marx, was determined to call attention to such abysmal conditions.

## Critics of Industrialism

It was not long before Engels and other socially conscious observers began to draw attention to the obvious abuses of the industrial movement and to stimulate reform of working conditions. Efforts to improve these sordid conditions were launched in Great Britain in the 1820s and 1830s and carried over into the 1870s.

**Socialists**    The plight of the working classes inspired many social activists to take up the fight for reform, among them French and English "utopian socialists"— a term originally used derisively to describe the presumed impracticality of their schemes. One of the earliest of these activists was Henri de Saint-Simon (1760–1825), whose view of humanity defied industrial society's competition for individual wealth. In Saint-Simon's view, private property should be more equally distributed, according to the notion "From each according to his abilities, to each according to his works." Louis Blanc (1811–1882) criticized the capitalist system in his *The Organization of Work* (1839), urging workers to agitate for voting rights and espousing radical ideas like the right to work. He reconfigured Saint-Simon's memorable phrase to read "From each according to his abilities, to each according to his needs." Charles Fourier (1772–1837) advocated the founding of self-sustaining model communities in which jobs were apportioned according to ability and interest, with a sliding scale of wages tailored to highly compensate those doing the most dangerous or unattractive jobs. Fourier's concept of such "phalanxes" was the one adopted by the North American Phalanx, in which Mary Paul spent time (see the opening of this chapter).

Robert Owen (1771–1858), a factory owner in the north of England, led a movement to establish the Grand National Consolidated Trades Union. Its objective was a national strike of all trade unions, but owing to a lack of participation among workers, the movement was disbanded. Owen had previously established a model community in Scotland called New Lanark, where more humane living and working conditions for workers resulted in greater profits. After campaigning for the formation of workers' unions, Owen left for America, where he set up a model socialist community in Indiana called New Harmony, which eventually dissolved amid internal quarrels when he returned to England.

Chartism was another organized labor movement in Britain. Taking its name from the People's Charter (1838), Chartism was formed by the London Working Men's Association, and its primary goal, among others, was universal male suffrage. Millions of workers signed petitions, which were presented to Parliament in 1839 and 1842; these were rejected. Nevertheless, the chartist movement galvanized for the first time workers' sentiments and aspirations, and it served as a model for future attempts at labor reform.

**Karl Marx**    By far the most famous of the social reformers was Karl Marx (1818–1883). The son of a prosperous German attorney, Marx proved a brilliant student, eventually earning a PhD in philosophy from the University of Berlin. Marx's activities, however, resulted in his being exiled from Germany and then from France. During a visit to the industrial center of Manchester, where he met and befriended Friedrich Engels, Marx observed both the miserable lives of factory workers and the patent inequities of industrialism. From this, Marx developed his theory, which he termed "scientific socialism," that all of history involved class struggles. Borrowing the dialectical schema of the German philosopher Georg Wilhelm Friedrich Hegel (1770–1831), Marx replaced its idealism with his own materialist concept based on economic class struggle: *dialectical materialism*. Moreover, Marx saw revolution as the means by which the industrial working classes will ultimately topple the capitalist order: Just as the Third Estate and bourgeoisie had overthrown the aristocracy during the French Revolution, the current struggle between the working classes and the capitalist entrepreneurs would ultimately result in the demise of capitalism.

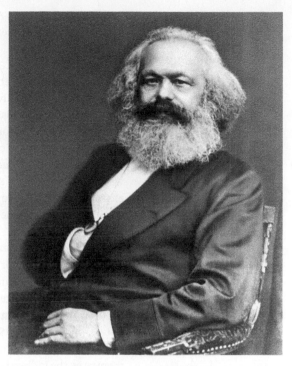

**Karl Marx.** In this photo, taken in London in 1875, Marx displays many of the character traits for which he is best known. Following the publication of his *Das Kapital* in 1871, Marx had established his reputation as a scholar of economic theory. Notice his self-satisfied and confident demeanor as he stares at the camera in an almost defiant manner. Notice as well his attire, ironically suggestive of a successful member of the bourgeoisie. After Marx's death, his longtime friend Friedrich Engels distributed 1,200 copies of this photo to communists around the world.

Convinced of the need to overthrow the capitalist system, Marx and Engels joined the nascent Communist Party in London. In preparation for a meeting in 1848, the two collaborators dashed off a pamphlet entitled *The Communist Manifesto* (1848), propaganda designed to rally support among the working classes, or *proletariat*, and to encourage them to rise up and overthrow the capitalist factory owners, or *bourgeoisie*. Compiled from a variety of French socialist, German philosophical, and personal interpretations of past history, the *Manifesto* reflects Marx's vision that "the history of all hitherto existing society is the history of class struggle" and that the time had come for the working classes to follow earlier examples and to overthrow the capitalists: "The proletarians have nothing to lose but their chains. They have a world to win. WORKING MEN OF ALL COUNTRIES, UNITE!"

**Inquiries and Reforms**    As critics of industrialism cried out against the abuses of the industrial movement, many—including some factory owners inspired by humanitarian concerns—called for governments to reform working conditions. In 1832 Parliament launched an inquiry into abuses within factories, resulting in the Sadler Report, which pointed out abuses related to child labor. In 1833 the Factory Act was passed, which set a minimum age of 9 for child employees and limited the workday to 8 hours for children between the ages of 9 and 13 and to 12 hours for those aged 13–18. Further reforms in 1847 and 1848 limited women and children to a maximum of 58 hours a week (the Ten Hours Act). Working conditions in mines were equally harsh, especially for women and children. Accordingly, similar inquiries were conducted concerning working conditions within mines, resulting in the Mines Act of 1842. It forbade the underground employment of all girls and women and set a minimum age of 10 for child laborers.

## Improved Standards of Living

Although still a matter of debate among historians, contemporary data suggest that in overall terms living and working conditions began to improve in Britain from around the 1830s to the end of the century. Thanks to the series of reforms already mentioned, conditions in factories and mines were substantially better than at the beginning of the century. Textile factories were now located in urban areas, and housing conditions for workers were more amenable. Most important, wage levels increased across the nineteenth century for industrial workers. For example, from 1850 to 1875 wages of British workers increased by around one-third and by nearly one-half by 1900.

**New Jobs for Women**    As a result of the second Industrial Revolution, many women fared far better in terms of employment. In overall terms, women represented around one-third of the workers in later nineteenth-century industrial jobs. The data from textile mills offer supporting evidence. While fewer than 2,000 women were employed in the mills in 1837, that figure nearly doubled by 1865, and by around 1900 the number of female textile workers had increased to nearly 6,000. But factory work in textile mills was not the only avenue open to women as the industrial era unfolded in the later years of the nineteenth century.

When new technologies and social trends created new employment possibilities, women constituted a readily available pool of workers. Inventions like the typewriter (perfected in the 1870s), the telephone (invented by Alexander Graham Bell in 1876), and calculating machines (in use in the 1890s), for instance, required workers to handle related jobs, the majority of which went mostly to single women and widows. As a result, women became particularly prominent in secretarial

**Women Working as Telephone Operators.** The first telephone exchange appeared in 1879. Women were selected as operators because their voices were considered pleasing to the ear and because they were considered more polite than men.

office jobs. In addition, the explosion of business firms created countless jobs for secretaries, while department stores opened up jobs for women as clerks.

**Women's Suffrage Movement**    Although many women were afforded new opportunities in business and in professions like nursing and education after 1871, in many other areas women remained second-class citizens. Women in both the United States and Europe did not begin to gain the right to own property or to sue for divorce until the third quarter of the nineteenth century, as exemplified by the passage of the English Married Woman's Property Act in 1882.

More urgent for many female reformers was the right to vote. Throughout Europe during the late nineteenth and early twentieth centuries, women formed political groups to press for the vote. The most active of these groups was in Britain, where in 1867 the National Society for Women's Suffrage was founded. The most famous—and most radical—of British political feminists was Emmeline Pankhurst (1858–1928), who together with her daughters formed the Women's Social and Political Union in 1903. They and their supporters, known as *suffragettes*, resorted to public acts of protest and civil disobedience in order to call attention to their cause. Although these tactics were of no avail prior to 1914, the right to vote was extended to some British women after the war.

Political feminists were also active on the Continent. The French League of Women's Rights was founded in the 1870s, and the Union of German Women's Organizations was formed in 1894; in neither country was the right to vote granted women until after World War I. Women in the United States pursued a parallel course with similar results: After decades of lobbying before the war, women's suffrage was finally granted by constitutional amendment in 1920.

## Improved Urban Living

Living conditions within the major urban areas in industrialized nations improved significantly during the late nineteenth and early twentieth centuries. Largely the result of the application of new technologies emerging from the industrial movement, there is no question that the lives of urban dwellers were improved in the second half of the nineteenth century.

**Sanitation and Electricity**    One measure of improved living conditions was in the provision of better sanitation. Beginning in the 1860s and 1870s large cities in Britain and Europe established public water services and began to construct underground sewage systems to carry waste from houses, outfitted with running water, to rivers and other locations beyond urban areas. By the latter part of the nineteenth century, the widespread use of gas lighting gradually began to give way to electrical varieties. Thomas Edison (1847–1931) perfected the incandescent light bulb in 1879, making the lighting of homes and business interiors more affordable and practical and gradually replacing gas lighting.

Paris represents a good example of the implementation of these reforms. In the 1850s and 1860s Napoleon III (r. 1852–1870) appointed the urban planner Georges Haussmann (1809–1891) to begin a massive reconstruction of the city. Haussmann tore down close-packed tenements in order to construct modernized buildings and wide boulevards. This was driven by a desire to beautify the city as well as the need to provide better access for government troops in the event of public demonstrations; barricaded streets, a feature of the revolutions of 1830 and 1848, thus became a thing of the past. And, like most cities of the industrialized West by the turn of the twentieth century, Paris featured lighted and paved streets, public water systems, parks, hospitals, and police. A dramatic symbol of both the newly redesigned city of Paris and the triumph of industry and science during the second Industrial Revolution was the Eiffel Tower, designed by Alexandre Gustave Eiffel (1832–1923). Erected for the Paris Exposition of 1889, the tower took years to construct, and at nearly 1,000 feet in height was the tallest structure in the world until the construction of the Empire State building in New York in 1931.

**Leisure and Sport**   Another advance in urban life in the "age of materialism" was an increase in leisure and sporting activities. The later nineteenth century saw the emergence of sporting organizations and clubs, along with the establishment of rules for play. Games played by professional teams, another innovation in sport, provided recreation for working-class men. In Britain, for example, rules for playing soccer were established in 1863 by the Football Association, and in 1888 the English Football League was established. In 1871 the Rugby Football Union was formed. In the 1870s and 1880s British cricket teams took the game abroad to compete with teams in their far-flung colonies. In 1901 the championship game of the British FA Cup competition drew over 100,000 spectators.

Nor was this trend confined to Britain. In 1896 the first modern Olympic Games took place in Athens, Greece. In 1903 the first Tour de France was run through the French countryside. In 1904 the game of soccer was given international rules by a meeting of the International Federation of Association Football in Paris. By the early 1900s the game of baseball in America had been formalized into two leagues, the National League and the American League.

## Big Business

As the scale of urban planning and renewal increased toward the end of the nineteenth century, business flourished. As manufacturing, transportation, and financing matured, entrepreneurs and businessmen became concerned about competition and falling profit rates. Since governments generally pursued hands-off liberalism (*laissez-faire*; see Chapter 22) in the economy, except for protective tariffs, entrepreneurs sought to establish cartels and monopolies, creating big business enterprises in the process.

**Large Firms**   As Britain industrialized, it gradually shifted from a closed mercantilist economy to the liberal free-trade policy Adam Smith advocated (see Chapter 22). Britain's competitors, especially Germany and the United States, by contrast, erected high tariff walls around their borders in order to help their fledgling industries. After the second wave of steel, chemical, and electrical industrialization in the second half of the nineteenth century, the scale of industrial investments rose exponentially. On domestic markets, governments did not interfere with business organization and practice, except for labor protection in Europe. As a result, in several branches of the economy, big businesses emerged during the second half of the nineteenth century that protected their profit rates through *cartels* (market-sharing agreements) or strove for outright monopolies.

Large firms typically developed in Germany and the United States, the leaders of the second wave of industrialization. By the 1890s, corporations like the Krupp steelworks in Germany and Standard Oil Company in the United States controlled large shares of their markets. Standard Oil at its height, for example, produced over 90 percent of the country's petroleum. The United States Steel Corporation, founded in 1901 by Andrew Carnegie (1835–1919), dominated the production of American steel. Carnegie himself amassed a huge personal fortune of almost $250 million, making him the richest man in the world at the time.

**New Management Styles**   In addition, new technologies in all industrial sectors offered more efficient means of production; the result was a series of significant changes in production processes during the second phase of European industrialism. One example is the implementation of the so-called American System, incorporating the use of interchangeable parts, which greatly enhanced mass production. A related development was the appearance of "continuous-flow production," wherein workers performed specialized tasks at stationary positions along an assembly line. In addition, new "scientific management" tactics were employed in mass-production assembly plants. Since no more than basic skills were required on many assembly lines, labor costs could be kept low.

The best known of the new management systems was Taylorism, named after Frederick W. Taylor (1856–1915), an American engineer. Its objective was to measure each factory worker's production based on how many units were completed in an hour's time. The result was that workers were not only more carefully managed by their superiors but also paid in accordance with their productivity. The combined result was a rapid escalation in the speed of production, which in turn contributed to a marked increase in the production of goods for daily consumption and, therefore, in the development of a consumer market at the turn of the twentieth century.

**The Assembly Line.** The American System of interchangeable parts for muskets of the early nineteenth century had evolved into the assembly line by the early twentieth. Here, Ford Model T automobiles are moved along a conveyor to different stations, where workers assemble them in simple, repetitive steps, resulting in production efficiency and low prices for the cars.

# Intellectual and Cultural Responses to Industrialism

The impressive achievements of industrialism contributed to social and cultural shifts in western society toward the close of the nineteenth century. The advent of modernity was initially celebrated as an age of progress in science, industry, and the development of a mass culture. Nevertheless, the new age of prosperity and materialism gradually provoked a growing sense of unease concerning what these advances had wrought. The rising chorus of doubt, initiated by new discoveries in the scientific community, generated similar reactions among intellectuals and artists. In the process alternative and startlingly innovative modes of cultural expression, particularly in the expressive arts, upset traditional and conventional forms. Taken together the intellectual and cultural scene in Europe was convulsive and chaotic, resulting in a mood of anxiety and uncertainty on the eve of the Great War.

## Scientific and Intellectual Developments

The latter half of the nineteenth century saw advances in both theoretical and empirical sciences that laid the basis for many of the staples of the twentieth century. Among the most far-reaching were atomic physics and relativity theory, Darwinism and evolution, and the foundations of modern psychology. Scientists also made great strides in medicine, although here the most important breakthroughs had to await the twentieth century.

**New Theories of Matter**    Quests for understanding the nature of matter, under way since Galileo (see Chapter 17), became systematic with the establishment of technical universities and science faculties in existing universities in the second half of the 1800s. Researchers made important discoveries in the 1890s that would have far-reaching consequences in the development of atomic physics and the theories of relativity. In 1892 the Dutch physicist Hendrik Lorentz (1853–1928) demonstrated that the atom, far from being a solid billiard ball, actually contained smaller particles, which he named "corpuscles"; these were later renamed electrons. A few years later, Wilhelm Roentgen (1845–1923) discovered a mysterious form of emission he called X-rays. The ability to generate these rays would shortly lead to the development of the X-ray machine. The following year, 1896, saw the first experiments in assessing radioactivity in uranium and radium by Antoine Becquerel (1852–1908) and Marie Curie (1867–1934).

As a result of these experimental findings, theoretical physics advanced new theories on the nature of light and energy. In 1900 Max Planck (1858–1947) proposed that instead of the accepted notion that energy is emitted in steady streams or waves, it is issued in bursts, or what he termed "quanta." This idea, later developed into quantum theory, suggested that matter and energy might be interchangeable. Ernest Rutherford (1871–1937), interested in this interchangeability, demonstrated in 1911 that radioactive atoms release a form of energy in the process of their disintegration. Thus, nearly three centuries of speculation about atoms as the building blocks of nature led to experimentally verified theories of subatomic particles.

**Albert Einstein**   These discoveries in the physical sciences set the stage for the appearance of perhaps the most sensational of the turn-of-the-century scientific theories: the theory of relativity of Albert Einstein (1879–1955). In 1905 and then again in 1915 Einstein published papers in which he destroyed the Newtonian notion of a certain, absolute, and mechanistic universe that obeys unvarying and objectively verifiable laws. Instead, Einstein argued that there are no absolutes of time, space, and motion; rather, these are relative to each other and depend on the position of the observer.

Moreover, Einstein demonstrated that Newton was incorrect in thinking that matter and energy were separate entities; they were, in fact, equivalent, and he developed the corresponding mathematical formula. In his equation $E = mc^2$, Einstein theorized that the atom contains an amount of energy equal to its mass multiplied by the square of the speed of light. In other words, relatively small amounts of matter could be converted into massive amounts of energy. This discovery, developed further in the twentieth century, provided the foundation for a better understanding of the forces among subatomic particles and the construction of nuclear weapons.

**Charles Darwin**   The basis of modern theories of evolution was first proposed by Charles Darwin (1809–1882). Darwin's *On the Origin of Species by Means of Natural Selection* (1859) argued that species gradually evolved from lower to higher forms. As a young man Darwin sailed on an exploratory mission on the HMS *Beagle* from 1831 to 1836 to the waters off the South American Pacific coast. Observing the tremendous variability of species on the string of the isolated Galapagos Islands, he found himself at a loss to explain why so many different species cohabited within such close geographical areas.

It occurred to Darwin—and independently to another English naturalist, Alfred Russell Wallace (1823–1913)—that an explanation for the appearance of new species in nature might lie in the struggle for food: Only those species equipped with the tools to survive in their environments would win out; those without these characteristics would become extinct.

The most controversial part of the Darwinian theory of evolution as spelled out in the *Origin* rests in the notion that characteristics are passed on by means of "natural selection." In other words, there is no intelligence or plan in the universe—only random chance and haphazard process, resulting in a pessimistic view of "nature, red in tooth and claw."

Although the *Origin* said nothing about the theory of evolution as applied to humankind—this appeared later in *The Descent of Man* (1871)—there were those who quickly applied it to society and nations. The English philosopher Herbert Spencer (1820–1903) was instrumental in proposing a theory that came to be called "social Darwinism," which sought to apply ideas of natural selection to races, ethnicities, and peoples. Spencer's ideas were frequently used to support imperial ventures aimed at the conquest and sometimes the "uplift" of non-European or American peoples as well as to justify increasingly virulent nationalism in the years leading to World War I.

**Sigmund Freud**   Victorians were especially concerned with apparently unconscious impulses for actions not subject to human will. The best known of the early

**Charles Darwin as Ape.**
Darwin's theories about the evolution of humankind aroused enormous scorn. In this scathing 1861 cartoon, Darwin, with the body of a monkey, holds a mirror to a simian-looking creature. The original caption quoted a line from Shakespeare's *Love's Labour's Lost*: "This is the ape of form."

psychologists was Sigmund Freud (1856–1939), an Austrian physician. Freud specialized in treating patients suffering from what was then called "hysteria," which he treated using a technique he labeled "psychoanalysis." In 1900 Freud published his highly influential *The Interpretation of Dreams*, in which he drew connections between dreams and the unconscious in humans. The sum total of Freudian psychological theories is that humans, so far from being rational creatures, are in fact irrational creatures, driven by subconscious, and not conscious, urges. Today, Freud's ideas no longer enjoy the unquestioned dominance they once did in the field, which has largely become a branch of medicine and, in particular, the study of brain chemicals. But his influence still survives on the practical level in the form of therapeutic counseling and behavior modification.

**The Meaning of the New Scientific Discoveries**
Physics, biology, and psychology were not the only sciences contributing to the emergence of scientific–industrial society at the end of the nineteenth century. Medicine began to acquire a scientific character, for example, with the discoveries of vaccines by Louis Pasteur (1822–1895). But it had to await the twentieth century before it reached maturity. With the arrival of the theories of relativity, Darwinian selection, and the psychological unconscious, however, the transition toward the scientific–industrial age was sufficiently under way to throw people into deep philosophical and religious confusion.

In a sense, the path of reductionism begun in the seventeenth century and discussed in Chapter 17 was being reached. In previous centuries, the Hobbesian embodied mind, fear of death, "war of all against all," and religious skepticism, secularism, and atheism of the Enlightenment were merely speculations that remained ultimately unproved. Now, the specter of a meaningless universe inhabited by beings devoid of free will and driven by biological forces over which they have no control seemed to many to be inescapable. Thus, the new era seemed to usher in a profoundly disturbing devil's bargain: The sciences had created so many useful things to ease the burdens of human life but had taken away the sense of purpose that made that life worth living. It was left to philosophers, religious leaders, intellectuals, and artists to wrestle with the implications of this central problem of scientific–industrial society.

## Toward Modernity in Philosophy and Religion
Despite the impressive achievements of Western industrialized society during the late nineteenth century, there were many who felt uneasy about the results. Scores

of detractors—mostly in the intellectual community of western Europe—decried the boastful claims of a "superior" scientific civilization. These voices ridiculed Western bourgeois values and advocated alternative approaches to personal fulfillment.

**Friedrich Nietzsche**   The most celebrated of these detractors was the German philosopher Friedrich Nietzsche (1844–1900), a brilliant but mentally unstable professor at the University of Basel. Nietzsche, who railed against the conventions of Western civilization and criticized the perceived decadence of modern culture, represents a tendency toward pessimism and doubt about the progress of Western culture near the end of the nineteenth century.

Nietzsche began his assault on Western culture in 1872 with the publication of *The Birth of Tragedy*, which was followed in later years by works like *Beyond Good and Evil* (1886) and *On the Genealogy of Morals* (1887). One object of derision for Nietzsche was the entire notion of scientific, rational thought as the best path toward intellectual truth. For Nietzsche, and for others of like mind, rational thought will not improve either the individual or the welfare of humankind; only recourse to "will" instead of intellect—what Nietzsche called the "will to power"—will suffice. The individual who follows this path will become a "superman" and will lead others toward truth. Another target of Nietzsche's wrath was Christianity, which in his eyes led its believers into a "slave morality"; he infamously declared that "God is dead."

> "I call Christianity the one great curse . . . the one immortal blemish of mankind."
>
> —Friedrich Nietzsche

## Toward Modernity in Literature and the Arts

As we have seen throughout this chapter, the creation of scientific-industrial society—modernity—was a slow and very traumatic process. The social realities of interacting and adapting to the new order were already on painful display in the postromantic period of realism in the arts and literature that marked the second half of the nineteenth century (see Chapter 22). The succeeding decades were to yield what in many ways was an even grimmer and more disjointed view of the new scientific-industrial society.

**Literature**   Literary expression was generally negative toward the popularization of "soulless" science and the materialism of the second half of the industrial revolution. Thomas Hardy (1840–1928), for example, in his *Far from the Madding Crowd* (1874) emphasized the despair resulting from the futility of fighting against the grinding forces of modernity. The plays of George Bernard Shaw (1856–1950) reflect the influence of Darwin, Nietzsche, and others and mock the shallowness and pretension of urban, bourgeois *fin de siècle* ("end of the century") society. In the mid-1880s two new movements in literature, decadence and symbolism, appeared. The decadents rejected prevailing bourgeois conventions and pretensions. For their part, symbolists preferred to revert to a form of the earlier romantic era and in the process to emphasize the ideal, the aesthetic, and the beautiful side of life.

**Modernism in Art**   Like their counterparts in literature, visual artists in the period 1871–1914 were confronted by the sweeping changes in life brought on by industrialism and science. The world of artistic expression in this period, often collectively labeled "modernism," in fact consisted of a great variety of successive movements, all of them skeptical of accepted middle-class conventions and truths. These movements became increasingly abstract and avant-garde as the Great War approached.

The first group of painters was known as the impressionists, and their style dominated from the 1870s until around 1890. The movement takes its name from a painting by Claude Monet (1840–1926) entitled *Impression, Sunrise* (1874). By around 1890 the impressionist school had been superseded by a more freewheeling style known as postimpressionism, which ran into the new century.

The period of art history from 1905 to 1914 saw numerous offshoots of the postimpressionists, each one more revolutionary and experimental than the last. These various artistic "schools" truly represent the beginnings of twentieth-century avant-garde art. Perhaps the best known of these, cubism, is represented in the works of Pablo Picasso (1881–1973). Picasso stretched fascination with geometric forms to their limits to deliberately fly in the face of accepted artistic conventions. In such works as *Les Demoiselles d'Avignon* (1907), for example, often considered the first of the cubist paintings, Picasso reveals his interest in African masks as an alternative to conventional European motifs.

**Modernism in Music**    During the 1870s, musical expression followed two separate tracks until 1914. One of these tracks is known as modernism, which was more attuned to cultural developments evolving in other fields during the waning years of the nineteenth century and early years of the twentieth.

An emerging trend in the period 1905–1914 was a movement in music often labeled "primitivism," in which composers abandoned the constraints of formal structure and convention to express their personal musical perceptions. Other musicians were even more outrageous and unconventional—and more typical of avant-garde rejections of Western musical conventions. In 1911 the Austrian composer and theoretician Arnold Schoenberg (1874–1951) published *Theory of Harmony*, in which he announced the inauguration of a new, modern style of musical composition featuring themes reflecting Freudian theories of the unconscious along with the noises and dissonances of engines, machines, and urban life.

**Modernism in Art.** Pablo Picasso's *Les Demoiselles d'Avignon* was unveiled in Paris in 1907. Its distorted and broken forms of expression set in a fractured and flattened space mark a conscious break with the Western artistic tradition. The painting's borrowing from "primitivist" African and ancient Iberian sources, and its forceful and unsettling depiction of *demoiselles*, a euphemism for prostitutes, unsettle the viewer.

# Putting It All Together

The series of dramatic and sweeping changes associated with the Industrial Revolution had profound implications for both the industrializing countries and the nonindustrialized world. Thanks in large part to new technologies and facilitated by advances in transportation and communication, the period from 1871 to 1914 saw world trade networks and empires dominated by the newly industrialized nations.

The Industrial Revolution began in Britain in the early eighteenth century and eventually spread to Europe and North America during the nineteenth century.

Britain began the revolution when it employed steam engines in the rapid production of textiles. The subsequent development of the factory system along with more efficient transportation systems facilitated by railroads greatly expanded British manufacturing. Not everyone benefited, however, from the emergence of the factory system; capitalist entrepreneurs were reluctant to share with workers their slice of the economic pie, which in turn led to social unrest and calls for reform.

During the second Industrial Revolution in the later nineteenth century, advanced technologies led to the development of steel, electricity, and chemicals, which in turn greatly expanded the industrial economies of highly industrialized countries beyond Britain, including those of America and Germany. The daily lives of most citizens in industrialized nations were also improved by the application of industrial technologies to advances in transportation, communication, and even safety and sanitation.

These same advances also contributed to a new and greatly expanded surge of European imperialism. The explosive growth of industry and commerce, aided and abetted by new technologies and inventions, resulted in a quest among highly industrialized nations for raw materials, cheap labor, and new markets in order to sustain and expand their developing industries. Moreover, Western industrial nations soon discovered that new needs required the importation of not only raw materials but also foodstuffs. It is important to point out that nineteenth-century imperialism was made possible in the first place by technological innovations associated with advances in science and industrialism. Steam-powered gunboats, rapid-firing breechloaders, and the machine gun provided the overwhelming firepower to subdue nonindustrial societies and to open up interior regions of continents to Western colonialism. By the 1880s sailing ships were eclipsed by faster ones powered by much more efficient steam engines, and submarine cables provided for more efficient overseas communications and for the setting of more exact timetables. After 1871, the world's economy was increasingly divided into those who produced the world's manufactured products and those who both supplied the requisite raw materials and made up the growing pool of consumers.

Amid this process the basis for many of the patterns of twentieth-century modernity was being laid, as well as the foundations of its opposition. With the coming of World War I, and in its aftermath, many of the cleavages created by modernity and its scientific–technological underpinnings were laid bare. Yet, as a new form of society, its interaction and adaptation with older forms continued unabated. Today, the two places that contain the largest number of "Mary Pauls"—young women migrating from their farms to find work in urban factories—are the successors to the agrarian–urban religious civilizations that held out against the new order most tenaciously: India and China, both of whose economies now increasingly set the pace for twenty-first-century industrial development. It is the story of the impact of modernity on these societies and others around the globe to which we now turn.

▶ For additional resources, including maps, primary sources, visuals, and quizzes, please go to www.oup.com/us/vonsivers. Please see the Further Resources section at the back of the book for additional readings and suggested websites.

# Against the Grain
# The Luddites

Although the mechanization of textile production during the early phase of the Industrial Revolution was welcomed by some as providing new opportunities for better lives, and by others as an indication of technological progress, still others were hardline opponents of the new industrial movement. Deeply skeptical of the new era in the production of cloth goods, one group of workers in early-nineteenth-century Britain, known as "Luddites," fiercely opposed the application of machines in the textile industry.

While the term "Luddite" now refers to those who oppose new technologies of any kind, the original Luddites feared the widespread use of new machinery that lowered their wages and threatened their livelihoods. Composed primarily of skilled artisans in the knitting and hosiery trades, Luddites mounted a series of violent protests against the use of vastly improved mechanical knitting frames and steam-powered looms. Referring to themselves as soldiers in the army of General Ludd, a mythical figure, Luddites began their assaults on the night of November 4, 1811. Breaking into the home of a weaver in Nottinghamshire containing several power looms, they smashed the machines to bits and then quickly dispersed under cover of darkness. During 1812 and 1813 Luddites expanded their assaults into neighboring Yorkshire and Lancashire. Across a span of only 14 months Luddite "armies" smashed and destroyed around 1,000 machines.

The British government was quick to respond. At the height of the disturbances around 14,000 troops were dispatched to suppress the Luddite movement, and in February of 1812 Parliament passed the Frame Breaking Act, which made attacks on textile machinery punishable by death. This was followed by the trial and hanging of eight Luddites later in the year. After a quick show trial in January of 1813 that was designed to serve as a stark lesson, 14 followers of the movement were executed. This event effectively ended the movement, although occasional outbreaks of Luddism lingered on for another few years.

Even though the Luddite movement was relatively short-lived, it nevertheless called attention to disparities and inequalities inherent in early industrialism, particularly related to factory workers. This in turn prompted a series of parliamentary reforms in the 1830s and 1840s, which when taken together improved working conditions for workers in factories, mines, and other occupations.

- **Why did the British government react with such urgency to suppress the Luddite movement?**

- **How does the Luddite revolt compare with other protest movements against modernity in the later nineteenth century?**

# Thinking Through Patterns

▶ **Where and when did the Industrial Revolution originate?**

Because of several advantageous factors, the Industrial Revolution began in Britain in the early eighteenth century. Among these were an earlier political revolution that empowered the merchant classes over the landed aristocracy, along with a prior agricultural revolution, and abundance of raw materials like coal.

Industrialization resulted in several social changes and adjustments. The capitalist middle classes were enriched and empowered by the growth of industrialism, as were the working classes, which did not exist as a group prior to industrialism. The benefits of industrialism were not evenly distributed across social strata; factory and mine workers were frequently exploited by the entrepreneurial and prosperous middle classes.

▶ **What were some effects of industrialization on Western society? How did social patterns change?**

▶ **In what ways did industrialization contribute to innovations in technology? How did these technological advances contribute to Western imperialism in the late nineteenth century?**

With the invention and perfection of the steam engine, capitalist entrepreneurs were able to substitute mechanical power for natural power and thus to develop the factory system. The factory system spread to the Continent and America as middle-class capitalism eclipsed mercantilism. Further advances contributed to a second Industrial Revolution beginning around 1850 based in steel, chemistry, and electricity.

Progress in industrial technology during the second Industrial Revolution led to innovations ranging from practical inventions like the light bulb to advances in communication and transportation. Inventions developed from industrial advances included the machine gun, new medicines, and startling developments in communications, to name a few. These tools facilitated the expansion of Western imperialism in Africa and Asia during the closing years of the nineteenth century

The new society that industrialism was creating not surprisingly spawned entirely new directions in science, philosophy, religion, and the creative fields such as literature and art. It generated new kinds of popular expression, from dime novels to photography. The advent of *mass society* also led to the beginnings of a mass culture, in which widespread literacy and public education allowed a far greater percentage of the populace access to what had largely been the province of elites. Yet there was also a profound disquiet among scientists, intellectuals, and artists. With so many of the old standards falling by the wayside, tremendous uncertainty lay present just under the surface of material progress. This disquiet would come to the surface with a vengeance in the immediate years after World War I.

▶ **What new directions in science, philosophy, religion, and the arts did industrialism generate? What kind of responses did it provoke?**

# Patterns of Evidence: Sources for Chapter 26

## SOURCE 26.1

## Charles Dickens, *Hard Times*

### 1854

Although his novels are beloved as works of fiction today, Charles Dickens (1812–1870) was also an acute observer of the ways in which industrialization fundamentally transformed economic conditions in England. Fully aware of the costs of economic dislocation (as a boy, Dickens had been confined in a debtors' prison with his family), the novelist described the residents of a fictional "Coketown" in one of his lesser-known works, *Hard Times*, published in 1854. The main industry in this town is a factory, owned and operated by the blowhard (and, it is ultimately revealed, self-created) Josiah Bounderby, and the people who work in the "manufactory" are the "Hands." The novel opens in a schoolroom, where children are being drilled, literally, in the acquisition of "facts, facts, facts." Their teacher is Mr. "M'Choakumchild" (Dickens was never very subtle in his nomenclature), and the director of the school is Mr. Gradgrind. The Gradgrind method will ultimately be proved a failure within Gradgrind's own family, but *Hard Times* reveals the actual "hardness" of conditions for so many in industrial Britain.

### Chapter 5: The Key-note

Coketown, to which Messrs Bounderby and Gradgrind now walked, was a triumph of fact; it had no greater taint of fancy in it than Mrs Gradgrind herself. Let us strike the key-note, Coketown, before pursuing our tune.

It was a town of red brick, or of brick that would have been red if the smoke and ashes had allowed it; but, as matters stood it was a town of unnatural red and black like the painted face of a savage. It was a town of machinery and tall chimneys, out of which interminable serpents of smoke trailed themselves for ever and ever, and never got uncoiled. It had a black canal in it, and a river that ran purple with ill-smelling dye, and vast piles of building full of windows where there was a rattling and a trembling all day long, and where the piston of the steam-engine worked monotonously up and down, like the head of an elephant in a state of melancholy madness. It contained several large streets all very like one another, and many small streets still

Source: Charles Dickens, *Hard Times, for These Times*, ed. David Craig (New York: Penguin, 1969), 65–66.

more like one another, inhabited by people equally like one another, who all went in and out at the same hours, with the same sound upon the same pavements, to do the same work, and to whom every day was the same as yesterday and tomorrow, and every year the counterpart of the last and the next.

These attributes of Coketown were in the main inseparable from the work by which it was sustained; against them were to be set off, comforts of life which found their way all over the world, and elegancies of life which made, we will not ask how much of the fine lady, who could scarcely bear to hear the place mentioned. The rest of its features were voluntary, and they were these.

You saw nothing in Coketown but what was severely workful. If the members of a religious persuasion built a chapel there - as the members of eighteen religious persuasions had done - they made it a pious warehouse of red brick, with sometimes (but this is only in highly ornamented examples) a bell in a bird-cage on the top of it. The solitary exception was the New Church; a stuccoed edifice with a square steeple over the door, terminating in four short pinnacles like florid wooden legs. All the public inscriptions in the town were painted alike, in severe characters of black and white. The jail might have been the infirmary, the infirmary might have been the jail, the town-hall might have been either, or both, or anything else, for anything that appeared to the contrary in the graces of their construction. Fact, fact, fact, everywhere in the material aspect of the town; fact, fact, fact, everywhere in the immaterial. The M'Choakumchild school was all fact, and the school of design was all fact, and the relations between master and man were all fact, and everything was fact between the lying-in hospital and the cemetery, and what you couldn't state in figures, or show to be purchaseable in the cheapest market and saleable in the dearest, was not, and never should be, world without end, Amen.

▶ **Working with Sources**

1. How does Dickens deploy imagery from the natural world to describe something as "unnatural" as Coketown?

2. In what specific ways is Coketown a "triumph of fact" over "fancy," and does he paint a convincing portrait of a typical town in a rapidly industrializing Britain?

## SOURCE 26.2

# The death of William Huskisson, first casualty of a railroad accident

September 15, 1830

Although William Huskisson (1770–1830) was a prominent member of the British Parliament and a cabinet member in several governments, he is more famous for the circumstances of his death in a rapidly industrializing

Great Britain. While attending the opening of the Liverpool and Manchester Railway in northern England, on September 15, 1830, Huskisson rode in a carriage with the Duke of Wellington, a political figure and venerated hero of the Napoleonic Wars. Exiting the train during a stop, he was attempting to shake hands with the duke when he failed to notice another locomotive, George Stephenson's *Rocket*, traveling down an adjacent track. Huskisson attempted to swing into the carriage but fell on the tracks in front of the *Rocket*. With his leg horribly mangled by the train, Huskisson was rushed to a hospital (in a train driven by George Stephenson), but he died of his injuries a few hours later. He is, therefore, the world's first reported railway casualty.

### Bangor, 19 September 1830

Jack Calcraft has been at the opening of the Liverpool rail road, and was an eye witness of Huskisson's horrible death. About nine or ten of the passengers in the Duke's car had got out to look about them, whilst the car stopt. Calcraft was one, Huskisson another, Esterhazy, Bill Holmes, Birch and others. When the other locomotive was seen coming up to pass them, there was a general shout from those within the Duke's car to those without it, to get in. Both Holmes and Birch were unable to get up in time, but they stuck fast to its sides, and the other engine did not touch them. Esterhazy being light, was pulled in by force. Huskisson was feeble in his legs, and appears to have lost his head, as he did his life. Calcraft tells me that Huskisson's long confinement in St George's Chapel at the king's funeral brought on a complaint that Taylor is so afraid of, and that made some severe surgical operation necessary, the effect of which had been, according to what he told Calcraft, to paralyse, as it were one leg and thigh. This, no doubt, must have increased, if it did not create, his danger and [caused him to] lose his life. He had written to say his health would not let him come, and his arrival was unexpected. Calcraft saw the meeting between him and the Duke, and saw them shake hands a very short time before Huskisson's death. The latter event must be followed by important political consequences. The Canning faction has lost its corner stone and the Duke's government one of its most formidable opponents. Huskisson, too, once out of the way, Palmerston, Melbourne, the Grants & Co. may make it up with the Beau [Wellington].

▶ **Working with Sources**

1. **What kind of commentary does Huskisson's death offer on the consequences of industrialization? Does this incident reveal another side of the history of industrialization?**

2. **Why does the author of this letter seem more interested in the political rather than the socioeconomic consequences of Huskisson's death?**

Source: Letter from Thomas Creevey to Miss Ord., available online at http://www.victorianweb.org/history/accident.html.

SOURCE 26.3

# Young miners testify to the Ashley Commission

## 1842

The British Parliament took on a series of initiatives to investigate the lives of women and children in the mid-nineteenth century, and the resulting testimonies presented by workers to the various parliamentary commissions make for fascinating—and uniquely visceral—reading. The lives of working children are rarely detailed in historical sources from any era, but these testimonies had a direct impact, if not a fully humane one, on the lives of British laborers. These documents were collected for Lord Ashley's Mines Commission of 1842, and the shocking testimony resulted in the Mines Act of 1842, which prohibited the employment in the mines of all females and of boys under 13 years of age.

### No. 116.—Sarah Gooder, aged 8 years.

I'm a trapper in the Gawber pit. It does not tire me, but I have to trap without a light and I'm scared. I go at four and sometimes half past three in the morning, and come out at five and half past. I never go to sleep. Sometimes I sing when I've light, but not in the dark; I dare not sing then. I don't like being in the pit. I am very sleepy when I go sometimes in the morning. I go to Sunday-schools and read Reading made Easy. She knows her letters, and can read little words. They teach me to pray. She repeated the Lord's Prayer, not very perfectly, and ran on with the following addition:— "God bless my father and mother, and sister and brother, uncles and aunts and cousins, and everybody else, and God bless me and make me a good servant. Amen." I have heard tell of Jesus many a time. I don't know why he came on earth, I'm sure, and I don't know why he died, but he had stones for his head to rest on. I would like to be at school far better than in the pit.

### No. 14—Isabella Read, 12 years old, coal-bearer

Works on mother's account, as father has been dead two years. Mother bides at home, she is troubled with bad breath, and is sair weak in her body from early labour. I am wrought with sister and brother, it is very sore work; cannot say how many rakes or journeys I make from pit's bottom to wall face and back, thinks about 30 or

Source: http://www.victorianweb.org/history/ashley. html, from *Readings in European History Since 1814*, ed. Jonathan F. Scott and Alexander Baltzly (New York: Appleton-Century-Crofts, 1930), drawing on *Parliamentary Papers*, 1842, vols. 25–27, Appendix 1, 252, 258, 439, 461; Appendix 2, 107, 122, 205.

25 on the average; the distance varies from 100 to 250 fathom.

I carry about 1 cwt. and a quarter on my back; have to stoop much and creep through water, which is frequently up to the calves of my legs. When first down fell frequently asleep while waiting for coal from heat and fatigue.

I do not like the work, nor do the lassies, but they are made to like it. When the weather is warm there is difficulty in breathing, and frequently the lights go out.

### No. 26.—Patience Kershaw, aged 17, May 15.

My father has been dead about a year; my mother is living and has ten children, five lads and five lasses; the oldest is about thirty, the youngest is four; three lasses go to mill; all the lads are colliers, two getters and three hurriers; one lives at home and does nothing; mother does nought but look after home.

All my sisters have been hurriers, but three went to the mill. Alice went because her legs swelled from hurrying in cold water when she was hot. I never went to day-school; I go to Sunday-school, but I cannot read or write; I go to pit at five o'clock in the morning and come out at five in the evening; I get my breakfast of porridge and milk first; I take my dinner with me, a cake, and eat it as I go; I do not stop or rest any time for the purpose; I get nothing else until I get home, and then have potatoes and meat, not every day meat. I hurry in the clothes I have now got on, trousers and ragged jacket; the bald place upon my head is made by thrusting the corves; my legs have never swelled, but sisters' did when they went to mill; I hurry the corves a mile and more under ground and back; they weigh 300 cwt.; I hurry 11 a-day; I wear a belt and chain at the workings, to get the corves out; the getters that I work for are naked except their caps; they pull off all their clothes; I see them at work when I go up; sometimes they beat me, if I am not quick enough, with their hands; they strike me upon my back; the boys take liberties with me sometimes they pull me about; I am the only girl in the pit; there are about 20 boys and 15 men; all the men are naked; I would rather work in mill than in coal-pit.

This girl is an ignorant, filthy, ragged, and deplorable-looking object, and such an one as the uncivilized natives of the prairies would be shocked to look upon.

### No. 72—Mary Barrett, aged 14, June 15.

I have worked down in pit five years; father is working in next pit; I have 12 brothers and sisters—all of them but one live at home; they weave, and wind, and hurry, and one is a counter, one of them can read, none of the rest can, or write; they never went to day-school, but three of them go to Sunday-school; I hurry for my brother John, and come down at seven o'clock about; I go up at six, sometimes seven; I do not like working in pit, but I am obliged to get a living; I work always without stockings, or shoes, or trousers; I wear nothing but my chemise; I have to go up to the headings with the men; they are all naked there; I am got well used to that, and don't care now much about it; I was afraid at first, and did not like it; they never behave rudely to me; I cannot read or write.

▶ **Working with Sources**

1. Do the employers of these workers seem to have taken into account the unique conditions of their age and gender?

2. How does the recorder of these interviews interject his own reactions to these narratives? Why does he do this?

## SOURCE 26.4

# Karl Marx, "Wage Labour and Capital"

## 1847

Karl Marx (1818–1883) and Friedrich Engels (1820–1895) are best known for their collaborative work *The Communist Manifesto* (1848). However, the two had been observing the real consequences of industrialization for factory workers, particularly in Manchester, England, for many years before this. Working in his father's cotton factory in England, Engels had witnessed the inequities imposed by industrial systems, and he composed a scathing attack on these systems in his *Condition of the Working-Class in England* (1845). When Marx befriended Engels in Manchester, he too came to see how local conditions could lead to wide-ranging theories about labor, wages, and the measurement of "costs." In this lecture, delivered in December 1847, Marx took his audience through the most basic elements of the philosophy that would culminate in *Das Kapital* (vol. 1, 1867).

If several workmen were to be asked: "How much wages do you get?", one would reply, "I get two shillings a day," and so on. According to the different branches of industry in which they are employed, they would mention different sums of money that they receive from their respective employers for the completion of a certain task; for example, for weaving a yard of linen, or for setting a page of type. Despite the variety of their statements, they would all agree upon one point: that wages are the amount of money which the capitalist pays for a certain period of work or for a certain amount of work.

Consequently, it appears that the capitalist buys their labour with money, and that for money they sell him their labour. But this is merely an illusion. What they actually sell to the capitalist for money is their labour-power. This labour-power the capitalist buys for a day, a week, a month, etc. And after he has bought it, he uses it

Source: http://www.marxists.org/archive/marx/works/1847/wage-labour/, first published in German in the *Neue Rheinische Zeitung* (April 5–8, 11, 1849), and edited and translated by Friedrich Engels for an 1891 pamphlet.

up by letting the worker labour during the stipulated time. With the same amount of money with which the capitalist has bought their labour-power (for example, with two shillings) he could have bought a certain amount of sugar or of any other commodity. The two shillings with which he bought 20 pounds of sugar is the price of the 20 pounds of sugar. The two shillings with which he bought 12 hours' use of labour-power, is the price of 12 hours' labour. Labour-power, then, is a commodity, no more, no less so than is the sugar. The first is measured by the clock, the other by the scales.

Their commodity, labour-power, the workers exchange for the commodity of the capitalist, for money, and, moreover, this exchange takes place at a certain ratio. So much money for so long a use of labour-power. For 12 hours' weaving, two shillings. And these two shillings, do they not represent all the other commodities which I can buy for two shillings? Therefore, actually, the worker has exchanged his commodity, labour-power, for commodities of all kinds, and, moreover, at a certain ratio. By giving him two shillings, the capitalist has given him so much meat, so much clothing, so much wood, light, etc., in exchange for his day's work. The two shillings therefore express the relation in which labour-power is exchanged for other commodities, the exchange-value of labour-power.

The exchange value of a commodity estimated in money is called its price. Wages therefore are only a special name for the price of labour-power, and are usually called the price of labour; it is the special name for the price of this peculiar commodity, which has no other repository than human flesh and blood.

Let us take any worker; for example, a weaver. The capitalist supplies him with the loom and yarn. The weaver applies himself to work, and the yarn is turned into cloth. The capitalist takes possession of the cloth and sells it for 20 shillings, for example. Now are the wages of the weaver a share of the cloth, of the 20 shillings, of the product of the work? By no means. Long before the cloth is sold, perhaps long before it is fully woven, the weaver has received his wages. The capitalist, then, does not pay his wages out of the money which he will obtain from the cloth, but out of money already on hand. Just as little as loom and yarn are the product of the weaver to whom they are supplied by the employer, just so little are the commodities which he receives in exchange for his commodity—labour-power—his product. It is possible that the employer found no purchasers at all for the cloth. It is possible that he did not get even the amount of the wages by its sale. It is possible that he sells it very profitably in proportion to the weaver's wages. But all that does not concern the weaver. With a part of his existing wealth, of his capital, the capitalist buys the labour-power of the weaver in exactly the same manner as, with another part of his wealth, he has bought the raw material—the yarn— and the instrument of labour—the loom. After he has made these purchases, and among them belongs the labour-power necessary to the production of the cloth he produces only with raw materials and instruments of labour belonging to him. For our good weaver, too, is one of the instruments of labour, and being in this respect on a par with the loom, he has no more share in the product (the cloth), or in the price of the product, than the loom itself has.

Wages, therefore, are not a share of the worker in the commodities produced by himself. Wages are that part of already existing commodities with which the capitalist buys a certain amount of productive labour-power.

. . .

The free labourer, on the other hand, sells his very self, and that by fractions. He auctions off eight, 10, 12, 15 hours of his life, one day like the next, to the highest bidder, to the owner of raw materials, tools, and the means of life—i.e., to the capitalist. The labourer belongs neither to an owner nor to the soil, but eight, 10, 12, 15 hours of his daily life belong to whomsoever buys them. The worker leaves the capitalist, to whom he has sold himself, as often as he chooses, and the capitalist discharges him as often as he sees fit, as soon as he no longer gets any use, or not the required use, out of him. But the worker, whose only source of income is the sale of his labour-power, cannot leave the whole class of buyers, i.e., the capitalist class, unless he gives up his own existence. He does not belong to this or that capitalist, but to the capitalist class; and it is for him to find his man—i.e., to find a buyer in this capitalist class.

▶ **Working with Sources**

1. **How does Marx describe wages as a commodity price, equivalent to other sorts of "prices" in the marketplace?**

2. **How does he contrast larger economic forces with the lived realities of workers in a factory?**

## SOURCE 26.5

# Charles Darwin, *The Origin of Species*

1859

The name of Charles Darwin (1809–1882) is inextricably linked to the earth-shattering and (even today) controversial theory he proposed in 1859. However, it is also important to remember that he was a writer of exceptional skill and a best-selling author—even though many of his observations and conclusions were certainly too difficult for nonspecialists to appreciate. The 200th anniversary of his birth—and the 150th anniversary of the appearance of *The Origin of Species*—in 2009 resulted in a series of

Source: Charles Darwin, *The Origin of Species by Means of Natural Selection, or the Preservation of Favored Races in the Struggle for Life* and *The Descent of Man, and Selection in Relation to Sex* (New York: Modern Library, 1936), 353, 372, 373–374.

commemorative events around the world, a brief sample of which can be viewed online at http://darwin-online.org.uk/2009.html. Among the most famous elements of the book is the tangled-riverbank image introduced in the long book's final paragraph, and Darwin's stimulating view of the "grandeur in this view of life."

As this whole volume is one long argument, it may be convenient to the reader to have the leading facts and inferences briefly recapitulated.

That many and serious objections may be advanced against the theory of descent with modification through variation and natural selection, I do not deny. I have endeavoured to give to them their full force. Nothing at first can appear more difficult to believe than that the more complex organs and instincts have been perfected, not by means superior to, though analogous with, human reason, but by the accumulation of innumerable slight variations, each good for the individual possessor. Nevertheless, this difficulty, though appearing to our imagination insuperably great, cannot be considered real if we admit the following propositions, namely, that all parts of the organisation and instincts offer, at least individual differences—that there is a struggle for existence leading to the preservation of profitable deviations of structure or instinct—and, lastly, that gradations in the state of perfection of each organ may have existed, each good of its kind. The truth of these propositions cannot, I think, be disputed.

It is, no doubt, extremely difficult even to conjecture by what gradations many structures have been perfected, more especially among broken and failing groups of organic beings, which have suffered much extinction; but we see so many strange gradations in nature, that we ought to be extremely cautious in saying that any organ or instinct, or any whole structure, could not have arrived at its present state by many graduated steps. There are, it must be admitted, cases of special difficulty opposed to the theory of natural selection; and one of the most curious of these is the existence in the same community of two or three defined castes of workers or sterile female ants; but I have attempted to show how these difficulties can be mastered.

. . .

A grand and almost untrodden field of inquiry will be opened, on the causes and laws of variation, on correlation, on the effects of use and disuse, on the direct action of external conditions, and so forth. The study of domestic productions will rise immensely in value. A new variety raised by man will be a far more important and interesting subject for study than one more species added to the infinitude of already recorded species. Our classifications will come to be, as far as they can be so made, genealogies; and will then truly give what may be called the plan of creation. The rules for classifying will no doubt become simpler when we have a definite object in view. We possess no pedigrees or armorial bearings; and we have to discover and trace the many diverging lines of descent in our natural genealogies, by characters of any kind which have long been inherited. Rudimentary organs will speak infallibly with respect to the nature of long-lost structures. Species and groups of species which are called aberrant, and which may fancifully be called living fossils, will aid us in forming a picture of the ancient forms of life. Embryology will often reveal to us the structure, in some degree obscured, of the prototypes of each great class.

When we can feel assured that all the individuals of the same species, and all the closely allied species of most genera, have, within a not very remote period descended from one parent, and have migrated from some one birth-place; and when we better know the many means of migration, then, by the light which geology now throws, and will continue to throw, on former changes of climate and of the level of the land, we shall surely be enabled to trace in an admirable manner the former migrations of the inhabitants of the whole world. Even at present, by comparing the differences between the inhabitants of the sea on the opposite sides of a continent, and the nature of the various inhabitants of that continent in relation to their apparent means of immigration, some light can be thrown on ancient geography.

. . .

It is interesting to contemplate a tangled bank, clothed with many plants of many kinds, with birds singing on the bushes, with various insects flitting about, and with worms crawling through the damp earth, and to reflect that these elaborately constructed forms, so different from each other, and dependent upon each other in so complex a manner, have all been produced by laws acting around us. These laws, taken in the largest sense, being Growth with Reproduction; Inheritance which is almost implied by reproduction; Variability from the indirect and direct action of the conditions of life, and from use and disuse; a Ratio of Increase so high as to lead to a Struggle for Life, and as a consequence to Natural Selection, entailing Divergence of Character and the Extinction of less-improved forms. Thus, from the war of nature, from famine and death, the most exalted object which we are capable of conceiving, namely, the production of the higher animals, directly follows. There is grandeur in this view of life, with its several powers, having been originally breathed by the Creator into a few forms or into one; and that, whilst this planet has gone cycling on according to the fixed law of gravity, from so simple a beginning endless forms most beautiful and most wonderful have been, and are being evolved.

▶ **Working with Sources**

1. How does Darwin manage to convey the excitement that he feels for this new scientific field and the possibilities for applying his theory to other disciplines?

2. How does his quest for common ancestors underscore the interconnected nature of all species on our planet?

# Chapter 27 1750–1914

# The New Imperialism in the Nineteenth Century

**THE NEW
IMPERIALISM**

A t the end of the Muslim month-long observance of Ramadan in 1827, Hussein (r. 1815–1830), the ruler (*dey*) of the autonomous Ottoman province of Algeria in North Africa, held a celebratory reception for the diplomatic corps of consuls at his palace in the capital, the port city of Algiers. When he saw the French consul, Pierre Deval, Hussein signaled him to come up to the throne. In a quite undiplomatic harangue, the dey accused the consul of deliberately defrauding him of a large sum of money owed by France for wheat deliveries between 1793 and 1798. He then demanded immediate payment of this long-overdue debt. To emphasize his demand, the dey struck the consul with his fan and declared him *persona non grata*, which, in terms of diplomatic protocol, meant that he had to leave the country immediately.

France's restored Bourbon king, Charles X (r. 1824–1830), found this insult by the Algerian dey to an appointee of the French court intolerably injurious to his own divinely ordained dignity. He dispatched a naval detachment to Algiers in 1828, demanding an apology, declaring the debt liquidated, and asking for reparations for a number of piracy depredations that had occurred in the preceding years. When the dey rejected the demands, the French mounted a blockade of the port. In 1830, they followed up on

*ABOVE: Illustrations from a French schoolbook (c. 1910) show the cultivation of rice in French colonies.*

this blockade with an expeditionary force that conquered Algiers, deposed the dey, and sent him into exile. Less than two decades later Algeria became a colony of France.

The incident illustrates the changing fortunes of those countries that were the beneficiaries of the new forces of modernity—in this case, France—and those like the Ottoman Empire and its territories in Algeria that largely were not. In this chapter, our focus will be on those parts of the world outside east Asia (see Chapter 24) that were unable to preserve, even in a tenuous fashion, their political independence while adapting to the colonial challenge through military, constitutional, and economic reforms. Here, we will study the victims of conquest and occupation in south and southeast Asia, the Middle East, Africa, and the Pacific Ocean that most clearly make visible the underlying patterns of imperialism and colonialism.

---

Two patterns characterize the evolution of imperialism–colonialism in the period 1750–1900. The first was a shift from coastal trade forts under chartered companies—the old imperialism on the cheap—to government takeover, territorial conquest, and **colonialism**. Great Britain pioneered this "new imperialism" in India but also prevented the other European countries from following in its footsteps for a century.

The second pattern was the rise of direct territorial imperialism–colonialism by European countries in the course of the disintegration of the Ottoman Empire, under assault by Russia since the end of the eighteenth century, and, in the course of the nineteenth century, in Asia and Africa. The Europeans first protected the Ottomans from Russia, only later to help themselves to Ottoman provinces, beginning with the capture of Algeria by France. Thus the dey's fan slap in Algeria may be viewed as the unlikely catalyst that launched the competitive European imperialism–colonialism in Asia and Africa that characterized the remainder of the nineteenth century.

## The British Colonies of India, Australia, and New Zealand

The transition in India from European trade-fort activities to governmental colonialism coincided with the decline of the Mughal dynasty (see Chapter 20). The British East India Company exploited the Mughal decline to become a government in all but name. Its notorious corruption and ultimate inability to conduct military affairs, however, forced the British government to assume direct control. As a result, Britain became a colonial power in the Eastern Hemisphere, making India its center for the delivery of the cotton on which early British industrialization depended. Later on, sparsely inhabited Australia and New Zealand began as small British settler colonies, the former as a penal colony and the latter against fierce indigenous resistance.

## Seeing Patterns

▶ What new patterns emerged in the transition from trade-fort imperialism to the new imperialism?

▶ How did European colonizers develop their colonies economically, given that they were industrializing themselves at the same time?

▶ What were the experiences of the indigenous people under the new imperialism? How did they adapt to colonialism? How did they resist?

Colonialism: A system in which people from one country settle in another, ruling it and maintaining connections to the mother country; term now used most often to describe the contemporary exploitation of weaker countries by imperial powers.

## The British East India Company

An important factor in the rise of British power in India was the Seven Years' War. As we have seen, the Seven Years' War could be considered a kind of "first world war" in that fighting took place in Europe, in the Americas, on the high seas, and in India. It was the war in India, along with the deepening political difficulties of the Mughals, that enabled the rise of the British to supremacy not only on the subcontinent but later in Burma and Malaya as well.

**The Seven Years' War**    By the early eighteenth century Britain emerged as a strong contender for a larger share of global commerce among European trading companies. As we saw in Chapter 20, the British had joined forces at Surat on the west coast of India with the Dutch in the lucrative spice trade. But they had also established their own posts in provincial cities that would over time be transformed into India's greatest metropolises: Madras (Chennai), Bombay (Mumbai), and one created from scratch: Calcutta (Kolkata). By 1750 their chief commercial competitors were the French, who were aggressively building up both trade and political power from a base in Pondicherry in the southern part of peninsular India.

For the British East India Company, its evolution into a kind of shadow government in the area around Calcutta in Bengal on the northeast coast would now bear dividends. The decline of Mughal central power meant that regional leaders were being enlisted as French or British allies. If they were more powerful, they sought to use the sepoy (from Persian *sipahi* [see-pa-HEE], "soldier") armies of the European companies as support in their own struggles. Out of this confused political and volatile military situation, the ambitious East India Company leader, Robert Clive (1725–1774), won a victory over the Indian French allies at Plassey in 1757 and soon eliminated the French from power on the subcontinent. By the terms of the treaty ending the war in 1763, the East India Company ended up as the sole European power of consequence in India, and Clive set about consolidating his position from Calcutta.

**Going Native: the Nabobs**    Clive's aggressive style of economic aggrandizement set the tone for what Indian scholars have often called the "rape of Bengal" in the latter eighteenth century. The East India Company began to expand its holdings across northern India, extorting funds from pliant local princes. The company men had no interest in changing India or reforming Indian institutions. Indeed, many, inspired by Enlightenment ideals of cosmopolitanism, became great admirers of Indian culture. Some went so far as to "go native": After making their fortunes, they took Indian wives, dressed as Indian princes, and on occasion wielded power as local magnates, or **nabobs** (from Urdu *nawwab* [naw-WAHB], "deputy," "viceroy").

The vast distances separating the company's London directors from operations in India, southeast Asia, and China made its local activities more or less autonomous. Its power, organization, and, most important, its army increasingly became the determining factors in local disputes across northern India; its attractiveness to ambitious young men on the margins of British society who wished to quickly "make their pile" left it vulnerable to corruption. This was particularly

**Nabob:** A person who acquired a large fortune in India during the period of British rule.

true because of the company's policy of paying low wages while turning a blind eye to employees trading locally for their private benefit.

By 1800, through the company's efforts to pacify turbulent territories adjacent to its holdings, British possessions extended across most of northern India (see Map 27.1). This extension prompted a shift in the variety of trading goods toward the beginning of the nineteenth century. Spices had been replaced by cotton goods—and, increasingly, by raw cotton—as the most lucrative commodity, due to Britain's mechanized textile revolution. Indian cotton would later be supplemented and eventually supplanted by cotton from the American South, Egypt, and Sudan.

**The Perils of Reform**　While the nineteenth century is commonly perceived as the beginning of Western supremacy, it is well to remember—as we have noted in previous chapters—that even at this late date India and China were still the primary economic engines of Eurasia. As late as 1800, for example, Indian goods and services accounted for perhaps 20 percent of the world's output, while Britain's came to only 3 percent. As the Industrial Revolution kicked into high gear by the mid-1800s, however, these numbers began to reverse (see Figure 27.1). As Britain's share of India's economy grew, moreover, the British increasingly sought to create markets for their own goods there and to shunt Indian exports exclusively into the British domestic market. As we saw in Chapter 24, the early acquisition of Patna by the British enabled the creation of the Chinese opium trade, which by 1830 accounted for nearly one-quarter of company revenues in India. In addition, officials of the East India Company arbitrated disputes among Indian rulers, taking over their lands as payment for loans, and strong-arming many into becoming wards of the British. Because of this continuous attrition, by the end of the Napoleonic Wars, the Mughal emperor's lands had been reduced to the region immediately surrounding Delhi and Agra.

**Perceptions of Empire.** The British East India Company's real ascent to power in India began with Robert Clive's victory at Plassey in 1757, the symbolism of which is depicted here. Note the deference with which the assorted Indian princes treat the conqueror (top). Below, the second-from-last Mughal emperor, Akbar Shah II (r. 1806–1837), receives the British resident, ca. 1815. Despite the fact that the British East India Company had extended its sway over much of northern India by this time, the Indian artist depicts the British government official in a pose of supplication to Akbar Shah—in almost a mirror image of the imagined Indian princes in the painting of Clive.

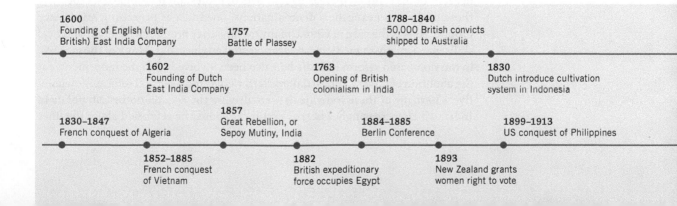

| | | | |
|---|---|---|---|
| **1600**<br>Founding of English (later British) East India Company | **1757**<br>Battle of Plassey | **1788–1840**<br>50,000 British convicts shipped to Australia | |
| | **1602**<br>Founding of Dutch East India Company | **1763**<br>Opening of British colonialism in India | **1830**<br>Dutch introduce cultivation system in Indonesia |
| **1830–1847**<br>French conquest of Algeria | **1857**<br>Great Rebellion, or Sepoy Mutiny, India | **1884–1885**<br>Berlin Conference | **1899–1913**<br>US conquest of Philippines |
| | **1852–1885**<br>French conquest of Vietnam | **1882**<br>British expeditionary force occupies Egypt | **1893**<br>New Zealand grants women right to vote |

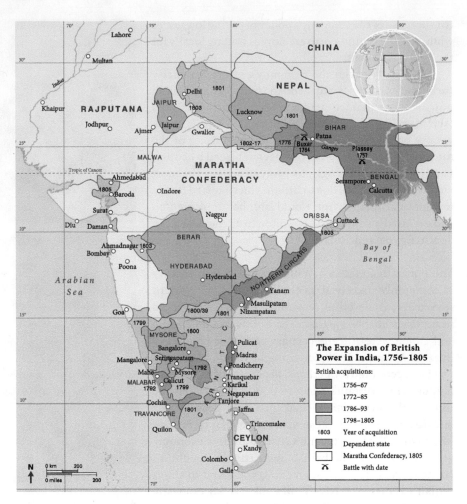

MAP 27.1 **The Expansion of British Power in India, 1756–1805.**

India's history, however, had long been marked by outsiders conquering large parts of the subcontinent, and while many chafed at company rule, its policy of noninterference with Indian customs and institutions softened the blow of the conquest somewhat. The period following the Napoleonic Wars, however, saw changes in this regard that had far-reaching consequences, by bringing the British government into a more direct role.

Clashes between factory owners and labor and the drive for political reform in Britain during this period found echoes in policy toward India. From the opening decades of the century, increasing numbers of Protestant missionaries, especially those of the new evangelical denominations, saw India as promising missionary ground. As was the case in China, many missionaries brought with them practical skills, particularly in medicine, education, and engineering. Many of those active in mission-based reform in India had also been involved with the movements for the abolition of slavery, industrial workers' rights, and electoral reform in Britain. By 1830 many of these individuals were driving the agenda on British policy in India, which increasingly asserted that India should be reformed along the lines

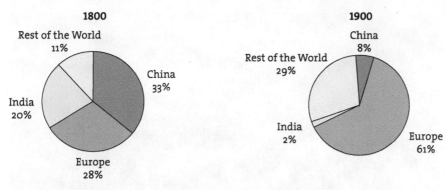

Figure 27.1 **Share of World Manufacturing Output, 1800 and 1900.**

they envisioned for Britain: better working conditions for the poor, free trade, the abolition of "barbaric" customs, and a vigorous Christian missionary effort.

In addition, the company reformed the tax system into a money-based land fee for greater efficiency of collection. At the same time, new industrial enterprises and transport and communication advances—steamboats, railroads, and telegraph lines—were constructed, benefiting the economy at large but also disrupting the livelihoods of many. Coupled with these changes was a perception on the part of opponents, and even some supporters, that these efforts in both India and England were characterized by smug righteousness and arrogance of the English toward Indian society. Perhaps the most famous expression of this was found in the parliamentary reformer and historian Thomas B. Macaulay's 1835 "Minute on Education," where he asserted that "a single shelf of European books is worth more than all the literatures of Asia and Arabia."

**The Great Mutiny**    The grim result of several decades of such wholesale change exploded in northern India in 1857. General disillusionment with the pace of change and the fear that British missionaries were attempting, with government connivance, to Christianize India came to a head among the company's sepoy troops. With the introduction of the new Enfield rifle, which required its operator to bite the end off a greased paper cartridge full of gunpowder, a rumor started that the grease had been concocted of cow and pig fat. Since this would violate the dietary restrictions of both Hindus and Muslims, the troops saw this as a plot to leave the followers of both religions ritually unclean and thus open to conversion to Christianity. Though the rumors proved untrue, a revolt raced through many of the sepoy barracks and in short order became a wholesale rebellion aimed at throwing the British out of India and restoring the aged Mughal emperor, Bahadur Shah Zafar (r. 1837–1857), to full power. The accumulated rage against the perceived insults to Indian religions and culture pushed the troops and their allies to frightful atrocities.

The Great Mutiny (also known by the British as the Sepoy Mutiny and by the Indians as the Great Rebellion, or First War of Independence) swiftly turned into a civil war as pro- and anti-British Indian forces clashed. The British shipped troops just sent to China for the Second Opium War back to India in a desperate attempt to crush the insurgency. Through a number of hard-fought engagements they were ultimately able to reassert control, but not without committing

**Execution of Indian Rebels.**
After British troops and loyalist Indian sepoys had restored order in northern India, retribution was unleashed on the rebels. Here, the most spectacular mode of execution is being carried out. Mutineers are tied across the mouths of cannons and blown to pieces while the troops stand in formation and are forced to watch.

atrocities of their own in retribution for the rebels' excesses. The occupation of many towns was accompanied by mass hangings and indiscriminate shootings of suspected rebels and collaborators.

## Direct British Rule

After assuming direct rule (Hindi *raj*, hence the term "Raj" for the colonial government), the British were crucially concerned to keep their apparatus of civilian administrators as small as possible while maintaining an army large enough to avoid a repeat of 1857. These administrators made use of Indian administrators who, however, did not have any real decision-making powers. The Raj functioned because of a "divide and rule" policy that exploited the many divisions existing in Indian society, which prevented the Indians from making common cause and challenging British rule.

**Creation of the Civil Service**    Even as the pacification was winding down, the British government conducted an investigation which led to sweeping reforms in 1858. The East India Company was dismantled, and the British government itself took up the task of governing India. In a proclamation to England and India, Queen Victoria announced that British policy would no longer attempt to "impose Our convictions on any of Our subjects." An Indian civil service was created and made open to British and Indians alike to administer the subcontinent's affairs. The incorporation of India as the linchpin of the British Empire was completed when Queen Victoria assumed, among her many titles, that of Empress of India in 1877. India had now become, it was said, the "jewel in the crown" of the empire (see Map 27.2).

Less than a decade later, the fruits of the new civil service and the Indian schools feeding it were already evident, though perhaps not in the way its creators envisioned or desired. In 1885, Indians first convened the National Congress, the

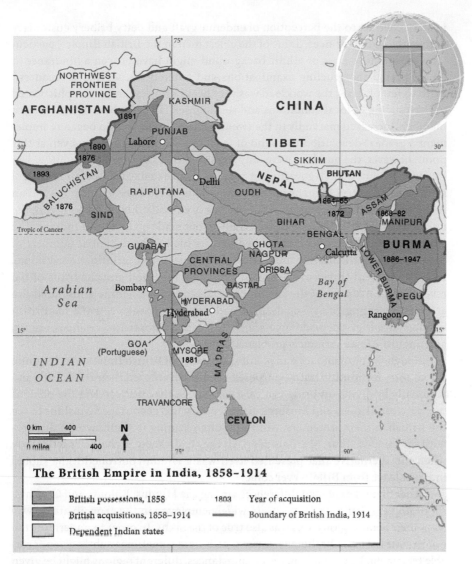

MAP 27.2 The British Empire in India, 1858–1914.

ancestor of India's present Congress Party. The congress's mission was to win greater autonomy for India within the structure of the British Empire and, by the opening decades of the twentieth century, to push for Indian independence. Already by the early 1890s, a young British-trained lawyer named Mohandas K. Gandhi (1869–1948) was actively campaigning for the rights of Indians in British-controlled South Africa. There, he developed the strategies that would make him among the most recognized world figures of the twentieth century as he pursued his quest to oust the British from India through nonviolence and noncooperation.

**Divide and Rule**    The Indian civil service, among the most difficult bureaucracies in the world into which to gain admission, seldom had more than 1,000 "Anglo-Indian" (ethnically British subjects who were either born in India or longtime residents there) and Indian officials to govern a quarter of a billion people. The civil service was intended as a showpiece of British incorruptibility and professionalism, in stark contrast to the perception of endemic graft and petty bribery customary among the Indian princes. Some of the ablest men in the British Empire, particularly those whose class or ethnic background might have proven a hindrance at home, passed the grueling examinations and entered the service as "readers." With so few officials, the workload was very heavy and demanded a sophisticated understanding of local conditions and sensibilities. The numbers of civil service members increased markedly in the twentieth century as Britain began to implement a gradual devolution to a kind of federated Indian autonomy. Even at this point, however, the numbers were only slightly above 3,000.

How did such a small government apparatus and expatriate population control such a large country? In many respects it was done by bluff and artifice. The Indian Army of Great Britain, the "thin red line" as it was called in the days before the uniforms were khaki, was small, well trained, but made up mostly of Indians. The British officers and noncommissioned officers included substantial numbers of Scots and Irish, themselves minorities often subject to discrimination at home. But the incipient threat of the army to suppress rebellion and the fruits of the revolution in weapons of the late nineteenth century—machine guns, rapid-fire artillery, repeating rifles—made any small revolt unthinkable, while the British divide-and-rule tactics made large-scale organization across caste, religious, ethnic, and linguistic lines extremely problematic.

Though the bureaucracy and political structure of British India served to unite the country for administrative purposes, the British secured their rule locally and regionally by divide-and-rule tactics. A key divide they utilized was the obvious one between Hindus and Muslims. British policy had encouraged Muslims to see the British as their protectors, while also often leaning in their favor in disputes with the Hindus. Thus, Muslims often felt they had a stake in the Raj, particularly when the alternative that presented itself was a Hindu-controlled India should independence from Britain ever come.

Other divides exploited differences among the Hindus. Rajputs and Gurkhas, for example, as military castes, were widely employed in the army in areas away from their home regions; this was also true of the Sikhs. In order to undermine the power bases of local Brahmans, lower castes were sometimes subtly given favorable treatment. Depending on the circumstances, different regions might be given preferential treatment as well.

The British also successfully exploited the sense of grandeur of the Indian elites, staging elaborate durbars (see Chapter 20) at the Raj's showpiece capital of New Delhi, built under the aegis of the British resident Lord Curzon (1859–1925). Curzon used these occasions to bolster the prestige, if not the actual power, of the Indian maharajas, and to reinforce traditional notions of deference and hierarchy.

The British administration created new systems of honorary ranks and revived older ones. By identifying British rule with India's historic past, it was hoped that the perception of strength and legitimacy would be enhanced. This effort to co-opt local rulers into upholding the British government as the historically destined status quo is sometimes called by historians a **subaltern** relationship. Yet a small but growing elite of Western-educated, often accomplished Indian leaders began to use the arguments of empire against their occupiers. By the 1920s many of these people—lawyers, journalists, and other professionals—would make up

**Subaltern:** A person or thing considered subordinate to another.

the burgeoning national movement associated with Gandhi's strategy of nonviolent noncooperation and the Indian National Congress's outlines for government when Britain was finally forced to "quit India."

## British Settler Colonies: Australia

India was merely one area in Asia and the Pacific where the British advanced from exploration and trade forts to imperial expansion and colonial settlement. In the continent of Australia and on the islands of New Zealand they colonized indigenous forager and agrarian populations. In contrast to India, the British also encouraged large-scale immigration of European settlers to these regions. The evolution of Australia from a colony to a white immigrant–dominated dominion is the topic of the discussion below.

**White Settlement in Australia**    Dutch navigators, blown off course on their way to Indonesia, initially discovered the western coast of Australia in 1606, but when profitable trade opportunities with the forager Aborigines (the name given to the indigenous Australians) failed to materialize, they did not pursue any further contacts. The British navigator James Cook (1728–1779), during one of his many exploratory journeys in the Pacific, landed in 1770 on the Australian east coast and claimed it for Great Britain. After the United States wrested its independence from Britain in 1783, the British government looked to Australia as a place where it could ship convicts. Between 1788 and 1840, some 50,000 British convicts were shipped to the penal colony.

Immigration by free British subjects, begun a decade before the end of convict shipments, led to a pastoral and agricultural boom. Settlers pioneered agriculture in south Australia, where rainfall, fluctuating according to dry and wet *El Niño/La Niña* cycles, was relatively reliable and provided the population with most of its cereal needs. Sugar and rice cultivation, introduced to the tropical northeast in the 1860s, was performed with indentured labor recruited from Pacific islands. Even during penal colony times, sheep ranching in the east and the exportation of wool developed into a thriving business; eventually, half of the wool needed by the British textile industry was supplied by Australia. Even more important for the evolution of the Australian colony was the mining of gold and silver, beginning in the east in 1851 and continuing thereafter in nearly all parts of the continent. Although a colony, Australia was very similar to independent Latin America (see Chapter 23) in that it was a labor-poor but commodity-rich region, seeking its wealth through export-led growth.

Mining generated several gold-rush immigration waves, not only from Britain but also from China, as well as internal migrations from mining towns to cities when the gold rushes ended. Cities like Sydney and Melbourne expanded continuously during the 1800s and encompassed more than two-thirds of the total white population of about 5 million by 1914. The indigenous population of Aborigines, who had inhabited the continent for over 50,000 years, shrank during the same time from several hundred thousand to 67,000, mostly as a result of diseases but also after confrontations with ranchers intruding on their hunting and gathering lands. As in North America, whites were relentless in taking possession of an allegedly empty—or expected soon to be empty—continent.

# Military Transformations and the New Imperialism

**French Defeat of the Mamluks at the Battle of the Pyramids, 1798.** This painting shows the clear advantage of the military innovation of the line drill. The orderly French forces on the right, commanded by officers on horseback, mow down the cavalry charges of the Mamluks.

Between 1450 and 1750 firearm-equipped infantries rose to prominence throughout Eurasia. Recently, scholars have hotly debated the significance of the differences among the infantries and military organization more generally during this age of empire.

Historians believed for a long time that western Europeans had superior firearms, cannons, and cannon-equipped ships that enabled them to embark on overseas expansion, establish trade-fort mercantile empires, and eventually achieve imperial conquest and colonization of the Middle East, Africa, and southeast Asia. However, most scholars are now of the opinion that, beginning in the late seventeenth century, it was the flintlock muskets, bayonets, and line drill that distinguished western European infantries from other armies in Asia and Africa and gave Europeans an advantage. (The *line drill* was the Swedish-introduced innovation of training infantry soldiers stretched out in long lines three to six deep to fire, step back, allow the next line to fire, reload their muzzle-loaded flintlock muskets, and so on with the third to sixth lines.) These advantages were manifested in the Ottoman–Russian War of 1768–1774 and in Napoleon's invasion of Egypt in 1798.

In the early 1730s, the Ottomans realized that they could not match other powers with their matchlock muskets and that their infantry, the Janissaries, lacked sufficient discipline. Although their gunsmiths switched to flintlocks, the largely part-time and poorly paid Janissaries resisted all efforts at drills. Lack of finances caused these military reforms to grind to a halt. The Russian military, by contrast, learned much from the Seven Years' War (1756–1763), in which it was allied with Austria and France against Prussia and Great Britain. Its sizeable line infantries were of great importance during the war of 1768–1774 against the uncoordinated and untrained Ottoman foot soldiers. Similarly, Napoleon successfully employed his small, highly mobile, and

**The Difficult Turn of the Century**   The boom years ended for Australia around 1890. During the last quarter of the nineteenth century, the economies of the three leading industrial countries of the world—Great Britain, the United States, and Germany—slowed, with first a financial depression in 1873–1879 and another more economy-wide one in 1890–1896. Australia had been able to ride out the first depression, mainly thanks to continuing gold finds. But in the 1890s, construction as well as banking collapsed and factories closed. Coincidentally, a dry El Niño cycle devastated free selection farming. Labor unrest followed; although widespread strikes failed, the newly founded Labor Party (1891) immediately became a major political force. The country adopted labor reforms, an old-age pension, fiscal reforms, and a white-only immigration policy. The discovery of huge gold deposits in western Australia in 1892–1894 helped to redress the

flexible units (composed of mixed infantry, cavalry, and artillery) in his victory against the lopsidedly cavalry-dominated Egyptian Mamluks in 1798.

The Mughals in India and the Qing in China did not have to worry about flintlock, bayonet, and line infantry attacks in the eighteenth century, either from their neighbors or from the faraway Europeans. Like the Ottomans, who continued to maintain large cavalry forces against their nomadic neighbors in the Middle East and central Asia, the Mughals and Qing privileged their cavalries. However, once British East India Company officers elevated indigenous infantry soldiers to the privileged ranks of the sepoy regiments, their efficiency ultimately created such problems for the company that the British Crown had to take over the governance of India in 1858.

When European innovators introduced workable breech-loading rifles and artillery in the late 1850s, the technological balance shifted decisively toward Europe. The addition of rapid-firing mechanisms in the second half of the 1800s to these improved weapons further cemented Europe's technological superiority.

Thus, in this shift from an initially slight to an eventually pronounced superiority of European arms during this period, the new imperialism and the Industrial Revolution were parallel developments engendered by the same modernity that also saw the rise of constitutional nationalism and the formation of a new type of polity, the nation-state. Certainly, industrially produced weapons in the later nineteenth century greatly enhanced Europe's ability to dominate much of the Middle East, Africa, and Asia.

**Ethiopian Forces Defeating an Italian Army at Adowa, 1896.** A hundred years after Napoleon's victory, the tables were turned when an Ethiopian army equipped with repeating rifles, machine guns, and cannon routed an Italian invasion force. In response to the defeat, the *Times* of London complained that "the prestige of European arms as a whole is considerably impaired."

## Questions

• Examine the painting showing French forces defeating the Mamluk cavalry. Are the military advantages of the line drill evident? If so, what are they?

• Does the painting of Ethiopian forces defeating an Italian army in 1896 show that indigenous peoples could adapt Western innovations to their own purposes? If so, how?

economic problems. In 1900, Australia finally adopted a federal constitution, which made the country the second fully autonomous British "dominion," after Canada (1867) but before New Zealand (1907), Newfoundland (1907), South Africa (1910), and Ireland (1922).

# European Imperialism in the Middle East and Africa

The British role in the Middle East during the eighteenth and early nineteenth centuries was much more modest, as was that of Europeans in general. Their function was limited to that of merchants, diplomats, or military advisors in an

Ottoman Empire with a long tradition of conquering European lands. The situation changed at the end of the eighteenth century when Russia adopted a plan of southern expansion designed to drive the Ottomans back into Asia, take Istanbul, and convert it back into an eastern Christian capital. The other European powers sought to slow the Russian advances, with Great Britain assuming the lead role in protecting the Ottomans. In the long run, this policy of containment failed. Under Russian pressure, Ottoman territory shrank, the Europeans joined Russia in dismembering the Ottoman Empire, and a general imperialist competition for carving up other parts of the world—notably south and east Asia as well as Africa—ensued.

## The Rising Appeal of Imperialism in the West

Empires (multiethnic, multilinguistic, and multireligious polities) were, as we have repeatedly seen, of old lineage in world history. Their current embodiments were the Ottoman, Habsburg, and Russian Empires. The Russian Empire, a late-comer, saw its mission as replacing the Ottoman Empire as the dominant eastern European power and, by expanding eastward across the steppe, becoming the leading Asian power. Its ambition became the catalyst for France, Great Britain, Belgium, Germany, and even late-industrializing Italy to embark on competitive imperialism in other parts of the world (see Map 27.3).

**The Ottoman, Russian, and British Empires**    After the failure in 1815 of Napoleon's imperial schemes in both Egypt and Europe, Great Britain was the

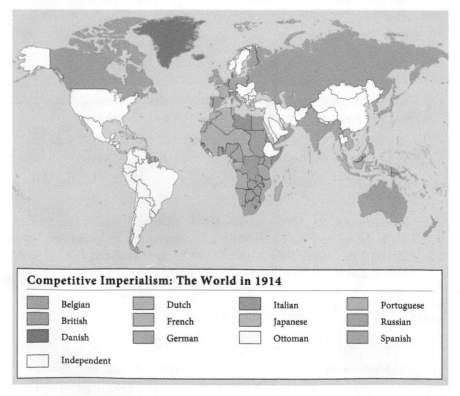

**Competitive Imperialism: The World in 1914**

| | | | |
|---|---|---|---|
| Belgian | Dutch | Italian | Portuguese |
| British | French | Japanese | Russian |
| Danish | German | Ottoman | Spanish |
| Independent | | | |

MAP 27.3  **Competitive Imperialism: The World in 1914.**

undisputed leading empire in the world. No country had a navy that could rival it, British trade posts and colonies were widely distributed over the world, and British colonialism in India provided Indian cotton to fuel British industrialization. On the European continent, Britain worked to restore the monarchies of France, Austria, Prussia, and Russia so that they would balance each other as "great powers" in a **Concert of Europe**. Britain would not tolerate any renewed European imperialism of the kind that Napoleon had pursued. Meeting more or less regularly in congresses, the great powers were remarkably successful at maintaining peace in Europe. For an entire century not a single war engulfed the continent as a whole.

The Concert of Europe, however, was less successful at curbing the imperial ambitions of its members reaching for lands outside of western Europe. Russia did not hide its goal of throwing the Ottoman Empire (admitted to the Concert for better protection of its integrity in 1856) back into "Asia"—that is, Asia Minor, or Anatolia. Great Britain, although it made itself the protector of the integrity of the Ottoman Empire, could at best only slow the ambitions of Russia. The movement to secure the independence of Greece (1821–1832) is a good example of this pattern. Russia, as the Greeks' coreligionist and protector, was centrally involved in initiating a pattern of ethnolinguistic nationalism that replaced constitutional nationalism as the organizing ideology for many Europeans in the nineteenth century.

**Concert of Europe:** International political system that dominated Europe from 1815 to 1914, which advocated a balance of power among states.

**The French Conquest of Algeria**   Britain, unable to prevent the renewal of French imperialism, directed it outside Europe against Ottoman Algiers. The French naval expedition—the circumstances of which were described at the beginning of this chapter—conveniently took place in 1830 while British attention was still focused on the negotiations for Greece's independence. In its North African expedition, France followed an earlier short-lived blueprint of Napoleon's, which envisaged the creation of a Mediterranean empire encompassing Algeria and/or Egypt, prior to his lightning imperialism in Europe, possibly to signal to Britain the ease of reaching India via the Mediterranean.

Algeria was the crucial first step of a European power—in this instance France—seizing provinces of the Ottoman Empire in competition with the Russians, while officially protecting its integrity. This first step was still full of hesitations and counter-maneuvers. At first, the French stayed on a small coastal strip around Algiers and other places, encouraging the rise of indigenous leaders to take over from the Ottoman corsairs and Janissaries and share the country with the French. The British discreetly supported Algerian leaders with weapons to be used against the French.

In the end, however, coexistence proved impossible, and the French military—against strong Algerian resistance—undertook an all-out conquest. The civilian colonial administration after 1870 encouraged large-scale immigration of French and Spanish farmers, who settled on small plots, as well as French corporate investments in vineyards and citrus plantations on the coast. The indigenous population of Arabs and Berbers, decimated by cholera epidemics in the 1860s, found itself largely reduced to less fertile lands in the interior.

**Britain's Containment Policy**   Great Britain sought to limit Russian ambitions not only in Europe; it also opposed Russia in its own backyard of central Asia,

**The Great Game:** Competition between Great Britain and Russia for conquest or control of Asian countries north of India and south of Russia, principally Afghanistan.

inaugurating what was called the **Great Game** against Russia in Asia with the first Anglo–Afghan war in 1838. Although Great Britain failed to occupy Afghanistan and make it an advance protectorate against the approaching Russians, it eventually succeeded in turning Afghanistan into a buffer state keeping Russia away from India. A little later, in 1853–1856, Britain and France teamed up in the Crimean War to stop Russia from renewing its drive for Istanbul. This defeat, demonstrating the superiority of new industrially produced rifles and breech-loading artillery, chastened Russia for the next two decades.

In the second half of the nineteenth century, however, the ethnic–nationalist unification of Germany in 1870–1871, engineered by Prussia through a successful war against France (the Franco–Prussian War), destroyed the balance of the European Concert. Germany, much larger than Prussia and strengthened further through the annexation of the French industrializing region of Alsace-Lorraine, was now the dominant power in western Europe. Russia promptly exploited the new imbalance in Europe during anti-Ottoman uprisings in the Balkans in 1876. Leaving the humiliation of the Crimean War behind, Russian troops broke through Ottoman lines of defense and marched within a few miles of Istanbul. However, Great Britain, although no longer the arbiter of the European Concert, still had enough clout to force Russia into retreating.

**Scottish Troops at the Sphinx, 1882.** The British occupied Egypt as a means to secure the Suez Canal and guarantee the repayment of Egyptian debts. Subsequent negotiations with the Ottoman sultan for the status of Egypt failed, and the province became an unofficial protectorate of Britain. Although granted internal independence in 1922, Egypt remained in a semicolonial relationship with Britain until 1956.

**British Imperialism in Egypt and Sudan**    To prevent a repeat of the Russian invasion, Britain and the Ottomans agreed in 1878 to turn the island of Cyprus over to the British as a protectorate. This protectorate would have British advisors and troops, ready to defend Istanbul against a renewed Russian invasion. Thus, in the name of curbing Russian imperialism, Great Britain became an imperial power itself in the Mediterranean.

Events after the occupation of Cyprus, however, followed a dramatically different course. Instead of watching Russia, the commanders of the British navy squadron in Cyprus had to turn their attention to Egypt. This province was the wealthiest part of the Ottoman Empire. It was governed by a dynasty of autonomous rulers, beginning with Muhammad Ali (r. 1805–1848), an Albanian officer in the Ottoman army who assumed political control after Napoleon's troops had evacuated Egypt. Although his efforts to use his new army to conquer Istanbul and take over the Ottoman Empire were thwarted by a Great Britain anxious to protect the sultans, Muhammad Ali had a huge impact on Egypt. In a major reform effort, similar to the Tanzimat constitutional reforms in Istanbul, Cairo and Alexandria became centers of adaptation to European arts and letters as well as a reformed Islam.

Muhammad Ali's successors were less able rulers who incurred considerable debts, in part for the French-led construction of the Suez Canal in 1869. Britain took over a large part of the canal shares from the debt-ridden Egyptian ruler in 1857. A year later, Britain and France imposed a joint debt commission that garnished a portion of Egyptian tax revenue. Opposition in Egypt to this foreign interference grew in the following years, both inside and outside the Egyptian government, and culminated in 1881 with a revolt in the Egyptian army that endangered the debt repayments.

British-initiated negotiations between the Ottoman sultan and the leader of the army revolt, Colonel Ahmad Urabi (1841–1911), over the issue of the debt collapsed after riots in Alexandria and a careless British bombardment of the port in response to Egyptian fortification efforts. Interventionists in London, fearing for their bonds and the supply of Egyptian cotton for the British textile industry, gained the upper hand. Overcoming the fiercely resisting Egyptian army, a British expeditionary force occupied Egypt in 1882.

> "I have always, and do now recommend it [the purchase of the Suez Canal shares] . . . which I believe is calculated to strengthen the Empire."
>
> —Benjamin Disraeli

The Ottoman sultan acquiesced to the occupation because the appointment of a British-appointed high commissioner, charged with the reorganization of the Egyptian finances, was supposed to be only temporary. Costly campaigns by British-led Egyptian troops in Sudan during 1883–1885, however, derailed any early departure plans. Egypt had occupied Sudan in the 1820s and, as in Egypt, had made cotton a major export crop for the British textile industry. Sudanese resentment over the occupation and anxiety over the accompanying social changes led to a religiously inspired uprising in Khartoum in 1883.

The leader of the uprising was Muhammad Ahmad Ibn Abdallah (1844–1885), head of an Islamic Sufi brotherhood and self-styled Mahdi ("rightly guided" or "Messiah"), sent to establish a realm of justice. After the Mahdi succeeded in driving the British–Egyptian forces from Sudan and establishing an independent state, he was left alone for the next decade.

Until the British slaughtered Abdallah's forces at the Battle of Omdurman in 1898, Egypt's finances, aggravated by problems in Sudan, were sufficiently in disarray to keep the British focused on Egypt. On the one hand, the British wanted to put Egyptian finances on a sound footing again, but on the other hand, they wanted out to avoid responsibility for the country's governance. They had no plans yet for a full-fledged Mediterranean imperialism. As a compromise, they conceived of a conditional departure, with the right of return at times of internal unrest or external danger. The Ottoman sultan, however, refused to sign this compromise. He was grateful to Britain for recognizing Ottoman sovereignty but sought to avoid the responsibility of governance. In the end, Britain stayed for almost three-quarters of a century, running Egypt as an undeclared colony for the first 40 years. Without a clear plan, Britain had nonetheless transplanted the pattern of imperialism–colonialism it had first experimented with in India.

**France's Tunisian Protectorate**    Similar to Algeria and Egypt, Tunisia was an autonomous Ottoman province, ruled by its own dynasty of *beys*. The dynasty had been founded by a Janissary officer in 1705 when the military ruling class began to shift from corsair raids against Christian shipping to the fiscal exploitation of the villages and nomadic tribes of the interior. Fertile northern Tunisia provided limited but fairly reliable tax revenues from olive oil, barley, wheat, fruits, and nuts. Annual tax expeditions to the south among the seminomadic sheep and camel tribes usually yielded few taxes and served mostly to demonstrate the dynasty's sovereignty.

The beys responded to the Western challenge early, being the first in the Muslim Middle East and North Africa to modernize their military and adopt a constitution (1857). With their more limited revenues, they hit the debt ceiling already in 1869, much earlier than the Ottomans and Egyptians, and had to accept a British–French–Italian debt commission for the reorganization of the country's revenues. When the French took over in 1881, they began with the same thankless task of balancing the budget as the British had in Egypt. Only later did they benefit from the French and Italian settlers they invited to the protectorate to intensify agriculture.

## The Scramble for Africa

Competitive European imperialism exploded beyond the Mediterranean in early 1884 as Germany claimed its first protectorates in Africa. Conveniently, after having secured lands for his country, the German chancellor Otto von Bismarck (in various offices 1862–1890) called a conference in Berlin, which met from late 1884 to early 1885. The main agenda of the Berlin conference was a discussion on how the 14 invited European countries and the United States should "define the conditions under which future territorial annexations in Africa might be recognized." Bismarck's proposed main condition was "effective occupation," with the creation of spheres of influence around the occupied places. The first protectorates, confirmed at the conference, were Cameroon in west central Africa for Germany and Congo as a private possession of King Leopold II of Belgium. The **Scramble for Africa** was on (see Map 27.4).

**Scramble for Africa:**
Competition among European powers from 1884 to 1912 to acquire African colonies.

**Explorers, Missionaries, and the Civilizing Mission**    Sub-Saharan Africa was still little known and often misunderstood by most Europeans in the 1800s. The Enlightenment had instilled curiosity about the geography, flora, fauna, and ethnology of Africa among the European reading public. As a result, intrepid explorers descended on the "Dark Continent," and in order to gain access to the interior explorers utilized trade routes and caravans, long in use by Africans. But enduring the hardships of traveling in the savanna, rain forest, and desert required strong commitment. David Livingstone (1813–1873), a tireless missionary and passionate opponent of slavery, was the best known among the pioneers who explored much of south central Africa. Livingstone's ultimate goals were not only to terminate trafficking in slaves but also to "civilize" Africans by broadcasting the blessings of Christianity and commerce.

The generation of explorers after Livingstone was better equipped, led larger expeditions, and composed more precise accounts. Here, the outstanding figure was Henry Morton Stanley (1841–1904), a Welsh journalist who worked in the United States and became famous for his encounter with Livingstone ("Dr. Livingstone, I presume?") at Lake Tanganyika in east central Africa. Still, in spite of extensive explorations, European politicians at the end of the century had only the vaguest idea of the geography of the "dark continent."

**Civilizing mission:**
Belief that European colonizers had a duty to extend the benefits of European civilization to "backward" peoples.

The exploits of Christian missionaries created a sense of both responsibility for and superiority to the Africans in the European public. They were at the forefront of the **civilizing mission**, the belief prevalent in the West in the nineteenth

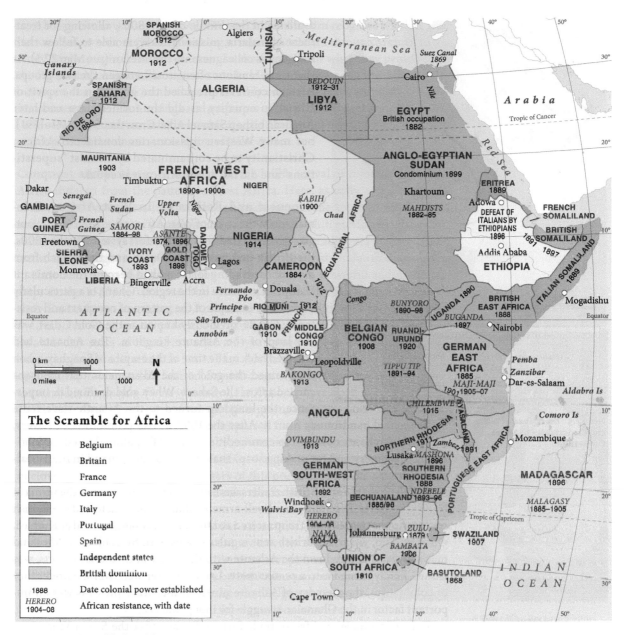

MAP **27.4** **The Scramble for Africa.**

century that colonists had a duty to extend the benefits of civilization (that is, European civilization) to the "backward" people they ruled.

In the early 1800s, malaria and yellow fever confined missionaries to the coasts of Africa. There, supported by missionary societies in Europe, they trained indigenous missionaries to translate tracts and scriptures for the conversion of Africans in the interior. When quinine (made from the bark of a Brazilian tree) became

"We must say openly that indeed the higher races have a right over the lower races . . . I repeat, that the superior races have a right because they have a duty. They have the duty to civilize the inferior races."

—Jules Ferry, French statesman

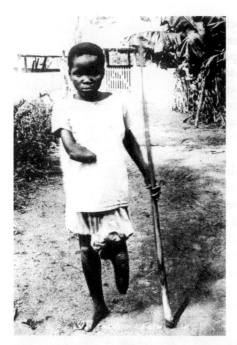

**Colonial Brutality in the Congo.** A young African boy whose hand and foot were severed by sentries after his village failed to meet its rubber quota. The Belgian Congo under King Leopold II employed mass forced labor of the indigenous population to extract rubber from the jungle. As the demand for rubber grew King Leopold's private army of 16,000 mercenaries was given leave to use any method to coerce the population into meeting quotas, including random killing, mutilation, village burning, starvation and hostage taking.

North of Namibia, King Leopold II (r. 1865–1909) of Belgium turned his personal colony of the Congo into a vast forced-labor camp for the production of rubber. The wild rubber tree, native to Africa, gained great importance in Europe for a variety of industrial applications. Leopold was particularly sadistic in his exploitation of the native workforce, using beatings and mutilations if collection quotas were not filled. Recent research indicates that an astonishing 10,000,000 Congolese were either killed or starved to death.

The scramble finally ended in 1912 with the French declaration of a protectorate over Morocco. By this time, the political competition in Europe had narrowed to the struggle between Germany and Great Britain for political predominance in western Europe. Italy's imperialist dreams were stymied by its crushing defeat at the battle of Adowa in 1896, in which one-third of its army was killed by Ethiopian forces (see "Patterns Up Close"). Ethiopia emerged from the scramble as the only noncolonized state in Africa. French and British rivalry in Africa, which had cropped up during the scramble and had even led to a confrontation at Fashoda over the control of Sudan in 1898, ended between 1905 and 1911, when Britain allied with France to counterbalance Germany. As a result of this alliance, Britain recognized France's interests in Morocco, adjacent to the two French territories of Algeria and Tunisia, over protests by Germany.

**European Colonization**   European colonial powers had many common interests as they plunged into the Scramble for Africa. They all participated in the exploitation of African raw materials and minerals, as well as the quest for overseas markets and territories in order to demonstrate their power and influence as rivalries among them heated up in the later nineteenth century.

But there were differences in the methods used to realize their ambitions. Portugal was the first European state to establish bases of power in Africa. In order to develop profitable plantations, the Portuguese adopted a policy of direct rule, administered by a centralized bureaucracy. In addition, by the policy of assimilation, qualified colonists could eventually attain citizenship status. Since the Portuguese had established port colonies in Angola and Mozambique in the 1600s, they attempted to expand their holdings during the early phase of the Scramble for Africa. As a result of the Berlin conference in 1884–1885, Portugal claimed a wide swath of sub-Saharan central Africa extending from Angola in the west to Mozambique in the east, in order to create a continent-wide swath across central Africa. Owing, however, to its relatively small size, its economy was not strong enough to sustain expansion, and as a result Portuguese interests were edged out by the larger colonial powers of Germany and Britain.

King Leopold of Belgium began the rush for African territories, concentrating on developing Belgian interests in Central Africa. After establishing the International Association for the Exploration and Civilization of Central Africa in 1876, the Belgian ruler commissioned Henry Morton Stanley to assist in the creation of the Congo Free State. Stanley trudged around the region, ostensibly making treaty arrangements with local rulers, but in reality "claiming" these lands for the Belgian crown. In order to convert these acquisitions into profitable commercial enterprises, Leopold set up vast plantations, adopting a policy of brutality in order to maintain control over their holdings.

Germany began to pursue its colonial ambitions in Africa in the 1880s and 1890s. Although Bismarck was initially reluctant, the growing need to make Germany competitive with other industrial powers, especially Britain, finally inspired Bismarck to join in the race for African possessions. Germany developed colonies in East Africa and West Africa, as well as in the Cameroons. The Germans quickly converted these lands into plantation economies, which in turn produced much-needed raw materials for burgeoning German industrialism. Like many other European colonizers, Germany relied upon brutality to render its plantations profitable.

Because it achieved unification as the Kingdom of Italy only in 1870, by the time Italian efforts were under way to establish colonies in Africa much of the continent had already been claimed. As a result, Italians had to settle for what was left, primarily regions in the Horn of Africa, increasingly important because of its proximity to the Suez Canal. In 1869 Italy acquired rights to the port of Assab on the coast of the Red Sea, and subsequently declared it a colony in 1882. From there Italians expanded their holdings into Somaliland in 1888, followed by Ethiopia in 1889; each of these was declared an Italian protectorate. But when the Ethiopian ruler discovered that he had been deceived, he mounted a fierce resistance movement that led to the defeat of Italian forces at the battle of Adowa in 1896.

**Resistance**    Resistance to European colonialism took different forms depending on a variety of factors. Among these were ongoing and systemic warfare among African societies, resulting in disunity and the resultant inability to mount an effective Africa-wide effort to oust the Europeans. A good example is afforded by Ghana, where opponents of the Ashante sided with the British in their effort to annex Ashante lands. Another form of resistance was the adoption of noncooperation tactics by colonized Africans. Termed "weapons of the weak" by a noted scholar of Africa, these included work slowdowns, desertion, arson, and even sabotage.

Resistance was also dependent on the size and power of assorted indigenous chiefdoms and kingdoms. For smaller communities, the preferred tactic was guerilla warfare; for larger and better-organized societies full-fledged armed confrontation was the method of choice. Many African rulers possessed European weapons, including rapid-fire rifles, through contacts with European traders. Moreover, some rulers also manufactured their own ammunition and gunpowder. Ethiopia, for example, amassed a huge fighting force of some 100,000 troops, which won a significant victory over Italian soldiers at the Battle of Adowa in 1896.

Although African societies mounted a variety of resistance movements, it was ultimately the superior technologies of Europeans that prevailed. The by-products of industrialization, these advances included gunboats, telegraph communications, and others. But by far the most lethal weapons in European arsenals were breech-loading rifles and especially machine guns. These advanced weapons proved far superior to the weapons available to Africans, weapons like bows and arrows, spears, and muskets. The disparity enabled relatively small contingents of European soldiers, numbering sometimes only in the hundreds, to fend off thousands of charging African warriors in pitched battles.

# Western Imperialism and Colonialism in Southeast Asia

Parallel to developments in Africa, the new imperialism made its appearance also in southeast Asia, specifically Indonesia, the Philippines, Vietnam, Cambodia, and Laos. While the new imperialism in southeast Asia was an outgrowth of the earlier trade-fort presence of Portugal, Spain, and the Netherlands, it also included the return of France to imperial glory.

## The Dutch in Indonesia

The Dutch were heirs of the Portuguese, who had set up forts that traded for spices in Indonesia during the sixteenth century and for the next 100 years were the middlemen for the distribution of spices from Portugal to northern Europe. But after liberating themselves from Habsburg–Spanish rule, the Netherlands displaced Portugal from its dominant position as a spice importer to Europe. From 1650 to 1750, the Netherlands was the leading naval power in the world. After 1750, they shifted from the trade of spices in their trade forts in Indonesia to the planting of cash crops, such as sugar, cacao, coffee, and tobacco—the mild- and warm-weather commodities that Europeans consumed in ever-larger quantities. The aim of the full colonization of Indonesia during the nineteenth century was to profit from European industrial demand for agricultural and mineral commodities.

**Portuguese and Dutch Trade Forts**   Portuguese sailors arrived in the strategic Strait of Malacca, which separates Sumatra from the Malay Peninsula and divides the Indian Ocean from the Chinese Sea, in 1511. They defeated the local sultanate and established a fort in the Malaysian capital, Malacca. Their main interest, however, given the power of Aceh on Sumatra, was to push onward to the spice-producing Maluku Islands (known in English as the Moluccas) in eastern Indonesia (between Sulawesi and New Guinea), where they established a trade fort in 1522, amid several Islamic island lords. From there, the Portuguese pushed on to China and finally Japan, where they arrived in the mid-1500s. Overall, their role in the Indonesian spice trade remained small, and indigenous Islamic merchants maintained their dominance.

After declaring their independence from Spain in 1581, the northern provinces of the Netherlands formed the Republic of the United Netherlands and pushed for their own overseas network of trade forts. In 1602, the Dutch government chartered the Dutch United East India Company (VOC), which spearheaded the expansion of Dutch possessions in India and southeast Asia. After a slow start, the company erected outposts on many Indonesian islands and in the mid-1600s founded Batavia (today Jakarta) on the island of Java as its main southeast Asian center. The VOC was by far the largest and wealthiest commercial company in the world during the seventeenth century, with a fleet consisting of nearly 5,000 merchant ships supported by large naval and land forces.

When the Dutch *stadhouder* (governor) of the Netherlands, William of Orange (1650–1702), became king of England after the English Glorious Revolution (see Chapter 17), the Dutch and English overseas trade interests were pooled. Great

Britain (as the country was known after England's union with Scotland in 1707) deepened its Indian interests through the British East India Company, and the Dutch pursued their engagements in Indonesia. Like the British company in India, the VOC was increasingly drawn during the early 1700s into local dynastic wars. Supported by some 1,000 Dutch soldiers and 3,000 indigenous auxiliaries, the VOC established peace in 1755 in the fragmenting Islamic sultanate of Banten (1527–1808). Thereafter, it became the de facto government on the island of Java over a set of pacified Islamic protectorates.

Several decades earlier than its British counterpart in India, the VOC fell on hard times. Governing and maintaining troops was expensive. VOC employees often paid their expenses out of their own pockets, since contact with the Netherlands in pretelegraph times was slow and sporadic. In the late eighteenth century, trade shifted from spices to bulk commodities, such as sugar, cacao, coffee, tobacco, indigo, and cotton. The inability of the VOC to shift from spices to commodities, which required investments in plantations and accompanying transportation infrastructures, was the decisive factor that led in 1799 to the liquidation of the VOC. Similar to the British experience in India, the government of the Netherlands then became the ruler of Indonesian possessions that had grown from trade forts into small colonies, surrounded by dependent indigenous principalities as well as independent sultanates.

**Dutch Colonialism**    The Dutch government took the decisive step toward investments in 1830 when Belgium separated from the large Dutch kingdom created after the Napoleonic Wars to form an independent Catholic monarchy. Faced with severe budgetary constraints and cut off from industrializing Belgium, the Dutch government adopted the **cultivation system** in Indonesia. According to this system, indigenous Indonesian subsistence farmers were forced into compulsory planting and labor schemes which required them to either grow government crops on 20 percent of their land or work for 60 days on Dutch plantations. Overnight, the Dutch and collaborating Indonesian ruling classes turned into landowners. They reaped huge profits while Indonesian subsistence farmers, having to replace many of their rice paddies with commercial crops, suffered in many places from famines. In the course of the nineteenth century, Indonesia became a major or even the largest exporter of sugar, tea, coffee, palm oil, coconut products, tropical hardwoods, rubber, quinine, and pepper to the industrial nations.

Cultivation system:
Dutch colonial scheme
of compulsory labor
and planting of crops
imposed on indigenous
Indonesian self-
sufficiency farmers.

To keep pace with demand, the Dutch pursued a program of systematic conquest and colonization. They conquered the Indonesian archipelago, finally subduing the most stubborn opponents, the Muslim guerillas of Aceh, in 1903 (see Map 27.6). Even then, the conquest was incomplete, and inland rain forests remained outside Dutch government control. Conquered lands were turned over to private investors who established plantations. To deflect criticism at home and abroad, the Dutch also introduced reform measures. In 1870 they liberated farmers from the compulsory planting of government crops, and in 1901 they issued an "ethical policy," announcing measures such as land distribution, irrigation, and education. Severe underfunding, however, kept these measures largely on paper, and it was clear that the profits from colonialism were more important than investment for indigenous people.

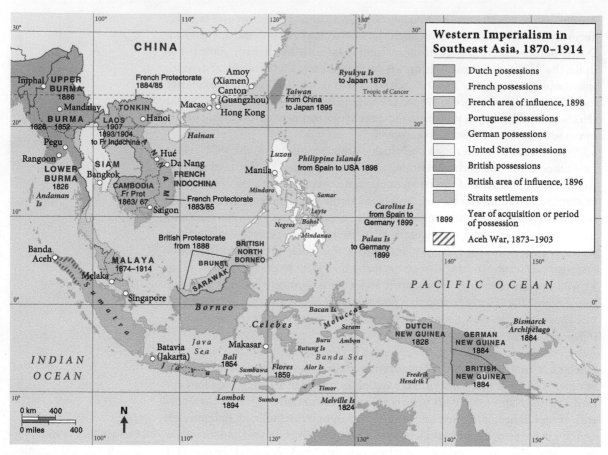

MAP 27.6 **Western Imperialism in Southeast Asia, 1870–1914.**

## Spain in the Philippines

The Philippines are adjacent to the Indonesian islands in the northeast. The Spanish had built their first trade fort of Manila there shortly after conquering Mexico from the Aztecs, using it as a port from which to trade Mexican silver with China for luxury manufactures. Manila expanded only slowly, suffering from constant raids by indigenous highlanders from the interior, Islamic rulers from the southern islands, and Dutch interlopers. Imperial conquest had to await the later eighteenth century, and colonization followed in the middle of the nineteenth century with the introduction of sugarcane.

**Galleons and Trade with China**    Spain expanded early on from the Americas farther west in order to prevent Portugal from claiming all the lucrative spice islands of Indonesia. A Portuguese explorer in Spanish service, Ferdinand Magellan (ca. 1480–1521), successfully crossed the sea channels at the southern tip of South America in 1520 and, on a journey that took his fleet eventually around the entire globe, discovered what later became known as the Philippines, in honor of King Phillip II of Spain. It took another half century, however, before Spain could spare ships and men for the construction of a first trade fort and small colony. This fort,

Manila, became the base for subsequent biannual silver fleets from Mexico. Spanish merchants based in Mexico, from which Manila was administered, benefited greatly from the trade of silver for Chinese silk, porcelain, and lacquerware. Thus, Manila began as a small subcolony of the large Spanish colony of Mexico, or New Spain.

As the Spanish gradually expanded their hold on the coastal lowlands outside Manila on Luzon and Visaya (where the local king had converted to Christianity), they established estates, thus advancing from trade-fort imperialism to the beginnings of territorial expansion.

**Incipient Colonialism**  The indigenous farmers on the Philippine estates were obliged to deliver rents, in the form of rice and animals, to ensure the food supply for some 30,000 inhabitants of Manila, mostly merchants of Spanish, Chinese, and Japanese origin. Warrior chieftains outside Spanish lands who converted to Catholicism were confirmed as owners on their lands and transformed themselves into a Hispanicized landowner class. By the early eighteenth century, the Spanish controlled a critical mass on the two islands of Luzon and Visaya such that they were able to establish a regular administration for fiscal and juridical matters. The beginnings of colonialism in the Philippines had emerged.

The balance sheet for the colonial administration was always in the red, however, since the fiscal revenue did not yield surpluses and villagers produced only small quantities of exportable ginger, cinnamon, and gold. Much money had to be invested in defending the Spanish-controlled territory from attacks by independent Filipinos in the mountainous upland interiors of Luzon and Visaya who resisted conquest and conversion. Even more vexing were raids supported by Islamic sultanates which had formed in the south based in trading hardwoods for luxuries with China.

**Full Colonialism**  Major reforms, shifting the economy from silver to commodity exports, began in the early 1800s, motivated by the Spanish loss of Mexico to independence. These reforms resulted in the liberalization of trade and the beginnings of commercial agriculture for export. Ports were opened to ships from all countries, discrimination against Chinese settlements ended, and Spanish administrators and churchmen lost their trade privileges. Foreign entrepreneurs cleared rain forests and exported hardwoods. On the new land they grew cash crops, such as sugar, tobacco, hemp (for ropes and sacks), indigo, coffee, and cotton. Large-scale rice farms replaced a great number of small-scale village self-sufficiency plots, and thus, commercialization even usurped subsistence agriculture.

Strong resistance by landowners against a reform of the land regime and tax system until the very end of the nineteenth century, however, ensured that Spain did not benefit much from the liberalization of trade. Additionally, Philippine society stratified rapidly into a wealthy minority and a large mass of landless rural workers and urban day laborers. Manila had over 100,000 inhabitants in the early nineteenth century. This stratification, however, was very different from that in the Americas. There was no real Creole class—that is, a Spanish–Philippine upper stratum of landowners and urban people. Although the French Revolution and subsequent Napoleonic upheavals in Spain had their impact on the islands, agitation for independence and constitutionalism was largely limited to urban intellectuals.

**American Soldiers in the Philippines.** The victory of the United States over Spain in 1898 and its decision to annex the Philippines created for the first time an American overseas empire. Resistance was immediate, and a brutal war against Philippine fighters lasted from 1902 until 1913, with isolated outbreaks continuing until Philippine independence in 1946. Here, American troops dig in and fortify an outpost in Luzon.

The Philippines remained a colony, producing no revenue and still demanding costly administrative (especially fiscal) reforms and infrastructural investments, both of which Spain was unable to afford.

The first stirrings of Filipino nationalism, primarily among Hispanicized Filipinos of mixed Spanish and indigenous or Chinese descent, made themselves felt in the second half of the nineteenth century. The principal spokesman was José Rizal (1861–1896), whose subversive novels were a response to the Spanish justification of continued colonialism.

Colonial authorities promptly arrested Rizal for his activities, banishing him to Hong Kong, but he returned to Manila in 1892, inspiring both overt and underground resistance groups. One of these groups, Katipunan, operated in secret, advocating Filipino independence through armed struggle. In 1896 the government discovered the existence of the organization in Manila and executed hundreds of revolutionaries, including Rizal, before firing squads. But it was unable to destroy Katipunan in the provinces, and the two sides agreed in 1897 to a truce which included the end of armed revolt in return for exile of the leadership to Hong Kong.

**Philippine–American War**   Although it appeared that the colonial government was successful in suppressing the Filipino revolt for independence, events took a dramatic turn when the Spanish–American War broke out in 1898. The mysterious explosion of an American warship in Cuba—newly autonomous under Spanish suzerainty—had led to mutual declarations of war. The two sides fought their first battle in Manila Bay, where the United States routed a Spanish squadron. An American ship fetched the exiled Filipino rebel Emilio Aguinaldo (1869–1964) from Hong Kong, and he quickly defeated the Spanish and declared independence. Over four centuries of Spanish colonialism in the Pacific had come to an end.

After 4 months of fighting, Spain was defeated not only in Cuba, Puerto Rico, and Guam but also in the Philippines. The United States and Spain made peace at the end of 1898, ignoring the independent Philippine government in their agreement. Accordingly, US forces took possession of Manila in 1899 and within a year defeated the troops of the protesting Filipino government under the elected president, Emilio Aguinaldo. The Filipinos shifted to guerilla war, but US troops were able to capture Aguinaldo in 1901. The United States declared the war over in 1902 but had to fight remnants of the guerillas as well as southern rebels until 1913. Thus, the United States had joined the European race for imperial and colonial control of the non-Western world.

## The French in Vietnam

North of Indonesia and west of the Philippines is Vietnam. Indochina, the peninsula on which Vietnam is located, also includes Cambodia, Laos, and Thailand. Portuguese monks in the sixteenth century were the first western Europeans to go to Indochina, seeking converts among the Buddhist, neo-Confucian, and animist indigenous inhabitants. French imperial and colonial involvement began in 1858, at a time when Europe was industrializing and competition in the Concert of Europe was beginning to spill over from the Balkans and Middle East into Africa. At first focusing on the south of Indochina, France gradually expanded northward, establishing protectorates over the Nguyen royal dynasty, which was the last of a succession of kingdoms that had begun in the third century CE.

**French Interests in Vietnam**  French royal efforts in the seventeenth and early eighteenth centuries to sponsor Catholic missions and trading companies were largely unsuccessful and ended altogether after their defeat in the Seven Years' War (1756–1763). When France renewed these efforts after the French Revolution and Napoleon, it was rebuffed by the Vietnamese kings, who shared Chinese concerns about the Western challenge. Both China and Vietnam adopted a policy of isolationism as their first answer to Western patterns of challenge.

The French, however, were not deterred. Napoleon had considered the idea of a Mediterranean empire that included either Algeria or Egypt before embarking on his campaign of European imperialism. The French then actually conquered Algeria in 1830–1847, as detailed earlier in this chapter. The ruler who was subsequently most active in pushing for the renewal of Napoleon's imperialism outside Europe was his nephew, Napoleon III (r. 1848–1870). This self-styled emperor involved himself in a variety of short-lived ventures in Mexico, China, and Japan. His one enduring conquest was that of Cochinchina, or southern Vietnam, in the late 1850s. Taking as a pretext the renewed torture and execution of French missionaries and Vietnamese converts, the French dispatched a squadron that occupied the sparsely inhabited Mekong River delta in 1858–1862, annexing it as a protectorate.

**Conquest and Colonialism**  Serious colonization efforts by the French had to await the scramble for the division of Africa and what remained unclaimed in Asia in the mid-1880s. After Napoleon III's fall from power as a result of the lost war against Prussia and the establishment of the Third Republic, opinions among politicians about the wisdom of a French empire were divided. But a year after pro-imperialists came to power in 1883, the French challenged and ultimately defeated China in a war for the control of northern Vietnam. In contrast to the thinly settled south, the Red River estuary in the north with the capital of the kingdom, Hanoi, was densely populated. When the imperialist frenzy was at its peak during the Berlin conference of 1884–1885 for the partition of Africa, the French conquerors united southern and northern Vietnam into the French colony of Indochina. Two members of the deposed Vietnamese dynasty took to the mountains and waged a guerilla war against the occupation, called the Black Flag Revolt. But by the early twentieth century the French had captured both and were in full control.

The French government and French entrepreneurs invested substantial sums in the Mekong delta, establishing plantations for the production of coffee, tea, and rubber. Indigenous rice farmers had to deliver 40 percent of their crops to the colonial government. Hanoi was made the seat of the colonial administration in 1902 and was enlarged as an architecturally French city. The port of Haiphong, downriver from Hanoi, became the main entry point for ships to load agricultural commodities for export. The commodities for the world market, which French West Africa largely lacked, existed in Vietnam, Cambodia, and Laos (the latter two added in 1893–1904).

**Early Nationalism**    Given Vietnam's long tradition of Confucian scholar-administrators, it was only a question of time before the pre-1858 spirit of antiforeign Vietnamese patriotism reasserted itself. The driving force in this reassertion was Phan Boi Chau (1867–1940), trained by his father and other scholars and an eyewitness to the crushing by the French of a protest by scholars in 1885. Phan Boi Chau's activities and writings inspired antitax demonstrations and a provincial uprising in Vietnam in 1908–1909, which the French suppressed harshly. Under French pressure, the Japanese expelled Phan Boi Chau from Japan in 1909. By 1912, he had given up his royalism, and from then on a newly formed nationalist grouping favored the expulsion of the French and the formation of a Vietnamese democratic republic.

# Putting It All Together

Ever since Vladimir Lenin, the founder of the Soviet Union, declared in 1916 that imperialism was "the highest stage of capitalism" (adopting a thesis first suggested by the English historian John A. Hobson in 1902), scholars have hotly debated the topic of whether or not the capitalist industrialization process in Europe, North America, and Japan needed colonies to sustain its growth. Most recent historians, beginning with David K. Fieldhouse in 1984, have concluded that imperialism and colonialism were not needed and that all the mineral and agrarian commodities crucial for industrialization during the first and second Industrial Revolutions could have been bought from independent countries on the world market. It so happened, of course, that Great Britain had transformed its activity in India from trade-fort imperialism to territorial imperialism just prior to its industrialization and used Indian cotton as raw material for its textile factories. But this raises the reverse question: Would industrialization have happened had Great Britain not conquered India? This counterfactual question has no easy answer.

Perhaps a better approach to the question is to think of trade-fort and territorial imperialism as world-historical patterns of long standing. By contrast, industrialization was a much later phenomenon that arose out of the application of the New Sciences to practical mechanical uses, of which steam engines and textile factories were the first examples, appearing around 1800. Thus, old patterns of imperialism persisted during the rise of the new pattern of industrialization. These old patterns were tremendously amplified by the new power that industrialization gave the European countries. Therefore, the new imperialism of the nineteenth century, and the colonialism that followed in its wake, can be seen as phenomena in which old patterns continued but were superimposed on and enlarged by new patterns of industrial power.

▶ For additional resources, including maps, primary sources, visuals, and quizzes, please go to www.oup.com/us/vonsivers. Please see the Further Resources section at the back of the book for additional readings and suggested websites.

# Against the Grain

# An Anti-Imperial Perspective

During the heyday of Western imperialism in the later nineteenth century, many popular European writers justified the conquest of foreign lands and the exploitation of native peoples by expressing attitudes reflected in social Darwinism. Seen from this perspective, Europeans were doing God's work by pursuing a "civilizing mission," thus exposing "lesser breeds" to the benefits of Christianity and commerce. For proponents of imperialism, it was fitting and just to pursue a policy of civilizing the "inferior races." Perhaps the best known of these condescending works was Rudyard Kipling's "The White Man's Burden," published in 1899 in response to America's takeover of the Philippines after their victory in the Spanish–American war of 1898. According to this poem it was the duty, or "burden," of Western imperialists to "serve your captives' need / Your new-caught, sullen peoples / Half-devil and half-child."

Not all Europeans, however, were of like mind; there were many who refused to follow suit, and who expressed views contrary to the majority opinion. Among the most outspoken critics of European imperialism was a contemporary of Kipling, the British journalist E. D. Morel (1873–1924). Initially employed as a clerk in an English trading firm with commercial interests in the Belgian Congo, Morel had access to records and documents that revealed the mistreatment and exploitation of African slave labor on Belgian rubber plantations. Determined to expose these atrocities, Morel published a series of scathing denunciations in 1900.

Forced to leave his job, Morel continued his activist campaign against Belgian atrocities by launching a newspaper, the *West African Mail*, in 1903, followed by his foundation of the Congo Reform Association in 1904. Two particularly trenchant books exposing Leopold II's brutal policies soon followed: *King Leopold's Role in Africa* (1904) and *Red Rubber* (1906). By far the most famous of Morel's indictments, however, was *The Black Man's Burden* (1920), a condemnation of the evils of European capitalism and industrialism: "Its destructive effects are . . . permanent. . . . It kills not the body merely, but the soul. It breaks the spirit." For his pacifist activities Morel was sentenced to prison in 1917, but subsequently went on to win a seat in Parliament in 1922 as a Labour candidate, defeating Winston Churchill in the process. Although he played only a minor role in Parliament, Morel is often considered the father of international activism on behalf of human rights.

- In what ways is Morel a good example of nonconformity with European imperialism in Africa?

- How would you compare Morel's actions with current protest movements around the world?

# Thinking Through Patterns

▶ **What new patterns emerged in the transition from trade-fort imperialism to the new imperialism?**

During the early modern period, European monarchs commissioned merchant marine companies, such as the British East India Company and the Dutch United East India Company, in order to avoid military expeditions of their own but still receive a share of the profits of trade. The mariner-merchants built coastal forts for storage and protection, granted to them by the local rulers with whom they traded. In the seventeenth and eighteenth centuries, much larger trading companies were formed, in which investors pooled their resources, and large numbers of mariner-merchants now served in dozens of trade forts overseas. In India and Indonesia, these companies became "too big to fail" and needed their governments in England and the Netherlands to rescue them. Thus, through the back door, governments found themselves forced to conquer and to colonize—they had become imperialist colonizers.

Great Britain was the pioneer in the development of exportable agricultural and mineral commodities in its colonies for the support of its expanding industries. By the middle of the nineteenth century, other industrializing countries either embarked on imperial conquests or shifted to full colonialism in order to obtain necessary commodities. As a rule, labor for the production of these commodities was scarce. Workers had to be recruited forcibly and were routinely paid low wages.

▶ **How did European colonizers develop their colonies economically, given that they were industrializing themselves at the same time?**

▶ **What were the experiences of the indigenous people under the new imperialism? How did they adapt to colonialism? How did they resist?**

Many imperial conquests involved protracted campaigns that claimed many indigenous victims. If one of the goals of the ensuing colonization was commodity production, the indigenous population was recruited, often forcibly and with low wages. Resistance to European colonialism manifested itself in ethnic nationalism, as demonstrated by the examples of José Rizal, Phan Boi Chau, and Emilio Aguinaldo discussed in this chapter. In Australia and New Zealand and other colonies where European settlement was encouraged, colonial governments or settlers ousted the indigenous population from the most fertile lands, often in the face of fierce resistance.

# Patterns of Evidence:
# Sources for Chapter 27

## SOURCE 27.1

## The Azamgarh Proclamation

**September 29, 1857**

This proclamation was published in the *Delhi Gazette* in the midst of the "Great Mutiny" of 1857. The author was most probably Firoz Shah, a grandson of the Mughal emperor Bahadur Shah Zafar (r. 1837–1857), whose restoration to full power was a main aim of the rebels. General disillusionment with the pace of change and the fear that British missionaries were, with government connivance, attempting to Christianize India came to a head among the British East India Company's sepoy troops. A rumor started that the grease used in the paper cartridges of the Enfield rifle contained both cow and pig fat, an affront to the sensibilities of both Hindus and Muslims. The resulting mutiny (known to Indians as the Great Rebellion or the First War of Independence) resulted in a war dominated by mass atrocities—and ultimately in the imposition of the British "Raj," or direct rule.

It is well known to all, that in this age the people of Hindustan, both Hindoos and Mahommedans, are being ruined under the tyranny and oppression of the treacherous and infidel and treacherous English. It is therefore the bounden duty of all the wealthy people of India, especially of those who have any sort of connexion with any of the Mohammedan royal families, and are considered the pastors and masters of their people, to stake their lives and property for the well-being of the public. With the view of effecting this general good, several princes belonging to the royal family of Delhi, have dispersed themselves in the different parts of India, Iran, Turan, and Afghanistan, and have been long since taking measures to compass their favourite end; and it is to accomplish this charitable object that one of the aforesaid princes has, at the head of an army of Afghanistan, &c., made his appearance in India—and I, who am the grandson of Abul Muzuffer Sarajuddin Bahadur Shah Ghazee, king of India, having in the course of circuit come here to extirpate the infidels residing in the eastern part of the country, and to liberate and protect the poor helpless people now groaning under their iron rule, have, by the aid of the Majahdeens, or religious fanatics, erected the standard of Mohammed, and persuaded the orthodox Hindoos who had been subject to my ancestors, and have been and are still accessories

Source: http://www.csas.ed.ac.uk/mutiny/Texts-Part2
.html.

in the destruction of the English, to raise the standard of Mahavir.

Several of the Hindoo and Mussulman chiefs who . . . have been trying their best to root out the English in India, have presented themselves to me, and taken part in the reigning Indian crusade, and it is more than probable that I shall very shortly receive succours from the west. Therefore, for the information of the public, the present Ishtahar, consisting of several sections, is put in circulation, and it is the imperative duty of all to take it into their careful consideration and abide by it. Parties anxious to participate in this common cause, but having no means to provide for themselves, shall receive their daily subsistence from me; and be it known to all, that the ancient works both of the Hindoos and the Mohammedans, the writings of the miracle-workers, and the calculations of the astrologers, pundits and rammals, all agree asserting that the English will no longer have any footing in India or elsewhere. Therefore it is incumbent on all to give up the hope of the continuation of the British sway, side with me, and deserve the consideration of the Badshahi, or imperial government by their individual exertion in promoting the common good and thus attain their respective ends.

. . .

Section II.—Regarding Merchants.— It is plain that the infidel and treacherous British government have monopolised the trade of all the fine and valuable merchandise, such as indigo, cloth, and other articles of shipping, leaving only the trade of trifles to the people, and even in this they are not without their share of the profits, which they secure by means of customs and stamp fees, &c., in money suits, so that the people have merely a trade in name. Besides this, the profits of the traders are taxed with postages, tolls, and subscriptions for schools, &c. Notwithstanding all these concessions, the merchants are liable to imprisonment and disgrace at the instance or complaint of a worthless man. When the Badshahi government is established, all these aforesaid fraudulent practices shall be dispensed with, and the trade of every article, without exception both by land end water, shall be open to the native merchants of India, who will have the benefit of the government steam-vessels and steam carriages for the conveyance of their merchandise gratis; and merchants having no capital of their own shall be assisted from the public treasury. It is therefore the duty of every merchant to take part in the war, and aid the Badshahi government with his men and money, either secretly or openly, as may be consistent with his position or interest, and forswear his allegiance to the British government.

. . .

Section V.—Regarding Pundits, Fakirs, and other learned persons.—The pundits and fakirs being the guardians of the Hindoo and Mohammedan religions respectively, and the European being the enemies of both the religions, and as at present a war is raging against the English on account of religion, the pundits and fakirs are bound to present themselves to me, and take their share in the holy war, otherwise they will stand condemned according to the tenor of the Shurrah and the Shasters; but if they come, they will, when the Badshahi government is well established, receive rent-free lands.

Lastly, be it known to all, that whoever, out of the above-named classes, shall, after the circulation of this Ishtahar, still cling to the British government, all his estates shall be confiscated, and his property plundered, and he himself, with his whole family, shall be imprisoned, and ultimately put to death.

parents in 1832, he lived briefly in Venezuela and the United States before emigrating to Liberia at the age of eighteen. Liberia had been founded by liberated African American slaves on the west coast of Africa in 1822, and Blyden was fully engaged in the project of establishing a Liberian identity, based on the intellectual and political development of the nation's citizens. Blyden was appointed professor of classics at Liberia College in 1862. In his quest to make the college (the first secular English-speaking institution of higher learning in sub-Saharan Africa) more relevant to Liberia, he began teaching Arabic in 1867. He was also a significant figure in Liberian politics, serving as secretary of state (1864–1866) and an advisor to the reformist President Roye after 1870. In this address, celebrating Liberian independence, Blyden compares his nation's constitution with that of the United States, promoting the benefits of reform and self-government for his fellow citizens.

Our Constitution needs various amendments. It is of very great importance that the utmost care should be exercised in interfering with the fundamental law of the land; but we must not attach to it such mysterious and unapproachable sacredness as to imagine that it must not be interfered with at all, even when circumstances plainly reveal to us the necessity of such interference. The Constitution is only a written document, and, like all written documents . . . it has many errors and omissions. It becomes us, then, who long for the prosperity of our country, calmly and deliberately to examine and consider such defects as may exist in that most important paper, and set ourselves to the work of remedying them to the best of our ability. It is the people's Constitution, and it is the work of the people to correct its deficiencies.

. . .

Another mistake in our Constitution and laws is the arrangement which causes several months to elapse between the election of the President and his inauguration—from May to January—which gives his predecessor, if he be of an opposing party, a long time during which to carry out his party's views. Our arrangement is alarmingly defective, for instead of four months as in the United States, we allow fully eight months to the dissentient minority to carry out their purposes. This is a defect that calls loudly for immediate remedy.

These changes . . . depend upon the will of the people; but we must remember that the people cannot be browbeaten into them. They have to be reasoned with and convinced by patient and persevering argument. The enterprise of persuading and convincing them deserves the utmost exertion of true patriots. The reward with which such efforts will be crowned is no less than the emancipation of the body politic from fatally injurious influences and the introduction among us of salutary conditions of national existence, under which we may go on prospering and to prosper.

. . .

Source: *Black Spokesman: Selected Published Writings of Edward-Wilmot Blyden,* ed. Hollis R. Lynch (London: Frank Cass, 1971), 77–79.

We are engaged here on this coast in a great and noble work. We cannot easily exaggerate the magnitude of the interests involved in the enterprise to which we are committed. Not only the highest welfare of the few thousands who now compose the Republic, but the character of a whole race is implicated in what we are doing. Let us then endeavour to rise up to the "height of this great argument." . . . Something has been done; but what is the little we have achieved compared to what has still to be done! The little of the past dwindles into insignificance before the mighty work of the future.

We are more eagerly watched than we have any idea of. The nations are looking to see whether "order and law, religion and morality, the rights of conscience, the rights of persons, the rights of property, may all be secured," by a government controlled entirely and purely by Negroes. Oh, let us not by any unwise actions compel them to decide in the negative.

. . .

We have made a fair beginning. . . . Here we are, with all our unfavourable antecedents, still, after eighteen years of struggle, an independent nation. We have the germ of an African empire. Let us, fellow-citizens, guard the trust committed to our hands. The tribes in the distant interior are waiting for us. We have made some impression on the coast; . . . we shall make wider and deeper impressions. . . .

▶ **Working with Sources**

1. **What does Blyden seem to have considered the proper relationship between a government and the people it governs?**

2. **Was Blyden right in his observation that the Liberian experiment was "more eagerly watched than we have any idea of"? Why?**

## SOURCE 27.4

# Rudyard Kipling, "The White Man's Burden"

## 1899

The phrase "the white man's burden" and its association with the British writer Rudyard Kipling (1865–1936) is well known today, but few realize that this exhortation was addressed to the American people, who had taken possession of the Philippines in 1899 as a result of the Spanish–American War (1898). Ignoring the independent Philippine government when signing a peace treaty with Spain, the United States occupied Manila and within a year defeated the troops of that government under its elected president Emilio Aguinaldo. US troops captured Aguinaldo in 1901, but a full-scale guerilla war continued—and tactics like the "waterboarding" of captured insurgents were introduced—until 1913. Kipling, however, consistently advocated the position that, as he claimed for the British in India, "East is East and West is West, and never the twain shall meet."

Source: http://www.fordham.edu/halsall/mod/kipling.asp

Take up the White Man's burden—
Send forth the best ye breed—
Go bind your sons to exile
To serve your captives' need;
To wait in heavy harness,
On fluttered folk and wild—
Your new-caught, sullen peoples,
Half-devil and half-child.

Take up the White Man's burden—
In patience to abide,
To veil the threat of terror
And check the show of pride;
By open speech and simple,
An hundred times made plain
To seek another's profit,
And work another's gain.

Take up the White Man's burden—
The savage wars of peace—
Fill full the mouth of Famine
And bid the sickness cease;
And when your goal is nearest
The end for others sought,
Watch sloth and heathen Folly
Bring all your hopes to nought.

Take up the White Man's burden—
No tawdry rule of kings,
But toil of serf and sweeper—
The tale of common things.
The ports ye shall not enter,

The roads ye shall not tread,
Go mark them with your living,
And mark them with your dead.

Take up the White Man's burden—
And reap his old reward:
The blame of those ye better,
The hate of those ye guard—
The cry of hosts ye humour
(Ah, slowly!) toward the light:—
"Why brought he us from bondage,
Our loved Egyptian night?"

Take up the White Man's burden—
Ye dare not stoop to less—
Nor call too loud on Freedom
To cloke your weariness;
By all ye cry or whisper,
By all ye leave or do,
The silent, sullen peoples
Shall weigh your gods and you.

Take up the White Man's burden—
Have done with childish days—
The lightly proferred laurel,
The easy, ungrudged praise.
Comes now, to search your
  manhood
Through all the thankless years
Cold, edged with dear-bought
  wisdom,
The judgment of your peers!

▶ Working
with Sources

1. Why, in Kipling's estimation, should the Americans expect to encounter "sullen" reactions among the Filipinos if they go out of their way to provide "aid"?

2. Why does Kipling consider the "civilizing" of Filipinos to be a burden and a duty, and not merely an opportunity to exploit the native people?

SOURCE 27.5

# Mark Twain, "To the Person Sitting in Darkness"

## 1901

To some extent, Kipling was wrong that "East is East and West is West, and never the twain shall meet," since the preeminent American man of letters Mark Twain (1835–1910) did meet the challenge posed by the poem "The White Man's Burden." Incensed by the blatant racism of Kipling's exhortation—as well as the role of racism in sparking the Civil War in his own United States—Twain lashed out with a brilliant satire of imperialist attitudes. This essay is emblematic of Twain's final years, during which he became increasingly embittered and pessimistic about the chances of "civilization" to overcome barbarism. It is posed in the form of a preacher's address to an American audience. The voice of the huckster-preacher conveys what to him seems the perfect alignment of financial and moral considerations; to his mind, it is just a matter of public relations to obtain the willing incorporation of the Filipinos into this (fraudulent) "Blessings-of-Civilization Trust."

Extending the Blessings of Civilization to our Brother who Sits in Darkness has been a good trade and has paid well, on the whole; and there is money in it yet, if carefully worked—but not enough, in my judgment, to make any considerable risk advisable. The People that Sit in Darkness are getting to be too scarce—too scarce and too shy. And such darkness as is now left is really of but an indifferent quality, and not dark enough for the game. The most of those People that Sit in Darkness have been furnished with more light than was good for them or profitable for us. We have been injudicious.

The Blessings-of-Civilization Trust, wisely and cautiously administered, is a Daisy. There is more money in it, more territory, more sovereignty, and other kinds of emolument, than there is in any other game that is played. But Christendom has been playing it badly of late years, and must certainly suffer by it, in my opinion. She has been so eager to get every stake that appeared on the green cloth, that the People who Sit in Darkness have noticed it—they have noticed it, and have begun to show alarm. They have become suspicious of the Blessings of Civilization. More—they have begun to examine them. This is not well. The Blessings of Civilization are all right, and a good commercial property; there could not be a better, in a dim light. In the right kind of a light, and at a proper distance, with the goods a little out of focus, they furnish this

Source: Mark Twain, *The Family Mark Twain* (New York: Harper & Brothers, 1935), 1390–1391, 1394–1395, 1397, 1398.

desirable exhibit to the Gentlemen who Sit in Darkness:

LOVE,
JUSTICE,
GENTLENESS,
CHRISTIANITY,
PROTECTION TO THE
WEAK,
TEMPERANCE,
LAW AND ORDER,
LIBERTY,
EQUALITY,
HONORABLE DEALING,
MERCY,
EDUCATION,

—and so on.

There. Is it good? Sir, it is pie. It will bring into camp any idiot that sits in darkness anywhere. But not if we adulterate it. It is proper to be emphatic upon that point. This brand is strictly for Export—apparently. *Apparently.* Privately and confidentially, it is nothing of the kind. Privately and confidentially, it is merely an outside cover, gay and pretty and attractive, displaying the special patterns of our Civilization which we reserve for Home Consumption, while inside the bale is the Actual Thing that the Customer Sitting in Darkness buys with his blood and tears and land and liberty. That Actual Thing is, indeed, Civilization, but it is only for Export. Is there a difference between the two brands? In some of the details, yes.

. . .

The more we examine the mistake, the more clearly we perceive that it is going to be bad for the Business. The Person Sitting in Darkness is almost sure to say: "There is something curious about this—curious and unaccountable. There must be two Americas: one that sets the captive free, and one that takes a once-captive's new freedom away from him, and picks a quarrel with him with nothing to found it on; then kills him to get his land."

The truth is, the Person Sitting in Darkness is saying things like that; and for the sake of the Business we must persuade him to look at the Philippine matter in another and healthier way. We must arrange his opinions for him. I believe it can be done; for Mr. Chamberlain has arranged England's opinion of the South African matter, and done it most cleverly and successfully. He presented the facts— some of the facts—and showed those confiding people what the facts meant. He did it statistically, which is a good way. He used the formula: "Twice 2 are 14, and 2 from 9 leaves 35." Figures are effective; figures will convince the elect.

. . .

We must bring him to, and coax him and coddle him, and assure him that the ways of Providence are best, and that it would not become us to find fault with them; and then, to show him that we are only imitators, not originators, we must read the following passage from the letter of an American soldier-lad in the Philippines to his mother, published in Public Opinion, of Decorah, Iowa, describing the finish of a victorious battle:

"WE NEVER LEFT ONE ALIVE. IF ONE WAS WOUNDED, WE WOULD RUN OUR BAYONETS THROUGH HIM."

. . .

Now then, that will convince the Person. You will see. It will restore the Business. Also, it will elect the Master of the Game to the vacant place in the Trinity of our national gods; and there on their high thrones the Three will sit, age after age, in the people's sight, each bearing the Emblem of his service: Washington, the Sword of the Liberator; Lincoln, the Slave's Broken Chains; the Master, the Chains Repaired.

. . .

[And as for a flag for the Philippine Province], it is easily managed. We can have a special one—our states do it: we can have just our usual flag, with the white stripes painted black and the stars replaced by the skull and crossbones.

▶ **Working with Sources**

1. How does Twain incorporate the language of the marketplace into this oration, and why?

2. Is Twain justified in seeing the conquest of the Philippines as a betrayal of American values and historical development?

# PART SIX

# From Three Modernities to One

## 1914–PRESENT

### World War I and the Interwar Period

The first great crisis in the evolution of modern scientific–industrial society was World War I (1914–1918). Although imperial competition in the Balkans triggered the war, there were even stronger forces at work in the background, together with other reasons still hotly contested by historians today.

For our purposes, the most dramatic effect of the war was that the single nineteenth-century pattern of modernity—constitutional and ethnic–linguistic nationalism and scientific–industrial society—splintered into the three subpatterns: capitalism–democracy, socialism–communism, and supremacist nationalism. The countries representing these subpatterns of modernity formed camps that were bitterly hostile to each other:

- Capitalist democracy (most notably in the United States, Britain, France, and parts of Latin America): support for the concepts of freedom (especially the free market), capitalism, and international institutions for maintaining peace

- Communism–socialism (the Soviet Union): professed support for equality over freedom and a command economy controlled from the top

- Supremacist nationalism (Italy, Germany, and Japan): contempt for both democracy and communism, the celebration of racial supremacy and authoritarian/dictatorial rule, a state-controlled economy, and territorial expansion through military conquest

In the period after World War I, the countries representing these three modernities moved in very different directions:

- The democratic victors, Great Britain and France, expanded their colonial empires by acquiring, under the rubric of "mandates," new territories taken from the liquidated Ottoman Empire in the Middle East and the Second German Empire in Africa. Since a variety of ethnolinguistic nationalisms in these territories were forming at the same time, future conflicts were inevitable.

**1908**
Oil discovered in the Middle East

**1914–1918**
World War I

**1919**
Versailles Treaty; League of Nations

**1937–1945**
World War II in China, the Pacific, and (from 1939) Europe

**1947**
Indian and Pakistani independence

**1950–1953**
Korean War

**1911–1912**
Revolution in China; fall of Qing Dynasty

**1917**
Bolshevik Revolution

**1929–1933**
Stock market crash; Great Depression

**1942**
Nazi Final Solution implemented

**1948**
State of Israel founded; first Arab–Israeli War

**1957**
USSR launch of Sputnik; decolonizatio begins in Afr

- In Russia, a small but highly disciplined Communist Party managed to engineer a political takeover, withdraw the nation from the war, and build a communist state: the Union of Soviet Socialist Republics (Soviet Union, or USSR). The Soviet Union achieved full industrial strength in the 1930s.

- The loser of World War I, Germany, together with Italy and Japan (both of which had joined the Allies in hopes of territorial gains), turned toward supremacist nationalism.

## World War II and the Rise of New Nations

In contrast to World War I, World War II was actively planned by the supremacist nationalists and was far less avoidable. Both World War I and the Great Depression effectively ended the global free trade that had characterized the nineteenth century. All countries, including the capitalist democracies, now subscribed to the idea that the future of industry lay in economic "spheres" dominated by one *autarkic*—that is, self-sufficient—industrial power. With the victory of the Allies, the United States and Soviet Union emerged after World War II as the leading examples of the two surviving patterns of modernity: capitalist democracy and socialism–communism. The proponents of each of these patterns competed with the other during the Cold War (1945–1991):

- The first, or "hot," phase, 1945–1962: The United States and Soviet Union surrounded themselves with allies in Europe and Asia and fought one another militarily through proxies—that is, smaller allied states. They also sought to align the new nations emerging in the wake of decolonization into their respective camps. The Cold War climaxed during the Cuban Missile Crisis of 1962.

- The second, "cooling" phase, 1962–1991: During this time, the two nuclear powers reduced tensions ("détente") and agreed on a mechanism to limit, and then to reduce, their nuclear arsenals. But they continued their proxy wars, in particular in Vietnam and Afghanistan.

## Capitalist Democratic Modernity

Perhaps the most significant event that put the United States on course for eventual victory over the Soviet Union in 1991 was the computer revolution—the third industrial revolution after those based on the steam engine (ca. 1800) and steel, electricity, and chemicals (ca. 1865). After fully adapting itself to this revolution, the United States became the unrivaled superpower, deriving its strength from its advanced computer technology, powerful financial services, and unmatched military strength.

# Thinking Like a World Historian

▶ How are the three patterns that emerged after World War I different adaptations to modernity? Despite their marked differences, what common features do they share?

▶ Why, after World War II, was socialism–communism in many ways a more attractive pattern to decolonizing countries than capitalism–democracy?

▶ Why was the United States better able to adapt to technological innovation than the Soviet Union?

▶ How do consumerism and the widespread use of social networking show the emergence of a global culture in the twenty-first century? Can we predict what future patterns will look like?

| 1958 Great Leap Forward in China | 1963 Nuclear Test Ban Treaty | 1966–1969 Cultural Revolution in China | 1979 Shah of Iran overthrown; USSR invades Afghanistan | 1989–1991 Collapse of communism in eastern Europe and Soviet Union |
|---|---|---|---|---|
| 1962 Cuban Missile Crisis | 1965–1973 Vietnam War | 1978 "Four Modernizations" in China | 1985–1989 Perestroika and Glasnost in the USSR | 1989 Tiananmen Square demonstrations in China; Berlin Wall torn down |

| 1990 German unification | 1990–2000 Civil war and ethnic cleansing in former Yugoslavia | 1994 End of apartheid and election of Nelson Mandela as president in South Africa; genocide in Rwanda | 2001 Al-Qaeda attack on United States | 2008–2011 Global financial crisis and economic recession | 2011 Arab Spring uprisings; world population reaches 7 billion |
|---|---|---|---|---|---|

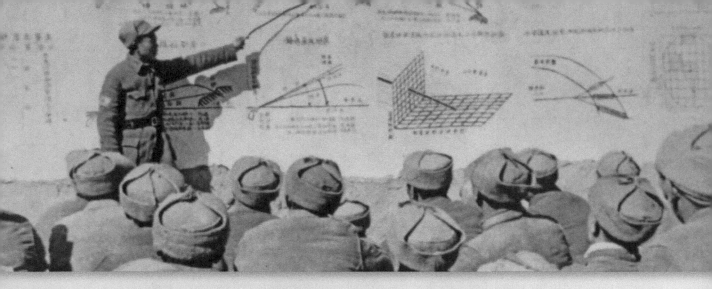

# Chapter 28 1900–1945

# World Wars and Competing Visions of Modernity

P rofessor Minobe seemed rattled. For 30 years he had been Japan's lead- ing jurist and constitutional theorist. His decades of work in the law school of Japan's leading academic institution, Tokyo Imperial University, were celebrated not just in Japan but among scholars throughout the world. Indeed, such was his prestige that he had received a noble rank and occu- pied an honored place in Japan's House of Peers, the upper chamber of its Diet, or parliament. A self-confident, even combative, man, he was not ordi- narily given to suffering fools or meekly taking a dressing down.

But today was different, and only later would Minobe Tatsukichi (1873– 1948) realize what a dramatic turning point it was for him and for the di- rection of Japanese law and politics. On this bleak February day in 1934, his fellow peer Baron Takeo Kikuchi had taken the floor and publicly denounced Minobe's most famous legal theory. Decades earlier, Minobe had posited that the relationship of the emperor to the constitution was one in which the emperor was an organ of the state. More than a generation of Japanese lawyers and scholars had internalized and practiced law according to this "organ theory." But now, the baron had accused Minobe of belittling the emperor's role in Japan's unique *kokutai*, or "national polity/essence." This concept, as

**A WORLD AT WAR, 1900–1945**

North America  Europe  Asia

Africa

South America

Australia

*ABOVE:* **Members of the Chinese People's Liberation Army undergo artillery training.**

we shall see, played a key role in Japanese supremacist nationalism during the 1930s.

Though Minobe defended his position skillfully, reminding his colleagues that to say the emperor was an organ of the state simply means that he rules for the state and not for himself, the damage had been done. Following more attacks in the Diet, Minobe resigned from his position, narrowly escaped being tried for his views, and was nearly assassinated in 1936. Already, however, in their drive to "clarify" the meaning of the "national essence," the cabinet had eliminated all of Minobe's writings and banned his works from study or circulation. Minobe's experience personalizes a struggle to come to grips with new visions of modernity not only in Japan but in much of the world as well.

## Seeing Patterns

▶ Which three patterns of modernity emerged after World War I? How and why did these patterns form?

▶ What were the strengths and flaws of each of the three visions of modernity?

▶ Why did supremacist nationalism disappear in the ashes of World War II?

By the 1930s, the liberal principles of modernity—constitutionalism, capitalism, science, and industry—were being tested in the crucible of the Great Depression and increasingly found wanting. In Japan, these values were already giving way to what we call "supremacist nationalism," offering close parallels to the ideologies of fascism in Italy and Nazism in Germany. In Russia, communism represented another new subpattern of modernity. Other nations—Spain, Portugal, and China, for example—struggled with variations of one or more of these competing ideologies.

In this chapter we will explore how the conflicts of spreading modernity spawned these new visions and how each fared through two world wars and the largest economic depression in history. We will also see how the supremacist nationalism that haunted Minobe, as embodied in the Axis powers, was utterly destroyed by the alliance of communism and capitalist democracy. Their interlude of victory, however, was destined to be short-lived. Within a few years the remaining two divisions of modernity renewed the struggle for dominance against each other under the shadow of potential nuclear annihilation.

## The Great War and Its Aftermath

On July 27, 1914, the nations about to plunge into the abyss of total war the following day represented a host of different conditions on their way to modernity. As we saw in the preceding chapters, some, like Great Britain, Germany, and France, were, along with the United States, among the world leaders in the development of what we call "scientific–industrial society." Others, like Austria-Hungary, the Ottoman Empire, the newly independent Balkan nations, Russia, and even Japan, were at various stages of industrialization, more or less along the lines of the leading powers. In most cases, this latter group had come to this condition somewhat reluctantly, often after violent interactions with the new industrial powers. In terms of political modernity, all of these initial members of what would shortly be known as the Allies and Central powers—with the exception of France—were monarchies, though a number had become modified over the course of the nineteenth century with the addition of constitutions and legislative assemblies. The larger powers were also imperial powers that collectively had reduced much of Asia and effectively the entire

**Total War.** By 1918, large swaths of northern France and Belgium resembled moonscapes from 4 years of destruction and carnage. One of the unluckiest places was the Belgian city of Ypres, which suffered three battles and was all but completely obliterated by war's end.

continent of Africa to the status of colonies. Over the next 4 years, this picture would change so completely that the old order could only be dimly glimpsed through the fog of memory of the diminished numbers who could recall it.

## A Savage War and a Flawed Peace

Time-honored imperial competition, tempered by the need for a balance of power among the major states, dominated Europe during the century following the Napoleonic Wars. This intersected with the two trends of nineteenth-century modernity we have identified in the last several chapters: the political patterns of constitutional nationalism and ethnolinguistic nationalism and the pattern of industrialization. The rise of the new imperialism in the nineteenth century, itself part of the growth of nationalism and industrialism accompanying modernity, carried a logic of its own that seemed destined to disrupt the ongoing efforts of statesmen to adjust the balance of power to ever-shifting political conditions.

**Empires and Nations in the Balkans**   After decades of consensus and revision, modern scholars have begun to emphasize German aspirations for expansion into eastern Europe as one of the prime catalysts for its support of Austria against Serbia in 1914. For its part, France had sought at various times *revanche*—revenge—for Germany's annexing of its "amputated provinces" of Alsace and Lorraine in 1870, though this was tempered by the painful awareness of Germany's superior might. In the first decade of the twentieth century, however, the key to the preservation of peace in Europe was seen as maintaining the balance among the three unequal empires that met in the Balkans.

The shrinking Ottoman Empire, beset by continuing demands from ethnic-nationalist minorities for independence, struggled to survive. The expanding Russian Empire, despite having suffered a defeat at the hands of Japan and an abortive revolution in 1904–1905, was rapidly recovering its aggressiveness, if not its military strength. For its part, the opportunistic Habsburg Empire of Austria-Hungary opposed Russian expansionism but also sought to benefit from Ottoman weakness. Germany had largely replaced Great Britain as the protector of the Ottomans and assisted the latter in strengthening their army. Though it had taken

Mediterranean territories from the Ottomans, Britain still had a stake in keeping the rest of the Ottoman Empire in existence, as did the other powers, all of whom feared the results of a territorial scramble if the Ottoman Empire collapsed altogether. Hence, as there had been in China during the scramble for concessions of the late 1890s, there was a rough community of interest aimed at strengthening the Ottoman Empire, whose leaders were themselves seeking to improve their military posture.

One unresolved ethnic-nationalist issue of concern to the three empires was Bosnia-Herzegovina. After the Balkan war of 1878, Austria-Hungary had become the territory's administrator—but not sovereign—as a compromise with the Ottomans, who were unable to keep Serbs, Croats, and Muslims apart. When Russia renewed its support for Serb ethnic nationalism in the Balkans after 1905, Austria-Hungary felt compelled to assume sovereignty of Bosnia-Herzegovina in a protective move in 1908. This in return offered Russia support for its demand for open shipping through the Bosporus. Britain and Germany, however, forced Russia to withdraw this demand. Russia, committed to a policy of pan-Slavism—support for the aspirations of Slavs everywhere—avenged itself by stirring up Serb nationalists. On June 28, 1914, members of a Bosnian Serb nationalist group assassinated the Austrian heir to the throne, Franz Ferdinand, and his wife while they toured the Bosnian city of Sarajevo. This assassination began the tragic slide of the two rival alliances that maintained the balance of power into the cataclysm of World War I. Yet even this occurred only after a month of intense diplomacy and increasing desperation among most of the politicians involved. In the end, each country's perceived military necessities were invoked to trump any diplomatic solution to the crisis.

**The Early Course of the War**    In contrast with past conflicts, this war was no longer limited and localized but comprehensive from the start: **total war**. In addition, the contingency plans of the combatants' general staffs in many cases relied on precise timing and speedy mobilization of their forces. Here, the most dramatic example was that of Germany. In order to avoid a two-front war, Germany, with its allies Austria-Hungary and the Ottoman Empire (the Central powers), had to defeat France before Russia's massive army was fully mobilized. The German Schlieffen Plan therefore called for a massive assault on northern France through Belgium that would take Paris in 6 weeks, while trapping and isolating the Allied armies seeking to invade Alsace and Lorraine, taken by Germany after the Franco–Prussian War of 1870.

Though the German plan came close to succeeding, it ultimately failed after the desperate French–British victory in the first Battle of the Marne in early September 1914, a more rapid Russian mobilization than expected, and a poor showing by the Austrians against Russia. After several months of seesaw fighting along

**Total war:** A type of warfare in which all the resources of the nation—including all or most of the civilian population—are marshaled for the war effort. As total war became elaborated, all segments of society were increasingly seen as legitimate targets for the combatants.

| 1908 Oil discovered in Middle East | | 1915–1916 Massacre of Armenians in Ottoman Empire | 1919 Versailles Treaty; founding of League of Nations | 1929 Stock market crash; Great Depression begins |
| | 1914–1918 World War I | | | |

1911–1912 Revolution in China; fall of Qing Dynasty

1917 Balfour Declaration promises Jews a homeland in Palestine

1917 Bolshevik Revolution

1922 Mussolini's March on Rome

1931 Japanese annexation of Manchuria

1932–1945 New Deal in United States

1936–1939 Spanish Civil War

1937 Rape of Nanjing

1942 Hitler implements the Final Solution: genocide of European Jews

1929–1932 Collectivization of agriculture in Soviet Union

1933 Hitler becomes chancellor in Germany

1937–1945 World War II in China and the Pacific

1939–1945 World War II in Europe, the Mediterranean, and North Africa

the lines of the initial German advance into France, the Germans and the French and British dug in. By 1915 the two sides were forced to conduct grinding trench warfare in northeastern France and an inconclusive war in the east.

The Germans, with superior firepower and mobility, were able to keep the Russians at bay and inflicted heavy losses on their troops—many of whom marched into battle without weapons, being expected to pick them up off their dead comrades. For its part, the Ottoman Empire suffered a crushing Russian invasion in the Caucasus, prompting it to carry out a wholesale massacre of its Armenian minority, which was alleged to have helped in the invasion. From official Turkish documents published in 2005 it can be concluded that the number of Armenians killed was close to 1 million. This planned massacre, the one large-scale atrocity of the war, still requires a full accounting today and is hotly debated by scholars, lawyers, and politicians.

> "Those three battalions [2,500 men] who went over were practically annihilated. Every man went to his death or got wounded without flinching. Yet in this war, nothing will be heard about it, the papers have glowing accounts of great British success."
>
> —British soldier Reginald Leetham, on the Battle of the Somme (July–November 1916)

As the war dragged on, both camps sought to recruit new countries to their sides. Italy, Greece, and Romania entered on the Allied side with the hope of gaining territory from Austria-Hungary and the Ottomans; Bulgaria joined the Central powers in the service of its own territorial ambitions. Japan declared war on Germany in 1914 as part of a previous alliance with Britain but used its occupation of German territories in the Pacific and China as a step toward expanding its own empire. The Allies also recruited volunteers from among their dominions and colonies in considerable numbers, some 800,000 from India alone. Thus, with soldiers from the mostly white dominions of Australia and New Zealand, as well as the African and Asian colonies of Britain and France fighting and dying in the trenches, the war became a true world war. With the token entrance of China in 1917 and the pivotal entrance of the United States that same year, the war now involved every major state in the world.

**The Turning Point: 1917**    By early 1917 the ever-intensifying slaughter took its first political toll. In March 1917, tsarist Russia collapsed in the face of horrendous casualties, crippled industry, extensive labor unrest, government ineptitude, and general internal weakness. The February Revolution (actually in March, so called because it took place during February in the old-style Julian calendar still in use in Russia at the time) forced Tsar Nicholas II to abdicate and created a provisional government. The new social-democratic government committed itself to carrying on the war, which now grew even more unpopular and impossible for Russia to manage. The communist Bolshevik Party of Vladimir Lenin (1870–1924), now liberated from persecution by the provisional government, steadily campaigned against continuing the war and in early November (October in the Julian calendar) launched a takeover of the government in the capital of Petrograd—as St. Petersburg had been renamed at the beginning of the war.

Seizing the reins of government, the Bolsheviks began tortuous negotiations with the Germans, which resulted in the disastrous Treaty of Brest-Litovsk in March 1918. Roughly one-third of the Russian Empire's population, territory, and resources were handed over to the Germans in return for Russia's peaceful withdrawal from the conflict. The Germans had now come close to achieving the secret war goal of the Supreme Army Command (*Oberste Heeresleitung*, OHL): the creation of *Lebensraum* (living space) for Germany in the industrialized European part of Russia.

**Supporting the Empire.** The colonies were drawn into the conflicts of their rulers. Over three-quarters of a million Indian troops such as the ones shown here fought with the British during World War I.

The United States had declared neutrality at the outset of the war, but despite President Woodrow Wilson's plea to Americans to stay "neutral in thought" as well as action, the course of the war had shifted US opinion decidedly toward the Allied side. The German violation of Belgian neutrality in the opening days of the war and extensive German use of the new technology of the submarine swung Americans toward a profound distaste for German actions. The German torpedoing and sinking of the British liner *Lusitania* on May 7, 1915, cost the lives of more than 100 Americans and brought the United States to the brink of war. Germany drew back for a while but then, in early 1917, resumed its unrestricted submarine warfare. Wilson had no choice but to ask Congress to declare war, which it did on April 6, 1917.

The entrance of the United States added the critical resources needed by the Allies to ultimately win the war. More important, Wilson's war aims, embodied in his war address to Congress and later in his Fourteen Points, sought to transform the conflict from one of failed diplomacy and territorial gain to a war to make "the world . . . safe for democracy." He called for freedom of the seas, the rights of neutral powers, self-determination for all peoples, and peace "without annexations or indemnities." These new causes not only represented American goals but now were presented as the Allies' war aims as well. For peoples in all the world's empires yearning for independence and self-determination, it appeared, briefly at least, that one side decisively championed their desires.

It was not until early 1918, however, that American troops began to land in France in appreciable numbers. This coincided with a spring offensive mounted by Germany. Bolstered by the addition of troops from the now-peaceful Russian front, the Germans threw everything they had at the Allies and once again came close to seizing Paris. But the new American troops in France gave the Allies the advantage they needed to stop the German effort, which soon collapsed. By June, more than 1 million Americans had arrived; by September, nearly 2 million; and by the end of fighting in November, 4 million more Americans were in various stages of progress to the western front. Faced with these new conditions and reeling from the Allies' September counteroffensive, which now threatened to advance into Germany, the Germans agreed to an armistice on November 11, 1918.

**The Versailles Peace**    As the staggering war toll sank in, the Allies settled down to make peace. About 20 million soldiers and civilians were dead, and 21 million were wounded. Military deaths were 5 million for the Allies and 4 million for the Central powers. Many more millions perished in the world's worst influenza pandemic, abetted by the massive transportation of goods and soldiers at war's end. The settlement, signed at Versailles on June 28, 1919—the fifth anniversary of the assassination of Franz Ferdinand—has been described unflatteringly as a "victor's peace."

The German, Austro-Hungarian, and Ottoman Empires were all dismantled, and new nation-states were created in their stead. Germany lost its overseas colonies, Alsace-Lorraine, and West Prussia. The Allies declared Germany responsible for the war and subjected it to substantial military restrictions and huge reparation payments. France did not prevail with plans to divide Germany again into its pre-1871 components but succeeded in acquiring temporary custody of the Saar province with its coal reserves and steel factories as a guarantee for the payment of war reparations. For a long time, historians considered the Allied-imposed reparations excessive, but more recent research has come to the conclusion that Germany, which was not destroyed by war, had the industrial-financial capacity to pay.

**League of Nations:** An international body of 58 states created as part of the Versailles Treaty and functioning between 1919 and 1946 that sought to ensure world peace.

A new supranational **League of Nations** was entrusted with the maintenance of peace. But since one of its clauses required collective military action in case of aggression, the US Senate refused ratification, rejecting this infringement on American sovereignty. Altogether, the Versailles peace was deeply flawed. Instead of binding Germany into a common western European framework, the Allies actually encouraged it to go it alone by flanking it in the east with small and weak countries that could be dominated in the future (see Map 28.1).

## America First: The Beginnings of a Consumer Culture and the Great Depression

The United States emerged from the war as by far the strongest among the Allied democracies. It had turned from a debtor country into a creditor country; a majority of Americans now lived in nonrural environments; and the war economy shifted relatively easily into a sustained peacetime expansion. Far less hampered by old traditions than its European counterparts, it espoused modernity with a brusque enthusiasm, although its writers and intellectuals were often all too aware of modernity's contradictions.

**Modernity Unfolding in the United States**    Increased mechanization in industries such as construction materials, automobile assembly lines, and electrical appliance manufacturing spurred the economic expansion. A new dream arose among Americans: to move from countryside to city and to own a house (with indoor plumbing), car, refrigerator, radio, and telephone. Once in the city, during the Roaring Twenties, as the 1920s came to be called, Americans wanted to be

**MAP 28.1** Europe, the Middle East, and North Africa in 1914 and 1923.

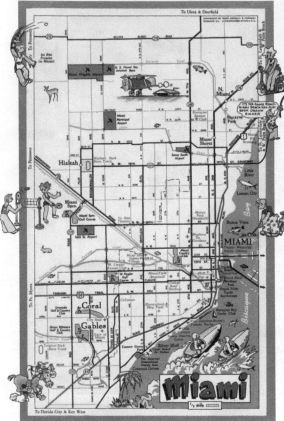

**A Vision of American Modernity.** This detail from a ca. 1930 Gulf Gasoline "Florida Info Map" vividly captures the vision of the American pattern of modernity—miles of roads and highways stretching in all directions, ample leisure opportunities, and a natural environment where the sun always shines.

entertained. A remarkable efflorescence of popular culture accompanied the rising urban prosperity. City and small-town dwellers alike were caught up in the mania of the movies, which, after 1927, came with sound. Americans frequented ballrooms to experiment with a wide range of dance steps and to listen to bands playing popular tunes. Jazz music in a large variety of styles found avid listeners. One could now listen to recorded sound on convenient 78-rpm records played on gramophones. The film industry of Hollywood and a recording industry came into being, churning out "hits," as their popular products came to be called, for the entertainment of the new consumers. And the rapid development of the radio now allowed news and entertainment to enter every household that could afford a set.

**The New Woman**  The Nineteenth Amendment of 1920 gave American women the right to vote, enormously expanding the promise of constitutional nationalism by half the population. In addition to winning political rights, American women heightened their social profile. Many colleges and universities went coed, although women often majored in education to become teachers, or in home economics to become good housewives for the husbands they met at school. Alternatively, they became secretaries skilled in shorthand and typing or nurses in hospitals. Indeed, the typewriter, developed in the late nineteenth century, directly contributed to the shift from secretaries being mostly men to overwhelmingly female. Its ease of operation and speed of copying and reproduction (through the use of carbon paper) was ideally suited to what were perceived to be women's skills and abilities. Similarly, women swiftly dominated the new occupation of telephone operator as the new century advanced.

For people of color, however, the situation was far different. Black women, if they were not agricultural laborers, rarely were able to become more than domestic servants or laundry workers in the growing urban economy. In larger segregated areas with more diversified economies, however, African American women often found similar kinds of opportunities as white women, though far more limited in scope and availability. Hence, although emancipation was expanding for white women, it clearly remained gendered, while the situation for black women continued to be additionally hampered by racism.

**High Artistic Creativity**  American intellectuals, writers, and artists viewed consumer and pop culture modernity with mixed feelings. On the one hand, they hailed what they viewed as the progress of liberal values. But on the other hand they were often uneasy about what they perceived as an increasing superficiality and materialism in modernity, furthered by ads, fashions, and fads. After World War I, the ambiguities of modernity engendered a veritable explosion of creativity in American culture.

The shattered illusions of the pre–world war era and search for a new beginning in modernity fueled much of this creativity. An entire cohort of artists and intellectuals viewed themselves as belonging to a "lost generation," referring to the sense that a generation that had lost its best years of life, or even life altogether, to a senseless world war. For African Americans, a new cultural touchstone was the Harlem Renaissance, featuring the leading innovators in jazz and literature (see "Patterns Up Close"). Few later authors plumbed modernity with the breadth of education as these "modernists" did, analyzing its contradictions, exposing its follies, articulating its inner emotional tensions in a "stream of consciousness," or offering counter-models of spirituality, naturalness, Greek classicism, or Chinese monism. Not only did the United States set the pace for mass culture; it also provided many of the literary tools to grapple with modernity and attempt to understand it, either by loathing it or by living with it critically.

**Business and Labor**    Just as much energy characterized American business. Presidents Harding, Coolidge, and Hoover along with the Congress exercised a minimum of political control, illustrated by Harding's campaign slogan "Less government in business and more business in government." While business boomed, trade and industrial unions stagnated. The American Federation of Labor (AFL), founded in 1886, was the largest trade union pushing for improved labor conditions. But, in contrast to European labor unions, it was always hampered by the fact that its members were unskilled workers of many ethnic, linguistic, and religious backgrounds and were therefore difficult to organize. Business easily quashed widespread strikes for the right to unionize in 1919. An anti-immigration hysteria followed, with laws that cut immigration by half. The hysteria, mixed with anticommunism, climaxed in 1927 with the trial of Ferdinando Nicola

**Lynching.** Outside the South, Indiana was the state that experienced the greatest surge in racial tensions in the period immediately after World War I. In 1925, the governor and half the state assembly were members of the Ku Klux Klan, as were about 30 percent of the state's white population. In this photo from August 1930, a crowd gathers to gawk at Tom Shipp and Abram Smith, two African American men who were lynched by a mob in Marion, Indiana, for allegedly committing robbery and rape.

## Patterns Up Close | The Harlem Renaissance and the African Diaspora

**Langston Hughes.** The noted poet and writer Langston Hughes first emerged on the literary scene during the Harlem Renaissance and went on to influence the shaping of African and African American literary identity for decades afterwards.

As we have seen, the modern period up to the early twentieth century saw some of the largest migrations in human history. Such "diasporas"—a term originally used to describe the scattering of the Jews around Europe, the Middle East, and North Africa—not only threw those affected into new and sometimes hostile environments but over time also created rich and complex cultural conditions in which new generations struggled to forge their identities. In the case of African Americans in the 1920s, now several generations removed from slavery yet still hobbled by legal and social impediments, a new and vital cultural touchstone was the Harlem Renaissance.

Growing—though still severely limited—educational opportunities, a rapid increase in urbanization stemming from the "Great Migration" of rural southern African Americans seeking work in northern factory cities during World War I, and a new political assertiveness in the face of racism all contributed to a cultural explosion in a wide array of areas. As the largest African American enclave in America's largest city, New York, Harlem became the most vital black cultural center. Jazz and its offshoots came to dominate popular tastes; young people of all ethnicities sought to take up the latest dances from "uptown"; and writers such as Claude McKay (1889–1948), Langston Hughes (1902–1967), James Weldon Johnson (1871–1938), Zora Neale Hurston (1891–1960), and dozens of others achieved national and international recognition on an unprecedented scale.

Sacco and Bartolomeo Vanzetti, two Italian anarchist immigrants who were convicted for murder on contradictory evidence and executed.

**The Backlash**  The antiforeigner and anticommunist hysteria was part of a larger unease with modernity. Fundamentalist religion, intolerance toward Catholics and Jews, and fear and violence directed at African Americans rose visibly. The revival of the Ku Klux Klan was at the center of repeated waves of lynchings in the South and attempts to control the local politics of a number of states, most prominently Indiana. The Klan remained a powerful force in the South and Midwest until World War II.

The most startling offenses against the modern principles of liberty and equality, however, came from ideologues wrapping themselves in the mantle of modern science. Researchers at the leading private universities lent respectability to the

For many of these writers, a vision of Africa as their homeland hovered over their work. Though relatively few (such as Langston Hughes) actually visited Africa, its resonance as the center of their self-defined identity was powerful, and the legacy of this vision remains so even today. To be African in this sense was to be beyond the history of slavery and oppression and to be part of larger and richer collective history extending to the first human beings. Not surprisingly, this solidarity was expressed in the Pan-African movement of which the educator, activist, and cofounder of the NAACP W. E. B. DuBois (1868–1963) was a prominent popularizer. Indeed, during the 1920s the most popular mass movement among African Americans was the Universal Negro Improvement Association led by Marcus Garvey (1887–1940), which sought to help those of the African diaspora repatriate to the continent with a view to creating a strong and prosperous Africa for the Africans.

For its part, the Harlem Renaissance also had a profound effect on people of African descent in places far removed from the United States. Drawing from the revolutionary history of Haiti as well as the poetry of Hughes, African expatriates in Paris in the 1930s championed a cultural movement called Négritude, which called for a new pride in African history, culture, and "blackness" itself. Influenced by such writers as Aimé Césaire (1913–2008) and Léopold Senghor (1906–2001), the movement was powerfully influential in French-speaking Africa. Senghor himself became Senegal's first president and served for two decades. Through it all, however, these writers ultimately wrestled with a timeless, universal question, now burdened with all the urgency of modernity: "Who am I?"

## Questions

- What were some of the factors that led to the Harlem Renaissance emerging in the 1920s, instead of some other time?

- Why were the questions these writers raised about identity so important to them? Why was this especially so in the new "modern" age?

pseudoscience of **eugenics**, conceptualizing an ideal of a "Nordic" race and searching for ways to produce more athletic, blond, and blue-eyed Americans. Foundations such as the Carnegie Endowment and businessmen such as Henry Ford financed research on how to prevent the reproduction of genetically "inferior" races. California and other states passed laws that allowed for the sterilization of nearly 10,000 patients—mostly women (black and white)—in state mental hospitals, and the Supreme Court in 1927 upheld these laws. Ironically, some of the practices that would inspire Hitler and the Nazis were already quietly put in place during the 1920s in the United States and actually regarded by some as progressive.

**Eugenics:** The discredited idea of the hereditary breeding of better human beings by genetic control.

**The Great Depression**    The Roaring Twenties came to a screeching halt in 1929, when saturation of the market for consumer goods behind high tariff walls during the later 1920s led to falling profit rates. Many of the wealthy had begun to shift their money from investments in manufacturing to speculation on the stock market. In addition, stocks began to be seen as a viable outlet for ordinary investors thanks to widespread margin borrowing with little money down. As long as the market boomed, investors made money, but if stocks went down, the margin calls went out, and investors could be wiped out.

By the late 1920s, a general slowdown in production shifted attention to unsustainable debt levels. Farmers were particularly deep in debt, having borrowed to mechanize while speculating wrongly on a continuation of high prices for commodities. In October 1929, the speculators panicked, selling their stock for pennies on the dollar. The panic rippled through both the finance and manufacturing sectors until it burst into a full-blown cascade. As banks began calling in loans at home and abroad, the panic swiftly became a worldwide crisis: the Great Depression of 1929–1933. Harrowing levels of unemployment and poverty put the American system of capitalist democratic modernity to a severe test.

Americans largely blamed their probusiness president, Herbert Hoover (in office 1929–1933), for failing to manage the crisis, and in 1932 they elected Franklin D. Roosevelt (in office 1933–1945). Hoover's approach had been one that previous administrations had turned to in times of economic crisis: cut government spending, raise tariffs to protect US industries, and let market forces correct themselves. But such measures only made things worse, while the Smoot-Hawley Tariff of 1930, with the highest tariff rates in American history, encouraged retaliatory tariffs in other countries and discouraged world commerce, thus contributing to a worldwide economic collapse.

Under Roosevelt's prodding, Congress immediately enacted what he called the "New Deal," in which the government engaged in deficit spending to enact a number of measures designed to help the unemployed and revive business and agriculture. One showpiece of the New Deal was the Tennessee Valley Authority, a government-owned corporation for the economic development of large parts of the southeastern United States particularly hard hit by the Depression. In addition, a social safety net was created for the first time, with unemployment benefits and the Social Security Act. Finally, a Securities and Exchange Commission (SEC) was created in 1934 to supervise and enforce regulations governing the stock market in order to prevent a number of the practices that had led to the collapse of 1929.

In 1937, however, a Congress frightened by the deficit slackened efforts to reduce unemployment, while the Supreme Court declared several of the New Deal programs unconstitutional. The result was a new slump, from which the economy finally recovered only with America's entry into World War II.

## Great Britain and France: Slow Recovery and Troubled Empires

While the impact of World War I on the United States was relatively small, Britain and France suffered severely. A lack of finances hampered the recovery, as did the enormous debt both countries took on during the war. Conservative politicians relinquished the state capitalism of the war period and returned to politics favorable to private investors, without, however, allowing for the same uncontrolled speculations as in the United States. Although socialist politicians gained in importance, they did not succeed in improving working-class conditions or the safety net. Britain benefited from the discovery of oil in its mandates in the Middle East. Accordingly, the demands of the League of Nations mandate system, in which the colonies were to be prepared for future independence, were not pursued vigorously by either France or Britain.

**Weak British Recovery**   As the economy shifted from state control during the war back to market capitalism, industry was still in a leading role; but Britain was also heavily dependent on world trade, carried by its merchant fleet. Unfortunately for Britain, world trade declined dramatically after the war. In addition, the country owed a war debt of $4.3 billion to the United States for war materiel, which the United States insisted on receiving back (relenting only during the Depression). Since much of Britain's ability to repay these debts rested upon Germany's ability to pay its reparations, the entire European economic system remained fragile throughout the 1920s.

With the restructuring of Germany's debts under the Dawes Plan in 1924, some stability finally came to the international capital markets. Still, close to half of the annual British budgets in the interwar period went to paying off the war debt. In this situation, industrial investments were low and unemployment was high, dipping below 10 percent of the workforce only once during the 1920s. In addition, business lowered wages, causing labor to respond with a massive general strike in 1926. The strike collapsed after only 9 days, but business, without capital to make industry competitive again, did not benefit either. The British economy remained stagnant.

The dominant conservatives in the government could not bring themselves in the 1930s to accept deficit spending. At a minimum, however, they went off the gold standard and devalued the currency to make exports competitive again. World trade, of course, had declined; but by lowering tariffs within the empire, Britain created the equivalent of the **autarky** that Nazi Germany and militaristic Japan were dreaming of with their planned conquests. A semblance of prosperity returned to the country in the 1930s.

**France: Moderate Recovery**   Together with Russia, France suffered devastating human losses and destruction of property during the war. For every 10 men of working age, two were dead, one was disabled, and three were recuperating from their wounds. The population drop and consequent lack of replacement during the interwar period prompted some French observers to talk about the "hollow years." Alsace-Lorraine, the most important industrial region and the territory that France desperately wanted to recover from the Germans, was now a wasteland. The war had been fought with war materiel borrowed from the United States and Great Britain ($5 billion), to be paid for after the war. Some money for the reconstruction of industry and housing came from increased taxes, German

**Down and Out in Wales.** The prosperity of the 1930s was largely limited to southern England. Most of the rest of the British Isles, such as this unemployed miner in Wales, who here perhaps consoled by his two children, were largely left out.

**Autarky:** The condition of economic independence and self-sufficiency as state policy.

reparations, and taxes from German provinces occupied after the war. But reconstruction could be completed only in 1926–1929, when taxes were once more increased and Germany finally made full reparation payments.

Although French governments were dependent on coalitions among parties and therefore less stable, labor was more often than not represented in the governments. France did not suffer a traumatic general strike like England did, and even though it also returned to the gold standard (1928–1936), it wisely avoided the prewar parity, thereby making the low wages for its workers a bit more bearable. Since it had to reconstruct so much from the ground up, France modernized more successfully in many ways than Britain in the interwar period.

Thanks to its successful reconstruction, France weathered the Depression until 1931. Even then, conservative politicians found the idea of deficit spending as a way to get out of the Depression too counterintuitive. Instead, like the Hoover administration in America, they slashed government spending and refused to devalue the currency. Unrest in the population and rapidly changing governments were the consequences which in 1933–1934 made supremacist nationalism an attractive model, especially for business, which was afraid of labor strife. When fascist–communist street fighting broke out in Paris, the Communist Party initiated the formation of a Popular Front coalition with the Socialist Party and others (1936–1938). Although this coalition prevented a further slide into supremacist nationalism, it was too short-lived to allow the centrist middle-class core to broaden, with disastrous consequences for France's ability to resist Hitler in World War II.

**Colonies and Mandates**    The carefree consumer modernity in France and Britain during the 1920s contrasted sharply with the harsh reality of sustaining expensive colonial empires covering much of the world's land mass. After World War I, the British Empire grew by 2 million square miles to 14 million, or one-quarter of the earth's surface, adding 13 million more to its 458 million subjects, or one-quarter of the world population. The French Empire at the same time measured 5 million square miles, with a population of 113 million. Although the wisdom of maintaining empires was widely debated in the interwar period, in view of increased subsidies that had to be given to many of the colonies, conservatives held fast to the prestige that square mileage was presumed to bestow on its holders. Defense of these far-flung empires, interpreted as the "strategic interest" of the colonial powers, dominated the policies of Britain and France toward their dependencies and mandates during the interwar period (see Map 28.2).

The most important area strategically for both the British and the French after World War I was the Middle East. Under the postwar peace terms, the British and French had received the Arab provinces of the former Ottoman Empire (other than Egypt and Sudan, acquired in 1881) as *mandates*—that is, as territories to be prepared for independence. After a British geologist had in 1908 discovered oil in southwestern Iran, however, Britain and France put a high premium on their new Middle Eastern imperial possessions. Neither was in a hurry to guide its mandates to independent nationhood.

**Twice-Promised Lands**    As would be expected, Arab leaders were strongly opposed to the British and French mandates. Nationalism was on the rise, ironically

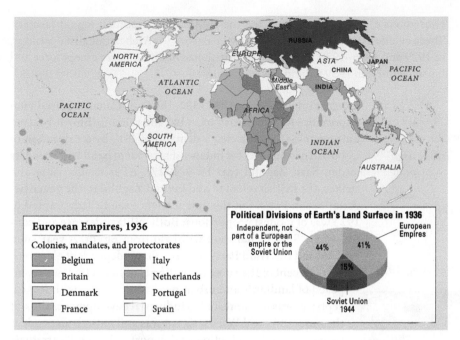

MAP 28.2 **European Empires, 1936.**

encouraged by the British during the war as they were searching for regional allies against the Ottomans. Their agent, T. E. Lawrence (1888–1935), the famous "Lawrence of Arabia," fluent in Arabic and Islamic customs, helped the members of a prominent family, the Hashemites from Mecca in western Arabia, to assume leadership of the Arabs for a promised national kingdom in Syria and Palestine in the so-called McMahon–Hussein correspondence of 1915–1916.

Since the British, seeking to rally support among Jews in Britain as well as Germany, Poland, and Russia, also promised the Jews a "national home" in Palestine in the Balfour Declaration of 1917, Arab nationalism was stymied even before it could unfold. The French ended a short-lived Arab-declared kingdom in 1920 in Damascus, and the British moved the Hashemites into their mandates of Iraq and Transjordan in 1921, in accordance with the Sykes–Picot agreement (1916) concerning the imperial division of the Middle East between the Allies. As Iraq was divided by majority Shiites and minority Sunnis, the British inaugurated a policy of divide and rule in their Middle Eastern mandates, while dangling the prospect of eventual independence in front of their populations.

In Palestine, the contradiction between the promises to Arabs and Jews during the war forced Britain to build an expensive direct administration under a high commissioner. In 1920, Palestine was inhabited by nearly 670,000 Arabs and 65,000 Jews. Many religious Jews had arrived as refugees from anti-Semitic riots, or pogroms, in Russia in the early 1880s and 1890s and the difficult postwar years in eastern Europe. When the Austrian Jewish journalist Theodor Herzl (1860–1904) made ethnic nationalism the ideology of secular Jews, early pioneers of **Zionism**, as secular Jewish nationalism was called, began to arrive as well. A Jewish National Fund collected money from Jews worldwide to buy land from willing Palestinian absentee landlords residing in Beirut and Jerusalem. As a

Zionism: The belief, based on the writings of Theodor Herzl, that European Jews—and by extension all Jews everywhere—were entitled to a national homeland corresponding to the territory of Biblical Israel. It grew into a form of ethnolinguistic-religious nationalism and ultimately led to the formation of the state of Israel in 1948.

consequence, Jewish settlers evicted the landlords' Palestinian tenant farmers. These evictions were the root cause of two Palestinian–Arab nationalist uprisings, in 1929 and 1936–1939, for which the British had no real answer except force and belated efforts in 1939 to limit Jewish immigration.

"We want it to be known—total independence is our goal! If only 'they' [the English] leave our nation! We could surpass Japan in civilization. Return to your country! Pick up your belongings! What audacity and rudeness. You are a true calamity! Do you have to stick to us like glue?"

—Popular Egyptian song, 1919

**Secularizing Turkey.** Atatürk was a committed educational reformer who sought to create a "public culture," and he was advised by the famous American philosopher of education John Dewey (1859–1952). Here, in 1928, dressed in a Western-style suit and necktie, he gives a lesson on the new Turkish alphabet, a variant of the Latin alphabet, whose use was mandated throughout the republic.

**Egypt and Turkey**   After 1882, the Suez Canal acquired vital importance for the British in India, and relinquishing it became unthinkable. They rejected a demand in 1919 by a delegation of Egyptian nationalists for independence out of hand and exiled its leader, Saad Zaghlul (ca. 1859–1927). After deadly riots and strikes, the British relented and invited Zaghlul to the peace negotiations in Paris. But the independence the British granted in 1923 was of modest proportions: Both military defense and control of the Suez Canal were withheld from Egypt. A year later, Zaghlul and the Wafd Party won the first independent elections, with 90 percent of the vote. The ruling class, as in Iraq, was composed of landlords and urban professionals and, with few exceptions, was uninterested in industrial development. Thus, at the onset of World War II, Egypt was still entirely dependent on agricultural production and exports, though its strategic position was absolutely vital to the British Empire.

The severe punishment meted out to the Ottoman Empire by the Allies provoked the rise of local grassroots resistance groups in Anatolia. These groups merged under the leadership of General Mustafa Kemal "Atatürk" ("Father of the Turks," 1881–1938) into a national liberation movement, driving out the Greeks from western Anatolia, occupying one-half of Armenia (the other half was taken by the new Soviet Union), and ending the Ottoman sultanate/caliphate (1921–1924) altogether. Atatürk, the son of an Ottoman customs official in Salonika in what is now Greece, was among the relative few of the empire's militarily successful officers in World War I, most notably in his defense of Gallipoli against the British. Atatürk was the driving force behind the creation of a modern, secular Turkey that was able to stand up against the European powers.

Although he was authoritarian, Atatürk saw to it that the new Turkish parliament remained open to pluralism. Parliament adopted the French model of separation of state and religion, European family law, the Latin alphabet, the Western calendar, metric weights and measures, modern clothing, and women's suffrage. During the Depression, Atatürk's economic advisors launched *étatism*, the Turkish version of deficit spending. State capitalism, rather than private domestic or foreign capital, provided for the construction of steel and consumer goods factories, including textile plants. Both modernism and étatism showed only modest successes by 1939, and the rural masses in Anatolia remained mired in small-scale self-sufficiency farming and wedded to religious tradition. But the foundation was laid in Turkey not only for a Westernized ruling class but also for a much larger urbanized middle class.

**Indian Demands for Independence** The compromises negotiated during the Versailles Peace Conference, as we have seen, had a profound effect on the colonial world. Nowhere was this truer than in India. In April 1919, frustrated by a British crackdown on political protest, a large crowd gathered in a walled square in the Sikhs' sacred city of Amritsar. The British responded with a wholesale slaughter of the assembled men, women, and children by an elite unit of Gurkha troops. As the international furor over this "Amritsar Massacre" raged, the British, giving in to the inevitable, reformed the Indian Legislative Assembly by enlarging the portion of elected members to nearly three-quarters and the property-based franchise to 5 million, out of a population of 250 million. The Indian National Congress was infuriated by this minimal improvement and called for full self-rule (Hindi *swaraj*), urging nonviolent noncooperation, which, among other measures, called for a refusal to pay the land tax, for a boycott of British goods, and for people to spin and weave textiles at home.

Inevitably, civil disturbances accompanied the congress's push for self-rule. Mohandas Gandhi (1869–1948), a trained lawyer and the most prominent advocate of nonviolence, suspended the push in 1921. The leaders—lawyers, doctors, journalists, and teachers—exited the cities and, with the help of a large influx of party workers, scoured the countryside preaching nonviolent civil disobedience. It was during the 1920s and 1930s that the National Congress transformed itself from a small Westernized elite into a mass party.

In 1929, the new Labour government in Britain explored the possibility of giving India dominion status, but there was strong opposition from the other parties. When Labour could not deliver, Gandhi responded with the demand for complete independence and, on March 12, 1930, embarked on his famous 24-day Salt March to the sea in order for his followers to pan their own salt, which the government refused to free from taxation. Crowds in other places also marched to the sea. Disturbances accompanied the marches, and in a massive crackdown, with 100,000 arrests, the government succeeded in repressing the National Congress.

Nevertheless, after lengthy discussions the British government in 1935 passed the Government of India Act, which devolved all political functions except defense and foreign affairs to India. The members of the National Congress were unhappy, however, because of the decentralized structure of the reformed Indian government and particularly because the act recognized the Muslim League of Muhammad Ali Jinnah (1876–1948), not the Congress, as the representative of the Muslims. The British viceroy further inflamed matters in 1939 when he declared India in support of the British World War II effort, without even asking the Congress. As in Egypt and Iraq, there was a profound reluctance by the Western powers to relinquish colonialism. The legacy of this unwillingness would haunt the capitalist democracies well into the later twentieth century.

**Swaraj:** Literally, "self-rule" [*swa-RAJ*]. Gandhi interpreted this term as meaning "direct democracy," while the Congress Party identified it with complete independence from Great Britain.

**Gandhi Leading the Salt March.** Perhaps the most famous act of civil disobedience in Gandhi's career was the Salt March in 1930 to protest the British salt monopoly in India. It was a perfect embodiment of Gandhi's belief in nonviolent civil disobedience, which he called *satyagraha*, "soul-" or "truth-force." Though it failed to win major concessions from the British, it focused worldwide attention on the Indian independence movement.

## Latin America: Independent Democracies and Authoritarian Regimes

Like Britain and France, Latin America remained faithful to its constitutional-nationalist heritage throughout the nineteenth century, though with a preference for authoritarian rule. In addition, a pattern of narrow elite rule had evolved in which large estate owners controlled the elections and politics of their countries and, through the military, kept rural black and indigenous Amerindian peoples, as well as the mixed urban populations, in check. Politicians in some countries realized the voting potential of the urban populations after World War I and pursued a new type of autocratic politics, called "populism," in conjunction with more or less extensive industrialization programs. Estate owner politics and populism, together with industrialization programs, characterized Latin America during the later interwar period.

**Postwar Recovery**    At the beginning of the 1900s, Mexico had enjoyed a long period of political stability and economic growth. It had a relatively diversified array of mineral and agricultural export commodities and began to exploit its mineral wealth to set up an iron and steel industry. But no change had taken place in agriculture, where the traditional oligarchy of rich ranching and plantation landowners continued to keep wages low. Thanks to US investments, railroad construction had progressed but more in order to support mining interests than agriculture, as there was no desire to improve the mobility of either the landless tenants or the indigenous Native American population engaged in subsistence farming.

**The Years of Depression**    In Mexico, a rapid urbanization process, begun in the late 1800s, continued during the interwar period. Immigration from overseas, mostly from southern and eastern Europe, as well as rural–urban migration fueled this process. In 1929 the newly created Institutional Revolutionary Party (Partido Revolucionario Institucional, PRI) brought the revolution of 1910–1917 to an end. A sufficiently strong government was in place again to complete land distribution to poor farmers, expand education, and begin social legislation. The PRI weathered the Depression with some difficulty, but thanks to increased state control of economic investments, it was able to maintain its footing until European and east Asian war preparations increased demand for commodities again.

Like Mexico, the countries with the largest internal markets, such as Argentina and Brazil, rode out the Depression more successfully than others. Nevertheless, overall the impact was substantial, with a reduction of commodity exports by over 50 percent. The Depression resulted in urban unrest, especially in countries with newly expanded mines or oil wells, such as Chile, Peru, and Venezuela, or expanded administrative bureaucracies, as in Brazil. At no time except the period of independence were there more coups, attempted coups, and uprisings than during 1930–1933.

An important shift away from landed oligarchies, however, began to appear among the ruling classes. Millions of people now lived in cities, although they did not have the clearly delineated social classes of workers or the nonindustrial lower classes that could be organized by communists, socialists, fascists, and militarists. Instead, a new generation of military officers, with urban backgrounds and no ties to the traditional oligarchy, appeared. They offered populist authoritarian programs that mixed elements from the prevailing European ideologies.

# New Variations on Modernity: The Soviet Union and Communism

Communism was the second pattern of modernity that arose out of the ashes of World War I. Following their coup in November 1917, the Bolsheviks under Lenin ultimately triumphed in a debilitating civil war and established the Union of Soviet Socialist Republics. Lenin's successor, Joseph Stalin (1879–1953), built the Communist Party into an all-powerful apparatus that violently shifted resources from agriculture into industry and dealt ruthlessly with opposition to its policies. By World War II, Stalin's brutal policies had lifted the Soviet Union into the ranks of the industrialized powers.

## The Communist Party and Regime in the Soviet Union

Karl Marx, the founder of communism, did not think that the underdeveloped Russian Empire, with its large majority of peasants, would be ready for a communist revolution for a long time to come. It was the achievement of Vladimir Lenin, however, as the leader of the Bolsheviks, a faction of the Russian Communist Party, to adapt Marxism to his circumstances. For him, the party was not the mass movement envisioned by Marx but rather the disciplined, armed vanguard that ruled with monopoly power and instilled the ideology of communism in a gradually expanding working class.

**The Bolshevik Regime**   Lenin was from a well-educated middle-class family; both of his parents were teachers, and his father had been given a patent of nobility; Lenin himself had a degree in law. The execution of his brother by the tsarist government for alleged complicity in the assassination of Tsar Alexander II (1881) imbued him with an implacable hatred for Russian autocracy. At the same time, he became steeped in the writings of Marx and radical thinkers across the political spectrum then circulating around Russia's intellectual underground. Contemplating the revolutionary potential of a communist party in Russia, he published a pamphlet in 1903 called *What Is to Be Done?* Here, he articulated for the first time the idea of professional revolutionaries forming an elite strike force. By eliminating the tsar and seizing control of the government, he argued, an ideologically trained communist party would be able, given Russia's highly centralized political structure, to implement its program of equality and industrialization from the top down.

The fall of the tsar's government in the spring of 1917 allowed Lenin and his fellow Bolsheviks to return from political exile. These included Leon Trotsky (1879–1940), the well-educated son of an affluent Ukrainian Jewish family, and Joseph Stalin, the hardnosed son of an impoverished Georgian cobbler who had escaped exile in Siberia seven times before the outbreak of World War I. Well aware of Lenin's subversive potential, the German government provided Lenin safe passage from Switzerland to Petrograd. By the summer of 1917, the Bolsheviks were mounting massive demonstrations with the slogans "Land, Peace, Bread" and "All Power to the Soviets" (councils of workers and soldiers that helped maintain order as the nation struggled to create a constitution). The collapse of a disastrous Russian summer offensive emboldened the Bolsheviks, who controlled the Petrograd Soviet, to make a bid for power. In early November 1917, the Bolsheviks staged a successful coup d'état in Petrograd.

**Civil War and Reconstruction**    The takeover of Russia by a tiny radical minority unleashed a storm of competing factions all across the political spectrum. For the Bolsheviks the first necessity therefore became building an army from scratch. Here, Trotsky proved a genius at inspiration and ruthless organization. From his armored train, flying the new "hammer and sickle" red flag, he continually rallied his forces against the far more numerous but utterly disunited "White" armies arrayed against his "Red" forces. From 1918 to 1921, the Ukraine, Georgia, Armenia, and Azerbaijan were each forced back into the new Bolshevik state.

The price for communist victory in the civil war was a complete collapse of the economy, amid a coincidental harvest failure. Lenin had initiated a policy of "war communism"—sending the Red Army into the countryside to requisition food, often with unrestrained brutality. Peasants fought back, and by 1922 a second civil war threatened. Only then did Lenin relent by inaugurating the temporary New Economic Policy (NEP), with a mixture of private and state investment in factories and small-scale food marketing by peasants. At the same time, however, the party—now several hundred thousand members strong—established an iron grip, with no deviation allowed. By 1928, a successful NEP had helped the Soviet Union to return to prewar levels of industrial production.

## The Collectivization of Agriculture and Industrialization

Lenin suffered a stroke in 1922 and recovered only for short periods before he died in 1924. His successor was Joseph Stalin, who had garnered the key position of general secretary of the Communist Party in 1922. He had to fight a long struggle, from 1924 to 1930, to overcome potential or imagined rivals, a struggle which left in him a deep reservoir of permanent suspicion. His chief victim was Trotsky, whom he outmaneuvered, forced into exile, and ultimately had assassinated in Mexico in1940.

**"Liquidation of the Kulaks as a Class"**    When Stalin finally felt more secure, he decided that industrialization through the NEP was advancing too slowly. The most valuable source of funds to finance industrialization came from the sale of grain on the world market. But farmers had lost all trust in the communist regime after the forcible requisitions during the civil war and hoarded their grain. Grain production had fallen off and created a so-called Crisis of 1928. In November 1929, therefore, the party decreed the collectivization of agriculture as the necessary step for an accelerated industrialization. Over the next two years , in a carefully laid out plan, 3–5 percent of the "wealthiest" farmers on grain-producing lands, called *kulaks* (Russian for "fist," indicating the tightfistedness of wealthier farmers vis-à-vis poor indebted ones), were "liquidated"—selected for execution, removal to labor camps, or resettlement on inferior soils. Their properties were confiscated, and the remaining peasants were regrouped as employees either of state farms (*sovkhozy*) or of poorer collective farms (*kolkhozy*). Animals were declared collective property, with the result that many farmers slaughtered their cherished livestock rather than turn them over to the collectives. Between 6 and 14 million farmers were forcibly removed, with the majority killed outright or worked and starved to death.

**Stalinism** The impact on agriculture was devastating. Grain, meat, and dairy production plummeted and failed to return to 1927 levels during the remainder of the interwar period. Food requisitions had to be resumed; bread had to be rationed on farms as well as in cities; and real wages on farms and in factories sank. On the other hand, the one-time transfer of confiscated wealth from the kulaks to industry was substantial. Income from accelerated oil exports and renewed grain exports from state farms in the 1930s was similarly poured into factory construction. By 1939, the rural population was down from 85 to 52 percent, and, for all practical purposes, industrialization had been accomplished, though at an unparalleled human cost.

The industrial and urban modernity that the Soviet Union reached was one of enforced solidarity without private enterprises and markets. The communist prestige objects were huge plant complexes producing the industrial basics of oil, coal, steel, cement, fertilizer, tractors, and farm combines. Little investment was left over for textiles, shoes, furniture, and household articles, not to mention cars, radios, and appliances. Consumers had to make do with shoddy goods, delivered irregularly to government outlets and requiring patient waiting in long lines.

The disaster of collectivization made Stalin even more concerned about any hidden pockets of potential resistance in the country. Regular party and army purges decimated the top echelons of the communist ruling apparatus. In 1937 alone, Stalin had 35,000 high-ranking officers shot, with disastrous effects for the conduct of World War II a few years later. Thus, in view of the enormity of Stalin's policies, scholars have since wondered about the viability of this attempt at accelerated modernity.

**"Comrade, Come Join Us at the Collective Farm!"** This is the call with which the woman on this wildly optimistic poster of 1930 is seen. In reality, Russian peasants experienced the collectivization program of 1929–1940 as a second serfdom, especially in the Ukraine, where private rather than collective village farming was widespread. They resisted it both passively and actively, through arson, theft, and especially the slaughtering of livestock.

# New Variations on Modernity: Supremacist Nationalism in Italy, Germany, and Japan

The third vision of modernity was an ideology of supremacist nationalism. In contrast to communism, which was a relatively coherent ideology, the systems of fascism, Nazism, and Japanese militarism were far more diffuse and cobbled together from a wide variety of nineteenth-century intellectual sources. Fascism became a persuasive alternative to democracy and communism in Italy right after World War I. The much more brutal German Nazi and Japanese militarist ideologies became acceptable only once the Depression hit and appeared to reveal capitalist democracy to be incapable of weathering the crisis.

## From Fascism in Italy to Nazism in the Third Reich

Benito Mussolini (1883–1945), the son of a blacksmith with anarchist leanings and a teacher, was well read in nineteenth-century philosophy and held positions as a journalist at various socialist newspapers. His support for the war as an instrument of radical change brought him into conflict with the majority of socialists, who bitterly opposed the war. As a result, he grew disillusioned with Marxism and founded the Italian Combat Squad (*Fasci italiani di combattimento*). War veterans, dressed in black shirts and organized in paramilitary units, roamed the streets and broke up communist labor rallies and strikes. The symbol of the movement was the *fasces* [FAS-sees]—derived from the old Roman emblem of authority in the form of a bundle of sticks and an ax, tied with a ribbon.

With their street brawls, the fascist "Blackshirts" contributed mightily to the impression of a breakdown of law and order, which the democratic government was apparently unable to control. Anticommunism thus was accompanied by denunciations of democracy as a chaotic form of government incapable of decisive action. Although Mussolini's party was still woefully behind the Socialist, Christian Democrat, and Conservative Parties in the parliament, he demanded and received the premiership by threatening a march on Rome by 10,000 Blackshirts. This turned into a victory parade, with the king acquiescing to the fascists' "third way" alternative to democracy and socialism.

Once given his chance, Mussolini transformed the Blackshirts into a militia for national security, paid for by the state. In 1923 he used the threat of their force again when he led his coalition government in the passing of a law that gave two-thirds of the seats in parliament to the party that garnered the most votes (at least 25 percent). A year later, Il Duce ("the Leader"), as he now styled himself, won his two-thirds and began to implement his fascist **corporate state**.

**Corporate state:**
Sometimes called an "organic state"; based on a philosophy of government that sees all sectors of society contributing in a systematic, orderly, and hierarchical fashion to the health of the state, the way that the parts of the body do to a human being.

By 1926, elections were abolished, strict censorship of the press was in place, and the secret police kept a close eye on the population. Fascist party officials, provincial governorships, and mayors were appointed from above, and labor unions were closed down. In the Ministry of Corporations, industrialists and bureaucrats, representing labor, met and sharply curtailed wages and labor regulations. The Lateran Accords of 1926–1929 made Catholicism the Italian state religion in return for full support by the Vatican for the fascists.

**Depression and Conquests**   Italy weathered the Depression through deficit spending and state investments. In 1933, Mussolini formed the Industrial Reconstruction Institute, which took over the industrial and commercial holdings of the banks that had failed earlier. This institute was crucial in efforts to revive the Italian industrial sector, which was still much smaller than elsewhere in Europe. Only in the mid-1930s did the urban population, concentrated mostly in the north, come to outnumber its rural counterpart. In spite of a few swamp-reclamation and grain-procurement reforms, the fascists had no answer for the endemic underdevelopment of southern Italy, which remained over-whelmingly rural and poor.

Nevertheless, Italy's military industry was sufficiently advanced for Mussolini to proclaim a policy of autarky with the help of overseas territories. First, the conquest of formerly Ottoman Libya was completed with utmost brutality in 1931. Declaring Libya to be the "Fourth Shore," the fascists encouraged emigration into the largely infertile Sahara colony, which eventually numbered some 100,000 settlers. The other major colony was the proud Christian kingdom of Ethiopia, conquered by Italy in 1935–1936 and merged thereafter with the earlier territories of Italian Eritrea and Somalia into Italian East Africa. Eager to avenge Italy's defeat by the Ethiopians forty years before, Mussolini's forces invaded with airplanes, tanks, and poison gas and, after crushing Ethiopian resistance, pacified the new colony with the settlement of 200,000 Italians.

The Ethiopian conquest prompted protests by the League of Nations. Although these were ineffective, Mussolini felt sufficiently isolated that he sought closer relations with Adolf Hitler and the Nazis. He had formerly treated Hitler as a junior colleague but now found him to be a useful counterweight against international isolation. An increasingly close cooperation began between the two dictators, who formed the nucleus of the Axis powers, joined in 1941 by Japan.

**The Founding of the Weimar Republic**    In September 1918, the German Supreme Army Command (OHL) came to the conclusion that Germany had lost World War I. In the subsequent 2 months unrest broke out in the navy and among workers. German soldiers melted away from the western front, and communist worker councils formed in a number of major cities. Alarmed civilian politicians in Berlin did everything in their power to bring about a peaceful transition from empire to republic. When the emperor eventually abdicated, his last chancellor (head of the government) appointed Friedrich Ebert (1871–1925), a prominent member of the German Social Democratic Party, on November 9, 1918, as his successor. This appointment was not quite legal, but Ebert immediately contacted the OHL for armed support, and in the following months the two cooperated in crushing the well-organized and armed communist workers' councils.

The first test for the new republic (founded in nearby Weimar during the height of communist unrest in Berlin) came in the summer of 1919 when the Allies presented their peace settlement. The French, concerned about both their military security and future German economic power, would have liked to have Germany divided into individual states again, as it was before 1871. The British and Americans, however, were opposed to such a drastic settlement. Germany was let off with what historians now see in retrospect as relatively moderate reparations for civilian casualties, along with the loss of two western provinces, although it was also forced to accept responsibility for beginning the war. The compromise settlement was satisfactory to no one. France's security remained uncertain, German conservatives and nationalists screamed defiance, and the democrats of Weimar who accepted the settlement were embittered by its immediate consequence: inflation.

Asked to begin the payments immediately, Germany was unable to correct the general inflation when pent-up consumer demand exploded with the onset of peace. Instead, the inflation accelerated to a hyperinflation in which the German

**Play Money.** German children in 1923 playing with bundles of money in the streets. Hyperinflation had made money in the Weimar Republic worthless: At the height of the inflation, in November 1923, $0.24 US was worth 1 trillion "paper marks." To overcome the hyperinflation, the German Central Bank cut the "trillions" off the mark and created the "reichsmark." This currency was tied again to the gold standard and was in circulation until 1948.

mark became virtually worthless and Germany had to suspend payments. France and Belgium responded by occupying the industrial Ruhr province in 1923. German workers in the Ruhr retaliated with passive resistance, and a deadlock was the result.

Faced with this crisis, the new Weimar Republic made peace with the French by recognizing the new borders. Recognizing, too, the dire financial implications of an economically crippled Germany, the American-crafted Dawes Plan of 1924 had US banks advance credits to European banks to refinance the now considerably reduced German reparation payments. France and Belgium withdrew from the Ruhr, inflation was curtailed, and the currency stabilized. The newly solvent Weimar Republic then experienced a considerable economic and cultural efflorescence during the rest of the decade.

**The Rise of the Nazis** This affluence disintegrated quickly in the months after the US stock market crash of 1929. American banks, desperate for cash, began to recall their loans made to Europe. Beginning in 1931 in Austria, European banks began to fail, and in the following 2 years world trade shrank by two-thirds, hitting an exporting nation like Germany particularly hard. Unemployment soared meanwhile to 30 percent of the workforce. The number of people voting for extremist opponents of democracy—communists and ultra-nationalists—rose from negligible to more than half of the electorate by July 1932. Among them, the National Socialist German Workers' Party (NSDAP, or Nazi Party), achieved 38 percent, becoming the largest party in parliament.

In early 1933, the Nazi leader, Adolf Hitler (1889–1945), a failed artist and son of an Austrian customs official, could look back on a checkered postwar political career. He had led a failed uprising in 1923, done time in prison, and in *Mein Kampf* (*My Struggle*), a book published in 1925, openly announced a frightening political program. Hitler advocated ridding Germany of its Jews, whom he blamed for World War I, and communists, whom he blamed for the Central powers losing the war, and sought to punish the Allies for the peace settlement they had imposed on Germany. In its most grandiose sections he supported the German conquest of a "living space" (*Lebensraum*) in Russia and eastern Europe for the superior "Aryan" (German) race, with the "inferior" Slavs reduced to forced labor. No one who followed politics in Germany during the 1920s could be in doubt about Hitler's unrestrained and violent supremacist nationalism. Throughout the decade, however, he remained marginalized and often ridiculed for his extreme views.

**The Nazis in Power** When the Nazis won a plurality in parliament, however, not only in the spring of 1932 but again in the fall, Hitler demanded the chancellorship. Upon the advice of his counselors, President Paul von Hindenburg (in office 1925–1934), one of Germany's heroes as a leading general during World War I, nominated Hitler to the post on January 30, 1933, in an effort to neutralize Nazism and keep Hitler under control. Hitler, however, wasted no time in escaping all restraints. Following a major fire in the Reichstag (German parliament) building in February 1933, the causes of which have never been fully explained, but which Hitler blamed on the communists, the president allowed his new chancellor the right to declare martial law for a limited time. Two months later, the Nazi Party in parliament passed the Enabling Act with the votes of the mostly Catholic Centrist Party; its leaders calculated that they could control Hitler and also reach a much-desired agreement between the Vatican and Germany parallel to the one of Mussolini. According to the constitution, Hitler now had the power to rule by emergency decree for 4 years.

Taking their cue from Mussolini's policies, the Nazis abolished the federalist structure of the Weimar Republic, purged the civil service of Jews, closed down all parties except the NSDAP, enacted censorship laws, and sent communists to newly constructed concentration camps. Other inmates of these camps were Roma (Gypsies), homosexuals, and religious minorities. In order to gain the support of Germany's professional army, Hitler replaced his *Sturmabteilung* (SA) militias of thugs with the smartly outfitted *Schutzstaffel* (SS). A new secret police force (abbreviated *Gestapo*) established a pervasive surveillance system in what was now called the Third Empire (*Drittes Reich*), following that of the Holy Roman Empire and Germany after its unification in 1871.

At the same time, Hitler succeeded in gaining enthusiastic support among the population. Aided by a general recovery of the economy, within a year of coming to power he lowered unemployment to 10 percent. He had the support of able economists who advised him to reduce unemployment through deficit spending and build a mixed economy of state-subsidized private industrial cartels. Enthusiastic Germans built freeways, cleared slums, constructed housing, and, above all, made arms, for minimal wages. Hitler also denounced the "decadence" of modern art and pushed his planners to create monumental buildings in older neoclassical or Art Deco styles. In all of these endeavors he advocated a personal vision of a stridently "nationalist" German art. In his appeal to the patriotic and economic aspirations of so many Germans, Hitler thus succeeded in making himself a genuinely popular leader (*Führer*) among the great majority of Germans.

German rearmament was initially secret but, after 1935, became public knowledge, with the introduction of the draft and the repudiation of the peace settlement cap on troop numbers. During 1935–1939, the army grew from 100,000 to 950,000 men, warships from 30 to 95, and, most startling of all, the air force from 36 to over 8,000 planes. France, realizing the danger this rearmament signified for its security, signed a treaty of mutual military assistance with the Soviet Union, which Hitler took as a pretext for the remilitarization of the Rhineland (one of the German provinces temporarily occupied by France after World War I) in 1936.

This first step of German military assertion was followed with unofficial support for General Francisco Franco (1892–1975), who rose against the legitimate republican government in the Spanish Civil War (1936–1939), and the incorporation of Austria into Nazi Germany in 1938. Now alarmed at Germany's growing appetite for expansion and committed by treaty to defend the eastern European states created after the war, the heads of state of Britain and France met with Hitler and Mussolini in Munich in the summer of 1938 to hammer out a general agreement on German and Italian territorial claims. In the Munich Agreement, Hitler was allowed to occupy the Sudetenland, an area in Czechoslovakia largely inhabited by ethnic Germans, with the understanding that it represented his final territorial demand. The British prime minister, Neville Chamberlain (in office 1937–1940), seeking to mediate between the less-compromising France and Hitler, claimed that this appeasement of Germany promised "peace in our time." Hitler went to war, however, in little more than a year.

**World War II in Poland and France**    In 1939 Hitler decided that the German armed forces were ready to begin the quest for *Lebensraum* in eastern Europe. In a first step, Poland needed to be taken; and in order for this to happen, Stalin had to be led to believe that it was in the best interest of the Soviet Union and Germany to share in the division of eastern Europe. Stalin, of course, was under no illusions about Hitler's plans but needed time to rebuild his army after the purges of 1937 and found the idea of a Russian-dominated Polish buffer against Germany appealing. Accordingly, the two signed a nonaggression pact on August 23, 1939, and German troops invaded Poland on September 1, triggering declarations of war by Poland's allies Britain and France 2 days later. World War II had begun in Europe.

Having removed the two-front problem that had plagued Germany in World War I, Hitler had to eliminate Britain and France before turning to the next phase in the east. This he did by attacking France on May 10, 1940. The German army in Poland had pioneered a new kind of warfare: *Blitzkrieg,* or "lightning war." Using aircraft to cripple rear area defenses and harass enemy troops, while smashing enemy lines with tanks and motorized infantry, the Germans turned warfare from the stagnant defensive posture of World War I into a fast, highly mobile conflict. The French, bled dry of manpower in the previous war, had since relied largely on the highly elaborate but fixed defenses of their Maginot Line. Now, the German troops simply went around these fortifications on a broad front, from the Netherlands and Belgium to Luxembourg. After breaking through the thick unprotected Ardennes Forest in southern Belgium, to the great surprise of the French and British, the German troops turned northward, driving the Allies toward the Atlantic coast. Establishing a desperate defensive perimeter at Dunkirk, the encircled French and British troops used every available vessel to escape across the English Channel to Britain as the Germans regrouped for their final thrust.

France surrendered and agreed to an armistice. Hitler divided the country into a German-occupied part, consisting of Paris and the Atlantic coast, and a smaller unoccupied territory under German control, with its capital in Vichy. The German follow-up effort of an invasion of Britain failed when the air force, having suffered more losses than anticipated in the invasion of France, was unable to deliver the final blow. During the worst air raids the Conservative politician Winston Churchill (in office 1940–1945) replaced Neville Chamberlain as prime minister. Churchill's inspirational and unbending will during the aerial Battle of Britain proved to be a turning point in rallying the Allied cause.

**The Eastern Front**    A year after finishing with France, and with Britain only desperately hanging on, Hitler launched an invasion of the Soviet Union on June 22, 1941, to the surprise of an unprepared Stalin. Although the Soviet forces were initially severely beaten, they did not disintegrate, thanks in part to a force of new T-34 tanks that proved superior to German models and were four times more numerous than the Germans expected. The Soviets held out against the German attacks on Leningrad (the renamed St. Petersburg/ Petrograd), Moscow, and the Ukraine. Neither side made much progress in 1942, until the Soviets succeeded in trapping a large force of Germans in Stalingrad on the lower Volga, near the vital Caspian oil fields. The Soviet victory on February 2, 1943, became the turning point in the European war. Thereafter, it was an almost relentless and increasingly desperate retreat for the Germans, particularly after the western Allies invaded the continent in Italy and France.

**The Final Solution**    As Hitler's *Mein Kampf* foretold, the war in the east became an ideological war of annihilation: Either the supremacist or the communist vision of modernity would prevail. The Soviets began early with their killings, when they massacred nearly 22,000 Polish prisoners of war in the forest of Katyn and sent hundreds of thousands of eastern Europeans to their eventual deaths in labor camps. The German SS and army, driven by their racism against Slavs, murdered soldiers and civilians alike, and German businesses worked their Slavic slave laborers to death. The so-called **Final Solution** (*Endlösung*), the genocide of the

**Genocide.** The spectera of the Holocaust that haunt us usually involve the infamous extermination camps—Auschwitz, Treblinka, Majdanek, Sobibor— but millions of Jews and other "undesirables"—Slavs, Gypsies (Roma), and homosexuals—were shot, such as this man calmly waiting for the bullet to penetrate his brain while SS executioners look on.

European Jews, was the horrendous culmination of this struggle. After Poland and the western Soviet Union were conquered, the number of Jews under German authority increased by several million. The Final Solution, set in motion in January 1942, entailed transporting Jews to extermination camps, the most infamous of which was at Auschwitz, in Poland, to be gassed in simulated shower stalls and their corpses burned in specially constructed ovens. In its technological sophistication in creating a kind of assembly line of death and the calm, bureaucratic efficiency with which its operators went about their business, the Holocaust (Hebrew *Shoah*) marks a milestone in twentieth-century inhumanity. It has since become the standard of genocide against which other planned mass murders are measured.

**The Turn of the Tide in the West**    The first counteroffensives of the Allies in the west after their defeat in 1940 came in November 1942. After fighting a desperate rearguard action against the German general Erwin Rommel (1891–1944), "the Desert Fox," British forces in Egypt and American forces landing in occupied French North Africa launched a combined offensive, capturing Rommel's forces in a pincer movement and driving them to capitulate 6 months later. But it took another 2.5 years of long campaigning to grind down the forces of the Axis powers. Here, the industrial capacity of the United States proved to be the determining factor. For example, between 1942 and 1945 American factories produced 41,000 Sherman M4 tanks alone, which was more than the production of all German tank types taken together. German aircraft production peaked in 1944 at 44,000 planes; US manufacturers produced more than 100,000 the same year. The United States enjoyed similar advantages in manpower. By war's end, over 16 million American men and women, or 10 percent of the entire population, had served in

**Final Solution:** German supremacist-nationalist plan formulated in 1942 by Adolf Hitler and leading Nazis to annihilate Jews through factory-style mass extermination in concentration camps, resulting in the death of about 6 million Jews, or roughly two-thirds of European Jewry.

the armed forces. Finally, the natural barriers of the Atlantic and Pacific Oceans and American naval power ensured against invasion, while the lack of a long-range strategic bombing force prevented Axis air attacks on North America.

Furthermore, starting in 1943, the US Army Air Force and Britain's Royal Air Force began a furious campaign of around-the-clock bombing of military and civilian targets in Germany. Despite heavy Allied losses in planes and men, by war's end there was scarcely a German city or industrial center of any size that had not been reduced to rubble by air attack—quite a contrast to World War I, when Germany's interior was unscathed. With the landing of troops in Sicily in July 1943, the Italian Peninsula in early September, and Normandy in June 1944, along with the steady advance of Soviet forces in the east, the eventual unconditional German surrender on May 8, 1945 (VE, or "Victory in Europe" Day) was inevitable (see Map 28.3).

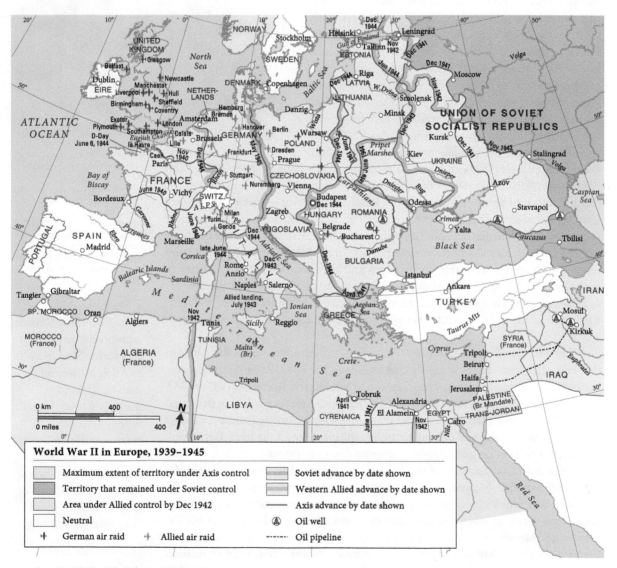

MAP **28.3 World War II in Europe, 1939–1945.**

## Japan's "Greater East Asia Co-Prosperity Sphere" and China's Struggle for Unity

The Japanese ruling class that implemented the Meiji industrialization consisted for the most part of lower-ranking samurai "oligarchs." After World War I, this generation retired, and for the first time commoners entered politics. They formed two unstable conservative party coalitions, representing small-business and landowner interests, but were financed by big-business cartels, the zaibatsus (see Chapter 24). By the mid-1920s Japan's interwar liberalizing era had reached perhaps its high point, with universal male suffrage for those over the age of 25. Thereafter, however, and at an accelerated pace during the Depression of 1929–1933, the military increased its power and ended the liberalizing era.

**Liberalism and Military Assertion**    In the midst of the middle-class ferment of "Taisho Democracy," as Japan's politics during the reign of Emperor Taisho (r. 1912–1926) was known, the government not only broadened the suffrage but also enacted the first of what would be a long line of security laws. Worried about communist influence, the Peace Preservation Law of 1925 drew a line against frequent labor strikes and general leftist agitation. Anyone violating the "national essence" (*kokutai*) in thought or action could be arrested. A branch of the secret services, the *Tokko*, made widespread use of this law, with some 70,000 mostly arbitrary arrests during 1925–1945. The law was the turning point when Western-inspired liberalism began to swing toward militarism. Nowhere was this more dramatically on display than in the saga of Professor Minobe, described at the beginning of this chapter, who would go in a few short years from being Japan's leading legal theorist to being denounced as a traitor.

Military officers of modest rural origin, trained prior to World War I and without much general education, were unable or unwilling to comprehend the democracy, cultural transformation, and labor strikes of the 1920s. They became intoxicated with the staples of supremacist nationalism, such as the absolutism of the emperor, above law and parliament, and the right of junior officers to refuse to execute parliamentary laws. These two points were decisive for actions through which the military achieved dominance over parliament in the 1930s.

**Militaristic Expansion**    The early 1930s saw the end of a period of diplomacy by which Japan sought to consolidate its gains in international prestige from the Washington Naval Treaty and subsequent treaties stabilizing Japan's position in China. The growth of the power of the Chinese Nationalist Party (Guomindang, GMD) and its creation of a relatively stable regime in China after 1927 altered the fragile balance of power among the contending warlord regimes that Japan had exploited for over a decade in order to expand its influence. The junior officers who chafed at the liberalization of Japan and hearkened back to samurai values increasingly found a home and opportunity in the colonial armies of Manchuria.

The first step in this new direction was taken in 1928 when the Japanese Kwantung Army (Japan's force in Manchuria) blew up the train of the Chinese warlord Zhang Zuolin because of his leanings toward the GMD. This was followed by the Mukden Incident of 1931, in which the Japanese military engineered another railroad bombing, which was blamed on local warlords and used as the pretext for the annexation of Manchuria. Politicians in Tokyo, cowed by the aggressiveness of supremacist nationalist ideologues and by the select assassinations of political opponents of Japan's expansion, acquiesced. By way of making it a puppet state, they installed the last Manchu Qing Chinese emperor (Henry) Pu-Yi (r. 1908–1912; 1932–1945), deposed as a boy in the Chinese Republican Revolution of 1911–1912. Over the next several years, the Japanese army in Manchuria systematically moved into northern China. In July 1937, after a clash between Chinese and Japanese forces near the Marco Polo Bridge outside Beijing, Japan launched a full-scale invasion of China.

**The Republican Revolution in China**   As we saw in Chapter 24, the Qing dynasty had failed to develop a sustained effort at reform in response to the Western challenge during the 1800s. Following belated attempts at institutional reform in the wake of the Boxer Rebellion in 1900, a variety of radical groups, aided by the growing numbers of overseas Chinese, began to work for the overthrow of the Qing. The most important figure among these groups was Sun Yat-sen (1866–1925), a medical doctor and son of peasants in south China, with his Revolutionary Alliance of 1905. Making common cause with a number of local revolutionary groups and Chinese secret societies, Sun's group formed an umbrella organization for a wide array of political ideas.

On October 10, 1911, an explosion in a Wuhan barracks signaled a takeover of the base. The movement quickly spread, and by the end of the year three groups of Qing opponents—provincial warlords, scholar-gentry, and nationalists—staged separate uprisings that reduced the Qing to a small territory in the north. The Qing commander, Yuan Shikai (1859–1916), struck a deal with the insurgents whereby he came over to them in return for the presidency of the new republic, formed upon the abdication of the Qing in February 1912. Sun was thus elbowed aside by the revolution he had done so much to begin. With Yuan's death in 1916, the remaining warlords feuded with each other for control of the country for the next decade.

**Reemergence of Nationalism**   Sun Yat-sen, however, was not quite finished. With the republic in shambles and the provinces hijacked by the warlords, Sun remained a profoundly inspirational figure for Chinese nationalists, mostly through his numerous publications issued from exile in the Western treaty port of Canton (Guangzhou). Meanwhile, the decision announced on May 4, 1919, by the Allies at Versailles to allow Japan to keep the German territory in China it had seized at the beginning of the war set off mass demonstrations and a boycott of foreign businesses. This May Fourth Movement, as it came to be called, is often cited as the modern beginning of Chinese nationalism. Shortly thereafter, inspired by the Bolshevik Revolution in Russia, the Chinese Communist Party (CCP) was founded in 1921.

By 1923, encouraged by support from the Third Communist International (Comintern), Sun's Nationalist Party was being reorganized and supplied with Russian help, in return for which the party agreed to allow members of the CCP to join with it to form what became known as the First United Front (1924–1927). Sun died in 1925, and a year later Chiang K'ai-shek (1887–1975) ascended to the leadership of the army. Chiang came from a wealthy salt-merchant family and was a military officer trained in the Nationalist Party academy and in Moscow. The most pressing objective in 1926 was the unification of China. The two parties mobilized an army of some 85,000 men, and the so-called Northern Expedition of 1926–1927 became a remarkably successful effort that brought about the unification of southern China as far north as the Yangzi River.

In the middle of the campaign, however, the bonds between the GMD and CCP ruptured. The socialist wing of the GMD and the CCP had taken the important industrial centers of Wuhan and Shanghai in the Yangtze Delta from warlords, setting the stage for a showdown with the nationalist wing. Though he had been trained in Moscow, Chiang had grown intensely suspicious of Comintern and CCP motives and thus launched a preemptive purge of communists in nationalist-held areas. Though much of the leftist opposition was eliminated, a remnant under Mao Zedong (1893–1976) fled to the remote province of Jiangxi in the south to regroup and create their own socialist state. Mao, a librarian by training from a wealthy peasant family, was an inspiring rural organizer, and he set about developing his ideas of Marxist revolution with the heretical idea of having peasants in the vanguard.

**Mao.** The images of Mao that dominate our consciousness are usually the old Mao, when his health was failing, his youthful vigor long gone, and his political power diminished. But it is in the young Mao, such as in this photo from 1938, that we can best see his leadership skills in action.

By the early 1930s Mao's Chinese communists had developed this crucial variant of rural communism, which Marx and Lenin had found impossible to envisage. Mao replaced the capitalists with the landlords as the class enemy and promised a much-needed land reform to the downtrodden peasants. Moreover, the peasants would be the leading participants in the "People's War"—a three-stage guerilla conflict involving the entire populace and borrowing from sources as diverse as Sun Zi's *Art of War* and the colonists' tactics against the British in the American War for Independence.

Believing the communist threat to be effectively eliminated, Chiang resumed his Northern Expedition in 1928, subjugating Beijing but failing to eliminate the strongest northern warlords. Nevertheless, China was now at least nominally unified, with the capital in Nanjing, the National Party Congress functioning as a parliament, and Chiang as president. Chiang made substantial progress with railroad and road construction as well as cotton and silk textile exports. Thanks to the silver standard of its money, rather than the fatal gold standard of many other countries, the financial consequences of the Depression of 1929–1933 remained relatively mild. Chiang made little headway, however, with land reform. Furthermore, the volatile relations with the remaining warlords made the government vulnerable to border violence and corruption. Hovering above all after 1931 was the Japanese annexation of Manchuria and creeping encroachment on northern China.

"The Comrade's style of work incorporates the modesty and pragmatism of the Chinese people; the simplicity and diligence of the Chinese peasants; the love of study and profound thinking of an intellectual; the efficiency and steadfastness of a revolutionary soldier; and the persistence and indomitability of a Bolshevik."

—Zhou Enlai (1898–1976) describing Mao Zedong, 1943

**The Long March and the Rape of Nanjing**    In the early 1930s, Chiang knew that Japan was the enemy to watch, but he was painfully aware of the need to completely eliminate his internal opponents. Following the old proverbial warning of "Disorder within, disaster without" he resolved to eliminate the remaining threat from Mao's "Jiangxi Soviet." He mounted increasingly massive "bandit extermination" campaigns from 1931 to 1934, but each one was defeated by the superior mobility, local loyalty, and guerilla tactics of Mao's growing People's Liberation Army. With the help of German advisors, Chiang turned to encircling the CCP areas with a ring of trenches and blockhouses to limit the mobility of his opponents. By the fall of 1934 he had tightened the noose around the communists and almost succeeded in destroying their army.

But Mao and about 100,000 soldiers broke out in October 1934. Once free, the majority of the Red Army embarked on its epic Long March of 6,000 miles, describing a semicircle from the south through the far west and then northeast toward Beijing. Along the way harassment by nationalist troops, warlords, and local people as well as hunger, famine, heat, swamps, bridgeless rivers, and desertion decimated the bedraggled marchers. In the fall of 1935 some 10,000 communists eventually straggled into the small enclave of Yan'an (Yenan), out of Chiang's reach.

The communists had seized upon Japan's aggression as a valuable propaganda tool and declared war against Japan in 1932. Chiang's obsession with eliminating his internal enemies increasingly made him subject to criticism of appeasement toward Japan. In 1936, a group of dissident nationalist generals arrested Chiang outside the city of Xi'an and spirited him off to CCP headquarters at Yan'an. After weeks of fraught negotiations, Chiang was released as the leader of a China now brought together under a Second United Front, this time against Japan.

Seeing their prospects for gradual encroachment quickly fading, Japan seized on the so-called Marco Polo Bridge Incident and launched an all-out assault on China. The bridge was a key point along the front between Japanese and Chinese forces just outside Beijing, and on the night of July 7, 1937, a brief exchange of fire accidentally took place between the two sides. When a Japanese soldier seeking to relieve himself during the exchange did not return to post, the Japanese used this as a pretext to move against the Chinese. Though Chinese resistance was stiff in the opening months, the Japanese were able to use their superior mobility and airpower to flank the Chinese forces and take the capital of Nanjing (Nanking) by December 1937. Realizing the need to defeat China as quickly as possible in order to avoid a war of attrition, they subjected the capital to the first major atrocity of World War II: the "Rape of Nanjing." Though scholars are still debating the exact number of casualties, it is estimated that between 200,000 and 300,000 people were slaughtered in deliberately gruesome ways: hacked to death, burned or buried alive, and beheaded. Over and above this brutality, however, rape was systematically used as a means of terror and subjugation.

The direct message of all of this was that other Chinese cities could expect similar treatment if surrender was not swiftly forthcoming. Like the British and Germans under aerial bombardment a few years later, however, the destruction only stiffened the will to resist of the Chinese. Continually harassed as they retreated from Nanjing, the Chinese adopted the strategy of trading space for time to regroup, as did the Soviets a few years later. In an epic mass migration, Chinese soldiers and civilians stripped every usable article and moved it to the region around the remote city of Chongqing (Chungking), which became the wartime capital of China until 1945. Thereafter, both nationalists and communists used the vast interior as a base for hit-and-run tactics, effectively limiting Japan to the northeast and coastal urban centers but remaining incapable of mounting large offensives themselves.

**World War II in the Pacific**   While Japan had used its control of Manchuria, Korea, and Taiwan in its quest for autarky and economic stability in the 1930s, it portrayed its imperial

**The Rape of Nanjing.** Of the many horrors of the twentieth century, few can match the Rape of Nanjing for its sadistic brutality, in which perhaps as many as 300,000 people lost their lives in a Japanese killing orgy.

bid in the Pacific as the construction of a "Greater East Asia Co-Prosperity Sphere." This expansion was considered essential because oil, metals, rubber, and other raw materials were still imported in large quantities from the United States and the Dutch and British possessions in southeast Asia. After Hitler invaded the Netherlands and France in 1940, the opportunity arrived for the Japanese could add to their power and remove the United States from the Pacific. Moreover, the stalemate in China was increasingly bleeding Japan of vital resources, while mounting tensions with the United States over China were already resulting in economic sanctions. Accordingly, in the summer of 1941, the Japanese government decided on extending the empire into the Dutch East Indies and southeast Asia, even if this meant war with the United States. Under the premiership of General Tojo Hideki (in office 1941–1944), Japan attacked Pearl Harbor in Hawaii, the Philippines, and Dutch and British territories on December 7–8, 1941. Within a few months, the Japanese completed the occupation of all the important southeast Asian and Pacific territories they had sought (see Map 28.4).

Japan's newfound autarky did not last long, however. Within 6 months, in the naval and air battle around Midway Atoll, American forces regained the initiative. The Japanese now exploited the populations of their new territories in extracting their raw materials with increasing urgency. As the American forces slowly deprived the Japanese of these resources through their highly effective "island-hopping" strategy, they came within bombing range of the Japanese home islands by late 1944. Starting in March 1945, they subjected Japan to the most devastating firebomb attacks ever mounted. Finally, President Harry S. Truman (in office 1945–1953) made the fateful decision to have two experimental atomic bombs dropped on Hiroshima and Nagasaki (August 6 and 9, 1945), effectively obliterating both cities. With the Soviets declaring war against Japan on August 8 and advancing into Manchuria, the Japanese were finally convinced that the war

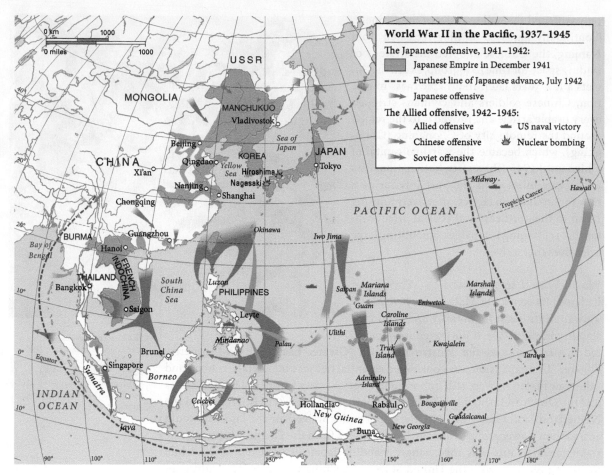

MAP **28.4** **World War II in the Pacific, 1937–1945.**

was lost. They surrendered on August 14, 1945, with the final ceremony taking place aboard the US battleship *Missouri* on September 2, 1945.

# Putting It All Together

As discussed in previous chapters, the patterns of constitutional nationalism and industrialization in the late eighteenth and early nineteenth centuries were most visibly manifested in Great Britain, the United States, and France. Subsequently, two further patterns complicated the evolution of nations engaging in the pursuit of modernity: ethnolinguistic nationalism and the rise of the industrial working class. Abetted by the imperialistic tendencies inherited from before 1800, all of these patterns collided in World War I. After the war, they recombined into the three ideologies of modernity analyzed in this chapter: capitalist democracy, communism, and supremacist nationalism.

For the most part, only democracy and communism are considered to be genuine ideologies of modernity, in the sense of being based on relatively coherent programs. More recent historians, however, have come to the conclusion that supremacist nationalism was a genuine variety of modernity as well, though one defined more by what it opposed than by what it supported. The adherents of the three modernities bitterly denounced the ideologies of their rivals. All three considered themselves to be genuinely "progressive" or modern.

What is very difficult to understand in a country like the United States, still deeply loyal to its foundational national constitutionalism, is that someone could be an ardent ethnic nationalist, have little faith in constitutional liberties, find the conquest of a large and completely self-sufficient empire perfectly logical, and think of all this as the ideal of a future modernity. Indeed, historians have customarily thought of these views as revolts *against* modernity. Yet, as we have seen so often, innovations frequently create a "gelling" effect in which opposition to the new clarifies and solidifies, often in unexpected ways. The "modern" notion of ethnolinguistic nationalism thus created ways of opposing other modern innovations such as constitutionalism and industrialism—with their messy uncertainties and feelings of rootlessness—by insisting on a purer, more mystical bond for the modern nation-state that, ironically, harkened back to a simpler, reimagined past. But Mussolini, Hitler, and the Japanese generals all aspired to the same scientific–industrial future as Roosevelt, Churchill, Stalin, Chiang K'ai-shek, and Mao Zedong.

▶ For additional resources, including maps, primary sources, visuals, and quizzes, please go to www.oup.com/us/vonsivers. Please see the Further Resources section at the back of the book for additional readings and suggested websites.

## Against the Grain
# Righteous among the Nations

Some 25,000 men and women bravely defied the German Nazi regime (1932–1945) during the Holocaust and saved Jews from arrest, deportation, and the gas chamber. Their acts of defiance are proof that ordinary citizens in Germany and the countries conquered by Germany during World War II carried out their human responsibility of saving other human beings. They did not cower before the seemingly all-powerful Gestapo, nor did they attempt to claim helplessness or ignorance regarding what was happening around them. They were aware, of course, that they risked their own lives by hiding Jews or smuggling them out of harm's way. Indeed, many were martyred at the hands of Nazi authorities. But they still acted as they did because they considered it their human calling.

Thousands of the saviors of Jews were Poles, Dutch, French, Ukrainians, and Belgians, all under German occupation during the war. By contrast, only 563 and 525 Italians and Germans, respectively, helped Jews to survive. The contrast in numbers illustrates the feelings of hatred among many in the conquered territories for the Germans on the one hand and the pervasiveness of the supremacist-nationalist fascist and Nazi ideologies in the populations of Italy and Germany on the other. Even if having the courage to help Jews was much easier in Nazi Germany than many Germans pretended after the war, their anti-Semitism prevented them from feeling any pangs of conscience.

Today, Israel recognizes 24,811 saviors of Jews as "Righteous among the Nations" and honors them in a special garden in the Yad Vashem Holocaust memorial museum in Jerusalem. One of them, Irena Sendler (1910–2008), may serve as an example for all. Sendler was a health worker, the daughter of a Polish physician who treated Jewish patients. When the Germans invaded she was an administrator for the Warsaw Social Welfare Department, responsible for providing food, clothing, medicine, and money for the poor and elderly. During the time of the Warsaw Ghetto (1940–1943), she was able to smuggle some 2,500 Jewish children out of the country, hiding them under loads of goods, in potato sacks or even in coffins. She provided them with false identities and had them taken to hiding places with Christian families. When the Nazis finally discovered her activities in 1943, they arrested and tortured her. But after members of the Polish resistance succeeded in bribing her would-be executioners, Sandler escaped and went into hiding until the end of the war. Yad Vashem honored Irena Sendler in 1965 as a righteous person and planted a tree in her name at the entrance of the Avenue of the Righteous among Nations.

- Faced with a situation similar to that of Irena Sendler, what would you do?

- Can you think of other 20th century mass atrocities in which people like Irena Sendler desperately tired to save innocent lives?

# Thinking Through Patterns

▶ **Which three patterns of modernity emerged after World War I? How and why did these patterns form?**

Ethnic nationalism was difficult to accommodate in the nineteenth century, which began with the more inclusive constitutional nationalism of Great Britain, the United States, and France. New nations like Italy, Germany, and Japan were formed on the basis of an ethnic nationalism that in a sense created nations but not necessarily ones with the ideals of equality embodied in constitutional nation-states. World War I set back Germany, Italy, and Japan, but afterward they elevated their ethnic nationalism into supremacist nationalism and adopted imperialism, all under the banner of modernity. In Russia, communists seized the opportunity offered by the turmoil of World War I to turn a constitutionally as well as industrially underdeveloped empire into a communist, one-party industrial empire. The United States, Britain, and France, each based on variations of constitutionalism, industry, and smaller or larger empires, became advocates of a capitalist democratic modernity.

Capitalist democracy was a modernity that upheld free enterprise, the market, and consumerism. It succeeded in providing the modern items of daily life, but it suffered a major setback in the Depression and had to be reined in through tightened political controls. It also withheld freedom, equality, and the staples of daily life from minorities and the colonized. Communism succeeded in industrializing an underdeveloped empire and providing the bare necessities for modern life; it did so with untold human sacrifices. Supremacist nationalism was attractive to nationalists who were not workers and therefore afraid of communism. Supremacist nationalists held democracies in disdain because they considered constitutions meaningless pieces of paper.

▶ **What were the strengths and flaws of each of the three visions of modernity?**

▶ **Why did supremacist nationalism disappear in the ashes of World War II?**

Supremacist nationalism was a modernity that failed because the conquest of new, self-sufficient empires proved to be impossible. The advocates of democratic capitalist and communist modernity—most notably the United States, Great Britain, France, and the Soviet Union—were dangerously threatened by Germany, Italy, and Japan and came together to destroy these supremacist-nationalist countries.

Thus ended the action at Hill 60. Birdwood believed that the actual knoll had been captured, and so reported to Hamilton, who wrote: "Knoll 60, now ours throughout, commands the Biyuk Anafarta valley with view and fire—a big tactical scoop." As a matter of fact half the summit—or possibly rather more—was still in possession of the Turks. The fighting of August 27th, 28th, and 29th had, however, given the troops on the left of Anzac a position astride the spur from which a fairly satisfactory view could be had over the plain to the "W" Hills. The cost was over 1,100 casualties. The burden of the work had been sustained by war-worn troops. The magnificent brigade of New Zealand Mounted Rifles, which was responsible for the main advances, had been worked until it was almost entirely consumed, its four regiments at the end numbering only 365 all told. The 4th Australian Infantry Brigade which, through defective co-ordination with the artillery, had been twice thrown against a difficult objective without a chance of success, was reduced to 968. General Russell and his brigade-major, Powles, had worked untiringly, the latter personally guiding almost every attacking party to its starting point in the dangerous maze of trenches. It was not their fault that at this stage of the war both staff and commanders were only learning the science of trench-warfare. Had the experience and the instruments of later years been available, the action at Hill 60 would doubtless have been fought differently.

## ▶ Working with Sources

1. **What factors, in Bean's estimation, led to the very high casualty figures among the Allied troops in this campaign?**

2. **Does Bean consider the loss of these troops a "useless waste of life"? Were the leaders of the effort incompetent?**

## SOURCE 28.2

# Vera Brittain, *Testament of Youth*

## 1933

**B**orn in 1893 into an upper-class family at a time when society expected neither intellectual nor professional achievement from such women, Vera Brittain obtained a scholarship to Somerville College at Oxford University in 1914. When the war began in August 1914, her brother, Edward, and his best friend, Roland Leighton, enlisted. Brittain left college the following year to study nursing, and she joined a VAD (Voluntary Aid Detachment)

Source: Vera Brittain, *Testament of Youth* (New York: Seaview, 1980), 239–241.

unit. Having become engaged to Leighton while he was home on leave in August 1915, Brittain learned in December of that year that he had been killed in action on the Western Front. Continuing her nursing work, Brittain experienced the loss of numerous other friends and relatives, including her brother, over the course of the war. After the war, she returned to Oxford and developed an important literary career in her own right, publishing her beautifully written and compelling wartime memoir *Testament of Youth* in 1933. Throughout the 1930s, she advocated international peace and women's rights, insisting that the shattering experiences of her youth should not be reinflicted on contemporary young people.

Perhaps ...
To R. A. L.

Perhaps some day the sun will shine
  again,
And I shall see that still the skies
  are blue,
And feel once more I do not live
  in vain,
Although bereft of You.

Perhaps the golden meadows at my
  feet
Will make the sunny hours of
  spring seem gay,
And I shall find the white May-blos-
  soms sweet,
Though You have passed away.

Perhaps the summer woods will
  shimmer bright,
And crimson roses once again
  be fair,
And autumn harvest fields a
  rich delight,
Although You are not there.

But though kind Time may
  many joys renew,
There is one greatest joy I shall
  not know
Again, because my heart for loss
  of You
Was broken, long ago.
V. B. 1916.
—From *Verses of a V.A.D.*

Whenever I think of the weeks that followed the news of Roland's death, a series of pictures, disconnected but crystal clear, unroll themselves like a kaleidoscope through my mind.

A solitary cup of coffee stands before me on a hotel breakfast-table; I try to drink it, but fail ignominiously.

Outside, in front of the promenade, dismal grey waves tumble angrily over one another on the windy Brighton shore, and, like a slaughtered animal that still twists after life has been extinguished, I go on mechanically worrying because his channel-crossing must have been so rough.

In an omnibus, going to Keymer, I look fixedly at the sky; suddenly the pale light of a watery sun streams out between the dark, swollen clouds, and I think for one crazy moment that I have seen the heavens opened. . . .

At Keymer a fierce gale is blowing and I am out alone on the brown winter ploughlands, where I have been driven by a desperate desire to escape from the others. Shivering violently, and convinced that I am going to be sick, I take refuge behind a wet bank of grass from the icy sea-wind that rushes, screaming, across the sodden fields.

It is late afternoon; at the organ of the small village church, Edward is improvising a haunting memorial hymn for Roland, and the words: "God walked in the garden in the cool of the evening," flash irrelevantly into my mind.

I am back on night-duty at Camberwell after my leave; in the chapel, as the evening voluntary is played, I stare with swimming eyes at the lettered wall, and remember reading the words: "I am the Resurrection and the Life," at the early morning communion service before going to Brighton.

I am buying some small accessories for my uniform in a big Victoria Street store, when I stop, petrified, before a vase of the tall pink roses that Roland gave me on the way to *David Copperfield*; in the warm room their melting sweetness brings back the memory of that New Year's Eve, and suddenly, to the perturbation of the shop-assistants, I burst into uncontrollable tears, and find myself, helpless and humiliated, unable to stop crying in the tram all the way back to the hospital.

It is Sunday, and I am out for a solitary walk through the dreary streets of Camberwell before going to bed after the night's work. In front of me on the frozen pavement a long red worm wriggles slimily. I remember that, after our death, worms destroy this body—however lovely, however beloved—and I run from the obscene thing in horror.

It is Wednesday, and I am walking up the Brixton Road on a mild, fresh morning of early spring. Half-consciously I am repeating a line from Rupert Brooke:

*"The deep night, and birds singing, and clouds flying . . ."*

For a moment I have become conscious of the old joy in rainwashed skies and scuttling, fleecy clouds, when suddenly I remember—Roland is dead and I am not keeping faith with him; it is mean and cruel, even for a second, to feel glad to be alive.

▶ Working with Sources

1. How did Brittain cope with the grief of losing her fiancé?

2. Did the Great War impose unique burdens on women? In what respects?

## SOURCE 28.3

# Benito Mussolini and Giovanni Gentile, "Foundations and Doctrine of Fascism"

## 1932

Through a series of small demonstrations and gatherings in 1919, Benito Mussolini (1883–1945) created, at least in his own estimation, a completely new political ideology. He named this philosophy for a symbol used in the ancient Roman empire: the fasces, which was a bundle of rods together with an ax and carried by lictors as a representation of power. Mussolini was installed as Italy's leader, or "Duce," in October 1922. He published an explanation of what he had achieved as well as a statement of his political beliefs in the *Enciclopedia Italiana* in June 1932. Reflecting on the decade of rule following his seizure of "totalitarian" power (the word itself was coined by this regime, and specifically with the collaboration of Mussolini's court philosopher, Giovanni Gentile), Mussolini justified the violence inflicted by his regime and emphasized its fundamentally "moral" basis.

Anti-individualistic, the fascist conception of life stresses the importance of the state. It affirms the value of the individual only insofar as his interests coincide with those of the state, which stands for the conscience and the universal will of man in history. It opposes classical liberalism, which arose as a revolt against absolutism and exhausted its historical function when the state became the expression of the conscience and will of the people. Liberalism denied the state in the name of the individual; fascism reasserts the state as the true reality of the individual. And if liberty is to be the attribute of living men and not of the sort of abstract dummies invented by individualistic liberalism, then fascism stands for liberty. Fascism stands for the only liberty worth possessing: the liberty of the state and of the individual within the state. The fascist conception of the state is all-embracing. Outside of it no human or spiritual values can exist, much less have value. Thus understood, fascism is totalitarian, and the fascist state—in which all values are synthesized and united—interprets, develops, and heightens the life of the people.

No individuals outside the state; no groups (political parties, associations, trade unions, social classes) outside the state. This is why fascism is opposed to socialism, which sees in history nothing but class struggle and

Source: Jeffrey T. Schnapp, ed., *A Primer of Italian Fascism*, trans. Jeffrey T. Schnapp, Olivia E. Sears, and Maria G. Stampino (Lincoln: University of Nebraska Press, 2000), 48–50.

neglects the possibility of achieving unity within the state (which effects the fusion of classes into a single economic and moral reality). This is also why fascism is opposed to trade unionism as a class weapon. But when brought within the orbit of the state, fascism recognizes the real needs that gave rise to socialism and trade unionism, giving them due weight in the corporative system in which divergent interests are harmonized within the unity that is the state.

Grouped according to their interests, individuals make up classes. They make up trade unions when organized according to their economic activities. But, first and foremost, they make up the state, which is no mere matter of numbers, or simply the sum of the individuals forming the majority. Accordingly, fascism is opposed to that form of democracy that equates a nation with the majority, reducing it to the lowest common denominator. But fascism represents the purest form of democracy if the nation is considered—as it should be—from the standpoint of quality rather than quantity. This means considering the nation as an idea, the mightiest because the most ethical, the most coherent, the truest; an idea actualizing itself in a people as the conscience and will of the few, if not of One; an idea tending to actualize itself in the conscience and the will of the mass, of the collective ethnically molded by natural and historical conditions into a single nation that moves with a single conscience and will along a uniform line of development and spiritual formation. Not a race or a geographically delimited region but a people, perpetuating itself in history, a multitude unified by an idea and imbued with the will to live, with the will to power, with a self-consciousness and a personality.

To the degree that it is embodied in a state, this higher personality becomes a nation. It is not the nation that generates the state (an antiquated naturalistic concept that afforded the basis for nineteenth-century propaganda in favor of national governments); rather, it is the state that creates the nation, granting volition and therefore real existence to a people that has become aware of its moral unity.

. . .

A higher, more powerful expression of personality, the fascist state embodies a spiritual force encompassing all manifestations of the moral and intellectual life of man. Its functions cannot be limited to those of maintaining order and keeping the peace, as liberal doctrine would have it. The fascist state is no mere mechanical device for delimiting the sphere within which individuals may exercise their supposed rights. It represents an inwardly accepted standard and rule of conduct. A discipline of the whole person, it permeates the will no less than the intellect. It is the very principle, the soul of souls [*anima dell'anima*], that inspires every man who is a member of a civilized society, penetrating deep into his personality and dwelling within the heart of the man of action and the thinker, the artist, and the man of science.

Fascism, in short, is not only a law giver and a founder of institutions but also an educator and a promoter of spiritual life. It aims to refashion not only the forms of life but also their content: man, his character, his faith. To this end it champions discipline and authority; authority that infuses the soul and rules with undisputed sway. Accordingly, its chosen emblem is the lictor's fasces: symbol of unity, strength, and justice.

▶ **Working with Sources**

1. How does Mussolini contrast fascism with "liberalism"? Is his contrast merely empty rhetoric?

2. Why does Mussolini pay so much attention to the "spiritual" elements that animate fascism? Why does he avoid attributing historical development to materialist causes?

## SOURCE 28.4

# Adolf Hitler, *Mein Kampf*

## 1925

As a result of the failure of his Beer Hall Putsch in Munich in November 1923, Adolf Hitler (1889–1945) was sent to a minimum security prison at Landsberg. However, he was paroled, four years before the completion of his sentence, in December 1924. Having met with the respect of his judges during his trial in February 1924 and with the approval of the Bavarian Supreme Court, although against the advice of state prosecutors, he had his sentence—after his conviction for a treasonable attempt to take over the state—commuted. Nevertheless, there were some restrictions, both in Bavaria and elsewhere in Germany, on Hitler's speaking and freedom of movement. In spite of these restrictions, he emerged from prison with the manuscript of a new political statement of his life and philosophy, a document he entitled *Mein Kampf* (*My Struggle*). As recently discovered documents reveal, Hitler hoped to use the proceeds from the sale of this book for a new car as well as to fund his political movement. The party growing out of this movement would be labeled the National Socialist German Workers' Party, and he would be installed as its unquestioned *Führer* (leader) by 1925. The following excerpt from *Mein Kampf* reveals what he had learned about rhetoric and political action in his nascent career.

I have already stated in the first volume that all great, world-shaking events have been brought about, not by written matter, but by the spoken word. This led to a lengthy discussion in a part of the press, where, of course, such an assertion was sharply attacked, particularly by our bourgeois wiseacres. But the very reason why this occurred confutes the doubters.

Source: Adolf Hitler, *Mein Kampf*, trans. Ralph Mannheim (Boston: Houghton Mifflin, 1998), 469–471.

For the bourgeois intelligentsia protest against such a view only because they themselves obviously lack the power and ability to influence the masses by the spoken word, since they have thrown themselves more and more into purely literary activity and renounced the real agitational activity of the spoken word. Such habits necessarily lead in time to what distinguishes our bourgeoisie today; that is, to the loss of the psychological instinct for *mass effect and mass influence*.

While the speaker gets a continuous correction of his speech from the crowd he is addressing, since he can always see in the faces of his listeners to what extent they can follow his arguments with understanding and whether the impression and the effect of his words lead to the desired goal— the writer does not know his readers at all. Therefore, to begin with, he will not aim at a definite mass before his eyes, but will keep his arguments entirely general. By this to a certain degree he loses psychological subtlety and in consequence suppleness. And so, by and large, a brilliant speaker will be able to write better than a brilliant writer can speak, unless he continuously practices this art. On top of this there is the fact that the mass of people as such is lazy; that they remain inertly in the spirit of their old habits and, left to themselves, will take up a piece of written matter only reluctantly if it is not in agreement with what they themselves believe and does not bring them what they had hoped for. Therefore, an article with a definite tendency is for the most part read only by people who can already be reckoned to this tendency. At most a leaflet or a poster can, by its brevity, count on getting a moment's attention from someone who thinks differently.

The picture in all its forms up to the film has greater possibilities. Here a man needs to use his brains even less; it suffices to look, or at most to read extremely brief texts, and thus many will more readily accept a *pictorial presentation* than *read* an *article* of any *length*. The picture brings them in a much briefer time, I might almost say at one stroke, the enlightenment which they obtain from written matter only after arduous reading.

The essential point, however, is that a piece of literature never knows into what hands it will fall, and yet must retain its definite form. In general the effect will be the greater, the more this form corresponds to the intellectual level and nature of those very people who will be its readers. A book that is destined for the broad masses must, therefore, attempt from the very beginning to have an effect, both in style and elevation, different from a work intended for higher intellectual classes.

Only by this kind of adaptability does written matter approach the spoken word. To my mind, the speaker can treat the same theme as the book; he will, if he is a brilliant popular orator, not be likely to repeat the same reproach and the same substance twice in the same form. He will always let himself be borne by the great masses in such a way that instinctively the very words come to his lips that he needs to speak to the hearts of his audience. And if he errs, even in the slightest, he has the living correction before him. As I have said, he can read from the facial expression of his audience whether, firstly, they *understand* what he is saying, whether, secondly, they can *follow the speech as a whole*, and to what extent, thirdly, he has *convinced* them of the *soundness* of what he has said. If—firstly—he sees that they do not understand him, he will become so primitive and clear in his explanations that even the last member of his audience has to understand him; if he feels—secondly—that they cannot follow him, he will construct his ideas so cautiously and slowly that even the weakest member of the audience is not left behind, and he will—thirdly—if he suspects that they do not seem convinced of the soundness of his argument, repeat it over and over in constantly new examples. He himself will utter their objections, which he senses though unspoken, and go on confuting them and exploding them, until at length even the last group of an opposition, by its very bearing and facial expression, enables him to recognize its capitulation to his arguments.

Here again it is not seldom a question of overcoming prejudices which are not based on reason, but, for the most part unconsciously, are supported only by sentiment. To overcome this barrier of instinctive aversion, of emotional hatred, of prejudiced rejection, is a thousand times harder than to correct a faulty or erroneous scientific opinion. False concepts and poor knowledge can be eliminated by instruction, the resistance of the emotions never. Here only an appeal to these mysterious powers themselves can be effective; and the writer can hardly ever accomplish this, but almost exclusively the orator.

▶ **Working with Sources**

1. What advantages does the orator have over the writer, in Hitler's assessment? Is he convincing on this point?

2. How does a skillful speaker manipulate an audience? Does the substance of the speech matter at all, according to Hitler's description of the process of public speaking?

## SOURCE 28.5

# Franklin D. Roosevelt, undelivered address planned for Jefferson Day

**April 13, 1945**

During his first inaugural address as the president of the United States in March 1933, Franklin D. Roosevelt had warned his fellow Americans, "The only thing we have to fear is fear itself." Through a series of radio broadcasts called "fireside chats," the president continued to reassure the

Source: Gerhard Peters and John T. Woolley, the American Presidency Project, http://www.presidency. ucsb.edu/ws/?pid=16602.

American public during the darkest days of the Depression. He would go on, in January 1941, to enumerate the "four freedoms" to which every American, and perhaps every person around the globe, was entitled. Among these were freedom of speech, freedom of worship, freedom from want, and, perhaps most importantly, freedom from fear.

Suffering from debilitating illness in the final years of the war, Roosevelt persisted in envisioning a world in which those four freedoms could be guaranteed—and in which the unprecedented and horrific suffering of World War II could be transformed into a new period of human development. As Thomas Paine had argued about the American Revolution, there was now a chance "to begin the world over again." Roosevelt prepared an oration on the subject to be delivered on the occasion of Thomas Jefferson's birthday. The war was drawing to its close in Europe, and would end several months later in Asia—but Roosevelt did not live to see the achievement of peace. Although he died on April 12, 1945, the day before he was to deliver this address, the prepared speech demonstrates the tenor of Roosevelt's thought at this point in his life.

Today this Nation which Jefferson helped so greatly to build is playing a tremendous part in the battle for the rights of man all over the world.

Today we are part of the vast Allied force—a force composed of flesh and blood and steel and spirit—which is today destroying the makers of war, the breeders of hatred, in Europe and in Asia.

In Jefferson's time our Navy consisted of only a handful of frigates headed by the gallant U.S.S. Constitution—Old Ironsides—but that tiny Navy taught Nations across the Atlantic that piracy in the Mediterranean—acts of aggression against peaceful commerce and the enslavement of their crews—was one of those things which, among neighbors, simply was not done.

Today we have learned in the agony of war that great power involves great responsibility. Today we can no more escape the consequences of German and Japanese aggression than could we avoid the consequences of attacks by the Barbary Corsairs a century and a half before.

We, as Americans, do not choose to deny our responsibility.

Nor do we intend to abandon our determination that, within the lives of our children and our children's children, there will not be a third world war.

We seek peace—enduring peace. More than an end to war, we want an end to the beginnings of all wars—yes, an end to this brutal, inhuman, and thoroughly impractical method of settling the differences between governments.

The once powerful, malignant Nazi state is crumbling. The Japanese war lords are receiving, in their own homeland, the retribution for which they asked when they attacked Pearl Harbor.

But the mere conquest of our enemies is not enough.

We must go on to do all in our power to conquer the doubts and the fears, the ignorance and the greed, which made this horror possible.

Thomas Jefferson, himself a distinguished scientist, once spoke of "the brotherly spirit of Science, which unites into one family all its votaries of whatever grade, and however widely dispersed throughout the different quarters of the globe."

Today, science has brought all the different quarters of the globe so close together that it is impossible to isolate them one from another.

Today we are faced with the pre-eminent fact that, if civilization is to survive, we must cultivate the science of human relationships—the ability of all peoples, of all kinds, to live together and work together, in the same world, at peace.

Let me assure you that my hand is the steadier for the work that is to be done, that I move more firmly into the task, knowing that you—millions and millions of you—are joined with me in the resolve to make this work endure.

The work, my friends, is peace. More than an end of this war—an end to the beginnings of all wars. Yes, an end, forever, to this impractical, unrealistic settlement of the differences between governments by the mass killing of peoples.

Today, as we move against the terrible scourge of war—as we go forward toward the greatest contribution that any generation of human beings can make in this world—the contribution of lasting peace, I ask you to keep up your faith. I measure the sound, solid achievement that can be made at this time by the straight edge of your own confidence and your resolve. And to you, and to all Americans who dedicate themselves with us to the making of an abiding peace, I say:

The only limit to our realization of tomorrow will be our doubts of today. Let us move forward with strong and active faith.

▶ **Working with Sources**

1. What did Roosevelt consider the root and ultimate causes of war?

2. How, in his belief, would a lasting peace be achieved and a "third world war" avoided?

# Chapter 29  1945–1962

# Reconstruction, Cold War, and Decolonization

B y any standard the event seemed symbolic of a new world order, one in which the emerging nonaligned nations would set the pace of innovation. Appropriately enough, it also marked the beginning of a new decade, one that would begin full of promise and peril and end in conflict and confusion for much of the world. The event was the 1960 election of the world's first female prime minister, Sirimavo Bandaranaike (1916–2000), of what was then called Ceylon (renamed Sri Lanka in 1972), a large island off the southeastern coast of India.

Coming from a prominent Buddhist family, she believed in a strong national foundation for her country as an independent nation beholden to neither West nor East. As a socialist, she continued the nationalization of the banking, insurance, and petroleum sectors begun by her husband, ordered the state to take over all Catholic schools, and joined the Non-Aligned Movement in 1961. The movement sought to bring India, Egypt, Yugoslavia, Indonesia, and a number of other states together as a bloc to retain their independence from the pressures of the Cold War between the two superpowers of the United States and the Soviet Union and their allies. Her strong commitment to a Sinhalese-only language policy, however, aroused considerable resistance in the country, especially

UNITED STATES  Europe  SOVIET UNION  Middle East  Africa  CHINA  India  South America  Australia

**THE COLD WAR AND DECOLONIZATION**

*ABOVE:* **Voters line up to cast their ballots in Ceylon (now Sri Lanka) on March 22, 1960. Sirimavo Bandaranaike was elected the world's first woman prime minister.**

from the Tamil minority in the north. The Theravada Buddhist Sinhalese compose about 74 percent and the Hindu Tamils 17 percent of the population. Only 2 years into Bandaranaike's tenure, the country was gripped by a Tamil civil disobedience campaign, and it rapidly became apparent that Ceylon was entering a time of political turbulence. Ultimately, anti-Tamil discrimination led to the abortive Tamil Tiger liberation war (1976–2009), pursued on both sides with the utmost brutality.

During her four terms as prime minister (1960–1965, 1970–1972, 1972–1977, and 1994–2000), Bandaranaike was a prominent leader on the world stage. Like her fellow female prime ministers Benazir Bhutto in Pakistan and Indira Gandhi in India and first-generation nonaligned leaders like Jawaharlal Nehru of India, Sukarno of Indonesia, and Gamal Abdel Nasser of Egypt, Bandaranaike tried to navigate the turbulent waters of ethnic and religious conflict, superpower pressure, and nation building in an increasingly competitive economic arena. The backdrop against which these nonaligned nations acted was woven from two main elements in the unfolding pattern of scientific–industrial modernity: the Cold War and decolonization. The capitalist–democratic and the socialist–communist spheres competed with each other for political, military, and economic dominance; at the same time, the West rid itself of what was now seen as its biggest curse—colonialism—which had severely detracted from its appeal during the interwar and early postwar periods.

## Superpower Confrontation: Capitalist Democracy and Communism

World War II was the most destructive war in human history. After nearly 6 years of fighting in Europe and 9 years in Asia, the total loss of life (including combatants, civilians, and victims of the Holocaust) is estimated at over 50 million, three times as many as in World War I. With the exception of the continental United States, which was unreachable by enemy aircraft, all combatant countries in World War II suffered widespread destruction. Most ominous was the use of the first atomic weapons by the United States against Japan in the final days of the war. Yet, while the war raged, the foundations of a new world organization to replace the old League of Nations— the **United Nations (UN)**, whose charter was later signed by 51 nations in October 1945—were being laid. Remarkably, within a few years, the world's remaining patterns of modernity—capitalism–democracy and socialism–communism—would reemerge from the ruins stronger than ever, each according to its own vision.

### The Cold War Era, 1945–1962
As the world rebuilt, the United States and the Soviet Union promoted their contrasting visions of modernity—capitalist–democratic and communist—with missionary fervor. For the next 45 years the two powers struggled to determine

## Seeing Patterns

▶ Why did the pattern of unfolding modernity, which offered three choices after World War I, shrink to just capitalist democracy and socialism–communism in 1945? How did each of these two patterns evolve between 1945 and 1962?

▶ What are the cultural premises of modernity?

▶ How did the newly independent countries of the Middle East, Asia, and Africa adapt to the divided world of the Cold War?

**United Nations:** Successor of the League of Nations, founded in 1945 and today comprising about 200 countries, with a Secretary General, a General Assembly meeting annually, and a standing Security Council composed of permanent members (United States, China, Russia, the United Kingdom, and France) as well as five rotating temporary members.

**Destruction and Despair in the Nuclear Age.** World War II was the most destructive human conflict in history, far exceeding the damage of what had only a short time before been considered to be "the war to end all wars"—World War I. Nowhere was the damage more complete than in Japan, where an aerial campaign of firebombing Japanese cities by American B-29s had destroyed nearly every major Japanese center. The culmination of this campaign was the first—and, to date, last—use of nuclear weapons in warfare on the Japanese cities of Hiroshima and Nagasaki in August 1945. Here, a mother and child who survived the nuclear destruction of Hiroshima sit amid the utter devastation of their city in December 1945.

which approach would prevail. While each on occasion engaged in brinkmanship—pushing crises to the edge of nuclear war—as a rule both sought to avoid direct confrontation. Instead, they pursued their aims of expanding and consolidating their respective systems, in a conflict dubbed the "Cold War," through ideological struggle and proxy states (that is, states acting as substitutes against each other). Two phases can be discerned in the early Cold War. The first lasted from 1945 to 1956, when the Soviet Union continued to pursue Stalin's prewar policy of "socialism in one country," which was now extended to include Eastern Europe. The second comprised the years 1956–1962, when Stalin's successor, Nikita Khrushchev (1894–1971, in office 1953–1964), reformulated the policy to include spreading aid and influence to new nationalist regimes in Asia and Africa that had won their independence from Western colonialism, even if these regimes were not (yet) communist. This new policy, applied to Cuba, produced the near-disaster of the Cuban Missile Crisis in 1962, during which the United States and the Soviet Union almost came to blows (see Map 29.1).

**Cold War:** Ideological struggle between the United States and its allies and the Soviet Union and its allies that lasted from 1945 to 1989.

**Cold War Origins**    The origins of the **Cold War** have been bitterly debated since the 1940s, with apologists for each side tending to blame its inception on the actions of the other. While it may not be possible at this point to establish an exact time or event marking the beginning of the Cold War, we can point to certain mileposts in its development. It is important to note that tensions and distrust between the United States and the Soviet Union began to emerge earlier in the twentieth century. As early as the Bolshevik Revolution, concerns mounted in the West regarding communist expansion, prompting fear of communism in America during the 1920s. Awareness of Joseph Stalin's policies in the 1930s contributed to increasing doubts that delayed American recognition of the Soviet government until 1933.

Another milepost came in the spring of 1945, when the Soviet Red Army occupied German-held territories in Eastern Europe and communist guerillas made rapid advances in the Balkans. In a secret deal between British prime minister Churchill and Soviet leader Stalin in May 1944, Greece became part of the British sphere, in return for Romania and Bulgaria being apportioned to the Soviet sphere of responsibility for occupation at war's end.

When it became increasingly clear that Stalin was determined to maintain the Russian presence in Eastern Europe, the United States formulated a policy designed to thwart Soviet expansion known as **containment**. First spelled out in 1946 by George F. Kennan, a diplomat in the State Department, the proposed policy served as the foundation for the administration's effort to confront communist expansion.

**Containment:** US foreign policy doctrine formulated in 1946 to limit as much as possible the spread of communism.

"It is clear that the United States cannot expect in the foreseeable future to enjoy political intimacy with the Soviet regime."

—George F. Kennan

**Confrontations, 1947–1949** The apportionment of spheres of interest in the Balkans did not work out well. In Yugoslavia, the anti-Nazi resistance hero Josip Broz Tito (1892–1980) took over the government in November 1945 with the help of Soviet advisors. He then provided Greek communists with aid to overthrow the royal government that had returned to rule with British support in 1946. The United States stepped in with supplies for the Greek government in 1947, assuming that Stalin was orchestrating aid from Yugoslavia, Bulgaria, and Romania. Under the **Truman Doctrine**, the United States announced its support of all "free peoples who are resisting attempted subjugation by armed minorities or by outside pressures."

A 2-year proxy civil war between East and West in Greece ended in a split between Tito and Stalin. In 1948, Tito claimed his right to regional communism, against Stalin's insistence on unity in the Communist Bloc. Although Stalin had never supported the Greek communists directly, given his agreement with Churchill, a surprising majority of them opted for Stalin. Tito withdrew his support for the pro-Stalin Greek communists, and the bid for communism in Greece collapsed in 1949.

In keeping with his doctrine, Truman announced the **Marshall Plan** of aid to Europe, for the recovery of the continent from the ruins of the war. The plan was named after its architect, secretary of state George C. Marshall (1880–1959). Although invited to take part, Stalin flatly rejected American aid and forbade Hungary, Czechoslovakia, and Poland to ask for it. In addition to the political reasons behind Stalin's injunction, the Marshall Plan's requirement of free markets and convertible currencies contradicted the communist ideology of a central command economy. Stalin instead engineered fledgling communist governments in Eastern Europe and the Balkans, transforming them into the Communist Bloc and integrating their economies with that of the Soviet Union. This was formalized in 1949 as the Council for Mutual Economic Assistance (COMECON).

**Truman Doctrine:** Policy formulated in 1947, initially to outline steps directed at preventing Greece and Turkey from becoming communist, primarily through military and economic aid.

**Marshall Plan:** Financial program of $13 billion to support the reconstruction of the economics of 17 European countries during 1948–1952, with most of the aid going to France, Germany, Italy, and the Netherlands.

| 1945 | 1947 | 1949 | 1952 |
|------|------|------|------|
| Yalta and Potsdam conferences | Indian and Pakistani independence | People's Republic of China; formation of NATO | Nasser assumes power in Egypt |

| 1946 | 1948 | 1950–1953 | 1953 |
|------|------|-----------|------|
| Churchill's "Iron Curtain" speech | State of Israel founded; first Arab–Israeli War | Korean War | CIA-inspired coup in Iran |

| 1955–1956 | 1957 | 1958 | 1961 |
|-----------|------|------|------|
| Morocco, Tunisia independent | USSR launches Sputnik satellite | Great Leap Forward in China | First earth orbit by Yuri Gagarin; erection of Berlin Wall |

| 1956 | 1957–1962 | 1959 | 1962 |
|------|-----------|------|------|
| Suez War of Great Britain, France, and Israel against Egypt | Independence for most African colonies | Castro assumes power in Cuba | Cuban Missile Crisis |

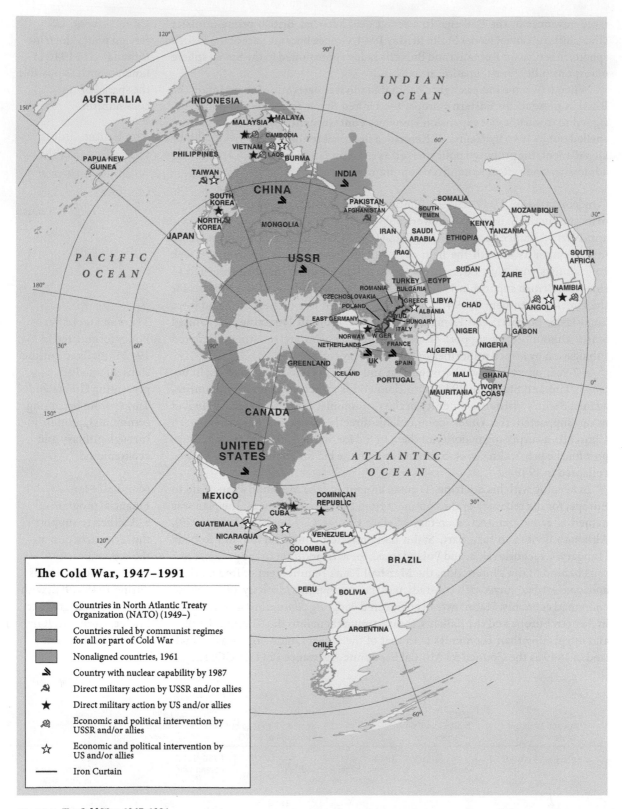

**The Cold War, 1947–1991**

Countries in North Atlantic Treaty Organization (NATO) (1949–)

Countries ruled by communist regimes for all or part of Cold War

Nonaligned countries, 1961

Country with nuclear capability by 1987

Direct military action by USSR and/or allies

Direct military action by US and/or allies

Economic and political intervention by USSR and/or allies

Economic and political intervention by US and/or allies

Iron Curtain

MAP **29.1 The Cold War, 1947–1991.**

**The Berlin Airlift.** From June 1948 to May 1949, US, British, and British Commonwealth airplanes delivered more than 2 million tons of food and supplies to Berlin after Stalin had blocked all land access to the city. Here, Berlin children eagerly await the next delivery of supplies.

The success of the American Marshall Plan further irritated Stalin because it made the Western sectors of Germany and Berlin magnets for Eastern Europeans fleeing to the West. In 1948, therefore, the Soviets took the provocative step of setting up a highway and rail blockade of food and supplies to Berlin. The United States and Britain responded with the "Berlin Airlift," a demonstration of technological prowess as well as humanitarian compassion. For nearly a year, food, fuel, and other supplies required by this large city were flown in until Stalin finally gave up the blockade.

So far, the Cold War in Europe had been confined to diplomatic maneuvering between Washington and Moscow. During the Berlin crisis, however, the confrontation assumed military dimensions. Thanks in part to an elaborate espionage network embedded inside the nuclear programs of Britain and the United States, the Soviets had accelerated their efforts to build a nuclear bomb. In 1949, they detonated their first device 4 years earlier than anticipated. Now, with its advantage in nuclear weapons eliminated and concern increasing over the possibility of a communist takeover in Western Europe, the United States formed a defensive alliance known as the North Atlantic Treaty Organization (NATO) in 1949. In response, the Soviet Union later formed the Warsaw Pact in 1955 among the states of the Eastern Bloc.

**The Central Intelligence Agency**    In addition to military and diplomatic initiatives to contain the spread of communism, the United States used alternative means to overthrow left-leaning and socialist movements and governments around the globe. For these purposes the government relied primarily on the Central Intelligence Agency (CIA), an offshoot of the Office of Strategic Studies (OSS)

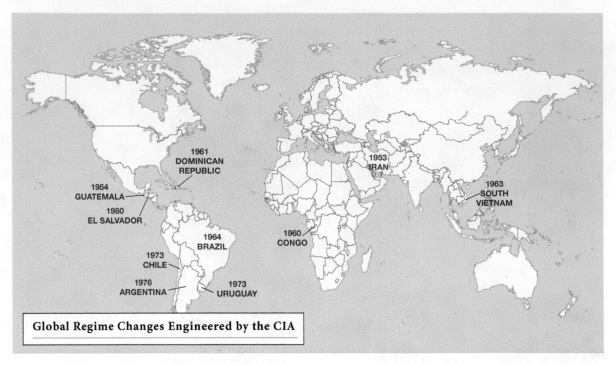

Global Regime Changes Engineered by the CIA

MAP 29.2 **Global Regime Changes Engineered by the CIA.**

developed during World War II. To carry out its mission the CIA employed a variety of covert operations including spy missions, electronic eavesdropping, photographs obtained by high-flying aircraft, and even outright assassination plots. As indicated in Map 29.2, CIA involvement in regime changes spanned the globe.

**Hot War in Korea** Emboldened by the development of the nuclear bomb and the victory of the Chinese communists over the nationalists in October 1949, Stalin ratcheted up the Cold War. After a series of raids and counter-raids between communist North Korea and nationalist South Korea and Stalin's blessing for an invasion by the north, the Cold War turned hot. In June 1950, large numbers of North Korean communist troops invaded South Korea in an attempt at forcible unification. South Korean troops fought a desperate rearguard action at the southern end of the peninsula. Under US pressure and despite a Soviet boycott, the UN Security Council branded North Korea as the aggressor, entitling South Korea to UN intervention. At first, in July 1950, the North Korean invaders trapped US troops arriving from Japan and what remained of the South Korean defense forces in the southeast. But by October US troops, augmented by troops from a number of UN members, had mounted a surprise amphibious invasion and fought their way into North Korea, occupied the capital (Pyongyang), and advanced to the Chinese border.

In the meantime, the United States had sent a fleet to the remnant of the Chinese nationalists who had formed the Republic of China on the southern island of Taiwan, to protect it from a threatened invasion by a newly communist China. Thwarted in the south at Taiwan, Mao Zedong took the pronouncements of General Douglas MacArthur, the commander of the UN forces in Korea, about raiding Chinese supply bases on the North Korean border seriously. Stalin, on the other hand, opposed escalation and gave Mao only token support.

Secretly marching to the border in October 1950, communist Chinese troops launched a massive surprise offensive into the peninsula, pushing the UN forces back deep into South Korea. Over the next 3 years, the war seesawed back and forth over the old border of the 38th parallel, while negotiations dragged on. Unwilling to expand the war further or use nuclear weapons, the new Eisenhower administration and the North Koreans agreed to an armistice in 1953. The armistice has endured since that date, and no official peace treaty was ever signed. For more than half a century, the border between the two Koreas has remained a volatile flashpoint, with provocative incidents repeatedly threatening to reopen the conflict.

**McCarthyism in the United States**    The strains of a hot war in Korea had a troubling domestic impact in the United States as well. Amid the general atmosphere of anticommunism, Joseph McCarthy (1908–1957), a Republican senator from Wisconsin, sensationally announced in 1950 that he had a lengthy list of members of the Communist Party employed by the State Department. Though he never produced the list, his smear tactics, together with denunciations made by the House Committee on Un-American Activities, ruined the careers of hundreds of government employees, movie actors and writers, and private persons in many walks of life. McCarthy went as far as accusing Presidents Truman and Eisenhower of tolerating communist "fellow travelers" in their administrations. After 4 years of anticommunist hysteria, enough voices of reason arose in the Senate to censure McCarthy and relegate him to obscurity. The legacy of bitterness engendered by the "McCarthy era" remained for decades and generated abundant political accusations on both sides.

**Revolt in East Germany**    In April 1953, at the height of the McCarthy drama and the ongoing Korean armistice negotiations at Panmunjom, Stalin died of a stroke. The death of this powerful and paranoid dictator was profoundly unsettling for the governments of the Eastern Bloc, especially in the German Democratic Republic (East Germany). The East German government was nervously watching the rising wave of defections to the Federal Republic (West Germany)—nearly a million persons during 1949–1953. It had sealed off the border through a system of fences and watchtowers, but Berlin—also divided into East and West sectors—was still a gaping hole. The population was seething over rising production quotas, shortages resulting from the shipment of industrial goods to the Soviet Union (in the name of reparations), and the beginnings of a West German economic boom in which it could not share.

In June 1953, a strike among East Berlin workers quickly grew into a general uprising, encompassing some 500 cities and towns. East German police and Soviet troops, stunned at first, quickly moved to suppress the revolt. The Politburo (the Communist Party's Central Committee Political Bureau) in Moscow, still trying to determine Stalin's successor, refused any concessions, except for a few cosmetic changes in the reparations. The German Stalinist government obediently complied.

In the fall of 1953 Nikita Khrushchev was chosen to succeed Stalin. Khrushchev, a metalworker from a poor farming family on the Russian–Ukrainian border, had worked his way up through the party hierarchy during the war. It took him a year and a half to consolidate his power as party secretary and premier, during which he made substantial investments in agriculture, housing, and consumer goods. In February 1956 he gave a much-noted speech in which he denounced Stalin's "excesses" during collectivization and the purges of the 1930s. Thousands were released from prisons and labor camps (*gulags*). In the Communist Bloc Khrushchev pushed to replace Stalinist hard-liners with new faces willing to improve general living conditions for the population. To balance the new flexibility within the Soviet Bloc, Khrushchev was careful to maintain toughness toward the West. He alarmed leaders of the West when he announced that he was abandoning Stalin's doctrine of socialism in one country for a new policy that supported anticolonial nationalist independence movements around the globe even if the movements were not communist.

**Revolt in Poland and Hungary**   Khrushchev's reforms awakened hopes in Eastern Europe that new leaders would bring change there as well. In Poland, where collectivization and the command economy had progressed only slowly and the Catholic Church could not be intimidated, Khrushchev's speech resulted in workers' unrest similar to East Germany 3 years earlier. Nationalist reformists gained the upper hand over Stalinists in the Polish Politburo, and Khrushchev realized that he had to avoid another Tito-style secession at all costs. After a few tense days in mid-October, pitting Soviet troops and an angry population against each other, Poland received its limited autonomy.

**Unrest in the Soviet Bloc.**
In the Hungarian uprising from October to November 1956, some 2,500 Hungarians and 700 Soviet troops were killed, while 200,000 fled to neighboring Austria and elsewhere in the West. Here, a young boy and older man watch while a Soviet tank rumbles through an intersection with barricades set up by Hungarian "freedom fighters."

In Hungary, the Politburo was similarly divided between reformers and Stalinists. People in Budapest and other cities, watching events in Poland with intense interest, took to the streets. The Politburo lost control, and the man appointed to lead the country to a national communist solution similar to that of Poland, Imre Nagy [noj] (1896–1958), felt emboldened by popular support to announce a multiparty system and the withdrawal of Hungary from the Warsaw Pact. This was too much for Khrushchev, who unleashed the Soviet troops stationed in Hungary to repress what had become a grassroots revolution.

Aware of British, French, and American preoccupation with the Suez Crisis, the Soviets crushed the uprising in November 1956. Nagy, finding sanctuary in the Yugoslav Embassy and promised safe conduct out of the country, was duped and arrested. The new pro-Moscow government executed him in 1958. During the brief uprising, perhaps a quarter of a million Hungarian citizens escaped to the West. For those who stayed, in the hopes of experiencing greater freedom, the events were a crushing blow.

**ICBMs and Sputniks**  The suppression of anticommunist unrest in the Eastern Bloc lessened the appeal of communism among many Marxists and revolutionary socialists in the West. But steady advancement in weapons technologies, including missiles and space flight, revealed a powerful military punch behind Soviet repression. In 1957 the Soviet Union announced the development of the world's first intercontinental ballistic missile (ICBM), with a range of around 3,500 miles, making it capable of reaching America's East Coast. In the same year, the Soviet Union launched the world's first orbiting satellite, named Sputnik, into space. Then, in 1961, Russian scientists sent the world's first cosmonaut, Yuri Gagarin (1934–1968), into space, followed 2 years later by Valentina Tereshkova (b. 1937), the world's first female cosmonaut.

These Soviet achievements frightened the Eisenhower administration and Congress as the implications of nuclear weapons descending from space with no practicable defense against them began to set in. Politicians played up the apparent technological leadership of the Soviet Union to goad Congress into accelerating the US missile and space program even at the risk of reheating the Cold War with the Soviet Union. Thus, in 1958 the United States successfully launched its first satellite, Explorer 1, and the following year its first ICBM, the Atlas. The space and missile races were now fully under way.

**Communism in Cuba**  In 1959, Fidel Castro (b. 1926), a nationalist guerilla fighter opposed to the influence of American companies over a government generally perceived as corrupt, seized power in Cuba. A lawyer, Castro was the son of a Spanish immigrant who had become a wealthy planter. About 6 months after the coup, Cuba was the new symbol of the Khrushchev government's widely hailed openness toward national liberation movements worthy of communist largesse. The Soviet Union lavished huge sums on the development of the island's economy. Khrushchev's instincts were proven right when Castro openly embraced communism in 1960.

To counter Khrushchev's overtures to national liberation movements, President Eisenhower and the head of the CIA, Allen Dulles (1893–1969), secretly supported and trained anticommunist dissidents in the Middle East, Africa, and

**Aiming for the Stars.** New scholarship sheds light on Sputnik's role in Russian cultural history. As this commemorative postcard reveals, the connection between the technological achievement of Sputnik and popular interest in space travel was strong. The legend reads in Russian: "4 October, the USSR launched Earth's first artificial satellite; 3 November, the USSR launched Earth's second artificial satellite."

Latin America. In the case of Latin America, a group of Cuban anticommunists trained in Guatemala with CIA support for an invasion and overthrow of Castro in Cuba. President John F. Kennedy (in office 1961–1963) inherited the initiative and, against his better judgment, decided to steer a middle course, sanctioning an invasion of Cuba by seemingly independent freedom fighters with no direct US military support. The so-called Bay of Pigs invasion in April 1961 (named for the small bay in southern Cuba where the anticommunist invasion began) was promptly intercepted and easily defeated by Castro's forces, to the great embarrassment of Kennedy.

**The Berlin Wall** Fortunately for the United States, Khrushchev suffered a severe embarrassment of his own. East Germany, which retained its Stalinist leadership, pressured Khrushchev to close the last opening in Berlin through which its citizens could escape to West Germany. Between 1953 and 1961, the East German "brain drain" reached 3 million defectors, or nearly one-fifth of the population, most of them young and ambitious people whose talent and skills the regime coveted. The East German Stalinists, allied with a few remaining Stalinists in the Politburo, prevailed over Khrushchev's opposition and built the Berlin Wall in 1961, effectively turning the German Democratic Republic into a prison.

**Post-War Eastern Europe** Behind the Iron Curtain eastern European countries freed from Nazism by advancing Red Armies, known collectively as the Eastern (or Soviet) Bloc, consisted of eight countries: Albania, Bulgaria, Czechoslovakia, East Germany, Hungary, Poland, Romania, and Yugoslavia. The social and cultural patterns of each of these nations were of different forms, but one theme that unites them all concerns their social and cultural experiences. Adherence to official Soviet policies was rigidly controlled by state centralization administered ultimately by the Communist Party in Moscow, enforced at the local level by Party committees.

Coercion was enforced through a network of secret police, the KGB, and concentration camps in the Russian gulag system. Although throughout the Stalinist era (1945–1953) and post-Stalinist period (1953–1968) industrialization was increased, often at the expense of agricultural production, shortages and even rationing of consumer goods were common. Employment opportunities were not on a par with those created by the Western economic postwar recovery, and although women were afforded jobs in the workforce, their principal responsibilities still lay within the home. State-sponsored educational programs stressed a program of Soviet propaganda and the sciences. The media were carefully monitored, cultural and religious expression was rigidly censored, and Western culture was condemned. Even so, some aspects of Western culture—especially jazz and rock music—found their way around the censors, along with diversions provided by television shows and athletic competitions.

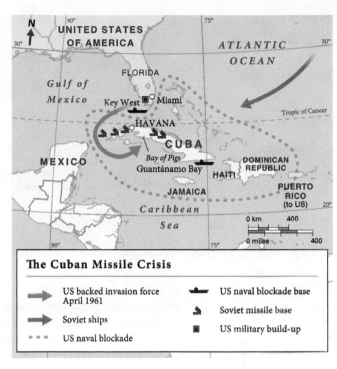

MAP 29.3 **The Cuban Missile Crisis.**

The playing field between East and West was now level, with setbacks on both sides, when the two reached the climax of the Cold War: the first direct confrontation between the Soviet Union and the United States, nearly two decades after the end of World War II. In October 1962, when US spy planes discovered the presence of missile launching pads in Cuba, President Kennedy demanded their immediate destruction and then followed up with a naval blockade of the island to prevent the arrival of Russian missiles. In defiance, Khrushchev dispatched Russian ships to Cuba; when it was discovered that they were bearing more missiles, President Kennedy demanded that Khrushchev recall the ships. The world held its breath for several days as the ships headed steadily for Cuba, raising the very real possibility of a nuclear exchange between the world's superpowers (see Map 29.3).

In the face of American determination, Khrushchev recalled the ships at the last minute. Kennedy, for his part, agreed to remove American missiles from Turkey. Realizing just how close the world had come to World War III, Kennedy and Khrushchev signed the Nuclear Test Ban Treaty in 1963, an agreement banning the aboveground testing of nuclear weapons. The treaty also sought to prevent the spread of these technologies to other countries. After this dramatic climax in the Cold War, relations gradually thawed.

## Society and Culture in Postwar North America, Europe, and Japan

In the years after World War II, veterans sought to pursue civilian lives of normalcy and comfort. Intellectuals and artists again cast a critical eye on modern culture, as the previous generation had after World War I. Now, however, the political and ideological options were narrower. Supremacist nationalism in the form of fascism, Nazism, or militarism had been thoroughly bankrupted, and the

**The GI Bill for African Americans.** Staff Sergeant Herbert Ellison explains the GI Bill to members of his company. The bill, enacted in 1944, provided soldiers returning from the war with support for training and education as well as subsidized home loans. Some 7.8 million veterans benefited from the training and education it provided.

**Modernism:** Any of various movements in philosophy and the arts characterized by a deliberate break with classical or traditional forms of thought or expression.

**Existentialism:** A form of thought built on the assumption that modern scientific–industrial society is without intrinsic meaning unless an answer to the question of what constitutes authentic existence is found.

choices had shrunk to communism and capitalist democracy. Still, among the emerging nations, artists and intellectuals struggled to forge new paths, often attempting synthesis among indigenous culture and socialist and democratic ideas.

**Mass Consumption Culture**    American soldiers returned to civilian life and started families, launching the so-called baby-boomer generation between 1945 and 1961. Families with four to six children were almost the norm. Medical advances and better diet and nutrition improved the health of parents and children. The growing population triggered increased consumer demand for such basics as food, clothes, and shelter, as well as consumer durables that increased the comfort of living, such as refrigerators, dishwashers, vacuum cleaners, radios, televisions, telephones, and cars. In the United States, the GI Bill supported not only a middle-class lifestyle but also university studies that led to better-paying jobs. In Europe, the Marshall Plan helped to provide Europeans with similar, if still somewhat lower, living standards. Americans increasingly took on credit to move into their middle-class lives, while Europeans tended to save first before purchasing consumer goods.

In the idealized family of the 1950s and early 1960s, husbands worked downtown from 9:00 to 5:00, while mothers and grandmothers were responsible for the household and children. Shopping was done in the new suburban mall, and everybody went to church or synagogue on weekends and occasionally treated themselves with a trip to the downtown department store and movie theater. This gendered and spatially segregated life was highly structured, corresponding to the yearning of the expanding middle classes for regularity and order after the years of economic depression and war. In Europe and Japan, with variations arising from cultural differences and a later suburbanization process, similar changes in consumer culture took place. An important minority of baby boomers eventually found this middle-class life so stultifying that they revolted in the 1960s, as we will see in Chapter 30.

**Artistic Culture**    Consumerism, a central element in the capitalist–democratic order, was based on the belief in the autonomous individual as the basic component of society. The Enlightenment ideas of materialism and the social contract continued to dominate the Anglo-American cultural sphere and also became dominant in the European arts. They formed the background for the search for ever new forms of **modernism** in thought, writing, theater, painting, music, and film, such as neorealism, **existentialism**, abstract expressionism (see the images on p. 907), and serialism. After two world wars, however, the nineteenth century's optimism in an eternal progress was thoroughly discredited. Although intellectuals and artists remained strongly committed to modernism, they were now much more sensitive to its contradictions.

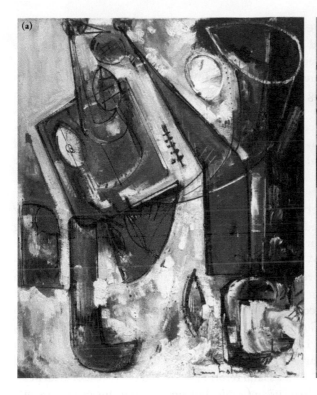

**Abstract Expressionism.**
(a) Hans Hofmann (1880–1966), *Delight*, 1947. (b) Willem de Kooning (1904–1997), *Montauk Highway*, 1958. Abstract expressionism was a New York–centered artistic movement that combined the strong colors of World War I German expressionism with the abstract art pioneered by the Russian-born Wassily Kandinsky and the artists of the Bauhaus school. Before and during the Nazi period, many European artists had flocked to New York, including Hofmann and de Kooning. The movement caught the public eye when Jackson Pollock, following the surrealists, made the creation of a work of art—painting a large canvas on the floor through the dripping of paint—an art in itself.

Thinkers and artists reflecting on modernity versus tradition focused on such themes as individualism, loneliness, and alienation; conformism, freedom, and personal fulfillment; family bonds and parental relations; class, race, and gender sensibilities; and political persecution, torture, and mass murder. All provided for rich artistic post–World War II cultures in Western countries. As culture-specific as many artists were, by not merely dwelling on the inevitability of modernity but rather confronting it with their multiple inherited premodern traditions, they created works that could be understood across cultures.

# Populism and Industrialization in Latin America

Western political and cultural modernity, as discussed above, was also a part of the Latin American experience. But the region also had a large population of Amerindians and blacks, who participated only marginally in this modernity and large majorities of whom were mired in rural subsistence. Since these populations increased rapidly after World War II, the region faced problems that did not exist in North America or Europe, where industry and its related service sector employed an overwhelmingly urban society. Latin America began to resemble Asia and Africa, which also had massive rural populations, small middle classes, and limited industrial sectors. Populist leaders relying on the urban poor thus sought to steer their countries toward greater industrialization, although with limited success.

## Slow Social Change

Latin America had stayed out of World War II. The postwar aftermath therefore neither disrupted nor offered new opportunities to its pattern of social and economic development. The region had suffered from the disappearance of commodity export markets during the Depression of the 1930s, and politicians realized that import-substitution industrialization, replacing imported manufactures with domestically produced ones, had to be adopted as a postwar policy. Tackling industrialization, however, was not easy, since landowners opposed it and the great majority of rural and urban Latin Americans were too poor to become consumers.

**Rural and Urban Society**   Prior to 1945, the rural population, though slowly decreasing, still composed about two-thirds of the total population. But during 1945–1962, the pace of urbanization picked up, with the proportions nearly reversing (see Map 29.4). While overall population growth during this period accelerated, poverty rates remained the same or even increased, making Latin America the world region with the greatest income disparities. The inequalities were exacerbated by the continuing presence of sizeable indigenous Amerindian farming populations in Guatemala, Ecuador, Peru, Bolivia, and parts of Mexico, as well as blacks in Brazil. Landowners continued to thwart efforts at land reform: Except for Mexico (in spurts after 1915) and Bolivia (1952) no country abolished landlordism prior to 1962. Cuba's land reform (1959) and the threat of local peasant revolutions made the issue urgent again, but agrarian reforms picked up only in the 1960s.

Much of the landless population migrated to the cities, making up nearly half of the arrivals. They settled in sprawling shantytowns with no urban services. Some migrants found employment in the expanding industrial sector, but more often than not they survived through occasional labor in the so-called informal sector, a new phenomenon of peddling, repairing, and recycling which composed the livelihood about one-third of the urban population. In contrast to the villages, rural–urban migrants benefited at least marginally from the health and education benefits that populist politicians introduced. The industrial labor force grew to about one-quarter of the total labor force, a growth that was far behind that of the east Asian "Tigers" or "Little Dragons" (terms meant to the connote rapid economic growth in this region) of Korea, Taiwan, and Hong Kong in the 1950s and reflected the hesitant attitude of the politicians toward industrialization in view of rebounding commodity exports in the 1950s.

At the end of World War II, industrialism was still confined mainly to food processing and textile manufacturing; only Mexico and Brazil had moved into basic goods, such as steel and chemicals. In the later 1940s and early 1950s, the larger Latin American countries moved to capital goods and consumer durables, such as machinery, tools, cars, and refrigerators. As a result, expanded production of manufactures reduced dependence on foreign imports. Unfortunately, however, very little private capital was available on the domestic market for risky industrialization ventures, requiring the state to allocate the necessary funds. Smaller countries, like Bolivia, Peru, and Paraguay, overextended themselves

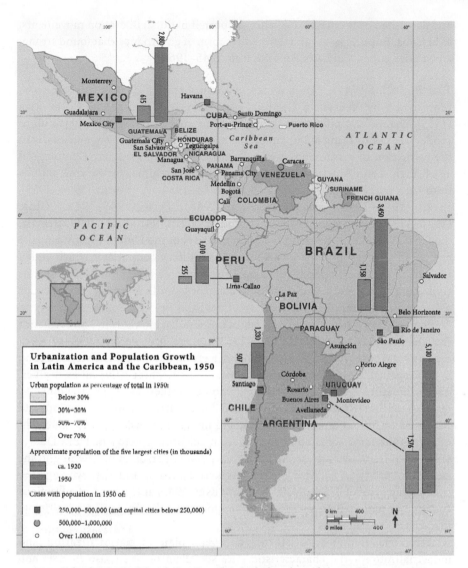

MAP 29.4 Urbanization and Population Growth in Latin America and the Caribbean, ca. 1950.

with industrial import substitution and, after a few years of trying, had to return in the early 1950s to a primacy of commodity exports.

## Populist Guided Democracy

During the period 1945–1962, the influence of fascism and Nazism faded, and only democracy and communism remained as political and ideological choices. The attraction of democracy in its constitutional-nationalist North American and European forms, however, was limited, since the United States, in the grip of the Cold War, was primarily interested in the professed loyalty of autocratic rulers in its Latin American backyard. Communism was initially also of limited appeal, given Stalin's preference for large, obedient communist parties that toed his line,

**Populism:** Type of governance in which rulers seek support directly from the population, through organizing mass rallies, manipulating elections, and intimidating or bypassing parliament.

and flourished only once Khrushchev supported national liberation movements, as in Cuba. **Populism** was an intermediate form of governance that found strong, albeit brief, support in Latin America from 1945–1962.

**The Populist Wave**    Democracy in Latin America during this time was represented by Venezuela (1958), Colombia (1953–1964), and Costa Rica (1953). Democratic politicians, however, were unable to put Venezuela's oil to productive use or bring about land reform in Colombia, resulting eventually in the formation of a communist guerilla underground in the latter country in 1964. Eight Latin American countries had populist regimes for varying periods from the mid-1940s onward: Guatemala (1944–1954), Argentina (1946–1955), Brazil (1946–1954), Venezuela (1945–1948), Peru (1945–1948), Chile (1946–1952), Costa Rica (1948–1953), and Ecuador (1948–1961). In Guatemala, the Cold War and the banana plantation interests of the United Fruit Company formed the background for a CIA-fomented military coup d'état which ended the rule of the elected populist Jacobo Árbenz and was the prelude to a vicious civil war (1960–1996). The remaining countries similarly saw waves of coups d'état and authoritarian or dictatorial regimes from 1945 to 1962.

Peronism is the best-known example of the populist interlude in Latin America that characterized the period of 1945–1962. Colonel Juan Perón (1895–1974), of modest rural background, was a member of a group of officers who staged a coup in 1943 against the traditional landowners and their conservative military allies. They sympathized with the urban population of workers as well as the poor. As minister of labor in the junta, Perón entered into an alliance with labor unions and improved wages, set a minimum wage, and increased pensions. After an earthquake, as the junta solicited donations from celebrities, Perón met Eva Duarte (1919–1952), a movie actress. An attractive, popular person in her own right, she headed a variety of social organizations and charities; and the two together became the symbol of Peronism. In elections in 1946, at the head of a fractious coalition of nationalists, socialists, and communists, Perón gained a legitimate mandate as president.

After the elections he started a 5-year plan of nationalization and industrialization—the characteristic state socialism pursued also in Asia and Africa. Banks, phone companies, railroads, and streetcars, mostly in the hands of British and French capital, were nationalized, as was the entire export of agricultural commodities. A year later, construction of plants for the production of primary and intermediate industrial goods got under way. During Perón's tenure, the economy expanded by 40 percent.

To get the national factories going, however, they had to be equipped with imported machinery. Initially, Perón paid for these imports with reserves accumulated from commodity exports during World War II. But soon the costs of the imported machinery exceeded the internal reserves and revenues of Argentina, leading to inflation and strikes. What eventually derailed Perón, however, was the Cold War. President Truman refused to include Argentina in the list of recipients for Marshall Plan aid. He disliked the presence in his own hemisphere of a populist regime that strove to leap into full industrialization through state socialism. Plagued by chronic deficits and unable to pay its foreign debts, Perón was overthrown by a conservative-led coup in 1955. Thus, Argentina, instead of leaping into industrialization, stumbled—not unlike China in the later 1950s.

# The End of Colonialism and the Rise of New Nations

Like Latin America, Asia and Africa also experienced rapid population growth and urbanization in the period 1945–1962. But in contrast to the politically independent American continent, colonialism was still dominant in Asia and Africa at the end of World War II. The governments of Great Britain and France had no inclination to relinquish their empires at this point, but both were too exhausted by the war to hold them completely. Thus, in a first wave after the end of war, a few independence movements succeeded, notably in the Middle East and Asia. A major shift in the perception of the benefits of colonialism during the mid-1950s, however, had to take place before Britain and France were willing to loosen their colonial grip in Africa.

## "China Has Stood Up"

Japan maintained a short and brutal colonial regime from 1937 to 1945 in China. Given Japan's defeat in World War II by the Allies, the Chinese did not have to fight for their independence; but they were not spared conflict. In 1949 the communists finally prevailed over the nationalists after more than a decade of civil war. China was still fundamentally a peasant-based economy with scant industrial resources. Mao's theories of revolution had adopted Marxist principles to put peasants instead of industrial workers at the forefront of the movement toward socialism. For Mao, this reinterpretation of Marxism opened up fresh possibilities of development, with the expropriation of landlords, the construction of communal farms, and the eventual leap into decentralized village industrialization. During the Stalin years, China depended heavily on Soviet material aid and advisors. After Khrushchev introduced his consumer-oriented reforms in the mid-1950s and refused to share nuclear and space technology, estrangement set in, culminating in the Soviet Union's withdrawal of all advisors from China in 1960.

**Victory of the Communists**   China emerged from World War II on the winning side but was severely battered militarily, economically, and politically. The brutal war with Japan had taken 10–20 million lives, according to various estimates. Moreover, the shaky wartime alliance between the communists under Mao Zedong and the nationalists under Chiang K'ai-shek unraveled in the later civil war. The communists, deeply entrenched in the countryside, were at a strategic advantage in China's overwhelmingly rural society. Despite the nationalists' superiority, resulting from modern arms and American support, the communists were able to systematically choke the cities, causing hyperinflation in Shanghai and other urban centers in 1947.

By 1948 the size of the two armies had reached parity, but Mao's People's Liberation Army had unstoppable popular momentum, and the United States cut back on its aid to Chiang as he faced imminent defeat. By 1949, Chiang and most of his forces had fled to Taiwan, Mao's forces took Beijing, and the new People's Republic of China set about reshaping the country according to the Maoist vision of the communist pattern of collectivist modernity. For millions of Chinese,

**Land Reform with a Vengeance, 1952.** A Chinese farmer kneels at gunpoint before a communist court enforcing land redistribution policies. Like thousands of others, the landowner was convicted of being a "class enemy" and was executed.

Mao's pronouncement on October 1, 1949, from atop the Gate of Heavenly Peace in Beijing that "China has stood up" and would never be a victim of imperialism again was a source of enormous pride. What would follow in the next decade, however, would be met with more selective enthusiasm.

**Land Reform**    During the 1950s, a central aspect of Mao's thinking was the idea that Chinese peasants were the country's only reliable resource. With China lacking a workable industrial and transportation base, the early Maoist years were marked by repeated mass mobilization campaigns. Aside from the "Resist America/Aid Korea" campaign in support of Chinese intervention in Korea, the most important of these was the national effort at land reform. Party cadres moved into the remaining untouched rural areas and expropriated land, dividing it among the local peasants. Landlords who resisted were "struggled"—abused by tenants who were egged on by party cadres—and often lynched. By some estimates, land reform between 1950 and 1955 took as many as 2 million lives. As hoped for, peasant landownership caused agricultural productivity to increase.

Several years into the land reform program, party leaders decided it was time to take the next step toward socialized agriculture. Mao wanted to avoid the chaos that had accompanied Soviet collectivization of agriculture in 1930–1932. The party leadership felt that by going slowly they could greatly ease the transition. Thus, in 1953 peasants were encouraged to form "agricultural producers' cooperatives" in which villages would share scarce tools and machinery. Those who joined were given incentives in the form of tax breaks and higher prices. By 1956, agricultural production had recovered to pre–World War II levels and was registering impressive gains.

**"Let a Hundred Flowers Bloom"**    By 1957, Mao was ready to evaluate the commitment of the nation's intellectuals, many of whom had initially been enthusiastic about the reforms. Mao, however, was not sure whether these people truly supported his programs or were simply being circumspect. Adopting a slogan from China's philosophically rich late Zhou period, "Let a hundred flowers bloom, let a hundred schools of thought contend," the party invited intellectuals to submit public criticism of the party's record, assuring the intellectuals that offering their critique was patriotic.

By mid-1957 the trickle of criticisms had become a torrent, but when some critics suggested forming an opposition party, Mao acted swiftly. The "Hundred Flowers" campaign was terminated and the "Anti-Rightist" campaign was launched. Calls for an opposition party were denounced as the worst kind of right-wing thinking—as opposed to the "correct" left-wing thinking of the monopoly Communist Party. Those accused of rightism were rounded up and subjected to "reeducation." Even Deng Xiaoping (1904–1997), an old companion of Mao's and later the architect of China's present market economy, was forced to endure 5 years on a hog farm. In addition to being imprisoned and made to endure endless "self-criticism" sessions, many intellectuals were sentenced to long stretches of "reform through labor" in remote peasant villages.

**The Great Leap Forward**    At about the same time, Mao was growing impatient with the pace of Chinese agricultural collectivization. If production could be ramped up sufficiently, the surplus agricultural funds could then be used to fund 5-year plans for industrial development along the lines of those in the Soviet Union. Moreover, China had been borrowing heavily from the Soviet Union through the 1950s and had availed itself of Soviet technicians and engineers. All of the progress of the decade might be radically slowed or halted if agricultural revenues could not keep pace.

Mao therefore prodded the Communist Party into its most colossal mass mobilization project yet: the Great Leap Forward (1958–1961). The entire population of the country was to be pushed into a campaign to communalize agriculture into self-sustaining units that would function like factories in the fields. Men and women would work in shifts and live in barracks on enormous collective farms. Peasants were to surrender all their iron implements to be melted down and made into steel to build the new infrastructure of these communes. The most recognizable symbol of the campaign was the backyard steel furnace, which commune members were to build and run for their own needs. Technical problems were to be solved by the "wisdom of the masses" through politically correct "red" (revolutionary) thinking. The entire country would therefore modernize its rural areas and infrastructure in one grand campaign.

Predictably, the Great Leap was the most catastrophic policy failure in the history of the People's Republic. Knowledgeable critics had been cowed into silence by the Anti-Rightist campaign, and the initial wave of enthusiasm that greeted the mobilization ground to a halt as peasants began to actively resist the seizure of their land and implements. So many were forced into building the communal structures and making unneeded steel that by 1959 agricultural production in China had plummeted and the country experienced its worst famine in modern times. By 1962 an estimated 30 million people had died.

Conditions became so bleak that Mao stepped down from his party chairmanship in favor of "expert" Liu Shaoqi (1898–1969) and retreated into semiretirement. Liu, from a well-off peasant background in south-central China, and the rehabilitated Deng Xiaoping were now reinstated. Together they tackled the task of rebuilding the shattered economy and political structures. The next 5 years saw impressive gains in China's technical, health, and education sectors as the country returned to something like normalcy. But Mao was soon plotting his return.

## Decolonization, Israel, and Arab Nationalism in the Middle East

Parallel to China ridding itself of Japanese colonialism after World War II, independence movements arose in the Middle East and North Africa against the British and French colonial regimes. Here, countries achieved their independence in two waves, the first following World War II and the second during

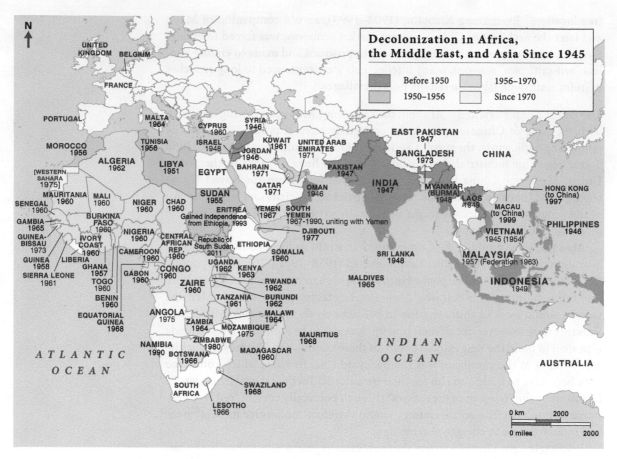

**MAP 29.5** **Decolonization in Africa, the Middle East, and Asia since 1945.**

1956–1970 (see Map 29.5). The first wave was the result of local pressures, which colonial authorities found too costly to resist, as in the cases of Syria, Lebanon, Iraq, Jordan, and Israel. The second wave had to await the realization of the British and French governments that they were no longer powerful enough to maintain their empires in a world dominated by the United States and the Soviet Union.

**Palestine and Israel**    As World War II ended, Britain found itself in a tight spot in Palestine. After the suppression of the uprising of 1936–1939, the Arab Palestinians were relatively quiet but Zionist guerilla action protesting the restrictions on Jewish immigration and land acquisitions had begun in the middle of the war. Sooner or later some form of transition to self-rule had to be offered, but British politicians and the top military were determined to hold on to the empire's strategic interests (oil and the Suez Canal), especially once the Cold War heated up in 1946.

When it became impossible to find a formula for a transition acceptable to the Arabs, in February 1947 Britain turned the question of Palestinian independence over to the United Nations. After the collapse of the Soviet Union in 1991, documents surfaced showing—interestingly, given the Soviet Union's later animosity toward the Jewish state and support of the Arabs—that during the 1940s Stalin had used the United Nations to push for a weakening of the British imperial position in the Middle East by favoring the creation of the state of Israel. Accordingly, the United Nations adopted a partition plan worked out with American assistance in November, and Israel declared its independence on May 14, 1948 (see Map 29.6).

The Soviet Union backed up its tactical, Cold War–motivated support for Israel by releasing 200,000 Jewish emigrants from the Soviet Bloc and having Czechoslovakia deliver rifles, machine guns, and World War II–vintage planes to Israel. Israel was victorious against the Arab armies that invaded from surrounding countries, which, although determined to contest the new state, were unable to obtain weapons as the result of British and American embargoes. Only Jordan was partly successful, conquering the West Bank and the Old City of Jerusalem. Between November 1947 and the end of fighting in January 1949, the territory in and around the new state experienced, albeit on a smaller scale, the same kind of tragic and chaotic population shift that took place at about the same time in India and Pakistan. Some three-quarters of a million Palestinians were either forced from their villages or fled, leaving only 150,000 in an Israeli territory now substantially larger than that of the original partition plan. In response, the Arab countries expelled about half a million Jews during the next decade from their countries. In the end, Stalin's early Cold War tactics were a grave miscalculation: Israel became a staunch Western ally. But the Western camp did not fare much better: The Arab "catastrophe" (Arabic *nakba*), as it was called, led to the replacement of liberal, landowning Arab nationalists by ardent military hard-liners of refugee background determined to end what remained of Western colonialism—which now, in their eyes, included the state of Israel.

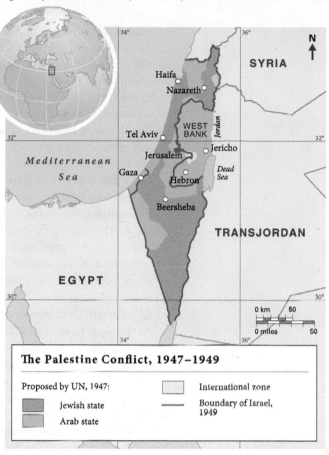

### The Palestine Conflict, 1947–1949

Proposed by UN, 1947:
- Jewish state
- Arab state
- International zone
- Boundary of Israel, 1949

MAP **29.6** **The Palestine Conflict, 1947–1949.**

**The Officer Coup in Egypt**　One Egyptian officer serving with distinction in the war against Israel was Colonel Gamal Abdel Nasser (1918–1970), the eldest son of a postal clerk from southern Egypt. Nasser had benefited from the opening of the officer corps to commoners. He was bitter toward the Egyptian royalty, supported by landowners who had done little to support the country with arms and supplies in the war. In the middle of a declining internal security situation—massive British retaliation against acts of sabotage in the Suez Canal Zone—the secret "Free Officers," with Nasser at the center, assumed power in a coup in July 1952. They closed down parliament and sent the king into exile on his private luxury yacht. The coup was bloodless, and there was little reaction in the streets.

Nasser quickly tightened the rule of his military regime. To break the power of the landowners, the Free Officers in 1952 initiated the first round of a land reform that eventually eliminated large estates. A rival for power was the Muslim Brotherhood, a militant organization founded in 1928 by the preacher Hasan al-Banna (1906–1949), who propagated a reformed Islam among poor and rural–urban migrants and advocated the establishment of an Islamic regime. Accusing the Brotherhood of an assassination attempt, Nasser outlawed it in 1954, driving it underground. In a plebiscite in 1956, Nasser made himself president, with a largely rubber-stamp parliament.

Once firmly in power, Nasser espoused the Arab nationalist cause. Palestinian Arab "freedom fighters" carried out raids against Israel from refugee camps in the Arab countries, which inevitably provoked Israeli reprisals. After the first raid and reprisal involving Egypt in February 1955, Nasser realized that the Egyptian military needed urgent improvements. When the United States would not sell weapons readily, Khrushchev jumped in 6 months later, based on his new Soviet strategy of supporting anticolonial nationalists. Where Stalin had failed, Khrushchev succeeded: After its failure in Israel, the Soviet Union was in the Middle Eastern Cold War struggle again.

At the same time, Nasser laid early plans for infrastructural improvements in advance of a later state-industrialization plan: He asked the World Bank for a loan to finance the Aswan High Dam. Initially, the United States and Britain, the main underwriters of the World Bank, were in support. But they withdrew this support in spring 1956 when Nasser pressured Egypt's neighbor Jordan into dismissing the British commander of its crack troops, the Arab Legion. Nasser responded with the nationalization of the Suez Canal (but with compensation of the share-holders) and closure of the Strait of Tiran (used by Israel for Indian Ocean shipping) in July 1956. Without the necessary loans, Nasser had to put the construction of the High Dam on hold.

Israel considered the closure of the Strait of Tiran an act of war and, with French participation, prepared for a campaign to reopen the straits. France, anxious to punish Nasser for weapons deliveries to Algerian fighters in the war of liberation that had begun in 1954, persuaded Britain to join in a plan that would be initiated with an attack on Egypt by Israel. If Nasser would close the Suez Canal, France and Britain would occupy it, ostensibly to separate the combatants but actually to reestablish Western control. The plan was hatched in secret because of US opposition to the use of force against Nasser. It unraveled badly when Israel ended its canal campaign victoriously on November 2 but the British and French troops were unable to complete the occupation of the Canal Zone before November 4, the day of the ceasefire called by the UN General Assembly and the United States. Although defeated militarily, Nasser scored a resounding diplomatic victory, effectively ending the last remnants of British and French imperialism in the Middle East.

After the Suez War, Nasser rode high on waves of pan-Arabism, nonalignment, and Arab socialism. The monarchical regimes in Arabia were on the defensive and maintained themselves only thanks to the United States, heir to the strategic oil interests of Britain after the demise of the latter's empire. Although unification with Syria as the United Arab Republic (1958–1961) did not work out, Egypt succeeded in establishing a cultural hegemony from North Africa to Yemen based on propaganda, movies, and music. The relationship with the Soviet Union deepened: Thanks to the Soviets, the Aswan Dam was completed, Soviet military and technical support grew, and Egyptian students received advanced educations in the Eastern Bloc. In 1961, the regime cofounded the **Non-Aligned Movement**, together with Indonesia's Sukarno, India's Nehru, Yugoslavia's Tito, and Ceylon's Bandaranaike. In the same year, Nasser announced his first 5-year plan, which included the nationalization of all large businesses and the construction of heavy steel, aluminum, cement, and chemical plants. Egypt embraced industrial modernity but under the aegis of state investments similar to what Stalin had pioneered in 1930. Nasser called this "Arab socialism."

**Non-Aligned Movement:** An international, anticolonialist movement of state leaders that promoted the interests of countries not aligned with the superpowers.

## Decolonization and the Cold War in Asia

Nationalist forces similar to those in the Middle East arose also in south and east Asia as a consequence of World War II. The war had either thoroughly destroyed or considerably diminished the colonial holdings of Great Britain, France, the Netherlands, and Japan in Asia. With the destruction of Japan, the Greater East Asia Co-Prosperity Sphere around the Pacific Rim and its islands dissolved. In several colonies, existing independence movements established nationalist governments or fought against the attempted reimposition of European rule. In quick succession India and Pakistan (1947), Burma (1948), Malaysia (1957), Ceylon (1948), Indonesia (1949), and Vietnam (1954) achieved independence from the British and French. India and Vietnam merit a closer look as countries that played important roles during the Cold War competition between the two patterns of communism and capitalist democracy.

**Independence and Partition on the Subcontinent** India, Pakistan, and Bangladesh form a prime example of the trials and tribulations encountered by the newly independent ethnic–religious nations in Asia. As the Indian crown colony emerged from the war, to which it had once again contributed huge numbers of volunteer soldiers, nationalists demanded nothing less than full independence. Gandhi, Nehru, and the majority of the Indian National Congress envisaged an Indian nation on the entire subcontinent in which a constitution, patterned after that of Britain, would trump any ethnic, linguistic, and/or religious identities, of which there were literally hundreds. For the Congress, to be an Indian meant adherence to the constitutional principles of equality before the law, due process, and freedom from oppression.

The Muslim minority, however, beginning in the 1930s, had drifted increasingly toward religious nationalism, demanding a separate state for themselves in regions where they formed a majority. The main advocate for this separatism was the Muslim League, led by Muhammad Ali Jinnah (1876–1948). Not surprisingly, there was also a small minority of Hindu religious nationalists who had already in the 1920s published pamphlets advocating independence under the banner of "Hindu-ness" (*hindutva*). To the dismay of the Indian National Congress, the British negotiators lent an ear to the demands of the Islamic religious nationalists and prevailed on Gandhi and Nehru to accept independence with partition— and the possibility of widespread disruption, given that even the northwest and northeast, with their Muslim majorities, were home to sizeable minorities of millions of Hindus.

When, on August 15, 1947, the two nations of India and Pakistan ("Land of the Pure") became independent, the jubilation of freedom was immediately mixed with the horrors of a population exchange on a massive scale. Desperate to save themselves, more than 2 million panicked people fled hundreds of miles on foot, by cart, or by railroad to settle in their respective countries. More than 100,000 Indians died in the accompanying communal violence. Gandhi himself fell victim 5 months later to an assassin from the hindutva supremacist-nationalist minority who was enraged by both the partition and Gandhi's principled adherence to constitutional nationalism, to which Hindu nationalism was to be subordinated.

While India settled into federal parliamentary democracy, Pakistan's constitution became disposable and the regime authoritarian. From the start, it was clear that religious nationalism was insufficient to define the identity of Pakistanis, distributed over two physically separated regions of the nation, Punjab in the west and East Bengal in the east. The capital, Islamabad, was in the west, and Urdu became the national language, relegating Bengali in the east to secondary status (to the dismay of its speakers, who eventually seceded in a bloody civil war and formed the nation of Bangladesh in 1971).

A decade into independence, a military officer, Field Marshal Ayub Khan (1907–1974) from the Pashtu minority in Waziristan on the western border, assumed power in a bloodless coup. Subsequently, he abrogated the 1948 British-style constitution and in 1962 imposed a new constitution, providing for a "guided democracy" of elected village councilors who voted for the president and the members of the national assembly. The constitution's definition of Islam as a national identity and its relationship to subsidiary ethnic and linguistic identities in the country, however, were so contentious that they remained unresolved.

Worst of all, given the role of Islam as the religious–nationalist foundation principle, Pakistan was in conflict with India over Kashmir, a province lying in the north between India and Pakistan. In 1947, its Hindu prince hesitated to join Pakistan, while its majority Muslim population demanded incorporation. In the ensuing first war between Indian and Pakistan, India succeeded in conquering most of the province, with Pakistan holding on to only a small sliver, but Kashmiri Muslims remained restive. As in so many other postcolonial territorial disputes, clashes between constitutional and ethnic–linguistic–religious nationalism became irresolvable.

**Independent India**    India's first prime minister, Jawaharlal Nehru (in office 1947–1964), had the formidable task of tying the subcontinent's disparate constituencies together into a united government. Within the British system, perhaps one-quarter of the territory had remained under the nominal rule of local princes, who now had to surrender their realms to the national government. The bewildering array of castes and the social inequalities built into the system also posed a powerful obstacle, especially since the British had frequently exploited these inequalities to divide and rule. The new government was itself in the uncomfortable situation of constitutionally mandating equality for women and outlawing caste discrimination, while being forced to acquiesce to the de facto absence of the former and continuation of the latter. In the end, the British parliamentary and court systems were adopted and the old civil service was retained, while the economy of the new government would officially be a modified, nonrevolutionary kind of socialism. Nehru's admiration for Soviet successes persuaded him to adopt the 5-year-plan system of development. Not surprisingly, India's first 5-year plan (1951–1955), like the early efforts in the Soviet Union and China, was geared toward raising agricultural productivity as a precondition for industrial development.

The most formidable problem was poverty. Though the cities were rapidly expanding beyond the ability of their local governments to keep pace with services, India, like China at the same time, was still fundamentally rural. The new nation's village population was second only to China's in size. The strains upon the land and reliance on the monsoon cycle meant a constant risk of famine. In the 1950s, India launched a family planning program, to encourage a slowing of the demographic expansion. As a democratic country, however, India had to rely on the voluntary cooperation of the villagers, a cooperation which was difficult to achieve as long as urbanization and industrialization were in their initial stages. For poor families, children were either important laborers in agriculture or, among the landless and the poor in city slums, crucial additional breadwinners as soon as they were old enough to work.

**Political and Economic Nonalignment**    Similar to the governments of the Soviet Union, China, and Egypt, Nehru and the Congress Party argued that the pressing rural poverty could be overcome only through rapid industrialization undertaken by the state. A hybrid regime of capitalist–democratic constitutionalism with private property (on a small scale) and guided "socialist" state investments came into being, which was officially aligned with neither the West nor the East. This nonalignment (Nehru coined this term in 1954) became the official policy of India and under its initiative also the founding principle of an entire organization, the Non-Aligned Movement, informally established in Bandung, Indonesia, in 1955, and formally inaugurated in 1961 (see "Patterns Up Close"). The Non-Aligned Movement, still in existence today, sought to maintain neutrality in the Cold War. It predictably incurred the wrath of Western Cold War warriors but was generally successful in maintaining its own course independent from the Western and Soviet Blocs.

Indian state socialism began with the state's second 5-year plan (1956–1961), which focused on state investments in heavy industry. Existing private enterprises were nationalized, and an immense hydroelectric complex and five steel plants were built, along with numerous cement works and an ambitious expansion of coal mines and railroads. In 1958, the Atomic Energy Commission was formed to pursue both peaceful and military applications of nuclear fission. With the iron, aluminum, cement, and chemicals from heavy industry, the planners hoped, private Indian investors, still minuscule in number but recipients of compensation for factories lost to nationalization, would buy the heavy industrial goods—iron, aluminum, and chemicals—to construct housing and build factories for the production of basic consumer goods. The giant domestic market of India was to become fully self-sufficient and independent of imports.

Though begun with much hope at a time of prosperity, the second plan failed to reach its goals. The government debt, owed both to domestic banks and to foreign lending institutions, grew astronomically. Tax collection was notoriously

# Bandung and the Origins
# of the Non-Aligned Movement

As we have noted in this chapter, one of the most momentous events of the post–World War II period was the dismantling of the vast colonial empires of the Western powers and Japan and the rapid emergence from them of dozens of new nation-states. While nationalist movements in these empires had long predated the war, the complete defeat of Japan accompanied by the exhaustion of Great Britain, France, and the Netherlands and the emergence of the Cold War proved powerful catalysts for independence—as had Allied propaganda during the war and the pronouncements and policies of the newly created United Nations after 1945.

As these new nations arrived on the scene in the 1940s and 1950s, however, they faced a host of unprecedented problems, ranging from poverty and developmental gaps to ethnic and religious conflicts. Looming over all of these emerging nations was the intensifying struggle between the United States and its allies in the capitalist camp and the Soviet Union and the Communist Bloc. As a result, many leaders of these new nations saw themselves as natural colleagues. They shared a common colonial experience, and many had also been fighters for national independence. Now, they also had to contend with both Cold War rivals attempting to enlist their support. By the early 1950s, the French scholar Alfred Sauvy had coined the term "third world" to describe these newly emergent nonaligned nations, whose situation he saw as parallel to the famous Third Estate of prerevolutionary France (Chapter 22).

Thus, led by the dynamic Indonesian president Sukarno and India's Prime Minister Nehru, Indonesia, India, Burma, Pakistan, and Ceylon (Sri Lanka) convened a conference in April 1955 attended by 25 countries, representing 1.5 billion people, at the Indonesian resort town of Bandung. Throughout the conference the words of Sukarno's opening speech seemed to sound a dramatic and prophetic note:

> The twentieth century has been a period of terrific dynamism. Perhaps the last fifty years have seen more development and more material progress than the previous five hundred years. . . . But has man's political skill marched hand-in-hand with his technical and scientific skill?

Indeed, although the Bandung Conference established the base on which Non-Aligned Movement was founded, politics proved a corrosive force in its interactions from the outset. Delegates on the whole agreed on the principle of Afro-Asian solidarity and cooperation, and were unanimous in their opposition to colonialism by any country. They were much less agreed, however, on exactly what constituted colonialism: Some equated the Soviet position in Eastern Europe with colonialism and worried about China's emergent predominance in east Asia. Others, more friendly toward Marxist developmental approaches and eager for aid from socialist countries, dismissed such ideas as Western propaganda. Zhou Enlai, the People's Republic of China's delegate, did much to calm the anxieties of those worried about his country's possible expansion and, indeed, attempted to place China firmly in the ranks of the nonaligned, despite China's close relationship with the Soviet Union at the time. The United States refused to attend, at least in part because of its policy of not recognizing the People's Republic, though American pronouncements offered aid and developmental expertise to the participants. (However, American congressman Adam Clayton Powell and the writer Richard Wright—both African American—did attend in unofficial capacities.) In the end, the conference unanimously adopted a 10-point declaration of "world peace and cooperation," very much in keeping with the tenets of the UN Charter.

Though regional rivalries and competing political aims, as well as the circumstances of the Cold War, never allowed the development of the kind of solidarity championed at Bandung, successive conferences in Cairo and Belgrade led to the official creation of the Non-Aligned Movement in 1961. Many of the leaders of Bandung, including Nehru, Sukarno, and Egypt's President Nasser, were there, as was the subject of this chapter's opening vignette, Sirimavo Bandaranaike. The movement marked the maturation of an important pattern that helped to regulate the behavior of the Cold War players to a considerable extent. The search for a third way beyond capitalism and Soviet communism spurred economic and developmental experimentation and encouraged both Cold War camps to woo nonaligned members into their respective ideological orbits. Politically, the growing number of new nations seeing security in a coalition opposed to superpower domination made the movement a genuine power of its own, particularly in international forums such as the UN General Assembly.

**Bandung Conference.**
(L-R) Dr. Ali Sastroamidjojo, Sir John Kotelawala, Pakistan's Premier Mohamed Ali, Jawaharlal Nehru, and U Nu at the Bandung Conference, April 1, 1955.

The pattern of resistance to superpower dominance continues today, decades after the end of the Cold War. The Non-Aligned Movement still casts itself as the champion of the developing "global south" in opposition to the economic power of the wealthy "north." Politically, however, its stance is now directed against membership in great power alliances such as NATO. With membership now including 120 countries and 17 observer nations, the Non-Aligned Movement's influence is arguably more widespread than ever, though the absence of the Cold War has made its focus more diffuse. One could say, however, that Sukarno's observation about politics remains as relevant and complex as ever: For the period 2012 to 2015, the presidency of the Non-Aligned Movement has moved to Iran, a country whose relationship with its neighbors and with the Western powers and the United States has been for decades one of extreme tension.

## Questions

- How does the Non-Aligned Movement reflect the pattern of postwar developments regarding the trend toward anticolonialism?

- In what ways does Sukarno's opening speech anticipate postwar political and diplomatic relations among emerging independent states?

**The Strains of Nonalignment.** India's determined stance to navigate its own course between the superpowers was a difficult one, especially during the height of the Cold War. Here, however, a degree of diplomatic warmth appears to pervade the proceedings in Geneva, Switzerland, as the People's Republic of China's foreign minister, Chen Yi (left), toasts his Indian colleague, defense minister V. K. Krishna Menon (right), and the Soviet foreign minister, Andrei Gromyko (center background), smiles at them both. The date of this conference, however, formally convened to discuss issues between the Soviet and American sides over influence in the southeast Asian nation of Laos in July 1962, also coincided with rising border tensions between India and China. This photo was specifically released to show that both sides were still on friendly terms. Within a few months, however, they were shooting at each other.

difficult and unproductive, and chronic national and federal budget deficits drove up inflation. Bad monsoon seasons caused food shortages. In democratic India it was not possible to use the draconian dictatorial powers that Stalin had employed. India's difficulties were experienced time and again in other countries after independence.

**Southeast Asia**    In contrast to India, where the postwar British imperialists gave in to the inevitable, the French under Charles de Gaulle (1890–1970) in 1944–1946 were determined to reconstitute their empire. De Gaulle and a majority of French politicians found it inconceivable that this new republic would be anything less than the imperially glorious Third Republic. To de Gaulle's chagrin, military efforts to hold on to Lebanon and Syria failed against discreet British support for independence and the unilateral establishment of national governments by the Lebanese and Syrians in 1943–1944. After these losses, the politicians of the Fourth Republic were determined not to lose more colonies.

"For more than eighty years, the French imperialists, abusing the standard of Liberty, Equality, and Fraternity, have violated our Fatherland and oppressed our fellow citizens."

—Ho Chi Minh

Unfortunately for the French, however, when they returned to Indochina (composed of Vietnam, Laos, and Cambodia) in the fall of 1945, the prewar communist independence movement had already taken over. With covert American assistance, the communists had fought the Japanese occupiers in a guerilla war, and on

September 2, 1945, the day of Japan's surrender to the United States, Ho Chi Minh, the leader, read a Vietnamese declaration of independence to half a million people in Hanoi.

Following protracted negotiations in early 1946 between Ho and the French, a stalemate ensued. Ho did not budge from his demand for independence, while the French insisted on returning to their "colony." The Vietminh promptly relaunched their guerilla war. Because of the rapid escalation of the Cold War, the French were successful at persuading the American administration that a Vietminh victory was tantamount to an expansion of communism in the world. By the early 1950s, the United States was providing much of the funding, and the French and allied Vietnamese troops did the actual fighting.

In May 1954, however, the Vietminh defeated the French decisively. During the Geneva negotiations carried out later that year, the French surrender resulted in a division of Vietnam into north and south along the 17th parallel, pending national elections, and the creation of the new nations of Laos and Cambodia.

The elections, however, never took place, and instead Ngo Dinh Diem [no deen jem] (in office 1955–1963), an authoritarian politician with a limited power base primarily composed of Catholics, emerged in the south. He legitimized his rule in 1955 through a fraudulent plebiscite. Although the new Kennedy administration (1961) was aware of Diem's unscrupulous rule, concerns about military successes being achieved by Laotian and South Vietnamese communists receiving North Vietnamese support led to the fateful American decision to carry the Western Cold War into Indochina. President Eisenhower had already sent several hundred military advisors to Diem, but President Kennedy, faced with the Bay of Pigs disaster in Cuba (April 1961) and the East German wall in Berlin (August 1961), increased the military presence to 16,000 by 1963. Since Diem was corrupt and unwilling to carry out much-needed land reforms, the United States engineered a coup in November 1963 that put a military government in place. This proxy regime was soon propped up by a growing American military presence that would reach a half-million men by 1967.

## Decolonization and Cold War in Africa

Only 7 months after their defeat at Dien Bien Phu, the French had to face the declaration of a war for independence by the Algerian Front of National Liberation (November 1, 1954). Algeria, a French colony of 10 million Muslim Arabs and Berbers, had a European settler population of nearly 1 million. The French army was determined to prevent a repeat of the humiliation it had suffered in Indochina. But that is precisely what happened only 2 years later in the Suez war of 1956, and British and French politicians began to realize that the maintenance of colonies was becoming too costly. France hung on to Algeria and was even able to largely repress the liberation war by the later 1950s. But in the long run, Algerian independence (in 1962) could not be prevented, even though French military elements and settlers did everything (including two revolts in 1958 and 1961 against Paris) to keep the country French. France's colonial interests were too costly to be maintained, and the United States took over the West's strategic interests in the world. Since the colonies required immense expenditures to support newly burgeoning populations, and the reconstruction of Europe was still far from complete, both Britain and France were forced to rethink the idea of colonialism.

Amid much soul-searching, European governments began to liquidate their empires, beginning in 1957. Only Portugal and Spain continued to maintain their colonies of Angola, Mozambique, and Rio de Oro. South Africa introduced its apartheid regime (1948–1994), designed to segregate the white Afrikaner (Dutch-descended) ruling class from the black majority. As the British, French, and Belgians decolonized, however, they ensured that the governments of the newly independent African countries would remain their loyal subalterns. For them, African independence would be an exchange for support in the Cold War and continued economic dependence.

**The Legacy of Colonialism**    Between 1918 and 1957, even though the governments of Britain, France, Belgium, and Portugal had invested little state money in their colonies, vast changes had occurred in sub-Saharan Africa. The population had more than doubled from 142 to 300 million, mostly as a result of the reduction of tropical diseases through better medicine. Urbanization was accelerating; economies were coming to rely too heavily on commodity exports; and an emerging middle class was becoming restless. Heavy investments were required, not merely in mining and agriculture but also in social services to improve the lot of the growing African population. Faced with this financial burden, most of the colonial powers decided to grant independence rather than divert investments badly needed at home.

**Ghana, the African Pioneer**    Once Britain had decided to decolonize, the governmental strategy toward African independence was to support nationalist groups or parties that adopted British-inspired constitutions and the rule of law, guaranteed existing British economic interests, and abided by the rules of the British Commonwealth of Nations. The first to fit these criteria was Ghana in 1957. Its leader, Kwame Nkrumah (1909–1972), held a master's degree in education from the University of Pennsylvania and appeared to be a sound choice.

> "Capitalism is too complicated a system for a newly independent nation. Hence the need for a socialistic society."
>
> —Kwame Nkrumah

Ghana sought to be the pioneer of sub-Saharan independence and development. It had a healthy economy based on cocoa production as well as some mineral wealth. Its middle class was perhaps the most vital of any African colony's. Nkrumah had had a long career as an activist for African independence and a leading advocate of pan-African unity. Although he was jailed during the 1950s for his activism in the Convention People's Party and therefore viewed with some concern, the British nevertheless also realized that Nkrumah wielded genuine authority among a majority of politically inexperienced Ghanaians.

Only 2 years into his rule, however, Nkrumah discarded the independence constitution. Exploiting ethnic tensions among Ashante groups, where an emerging opposition to his rule was concentrated, he promulgated a new republican constitution, removing the country from the British Commonwealth. A year later, he turned to socialist state planning, similar to that of Egypt and India.

The construction of a massive hydroelectric dam on the Volta River, begun in 1961, was supposed to be the starting point of a heavy industrialization program, including aluminum, steel, glass, and consumer goods factories. But the country soon ran into financing problems, since prices for cocoa, the main export commodity, were declining on the world market and large foreign loans were required to continue the program. On the political front, Nkrumah in 1964 amended the constitution again, making Ghana a one-party state with Nkrumah himself as leader for life. An unmanageable foreign debt eventually stalled development, and an army coup, supported by the CIA in the name of Cold War anti-communism, ousted Nkrumah in 1966.

**Resistance to Independence in Kenya**  In some regions of Africa, particularly in Kenya, decolonization was not achieved as easily as in Ghana. Efforts to terminate British colonialism were advanced by Jomo Kenyatta (1894–1978), who founded the Kenya African National Union earlier in the 1940s. Interrupted by the war, Kenyatta's movement gathered momentum after the liberation of Ghana in 1957. But this was met with resistance by British settlers who had established profitable agricultural plantations earlier in the twentieth century, and who were therefore reluctant to relinquish control of their economic and political interests. In the face of British opposition, the African nationalists formed the Mau Mau movement, which resorted to terrorist attacks on British estates to achieve their ends. Finally, independence was granted Kenya in 1963, and in the following year Kenyatta was named as the first president of the newly created republic.

**The Struggle for the Congo's Independence**  Among the large group of sub-Saharan colonies achieving independence between 1957 and 1960, the Belgian Congo is an important case study because, like Vietnam, it became a battleground of the Cold War. The Belgian Congo had been under the authority of the Belgian government since the beginning of the twentieth century, when it took over from the king (see Chapter 27). During the interwar period, concession companies invested in mining, especially in the southern and central provinces of Katanga and Kisaï, where huge deposits of copper, cobalt, iron, uranium, and diamonds were discovered. Little money went into human development until after World War II, when Catholic mission schools, with state support, expanded the health and the primary school systems. The urban and mine workforce expanded considerably, but no commercial or professional middle classes existed.

Serious demands for independence arose in the Congo only after Ghana became independent in 1957. Several groups of nationalists, some advocating a federation and others a centralized state, competed with each other. The urban and mine worker-based National Congolese Movement (*Mouvement National Congolais*, MNC), founded in 1958 by the former postal clerk and salesman Patrice Lumumba (1925–1961), was the most popular group, favoring a centralized constitutional nationalism that transcended ethnicity, language, and religion. After riots in 1959 and the arrest of Lumumba, accused of stirring up the riots, Belgian authorities decided to act quickly so as not to lose control over events: They needed compliant nationalists who would continue existing economic arrangements. A Brussels conference with all nationalists—including Lumumba, freed from prison—decided to hold local and national elections in early 1960. To the dismay of Belgium, the centralists, led by Lumumba, won. On June 30, 1960, the Congo became independent, with Lumumba as prime minister and the federalist Joseph Kasa-Vubu (ca. 1910–1969) from Katanga as president.

Lumumba's first political act was the announcement of a general pay raise for state employees, which the Belgian army commander undermined by spreading a rumor that the Congolese foot soldiers would be left out. Outraged, the soldiers mutinied, and amid a general breakdown of public order, Katanga declared its independence. Lumumba fired the Belgian officers, but to restore order he turned to the United Nations. Order was indeed restored by the United Nations, but Belgium made sure that Katanga did not rejoin the Congo. To force Katanga, Lumumba turned for support to the Soviet Union, which airlifted advisors and equipment into the country. The Cold War had arrived in Africa.

Kasa-Vubu and Lumumba dismissed each other from the government on September 5, giving the new Congolese army chief, Mobutu Sese Seko (1930–1997), the opportunity to seize power on September 14. Mobutu was a soldier turned journalist and member of the MNC whom Lumumba had appointed as army chief, even though it was general knowledge that he was in the pay of the Belgians and the CIA. (Mobutu went on to become the dictator of the Congo, renamed Zaire, and was a close ally of the United States during the period he held power, 1965–1996.) He promptly had Lumumba arrested. Eventually, Belgian agents took Lumumba to Katanga, where they executed him on January 17, 1961.

At that time, as it is now known from documentary investigations in the 1990s, the Belgian government and the Eisenhower White House were convinced that Lumumba was another Castro in the making, a nationalist who would soon become a communist, influenced by Khrushchev's charm offensive among the African nationalists about to achieve independence. In the Cold War between the United States and the Soviet Union, the fierce but inexperienced Lumumba was given no chance by the Belgian and American governments acting with mutual consultation. At all costs, the Congo had to remain in the Western camp as a strategic, mineral-rich linchpin in central Africa.

## Putting It All Together

Rapid, dizzying change characterized the pattern of modernity as it unfolded in the middle of the twentieth century. After only 150 years of constitutionalism and industry, 75 years of worldwide imperialism, and 15 years of a three-sided competition among the modernist ideologies of capitalist democracy, communism, and supremacist nationalism, the world changed drastically once more. An intense Cold War competition between the proponents of the ideologies of capitalist democracy and communism ensued. Imperialism and colonialism collapsed within a mere 17 years. And nearly 200 nations came to share the globe in the United Nations. Compared to the slow pace of change in the agrarian–urban period of world history for 5,300 years, the speed of development during just 145 years of scientific–industrial modernity was dizzying.

Perhaps the most noteworthy series of events characterizing the 17 years of the early and intense Cold War between capitalist democracy and communism in 1945–1962 was the sad fate of many countries as they emerged into independence or as they struggled to accommodate themselves as best they could in the Western camp, Eastern Bloc, or Non-Aligned Movement. As we have seen in this chapter, US and Soviet leaders were ruthless wherever they perceived communist or capitalist influence in their ranks. But even when new nations pursued a policy of nonalignment, there were subtler ways through which both West and East could apply financial pressures with devastating consequences: Egypt lost its finances for the Aswan Dam, and China lost its Soviet advisors during the Great Leap Forward.

Not that capitalist democracy and communism were on the same plane: The former, even if it did not readily offer meaning or equality to its adherents, provided greater political participation than the latter, which paid only lip service to its notions of equality, as became obvious in 1989. But the period of the early, active Cold War and decolonization from 1945 to 1962 was far less brutal than the preceding interwar period. Although several confrontations between East and West were hot, and nuclear war on one occasion posed a serious threat, humanity was spared the cataclysms of World War III.

▶ For additional resources, including maps, primary sources, visuals, and quizzes, please go to www.oup.com/us/vonsivers. Please see the Further Resources section at the back of the book for additional readings and suggested websites.

## Against the Grain

# Postwar Counterculture

Postwar Europe and North America during the 1950s embarked on programs of reconstruction, reflecting a yearning for normalcy following years of deprivation and hardship. Central to this agenda was a mood of conservatism and traditionalism. In America, however, fear of socialism and communism amid Cold War tensions generated a new element, provoked by fear of left-wing socialism and communism. Crackdowns on suspicious groups by the House Committee on Un-American Activities promoted a prevailing trend toward conformity with traditional Western social and cultural values.

Not everyone fell in line with this trend. The early 1950s witnessed the emergence of a countercultural movement known as the "Beat Generation," initiated by a group of writers and students affiliated with Columbia University. Finding prevailing conformity and uniformity stultifying and restrictive, Jack Kerouac, Allen Ginsberg, William Burroughs, and others sought new avenues of nonconformist expression, including experimentation with addictive drugs, alternative sexuality, and a fascination with Eastern religions—especially Buddhism—and music. Ginsberg's *Howl and Other Poems* (1956), an indictment of traditional societal and cultural norms, represents the earliest expression of the Beat ethic. *Howl* was followed by Kerouac's *On the Road* (1957); drawn from a series of road trips around America, the work expresses the emptiness of current culture.

Interestingly, Beats roamed the globe in quest of non-Western intellectual inspiration. Kerouac, Burroughs, and Ginsberg traveled widely; Ginsberg's visits to India introduced him to Eastern religions, particularly Buddhism and Krishnaism. In turn, Beat culture transcended American borders, and was assimilated into countercultural movements in Vienna, Prague, Istanbul, and Tokyo. Among the more telling instances of Beat influence abroad was John Lennon's meeting with a Beat poet in 1960, which resulted in changing the spelling of his famous rock group from "Beetles" to "Beatles."

The Beat Generation nurtured the emergence of later countercultures, including the hippies of the 1960s. Whereas the Beats simply explored alternative lifestyles, later exemplars were more motivated by, and interested in, political expressions. Their reach even extended to musical expressions of the 1960s; Bob Dylan, Jim Morrison, and the Beatles are among their many devotees.

- **What did the Beat Generation find so offensive and alienating about America during the postwar era of the 1950s?**

- **How does the Beat countercultural movement following World War II compare with expressions of the Lost Generation in the aftermath of World War I?**

# Thinking Through Patterns

▶ **Why did the pattern of unfolding modernity, which offered three choices after World War I, shrink to just capitalist democracy and socialism–communism in 1945? How did each of these two patterns evolve between 1945 and 1962?**

The pattern of modernity evolved in the nineteenth century with four major ingredients: constitutional nationalism, ethnic–linguistic–religious nationalism, industrialism, and communism. However, traditional institutions such as monarchies and empires from times prior to 1800 continued to flourish. World War I wiped out most monarchies, but capitalist democracy continued, communism came into its own in the Soviet Union, imperialism and colonialism survived, and supremacist nationalism attracted all those who found democracy and communism wanting. World War II eliminated supremacist nationalism and, after a delay of 17 years, also imperialism and colonialism. The remaining choices of capitalist democracy and communism were divided between two power blocs, which during the early Cold War period of 1945–1962 shared the world almost evenly among themselves.

Modernity grew out of the philosophy of the New Sciences in the 1600s, with its assumptions of materialism and the social contract. After acquiring mass support, modernity with its twin ideologies of constitutional nationalism and industrialism evolved into scientific–industrial modernity, with profound cultural consequences. On the one hand, waves of increasingly modern artistic movements appeared, from early-nineteenth-century romanticism to mid-twentieth-century existentialism. On the other hand, these consecutive waves of newness were insufficient to address the basic materialist flaw of modernity, which in each generation gave rise to the question of the meaning of it all. Did a modern world of rampant consumerism and gaping social inequities have intrinsic meaning even if people continued to find thrilling possibilities in material and intellectual–artistic life? The question still haunts us today.

▶ **What are the cultural premises of modernity?**

▶ **How did the newly independent countries of the Middle East, Asia, and Africa adapt to the divided world of the Cold War?**

During 1945–1962 the number of nations on earth quadrupled to total (in 2011) approximately 200. The new nations, emerging from colonialism, were in theory, like the older nations of early modernity in the nineteenth century, countries with ethnic–linguistic–religious cores and functioning constitutional institutions. In fact, many were not. Since most, furthermore, were still overwhelmingly agrarian, industrialism was beyond reach. With great hope, the ruling elites in a number of large new nations embraced a mixed capitalist–democratic and socialist regime, with heavy state investments in basic industries. However, in contrast to Stalin, who introduced these types of investments under the label of state-guided socialism, none of the elites in the new nations had the will to collect the money for these investments from their rural population. Instead, they borrowed heavily from the capitalist–democratic countries. True independence remained elusive.

# Patterns of Evidence: Sources for Chapter 29

## SOURCE 29.1

## The Universal Declaration of Human Rights

**December 10, 1948**

The Universal Declaration of Human Rights, adopted by the United Nations General Assembly on December 10, 1948, was one of the most significant and lasting results of the World War II. The League of Nations, created after the World War I, had failed to prevent the beginning of another, even more catastrophic and costly conflict. The United Nations was planned throughout the war as a substitute mechanism for global peace and security, but world leaders also believed that a document was necessary to affirm the rights of individuals throughout the entire world. A formal drafting committee, consisting of members from eight countries, was charged with the task. The committee chair was Eleanor Roosevelt, the widow of President Roosevelt and a strong advocate for human rights in her own right. By its resolution 217 A (III), the General Assembly, meeting in Paris, adopted the Universal Declaration of Human Rights. Eight nations abstained from the vote, but none dissented.

### PREAMBLE

Whereas recognition of the inherent dignity and of the equal and inalienable rights of all members of the human family is the foundation of freedom, justice and peace in the world,

Whereas disregard and contempt for human rights have resulted in barbarous acts which have outraged the conscience of mankind, and the advent of a world in which human beings shall enjoy freedom of speech and belief and freedom from fear and want has been proclaimed as the highest aspiration of the common people,

Whereas it is essential, if man is not to be compelled to have recourse, as a last resort, to rebellion against tyranny and oppression, that human rights should be protected by the rule of law,

Whereas it is essential to promote the development of friendly relations between nations,

Whereas the peoples of the United Nations have in the Charter reaffirmed their faith in fundamental human rights, in the dignity and worth of the human person and in the equal rights of men and women and have determined to promote social progress and better standards of life in larger freedom,

Whereas Member States have pledged themselves to achieve, in co-operation with the United Nations, the promotion of universal respect for and observance of human rights and fundamental freedoms,

Whereas a common understanding of these rights and freedoms is of the greatest importance for the full realization of this pledge,

**Now, Therefore THE GENERAL ASSEMBLY** proclaims **THIS UNIVERSAL DECLARATION OF HUMAN RIGHTS** as a common standard of achievement for all peoples and all nations, to the end that every individual and every organ of society, keeping this Declaration constantly in mind, shall strive by teaching and education to promote respect for these rights and freedoms and by progressive measures, national and international, to secure their universal and effective recognition and observance, both among the peoples of Member States themselves and among the peoples of territories under their jurisdiction.

**Article 1.**
All human beings are born free and equal in dignity and rights. They are endowed with reason and conscience and should act towards one another in a spirit of brotherhood.

**Article 2.**
Everyone is entitled to all the rights and freedoms set forth in this Declaration, without distinction of any kind, such as race, colour, sex, language, religion, political or other opinion, national or social origin, property,

birth or other status. Furthermore, no distinction shall be made on the basis of the political, jurisdictional or international status of the country or territory to which a person belongs, whether it be independent, trust, non-self-governing or under any other limitation of sovereignty.

**Article 3.**
Everyone has the right to life, liberty and security of person.

**Article 4.**
No one shall be held in slavery or servitude; slavery and the slave trade shall be prohibited in all their forms.

**Article 5.**
No one shall be subjected to torture or to cruel, inhuman or degrading treatment or punishment.

**Article 6.**
Everyone has the right to recognition everywhere as a person before the law.

. . .

**Article 15.**
(1) Everyone has the right to a nationality.
(2) No one shall be arbitrarily deprived of his nationality nor denied the right to change his nationality.

**Article 16.**
(1) Men and women of full age, without any limitation due to race, nationality or religion, have the right to marry and to found a family. They are entitled to equal rights as to marriage, during marriage and at its dissolution.
(2) Marriage shall be entered into only with the free and full consent of the intending spouses.
(3) The family is the natural and fundamental group unit of society and is entitled to protection by society and the State.

**Article 17.**
(1) Everyone has the right to own property alone as well as in association with others.

(2) No one shall be arbitrarily deprived of his property.

**Article 18.**

Everyone has the right to freedom of thought, conscience and religion; this right includes freedom to change his religion or belief, and freedom, either alone or in community with others and in public or private, to manifest his religion or belief in teaching, practice, worship and observance.

**Article 19.**

Everyone has the right to freedom of opinion and expression; this right includes freedom to hold opinions without interference and to seek, receive and impart information and ideas through any media and regardless of frontiers.

. . .

**Article 23.**

(1) Everyone has the right to work, to free choice of employment, to just and favorable conditions of work and to protection against unemployment.

(2) Everyone, without any discrimination, has the right to equal pay for equal work.

(3) Everyone who works has the right to just and favorable remuneration ensuring for himself and his family an existence worthy of human dignity, and supplemented, if necessary, by other means of social protection.

(4) Everyone has the right to form and to join trade unions for the protection of his interests.

**Article 24.**

Everyone has the right to rest and leisure, including reasonable limitation of working hours and periodic holidays with pay.

**Article 25.**

(1) Everyone has the right to a standard of living adequate for the health and well-being of himself and of his family, including food, clothing, housing and medical care and necessary social services, and the right to security in the event of unemployment, sickness, disability, widowhood, old age or other lack of livelihood in circumstances beyond his control.

(2) Motherhood and childhood are entitled to special care and assistance. All children, whether born in or out of wedlock, shall enjoy the same social protection.

**Article 26.**

(1) Everyone has the right to education. Education shall be free, at least in the elementary and fundamental stages. Elementary education shall be compulsory. Technical and professional education shall be made generally available and higher education shall be equally accessible to all on the basis of merit.

(2) Education shall be directed to the full development of the human personality and to the strengthening of respect for human rights and fundamental freedoms. It shall promote understanding, tolerance and friendship among all nations, racial or religious groups, and shall further the activities of the United Nations for the maintenance of peace.

(3) Parents have a prior right to choose the kind of education that shall be given to their children.

▶ **Working with Sources**

1. According to the Universal Declaration of Human Rights, what would be the practical benefits of guaranteeing human rights for the entire human family?

2. How likely were these goals to be applied globally in 1948? Which articles remained to be fulfilled at that point—and perhaps even today?

SOURCE 29.2

# Winston Churchill, "The Iron Curtain Speech"

## March 5, 1946

Throughout the 1930s, Churchill had opposed the policy of "appease-ment" advocated by Prime Minister Neville Chamberlain and his allies in the British Parliament. His rise to the highest political office was facili-tated by Chamberlain's failure to deliver on the "peace in our time" he had promised after the Munich Agreement in September 1938. However, it was not until May 1940 that Churchill got his chance. Having calmed, encour-aged, and directed the British people—and others—throughout the war years, Churchill was himself removed from power in 1945. Nevertheless, at this famous address delivered at Westminster College in Missouri in 1946, Churchill warned of a new regime that also could not, and should not, be appeased. It is considered one of the first salvos in the developing Cold War between the West and the Soviet bloc.

The safety of the world, ladies and gentlemen, requires a unity in Europe, from which no nation should be per-manently outcast. It is from the quar-rels of the strong parent races in Europe that the world wars we have witnessed, or which occurred in former times, have sprung. Twice the United States has had to send several millions of its young men across the Atlantic to fight the wars. But now we all can find any nation, wherever it may dwell, between dusk and dawn. Surely we should work with conscious purpose for a grand pacification of Europe within the structure of the United Nations and in accordance with our Charter. In a great number of countries, far from the Russian frontiers and throughout the world, Communist fifth columns are established and work in com-plete unity and absolute obedience to the directions they receive from the Communist center. Except in the British Commonwealth and in the United States where Communism is in its infancy, the Communist parties or fifth columns constitute a growing challenge and peril to Christian civi-lization. The outlook is also anxious in the Far East and especially in Manchuria. The agreement which was made at Yalta, to which I was a party, was extremely favorable to Soviet Russia, but it was made at a time when no one could say that the German war might not extend all through the summer and autumn of 1945 and when the Japanese war was expected by the best judges to last for a further eighteen months from the end of the German war. I repulse the idea that a new war is inevitable—still more that it is im-minent. It is because I am sure that our fortunes are still in our own hands and that we hold the power to save the future, that I feel the duty to speak out now that I have the occasion and the opportunity to do so. I do not believe that Soviet Russia desires war. What they desire is the fruits of war and the indefinite expansion of their power and doctrines. But what we have to consider here today while time remains, is the permanent prevention of war and the establishment of conditions of freedom and democracy as rapidly as possible in all countries. Our difficulties and dangers will not be removed by closing our eyes to them. They will not be removed by mere waiting to see what happens; nor will they be removed by a policy of appeasement. What is needed is a settlement, and the longer this is delayed, the more difficult it will be and the greater our dangers will become. From what I have seen of our Russian friends and allies during the war, I am convinced that there is nothing they admire so much as strength, and there is nothing for which they have less respect than for weakness, especially military weakness. For that reason the old doctrine of a balance of power is unsound. We cannot afford, if we can help it, to work on narrow margins, offering temptations to a trial of strength.

. . .

If the population of the English-speaking Commonwealth be added to that of the United States, with all that such cooperation implies in the air, on the sea, all over the globe, and in science and in industry, and in moral force, there will be no quivering, precarious balance of power to offer its temptation to ambition or adventure. On the contrary there will be an overwhelming assurance of security. If we adhere faithfully to the Charter of the United Nations and walk forward in sedate and sober strength, seeking no one's land or treasure, seeking to lay no arbitrary control upon the thoughts of men, if all British moral and material forces and convictions are joined with your own in fraternal association, the high roads of the future will be clear, not only for us but for all, not only for our time but for a century to come.

▶ **Working with Sources**

1. **What does this speech reveal about changing commitments and alliances after the end of the war in 1945? What factors caused a change in policy in Western countries toward the Soviet Union?**

2. **Why was Churchill commenting on the dangers of appeasement with regard to Soviet foreign policy?**

## SOURCE 29.3

# Letters on the Cuban Missile Crisis between Fidel Castro and Nikita Khrushchev

### October 28 and 30, 1962

The Cuban Missile Crisis of October 1962 marked the climax, and the most dangerous point, of the Cold War between the United States and the Soviet Union. When US spy planes discovered the presence of missiles and launching pads in Cuba, President John F. Kennedy demanded their immediate destruction and followed up this demand with a naval blockade of the island—and continued reconnaissance missions in Cuban airspace—to prevent the arrival of Russian reinforcements. The world held its breath for several days as Soviet ships, bearing more nuclear missiles, sailed steadily for Cuba. The globe teetered on the brink of nuclear annihilation, and this exchange of letters reveals, from the Soviet and Cuban side, how very close to that brink the world actually came.

### Letter to Nikita Khrushchev from Fidel Castro regarding defending Cuban air space

October 28, 1962

Dear Comrade Khrushchev:

I have just received your letter.

The position of our Government regarding your statement can be found in the text of the declaration announced today, with which you are surely familiar.

I must clarify a point relating to the anti-aircraft measures which we adopted. You said: "Yesterday you shot down one of them, yet previously you did not when they flew over your territory."

Previously, there were isolated violations with no particular military purpose, and they did not result in real danger.

This is no longer the case. There was the danger of a surprise attack on certain military sites. We decided that we could not remain idle because of the danger of a surprise attack. With our warning radars turned off, the potential attackers could fly with impunity over the sites and totally destroy them. We did not believe that we should allow this, given the cost and effort which we have expended, and because an attack would have gravely weakened our morals and military capability. Because of this, Cuban forces mobilized fifty anti-aircraft batteries, our entire reserves, on October 24 in order to support the positions of the Soviet forces. If we wanted to prevent the risk of a surprise attack, the crews had to have orders to shoot. The Soviet Forces Command can give you further details on what happened with the plane that was shot down.

In the past, violations of our airspace were de facto and were conducted furtively. Yesterday the American Government tried to make official the privilege of violating our air space at any time, day and night. This we could not accept because it would mean renouncing our sovereign prerogative. Nevertheless, we agree to avoid an incident at this moment that could gravely harm the negotiations. We will instruct the Cuban batteries to hold their fire while the negotiations last, without reversing the decision we announced yesterday to defend our air space. We must consider the dangers of possible incidents in the present conditions of high tension.

I also wish to inform you that we are opposed, by principle, to inspections on our territory.

I appreciate the enormous efforts which you have made to maintain the

Source: http://www.cubanet.org/htdocs/ref/dis/10110201.htm.

peace, and we totally agree with the necessity to fight for this aim. If we achieve it in a just, solid, and permanent way it will be an enormous service to humanity.

Fraternally,
*Fidel Castro*

### Letter to Fidel Castro from Nikita Khrushchev stating Khrushchev will help to defend Cuba
October 30, 1962
Dear Comrade Fidel Castro:

We have received your letter of October 28, along with the reports of the conversations that you and President Dorticos had with our ambassador.

We understand your situation and are taking into account your difficulties in this first stage following the elimination of the maximum tension that resulted from the threat of an attack by American imperialists which you expected at any moment.

We understand that for you certain difficulties may have emerged as a consequence of the promises we made to the United States to withdraw the missile bases from Cuba in exchange for their promise to abandon their plans to invade Cuba and to prevent their allies in the Western hemisphere from doing so, to end their so-called "quarantine"—their blockade of Cuba. This commitment has led to an end to the conflict in the Caribbean, a conflict which implied, as you can well understand, a superpower confrontation and its transformation into a world war where the missiles and thermonuclear weapons would have been used. According to our ambassador, certain Cubans feel that the Cuban people would prefer a different kind of statement, one that would not deal with the withdrawal of the missiles. It is possible that such feelings exist among the people. But we, politicians and heads of state, are the people's leaders and the people do not know everything. This is why we must march at the head of the people. Then they will follow and respect us.

If, by giving in to popular sentiment, we had allowed ourselves to be swept up by the more inflamed sectors of the populace, and if we had refused to reach a reasonable agreement with the government of the USA, war would have probably broken out, resulting in millions of deaths. Those who survived would have blamed the leaders for not having taken the measures that would have avoided this war of extermination.

The prevention of war and of an attack on Cuba did not depend only on the measures taken by our governments, but also on the analysis and examination of the enemy's actions near your territory. In short, the situation had to be considered as a whole.

Some people say that we did not consult sufficiently with each other before taking the decision of which you know.

In fact, we consider that consultations did take place, dear Comrade Fidel Castro, since we received your cables, one more alarming than the other, and finally your cable of October 27 where you said that you were almost certain that an attack against Cuba was imminent. According to you it was only a matter of time: 24 or 72 hours.

Having received this very alarming cable from you, and knowing of your courage, we believed the alert to be totally justified.

Wasn't that consultation on your part? We interpreted that cable as a sign of maximum alert. But if we had carried on with our consultations in such conditions, knowing that the bellicose and unbridled militarists of the United States wanted to seize the occasion to attack Cuba, we would have been wasting our time and the strike could have taken place.

We think that the presence of our strategic missiles in Cuba has polarized the attention of the imperialists. They were afraid that they would be used, which is why they risked wanting to eliminate them, either by bombing them or by invading Cuba. And we must recognize that they had the capability to put them out of action. This is why, I repeat, your sense of alarm was totally justified.

In your cable of October 27 you proposed that we be the first to carry out a nuclear strike against the enemy's territory. Naturally you understand where that would lead us. It would not be a simple strike, but the start of a thermonuclear world war.

Dear Comrade Fidel Castro, I find your proposal to be wrong, even though I understand your reasons.

We have lived through a very grave moment, a global thermonuclear war could have broken out. Of course the United States would have suffered enormous losses, but the Soviet Union and the whole socialist bloc would have also suffered greatly. It is even difficult to say how things would have ended for the Cuban people. First of all, Cuba would have burned in the fires of war. Without a doubt the Cuban people would have fought courageously but, also without a doubt, the Cuban people would have perished heroically. We struggle against imperialism, not in order to die, but to draw on all of our potential, to lose as little as possible, and later to win more, so as to be a victor and make communism triumph.

The measures which we have adopted have allowed us to reach the goal which we had set when we decided to send the missiles to Cuba. We have extracted from the United States the commitment not to invade Cuba and not to allow their Latin American allies to do so. We have accomplished all of this without a nuclear war.

▶ **Working with Sources**

1. Why was Castro so insistent in drawing Khrushchev's attention to violations of Cuba's sovereignty by the United States?

2. How did Khrushchev attempt to calm Castro down? Why did he do so, and what does the document reveal about his intentions during this crisis?

## SOURCE 29.4

# Ho Chi Minh, "The Path Which Led Me to Leninism"

**April 1960**

On September 2, 1945, the day of Japan's surrender to the United States, the leader of the communist resistance in Indochina, Ho Chi Minh, read a Vietnamese declaration of independence to half a million people in

Hanoi. Newly liberated from occupation by Nazi Germany, France hoped to reassert its power in the region it had colonized in the previous century, but the communist Vietminh refused to budge from their demands for independence. The French persuaded the United States that this colonial conflict was an outgrowth of the larger Cold War between the West and the Soviet Union, and the American administrations of Presidents Truman and Eisenhower (1945–1961) provided financial and moral support to the French as they clashed with Vietnamese insurgents. The French surrendered in 1954, but Vietnam was divided. The United States continued its involvement in South Vietnam—soon to be accelerated with the dispatch of military advisors and military personnel by Presidents Eisenhower and Kennedy (1961–1963). Published in April 1960 in a Soviet journal entitled *Problems of the East*, this statement by Ho Chi Minh encapsulates his thinking on the example of Vladimir Lenin in his own struggle against Western imperialism.

After World War I, I made my living in Paris, now as a retoucher at a photographer's, now as painter of "Chinese antiquities" (made in France!). I would distribute leaflets denouncing the crimes committed by the French colonialists in Viet Nam.

At that time, I supported the October Revolution only instinctively, not yet grasping all its historic importance. I loved and admired Lenin because he was a great patriot who liberated his compatriots; until then, I had read none of his books.

The reason for my joining the French Socialist Party was that these "ladies and gentlemen"—as I called my comrades at that moment—had shown their sympathy towards me, towards the struggle of the oppressed peoples. But I understood neither what was a party, a trade-union, nor what was socialism nor communism.

Heated discussions were then taking place in the branches of the Socialist Party, about the question whether the Socialist Party should remain in the Second International, should a Second and a half International be founded or should the Socialist Party join Lenin's Third International? I attended the meetings regularly, twice or thrice a week and attentively listened to the discussion. First, I could not understand thoroughly. Why were the discussions so heated? Either with the Second, Second and a half or Third International, the revolution could be waged. What was the use of arguing then? As for the First International, what had become of it?

What I wanted most to know—and this precisely was not debated in the meetings—was: which International sides with the peoples of colonial countries?

I raised this question—the most important in my opinion—in a meeting. Some comrades answered: It is the Third, not the Second International. And a comrade gave me Lenin's "Thesis on the national and colonial

Source: Ho Chi Minh, *Selected Works*, vol. 4 (Hanoi: Foreign Languages Publishing House, 1962), available online at http://www.marxists.org/reference/archive/ho-chi-minh/works/1960/04/x01.htm.

questions" published by l'Humanité to read.

There were political terms difficult to understand in this thesis. But by dint of reading it again and again, finally I could grasp the main part of it. What emotion, enthusiasm, clear-sightedness and confidence it instilled into me! I was overjoyed to tears. Though sitting alone in my room, I shouted out aloud as if addressing large crowds: "Dear martyr compatriots! This is what we need, this is the path to our liberation!"

After then, I had entire confidence in Lenin, in the Third International.

Formerly, during the meetings of the Party branch, I only listened to the discussion; I had a vague belief that all were logical, and could not differentiate as to who were right and who were wrong. But from then on, I also plunged into the debates and discussed with fervour. Though I was still lacking French words to express all my thoughts, I smashed the allegations attacking Lenin and the Third International with no less vigour. My only argument was: "If you do not condemn colonialism, if you do not side with the colonial people, what kind of revolution are you waging?"

. . .

At first, patriotism, not yet communism, led me to have confidence in Lenin, in the Third International. Step by step, along the struggle, by studying Marxism-Leninism parallel with participation in practical activities, I gradually came upon the fact that only socialism and communism can liberate the oppressed nations and the working people throughout the world from slavery.

▶ **Working with Sources**

1. **What did Ho make of the inner divisions among socialists? How did these divisions affect the interests of the Vietnamese, as he saw them?**

2. **In what respects did Ho see Lenin as a liberator of all "colonized" peoples? Was he justified in this conclusion?**

## SOURCE 29.5

# Indira Gandhi, "What Educated Women Can Do"

### November 23, 1974

The only child of Jawaharlal Nehru, the first prime minister of India, Indira Gandhi served in turn as prime minister between 1966 and 1977 and again from 1980 until her assassination in 1984. She was the third of the country's prime ministers and the first female to hold the position. Gandhi pursued many of the same policies as her father, supported the Non-Aligned

Source: http://www.edchange.org/multicultural/ speeches/indira_gandhi_educated.html.

Movement, and was especially concerned to promote the interests of the women and girls of her nation and of the world. This speech, delivered to students in a women's college, reveals her concern to combine women's rights with India's drive for modernization.

An ancient Sanskrit saying says, woman is the home and the home is the basis of society. It is as we build our homes that we can build our country. If the home is inadequate—either inadequate in material goods and necessities or inadequate in the sort of friendly, loving atmosphere that every child needs to grow and develop—then that country cannot have harmony and no country which does not have harmony can grow in any direction at all.

That is why women's education is almost more important than the education of boys and men. We—and by "we" I do not mean only we in India but all the world—have neglected women's education. It is fairly recent. Of course, not to you but when I was a child, the story of the early days of women's education in England, for instance, was very current. Everybody remembered what had happened in the early days.

I remember what used to happen here. I still remember the days when living in old Delhi even as a small child of seven or eight. I had to go out in a **doli** if I left the house. We just did not walk. Girls did not walk in the streets. First, you had your sari with which you covered your head, then you had another shawl or something with which you covered your hand and all the body, then you had a white shawl, with which every thing was covered again although your face was open fortunately. Then you were in the doli, which again was covered by another cloth. And this was in a family or community which did not observe **purdah** of any kind at all.

**Doli:** A covered litter.

**Purdah:** Ritual seclusion of females.

In fact, all our social functions always were mixed functions but this was the atmosphere of the city and of the country.

Now, we have got education and there is a debate all over the country whether this education is adequate to the needs of society or the needs of our young people. I am one of those who always believe that education needs a thorough overhauling. But at the same time, I think that everything in our education is not bad, that even the present education has produced very fine men and women, especially scientists and experts in different fields, who are in great demand all over the world and even in the most affluent countries. Many of our young people leave us and go abroad because they get higher salaries, they get better conditions of work.

. . .

Sometimes, I am very sad that even people who do science are quite unscientific in their thinking and in their other actions—not what they are doing in the laboratories but how they live at home or their attitudes towards other people. Now, for India to become what we want it to become with a modern, rational society and firmly based on what is good in our ancient tradition and in our soil, for this we have to have a thinking public, thinking young women who are not content to accept what comes from any part of the world but are willing to listen to it, to analyse it and to decide whether it is to be accepted or whether it is to be thrown out and this is the sort of education which we want, which enables our young people to adjust to this changing world and to be able to contribute to it.

Some people think that only by taking up very high jobs, you are doing something important or you are doing national service. But we all know that the most complex machinery will be ineffective if one small screw is not working as it should and that screw is just as important as any big part. It is the same in national life. There is no job that is too small; there is no person who is too small. Everybody has something to do. And if he or she does it well, then the country will run well.

In our superstition, we have thought that some work is dirty work. For instance, sweeping has been regarded as dirty. Only some people can do it; others should not do it. Now we find that manure is the most valuable thing that the world has today and many of the world's economies are shaking because there is not enough fertilizer—and not just the chemical fertilizer but the ordinary manure, night-soil and all that sort of thing, things which were considered dirty.

Now it shows how beautifully balanced the world was with everything fitted in with something else. Everything, whether dirty or small, had a purpose. We, with our science and technology, have tried to —not purposely, but somehow, we have created an imbalance and that is what is troubling, on a big scale, the economies of the world and also people and individuals. They are feeling alienated from their societies, not only in India but almost in every country in the world,

except in places where the whole purpose of education and government has to be to make the people conform to just one idea. We are told that people there are very happy in whatever they are doing. If they are told to clean the streets, well, if he is a professor he has to clean the streets, if he is a scientist he has to do it, and we were told that they are happy doing it. Well, if they are happy, it is alright.

But I do not think in India we can have that kind of society where people are forced to do things because we think that they can be forced maybe for 25 years, maybe for 50 years, but sometime or the other there will be an explosion. In our society, we allow lots of smaller explosions because we think that that will guard the basic stability and progress of society and prevent it from having the kind of chaotic explosion which can retard our progress and harmony in the country.

So, I hope that all of you who have this great advantage of education will not only do whatever work you are doing keeping the national interests in view, but you will make your own contribution to creating peace and harmony, to bringing beauty in the lives of our people and our country. I think this is the special responsibility of the women of India. We want to do a great deal for our country, but we have never regarded India as isolated from the rest of the world. What we want to do is to make a better world. So, we have to see India's problems in the perspective of the larger world problems.

▶ **Working with Sources**

1. **What were the parameters of the "modern, rational society" that Gandhi envisioned?**

2. **In what terms did she contrast ancient superstitions and modern science, and how did she relate this dichotomy to Indian history and cultural identity?**

# Chapter 30 1963–1991

# The End of the Cold War, Western Social Transformation, and the Developing World

A s the helicopter slowly approached the snow-capped mountain, the fighter on the ground recognized it immediately: *Shaitan Arba*— "Satan's Chariot," the Soviet MI-5 "Hind" attack helicopter. This new, heavily armed and armored helicopter gunship had proven largely impervious to the rifle and small arms fire with which the fighter and his *mujahideen* Afghan warriors vainly attempted to bring it down. Worse still, it carried a devastating array of rockets and machine cannon; the fighter had seen these gunships wipe out entire squads of his comrades. In this desperate fight in the Afghan high country, the Soviets, it appeared, had acquired a decisive technological edge as they sought to eliminate resistance to the client regime they had installed in the capital of Kabul in 1979.

But just before the soldier took cover, the helicopter exploded in a red and orange fireball, plummeting swiftly into the mountainside. A rapidly dissolving vapor trail marked a spot about 200 meters away from where it appeared a rocket had been fired. A small group of men shouted "God is great!" and cheered lustily at their victory.

North America  Europe  Asia

Africa

South America

Australia

**THE WORLD, 1963–1991**

*ABOVE: Afghan Mujahideen soldiers, battling the Soviet invasion, celebrate the downing of a Russian helicopter in January 1980.*

Similar scenes were repeated more than 300 times during the coming years. The weapon that had downed the helicopter was a new American "Stinger" shoulder-fired missile, which the United States was clandestinely supplying to the Afghan Muslim fighters attempting to expel the Soviet occupying forces. Perhaps more than any other weapon, the Stinger neutralized the Soviet technological advantage in airpower and enabled an international force of mujahideen to ultimately push the Soviets out of Afghanistan in this last contest of the Cold War, in much the same way that the United States had been forced from South Vietnam. In fact, as we will see in more detail in this chapter, the immense cost of the Soviet–Afghan War, added to the even higher price of trying to match the American effort to create a missile defense system against intercontinental ballistic missiles (ICBMs), contributed to the collapse of the Soviet economy by the end of the 1980s and led to the end of the Eastern Bloc and the Soviet Union itself. It thus appeared that the West and its version of modernity—capitalist democracy—had convincingly won both the physical and ideological contests of the Cold War.

## Seeing Patterns

▶ How did the political landscape of the Cold War change from 1963 to 1991?

▶ Why did such radically different lifestyles emerge in the United States and the West during the 1960s and 1970s? What is their legacy today?

▶ Why did some nations that had emerged from colonialism and war make great strides in their development while others seemed to stagnate?

In this chapter we will trace the progress of this struggle and the immense social changes associated with the period from 1963 to 1991 in the West and the progress of the struggle in the developing world. Although the end result was an apparent victory for democracy and capitalism—both of which were to be introduced into the successor states of the Soviet Union in the 1990s—the contest in the developing world was still active. From the triumph of Muslim resistance to the secular communist vision of modernity in Afghanistan would emerge a new global movement of resistance to the secular West and democratic capitalism: al-Qaeda and its affiliates.

## The Climax of the Cold War

The Cold War continued into the 1980s when the power of the Soviet Union began to ebb. During the 1960s, despite the enactment of the Nuclear Test Ban Treaty, the United States and the Soviet Union remained bitter ideological enemies. The Soviet Union and the People's Republic of China both sent aid to Ho Chi Minh's forces fighting the Americans in Vietnam. The Soviets also supported the Arab efforts against US-backed Israel in 1967 and 1973. Moreover, both sides upgraded and expanded their nuclear arsenals. Despite this continuing hostility, the late 1960s and early 1970s also witnessed the era of *détente*: a downplaying of overt aggression toward one another and the pursuit of competition through diplomatic, social, and cultural means. The Soviet invasion of Afghanistan in 1979, however, ushered in a final phase of both openly hostile competition and covert warfare. In the end, the Soviet Union's resources were simply not sufficient to outlast those of the West in the struggle.

## The Soviet Superpower in Slow Decline

In 1963, only a few months after the Cuban Missile Crisis, it still appeared that the Soviet Union was an adversary more or less equal to the United States. Indeed, in many respects, it seemed to have the momentum of history on its side. Yet, in less than 30 years the Soviet Union would fall apart, to be replaced by its core political unit of Russia and a host of newly independent former Soviet republics. What set this unexpected course of events in motion?

**From the Brink of War to Détente**   Nikita S. Khrushchev had cultivated a down-to-earth image that contributed to his popularity in the Soviet Union and, to some extent, on the international stage. But his initial success in rolling back some of the worst abuses of Stalinism had been overshadowed by three failures during the early 1960s. The first was allowing the Sino–Soviet split of 1960 to become a complete break. Moreover, Khrushchev's building of the Berlin Wall, though largely effective in its immediate objective of stopping the flood of refugees from East Berlin, had been a propaganda failure. His American counterpart, the youthful, charismatic president John F. Kennedy (in office 1961–1963), had rallied world opposition to the wall when he proclaimed, "Ich bin ein Berliner" ("I am a Berliner").

But Khrushchev's key blunder had been in appearing to back down during the Cuban Missile Crisis in October 1962. Seeking to test the resolve of the young American president by installing nuclear missiles on America's doorstep, the premier instead was forced to dismantle Soviet bases in Cuba. Though the United States also agreed to the face-saving gesture of dismantling its own medium-range missiles in Turkey, the Soviet Politburo shortly acted to oust Khrushchev, who duly resigned in October 1964.

The years of Leonid Brezhnev (in office 1960–1964; 1977–1982) were marked by actions demonstrating just how shaken the Soviet Union and United States were by how close they had come to all-out nuclear war in October 1962. One way that this danger had been partially defused was by the Nuclear Test Ban Treaty, signed in October 1963. Alert to the toxic effects of nuclear fallout and the possibility that tests may raise false alarms about attacks, the signatories agreed to abandon all aboveground nuclear testing. Nonnuclear nations were severely discouraged from developing their own weapons in subsequent "nonproliferation" treaties. Additional safeguards were built into the detection and early warning systems both sides used as part of missile defense. Finally, a hotline—a direct telephone link between the White House and the Kremlin—was created so that American and Soviet leaders could alert each other if an accident or false attack signal had been issued. Nonetheless, the mood of the 1960s remained one of nuclear tension on both sides, and American popular culture was rife with doomsday fantasies of the catastrophic effects of nuclear war.

By the late 1960s, the United States and the Soviet Union had entered into a period of relatively tranquil relations often referred to by historians as "**détente**," from the French term for "release of tension." However, for the Soviets, tensions were mounting with the People's Republic of China over disputed borders along the Amur River and the rising chaos of the Cultural Revolution. At several points, military engagements took place, and at least once, the Americans were approached by the Soviets about the possibility of a preemptive nuclear strike against China.

**Détente.** Following closer diplomatic contact between the United States and the Soviet Union in the wake of the Arab–Israeli War in the beginning of June 1967, President Lyndon Johnson and Soviet Premier Andrei Gromyko met at Glassboro State College (now Rowan University). The talks centered around the US position in Vietnam and the possibility of opening talks on lessening nuclear tensions. Here, President Johnson and Premier Gromyko are engaged in a frank discussion.

The era of détente abruptly ended in the fall of 1973, however, with the Egyptian and Syrian surprise attack on Israel, which coincided with both the Jewish holy day of Yom Kippur and the Muslim month of Ramadan and sparked the largest Arab–Israeli conflict to date. The Soviets actively supported the boycott by the largely Arab Organization of the Petroleum Exporting Countries (OPEC) of oil shipments to the United States during the mid-1970s and resumed support for North Vietnam's final drive to conquer South Vietnam after the American withdrawal in 1973.

**"Prague Spring" in Czechoslovakia and "Solidarity" in Poland**    The Brezhnev years were also marked by increasing dissent, both in the Soviet Union and, even more markedly, in its Eastern European client states (see Map 30.1). Since the uprising in Hungary in 1956, for example, government efforts to stifle dissent and reform had been increasingly difficult and threatened to stir up latent nationalistic feeling. One result was the evolution under János Kádár (in office 1956–1988), the Hungarian party secretary, of what came to be called "goulash communism": a relatively relaxed attitude toward criticism of the regime, the introduction of limited market reforms, some attention to consumer demands, and limited trade with the West.

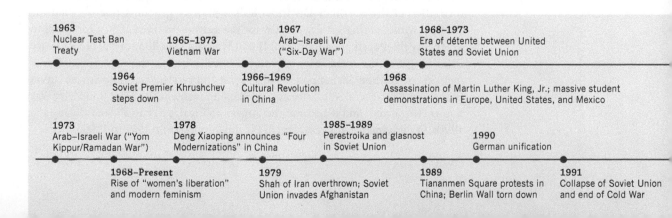

| 1963 | | 1967 | 1968–1973 |
|---|---|---|---|
| Nuclear Test Ban Treaty | 1965–1973 | Arab–Israeli War ("Six-Day War") | Era of détente between United States and Soviet Union |
| | Vietnam War | | |

| | 1964 | 1966–1969 | 1968 |
|---|---|---|---|
| | Soviet Premier Khrushchev steps down | Cultural Revolution in China | Assassination of Martin Luther King, Jr.; massive student demonstrations in Europe, United States, and Mexico |

| 1973 | 1978 | 1985–1989 | |
|---|---|---|---|
| Arab–Israeli War ("Yom Kippur/Ramadan War") | Deng Xiaoping announces "Four Modernizations" in China | Perestroika and glasnost in Soviet Union | 1990 German unification |

| 1968–Present | 1979 | 1989 | 1991 |
|---|---|---|---|
| Rise of "women's liberation" and modern feminism | Shah of Iran overthrown; Soviet Union invades Afghanistan | Tiananmen Square protests in China; Berlin Wall torn down | Collapse of Soviet Union and end of Cold War |

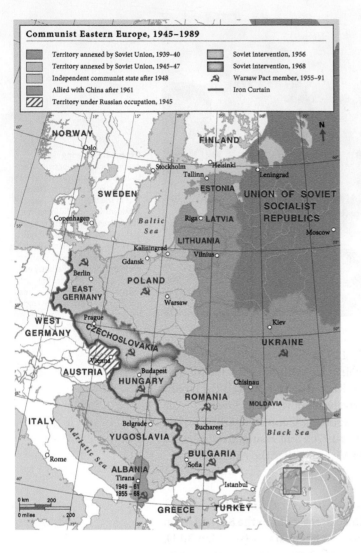

**Communist Eastern Europe, 1945–1989**

- Territory annexed by Soviet Union, 1939–40
- Territory annexed by Soviet Union, 1945–47
- Independent communist state after 1948
- Allied with China after 1961
- Territory under Russian occupation, 1945
- Soviet intervention, 1956
- Soviet intervention, 1968
- ☭ Warsaw Pact member, 1955–91
- Iron Curtain

MAP **30.1 Communist Eastern Europe, 1945–1989.**

In 1968, dissent took a more direct course in Czechoslovakia, in what came to be called the "Prague Spring." With the rise to power of Alexander Dubček (in office 1968–1969) in January 1968, a sweeping set of reforms, more extensive than those by Kádár in Hungary, was introduced. There were calls for a new decentralized administrative structure, relaxation of censorship, free speech, and opposition political parties. An atmosphere of excitement and expectation prevailed in the capital of Prague. Brezhnev's government, however, saw this as evidence of the Czechoslovak Communist Party's power slipping and entered into negotiations in order to bring the country back into line. By August, as the push for reform became more persistent, the Soviets sent Warsaw Pact forces into Czechoslovakia, where they ousted Dubček, installed Gustáv Husák (1913–1991), and dismantled the reforms of the previous 7 months. The Soviet move demonstrated what became known as the "Brezhnev Doctrine"—the right of the Soviets and Warsaw Pact to forcibly restrain any member country attempting to abandon socialism and the alliance with the Soviet Union.

With the shadow cast by the Brezhnev Doctrine, dissent once again went underground. In 1980, however, it reemerged in Poland with a strike by electrical workers at the Lenin Shipyard in Gdansk, which quickly spread to other port cities. A labor union was formed called "Solidarity," led by an electrician named Lech Walesa (b. 1943), which called for an end to censorship, the lifting of economic restrictions, and the right of workers to organize outside of the Communist Party. Despite arrests and government threats, by the end of 1980 one-fourth of Poland's population had joined the movement, including 80 percent of the country's workers.

The Polish government declared martial law in an attempt to stave off a Soviet invocation of the Brezhnev Doctrine. Still, a massive general strike crippled the country, while international sympathy for the movement intensified after a visit to Poland by the Polish pope John Paul II and Walesa's selection for the Nobel Peace Prize in 1983. The installation of Mikhail Gorbachev as the new Soviet leader in 1985 and his liberalizing policies of *glasnost* and *perestroika* in the Soviet Union ensured the future of Solidarity as a political movement. In 1989 Solidarity was finally relegalized, and it became the largest political party in Poland during the 1990s. Walesa was elected president of Poland, serving from 1991 to 1995.

**The 1980s: Afghanistan and "Star Wars"**   Despite the tensions following the collapse of détente and the Brezhnev Doctrine, some genuine progress on strategic arms limitation was achieved between the superpowers. The progress was motivated in part by the concept of "mutually assured destruction," which meant that nobody would "win" in an all-out atomic war. During the SALT II talks from 1977 to 1979, a historic agreement was reached in 1979 that would, for the first time, require the United States and the Soviet Union to limit certain types of nuclear weapons and begin a process of actually reducing them—a process that would later be known as START (Strategic Arms Reduction Talks/Treaty).

Much of the sense of progress achieved by this breakthrough was checked, however, by the Soviet invasion of Afghanistan in December 1979. The Egyptian–Israeli peace treaty of 1979 and the tilting of Saudi Arabia and Iraq toward the United States had altered the Middle Eastern landscape radically in favor of the West. Fearful of a weak, nominally communist Afghan government on its flank, adjacent to pro-American Pakistan and a China that appeared to have shifted toward the United States, the Soviets launched a swift coup in Afghanistan and installed a communist leader with a massive military force to back him up. The Soviets were immediately subjected to international condemnation, and the United States boycotted the 1980 Summer Olympics, which took place in Moscow.

At the same time, the new administration of President Ronald Reagan (in office 1981–1989) in the United States sought a more assertive policy toward the Soviet Union. The administration felt that the previous president, Jimmy Carter (in office 1977–1981), had been somewhat soft in response to both the Iranian taking of American hostages and the Soviet invasion of Afghanistan. At the same time, technological breakthroughs in computers and satellite communications made it theoretically possible for the United States to create an antiballistic missile system in outer space. Such a system was in violation of the antiballistic missile provisions of the 1969 SALT I accords, but the advantages of having a reliable missile defense in space—while at the same time retaining "first strike capability"—were overwhelming to American defense planners. Thus, over Soviet protests, the United States began to develop its Strategic Defense Initiative (SDI), nicknamed "Star Wars" after the popular movie of the same name.

From the mid-1980s, both superpowers thus began an enormously expensive strategic arms development race. For the Soviets, however, the drain of this new arms race, combined with the increasingly costly and unpopular war in Afghanistan, was simply unsustainable.

**Glasnost and Perestroika**   The death of Leonid Brezhnev in 1982 ushered in two short-lived successors before the relatively young Mikhail Gorbachev (b. 1931) took office as general secretary in the Politburo in 1985. Faced with growing dissent in Poland and other Eastern Bloc countries, an increasingly inefficient economy (the problems of which seemed to be highlighted by successful Chinese experiments with market economics), the endless war in Afghanistan,

**Lech Walesa and Solidarity.**
The strike at the Gdansk shipyard in Poland in 1980 brought to the fore an obscure electrician but able leader named Lech Walesa. Here, he is shown at a 1981 meeting of the organization he helped found, Solidarity, which ultimately helped topple Poland's communist government. Walesa himself went on to win the Nobel Peace Prize and was elected president of Poland in 1990.

and now the expensive arms race with the United States, Gorbachev called for large-scale structural reforms in the Soviet system.

Up until the 1980s, the Soviet economy had functioned as a giant economic command pyramid. Some 100 ministries in Moscow and 800 in the provinces oversaw some 50,000 enterprises, which produced some 24 million individual products. An army of ministerial bureaucrats oversaw every detail of the production and distribution process. The bureaucrats could never count on accurate figures, however, since both workers and managers had every incentive to overreport production figures and manufacture shoddy consumer goods as cheaply as possible. Periodic shortages were inevitable. As the saying on factory floors went, "They pretend to pay us and we pretend to work."

By the mid-1980s, however, Soviet planners had realized that their command system was delivering diminishing returns. Overall growth rates—in the 1950s and 1960s hovering around an impressive 10 percent—had declined to 3 percent. Several factors were responsible for the decline: fewer people were working in the factories; a lack of investment in new technologies and labor-saving machinery meant that factories were becoming less productive; and the percentage of people over 60 years of age had doubled between World War II and the mid-1980s, requiring the labor force to support more and more retirees.

Two years after becoming secretary of the Politburo in 1985, Gorbachev launched his two trademark economic and political programs, "restructuring" (**perestroika**) and "openness" (**glasnost**), which were intended to revitalize communism. Restructuring entailed the partial dismantling of the command economy. Freed to some degree from the planners' oversight, managers could sell up to one-third of what their factories produced on the market, instead of delivering everything to the state. Citizens were free to establish "cooperatives," the communist euphemism for private business enterprises. By the end of the 1980s, the law permitted co-ops in practically all branches of the economy. Gorbachev promoted the new mixed command and market economy as a "socialist" or "regulated" system, advertising it as the same order once pursued by Lenin (then called the New Economic Policy, or NEP).

In practice, perestroika did not work out as intended. Market production rose to a meager 5 percent of total production. Many managers were stuck with the manufacture of unprofitable goods, such as soap, toothpaste, matches, and children's clothes. Consumers complained about continued or even worse shortages in the stores. Other managers, eager to increase production, granted irresponsible wage increases to their workers as incentives. People of modest means established small businesses, charging outrageous prices and evading payment of taxes. Support structures for the co-ops, such as credit, banking, contract law, wholesale distribution centers, and wage bargaining mechanisms, were lacking. Gorbachev's measures, therefore, did little to end the stagnation of state factories and encouraged the rise of wild "carpetbagger" capitalism.

Parallel to economic restructuring, Gorbachev introduced political "openness," or glasnost. The catalyst for glasnost was the nuclear accident at Chernobyl in the Ukraine in April 1986. When it was impossible to conceal the magnitude of the disaster, reporting in the media became remarkably frank. This openness quickly extended to other hitherto suppressed topics. Gorbachev's glasnost was supposed to produce a "socialist pluralism," but the unintended result was a more

**Perestroika:** "Restructuring" of the Soviet bureaucracy and economic structure in an attempt to make it more efficient and responsive to market demand.

**Glasnost:** "Openness"; an attempt to loosen restrictions on media in the Soviet Union with an aim at more accurate reporting of events and the creation of "socialist pluralism."

spontaneous pluralism, reducing communism to just one of many competing ideologies in the rapidly evolving Soviet political scene.

**Transformations in the Soviet Bloc**    The countries of the Soviet Bloc, which were not oil producers, had borrowed heavily from the West in the 1970s and early 1980s for their costly oil imports and the renewal of their industrial base. Others borrowed to build oil and gas pipelines from Russia via their territories to Western Europe. But the oil price collapse of 1985–1986 forced all Soviet Bloc countries to reschedule their debts and cut their budgets, especially expenditures for their social safety nets and subsidies for basic consumer goods. Popular protests against these cuts in 1989 and 1990 in Poland, Hungary, and Czechoslovakia were accompanied by demands for power sharing.

As a result, dramatic and successful establishments of independent governments took place in Poland and Czechoslovakia. Yielding to increasing pressure, in 1989 the Communist Party in Poland permitted the first free elections in over 40 years, in which Solidarity won a landslide victory. Secure in its electoral majority, Solidarity formed a new coalition government, in which communists were a minority. When no reprisals from Moscow were forthcoming, Lech Walesa was elected Poland's president in 1990, a precedent which unleashed a wave of independence movements in the Soviet Bloc. In Czechoslovakia massive demonstrations in Prague and other cities toppled the ruling communist regime of President Husák in 1989 without bloodshed (the so-called Velvet Revolution). In its place, a coalition government consisting of the Party and members of the noncommunist Civic Forum was established. Its interim president was Vaclav [VATS·lav] Havel (1936–2011), a popular writer and dissident; in 1990 Havel was officially named president.

In the German Democratic Republic (GDR, East Germany), a particularly dramatic shift occurred. East Germans, after their summer vacations at the Black Sea in 1989, refused to return home, gathering instead at the Hungarian-Austrian border in hopes of being permitted to leave. Hungary, at that moment pursuing its own reforms, let the vacationers cross the border. Back in the GDR, massive demonstrations led to the fall first of the communist government and then of the Berlin Wall on the night of November 9, 1989. A year later, with Gorbachev's blessing, the two Germanys united, ending nearly a half century of division.

"We were walled in, things were kept away from us, we were lied to. And then, all of a sudden, we realized things could also be done or organized differently, and that's when it all began, when we began to rethink everything . . ."

—former East German factory worker, describing the events of 1989

Communist governments now fell in other Soviet Bloc countries as well (see Map 30.2). The governments of the Baltic states of Estonia, Latvia, and Lithuania, as well as that of Bulgaria, gave way more or less voluntarily to democracy. Albania followed suit in 1992. The only exception was Romania, where Nicolae Ceauşescu [chow-SHESS-coo] (in office 1974–1989) had built a strong personality cult and had put family members into key party and government offices. The botched eviction by the police of a Hungarian-minority Protestant pastor from his parish in western Romania in November 1989 resulted in scores of deaths. Following a mass demonstration in Bucharest protesting the deaths, portions of the army defected and arrested the fleeing Ceauşescu and his wife, Elena. Army elements assembled a tribunal, sentenced the two to death, and executed them summarily on

## The Fall of Communism in Eastern Europe and the Soviet Union

Former republics of the Soviet Union gaining independence in 1991

Boundary of Russian Federation after December 1991

Independence from Soviet Union declared 1991; at war with Russia, 1994–2000

Former Warsaw Pact country holding free elections, 1990–1992

—— Boundary of the former Soviet Union to 1991

⚜ Violent ethnic conflicts

MAP 30.2 **The Fall of Communism in Eastern Europe and the Soviet Union.**

December 25, 1989. Subsequently, however, the army and the Communist Party reconciled, and the country returned to a dictatorship. It was not until 1996 that Romania adopted a democratic system.

The dissolution of communism in the Eastern Bloc eventually caught up with the 15 states making up the Soviet Union, most of which declared their sovereignty or independence in 1990. After arduous negotiations, Gorbachev agreed with President Boris Yeltsin and the other state presidents to a new federal union treaty for the Soviet Union in spring 1991, to be signed in August. This treaty triggered an abortive plot by eight communist hardliners who briefly succeeded in arresting Gorbachev as he was vacationing for a few days in his dacha on the Black Sea. The conspirators, however, showed their ineptitude by failing to arrest Yeltsin. In a tense showdown with troops sent to occupy the Russian parliament, Yeltsin and a large crowd of Muscovites forced the hardliners to relent. Officially, the Soviet Union ended on Christmas Day, 1991, replaced by the Commonwealth of Independent States with a democratic Russia under Yeltsin at its center.

# Transforming the West

While North America and Western Europe enjoyed impressive growth and social change from the late 1940s through the early 1960s, scholars of popular culture have singled out the period from 1963 through the early 1970s as particularly dynamic. Social movements such as the African American civil rights movement in the United States moved to the center of the national agenda; the movements for equal rights for women and other historically marginalized groups also rose in prominence. Nearly all of these movements involved peaceful protests and civil disobedience, some borrowing directly from the strategies and philosophy of Gandhi and the powerful actions of Dr. Martin Luther King, Jr. Some, however, advocated violent confrontation.

## Civil Rights Movements

The massive mobilization of Americans during World War II accelerated civil rights efforts. Vast numbers of African Americans serving in the armed forces, along with professed US and Allied repugnance regarding Nazi racial policies, made segregation in the military increasingly untenable. In 1947, therefore, President Truman signed an executive order desegregating the American armed forces. In 1954, the Supreme Court reversed its earlier stand on segregation in education in the momentous *Brown v. Board of Education* ruling. Overturning the 1896 *Plessy v. Ferguson* decision that "separate but equal" facilities were constitutional, the court now ruled that the separate facilities were by definition not equal. Schools were therefore ordered to desegregate "with all deliberate speed." This met with determined resistance in many communities; in 1957, President Dwight D. Eisenhower (in office 1953–1961) was compelled to deploy US Army troops to Little Rock, Arkansas, to enforce the ruling. Still, by the early 1960s there was a dramatic movement under way for civil rights and equal treatment for African Americans in the American south.

**The Civil Rights Struggle.** The career of the charismatic minister Dr. Martin Luther King, Jr., was launched during the 1955 Montgomery, Alabama, bus boycott. By the early 1960s he had emerged as America's preeminent civil rights leader. Here, he is shown at the peak of his influence, delivering his famous "I Have a Dream" speech on the Mall in Washington, DC, in August 1963.

**The Postwar Drive for Civil Rights**   The movement for desegregation was prompted by a domestic sense of urgency as well as international conditions. Postwar anticolonialism, particularly in Africa, where former European colonies secured their independence, had a powerful influence on the American civil rights movement. The Cold War also played a vital role, as Soviet propaganda had exploited the discrepancies between American claims of freedom and equality and its treatment of African Americans. Desegregation and guaranteeing civil rights would render that Soviet argument obsolete. Finally, when participants in civil rights marches and protests were brutally attacked by private citizens as well as law enforcement in some cities in the early 1960s, President John F. Kennedy reacted by sponsoring civil rights legislation to end discrimination.

> "I have a dream that one day this nation will rise up and live out the true meaning of its creed: 'We hold these truths to be self-evident; that all men are created equal.'"
>
> —Martin Luther King, Jr.

A high point of the civil rights movement occurred in August 1963 when the Reverend Martin Luther King, Jr. (1929–1968) delivered his electrifying "I Have a Dream" speech before a huge crowd at the Lincoln Memorial in Washington, DC.

After the assassination of Kennedy in November, his successor, Lyndon B. Johnson (in office 1963–1969), secured the passage of the Civil Rights Act of 1964, which provided significant protections for African Americans, including the prohibition of segregation in public places. This was followed by the 1965 Voting Rights Act, aimed at outlawing the poll taxes, literacy tests, and other means by which states attempted to limit their citizens' ability to vote. With legal remedies now in place for past discrimination, civil rights leaders increasingly turned their attention to economic and social justice. The Johnson administration program called "The Great Society" was aimed at eliminating poverty in America. Civil rights advocates lobbied for jobs, educational opportunities, and poverty-relief programs for their constituents.

**Civil Rights for Native Americans**    Native American activists in the 1960s and 1970s campaigned for social justice and to rectify previous abuses, including past treaty violations. Begun in Minneapolis in 1968, the American Indian Movement (AIM) initiated actions to end police mistreatment and harassment and advocate for better housing and other issues. In 1972, after a cross-country protest march, AIM activists occupied the Bureau of Indian Affairs offices in Washington, DC, to publicize a list of demands for change. In the following year armed AIM members laid siege to Wounded Knee, South Dakota, to commemorate the massacre of hundreds of Native Americans in 1890. After a 71-day standoff with federal troops, several AIM leaders were charged with numerous violations of federal laws; a negotiated settlement was finally reached when these charges were dismissed. The end result, however, was improved conditions for Native Americans.

**Women's Rights and the Sexual Revolution**    The success of the civil rights and antiwar movements encouraged the movement for women's rights. While the suffragist movement during World War I had led to voting rights for women in both Great Britain and the United States, the more sweeping social changes brought on by World War II and the Cold War advanced the movement for equality in gender relations further. A leading voice was that of Simone de Beauvoir (1908–1986), whose work *The Second Sex* (1949) challenged women to take more self-assertive actions in order to gain full equality with their male counterparts. De Beauvoir and other influential feminists also contributed to the so-called sexual revolution of the 1960s. European and American women now openly demanded an end to restrictions placed upon their reproductive and sexual freedoms. Laws prohibiting contraception and abortion were overturned in several Western countries during the 1960s and 1970s. The development and widespread use of oral contraceptives became commonplace, and the 1973 Supreme Court decision *Roe v. Wade* protected a woman's right to have an abortion. The loosening of postwar moral standards, along with relaxed censorship in the media as well as an increased emphasis on sex and eroticism in popular culture, also played a part in new attitudes toward female sexuality. By the late 1960s, the "women's liberation" movement worked toward equal pay for equal work and more social freedom for women to pursue careers outside the home.

**Gay Rights Movement**    Gay and lesbian Americans, whose push for equality and acceptance emerged during the countercultural era in the 1950s, also fought for their civil rights during this era. A single event in 1969, the so-called Stonewall Riot, is considered the flashpoint of the contemporary gay rights movement. On the night of June 28, 1969, New York City police raided the Stonewall Inn, a gay bar in Greenwich Village. (Police raids on gay bars were common at the time.) Accounts differ on what happened next, but for the first time gay patrons took the unusual step of fighting back, pelting police with coins and other objects and shouting "Gay power!" Large numbers of gay activists and protesters converged on the scene in subsequent days, demanding an end to discrimination against gays and lesbians. In the months that followed gay and lesbian activists launched the Gay Liberation Front (GLF), along with the publication of the first gay newspaper. The movement quickly spread around the globe, and gay pride parades are held annually around the end of June in New York and elsewhere in commemoration of Stonewall. These and other factors have produced greater social and legal equality, including same-sex marriages, for LGBT people, but subtle discrimination against them is still in evidence.

**Stonewall Inn.** Venerated by gays and lesbians, the Stonewall Inn in New York City was the site of the Stonewall riots. On June 28, 1970, the first annual gay pride (or simply "pride") parade was organized by gay-rights activists to commemorate the first demonstration of resistance to harassment and intimidation by New York City police. Here, unidentified revelers line up along the parade route at the Stonewall Inn on June 26, 2011.

**Woodstock.** The iconic event of the "hippie" or "counterculture" era of the late 1960s was the Woodstock music and art festival held in August 1969 in upstate New York. It was a massive event, attended by perhaps as many as 400,000 people. Of the dozens of performers playing over the 3 days of the event, one of the most electrifying was the guitarist Jimi Hendrix. Hendrix pioneered a wild, free-form, blues-inflected style that is still widely admired and imitated today.

**The Global Youth Movement**   A new global generation, known as "baby boomers" (those born during the postwar "baby boom" between 1945 and 1961), emerged during the postwar era. United by common bonds expressed in terms of dress, pop music, and shared ideologies, this new generation repudiated the rigidity of their parents by growing their hair long—in imitation of the Beatles and other rock bands—wearing jeans, T-shirts, and "workers'" clothing; dabbling in Asian philosophies; taking drugs; and engaging in sexual experimentation.

The early center for this movement of "hippies" was San Francisco, in which 1967 was proclaimed the "summer of love." Musical groups espousing hippie values—often crudely summed up as "sex, drugs, and rock and roll"—dominated much of the popular music scene during this time. Perhaps the peak of this movement came in August 1969, when the Woodstock Festival in New York State drew an estimated 300,000–500,000 attendees and sparked a decade of giant musical and cultural festivals attempting to capture the spirit of what became known as the "Woodstock generation." Though the hippie movement as a force for liberation from confining mainstream values had largely spent itself by the early 1970s, its influence in fashion, sexual attitudes, music, and drug use continues to some extent even today.

**Student Demonstrations in the 1960s**   Pent-up passions and discontent burst forth in a global movement of student demonstrations in the 1960s and 1970s. In protest against what they perceived as the excessive materialism, conformism, and sexual prudishness of the previous generation, student activists held marches, demonstrations, and protests in the United States, Japan, and several European and South American countries. Even third-world countries like Cuba and China, as well as Eastern Bloc countries, experienced similar protests. In each instance student activists shared similar ideologies and goals informed by the common thread of protest against existing polices on gender roles, abortion, gay rights, and other issues.

A prime example of global student activism is afforded by the antiwar movement. For many of the thousands of idealistic students who had taken part in civil rights demonstrations and programs to register African American voters in southern states in the early 1960s, it seemed to be a natural transition from activism in favor of civil rights to activism for other causes. By 1965, the American military effort in Vietnam began to attract protests against US involvement in southeast Asia. This was particularly true for young people of draft age, whether they had college deferments or not. The antiwar movement, initially limited to college campuses and other centers of left or liberal political leaning, increasingly became more mainstream over the next several years.

By 1968 additional factors adding to tensions on both sides were the assassinations of civil rights leaders Martin Luther King, Jr., and the antiwar presidential candidate Robert Kennedy in the spring of that year. In addition to anger and despair about creating change in the United States, student demonstrations now shook much of the Western world. The most serious of these took place in Paris, where rebelling students calling for major education reforms at the University of Paris took to the streets, a rebel movement that spread beyond the students to the labor sector and eventually brought down the French government. Massive demonstrations also took place in Mexico City in advance of the Olympic Games there that summer. In the wake of the quelling of these riots in Europe and the frustration felt by American radicals at their failure to stop the war, many now called for revolutionary violence directed against governments and programs funded by the military.

In Italy and West Germany, some rebel students joined violent revolutionary organizations such the Red Brigades and the Baader-Meinhof Gang. The most radical students expressed solidarity with third-world revolutionary efforts and such figures as Ernesto "Che" Guevara (1928–1967), Ho Chi Minh, and Mao Zedong. With the end of American involvement in Vietnam and the draft in the early 1970s, however, these groups either disbanded, went fully underground, or were dismantled by the authorities.

### Economics and Politics in the 1970s and 1980s

Whereas the 1950s and 1960s represented unprecedented growth and prosperity, a sudden economic downturn in the early 1970s initiated a prolonged period of economic stagnation. Several factors were at work here. One cause was the ramping down of the Vietnam War effort, which had driven the US defense industry. Another cause stemmed from renewed hostilities between Arab and Israeli factions in 1973. In retaliation for American support of Israel, the newly formed OPEC, led by Arab states, dramatically increased the price of oil for export to America. The price per barrel of oil rose dramatically from $1.73 in 1973 to nearly $35 in 1981. The consequences of these economic downturns were at first inflation and then by the late 1970s **stagflation**. The emergence of developing economies in Asia and South America also began to lure American manufacturers to relocate to these countries in order to take advantage of lower labor costs, resulting in the decline of major industries in the United States.

**Stagflation:** Increased prices and record high interest rates but a stagnant economy overall.

The combined effect of these economic circumstances caused corresponding realignments in politics in the 1970s and 1980s. In some Western countries— the United States, Britain, and Germany—the trend shifted toward the adoption of more conservative policies. The most notable examples of what has been termed the "New Conservatism" were the policies of the American president Ronald Reagan and Britain's prime minister Margaret Thatcher (in office 1979–1990). Reagan's fiscal policies, by way of example (sometimes termed "Reaganomics"), featured lower taxes as a way to increase jobs, along with lower interest rates, and offset deficit spending. Although the subject of considerable debate, these policies have been credited with producing a period of sustained economic growth during his presidency. Both leaders orchestrated cutbacks in governmental spending for social services and welfare programs, and in both countries industrial strikes and the power of labor unions were restricted and the nationalization of major industries was replaced by privatization.

# From Women's Liberation to Feminism

Historians often consider the 1960s and 1970s as particularly important. Indeed, the period is often considered to mark the beginning of "second-wave feminism," a renewal of the push that crested with "first-wave" feminism's achievement of suffrage and full political rights (see Map 30.3). A key reason for the importance of the period is that women seeking change had the examples of the African American civil rights movement and the growing antiwar movement on which to draw. Within both of these movements some attention was given to women's rights as part of a larger rubric of emancipation, but it remained largely a secondary issue.

By the mid-1960s growing numbers of American women were becoming dissatisfied with what they perceived as the latent *sexism*—the gender equivalent of racism—of other progressive organizations. In response, they founded the National Organization for Women (NOW) in 1966. At about this time the term "women's liberation" began to appear, first in the radical media and shortly thereafter in more mainstream media. At first, leaders of the movement agitated for such things as equity in the workplace. In the cultural realm, they led the call for women's studies and less gendered forms of address like "Ms." As the stakes of the movement turned toward more personal issues in women's lives, these became political and medical issues as well; for example, the availability of birth control and abortion was advocated by physicians in America and by population scientists in nondeveloped countries. Laws governing marriage became hot-button issues, reflected in the movement's motto, "The personal is political."

Although a "third wave" of feminism took hold in the 1990s and often projected a less restrictive attitude toward sexuality of all types than earlier feminism, feminist

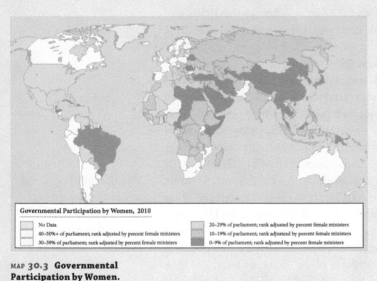

Governmental Participation by Women, 2010

| | |
|---|---|
| No Data | 20–29% of parliament; rank adjusted by percent female ministers |
| 40–50%+ of parliament; rank adjusted by percent female ministers | 10–19% of parliament; rank adjustezd by percent female ministers |
| 30–39% of parliament; rank adjusted by percent female ministers | 0–9% of parliament; rank adjusted by percent female ministers |

MAP 30.3 **Governmental Participation by Women.**

# From "Underdeveloped" to "Developing" World, 1963–1991

As the Cold War reached its peak in the 1960s, the drive for independence in Africa also crested, with the last colonies finally achieving nationhood in the 1970s. At the same time the drive for economic development, national prestige, and

concerns became part of the ordinary political landscape of many countries. Indeed, "feminism" completely supplanted "women's liberation" as the term for a constellation of values and causes that includes equal pay in the workplace, free and full reproductive rights, greater sexual freedom for women, and a thoroughgoing lack of discrimination in society on the basis of gender. During this period, there was much theoretical groundwork laid for the problem of the "feminization of poverty" in the developing world: According to a United Nations report, women did 66 percent of the world's work, produced at least half of the food, but made only 10 percent of the income and owned a scant 1 percent of the property. Thus, female poverty was intricately linked with the patriarchy embedded in long-standing cultural practices.

Cross-cultural interactions and subsequent assimilations have greatly enhanced worldwide movements to advance women's rights. In 1977 the UN General Assembly declared the first annual International Women's Day. Similar initiatives were then undertaken in countries around the globe: the Progressive Organization for Women (POW) in India; the organization of feminist groups in Israel and Turkey; and the Japanese Equal Employment Opportunity Law, which outlawed gender discrimination in hiring. Feminist authors and activists found increasing audiences in countries around the world, Ding Ling in China, Huda Shaarawi and Nawal El-Saadawi in Egypt, Madhu Kishwar in India, and Fatima Mernissi in Morocco among them. As a measure of women's increasing importance in global politics, many countries have had female prime ministers and presidents; among them are Argentina, Bolivia, the United Kingdom, India, Israel, Liberia, Pakistan, Sri Lanka, and Turkey.

**Women's Liberation in India.** Members of the National Federation of Dalit Women demonstrate in support of rights for women of the dalit ("untouchables") caste in New Delhi, India, in 2008. While discrimination against dalit is proscribed by law in India, bias against dalit women is still widespread.

## Questions

- How does the women's liberation movement demonstrate many of the characteristics of evolving modernity?

- Why does feminism promise to be the great emancipation movement of the twenty-first century?

national power continued to grow among newly independent nations everywhere. The 1960s through the 1980s marked the height of the contest among the nonaligned nations for preeminence between our two competing modernisms: market capitalism with democratic governments and variants of communism, based on the Soviet or Chinese model. Some newly independent governments attempted combinations of both forms of modernity as paths to development. Although many countries remained in dire poverty and were scarred by internal and external wars, the period also witnessed many more moving from the catchall category of "underdeveloped" to the more optimistic one of "developing."

While the unsurpassed prosperity of the West in this period impressed leaders in the developing world, many, if not most, continued to question whether capitalism was appropriate for their nations as an economic system. As we saw in Chapter 29, the socialist road also had a powerful theoretical appeal to many leaders in these emerging nations. The examples of the Soviet Union and China, and implicitly the Communist Bloc countries, appeared to show that formerly poor countries could quickly become rich and powerful—even to the point of being superpowers. Moreover, they were without the fatal stain of having been colonialists—at least in the sense that they had not created overseas empires—and thus could be perceived to be without a long-standing ulterior motive. Finally, one key development worth mentioning in this regard revolves around the ideological approaches of the rival camps. Marxist theorists had long argued that underdevelopment was *caused* by capitalism and imperialism.

> "Imperialism leaves behind germs of rot, which we must clinically detect and remove from our land, but from our minds as well."
>
> —Frantz Fanon

## China: Cultural Revolution to Four Modernizations

Of all the major world powers, the People's Republic of China experienced perhaps the most wrenching policy changes during the period 1963–1991. Having just emerged from the first Maoist era of the 1950s, it entered into a relatively calm few years of Soviet-style socialist development, only to be catapulted into the frenzy of the Cultural Revolution in the late 1960s. The death of Mao in 1976, however, ushered in a complete reversal of economic course. In 1978, the Four Modernizations of Deng Xiaoping called for opening the country to foreign experts, aid, and investment and creating a market economy—that is, introducing capitalism. To this day, China's economic policy is officially called "socialism with Chinese characteristics."

**China's "Thermidorean Reaction," 1960–1966**     The turbulence of the first round of the Maoist years died down considerably under the leadership of Liu Shaoqi [shao-CHEE]. The decade began, however, with the "Sino–Soviet split," in which Soviet apprehensiveness about China's radical programs and Mao's distrust of Soviet policy changes under Khrushchev led to a complete withdrawal of Soviet aid and advisors in 1960. By the end of the decade, Chinese and Soviet forces would be exchanging fire at several disputed border crossings.

Nonetheless, the early 1960s saw a reassertion of the need for education and technical training in China under Liu, and China made several important technological advances with military implications: the detonation of China's first nuclear device in October 1964, the testing of a thermonuclear (hydrogen) device in 1966, and advances in missile technology that would yield the first Chinese satellites in the following decade. In addition, Liu's regime engaged in a more assertive policy of border rectification. Chinese forces had entered Tibet in 1959 to suppress an independence movement, resulting in the flight of the Dalai Lama to India. In securing Tibet, however, disputes arose regarding the actual border with India. In 1962, Chinese forces moved into the disputed regions and fought a brief undeclared war until withdrawing and submitting

**Red Guards on the March.** Mao Zedong's injunction to the youth of China to question the authority of party bureaucrats had swift effects on everything from the school system to factory production. The students banded together into Red Guard units and challenged their elders, often violently, on their adherence to Mao's thought as expressed in the famous "little red book," *Quotations from Chairman Mao Zedong.* In this photo from 1967, Red Guards parade with a portrait of Mao, while many carry the red book in their hands.

the issue to negotiation. This kind of display of force in order to make a point would be seen again in China's attack on Vietnam in 1979, though with far less effectiveness.

**The Cultural Revolution**   As China's Communist Party and government assumed a more Soviet-style approach to running the People's Republic, Mao Zedong grew uneasy about the direction of policy. For Mao, the party was reverting to a bureaucracy, uninterested in pushing the revolution forward toward a pure communism. Mao's position of politics taking command was in direct opposition to the increasingly technocratic stance he saw in Liu Shaoqi's policies. Thus, Mao spent several years writing widely circulated essays extolling the virtues of devoted communists and plotting his comeback. An important step was the publication of his famous "little red book," *Quotations from Chairman Mao Zedong,* in 1964. His ideological ally Lin Biao (in office 1954–1971), as vice premier and head of the People's Liberation Army, made it required reading for the troops and helped Mao establish an important power base.

In the spring of 1966, Mao launched a violent critique of the new direction of the party and called on the nation's youth to rededicate themselves to "continuous revolution." Young people were encouraged to criticize their elders and form their own pure "red" ideological path to socialism. Mao announced the launching of the Great Proletarian Cultural Revolution, the purpose of which was to stamp out the last vestiges of "bourgeois" and "feudal" Chinese society. Students formed squads of Red Guards with red armbands and attacked their teachers and elders. By August, millions of Red Guards converged on Beijing, where Mao addressed over 1 million of them in Tiananmen Square and symbolically donned their red armband as a show of solidarity.

From 1966 until 1969, when the Cultural Revolution was officially declared over, millions of people were persecuted or murdered by Red Guards and their allies. The "little red book" became the talisman of the movement, with people struggling to interpret it correctly to prove their ideological fitness. China's official ideology was now listed as "Marxism–Leninism–Mao Zedong Thought." Despite the atrocities committed by Mao, a cult of personality surrounding him and his book sprang up as people waved it at mass rallies and even attributed magical powers to it. By 1968 the country was in complete chaos as pro– and anti–Cultural Revolution factions battled each other in several regions. It was chiefly to end this endemic civil war that Mao declared the Cultural Revolution over in 1969. Its aftermath, however, continued until Mao's death in 1976.

**"To Get Rich Is Glorious": China's Four Modernizations**    The final years of Mao's tenure as party chair saw at least one important change in policy. Despite the Sino–Soviet split, the People's Republic had maintained a strong anti-American posture in its domestic and foreign policy. This was matched by American Cold War antipathy toward "Red China" as a linchpin of the Communist Bloc. By the early 1970s, however, with the Vietnam War winding down and Soviet–Chinese tensions still high, President Richard Nixon made a bold visit to the People's Republic, which resulted in the Shanghai Communiqué of 1972. In this document, the United States and the People's Republic of China announced plans to initiate formal diplomatic and cultural relations (which went into effect in 1979), the United States pledged to no longer block the People's Republic's bid for a seat in the United Nations, and the United States agreed to downgrade its diplomatic presence in Taiwan.

The death of Mao Zedong in September 1976 opened the way for a new generation of Communist Party leadership in China. The result was a repudiation of the Cultural Revolution and those who promoted it and an entirely different direction in strategy for building a new China. After some jostling among the party factions, Deng Xiaoping ([hee-yao-PING]; in office 1978–1992) emerged in 1978 with the title of "vice premier" but in fact held the real power in the regime. The pragmatic Deng, whose motto was "It doesn't matter whether the cat is black or white, as long as it catches mice," implemented the fundamental policies that remain in force in China to the present: the Four Modernizations.

Aware of the difficulties of pursuing socialism in a country with little wealth to share, Deng's strategy relied on upgrading the quality of agriculture, industry, science, technology, and the military. China would pursue a new "open-door" policy with regard to foreign expertise from the West; it would allow its own students to study abroad and, most tellingly, allow the market forces of capitalism to create incentives for innovation in all sectors of the economy. China's new motto became "To get rich is glorious!"

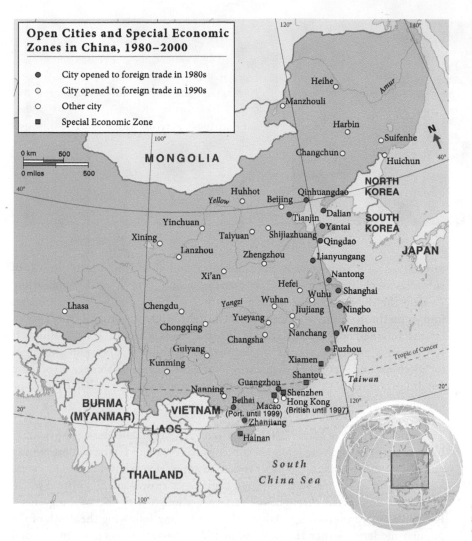

MAP 30.4 **Open Cities and Special Economic Zones in China, 1980–2000.**

The "responsibility system," as it was called, was introduced in a special economic zone set up in south China at Shenzhen to take advantage of capital and expertise from Hong Kong. The experiments in capitalism would then be expanded to the country at large once any flaws had been corrected. Peasants were among the first beneficiaries as the communes were disbanded, individual plots assigned, and market incentives introduced. By the mid-1980s China, which had long been a byword in the West for hunger, was rapidly approaching self-sufficiency in food production and, by the 1990s, would register surpluses (see Map 30.4). Through the 1980s and 1990s China's gross domestic product (GDP) grew at an astonishing double-digit rate. In 2010 it surpassed Japan as the second largest economy in the world, after the United States.

Another more controversial innovation was the "one-child" policy. Mao felt that China's huge and growing population was an advantage because of its potential manpower and as a hedge against catastrophic losses from nuclear war. But population pressures were also a powerful brake on China's development. Thus, a policy was inaugurated in 1979 mandating that families (excluding those of most

**Tiananmen Square Demonstrations.** At their peak in May 1989, the demonstrations by students seeking greater government accountability and a more open political system were joined by workers and people from all walks of life (left). In this memorable image of the suppression of the demonstration, a lone man confronts a tank (right). The driver of the tank tried to get around the man and eventually stopped, together with the other tanks. At that point, demonstrators pulled the man back to safety. His subsequent fate is unknown. Both images were widely broadcast throughout the world.

minorities) were to have only one child. A second child would result in loss of subsidies for childrearing; a third pregnancy would result in mandatory abortion. Despite the many problems in enforcing such a policy, and its severe cultural impact on the male-centered traditional Chinese family structure, China's population has remained remarkably stable since the 1980s at around 1.3–1.5 billion. It has, however, abetted problems of selective female abortion, giving up girl babies for adoption, and even, in extreme cases, female infanticide. Moreover, all of these conditions have lent themselves to a large and growing gender imbalance: China currently has 117 male births for every 100 female births.

**Tiananmen Square Massacre**    The Chinese government managed a delicate balance between allowing foreign technology to come into China and preventing cultural items "injurious to public morals" to enter. Hence, IBM computers were welcome, but MTV was not. Repeated campaigns against such "spiritual pollution" were conducted throughout the 1980s, though with diminishing effect. Prodemocracy protests began taking place in Beijing following the death of the popular moderate leader Hu Yaobang in 1989. The gatherings grew in size and force as the seventieth anniversary of the May Fourth nationalist movement grew closer. At one point students constructed a large statue they called the Goddess of Democracy, which dominated the center of the square near the Monument to the People's Revolutionary Martyrs. By the beginning of June workers and citizens had joined the students in a generalized protest.

During the period of April 25 to May 19, the members of the Politburo engaged in intense discussions on how to deal with the protests. The hardliners eventually prevailed, but when they prepared the declaration of martial law, a number of high-ranking army officers weighed in with grave doubts. They argued that the People's Army could not possibly shoot on its own people. The most prominent figure refusing any order to shoot was Major General Xu Qinxian [hoo chin-HEEYAN], according to new documents publicized by the *New York Times* in June 2014 at the occasion of the twenty-fifth anniversary of the Tiananmen Massacre. But the Politburo prevailed and during June 2–4 soldiers crushed what to many among the leaders seemed to be an incipient rebellion. To this day, the number of killed is unknown, ranging between 300 (official number) to thousands. General Xu was court-martialed and imprisoned for four years, living in 2014 in a military sanatorium in northern China.

## Vietnam: War and Unification

As we noted in Chapter 29, by the early 1960s Vietnam, having thrown off French colonialism in the 1950s, had failed to achieve final unification because of Cold War politics and remained divided into North and South Vietnam. The development of communist guerilla fighters, the Vietcong, in South Vietnam and similar guerilla threats in Laos had prompted the United States to send aid and military advisors to the shaky government of the Republic of Vietnam (South Vietnam) through the late 1950s. Rocked by clashes between Catholics and Buddhists, the government of South Vietnam was ousted in a coup with help from the American Central Intelligence Agency (CIA) in late 1963. Several weak governments took its place until a more stable one under Nguyen Van Thieu emerged and lasted from 1965 to 1975.

**The American War** In the summer of 1964 several alleged attacks on American ships in the Gulf of Tonkin (the truth of these allegations is still murky today) resulted in the United States radically ramping up its presence in Southeast Asia, effectively beginning what became known in Vietnam as the American War and in the United States as the Vietnam War. In retaliation for the attacks, American planes bombed

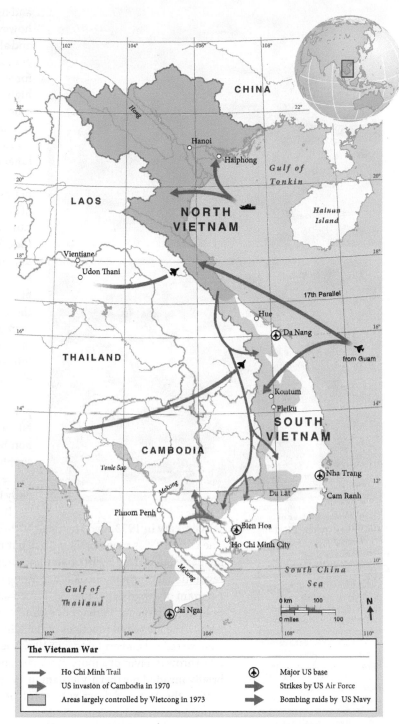

MAP **30.5** **The Vietnam War.**

sites in North Vietnam. By 1965 tens of thousands of American combat troops were being sent to support the South Vietnamese against the Vietcong. But, as in Korea, the Americans and their allies were plagued by unclear goals and the impatience of a public hoping for quick, decisive results. The task of "winning the hearts

**The Arab–Israeli War of June 1967.** The stunning victory of Israel over the combined armies of Syria and Egypt generated both admiration in the West and consternation in the Arab world and the Soviet Bloc. The Israelis' preemptive use of air power against Egyptian and Syrian air forces and tank and troop concentrations and their expert use of armor proved the deciding factors in the conflict. Here, Egyptian prisoners (in white underclothes in the truck to the right) are being transferred to holding camps (*top*). The war also led to a dramatic rise in the popularity of the Palestinian cause in the Arab and communist spheres. Here, Yasir Arafat marches with members of Fatah in 1970 (*bottom*).

and minds of the people," as the slogan went, however, was a long and tortuous one at best and always hampered by being a foreign presence in someone else's land. Thus, American forces were increased until they reached a high of over a half-million by 1967. Despite official optimism, there was little evidence that the war was being won (see Map 30.5).

In February 1968, on the Vietnamese lunar new year (*Tet*), the Vietcong, supported by North Vietnamese forces, launched an all-out assault on the South Vietnamese capital of Saigon and a number of other cities. American and Army of the Republic of Vietnam (South Vietnam) forces reeled for several days but launched a successful counterattack, finally destroying the Vietcong as an effective fighting force. In the United States, however, the Tet Offensive, as it came to be called, was seen as an American defeat. In the wake of massive protests against the war, President Johnson announced he would not seek reelection, and the way was clear for the United States to begin negotiations to end the war by political means. With the election of Richard Nixon in 1968, a combination of massive bombings of North Vietnam and Cambodian supply lines for North Vietnamese forces and peace talks in Paris over the next 5 years finally brought the war to an end.

Though South Vietnam survived the peace treaty in 1973, the American withdrawal spelled its demise within 2 years. The country was now finally united, but much of Vietnam, Cambodia, and Laos lay devastated from fighting and bombing. Over the next 2 years a Cambodian revolutionary group, the Khmer Rouge ("Red Khmers"), launched a radical program of urban depopulation, forced labor, and genocide against religious and political opponents. Perhaps one-third of the country's population was killed as a result. The ideas and practices of the Khmer Rouge leader, Pol Pot (1925–1998), were so radical and brutal that in 1977 Vietnam invaded the state and initiated his overthrow in favor of a more moderate and pliable candidate. In response, China briefly invaded northern Vietnam in 1979 but was soon repulsed by Vietnamese forces, the last and least successful of the many Chinese invasion attempts launched over two millennia.

## The Middle East

One of the most troubled areas of the world during the twentieth century was also one that, as we have seen over the course of this book, has been the cradle of many influential religions: the Middle East. Since 1945, the area encompassing the

Arabian Peninsula, Iran, Iraq, and the eastern shores of the Mediterranean has seen a number of major wars and minor conflicts, innumerable guerilla raids and assaults, and attacks directed against the religious symbols of Judaism, Christianity, and Islam. As of this writing, despite peace talks that have been conducted over the course of decades, no comprehensive settlement has been reached.

**Israeli and Arab Conflict**   In addition to competition arising from the demand for petroleum as a strategic commodity and Shiite–Sunni conflict within the context of Persian–Arab competition, by far the most contentious issue in the Middle East has been the presence of the Jewish state of Israel. During the 1950s and 1960s, Israel was largely seen in the West as a young country fighting democracy's battles against an array of authoritarian Arab states supported by the Soviet Union. A significant number of highly educated immigrants in the postwar decades helped the new state to build an efficient agriculture—often through the socialist device of the communal farm, or *kibbutz*—and an increasingly sophisticated manufacturing sector. West German reparations, compensating for Jewish losses during the Third Reich, helped financially. Mandatory military service and generous American support also contributed to the creation of superior armed forces equipped with the latest military technology.

MAP 30.6 **The Arab–Israeli Wars, 1967 and 1973.**

**The "Six-Day War"**   For the Palestinian Arabs and their allies, however, the perspective was very different. For them it was "the disaster." Hundreds of thousands displaced since 1948 awaited their return in surrounding countries—often in camps—for decades, a situation that grew worse when new refugees arrived after every Arab–Israeli conflict. In the polarized Cold War climate, the Arab states viewed Israel as simply a new Western imperial outpost in what was rightfully Arab territory. Consequently, many subsequent attempts at Arab unity were premised on war with Israel. While Arab nationalism was largely secular, and often socialist-leaning with Soviet support, Muslim fundamentalist groups such as Egypt's Muslim Brotherhood gained adherents, despite government repression, as Western secular values came to be seen as causing Muslim difficulties.

In 1964, Yasir Arafat (1929–2004) and other like-minded Palestinian nationalists formed the Palestine Liberation Organization (PLO), whose militant wing, Fatah, began a guerilla war against Israel and its backers. Matters came to a head on May 22, 1967, when Egypt closed the Gulf of Aqaba to Israeli shipping, preventing the importation of oil. Following an Egyptian military buildup along the Sinai border and the expulsion of UN forces there, Iraq sent troops to Jordan at its invitation, and local Muslim leaders began to call for holy war against Israel. On June 5 the Israelis launched a massive preemptive air assault to neutralize the Egyptian and Syrian air forces. With an overwhelming advantage in number and quality of aircraft, Israel took out the Arab armor and ground troops with astonishing skill. The Six-Day War, as it came to be called, established Israel's reputation for military prowess and enlarged the state by conquering the eastern side of the Jordan River, the Golan Heights, and the Gaza Strip—territories belonging to Jordan, Syria, and Egypt, respectively. For many observers, Israel had now moved from a state simply fighting for its existence to one bent on expansion.

**The Yom Kippur/Ramadan War**    In early October 1973, Egypt, Syria, and a coalition of Arab states, stung by their defeat in 1967, launched a massive attack during the Jewish holy day of Yom Kippur, which in 1973 coincided with the Muslim holy month of Ramadan. This time, with Israel, the United States, and the Soviet Union caught unawares, Egyptian tanks crossed the Suez Canal on pontoon bridges and attacked Israel (see Map 30.6). Syria attacked the Golan Heights and contributed to the Egyptian crossing of the Canal. After taking severe losses and conceding ground for a week, Israeli forces managed to ultimately defeat the combined Arab armies once again. Having trapped Egyptian forces along the Suez Canal, Israeli units occupied the west bank of the Canal, pushing within 63 miles of Cairo. Other units drove 25 miles into Syria. A ceasefire was brokered by the United Nations, but the intensity of the fighting and the resupply efforts by the United States and Soviet Union moved both countries dangerously close to direct confrontation. For their part, the Arab oil producers and Iran immediately launched an oil embargo of the United States. Stringent measures and a degree of rationing and sharply higher gasoline prices drove home to Americans how dependent they had become on foreign oil, and encouraged new interests in solar and other alternative forms of energy.

For Egypt, the defeat resulted in a transformation of policy toward Israel. Under President Anwar el-Sadat (in office 1970–1981), Egypt took the initiative in undertaking peace talks by visiting Israel in 1977. The following year, the two sides reached an understanding about a basic framework for peace; and with the backing of the American president Jimmy Carter, Egypt and Israel signed the first treaty between an Arab country and the Jewish state at Camp David, Maryland, in 1979. Egypt and Jordan are the only Arab states to date to maintain diplomatic and cultural relations with Israel. While Egyptian–Israeli relations remained relatively cordial on the surface, no other Arab countries followed suit. Syria remained hostile, having lost the Golan Heights again, while the PLO stepped up its efforts throughout the 1980s. Profound resentment of Sadat for signing the treaty festered among many Egyptians. Despite some concessions to increasingly vocal fundamentalist Muslim groups—for example, agreeing to base Egyptian legislation on Islamic Sharia law—Sadat was killed by assassins in 1981.

## Africa: From Independence to Development

During the period 1963–1991, the main struggles in Africa moved from ones mainly concerned with completing the pattern of decolonization and independence to ones involving development. As with other parts of the postcolonial world, vigorous internal debates were conducted about strategies for economic development, how best to deploy scarce resources, and the relative merits of a planned economy versus one governed by market forces. But in nearly all cases, the economies of the newly independent states, regardless of which economic system they favored, were problematic. In most cases they were tied to their former colonial regimes by means of the same raw materials—minerals, petroleum, agricultural or forest products—that had been exploitatively extracted during their colonial days. Moreover, they were more frequently than not competing in the markets for these products with other former colonies. Thus, they were at the mercy of world commodity prices but not insulated from the worst ups and downs by their former colonial regimes.

As in Chapter 29, far too many new nations emerged in Africa during this period for this chapter to cover them all. Therefore, we will focus on Nigeria, Zimbabwe, and South Africa as representative of the problems and prospects of the era.

**Nigeria: Civil War and Troubled Legacies**   While in the Congo the Cold War played out in dramatic fashion with the United States supporting the overthrow of Patrice Lumumba in favor of Mobutu Sese Seko in the early 1960s, Nigeria's independence had a more promising start. With a large and fairly prosperous population, sound agriculture, and abundant resources, it entered the postcolonial era as a republic with a British parliamentary system, Commonwealth membership, and a federal-style constitution. Like many African former colonies, however, it soon became apparent that Nigeria was also saddled with ethnic and religious conflicts that were a legacy from the old colonial divisions of the continent. Thus, its growing pains were marked by clashes between its established system of constitutional nationalism and the desires of its major constituent groups for their own nation states more reflective of Nigeria's ethnic, linguistic, and religious makeup.

The new nation was marked by occasional conflicts and cooperation among three major antagonistic groups, the Hausa, Igbo, and Yoruba, divided by history, culture, religion, and language. The largest, the Hausa, were Muslims from the northern region who constituted nearly 30 percent of Nigeria's population. The Igbo, mostly living in the eastern region where valuable oil deposits had been recently discovered, were predominantly Christian or African-spiritual. The Yoruba, who controlled most of the national offices, were predominantly Muslim, although there were also Christian Yoruba.

Starting in 1966, the central government under strongman Yakubu Gowon (in office 1966–1975) had authorized raids to bring Igbo areas under greater control. In 1967, the eastern Igbo region declared itself independent as the state of Biafra under Colonel Chukwuemeka Odumegwu Ojukwu (b. 1933). What followed was perhaps the bloodiest civil war of the era. Both sides fought determinedly, and when a military stalemate was reached the Nigerian forces attempted to starve Biafra into submission. More than 1 million Biafrans died, mostly of starvation and malnutrition, before Biafra surrendered in early 1970. In the remainder of the period to 1991, Nigeria was ruled by a series of military strongmen, each in turn attempting to stabilize the volatile political situation of the central government. By 1991, the prosperous future that seemed so promising in 1960 seemed impossible to all but the most optimistic observers.

**Zimbabwe: The Revolution Continued**   Some of the former European colonies in Africa came to independence with substantial populations of white settlers, some of whose families had been there for several generations. Accustomed to a life of relative privilege, they had, in many cases, opposed independence, and when it came, they sought guarantees from the new governments against expropriation of land, discrimination, and reprisals. In 1964 the old colony of Northern Rhodesia gained independence as Zambia, breaking up a federation of the two colonies and Nyasaland, which subsequently became independent as Malawi. Threatened by the independence of nearby black African nations and confident of support from apartheid-based South Africa, the white leaders of the territory that now called itself simply "Rhodesia" declared unilateral independence in 1965 and set up a government in the colonial capital of Salisbury under Ian Smith (in office 1965–1970). Distressed at this move, Britain refused to recognize the new government and expelled Rhodesia from the Commonwealth. Few countries outside of South Africa recognized the regime, which now faced international sanctions and a guerilla movement from within.

Two rival groups, the Zimbabwe African National Union (ZANU) under Robert Mugabe (b. 1924) and the Zimbabwe African People's Union (ZAPU) led by Joshua Nkomo (1917–1999), struggled to bring Smith's regime down and create a majority-rule state. The long and bitter war lasted throughout the 1960s and 1970s, until Mugabe and ZANU finally triumphed and created a new state called "Zimbabwe" in 1980. Mugabe's regime pledged fairness to the remaining white settlers and, after changing the name of the capital to Harare, set about creating a socialist state. In this sense, despite constant condemnations of Africa's imperial legacy, Mugabe has been in constant need of the economic power of the country's white minority and thus initially trod fairly lightly on their rights. By the 1990s, however, vigilante seizures of white lands by "revolutionary veterans" became a regular occurrence. By the early 2000s, the chaotic agricultural sector combined with repression of opposition to ZANU one-party rule had plunged the country into a serious economic crisis.

**Angola and Mozambique**   Two colonies under Portuguese control, Angola and Mozambique, were among the last to gain independence from European rule. In spite of a series of uprisings in the early 1960s, the authoritarian government of Portugal refused to relinquish control of its possessions along the southwestern and southeastern coasts of Africa, respectively. Following a military coup in Portugal in 1974, however, during which the regime was overthrown, each was granted independence in the following year.

**South Africa: From Apartheid to "Rainbow Nation"**   South Africa, the richest of the continent's countries, also had the most complex and restrictive racial relations. From the seventeenth century, first Dutch, then English, settlers came to service the maritime traffic around the Cape of Good Hope. By the nineteenth century, the Dutch-descended Boers had moved inland from Cape Town to

**Black Commuters in South Africa.** The regime of apartheid (the strict separation of the races) that had been inaugurated by the white minority government in South Africa in 1948 obliged all black citizens, such as these workers congregating in a Johannesburg train station in the late 1950s, to carry "passbooks" that specified what areas they were permitted to enter. Resentment at the passbook requirement prompted mass demonstrations that resulted in the Sharpeville Massacre of March 21, 1960, which in turn sparked widespread protests against the apartheid system.

establish farms, ranches, and vineyards, pushing out the local people. The expansion of Zulu power at roughly the same time forced the British rulers and Dutch settlers into protracted Zulu wars that, climaxing in 1879, broke the last black empire in the region. By the end of the nineteenth century, the discovery of vast mineral wealth in gold and diamonds led to both the expansion of the colony's holdings and an influx of immigrants, including Chinese and Indians.

In the early twentieth century, the social divisions among whites, Africans, and "coloureds"—south and east Asians and peoples of mixed descent—were hardened into legal classifications. The Indian nationalist leader Mohandas Gandhi, for example, developed his successful nonviolent strategies by leading protests in South Africa for Indian rights. After 1910, immigration restrictions on Asians went into effect along with ever-more-restrictive laws governing relations between whites and Africans. This trend culminated in the institution of apartheid (Afrikaans, "apartness") in 1948. Black South Africans were relegated to a legal second-class status and were to live in designated "Bantustans"—that is, separate territories. They were required to carry passes when traveling; those commuting to work in white urban areas had to leave by sunset; and they were subject to curfew regulations.

Through the 1950s South Africa faced international criticism for its policies, which the white government justified as necessary to maintain its rule, since whites made up less than one-sixth of the population. Moreover, as newly independent black majority countries came into being and completed the pattern of decolonization, the white government—resisting this pattern—felt itself increasingly besieged. It pointed out with some justification that a few of these emerging states were Marxist and thus claimed that it was fighting the free world's battle against the expansion of the Soviet Bloc in Africa. Nonetheless, it withdrew from the British Commonwealth in 1961, and a number of black political organizations—most prominently the African National Congress (ANC)—campaigned for the

**Apartheid:** System of social and legal segregation by race enforced by the government of South Africa from 1948 until 1994.

dismantling of apartheid. The brutality of the white armed forces and police and the constant harassment of dissenters, both white and black, added to the oppressive atmosphere.

By the 1980s it was clear that events in and outside the country would eventually force the dismantling of apartheid. International boycotts of South Africa had gained momentum, particularly after the public call for sanctions by the African Anglican bishop Desmond Tutu (b. 1931), who was awarded the Nobel Peace Prize in 1984. In the townships, the ANC, through a political and guerilla campaign, was making gradual gains. Massive strikes by black workers in 1987 and 1988 also led to increasing paralysis of the government. Finally, amidst the collapse of communism in the Soviet Bloc in 1990, the newly elected president, Frederik Willem de Klerk (b. 1936), began a set of sweeping reforms aimed ultimately at dismantling apartheid. In quick succession, the ANC was legalized and became South Africa's largest political party; its leader, Nelson Mandela (1918–2013), was released from prison; in 1991 all apartheid laws were repealed; and finally, in 1992 white voters amended the constitution to mandate racial equality among all citizens. By 1994, the first multiracial elections were held, and Mandela became president of the new South Africa, which Archbishop Tutu dubbed the "Rainbow Nation" in honor of its newly recognized diversity. Thus, the pattern of decolonization was completed.

## Latin America: Proxy Wars

As in Africa, the 1960s in Latin American politics were marked in many ways by the forces contending for dominance against the backdrop of the Cold War. Here, however, because the countries in question had long since achieved their independence—if not yet long-term stability in government—the issues guiding the respective sides were largely ideological and economic, as well as centering around revolutionary politics.

By the 1970s, dissatisfaction with the authoritarian regimes of the region, particularly in Central America, resulted in several revolutionary efforts, the most notable being in Nicaragua and El Salvador. Since the mid-1930s, the United States had supported the family of the authoritarian Nicaraguan strongman Anastasio Somoza García (collectively in office from 1936–1979). Landlordism and rural poverty had been particularly acute problems in Nicaragua, and from the early 1960s a guerilla insurgency called the Sandinista National Liberation Front (FSLN) had sought to overthrow the Somozas and mount a socialist land-reform scheme. The Somoza regime fell in 1979, and a new government under the Sandinistas (invoking the name of Emilio Sandino, one of the original Somoza opponents) was led by Daniel Ortega (in office 1979–1990; 2007–).

The socialist direction of the new regime prompted the American administration of President Ronald Reagan to cut off aid to Nicaragua, begin a covert operation to destabilize Ortega through the funding and arming of opposition groups known collectively as the Contras, and end trade with the regime. With US support and fading aid from Cuba and the Soviet Bloc in the late 1980s, the two sides agreed to elections in 1990. These resulted in the presidency of the conservative opposition candidate, Violeta Barrios de Chamorro (in office 1990–1997).

In similar fashion, guerilla groups in El Salvador fought US-backed government forces, whose actions were sometimes directed against Catholic clergy believed to support the insurgents, in a bloody conflict throughout the 1980s, until elections were finally held in 1992. The death toll in this tiny country is estimated to be as high as 75,000. By the early 1990s, however, the two sides, as in Nicaragua, had resolved to work within the new political system.

The commitment of the United States to opposing any groups espousing Marxist or communist beliefs in Latin America also revealed itself in covert policy toward governments recognized as legitimate. As we saw in Chapter 29, for example, the CIA helped engineer a coup against Guatemalan leader Jacobo Árbenz (in office 1951–1954) in 1954 because he permitted the existence of a communist labor union. The most spectacular instance of American Cold War covert action, however, was directed at Chilean President Salvador Allende (in office 1970–1973) in 1973. Allende had led a coalition of socialists, communists, and liberal Christian Democrats to a plurality win in 1970. Many of his policies met opposition within Chile, while his ideology and nationalization of American interests in Chile's mines pushed the Nixon administration to back his opposition.

With American blessings and CIA help, Allende was overthrown, and the repressive regime of General Augusto Pinochet (in office 1973–1990) installed. Determined to suppress leftist groups and their sympathizers Pinochet launched Operation Colombo in 1975, resulting in the disappearance of over 100 activists and others perceived as threats to the government's plan to restore a capitalist economy. Throughout Pinochet's term of 16 years in power, his rule remained repressive, but Chile also became increasingly economically vibrant and slowly began to move toward a more open and democratic government. In 1998 Pinochet was arrested in London on charges of human rights violations and torture. After a lengthy court battle, he was ultimately released and returned to Chile, where he died in 2006.

**"The Dirty War" and the "Disappeared"**    As we have seen in this section, the damage inflicted by the Cold War and the actions of its combatants, real and proxy, upon Latin America was considerable. One of the most tragic and internationally condemned episodes of this struggle was the "Dirty War" (*Guerra Sucia*) carried out in Argentina from 1976 to 1983. The tangled politics of the post-Perón era resulted in a smoldering guerilla war against various regimes from the 1960s onward. By the early 1970s, many of these groups had coalesced into the Peronist Montoneros and the Marxist People's Revolutionary Army (ERP). While the Montoneros were essentially crushed in 1977, the ERP remained active, and under the cover of "Operation Condor" tens of thousands of Argentinians were kidnapped, imprisoned, and killed. Many of these men and women were not guerillas but writers, editors, labor organizers, teachers, and others suspected of having left-wing leanings or whom the government sought to eliminate for other reasons.

These victims became known as the "disappeared." Their fate is still poignantly brought to light by the Mothers of Plaza de Mayo, a group of women who have kept vigil for lost friends and relatives in that plaza in Buenos Aires since 1977 and grown into an internationally recognized human rights movement, spreading in the mid-1970s to other countries also suffering instances of "disappearances" under authoritarian rule such as Bolivia, Chile, Paraguay, and Uruguay. Already by 1979 the wholesale imprisonments prompted US president Carter to offer asylum to those languishing in Argentine jails.

In 1983, having deeply miscalculated in provoking and losing the Falklands War with Great Britain, the junta stepped down, elections were held, and a National Commission on the Disappearance of Persons (CONADEP) was established in December. While the figures vary greatly, from 15,000 to perhaps 30,000 "disappeared," the progress of the commission and its findings of torture, killing, and indefinite incarceration caused an international sensation. Today, most of the surviving military and political leaders held responsible are in prison or have already served lengthy terms.

# Putting It All Together

During the years 1962 to 1991, from the Cuban Missile Crisis to the dissolution of the Soviet Union, the Cold War contest between the two remaining twentieth-century versions of modernity—capitalist democracy and the different varieties of communism–socialism—reached its climax. At the beginning of the period it seemed that communism was competing evenly, perhaps even winning, in its appeal to so many developing nations and their leaders. But in the end, the wealth and power of the West, particularly the United States, ultimately wore the Soviet Bloc down. Along the way, the most populous communist state, China, abruptly changed from extreme radical leftist programs during its Cultural Revolution to a capitalist style of market economics by 1991. Many other countries were now looking for some mixture of the two systems or a third way between the two for their own development. As the period drew to a close, it was, ironically, the two iconic communist regimes, the Soviet Union and the People's Republic of China, that were pioneering the way *out* of Marxist socialism. The Chinese sought to do this by retaining a powerful authoritarian government while embracing market economics. The former Soviet Union adopted democratic political values and guardedly introduced capitalism.

For the people of the world observing these changes it might indeed have seemed as if the triumphant words of Francis Fukuyama's 1989 essay "The End of History?" actually did sum up the age:

> A remarkable consensus concerning the legitimacy of liberal democracy as a system of government had emerged throughout the world over the past few years, as it conquered rival ideologies like hereditary monarchy, fascism, and most recently communism. More than that, however ... liberal democracy may constitute the "end point of mankind's ideological evolution" . . . and as such . . . the end of history.

The next two decades, however, would see the emergence of new and unanticipated challenges to the domination of the capitalist-democratic order. For many, its secular character and its breaking down of traditional norms in the West was evidence that the evolving culture of this version of modernity would undermine the core values of their own societies. Hence, like the reformers in many of the old empires of the nineteenth century, they struggled to acquire the material advantages of modernity while isolating themselves from the cultural threat it presented. Still others in both the West and elsewhere had come to see the forces of modernity as threats to the delicate balance between human beings and the environment. They therefore sought to curtail the rapacity of capitalist-democratic countries and corporations in their contest for resources. In the final chapter of this book, both these trends—and the devil's bargain they present to so many—will occupy a considerable amount of our attention.

▶ For additional resources, including maps, primary sources, visuals, and quizzes, please go to www.oup.com/us/vonsivers. Please see the Further Resources section at the back of the book for additional readings and suggested websites.

## Against the Grain
# The African National Congress

In the early 1900s, the Union of South Africa adopted laws which formed the backbone of what in 1948 was to become apartheid, an official program of racial segregation. According to these laws, blacks (who made up 5 million of the 6 million inhabitants of the country) were to be removed from the villages, towns, and cities of western South Africa to reservations and trust lands in the less fertile eastern part of the country, called "Bantustans."

In protest against segregation and demanding equal rights, in 1912 a few black professionals organized what was to become the African National Congress (ANC). Their demands were similar to those voiced by Indians and Egyptians around World War I and set the beginnings of the pattern of decolonization in the twentieth century. It required, however, another generation of younger professionals, including the law partners Oliver Thambo (1917–1993) and Nelson Mandela (1918–2013), before the ANC was able to become a mass movement among the impoverished and illiterate masses. They created a youth league within the ANC and formulated demands for land distribution, labor organization, and mass education.

After the Afrikaner nationalists came to power in 1948 and established outright apartheid, black South Africans were increasingly driven to join the ANC. During the 1950s, the government introduced race-marked passports, outlawed interracial marriages and sexual relations, demolished black shantytowns, resettled blacks, banned communism, and decreed segregated parks, beaches, buses, hospitals, schools, and universities. Determined to enforce apartheid, the government built up a massive bureaucracy, including an effective secret service.

Even though the events of the 1950s made the ANC a true representative of South African blacks, it held fast to its original program of multiracial and ideologically varied (including communism) integration, resisting any more narrowly defined black nationalist political orientation. Its mass protests and acts of sabotage through a newly created armed wing in 1961–1964 were met by the government with brutal acts of repression and mass arrest. In the so-called Rivonia trial, the arrested ANC leadership, including Mandela, was condemned to life or long-term imprisonment on Robben Island.

Courageous protests by student and labor organizations, churches, and white liberals continued, as did undiminished government brutality in response. The ANC was driven underground, from where it sought to make townships ungovernable. It also operated from abroad, where it helped in the creation by the 1980s of a broad coalition of Western states and organizations which sought to force South Africa to abolish apartheid through sanctions and boycotts. Ultimately, the ANC prevailed because of the collapse of the Soviet Bloc in 1989–1991; the apartheid regime could no longer claim that it was the final bulwark against world communism. In 1994, South Africa became a black-governed nation under the rule of the ANC.

- How does the ANC's support for racial integration, and its acceptance of differing political views, contrast with other nationalist and liberation movements from this period?

- Compare and contrast South African apartheid and segregation in the United States between 1918 and 1964. What are the similarities? What are the differences?

# Thinking Through Patterns

▶ **How did the political landscape of the Cold War change from 1963 to 1991?**

Perhaps the biggest changes came in the 1980s. Though the United States had been defeated politically in Vietnam and was facing a recession at home, it still was the world's largest economy and could weather a protracted arms race. Though it was not fully perceived at the time, the Soviet Union was far more economically fragile—which ultimately made it ideologically fragile as well. The strains of Polish dissent, the Afghan War, and a renewed arms race with the United States simply wore the Soviet state down.

The unprecedented prosperity of the United States and the West more generally allowed younger people to attend universities in record numbers, experiment with new ideas of living, and simply indulge their desires for fun and new experiences. The idealism of the era also played a role, as did the threat of the military draft and the larger threat of nuclear war. For many, the materialism of the age repelled them and made them long for a simpler, more "authentic" existence. Thus, a popular motto from the time was "Turn on, tune in, drop out."

▶ **Why did such radically different lifestyles emerge in the United States and the West during the 1960s and 1970s? What is their legacy today?**

▶ **Why did some nations that had emerged from colonialism and war make great strides in their development while others seemed to stagnate?**

By and large, the nations that prospered were the ones that had already achieved self-sufficiency in agriculture, had at least a basic transportation and communications infrastructure, and were resourceful in adopting policies that maximized their labor force. Taiwan, South Korea, and Singapore are good examples of countries that made great strides in their development during this period. China, under Deng Xiaoping, followed a modified version of this strategy and was already growing at record levels by 1991. In the following decades, nearly all Asian countries (an exception being North Korea) would follow suit, with India moving into the top ranks of development and growth. Many Latin American countries—in particular, Brazil—also made great strides, and the drive to follow the example of using cheap labor to create a successful export manufacturing base also took hold in Africa.

In all cases, culture and ideology could and did play a powerful role in setting the psychological conditions for citizens to believe that progress was possible. Peace and stability also played an important role, for obvious reasons. The many internal conflicts that pockmarked Latin America and Africa held back development during this period.

# Patterns of Evidence: Sources for Chapter 30

SOURCE 30.1

## Mikhail Gorbachev, *Perestroika: New Thinking for Our Country and the World*

**1987**

Two years after becoming first secretary of the Soviet Politburo in 1985, Mikhail Gorbachev (b. 1931) launched his two trademark economic and political programs, perestroika ("restructuring") and glasnost ("openness"). Hoping to revitalize communism, he restructured and partially dismantled the command economy that had dominated the Soviet Union since the Bolshevik Revolution. While perestroika did not work out as intended, glasnost, which permitted frank commentary and the exposure of incompetence and cover-ups by the Soviet leadership, had more wide-ranging consequences for the Soviet Union, which finally collapsed in 1991. Gorbachev summarized his attitude toward domestic politics for Western readers in a book published in English in 1987. However, a significant portion of the book also deals with Cold War tensions, as he was negotiating with President Reagan (1981–1989) of the United States, especially over the destruction of nuclear weapons.

### Who Needs the Arms Race and Why?

Pondering the question of what stands in the way of good Soviet-American relations, one arrives at the conclusion that, for the most part, it is the arms race. I am not going to describe its history. Let me just note once again that at almost all its stages the Soviet Union has been the party catching up. By the beginning of the seventies we had reached approximate military-strategic parity, but on a level that is really frightening. Both the Soviet Union and the United States now have the capacity to destroy each other many times over.

It would seem logical, in the face of a strategic stalemate, to halt the arms race and get down to disarmament. But the reality is different. Armories already overflowing continue to be

Source: Mikhail Gorbachev, *Perestroika: New Thinking for Our Country and the World* (New York: Harper & Row, 1987), 218–221.

filled with sophisticated new types of weapons, and new areas of military technology are being developed. The US sets the tone in this dangerous, if not fatal pursuit.

I shall not disclose any secret if I tell you that the Soviet Union is doing all that is necessary to maintain up-to-date and reliable defenses. This is our duty to our own people and our allies. At the same time I wish to say quite definitely that this is not our choice. It has been imposed upon us.

All kinds of doubts are being spread among Americans about Soviet intentions in the field of disarmament. But history shows that we can keep the word we gave and that we honor the obligations assumed. Unfortunately, this cannot be said of the United States. The administration is conditioning public opinion, intimidating it with a Soviet threat, and does so with particular stubbornness when a new military budget has to be passed through Congress. We have to ask ourselves why all this is being done and what aim the US pursues.

It is crystal clear that in the world we live in, the world of nuclear weapons, any attempt to use them to solve Soviet-American problems would spell suicide. This is a fact. I do not think that US politicians are unaware of it. Moreover, a truly paradoxical situation has now developed. Even if one country engages in a steady arms build up while the other does nothing, the side that arms itself will all the same gain nothing. The weak side may simply explode all its nuclear charges, even on its own territory, and that would mean suicide for it and a slow death for the enemy. This is why any striving for military superiority means chasing one's own tail. It can't be used in real politics.

Nor is the US in any hurry to part with another illusion. I mean its immoral intention to bleed the Soviet Union white economically, to prevent us from carrying out our plans of construction by dragging us ever deeper into the quagmire of the arms race.

. . .

We sincerely advise Americans: try to get rid of such an approach to our country. Hopes of using any advantages in technology or advanced equipment so as to gain superiority over our country are futile. To act on the assumption that the Soviet Union is in a "hopeless position" and that it is necessary just to press it harder to squeeze out everything the US wants is to err profoundly. Nothing will come of these plans. In real politics there can be no wishful thinking. If the Soviet Union, when it was much weaker than now, was in a position to meet all the challenges that it faced, then indeed only a blind person would be unable to see that our capacity to maintain strong defenses and simultaneously resolve social and other tasks has enormously increased.

I shall repeat that as far as the United States foreign policy is concerned, it is based on at least two delusions. The first is the belief that the economic system of the Soviet Union is about to crumble and that the USSR will not succeed in restructuring. The second is calculated on Western superiority in equipment and technology and, eventually, in the military field. These illusions nourish a policy geared toward exhausting socialism through the arms race, so as to dictate terms later. Such is the scheme; it is naïve.

Current Western policies aren't responsible enough, and lack the new mode of thinking. I am outspoken about this. If we don't stop now and start practical disarmament, we may all find ourselves on the edge of a precipice. Today, as never before, the Soviet Union and the United States need responsible policies. Both countries have their political, social and economic problems: a vast field for activities. Meanwhile, many brain trusts work at strategic plans and juggle millions of lives. Their recommendations boil down to this: the Soviet Union is the most horrible threat for the United States and the world. I repeat: it is high time this caveman mentality was given up. Of course, many political leaders and diplomats have engaged in just such policies based on just such a mentality for decades. But their time is past. A new outlook is necessary in a nuclear age. The United States and the Soviet Union need it most in their bilateral relations.

We are realists. So we take into consideration the fact that in a foreign policy all countries, even the smallest, have their own interests. It is high time great powers realized that they can no longer reshape the world according to their own patterns. That era has receded or, at least, is receding into the past.

▶ **Working with Sources**

1. **Why does Gorbachev describe American foreign policy as being dictated by "illusions" and "delusions"? Was he being disingenuous or hypocritical in this assertion?**

2. **In what ways was Gorbachev advocating a global position on the problems of the world? Was he also guided by "delusions" in this advocacy?**

## SOURCE 30.2

# Martin Luther King, Jr., "I Have a Dream"
### August 28, 1963

Under the accelerating pressure of the American civil rights movement—and with images of African Americans being attacked and beaten as they demanded equality beaming across television screens—President Kennedy introduced civil rights legislation during his administration. Realizing that advocacy of this position might endanger the position of his Democratic Party, particularly in the South, in the elections of 1964, Kennedy continued to find ways to shape American public opinion while also cajoling Congress to implement this legislation. Civil rights advocates, spearheaded by the

Reverend Dr. Martin Luther King, Jr. (1929–1968), convened in a march on Washington, DC, in August 1963. Marchers explicitly demanded "jobs and freedom." While the electrifying speech King gave on that day is more remembered for its stirring conclusion about his "dream" and about letting "freedom ring," the prepared remarks at the beginning of the speech reveal even more of King's brilliance and the depth of his political thought.

I am happy to join with you today in what will go down in history as the greatest demonstration for freedom in the history of our nation.

Five score years ago, a great American, in whose symbolic shadow we stand today, signed the Emancipation Proclamation. This momentous decree came as a great beacon light of hope to millions of Negro slaves who had been seared in the flames of withering injustice. It came as a joyous daybreak to end the long night of their captivity.

But one hundred years later, the Negro still is not free. One hundred years later, the life of the Negro is still sadly crippled by the manacles of segregation and the chains of discrimination. One hundred years later, the Negro lives on a lonely island of poverty in the midst of a vast ocean of material prosperity. One hundred years later, the Negro is still languished in the corners of American society and finds himself an exile in his own land. And so we've come here today to dramatize a shameful condition.

In a sense we've come to our nation's capital to cash a check. When the architects of our republic wrote the magnificent words of the Constitution and the Declaration of Independence, they were signing a promissory note to which every American was to fall heir. This note was a promise that all men, yes, black men as well as white men, would be guaranteed the "unalienable Rights" of "Life, Liberty and the pursuit of Happiness." It is obvious today that America has defaulted on this promissory note, insofar as her citizens of color are concerned. Instead of honoring this sacred obligation, America has given the Negro people a bad check, a check which has come back marked "insufficient funds."

But we refuse to believe that the bank of justice is bankrupt. We refuse to believe that there are insufficient funds in the great vaults of opportunity of this nation. And so, we've come to cash this check, a check that will give us upon demand the riches of freedom and the security of justice.

We have also come to this hallowed spot to remind America of the fierce urgency of Now. This is no time to engage in the luxury of cooling off or to take the tranquilizing drug of gradualism. Now is the time to make real the promises of democracy. Now is the time to rise from the dark and desolate valley of segregation to the sunlit path of racial justice. Now is the time to lift our nation from the quicksands of racial injustice to the solid rock of brotherhood. Now is the time to make justice a reality for all of God's children.

It would be fatal for the nation to overlook the urgency of the moment. This sweltering summer of the Negro's legitimate discontent will not pass until there is an invigorating autumn of freedom and equality. Nineteen sixty-three is not an end, but a beginning. And those who hope that the Negro needed to blow off steam and will now be content will have a rude awakening if the nation returns to business as usual. And there will be neither rest nor tranquility in America until the Negro is granted his citizenship rights. The whirlwinds of revolt will continue to shake the foundations of our nation until the bright day of justice emerges.

But there is something that I must say to my people, who stand on the warm threshold which leads into the palace of justice: In the process of gaining our rightful place, we must not be guilty of wrongful deeds. Let us not seek to satisfy our thirst for freedom by drinking from the cup of bitterness and hatred. We must forever conduct our struggle on the high plane of dignity and discipline. We must not allow our creative protest to degenerate into physical violence. Again and again, we must rise to the majestic heights of meeting physical force with soul force.

The marvelous new militancy which has engulfed the Negro community must not lead us to a distrust of all white people, for many of our white brothers, as evidenced by their presence here today, have come to realize that their destiny is tied up with our destiny. And they have come to realize that their freedom is inextricably bound to our freedom.

We cannot walk alone.

And as we walk, we must make the pledge that we shall always march ahead.

We cannot turn back.

There are those who are asking the devotees of civil rights, "When will you be satisfied?" We can never be satisfied as long as the Negro is the victim of the unspeakable horrors of police brutality. We can never be satisfied as long as our bodies, heavy with the fatigue of travel, cannot gain lodging in the motels of the highways and the hotels of the cities. We cannot be satisfied as long as the Negro's basic mobility is from a smaller ghetto to a larger one. We can never be satisfied as long as our children are stripped of their self-hood and robbed of their dignity by signs stating: "For Whites Only." We cannot be satisfied as long as a Negro in Mississippi cannot vote and a Negro in New York believes he has nothing for which to vote. No, no, we are not satisfied, and we will not be satisfied until "justice rolls down like waters, and righteousness like a mighty stream."

▶ Working with Sources

1. How and why did King use financial metaphors to describe the position of African Americans a century after their supposed "emancipation"?

2. How did he describe the rights and equality of African Americans as being in the interests of *all* Americans?

## SOURCE 30.3

# Simone de Beauvoir, *The Second Sex*

### 1949

Encouraged by the successful strategy and tactics of the civil rights and antiwar movements, a new assertiveness also marked the drive for women's rights after the conclusion of the World War II. One important voice in the movement for women's freedoms was that of a leading French philosopher and intellectual, Simone de Beauvoir (1908–1986). Her lengthy, detailed, and compelling study *The Second Sex*, published in 1949, challenged women to take action on their own behalf in order to gain full equality with their male counterparts. Her analysis traced the origins of sexism and a sense of women's inferiority to the unique circumstances of girlhood and to society's instilling of "feminine" characteristics in young women. Only by breaking the barriers of societal expectations for "well-bred young girls," she argued, could women achieve the goal of true and complete equality with men.

The housekeeping chores and common drudgery, which mothers do not hesitate to impose on schoolgirls or apprentices, overwork them in the end. During the war I saw students in my classes at Sèvres overburdened with family tasks superimposed upon their schoolwork: one came down with Pott's disease, another with meningitis. The mother, as we shall see, is secretly hostile to her daughter's liberation, and she takes to bullying her more or less deliberately; but the boy's effort to become a man is respected, and he is granted much liberty. The girl is required to stay at home, her comings and goings are watched: she is in no way encouraged to take charge of her own amusements and pleasures. It is unusual to see women organize by themselves a long hike or a trip on foot or by bicycle, or devote themselves to games such as billiards or bowling.

Beyond the lack of initiative that is due to women's education, custom makes independence difficult for them. If they roam the streets, they are stared at and accosted. I know young girls who, without being at all timid, find no enjoyment in taking walks alone in Paris because, importuned incessantly, they must be always on the alert, which spoils their pleasure. If girl students run in gay groups through the streets, as boys do, they make a spectacle of themselves; to walk with long strides, sing, talk, or laugh loudly, or eat an apple, is to give provocation; those who do

Source: Simone de Beauvoir, *The Second Sex*, trans. and ed. H. M. Parshley (New York: Alfred A. Knopf, 1953), 334–336.

will be insulted or followed or spoken to. Careless gaiety is in itself bad deportment; the self-control that is imposed on women and becomes second nature in "the well-bred young girl" kills spontaneity; her lively exuberance is beaten down. The result is tension and ennui.

This ennui is catching: young girls quickly tire of one another; they do not band together in their prison for mutual benefit; and this is one of the reasons why the company of boys is necessary to them. This incapacity to be self-sufficient engenders a timidity that extends over their entire lives and is marked even in their work. They believe that outstanding success is reserved for men; they are afraid to aim too high. We have seen that little girls of fourteen, comparing themselves with boys, declared that "the boys are better." This is a debilitating conviction. It leads to laziness and mediocrity. A young girl, who had no special deference for the stronger sex, was reproaching a man for his cowardice; it was remarked that she herself was a coward. "Oh, a woman, that's different!" declared she, complacently.

The fundamental reason for such defeatism is that the adolescent girl does not think herself responsible for her future; she sees no use in demanding much of herself since her lot in the end will not depend on her own efforts. Far from consigning herself to man because she recognizes her inferiority, it is because she is thus consigned to him that, accepting the idea of her inferiority, she establishes its truth.

And, actually, it is not by increasing her worth as a human being that she will gain value in men's eyes; it is rather by modeling herself upon their dreams. When still inexperienced, she is not always aware of this fact. She may be as aggressive as the boys; she may try to make their conquest with a rough authority, a proud frankness; but this attitude almost surely dooms her to failure. All girls, from the most servile to the haughtiest, learn in time that to please they must abdicate. Their mothers enjoin upon them to treat the boys no longer as comrades, not to make advances, to take a passive role. If they wish to start a friendship or a flirtation, they must carefully avoid seeming to take the initiative in it; men do not like *garçons manqués*, or bluestockings, or brainy women; too much daring, culture, or intelligence, too much character, will frighten them. In most novels, as George Eliot remarks, it is the blonde and silly heroine who is in the end victorious over the more mannish brunette; and in *The Mill on the Floss* Maggie tries in vain to reverse the roles; but she finally dies and the blonde Lucy marries Stephen. In *The Last of the Mohicans* the vapid Alice gains the hero's heart, not the valiant Clara; in *Little Women* the likable Jo is only a childhood playmate for Laurie; his love is reserved for the insipid Amy and her curls.

▶ Working with Sources

1. **How, in de Beauvoir's estimation, do young women internalize feelings of inferiority and carry these ideas with them into adulthood?**

2. **What role do the practical, daily experiences of women in the wider world play in the development of "feminine" expectations? Can these be overcome?**

SOURCE 30.4

# Coverage of the Tiananmen Square Protests

## 1989

I n May 1989, a protest movement gathered strength in Tiananmen Square in Beijing, as students convened and constructed a large statue called the Goddess of Democracy. By the beginning of June, the movement had turned into a generalized protest by workers and ordinary citizens in addition to the students. When they refused to disperse, the government sent in the army on June 4 to crush what, to many in the Communist Party, had become an incipient rebellion. The image of a lone man attempting to face down an approaching tank became the instant icon of the movement, but there are many other arresting narratives of the events that occurred during this protest. On the 15th anniversary of the suppression of these protests, the British Broadcasting Corporation interviewed survivors and eyewitnesses, gathering their testimonies into the report excerpted below.

### Witnessing Tiananmen: Clearing the Square

*The BBC's Chinese Service has interviewed some of those who witnessed the protests and subsequent bloodshed.*

Zhang Boli was deputy director of the students' hunger strike at Tiananmen Square. He then spent two years on the run before fleeing to the United States, where he now lives

While we were making preparations news came from all sides saying that the troops had started to open fire.

I remember many students ran to the square with blood running down their faces.

In some places, troops were shooting and in some places there were clashes. Zhang Huajie had actually been beaten up. When he ran to the square his face was full of blood.

He grabbed the microphone and spoke into it: "Fellow students, they have really opened fire now. They are really shooting! They are using their guns and using real bullets!"

I couldn't believe it. We at the square at the time could not really believe it.

There was a speaker's platform under the statue of the Goddess of Democracy. It was at the time when Yan Jiaqi and I had just started to speak, the troops arrived. And they were moving into Tiananmen Square.

Under the floodlight I could see all those dark helmets moving like waves into the square towards us. I felt that the final moment must have come.

So I spoke to the students, telling them that we should still behave in the spirit we had adopted all along: "We will not fight back even if we are beaten up, and we will not talk back even if we are cursed upon."

We decided to retreat to the Monument of Heroes to wait there for instructions from our command centre. Finally we reached the Monument.

Later, Zhou Duo and Hou Dejian removed their white vests and, using them as white flags, they walked over to the troops to negotiate. After all, Hou Dejian was a famous singer of some influence. He couldn't be cast as an anti-revolutionary rebel.

When Zhou Duo returned he told the students: "They say over there 'We'll give you only half an hour to leave, to evacuate. If you don't, you will have to bear the consequences.'"

So a very important decision was to be made at the time. What are we going to do with the several thousand students here? To leave, to evacuate, or not? Actually it was quite obvious at the time that it was time that we should leave. So when Feng Congde took over the microphone he knew that a heavy burden of history was handed to him.

Finally, the lights (at the square) were switched off. When the lights were out the students thought the troops would start shooting. So, many students huddled together. When the lights were out the microphone was also cut off.

Feng Congde then used a loudspeaker to speak to the students: "Fellow students, we have two opinions here. One says we should leave now. Another says we should stay put. As I can't see you, please speak aloud to respond. I will first say "WE WILL NOT LEAVE." If you agree, please say aloud WE AGREE. Then I will say "WE WILL LEAVE." If you agree, please say "AGREE." I'll see which response is louder."

Actually it was not easy to tell which response from the crowd was louder.

Feng Congde quickly made a wise decision: "I am standing here. This is the highest place. I could hear the response for us TO LEAVE was louder. So the command centre have now decided WE SHOULD LEAVE."

After it was decided that we should leave, they left only a very small gap for us to leave—just about as wide as this room. But nobody dared to move first.

. . .

The guns of the People's Army were pointing at [us] and they were loaded. They were holding machine guns. With one pull of the finger they could fire on us.

Hou Dejian went over to say: "Would it be OK for you people to raise your guns a bit higher and point at the sky?"

It was quite a painful experience. But we came out of the Square. And they didn't fire on us. I think that was because they also had to consider the opinions of the people of the nation and of the whole world.

If they were rash enough to decide to finish the lot of us on the spot, they could, but it would not do them any good at all. So it was still quite peaceful when we left Tiananmen Square.

But when we reached Liulukou suddenly there was trouble.

It was already dawn. A speeding tank came upon us like a gust of wind trying to cut through the lines of people. It was not just trying to run over people, it was also throwing out tear gas.

I remember we were all choking and couldn't open our eyes. We just heard the loud rumblings of the tanks.

About a dozen metres behind me people were crying in hysteria. I think more than 12, or 20-odd people were in a mess of blood and flesh.

It was said later that 11 people were killed there."

▶ **Working with Sources**

1. **What did the Goddess of Democracy mean to the students, and how did they envision their protest?**

2. **What do the varying reactions of the soldiers sent to quell the protests suggest about the pro-democracy movement in China at that time?**

## SOURCE 30.5

# Salvador Allende, "Last Words to the Nation"

**September 11, 1973**

Salvador Allende led a coalition of socialists, communists, and liberal Christian Democrats to a plurality win as president of Chile in 1970. Many of his policies met opposition within Chile, while his ideology and nationalization of American interests in the country's mines prompted the administration of US president Nixon (1969–1974) to back Allende's opposition. With American blessings and CIA help, Allende was overthrown and murdered in 1973. He would be replaced with the repressive but friendlier (to the United States) regime of General Augusto Pinochet, who remained in office and repeatedly violated the human rights of Chileans until 1990. Nevertheless, the coup that toppled Allende ended with a riveting address by the deposed leader to his people.

Source: https://www.marxists.org/archive/allende/1973/september/11.htm.

My friends,

Surely this will be the last opportunity for me to address you. The Air Force has bombed the towers of Radio Portales and Radio Corporación.

My words do not have bitterness but disappointment. May they be a moral punishment for those who have betrayed their oath: soldiers of Chile, titular commanders in chief, Admiral Merino, who has designated himself Commander of the Navy, and Mr. Mendoza, the despicable general who only yesterday pledged his fidelity and loyalty to the Government, and who also has appointed himself Chief of the Carabineros [national police].

Given these facts, the only thing left for me is to say to workers: I am not going to resign!

Placed in a historic transition, I will pay for loyalty to the people with my life. And I say to them that I am certain that the seed which we have planted in the good conscience of thousands and thousands of Chileans will not be shriveled forever.

They have strength and will be able to dominate us, but social processes can be arrested neither by crime nor force. History is ours, and people make history.

Workers of my country: I want to thank you for the loyalty that you always had, the confidence that you deposited in a man who was only an interpreter of great yearnings for justice, who gave his word that he would respect the Constitution and the law and did just that. At this definitive moment, the last moment when I can address you, I wish you to take advantage of the lesson: foreign capital, imperialism, together with the reaction, created the climate in which the Armed Forces broke their tradition, the tradition taught by General Schneider and reaffirmed by Commander Araya, victims of the same social sector which will today be in their homes hoping, with foreign assistance, to retake power to continue defending their profits and their privileges.

I address, above all, the modest woman of our land, the campesina who believed in us, the worker who labored more, the mother who knew our concern for children. I address professionals of Chile, patriotic professionals, those who days ago continued working against the sedition sponsored by professional associations, class-based associations that also defended the advantages which a capitalist society grants to a few.

I address the youth, those who sang and gave us their joy and their spirit of struggle. I address the man of Chile, the worker, the farmer, the intellectual, those who will be persecuted, because in our country fascism has been already present for many hours—in terrorist attacks, blowing up the bridges, cutting the railroad tracks, destroying the oil and gas pipelines, in the face of the silence of those who had the obligation to protect them. They were committed. History will judge them.

. . .

Workers of my country, I have faith in Chile and its destiny. Other men will overcome this dark and bitter moment when treason seeks to prevail. Go forward knowing that, sooner rather than later, the great avenues will open again where free men will walk to build a better society.

Long live Chile! Long live the people! Long live the workers!

These are my last words, and I am certain that my sacrifice will not be in vain, I am certain that, at the very least, it will be a moral lesson that will punish felony, cowardice, and treason.

▶ Working with Sources

1. How did Allende combine the notions of "patriotism" and resistance to "foreign capital"?

2. What forces and institutions were most guilty, in his assessment, of betraying the economic and political interests of ordinary Chileans?

# Chapter 31 1991–2014

# A Fragile Capitalist-Democratic World Order

It was a scene that had been repeated hundreds of times across North Africa and the Middle East during the months of winter and spring of 2010–2011. First in Tunisia in December, then with daily regularity in Egypt, Libya, Bahrain, Yemen, and Syria, growing crowds gathered to remonstrate with authoritarian governments over a wide range of issues that had marked the process of modernity for two centuries: the constitutional rights of life, liberty, security, economic opportunity, emancipation of minorities and women, freedom of expression, and the rights of ethnic and religious groups to nationhood, autonomy, or even mere existence.

The governments challenged by these movements had long been propped up by brutal and repressive security services. Unable or unwilling to broaden political participation, aging authoritarian rulers had groomed their sons or favorites to succeed them. The rulers pretended to have liberalized the economies of their countries, but instead "crony capitalism" benefited their relatives and followers and discouraged entrepreneurial innovation. Chronic unemployment and underemployment left both the poor and the middle class in despair over their future. For many years, the unemployed youth of the Middle East had found solace in an Islamism whose preachers promised the

Population increase, 1950–2010
Country where population increased by:
- 0–100%
- 200–300%
- 100–200%
- over 300%

*ABOVE:* Activist and 2011 Nobel Peace Prize recipient Tawakkol Karman leads a rally for democracy in Sana, Yemen.

solution for all ills. But these preachers had not turned out to be any more able than the increasingly despised rulers to improve the daily lives of the people. A general stagnation had set in throughout the region.

By mid-spring 2011 the relentlessly repeated, massive, and unarmed street protests had toppled the governments of Tunisia and Egypt. Crowds massed as well in Syria, Bahrain, Libya, and Yemen. Syria and Bahrain sought to suppress the democracy movements, while in Libya, Yemen, and Syria civil wars tore the populations apart. More remarkably, however, was that in Yemen, one of the many male-dominated bastions of conservative Islam, the movement was led by a charismatic female journalist and grassroots organizer. Armed with computers, smart phones burgeoning with apps such as Twitter, Facebook, and all the latest tools of social networking, Tawakkol Karman, 32, the leader of Women Journalists Without Chains and a mother of three, harangued mostly male crowds of thousands with calls for revolution. "We will make our revolution or we will die trying," she thundered, her words echoing those of so many insurgents of the recent past. "We are in need of heroes," said one Yemeni observer. "She manages to do what most men cannot do in a society that is highly prejudiced against women." But with her personal role models including Nelson Mandela of South Africa, Mohandas Gandhi of India, and Martin Luther King, Jr., and Hillary Clinton of the United States, Karman as much as any woman of her time embodied the choices and challenges marking the patterns of world history in the rapidly globalizing early twenty-first century. Not surprisingly, the Norwegian Nobel Committee made her the cowinner of the Peace Prize in 2013.

---

In the largest sense, achieving modernity through urbanization, science, industrialization, the accumulation of capital, and grassroots participation in political pluralism has become close to a universal goal in the world. Where it will lead is anyone's guess. But the story of how this pattern of modernity has grown to become nearly universal—and the old and new forces that oppose it—is the focus of this final chapter in our survey of world history.

## Capitalist Democracy: The Dominant Pattern of Modernity

With the demise of communism, the struggle among the three ideologies of modernity that had characterized much of the twentieth century was now over. In the first flush of enthusiasm, some Western observers declared history to have ended, henceforth to be written merely as a series of footnotes to the triumph of capitalism and democracy. Other viewers argued that modernity had ended and we were

## Seeing Patterns

▶ How did the United States demonstrate its dominant economic position toward the end of the twentieth century? How did it accelerate the pattern of globalization?

▶ What made capitalist democracy so attractive toward the end of the twentieth century that it became a generic model for many countries around the world to strive for?

▶ Which policies did China and India pursue so that they became the fastest industrializing countries in the early twenty-first century?

▶ How have information technology and social networking altered cultural, political, and economic interactions around the world?

▶ What is global warming, and why is it a source of grave concern for the future?

Postmodernism and postculturalism: Cultural movements influential across the world from ca. 1970 to 2010 which began with the adoption of eclectic styles in architecture. They evolved into a general "critical theory," according to which reality is constructed through discourse, the will to power determines society's institutions, and subaltern minorities in the new nations strive to overcome the hegemony of Western-centric culture.

at the beginning of a new age of **postmodernism** and **postcolonialism**. Less triumphant observers expressed the hope that capitalist modernity in the coming decades would become an increasingly generic pattern, adoptable in non-Western cultures. But they also realized that democracy would not spread rapidly as long as countries remained poor and stuck in inherited forms of authoritarianism or even autocracy.

More than a decade into the twenty-first century it has become clear that history not only did not end but is still in the middle of its scientific–industrial stage of modernity, which began around 1800. This stage of modernity, Western-centric during 1800–2000, has evolved into a generic modernity composed of capitalism, democracy, and consumerism spread across the globe.

## A Decade of Global Expansion: The United States and the World in the 1990s

In the aftermath of the oil crisis of 1985–1986, and with even greater vigor after the collapse of communism in 1991, the United States advocated free trade, fiscal discipline, and transnational economic integration as the proper course for world development. It did so as the most economically and politically powerful country. Two characteristics made the United States the sole superpower it currently is. First, the United States dominated the so-called dollar regime—that is, dollars functioned as the currency for all oil sales and purchases. In fact, despite the growth in popularity of the European Union's euro and other major currencies like the English pound, Swiss franc, and Japanese yen, the dollar remained in a very real sense the world's currency. Second, with its giant consumer economy, the United States functioned as the world's favored destination for manufactured goods, particularly from east Asia. The leverage which the United States gained from these two economic functions was bolstered by overwhelming military force, which made the United States the principal enforcer of peace in the world. This enforcement function has earned the United States the opprobrium of many who criticize it for imperialism, materialism, and unrestrained spying.

**A Hierarchy of Nations**   During the 1990s, there were some 190 sovereign countries in the world, forming a three-tier hierarchy. At the top of the first tier, almost in a category of its own, was the United States. It was the richest, most evolved constitutional nation-state, based on a mature scientific–industrial society, sophisticated financial institutions, and by far the most powerful military. It boasted the densest infrastructure of universities, colleges, public libraries, museums, theaters, and other cultural institutions. Below the United States, the fully industrialized democracies in Europe, North America, and Australia occupied the rest of the first tier. In the course of the 1990s, four "newly industrialized countries" joined this tier, the Asian "Tigers" or "Dragons": Taiwan, South Korea, Hong Kong, and Singapore. Since the early 2000s, the so-called BRIC countries, Brazil, Russia, Indonesia, and China, as well as Turkey and Mexico, can be added. Such was the economic power of the fully industrialized and largely democratic countries (except for China) in the top tier that they alone still conducted nearly 60 percent of all world trade in goods and services.

In the second tier of the world hierarchy were 88 "middle-income countries," according to the United Nations' definition. These were developing countries in economic and democratic "transition." They were either industrializing states in the Middle East, south Asia, east Asia, and Latin America or reindustrializing states located in the former Communist Bloc. The reindustrializing states were replacing their obsolete communist-era manufacturing infrastructures with modern systems. In the broad bottom tier were 66 countries defined as "low-income" or "poor," located for the most part in sub-Saharan Africa and southeast Asia. Many of these countries were in early stages of economic development, with little or no democratization (see Map 31.1).

In 2000, about one-fifth of the world's population of 6 billion lived in fully industrialized countries, two-thirds in middle-income countries, and 15 percent in poor

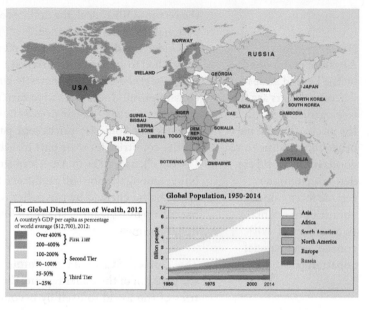

MAP 31.1 **The Global Distribution of Wealth, 2012.**

countries. The world population was still expanding, but the pace of the expansion was slowing, largely as a result of improved female education and contraceptives. The dominance of scientific–industrial society was such that only two centuries after its beginnings 90 percent of the world population was more or less integrated into the pattern of capitalist modernity characterized by market exchange and consumerism and no longer by traditional agrarian–urban subsistence agriculture.

**The Dollar Regime** The United States stood at the top of the world hierarchy thanks largely to the power of its financial system. The beginnings of this system date back to the years following 1971 when President Richard Nixon took the dollar off the gold standard. At that time, in a period of war expenditures in Vietnam and high inflation, the United States was running out of gold payable for dollars at the internationally agreed price of $35 an ounce. Two years later, Nixon persuaded the Middle East–dominated Organization of the Petroleum Exporting Countries (OPEC) to accept only dollars as payment for oil. In support of Egypt and Syria against Israel in the October War of 1973, OPEC had just quadrupled oil prices. Despite American support for Israel, however, OPEC was anxious to remain in the good graces of the United States as its largest buyer. As a result of

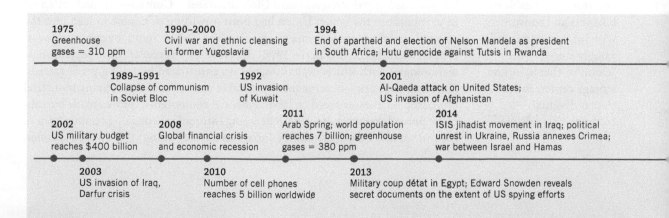

| 1975 Greenhouse gases = 310 ppm | 1990–2000 Civil war and ethnic cleansing in former Yugoslavia | 1994 End of apartheid and election of Nelson Mandela as president in South Africa; Hutu genocide against Tutsis in Rwanda |
| | 1989–1991 Collapse of communism in Soviet Bloc | 1992 US invasion of Kuwait | 2001 Al-Qaeda attack on United States; US invasion of Afghanistan |
| 2002 US military budget reaches $400 billion | 2008 Global financial crisis and economic recession | 2011 Arab Spring; world population reaches 7 billion; greenhouse gases = 380 ppm | 2014 ISIS jihadist movement in Iraq; political unrest in Ukraine, Russia annexes Crimea; war between Israel and Hamas |
| 2003 US invasion of Iraq, Darfur crisis | 2010 Number of cell phones reaches 5 billion worldwide | 2013 Military coup détat in Egypt; Edward Snowden reveals secret documents on the extent of US spying efforts | |

the Nixon–OPEC deal, the dollar took over from gold as the acknowledged international standard of exchange.

**Dollar regime:**
A system maintained by the United States whereby dollars are the sole currency in which the price of oil and most other commodities and goods in the world are denominated; the regime forces most countries to maintain two currencies, with consequent financial constraints.

Under the **dollar regime**, all oil-importing countries, except for the United States, had to manage two currencies. One, denominated in dollars, was for energy purchases; the other, in domestic currencies, was for the internal market of oil consumption. Countries had to carefully look after the strength of their domestic currency, as rising dollar prices could lead to severe crises in efforts to control inflationary domestic prices and pay back foreign, dollar-denominated loans. OPEC countries for their part invested their "petrodollars" in US Treasury bills ("T-bills"), as well as in American stocks and bonds. There were repeated grumblings among the non–oil producers of the world, both developed and developing, about being cheated by the dollar regime. But the US–OPEC deal did endure, backed up by a gigantic American financial system that emerged as a result of the dollar regime.

**The United States as an Import Sinkhole**   In a development parallel to the creation of the dollar regime, the United States tied the industrializing countries of the world to itself by becoming the country to which everyone wanted to export. Building this tie was particularly important in east Asia. During the Cold War, the United States had encouraged import substitution industrialization along the lines of Japan in Korea, Taiwan, Hong Kong, Thailand, and southeast Asian countries. By becoming prosperous, so it was assumed, these countries would be less susceptible to the expansion of communism. Although uneven, the industrialization process advanced apace in most east Asian countries. In the 1990s, it reached levels where the United States began to pressure the Asian Tigers to reduce import substitution protectionism and replace it with free trade. In return for the United States buying their industrial goods, the countries of east Asia agreed to give free access to American financial institutions, such as banks and hedge funds.

"Although nobody loves the dollar standard, it is a remarkably robust institution that is too valuable to lose and too difficult to replace."
—Economist Ronald McKinnon, 2010

In the meantime, communism collapsed, and China, pushing its own import substitution industrialization, began to export cheap industrial goods as well to the United States. In the 1990s, aided by abundant cheap labor, these goods undercut those produced by the Asian Tigers, and the United States became an even deeper "sinkhole," this time for textiles, toys, and simple electrical and electronic devices made in the People's Republic of China. The United States in effect underwrote China's industrialization, binding the country's economic interests closely to its own financial interests within the dollar regime (see Map 31.2).

**Information technology:**
The array of computers, information, electronic services, entertainment, and storage available to business and consumers, with information increasingly stored in the "cloud"—that is, online storage centers rather than individual computer hard drives.

**US Technological Renewal and Globalization**   Communism had collapsed in part because the Soviet Union had been unwilling or unable to leap into the new industrial age of consumer electronics. The United States, by contrast, transformed itself thoroughly in the 1990s. Electronics was one of those periodic new technologies with which capitalism, always threatened by falling profit rates in maturing industries, became more profitable again. By computerizing industrial processes, businesses saved on labor. Personal computers in offices made bureaucratic procedures more efficient. A fledgling Internet speeded up communication. An entirely new branch of industry, **information technology (IT)**, put cell phones,

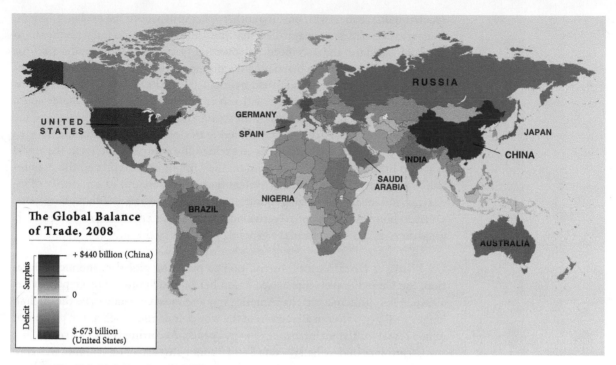

The Global Balance
of Trade, 2008

Surplus
+ $440 billion (China)

0

Deficit
$-673 billion
(United States)

RUSSIA
UNITED STATES
GERMANY
SPAIN
JAPAN
CHINA
INDIA
SAUDI ARABIA
NIGERIA
BRAZIL
AUSTRALIA

MAP 31.2 **The Global Balance of Trade, 2008.**

online delivery of music and entertainment, and a vast array of other services into the hands of consumers.

During this decade, the national budget was balanced; America became the leader in what was now called the "high-tech industry" of electronics, biotechnology, and pharmacology; unemployment shrank; inflation remained low; and the foreign debt was moderate. Worldwide, the volume of trade goods doubled and the volume of capital flows quadrupled. The US Federal Reserve kept up with demand and printed more than half as many dollars in the course of the 1990s as were already in circulation.

The only blemishes in the **globalization** process, from an American perspective, were continued protectionism and low consumption in many Asian countries. The closest economic advisors of President Bill Clinton (in office 1993–2001) were bankers and investors who had greatly expanded the size and influence of the financial services sector since the Nixon years. This sector handled the spectacularly enlarged volume of dollars floating around in the world. Alongside the traditional means of investment—stocks and bonds—new, more speculative instruments called "derivatives" gained in popularity. Derivatives were complex bets on higher or lower future prices of stocks, bonds, commodities, currencies, or anything else traded on the world market. The US globalization offensive in the 1990s was thus in large part an effort to open protected foreign markets to American financial institutions.

**Globalization:** The ongoing process of integrating the norms of market economies throughout the world and binding the economies of the world into a single uniform system.

**Globalization and Its Critics**    In many ways, the dollar- and import-sinkhole regimes were so complex that they attracted critics from the entire political spectrum dissatisfied with one or another specific aspect of the evolving system. Conservative critics were appalled that the United States no longer adhered to the gold standard and sacrificed its sovereignty to oil sheikhs trading oil for dollars. They furthermore bemoaned the disappearance of the traditional manufacturing sector and its replacement by financial institutions and Internet start-ups that produced nothing tangible. In their judgment, the United States could be held hostage to policy dictates by the foreign holders of T-bills.

Progressive critics accused the United States of using its arrangements with OPEC and the east Asian countries to exclude the poorer countries in the world that had little to offer. In their opinion, the United States pursued the maintenance of an imperialist capitalist system that limited wealth to a minority of industrialized and industrializing countries and refused to share it with the have-nots. Overall, however, both conservative and progressive criticisms remained marginal during the 1990s, given the general prosperity of the industrial countries.

**US Military Dominance**    In addition to pursuing global economic integration, the United States emphasized a number of basic political principles in the 1990s. A first principle was that America was and must continue to be the unchallenged military power in all regions of the world. It defined itself as the guarantor of last resort for the maintenance of world peace. Accordingly, by the year 2002, the US military budget had risen to $400 billion. This astronomical sum was considerably smaller than during the Cold War but still larger than the defense budgets of the next eight countries combined. On the basis of this military machine, President Bill Clinton operated from a position of de facto world dominance.

His successor, President George W. Bush (in office 2001–2009), articulated this dominance in an official doctrine, the National Security Strategy of 2002. American might was highly visible in all parts of the world, generating considerable resentment among those for whom the combined economic–military power of the United States amounted to a new kind of world dominance. Since 2009, however, President Barack Obama (in office 2009–) sought to reduce the American military posture by withdrawing troops from Iraq and Afghanistan and reducing the now-unsustainable military budget. In spite of these reductions, American predominance remained undiminished (see Map 31.3).

**Intervention in Iraq**    The National Security Strategy elevated two policies already in practice into doctrine: preventing countries from establishing dominance in a region and destroying terrorist organizations bent on destruction in the United States. The first policy was enacted after Saddam Hussein (1937–2006) and his Baath regime occupied Kuwait (1990–1991). President George H. W. Bush (in office 1989–1993) intervened when it became clear that Saddam Hussein, by invading Kuwait, sought dominance over Middle Eastern oil exports from Saudi Arabia and that the region was unable or unwilling to prevent him from achieving it. At the head of a coalition force and with UN backing, in 1992 Bush ordered US troops to evict the Iraqis from Kuwait in Operation Desert Storm. In a devastating combined air and ground war of 6 weeks, the coalition force drove the Iraqi occupiers from Kuwait.

In the following decade, the United States and United Nations subjected Iraq to a stringent military inspection regime to end Saddam Hussein's efforts to acquire nuclear and chemical weapons. The inspectors discovered large quantities of weapons and supervised their destruction. But in the face of massive Iraqi efforts at obstruction, the inspectors eventually left. Their departure was followed by a retaliatory US bombardment of Baghdad in 1998. After the US invasion of Afghanistan in 2001, a chastened Saddam Hussein readmitted the inspectors. Their inability to find anything significant touched off an intense debate among the members of the UN Security Council. The United States and Great Britain considered further inspections worthless, while France, Russia, and China argued that these inspections should be given more time. A stalemate ensued, and in an extraordinarily passionate worldwide discussion the multilateralists who advocated continued United Nations–led sanctions squared off against the unilateralists favoring a preemptive United States–led invasion of Iraq.

In the end, in March 2003, President George W. Bush espoused the unilateralist cause and ordered a preemptive invasion without Security Council backing, arguing that Iraq had once more become a regional threat. To the surprise of many, Saddam Hussein's regime put up little resistance and fell after just 3 weeks to the vastly superior US armed forces. Afterward, no weapons of mass destruction were discovered, in spite of an intense scouring of every corner of the country.

**Intervention in Afghanistan**   The second US principle announced in President George W. Bush's national security strategy was swift retaliation, prevention, and even preemption against nonstate challengers of American supremacy. This doctrine was a response to the rise of Islamic terrorism. In 1992, al-Qaeda ("the Base") under the leadership of Osama bin Laden (1957–2011) had emerged as the principal terrorist organization operating on an international scale.

Al-Qaeda's campaign of terrorism climaxed on September 11, 2001. Suicide commandos hijacked four commercial airliners in the northeastern United States and crashed them into the World Trade Center's Twin Towers in New York City, the Pentagon outside Washington, DC, and (after passengers on the plane disrupted the attempted hijacking) a field near Shanksville, Pennsylvania. Nearly 3,000 people died in the disasters. In response, US troops invaded Afghanistan on October 7, 2001, in an effort to eliminate bin Laden, who was protected by the regime in power. They destroyed the pro–al-Qaeda government of the Taliban, receiving support from anti-Taliban Afghans, and drove the al-Qaeda terrorists to western Pakistan. It took another decade for the United States to track down and assassinate bin Laden (May 2011) and several of his close collaborators and to come to grips with the resurgent Taliban terrorists in its ongoing war in Afghanistan.

**Day of Infamy.** Smoke billowing from the south tower of the World Trade Center in New York City on September 11, 2001. The north tower had already collapsed. Nearly 2,600 people died in the inferno, in which the heat of the exploding commercial airplanes in the interior of the high rises melted the steel girders supporting the buildings.

**The United Nations and Regional Peace**   Even though it was the United States and sometimes the North Atlantic Treaty Organization (NATO) that guaranteed peace in the 1990s and early 2000s and not the United Nations, the United Nations nevertheless fulfilled vital, if not always successful, peace

MAP 31.3  **US Security Commitments since 1945.**

missions in regional conflicts. An important example of a failure in this regard was the Rwandan civil war of 1994, in which mostly French peacekeeping troops serving under UN auspices stood by as the Hutu ethnic majority massacred the Tutsi ethnic minority by the hundreds of thousands.

On the other hand, despite the bloodshed on both sides, the crisis in the Sudan saw the United Nations fare somewhat better. Two vicious civil wars raged between Arab Muslim northern Sudan on the one hand and Christian and

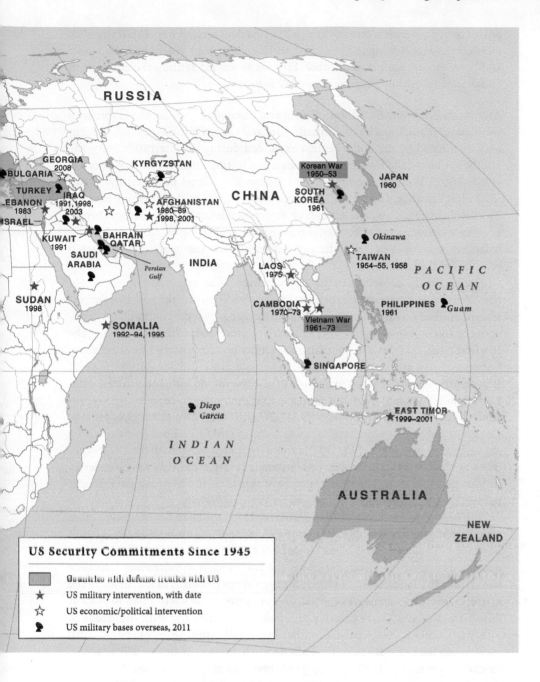

**US Security Commitments Since 1945**

Countries with defense treaties with US

★ US military intervention, with date

☆ US economic/political intervention

US military bases overseas, 2011

African-spiritual southern Sudan (1983–2005) and the non-Arab Muslim region of Darfur in western Sudan (2003–present), on the other. After lengthy efforts under UN mediation, the two sides in the first conflict agreed to the secession of South Sudan as an independent country in 2011. The Darfur conflict continued to smolder, with the United Nations pursuing criminal charges against the president of Sudan and an African Union force seeking to protect the refugees from Arab-inspired attacks. After barely two years of independence in South Sudan, the power struggle between two leading politicians degenerated into a civil war with ethnic overtones, pitting the president and former vice president and the Dinka and Nuer groups against each other. First steps toward settling the conflicts in Sudan were taken, but much more needed to follow.

**American Finances Go Global: Crisis and Recovery**    Under the umbrella of world peace maintained by the United States and United Nations, the world economy dominated by the dollar regime expanded during the late 1900s and early 2000s. In the so-called Washington Consensus, lasting a little more than a decade (1989–2002), Western economists and foreign aid officers preached the motto "Stabilize, Privatize, and Liberalize" to the governments of the emerging nations. To receive investments, foreign aid, or emergency loans to overcome recurrent economic crises, recipient countries had to submit to stringent rules concerning balanced budgets, the privatization of state firms, and the opening of protected branches of the economy.

Spurred by the consensus in the 1990s, private US investors had nearly tripled the value of their assets abroad, to a total of over $6.5 trillion. The now more accessible public and private financial systems in many newly industrialized and developing countries, however, were often not sufficiently robust to respond adequately. In a first crisis, the Mexican government—under pressure in 1994 from inflation, budget deficits, and political instability—could not avoid devaluing the peso. It promptly ran out of pesos to service its short-term, dollar-denominated debt. Fortunately, President Bill Clinton was at that time eager to complete the North American Free Trade Agreement (NAFTA) with Canada and Mexico. He had Congress and the International Monetary Fund (IMF) bail out Mexico with a massive infusion of loans. (The IMF is an international bank, with the US government as the largest shareholder, that provides emergency loans to countries in sudden financial distress.) With the help of this loan, the Mexican government paid off the foreign lenders and steadied its financial system.

The next crisis began in 1997 in Thailand. Here, the state finances were more solid than in Mexico. The liberalized private banking sector was still in its infancy, however, with huge unpaid loans on its books. When many private banks could not pay back their American creditors, the latter began withdrawing what they could from Thailand. American funds for derivatives moved in to speculate on the distress. Derivative managers specializing in currency bets sensed an imminent devaluation of the Thai currency, the *baht*. Since they bet with hundreds of billions of dollars, their speculation became a self-fulfilling prophecy. Accordingly, when the devaluation of the baht finally happened, it stripped Thailand of its currency reserves. Thailand—in good times one of the world's leading tourist destinations—scraped along the edge of bankruptcy, recovered in 1999, but was thrown again into turmoil in 2010–2011 and 2013–2014 in a near–civil war over allegations of corruption in the government.

From Thailand the crisis quickly expanded in 1998 to Malaysia, Indonesia, and finally even the newly industrialized Korea, Singapore, and Taiwan. These countries suffered from variations of the same problem of overcommitted banks with nonperforming portfolios. They thereby also made themselves vulnerable to American derivatives speculators invading their financial markets. The IMF had to move in with massive loans to the southeast and east Asian countries. In return, these countries had to tighten credit, close unprofitable banks and factories, tolerate higher unemployment, and promote increased exporting. Newly industrialized South Korea was relatively successful with its reforms and quickly cranked up its exports again.

**Russia's Crisis and Recovery**   Russia defaulted in 1998 on its internal bonds and from 1999 to 2001 on several of its external loans. These defaults were a culmination of the disastrous postcommunist economic free fall. In the decade after 1991, Russia's gross domestic product (GDP) dropped by nearly half, a decline far worse than that experienced by the United States during the Great Depression of the 1930s. Ordinary Russians had to reduce their already minimal consumption to half of what they had been used to under communism. Moreover, the government had yet to dismantle the system of unproductive former state enterprises financing themselves through local tax collection. Consequently, the state was periodically starved of funds needed for the repayment of its external loans. Fortunately, higher oil prices after 2001 eased the debt situation of Russia somewhat.

The oil and gas revenues from state firms available directly to the government, however, strengthened its autocratic tendencies. The former KGB officer Vladimir Putin, president of Russia 2000–2008 and again after 2012, was the principal engineer of this autocracy. Pervasive corruption and obedience to state directives undermined the legal system so severely that it was no longer possible to speak of the rule of law in Russia. Given the small size of the private sector in the early 2000s, the country was still years away from subjecting its state enterprises to market rules and creating a comprehensive market economy.

In addition, Putin has sharply curtailed civil rights, restricted press freedom, and made it difficult for NGOs and human rights organizations to operate in Russia. Putin has also encouraged a resurgent nationalism, a desire to restore the country to its former imperial greatness he exploits to promote his agenda of reasserting Russian hegemony. In August 2008, Putin provoked the former Soviet republic of Georgia, which was on track for admission into NATO, into a conflict that resulted in Russian control over both South Ossetia and Abkhazia. The biggest prize in Putin's imperial land grab so far is Crimea, part of Ukraine since 1954. When massive protests erupted in early 2014 against the pro-Russian Ukrainian president Viktor Yanukovych, who had scuttled a popular agreement to increase Ukraine's ties to the European Union, Yanukovych was overthrown. Putin used this opportunity to invade and seize Crimea in March 2014. A separatist, pro-Russian rebellion in eastern Ukraine has been strongly condemned by the international community.

**Globalization and Poor Countries**   The mixed record of development in the middle-income countries was mirrored in the bottom tier of poor countries. Since these countries still had weak manufacturing bases, their governments relied on the export of mineral or agricultural commodities to finance development. Apart from the oil-rich desert states of the Middle East, some 50 poor states depended on three or fewer commodities for over half of their export earnings. In about 20 of these states, these commodities even made up over 90 percent of export earnings. As a result of overproduction on the world market, commodity prices were depressed through most of the 1990s. The price depression imposed severe budget cutbacks on many poor countries, with consequent unemployment, middle-class shrinkage, reduction in education, and a rise in HIV infections.

In a world perspective, however, the developing world benefited from the globalization of the 1990s. Poverty declined up until the recession of 2008, although this decline was unevenly distributed among the regions of the world. The World Bank defines as "absolutely poor" a man or woman who has to live on less

than $1.25 a day. According to statistics compiled during 1990–2000, the total number of the poor went down from 29 to 24 percent, even though the world population grew by nearly 1 billion. As encouraging as this figure was, the gains were concentrated almost exclusively in east and south Asia, particularly China, Vietnam, and India. The number of the absolute poor actually increased in sub-Saharan Africa, southeast Asia (except Vietnam), Russia and central Asia, and Latin America. Thus, while globalization benefited an absolute majority of humans, its uneven geographical distribution made the benefits look substantially smaller in many regions.

## Two Communist Holdouts: China and Vietnam

Communism or socialism as an official ideology survived in North Korea, Cuba, China, Vietnam, North Korea, and Cuba. China and Vietnam opened their command economies to the market quite dramatically but maintained many large state firms and single-party control. In both cases, the parties remained communist in name but became in fact ordinary autocracies presiding over capitalist economies.

**Two Views of China.** Despite attempts to regulate its pace, China's economic acceleration continued at a torrid pace. In 2010, its GDP surpassed that of Japan to become second only to that of the United States. The new prosperity created startling contrasts and a growing diversity of lifestyles in the People's Republic. In the image above, young Chinese hipsters sport T-shirts harkening back with deliberate irony to revolutionary leaders Mao Zedong and Cuba's romantic figure of Che Guevara. In the lower panel, China's leadership—smartly decked out in Western suits and "power ties"—strive to steer the country toward continued growth as the means to preserve the ascendancy of the Chinese Communist Party.

**The Chinese Economic Boom**    After the crushing experience of Tiananmen Square in 1989, the new Chinese middle class, benefiting from the economic reforms of the Open Door and Four Modernizations, had to accommodate itself as best it could to a repressive top layer and a corrosively corrupt bottom layer of a monopoly party that was communist in name but autocratic in practice. The basic characteristics of the middle class were remarkably similar to those of India and Turkey, discussed later in this chapter. Socially conservative migrants from the provinces to the cities found unskilled jobs in the early 1980s. They acquired skills and earned enough to send their children to school. From around 2005, the children, now with college degrees, took jobs as managers, technicians, professionals, and entrepreneurs in state companies, private firms, and Chinese branches of foreign firms. They began to flex their muscles as consumers.

To keep the middle class from demanding political participation outside the Communist Party, the government pursued accelerated annual GDP growth, which in some years went into double digits. Wages rose beyond those paid in

Vietnam, Bangladesh, India, and Pakistan. Instead of spending its earnings, however, the middle class saved at rates double those in Japan or Europe prior to the recession of 2008–2011. The only partially subsidized new health care and education systems consumed many of those savings, even though the payments were bearable under the continued conditions of the one-child law (relaxed somewhat in 2013). In addition, urban real estate and rental apartments became increasingly unaffordable in many Chinese cities during the early 2000s. Under the slogan of the "harmonious society"—in which all segments of the populace worked together with no toleration for "disruptive elements" or those advocating independence for Tibet or the ethnically Uighur region of Xinjiang—the government and party staked its continued legitimacy to ongoing economic progress.

**Vietnam Taking Off**   With stellar double-digit growth rates in the 1990s, Vietnam outpaced other poor Asian neighbors, such as Cambodia and Bangladesh, diversifying its manufacturing sector from textiles to footwear and electronics. Hong Kong, Taiwanese, and Korean companies, the principal foreign investors, showed a strong preference for Vietnam, on account of its advanced literacy rate and lower wages compared to China. A major new export sector from the later 1990s onward was aquaculture, the farming of shrimp, catfish, and tilapia. Vietnam moved in 2010 from the poor to the intermediate countries on the world list of nations.

## A Decade of Global Shifts: Twenty-First-Century Currents and Cross Currents

In the first and early second decade of the 2000s, there was a palpable swing toward pessimism in the West. Two recessions framed the decade, the Washington consensus fell apart over protests from borrower countries, and the problematic postwar settlement in Iraq demonstrated the limits of US power. The Middle East fared even worse, with terrorism, suicide bombings, the Syrian (2011–) and Iraqi (2014–) civil wars, no Arab–Israeli peace, and a potential Iranian nuclear bomb. By contrast, China and India, with strong economic growth rates, expanded their educated and entrepreneurial middle classes. Africa and Latin America, benefiting from the voracious demand for oil and minerals in China and India, experienced similarly strong growth. By the second decade of the 2000s, it was clear that, while there might be doubts about the course of modernity in the West, the commitment to it was growing everywhere else.

**Unease in the West**   Two recessions in the first decade of the 2000s in the United States sapped much of the enthusiasm about the future of modernity that had ridden so high after the fall of communism. The first—relatively mild—recession, of 2001–2003, was the so-called dot-com crisis, which had its origins in uncontrolled speculation about the expansion of the new medium of the Internet. The second—much more severe—recession of 2008–2011 began with the collapse of the housing market, as a result of the overly risky granting of real-estate mortgages to buyers with insufficient funds. Mortgage-backed uncollectable securities became "toxic," getting the banks holding them into deep financial trouble. The mortgage crisis snowballed into a general credit, credit card, and auto loan crisis, reducing consumer demand. Manufacturers, especially in the auto industry (General

Motors and Chrysler), became insolvent and mass unemployment deepened the recession. The unemployment rate reached 9.6 percent in 2010, compared to half the rate in 2000–2008. There were signs suggesting the recession of 2008–2011 could have reached the dimensions of the Great Depression of 1929–1932, had it been left unchecked.

The crisis of 2001–2003 hit the African American and Hispanic working class particularly hard; in the following recession of 2008–2011 many white workers lost their jobs. By contrast, a majority of employees in the financial sector, the upper management of large corporations, and in the information technology industry survived the recession relatively unscathed. The American public became increasingly aware of the gap that separated the top one percent of income earners and asset owners from the rest of the population.

In addition to the unease about economic inequalities, unhappiness about political and social issues grew, especially among white, middle-class, older, and evangelical voters. The Tea Party movement ("Taxed Enough Already") founded by these voters in 2009 introduced radically populist antiestablishment and anti-foreigner agendas into the political debate. This movement opted to work inside the Republican Party, seeking to reform it from within. It thereby began to push the party to the right, polarizing American politics as a result.

At first, the successful presidential campaign of Barack Obama (President 2009–), a law professor and the first African American president of the nation, gave a majority of Americans a much-needed boost of optimism to emerge from the depression. It appeared initially that the president's deficit spending helped in steadying the economy. But given the strong opposition of Congress, this spending turned out to be insufficient, and the grind of a continuing recession dragged the ebullient mood down again. Meanwhile, conservatives and Tea Party activists relentlessly criticized government spending, health-care reform, illegal immigration, and especially the slow economic recovery. In the 2010 elections, the Republicans regained the House and rejected tax increases to offset budget deficits out of hand.

A year later the Tea Party wing of the Republican Party held the nation hostage in the negotiations for an increase of the national debt ceiling. It nearly drove the country into default, and the creditworthiness of the United States was damaged. In 2013 Tea Party members repeated the action and, simultaneously, shut the government down for 16 days in a failed effort to defund the Affordable Health Care Act passed in 2010, which guaranteed health insurance for the large majority of Americans. Given the unwillingness of lawmakers to reform the tax code, the gap between the wealthy and poor continued to widen. This gap increasingly threatened the ability of middle-class Americans to consume and thereby sustain the capitalist system, given that 70 percent of the GDP was consumer-generated.

Europe saw a similar trend of rising income disparities, although this was mitigated by a stronger manufacturing sector (around 20 percent of GDP versus 11 percent in the United States in 2010) and a more generous social safety net. But the costs of this net weighed heavily on the budgets of many countries, seriously imperiling the future not only of Greece, Portugal, Spain, and Ireland (all of which fell into near-bankruptcy during the recession of 2008–2011), but also of the European Union itself. Questions arose whether the euro, which was launched with great fanfare in 1999, could be maintained as the common currency.

Since the unemployed (6.8–12 percent during 2008–2014) were entitled to long-term support in most European countries, the Tea Party-type angry populist debate was more muted during the early stages of the recession. But the rigorous policy of budget-cutting and public savings, largely imposed by Germany, slowed the recovery in 2011 to a crawl. Antiestablishment and antiforeign populism finally broke into the open in 2014 when between 19 and 27 percent of the electorate in Austria, Denmark, France, Italy, and the United Kingdom voted for anti-European candidates running for the European parliament. As in the United States, optimism about the future of modernity was at a low ebb in the second decade of the twenty-first century.

**A Bloody Civil War in Yugoslavia**    Eastern Europe and the Balkans went through an economic collapse and political restructuring during the 1990s similar to Russia, Ukraine, Belarus, and the other former Soviet republics. This collapse and restructuring was mostly peaceful except in Yugoslavia, where a civil war raged from 1990 to 1995. Until the 1980s, communism was the main ideology in Yugoslavia, through which the country's ethnic nationalisms of the Orthodox Christian Serbs (one-third of the population), Catholic Croats (20 percent), Muslim Bosnians (9 percent), Catholic Slovenes (8 percent), and mostly Muslim Kosovar Albanians (8 percent) were subsumed under the mantle of a federal constitution granting these ethnic groups a degree of autonomy. The main enforcer of communist unity, through carrot and stick, was President Josip Tito (1892–1980), a Croat whose authority—based on his legitimacy as an underground fighter against the Nazi occupation during World War II—was unimpeachable. After his death, however, the Serb president Slobodan Milošević ([mee-LOSH-e-vich], 1941–2006) exploited the demographic superiority of his ethnic community for the establishment of political dominance while holding on to communism as the pro forma ideology.

Yugoslavia, like many Eastern European communist states, had borrowed heavily from Western countries to keep its industries from collapsing during the oil price slump of 1985–1986. At the end of the 1980s it was practically bankrupt, with hundreds of thousands of unemployed workers carrying their dashed hopes for the good life of consumerism in the city back to their native villages. This disappointment exploded in 1990 with extraordinary fury into deadly religious–nationalist hatred, led by the smaller ethnic groups against Serbs on their territories. The Serb supremacist-nationalist backlash, with an effort to "cleanse" minorities from "greater Serbian" territory, was no less explosive. It took more than a decade for the European Union and the United States to stop the Orthodox Serbs from murdering Muslim Bosnians and Albanians and enforce a semblance of peace in the Balkans.

Since then, the five successor states of Yugoslavia have struggled to adapt to capitalism and democracy. Slovenia has done so relatively successfully, while others like Bosnia-Herzegovina, Serb-controlled Bosnia, and Kosovo have yet to master the basics, much less implement them. Serb supremacist nationalism survived the longest and only gradually began to subside when the democratically elected pro-European government decided to arrest the main perpetrators of ethnic cleansing, Radovan Karadžić ([KA-ra-jich], b. 1945) and Ratko Mladić ([my-LA-dich], b. 1943) in 2008 and 2011, respectively. The two had lived more or less openly in Serbia for years, protected by diehard followers. With these arrests and much relief, the Serbian government opened the way toward joining the European Union.

**The Middle East: Paralysis, Liberation, and Islamism**    As in the United States and Europe, the momentum that was generated after the collapse of communism had largely dissipated in the Middle East and North Africa by the early 2000s. In fact, with the exception of Turkey, a pall of economic and political paralysis hung over the region. The republics in the 1990s and early 2000s (e.g., Egypt, Syria, Algeria, Tunisia, and Yemen) inched intermittently toward privatization of state-run businesses but not at all toward democratization. Monarchies (Saudi Arabia, Jordan, Oman, and the Gulf sheikhdoms) actively encouraged private investment, especially in the oil sector, but were extremely cautious, if not altogether hostile, toward democratic reforms. Under the impact of the Arab Spring, in 2011 the kingdom of Morocco adopted constitutional reforms allowing for greater democracy. The "rejection front" of autocratic regimes in Iran and Syria, as well as the guerilla terrorist organizations Hezbollah in southern Lebanon and Hamas in the Gaza Strip, rejected Washington and globalization out of hand. Syria did, however, open its state-controlled economy ever so cautiously to privatization in the early 2000s.

**Islamism:** Religious-nationalist ideology in which the reformed Sunni or Shiite Islam of the twentieth century is used to define all institutions of the state and society.

Fear of **Islamism** was a major factor accounting for the immobility of "republican autocrats" as well as monarchs. Western secular observers often expressed surprise at the strength of the religious resurgence in the Middle East after watching its apparent demise with the rise of secular Arab nationalism and Arab socialism during the period 1952–1970. In this case, however, while Islam was less visible in the region in the twentieth century when the political elites consisted of secular liberals and nationalists, it had not receded at all from the villages and poor city quarters, where it remained as vital as ever.

The key to understanding the rise of Islamism lay in the acceleration of rural–urban migration in the Middle East in the late 1990s and early 2000s. Ever since the 1960s, when Middle Eastern and North African governments built the first large state-run manufacturing plants in their cities, the workers were largely peasants arriving from villages with highly localized cultures of saintly Sufi (mystical) Islam. They encountered militant preachers in the cities who—representing a reformed, standardized, urban Sunni Islam—were appalled by the "un-Islamic" saint cults among the workers. The children of these workers learned a similar standardized Islam in the schools, intended to buttress Arab nationalism, in which the Prophet Muhammad was the first nationalist. Standard Islam and militant urban Islamism gradually crowded out the rural saintly Islam and eventually produced small but potent offshoots of Islamist terrorism, such as al-Qaeda, the Taliban, and the Salafists.

In the 1990s and early 2000s Middle Eastern governments essentially barricaded themselves behind their secret services and armies against the onslaughts of these Islamists. Terrorists attacked tourists, as happened periodically in Egypt, seeking to bring down a government that relied heavily on Western tourism. Sometimes they picked weak states such as Yemen, which, relying on dwindling oil revenues, began to lose control of its nomadic groups in the east, agricultural minorities in the north, and urban secessionists in the south. In this condition, it became a haven for al-Qaeda terrorists. Even a stronger state, Algeria, suffered a devastating civil war that claimed 150,000 victims from 1992 to 2002. Under the threat of Islamist terrorism, Middle Eastern and North African governments found it impossible to pursue bold new initiatives of the kind that China or India advanced.

**The Growth of Hezbollah**   One area where Islamists achieved a breakthrough was Lebanon. Hezbollah ("Party of God"), an Islamist guerilla organization with attendant social services and recruiting from among the Shiite majority of Lebanese Muslims, waged an underground war against Israel. It succeeded in 2000 at driving Israel from southern Lebanon after an 18-year occupation that had begun with Israel expelling the Palestine Liberation Organization (PLO) from the country. Thereafter, it periodically fired rockets into Israel and repelled a retaliatory Israeli raid in 2006. During this time, Hezbollah was apparently also active abroad: It was accused of bombing the US embassy in Beirut in 1983, hijacking an American airliner in 1985, and carrying out two bombings against Jews in Argentina in 1992 and 1994 and the bombing of an Israeli tour bus in Bulgaria in 2012. By the second decade of the 2000s, Hezbollah had evolved into the most formidable enemy of Israel.

In 2013, Hezbollah even grew into the role of a regional, quasi-state actor. Not only did it come to dominate the Lebanese administration, it became a decisive force strengthening Bashar al-Assad in his civil war against his Arab Spring challengers (see below). Increasingly, Sunni terrorist groups were elbowing the challengers aside, seeking to turn the Syrian civil war into a sectarian conflict. Hezbollah and its patron, Iran, were determined to assert the role of Shiism in the contemporary Middle East. Given the internal conflicts in Egypt, Iran emerged as a main power in Middle Eastern politics.

**Israel and Gaza**   During the globalization of the 1990s, Israel developed an advanced economy specializing in high-tech software and microbiology. In 1994, it was officially at peace with two Arab neighbors, Egypt and Jordan. But it continued to face a hostile Arab Middle East in general and restless Palestinians in the occupied territories on the West Bank and in Gaza, in particular. To protect its citizens from guerilla attacks, the Israeli government built a border fence in 2002–2013, supplemented in places by a wall of concrete slabs, inside the entire length of the occupied West Bank. In many places, this fence veered into West Bank territory, separating Palestinian villagers from their farmland. In a parallel move it withdrew from the fenced-in Gaza Strip in 2005. Suicide attacks were fewer, but cross-border rocket attacks from Gaza increased, trapping Israel in a cat-and-mouse game of low-level cross-border warfare.

After 2006, Israel slid into an even worse trap. In the first-ever Palestinian elections the victory in Gaza went to the Islamic guerilla organization Hamas, founded in 1988, over the older, secular, ethnic-nationalist PLO. The PLO, deprived of its inspiring leader Yasir Arafat, was able to prevail only in the West Bank. The PLO refused to recognize the elections, and a civil war broke out, in which Hamas was victorious, forcing the PLO to retreat to the West Bank. Israel imposed a complete embargo on Hamas-ruled Gaza in an attempt to bring the organization down.

For those in Israel who wished to renew the Camp David peace process, left incomplete in 2000, the PLO–Hamas split was a disaster, since it threw the entire idea of a two-state solution into doubt. Hamas was happy to deepen this doubt in the following years by launching thousands of rockets against Israel. In retaliation, Israel invaded Gaza in December–January 2008–2009, causing unmitigated misery for the Palestinian population of Gaza, but was not able to defeat Hamas. Efforts at healing the split between PLO and Hamas produced no results. In the summer of 2014 vicious war between Israel and Hamas erupted once again.

**Israel's Predicament and Iranian Ambitions**    The failure of the Lebanon invasion in 2009 brought a conservative government into power in Israel. The government renewed the open pursuit of Israeli settlement construction in the West Bank while tightening the embargo on Gaza. But neither more Jewish settlements in the West Bank (making the two-state solution illusory) nor punishing Israel's neighbors Hezbollah and Hamas with invasions and/or embargoes brought the country closer to peace. In fact, a major US push toward a peace settlement in 2013–2014 ended not only without results but also with renewed mutual accusations. The formation of a PLO–Hamas unity government of technocrats in 2014 was greeted by Israel with further settlement plans. Israel's long dominance over its neighbors, gradually acquired in the last half of the twentieth century, appeared to have reached its limits in the early years of the twenty-first.

Hezbollah and Hamas were able to assert themselves against Israel thanks to Iran, which supplied them with rockets. Iran, a leader of the rejectionist front against Israel, had experienced a "pragmatic" period after the death of its spiritual guide, Ruhollah Khomeini, in 1989. This pragmatism had raised the hope that the Shiite Islamist regime was lessening its policy of fighting what it viewed as the "satanic" Western culture of secularism, liberalism, and pop culture. But the reformers were timid, and the still-powerful clerics systematically undermined attempts at democratic and cultural reforms.

Any remaining hopes for reform were dashed when Mahmoud Ahmadinejad [ah-ma-DEE-nay-jahd] (b. 1956), an engineer from a modest rural background, was elected president. He renewed the anti-Western crusade and adopted a policy of populism, with subsidies for food and gas as well as distributions of cash by the suitcase on his cross-country trips. Most important, under his leadership, the Revolutionary Guard became not only the most effective military organization but, by investing in a wide variety of businesses, also a huge patronage machine.

The precipitous decline of revenues from oil exports during the recession of 2008–2011, however, seriously reduced Ahmadinejad's populist appeal. Hence, he needed the Revolutionary Guard commanders to falsify the elections of 2009 to stay in power. Suspected Iranian ambitions for acquiring a nuclear bomb, coupled with North Korea's already existing nuclear arsenal, created recurrent nightmares in the world about nuclear proliferation, "dirty" nuclear material in the hands of terrorists, and the possibility of nuclear war by "rogue" nations. Put under a severe economic sanctions regime by the United Nations, Iran elected a less populist and more pragmatic president, Hasan Rouhani (b. 1948), in 2013 and began to search for ways to stabilize the dire economic situation. Rouhani negotiated an initial easing of some sanctions in return for increased inspections and a limitation on nuclear enrichment in November 2013.

**The Ascent of Turkey**    Turkey was the one Middle Eastern country to have largely escaped Islamist militancy and had become one of the most dynamic newly industrialized countries in the world. In contrast to other regimes in the Middle East, Turkish Muslims found access to the political process, thanks to a well-established and functioning multiparty system. After many false starts and interruptions by military coups d'état, a right-of-center party with a strong contingent of Islamists in 1983 not only captured the premiership of the country but simultaneously implemented bold new initiatives of economic privatization and industrial export orientation. Benefiting from these initiatives, an entire new middle class of socially conservative but economically liberal entrepreneurial businesspeople arose.

In an even more effective second wave of Islamist middle-class expansion after 2003 under Prime Minister Recep Erdoğan [RAY-jep er-dow-AHN] (b. 1954), Turkey's GDP grew to become the world's fifteenth largest. Elections in June 2011 enabled Erdoğan's party to garner slightly more than half of the vote and, on the basis of this vote, enacted constitutional reforms which rescinded the military's power in politics. His electoral strength, however, misled Erdoğan into believing that he could repress environmentally motivated popular protests in Istanbul in 2013 without damaging the democratic process. Even more damage occurred soon thereafter when he sought to quash a corruption scandal among a number of ministers and their sons by removing investigating police and state attorneys from their positions. The repression revealed a deep rift among factions in the ruling party. Thus, while Turkey largely completed its arrival in capitalist modernity, it has yet to complete the democratic counterpart.

**The Arab Spring of 2011**    Turkey was a model example for the compatibility of Islam and beginning democracy. But in spring 2011 Tunisia and Egypt each saw constitutional-nationalist revolutions, which demonstrated that democracy could sprout in Arab countries as well. On December 17, 2010, 26-year-old Mohamed Bouazizi set himself ablaze in a last spectacular act of despair brought about by the humiliations he had suffered at the hands of a Tunisian policewoman.

**Democracy's Martyr.**
A refashioned monument in the city of Sidi Bouzid, Tunisia, in honor of Mohamed Bouazizi, whose portrait is visible on top of the monument. Bouazizi was a street vendor, selling fruits and vegetables. After months of harassment by the police, he set himself afire in despair. His example galvanized young, educated, and social network–savvy Tunisians into their peaceful Arab Spring revolution.

Bouazizi's death touched off the mostly peaceful democratic revolutions dubbed the "Arab Spring," on which we centered this chapter's opening vignette. Beginning in Tunisia, they snowballed into Egypt, Libya, Bahrain, Yemen, and Syria in the course of early 2011. In Tunisia and Egypt they ousted longtime and aging autocrats, Tunisia's Zine El Abidine Ben Ali (r. 1987–2011) and Egypt's Hosni Mubarak (r. 1981–2011). After months of fighting, Libya's Muammar el-Qaddafi (r. 1969–2011) was finally toppled in September 2011 and killed a month later. Autocratic rulers in countries seeing similar protests held on with iron nerves and unrestrained brutality. Central to the nonviolent daily rallies in Tunisia and Egypt, continuing for days and weeks, were demands for freedom, equality, fair elections, the end of corruption (especially crony capitalism), new democratic constitutions, the rule of law, and, last but not least, jobs.

The demonstrators, for the most part young, Internet-savvy, educated, and fully conversant with international youth culture, documented the events through pictures, videos, and blogs and revealed police violence for the world to instantly see. Social connectedness and the direct transmission of facts on the ground gave these constitutional revolutions a new character. Now a world public watching these events could declare solidarity with the demonstrators and demand action from its own politicians. As these democratic revolutions were beginning to be implemented, however, they raised the question of how closely the young demonstrators were integrated into the rest of the population, such as Islamists, as well as the urban and rural traditional Muslims. Would they be able to relate to the population at large with their demonstrations?

"When we took part in the protests it was just a protest for our basic human rights, but they [the regime] escalated it to a revolution . . . They empowered us through their violence; they made us hold onto the dream of freedom even more."

—Egyptian filmmaker Salma El Tarzi, 2011

Unfortunately, the Arab Spring activists were too diverse in their interests to be able to translate their newfound power into electoral victories. In both Tunisia and Egypt, elections brought organizationally more unified Islamist parties to power, even if only by slim margins. These parties went to work immediately to Islamize Tunisia and Egypt, even though they had not participated much in the Arab Spring demonstrations. Renewed mass demonstrations in 2013, this time against the Islamization measures, became unmanageable, and in Egypt the military stepped in. In a coup d'état, the military ended both the tenure of President Muhammad Morsi (r. 2012–2013) and the Arab Spring. In Tunisia, the political process broke down as well in 2013, but in the absence of a large army the opponents sought to resolve the breakdown through negotiations. In Egypt, the military deepened its rule in 2014 through the adoption of a new constitution and the election of a new president, Abdel Fattah Sisi (b. 1954), even though only 38 and 46 percent of the citizens, respectively, voted. In Tunisia, by contrast, the Islamist government stepped aside in favor of a government of technocrats that is to complete work on a new constitution and hold new elections. Thus, Islamism entered a period of crisis, with further democratization slowing down.

In Syria, hopes for an Arab Spring were dashed almost immediately. The first pro-democracy protests began in mid-March, but the president, Bashar al-Assad (b. 1965), sought to suppress them with an iron fist, beginning in the end of April and continuing until early June when the protests turned into an armed rebellion. Assad was the heir of the secular Arab-socialist regime of the Baath Party in which members of the small Shiite sect of the Alawites from northwestern Syria held the key army and secret service positions. Baath bureaucrats pursued a policy of state capitalism as late as 1991 when first concessions to economic liberalization were finally granted.

Although a large majority of Sunni Arabs (64 percent of the population of 22 million), Sunni Kurds (10 percent), and Christian Arabs (9 percent) benefited from the Baath's policies of industrialization, urbanization, and education, income disparities grew during the period of economic liberalization in the 1990s and early 2000s. An uprising in 1982 by Islamists in Hama had been bloodily suppressed at the cost of some 20,000 lives and a brief "Damascus Spring" at the beginning of Assad's rule (2000–2001), during which prisoners were released and political pluralism was discussed, ended with rearrests and repression. Although Syria was led by a young president, it did not differ much from the old-men regimes of Tunisia and Egypt in early 2011.

During the summer of 2011, the Arab Spring uprising grew into a full-fledged civil war. The initially untrained rebels were increasingly joined in 2012 by hardened Sunni jihadists with battle experience from Afghanistan, Iraq, Yemen, and the Russian Caucasus. At the same time, Assad released Islamists from his own prisons to the rebels, so as to discourage the United States and Europe from arming the secular wing of the opposition, for fear of their weapons falling into the hands of the jihadists. The brutality with which Assad battled his opponents—he used chemical weapons (until stopped in 2013 by the United States) as well as indiscriminate barrel bombs, in addition to heavy artillery, airplanes, and helicopters—caused a mass exodus of refugees (over 9 million) to neighboring countries. Until the end of 2013 Assad was on the defensive, but thanks to unwavering support from Russia and Iran, as well as soldiers from Iran and the Lebanese Hezbollah, he regained the initiative. Even though he gave up large swaths of land in the north and northeast he made major gains in the populated corridor between Damascus and Aleppo.

In the northeast, Assad discreetly gave some of the most radical jihadists free rein, even though this meant allowing them to control Syria's oil wells in the region. The organization "Islamic State in Iraq and al-Sham [historical Syria]" or ISIS took advantage of Assad's ploy in 2013. Aiming not merely at terrorism but the reconstruction of the seventh-century caliphate allegedly based on the pristine Islam of the Quran and Sunna, ISIS developed its own forms of brutality which alienated it from the other anti-Assad jihadist groups in northern Syria. Led by the former Iraqi al-Qaeda operative Abu Bakr al-Baghdadi (b. 1971), a man from Samarra with a religious education, ISIS built a state in northeastern Syria based on draconic Islamic laws, steep taxes on non-Muslims, as well as money from hostages, bank heists, and oil.

In early 2014, well-paid and highly disciplined ISIS units crossed into Iraq and occupied parts of the cities of Falluja and Ramadi. In the middle of the year they followed up with a lightning campaign that netted them central Iraq, with the city of Mosul as the major prize. The troops of the largely impotent Iraqi government fled with hardly a shot fired. The result of this unexpected turn of events was not only the de facto division of Iraq into a triad of Kurdish, Sunni, and Shiite polities but also the utter evaporation of what were even the minimal achievements of the humanly and financially expensive US war in Iraq during 2003–2011.

**Driving Toward Prosperity.** The Bajaj scooter was the early status symbol of the emerging Indian middle class. On account of their size, the Indian and Chinese middle classes, numbering perhaps in the hundreds of millions, are powerful groups, representing a huge reservoir of ever-more-demanding consumers. This picture is from 2010, when the Indian middle class had come of age.

**The New Middle Class in India**    The rise of a conservative Islamic middle class in Turkey and other Middle Eastern countries had its parallel in India in the rise of a religiously conservative Hindu middle class of shopkeepers, traders, merchants, and small manufacturers. The new Indian middle class—defined by a cell phone, motorized transportation, and a color TV—includes anywhere between 60 and 300 million Indians, in a population of 1.2 billion in 2010. During the 1990s and early 2000s, the secular Congress Party enjoyed the trust of the new middle class. But an economic slowdown in 2013 and the perception of bureaucratic immobility, cronyism, and corruption returned the religiously oriented Bharatiya Janata Party to power in the 2014 elections.

The most dynamic members of the new middle class live and work in the southern heavy industry and high-tech hub of Bangalore. Because the city is 12.5 hours ahead of California, it is perfect for effecting linkages to maintain around-the-clock computing with Silicon Valley. By the second decade of the 2000s, these two leading world centers of information technology on opposite sides of the globe had become closely integrated.

The rapid expansion of urban centers such as Bangalore greatly contributed to the decline of the traditional caste divisions in Hinduism within the urban and even, to some degree, rural contexts. Widespread protests in 2006 against the complex affirmative action system introduced in the 1990s in favor of less-privileged social groups indicated the beginning of a dissolution of the caste divisions in the urban environment. Since descent could be hidden in the cities, even the untouchable caste (*dalit*) began to enter the new middle class.

The success of the middle class in India, impressive as it is, must be measured against conditions in the countryside, much of which is still largely outside the market economy. Almost three-quarters of the population lived in villages with poor or no water, electricity, and roads at the beginning of the twenty-first century. An overwhelming majority of villagers lived in extreme poverty (less than $1.25 per day), existing completely outside the market circuit and depending on handouts. This majority declined in the first decade of the 2000s, perhaps by one-quarter, helped by a sinking birth rate that stood at 2 percent in 2013. A major factor in the persistence of poverty was an incomplete land reform. Landlordism and tenancy continued to encompass nearly half of the rural population. Large landholdings had been abolished after independence, but medium and small landlordism persisted undiminished. As a major voting bloc in the Congress Party, the landlords were successful in resisting further land reform.

African Transformations    The half-decade between the oil price slump, debt crisis, and disappearance of communism (1985–1991) was as challenging for sub-Saharan Africa as it was for India. The continent's GDP in the early 1990s was down by almost half from what it was in 1975 when all main social and economic indicators were at their peak. The decline of living conditions was particularly devastating in the health services sector, cut back by half in almost all countries, in spite of a steady increase in HIV/AIDS. Many countries expended more hard currency on their debt services than on education. With a doubling of the population at the absolute poverty level ($1.25 per day), sub-Saharan Africa became by far the poorest region in the world.

During this time, the urban population of sub-Saharan Africa increased to almost one-third of the total population, making it more numerous than that of India but still smaller than that of China, where nearly half of the population was urban. The urbanization process was an important factor for the political consequences of the crisis: Students, civil servants, and journalists became restless and demanded political reforms. Up until the early 1990s, almost everywhere state structures were patronage hierarchies: The civilian or military rulers in power provided cushy government jobs for the ethnic groups from which they hailed. Although all 61 African countries were officially "nations" with seats in the United Nations, none (except South Africa) was either a functionally constitutional or ethnically uniform nation. Urban dwellers, however, were less tied to ethnicity and more committed to constitutionalism. They felt little sympathy for autocratic rulers and their kin running the states into financial ruin and pushed for democratic reforms in the late 1990s and early 2000s.

Unfortunately, the push for reforms had mixed results. On the one hand, while a majority of rulers in power prior to 1991 had exited office as a result of coups or assassinations, after 1991 they either resigned voluntarily or stepped down after losing elections. On the other hand, incumbents still won more often than not, and honest elections were rare. Some regime changes were truly thrilling, notably the end of apartheid and the election of Nelson Mandela (1918–2013, president 1994–1999) in the Republic of South Africa; three cycles (2004–2012) of clean multiparty elections in Ghana; the first election of a female African president, the Harvard-trained economist Ellen Johnson Sirleaf (b. 1938, elected 2006 and

# Patterns Up Close | Social Networking

As we have seen, the Tunisian revolution sparked a wave of revolts across North Africa and the Middle East in what has come to be called the Arab Spring. What makes these movements unique, however, is that they were organized and carried out by means of *social networking sites* (SNSs) like Twitter, Facebook, and YouTube, supported by cell phones and other modern communication technologies. But what are the origins of these devices, and how have they developed into such important tools of political and social revolution?

SNSs can ultimately be traced back to the origins of the Internet and the World Wide Web. The Internet is a product of the Cold War. In 1969 the US government initiated the Advanced Research Projects Agency (ARPA), which created a system linking computers at major universities into a network that allowed them to share vital information. From this small step the Internet expanded during the 1990s into a global computer network. The World Wide Web was conceived in 1989 and launched two years later as a part of the Internet. Simply put, the "web" uses the Internet to gain access to categories of data, documents, and other resources found within the larger network.

**The Face of Revolution.** Perhaps the most novel aspect of the ongoing "Arab Spring" has been the widespread use of social media in recruiting; organizing, and popularizing the efforts of activists in various countries. The inventiveness of the participants in avoiding government scrutiny and bypassing restrictions on SNSs has become legendary. Here a Syrian man logs into his Facebook account "legally" for perhaps the first time in February, 2011.

reelected 2011) in Liberia; and the relatively clean Nigerian presidential elections of 2007 and 2011.

Setbacks in 2012 and 2013, however, with coups d'état and armed revolts in Guinea Bissau, Mali, the Central African Republic, and South Sudan, were stark reminders that African democratization is still fragile. For a short period, Mali even split apart into a rump republic in the populated south and an Islamist state in the north (2012–2013). It was eventually reunited only after an armed intervention by France.

Islamism was also a factor in bloody conflicts engulfing the Central African Republic and northern Nigeria. In the Central African Republic, a rebellion by leaders from the Muslim minority in the north led to a ferocious backlash from the Christian majority in the south, requiring the intervention of a European Union peace contingent to establish a tenuous truce in 2014. In Northern Nigeria, the

SNSs sprang up in the 1990s when it was recognized that the Internet provided social groups the means to easily communicate with each other and to share information. By the 2000s, social networking sites represented a global explosion of instantaneously distributed information that revolutionized the nature of communication.

An early example of the power of SNSs to effect change was the so-called Twitter Revolution in Iran in 2009, during which antigovernment activists used the full range of SNSs while engaged in an ultimately futile effort to overthrow the Iranian regime. Following the success of the Tunisian revolution, however, an even more spectacular display of the power of SNSs erupted in Egypt on January 25, 2011, when thousands of protesters took to the streets to demand the ouster of the authoritarian president Hosni Mubarak. This "Facebook Revolution," was launched by the April 6 Youth Movement, a Facebook group composed of social and political activists.

For all their success in facilitating uprisings against authoritarian governments, however, SNSs are used with equal effectiveness by extremist terrorist groups. Al-Qaeda and the Taliban have learned to take advantage of Facebook and Twitter to broadcast their calls for global *jihad*. SNSs are also used to solicit financial support and share information concerning plans for forthcoming attacks. Moreover, SNSs—particularly Facebook—serve as effective recruitment tools. How ironic that Internet websites originally intended for exchanges among friends have been transformed into tools to spread revolution, violence, and terrorism.

## Questions

- How do SNSs show how an innovation can be adapted for purposes wholly different from the original purposes for which they were intended?

- Do you believe SNSs have allowed young people around the world to make their wishes and aspirations more powerfully felt? If so, what does this say about the connection between technology and youth?

---

government proved to be completely incompetent against the rapidly expanding Islamist movement Boko Haram ("Western education is sin"). Founded in 2002, this jihadist organization intent on introducing Sharia law staged increasingly daring raids, beginning in 2009 and culminating in 2014 with the abduction of over 300 Christian schoolgirls. African as well as foreign observers note the rise in sectarian conflicts on the continent with growing concern.

The African economy picked up in the early 2000s, mostly because of rising commodity prices. The main oil exporters (Nigeria, Angola, Chad, Sudan, Gabon, Cameroon, Equatorial New Guinea, and the two Republics of the Congo) benefited from higher oil prices, as did the mining countries of South Africa, Zambia, both Congos, and Malawi with their diamonds, gold, copper, silver, zinc, lead, and other rare metals. In a United Nations–sponsored scheme in 1998, "blood diamonds" mined to finance civil wars, as in Angola, Sierra Leone, Liberia, Ivory

**Freedom, Justice, and Dignity.** The end of apartheid in 1994 and the election of Nelson Mandela (1918–2013), seen here visiting his former prison cell, was an inspiring event in Africa and the rest of the world. South Africa is the richest and most industrialized country of Africa, with large mineral and agricultural resources. Nearly 80 percent of the population is black, speaking its own languages, including isiZulu and isiXhosa. But Afrikaans (a Dutch-originated language) remained the dominant media language, with English being only the fifth most spoken language. In spite of South Africa's relative wealth, years of apartheid have resulted in vast income disparities.

Coast, and both Congos, were subjected to certification so as to prevent future wars. (Diamonds mined in Zimbabwe were exempted, since Zimbabwe's disintegration into a failed state was not considered to be the effect of a civil war.) Apart from minerals, agricultural products, such as coffee, cotton, and fresh flowers for the European market, also regained significance in the early 2000s. The global recessions of 2001 and 2008 did not have a major impact, largely because of the arrival of China on the scene as a major buyer and investor. Optimism about a sustained recovery and modernity within reach was clearly visible on the continent, even if tempered by continuing ethnic and sectarian conflicts.

**Latin American Expansion**   Elections after the scare of the financial meltdowns in the freewheeling 1990s produced more fiscally restrained, socially engaged governments in the large Latin American countries during the early 2000s. Democratic transitions in Mexico, Brazil, Argentina, and Chile (the latter three with socially oriented governments) demonstrated that the unhappy years of military dictatorships in the 1980s had been left behind. In Mexico the long rule of the Institutional Revolutionary Party (PRI) was interrupted from 2000 to 2012, with an orderly transition to less socially engaged Christian Democratic presidents. Only in 2012 did a markedly rejuvenated PRI return to power. It continued the pattern of economic liberalization begun at the beginning of the century.

Two extraconstitutional events in smaller Latin American countries, however, demonstrated that authoritarian temptations still survived. The first was an abortive uprising in 2002 of army units in Paraguay, allegedly instigated by a former commander outside the country who was wanted for an earlier coup attempt. The second, in Honduras in 2009, was the forcible removal of the president, who intended to hold a referendum on his plan for reelection, even though it had been forbidden by the Honduran constitutional court. More disruptive were continued efforts by revolutionary Marxists in Colombia to overthrow the government, even though their liberation movement, founded in 1964, declined in the early 2000s. In neighboring Venezuela, President Hugo Chávez (1954–2013), a former officer from a working-class background, was alone in mainland Latin America in his adherence to state socialism, encountering periodic middle-class resistance.

Industrialization, largely through foreign investments but increasingly also through internal financing, stimulated state-run firms to become competitive and even to privatize in several large Latin American countries. In some cases, as with Brazilian Embraer commercial airplanes or the electronics and information technology industry of Guadalajara in Mexico, Latin American countries have become world competitors. All four large economies—Brazil, Mexico, Argentina, and Chile—exported more manufactured goods than commodities by 2008. These countries clearly displayed the features of scientific–industrial modernity by the second decade of the 2000s.

# The Environmental Limits of Modernity

What we have defined in the last two parts of this book as *modernity*—the political systems marked by constitutional and ethnic nationalism, as well as the economic systems propelled by science and industrialism—has now become not simply a regional or "Western" phenomenon but a global one. In the absence of the competing subpatterns of modernity—communism and supremacist nationalism—the systems of capitalism, consumerism, and democracy embodied by the United States, Canada, western Europe, and Australia have increasingly become the ones to emulate. All new nations in the world either are industrializing or seeking to do so if they have the financial means. The principal obstacle for these nations is the debilitating poverty of the great majority of their inhabitants, who are still mired in either subsistence farming or marginal work in the shantytowns of sprawling cities. The poorest are unskilled and uneducated and, because of high infant mortality rates and the need for farm labor and old-age support, still view large families as a necessity. Improved public health care is helping to raise life spans for the poorest people, but the combination of modern medicine and the desire for large families has caused a startling increase in the world population since the middle of the twentieth century.

**Sustainability and Global Warming**   In 1800, there was only one country (Great Britain) embarking on industrialization; by 1918, there were about a dozen countries (Europe and Japan), and by 1945 about three dozen countries (on three continents) had industrialized themselves. Today, about two-thirds of the 194 independent countries of the world are either industrialized or on the way toward full industrialization. We are only now, however, beginning to grasp the environmental consequences of this move to scientific–industrial modernity. Until about the last quarter of the twentieth century the carbon footprint of these countries had risen from 280 parts per million (ppm) of atmospheric carbon dioxide and

**A Smoggy Future.** China, the world's worst emitter of greenhouse gases, has large numbers of coal-fed power plants and factories which continue to belch out carbon dioxide as well as toxic substances into the air, with little scrubbing or other devices to clean the emissions before they reach the atmosphere. Here, a power plant on the outskirts of Linfen in Shanxi Province southwest of Beijing fouls the environment in 2009.

other chemical compounds—commonly called "greenhouse gases"—to 330 ppm. Between 1975 and 2010 the concentration of greenhouse gases in the atmosphere climbed to 380 ppm. In other words, a rise of 50 ppm in 175 years was followed by a rise of 70 ppm in only 35 years.

While there has been considerable debate over the last several decades on the nature and degree of global warming—whether it is a natural cyclical phenomenon or human-produced or even if it exists at all—there is a general scientific consensus that greenhouse gases are the main contributors to temperature increases on earth. Scientists generally assume that at current rates of greenhouse gas production the earth will reach a "tipping point" of 450 ppm, with irreversible consequences for the planet's climate, before the middle of this century.

What will happen when this tipping point is reached? If projections hold true, the polar ice caps and high mountain glaciers will melt. Ocean levels, rising from the melted ice, will submerge many islands and make inroads on the coasts of all continents. Widespread droughts and violent storms will regularly hit various parts of the earth, eroding by wind and flood what in many places had previously been fertile land. The world's tropical forests, already considerably reduced from timber harvesting and agricultural expansion, may well be wiped out, removing the most important agents for cleaning the atmosphere of greenhouse gases. Pollution and overfishing will leave little of the world's marine life. Biodiversity will be dramatically reduced, with many animal and plant species dying out. The consequence of these grim developments will likely be a severe reduction of the earth's arable land and fisheries needed for the production of food.

The ultimate outcome of this prospective climate transformation will be much worse for the new countries with less wealth to cushion them than for the older ones that industrialized early and have the resources to adjust. The crushing irony of such projections, therefore, is that the nations that viewed their adaptation to modernity as their salvation may well find themselves among the first to be doomed.

**Scientific and Political Debate**    There is a consensus among scientists that the warming trend in the world from greenhouse gases is real. Very few scientists still hold a skeptical view. The general public is gradually coming around to taking global warming seriously, though less so in the United States than in Europe. But vocal minorities still vociferously denounce climate warming as a hoax or conspiracy. So far, political responses have been tepid and largely divided.

By 2013, a total of nine UN conferences had been convened since the 1997 Kyoto Protocol that established benchmarks for the reduction of greenhouse gases in the European Union and 38 industrialized countries. But only the European Union was on track to meet its provision, mandating an annual reduction of 5.2 percent. The remaining countries were substantially off the mark. The 2013 Warsaw conference saw bitter conflicts over the inclusion of newly industrialized countries into the Kyoto Protocol and financial compensation demanded by

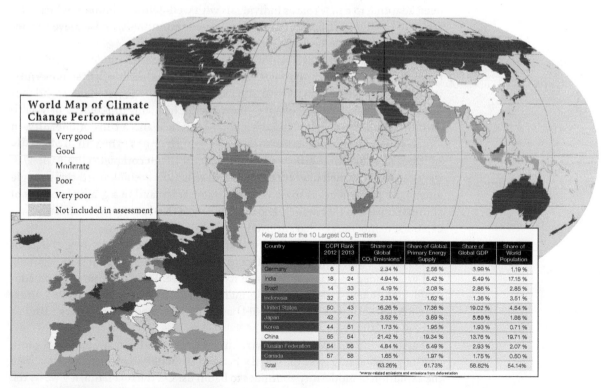

**World Map of Climate Change Performance**

- Very good
- Good
- Moderate
- Poor
- Very poor
- Not included in assessment

| Country | CCPI Rank 2012 | CCPI Rank 2013 | Share of Global $CO_2$ Emissions* | Share of Global Primary Energy Supply | Share of Global GDP | Share of World Population |
|---|---|---|---|---|---|---|
| Germany | 6 | 8 | 2.34 % | 2.56 % | 3.99 % | 1.19 % |
| India | 18 | 24 | 4.94 % | 5.42 % | 5.49 % | 17.15 % |
| Brazil | 14 | 33 | 4.19 % | 2.08 % | 2.86 % | 2.85 % |
| Indonesia | 32 | 36 | 2.33 % | 1.62 % | 1.36 % | 3.51 % |
| United States | 50 | 43 | 16.26 % | 17.36 % | 19.02 % | 4.54 % |
| Japan | 42 | 47 | 3.52 % | 3.89 % | 5.59 % | 1.86 % |
| Korea | 44 | 51 | 1.73 % | 1.95 % | 1.93 % | 0.71 % |
| China | 55 | 54 | 21.42 % | 19.34 % | 13.76 % | 19.71 % |
| Russian Federation | 54 | 56 | 4.84 % | 5.49 % | 2.93 % | 2.07 % |
| Canada | 57 | 58 | 1.65 % | 1.97 % | 1.75 % | 0.50 % |
| Total | | | 63.26% | 61.73% | 58.82% | 54.14% |

*energy-related emissions and emissions from deforestation

MAP 31.4  **World Map of Climate Change Performance.**

developing countries for damages suffered from extreme weather. As agreed upon in Warsaw, governments are now supposed to formulate new targets for greenhouse gas emission curbs by 2015—curbs to begin in 2020.

At present, the consensus is that if the European 5.2 percent reduction rate were to continue after 2013 and everyone would sign on to this rate, the eventual decline in temperature by the middle of the twenty-first century would be 0.2 degree Fahrenheit below the current average temperature. Whether this would be sufficient to reverse the melting of polar ice and the onset of irregular weather patterns is debatable. But if present trends with minimal or no reductions continue, the projected temperature increase in 2050 will be more likely in the range of 3–4 degrees Fahrenheit—enough for the projections to indicate the catastrophic consequences we have mentioned, which are widely agreed to be irreversible.

> "Go back in your life to think about the hottest, most traumatic event you have experienced. What we're saying is that very soon [between 2047 and 2069], that event is going to become the norm."
>
> —Biogeographer Camilo Mora

## Putting It All Together

The first decade of the twenty-first century witnessed the final transformation of the world from a millennia-old agrarian–urban pattern of life to a new scientific–industrial pattern. All of this was accomplished in the breathtakingly short span of 200 years. What had begun as a culturally specific, western European–pioneered transition, first from descriptive to mathematical science and then from agriculture to industry, had become ubiquitous. Everywhere in the world people have been adapting to a new role as individuals with well-defined "human rights," who aspire to be educated, find fulfilling jobs, become consumers, and achieve a materially secure life—in short, they are becoming *modern*.

The twentieth century also saw the original pattern of modernity split into three. World War I was a cataclysm that produced proponents of a first modernity, who sought to create competitive, capitalist, democratic societies; a second modernity, which sought to collapse power hierarchies and differences of wealth through equality in socialist–communist societies; and a third modernity, in which supremacist-nationalist societies sought to impose the will of allegedly superior races or ethnic groups through conquest (if not complete elimination) of inferior ones. Tremendous suffering and destruction accompanied the struggle among the proponents of these visions of modernity, and in a gradual process of elimination, it was the messiest and most unruly of the three forms of modernity—capitalist democracy—that survived.

Today, the faith in democracy that marked the exuberant beginnings of modernity at the end of the eighteenth century appears to be just as vigorous and unbounded in places far outside its birthplace. People—young, poor, educated, ambitious—continue to be its martyrs (Tiananmen Square, 1989; Tehran, 2009; Arab Spring, 2011; Kiev, 2014) as well as its proud flag bearers (Tunisia and Egypt, 2011).

Faith in the future of the environment at this point is a good deal more cautious, however. Here, the devil's bargain of materialism that accompanied the evolution of modernity continues to haunt us: On the one hand, it gave us the human right to a decent existence in material security; on the other hand, the means of achieving that security through exploitation of the earth's material resources has given us the nightmare prospect of an irreversibly changed nature that may allow for fewer and fewer of the comforts we currently enjoy. The pattern of modernity and the scientific–industrial society that supports it will no doubt continue, but its future shape will be just as unknowable to us as the patterns of society in the past were to those living through them.

▶ For additional resources, including maps, primary sources, visuals, and quizzes, please go to www.oup.com/us/vonsivers. Please see the Further Resources section at the back of the book for additional readings and suggested websites.

## Against the Grain

# North Korea: Lone Holdout against the World

In the second decade of the 2000s, North Korea was the laggard among the few countries that remained committed to socialism, such as China, Vietnam, and Cuba. While these latter countries enacted ambitious economic reforms since 1991, North Korea dragged its feet. Although it formally abandoned the ideologies of Marxism-Leninism and communism in its constitutions of 1972 and 2009, respectively, as unfulfillable, it retained its commitment to socialism, self-sufficiency, isolation, and militarism. The disappearance of all-important aid from the Soviet Bloc in 1991 plunged North Korea into hunger and starvation from which it barely reemerged after 2002.

The disappearance of Soviet Bloc aid, in combination with bad weather and several harvest failures during the 1990s, led to mass starvation on a scale similar to famines earlier in the century in the Soviet Union and China. It is estimated that hundreds of thousands died in this nation of 24.5 million inhabitants. Chinese, South Korean, and international food aid brought only minimal relief. Thereafter, massive malnourishment remained, accompanied by associated diseases. Reportedly, children were stunted in their growth by 1–3 inches in comparison to their South Korean counterparts. Adults had to subsist on 700 calories daily, as compared to 2,000–2,500 calories among Europeans. The constitutional principle of food self-sufficiency was a cruel joke.

In 2002 the regime enacted the first small steps of economic reform, recognizing the existence of the informal sector of private garden plots, mechanical workshops, and neighborhood markets. An economic free zone with South Korean factories was established near the border, and some foreign investment was allowed. Collective farmers were entitled to their own produce, in return for a steep 15 percent "rent" on their state-owned lands. After Kim Jong-un's succession to his father's position of supreme leader in 2013, reforms accelerated and North Korean businesses began to export cheap consumer products.

But sanctions imposed after the country's three nuclear tests in 2006 significantly slowed its small arms and missile exports to developing countries, which had provided revenue for keeping the regime in power and feed its outsized military program. With the country ranking lowest in the democracy index, around no. 70 in the poverty index (according to GDP), and no. 29 in military expenditures among the 194 nations in the world, North Korea is the most extreme example of a nation going against the grain of the twenty-first century.

- **Which factors explain the spectacular agricultural collapse in North Korea during the 1990s?**

- **Why is North Korea so steadfastly devoted to its military program? Why is this military program so worrisome for the world?**

# Thinking Through Patterns

▶ **How did the United States demonstrate its dominant economic position toward the end of the twentieth century? How did it accelerate the pattern of globalization?**

The United States demonstrated its dominant economic position through the dollar regime and by becoming the sinkhole for industrial exports from developing countries. In compensation for the latter, it expanded the reach of its financial system worldwide. The result was the globalization of the world economy.

Capitalist democracy became the universal model of modernity in part because growing middle classes in cities demanded liberalized markets where they could develop personal initiative and accumulate capital for business ventures. Socially conservative new middle classes became the engines that powered more than half a dozen successful industrialization processes throughout Asia, Latin America, and Africa.

▶ **What made capitalist democracy so attractive toward the end of the twentieth century that it became a generic model for many countries around the world to strive for?**

▶ **Which policies did China and India pursue so that they became the fastest industrializing countries in the early twenty-first century?**

China and India accelerated their industrialization by systematically encouraging the expansion of their middle classes as the engines of investment and innovation. China, however, did not allow the development of a multiparty system, fearing the chaos of popular agitation. India, by contrast, possessed constitutional-nationalist traditions reaching back to the nineteenth century that included constraints against populism and allowed for peaceful democratic competition.

Perhaps more than any other innovation in the last 20 years, or even the last 200 years, the communications revolution has reshaped the way humans interact with each other. The exponential growth of networking boggles the mind. In 2006, 50 billion e-mails were sent. Just 4 years later, that number had risen to 300 billion. Because of this connectedness, politics, culture, and economic activity now mutate more rapidly—and with more volatility—than ever before.

▶ **How have information technology and social networking altered cultural, political, and economic interactions around the world?**

▶ **What is global warming, and why is it a source of grave concern for the future?**

Global warming is caused by carbon dioxide and other gases that accumulate in the upper atmosphere and trap the sun's heat in the lower atmosphere. Warming and cooling trends have occurred periodically since the end of the last ice age, and for a long time scientists labored to distinguish clearly between a temporary trend toward warmer temperatures and a permanent, greenhouse gas–caused trend toward a decisive tipping point that will permanently alter nature as we know it. Today, there is an overwhelming scientific consensus concerning the reality of global warming. But politicians and the general public are not yet entirely convinced that the efforts begun with the Kyoto Protocol of 2005 should be intensified.

# Patterns of Evidence: Sources for Chapter 31

## SOURCE 31.1

## Osama bin Laden, "Declaration of War against the Americans Occupying the Land of the Two Holy Places"

**August 23, 1996**

In 1992, al-Qaeda ("the base") under the leadership of Osama bin Laden (1957–2011) had emerged as a significant terrorist organization operating on an international scale. Bin Laden, the multimillionaire son of a Yemeni-born Saudi Arabian contractor, had fought the Soviet occupation of Afghanistan (1979–1989). He now turned his attention to the United States (who had covertly funded the "mujahid" Afghan resistance in the interest of its own Cold War ambitions). In bin Laden's eyes, America was a godless country without moral principles, bent on a Western crusade to destroy Muslim independence. The al-Qaeda campaign of terrorism climaxed on September 11, 2001, but bin Laden had already ordered bombings and terrorist attacks in several parts of the world in the 1990s. This fatwa (an opinion or ruling based on Islamic law) was issued by bin Laden against the "Zionist-Crusader alliance" in 1996.

It should not be hidden from you that the people of Islam had suffered from aggression, iniquity and injustice imposed on them by the Zionist-Crusaders alliance and their collaborators; to the extent that the Muslims' blood became the cheapest and their wealth as loot in the hands of the enemies. Their blood was spilled in Palestine and Iraq. The horrifying pictures of the massacre of Qana, in Lebanon are still fresh in our memory. Massacres in Tajikistan, Burma, Kashmir, Assam, the Philippines, Fatani, Ogaden, Somalia, Eritrea, Chechnya and in Bosnia-Herzegovina took place, massacres that send shivers in the body and shake the conscience. All of this and the world watch and hear, and not only didn't respond to these atrocities, but also with a clear conspiracy between the USA and its allies and under the cover of the iniquitous United Nations, the dispossessed people were even prevented from obtaining arms to defend themselves.

Source: http://www.pbs.org/newshour/updates/military-july-dec96-fatwa_1996/

The people of Islam awakened and realised that they are the main target for the aggression of the Zionist-Crusaders alliance. All false claims and propaganda about "Human Rights" were hammered down and exposed by the massacres that took place against the Muslims in every part of the world.

. . .

Utmost effort should be made to prepare and instigate the Ummah against the enemy, the American-Israeli alliance—occupying the country of the two Holy Places [Saudi Arabia] and the route of the Apostle (Allah's Blessings and Salutations may be on him) to the Furthest Mosque (Al-Aqsa Mosque). Also to remind the Muslims not to be engaged in an internal war among themselves, as that will have grieve consequences namely:

1-consumption of the Muslims' human resources as most casualties and fatalities will be among the Muslim people.

2-Exhaustion of the economic and financial resources.

3-Destruction of the country infrastructures

4-Dissociation of the society

5-Destruction of the oil industries. The presence of the USA Crusader military forces on land, sea and air of the states of the Islamic Gulf is the greatest danger threatening the largest oil reserve in the world. The existence of these forces in the area will provoke the people of the country and induces aggression on their religion, feelings and pride and push them to take up armed struggle against the invaders occupying the land; therefore spread of the fighting in the region will expose the oil wealth to the danger of being burned up. The economic interests of the States of the Gulf and the land of the two Holy Places will be damaged and even greater damage will be caused to the economy of the world. I would like here to alert my brothers, the Mujahideen, the sons of the nation, to protect this (oil) wealth and not to include it in the battle as it is a great Islamic wealth and a large economic power essential for the soon to be established Islamic state, by Allah's Permission and Grace. We also warn the aggressors, the USA, against burning this Islamic wealth (a crime which they may commit in order to prevent it, at the end of the war, from falling in the hands of its legitimate owners and to cause economic damages to the competitors of the USA in Europe or the Far East, particularly Japan which is the major consumer of the oil of the region).

6-Division of the land of the two Holy Places, and annexing of the northerly part of it by Israel. Dividing the land of the two Holy Places is an essential demand of the Zionist-Crusader alliance. The existence of such a large country with its huge resources under the leadership of the forthcoming Islamic State, by Allah's Grace, represent a serious danger to the very existence of the Zionist state in Palestine. The Nobel Ka'ba,—the Qiblah of all Muslims—makes the land of the two Holy Places a symbol for the unity of the Islamic world. Moreover, the presence of the world largest oil reserve makes the land of the two Holy Places an important economical power in the Islamic world. The sons of the two Holy Places are directly related to the life style (Seerah) of their forefathers, the companions, may Allah be pleased with them. They consider the Seerah of their forefathers as a source and an example for re-establishing the

**Kufr**: Unbelief.

greatness of this Ummah and to raise the word of Allah again. Furthermore the presence of a population of fighters in the south of Yemen, fighting in the cause of Allah, is a strategic threat to the Zionist-Crusader alliance in the area. The Prophet (ALLAH'S BLESSING AND SALUTATIONS ON HIM) said: (around twelve thousands will emerge from Aden/Abian helping—the cause of—Allah and His messenger, they are the best, in the time, between me and them) narrated by Ahmad with a correct trustworthy reference.

7-An internal war is a great mistake, no matter what reasons there are for it. The presence of the occupier—the USA—forces will control the outcome of the battle for the benefit of the international **Kufr**.

. . .

Our Lord, guide this Ummah, and make the right conditions (by which) the people of your obedience will be in dignity and the people of disobedience in humiliation, and by which the good deeds are enjoined and the bad deeds are forebode.

Our Lord, bless Muhammad, Your slave and messenger, his family and descendants, and companions and salute him with a (becoming) salutation.

And our last supplication is: All praise is due to Allah.

▶ **Working with Sources**

1. How did bin Laden conflate oil interests with the goals of religious regeneration?

2. How and why did he address the Israeli–Palestinian conflict in this document?

## SOURCE 31.2

# Vladimir Putin, Address to the Duma concerning the annexation of Crimea

### March 19, 2014

Vladimir Putin, the former KGB officer who has dominated Russian political life since 2000, delivered this remarkable oration after annexing the Crimea region from the nation of Ukraine in March 2014. This move came after a protest movement had driven the pro-Russian president of Ukraine out of office, and as tensions between ethnic Ukrainians and ethnic Russians in the country had erupted into violence in several Ukrainian cities. Once a referendum was held in the Crimean Peninsula about whether to remain within Ukraine or to be united to Russia, Putin, believing that "the

Source: http://rt.com/politics/official-word/vladimir-putin-crimea-address-658/

numbers speak for themselves," authorized the annexation of the region as Russian territory. In this speech, justifying his country's move against a fellow former Soviet Socialist Republic, Putin appealed to both recent and distant history—and, perhaps, signaled his further intentions for the future.

Dear friends, we have gathered here today in connection with an issue that is of vital, historic significance to all of us. A referendum was held in Crimea on March 16 in full compliance with democratic procedures and international norms.

More than 82 percent of the electorate took part in the vote. Over 96 percent of them spoke out in favour of reuniting with Russia. These numbers speak for themselves.

To understand the reason behind such a choice it is enough to know the history of Crimea and what Russia and Crimea have always meant for each other.

Everything in Crimea speaks of our shared history and pride. This is the location of ancient Khersones, where Prince Vladimir was baptised. His spiritual feat of adopting Orthodoxy predetermined the overall basis of the culture, civilisation and human values that unite the peoples of Russia, Ukraine and Belarus. The graves of Russian soldiers whose bravery brought Crimea into the Russian empire are also in Crimea. This is also Sevastopol—a legendary city with an outstanding history, a fortress that serves as the birthplace of Russia's Black Sea Fleet. Crimea is Balaklava and Kerch, Malakhov Kurgan and Sapun Ridge. Each one of these places is dear to our hearts, symbolising Russian military glory and outstanding valour.

Crimea is a unique blend of different peoples' cultures and traditions. This makes it similar to Russia as a whole, where not a single ethnic group has been lost over the centuries. Russians and Ukrainians, Crimean Tatars and people of other ethnic groups have lived side by side in Crimea, retaining their own identity, traditions, languages and faith.

. . .

In people's hearts and minds, Crimea has always been an inseparable part of Russia. This firm conviction is based on truth and justice and was passed from generation to generation, over time, under any circumstances, despite all the dramatic changes our country went through during the entire 20th century.

After the revolution, the Bolsheviks, for a number of reasons—may God judge them—added large sections of the historical South of Russia to the Republic of Ukraine. This was done with no consideration for the ethnic make-up of the population, and today these areas form the southeast of Ukraine. Then, in 1954, a decision was made to transfer Crimean Region to Ukraine, along with Sevastopol, despite the fact that it was a city of union subordination. This was the personal initiative of the Communist Party head Nikita Khrushchev. What stood behind this decision of his— a desire to win the support of the Ukrainian political establishment or to atone for the mass repressions of the 1930's in Ukraine—is for historians to figure out.

What matters now is that this decision was made in clear violation of the constitutional norms that were in place even then. The decision was made behind the scenes. Naturally, in a totalitarian state nobody bothered to ask the citizens of Crimea and Sevastopol. They were faced with the fact. People, of course, wondered why all of a sudden Crimea became part of Ukraine. But on the whole—and we must state this clearly, we all know it—this decision was treated as a formality of sorts because the territory was transferred within the boundaries of a single state. Back then, it was impossible to imagine that Ukraine and Russia may split up and become two separate states. However, this has happened.

Unfortunately, what seemed impossible became a reality. The USSR fell apart. Things developed so swiftly that few people realised how truly dramatic those events and their consequences would be. Many people both in Russia and in Ukraine, as well as in other republics hoped that the Commonwealth of Independent States that was created at the time would become the new common form of statehood. They were told that there would be a single currency, a single economic space, joint armed forces; however, all this remained empty promises, while the big country was gone. It was only when Crimea ended up as part of a different country that Russia realised that it was not simply robbed, it was plundered.

At the same time, we have to admit that by launching the sovereignty parade Russia itself aided in the collapse of the Soviet Union. And as this collapse was legalised, everyone forgot about Crimea and Sevastopol—the main base of the Black Sea Fleet. Millions of people went to bed in one country and awoke in different ones, overnight becoming ethnic minorities in former Union republics, while the Russian nation became one of the biggest, if not the biggest ethnic group in the world to be divided by borders.

Now, many years later, I heard residents of Crimea say that back in 1991 they were handed over like a sack of potatoes. . . .

Like a mirror, the situation in Ukraine reflects what is going on and what has been happening in the world over the past several decades. After the dissolution of bipolarity on the planet, we no longer have stability. Key international institutions are not getting any stronger; on the contrary, in many cases, they are sadly degrading. Our western partners, led by the United States of America, prefer not to be guided by international law in their practical policies, but by the rule of the gun. They have come to believe in their exclusivity and exceptionalism, that they can decide the destinies of the world, that only they can ever be right. They act as they please: here and there, they use force against sovereign states, building coalitions based on the principle *"If you are not with us, you are against us."* To make this aggression look legitimate, they force the necessary resolutions from international organisations, and if for some reason this does not work, they simply ignore the UN Security Council and the UN overall.

This happened in Yugoslavia; we remember 1999 very well. It was hard to believe, even seeing it with my own eyes, that at the end of the 20th century, one of Europe's capitals, Belgrade, was under missile attack for several weeks, and then came the real intervention. Was there a UN Security Council resolution on this matter, allowing for these actions? Nothing of the sort. And then, they hit Afghanistan, Iraq, and frankly violated the UN Security Council resolution on Libya, when instead of imposing the so-called no-fly zone over it they started bombing it too.

. . .

Let me say one other thing too. Millions of Russians and Russian-speaking people live in Ukraine and will continue to do so. Russia will always defend their interests using political, diplomatic and legal means. But it should be above all in Ukraine's own interest to ensure that these people's rights and interests are fully protected. This is the guarantee of Ukraine's state stability and territorial integrity.

We want to be friends with Ukraine and we want Ukraine to be a strong, sovereign and self-sufficient country. Ukraine is one of our biggest partners after all. We have many joint projects and I believe in their success no matter what the current difficulties. Most importantly, we want peace and harmony to reign in Ukraine, and we are ready to work together with other countries to do everything possible to facilitate and support this. But as I said, only Ukraine's own people can put their own house in order.

▶ **Working with Sources**

1. In what specific ways, and for what purpose, did Putin appeal to the historical past?

2. What does he believe will be the consequences of the end of "bipolarity" in global politics—and of the belief in American "exceptionalism" demonstrated by US military action since 1999?

## SOURCE 31.3

# Mohamed Bouazizi triggers the Arab Spring, Tunisia

**January 2011**

On December 17, 2010, 26-year-old Mohamed Bouazizi set himself on fire in a spectacular act of despair that triggered the "Arab Spring," the initial results of which continue to reverberate throughout the Middle East and the wider world. His act of defiance, and the reactions to it, led to the ouster of Tunisia's dictator Zine El Abidine Ben Ali (ruled 1987–2011), and, once the revolt had spread to Egypt, of Hosni Mubarak (ruled 1981–2011).

Source: Marc Fisher, "In Tunisia, Act of One Fruit Vendor Unleashes Wave of Revolution through Arab World," *Washington Post*, March 26, 2011, available online at http://www.washingtonpost.com/world/in-tunisia-act-of-one-fruit-vendor-sparks-wave-of-revolution-through-arab-world/2011/03/16/AFjfsueB_story.html

While this article profiles Bouazizi, and the confrontation with a policewoman that led to his action, at greater length than most portraits, it also connects the street vendor with the media-savvy young leaders of the revolt in Tahrir Square that brought down Mubarak.

On the evening before Mohammed Bouazizi lit a fire that would burn across the Arab world, the young fruit vendor told his mother that the oranges, dates and apples he had to sell were the best he'd ever seen. "With this fruit," he said, "I can buy some gifts for you. Tomorrow will be a good day."

For years, Bouazizi had told his mother stories of corruption at the fruit market, where vendors gathered under a cluster of ficus trees on the main street of this scruffy town, not far from Tunisia's Mediterranean beaches. Arrogant police officers treated the market as their personal picnic grounds, taking bagfuls of fruit without so much as a nod toward payment. The cops took visible pleasure in subjecting the vendors to one indignity after another—fining them, confiscating their scales, even ordering them to carry their stolen fruit to the cops' cars.

Before dawn on Friday, Dec. 17, as Bouazizi pulled his cart along the narrow, rutted stone road toward the market, two police officers blocked his path and tried to take his fruit. Bouazizi's uncle rushed to help his 26-year-old nephew, persuading the officers to let the rugged-looking young man complete his one-mile trek.

The uncle visited the chief of police and asked him for help. The chief called in a policewoman who had stopped Bouazizi, Fedya Hamdi, and told her to let the boy work.

Hamdi, outraged by the appeal to her boss, returned to the market. She took a basket of Bouazizi's apples and put it in her car. Then she started loading a second basket. This time, according to Alladin Badri, who worked the next cart over, Bouazizi tried to block the officer.

"She pushed Mohammed and hit him with her baton," Badri said.

Hamdi reached for Bouazizi's scale, and again he tried to stop her.

Hamdi and two other officers pushed Bouazizi to the ground and grabbed the scale. Then she slapped Bouazizi in the face in front of about 50 witnesses.

Bouazizi wept with shame.

"Why are you doing this to me?" he cried, according to vendors and customers who were there. "I'm a simple person, and I just want to work."

Revolutions are explosions of frustration and rage that build over time, sometimes over decades. Although their political roots are deep, it is often a single spark that ignites them—an assassination, perhaps, or one selfless act of defiance.

. . .

Bouazizi returned to the market and told his fellow vendors he would let the world know how unfairly they were being treated, how corrupt the system was.

He would set himself ablaze.

"We thought he was just talking," said Hassan Tili, another vendor.

A short while later, the vendors heard shouts from a couple of blocks away. Without another word to anyone, Bouazizi had positioned himself in front of the municipal building, poured paint thinner over his body and lit himself aflame.

The fire burned and burned. People ran inside and grabbed a fire extinguisher, but it was empty. They called for police, but no one came. Only an hour and a half after Bouazizi lit the match did an ambulance arrive.

Manoubya Bouazizi said her son's decision "was spontaneous, from the humiliation." Her clear blue eyes welled as her husband placed at her feet a small clay pot filled with a few white-hot pieces of charcoal, their only defense against a cold, raw, rain-swept day. The Bouazizi family has no money, no car, no electricity, but it was not poverty that made her son sacrifice himself, she said. It was his quest for dignity.

. . .

In the days after the revolution in Tunisia, Egypt's state security agents were on high alert. They knew whom to watch. They'd been onto Ahmed Maher for a long time. They'd tapped his phones, recruited informants among his friends, plugged into his e-mail. They knew he was planning something far bigger than the marches of a few dozen people he'd organized in recent years.

But Maher, 30, was smarter this time. He stayed off e-mail and his cellphone so the authorities couldn't track him. And he worked through Facebook, a phenomenon that seemed to mystify the secret police. (The last time they took him into custody, they asked Maher questions about people who had commented on his Facebook page, apparently thinking he must know every random person who had left a posting.)

In the past, Maher, a soft-spoken civil engineer who looks as if he'd be more at home in a design studio than a demonstration, had spent much of his energy persuading Egyptians that they could speak out against Hosni Mubarak without sacrificing their careers. This time, he had Tunisia on his side.

"Everybody said, 'How come we're not like them?'" Maher said. "We'd just been waiting for something to trigger us."

The contagion of revolution has a way of wiping away differences that usually divide people. History has provided evidence of the phenomenon again and again, in years that became shorthand for waves of change—1848, 1989, and now, in the Arab world, 2011. In each case, corrupt regimes fell to people who suddenly felt free to push back. Stifling job markets, near-absolute political power and a frustrated middle class combined to create a perfect storm in which formerly divided classes joined to rise up against their rulers.

In many revolutions, the tools of oppression seem to crumble in an instant. But no one can be sure in the moment. In Egypt, the security service had foiled Maher before. Back in 2008, they'd read his blog every day as he planned a general strike to protest Mubarak's regime.

On the morning of the strike, "the security apparatus arrested everyone I knew," Maher said, erasing the protest before it could start. The authorities caught up with Maher one morning soon thereafter. Unmarked cars surrounded him. Agents blindfolded Maher, tied his hands and beat him with fists and batons.

"You think you can hide from us?" an agent said. "We can make you disappear."

Before they let him go two days later, Maher had suffered electric shock and beatings—and then the agents pivoted. "You can be head of a small political party," a "good cop" promised. "We can be friends."

Maher instead announced his ordeal to the world. He resumed blogging, writing about educated Egyptians who couldn't get work because they lacked connections, about censorship, about corruption such as that which initially drove him to activism: At his first job, he was crushed to learn that his design firm's plans for modern roads would be ignored because public contracts went to the president's cronies.

Now, Maher watched the news from Tunisia as it hopped across hundreds of Facebook pages. He decided to capitalize on the moment, recruiting friends to help plan the first big protests in Tahrir Square, the sprawling traffic circle between Cairo's colonial-era downtown and the banks of the Nile. They used Facebook to consult with Tunisians, learning how to defend themselves against tear gas (vinegar and Pepsi, applied to the eyes).

It was all about momentum, Maher believed. If the crowds kept growing, the pressure on the regime would become unbearable. They picked a day to strike—Jan. 28. To disperse the police, he devised a plan to enter the square from a dozen directions.

▶ **Working with Sources**

1. **How do the author of the article and the people he interviewed connect Bouazizi's personal humiliation with his resistance to the regime?**

2. **To what extent was the fall of Mubarak the result of the inability of the regime to react to emerging technologies and to counter resistance fostered by Facebook?**

## SOURCE 31.4

# Arundhati Roy, "Capitalism: A Ghost Story"

### March 26, 2012

Indian writer Arundhati Roy (b. 1961) won the Man Booker Prize for her brilliant novel *The God of Small Things* (1997), but she is better known today for her speaking and writing on political causes. A strong advocate for the rights of lower-caste people in Indian society, she has extended her concern to matters of Indian domestic and foreign policy, protesting in particular the speed and direction of globalization in her own and in other countries. In the aftermath of the 2008 financial crisis, Roy has continued her criticism of global capitalism and has often come into conflict with the Indian government and leading figures in the Indian business world.

Source: Arundhati Roy, "Capitalism: A Ghost Story," *Outlook India*, March 26, 2012, available online at http://www.outlookindia.com/article.aspx?280234.

Indian poverty, after a brief period in the wilderness while India "shone," has made a comeback as an exotic identity in the Arts, led from the front by films like *Slumdog Millionaire*. These stories about the poor, their amazing spirit and resilience, have no villains—except the small ones who provide narrative tension and local colour. The authors of these works are the contemporary world's equivalent of the early anthropologists, lauded and honoured for working on "the ground," for their brave journeys into the unknown. You rarely see the rich being examined in these ways.

Having worked out how to manage governments, political parties, elections, courts, the media and liberal opinion, there was one more challenge for the neo-liberal establishment: how to deal with growing unrest, the threat of "people's power." How do you domesticate it? How do you turn protesters into pets? How do you vacuum up people's fury and redirect it into blind alleys?

Here too, foundations and their allied organisations have a long and illustrious history. A revealing example is their role in defusing and de-radicalising the Black Civil Rights movement in the US in the 1960s and the successful transformation of Black Power into Black Capitalism.

The Rockefeller Foundation, in keeping with J.D. Rockefeller's ideals, had worked closely with Martin Luther King Sr (father of Martin Luther King Jr). But his influence waned with the rise of the more militant organisations—the Student Non-violent Coordinating Committee (SNCC) and the Black Panthers. The Ford and Rockefeller Foundations moved in. In 1970, they donated $15 million to "moderate" black organisations, giving people grants, fellowships, scholarships, job training programmes for dropouts and seed money for black-owned businesses. Repression, infighting and the honey trap of funding led to the gradual atrophying of the radical black organisations.

Martin Luther King Jr made the forbidden connections between Capitalism, Imperialism, Racism and the Vietnam War. As a result, after he was assassinated, even his memory became a toxic threat to public order. Foundations and Corporations worked hard to remodel his legacy to fit a market-friendly format. The Martin Luther King Junior Centre for Non-Violent Social Change, with an operational grant of $2 million, was set up by, among others, the Ford Motor Company, General Motors, Mobil, Western Electric, Procter & Gamble, US Steel and Monsanto. The Center maintains the King Library and Archives of the Civil Rights Movement. Among the many programmes the King Center runs have been projects that "work closely with the United States Department of Defense, the Armed Forces Chaplains Board and others." It co-sponsored the Martin Luther King Jr Lecture Series called 'The Free Enterprise System: An Agent for Non-violent Social Change'. Amen.

. . .

In the United States, as we have seen, corporate-endowed foundations spawned the culture of NGOs. In India, targeted corporate philanthropy began in earnest in the 1990s, the era of the New Economic Policies. Membership to the Star Chamber doesn't come cheap. The Tata Group donated $50 million to that needy institution, the Harvard Business School, and another $50 million to Cornell University. Nandan Nilekani of Infosys and his wife Rohini donated $5 million as a start-up endowment for the India Initiative at Yale. The Harvard Humanities Centre is now the Mahindra Humanities Centre after it received its largest-ever donation of $10 million from Anand Mahindra of the Mahindra Group.

At home, the Jindal Group, with a major stake in mining, metals and power, runs the Jindal Global Law School and will soon open the Jindal School of Government and Public Policy. (The Ford Foundation runs a law school in the Congo.) The New India Foundation funded by Nandan Nilekani, financed by profits from Infosys, gives prizes and fellowships to social scientists. The Sitaram Jindal Foundation endowed by Jindal Aluminium has announced five cash prizes of Rs 1 crore each to be given to those working in rural development, poverty alleviation, environment education and moral upliftment. The Reliance Group's Observer Research Foundation (ORF), currently endowed by Mukesh Ambani, is cast in the mould of the Rockefeller Foundation. It has retired intelligence agents, strategic analysts, politicians (who pretend to rail against each other in Parliament), journalists and policymakers as its research "fellows" and advisors.

ORF's objectives seem straightforward enough: "To help develop a consensus in favour of economic reforms." And to shape and influence public opinion, creating "viable, alternative policy options in areas as divergent as employment generation in backward districts and real-time strategies to counter nuclear, biological and chemical threats."

I was initially puzzled by the preoccupation with "nuclear, biological and chemical war" in ORF's stated objectives. But less so when, in the long list of its 'institutional partners', I found the names of Raytheon and Lockheed Martin, two of the world's leading weapons manufacturers. In 2007, Raytheon announced it was turning its attention to India. Could it be that at least part of India's $32 billion defence budget will be spent on weapons, guided missiles, aircraft, warships and surveillance equipment made by Raytheon and Lockheed Martin?

Do we need weapons to fight wars? Or do we need wars to create a market for weapons? After all, the economies of Europe, US and Israel depend hugely on their weapons industry. It's the one thing they haven't outsourced to China.

In the new Cold War between US and China, India is being groomed to play the role Pakistan played as a US ally in the cold war with Russia. (And look what happened to Pakistan.) Many of those columnists and "strategic analysts" who are playing up the hostilities between India and China, you'll see, can be traced back directly or indirectly to the Indo-American think-tanks and foundations. Being a "strategic partner" of the US does not mean that the Heads of State make friendly phone calls to each other every now and then. It means collaboration (interference) at every level. It means hosting US Special Forces on Indian soil (a Pentagon Commander recently confirmed this to the BBC). It means sharing intelligence, altering agriculture and energy policies, opening up the health and education sectors to global investment. It means opening up retail. It means an unequal partnership in which India is being held close in a bear hug and waltzed around the floor by a partner who will incinerate her the moment she refuses to dance.

In the list of ORF's 'institutional partners', you will also find the RAND Corporation, Ford Foundation, the World Bank, the Brookings Institution (whose stated mission is to "provide innovative and practical recommendations that advance three broad goals: to strengthen American democracy; to foster the economic and social welfare, security and opportunity of all Americans; and to secure a more open, safe, prosperous and cooperative international system.") You will also find the Rosa Luxemburg Foundation of Germany. (Poor Rosa, who died for the cause of Communism, to find her name on a list such as this one!)

Though capitalism is meant to be based on competition, those at the top of the food chain have also shown themselves to be capable of inclusiveness and solidarity. The great Western Capitalists have done business with fascists, socialists, despots and military dictators. They can adapt and constantly innovate. They are capable of quick thinking and immense tactical cunning.

But despite having successfully powered through economic reforms, despite having waged wars and militarily occupied countries in order to put in place free market "democracies," Capitalism is going through a crisis whose gravity has not revealed itself completely yet. Marx said, "What the bourgeoisie therefore produces, above all, are its own grave-diggers. Its fall and the victory of the proletariat are equally inevitable."

▶ **Working with Sources**

1. What does Roy assert that the Western and Indian foundations and think tanks are gaining from the money they spend?

2. What does she believe will ultimately result from the global financial crisis that began in 2008?

## SOURCE 31.5

# United Nations Framework Convention on Climate Change, Copenhagen

2009

While there has been considerable debate over the last several decades on the nature and degree of global warming, there is general scientific consensus that greenhouse gases are the main contributors to temperature increases on earth. Scientists generally assume that at current rates of greenhouse gas production the earth will reach a "tipping point" of 450 parts per million, with catastrophic consequences for the planet's climate, before the middle of this century. Although 169 nations joined the 2005 Kyoto Protocol to reduce greenhouse emissions, the United States refused to sign the agreement. However, the United States did eventually sign on to an international agreement regarding climate change and the reduction of its

Source: http://unfccc.int/resource/docs/2009/cop15/eng/11a01.pdf.

global threat under President Barack Obama. This framework document, resulting from a conference held in Copenhagen in 2009, pledges the international community to action on the environment, in both specific and principled terms.

*[The signatory nations] have agreed* on this Copenhagen Accord which is operational immediately.

**1.** We underline that climate change is one of the greatest challenges of our time. We emphasise our strong political will to urgently combat climate change in accordance with the principle of common but differentiated responsibilities and respective capabilities. To achieve the ultimate objective of the Convention to stabilize greenhouse gas concentration in the atmosphere at a level that would prevent dangerous anthropogenic interference with the climate system, we shall, recognizing the scientific view that the increase in global temperature should be below 2 degrees Celsius, on the basis of equity and in the context of sustainable development, enhance our long-term cooperative action to combat climate change. We recognize the critical impacts of climate change and the potential impacts of response measures on countries particularly vulnerable to its adverse effects and stress the need to establish a comprehensive adaptation programme including international support.

**2.** We agree that deep cuts in global emissions are required according to science, and as documented by the IPCC Fourth Assessment Report with a view to reduce global emissions so as to hold the increase in global temperature below 2 degrees Celsius, and take action to meet this objective consistent with science and on the basis of equity. We should cooperate in achieving the peaking of global and national emissions as soon as possible, recognizing that the time frame for peaking will be longer in developing countries and bearing in mind that social and economic development and poverty eradication are the first and overriding priorities of developing countries and that a low-emission development strategy is indispensable to sustainable development.

**3.** Adaptation to the adverse effects of climate change and the potential impacts of response measures is a challenge faced by all countries. Enhanced action and international cooperation on adaptation is urgently required to ensure the implementation of the Convention by enabling and supporting the implementation of adaptation actions aimed at reducing vulnerability and building resilience in developing countries, especially in those that are particularly vulnerable, especially least developed countries, small island developing States and Africa. We agree that developed countries shall provide adequate, predictable and sustainable financial resources, technology and capacity-building to support the implementation of adaptation action in developing countries.

**4.** Annex I Parties commit to implement individually or jointly the quantified economy-wide emissions targets for 2020, to be submitted in the format given in Appendix I by Annex I Parties to the secretariat by 31 January 2010 for compilation in an INF document. Annex I Parties that are Party to the Kyoto Protocol will thereby further strengthen the emissions reductions initiated by the Kyoto Protocol. Delivery of reductions and financing by developed countries will be measured, reported and verified in accordance with existing and any further guidelines adopted by the Conference of the Parties, and will ensure that accounting of such targets and finance is rigorous, robust and transparent.

**5.** Non-Annex I Parties to the Convention will implement mitigation actions, including those to be submitted to the secretariat by non-Annex I Parties in the format given in Appendix II by 31 January 2010, for compilation in an INF document, consistent with Article 4.1 and Article 4.7 and in the context of sustainable development. Least developed countries and small island developing States may undertake actions voluntarily and on the basis of support. Mitigation actions subsequently taken and envisaged by Non-Annex I Parties, including national inventory reports, shall be communicated through national communications consistent with Article 12.1(b) every two years on the basis of guidelines to be adopted by the Conference of the Parties. Those mitigation actions in national communications or otherwise communicated to the Secretariat will be added to the list in appendix II. Mitigation actions taken by Non-Annex I Parties will be subject to their domestic measurement, reporting and verification the result of which will be reported through their national communications every two years. Non-Annex I Parties will communicate information on the implementation of their actions through National Communications, with provisions for international consultations and analysis under clearly defined guidelines that will ensure that national sovereignty is respected. Nationally appropriate mitigation actions seeking international support will be recorded in a registry along with relevant technology, finance and capacity building support. Those actions supported will be added to the list in appendix II. These supported nationally appropriate mitigation actions will be subject to international measurement, reporting and verification in accordance with guidelines adopted by the Conference of the Parties.

**6.** We recognize the crucial role of reducing emission from deforestation and forest degradation and the need to enhance removals of greenhouse gas emission by forests and agree on the need to provide positive incentives to such actions through the immediate establishment of a mechanism including REDD-plus, to enable the mobilization of financial resources from developed countries.

**7.** We decide to pursue various approaches, including opportunities to use markets, to enhance the cost-effectiveness of, and to promote mitigation actions. Developing countries, especially those with low emitting economies should be provided incentives to continue to develop on a low emission pathway.

▶ **Working with Sources**

1. In what terms does the document attempt to reconcile national policies with international environmental goals?

2. How does the document recognize, and try to account for, the differences in economic development among the world's countries?

# Further Resources

## Chapter 1

Burroughs, William J. *Climate Change in Prehistory: The End of the Reign of Chaos.* Cambridge, UK: Cambridge University Press, 2005. Very well-researched and up-to-date discussion of climate and human evolution.

Finlayson, Clive. *The Humans Who Went Extinct: Why Neanderthals Died Out and We Survived.* Oxford: Oxford University Press, 2010. A comprehensive history of human evolution in the context of geological and climatic changes, by the excavator of the last Neanderthal traces in Europe.

Flood, Josephine. *Archaeology of the Dreamtime: The Story of Prehistoric Australia and Its People.* New Haven, CT: Yale University Press, 1989. Overview of the Australian archaeological record; short on discussion of Aboriginal Dreamtime and myths.

Johanson, Donald, and Kate Wong. *Lucy: The Quest for Human Origins.* New York: Three Rivers, 2009.

Lawson, Andrew J. *Painted Caves: Palaeololithic Rock Art in Western Europe.* Oxford: Oxford University Press, 2012. Presents an extensive overview ("gazetteer") of the various sites and analyzes the rock art phenomenon in great detail.

McBrearty, Sally, and Allison S. Brooks. "The Revolution that Wasn't: A New Interpretation of the Origin of Modern Human Behavior." *Journal of Human Evolution* 39 (2000): 453–463. Crucial, pioneering article in which the authors grounded anatomically and intellectually modern *H. sapiens* in Africa.

Pauketat, Timothy, ed. *The Oxford North American Handbook of Archaeology.* New York: Oxford University Press, 2012. Very detailed coverage of Paleo-Indian migrations and settlements. Needs to be supplemented with the March 2014 article in *Science* by Dennis O'Rourke, John Hoffecker, and Scott Elias on humans being trapped for 10,000 years on the habitable south coast of Beringia.

Renfrew, Colin,. *Prehistory: The Making of the Human Mind.* New York: Modern Library, 2008. Renfrew, a senior British archaeologist, incorporates the history of human evolution into the process of world history.

Tattersall, Ian. *Masters of the Planet: The Search for Human Origins.* New York: Palgrave Macmillan, 2012. A scholarly well-founded overview for the general reader, by one of the leading senior paleoanthropologists.

### WEBSITES

Bradshaw Foundation, http://www.bradshawfoundation.com/. The Bradshaw Foundation has a large website on human evolution and rock art, with many images, and a link to Stephen Oppenheimer's website Journey of Mankind: The Peopling of the World, an important overview of *Homo sapiens'* migrations.

Institute of Human Origins, Arizona State University, http://iho.asu.edu/. Arizona State University's Institute of Human Origins runs the popular but scholarly well-founded website Becoming Human (http://www.becominghuman.org/).

## Chapter 2

Alcock, Susan E., John Bodel, and Richard J. A. Talbert, eds. *Highways, Byways, and Road Systems in the Pre-Modern World.* Chichester, UK: John Wiley & Sons, 2012. Fascinating global survey of methods of transport and communication.

Assmann, Jan. *The Search for God in Ancient Egypt.* Ithaca, NY: Cornell University Press, 2001. Reflective investigation of the dimensions of Egyptian polytheism by a leading Egyptologist.

Bottéro, Jean. *Mesopotamia: Writing, Reasoning, and the Gods.* Chicago: University of Chicago Press, 1992. Classic intellectual history of ancient Mesopotamia.

Drews, Robert. *The End of the Bronze Age: Changes in Warfare and the Catastrophe ca. 1200 B.C.* Princeton, NJ: Princeton University Press, 1993. Closely argued essay on the destruction of Mycenaean culture and its consequences for the eastern Mediterranean.

Finkelstein, Israel. *The Archaeology of the Israelite Settlement.* Jerusalem: Israel Exploration Society, 1988. Authoritative presentation of the archaeology of the earliest period of Israelite social formation.

Kuhrt, Amélie. *The Ancient Near East, c. 3000–330 BCE,* 2 vols. London: Routledge, 1994. Comprehensive handbook surveying all regions of the Middle East.

Mithen, Steven. *After the Ice: A Global Human History, 20,000–5000 B.C.* Cambridge, MA: Harvard University Press, 2003. Engagingly written story of humans settling, becoming farmers, and founding villages and towns, as seen through the eyes of a modern time traveler.

Podany, Amanda H. *The Ancient Near East: A Very Short Introduction.* New York: Oxford University Press, 2014. Readable survey of the origin and development of Near Eastern civilizations.

Van de Mieroop, Marc. *The Ancient Mesopotamian City.* Oxford: Clarendon, 1997. Full examination of Mesopotamian urban institutions, including city assemblies.

### WEBSITES

British Museum. Ancient Egypt, http://www.ancientegypt.co.uk/menu.html. Pictorial introduction, with short texts.

Livius.org. "Mesopotamia," http://www.livius.org/babylonia.html. A large collection of translated texts and references to philological articles, with portals on Mesopotamia, Egypt, Anatolia, and Greece.

Oriental Institute, University of Chicago. Ancient Mesopotamia, http://mesopotamia.lib.uchicago.edu/. A user-friendly portal to the world-renowned Mesopotamia collection of the Oriental Institute.

## Chapter 3

Bryant, Edwin. *The Quest for the Origins of Vedic Culture: The Indo-Aryan Migration Debate.* Oxford: Oxford University Press, 2001. A scholarly yet readable attempt to address the linguistic and archaeological evidence surrounding the thesis of Aryan migration versus the more recent theory of indigenous Vedic development.

Embree, Ainslee T., ed. *Sources of Indian Tradition,* vol. 1, 2nd ed. New York: Columbia University Press, 1988. Though the language is dated in places, this is still the most comprehensive sourcebook of Indian thought available. Recent additions on women and gender make it even more so. Sophisticated yet readable introductions, glosses, and commentary.

Eraly, Abraham. *Gem in the Lotus: The Seeding of Indian Civilization.* London: Weidenfeld & Nicholson, 2004. Readable, comprehensive survey of recent scholarship from prehistory to the reign of Ashoka during the Mauryan dynasty of the fourth and third centuries BCE. Emphasis on transitional period of sixth-century religious innovations, particularly Buddhism.

Fairservis, Walter A. *The Roots of Ancient India: The Archaeology of Early Indian Civilization.* New York: Macmillan, 1971. Classic, well-detailed, and well-documented treatment of Indian archaeology and history to 500 BCE. Particularly well done on the so-called Vedic dark ages to 800 BCE. More useful in general for experienced students.

Kenoyer, Jonathan Mark. *Ancient Cities of the Indus Valley Civilization.* New York: Oxford University Press, 1998. Comprehensive work by team leader of Harappan Research Project. Particularly good on Lothal.

Kinsley, David R. *Hinduism: A Cultural Perspective.* Englewood Cliffs, NJ: Prentice Hall, 1993. Short, highly accessible overview of the major traditions within the constellation of belief systems called by outsiders "Hinduism." Sound treatment of the formative Vedic and Upanishadic periods.

Possehl, Gregory L., ed. *Harappan Civilization: A Recent Perspective,* 2nd ed. New Delhi: Oxford University Press, 1993. Sound and extensive treatment of recent work and issues in Indus valley archaeology by one of the leading on-site researchers and a former student of Fairservis. Used to best advantage by experienced students.

Singh, Upinder. *A History of Ancient and Early Medieval India: From the Stone Age to the 12th Century.* New Delhi: Pearson, 2008. Sweeping text by a longtime instructor of Indian history at the University of Delhi. Suitable for undergraduates and current on the latest debates on ancient origins.

Trautmann, Thomas. *India: Brief History of a Civilization.* New York: Oxford University Press, 2011. A succinct and lucid account of 4,000 years of Indian history, with particular emphasis on early developments.

Wolpert, Stanley. *A New History of India,* 5th ed. New York: Oxford University Press, 2004. Another extremely useful, readable, one-volume history from Neolithic times to the present. Excellent first work for serious students.

WEBSITES

Columbia University Libraries. South and Southeast Asian Studies, www.columbia.edu/cu/lweb/indiv/southasia/cuvl/history.html. Run by Columbia University, this site contains links to "WWW .Virtual Library: Indian History"; "Regnal Chronologies"; "Internet Indian History Sourcebook"; and "Medical History of British India."

Harappa, http://www.harappa.com. Contains a wealth of images of artifacts and other archaeological treasures from the Indus Valley.

## Chapter 4

Chang, Kwang-chih. *The Archaeology of Ancient China,* 4th ed. New Haven, CT: Yale University Press, 1986. Sophisticated treatment of archaeology of Shang China. Prime exponent of the view of overlapping periods and territories for the Sandai period. Erudite, yet accessible for experienced students.

Ebrey, Patricia Buckley, ed. *Chinese Civilization: A Sourcebook,* 2nd ed. New York: Free Press, 1993. Wonderful supplement to the preceding volume. Some different classical sources and considerable material on women and social history. Time frame of this work extends to the modern era.

Keightly, David N., ed. *The Origins of Chinese Civilization.* Berkeley: University of California Press, 1983. Symposium volume on a variety of Sandai topics by leading scholars. Some exposure to early Chinese history and archaeology is necessary in order to best appreciate these essays.

Keightly, David N., ed. *Sources of Shang History: The Oracle-Bone Inscriptions of Bronze Age China.* Berkeley: University of California Press, 1978. Benchmark in the authoritative interpretation and contextualization of ritual inscriptions. Some grounding in ancient Chinese history is helpful.

Linduff, Katheryn M., and Yan Sun, eds. *Gender and Chinese Archaeology.* Walnut Creek, CA: Altamira, 2004. Reexamines the role of gender in ancient China in the context of a critique of the general lack of gendered research in archaeology as a whole.

Lowe, Michael, and Edward L. Shaughnessy, eds. *The Cambridge History of Ancient China: From the Origins of Civilization to 221 B.C.*

Cambridge, UK: Cambridge University Press, 1999. The opening volume of the Cambridge History of China series, this is the most complete multiessay collection on all aspects of recent Chinese ancient historical and archaeological work. The place to start for the serious student contemplating in-depth research.

Schirokauer, Conrad. *A Brief History of Chinese Civilization.* New York: Harcourt Brace Jovanovich, 1991. Readable one-volume text on Chinese history up to the late twentieth century. More thorough treatment of Sandai period than is generally the case with other one-volume texts.

Thorp, Robert L. *China in the Early Bronze Age: Shang Civilization.* Philadelphia: University of Pennsylvania Press, 2006. Comprehensive yet accessible survey of recent archaeological work on the period 2070–1046 BCE, including traditional Xia and Shang periods under the heading of China's "bronze age."

Wang, Aihe. *Cosmology and Political Culture in Early China.* Cambridge, UK: Cambridge University Press, 2000. Part of the Cambridge Studies in Chinese History, Literature, and Institutions series. Wang argues that control of *cosmology*—how the world and universe operate—was a vital key to the wielding of power by the Shang and Zhou rulers. Recommended for serious students.

Watson, Burton, trans. *The Tso Chuan: Selections from China's Oldest Narrative History.* New York: Columbia University Press, 1989. Elegant translation by one of the most prolific of scholars working today. Excellent introduction to Zhou period and politics. Appropriate for beginning students, though more useful for those with some prior introduction to the period.

WEBSITES

http://lucian.uchicago.edu/blogs/earlychina/ssec/. This is the site of the journal *Early China*, published by the Society for the Study of Early China.

British Museum. Ancient China, http://www.ancientchina.co.uk. This site provides access to the British Museum's ancient Chinese collections and is highly useful for students seeking illustrations of assorted artifacts in a user-friendly environment.

## Chapter 5

### The Americas

Bellwood, Peter. *First Migrants: Ancient Migration in Global Perspective.* Chichester, UK: John Wiley & Sons, 2013. An intriguing study of prehistoric migration and its role in shaping the emergence of civilization.

Benson, Sonia, and Deborah J. Baker. *Early Civilizations in the Americas Reference Library,* 3 vols. Farmington Hills, MI: Gale UXL, 2009. Extensive three-volume encyclopedia available as a download or in hard copy. Contains an almanac of historical information and one of biographies and primary sources. Recommended for beginning and experienced students.

Bruhns, Karen Olsen, and Karen E. Stothert. *Women in Ancient America.* Norman: University of Oklahoma Press, 1999. A comprehensive account of women's roles in daily life, religion, politics, and war in foraging and farming as well as urban societies in the Americas.

Fiedel, Stuart J. *Prehistory of the Americas,* 2nd ed. Cambridge, UK: Cambridge University Press, 1992. Accessible, detailed survey of the archaeology of the Americas by a leading American scholar.

Thomas, David Hurst. *Exploring Native North America.* Oxford: Oxford University Press, 2000. Selected chapters are useful on the major early North American sites, particularly Adena and Hopewell.

Trigger, Bruce G., Wilcomb E. Washburn, Richard E. W. Adams, Murdo J. MacLeod, Frank Salomon, and Stuart B. Schwartz, eds. *Cambridge History of the Native Peoples of the Americas,* 3 vols. Cambridge, UK: Cambridge University Press, 1996–2000. As with all of the Cambridge histories, this is a highly useful set for beginner and accomplished scholar alike. Useful bibliographies with the article entries.

von Hagen, Adriana, and Craig Morris. *The Cities of the Ancient Andes.* New York: Thames & Hudson, 1999. While more geared to later periods, still a useful overview, with illustrations, by specialists on Andean cultures.

## Oceania

Bellwood, Peter S. *Man's Conquest of the Pacific: The Prehistory of Southeast Asia and Oceania.* New York: Oxford University Press, 1979. Along with Bellwood's earlier volume, *The Polynesians* (1978), traces the migrations of succeeding groups through the archipelagoes of the Pacific. Balanced treatment of controversies over gradual versus episodic migrations of Lapita cultures. For advanced students.

Fagan, Brian M., ed. *The Oxford Companion to Archaeology.* New York: Oxford University Press, 1996. Perhaps the best place to start for students interested in archaeological and historical overviews of the peopling of the Pacific. Extensive coverage of Lapita culture and expansion into Micronesia and Polynesia.

Kirch, Patrick V. *The Lapita Peoples: Ancestors of the Oceanic World.* Cambridge, MA: Blackwell, 1997. Basic introduction by one of the pioneers of Polynesian research.

Vlchek, Andre. *Oceania: Neocolonialism, Nukes and Bones.* Auckland, New Zealand: Atuanui, 2013. Analysis and discussion of the harmful effects of colonialism and neocolonialism on the development of Oceania.

### WEBSITES

Foundation for the Advancement of Mesoamerican Studies (FAMSI), http://www.famsi.org/. Home page for the foundation, which has recently begun collaboration with the Los Angeles County Museum of Art and runs a wide range of scholarly, funding, and educational outreach programs aimed at advancing studies of Mesoamerica.

http://www.britannica.com/EBchecked/topic/468832/Polynesian-culture. Good link leading to an 8,000-word essay on leading topics concerning Polynesia and Oceania. In order to access the complete essay the reader must apply for a free trial on the online *Encyclopedia Britannica*

## Chapter 6

### Sub-Saharan Africa

Chami, Félix. *The Unity of African Ancient History: 3000 BC to 500 AD.* Dar es Salaam: E&D, 2006. General overview by one of the leading archaeologists of East Africa.

McIntosh, Roderick J. *Ancient Middle Niger: Urbanism and the Self-Organizing Landscape.* Cambridge, UK: Cambridge University Press, 2005. Important revisionist work on the origins of urbanism and kingship in West Africa.

Mitchell, Peter, and Paul Lane. *The Oxford Handbook of African Archaeology.* Oxford: Oxford University Press, 2013. A total of 70 essays by specialists on all aspects of human culture in Africa, with an emphasis on hunter-gatherers, agriculturalists, and early urbanists.

Vansina, Jan. *Paths in the Rainforests: Toward a History of Political Tradition in Equatorial Africa.* Madison: University of Wisconsin Press, 1990. Magisterial presentation of the Bantu dispersal and village life in the rain forest.

### Mesoamerica and the Andes

Aveni, Anthony F. *Skywatchers,* rev. ed. Austin: University of Texas Press, 2001. Classic study on astronomy and calendars of pre-Columbian Americans, including a discussion of the Nazca lines.

Evans, Susan Tobey. *Ancient Mexico and Central America: Archaeology and Culture History.* London: Thames & Hudson, 2004. Densely

but clearly written and detailed, with many sidebars on special topics.

Grube, Nikolai, ed. *Maya: Divine Kings of the Rain Forest.* Cologne, Germany: Könemann, 2001. Lavishly illustrated book with short contributions by many hands.

Schele, Linda, and David Freidel. *A Forest of Kings: The Untold Story of the Ancient Maya.* New York: Quill-William Morrow, 1990. Classic study summarizing the results of the decipherment of Maya glyphs, by two pioneers.

Sharer, Robert J., *The Ancient Maya,* 6th ed. Stanford, CA: Stanford University Press, 2006. Standard academic work on the civilization of the Maya, by one of the leading Maya scholars until death in 2012.

### WEBSITES

Museum of Native American History. http://www.monah.us/precolumbian: Basic but fairly comprehensive website on pre-Columbian peoples and civilizations.

Stanford University Libraries. Africa South of the Sahara, http://www-sul.stanford.edu/depts/ssrg/africa/history.html. A large, resource-filled website based at Stanford University.

## Chapter 7

Boatwright, Mary, Daniel J. Gargola, and Richard J. A. Talbert. *The Romans: From Village to Empire.* New York: Oxford University Press, 2004. Clearly written, comprehensive introduction to Roman history.

Boyce, Mary. *A History of Zoroastrianism.* Vol. 1, *The Early Period,* rev. ed. Handbuch der Orientalistik. Leiden, the Netherlands: E. J. Brill, 1989. Standard work by the leading scholar on the subject.

Briant, Pierre. *From Cyrus to Alexander: A History of the Persian Empire.* Winona Lake, IN: Eisenbrauns, 2000. Monumental work; the most detailed and authoritative study of the topic to date.

Cameron, Averil. *The Mediterranean World in Late Antiquity, AD 395–600.* London: Routledge, 1993. New perspective on the strengths and weaknesses of the late empire.

Dignas, Beate, and Engelbert Winter. *Rome and Persia in Late Antiquity: Neighbours and Rivals.* Cambridge, UK: Cambridge University Press, 2007. Detailed historical investigation of the rivalry between Rome and Persia.

Freeman, Phillip. *Alexander the Great.* New York: Simon & Schuster, 2011. Illuminating study of Alexander the Great intended for a general audience.

Hubbard, Thomas K., ed. *A Companion to Greek and Roman Sexualities.* Chichester, UK: John Wiley & Sons, 2014. Far-ranging and informative collection of essays on all aspects of sexuality in ancient Greece and Rome.

Lehoux, Daryn. *What Did the Romans Know?: An Inquiry into Science and Worldmaking.* Chicago: University of Chicago Press, 2012. Sophisticated analysis of Roman science in both its derivative and unique aspects.

Shaked, Shaul. *Dualism in Transformation: Varieties of Religion in Sasanian Iran.* London: School of Oriental and African Studies, 1994. Short history of the different religions in Sasanid Persia.

Smith, Mark S. *The Early History of God: Yahweh and the Other Deities in Ancient Israel.* San Francisco: Harper & Row, 1990. Very readable introduction to the problem of early monotheism among Israelites.

### WEBSITES

British Museum. Ancient Greece, http://www.ancientgreece.co.uk/menu.html. Open the door to the compelling world of Ancient Greece. The British Museum has compiled a collection of images and information on various aspects of Greek history such as the Acropolis, Athens, daily life, festivals and games, Sparta, war, and gods.

Harvard University. Digital Atlas of Roman and Medieval Civilizations, http://darmc.harvard.edu/icb/icb.do?keyword=k40248&pageid=icb.page188868. Harvard University allows students to tailor searches in order to access specific geopolitical and spatial cartographical representations of the Roman and medieval worlds.

Perseus Digital Library, http://www.perseus.tufts.edu/hopper/. Probably the largest website on Greece and Rome, with immense resources, hosted by Tufts University.

## Chapter 8

Auboyer, Jeannine. *Daily Life in Ancient India*. London: Phoenix, 2002. Overview consisting of sections on social structures/religious principles; individual/collective existence; and royal and administrative existence. Multidisciplinary approach appropriate for most undergraduates.

Carter, John Ross, and Mahinda Palihawadana trans. *The Dhammapada*. New York: Oxford University Press, 1987. Erudite but accessible translation of one of the key texts in the Buddhist corpus. Students with some exposure to the introductory ideas of Buddhism will find it very useful in its step-by-step elucidation of a number of central concepts.

Chakravarti, Uma. *The Social Dimensions of Early Buddhism*. New Delhi: Oxford University Press, 1987. Thorough analysis, with extensive glossary, of the influence of the north Indian economic transition to peasant market farming on the social milieu of early Buddhism.

Doniger, Wendy. *The Hindus: An Alternative History*. New York: Penguin, 2009. Vivid but controversial new interpretation of the history of Hinduism by one of the leading scholars of Indian history. The book's portrayals of Hindu history, particularly in the area between myth and history, have prompted a lawsuit in India, which resulted in the withdrawal of the book there in early 2014.

Embree, Ainslee T. *Sources of Indian Tradition*, 2 vols, 2nd ed. New York: Columbia University Press, 1988. The latest edition contains a number of new selections useful for the study of social relations in addition to the older religious material. As with all of the works in this series, the level of writing is sophisticated, though accessible; the overviews are masterly; and the works are ably translated.

Keay, John. *India: A History*. New York: Grove, 2000. Lively, highly detailed narrative history, with a number of highly useful charts and genealogies of ruling houses. Sympathetic treatment of controversial matters.

Knott, Kim. *Hinduism: A Very Short Introduction*. New York: Oxford University Press, 1998. Sound, brief discussion of modern Hinduism and its formative influences. Asks provocative questions such as "What is a religion?" and "Is Hinduism something more than the Western conception of religion?"

Nikam, N. A., and Richard McKeon, eds. and trans. *The Edicts of Asoka*. Chicago: University of Chicago Press, 1959. Slim but useful volume for those interested in reading the entire collection of Ashoka's Pillar, Cave, and Rock Edicts. Short, accessible introduction.

Willis, Michael. *The Archaeology of Hindu Ritual*. Cambridge, UK: Cambridge University Press, 2009. Best utilized by experienced students, this book uses site archaeology, Sanskrit documents, and studies of ancient astronomy to plot the development of Hinduism under the Guptas and their use of it in statecraft as they created their vision of a universal empire.

Wolpert, Stanley. *A New History of India*, 6th ed. New York: Oxford University Press, 2000. The standard introductory work to the long sweep of Indian history. Evenly divided between the period up to and including the Mughals and the modern era. Good coverage of geography and environment, as well as social and gender issues. Good select bibliography arranged by chapter; highly useful glossary of Indian terms.

Digital Library of India, http://www.dli.ernet.in. This online resource, hosted by the Indian Institute of Science, Bangalore, contains primary and secondary sources not only for history but also for culture, economics, literature, and a host of other subjects.

## Chapter 9

Ebrey, Patricia Buckley, ed. *Chinese Civilization: A Sourcebook*, 2nd ed. New York: Free Press, 1993. Varied primary sources with an accent on social history material: letters, diary excerpts, etc. Particularly strong on women's history sources.

Hinsch, Bret. *Women in Early Imperial China*. Lanham, MD: Rowman & Littlefield, 2002. Broad examination of the place of women, and transition of the place of women, during the crucial early Chinese dynasties.

Huang, Ray. *China: A Macro History*. Armonk, NY: M. E. Sharpe, 1997. Readable, entertaining, and highly useful one-volume history. Particularly good on the complex politics of the post-Han and Song–Yuan periods.

Keay, John. *China: A History*. New York: Basic Books, 2009. Adventurous and well-written general history of China from prehistory to the present. Especially good for students with some previous grounding in the essentials of Chinese history.

Lewis, Mark Edward. *The Early Chinese Empires: Qin and Han*. Cambridge, MA: Harvard University Press, 2007. Detailed exploration of the rise and adaptations of China's initial empires. Better for advanced students.

Loewe, Michael. *Everyday Life in Early Imperial China during the Han Period, 202 B.C.–A.D. 220*. New York: Harper & Row, 1968. Short, highly useful one-volume survey of Han social history by a pre-eminent scholar. Especially good on details of peasant and elite daily existence.

Qian, Sima. *Records of the Grand Historian*. Translated by Burton Watson. 3 vols. Revised edition. New York: Columbia University Press, 1993. Complete, powerful translation of China's supreme historical work by one of its best interpreters. Includes material from the Qin and Han Dynasties. Invaluable source for serious students.

Snow, Philip. *The Star Raft: China's Encounter with Africa*. Ithaca, NY: Cornell University Press, 1988. Important, accessible study of the little-known area of China's maritime trade with Africa from Han times to the epic fifteenth-century voyages of Zheng He and beyond.

Asian Topics for Asian Educators. "Defining 'Daoism': A Complex History," http://afe.easia.columbia.edu/cosmos/ort/daoism.htm. Looks at Daoism as a term, its use, and its practice in terms of morality, society, nature, and the self.

http://bulldog2.redlands.edu/Dept/AsianStudiesDept/index.html. *East and Southeast Asia: An Annotated Directory of Internet Resources*. One of the most complete guides to websites dealing with all manner of Chinese and East Asian history and society.

## Chapter 10

*The Arabian Nights*. Translated by Husain Haddawy. New York: Norton, 1990. Translation of the critical edition by Muhsin Mahdi, which reconstitutes the original thirteenth-century text.

Barry, Michael. *Figurative Art in Medieval Islam and the Riddle of Bihazâd of Herât (1465–1535)*. Paris: Flammarion, 2004.

Chaudhuri, K. N. *Trade and Civilization in the Indian Ocean.* Cambridge, UK: Cambridge University Press, 1985. Discusses the historical evolution of the trade and its various aspects (sea route, ships, commodities, and capital investments).

Fryde, Edmund. *The Early Palaeologan Renaissance (1261–c. 1360).* Leiden, the Netherlands: E. J. Brill, 2000. Detailed presentation of the main philosophical and scientific figures of Byzantium after the recovery from the Latin interruption.

Khalili, Jim al-. *The House of Wisdom: How Arabic Science Saved Ancient Knowledge and Gave Us the Renaissance.* New York: Penguin, 2010. In spite of the somewhat overwrought title, an expertly written introduction to the golden age of Arabic science by a scientist.

Laiou, Angeliki E., and Cécile Morrisson. *The Byzantine Economy.* Cambridge, UK: Cambridge University Press, 2007. Comprehensive and well-researched study of ups and downs in the demography, productive capacity, and long-distance trade of Byzantium.

Lapidus, Ira. *Muslim Cities in the Later Middle Ages.* Cambridge, UK: Cambridge University Press, 1984. Seminal work and still the only study of Muslim urban society, although it should be supplemented by Shlomo D. Goitein's monumental study of Jews, *A Mediterranean Society* (1967–1993).

Rippin, Andrew. *Muslims: Their Religious Beliefs and Practices,* 2nd ed. London: Routledge, 2001. One of the best and most accessible introductions to the basic beliefs and practices of Islam, based on the reevaluation of Islamic origins also presented in this chapter.

Tyerman, Christopher. *God's War: A New History of the Crusades.* Cambridge, MA: Belknap, 2006. Persuasive revisionist history by a leading Crusade historian.

Whittow, Mark. *The Making of Byzantium, 600–1025.* Berkeley: University of California Press, 1996. Revisionist study of the Byzantine struggle for survival in the early years.

WEBSITES

BBC—Religion: Islam. http://www.bbc.co.uk/religion/religions/islam/. A very basic overview of Islamic Civilization. Most websites on Islam and Islamic civilization are apologetic (pro-Muslim or pro-Christian) and earlier scholarly websites are no longer available.

Asian Topics in World History "The Mongols in World History," http://afe.easia.columbia.edu/mongols/. With a timeline spanning 1000–1500, "The Mongols in World History" delivers a concise and colorful history of the Mongols' impact on global history.

## Chapter 11

Bartlett, Robert. *The Making of Europe: Conquest, Colonization, and Cultural Change, 950–1350.* Princeton, NJ: Princeton University Press, 1993. Analyzes the expansion of Europe from a cultural perspective.

Berend, Norma, Przemyslaw Urbanczlyk, and Przemyslaw Wiszewski. *Central Europe in the High Middle Ages: Bohemia, Hungary and Poland, ca. 900–ca. 1300.* New York: Cambridge University Press, 2013. Learned and insightful study that explores frequently overlooked aspects of medieval Europe.

Brown, Peter. *The Rise of Western Christendom: Triumph and Diversity, A.D. 200–1000,* 2nd ed. Oxford: Wiley-Blackwell, 2003. Traces the development of Christian Europe from the perspective of the church.

Grant, Edward. *The Foundation of Modern Science in the Middle Ages.* Cambridge, UK: Cambridge University Press, 1996. Seminal study of the contributions of medieval science to the scientific revolution of the seventeenth century.

Lawrence, C. H. *Medieval Monasticism: Forms of Religious Life in Western Europe in the Middle Ages,* 2nd ed. New York: Longman, 1984. Thorough survey of the development of the Western monastic tradition.

McKitterick, Rosamond. *Charlemagne: The Formation of a European Identity.* Cambridge, UK: Cambridge University Press, 2008. An examination of how Charlemagne's policies contributed to the idea of Europe.

Platt, Colin. *King Death: The Black Death and Its Aftermath in Late-Medieval England.* Toronto: University of Toronto Press, 1997. Riveting analysis of the effects of the Black Death on all aspects of society.

Reynolds, Susan. *Fiefs and Vassals: The Medieval Evidence Reinterpreted.* Oxford: Oxford University Press, 1994. Important revisionist study of medieval feudal institutions.

Riley-Smith, Jonathan, ed. *The Oxford Illustrated History of the Crusades.* New York: Oxford University Press, 1995. A very useful and readable history of the crusading movement.

Turner, Denys. *Thomas Aquinas: A Portrait.* New Haven, CT: Yale University Press, 2013. Up-to-date biography of one of the greatest figures in medieval philosophy.

WEBSITES

British Library. Treasures in Full: Magna Carta, http://www.bl.uk/treasures/magnacarta/virtual_curator/vc9.html. An excellent website that makes available a digitized version of Magna Carta. Audio files answer many FAQs about the manuscript and its significance.

Howe, Jeffery. A Digital Archive of Architecture, http://www.bc.edu/bc_org/avp/cas/fnart/arch/gothic_arch.html. Jeffery Howe's Digital Archive of Architecture has a quick index reference guide, which links to images of both early and high Gothic architecture.

## Chapter 12

Bulag, Uradyn Erden. *The Mongols at China's Edge: History and the Politics of National Unity.* Lanham, MD: Rowman & Littlefield, 2002. New historical overview of the Mongols through historical and anthropological lenses that seeks to demythologize their experience and interactions with China and central Asian peoples.

De Bary, William T., ed. *Sources of Chinese Tradition,* vol. 1. New York: Columbia University Press, 1960. Excellent introduction to major Chinese philosophical schools. Extensive coverage of Buddhism and Neo-Confucianism with accessible, highly informative introductions to the documents themselves.

Ebrey, Patricia Buckley, ed. *Chinese Civilization: A Sourcebook,* 2nd ed. New York: Free Press, 1993. More varied than de Bary, with more social history material: letters, diary excerpts, etc. Particularly strong on women's history sources.

Ebrey, Patricia Buckley, ed. *The Inner Quarters.* Berkeley: University of California Press, 1993. Perhaps the best scholarly exploration of the roles of women in Song China.

Hansen, Valerie. *The Open Empire: A History of China to 1600.* New York: W. W. Norton, 2000. A fresh and accessible synthesis of pre-modern Chinese history.

Levathes, Louise. *When China Ruled the Seas: The Treasure Fleet of the Dragon Throne 1405–1433.* New York: Simon & Schuster, 1994. Delightful coverage of the voyages of Zheng He from 1405 to 1433. Particularly good on the aftermath of the voyages.

Mujeeb, M. *The Indian Muslims.* London: Allen & Unwin, 1967. Thorough historical overview from the eighth century to the twentieth. Especially useful on political and administrative systems of the early and middle periods of Muslim hegemony in north India.

Robinson, Francis. *Islam and Muslim History in South Asia.* New York: Oxford University Press, 2004. Compendium of essays and reviews by the author on a variety of subjects concerning the history and status of Islam in the subcontinent. Of particular interest is his response to Samuel Huntington's famous "clash of civilizations" thesis.

Singh, Patwant. *The Sikhs*. London: John Murray, 1999. Readable popular history of the Sikh experience to the present by an adherent. Especially useful on the years from Guru Nanak to the changes of the early eighteenth century and the transition to a more militant faith.

## WEBSITES

Fordham University. Internet Indian History Sourcebook, http://www.fordham.edu/halsall/india/indiasbook.asp. One of series of online "sourcebooks" by Fordham containing links to important documents, secondary literature, and assorted other web resources.

Fordham University. Internet East Asian History Sourcebook, http://www.fordham.edu/halsall/eastasia/eastasiasbook.asp. As with its counterpart above, this is one in the series of useful online sources and links put together by Fordham, in this case about East Asia, with particular emphasis on the role of China as a center of cultural diffusion.

# Chapter 13
## General

Mann, Susan. *East Asia (China, Korea, Japan)*. Washington, DC: American Historical Association, 1999. The second volume in the Women's and Gender History in Global Perspective series. Short, informative volume with historiographic overviews and cross-cultural comparisons among the three countries named in the title. Critical annotated bibliographies on the use of standard texts in integrating women and gender into Asian studies.

Murphey, Rhoads. *East Asia: A New History*. New York: Longman, 1997. One of the few one-volume histories that include material on China, Japan, Korea, Vietnam, and southeast Asia. Written by a leading scholar of modern China and east Asia. Appropriate for beginning students but more useful for those with some background on the area.

Ramusack, Barbara N., and Sharon Sievers. *Women in Asia*. Bloomington: Indiana University Press, 1999. Part of the series Restoring Women to History. Far-ranging book divided into two parts, "Women in South and Southeast Asia" and "Women in East Asia." Coverage of individual countries, extensive chronologies, valuable bibliographies. Most useful for advanced undergraduates.

## Korea

De Bary, William T., ed. *Sources of Korean Tradition*, vol. 1. Introduction to Asian Civilizations. New York: Columbia University Press, 1997. Part of the renowned Columbia series on the great traditions of east Asia. Perhaps the most complete body of accessible sources for undergraduates.

Korean Overseas Information Service. *A Handbook of Korea*. Seoul: KOIS, 1993. Wonderfully complete history, geography, guidebook, and sociology text. Excellent source, but students should keep in mind its provenance and treat some of its historical claims to uniqueness accordingly.

## Japan

De Bary, William T., ed. *Sources of Japanese Tradition*, vol. 1. Introduction to Asian Civilizations. New York: Columbia University Press, 2002. Like the volume above on Korea and the others in this series on India and China, the sources are well selected, the glossaries are sound, and the overviews of the material are masterful. As with the other east Asia volumes, the complexities of the various Buddhist schools are especially well drawn. As with the others in the series, students with some previous experience will derive the most benefit from this volume.

Reischauer, Edwin O., and Albert Craig. *Japan: Tradition and Transformation*. Boston: Houghton Mifflin, 1989. The companion volume to J. K. Fairbank's *China*, by the leading American scholar of and former US ambassador to Japan. A one-volume history but with more emphasis on the modern than ancient periods.

Totman, Conrad. *A History of Japan*. Oxford: Blackwell, 2000. Part of Blackwell's History of the World series. A larger, more balanced, and comprehensive history than the Reischauer and Craig volume. More than half of the material is on the pre-1867 period, with extensive coverage of social history and demographics.

## Vietnam

Steinberg, Joel David, ed. *In Search of Southeast Asia*, rev. ed. Honolulu: University of Hawaii Press, 1987. Extensive coverage of Vietnam within the context of an area study of southeast Asia. Though weighted toward the modern period, very good coverage of agricultural and religious life in the opening chapters.

Taylor, Keith W. *The Birth of Vietnam*. Berkeley: University of California Press, 1983. Comprehensive, magisterial volume on early Vietnamese history and historical identity amid the long Chinese occupation. Best for students with some background in southeast Asian and Chinese history.

## WEBSITES

Department of Prints and Drawings, British Museum, http://www.britishmuseum.org/the_museum/departments/prints_and_drawings.aspx. A comprehensive source for all manner of interests related to Asian studies.

Public Broadcasting Service, Hidden Korea, http://www.pbs.org/hiddenkorea/history.htm, Sound introduction to the geography, people, history and culture of Korea, with links to additional source material.

Cambridge Journals Online, Journal of Southeast Asian Studies, http://journals.cambridge.org/action/displayJournal?jid=SEA. Online version of the scholarly publication of the same name, features articles on the history, sociology, cultural studies, and literature of the region. It aims for scholarly but accessible presentations. Recommended for advanced students.

# Chapter 14

Birmingham, David, and Phyllis M. Martin, eds. *History of Central Africa*, vol. 1. London: Longman, 1983. The first chapter, by Birmingham, provides an excellent summary of the history of Luba prior to 1450.

Collins, Robert O., and James M. Burns. *A History of Subsaharan Africa*, 2nd ed. Cambridge, UK: Cambridge University Press, 2014. Updated authoritative history by two well-known Africanists.

Crummey, David. *Land and Society in the Christian Kingdom of Ethiopia: From the Thirteenth to the Twentieth Century*. Urbana: University of Illinois Press, 2000. The first book in which the rich land records of the church have been used for a reconstruction of agriculture and land tenure.

Horton, Mark, and John Middleton. *The Swahili: The Social Landscape of a Mercantile Society*. Oxford: Blackwell, 2000. A study that gives full attention to the larger context of East Africa in which the Swahilis flourished. Middleton is the author of another important study, *The World of the Swahili: An African Mercantile Civilization* (Yale University Press, 1992).

Huffman, Thomas N. *Mapungubwe: Ancient African Civilization on the Limpopo*. Johannesburg: Witwatersrand University Press, 2005. Short but illuminating summary of the archaeological record by a leading South African expert, although his interpretation of Zimbabwe in an earlier work (*Snakes and Crocodiles*, Witwatersrand University Press, 1996) is controversial.

Levtzion, Nehemia. *Ancient Ghana and Mali*. New York: Africana, 1980. Originally published London: Methuen, 1973. Standard history of ancient Ghana, Mali, and Songhay based on a thorough knowledge of the Arabic sources; a revision by David Conrad, Paulo Farias, Roderick J. McIntosh, and Susan McIntosh has been announced but has yet to appear.

Robinson, David. *Muslim Societies in African History*. Cambridge, UK: Cambridge University Press, 2004. Advertised as part of a series of new approaches, this book nevertheless presents a conventional view of Islam, albeit in its African context.

Trigger, Bruce. *History and Settlement in Lower Nubia*. Yale University Publications in Anthropology 69. New Haven, CT: Yale University Press, 1965. Chapter 9 is still the best overview of Nubian history, by a scholar with a broad understanding of early civilizations.

WEBSITES

Heilbrunn Timeline of Art History. "Ife (from ca. 350 B.C.)," http://www.metmuseum.org/toah/hd/ife/hd_ife.htm. An excellent introductory website hosted by the Metropolitan Museum of Art. It contains many links and presents clear overviews.

For a website by Patrick Darling, the principal archaeological investigator of the Nigerian earthworks, see http://cohesion.rice.edu/CentersAndInst/SAFA/emplibrary/49_ch09.pdf for a copy of a 1998 article.

## Chapter 15

Bruhns, Karen Olsen, and Karen E. Stothert. *Women in Ancient America*. Norman: University of Oklahoma Press, 1999. Comprehensive account of women's role in daily life, religion, politics, and war in hunter-gatherer and agrarian-urban societies.

Brumfield, Elizabeth M., and Gary F. Feinman, eds. *The Aztec World*. New York: Abrams, 2008. Collection of expert short chapters on a variety of topics, richly illustrated.

Carrasco, David. *The Aztecs: A Very Short Introduction*. Oxford: Oxford University Press, 2012. Clear, compressed account by a specialist, containing all essential information.

D'Altroy, Terence. *The Incas*. Malden, MA: Blackwell, 2002. Well-organized, comprehensive, and up-to-date overview.

Hassig, Ross. *War and Society in Ancient Mesoamerica*. Berkeley: University of California Press, 1992. Best study of the rising importance of militarism in Mesoamerican city-states, up to the Aztec Empire.

Julien, Catherine. *Reading Inca History*. Iowa City: University of Iowa Press, 2000. Ambitious "reading" of "genres" of memory in the available, mostly Spanish sources.

Malpass, Michael A. *Daily Life in the Inca Empire*, 2nd ed. Westport, CT: Greenwood, 2009. Clear, straightforward, and readable account of ordinary people's lives by a specialist.

Smith, Michael E., *The Aztecs*, 3rd ed. Hoboken, NJ: Wiley, 2013. Up-to-date, extensive account of all aspects of Inca history and civilization.

WEBSITE

Aztec History, http://www.aztec-history.com/. Introductory website, easily navigable, with links.

## Chapter 16

Ágoston, Gábor. *Guns for the Sultan: Military Power and the Weapons Industry in the Ottoman Empire*. Cambridge, UK: Cambridge University Press, 2005. Thorough study, which is based on newly accessible Ottoman archival materials and emphasizes the technological prowess of Ottoman gunsmiths.

Casale, Giancarlo. *The Ottoman Age of Exploration*. New York: Oxford University Press, 2010. Detailed correction, based on Ottoman and Portuguese archives, of the traditional characterization of the Ottoman Empire as a land-oriented power.

Casey, James. *Early Modern Spain: A Social History*. London: Routledge, 1999. Detailed, well-documented analysis of rural–urban and royal–nobility tensions.

Elliott, John Huxtable. *Spain, Europe, and the Wider World: 1500–1800*. New Haven, CT: Yale University Press, 2009. A comprehensive overview, particularly strong on culture during the 1500s.

Glete, Jan. *War and the State in Early Modern Europe: Spain, the Dutch Republic, and Sweden as Fiscal–Military States, 1500–1660*. London: Routledge, 2002. A complex but persuasive construction of the forerunner to the absolute state. Unfortunately leaves out the Ottoman Empire.

Murphy, Rhoads. *Ottoman Warfare, 1500–1700*. New Brunswick, NJ: Rutgers University Press, 1999. Author presents a vivid picture of the Janissaries, their discipline, organization, campaigns, and voracious demands for salary increases.

Pamuk, Sevket. *A Monetary History of the Ottoman Empire*. Cambridge, UK: Cambridge University Press, 2000. Superb analysis of Ottoman archival resources on the role and function of American silver in the money economy of the Ottomans.

Ruiz, Teofilo R. *Spanish Society, 1400–1600*. London: Longman, 2001. Richly detailed social studies rewarding anyone interested in changing class structures, rural–urban movement, and extension of the money market into the countryside.

Subrahmanyam, Sanjay. *The Career and Legend of Vasco da Gama*. Cambridge, UK: Cambridge University Press, 1997. Focuses on the religious motivations in Vasco da Gama and the commercial impact of his journey to India.

WEBSITES

*Frontline*, "Apocalypse! The Evolution of Apocalyptic Belief and How It Shaped the Western World," PBS, 1995, http://www.pbs.org/wgbh/pages/frontline/shows/apocalypse/. The contribution by Bernard McGinn, University of Chicago, under the heading of "Apocalypticism Explained: Joachim of Fiore," is of particular relevance for the understanding of Christopher Columbus viewing himself as a precursor of Christ's Second Coming.

Islam: Empire of Faith: Timeline, http://www.pbs.org/empires/islam/timeline.html. Comprehensive and informative, this PBS website on the Ottoman Empire examines the various facets of this Islamic culture such as scientific innovations, faith and its leaders.

## Chapter 17

Biro, Jacquelin. *On Earth as in Heaven: Cosmography and the Shape of the Earth from Copernicus to Descartes*. Saarbrücken, Germany: VDM Verlag Dr. Müller, 2009. Short study establishing the connection between geography and cosmology in Copernicus. Uses the pathbreaking articles by Thomas Goldberg.

Black, Jeremy. *Kings, Nobles, and Commoners: States and Societies in Early Modern Europe—A Revisionist History*. London: Tauris, 2004. Available also electronically on ebrary; persuasive thesis, largely accepted by scholars, of a continuity of institutional practices in Europe across the sixteenth and seventeenth centuries, casting doubt on absolutism as being more than a theory.

Cañizares-Esguerra, Jorge. *Nature, Empire, and Nation: Explorations of the History of Science in the Iberian World*. Stanford, CA: Stanford University Press, 2006. A collection of essays that provides new perspectives on the history of science in early modern Iberia.

Geanakoplos, Deno John. *Constantinople and the West: Essays on the Late Byzantine (Palaeologan) and Italian Renaissances and the Byzantine and Roman Churches*. Madison: University of Wisconsin Press, 1989. Fundamental discussion of the extensive transfer of texts and scholars during the 1400s.

Jacob, Margaret C. *Scientific Culture and the Making of the Industrial West*. Oxford: Oxford University Press, 1997. Widely cited short book emphasizing the connections between New Science, scientific societies, and the steam engine.

Margolis, Howard. *It Started with Copernicus: How Turning the World Inside Out Led to the Scientific Revolution*. New York: McGraw-Hill, 2002. Important scholarly study of the connection between the discovery of the Americas and Copernicus's formulation of a sun-centered planetary system.

Nexon, Daniel H. *The Struggle for Power in Early Modern Europe: Religious Conflict, Dynastic Empires and International Change*. Princeton, NJ: Princeton University Press, 2009. Charles Tilly–inspired reevaluation of the changes occurring in sixteenth- and seventeenth-century Europe.

Park, Katharine, and Lorraine Daston, eds., *The Cambridge History of Science*. Vol. 3, *Early Modern Science*. Cambridge, UK: Cambridge University Press, 2006. Voluminous coverage of all aspects of science, under the currently paradigmatic thesis that there was no dramatic scientific revolution in Western Christian Civilization.

Rublack, Ulinka. *Reformation Europe*. Cambridge, UK: Cambridge University Press, 2006. Cultural history approach to the effects of Luther and Calvin on western Christians.

Schiebinger, Londa. *The Mind Has No Sex? Women in the Origins of Modern Science*. Cambridge, MA: Harvard University Press, 1989. A pioneering study presenting biographies and summaries of scientific contributions made by women. Discusses the importance of Marie Cunitz.

## WEBSITES

Ames Research Center. "Johannes Kepler: His Life, His Laws and Times," http://kepler.nasa.gov/Mission/JohannesKepler/. This NASA website looks at the life and views of Johannes Kepler. It examines his discoveries, his contemporaries, and the events that shaped modern science.

Howard, Sharon. "Early Modern Resources," http://sharonhoward.org/earlymodern.html. Website with many links on the full range of institutional and cultural change.

## Chapter 18

Alchon, Suzanne A. *A Pest in the Land: New World Epidemics in a Global Perspective*. Albuquerque: University of New Mexico Press, 2003. A broad overview, making medical history comprehensible.

Behringer, Wolfgang. *Witches and Witch-Hunts: A Global History*. Cambridge, UK: Polity, 2004. A well-grounded overview of the phenomenon of the fear of witches, summarizing the scholarship of the past decades.

Bulmer-Thomas, Victor, John S. Coatsworth, and Roberto Cortés Conde, eds. *The Cambridge Economic History of Latin America*. Vol. 1, *The Colonial Era and the Short Nineteenth Century*. Cambridge, UK: Cambridge University Press, 2006. Collection of specialized summary articles on aspects of Iberian colonialism.

Burkholder, Mark A., and Lyman L. Johnson. *Colonial Latin America*, 6th ed. Oxford: Oxford University Press, 2008. A well-established text, updated multiple times.

Eastman, Scott, *Preaching Spanish Nationalism across the Hispanic Atlantic, 1759–1823*. Baton Rouge: Louisiana State University Press, 2012. Close look at the national reform debates in the Iberian Atlantic world at the close of colonialism.

Ekberg, Carl J. *French Roots in the Illinois Country: The Mississippi Frontier in Colonial Times*. Urbana: University of Illinois Press, 1998. Detailed, deeply researched historical account.

Socolow, Susan M. *The Women of Latin America*. Cambridge, UK: Cambridge University Press, 2000. Surveys the patriarchal order and the function of women within it.

Stein, Stanley J., and Barbara H. Stein. *Silver, Trade, and War: Spain and America in the Making of Early Modern Europe*. Baltimore: Johns Hopkins University Press, 2000. Covers the significance of American silver reaching as far as China.

Taylor, Alan. *American Colonies*. London: Penguin, 2001. History of the English colonies in New England, written from a broad Atlantic perspective.

Wood, Michael. *Conquistadors*. Berkeley: University of California Press, 2000. Accessible, richly illustrated history of the conquest period.

## WEBSITE

Conquistadors, http://www.pbs.org/conquistadors/. Wonderful interactive website that allows you to track the journeys made by the Conquistadors such as Cortés, Pizarro, Orellana, and Cabeza de Vaca. Learn more about their conquests in the Americas and the legacy they left behind them.

## Chapter 19

Carney, Judith A. *Black Rice: The African Origins of Rice Cultivation in the Americas*. Cambridge, MA: Harvard University Press, 2001. Study which goes a long way toward correcting the stereotype that black slaves were unskilled laborers, and carefully documents the transfer of rice-growing culture from West Africa to the Americas.

Dubois, Laurent, and Julius S. Scott. *Origins of the Black Atlantic: Rewriting Histories*. New York: Routledge, 2009. Book that focuses on African slaves in the Americas as they had to arrange themselves in their new lives.

Gray, Richard, and David Birmingham, eds. *Pre-Colonial African Trade*. London: Oxford University Press, 1970. Collective work in which contributors emphasize the growth and intensification of trade in the centuries of 1500–1800.

Hall, Gwendolyn Midlo. *Slavery and African Ethnicities in the Americas: Restoring the Links*. Chapel Hill: University of North Carolina Press, 2005. Study that focuses on slaves in the Americas according to their regions of origin in Africa.

Heywood, Linda M., and John K. Thornton. *Central Africans, Atlantic Creoles, and the Foundation of the Americas*. Cambridge, UK: Cambridge University Press, 2007. Pathbreaking investigation of the creation and role of Creole culture in Africa and the Americas.

Iliffe, John. *Africans: The History of a Continent*. Cambridge, UK: Cambridge University Press, 1995. Standard historical summary by an established African historian.

Kriger, Colleen E. *Cloth in West African History*. Lanham, MD: Altamira, 2006. Detailed investigation of the sophisticated indigenous West African cloth industry.

Oliver, Roland, and Anthony Atmore. *Medieval Africa, 1250–1800*. Cambridge, UK: Cambridge University Press, 2001. Revised and updated historical overview, divided into regions and providing detailed regional histories on the emerging kingdoms.

Thornton, John. *The Kongolese Saint Anthony: Dona Beatriz Kimpa Vita and the Antonian Movement, 1684–1706*. Cambridge, UK: Cambridge University Press, 1998. Detailed biography of Dona Beatriz, from which the vignette at the beginning of the chapter is borrowed; includes a general overview of the history of Kongo during the civil war.

## WEBSITES

British Museum. "Benin: An African Kingdom," www.britishmuseum.org/PDF/british_museum_benin_art.pdf. In addition to offering a brief historical backdrop to the art of the Benin kingdom, the British Museum's PDF also depicts various artifacts taken by the British from the Royal Palace.

Voyages: The Atlantic Slave Trade Database, http://www.slavevoyages.org/tast/index.faces. A large electronic website based at Emory

University and sponsored by a number of American universities, presenting up-to-date demographic tables.

# Chapter 20

Bernier, François. *Travels in the Mogul Empire, A.D. 1656–1668.* Translated by Archibald Constable. Delhi: S. Chand, 1968. One of many fascinating travel accounts by European diplomats, merchants, and missionaries.

Eaton, Richard M. *Essays on Islam and Indian History.* New York: Oxford University Press, 2002. A compendium of the new scholarly consensus on, among other things, the differences between the clerical view of Islamic observance and its actual impact in rural India. Contains both historiography and material on civilizational and cultural issues.

Gommans, J. J. L. *Mughal Warfare: Indian Frontiers and Highroads to Empire 1500–1700.* New York: Routledge, 2002. Sound examination of the Mughal Empire as a centralizing state increasingly reliant on a strong military for border defense and extending its sway. Examination of the structure of Mughal forces and the organization and weapons of the military.

Kearney, Milo. *The Indian Ocean in World History.* New York: Routledge, 2003. Long view of the history of Indian Ocean trade from ancient times. Particularly relevant in examining the vital period in which the Portuguese and later East Indian Companies come to dominate the trade.

Nizami, Khaliq A. *Akbar and Religion.* Delhi: IAD, 1989. Extensive treatment of Akbar's evolving move toward devising his Din-i Ilahi movement, by a leading scholar of Indian religious and intellectual history.

Richards, John F. *The Mughal Empire.* Cambridge, UK: Cambridge University Press, 1993. Comprehensive volume in the New Cambridge History of India series. Sophisticated treatment; best suited to advanced students. Extensive glossary and useful bibliographic essay.

Schimmel, Annemarie. *The Empire of the Great Mughals: History, Art, and Culture.* London: Reaktion, 2004. Revised edition of a volume published in German in 2000. Lavish illustrations, wonderfully drawn portraits of key individuals, and extensive treatment of social, family, and gender relations at the Mughal court.

Srivastava, M. P. *The Mughal Administration.* Delhi: Chugh, 1995. Solid overview and analysis of the development and workings of the Mughal bureaucracy. Best utilized by advanced students.

## WEBSITES

Association for Asian Studies http://www.asian-studies.org/ As with other Asian topics, one of the most reliable websites are sponsored by the Association for Asian Studies, the largest professional organization for scholars of Asia.

BBC: Religions. "Mughal Empire (1500s, 1600s)" http://www.bbc.co.uk/religion/religions/islam/history/mughalempire_1.shtml. The Mughal Empire ruled most of India and Pakistan in the sixteenth and seventeenth centuries. Learn more about the religious divides and governance of Muslim Mughals in a country with a majority of Hindi populace.

# Chapter 21

## China

De Bary, William T., and Irene Bloom, comps. *Sources of Chinese Tradition,* 2 vols., 2nd ed. New York: Columbia University Press, 1999. Thoroughgoing update of the classic sourcebook for Chinese literature and philosophy, with a considerable amount of social, family, and women's works now included.

Fairbank, John K., and Edwin O. Reischauer. *China: Tradition and Transformation.* Boston: Houghton Mifflin, 1989. A complete textbook on Chinese history, with the majority of the material geared toward the modern era. Emphasis on the "change within tradition" model of Chinese history.

Mungello, D. E. *The Great Encounter of China and West.* Lanham, MD: Rowman & Littlefield, 1999. Sound historical overview of the period marking the first European maritime expeditions into East Asia and extending to the height of the Canton trade and the beginnings of the opium era.

Pomeranz, Kenneth. *The Great Divergence: China, Europe, and the Making of the Modern World Economy.* Princeton, NJ: Princeton University Press, 2001. Pathbreaking work mounting the strongest argument yet in favor of the balance of economic power remaining in east Asia until the Industrial Revolution was well under way.

Spence, Jonathan. *The Memory Palace of Matteo Ricci.* New York: Penguin, 1984. Highly original treatment of Ricci and the beginning of the Jesuit interlude in late Ming and early Qing China. Attempts to penetrate Ricci's world through the missionary's own memory techniques.

## Japan

De Bary, William T., ed. *Sources of Japanese Tradition,* 2 vols. New York: Columbia University Press, 1964. The Tokugawa era spans volumes 1 and 2, with its inception and political and philosophical foundations thoroughly covered in volume 1 and the Shinto revival of national learning, the later Mito school, and various partisans of national unity in the face of foreign intrusion covered in the beginning of volume 2.

Duus, Peter. *Feudalism in Japan,* 3rd ed. New York: McGraw-Hill, 1993. Updated version of a short, handy volume spanning all of Japanese history to 1867, with special emphasis on the shogunates. Good introduction on the uses and limitations of the term "feudalism" with reference to Japan within a comparative framework.

Gordon, Andrew. *A Modern History of Japan from Tokugawa Times to the Present.* New York: Oxford University Press, 2009. One of the few treatments of Japanese history that spans both the Tokugawa and the modern eras, rather than making the usual break in either 1853 or 1867/1868. Both the continuity of the past and the novelty of the new era are therefore juxtaposed and highlighted. Most useful for students with a background at least equivalent to that supplied by this text.

## WEBSITE

National Geographic. *China's Great Armada,* http://ngm.nationalgeographic.com/ngm/0507/feature2/map.html. Track the voyages made by Zheng He to southeast Asia, India, Arabia, and Africa.

# Chapter 22

Herb, Guntram H. *Nations and Nationalism: A Global Historical Overview.* Santa Barbara, CA: ABC-Clio, 2008. Contains a large number of articles on the varieties of ethnic nationalism and culture and the proliferation of nationalism in Europe and Latin America.

Israel, Jonathan I. *A Revolution of the Mind: Radical Enlightenment and the Origins of Modern Democracy.* Princeton, NJ: Princeton University Press, 2010. Israel is a pioneer of the contemporary renewal of intellectual history, and his investigations of the Enlightenment tradition are pathbreaking.

Kaiser, Thomas E., and Dale K. Van Kley, eds. *From Deficit to Deluge: The Origins of the French Revolution.* Stanford, CA: Stanford University Press, 2011. Thoughtful reevaluation of the scholarly field that takes into account the latest interpretations.

Kitchen, Martin. *A History of Modern Germany: 1800 to the Present.* Hoboken, NJ: Wiley-Blackwell, 2011. A broadly conceived historical overview, ranging from politics and economics to culture.

Rakove, Jack. *Revolutionaries: A New History of the Invention of America.* Boston: Houghton Mifflin, 2010. A new narrative history focusing on the principal figures in the revolution.

Riall, Lucy. *Risorgimento: The History of Italy from Napoleon to Nation-State*. New York: Palgrave Macmillan, 2009. Historical summary, incorporating the research of the past half-century, presented in a clear overview.

West, Elliott. *The Last Indian War: the Nez Perce Story*. Oxford and New York: Oxford University Press, 2009. Vivid story of the end of the US wars for the subjugation of the Native Americans.

Wood, Gordon S. *The American Revolution: A History*. New York: Modern Library, 2002. A short, readable summary reflective of many decades of revisionism in the discussion of the American Revolution.

## WEBSITES

Liberty, Equality, Fraternity: Exploring the French Revolution, http://chnm.gmu.edu/revolution/. This website boasts 250 images, 350 text documents, 13 songs, 13 maps, and a timeline all focused on the French Revolution.

Nationalism Project, http://www.nationalismproject.org/. A large website with links to bibliographies, essays, new books, and book reviews.

## Chapter 23

Adelman, Jeremy. *Sovereignty and Revolution in the Iberian Atlantic*, Princeton, NJ: 2006. A leading study in a group of recent works on the transatlantic character of colonial and postcolonial Latin America.

Brown, Matthew. *The Struggle for Power in Post-Independence Colombia and Venezuela*. New York: Palgrave Macmillan, 2012. Detailed history of the forces pulling for democracy as well as authoritarianism on the north coast of South America.

Bulmer-Thomas, Victor. *The Economic History of Latin America since Independence*, 2nd ed. Cambridge, UK: Cambridge University Press, 2003. A highly analytical and sympathetic investigation of the Latin American export and self-sufficiency economies, calling into question the long-dominant dependency theories of Latin America.

Burkholder, Mark, and Lyman Johnson. *Colonial Latin America*, 6th ed. New York: Oxford University Press, 2008. Overview, with focus on social and cultural history.

Dawson, Alexander. *Latin America since Independence: A History with Primary Sources*. New York: Routledge, 2011. Selection of topics with documentary base; for the nineteenth century covers the topics of the nation-state, caudillo politics, race, and the policy of growth through commodity exports.

Drake, Paul W. *Between Tyranny and Anarchy: A History of Democracy in Latin America*. Stanford, CA: Stanford University Press, 2009. The author traces the concepts of constitutionalism, autocracy, and voting rights since independence in clear and persuasive strokes.

Girard, Philippe, *The Slaves Who Defeated Napoléon: Toussaint Louverture and the Haitian War of Independence, 1801–1804*. Tuscaloosa: University of Alabama Press, 2011. Thoroughly researched study of the leader of the revolution, with a number of revisionist conclusions.

Hämäläinen, Pekka. *The Comanche Empire*. New Haven, CT: Yale University Press, 2008. A revisionist account that puts the extraordinary importance of the Comanche empire for the history of Mexico and the United States in the 19th century into the proper perspective.

Moya, Jose C., ed. *The Oxford Handbook of Latin American History*. New York: Oxford University Press, 2011. Important collection of political, social, economic, and cultural essays by leading specialists on nineteenth-century Latin America.

Popkin, Jeremy D. *The Haitian Revolution and the Abolition of Slavery*. Cambridge, UK: Cambridge University Press, 2010.

Sater, William F. *Andean Tragedy: Fighting the War of the Pacific, 1879–1884*. Lincoln: University of Nebraska Press, 2007. Close examination of this destructive war on the South American west coast.

Skidmore, Thomas. *Brazil: Five Centuries of Change*, 2nd ed. New York: Oxford University Press, 2010. Short but magisterial text on the history of Brazil, with a detailed chapter on Brazil's path toward independence in the nineteenth century.

Wasserman, Mark, and Cheryl English Martin. *Latin America and Its People*, 2nd ed. New York: Pearson Longman, 2007. Thematic approach, drawing general conclusions by comparing and contrasting the individual countries of Latin America.

## WEBSITE

Casahistoria. "19th Century Latin America," http://www.casahistoria.net/latin_american_history19.html. Website on nineteenth-century Latin America, for students.

## Chapter 24

### China

Cohen, Paul. *Discovering History in China*. New York: Columbia University Press, 1984. Important work on the historiography of American writers on China. Critiques their collective ethnocentrism in attempting to fit Chinese history into Western perspectives and approaches.

Fairbank, John K., and Su-yu Teng. *China's Response to the West*. Cambridge, MA: Harvard University Press, 1954. Though dated in approach, still a vitally important collection of sources in translation for the period from the late eighteenth century till 1923.

Kang, David C. *East Asia before the West: Five Centuries of Trade and Tribute*. New York: Columbia University Press, 2010. An excellent companion piece to D. E. Mungello's work covering the period from 1500–1800. Especially good on the Ming era.

Platt, Stephen R. *Autumn in the Heavenly Kingdom*. New York: Knopf, 2012. Reinterpretation of the Taiping era as a global political and economic phenomena involving the curtailing of US cotton exports during its civil war, their effects on the British textile industry, and the loss of Chinese markets during the Taiping Rebellion.

Spence, Jonathan D. *The Search for Modern China*. New York: Norton, 1990. Extensive, far-reaching interpretation of the period from China's nineteenth-century decline in the face of Western imperialism, through its revolutionary era, and finally to its recent bid for global preeminence.

### Japan

Beasley, W. G. *The Meiji Restoration*. Stanford, CA: Stanford University Press, 1972.

Reischauer, Edwin O., and Albert M. Craig. *Japan: Tradition and Transformation*. Boston: Houghton Mifflin, 1989.

Totman, Conrad. *A History of Japan*. Oxford: Blackwell, 2000.

Totman, Conrad. *Japan before Perry*. Berkeley: University of California Press, 1981.

## WEBSITES

Association for Asian Studies, http://www.asian-studies.org/. This website of the Association for Asian Studies has links to sources more suited to advanced term papers and seminar projects.

Education about Asia, http://www.asian-studies.org/eaa/. This site provides the best online sources for modern Chinese and Japanese history.

Sino-Japanese War 1894–5, http://sinojapanesewar.com/. Packed with maps, photographs and movies depicting the conflict between Japan and China at the end of the nineteenth century, students can learn more about causes and consequences of the Sino-Japanese War.

## Chapter 25

Gaudin, Corinne. *Ruling Peasants: Village and State in Later Imperial Russia.* DeKalb: Northern Illinois University Press, 2007. A close and sympathetic analysis of rural Russia.

Inalcik, Halil, and Donald Quataert, eds. *An Economic and Social History of the Ottoman Empire.* Vol. 2, *1600–1914.* Cambridge, UK: Cambridge University Press, 1994. A pioneering work with contributions by leading Ottoman historians on rural structures, monetary developments, and industrialization efforts.

Kasaba, Resat, ed. *The Cambridge History of Turkey.* Vol. 5, *Turkey in the Modern World.* Cambridge, UK: Cambridge University Press, 2008. An ambitious effort to assemble the leading authorities on the Ottoman Empire and provide a comprehensive overview.

Lieven, Dominic. *Empire: The Russian Empire and Its Rivals.* New Haven, CT: Yale University Press, 2002. Broad, comparative history of the Russian Empire, in the context of the Habsburg, Ottoman, and British Empires.

Nikitenko, Aleksandr. *Up from Serfdom: My Childhood and Youth in Russia, 1804–1824.* Translated by Helen Saltz Jacobson. New Haven, CT: Yale University Press, 2001. Touching autobiography summarized at the beginning of the chapter.

Poe, Marshall T. *Russia's Moment in World History.* Princeton, NJ: Princeton University Press, 2003. A superb scholarly overview of Russian history, written from a broad perspective and taking into account a good number of Western stereotypes about Russia, especially in the nineteenth century.

Quataert, Donald. *Manufacturing in the Ottoman Empire and Turkey, 1500–1950.* Albany: State University of New York Press, 1994. The author is still the leading American historian on workers and the early industrialization of the Ottoman Empire.

Riasanovsky, Nicholas, and Mark Steinberg. *A History of Russia,* 8th ed., 2 vols. New York: Oxford University Press, 2011. A comprehensive, fully revised history, ranging from politics and economics to literature and the arts.

Uyar, Mesut, and Edward J. Erickson. *A Military History of the Ottomans: From Osman to Atatürk.* Santa Barbara, CA: Praeger Security International, 2009. A detailed, well-documented history of the Ottoman Empire from the perspective of its imperial designs and military forces, by two military officers in academic positions.

Zurcher, Erik J. *The Young Turk Legacy and Nation Building: From the Ottoman Empire to Atatürk's Turkey.* London: I. B. Tauris, 2010. Detailed yet readable account of how the Young Turk movement laid the foundation for the Kemal Ataturk's Republic of Turkey.

WEBSITE

Russian Legacy. "Russian Empire (1689–1825)," http://www.russian-legacy.com/en/go_to/history/russian_empire.htm. Russian Legacy, a website devoted to the Russian Empire, organized as a timeline with links.

## Chapter 26

Allen, Robert C. *The British Industrial Revolution in Global Perspective.* Cambridge, UK: Cambridge University Press, 2009. An in-depth analysis, well supported by economic data, not only of why the Industrial Revolution occurred first in Britain but also of how new British technologies carried industrialism around the world.

Dublin, Thomas, ed. *Farm to Factory: Women's Letters, 1830–1860.* New York: Columbia University Press, 1981. A fascinating collection of correspondence written by women who describe their experiences in moving from rural areas of New England to urban centers in search of work in textile factories.

Griffin, Emma. *Liberty's Dawn: A People's History of the Industrial Revolution.* New Haven, CT: Yale University Press, 2013. Riveting study of the impact of the Industrial Revolution on the lives of working men and women in Britain, as told in autobiographies and memoirs.

Headrick, Daniel R. *The Tools of Empire: Technology and European Imperialism in the Nineteenth Century.* Oxford: Oxford University Press, 1981. A fascinating and clearly written analysis of the connections between the development of new technologies and their role in European imperialism.

Hobsbawm, Eric. *The Age of Revolution: 1789–1848.* London: Vintage, 1996. A sophisticated analysis of the Industrial Revolution (one element of the "dual revolution," the other being the French Revolution) that examines the effects of industrialism on social and cultural developments from a Marxist perspective.

Mokyr, Joel. "Accounting for the Industrial Revolution." In *The Cambridge Economic History of Modern Britain,* vol. 1, edited by Roderick Floud and Paul Johnson, pp. 1–27. Cambridge, UK: Cambridge University Press, 2004. An analysis of the industrial movement that emphasizes its intellectual sources, embraced in the term "Industrial Enlightenment."

More, Charles. *Understanding the Industrial Revolution.* London: Routledge, 2000. A comprehensive explanation of how theories of economic growth account for the development of the industrial movement in Britain.

Rosen, William. *The Most Powerful Idea in the World: A Story of Steam, Industry, and Innovation.* Chicago: University of Chicago Press, 2012. Absorbing history of the importance of steam technologies in the development of industrialism.

WEBSITES

Claude Monet: Life and Paintings, http://www.monetpainting.net/. A visually beautiful website which reproduces many of Monet's masterpieces; this site also includes an extensive biographical account of the famous painter's life and works. It also includes information about his wife Camille, his gardens at Giverny, and a chronology.

Darwin Online, http://darwin-online.org.uk/. This website has reproduced, in full, the works of Charles Darwin. In addition to providing digitized facsimiles of his works, private papers, and manuscripts, it has also added a concise biographical account and numerous images of Darwin throughout his life.

Einstein Archives Online, http://www.alberteinstein.info/. Fantastic and informative website that houses digitized manuscripts of Einstein's work. Also includes a gallery of images.

ThomasEdison.org, http://www.thomasedison.org/. Remarkable website that explores Thomas Edison's impact on modernity through his innovations and inventions. This site also reproduces all of Edison's scientific sketches, which are available to download as PDF files.

## Chapter 27

Belich, James. *Replenishing the Earth: The Settler Revolution and the Rise of the Anglo-World, 1783–1939.* Oxford: Oxford University Press, 2009. Important study by an Australian historian, focusing on the British settler colonies.

Burbank, Jane, and Frederick Cooper. *Empires in World History: Power and Politics of Difference.* Princeton, NJ: Princeton University Press, 2010. Well-written and remarkably comprehensive comparative work.

Chamberlain, M. E. *The Scramble for Africa.* New York: Routledge, 2013. Insightful account of the European colonization of Africa during the period 1870 to 1914.

Ferguson, Niall. *Empire: The Rise and Demise of the British World Order and the Lessons for Global Power.* New York: Perseus, 2002. Controversial but widely acknowledged analysis of the question of whether imperialism deserves its negative reputation.

Hobsbawm, Eric. *The Age of Empire, 1875–1914*. New York: Vintage, 1989. Immensely well-informed investigation of the climactic period of the new imperialism at the end of the nineteenth century.

Hochschild, Adam. *King Leopold's Ghost: A Story of Greed, Terror, and Heroism in Colonial Africa*. New York: Houghton Mifflin, 1998. A gripping exposé of Leopold II's brutal tactics in seizing territory and exploiting African labor in the Congo.

Jefferies, Matthew. *Contesting the German Empire, 1871–1918*. Malden, MA: Blackwell, 2008. Up-to-date summary of the German historical debate on the colonial period.

Ricklefs, Merle Calvin. *A History of Modern Indonesia Since c. 1200*, 3rd ed. Stanford, CA: Stanford University Press, 2001. Standard history with relevant chapters on Dutch imperialism and colonialism.

Singer, Barnett, and John Langdon. *Cultured Force: Makers and Defenders of the French Colonial Empire*. Madison: University of Wisconsin Press, 2004. Study of the principal (military) figures who helped create the French nineteenth-century empire.

### WEBSITES

The Colonization of Africa, http://exhibitions.nypl.org/africanaage/essay-colonization-of-africa.html. An academically based summary with further essays on African topics, as well as multimedia functions.

South Asian History—*Colonial* India, http://www.lib.berkeley.edu/SSEAL/SouthAsia/india_colonial.html. Very detailed website with primary documents and subtopics of nineteenth-century British India.

## Chapter 28

Berend, Ivan T. *An Economic History of Twentieth-Century Europe: Economic Regimes from Laissez-Faire to Globalization*. Cambridge, UK: Cambridge University Press, 2006. Includes Europe-wide, comparative chapters on laissez-faire and state-directed economies, including deficit spending.

Bose, Sugata, and Ayesha Jalal. *Modern South Asia: History, Culture, Political Economy*. New York: Routledge, 2004. Well-informed analyses by two of the foremost South Asia specialists.

Clark, Christopher. *The Sleepwalkers: How Europe Went to War in 1914*. New York: HarperPerennial, 2014. One of a slew of new investigations into the origins of the war published to mark its centennial; emphasizes the Austrian-Serbian roots of the war.

Fritzsche, Peter. *Life and Death in the Third Reich*. Cambridge, MA: Harvard University Press, 2008. Book that seeks to understand the German nation's choice of arranging itself to Nazi rule.

Gelvin, James L. *The Modern Middle East: A History*, 3rd ed. Oxford: Oxford University Press, 2011. Contains chapters on Arab nationalism, British and French colonialism, and Turkey and Iran in the interwar period.

Gordon, Andrew. *A Modern History of Japan: From Tokugawa Times to the Present*, 2nd ed. Oxford: Oxford University Press, 2009. Detailed overview of Japan's interwar period in the middle chapters.

Grasso, June M., J. P. Corrin, and Michael Kort. *Modernization and Revolution in Modern China: From the Opium Wars to the Olympics*, 4th ed. Armonk, NY: M. E. Sharpe, 2009. General overview with a focus on modernization, in relation to the strong survival of tradition.

Lombardo, Paul A., ed. *A Century of Eugenics in America: From the Indiana Experiment to the Human Genome Era*. Bloomington: Indiana University Press, 2011. Study of a dark chapter in US history.

Martel, Gordon, ed. *A Companion to Europe 1900–1945*. Malden, MA: Wiley-Blackwell, 2010. Collective work covering a large variety of cultural, social, and political European topics in the interwar period.

Meade, Teresa A. *A History of Modern Latin America: 1800 to the Present*. Malden, MA: Wiley-Routledge, 2010. Topical discussion of the major issues in Latin American history, with chapters on the first half of the twentieth century.

Snyder, Timothy. *Bloodlands: Europe between Hitler and Stalin*. New York: Basic Books, 2010. Book that chronicles the horrific destruction left behind by these two dictators.

### WEBSITES

BBC. World War One, http://www.bbc.co.uk/ww1, and World War Two, http://www.bbc.co.uk/history/worldwars/wwtwo/. The BBC's treatment of the causes, course, and consequences of both WWI and WWII from an Allied position.

Marxists Internet Archive. "The Bolsheviks," http://www.marxists.org/subject/bolsheviks/index.htm. A complete review of the Bolshevik party members, including biographies and links to archives which contain their works.

1937 Nanking Massacre, http://www.nanking-massacre.com/Home.html. A disturbing collection of pictures and articles tell the gruesome history of the Rape of Nanjing.

United States Holocaust Memorial Museum. Holocaust Encyclopedia, http://www.ushmm.org/wlc/en/article.php?ModuleId=10005151. The US Holocaust Memorial Museum looks back on one of the darkest times in Western history.

U.S. History, http://www.ushistory.org/us/. Maintained by Independence Hall Association in Philadelphia, this website contains many links to topics discussed in this chapter.

## Chapter 29

Baret, Roby Carol. *The Greater Middle East and the Cold War: US Foreign Policy under Eisenhower and Kennedy*. London: Tauris, 2007. Thoroughly researched analysis of American policies in the Middle East, North Africa, and south Asia.

Birmingham, David. *Kwame Nkrumah: Father of African Nationalism*. Athens: University of Ohio Press, 1998. Short biography by a leading modern African historian.

Conniff, Michael L. *Populism in Latin America*. Tuscaloosa: University of Alabama Press, 1999. The author is a well-published scholar on modern Latin America.

Damrosch, David, David Lawrence Pike, Djelal Kadir, and Ursula K. Heise, eds. *The Longman Anthology of World Literature*. Vol. F, *The Twentieth Century*. New York: Longman/Pearson, 2008. A rich, diverse selection of texts. Alternatively, Norton published a similar, somewhat larger anthology of world literature in 2003.

De Witte, Ludo. *The Assassination of Lumumba*. Translated by Ann Wright and Renée Fenby. London: Verso, 2002. An admirably researched study of the machinations of the Belgian government in protecting its mining interests, with the connivance of CIA director Allen Dulles and President Dwight F. Eisenhower.

Goscha, Christopher E., and Christian F. Ostermann. *Connecting Histories: Decolonization and the Cold War in Southeast Asia, 1945–1962*. Stanford, CA: Stanford University Press, 2009.

Guha, Ramachandra. *India after Gandhi: A History of the World's Largest Democracy*. New York: Harper Collins, 2007. Highly readable, popular history with well-sketched biographical treatments of leading individuals, more obscure cultural figures, and ordinary people. Accessible to even beginning students.

Hasegawa, Tsuyoshi. *The Cold War in East Asia, 1945–1991*. Stanford, CA: Stanford University Press, 2011. A new summary, based on archival research by a leading Japanese historian teaching in the United States. New insights on the Soviet entry into World War II against Japan.

Herman, Arthur. *Joseph McCarthy: Reexamining the Life and Legacy of America's Most Hated Senator*. New York: Free Press, 2000. A fascinating study of the Wisconsin senator whose virulent campaign against communism launched decades of fear and reprisals in America during the Cold War era.

Meredith, Martin. *The Fate of Africa: A History of the Continent since Independence.* Philadelphia: Perseus, 2011. A revised and up-to-date study of a fundamental analysis of Africa during the modern era.

### WEBSITES

*Economist.* "The Suez Crisis: An Affair to Remember," http://www.economist.com/node/7218678. The *Economist* magazine looks back on the Suez Crisis.

NASA. "Yuri Gagarin: First Man in Space," http://www.nasa.gov/mission_pages/shuttle/sts1/gagarin_anniversary.html. In addition to information and video footage regarding Yuri Gagarin's orbit of the earth, students will also find information on America's space history.

Newseum. The Berlin Wall, http://www.newseum.org/berlinwall/. The Newseum's interactive website looks at what life was like on both sides of the Berlin Wall.

## Chapter 30

Ash, Timothy Garton. *The Magic Lantern: The Revolution of '89 Witnessed in Warsaw, Budapest, Berlin, and Prague.* New York: Random House, 1999. A gripping first-hand account of the wave of anticommunist revolutions that rocked Eastern Europe after 1989.

Duara, Prasenjit. *Decolonization: Perspectives from Now and Then.* London: Routledge, 2004. A leading scholar of China and postcolonial studies edits essays in this offering in the Rewriting Histories series on the fall of the colonial empires by scholars such as Michael Adas and John Voll and activists and leaders such as Frantz Fanon and Kwame Nkrumah.

Fanon, Frantz. *The Wretched of the Earth.* New York: Grove, 1961. One of the most provocative and influential treatments of theoretical and practical issues surrounding decolonization. Fanon champions violence as an essential part of the decolonization process and advocates a modified Marxist approach that takes into consideration the nuances of race and the legacies of colonialism.

Frieden, Jeffrey. *Global Capitalism: Its Fall and Rise in the Twentieth Century.* New York: W. W. Norton, 2006. Despite the title, a comprehensive history of global networks from the days of mercantilism to the twenty-first century. Predominant emphasis on twentieth century; highly readable, though the material is best suited for the nonbeginning student.

Gaddis, John Lewis. *The Cold War: A New History.* New York: Penguin, 2005. Though criticized by some scholars for his pro-American positions, America's foremost historian of the Cold War produces here a vivid, at times counterintuitive, view of the Cold War and its global impact. Readable even for beginning students.

Gitlin, Todd. *The Sixties: Years of Hope, Days of Rage,* rev. ed. New York: Bantam, 1993. Lively, provocative account of this pivotal decade by the former radical, now a sociologist. Especially effective at depicting the personalities of the pivotal period 1967–1969.

Harmer, Tanya. *Allende's Chile and the Inter-American Cold War.* Chapel Hill: University of North Carolina Press, 2014. A reinterpretation of American determination to overturn Allende's leftist government and its subsequent results.

Liang Heng and Judith Shapiro. *After the Nightmare: A Survivor of the Cultural Revolution Reports on China Today.* New York: Knopf, 1986. Highly readable, poignant, first-person accounts of people's experiences during the trauma of China's Cultural Revolution by a former husband-and-wife team. Especially interesting because China was at the beginning of its Four Modernizations when this was written, and the wounds of the Cultural Revolution were still fresh.

Raleigh, Donald J. *Soviet Baby Boomers: An Oral History of Russia's Cold War Generation.* New York: Oxford University Press, 2012. A revealing and entertaining account of new social and cultural trends among Russia's youth, as told in a series of interviews.

Smith, Bonnie. *Global Feminisms since 1945.* London: Routledge, 2000. Part of the Rewriting Histories series, this work brings together under the editorship of Smith a host of essays by writers such as Sara Evans, Mary Ann Tetreault, and Miriam Ching Yoon Louie on feminism in Asia, Africa, and Latin America, as well as Europe and the United States. Sections are thematically arranged under such headings as "Nation-Building," "Sources of Activism," "Women's Liberation," and "New Waves in the 1980s and 1990s." Comprehensive and readable, though some background in women's history is recommended.

### WEBSITES

Cold War International History Project, http://www.wilsoncenter.org/program/cold-war-international-history-project. Run by the Woodrow Wilson International Center for Scholars. Rich archival materials including collections on the end of the Cold War, Soviet invasion of Afghanistan, Cuban Missile Crisis, and Chinese foreign policy documents.

College of DuPage Library, http:codlibrary.org. Entering "Research guide to 1960s websites" in the search box yields a wide-ranging set of relevant topics.

## Chapter 31

Chau, Adam Yuet, ed. *Religion in Contemporary China.* New York: Routledge, 2011. Collection of fascinating chapters on the revival of Daoist, Confucian, and Buddhist traditions and their adaption to middle-class modernity, with their proponents operating often in a gray zone between official recognition and suppression.

Daniels, Robert V. *The Rise and Fall of Communism in the Soviet Union.* New Haven, CT: Yale University Press, 2010. A magisterial summary of the communist period by a specialist.

Dillon, Michael. *Contemporary China: An Introduction.* New York: Routledge, 2009. Concise yet quite specific overview of the economy, society, and politics of the country.

Eichengreen, Barry. *Exorbitant Privilege: The Rise and Fall of the Dollar and the Future of the Monetary System.* New York: Oxford University Press, 2011. The author is an academic specialist on US monetary policies, writing in an accessible style and presenting a fluctuating picture of the role of something as prosaic as greenbacks.

Gelvin, James L. *The Arab Uprisings: What Everyone Needs to Know.* New York: Oxford University Press, 2012. Concise overview of the Arab Spring events with carefully selected background information.

Jacka, Tamara, Andrew Kipnis, and Sally Sargeson. *Contemporary China: Society and Social Change.* Cambridge, UK: Cambridge University Press, 2013. Ambitious sociological-historical study focusing on the many differences within Chinese society and the forces that drive change in contemporary China.

Meade, Teresa A. *A History of Modern Latin America: 1800 to the Present.* Malden, MA: Wiley-Blackwell, 2010. The book is an excellent, comprehensive analysis and has a strong final chapter on recent Latin America.

Saxonberg, Steven. *The Fall: A Comparative Study of the End of Communism in Czechoslovakia, East Germany, Hungary, and Poland.* Amsterdam: Harwood Academic, 2001. A well-informed overview of the different trajectories by an academic teaching in Prague.

Speth, James Gustav. *The Bridge at the Edge of the World: Capitalism, the Environment, and Crossing from Crisis to Sustainability.* New Haven, CT: Yale University Press, 2008. A strong plea to change our capitalist system.

Swanimathan, Jayshankar M. *Indian Economic Superpower: Fact or Fiction?* Singapore: World Scientific Publishing, 2009. A thoughtful evaluation of the pros and cons of economic growth in India, in concise overviews.

Wapner, Kevin. *Living through the End of Nature: The Future of American Environmentalism.* Cambridge, MA: MIT Press, 2010. A specialist's look at the vast transformation of nature which is taking place according to the best evidence science can marshal.

### WEBSITES

BBC. Nelson Mandela's Life and Times, http://www.bbc.co.uk/news/world-africa-12305154. The BBC News looks back at the life and career of Nelson Mandela.

Environmental Protection Agency. Climate Change, http://www.epa.gov/climatechange/. The US Environmental Protection Agency's website on climate change reviews the threat to the world's climate and the implications of consistent abuse. The site also looks at various initiatives to help reverse some of the damage already done.

Sierra Club, http://sierraclub.org/. Balanced and informative environmental websites.

# Credits

by permission of The State Hermitage Museum, St. Petersburg, Russia/CORBIS, 783; Museum of the Revolution, Moscow, Russia/RIA Novosti/Bridgeman Images, 786.

**Chapter 26:** Courtesy of the Library of Congress, 790; SSPL via Getty Images, 798; Peter Newark Military Pictures, 802; © The Print Collector/Alamy, 807; Private Collection/The Stapleton Collection/Bridgeman Images, 808; © Bettmann/CORBIS, 809; Private Collection/Archives Charmet/Bridgeman Images, 810; Private Collection/Peter Newark Pictures/Bridgeman Images, 813; Natural History Museum, London, UK/Bridgeman Images, 816; Giraudon, 818.

**Chapter 27:** Kharbine Tapabor, 822; (top) © National Portrait Gallery, London, 825; (bottom) ©The British Library Board, Add. Or.3079, 825; © CORBIS, 828; RMN-Grand Palais/Art Resource, NY, 832; Private Collection/Archives Charmet/Bridgeman Images, 833; © Hulton-Deutsch Collection/CORBIS, 836; UniversalImagesGroup/Getty Images, 841; Anti-Slavery Internation/Panos Pictures, 842; Courtesy of the Library of Congress, 848.

**Chapter 28:** Courtesy of the Library of Congress, 856; © Hulton-Deutsch Collection/CORBIS, 858; Popperfoto/Getty Images, 861; Courtesy of the Library of Congress, 864; Huton Archive /Getty Images, 865; Courtesy of the Library of Congress, 866; The Granger Collection, NYC — All rights reserved, 869; Getty Images, 872; Central Press/Getty Images, 873; © Heritage Image Partnership Ltd/Alamy, 877; © Hulton-Deutsch Collection/CORBIS, 880; Courtesy of the Library of Congress, 883; Hulton Archive/Getty Images, 887; © Bettmann/CORBIS, 889.

**Chapter 29:** Getty Images, 894; Time & Life Pictures/Getty Images, 896; AP Photo, 899; © Bettmann/CORBIS, 902; © Rykoff Collection/CORBIS, 904; © CORBIS, 906; (left) The Museum of Modern Art/SCALA/Art Resource, NY, 907; (right) © 2015 Museum Associates/LACMA. Licensed by Art Resource, NY, 907; Courtesy of the Library of Congress, 912; Lisa Larsen/The LIFE Picture Collection/Getty Images, 921; Courtesy of the Library of Congress, 922.

**Chapter 30:** © Alain DeJean/Sygma/CORBIS, 930; © CORBIS, 933; © Robert Maass/CORBIS, 935; © Bettmann/CORBIS, 939; lev raden/Shutterstock, 941; © Henry Diltz/CORBIS, 942; India Today Group/Getty Images, 945; © Bettmann/CORBIS, 947; (left) © Jacques Langevin/Sygma/Corbis, 950; (right) © Reuters/CORBIS, 950; (top) © Tim Page/CORBIS, 952; (bottom) © Bettmann/CORBIS, 952; Courtesy of the Library of Congress, 957.

**Chapter 31:** Getty Images Europe, 964; © Hubert Boesl/dpa/Corbis, 971; (top) AP Photo/str, 976; (bottom) AP Photo/Xinhua, Liu Weibing, 976; © Samuel Aranda /Corbis, 983; AP Photo/Manish Swarup, 986; Associated Press, 988; © Louise Gubb/CORBIS SABA, 990; AFP/Getty Images, 992.

# Source Index

Page numbers of the form S8-7–S8-8 indicate, in this case, a source document in chapter 8 on pages 7–8 in the source documents at the end of chapter 8. If the page number for the source document is followed by (d) this indicates a text source document. If the page number for the source document is followed by (v) this indicates a visual source document.

# Subject Index

Page numbers followed by *f* denote a figure or illustration. Page numbers followed by *m* denote a map.